Tutorial Guide to AutoCAD 2027

Shawna Lockhart

SDC PUBLICATIONS

SDC Publications
P.O. Box 1334
Mission, KS 66222
913-262-2664
www.SDCpublications.com
Publisher: Stephen Schroff

ISBN-13: 978-1-63057-821-3
ISBN-10: 1-63057-821-5

Printed and bound in the United States of America.

PREFACE

The AutoCAD® program is the most widely used design and drafting software in the world. Its position as the industry standard makes it an essential tool for anyone preparing for a career in engineering, design, or technology.

Key Features

This tutorial guide includes:

- Step-by-step tutorials written for the novice user to become proficient using AutoCAD.
- Getting Started chapters for configuring AutoCAD for use with the tutorials.
- Organization that parallels an introductory engineering graphics course.
- Tips offering suggestions and warnings as you progress through the tutorials.
- Key Terms and Key Commands listed to recap important topics and commands learned in each tutorial.
- Glossary of terms and Command Summary lists the key commands used in the tutorials.
- An Index to help you locate topics throughout the manual.
- Exercises at the end of each tutorial providing challenges to a range of abilities.

Exercises

The exercises included at the end of each chapter give you the chance to practice using AutoCAD to create practical technical drawings. A variety of problems using either metric or US Standard units (inches) are provided. Icons identify them as relating to the following areas:

- Mechanical
- Civil
- Electrical
- Architectural
- General (general exercises have no icon)

Acknowledgments

Thanks to my many colleagues who helped to shape the tutorials in this book. I cannot list all of the individuals who have contributed their encouragement, assistance, and ideas for this text, but I am grateful to the people listed below for their help in this and previous editions.

Special thanks go to Cindy Johnson, Amy E. Monte, Michigan Technological State University, Mary Tolle, South Dakota State University, Joseph A. Gosselin, Central Connecticut State University, S. Kant Vajpayee, University of Southern Mississippi, James G. Raschka, Reuben Aronovitz, John Matson, Craig L. Miller, Michael H. Gregg, Steve Bachman, Tom Bryson, Karen Coen-Brown, Mary Ann Koen, D. Krall, Kim Manner, John Walker, Danny Hubbard, Edward C. Livingston, Mitchell Stockdale, Barry Duke, Gian-Paul Piane, James J. Van Schaffel, Jr., and Susan Zimmer; Kristi Bain, P. Devin Leahy, Don Rabern, Denis Cadu and the many fine people at Autodesk; to Shannon Kyles and James Bethune, authors of previous editions of tutorial guides from which some material was adapted for this manual. I would like particularly to thank the following individuals for providing exercises used in the text: James Earle, Spocad Centers of Gonzaga University School of Engineering, Karen L. Coen-Brown, D. Krall, Tom Bryson, Kyle Tage, Amy E. Monte, Mary Ann Koen, Kevin Berisso, and Mary Tolle.

Finally, I would like to once again thank all of the great students I had the pleasure to teach at Montana State University and Embry Riddle Aeronautical University and from whom I am still learning.

I am happy to once again be able to provide frequent revision to this text, as each new software release is available. My sincere thanks to SDC Publishing for giving me this opportunity. I would like to specially thank Stephen Schroff, Zach and Karla Werner.

SHAWNA LOCKHART

BRIEF TABLE OF CONTENTS

TABLE OF CONTENTS

PREPARING FOR THE TUTORIALS

G1

Objectives

This chapter describes how to prepare your computer system and the AutoCAD 2027 software for use with the tutorials in this manual. As you read this chapter, you will

1. Understand how to use a mouse during the completion of these tutorials.
2. Recognize the typographical conventions used in this book.
3. Create and prepare data file and working directories.
4. Configure your copy of AutoCAD for use with these tutorials.

Introduction to the Tutorials

The tutorials in this guide help you learn to use the AutoCAD® 2027 software through a series of step-by-step exercises.

These tutorials assume that you are using the software's default settings. If your system has been customized, some of the settings may not match those used in these step-by-step instructions. Please check your system against the configuration in this chapter so that the tutorial instructions will match what you see on your screen.

If you are using the AutoCAD software on a network or the web, ask your instructor or system administrator about how the software is configured. You should not try to reconfigure the software unless instructed to do so by network personnel. Read about mouse techniques, typographical conventions, and end-of-tutorial exercises in this chapter, and then go on to GS-2, Getting Started with AutoCAD Basics.

Your system should be running 64-bit Microsoft Windows 10 Enterprise or Professional edition, version 1903 or Windows 11 or higher. You may notice some slight differences in the screens in this manual based on your operating system. To run AutoCAD as a web app for Windows or Mac, you must use the 64-bit version of Google Chrome, Mozilla Firefox, or Microsoft Edge (Chromium-based). A range of other browsers can be used to access help and other online resources.

Basic Mouse Techniques

These tutorials assume that you are using a mouse with a middle roller-button. The following terms describe use of the mouse. (These directions are given for right-handed mouse buttons.) If you are using a touchscreen substitute the corresponding gesture for the mouse directions given in the tutorial.

Term	Meaning
Pick or Click	Quickly press and then release the left mouse button
Right-click	Quickly press and release the right mouse button
Double-click	Rapidly click the left mouse button twice
Drag	Press and hold down the left mouse button while you move the mouse
Point	Move the mouse until the mouse pointer (cursor) on the screen is positioned over the item you want
Select	Position the mouse pointer/drawing cursor over an item and click the left mouse button

Tip: *To click (or pick) in Windows and AutoCAD, use the left mouse button. This button is also referred to as the pick button. To show short-cut menus, enter or return, click the right mouse button. The middle or scroll button on your mouse is typically set to pan or zoom.*

Tip: *You can use the Mouse Properties selection in the Windows control panel to switch your mouse to a left-handed configuration. This will switch your pick button to the right button on the mouse. The left mouse button will then act as the enter or return button.*

Tip: *The right button on your mouse and the spacebar often perform the same function as the [Enter] key. Pressing the right mouse button can also pop up a context menu from which you can pick Enter.*

Recognizing Typographical Conventions

During these tutorials, you'll use your keyboard and mouse to input information. As you read this book, you'll see special type styles to help you determine the information to input. Some of the special type illustrates computer keys, for example, the Enter or Return key is represented by [Enter].

Some special typefaces present instructions you will perform. These instructions are indented from the main text and indicate a series of actions or the AutoCAD command prompts you see on your screen.

Bold type (often in all capital letters) is used for the letters and numbers to be input by you.

Bold italic type indicates actions you are to take.

Sans Serif Font shows text you see on your computer screen, for example, messages and command prompts.

Here are some examples:

Command: ***LINE [Enter]***

instructs you to type "Line" then press [Enter] using the input box where you see "Type a command". This will start the Line command. Once the Line command is started, the input box shows a new prompt.

Specify first point: ***click point A***

instructs you to select point A on your screen by clicking with the mouse. The words "Command" and "Specify first point" represent the AutoCAD command prompts that you would see on your screen. The command prompt line is in sans serif type followed by a colon (:).

Instruction words, such as "*Click*," "*Type*," "*Select*," and "*Press,*" also appear in sans serif font and are italicized. For example, "*Type*" instructs you to press several keys in sequence. For the following instruction,

Type: ***4,4***

you would type 4,4 in that order on your keyboard. Remember to type exactly what you see, including spaces, if any. (Coordinate pairs do not have spaces between them in AutoCAD.)

"*Click*" tells you to click an object or an icon or to choose commands from the menu. For example,

Click: ***Line button***

instructs you to use your mouse to select the Line icon from the toolbar on your screen. To select an icon, move the pointer until the cursor is over the icon and click the left mouse button.

An Instruction shown like this:

Press: ***[Enter]***

means you should press the Enter or Return on your keyboard once.

Sometimes "press" is followed by two keys, such as

Press: ***[Ctrl]+[F1]***

In this case, press and hold down the first key, press the second key once and release it, and then release the first key.

Default values that are displayed as part of a command or prompt are represented in angle brackets: < >.

For example,

```
Specify inside diameter of donut <0.5000>:
```

is the command prompt when the Donut command has a default value of 0.5 for the inside diameter.

You will sometimes be instructed to perform some steps on your own. These instructions will be listed in a different font like this:

On your own, use the line command to draw a triangle.

Glossary

New terms are in italics in the text when they are introduced and are defined in the Glossary at the end of the book.

End-of-Tutorial Exercises

Exercises at the end of the tutorials provide practice for you to apply what you have learned during the tutorial. To become proficient at using AutoCAD, it is important to gain independent practice creating drawings such as those in the exercises.

Configuring Windows for the Tutorials

AutoCAD 2027 takes advantage of common Windows file operations and allows you to run the AutoCAD software while running other applications.

Windows 11

This guide uses Windows 11 which is now required for the Windows version of AutoCAD 2027. To run AutoCAD you need at least 16 GB RAM with 32 recommended, and display resolution of 1920 x 1080 with True Color. Higher resolution is supported on systems with a suitable video card. At least 10 GB of free hard drive space is required for the software. (Of course you will need additional space for creating files.) 3D modeling may require additional free space on the hard drive. You should have Internet Explorer or another browser with equivalent capabilities available.

Note: *The screens in this book were captured on a Lenovo IdeaPad 5 Pro laptop with 16 GB of RAM running Microsoft Windows 11.*

Screen Resolution

You can change your screen resolution from the Windows Display Settings. You can skip this step if you have already set up your system and do not need to make any changes.

Right-click an empty area of your Windows Desktop to show the pop-up menu

Click: ***Display Settings***

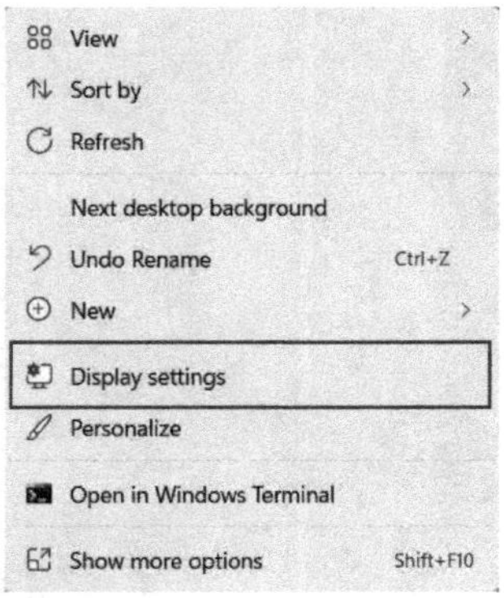

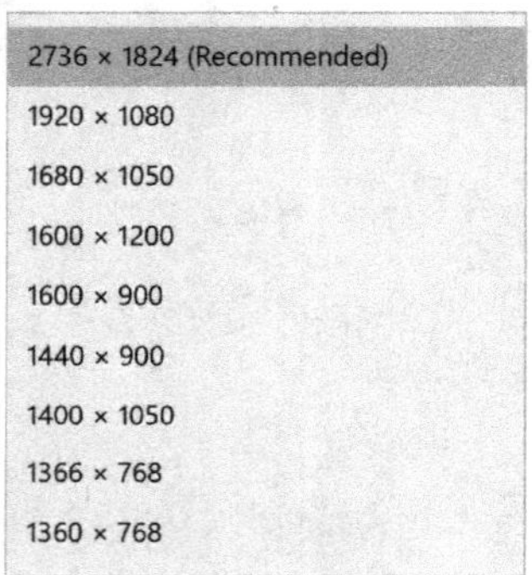

Note: *You can use the Scale selection to increase the relative size of text and icons to make them easier to see.*

The Display dialog box appears on your screen similar to Figure GS1.1,

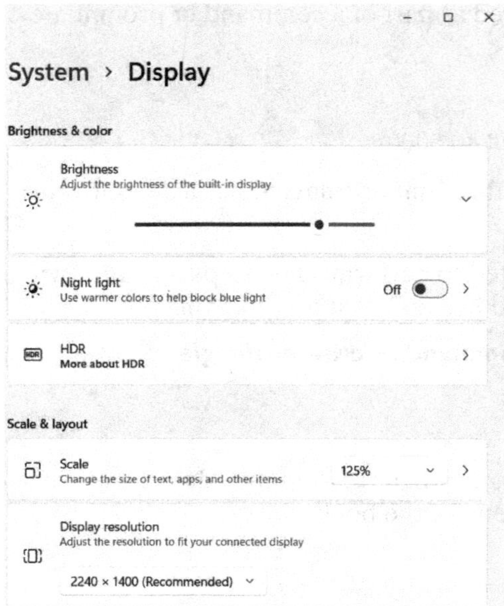

Figure GS1.1

Scroll to show the Resolution selection.

Expand the selections for resolution from the new dialog box, and select ***a resolution of at least 1920 x 1080 pixels.***

Be sure to test the setting to make sure it works. Not all monitors and video cards are capable of every resolution setting displayed. (Refer to your system documentation if you have trouble with your screen resolution settings.) Depending on your screen resolution selected, your screens will look slightly different from the ones captured for this book, but it should not affect the overall operation of the commands as described.

Close the dialog box and control panel on your own. If you are prompted to restart Windows do so now.

Creating a Work Folder

To make saving and opening files easier as you complete the tutorials, you will create and specify a new folder to use with AutoCAD. The working directory is the default folder used to open and save files. Directory is just another name for a folder. By setting a working directory, you will not have to search through all of the computer's folders every time you are asked to save a file.

This is a good practice in general for organizing your files. You should not save your drawing files and other work files in the same folder as the AutoCAD software because doing so makes it likely that they will be overwritten or lost when you install software upgrades. It is also easier to organize and back up your project files and drawings if they are in a separate folder. Making subdirectories within this folder for different projects will organize your drawings even further. Windows operating system often suggests you save into the Documents folder.

You will create a new shortcut for launching the AutoCAD 2027 software that will use a folder named *work* as the starting folder. If you are used to keeping your files in the Documents folder on your computer, then make a new folder named *work* inside your Documents folder. Often in work environments files are shared on a network drive space and automatically backed up, in which case, you would want your work folder to be on that network drive. These directions describe creating a folder named work at the root level of the c: drive (c:\work). If you locate your work folder some other place, just remember to browse to the correct location for your files.

On your own, use your File Explorer to create a new folder* named work *at this time.

work

Installing Data Files for the Tutorials

The next step is to create a folder for the data files used in the tutorials and install them. Throughout the tutorials, you will be instructed to use files already prepared for you. You will not be able to complete the tutorials without these files. You can download these files using a browser such as Chrome, Mozilla Firefox or Internet Explorer.

Tip: *You can add a new shortcut to your Start menu by using the Properties for the Start menu and choosing Taskbar & Start Menu.*

Warning: *If you are working on a networked system or on a workstation in a classroom or lab, your system has already been configured for you. Please skip to Getting Started 2, AutoCAD Basics.*

Navigate to *www.sdcpublications.com*

Click: ***Authors*** *tab, then choose letter L*

Choose: ***Lockhart, Shawna*** *to show these tutorial guides*

Choose: ***your edition of the text*** *by clicking on the picture of its cover*

From the book's page, choose the ***Download*** *tab*

Click: ***Download File*** *button*

Follow the instructions on screen to download the data files.

After you have retrieved the files, use Windows to create a new folder and name it *datafiles*. Copy *datafile2027.zip* into the folder and use a utility such as WinZip to uncompress it. When the file is uncompressed, you will see an assortment of files in the folder, most of which have the *.dwg* extension.

These tutorials assume you will make this *datafiles* folder. If you create it somewhere else, browse to your location during steps that list the *datafiles* folder.

Configuring AutoCAD for the Tutorials

Next you will set up your AutoCAD software so that you can work through the tutorials as instructed. The software is easy to customize, but it is good to start out with a standard look, so you know the typical arrangement of the menus and buttons. As you work through the tutorials, you will learn how to customize the software for your preferences.

Tip: *You may have to double-click the icon to start the software depending on your settings.*

To start the AutoCAD software,

*Click: **AutoCAD 2027 shortcut from the desktop***

The AutoCAD landing screen appears as shown in Figure GS1.2.

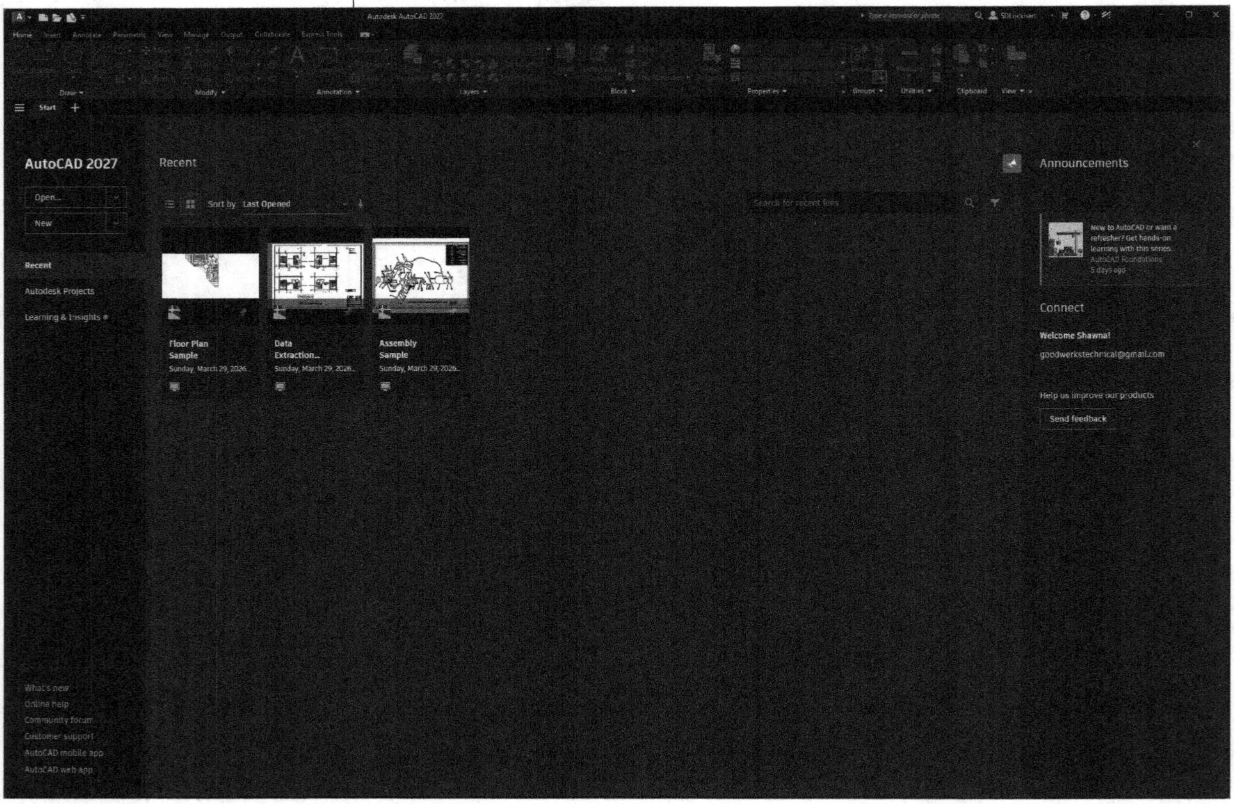

Figure GS1.2

*Click: **New** from the upper left of the landing screen.*

The AutoCAD graphics screen appears with its ribbon and commands.

Software written for the Windows operating system often has a large icon used to access commands related to opening and saving files, and other more general application wide functions. It is called the Application icon or button.

*Click: **Application icon** from the upper left of the AutoCAD software window*

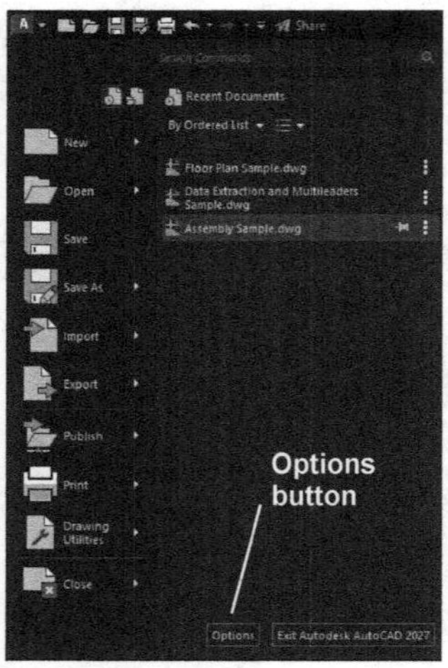

*Click: **Options** button from the bottom right of the list that expands*

The Options dialog box appears on your screen, as shown in Figure GS1.3. The Options dialog box uses the Windows interface to set up search paths, performance, display, pointer, and printer configurations, and various general items. When you make changes to the Options dialog box and click Apply, AutoCAD updates the system to use those features.

To change from one card to the next, you click on the named tab at the top of the dialog box. That tab will then appear on top of the stack.

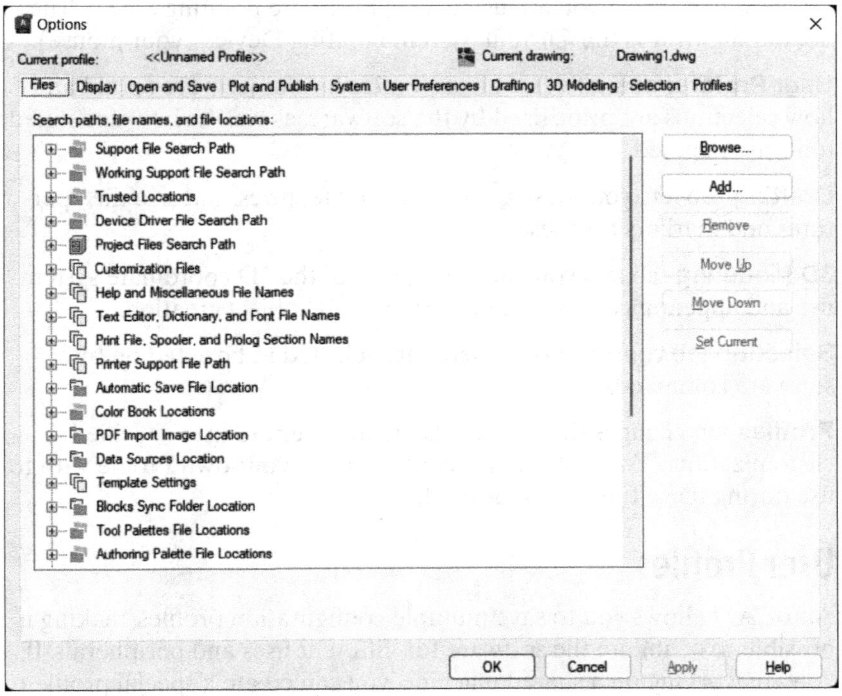

Figure GS1.3

Tip: *Connected support files allow members of an Autodesk Forma Data Management project to share support files. When Connected support files are set up by a member of an Autodesk project with Project Administrator level access, AutoCAD can find project fonts, plot styles, drawing templates, and more without you having to configure each AutoCAD installation. This lets you quickly use company approved up-to-date support files.*

Setting the system variable PROJECTAWARE to 1 turns on the use of Connected support files. This text is intended as a quick way to learn to use AutoCAD, so leave PROJECTAWARE set to 0 so the path settings are defined in your AutoCAD user profile.

The Options Dialog Tabs

These tutorials generally expect that you have AutoCAD installed using the defaults. If you have customized your software, it may behave differently than described here. Refer to AutoCAD's Help if you need to reset your system to the default settings. The following tabs are available from the options dialog box:

Files tab shows the search paths used during many software operations. They are how the software finds the configuration, menu, and toolbar files.

Display tab allows for changes to the display, including fonts and colors. You can use the Crosshair size slider to adjust the size of the cursor relative to the screen.

Open and Save tab allows you to change the default type of file created when you save, to set an automatic save time, and to control how externally referenced files are handled.

Plot and Publish tab allows you to change the current printer and modify its settings. If you did not select a printer when you installed the AutoCAD software, the simplest way to print your drawings is to click Add or Configure Plotters and then use the Add a Plotter Wizard to select the System Printer. Doing so allows you to use any printer that you have already set up to work with Windows. If you want to choose one of the other plotter options, refer to your documentation.

System tab allows you to select which video display driver is used and to select the pointing device, as well as other settings. Double check this card to see that you are using an appropriate pointing device. The default digitizer is the Current System Pointing Device (your mouse).

User Preferences tab lets you customize how objects are sorted and how selections are prioritized by the software, as well as how undefined units are handled.

Drafting tab lets you set snap and tracking features, and size the apertures and markers for these.

3D Modeling tab lets you control aspects of the 3D coordinate system use and appearance, navigation in 3D, and 3D object creation.

Selection tab controls how objects are selected to be acted on by software commands.

Profiles tab changes the AutoCAD environment to user-specified customizations. You will use this card to create your own Profile with to use during these tutorials, if desired.

User Profiles

AutoCAD allows you to save multiple configuration profiles, making it possible to configure the software for different uses and peripherals. If you are working on a shared machine, you can create a special profile to use for these tutorials so that another user doesn't change your settings and defaults between sessions. If you're working on a networked computer, your professor or system administrator has probably configured the system already. Ask which profile you should use, if any. To create a user-defined profile or configuration, first

Warning: *Changes to AutoCAD's configuration can affect its performance. If you are working on a networked system, you must check with the network administrator before creating your own profile. Whatever changes you make must be made only to your user Profile setting.*

*Click: **Profiles tab***

The Profiles tab appears on top of the stack, similar to Figure GS1.4.

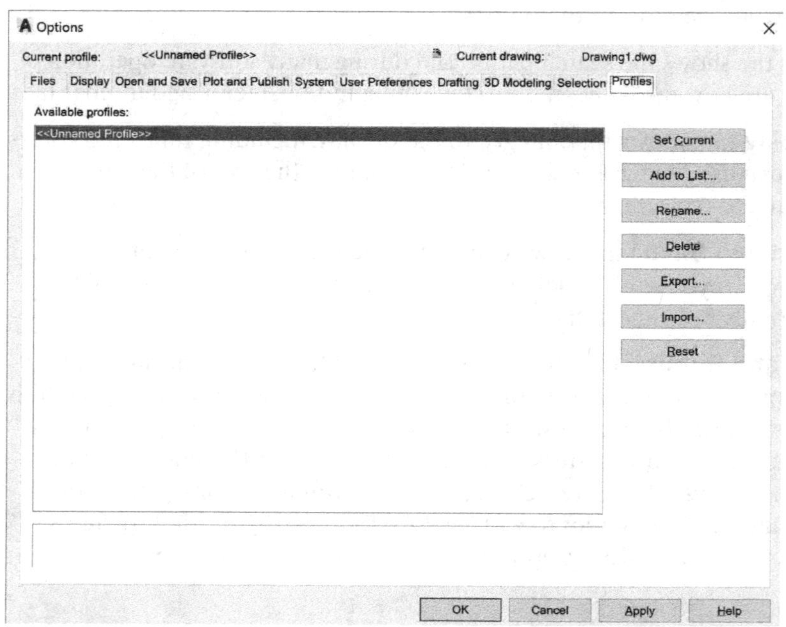

Figure GS1.4

The default profile is <Unnamed Profile>. Any changes made to items on the other tabs will be stored in this Profile because it is selected as current. You will make a new profile for the tutorials, set it as current, and then make changes to the other tabs.

Click: ***Add to List***

The Add Profile dialog box appears where you will enter the name of your new Profile. A description is optional, but not necessary.

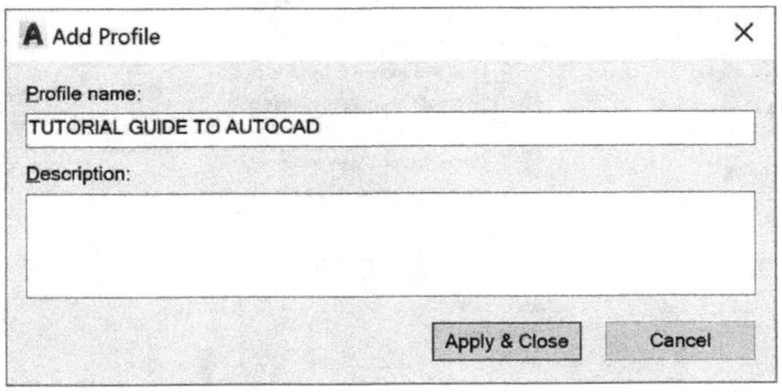

Figure GS1.5

Type: ***TUTORIAL GUIDE TO AUTOCAD*** *as shown in Figure GS1.5*

Click: ***Apply & Close***

You will see "TUTORIAL GUIDE TO AUTOCAD" appear in the list of profiles.

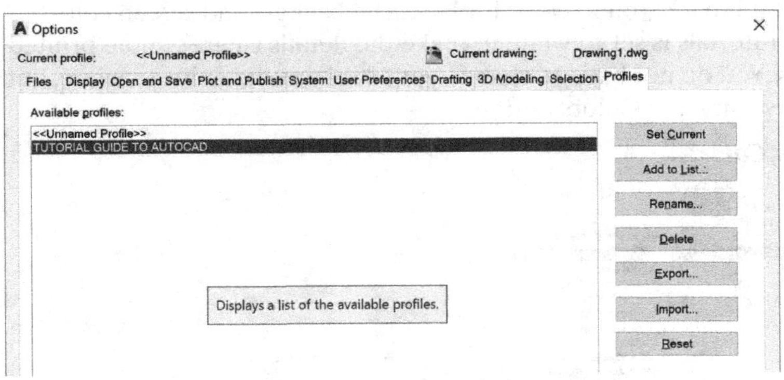

Figure GS1.6

Click: ***to highlight the new Tutorial Guide to AutoCAD profile***

Click: ***Set Current***

The software in the background should not change because the configuration settings for this Profile are the same as for the Unnamed Profile.

Tip: *You can also export your profile and save it in a separate directory where it will not be changed by other users. To do this, pick Export from the Profiles tab and use the dialog box to save the file ending in .arg to a secure folder. When you need to restore it, pick Import from the Profiles tab and select your file ending in .arg to import.*

Changing the Configuration Options

Now you will make changes to the other tabs, as necessary, to follow the tutorials in this guide.

Click: ***Display tab***

The Display tab appears as shown in Figure GS1.7.

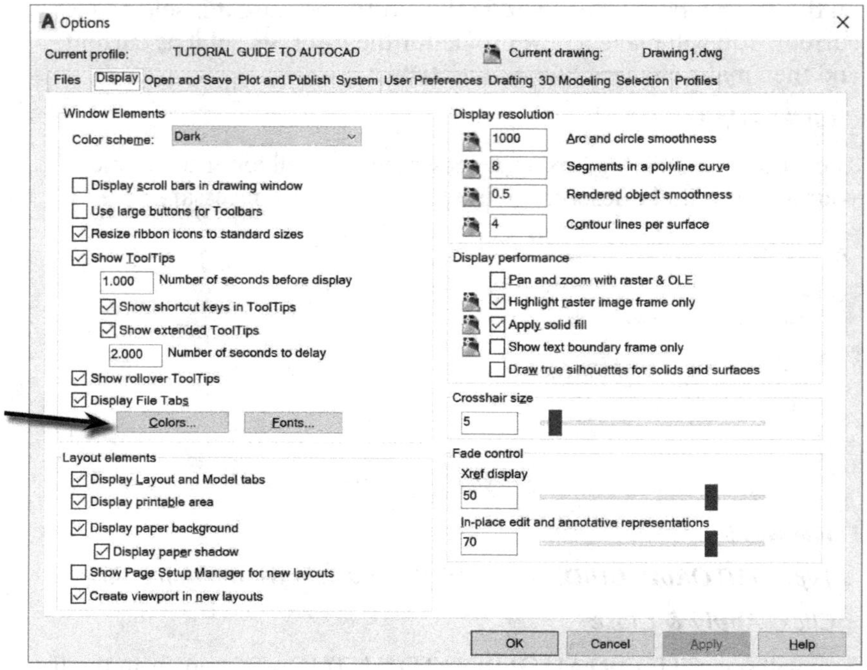

Figure GS1.7

The default background color is black. The background screen color for the tutorials is set to white to make the details clearer in the printed screens. You do not have to change your background color to white, but you may using the Colors option.

Click: ***Colors...***

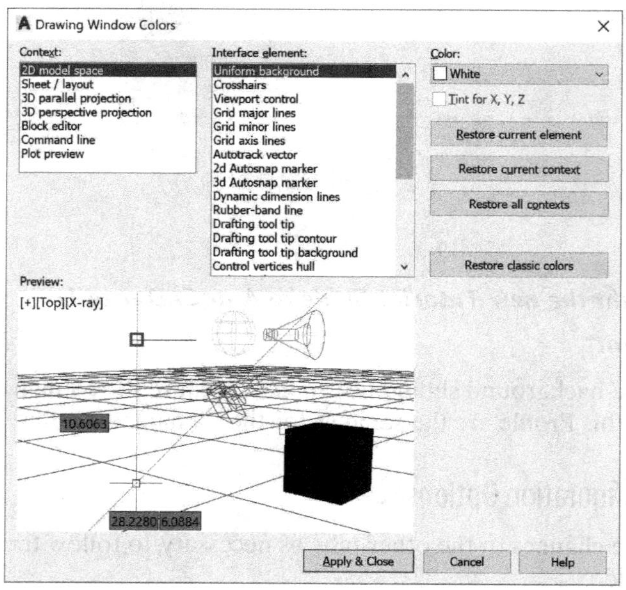

Figure GS1.8

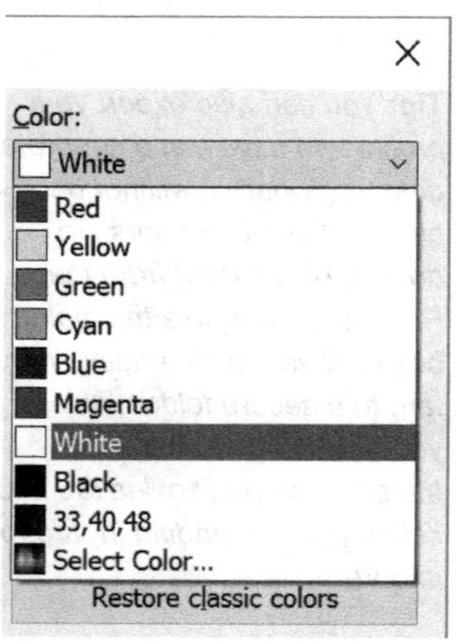

Click: ***2D model space, Uniform background***

Click: ***White*** *from the color list that expands from the top right*

Click: ***3D parallel projection, Uniform background***

Click: ***White*** *from the color list at the top right*

Click: ***3D parallel projection, Viewport control***

Click: ***Select Color from the color list***

Click: ***True color tab, color model RGB and choose color 102, 102, 102*** *(a dark gray), then pick OK from Select Color dialog box.*

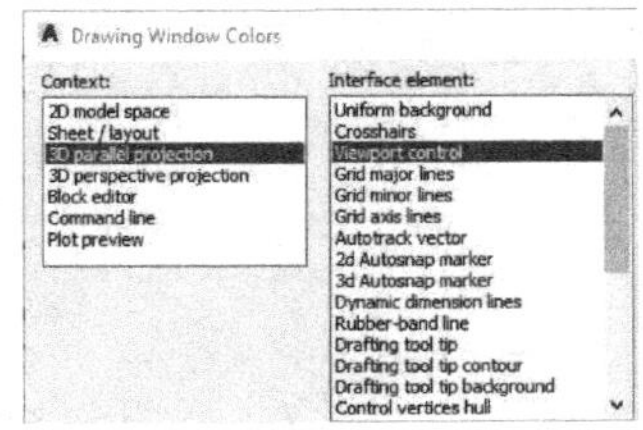

To accept the changes that you have just made (if any),

Click: ***Apply and Close***

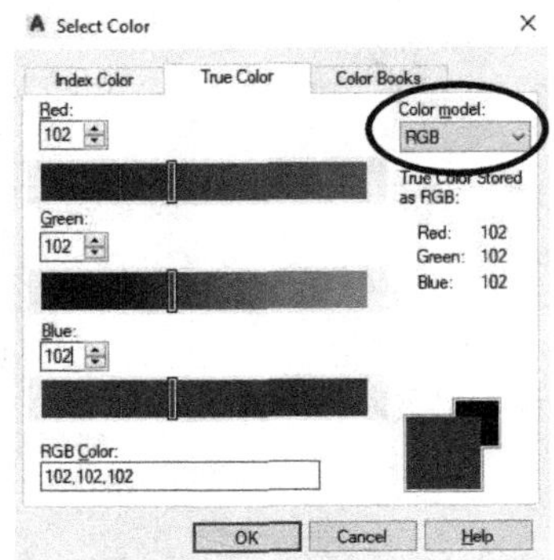

You return to the Options dialog box. To have your menu appearance match that of the book (light to appear better on the printed page), from the Display tab, Windows Elements area,

Click: ***Light*** *from the pull down list for Color scheme*

Click: ***Apply***

Backing Up AutoCAD Defaults

If you want to back up your configuration and menu files, you can do this by copying the customizable files listed below to a USB drive, separate location on your hard disk, or a remote network drive where they will not be overwritten.

To locate these files, you must determine where they are stored on your computer.

Click: ***the Files tab***

Expand the list by clicking on the plus signs to see paths, settings, and file locations. Examine the file locations.

You are finished with the Options dialog box. To exit the dialog box,

Click: ***OK***

The software screen appears again, with no significant changes, except the background color, if you decided to change it. Now whenever you launch the AutoCAD software, you can go to the Options dialog box and select the Tutorial Guide to AutoCAD profile to use with this guide.

After you have located the files, close the AutoCAD software.

Click: ***[X] Windows close button*** *(which appears like an X in the upper right corner of the software screen)*

At the prompt as to whether you wish to save the drawing file,

Click: ***No***

You return to the Windows desktop.

If you want to back up the configurable files, use Windows to copy them to a separate location as you would any file.

When you want to restore the AutoCAD software defaults, you can copy these files back to the directories where you found them or your working folder and overwrite the files there. If you are on a networked system, contact your network administrator about backing up these files. You can find the support files locations using the Files tab of the Options dialog.

Customizable Support Files

File	Description
**.cif*	An *.xml* file that defines most user interface elements. The file *acad.cui* is automatically loaded when you start the AutoCAD program. This file type replaces the *.mnu*, *.mns*, and *.mnc* menu file types used in previous versions.
**.cus*	Custom dictionary files.
**.dcl*	AutoCAD Dialog Control Language (DCL) descriptions of dialog boxes.
acad.dcl	Describes the AutoCAD software standard dialog boxes.
**.lin*	AutoCAD linetype definition files.
acad.lin	The standard AutoCAD linetype library file.
**.lsp*	AutoLISP® program files.
acad.lsp	A user-defined AutoLISP routine that loads each time you start a drawing.
**.mln*	A multiline library file.
**.mnl*	AutoLISP routines used by AutoCAD menus. A *.mnl* file must have the same filename as the *.mnu* file it supports.
acad.mnl	AutoLISP routines used by the standard AutoCAD menu.
**.mnr*	AutoCAD menu resource files. Contain the bit maps used by AutoCAD menus.
**.pat*	AutoCAD hatch pattern definition files.
acad.pat	The standard AutoCAD hatch pattern library file.
**.pc3*	AutoCAD plot configuration parameters files. Each *.pc3* file stores configuration information for a specific plotter.
acad.pgp	The AutoCAD program parameters file. Contains definitions for external commands and command aliases.
acad.fmp	The AutoCAD Font Map file.
acad.psf	AutoCAD PostScript Support file; the master support file for the PSOUT and PSFILL commands.
acad.rx	Lists ARX applications that load when you start the AutoCAD software.
**.scr*	AutoCAD script files. A script file contains a set of Auto-CAD commands processed as a batch.
**.shp*	AutoCAD shape/font definition files. Compiled shape/font files have the extension *.shx*.
acad.unt	AutoCAD unit definition file. Contains data that lets you convert from one set of units to another.

You have completed the setup steps.

AUTOCAD® BASICS

G2

Introduction

In this chapter, you will learn the basics of the AutoCAD software's screen display, menus, and on-line help. The chapter also describes the look of instructions you'll encounter in the tutorials.

Starting the AutoCAD 2027 Software

To start the AutoCAD software,

Click: ***AutoCAD 2027 shortcut from the Windows desktop***

The application start window shows on your screen, similar to Figure GS2.1.

When you first start the software, the left area has a large Start Drawing button. Below it at the left are options for opening files, sheet sets, getting drawing templates, and exploring sample drawings.

The center area has recent drawings you can click to open. If you are starting the software for the first time sample drawings are shown. At the right are options for reading messages or connecting with your Autodesk account.

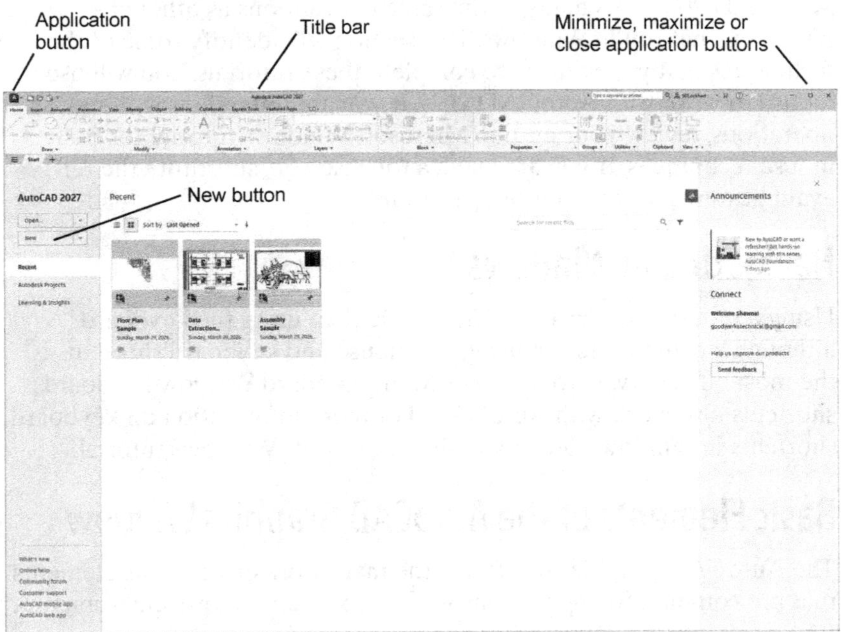

Figure GS2.1

Click: ***New button***

The main drawing window appears on your screen similar to Figure GS2.2.

Objectives

In this chapter you will:

1. Minimize your drawing session and switch between other Windows applications.
2. Start a new drawing.
3. Recognize buttons, palettes, and commands.
4. Use the mouse to select commands, options, and expand palettes.
5. Work with a dialog box.
6. Access on-line help.
7. Exit from the AutoCAD software and return to the Windows operating system desktop.

Warning: *If you are working on a network, ask your technical support person about the software configuration. Changes from the standard configuration might have been made; for example, the program might be under a different folder name or require a special command or password to launch.*

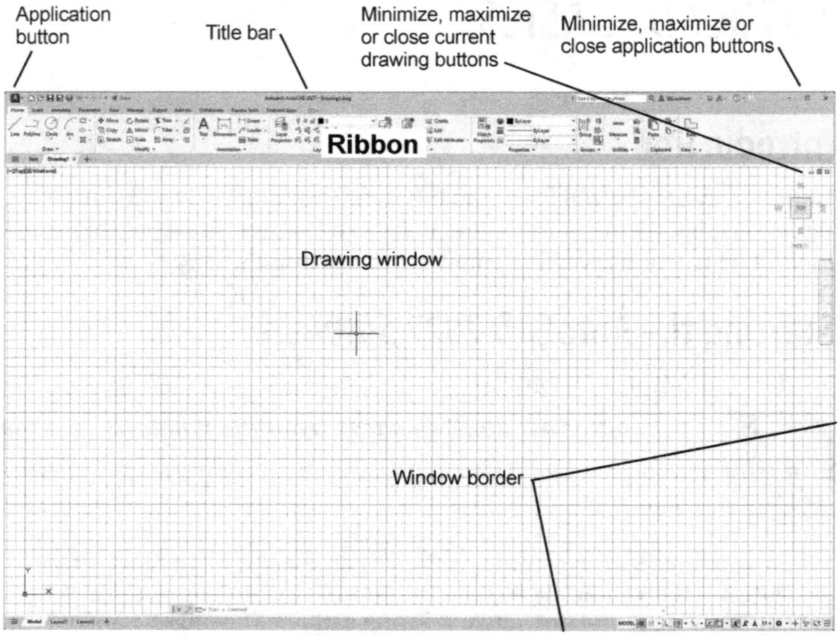

Figure GS2.2

Tip: *If your drawing window doesn't fill the screen area, or overlaps the ribbon, use the button to maximize the current drawing.*

If your screen doesn't appear similar to the figure, refer to the Preparing for the Tutorials chapter for information on setting your default environment.

Microsoft Windows Conventions

AutoCAD 2027 uses many of the same conventions as other applications that run in Windows. This section will identify some of the techniques that you will use to complete these tutorials. You will use a mouse to work with AutoCAD 2027. If you are unfamiliar with mouse operations, review your on-line Microsoft Windows tutorial for basic mouse techniques. If you are using a touchscreen, substitute the relevant gestures for the mouse operations.

Tip: *Some useful Windows shortcuts that work in AutoCAD are:*

Ctrl+C *copy to clipboard*

Ctrl+N *new file*

Ctrl+O *open file*

Ctrl+P *print*

Ctrl+S *save*

Ctrl+V *paste*

Ctrl+X *cut to clipboard*

Ctrl+Y *redo previous item*

Ctrl+Z *undo previous item*

Navigating in Windows

Using a mouse is easier for many people than using the keyboard, although a combination of using the mouse and keyboard shortcuts is the most efficient way to navigate. Many standard Window keyboard shortcuts also work with AutoCAD. For more information on keyboard shortcuts in Windows, see any on-line Microsoft Windows tutorial.

Basic Elements of the AutoCAD Graphics Window

The AutoCAD graphics window is the main workspace. It has elements that are common to applications written for the Windows environment.

These elements are labeled in Figure GS2.2 and described as follows.

-  The close button is in the upper right corner of each window. Clicking this button closes the window.
- The title bar shows the name of the document (in this case, Drawing1).
- The window border is the outside edge of a window. You can change the window size by moving the cursor over the border

until it becomes a double-ended arrow. Holding the mouse button down while you move the mouse (dragging) resizes the window.

- The maximize and minimize buttons are in the upper right corner of the window. Clicking the maximize button with the mouse enlarges the active window so that it fills the entire screen; this condition is the default for the AutoCAD software. You will learn to use the minimize button in the next section.

Minimizing and Restoring an Application

At times you may want to leave the AutoCAD software temporarily while you are in the middle of a work session, perhaps to access another application. Minimizing allows you to leave the program running and return to it quickly.

Clicking the minimize button reduces the AutoCAD window to a title button on the taskbar and makes the Windows desktop accessible.

Click: ***the minimize application button***

The AutoCAD software is reduced to a button at the bottom of your screen. (In a working AutoCAD session, you should usually save your work before minimizing the program.)

The AutoCAD software is still running in the background, but other applications are accessible to you. When you are ready to return, click the minimized AutoCAD 2027 button.

Click: ***the minimized AutoCAD 2027 button from the taskbar to restore AutoCAD***

Minimized AutoCAD applicaiton

The AutoCAD graphics window returns to your screen.

Microsoft Windows Multitasking Options

Microsoft Windows allows you to have several applications running and to multitask between them. To switch between active applications, you press [Alt]-[Tab]. You will minimize the AutoCAD window and open another application to see how this works.

Click: ***the minimize button***

Click: ***to launch a different application, so that you have another software open in addition to AutoCAD.***

Press: ***[Alt]-[Tab]*** *twice*

Small windows appear on your screen with the names of the applications you have running. Press [Alt]-[Tab] to toggle through them until you have your AutoCAD drawing session showing on your screen. (If it is not, continue pressing [Alt]-[Tab] until it appears.)

Press: ***[Alt]-[Tab]***

You should have returned to your other application. (If not, continue pressing [Alt]-[Tab] until you do.)

Quit the other application now.

You will return to your AutoCAD drawing session automatically if it was the last application you were in. (If you do not see it on your screen, press [Alt]-[Tab] until you return to your AutoCAD session.)

Clicking Commands and Menu Options

A drawing is made up of separate elements, called objects, that consist of lines, arcs, circles, text, and other elements that you create using AutoCAD commands and menu options. The mouse is the most common means of selecting commands and menu options, selecting objects, or locating points in AutoCAD.

The left mouse button is referred to as the click button. AutoCAD menus let you choose a command by simply positioning the cursor over a command and clicking to select it. In this way you are instructed to "click" specific commands. Clicking the right mouse button often pops up a short-cut menu used to pick recent commands, options, or act as the [Enter] key.

Entering Points

You can specify points in a drawing either by typing in the coordinates from the keyboard or by clicking your mouse to locate the desired points in the graphics window.

When you move the mouse around on the mouse pad or surface, "crosshairs" (the small intersecting vertical and horizontal lines on the screen) follow the motion of the mouse. These crosshairs form the AutoCAD cursor in the graphics window. You can select points from the screen by positioning the crosshairs at the desired location and then clicking. The crosshairs change to arrows or boxes with target areas during the execution of certain commands. You will learn about these modes in the tutorials.

Dragging

Many AutoCAD commands permit dynamic specification, or dragging, of an image of the object on the screen. You can use your mouse to move an object, rotate it, or scale it graphically. After you have selected an object in drag mode, the AutoCAD software draws tentative images as you move your pointing device. When you are satisfied with the appearance of the object, click to confirm it.

Object Selection

Tip: *You can unselect an item by holding down [Shift] and clicking on it.*

Many editing commands ask you to select one or more objects for processing. This collection of objects is called the *selection set.* You can use your mouse to add objects to the selection set or remove objects from it. You often use the cursor to point to objects in response to specific prompts. The objects highlight as you select them. You will learn about the various ways to select objects in the tutorials.

AutoCAD Commands and Options

There are several ways to enter commands. You can select commands from the ribbon, from toolbars, from the menus, or type them at the command prompt. You can also click commands and their options from the command prompt area to select them. You can also use dynamic and pointer input, which you will learn about in Tutorial 1.

How you start a command may affect the order and wording of the prompts displayed on the screen. These differences offer you options for more efficient use of the software. Most AutoCAD commands can be typed at the command prompt, but clicking them from the ribbon or a toolbar may be easier for you.

The command selection location you should use will be indicated. When you are supposed to type a command it will appear in all capital letters and bold (e.g., ***NEW***). You must press the [Enter] key to activate the command once typed. When you are supposed to start a command by clicking its button, the button name appears in the instruction line (e.g., *Click:* ***New button***).

You will learn about the benefits of choosing commands in different ways in different situations. For the purposes of the tutorials in this manual, you should click or type commands exactly as instructed.

Typing Commands

The command window at the bottom of your screen is very important for using AutoCAD. All commands that you select by any means are echoed there, and additional prompts inform you what to do next.

You can expand the command history by clicking the small arrow at the right of the command window as shown in Figure GS2.3 or you can press the [F2] function key.

The prompt "Command:" in this window is a signal that the program is ready for a command.

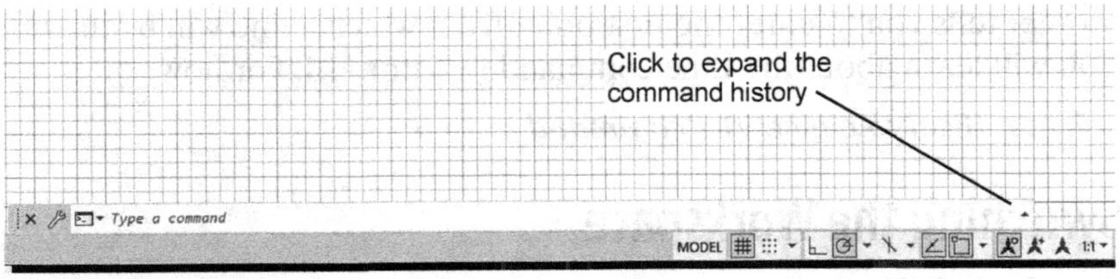

Figure GS2.3

Click: ***the small arrow to expand the command history***

You can drag the command window to a different location on your screen or dock it to the top or bottom of the drawing window. To do so, click and drag on the bar at the left of the command window as shown in Figure GS2.4.

Tip: *These dots are like sandpaper to let you "grip" the item so you can move it.*

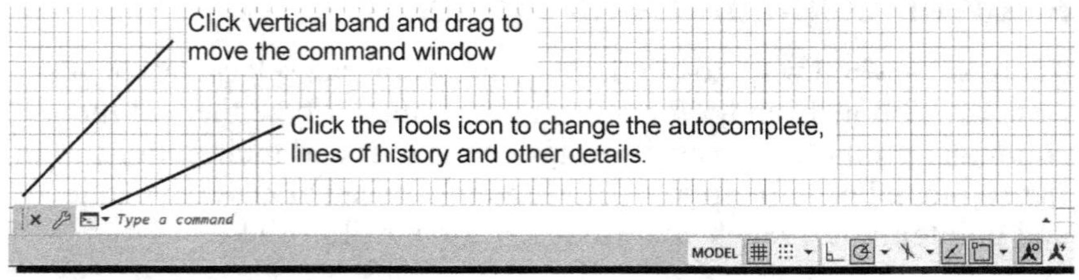

Figure GS2.4

***Move the command window** and then return it to its original location on your own.*

Tip: *If you accidentally close the command window, you can press [CTRL]+9 to show it again.*

You can also show an AutoCAD text window (Figure GS2.5). Press the[Ctrl]+ [F2] keys to toggle to the text window. This shows the command window information in a text window. To return to your graphics window, use the Windows close button in the upper right of the Text Window.

Tip: *You may want to drag the command window to the top of the drawing area. This may make it easier for you to notice the command prompts.*

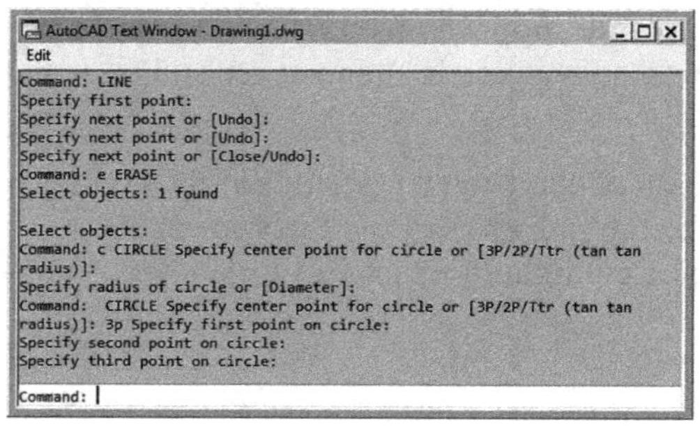

Figure GS2.5

In the tutorial, when you are asked to type a command, it will appear in all capital letters for example: LINE. AutoCAD is not actually case-sensitive; the capital letters in the book just help you identify what to type. Generally it is easiest to type the commands in lower case letters. Watch the command line in the window as you type. Try it now.

Command: ***LINE [Enter]***

The Line command is activated when you press [Enter], and the Line command prompt "Specify first point:" is in the command window. This prompt tells you to enter the first point from which a line will be drawn. You will learn about the Line command in Tutorial 1. For now,

*Press: **[Esc]** to cancel the command*

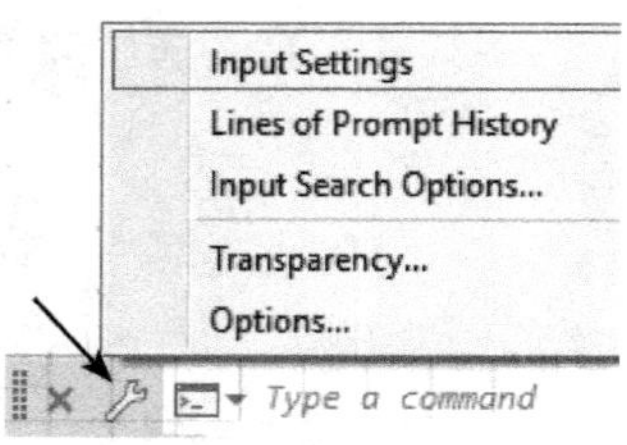

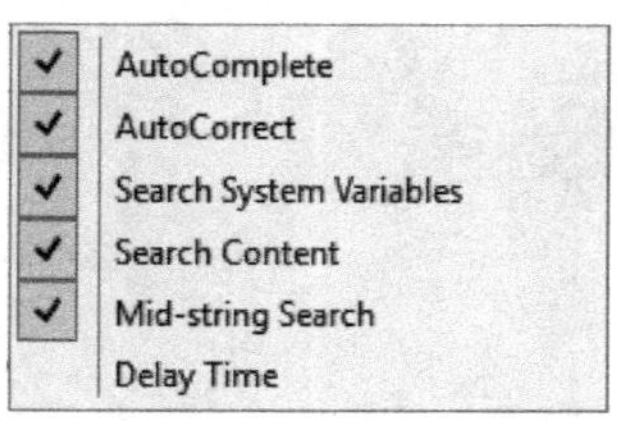

Tip: *Clicking the tool icon produces a menu of selections useful for controlling the appearance and function of the command window.*

Switching the Workspace

AutoCAD 2027 can be customized to your preferences. Customization is great when you are familiar with the software. While you are starting out, it is helpful to locate the commands in standard positions on the ribbon. The ribbon is the main toolbar which appears by default across the top of the screen. To provide some quick customizations for different purposes, you can select from pre-made workspaces. If you are using a different workspace, you will not see the same tabs and palettes on the ribbon as are shown in this book.

To view the workspace,

Click: ***Workspace Switching*** *from the Status bar at the bottom of the screen*

Click: ***3D Basics***

Notice the ribbon changes to display a different set of palettes and tools.

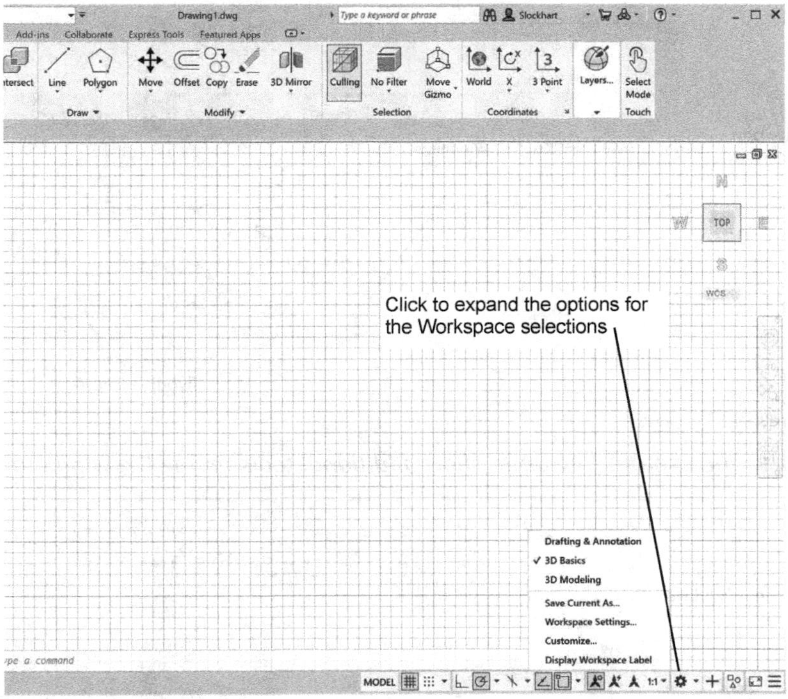

Figure GS2.6

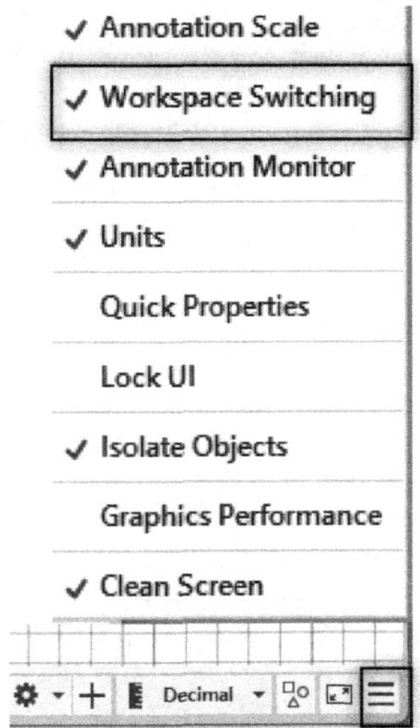

If you do not see the Work-space Switching icon, check that it is shown on the Status bar by clicking Customization.

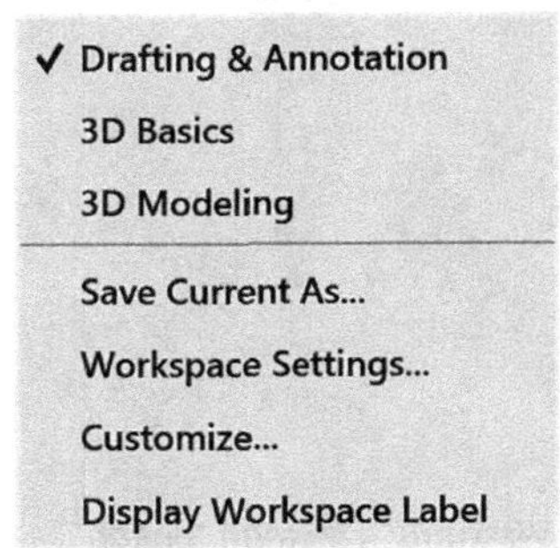

For the tutorials you will start with the 2D Drafting and Annotation workspace. Verify that it is selected.

Click: ***Workspace Switching*** *again to show the list*

Click: ***2D Drafting and Annotation*** *(Figure GS2.6)*

So that you can find the commands as directed, make sure to use the 2D Drafting and Annotation Workspace unless you are instructed other-wise in the tutorial.

Using the Ribbon

The ribbon contains tabs, palettes and buttons that are used to select commands and tools. You can "tear off" palettes from the ribbon and "float" them on your screen.

Click and Drag: ***on the title bar of the Draw palette*** *from the Home tab and move it off of the ribbon as shown in Figure GS2.7*

Warning: *You must use the* ***2D Drafting and Annotation*** *workspace for the palettes and tools shown on the ribbon to match those shown in the next steps.*

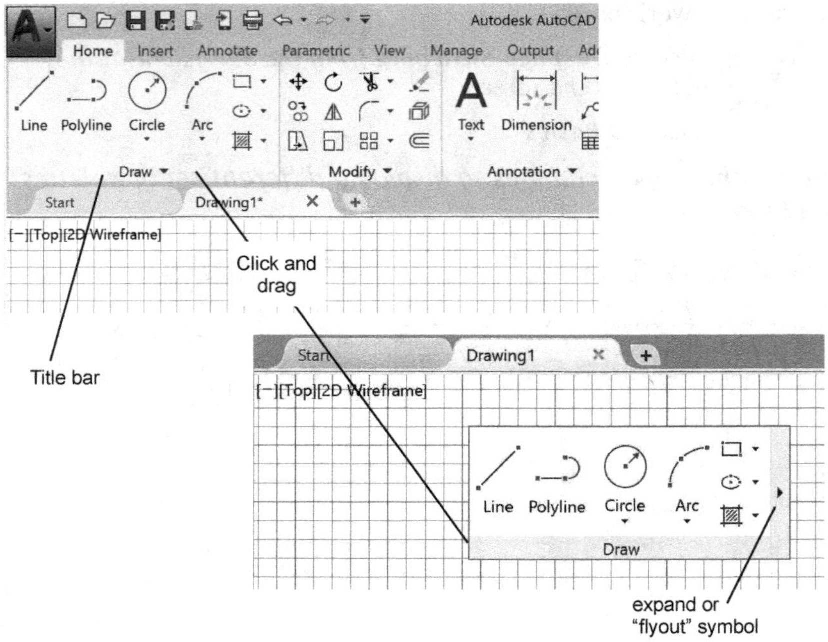

Figure GS2.7

Click: the ***expand button*** *to show additional tools on the Draw palette*

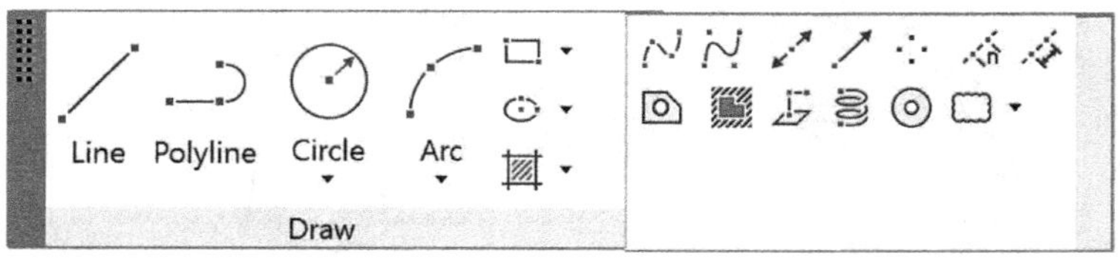

Figure GS2.8

The floating palette has a toolbar that appears at its right side. This bar has very small buttons on it. You can use them to return the panel to the ribbon or to toggle the toolbar's orientation. You can also drag the panel back onto the ribbon.

Move your cursor over the right side of the Draw palette

Additional buttons show along its edges.

Click: ***Return panels to ribbon button***

Warning: *The term "button" used in conjunction with a dialog box refers to these selection options and should not be confused with the buttons on your mouse.*

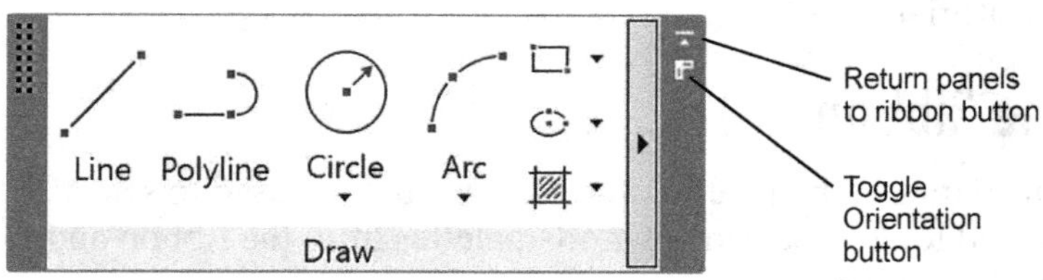

Figure GS2.9

When pointing to a button, the cursor changes to an arrow that points up and to the left. You use this arrow to select command buttons. When you move the pointing device over a button, the name of the button appears below the cursor. This feature is called a *tool tip* and is an easy way to identify buttons.

Icons with a small black triangle expand or *flyout* to show associated commands or subcommands.

***Click the mouse near the triangle in the lower portion of the Circle item** on the Draw panel to show the additional options, as shown in Figure GS2.10.*

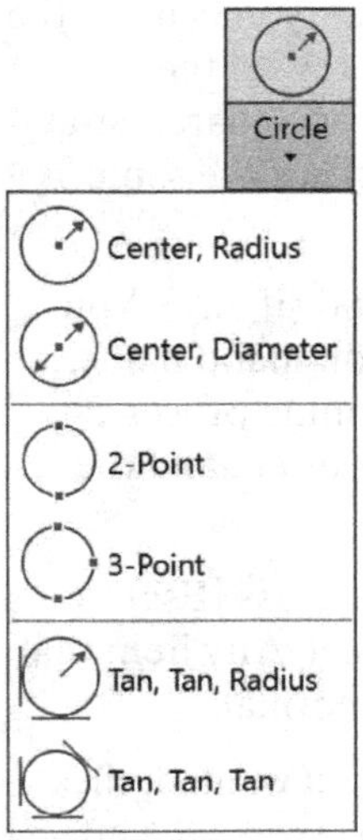

Figure GS2.10

Next you will try the Circle Center Radius command to see the options that appear. As you position the cursor over a command button, the command name is confirmed by the tool tip that appears. Sometimes the tool tip name is slightly different from the name that you would type at the command prompt. If you are confused about a specific command name, check the AutoCAD Help.

As new commands are introduced in the tutorials in this manual, their toolbar buttons will appear as the Circle button does here.

Click: ***Circle Center Radius***

The following options appear at the command line.

Specify center point for circle or [3P/2P/Ttr (tan tan radius)]: ***press [Esc] to cancel the command***

The letters that appear at the command prompt, 3P/2P/Ttr, are command options for the Circle command. Subcommands and command options function only when entered in response to the appropriate prompts on the command line. When a subcommand or option includes one or more uppercase letters in its name, it is a signal that you can type those letters at the prompt as a shortcut for the option name; for example, X for eXit. If a number appears in the option name—for example, 2P for Circle 2 Points—which creates a circle using two endpoints of the diameter—you need to type both the number and the capital letter(s). You can also just click on the option name or subcommand shown in the command prompt to select it.

Many buttons on the panels select suboptions for you automatically. For example, clicking on 2-Point from the Circle flyout will select that command suboption.

Backing Up and Backing Out of Commands

When you type a command name or any data in response to a prompt on the command line, the typed characters "wait" until you press the spacebar or [Enter] to act on the entered data.

If you have not already pressed [Enter] or the spacebar, you can use the [backspace] key (generally located above the [Enter] key on the keyboard and represented by a back arrow) to delete one character at a time from the command line. Pressing [Ctrl]-H often has the same effect as pressing [backspace].

Pressing [Esc] terminates the currently active command (if any). You can cancel a command at any time: while typing the command name, during command execution, or during any time-consuming process. A short delay may occur before the cancellation takes effect and the prompt *Cancel* confirms the cancellation.

If you are in the middle of selecting an object, you can press [Esc] to cancel the selection process and discard the selection set. Any item that was highlighted because you selected it will return to normal.

If you complete a command and the result is not what you wanted, click the Undo button or type U [Enter] or press [Ctrl]+Z to reverse the effect.

Repeating Commands

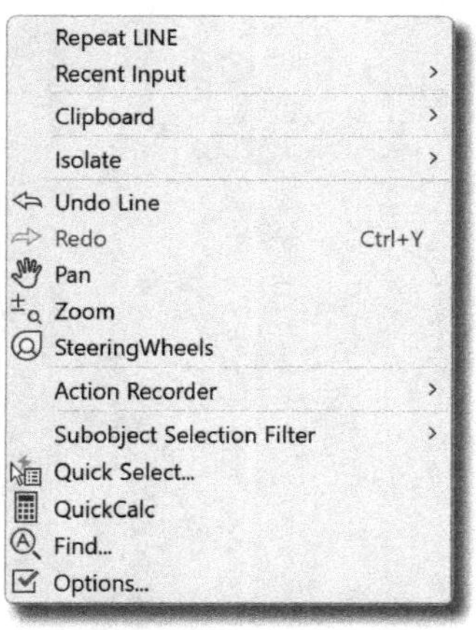

Figure GS2.11

You can press the spacebar or [Enter] at the command prompt to repeat the previous command, regardless of the method you used to enter that command. You can also right-click and use the short-cut menu to repeat the command. You will try this now by starting a command and then press [Esc] to cancel it. Then you will repeat the command.

Type: ***LINE [Enter]***

Specify first point: ***[Esc]***

Right-click: ***to show the short-cut menu***

A menu will appear as shown in Figure GS2.11. It can be used to repeat the command.

To remove the menu from your screen,

Press: ***[Esc]***

Working with the Ribbon

Tip: *Don't confuse the Annotate tab with the Annotation panel on the Home tab. The tab names are along the top of the ribbon. Panel names are below the panel icons.*

Clicking on a tab changes the list of palettes shown on the ribbon to those associated with that tab.

Click: ***Annotate tab*** *from the ribbon*

The ribbon appearance changes to show a new set of palettes and tools as shown in Figure GS2.12. Some common commands may be selected from more than one tab to minimize the time spent switching between tabs.

Tabs that have a down pointing arrow next to their title will expand to show more tools.

Move the mouse to the small downward right-pointing arrow in the right of the Dimension panel title bar, but don't click the mouse button

At first the tool tip shows, then as the cursor sits there longer, the expanded contextual help shown in Figure GS2.12 appears.

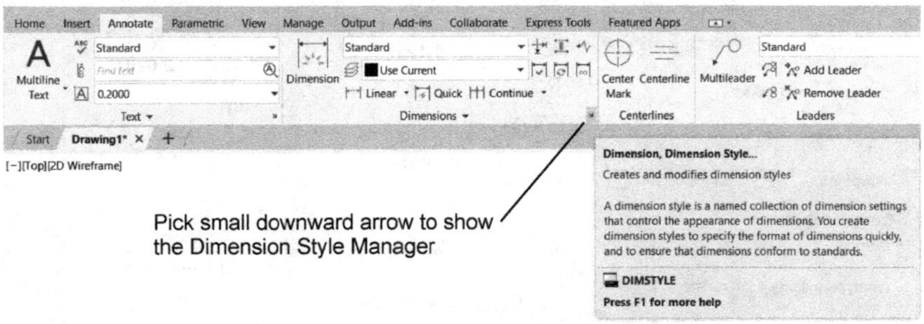

Figure GS2.12

Working with Dialog Boxes

Clicking the small downward right-pointing arrow next to a palette title bar opens the associated manager dialog box. An ellipsis (...) after a menu item also indicates that it will open a dialog box.

Click: the small downward right-pointing arrow at the bottom right of the Dimension palette ***to show the Dimension Style Manager*** *as shown in Figure GS2.13.*

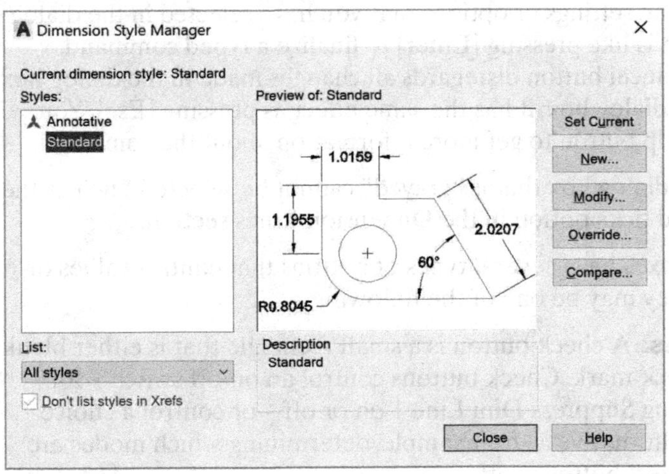

Figure GS2.13

When a dialog box is displayed, the cursor changes to an arrow that you use to select items. Some dialog boxes have subboxes that pop up in front of them. When this occurs, you must respond to the "top" dialog box and close it before the underlying one can continue. The New, Modify, Override, and Compare buttons at the right of the dialog box bring up such subboxes.

Click: ***Modify***

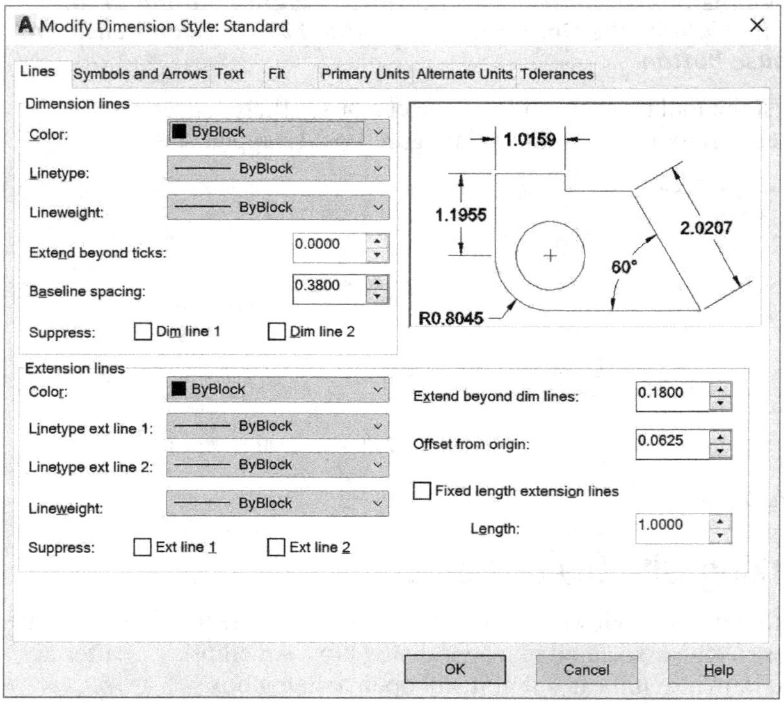

Figure GS2.14

The Modify Dimension Style dialog box shown in Figure GS2.14 is a typical dialog box. Most dialog boxes have an OK (or Close) button that confirms the settings or options that you have selected in the dialog box. Clicking it is like pressing [Enter] to finalize a typed command. Clicking the Cancel button disregards all changes made in the dialog box and closes the dialog box; it has the same effect as pressing [Esc]. You can use the Help button to get more information about the command.

Any item in a dialog box that is "grayed" cannot be selected, such as the Extend beyond ticks option in the Dimension Lines section.

Most dialog boxes have several types of buttons that control values or commands. They may be one of the following:

Check buttons: A check button is a small rectangle that is either blank or shows a check mark. Check buttons control an on/off switch—for example, turning Suppress Dim Line 1 on or off—or control a choice from a set of alternatives—for example, determining which modes are on. A blank check button is off.

Radio buttons: A radio button looks like a circle with a dot at the center. It also turns an option on or off. A filled-in radio button is on. You can select only one radio button at a time; clicking one button automatically turns any other button off. Click on the Fit tab of the Modify Dimension Style dialog box to see radio buttons.

Action buttons: An action button doesn't control a value but causes an action. The OK action button causes the dialog box to close and all the selected options to go into effect. When an action button is highlighted (outlined with a heavy rule), you can press [Enter] to activate it.

Text boxes: A text box allows you to specify a value, such as Baseline Spacing in Figure GS2.14. Clicking a text box moves the cursor into it and lets you type in values or alter values already there. If you enter an invalid value, the OK button has no effect; you must highlight the value, correct it, and select OK again.

Input buttons: An input button chooses among preset options, such as the Color button in Figure GS2.14. Input buttons have a small arrow at the right end. Clicking the arrow causes the value area to expand into a menu of options that you can use to select the value for the button.

You can also use the keyboard to move around in dialog boxes.

Tab key - Pressing [Tab] moves among the options in the dialog box.

Try this by pressing [Tab] several times now.

Arrow keys - Once you have highlighted a text box or input button, you can use the arrow keys to move the cursor in text boxes or to cycle among input options.

Spacebar - The [spacebar] toggles options on and off. (When you are not in a dialog box, it acts like pressing the [Enter] key.)

Scroll bar - Another common feature of dialog boxes is the scroll bar. A dialog box may contain more entries than can be displayed at one time. You use the scroll bars to move (scroll) the items up or down.

Most dialog boxes save changes to the current drawing only. Two exceptions to this rule are the Options dialog box and the Plot dialog box; these dialog boxes change the way AutoCAD operates, not just the current drawing itself.

Tip: *For information on what's new in the AutoCAD 2027 software, you can search for "New Commands and System Variables Reference" from the Help search box.*

The Cancel button ignores all the selections that you made while this dialog box was open and returns you to the most recent settings. To return to the graphics window without making any changes,

Click: ***Cancel***

Click: ***Close***

You return to the graphics window.

Accessing On-Line Help

AutoCAD has context-sensitive on-line help.

You can get help in a number of ways. You can click the Help button, type HELP or ? at the command prompt, or press [F1] to bring up the Help window.

Tip: *A feature of many Windows dialog boxes allows you to double-click on the desired selection to select it and exit the dialog box in one action.*

You will use the Help button, which looks like a question mark, from the Quick Access toolbar at the top right of the application window to open AutoCAD on-line help.

Click: ***Help button***

The AutoCAD 2027 Help window is shown in Figure GS2.15.

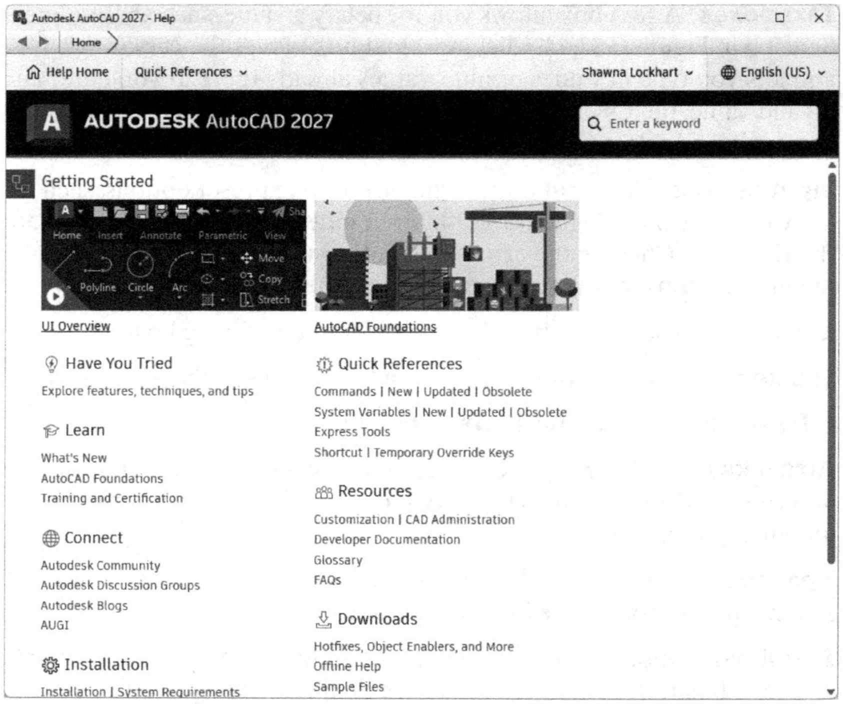

Figure GS2.15

The left panel of the window shows a list of links for learning, quick references, resources, downloads, and connecting to the support community. You can also type a search term in the input box at the upper left where it says, "Enter a keyword."

Click items on the screen at the right to tour basic information about using the software.

Click: ***AutoCAD Foundations*** *under Learn*

To return to the previous screen (if there was a previous screen), you can select the back arrow from the top left of the menu bar.

You will use the Windows close button to close the Help window and return to the AutoCAD graphics window.

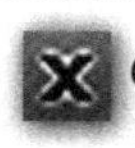

Click: ***the Windows close button*** *in the top right of the Help window*

On-line help is a great resource for learning how to use the powerful AutoCAD software. You should use help whenever you want more information about commands and options.

Working with Documents

All the documents that you will be instructed to use are held in the folders named *datafiles* and *work*, which you should have already created in Getting Started-1. The best procedure is to save all files on your hard drive, network drive, or cloud storage. Saving from AutoCAD to a removable drive can result in unrecoverable, corrupted drawing files if you remove the drive before the software is fully closed.

Exiting an AutoCAD Session

When you have finished an AutoCAD session, you will exit the program by choosing the Application icon and then clicking Exit or by using the Window close box for the application.

Click: ***Application icon, Exit Autodesk AutoCAD 2027***

Because quitting unintentionally could cause the loss of a lengthy editing session, the AutoCAD software prompts you to save the changes if you want to. An AutoCAD dialog box appears that contains the message Save Changes to DRAWING1.dwg? It gives you three options: Yes, No, and Cancel.

Click: ***No***

You are returned to Windows.

You are now ready to complete the tutorials in this manual.

Tip: *If you have made some irreversible error and want to discard all changes made in an AutoCAD session, you can choose Exit from the File menu (or type QUIT at the command prompt) and select No so that the changes are not saved to your file.*

STUDYING FOR THE BASIC AUTOCAD® CERTIFICATION EXAM

G3

Objectives

This chapter describes how to use this text to study for the AutoCAD Certication Exam. As you read this section you will:

1. Get general study tips for the exam.
2. Find web resources for studying for and taking the certification exam.
3. Learn how to identify which topics in this text may appear on the certification exam.

General Study Tips

Good exam taking strategies are helpful to keep in mind. Be well rested, comfortable, and ready at exam time.

Prepare – The exam includes performance based testing for which you need hands-on experience. Use the software, and study the written material. Practice your skills by making drawings. During the test you may not use calculators, books, or other electronic equipment, so don't plan to rely on them. But, keep in mind the useful functions built into the software: the *Help* command is key, but don't forget the *Quick Calculator* and reading the *command prompts*.

Review the information available at: *https://www.autodesk.com/learn/ondemand/course/autocad-design-drafting-cert-prep*. This provides information about the exam. You can also purchase practice exams here.

Look for free practice exams, which though not identical to the official exam, can show you areas where you need more practice. Check out *https://www.proprofs.com/quiz-school/story.php?title=autocad-2010-certified-associate-practice-questions. Or u*se an AI prompt, such as "*Write 10 study questions for an AutoCAD certification exam.*" to generate practice content for yourself.

Manage your time during the exam – Specific objectives are being tested, so read the questions carefully and make sure you know what is asked for. Pay attention to the introductory tutorial giving information on using the online testing system, **location of files**, instructions for answering questions, and general test information.

Make a quick judgement about how long it will take to answer the question. During the exam, you are often able to save datafiles and mark questions to return to later. Do the questions that are quick and easy for you first and mark the more difficult questions to work on later if time permits. You do not have to earn 100% to pass.

Review your answers – Review your answers before submitting your exam to make sure you have answered all of the items. If you don't know and have time, make educated guesses. Use the strategy of ruling out answers you know to be incorrect or unlikely and select from the remaining ones. Sometimes you may have to select the answer that is the least incorrect from a number of poor answer options.

Have a good attitude – Regardless of your performance on the exam, you will get valuable feedback about which areas you have mastered and which you still need to work on. Look at the exam as a learning opportunity, as well as a chance to show your abilities.

Certification Exam

The Autodesk Certified User (ACU) entry-level certification exam is delivered via Certiport. It generally contains 30 to 40 questions, in which you use AutoCAD to create drawings or modify data files. You will typically type your resulting answer into an input box, or select from multiple choice, matching, or point and click screen elements. A 75 minute time limit is typically given. The following items categorize the skills you will be expected to demonstrate on the entry-level exam. Your particular exam may not test you on all of the topics. Prepare to demonstrate your understanding of the following:

Exam Topic	In this text...
Basics	Tutorial 1
Interface	Tutorial 1
Inquiry	Tutorial 3
Draw Order	Tutorial 9
Help	Tutorial 1
Draw and modify objects	Tutorial 1
Create basic drawing objects; Lines, circles, rectangles, arcs, polygons, rays, etc.	Tutorial 1, 2, 3, 4
Edit geometric shapes	Tutorial 3, 4
Create 2D isometric drawings	Tutorial 4
Draw open or closed polylines	Tutorial 3
Edit a polyline, convert lines and arcs to polyline	Tutorial 3
Join polylines	Tutorial 3
Select and deselect objects	Tutorial 1
Use a selection or crossing windows to select objects	Tutorial 1
Remove objects from a selection set	Tutorial 1
Manage layers	Tutorial 2
Set the current layer	Tutorial 2
Create and/or remove layers	Tutorial 2
Edit the properties of a layer	Tutorial 2
Name, color, linetype, and lineweight	Tutorial 2
Freeze, thaw, lock, unlock, on, and off	Tutorial 2
Identify the objects on a specific layer	Tutorial 2
Work with blocks	Tutorial 5, 10
Create a basic block	Tutorial 10
Define the base point	Tutorial 10
Understand the significance of creating a block on layer 0	Tutorial 10
Insert and modify instances of a block	Tutorial 5, 10
Basepoint, Scale, Rotate, and Explode	Tutorial 10
Blocks palette, Tool palettes, and the Design Center	Tutorial 10
Transfer information between drawing files	Tutorial 5, 10
Copy with Basepoint	Tutorial 5, 10

Exam Topic	**In this text...**
Drag and drop across multiple open drawings	Tutorial 1
Draw with Accuracy	Tutorial 1, 4
Apply basic object snaps	Tutorial 4
Use object snaps and object snap tracking	Tutorial 4
Endpoint, midpoint, center, nearest, intersection, perpendicular, quadrant, extension, parallel, geometric center, and tangent	Tutorial 4
Midpoint between two points (M2P) combined with object snap tracking and polar tracking	Tutorial 4
Identify and use coordinates	Tutorial 1
Enter coordinate values on the Command Line	Tutorial 1
Relative, absolute, and polar coordinates	Tutorial 1
Use dynamic input and direct distance entry	Tutorial 1
Basic Editing	Tutorial 3, 4
Modify object properties	Tutorial 4
Identify and alter layer assignments, color, lineweight, and linetype	Tutorial 2
Properties palette and Quick Properties	Tutorial 3
Match the properties of one object to other objects	Tutorial 3
Use basic editing commands to modify objects	Tutorial 3
Move, copy, rotate, mirror, scale, and stretch objects	Tutorial 4
Move, copy, and stretch objects using grips	Tutorial 4
Trim, extend, or lengthen objects	Tutorial 3
Create rectangular and polar arrays	Tutorial 4
Offset objects at a specific distance	Tutorial 3
Apply a fillet or chamfer to objects	Tutorial 3
Rounded corners	Tutorial 3
Chamfered corners	Tutorial 3
Square corners (zero radius fillet)	Tutorial 3
Annotation	Tutorial 1, 5
Create and modify text/multiline text	Tutorial 1, 5
Apply text and multiline text properties	Tutorial 1, 5
Text height, justification, rotation, text wrapping, and text style	Tutorial 1, 5
Add and modify leaders and/or multileaders	Tutorial 9,10
Create and edit dimensions	Tutorial 7
Add dimensions	Tutorial 7
Linear, aligned, angular, radius, diameter	Tutorial 7
Create multiple dimensions with a single command	Tutorial 7
Continue and baseline dimensions	Tutorial 7
Modify and apply dimension styles	Tutorial 7

Exam Topic	In this text...
Precision, primary units, using overall scale, etc.	Tutorial 7
Apply hatches or fill patterns	Tutorial 9
Create a hatch or fill pattern	Tutorial 9
Pick points or select	Tutorial 9
Specify hatch or fill options	Tutorial 9
Angle, scale, pattern, match properties, inherit, and color	Tutorial 9
Layouts and Printing	Tutorial 5
Work with layouts and viewports	Tutorial 5, 11
Activate a layout	Tutorial 5
Modify viewports on a layout	Tutorial 5
Set the viewport properties so the geometry plots to scale	Tutorial 5
Add a title block to the layout	Tutorial 5
Manage output formats	Tutorial 5
Publish a drawing to a plotter, printer, or PDF file	Tutorial 5
Set printing and plotting options	Tutorial 5
Use the Page Setup Manager to apply plot settings to a layout	Tutorial 5

INTRODUCTION TO AUTOCAD®

1

Introduction

This tutorial introduces the fundamental operating procedures and drawing tools of AutoCAD 2027. It explains how to create a new drawing; draw lines, circles, and rectangles; and save a drawing to a new name. You will learn how to erase items and select groups of objects. This tutorial also explains how to add text to a drawing.

Starting

Launch the AutoCAD 2027 software. If you need assistance with this, refer to Getting Started 1 and 2.

The AutoCAD Screen

Figure 1.1 shows the AutoCAD application window. It should be open on your screen. When you first launch AutoCAD, the screen shows the Application icon, the Quick Access toolbar, and a button for creating new drawing tabs.

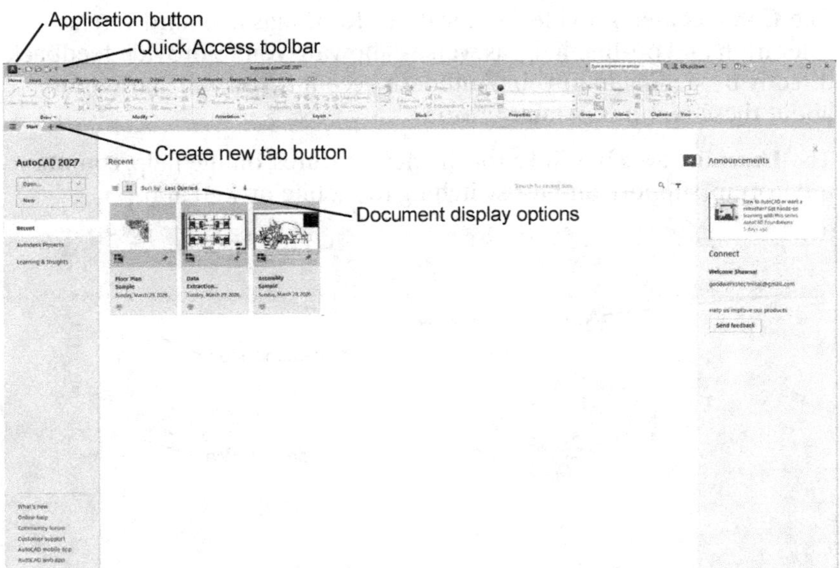

Figure 1.1 The Initial AutoCAD Application Window

When you launch the software, the screen shows the Start tab which has a clean new look in this version.

The **Open** button lets you lets you quickly find an existing drawing, sheet set, or sample drawings. The **New** button lets you begin a new drawing from a default template or from an existing drawing.

The central **Recent Documents** area lets you view and open recent files. Small buttons below the title for the Recent documents (Figure 1.2) let you change the style of that area from an image preview with details

Objectives

When you have completed this tutorial, you will be able to

1. Use the Ribbon to select commands.
2. Create new drawing files.
3. Work with multiple drawings.
4. Use the Help command.
5. Enter coordinates.
6. Draw lines, circles, and rectangles.
7. Erase objects.
8. Select objects using Window and Crossing.
9. Add and edit drawing text.
10. Save a drawing and transfer it from one drive to another.

Warning

If your screen does not look generally like Figure 1.4, verify that you configured the AutoCAD software properly. Screens in this book are shown with a white background for the best visibility. You may prefer to use other colors on your system. Refer to Getting Started 1 and 2 of this manual.

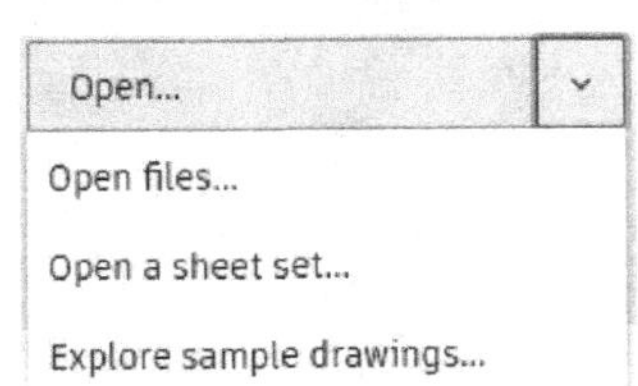

(the default) or a list. You can search within the recent documents, or list them by name rather than last open using the selections in this area.

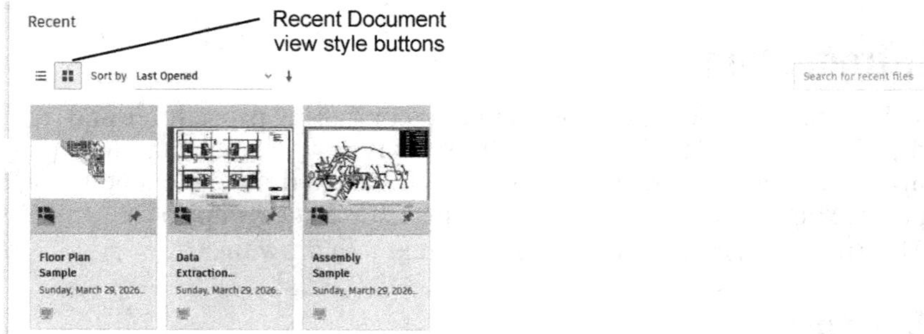

Figure 1.2 Recent Documents

*Click: each of the **Recent Document style buttons** to see the change in appearance of the recent documents panel. When you have finished return it to the default view showing the preview.*

The **Announcements** area shows information and messages. You can also close the panel with the X in its upper right corner. If you do not see it, click the red Announcements icon to show it.

The **Connect** area provides notifications for things like hardware acceleration and off-line help, as well as allowing you to provide feedback directly by signing in to your Autodesk account. You will learn more about these features in later tutorials.

The **Learning area** has links for the new features, online help, community forum, support, and for switching to mobile or web app.

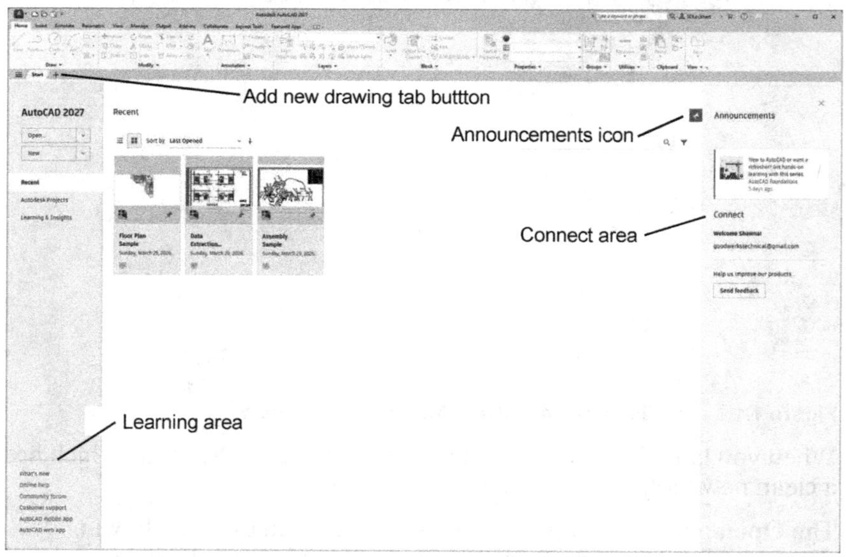

Figure 1.3 The AutoCAD Landing Page

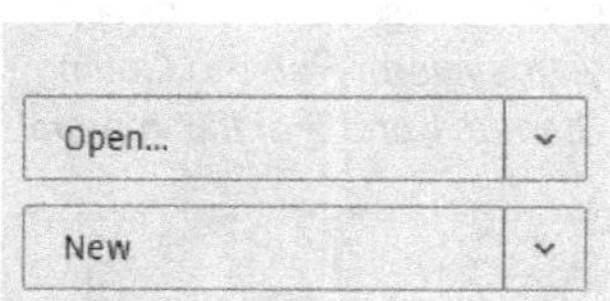

*Click: **New***

The screen changes to show the ribbon and a blank drawing (Figure 1.4). Next, familiarize yourself with the areas of the AutoCAD drawing screen.

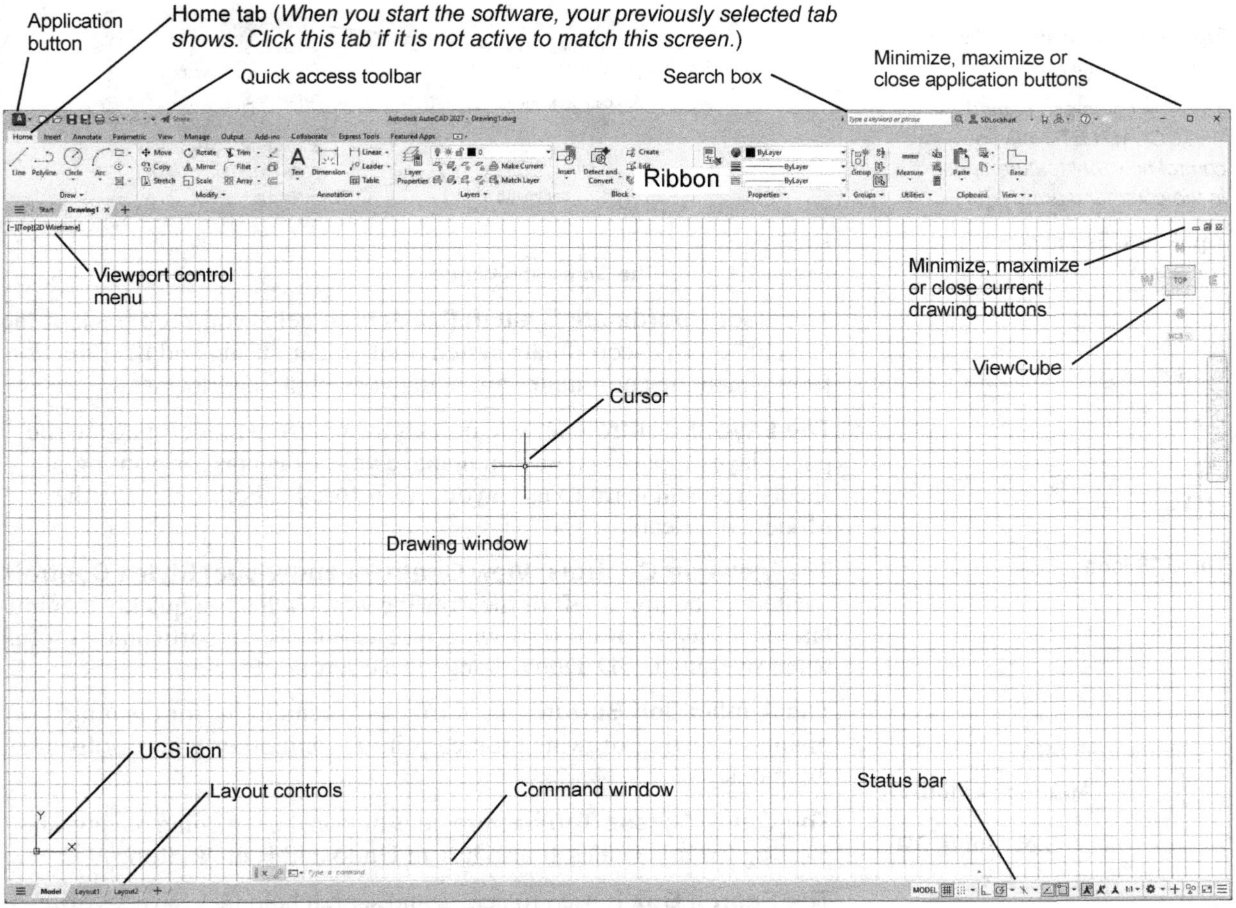

Figure 1.4 **The AutoCAD Drawing Window Main Features**

The Drawing Window is the central part of the screen, which you use to create and display drawings. The drawing's title bar appears above the blank area of the screen listing the drawing's name. *Windows control buttons* are located at the right of the title bar allowing you to minimize, maximize/tile, or close the drawing window.

The Graphics Cursor, or Crosshairs shows the location of your cursor in the graphics window. You use the graphics cursor to draw, select objects, or pick command items. The cursor's appearance depends on the command or option you select.

The Command Window (Figure 1.5) is usually located at the bottom of the screen. It is a *floating window* you can move anywhere on your screen.

As you start typing a command, the entry is auto-completed. The selection list shows commands that have the letters you typed. Command options also appear listed here.

You can use the small up triangle at its right to show command history. Pay close attention to the command window because that is where you are prompted to enter information or make selections.

Tip: *Check that the* **2D Drafting and Annotation** *workspace is selected. See page 6.*

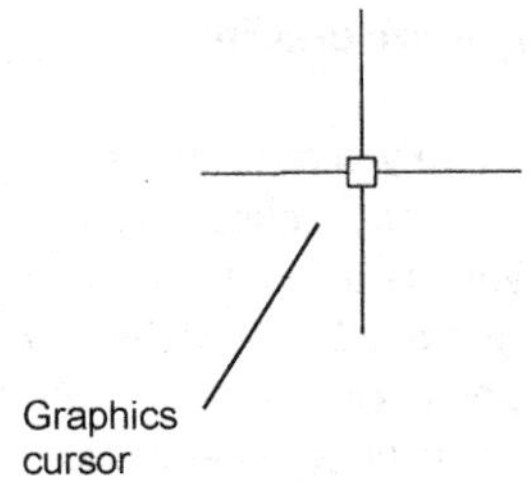

Tip: *Pressing F2 shows the full command history window.*

Tip: *The command named AUTOCOMPLETE lets you control how that feature appears in the command area.*

Tip: *Press [Esc] to cancel a command.*

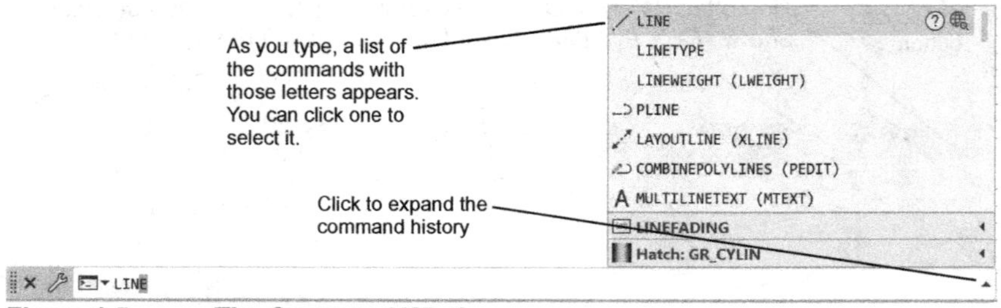

Figure 1.5 **The Command Window**

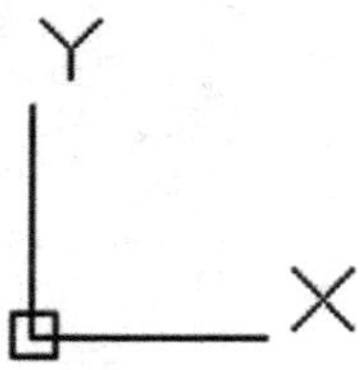

The UCS Icon

The User Coordinate System (UCS) Icon helps you keep track of the current X-, Y-, Z-coordinate system that you are using and the direction from which the coordinates are being viewed in 3D drawings.

The Layout Controls let you quickly switch from model space to the paper layout space, where you manage your drawings for printing on sheets. You will learn to use layouts in Tutorial 5. For now, leave the Model tab selected.

The Viewport Controls, View Controls, and Visual Styles Controls located at the upper left of the drawing window let you quickly manipulate the *viewport* or drawing window. These tools are particularly useful when working in 3D. Don't change these settings for now.

The Application Button is used to select menu items for opening, saving, exporting, drawing utilities, printing, and other typical software functions.

The Quick Access Toolbar provides buttons for opening, saving, and plotting (printing) files. It also has an Undo and Redo button.

The Search Box is used to access and search help files, save favorite search results, and access product information.

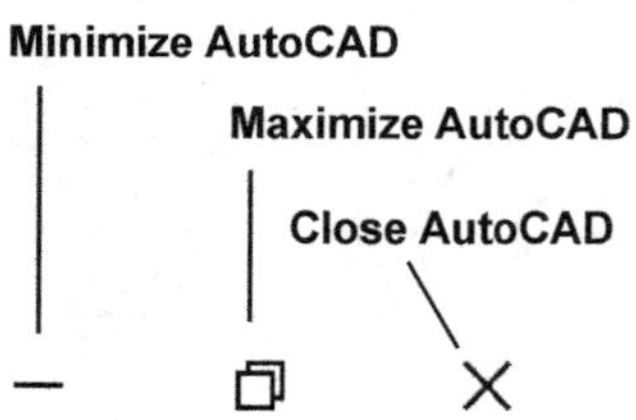

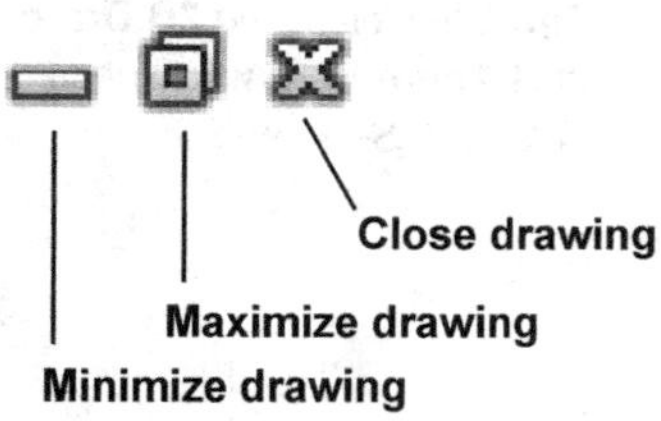

Minimize, maximize or close application buttons for the **AutoCAD software** are located in the upper right of the application window. Use these buttons to minimize, maximize or close the AutoCAD software.

Minimize, maximize or close buttons for the **drawing window** are located in the upper right of the drawing window. Use these buttons to minimize, maximize or close the drawing currently open.

The Status Bar

The Status Bar (Figure 1.6) at the bottom of the application window shows important settings and modes that may be in effect. The Customization item at the right of the status bar lets you pick which tools will appear.

The following are items that can be shown on the status bar: Coordinates, Model Space, Grid, Snap Mode, Infer Constraints, Dynamic Input, Ortho Mode, Polar Tracking, Isometric Drafting, 2D Object Snap, Lineweight, Transparency, Selection Cycling, 3D Object Snap, Dynamic UCS, Selection Filtering, Gizmo, Annotation Visibility, AutoScale, Annotation Scale, Workspace Switching, Annotation Monitor, Units, Quick Properties, Lock UI, Isolate Objects, Graphics Performance, and Clean Screen.

Tip: *When you are closing a drawing, double check to make sure you are using the drawing window close box. Accidentally choosing to close the AutoCAD application may cause you to lose unsaved work and takes time to restart the software.*

The buttons on the status bar turn these special modes on and off. When these modes are in effect, their buttons are highlighted.

Tip: *Switching on or off modes from the status bar changes the display and function of some commands. If you have trouble following the steps in these tutorials, make sure your status bar modes are set the same as those shown in the tutorial.*

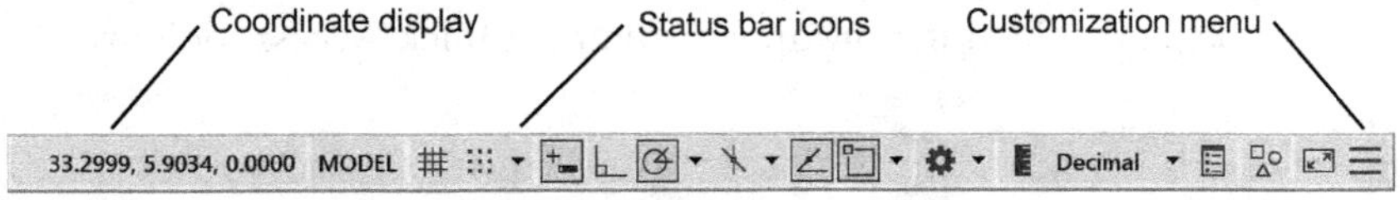

Figure 1.6 **The Status Bar and Coordinate Display**

Click the Customization button *(from the right of the status bar)*

The pop-up menu shows items you can select to show on the status bar.

Select: ***Coordinates, Model Space, Grid, Snap Mode, Dynamic Input, Ortho Mode, Polar Tracking, Object Snap Tracking, 2D Object Snap, AutoScale, Viewport Lock, Viewport Scale, Viewport Scale Sync, Workspace Switching, Units, Quick Properties, Isolate Objects, and Clean Screen*** *(so that they appear checked). Make sure all of the remaining items are unchecked.*

Click a location in the blank drawing area *(to remove the menu from the screen).*

Coordinates at the left of the status bar show the crosshairs' location as three numbers with the general form X.XXXX, Y.YYYY, and Z.ZZZZ. The specific numbers displayed on your screen tell you the location of your crosshairs.

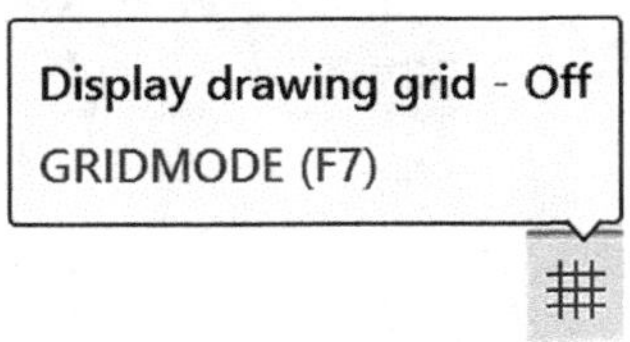

Figure 1.7 **Grid Button on the Status Bar**

Click the Grid button *to turn it off as shown in Figure 1.7*

Hover your mouse cursor over the Grid button but do not click *(to show the tool tip).*

A tip box appears with a description of the tool, its current state, command name, and shortcut key. Until you are familiar with the icons, these tips help you understand the tools and learn their shortcuts.

The Quick Access Toolbar

The Quick Access Toolbar (Figure 1.8) is used to select common commands, such as New, Open, Save, Save As, Open from Web, Save to Web, Plot, Undo, and Redo. Clicking the down-arrow button at its right allows you to select which commands are shown.

Figure 1.8 **The Quick Access Toolbar**

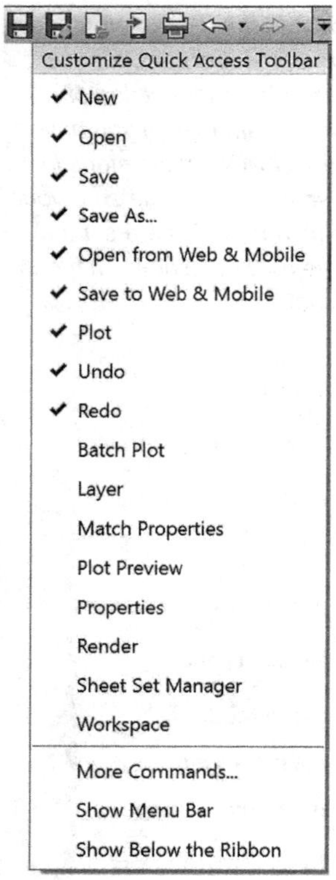

Click the down-arrow to show the customization options.

***Click Workspace** (if it is not already selected).*

The workspace selection now appears on the Quick Access toolbar.

Verify the workspace shown is Drafting and Annotation.

Workspaces make it easy to save your custom menu preferences. Different commands and tools will show in AutoCAD depending on the workspace selected. The ability to customize AutoCAD is great when you are working in a production environment, but it can make learning the software confusing when the tools are not where you expect them to be. If you are using a custom workspace, you will find it hard to match the steps in these tutorials. For now, you will use a standard workspace. In later tutorials you will learn how to customize your workspace.

The Ribbon

The Ribbon (Figure 1.9) is used to select commands and tools. It is grouped into *tabs* and *panels*, which include buttons for frequently used commands. (Right-clicking on the ribbon allows you to select which tabs and panels are shown there.)

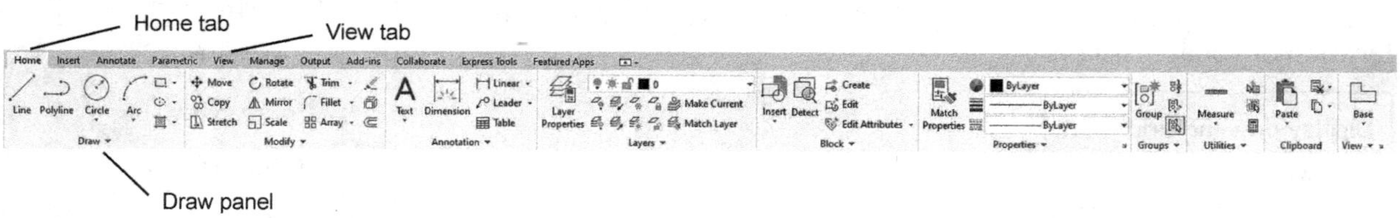

Figure 1.9 The Ribbon

Move the graphics cursor up into the Ribbon area.

Note that the cursor changes from the crosshairs to an arrow when it moves out of the graphics window.

Click on the View tab.

The ribbon changes to display a new set of panels used to select commands and tools for viewing your drawing as shown in Figure 1.10.

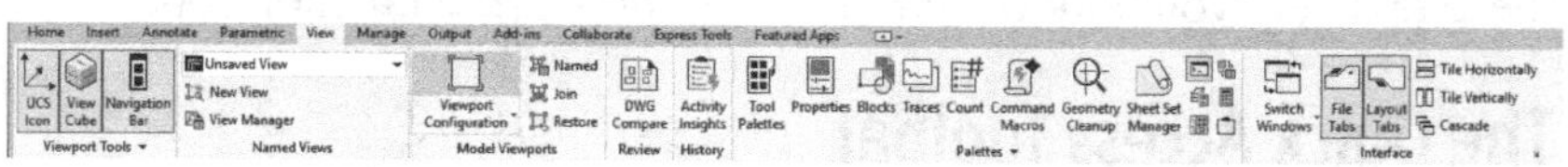

Figure 1.10 The View Tab

Tip: *Panels at the right of the ribbon automatically minimize as you resize your software window smaller. You may see minimized panels, which expand automatically when you move your cursor over them.*

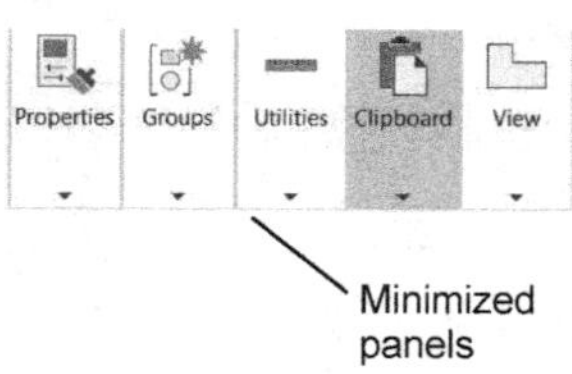

Click on the Home tab to show it on the ribbon.

Hover the arrow cursor over the Line button on the Draw panel, but do not click the mouse button.

After the arrow cursor remains over a button for a few seconds, the button's tool tip appears below it as shown in Figure 1.11.

If you are unsure about which command an icon represents, use the tool tip to help identify it. Leaving the cursor over the item even longer displays more detailed help for the command.

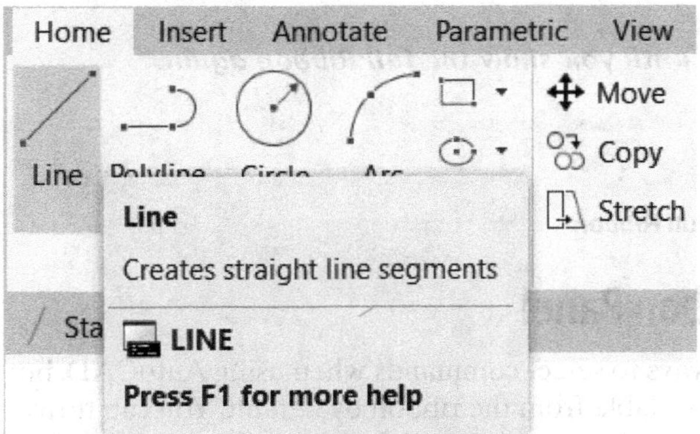

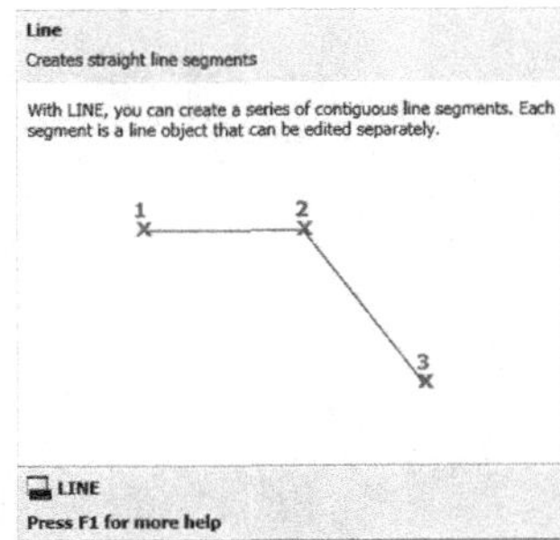

Figure 1.11 The Line Command Tool Tip

Move the arrow cursor over each button in turn to familiarize yourself with the buttons on the Draw panel.

The Ribbon can quickly be minimized to tabs, titles, buttons or cycled through these appearances using the tool shown in Figure 1.12. This tool is a toggle. Clicking it once changes the appearance of the Ribbon. Click it a second time to change the appearance of the Ribbon again.

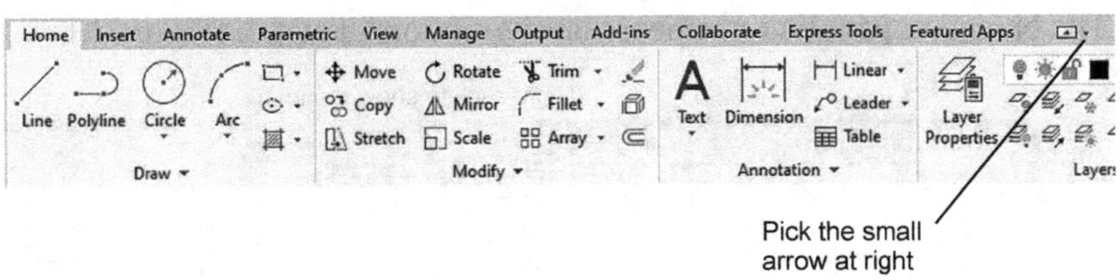

Figure 1.12 Expanding the Menu Choices for the Ribbon Appearance

Click: ***the small downward arrow at the right of the Ribbon tabs to expand the menu choices.***

Click: ***Minimize to Panel Buttons***

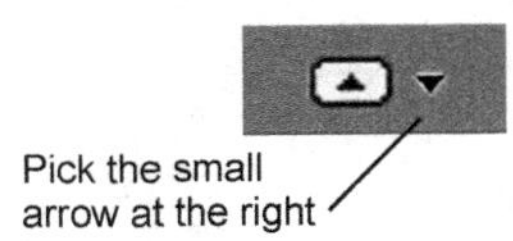

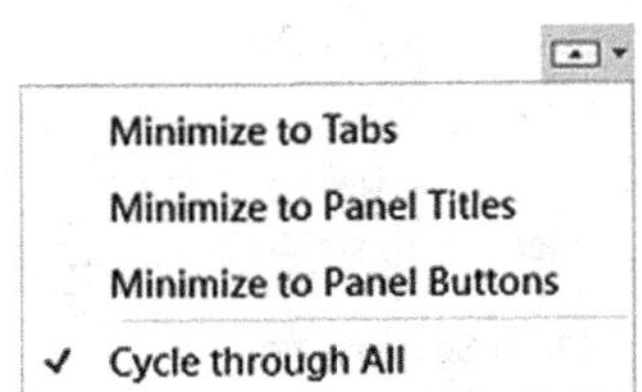

The Ribbon minimizes to a button for each tab as shown in Figure 1.13.

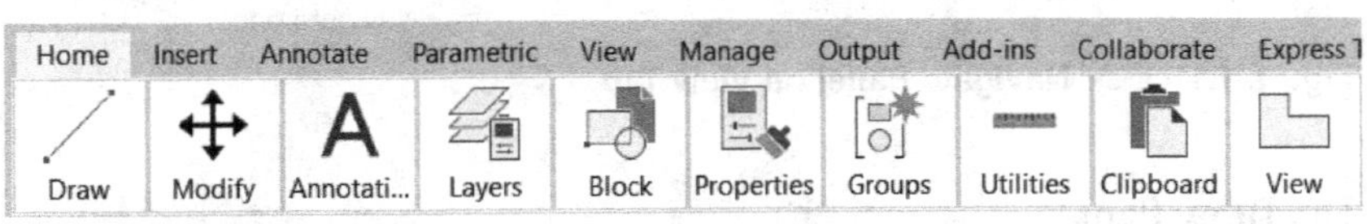

Figure 1.13 The Ribbon Minimized to Panel Buttons

Click: ***the small downward arrow at the right of the Ribbon tabs to expand the menu choices as shown in Figure 1.12.***

Click: ***Cycle through All***

Click: ***the left small arrow at the right of the Ribbon tabs to toggle the appearance of the Ribbon.***

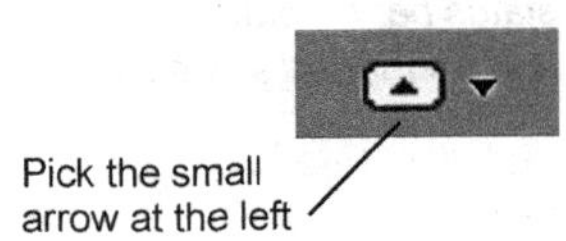

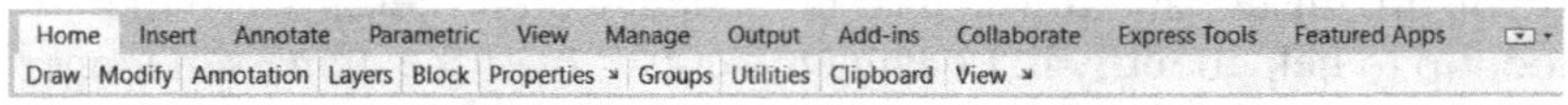

Figure 1.14 **The Ribbon Minimized to Titles**

Continue to click until you show the full Ribbon again.

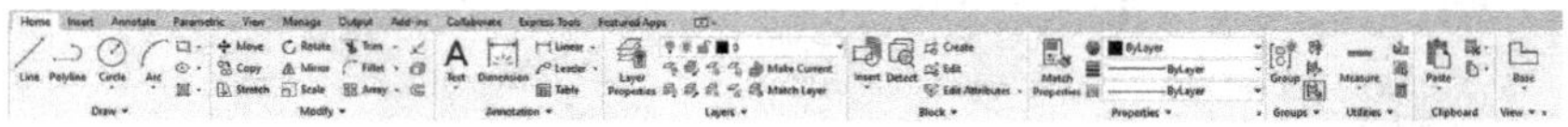

Figure 1.15 **The Full Ribbon**

Showing a Ribbon Panel

There are so many ways to select commands when using AutoCAD, but not all of them are available from the ribbon by default. You can turn on groups of commands that you find useful when you need them. Your customizations are saved in the user profile so that they are available the next time you launch AutoCAD.

Click: ***View tab*** *from the ribbon*

Right-click in the gray space at the right of the View tab (Figure 1.16)

Click: ***Show panels*** *from the context menu*

Click: ***Navigate***

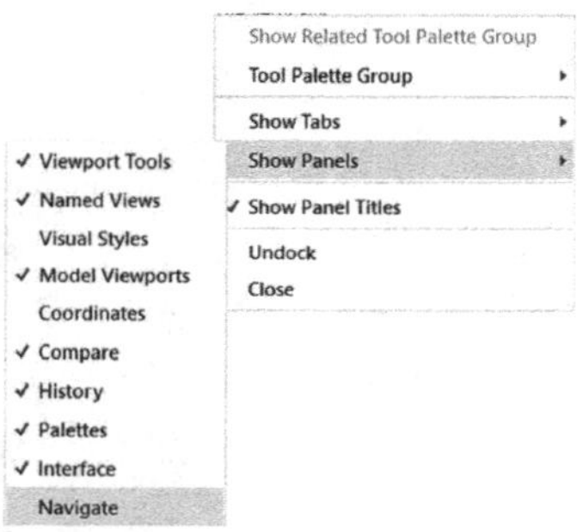

The Navigate panel now appears on the ribbon View tab (Figure 1.17).

Figure 1.16 **View Tab Context Menu**

Figure 1.17 **Navigate Panel on View Tab**

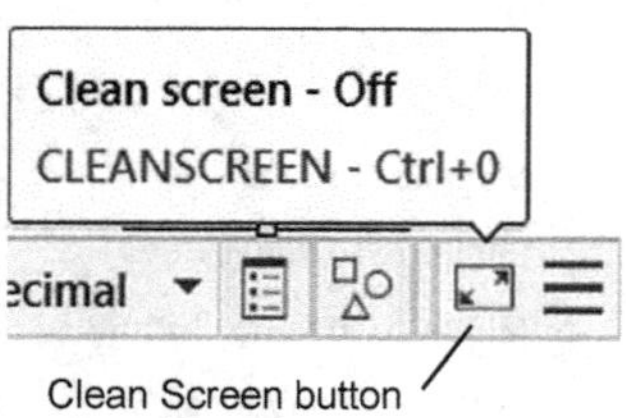

Tip: *Pick the Clean Screen button from the lower right of the status bar to remove the menus and go to a full screen look.*

The Draw Panel

The Draw panel (Figure 1.18) is on the Home tab of the Ribbon by default. The Draw panel provides commands to create new drawing objects, such as lines, circles and other drawing geometry. You also use it to create helices, insert hatch patterns, revision clouds and other objects.

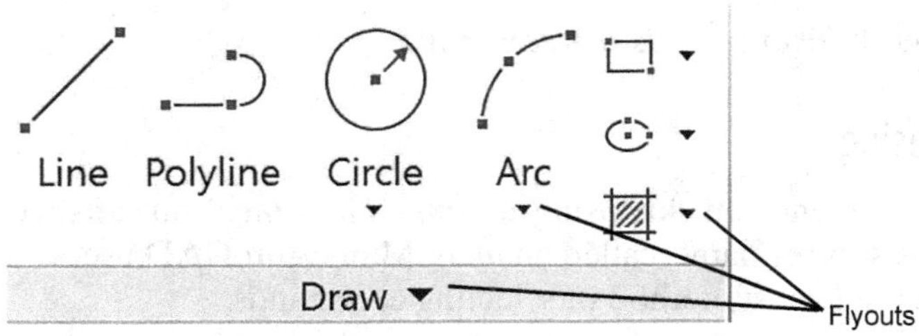

Figure 1.18 The Draw Tab

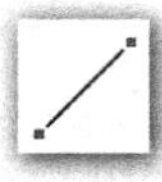

*Click: **Line***

The command window displays "LINE Specify first point:" indicating that the software is ready for you to select an endpoint to start your line.

*Click: **Dynamic Input button** from the status bar to turn it on, if it is not already on*

The Dynamic Input box appears near the cursor on the screen as shown in Figure 1.19. Dynamic input is a toggle. It may be useful when you are starting out to see the input boxes near the cursor. Toggle it off if it is in the way of your drawing.

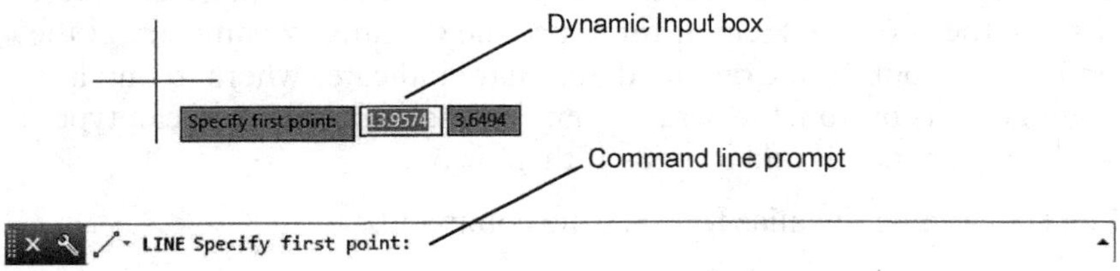

Figure 1.19 The Dynamic Input Box Appears Near the Cursor

Canceling Commands

You can easily cancel commands by pressing [Esc]. If you make a selection by mistake, press [Esc] to cancel it. Sometimes you may have to press [Esc] twice to cancel a command, depending on where you are in the command sequence.

*Press: **[Esc]** to cancel the Line command*

Tip: *If you drew some lines before canceling the command, they will not be erased. You can delete the lines by clicking them so they are selected and then pressing the Delete key on your keyboard.*

Typing Commands

You can type a command name or its shorter *alias* directly using *command prompt* in the command window. Keep in mind that many of the words on the tool tips are tool names, not command names. Only the actual command name or its alias may be typed to activate a command.

AutoCAD commands are not *case-sensitive;* you may type all capitals, capitals and lowercase, or all lowercase letters. As you type notice the list of likely commands appearing near the command window. As soon as you see the command name you want, you may click to select it. Try it next.

Command: ***LINE [Enter]***

Specify first point: ***[Esc]*** *cancels the command*

Command Aliasing

You can type commands quickly using *command aliasing.* You can give any command a shorter name, called an *alias.* Many AutoCAD users feel that this is the fastest method of selecting commands.

Many commands already have aliases assigned to them to help you get started. They are stored in the file *acad.pgp*, which is found in the folder you have set in your support files search path.

You can edit the file *acad.pgp* with a text editor and add lines with your own command aliases. (These lines take the form ALIAS, *COMMAND in the *acad.pgp* file.) After doing so, you can use the shortened name at the AutoCAD command prompt.

The commands in the margin are some for which aliases have already been created. When you need one of these commands, you can type its alias at the command prompt instead of the entire command name. To edit the *acad.pgp* file, click the Manage tab, then select Edit Aliases from the Customization panel.

Command	Alias
A	*ARC*
AA	*AREA*
AL	*ALIGN*
AR	*ARRAY*
B	*BLOCK*
C	*CIRCLE*
CH	*PROPERTIES*
CP	*COPY*
D	*DIMSTYLE*
DI	*DIST*
DIV	*DIVIDE*
E	*ERASE*
F	*FILLET*
G	*GROUP*
H	*HATCH*
I	*INSERT*
L	*LINE*
LA	*LAYER*
L	*LIST*
M	*MOVE*
MI	*MIRROR*
O	*OFFSET*
P	*PAN*
PE	*PEDIT*
PL	*PLINE*
PO	*POINT*
PR	*PROPERTIES*
R	*REDRAW*
RA	*REDRAWALL*
RE	*REGEN*
RO	*ROTATE*
SN	*SNAP*
SP	*SPELL*
SPL	*SPLINE*
T	*MTEXT*
TR	*TRIM*
UC	*UCSMAN*
UN	*UNITS*
W	*WBLOCK*
X	*EXPLODE*

This list shows only a few of the aliases available. For a more complete list, use the software Help or reference the Command Summary at the end of this book. The Command Summary indicates where to find a command, its button, the actual command name (which you can type to start the command) and its alias, if there is one.

Next, try typing the alias for the Line command.

Command: ***L [Enter]***

Specify first point: ***[Esc]***

There are many different ways to select each command. After you have worked through the tutorials in this book, decide which methods work best for you. While you are working through the tutorials, however, be sure to select the commands from the locations specified. The subsequent command prompts and options may differ, depending on how you selected the command.

Tip: *If you select a command by accident, press the [Esc] key on your keyboard to cancel the command.*

Dynamic Entry

Another way to give input and select command options is to enter values and options using the dynamic input boxes that appear near the cursor location. Dynamic input allows you to type input at your pointer location, specify dimensions during many draw commands and to select from command option prompts.

Right-click: ***Dynamic Input*** *button on the status bar (see Figure 1.20)*

Click: ***Dynamic Input Settings...***

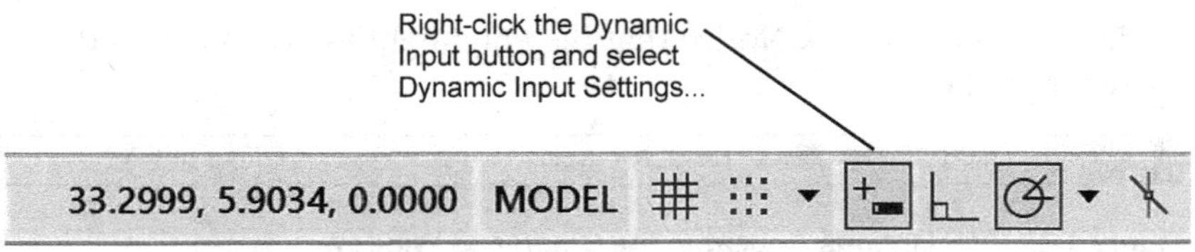

Figure 1.20 Dynamic Input Button and Menu

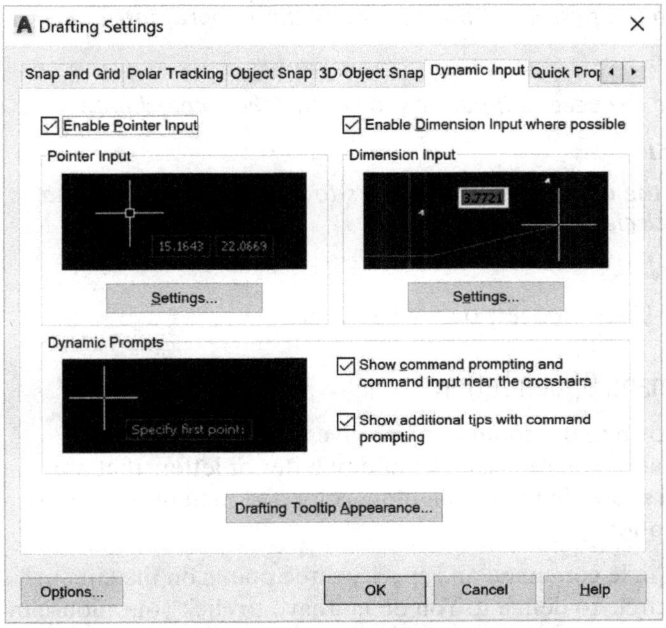

Figure 1.21 Drafting Settings Dynamic Input Tab

The Drafting Settings dialog box appears on your screen with the Dynamic Input tab uppermost as shown in Figure 1.21. You can use this dialog box to customize which dynamic input options are shown at the cursor location. Do not change any settings now.

*Click: **Cancel** to close the dialog box*

Check to see that the Dynamic Input button on your status bar is on.

Command: ***C [Enter]***

You should see the Circle command prompts appear on your screen along with the dynamic input boxes at the cursor location as shown in Figure 1.22.

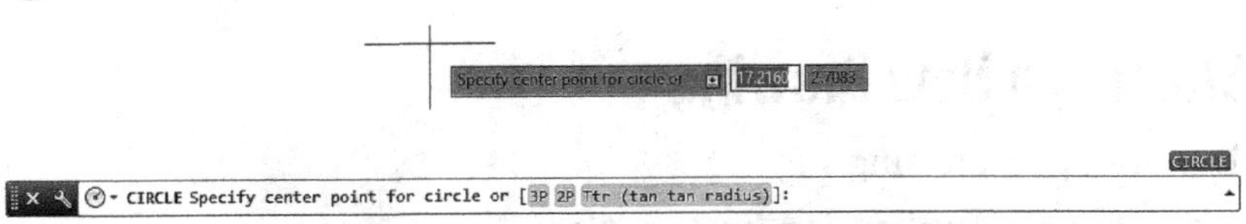

Figure 1.22 Circle Command Prompts and Dynamic Input Box

Once you have selected a command, a number of options may appear at the command prompt. For the circle command the options are 3P, 2P and Ttr (tangent, tangent, radius).

The options for the circle command appear in the command window

Tip: *When you see the [Enter] key in an instruction in this manual, you must press [Enter], (sometimes labeled Return) on your keyboard, to finalize the command or response. A quick shortcut is to press the space bar on your keyboard or click the right mouse button and select Enter from the menu that pops up. When you are entering text during a text command you must press the actual [Enter] key.*

as shown in Figure 1.23. Notice that they highlight as you position the cursor over them.

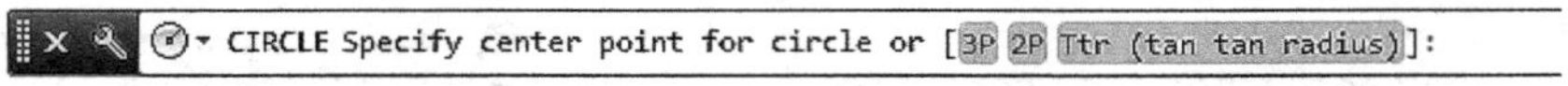

Figure 1.23 Options Appear in the Command Window

Tip: *During these tutorials take care to select the commands as directed, otherwise you may see different prompts than those in the directions.*

Click: ***2P from the options that appear in the command window***

Type: ***10 into the first input box to specify the x-coordinate***

Press: ***[Tab]***

Type: ***10 into the second input box to specify the y-coordinate***

Press: ***[Enter]***

Type: ***8 into the input box that appears to specify the second end-point of the circle's diameter***

Press: ***[Enter]***

The completed Circle appears on your screen.

Typing a Command Option Letter

The prompt shown in the command line gives the options for the selected command. You can type the option letter or letters that are capitalized and shown in the highlighting color and then press [Enter] to select that option.

Next, use the Circle command and specify three points on the circumference of the circle to define it. You do not have to click your mouse in the command area before you type. It is always ready for input.

Tip: *The status bar buttons appear gray when they are off. When they are turned on they appear in the highlighting color (the default is blue).*

Click: ***to turn off the Dynamic Input button on your status bar.***

Command: ***C [Enter]***

Specify center point for circle or [3P/2P/Ttr (tan tan radius)]: ***3P [Enter]***

Specify first point on circle: ***pick a point from the screen***

Specify second point on circle: ***pick a second point from the screen***

Specify third point on circle: ***pick a third point from the screen***

A second circle appears on your screen.

Next, you will practice with multiple drawing windows by creating a second drawing. Do not close this circle drawing.

Starting a New Drawing

To start a new drawing,

Tip: *You can also select New from the Quick Access toolbar.*

Click: ***Application button, New***

The Select template dialog box (shown in Figure 1.24) allows you to select a pre-existing template file as a starting point for the new drawing. A *template* can contain useful settings, borders, and other items that then become a part of the new drawing. A number of standard templates are available and you can create your own from any Auto-CAD drawing.

You will learn more about creating and using templates in Tutorial 5. The default option, *acad.dwt*, is a template with minimal settings for starting an essentially blank drawing.

Tip: *Clicking New directly opens the Select template dialog box. Notice there is also a flyout triangle indlcating more selections. Hovering your mouse on New will show options for Drawing or Sheet Set. You may also start the Select Template dialog box by selecting Drawing from this expanded menu.*

Tip: *Windows operating system settings control how you view file extensions (like the .dwt for template files). Use the Windows Explorer Tools menu to pick Folder options and then View to see where you can change the settings.*

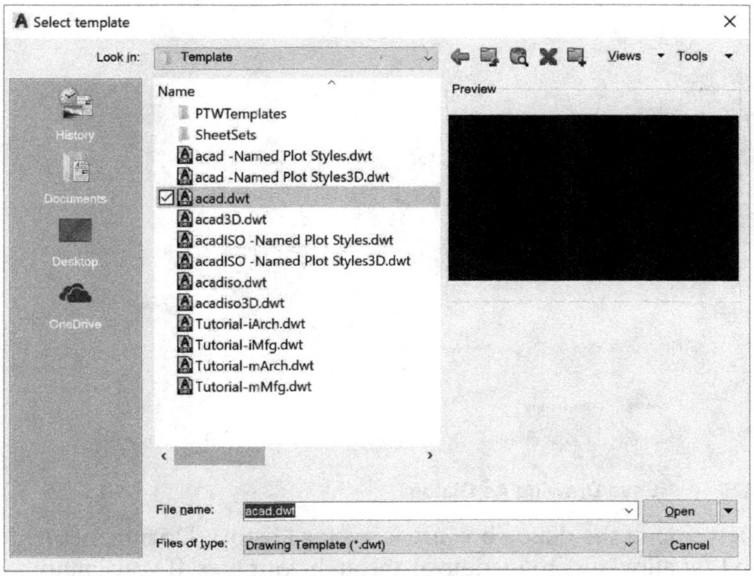

Figure 1.24 **Select Template Dialog Box**

Click: ***acad.dwt*** *(if it is not already highlighted), then click* ***Open***

Tip: *Double-clicking on a file name or template name opens it in one step.*

Naming Drawing Files

After the Select template dialog box closes, you should see the name of the new drawing, *Drawing2.dwg*, in the title bar at the top of the application window. Next, you will save the drawing and name it *shapes.dwg*.

Click: ***Application button, Save***

The Save Drawing As dialog box shown in Figure 1.25 appears, which you can use to name your file and select the drive and folder.

Type: ***SHAPES***

AutoCAD follows the Windows rules for naming a file. Names may include as many characters and/or numbers as you choose, along with other characters: underscores (_), dashes (-), commas (,), and periods (.). However, forward slashes (/) and backward slashes (\) aren't allowed in the drawing name.

Tip: *Backslash (/) is used to indicate a path or folder. Remember directory is another name for a folder.*

Drawing files are automatically assigned *file extension .dwg*, so typing the extension is unnecessary. Use names that are descriptive of the drawing being created to make recognizing your completed drawings easier.

Drawing names can include a drive and folder specification. If you don't specify a drive, the drawing is saved in the *default directory.* Keeping your files organized so that you can retrieve them later is an important aspect of using CAD. In Getting Started 1 of this manual, you should have already created a folder, called *work*, where you will save your drawing files.

Tip: *It is not generally good practice to include periods (.) or spaces in your AutoCAD drawing names. Periods are generally used to divide the file name from the file extension (for example, shapes.dwg). Using a period within the name of the file may cause confusion with the extension and can make it difficult to use the file with other operating system versions, or inside other AutoCAD drawings.*

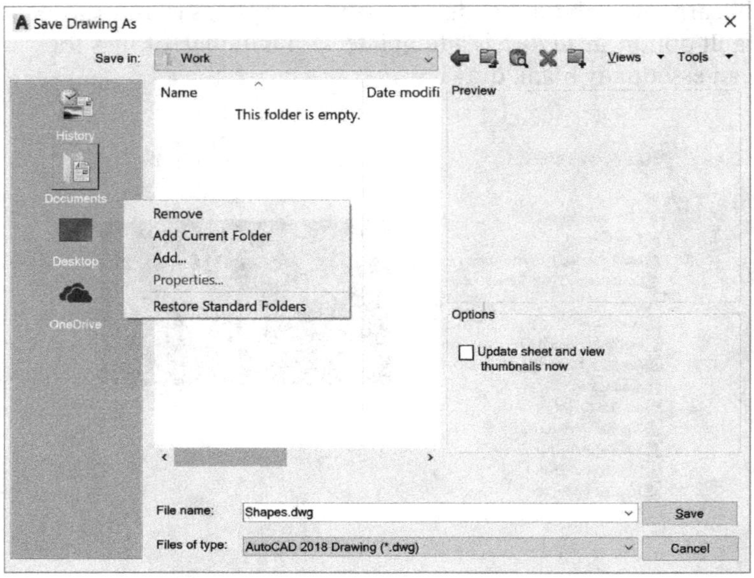

Figure 1.25 Save Drawing As Dialog

On the left side of the dialog box are icons for History, Documents, and Desktop that allow you to maneuver through your files. If you cannot see the full set of icons, use the scroll bars to enlarge the Save Drawing As window. If necessary, click the Desktop icon and use the resources there to help you browse to the folder where you want to store your files.

Tip: *When a drawing has not been saved previously, the Save command allows you to specify the filename, similar to using SaveAs.*

Navigate to your ***work*** *folder*

Right-click: ***in the folders area at the left of the dialog box***

Click: ***Add Current Folder*** *so your folder appears on the list*

Click: ***Save***

This action returns you to the drawing editor, where you can work on your drawing, *shapes.dwg.* Unless you are using a different drive or working directory on your system, the entire default name of your drawing is *\work\shapes.dwg.* Note that *shapes.dwg* now appears in the title bar as the current file name. Depending on your system, the *.dwg* extension may not show up in the title bar; however, AutoCAD recognizes it as such.

Working with Multiple Drawings

You should now have two open drawings: *Shapes,* the drawing you just created, and *Drawing1*, the previous drawing, where you drew circles using the 2P and 3P options of the Circle command. The open drawings show as tabs just below the ribbon as you see in Figure 1.26. You can click on a drawing's tab to make it the active drawing. You can also click the tab with the (+) plus sign to quickly start a new drawing. The Start tab returns you to the starting screen.

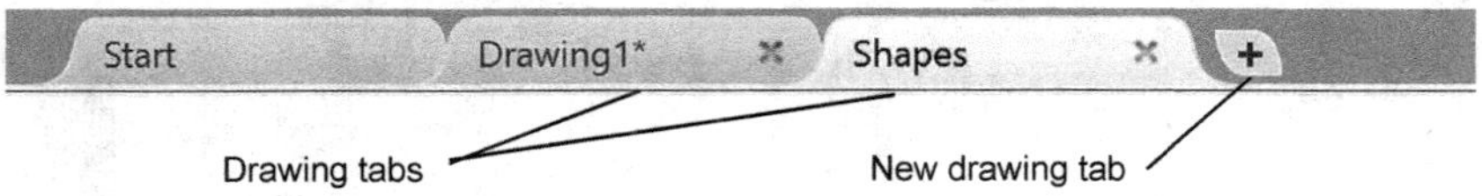

Figure 1.26 Multiple Drawing Tabs

*Click: **Drawing1** to make it active*

Drawing1.dwg is now the "top" active drawing window. Its name is now in the AutoCAD title bar. You can show both Shapes.dwg and *Drawing1.dwg* at the same time. You can use the Model Viewports panel from the ribbon View tab to tile the drawings *horizontally* or *vertically*, or cascade the drawings so that they appear in a neat stack. To do this,

*Click: **View tab** from the ribbon*

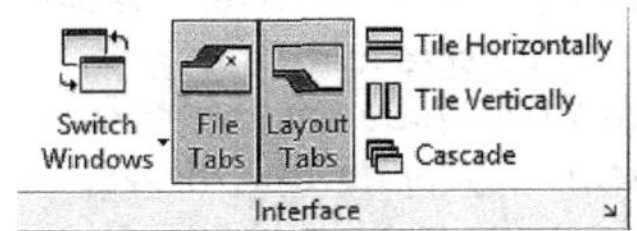

 *Click: **Tile Vertically button** from the Interface panel*

Both drawings now appear on your screen arranged side by side vertically as shown in Figure 1.27. If the Start tab shows, use its minimize window button to shrink it down.

Next you will make *shapes.dwg* the active drawing. The border and title bar of the active drawing appear darker.

*Click: **on the title bar for shapes.dwg***

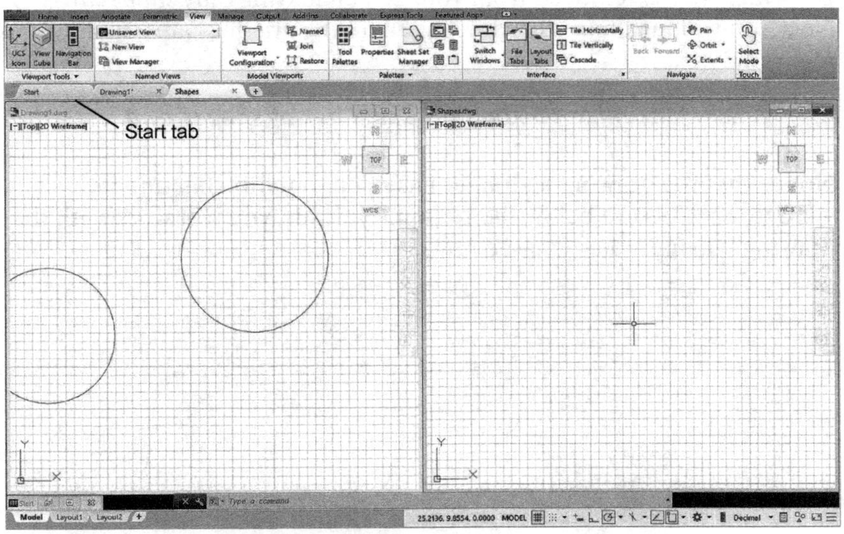

Figure 1.27 Two Drawings Tiled Vertically

Tip: *You may have to minimize the Start pane if it is showing when your drawings are tiled.*

Tip: *You can cut, or copy and paste objects from one drawing window to another.*

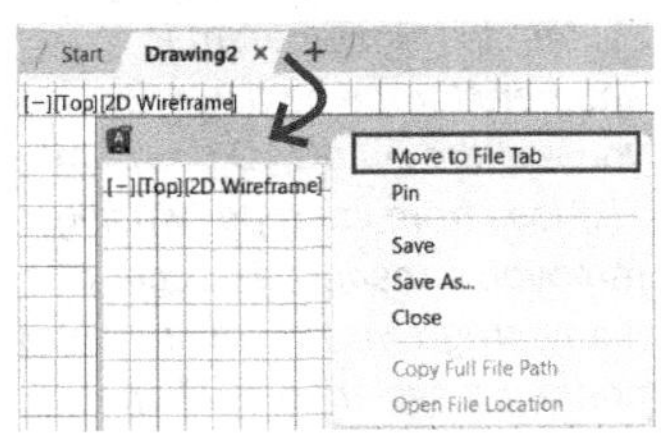

Tip: *You can drag drawing windows from the file tab to float them on your screen. Right-click on a floated window title bar to show the short-cut menu. You can use this to return the drawing file back to the file tab, or pin it in front of the other drawing(s). Cutting and pasting between windows can save you lots of time.*

 *Click: **Cascade button from the View tab Window panel***

The drawings now appear stacked and you can see the window controls for each drawing as shown in Figure 1.28.

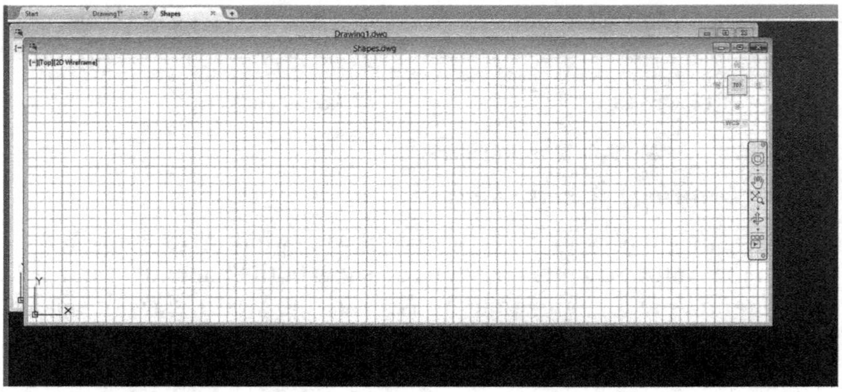

Figure 1.28 **Cascaded Drawings**

Next you will close Drawing1 by clicking its Windows Close button. Make sure not to close the application window.

*Click: **Drawing1** so that it becomes active*

 *Click: **Close button** for Drawing1.dwg*

At the prompt, "Save changes to *Drawing1.dwg*?",

*Click: **No***

Drawing1.dwg is removed from your screen leaving only *shapes.dwg*. Next you will maximize this drawing to fill the graphics area as shown in Figure 1.29.

 *Click: **Maximize button** in the title bar of shapes.dwg*

Notice that the drawing no longer has a separate title bar and its window controls are below the ribbon. Typically, you will work with the drawing maximized as you see now.

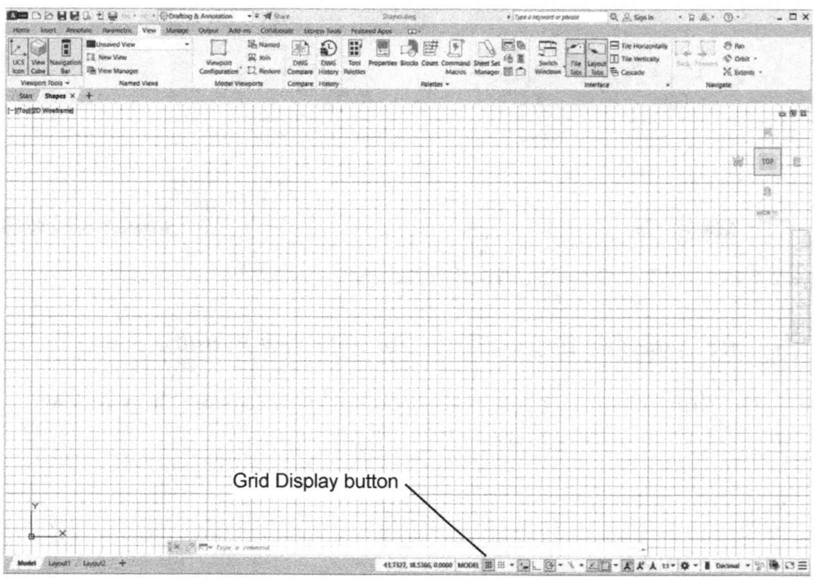

Figure 1.29 **Shapes Drawing Maximized to Fill Screen**

Tip: *If you cannot open your drawing for use with the AutoCAD program because it is corrupted, you may be able to recover it with the selection Application icon, Drawing Utilities, Recover from the menu bar.*

Warning *Saving a drawing directly to a removable USB drive can lead to problems. If you named your drawing so that it is stored on a removable disk, be sure to exit the AutoCAD program before you remove your device. Always leave the same memory device in the drive for the entire AutoCAD session. Otherwise, you can end up with part of your drawing not saved, which will result in an unrecoverable, corrupted drawing file.*

As you create a drawing, more and more data are stored in the drawing file. If the file size exceeds the remaining capacity of a disk, a FATAL ERROR may occur, resulting in the loss of the drawing file. To prevent problems with files that may become too large for your removable storage media, create all drawings on the hard drive or a network drive and then use your operating system to transfer them to another storage device after you exit the AutoCAD program. File loss from improperly using removable media can occur in many programs and even some operating system operations.

Tip: *Drawings may also be minimized or maximized. Minimized drawings appear at the bottom of the drawing window. Use the buttons on the title bar of the minimized drawing to maximize it if needed.*

Using Grid

Adding a grid to the graphics window gives you a helpful reference for drawing. A *grid* is a background of regularly spaced lines or dots. The grid does not show up in your drawing when you print. The grid is a toggle button, so clicking it when it is on will turn it off, and vice-versa.

Click: ***Display drawing grid*** *button (from the status bar or press [F7])*

The grid disappears on your screen (or appears if it was already off).

Click: ***Display drawing grid*** *button (to turn the grid on)*

The Grid Display button should now be highlighted to let you know that the grid is turned on. (At times the grid may be too large or small to be visible.)

You can also type the Grid command which turns it on and shows you options for setting the grid spacing.

Command: ***GRID [Enter]***

The prompt displays the options available for the command. The default option, in this case <0.5000>, appears within angle brackets. Pressing [Enter] accepts the default selection shown in the angled brackets.

To set the size of a grid, you type in the numerical value of the spacing and then press [Enter].

Specify grid spacing(X) or [ON/OFF/Snap/Major/aDaptive/Limits/Follow/Aspect] <0.5000>: ***1 [Enter]***

Notice that the grid in the drawing window changes to a spacing with grid lines 1 unit apart.

Using Zoom

The Zoom command enlarges or reduces areas of the drawing on your screen. It is different from the Scale command, which actually makes the selected items larger or smaller in your drawing database. Use Zoom when you want to enlarge something on the screen so that you see the details clearly. You can also zoom out so objects appear smaller to fit on your display.

Using Zoom All

The *Zoom All* option displays the *drawing limits* or shows all of the drawing objects on the screen, whichever is larger. Zoom All is located on the Zoom flyout on the View tab Navigate panel.

Click: ***Zoom, All*** *from the Navigate panel on the View tab*

Your screen should look like Figure 1.30, which shows a background grid drawn with 1-unit spacing.

Tip: *The flyouts show the last button you selected as the upper button. This is done to make it quick to reselect commands you use frequently. It can be confusing at first.*

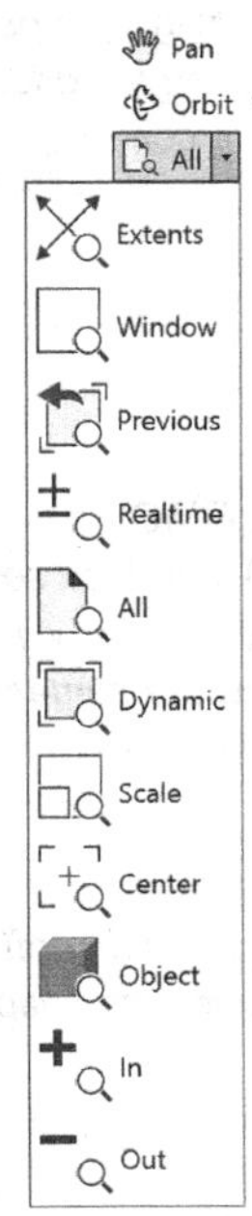

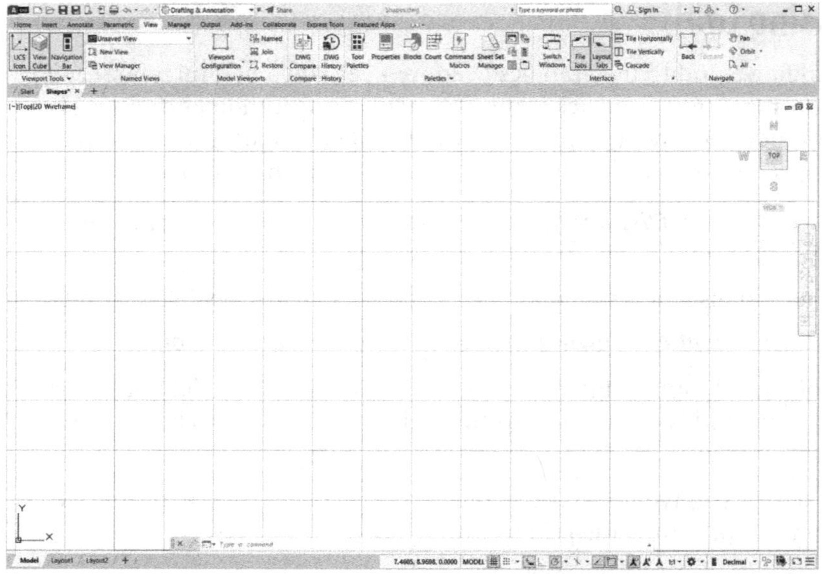

Figure 1.30

Using Snap Mode

When *Snap Mode* is on, your cursor jumps to the specified intervals. This is helpful for locating objects or distances in a drawing. If each jump on the snap interval were 0.5 unit (horizontally or vertically only, not diagonally), you could draw a line 2.00 units long by moving the cursor four snap intervals. To be useful, align the snap spacing with the grid size so it is the same as the grid spacing, at half the grid spacing, or some other even fraction of the grid spacing. Since the grid spacing is now set to 1, you will accept the snap default value of <0.5000> resulting in a snap increment that is one-half of the grid spacing.

Tip: *The Legacy option of the Snap command lets you select to use the older snap behavior where the cursor always jumps to the snap interval on the grid, whether you have a command active or not.*

Command: ***SNAP [Enter]***

Snap spacing or [ON/OFF/Aspect/Legacy/Style/Type] <0.5000> : ***[Enter]***

Note that Snap Mode is highlighted on the status bar to let you know that Snap is in effect. Once you start a command, instead of the smooth movement that you saw previously, the crosshairs jump or "snap" from point to point on the snap spacing.

Command: ***L [Enter]*** *(the alias for the Line command)*

Specify first point: ***move the cursor around on the screen***

Notice the cursor now jumps to stay on the snap interval.

Tip: *If you set the GRID spacing to 0.0000, and then set the SNAP, the grid spacing will automatically follow the same spacing as Snap Mode.*

Grid and Snap Toggles

Tip: *Pressing [Ctrl]-G or [F7] also toggles the grid on and off; [Ctrl]-B or [F9] toggles the snap function.*

You can quickly turn Grid Display and Snap on and off by clicking their buttons on the status bar. If their buttons on the status bar appear *highlighted* they are on; otherwise they are off. (If you can't tell, hover your mouse cursor over the button to show its tool tip where on/off is also listed.)

Each button on the status bar acts as a *toggle*: that is, clicking it once turns the function on; clicking it a second time turns the function off.

You can toggle Grid and Snap on and off during other commands.

Click: ***Snap Mode*** *button*

Now move the crosshairs around on the screen. Note that they have been released from the snap constraint. To turn Snap on again,

Click: ***Snap Mode*** *button*

The crosshairs jump from snap location to snap location again.

Click: ***Grid Display*** *button*

The grid disappears from your screen, but the snap constraint remains. To show the grid again,

Click: ***Grid Display*** *button*

Notice how the command window keeps a record of all past commands. You should still see the prompt for the line command.

Specify first point: ***press [Esc] to cancel the command.***

Tip: *You must have a command active to notice the snap behavior unless you set the Snap, Legacy option.*

Drafting Settings

You can also adjust Snap and Grid using the Drafting Settings dialog.

Right-click: ***Snap button*** *to show the context menu*

Click: ***Snap Settings***

The Drafting Settings dialog box appears on your screen as shown in Figure 1.31. The Snap and Grid tab should appear on top. You will learn about Polar Tracking and Object Snap in later tutorials.

Type: ***.25 into the Snap X spacing input box***

The Y Spacing box automatically changes to match the X Spacing box when you click in the Snap Y Spacing input box. If you want unequal spacing for X and Y, you can change the Y spacing separately.

Click: ***OK*** *(to exit from the dialog box)*

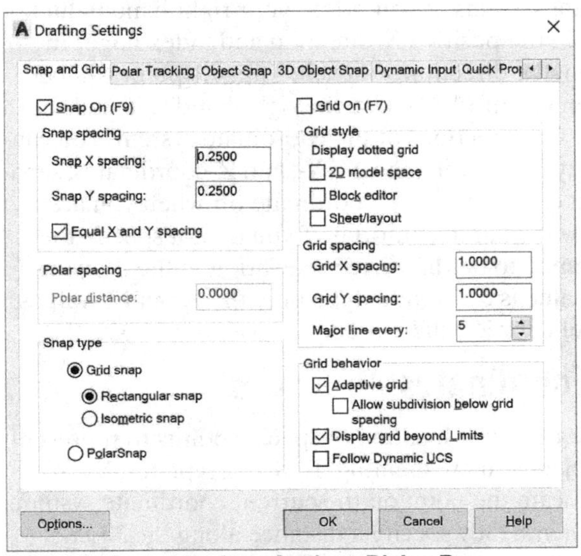

Figure 1.31 **Drafting Settings Dialog Box**

Tip: *Pressing [Enter] automatically closes the Drafting Settings dialog box. To quickly set a new snap or grid increment, type the value in the appropriate input box and then press [Enter] to close the dialog box.*

Using Line

The Line command draws straight lines between endpoints that you specify. For the next sequence of commands, you will use the ribbon Home tab Draw panel to select the Line command. (The toolbars, panels and menus are similar to spoken English. This is helpful when you are trying to remember where commands are located. For example, you might say, "I want to draw a line.") When selecting the Line command, be sure to click the button that shows dots at both endpoints. This icon indicates that the command draws a line between the two points selected. You can continue drawing lines from point to point until you press [Enter] to end the command.

Verify that the status bar Dynamic Input, Object Snap, Orthomode, Object Snap Tracking, Polar Tracking are turned* OFF.** ***Only Grid and Snap should be turned on.

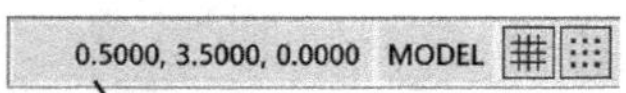

Coordinates may display at the left of the status bar. Right-click and use the context menu to change between absolute, relative, geographic and specific modes during commands.

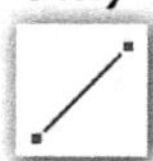

Click: ***Line button*** *(from the ribbon Home tab)*

You are prompted for the starting point of the line. You can answer prompts requesting the input of a point:

- By moving the cursor into the graphics window and clicking to choose a screen location (Grid and Snap help locate specific points.)
- By entering X-, Y-, and Z-coordinate values for the point

Tip: *If you don't see the coordinate display, check the customization options for your status bar. Refer to page 4.*

Entering Coordinates

Your drawing geometry is stored using *World Coordinates*, which is the AutoCAD default *Cartesian coordinate system*, where X-, Y-, and *Z-coordinate values* specify locations in your drawing. The UCS icon near the bottom left corner of your screen shows the positive X- and positive Y-directions on the screen. The default orientation of the Z-axis is as though in front of the monitor are positive values and inside the monitor are negative values. The AutoCAD software uses the right-hand rule for coordinate systems. If you orient your right hand palm up and point your thumb in the positive X-direction and index finger in the positive Y-direction, the direction your other fingers point will be the positive Z-direction (Figure 1.32). Use the right-hand rule and the UCS icon to figure out the directions of the coordinate system. You can specify a point explicitly by entering the X-, Y-, and Z-coordinates, separated by a comma. You can leave the Z-coordinate off when you are drawing in 2D, as you will be in this tutorial. If you do not specify the Z-coordinate, it is assumed to be the current elevation in the drawing, for which the default value is 0. For now, type only the X- and Y-values, and the default value of 0 for Z will be used.

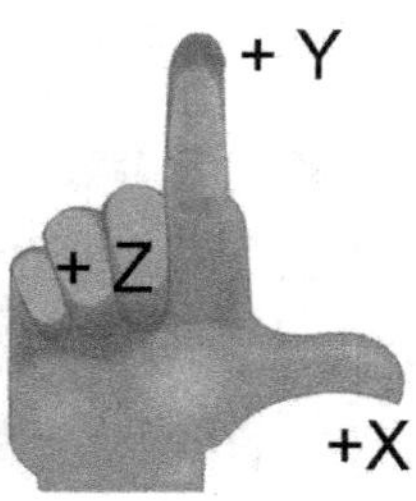

Figure 1.32

Using Absolute Coordinates

You often need to type the exact location of specific points to represent the geometry of the object you are creating. To do so, type the X-, Y-, and Z-coordinates to locate the point on the current coordinate system. Called *absolute coordinates*, they specify a distance along the X-, Y-,

Z-axes from the *origin* (or point (0, 0, 0) of the coordinate system).

Resume use of the Line command and use absolute coordinates to specify endpoints for the line you will draw. (Restart the Line command if you do not see the Specify first point: prompt.)

Specify first point: ***5.26,5.37 [Enter]***

As you move your cursor, you will see a line rubberbanding from the point you typed to the current location of your cursor. The next prompt asks for the endpoint of the line.

Specify next point or [Undo]: ***8.94,5.37 [Enter]***

After you enter the second point, the line appears on the screen. The rubberband line continues to stretch from the last endpoint to the current location of the cursor, and you are prompted for another point. This feature allows lines to be drawn end to end. Continue as follows:

Specify next point or [Undo]: ***8.94,8.62 [Enter]***

Specify next point or [Close/Undo]: ***5.26,8.62 [Enter]***

The Close option of the Line command joins the last point drawn to the first point drawn during that instance of the Line command. To close the figure, you will type C in response to the prompt.

Specify next point or [Close/Undo]: ***C [Enter]***

Drawing Using Grid and Snap

Use the grid and snap settings to draw another rectangle to the right of the one you just drew, as shown in Figure 1.33.

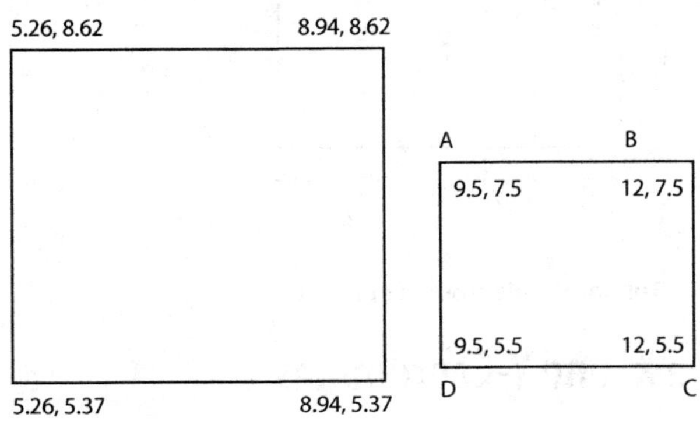

Figure 1.33

Click: ***Line button***

On your own, choose the starting point on the grid by moving the cursor to point A (Figure 1.33) and clicking the mouse. Use the coordinate display on the status bar to help you find the points.

Create the 2.5 horizontal line by moving the cursor 10 snap increments to the right and clicking to select point B.

Complete the rectangle by drawing a vertical line 8 snap increments (2.00 long) to point C and another horizontal line 10 snap increments (2.5 long) to point D.

Use the Close option to complete the rectangle, then press [Enter] to end the Line command.

Tip: *When typing in coordinates, enter only commas between them. Do not enter a space between the comma and the following coordinate of a coordinate pair because a space has the same effect as [Enter].*

Tip: *Recall that you can press the spacebar to enter commands quickly.*

Tip: *If you enter a wrong point while still in the Line command, you can back up one endpoint at a time with the Undo option by typing the letter U and pressing [Enter].*

Warning: *Undo functions differently if you pick it as a command. If you select Undo at the command prompt, you may undo entire command sequences. If necessary, you can use Redo to return something that has been undone.*

Tip: *The default setting displays an "adaptive" grid. If you set a grid size that is smaller than could be seen on the display, the grid is adapted to show larger subdivisions. To turn on or off the adaptive grid feature, type the Grid command at the prompt.*

Command: grid [Enter]
Specify grid spacing(X) or [ON/OFF/Snap/Major/aDaptive/Limits/Follow/Aspect] <0.0010>: **D [Enter]**
Turn adaptive behavior on [Yes/No] <Yes>: N [Enter]
turns off the adaptive grid.

Tip: *You can also click the Close option in the command prompt, instead of typing "C".*

Tip: *Be sure that Snap is highlighted on the status bar. If it is not, pick Snap Mode on the status bar or press [F8] to turn it on.*

Using Last Point

The software remembers the last point that you specified. Often you will need to specify a point that is exactly the same as the preceding point. The @ symbol on your keyboard is the AutoCAD name for the last point entered. You will use last point entry with the Line command. This time you will restart the Line command by pressing [Enter] at the blank command prompt to restart the previous command.

Command: ***[Enter]***

Specify first point: ***2,5 [Enter]***

Specify next point or [Undo]: ***4,5 [Enter]***

Specify next point or [Undo]: ***[Enter]***

Press: ***[Enter]*** *(or the right button on your mouse and use the menu to select Repeat Line)*

Specify first point: ***@ [Enter]***

Your starting point is now the last point you entered in the previous step (4,5). Note the line rubberbanding from that point to the cursor as shown in Figure 1.34.

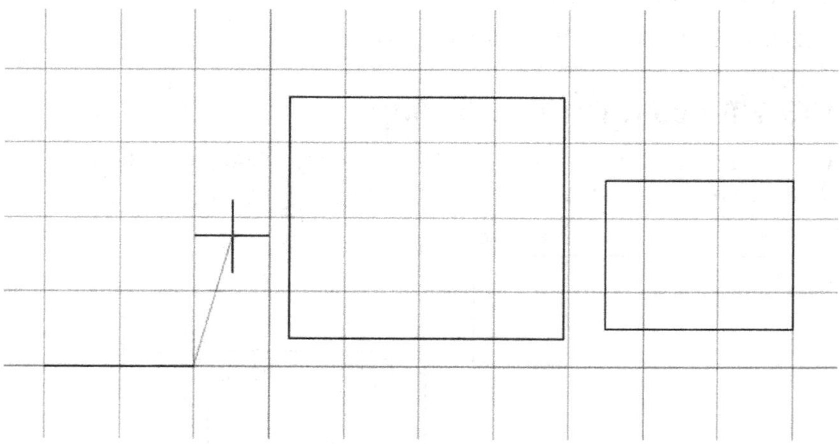

Figure 1.34 Line Rubber Bands from Last Point

Tip: *Because Line was the last command used, you could restart the command by pressing the [Enter] key, the spacebar, or right-clicking and selecting Repeat Line from the pop-up menu.*
Using these shortcuts will help you produce drawings in less time. Keep in mind that restarting a command has the same effect as typing the command name at the prompt. Some toolbar and menu selections contain special programming to select certain options for you automatically, so they may not function exactly the same when restarted by pressing [Enter].

Tip *Once in the Line command, you can also press the spacebar or [Enter] at the Specify first point: prompt to start your new line from the last point. Or you can press the right mouse button to return to the last point.*

Tip: *When drawing, moving the cursor away from the point you have selected can help you see the effect of the selection. You will not notice rubberband lines if you leave the cursor over the previously selected point.*
If it is hard to see the lines as you draw, you can turn off the grid briefly. You can also choose Display dotted grid in 2D model space from the Grid Settings dialog.

Using Relative X- and Y-Coordinates

Relative coordinates allow you to select a point at a known distance from the last point specified. To do so, use the @ symbol before your X- and Y-coordinate values. Now, continue the Line command.

Specify next point or [Undo]: ***@0,3 [Enter]***

Your line is drawn 0 units in the X-direction and 3 units in the positive Y-direction from the last point specified (4,5). Complete the shape.

Specify next point or [Undo]: ***@-2,0 [Enter]***

Specify next point or [Close/Undo]: ***@0,-3 [Enter]***

Specify next point or [Close/Undo]: ***[Enter]***

Your drawing should look like Figure 1.35. You may need to scroll your screen to see all three rectangles.

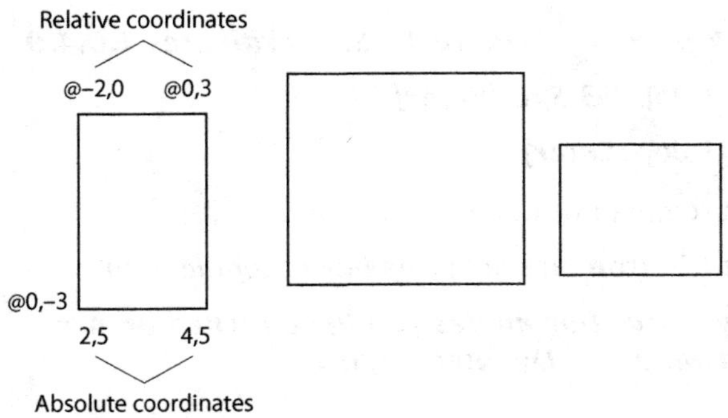

Figure 1.35

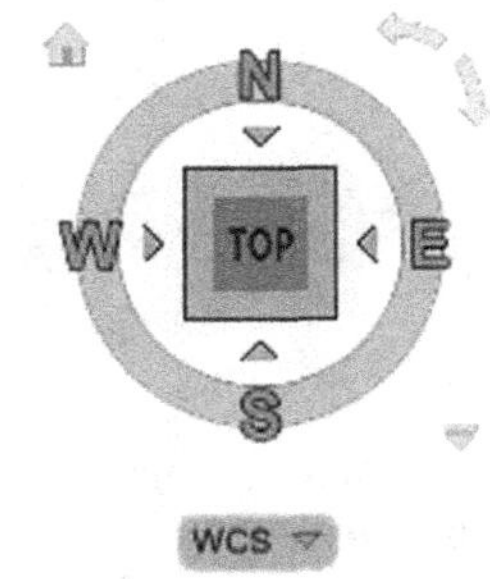

Tip: *If the View Cube is in your way making it difficult to select the points from the screen, hold down the middle button on your mouse and drag to pan your drawing area away from the View Cube location.*

Using Polar Coordinates

Polar coordinate values use the format @DISTANCE<ANGLE. Later on, you will learn how to select different units for lengths and angles. When using the default decimal units, you don't need to specify any units when typing the angle and length. When you are using polar coordinates, each new input is calculated relative to the last point entered. The default for measuring angles defines a horizontal line to the right of the current point as 0°. As shown in Figure 1.36, angular values are positive counterclockwise. Both distance and angle values may also be negative.

Figure 1.37 shows an example of lines using relative coordinate entry. In the figure, line 1 extends 3 units from the starting point at an angle of 30°. Angle 0° is at a horizontal line to the right of the starting point. Line 2 starts at the last point of line 1 and extends 2 units at an angle of 135°, again measured from a horizontal line to the right of that line's starting point. Polar coordinates are often useful for creating drawings.

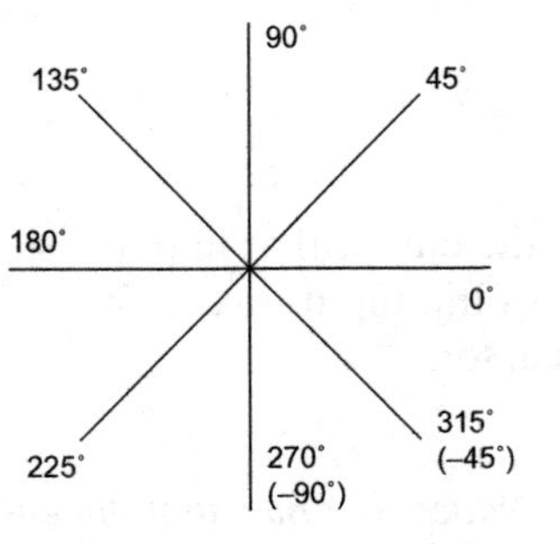

Figure 1.36 **Angle Values**

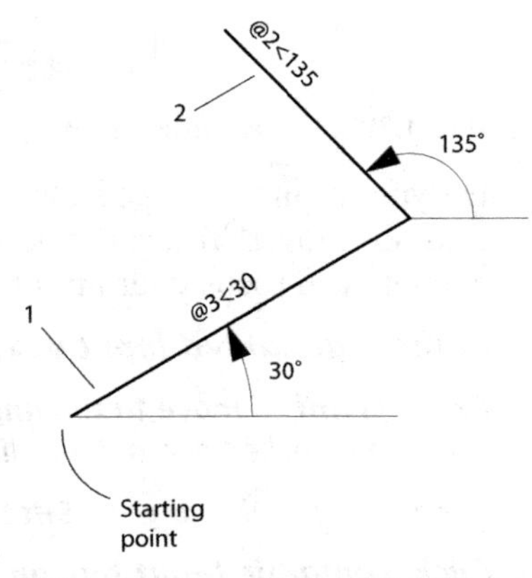

Figure 1.37 **Polar Coordinates**

Next, draw a rectangle using polar coordinate values. The starting point is point A in Figure 1.38. Use the toolbar to select the Line command.

You will draw a horizontal line 3.5 units to the right of the starting point by responding to the prompts.

Click: ***Line button***

Specify first point: ***pick point A in Figure 1.38, coordinates 1.0,4.0***

Specify next point or [Undo]: ***@3.5<0 [Enter]***

Specify next point or [Undo]: ***[Enter]***

Tip: *You can turn Dynamic Input off by pressing the F12 key. You can turn it off temporarily by holding down the F12 key. This is useful when you want to see what is below the dynamic input box.*

You will draw the next segment using dynamic input.

Click: ***Dynamic Input button*** *on the Status bar to toggle it on*

Check that the only status bar modes you have turned on are Snap Mode, Grid Display and Dynamic Input.

Click: ***Line button***

Specify next point or [Undo]: ***[Enter]*** *(a quick way to return to the last endpoint)*

The dynamic entry inputs appear near the cursor location as shown in Figure 1.38.

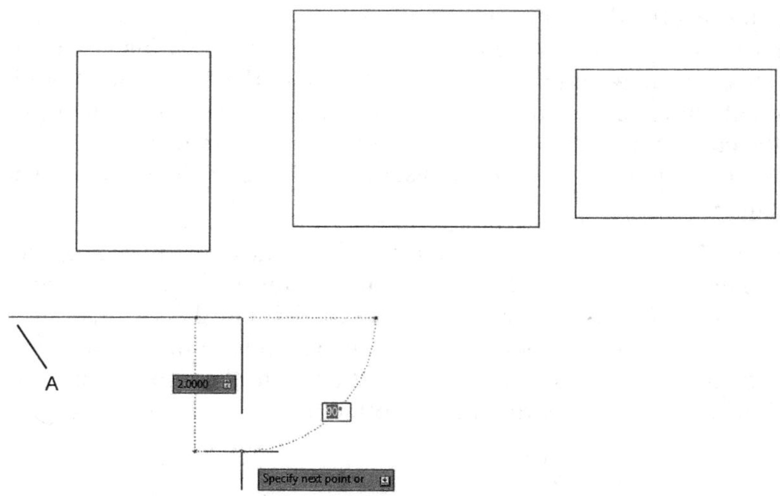

Figure 1.38 Dynamic Input

The dynamic input mode shows tooltips near the cursor that update as the cursor moves. You can type values in the tooltip input boxes. This mode lets you focus your attention near the cursor.

In the highlighted input box, type 2.00

Press [Tab] to move to the angle input box. *Notice that now that dimension shows locked and a 2-unit line extends toward the mouse location.*

Type: ***90*** *(for the angle)* ***[Enter]***

Click: ***Dynamic Input button*** *to toggle it off*

Click: ***Polar Tracking button*** *to toggle it on*

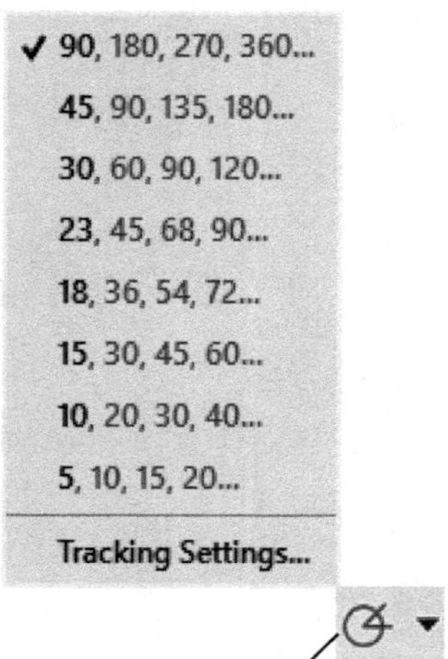

Right-clicking on the Polar Tracking button shows this menu which you can use to set the angle or adjust the tracking settings.

With Polar Tracking turned on, as you move your cursor near preset angles, an alignment and tooltip appears near the cursor as shown in Figure 1.39. The default angle for the alignment path is 90°.

Figure 1.39 Polar Tracking

On your own, complete the rectangle using polar tracking.

Your drawing should look like that in Figure 1.40.

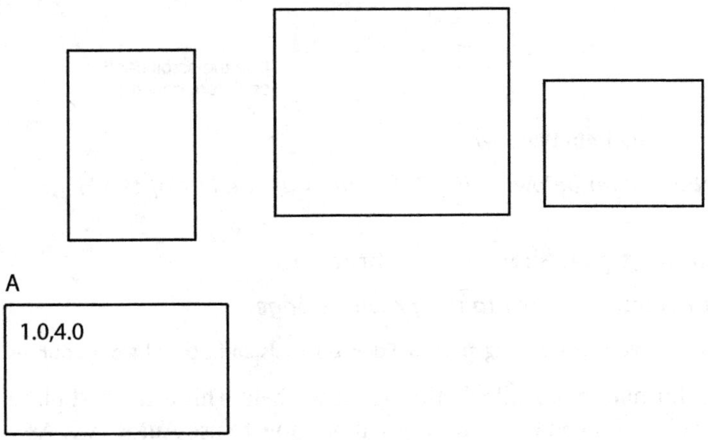

Figure 1.40

Using Help

AutoCAD's Help feature provides a wide variety of assistance. You can use it to find information about commands, how to use them, ways to select them, installation and customization information, and lots more.

Click: ***Help button***

The Help window opens in a standard browser (Figure 1.34). The Help window provides general help, training tips, advice and much more for the AutoCAD user community. You can use the back and forward arrows to return to previous topics from that session. You can click Home to return to the main page, which also provides useful links and information, such as the learning resources.

Tip: *You can press and drag with the middle mouse button to position your view (Pan). Scrolling with the middle mouse enlarges and reduces your view scale (Zoom).*

Tip: *You can get help during any command by using the transparent Help command. A transparent command is one that you can use during execution of another command. When transparent commands are entered at the command line, they are preceded by an apostrophe ('). You can type '? or 'Help, press [F1], or select the Help button during a command to show the Help dialog box. The Help button is in the upper right of the application window and looks like a question mark (?).*

Tip: *Clicking on the coordinates displayed on the status bar toggles their display off or on. When you toggle the coordinate display off, the coordinates do not change when you move the crosshairs and they appear grayed out on the status bar. When you toggle the coordinates back on, they once again display the X-, Y-, and Z-location of the crosshairs.*

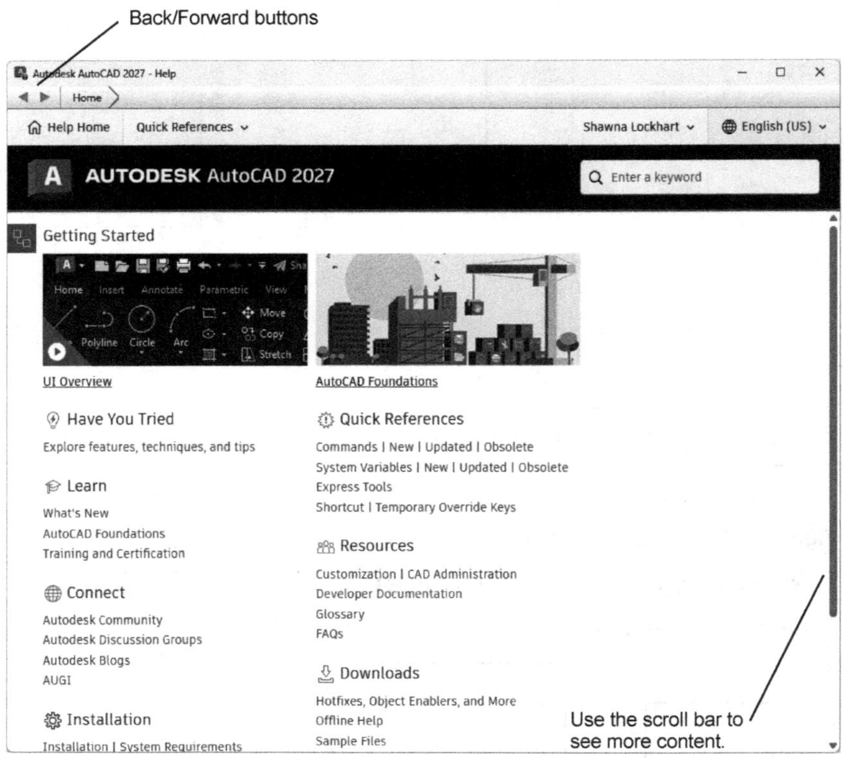

Figure 1.41 The Help Window

*Click: **Shortcut** from below Quick References at the left of the Help window*

The Shortcut Keys page shows in your browser.

*Click: **Back arrow** to return to the previous page*

On your own, explore the getting started video tutorials and other help resources.

Up-to-date information is available through using help. This is the first place you should look when you have questions about how to use AutoCAD. As you work through this book, use Help to find additional information.

As with other Windows applications, you may use the Close button in the upper right-hand corner to close the Help window.

*Click: **Close button***

Finding Help Using Search

The Search box is located at the top of the application window as shown in Figure 1.42.

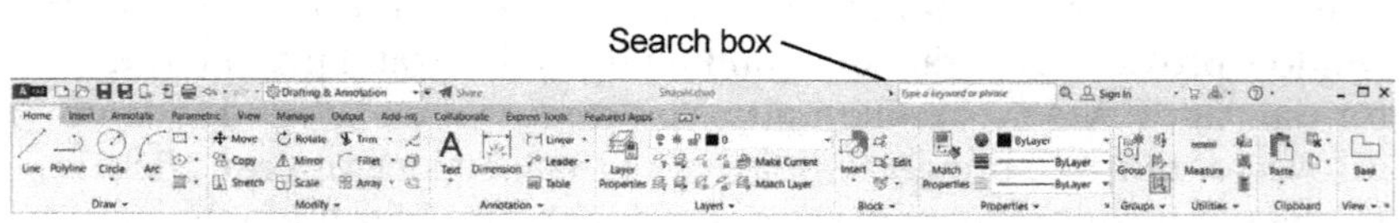

Figure 1.42 Search Box Location

*Type: **GRID [Enter]***

The Help opens showing information for the Grid command (Figure 1.41).

*Click: **Filter icon** from the left of the Help window to expand the options.*

The window expands to list choices for filtering the type of results shown.

*Click: **Product Documentation** from the Knowledge Source area.*

The right-side of the window is filtered to show only the search results from the product documentation.

*Click: **Clear All** from the Help window.*

*Click: **Help Window Close button***

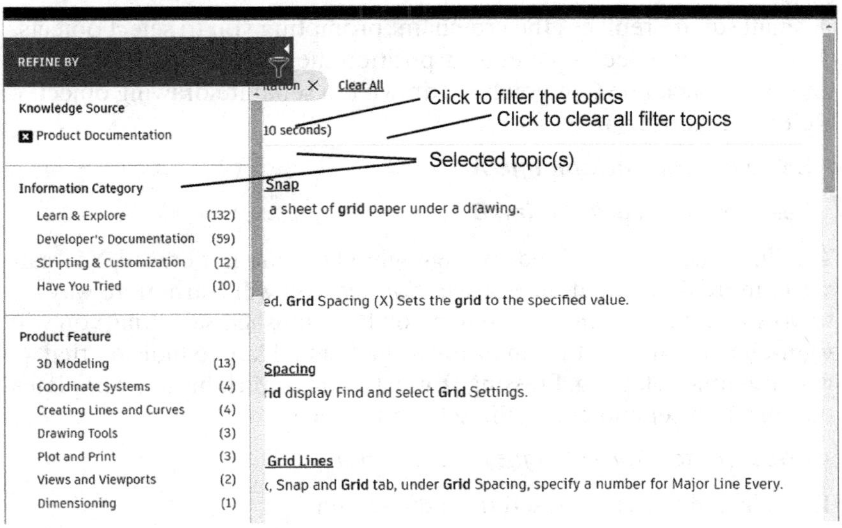

Figure 1.43 Grid Search Results

The AutoCAD Assistant

You can use the Autodesk Assistant's AI-enhanced chat to ask for information using ordinary language as well as query the drawing database such as layers list, block usage, and compare your drawing to company standards. It is very hard to see the icon in the light user interface. It is located just to the right of the help icon in the Info Center area. Try it on your own by entering a question in the prompt window or use an example provided in the list.

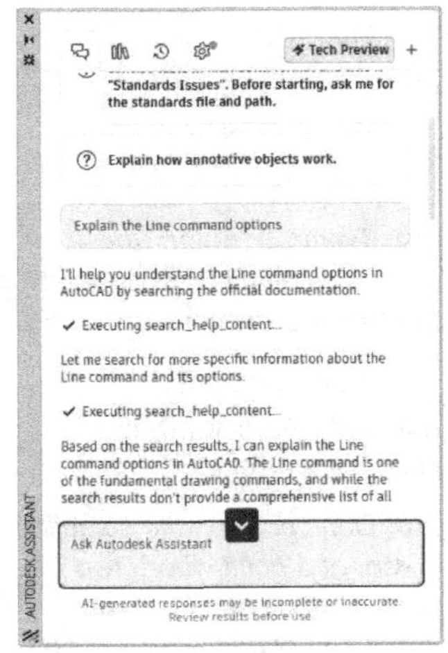

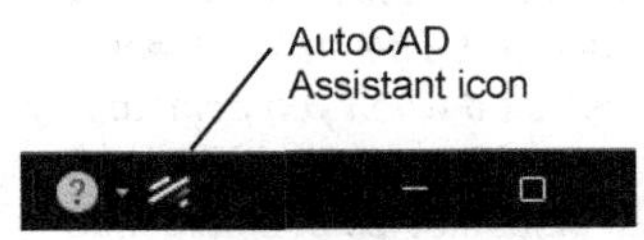

Dark Interface

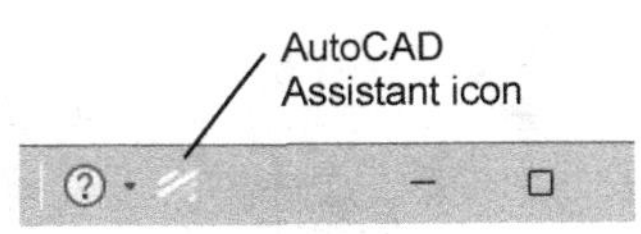

Light Interface

Tip: *You can use the Options dialog box to specify a time period and set up automatic saves, as well as controlling whether back-up files are created. But, it is still best to save your work periodically and not rely only on automatic saving. Why not use both? It is like wearing a belt and suspenders. To access the Options dialog box, click the Application button (which looks like a large A at the top left of the application window) then the Options button at the bottom right of the expanded list. From the Open and Save tab set a time for Automatic save and make sure the box for it is checked.*

Using Save

The *Save* command lets you save a drawing to the file name you have previously specified, in this case *shapes.dwg*. You should save your work frequently. If the power went off or your computer crashed, you would lose all the work that you had not previously saved. This time use the Save button on the Quick Access toolbar.

*Click: **Save button***

Your work will be saved to *shapes.dwg*. If you had not previously named your drawing, the Save Drawing As dialog box would appear, allowing you to specify a name for the drawing. Save your work periodically as you work through these tutorials.

Using Erase

The *Erase* command removes objects from a drawing. You can find the Erase command on the ribbon Home tab, Modify panel.

Click: ***Erase button***

Use the status bar to turn Snap off to make selecting easier.

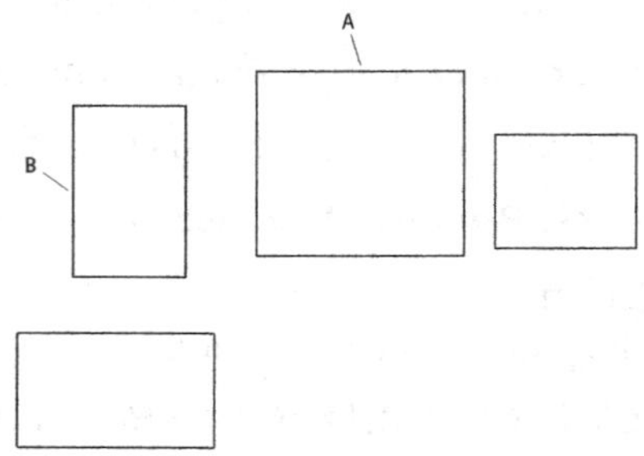

Figure 1.44

Tip: *Typing E [Enter] (the command alias) will also start the Erase command.*

Tip: *If Snap is turned on, turning it off makes object selection easier.*

Tip: *Don't position the selection cursor at a point where two objects cross because you cannot be certain which will be selected. The entire object is selected when you point to any part of it, so select the object at a point that is not ambiguous.*

A small square replaces the crosshairs, prompting you to select objects. To identify an object to be erased, position the cursor over the object and click. Each line that you have drawn is a separate drawing object. Refer to Figure 1.44.

Select objects: ***click on line A***

Select objects: ***click on line B***

The lines you have selected are highlighted but are not erased. You can select more than one item as a *selection set*. You will learn more ways to do so later in this tutorial. When you have finished selecting, you will right-click the mouse button or press the [Enter] key to indicate that you are done selecting. Pressing [Enter] or the return button completes the selection set and erases the selected objects.

Press: ***[Enter]*** *(or the right mouse button)*

The selected lines are erased from the screen.

If you erase an object by mistake, you may use the OOPS command at the command prompt.

Type: ***OOPS [Enter]***

The lines last erased are restored on your screen. OOPS restores only the most recently erased objects. However, it will work to restore erased objects even if other commands have been used in the meantime, which can be handy.

Erasing with Window or Crossing

Tip: *You can turn implied Windowing on and off and set its appearance using the Application button, Options button (lower right). From the Options dialog box, click: the Selection tab. For implied Windowing to work, it must be selected (a check must appear in the box to the left of Implied windowing). You can select Visual Effects settings to change the color of the windowing highlight.*

Next you will clear your graphics window to make room for new shapes by erasing all the rectangles on your screen. Selecting multiple objects is easy using the Window or Crossing modes.

To use implied Windowing mode, click a point on the screen that is not on an object and move your pointing device from left to right. A window-type box will start to rubberband from the point you selected. In the *implied Windowing* mode (a box drawn from left to right), the window formed selects everything that is entirely enclosed in it. However, drawing the box from right to left causes the *implied Crossing* mode to be used. Everything that either crosses the box or is enclosed in the box is selected. You can use implied Windowing and implied Crossing to select objects during any command in which you are prompted to select objects.

Click: ***Erase button***

Select objects: ***click above and to the left of your upper three rectangles, identified as A in Figure 1.45***

Other corner: ***click a point below and to the right of your upper three rectangles, identified as B***

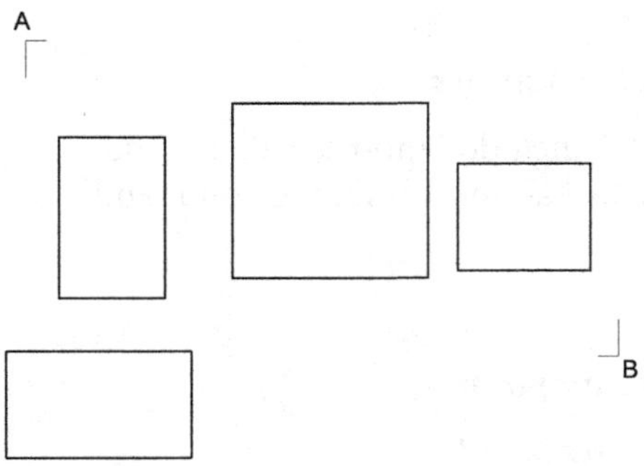

Figure 1.45

Note the "window" box formed around the area specified by the upper left and lower right corners. Your screen should look like that in Figure 1.46.

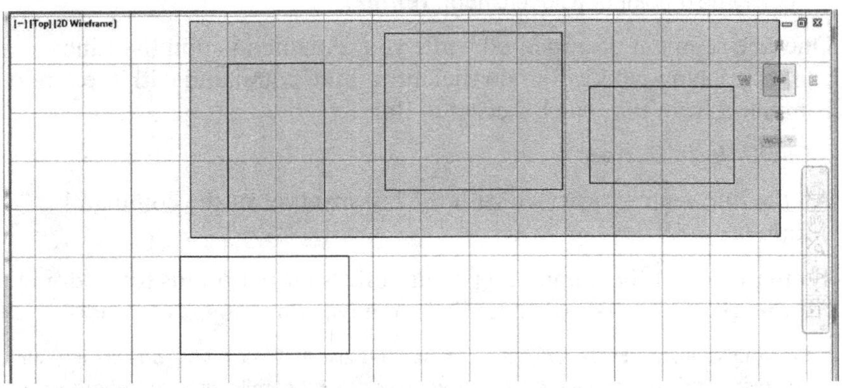

Figure 1.46 Selecting Using Window

When you chose the second corner of the window (point B), the objects entirely enclosed in the window became highlighted. Next end object selection to erase the selected objects.

Select objects: ***[Enter]*** *or* ***right-click***

Only objects entirely within the window were erased. The fourth rectangle was not completely enclosed and so it was not erased.

Next, restart the Erase command using the *context menu,* which appears when you right-click.

Right-click: ***in a blank area of the screen to show the menu***

Click: ***Repeat Erase*** *(from the context menu)*

Select objects: ***click below and to the right of the remaining rectangle*** *(to use crossing)*

Other corner: ***click above and to the left of the rectangle***

Select objects: ***[Enter]***

The remaining rectangle is erased from the drawing.

Tip: *As you work you may notice the Activities Insights panel with information about past actions in your drawing. You can close it with the X in the upper left corner and turn it off/on using the command Activityinsightsclose or Activityinsightsopen or select click the View tab, History panel, Activity Insights.*

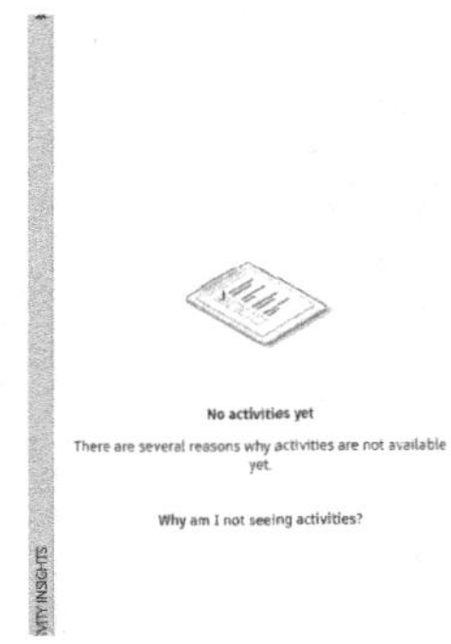

Tip: *A helpful visual cue when you are drawing a crossing box (right to left) is that the box is drawn with a dashed line and filled in green. When drawing a window box (left to right) the box is drawn with a solid line and filled in blue. You can use the dialog box to change to colors.*

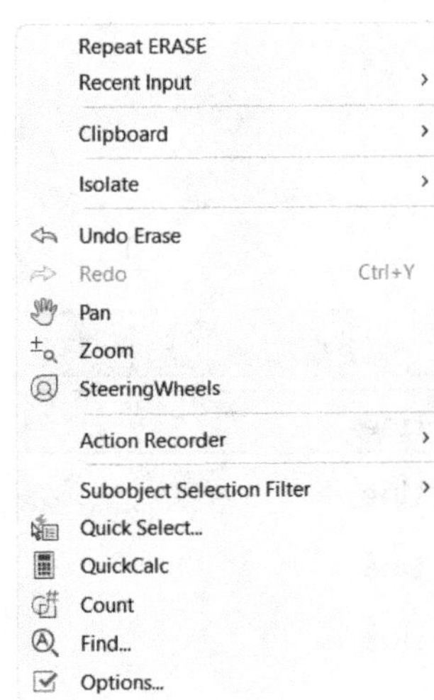

Using Undo

The *Undo* command removes the effect of previous commands. If you make a mistake, select the Undo command from the Quick Access toolbar, and the effect of the previous command will be undone.

Tip: *If you undo the wrong object, the Redo command lets you restore the items you have undone. It is the icon to the right of Undo on the Quick Access toolbar.*

Click: ***Undo button***

The last rectangle you erased reappears.

Line and some other commands also include Undo as a command option that allows you to undo the last action within the command.

Click: ***Line button***

Specify first point: ***click any point***

Specify next point or [Undo]: ***click any point***

Specify next point or [Undo]: ***click any point***

Specify next point or [Close/Undo]: ***click any point***

Specify next point or [Close/Undo]: ***U [Enter]***

Specify next point or [Close/Undo]: ***[Enter]***

One line segment disappeared while you remained within the Line command. Now, you will undo the entire Line command with the Undo command from the Quick Access toolbar.

Click: ***Undo button***

All the line segments drawn with the last instance of the command disappear.

Typing Undo at the command prompt offers more options for undoing your work. You will draw some lines to have some objects to undo.

On your own, use Erase from the toolbar and erase all remaining objects in your graphics window. Use Line on your own to draw six parallel lines anywhere on your drawing screen. Use Snap and Grid as needed.

In the next step, you will type the Undo command to remove the last three lines that you drew.

Type: ***UNDO [Enter]***

Enter the number of operations to undo or [Auto/Control/BEgin/End/Mark/Back] <1>: ***3 [Enter]***

The last three lines drawn should disappear, corresponding to the last three instances of the Line command. You could have selected any number, depending on the number of command steps you wanted to undo.

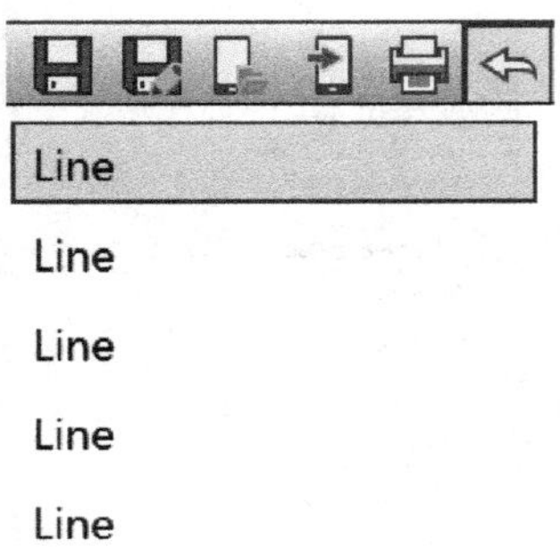

Using the Undo Flyout

The flyout symbol next to the Undo command on the Quick Access toolbar lets you view the command history of selections you have made. You can undo them one by one using this option.

Click: ***on the flyout triangle*** *next to the Undo button*

Click: ***on the first Line command*** *in the Undo flyout*

The line is undone from your screen.

*Click: **on the flyout triangle** next to the Undo button* to show the command history

*Click: **on the second Erase command** listed in the history*

The Erase command is undone and the boxes that you erased earlier return to the screen.

Using Redo

If the last command undid something you really did not want to undo, you can use the *Redo* command to reverse the effects. The Redo button appears on the Quick Access toolbar to the right of Undo.

*Click: **Redo button***

The erased boxes are removed again as the Erase command is Redone.

*Click: **the flyout triangle next to Redo***

You should see a command history of the items that you have Undone. You can choose from the list to redo them.

Using Undo Back

The Back option of the Undo command takes the drawing back to a mark that you set with the Mark option or to the beginning of the *drawing session* if you haven't set any marks. Be careful when selecting these options or you may undo too much.

*Type: **UNDO [Enter]***

Enter the number of operations to undo or [Auto/Control/BEgin/End/Mark/Back] <1>: ***B [Enter]***

This will undo everything. OK? <Y>: ***[Enter]***

All operations back to the beginning of the drawing session (or mark, if you had previously set one with the Mark option of the Undo command) will be undone. (You can use Help to find out what the remaining options, Auto, Control, Begin, and End, are used for.)

*Click: **to flyout the command history next to Redo***

The list of commands that you have selected in the drawing should appear in the command history window.

On your own, select some of the commands from the list to Redo.

Next, close drawing *Shapes.dwg*.

*Click: **Application button, Close***

You will be prompted "Save changes to *c:\work\shapes.dwg*?"

*Click: **No***

The drawing will close, and the graphics area will appear gray to indicate that there is no drawing open. Notice that now there are only the New, Open, Open from Web & Mobile, and Sheet Set Manager buttons available on the Quick Access toolbar.

Tip: *You can also just click the X at the corner of the Shapes drawing tab to close it.*

Drawing a Plot Plan

Next, you will create a new drawing showing a plot plan. A plot plan is a plan view of a lot boundary and the location of utilities.

The *New* button on the Quick Access toolbar is a quick way to start new drawings. It is the left-most button.

Click: ***New button***

The Select template dialog box appears on your screen. The default template *acad.dwt* should be highlighted.

Double-click: ***acad.dwt*** *(to select it and open the new drawing)*

Click: ***Application button, Save As*** *and save this drawing as* ***plotplan.dwg****. Be sure to create the new drawing in your* ***work*** *folder.*

Click: ***Save*** *(to exit the dialog box)*

Setting the Units

When you create a drawing, work in the type of units that are appropriate for that drawing. The *default units* are decimal. The units represent any type of real-world measurement you want to consider: decimal miles, furlongs, inches, millimeters, microns, or anything else.

When the time comes to plot the drawing, you determine the final relationship between your drawing database, in which you create the object the actual size it is in the real world, and the paper plot.

You can change the type of units for lengths to *architectural units* that appear in feet and fractional inches, *engineering units* that appear in feet and decimal inches, *scientific units* that appear in exponential format, or *fractional units* that are whole numbers and fractions.

When you use architectural or engineering units, one drawing unit is considered to be one inch. You specify feet by typing the feet mark after the numerical value (e.g., 50.5' or 20'2" or 35'-4").

Angular measurements can be given in decimal degrees; degrees, minutes, and seconds; gradians; radians; or *surveyor units*, such as the bearing N45°0'00"E.

Click: ***Application icon, Drawing Utilities, Units*** *as shown in Figure 1.47*

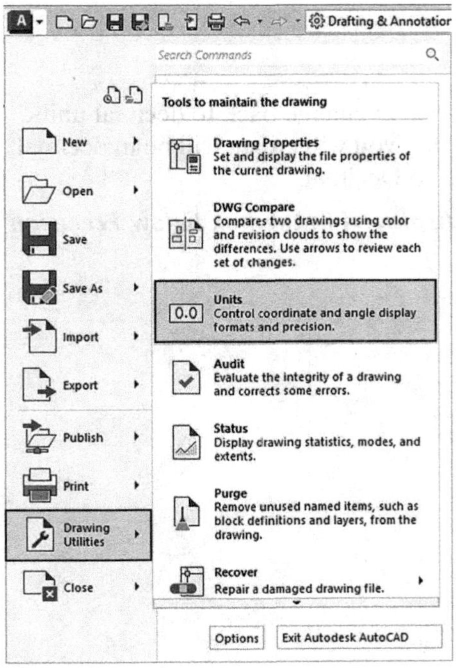

Figure 1.47

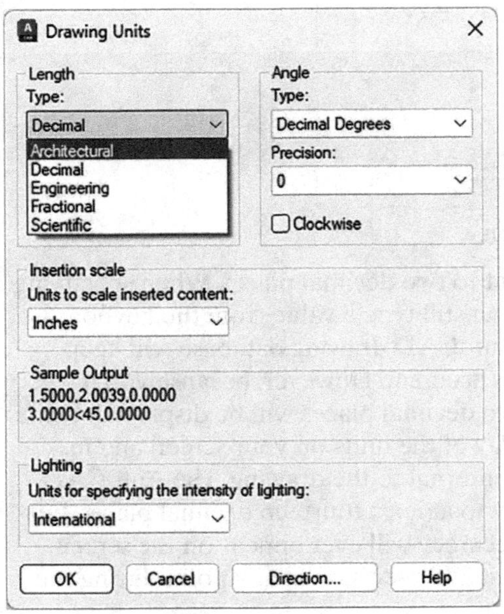

Figure 1.48 Unit Types

The Drawing Units dialog box appears on your screen. Use the Length area, Type pull down list to select from the available length units for the drawing. Figure 1.48 shows the types of length units expanded.

Click: ***to expand the list of available unit types***

Click: ***Architectural*** *(from the list)*

The dialog box changes to show Architectural as the type of units. You can select only one type at a time. Note that the units displayed under the heading Precision change to architectural units.

From the Length Type area

Click: ***Decimal***

Note that the units in the Precision area change back to decimal units. The dimensions for the plot plan that you will create will be in decimal feet, so you will leave the units set to Decimal.

Click: ***to expand the choices displayed in the box below Precision***

Click: ***0.00*** *(as shown in Figure 1.49)*

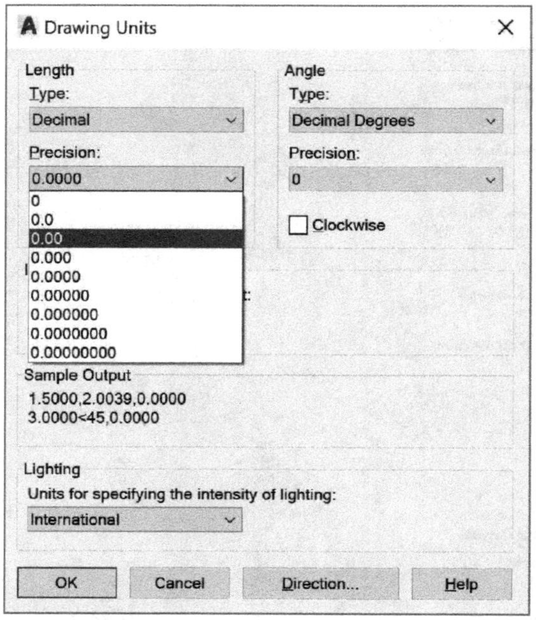

Figure 1.49 **Decimal Precision**

Now the display precision is set to two decimal places. When specifying coordinates and lengths, you can still type a value from the keyboard with more precision and the AutoCAD drawing database will keep track of your drawing with this accuracy. However, because you have selected this precision, only two decimal places will be displayed. Units precision determines the *display* of the units on your screen and in the prompts, not the accuracy internal to the drawing. The AutoCAD software keeps track internally to at least fourteen decimal places, but only eight decimal places of accuracy will ever appear on the screen. You can change the type of unit and precision at any point during the drawing process.

The right side of the dialog box controls the type and precision of angular measurements. Remember that the default measurement of angles is counterclockwise, starting from a horizontal line to the right as 0°. You can change the default setting by clicking on the Direction button and making a new selection. Leave the direction set at the default of 0 degrees toward East. Use the Type setting in the Angle area to:

Click: ***Surveyor's Units***

Note that the display in this Precision area changes to list the angle as a bearing. When this mode is active, you can type in a surveyor angle and the program will measure the angle from the specified direction, North or South, toward East or West, as specified. The default direction, North, is straight toward the top of the screen. If you want to view greater angle precision, click on the box containing the precision N 0d E. The list of the available precisions pops down, as shown in Figure 1.50, allowing you to choose to display degrees, minutes, and seconds.

To display degrees, minutes, and seconds:

Click: ***N0d00’00”E***

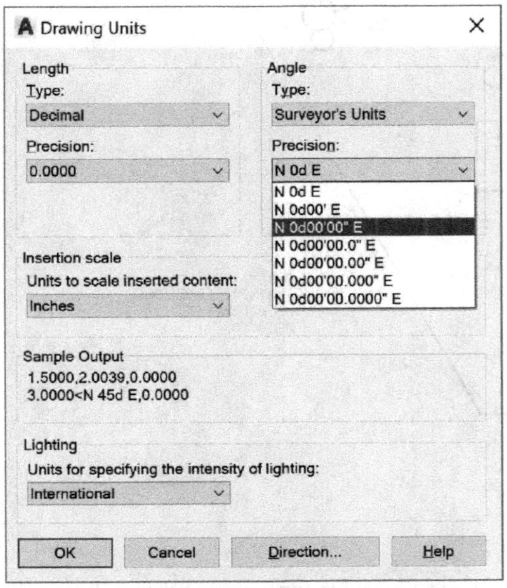

Figure 1.50 Surveyor’s Unit Precision

The Insertion scale area of the dialog box controls the scaling factor for blocks that are dragged into the current drawing from Tool palettes. You will learn more about the Tool palettes in Tutorial 10. You can also use the Drawing Units dialog box to change the units for lighting in international drawings.

Since this drawing will be created in decimal feet,

Click: ***Feet***

Click: ***OK*** *(to exit)*

Look at the status bar: The coordinate display has changed to show two instead of four places after the decimal.

Sizing Your Drawing

Create your AutoCAD drawing geometry in *real-world units.* In other words, if the object is 10” long, make it exactly 10” long in the drawing. If it is a few millimeters long, you create the drawing to those lengths. You can think of the decimal units as representing whatever decimal measurement system you are using. For this drawing, the units will represent decimal feet, so 10 units will equal 10 feet in the drawing. After you have created the drawing geometry, you can decide on the scale at which you want to print your final drawing on the sheet of paper. The ability to create drawings from which you can make accurate measurements and calculations is one of the powerful features of CAD. Also, you can plot the final drawing to any scale, saving time because you don't have to remake drawings just to change the scale.

For your plot plan, you will need a large drawing area to accommodate the site plan shown in Figure 1.51.

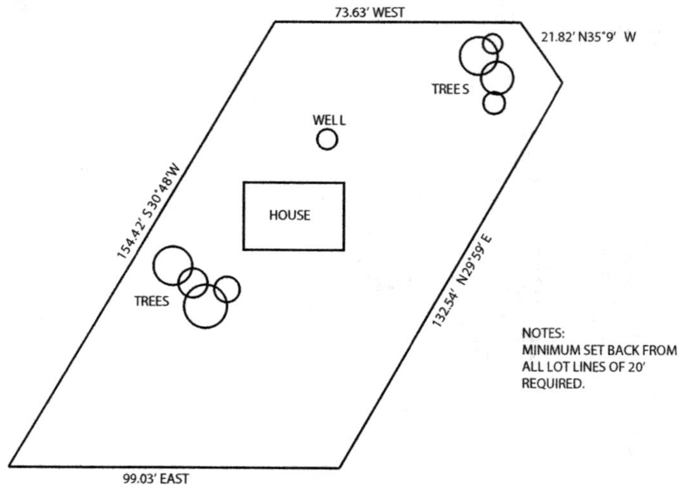

Figure 1.51 **Plot Plan**

Using Limits

The *Limits* command sets the size of your drawing area, where the grid is displayed. You can also turn off Limits if you do not want to preset the size of the drawing. You will use the command window.

Command: ***LIMITS [Enter]***

Specify lower left corner or [ON/OFF] <0.00,0.00>: ***[Enter]*** *(to accept default of 0,0)*

Specify upper right corner <12.00,9.00>: ***300,225 [Enter]***

Tip: *If the coordinate display does not show a larger size, check to see that you set the limits correctly and that you picked Zoom All. Be sure that the coordinates are turned on by clicking on the coordinates located on the status bar until you see them change as you move the mouse.*

The default space in which you create your drawing geometry or model is called model space. It is where you accurately create real-world models. In Tutorial 5, you will learn to use paper space, where you lay out views, as you do on a sheet of paper. You can set different sizes for model space and paper space with the Limits command.

Show your new larger area on your display.

Click: ***View tab, Navigate panel, All*** *(from the Zoom flyout)*

Tip: *Double-clicking the middle mouse button with the cursor positioned inside the drawing area is a quick way to fit the drawing extents on the screen.*

Move the crosshairs to the upper right-hand corner of the screen. The status bar displays the coordinate location of the crosshairs indicating that the graphics window has changed to reflect the drawing limits.

A larger grid spacing value will help you better relate to the sizes in your drawing.

Command: ***GRID [Enter]***

Specify grid spacing(X) or [ON/OFF/Snap/Major/aDaptive/Limits/Follow/Aspect] <0.50>: ***10 [Enter]***

To draw the site boundary, you will use absolute and polar coordinates as appropriate. You will be using surveyor angles to specify the directions for the lines. The AutoCAD surveyor angle units are given in bearings.

A *bearing* specifies the angle to turn from the first direction stated toward the second direction stated. For example, a bearing of *N29°59'E* means to start pointed in the direction of North and turn an angle of 29°59' toward the East. Type letter *"d"* instead of a degree symbol when you are entering bearings from the keyboard.

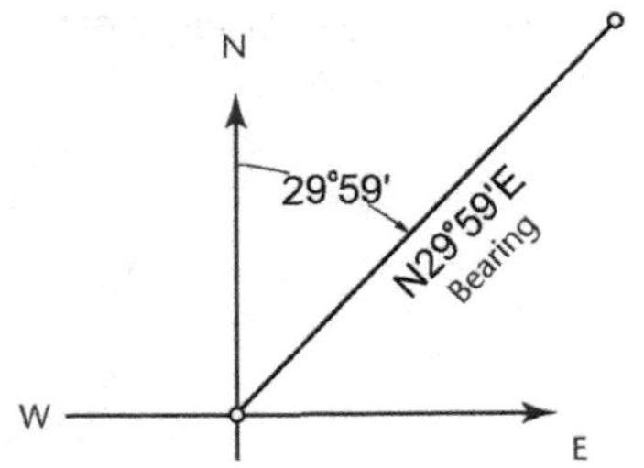

Now you are ready to start drawing the lines of the site boundary. Use the Draw panel from the ribbon Home tab.

On your own, check that Dynamic Input, Polar Tracking, Object Snap, and other modes are turned **OFF.** Use the status bar to turn them off if needed. Only the grid should be on.

Click: ***Line button***

Specify first point: ***50,30 [Enter]***

Specify next point or [Undo]: ***@99.03<E [Enter]***

Specify next point or [Close/Undo]: ***@132.54<N29d59'E [Enter]***

Specify next point or [Close/Undo]: ***@21.82<N35d9'W [Enter]***

Specify next point or [Close/Undo]: ***@73.63<W [Enter]***

Specify next point or [Close/Undo]: ***C [Enter]***

Your screen should look like Figure 1.52.

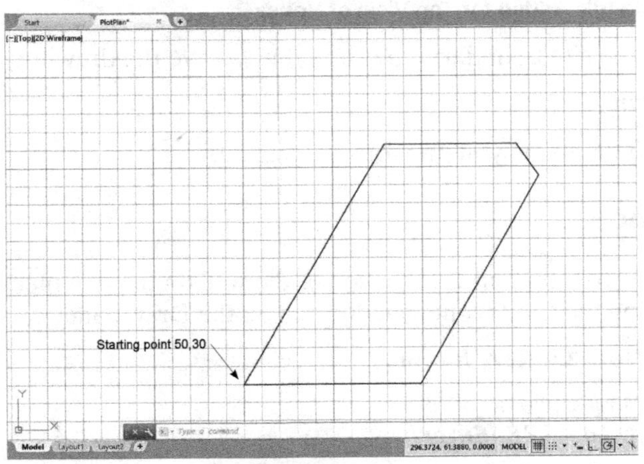

Figure 1.52 Plot Boundary Lines

Using Rectangle

The *Rectangle* command has several options: Chamfer, Elevation, Fillet, Thickness, and Width as well as a prompt for the corners of the rectangle. These options allow you to manipulate the appearance and placement of the rectangle before it is drawn. Chamfer and Fillet are options that change the corners of the rectangle (covered in Tutorial 3). Elevation and Thickness are options best used in 3D modeling. The Width option allows you to specify a width for the lines making up the rectangle.

A rectangle will represent a house on the plot plan. You will use coordinate values to place a rectangle roughly in the center of your plot plan. You will use the Width option to make wider than normal lines.

Tip: *You can also draw a rectangle by picking the corners directly from the screen using your mouse.*

Click: ***Rectangle button***

Specify first corner point or [Chamfer/Elevation/Fillet/Thickness/Width]: ***W [Enter]***

Specify line width for rectangles <0.00>: ***.5 [Enter]***

Specify first corner point or [Chamfer/Elevation/Fillet/Thickness/Width]: ***120,95 [Enter]***

Specify other corner point or [Area/Dimensions/Rotation]: ***150,115 [Enter]***

Your drawing should be similar to the one in Figure 1.53.

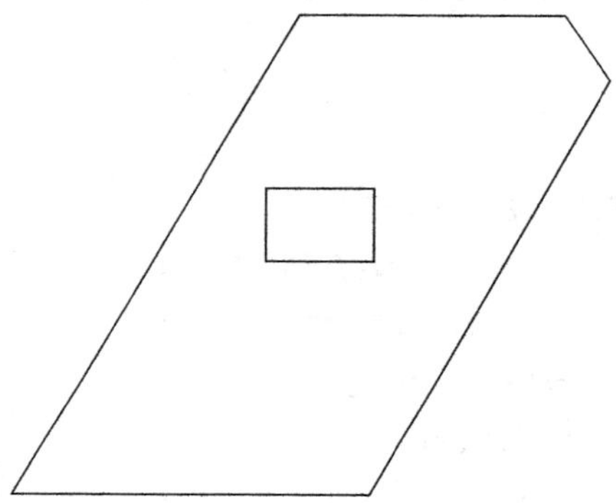

Figure 1.53 Rectangle Added for Top View of House

Tip: *Notice that when you select the Circle button, the last used option is the default button the next time the command is used. If you want that option, you only need to click the upper button. If not, expand the flyout options and make your selection. Then that option will become the top, default button.*

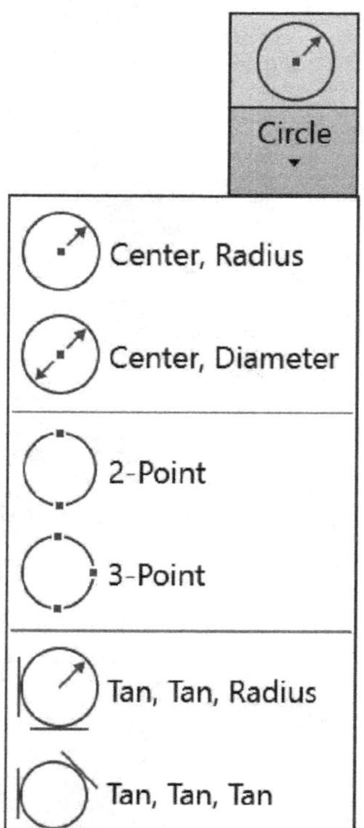

Having completed the site boundary, you should now save the drawing.

Click: ***Save button***

Your file is saved to the name you previously assigned.

Drawing Circles

You will draw a circle to represent the location of the well on the plot plan. You draw circles using the *Circle* command located on the Draw panel.

Click: ***Circle button, Center, Radius***

Specify center point for circle or [3P/2P/Ttr (tan tan radius)]: ***145,128 [Enter]***

As you move the cursor away from the center point, a circle continually re-forms, using the distance from the center to the cursor location as the radius value. You will type the value to specify the exact size for the circle's radius.

Specify radius of circle or [Diameter]: ***3 [Enter]***

Before continuing, check that the Grid Display is the only Status bar mode which is turned on. It can be difficult to draw freehand with other modes turned on. Some of the other modes, like Transparency, will not make any difference. You will learn more about these modes in Tutorial 4.

For now the only button that should appear highlighted is Grid Display.

Next, you will draw some circles to represent trees or shrubs in the plot plan. You will specify the locations for the trees by picking them from the screen.

Click: ***Circle button***

Specify center point for circle or [3P/2P/Ttr (tan tan radius)]: ***click on a point for the center of circle 1 (as shown in Figure 1.44)***

Specify radius of circle or [Diameter]: ***move the crosshairs away until the circle appears similar to that shown in Figure 1.54, then click***

On your own, draw the remaining circles representing trees using this method, so that you are pleased with their appearance.

Your drawing should look like that in Figure 1.54.

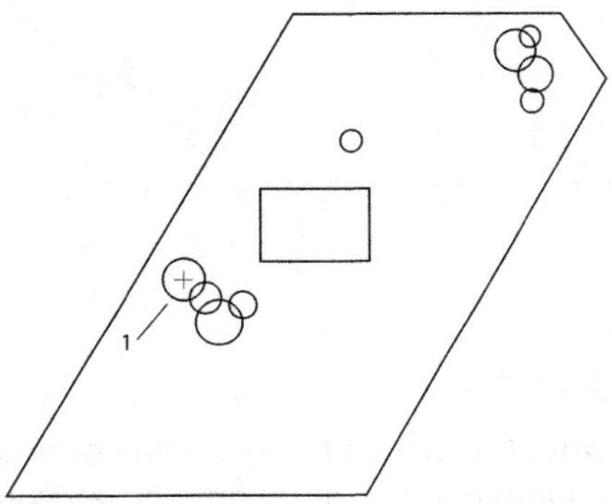

Figure 1.54 Circles for the Well and Trees Added

Tip: *Try typing the alias* **C** *to start the Circle command. You might find it to be faster than picking from the menu. Remember you can also right-click and select to restart commands.*

Adding Text

Use the Text (*formerly Dtext*) command to add single lines of text, words, or numbers to a drawing. Text, or Single Line Text, is located on the ribbon Home tab, Annotation panel, under Text.

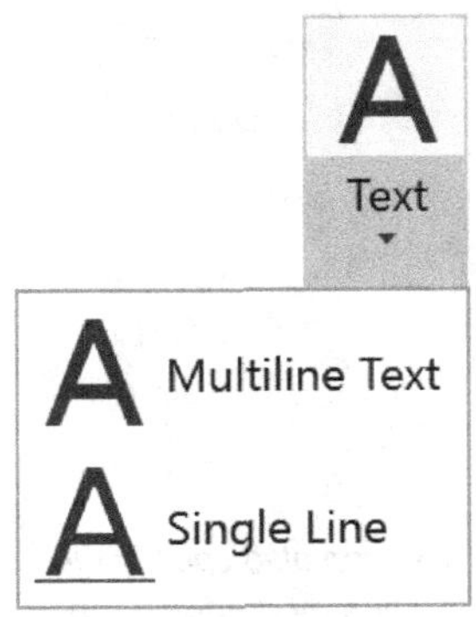

Unless you specify otherwise, text is added to the right of a designated starting point. You can use the Justify option to center text about a point or add it to the left of a point. For now, just add text to the right of the starting point.

Click: ***Single Line button*** *from the Home tab Annotation panel*

Specify start point of text or [Justify/Style]: ***select a point at about coordinates 90,25***

Specify height <0.20>: ***3 [Enter]***

Specify rotation angle of text <E>: ***[Enter]***

You should see the typing cursor at the location you selected for the text start point indicating the software is now ready to accept typed-in text.

Tip: *There is a tab named Annotate on the ribbon. There is also a panel named Annotation on the ribbon Home tab. If you have trouble finding the commands in the next section, make sure you are selecting them as directed. The tab and panel contain many of the same tools.*

Tip: *To determine the actual text height necessary, you must know the size of paper and scale you will use to plot the final drawing. In Tutorial 5 you will learn to use paper space to set up scaling and text for plotting. For now, if you are unsure about what text height to use, move the crosshairs on the screen and read the coordinate display on the toolbar. Use the lengths shown to get an appropriate size for your text. You can also use the rubberband line that appears during the text height portion of the Text command to set the height visually.*

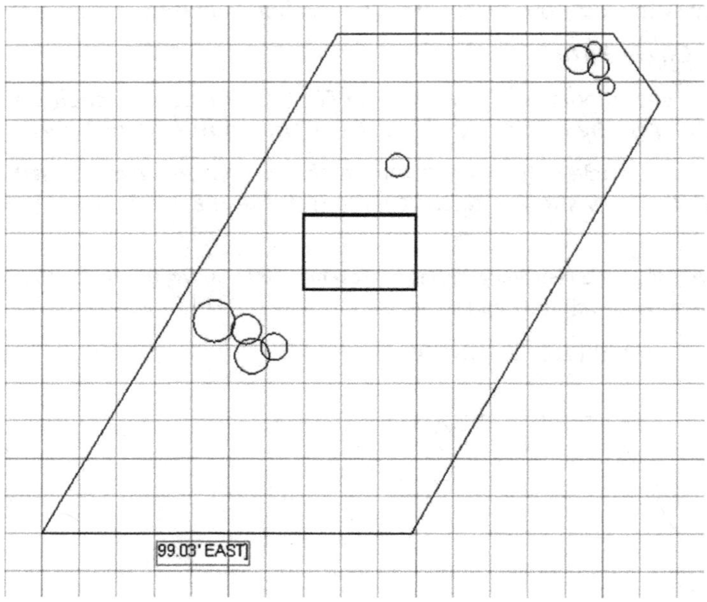

Figure 1.55 The Typing Cursor

Type: ***99.03' EAST [Enter] [Enter]***

You can type the text just as you would with a word processing program as shown in Figure 1.55. The Text command does not wrap text, so you must designate the end of each line by pressing [Enter]. To end the Text command, press [Enter] at the beginning of a blank line (a null reply to the prompt). (You must use the keyboard, not the return button on your pointing device.)

Tip: *If you make a mistake before exiting the Text command, backspace to erase the text. (After exiting the Text command, you can double-click the line of text to make corrections.)*

Using Special Text Characters

You will add the text labeling the length and angle for the right-hand lot line. When you are using the standard AutoCAD fonts, the special text item %%d creates the degree symbol. Type the line of text with %%d in place of the degree symbol. When you have finished typing in the text and press [Enter], %%d will be replaced with a degree symbol. (You will use more special text characters in Tutorial 7.) You will also specify a rotation angle for the text so that it is aligned with the lot line. This time, try typing the command.

Tip: *You can also specify the text rotation by dragging the line that appears during the Specify rotation angle prompt to show the orientation for your text and then click the mouse (parallel to the right lot line for this example). As you are typing the text still appears horizontal, but once you press [Enter] twice, the text aligns in the direction you specified.*

Command: ***TEXT [Enter]***

Specify start point of text or [Justify/Style]: ***click slightly to the right of the right-hand lot line***

Specify height <3.00>: ***[Enter]***

Specify rotation angle of text <E>: ***N29d59'E [Enter]***

Type: ***132.54' N29%%d59'E [Enter] [Enter]***

Once you press the final [Enter], the text should align with the lot line in your drawing.

Copying Text

Next you will learn how to copy a text object and edit it to quickly create labels for other items in your drawings. This is generally faster than placing text items one by one.

Click: Home tab, Modify panel, Copy button

Select objects: ***click on the bottom text 99.03' EAST [Enter]***

Specify base point or [Displacement] <Displacement>: ***click on the middle of that text object***

Specify second point or <use first point as displacement>: ***click above the upper line as shown in Figure 1.56***

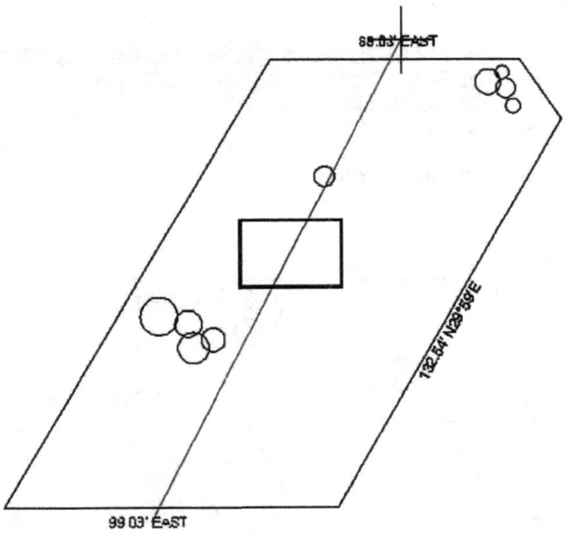

Figure 1.56 Copying a Text Object

Copied items can also be placed using the array option. Arrays are handy for copying things in rows or columns. You will learn more about arrays in Tutorial 4. Give the Array option of the Copy command a try next. The original item is counted in the number of items to array. You should still have the Copy command active. If not, restart it and continue from the following prompt:

Specify second point or [Array/Exit/Undo] <Exit>: ***A [Enter]***

Enter number of items to array: ***4 [Enter]***

Specify second point or [Fit]: ***as you move your cursor away from the basepoint, you will see the text items attached to a "rubber-band line" similar to that shown in Figure 1.57. Click to place the copied text items.***

Specify second point or [Array/Exit/Undo] <Exit>: ***On your own continue to place copied text items similar to that shown in Figure 1.58.***

Press: ***[Enter]*** *to end the command*

Choosing Fit when placing the copied items causes them to be fit between the cursor location and the basepoint instead of using that as the distance between the items.

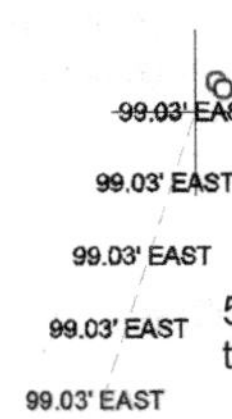

5 arrayed items with the Fit option

Tip: *If you don't see the copies of the text item on your screen, your cursor may be too far from the basepoint. The distance between the items is based on the distance and angle the cursor is from the basepoint. Move the cursor closer to the original text until you see the items.*

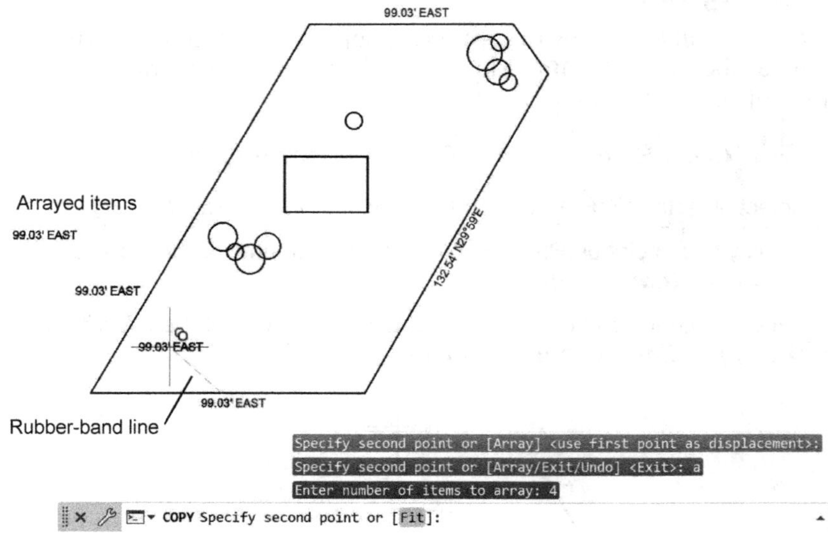

Figure 1.57 Copied Text with Array Option

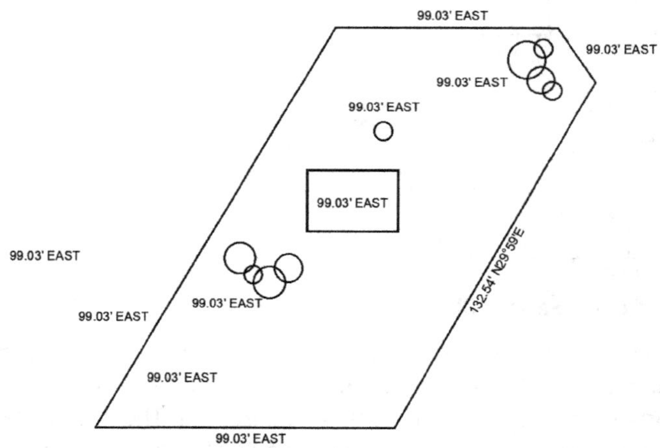

Figure 1.58 Copied Text Placed in Drawing

In Place Text Editing

Next you will change the text so that the drawing displays the correct information.

Double-click: ***on the text in the rectangle so that it appears in the text editor as shown in Figure 1.59***

Type: ***HOUSE [Enter]***

On your own, change the text identifying the trees, well locations, and remaining bearings and distances. See Figure 1.51 on page 36.

Press [Enter] to exit the command when done editing.

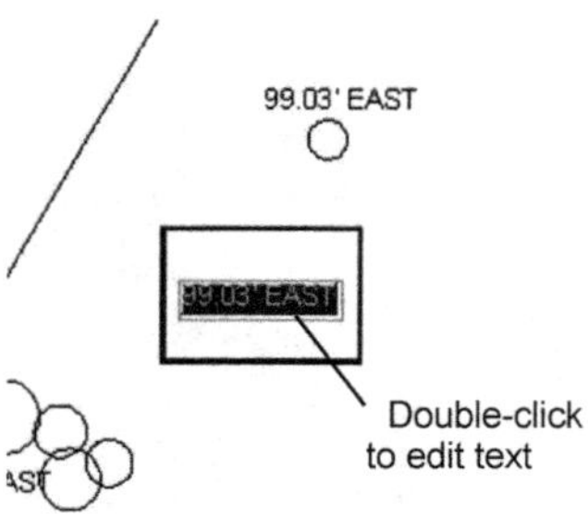

Figure 1.59
Text Editing Box Open

Moving and Rotating Text

Rotating and moving text is easy with the text object's grips.

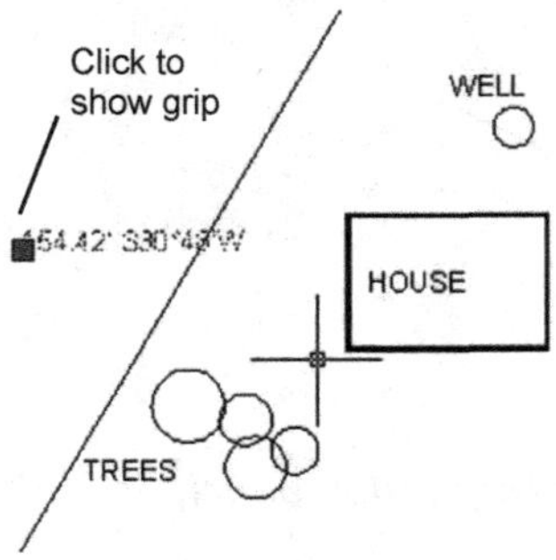

Figure 1.60 **Click to Show the Grip**

Click: ***on the closest copied text along the left lot line*** *so that its grip appears as shown in Figure 1.60*

Click: ***in the small grip box at the left of the text so that it appears "hot" or active****—its color should change*

Right-click: ***with your cursor over the grip*** *to show the grip editing menu*

Click: ***Rotate***

On your own, use the mouse to rotate the text into alignment with the left lot line and click to select the desired angle.

Press: ***[Esc]*** *to unselect the grips*

Notice that as you rotate items, the further away you move the mouse from the grip, the easier it is to control the rotation angle.

You can move items directly using the grips without selecting from the menu. To do this,

Click: ***the grip to make it active; then move the item to a new location using your mouse and click.***

On your own, position the remaining text items for the plot plan.

Tip: *If you have trouble showing the grip, check that you have exited the Textedit command.*

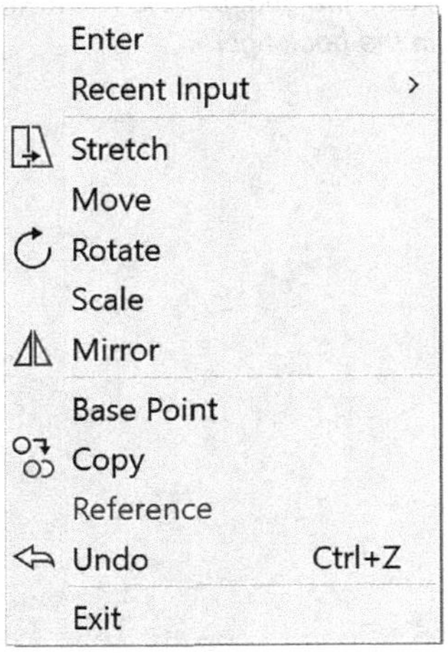

Setting the Text Style

The *Style* command allows you to create a style specifying the font and other characteristics for the shapes of the text in your drawing. A *font* is a set of letters, numbers, punctuation marks, and symbols of a distinctive style and design. AutoCAD supplies several *shape-compiled fonts* that you can use to create text styles. In addition to these shape-compiled fonts, you can also use your own True Type, Type 1 Postscript, or Unicode fonts. Some sample True Type fonts are provided with the AutoCAD software.

The Style command allows you to control the appearance of a font so that it is slanted (oblique), backwards, vertical, or upside-down. You can also control the height and proportional width of the letters.

To create a style, you will select Text Style by expanding the Annotation panel on the ribbon Home tab.

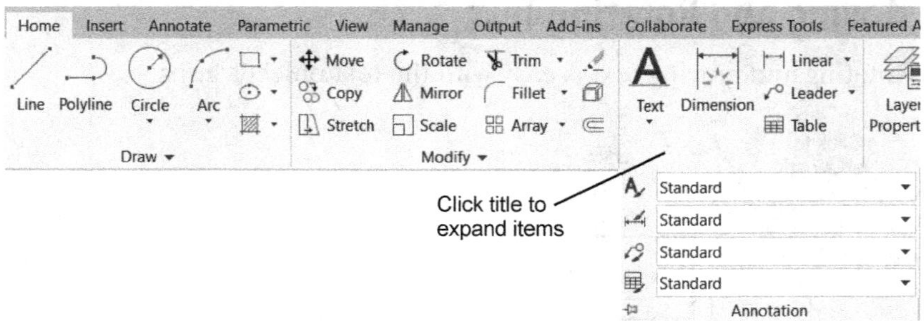

Figure 1.61 **The Annotation Flyout**

Tip: *Images often show clearly in this book when the grid is off, so don't be alarmed if you are using the grid, but it isn't shown in the book figure.*

Click: ***Text Style*** *from the Home tab, Annotation panel, as shown in Figure 1.61*

The dialog box shown in Figure 1.62 appears on your screen. It is divided into four different sections: Style Name, Font, Effects, and Preview. All of the text in a drawing has a style applied to it. So far, your drawing has been using the style called Standard, which is the default.

You can create a new style and set it as the current style to be used for any subsequently entered text.

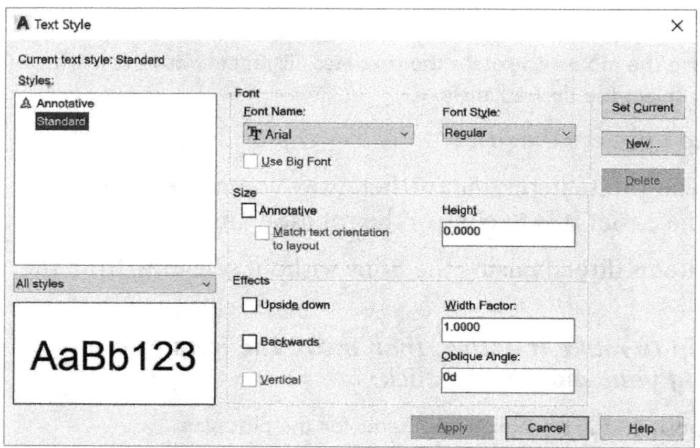

Figure 1.62 **Text Style Dialog Box**

Click: ***New***

Type: ***MyStyle*** *in the New Text Style dialog box*

Click: ***OK***

Font Area

Your system may have many fonts available in addition to the standard AutoCAD shape-compiled fonts.

Click: ***to expand the box below Font Name***

Click: ***on one of the fonts listed*** *and note the changes in the Preview area of the dialog box as in Figure 1.63.*

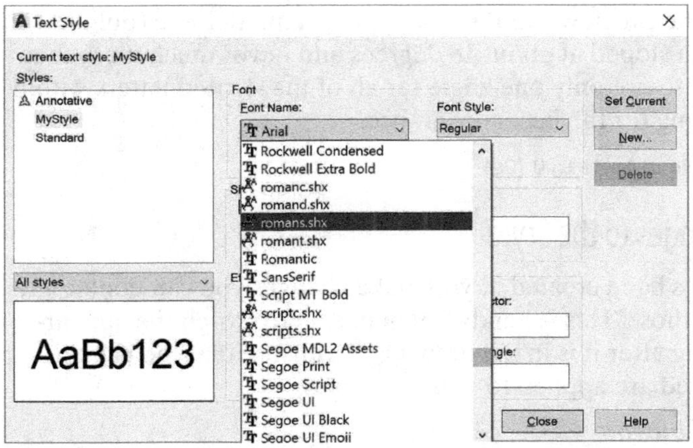

Figure 1.63 **Preview Area Shows Selected Font Shape**

An AutoCAD shape-compiled font that works well for engineering drawings is the Roman Simplex (romans.shx) font.

On your own, scroll through the list until you see the romans.shx font, preceded by the calipers symbol, and select it.

The Font Style option only allows changes to True Type fonts, not to shape-compiled fonts (**.shx*) so it appears grayed out.

Tip: *Keep in mind that if you use a font in your drawing and another person is going to open that drawing on a different computer system, they must have that font or a different font will be substituted. As different fonts have different horizontal spacing, this can cause the text to be misaligned. Stick to easy to read, common fonts, like Arial or romans.shx font. Romans is part of AutoCAD, so every user should have it.*

Size Area

Leaving the text height for a style set to zero causes the software to prompt for the height when you place text. This way you can set the height when you place the text.

Leave the default text height set to 0.00.

Warning: *Setting the text height in the Text Style dialog box causes you not to be prompted for the height of the text when you use the Text command.*

The Annotative selection in the Size area allows the text to be scaled automatically to show correctly at different layout scales. This is a very useful feature which you will learn more about in Tutorial 5. For now leave Annotative unchecked.

Effects Area

Upside down, Backwards, and Vertical are effects that can be applied to the font.

Click: ***to select Upside down,*** *so that it appears checked*

Notice that the preview now shows the lettering upside down.

Click: ***to deselect Upside down*** *(remove the check)*

Entering a value for Width Factor allows you to make compressed and expanded letters.

On your own, change the Width Factor to 2 and notice the change in the preview area. The letters should appear stretched out. Change the value to .8 and look at the preview. This time the letters should appear compressed.

Return the Width Factor to a value of 1.00.

Change the Oblique Angle to 20 *(20d)*.

The letters in the preview should now appear slanted. Italic (oblique) letters are often sloped at about 18 degrees and never much more than 20 degrees. Try to use only one angle for all of the slanted letters within the same drawing for the best appearance.

Return the Oblique Angle to 0 (0d)

Apply the Changes to the Style

Once a style has been created, if you make changes you can update the style to reflect those. This is handy if you decide to switch the appearance of lettering after it is in the drawing. To ensure that the changes you have entered are applied to your new style,

Click: ***Apply button***

To change an existing style, first select it from the list of styles, make the changes, and then apply them.

Setting Current Style

Any new text added to your drawing will apply the current text style until you set a different style as current.

Click: ***Set Current***

Click: ***Close*** *(to exit the dialog box)*

You will now add a title to the bottom of the drawing.

Command: ***TEXT [Enter]***

Specify start point of text or [Justify/Style]: ***J [Enter]***

Enter an option [Align/Fit/Center/Middle/Right/TL/TC/TR/ML/MC/MR/BL/BC/BR]: ***C [Enter]***

Specify center point of text: ***select a point near the middle bottom of the drawing***

Specify height <3.00>: ***[Enter]***

Specify rotation angle of text<E>: ***E [Enter]*** *(be sure that your rotation angle is set to E)*

Type: ***PLOT PLAN [Enter] [Enter]***

You can use the Help command to discover how the Justify options of the Text command work.

Click: ***Help button***

The Help window appears on your screen.

Type: ***TEXT*** *(into the search box, use all capitals)* ***[Enter]***

Click: ***Text (Command)*** *from the listed items*

Scroll down to see the help for aligning text *(Figure 1.64).*

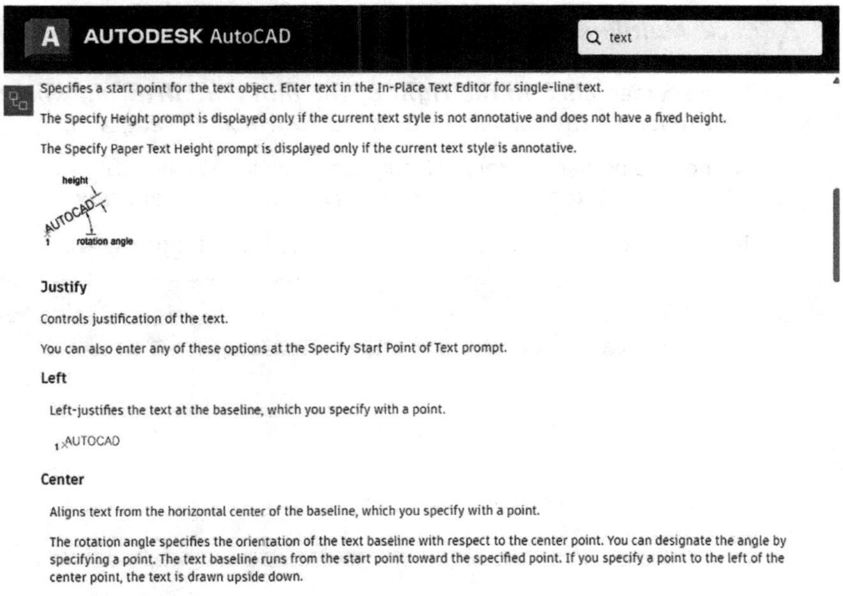

Figure 1.64 **Help Window Information for Text Justification**

Take a minute to familiarize yourself with the text justification options. You can return to the help screen whenever you want more information about how commands work.

Click: ***to close the Help window***

Setting a Style Current

You can quickly make a style current using the Text Style drop-down list as shown in Figure 1.65.

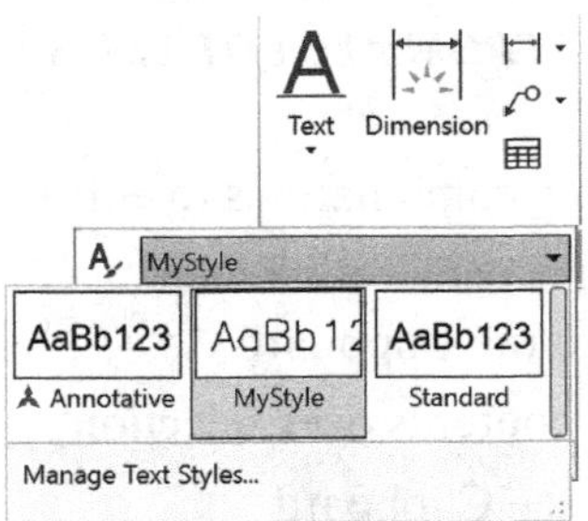

Figure 1.65 **Text Style Drop-Down List**

Click: ***to show the Text Style drop-down list***

Click: ***Standard** from the list of styles*

Now new text added to the drawing will use the style named Standard.

Using Mtext

Unlike Text, the Mtext command automatically adjusts text within the width you specify. You can also create text with your own text editor and then import it with the Mtext command. As with Text, you can easily edit Mtext by double-clicking it to use the DDEdit command.

A *Click:* ***MultilineText button***

Specify first corner: ***click to the right of the plot plan drawing** where you want to locate the corner of the notes; a window area forms*

Specify opposite corner or [Height/Justify/Line spacing/Rotation/Style/Width/Columns]: ***click to set the second corner of the window***

The ribbon changes to show the In-Place Text Editor (Figure 1.66).

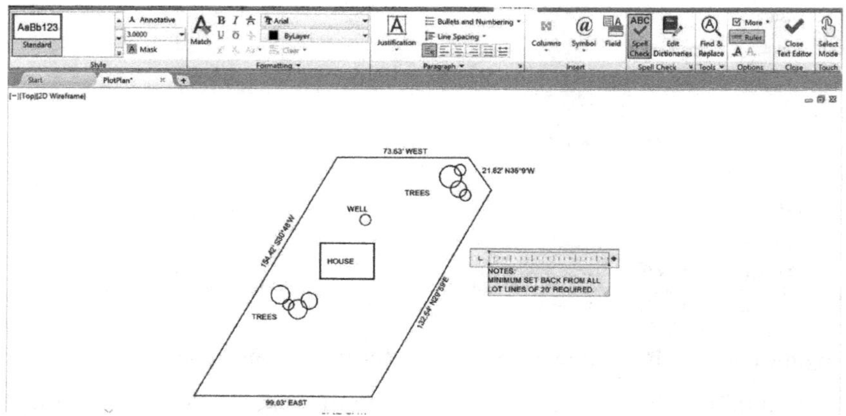

Figure 1.66 The In-Place Text Editor

The ruler along the top of the area you selected for text entry allows you to size the area where the text will appear in your drawing. The pointers on the left side of the ruler control the indent and margin. Holding down your mouse button and dragging the right end of the ruler controls the width of the box (corresponding to the width of the text area). The large blank area of the dialog box is where you will type in the notes for the plot plan.

Type: ***NOTES: [Enter] MINIMUM SET BACK FROM ALL LOT LINES OF 20' REQUIRED.***

You can use the standard Windows Control key combinations to edit text in the Text Formatting dialog box.

[Ctrl]-C	Copy selection to the Clipboard
[Ctrl]-V	Paste Clipboard contents over selection
[Ctrl]-X	Cut selection to the Clipboard
[Ctrl]-Z	Undo and Redo
[Ctrl]-[Shift]-[Spacebar]	Insert a nonbreaking space
[Enter]	End current paragraph and start a new line

Special Symbols

It is easy to add special symbols within a block of text using the Symbol flyout as shown in Figure 1.67. If you know the symbol's code, you can type it directly, but remembering the codes for symbols that you use infrequently can be difficult. Using the flyout, you can quickly select a symbol from the list.

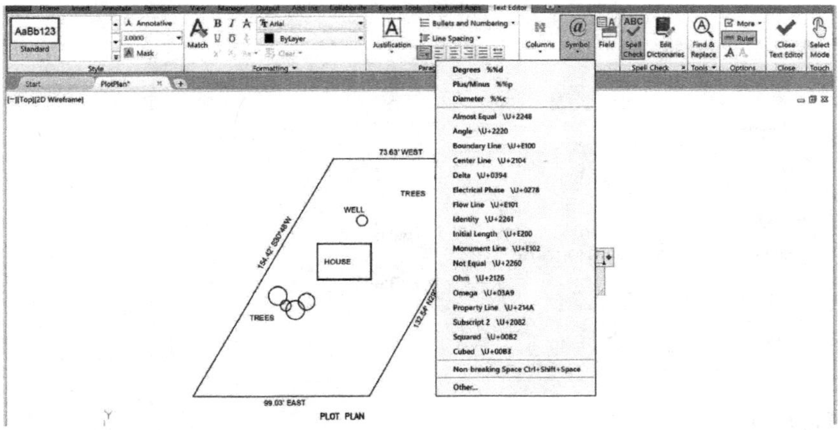

Figure 1.67 **Symbol Flyout**

Formatting

To change the current font, style of text (bold or italic), or color of text, use the text formatting options. These appear similar to that of your word processor. You can also cut and paste text between the In-Place Text Editor and your word processor. Experiment with them on your own.

Stacked Text for Fractions

You can create stacked fractions or stacked text with the Mtext command. To do so, separate the text to be stacked with a forward slash (/) for the text to stack automatically.

Type: ***5/8*** *into the Multiline Text at the end of the typed notes (the text must be followed by a space before it will "stack").*

Select: the ***5/8*** *text so it appears highlighted*

Click the icon as shown in Figure 1.68.

Click: ***Diagonal***

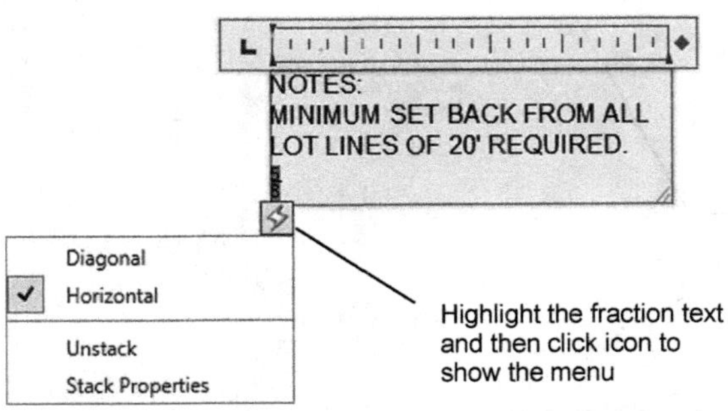

Figure 1.68

Select: the ***5/8*** *text so it appears highlighted*

Right-click and choose Stack from the list (Figure 1.68).

Click: ***Stack Properties***

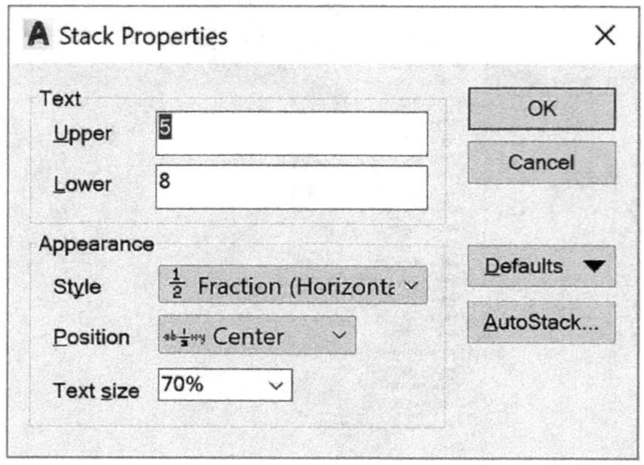

Figure 1.69

The Stack Properties dialog box appears as shown in Figure 1.69. This dialog box provides a variety of options for making stacked fractions.

Click: ***Cancel*** *to close the Stack Properties dialog box.*

Highlight the 5/8 text and click the icon to show the context menu.

Click: ***Unstack***

On your own, delete the 5/8 text.

Click: ***Close Text Editor*** *(from the upper right of the ribbon area)*

The notes are placed in your drawing, similar to Figure 1.70.

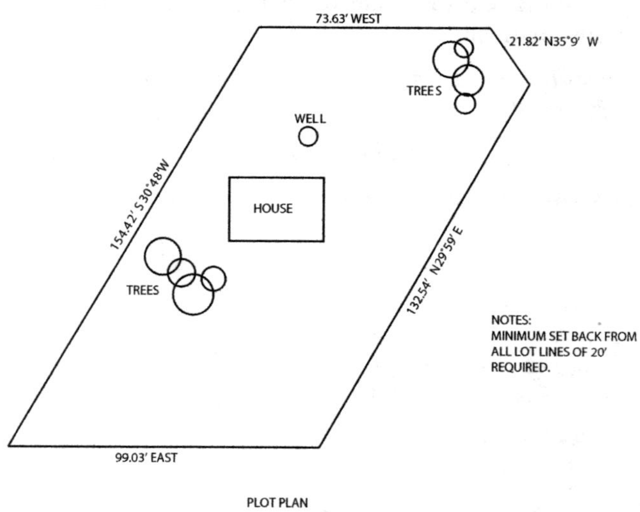

Figure 1.70

Spell Checking Your Drawing

You can use AutoCAD's spell checker to detect spelling errors.

Click: ***Annotate tab, Check Spelling button***

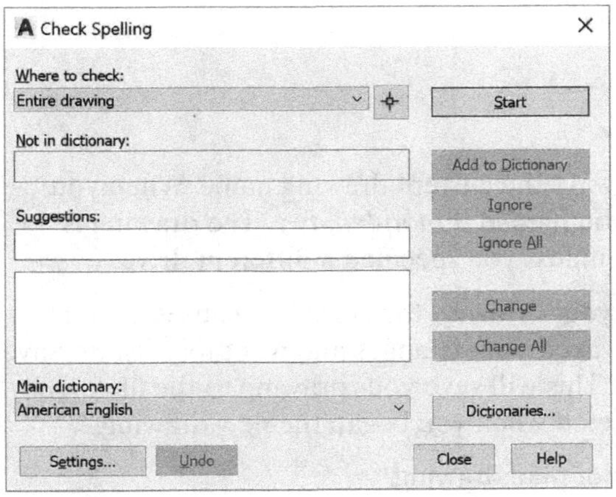

Figure 1.71

Tip: While you have the Text Editor open you can turn on the Check Spelling button so that errors will be highlighted as you type.

The Check Spelling dialog box appears on the screen as shown in Figure 1.71.

Click: ***Selected Objects*** *from the pull-down list in the Where to check area.*

Click: ***Select objects button*** *to the left of Where to check*

Select objects: ***click on the minimum set back note [Enter]***

Click: ***Start***

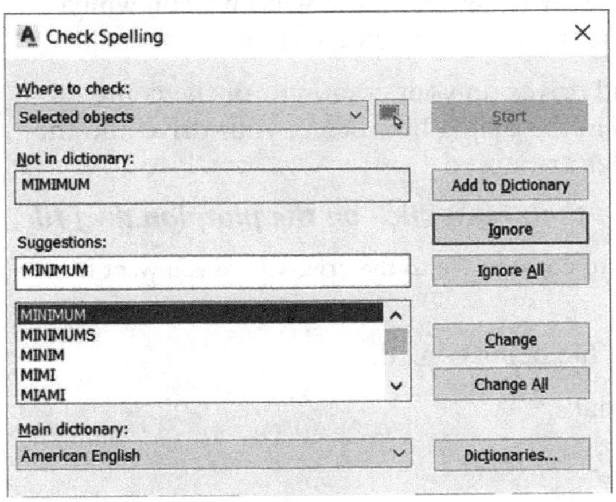

Figure 1.72 Spelling Error

If the text contains spelling errors, the Check Spelling dialog box will show them (Figure 1.72) and the incorrect item will be located and enlarged on your screen to make it easier to correct. If your drawing does not contain any misspellings, the message "Spelling check complete" will appear.

Click: ***Close***

You may have noticed that spelling errors are underlined in red in the text editor as you type.

Saving Your Drawing

Now, save your drawing.

Click: ***Save button***

The default file name is always the current drawing name. When you started the new drawing, you named it *plotplan.dwg.* The drawing is saved on the default drive unless you specified a different drive.

If you have already saved your drawing, the close box causes an immediate exit. If you have not saved your changes and want to, click on Save Changes in the dialog box. This will save your drawing to the file name *plotplan.dwg* that you selected when you began the new drawing.

You have completed the plot plan drawing.

Click: ***to close the AutoCAD program***

You should now see the Windows desktop.

Transferring Files

Use your operating system to copy or transfer files from one drive to another. To transfer the file named *plotplan.dwg* from the hard drive to a portable USB drive, use the Windows File Explorer.

Warning: *The appearance of Windows Explorer may depend on your operating system version and your individual settings.*

You should have a File Explorer located on the task bar that you can use to transfer and copy files. Windows 8.1 has a window icon which you can right-click to show a menu to open the File Explorer.

The various directories and drives on your computer or the contents of the current folder show in the dialog box. Select your drive and the *work* folder where your files are stored.

Tip: *Use the Windows File Explorer to check that your file has copied to the destination correctly.*

Click once to select and then right-click on the plotplan.dwg file.

On your own use this menu to copy the file to the drive where you want to save the file.

You see a box showing the file being copied.

You have completed Tutorial 1.

Key Terms

absolute coordinates
alias
angle brackets
architectural units
array
bearing
Cartesian coordinate system
case-sensitive
command aliasing
command prompt
command window
context-sensitive
context-sensitive menu
coordinate values
default directory
default units
docked
drag
drawing session
engineering units
file extension
floating
floating window
flyout
font
fractional units
graphics cursor (cross-hairs)
graphics window
grid
highlight
implied Crossing mode
implied Windowing mode
menu bar
origin
polar coordinates
real-world units
relative coordinates
scientific units
scroll bars
selection set
shape-compiled font
Sheet Set Manager
Standard toolbar
status bar
surveyor units
template
title bar
toggle
tool tip
tool palette
toolbar
transparent command
UCS icon
unidirectional text
window, cascade
window, tile horizontally
window, tile vertically
Windows control buttons
world coordinates

Key Commands (keyboard shortcut)

Circle (C)
Circle, 3 Points
Circle, Center Radius
Copy (CP)
Erase (E)
Grid (F7)
Help (?)
Limits (LIM)
Line (L)
Multiline Text (MT)
New Drawing (NEW)
OOPS
Rectangle (RECT)
REDO
REDRAWALL
Save (CTRL+S)
Single Line Text (TEXT)
Snap (F9)
Style (ST)
Text Editing (TEXTEDIT)
Undo (U)
Units (UNI)
Zoom (Z)
Zoom All

Exercises

Redraw the following shapes. If dimensions are provided, use them to create your drawing, showing the exact geometry of the part. The letter M after an exercise number means that the dimensions are in millimeters (metric units). If no letter follows the exercise number, the dimensions are in inches. The Ø symbol indicates that the following dimension is a diameter. Do not include dimensions on the drawings.

Exercises are marked with an icon indicating their subject area. Unmarked exercises are of a general nature.

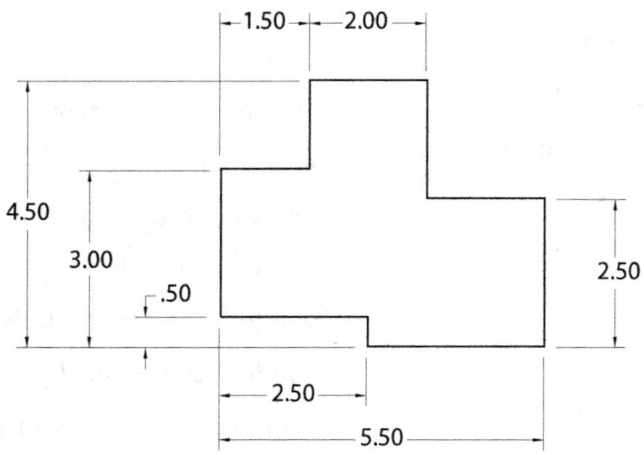

Exercise 1.1 Baseplate

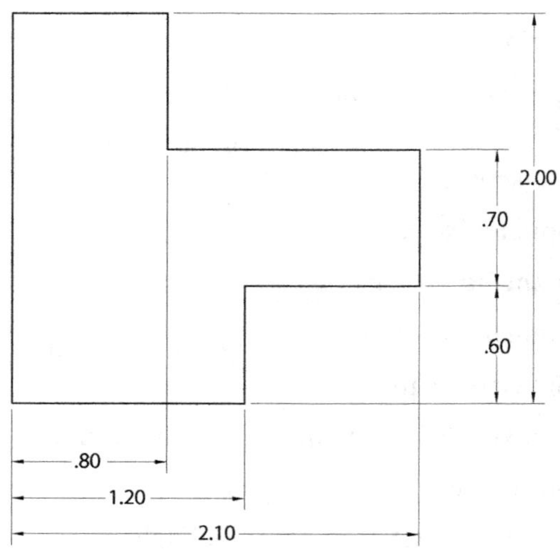

Exercise 1.2 Rectangular Bracket

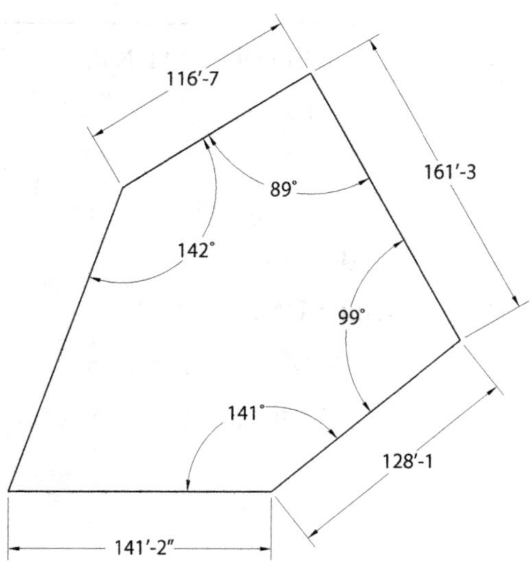

Exercise 1.3 Site Boundary

Tip: *Solve angle relative to 0° toward East or use Help to set Polar into relative mode.*

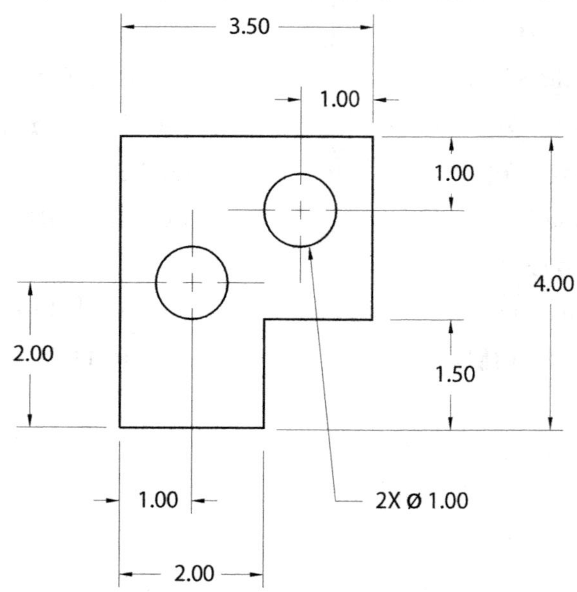

Exercise 1.4 Filter Plate

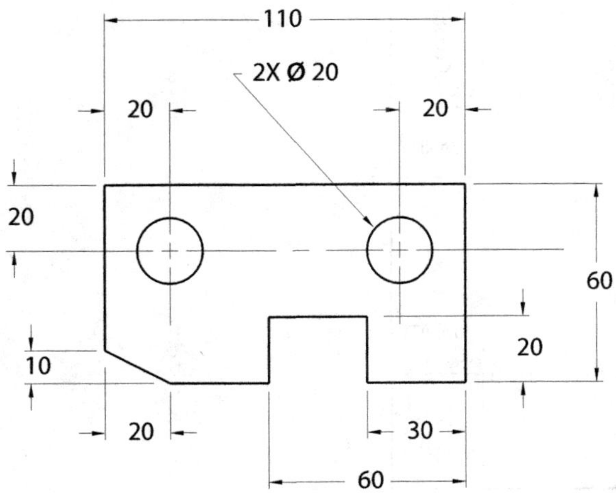

Exercise 1.5M Gasket

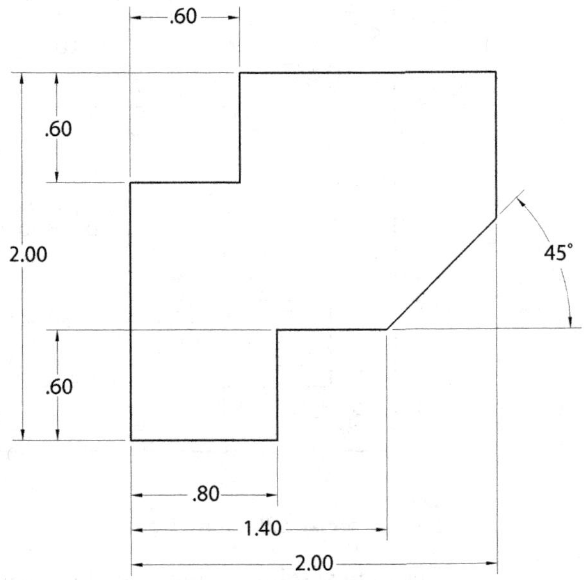

Exercise 1.6 Spacer

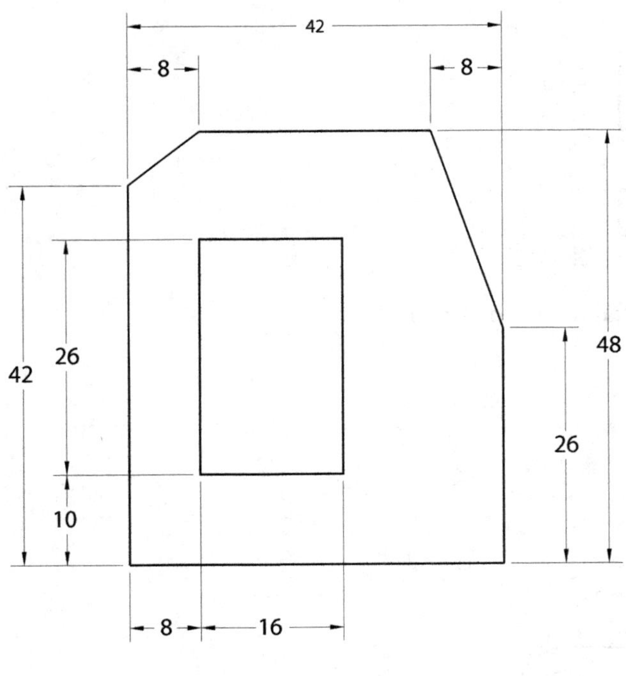

Exercise 1.7M Guide Plate

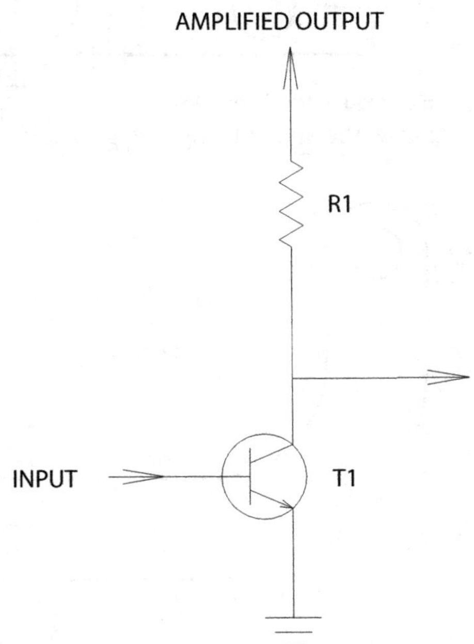

Exercise 1.8 Amplifier

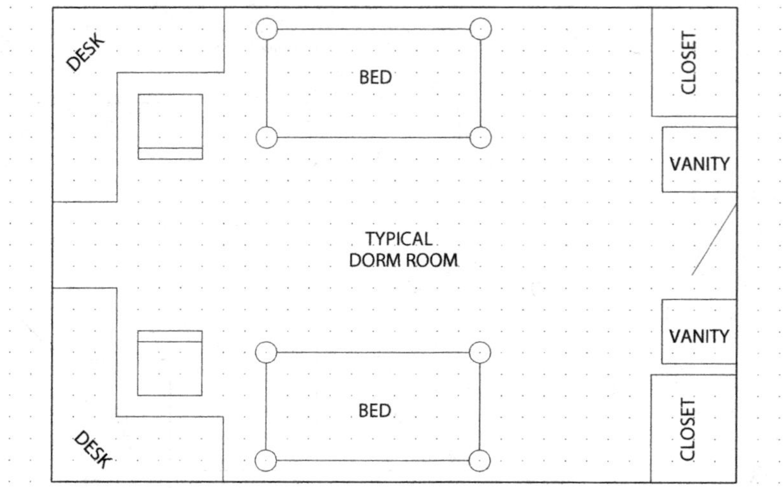

Exercise 1.9 Dorm Room

Reproduce this drawing using Snap and Grid. Use Text to label the items.

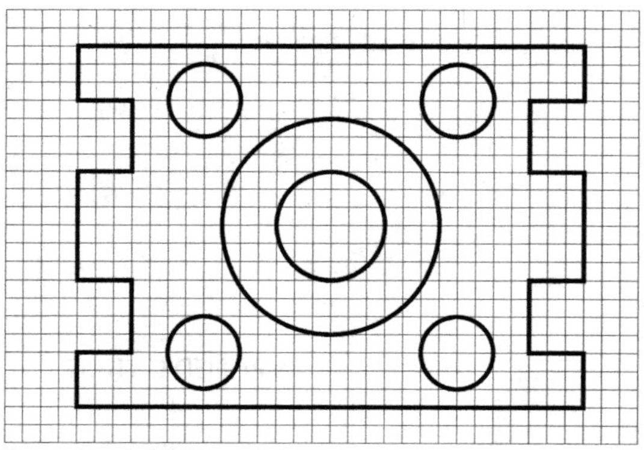

Exercise 1.10 Template

Draw the shape using one grid square equal to 1/4" or 10 mm.

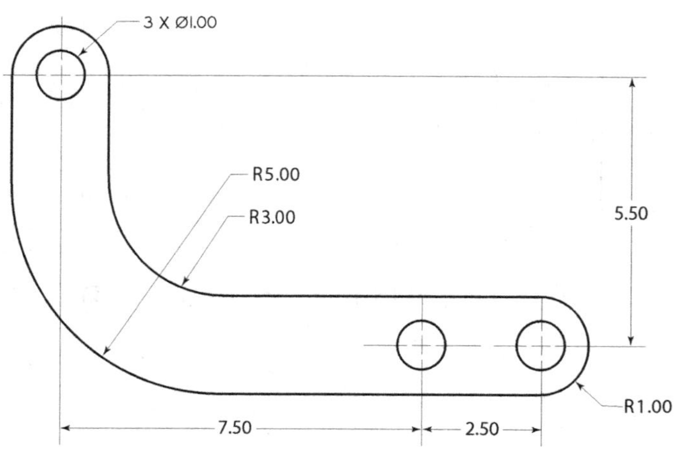

Exercise 1.11 Bracket

Redraw the following shape. Use the dimensions to create your drawing showing the exact geometry of the part.

BASIC CONSTRUCTION TECHNIQUES

2

Introduction

You usually create drawings by combining and modifying several different basic *primitive* shapes, such as lines, circles, and arcs, to create more complex shapes. This tutorial will help you learn how to draw shapes. Keep in mind that one of the advantages of using CAD over drawing on paper is that you are creating an accurate model of the drawing geometry. In Tutorial 3, you will learn to list information from the drawing database. Information extracted from the drawing is accurate only if you create the drawing accurately in the first place.

Starting

Before you begin, **launch AutoCAD 2027.**

Opening an Existing Drawing

This tutorial shows you how to add arcs and circles to the subdivision drawing provided with the datafiles that came with this guide. In Tutorial 3 you will finish the subdivision drawing so that the final drawing will look like Figure 2.1.

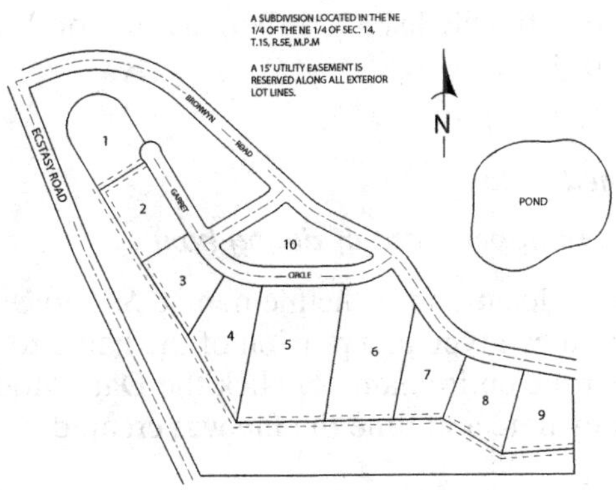

Wannabe Heights Estates

Figure 2.1

To open an existing drawing, use the Application icon, Open selection or click the button that looks like an open folder from the Quick Access toolbar.

Click: Open button

The Select File dialog box appears on your screen. Use the center portion, which shows the default directory and drive, to select the location where your datafiles have been stored. You should have already created a folder called *datafiles*, and copied all the datafiles for this book into it. If you have not done so, you may want to review the Getting Started chapters. If the correct folder is not showing in the Look In box, use the

Objectives

When you have completed this tutorial, you will be able to

1. Open existing drawings.
2. Work with new and existing layers.
3. Draw, using the Arc and Circle commands.
4. Set and use running Object snaps.
5. Change the display, using Zoom and Pan.
6. Use Dynamic View.
7. Draw ellipses.

Tip: *It is easy to download the datafiles. Use your browser to navigate to www.sdcpublications.com/Authors/Shawna-Lockhart. From there select the text you are using. Find and click the Download button on the page for your text.*

Up One Level icon or expand the choices by clicking on the downward arrow for the Look In box. Use the scroll bars if necessary to scroll down the list of directories and open the appropriate one so the files appear in the dialog box as in Figure 2.2. Scroll down the list of files until you see the file named *subdivis.dwg.* When you select a file, a preview of the file appears in the box to the right. (Older files may not show a preview.)

Tip: *Use the buttons at the left of the dialog box to show the History (recently used files), My Documents folder contents, or Favorites you have added. To add a favorite, find the folder and then right-click the Favorites button. Pick Add Current Folder from the pop-up menu that appears. To add a folder as a button, pick Tools, Add Current Folder to Places.*

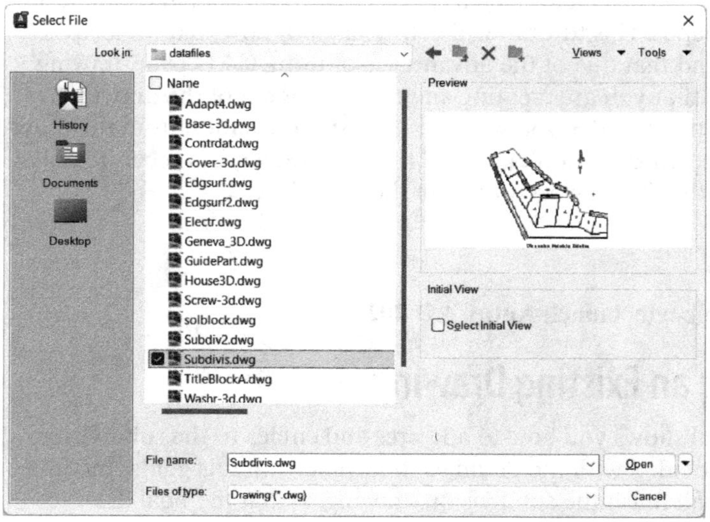

Figure 2.2

Menu choices at the top right of the Select File dialog box let you select different views to be displayed in the file list and other useful tools, such as a Find selection to search for files.

Click: ***Tools, Find***

Type: ***subdivis*** *(in the Named area)*

Click: ***Find Now button*** *(from upper right of dialog box)*

The Find dialog box displays the location for the file named *Subdivis. dwg*, as shown in Figure 2.3. You can type in a portion of the name to match if you cannot remember the entire name or click the Date Modified tab if you want to search by date and time the file was created.

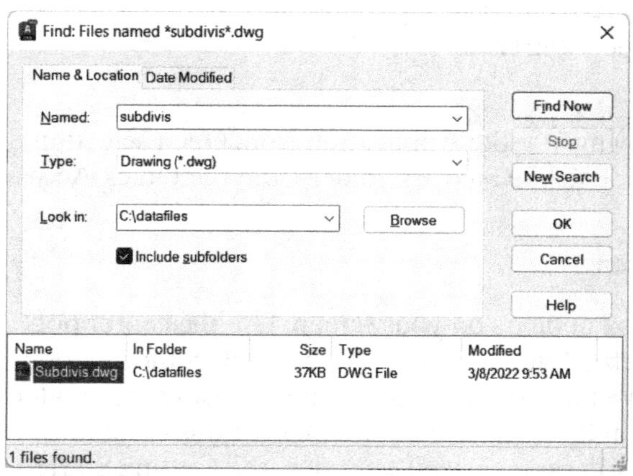

Figure 2.3

Double-click: ***Subdivis.dwg*** *(to select it from the list at the bottom)*

You return to the Select File dialog box.

Click: ***Open***

Double-click: in the center of the screen to zoom to the drawing extents

When you have opened the file, it appears on your screen, as shown in Figure 2.4. It opens with its own defaults for Grid, Snap, and other features. These settings are saved in the drawing file.

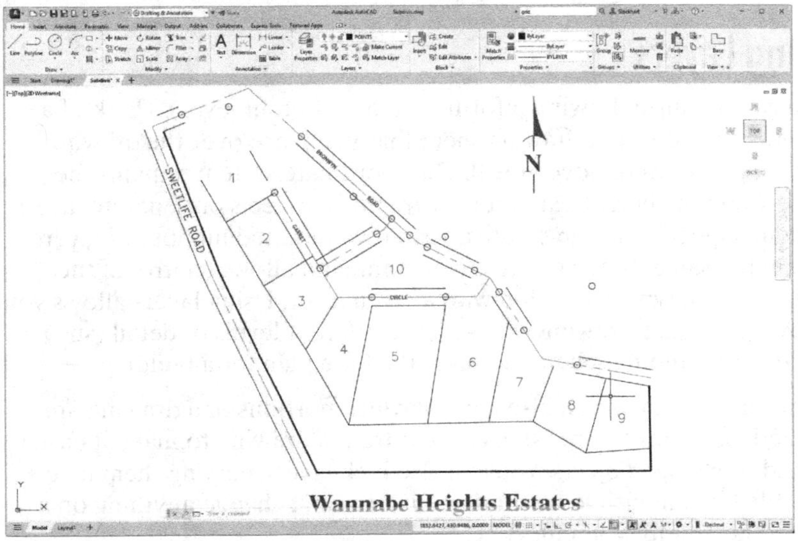

Figure 2.4

Saving as a New File

The Save As command allows you to save your drawing to a new file name and/or different drive or folder. You can select this command from the Application icon or from the Quick Access toolbar.

Click: ***Save As button***

The Save Drawing As dialog box appears similar to Figure 2.5.

Tip: *Don't use the Save command because that will save your changes into the original datafile.*

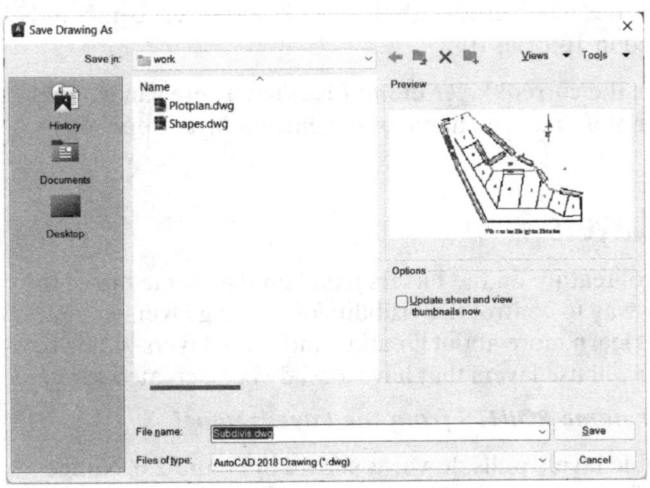

Figure 2.5

Tip: *Notice that if you have set up an account, you can use the OneDrive selection to save your files to storage in the "cloud."*

Warning: *If you save a file with the same name as one already in the directory, you will see a message the file "already exists. Do you want to replace it?" Choose No unless you want to replace the file.*

On your own, select the drive and folder *work* and specify the name for your drawing, *subdivis.dwg*.

In this case, the new file name is the same as the previous file name, but the folder is different. This creates a new copy of drawing *subdivis.dwg* saved in the folder named *work*.

The original *subdivis.dwg* remains unchanged on your drive. When you use the Save As command and specify a new file name, the software sets the newly saved file as current.

Using Layers

You can organize drawing information on different layers. Think of a *layer* as a transparent drawing sheet that you place over the drawing and that you can remove at will. The coordinate system remains the same from one layer to another, so graphical objects on separate layers remain aligned. You can create a virtually unlimited number of layers within the same drawing. The Layer command allows control of the color and linetype associated with a given layer. Using layers allows you to overlay a base drawing with several different levels of detail (such as wiring or plumbing schematics over the base plan for a building).

By using layers, you can also control which portions of a drawing are plotted, or remove dimensions or text from a drawing to make it easier to add or change objects. You can also lock layers, making them inaccessible but still visible on the screen. You can't change anything on a locked layer until you unlock it.

Current Layer

The *current layer* is the layer you are working on. Any new objects you draw are added to the current layer. The default current layer is layer 0. If you do not create and use other layers, your drawing will be created on layer 0. You used this layer when drawing the plot plan in Tutorial 1. Layer 0 is a special layer provided in the AutoCAD program.

You cannot rename or delete layer 0 from the list of layers. Layer 0 has special properties when used with the Block and Insert commands, which are covered in Tutorial 10.

Layer POINTS is the current layer in *subdivis.dwg*. There can be only one current layer at a time. The name of the current layer appears on the Layer toolbar.

Controlling Layers

The Layer Control feature on the Layers panel on the Home tab of the ribbon is an easy way to control the visibility of existing layers in your drawing. You will learn more about creating and using layers in this tutorial. For now, you will use layers that have already been created for you.

Click: ***on layer name POINTS from the Layers panel***

The list of available layers pulls down, as shown in Figure 2.6. Notice the special layer 0 displayed near the top of the list.

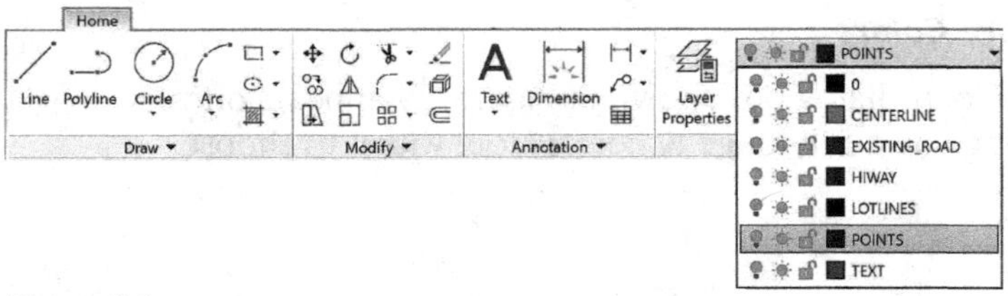

Figure 2.6

*Click: **on the layer name CENTERLINE from the Layer Control list***

It becomes the current layer shown on the toolbar. Any new objects will be created on this layer until you select a different current layer. The Layer Control now should look like Figure 2.7, showing the layer name CENTERLINE.

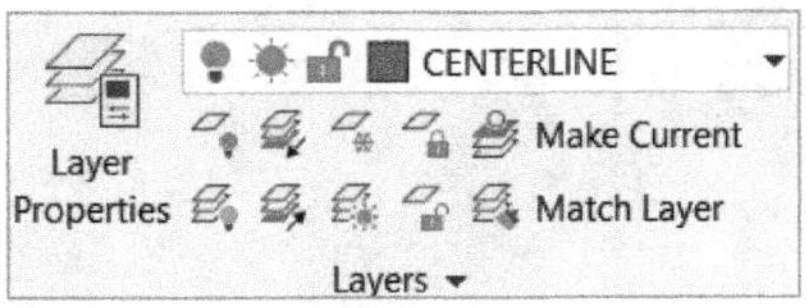

Figure 2.7

Use the Line command you learned in Tutorial 1 to draw a line off to the side of the subdivision drawing.

Note that it is green and has a centerline linetype (long dash, short dash, long dash). The line you drew is on Layer CENTERLINE.

Erase or Undo the line on your own.

Controlling Colors

Each layer has a color associated with it. Using different colors for different layers helps you visually distinguish different information in the drawing. An object's color also may control appearance during printing.

There are two different ways of selecting the color for objects on your screen. The best way is usually to set the layer color and draw the objects on the appropriate layer. This method keeps your drawing organized. The other method is to use the Color Control feature on the Properties panel. To select the Color Control pull-down feature,

Tip: *If your panels are minimized, you may need to click Properties to expand the panel (see Figure 2.8).*

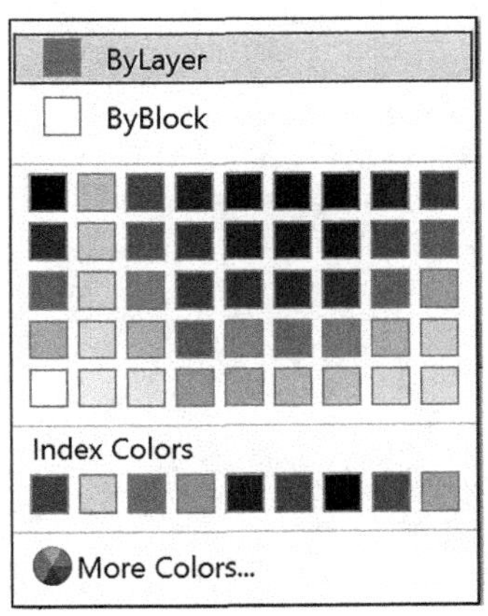

*Click: **ByLayer** from the Properties panel to pull down the Color Control*

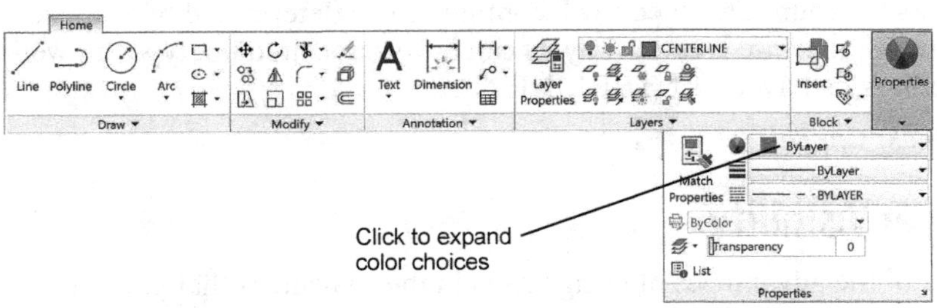

Figure 2.8

Note that the standard colors (yellow, red, green, blue, etc.) are shown. You can also choose More Colors to view the full color palette.

Click: ***More Colors***

Tip: *On a black background, color 7 used for layer 0 appears as white; on a white background it appears black.*

The Select Color dialog box shown in Figure 2.9 appears on your screen, giving you a full range of colors from which to choose.

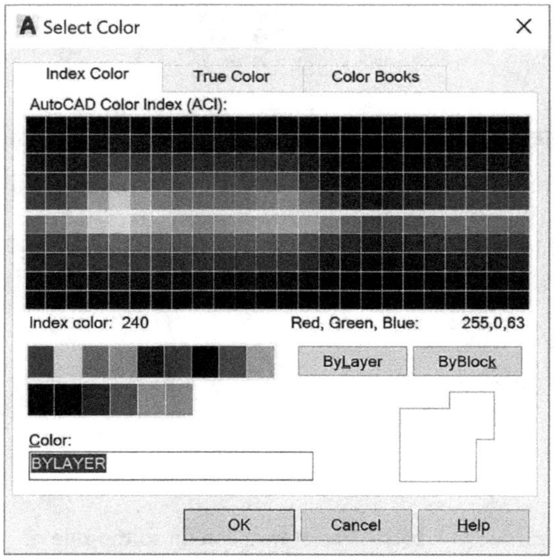

Figure 2.9

The three tabs of the Select Color dialog box allow you to choose among different methods to determine the color for your drawing entities. The True Color tab allows you to set color to either RGB, which stands for Red, Green, Blue, the primary colors of light, or HSL, which stands for the Hue, Saturation, and Luminance of the color. The Color Books tab lets you select from among different standard ink manufacturer's predefined colors so that you can match print colors very closely to the colors you choose on your screen. In this text you will use Index Color (AutoCAD Color Index) as the method for selecting color.

Make sure the ***Index Color*** *tab is selected.*

The default option for the Color (and also for the Linetype) command is BYLAYER. It's the best selection because, when you draw a line, the color and linetype will be those of the current layer. Otherwise, the color in your drawing can become very confusing. You will click Cancel to exit the Select Color dialog box without making any changes. The colors for your new objects will continue to be determined by the layer on which they are created. Layers can have associated linetypes, as well as colors, as Layer CENTERLINE does.

Click: ***Cancel***

Layer Visibility

One of the advantages of using layers in the drawing is that you can choose not to display selected layers. That way, if you want to create projection lines or even notes about the drawing, you can draw them on a layer that you will later turn off, so that it isn't displayed or printed. Or you may want to create a complex drawing with many layers, such as a building plan that contains the electrical plan on one layer and the mechanical plan on another, along with separate layers for the walls, windows, and so on. You can store all the information in a single drawing, and then plot different combinations of layers to create the electrical layout, first-floor plan, and any other combination you want.

Next you will use the Layer Control to lock, freeze, and turn off some of the layers in this drawing.

Click: ***on CENTERLINE*** *to show the list of layers*

The list of layers pulls down. Refer to Figure 2.10 as you make the following selections.

Click: ***the On/Off icon,*** *which looks like a lightbulb, to the left of Layer EXISTING_ROAD*

Click: ***any blank area of the screen*** *away from the Layer list to return to the drawing*

Note that the blue roadway lines have been turned off so that they no longer appear. Invisible (off) layers are not printed or plotted, but objects on these layers are still part of the drawing.

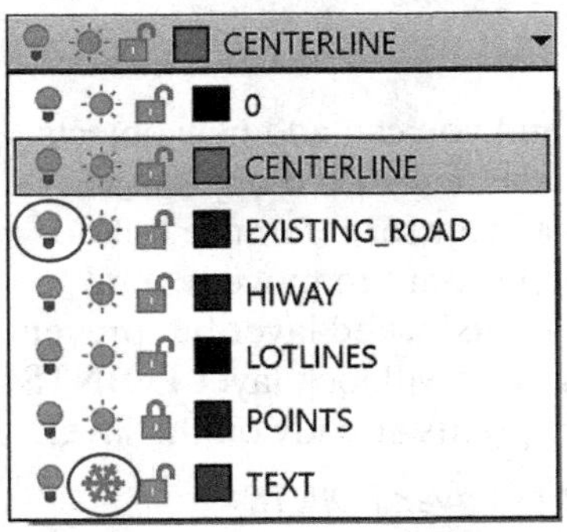

Figure 2.10 **Layer Control**

Freezing Layers

Freezing a layer is similar to turning it off. You use the *freeze* option not only to make the layer disappear from the display, but also to cause it to be skipped when the drawing is regenerated. This feature can noticeably improve the speed with which the software regenerates a large drawing. You should not freeze the current layer because that would create a situation where you would be drawing objects that you couldn't see on the screen. The icon for freezing and thawing layers looks like a snowflake when frozen and a shining sun when thawed.

Click: *to* ***expand the Layer Control*** *list*

Click: ***the Freeze/Thaw icon*** *to the left of Layer TEXT*

Click: ***any blank area in the graphics window*** *to return to the drawing*

Layer TEXT is still on, but it is frozen and therefore invisible. A layer can both be turned off and frozen; the effect is similar. You should either freeze a layer or turn it off, but there is no point in doing both. Your screen should now be similar to Figure 2.11.

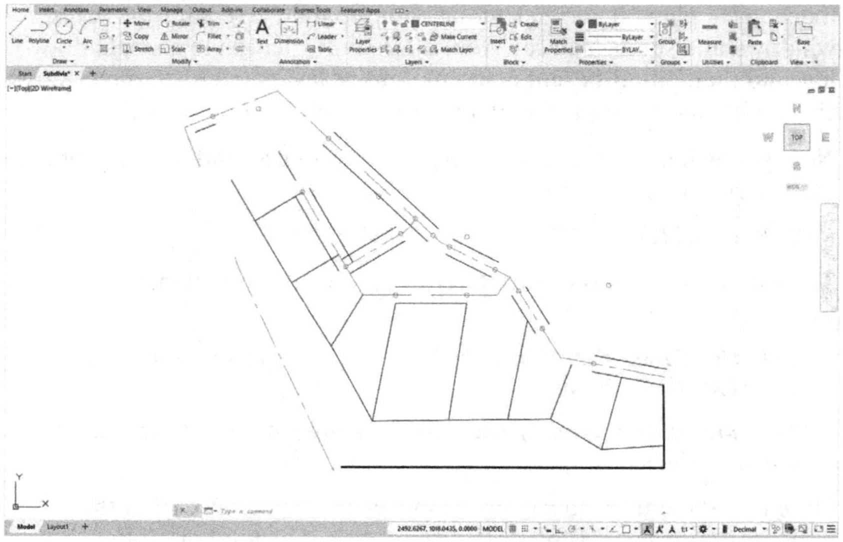

Figure 2.11

Locking Layers

You can see a *locked layer* on the screen, and you can add new objects to it. However, you can't make changes to the new or old objects on that layer. This is useful when you need the layer for reference but do not want to change it. For example, you might want to move several items so that they line up with an object on the locked layer but prevent anything on the locked layer from moving. You will lock layer POINTS so that you cannot accidentally change the points already on the layer.

Click: ***the Lock/Unlock icon*** *to the left of Layer POINTS*

Layer CENTERLINE should still be the current layer. (If for some reason it is not the current layer, set it current at this time.) Layer TEXT is frozen and does not appear. Layer EXISTING_ROAD is turned off and does not appear. Layer POINTS is locked so that you can see and add to it, but not change it.

On your own, try erasing one of the circled points in the drawing.

```
Command: _erase
Select objects: Specify
1 was on a locked layer.
```

A message appears, stating that the object is on a locked layer. The object won't be erased.

Making Object's Layer Current

The Make Current button is located above the Layer Control pull-down (Figure 2.11). This command lets you select an object and then click on the icon to make that object's layer the current layer.

Click: ***a black lot line*** *(white if your background color is black) representing a lot boundary*

Note that the Layer Control now shows LOTLINES, the layer of the line you selected. This name is only temporary, for if you drew a new line, the layer name changes back to the current layer (CENTERLINE). This is useful when you are unsure which layer a particular object is on.

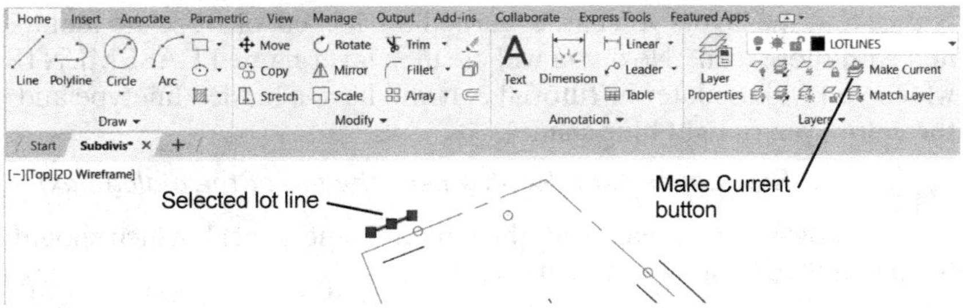

Figure 2.12

Next you will use the Make Current button to set LOTLINES as the current layer.

Make sure a black lot line is still highlighted

Click: Make Object's Layer Current icon

The current layer is changed to LOTLINES, and any new objects will be added to this layer. In the command prompt is the message: LOTLINES is now the current layer.

Now you will change the current layer back to CENTERLINE by using the Layer Previous button. If you are not sure which button to select, hover your mouse over the buttons to show the tooltips.

Click: ***to expand the Layer panel*** *(down arrow near panel name)*

Click: ***Layer Previous button***

Layer CENTERLINE returns as the current layer.

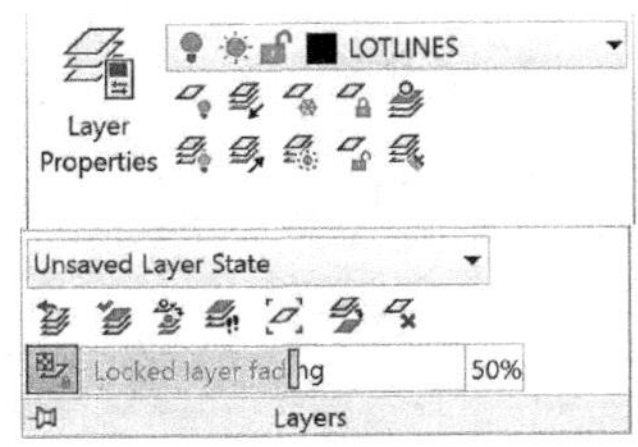

Using Layer

The Layer command lets you create new layers and control the color, line-type, and other properties of a layer. You can also use Layer to control which layers are visible or can be plotted and to set the current layer. Remember, only one layer at a time can be current. New objects are created on the current layer. Use the Layer Properties Manager icon from the Layer panel to create new layers and set their properties. (Its command alias is LA.)

Click: ***Layer Properties Manager button***

The Layer Properties Manager appears on the screen, showing the list of existing layers (Figure 2.13).

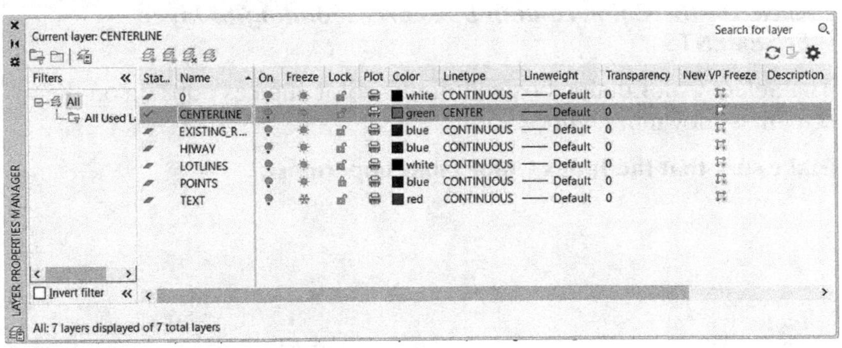

Figure 2.13

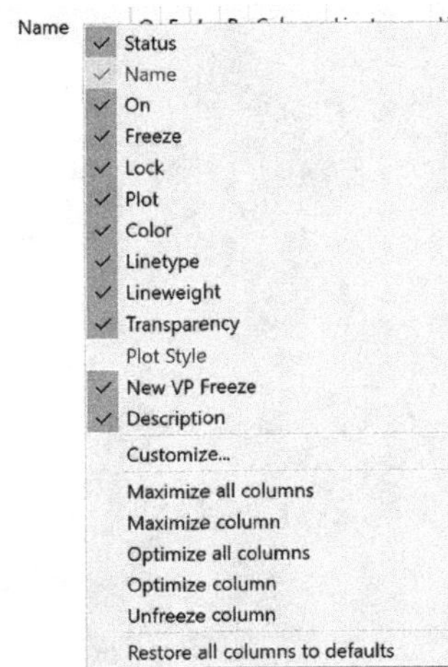

Tip: *Right-click on the column headings to show the context menu. Maximize all columns to show the full names.*

You can resize the Layer Properties Manager by dragging on its corners.

Notice that the layers you earlier turned off, locked, or froze are identified with those icons. Next you will create a layer named EASEMENTS which you will use later in Tutorial 3. It will have a hidden linetype and the color cyan (a light blue shade).

Click: ***New Layer icon (located near the top of the dialog box)***

A new layer appears with the default name Layer1, which should be highlighted as shown in Figure 2.14.

Tip: *You can right-click on a heading in the Layer Properties Manager, and select Maximize All Columns from the pop-up menu that appears.*

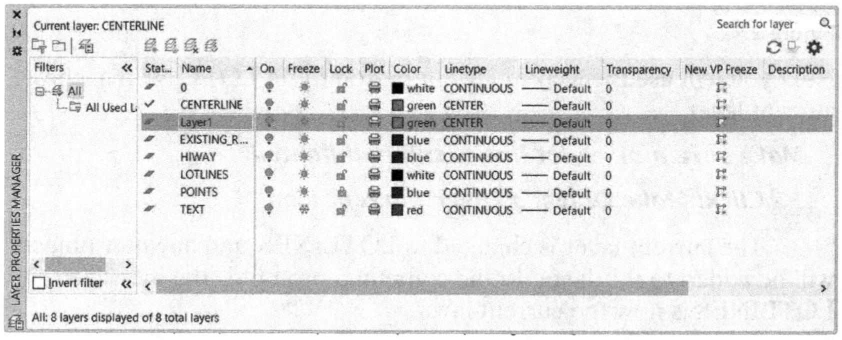

Figure 2.14

By default it has the same properties as the currently selected layer (CENTERLINE). You will change the layer name, color and linetype for the new layer next.

Layer names can be as long as 255 characters. Layer names can contain almost any characters, except for restricted operating system characters like comma (,) and others like <>/"?:*|'=. Letters, numbers, spaces, and the characters dollar sign ($), period (.), number sign (#), underscore (_), and hyphen (-) are valid. While Layer1 is still highlighted,

Type: ***EASEMENTS [Enter]***

Next, set the color for layer EASEMENTS. To the right of the layer names are the various layer controls mentioned previously. Each column title is labeled with the name of the function: On (light bulb), Freeze (sun), Lock/Unlock (lock), Color (small color box), Linetype, Lineweight, Plot Style, Plot, and Description. You can resize these columns to show more or less of the names by dragging the line between the name headings.

To change the color for layer EASEMENTS,

Click: ***on the Color column box corresponding to layer EASEMENTS***

The Select Color dialog box containing color choices pops up on the screen as shown in Figure 2.15.

Make sure that the Index Color tab is uppermost.

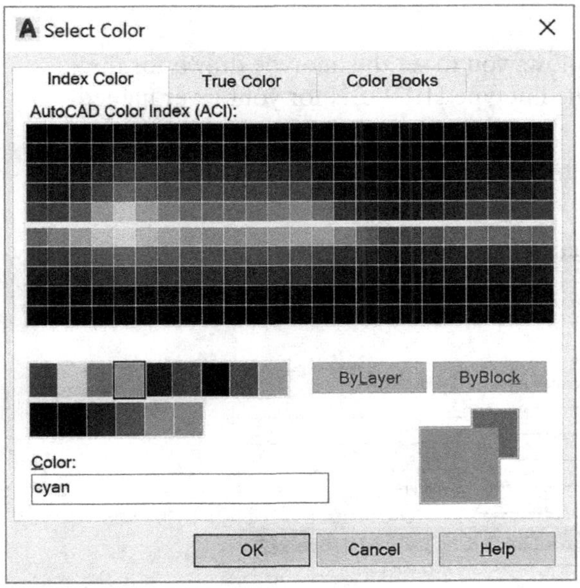

Figure 2.15

Color in Layers

The Select Color dialog box allows you to specify the color for objects drawn on a layer. You will select the color cyan for the easement layer that you are creating. The color helps you visually distinguish linetypes and layers in drawings. You also use color to select the pen and pen width for your printer or plotter. Tabs for Index Color, True Color and Color Books are arranged across the top of the dialog box, providing a wide array of options. Explore these on your own, and for now use the Index Colors.

The Select Color dialog box on the Index tab has the choices BY-LAYER and BYBLOCK on the right side. As you are specifying the color for layer EASEMENTS only, you can't select these choices, so they are shown grayed. Move the arrow cursor over the named color boxes, where cyan is the fourth color from the left.

*Click: **cyan** from the named color boxes to the left of the ByLayer button*

The name of the color that you have selected appears in the Color: box at the bottom of the screen. (If you select one of the standard colors, the name appears in the box; if you select one of the other 255 colors from the palette, the color number appears.)

*Click: **OK***

Now the color for layer EASEMENTS is set to cyan. Check the listing of layer names and colors to verify that cyan has replaced green in the Color column to the right of the layer name EASEMENTS.

Linetype in Layers

The linetype column allows you to set the linetype drawn for the layer. You will select the linetype HIDDEN for your layer named EASEMENTS.

Click: on Center in the Linetype column across from layer EASEMENTS

The Select Linetype dialog box appears on your screen.

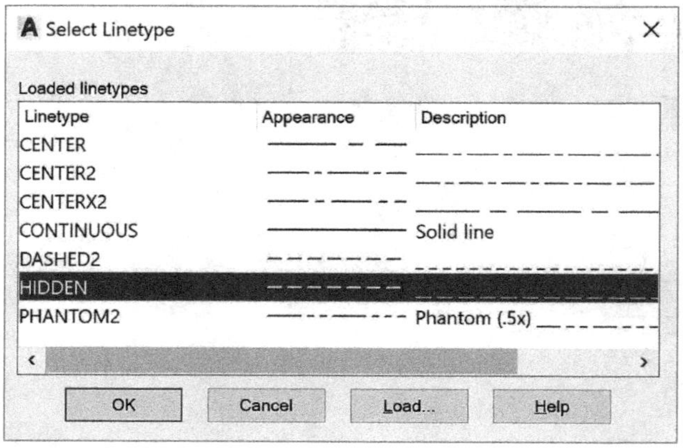

Figure 2.16

*Click: **HIDDEN** as shown in Figure 2.16*

*Click: **OK***

You return to the Layer Properties Manager. Layer EASEMENTS should have the properties set as shown in Figure 2.16.

*Click: **[X] from its upper left to close the Layer Properties Manager***

CENTERLINE should still be the current layer on the Layer toolbar, showing a green square to the left of the layer name. You will use the EASEMENTS layer you created later in this tutorial.

Using layers to control the color and linetype of new objects that you create will work only if BYLAYER is active as the method for establishing object color, object linetype, and lineweight.

On your own, examine the Color Control, Linetype Control, and the Lineweight Control on the Properties panel. All three should be set to BYLAYER.

Now that you know the basics of using and creating layers, you will begin creating the curved sections of the road centerline for the subdivision. The straight-line sections that the curves are tangent to have been drawn to get you started.

Using Object Snap

The object snap feature accurately selects locations based on existing objects in your drawing. When you click points from the screen without using object snaps, the resolution of your screen makes it impossible for you to select points with the accuracy stored in the drawing database. You have learned how to click accurately by snapping to a grid point. *Object snap* makes it possible for you to click points accurately on your drawing geometry by snapping to an object's center, endpoint, midpoint, and so on. Whenever prompted to select a point or location, you can use an object snap to help make an accurate selection. Without this command, locating two objects with respect to each other in correct and useful geometric form is virtually impossible. Object snap is one of the most important CAD tools. There are several different ways to access and use the Object Snaps.

Tip: *You can click the arrow to the right of the Object Snap button to expand the options.*

Right-click: ***the Object Snap button*** *on the Status bar*

The menu of Object Snap modes appears on your screen as shown in Figure 2.17.

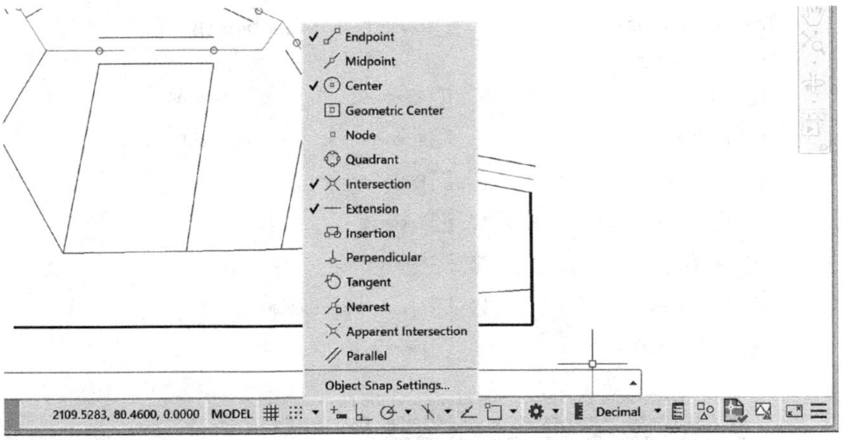

Figure 2.17

Object Snap can operate in two different ways. The first is called *override mode.* With this method, you select the object snap during a command. The object snap acts as a modifier within the command string to *target* the next point you select. You activate object snaps from within other commands by clicking the appropriate icon from the Object Snap toolbar. The object locations they select are indicated by small circles on the icons. When you activate an object snap in this manner, it is active for one click only. Remember, you can use this method only during a command that is prompting you to select points or objects.

Tip: *You can also activate an object snap by typing the three-letter name any time you are prompted to enter points or select objects. Refer to the Command Summary for the three letter codes.*

A special feature is active when Object Snap is in use. It displays a marker and description (SnapTip) when the cursor is placed near or on a snap point. This feature helps you to determine what location on the object will be selected.

The second method for using Object Snap is called *running mode.* With this method, you turn on the object snap and leave it on before using commands. When a running mode object snap is on, the marker box and SnapTip will appear during any future command when you are prompted for a point location, object selection, or other choice. The SnapTip will tell you which object snap location is being targeted.

*Click: **Object Snap Settings** from the menu (see Figure 2.17)*

The Drafting Settings dialog box you used to set the snap and grid appears on your screen. Notice it has many tabs: Snap and Grid, Polar Tracking, and Object Snap, and so on. Object Snap should be on top.

*Click: **Clear All** (to unselect any current modes)*

*Click: **Node***

A check appears in the box when it is selected, as shown in Figure 2.18. Node snaps to objects drawn with the AutoCAD Point command. The symbol next to the Node setting represents the AutoSnap marker shape that will appear in the drawing.

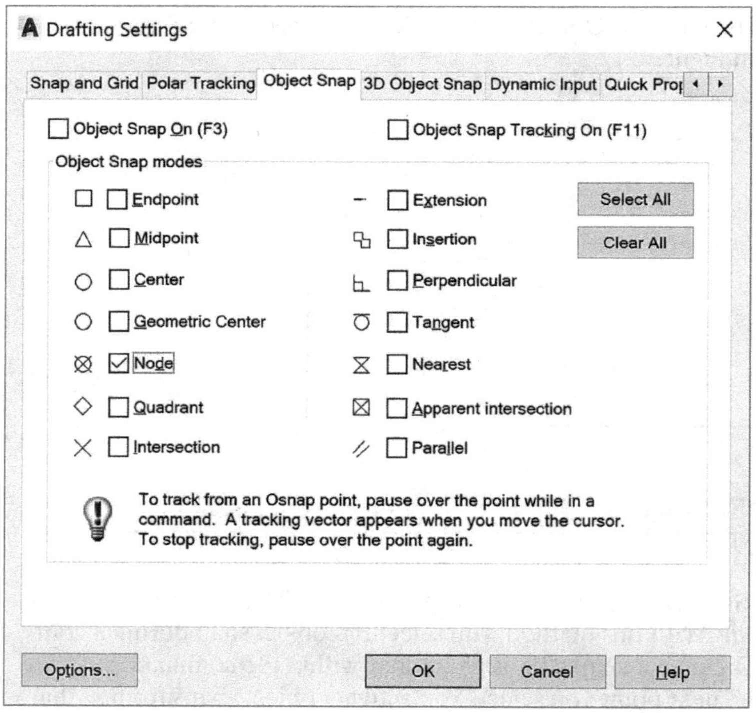

Figure 2.18

*Click: **Options** (from the lower left of the dialog box)*

The Options dialog box appears on your screen as shown in Figure 2.19. You can use it to change Marker size, color, and settings. You may want to make the Marker box smaller or larger, depending on your drawing's complexity and size.

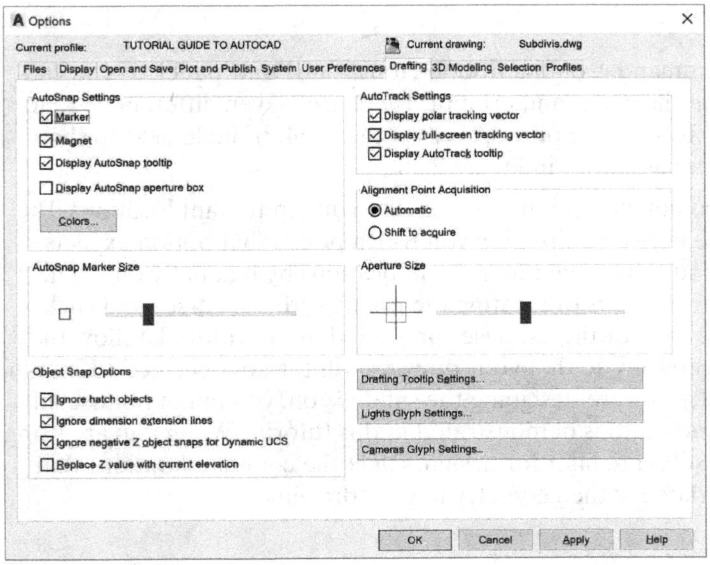

Figure 2.19

On your own, try using the slider to make the box smaller and then larger. Next, you may want to change the Marker color to a more noticeable color, such as red. When you have finished,

Click: ***OK*** *(to exit the Options dialog box)*

Click: ***OK*** *(to exit the Drafting Settings dialog box)*

Click: ***Object Snap button*** *to turn it on, if it is not already on*

On your own, click the small downward arrow to the right of the Object Snap button on the status bar to expand the options. Notice that now Node is checked and the other modes do not have check marks. You can also set the object snap modes quickly by checking or unchecking them from this list.

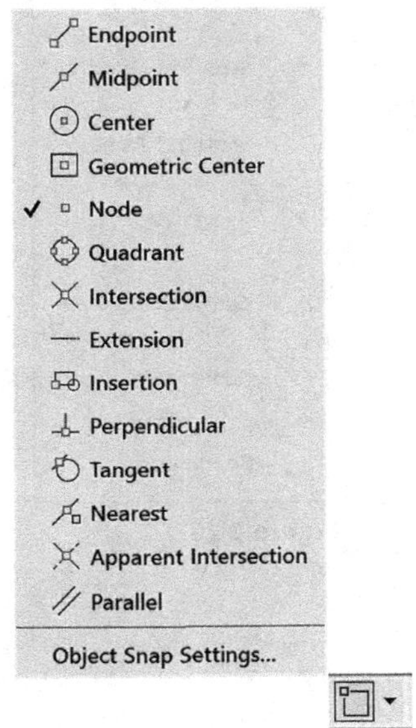

Make sure that **Ortho mode, Polar tracking, and Object snap tracking** are **off**.

Object Snap is a very useful tool and you will use it frequently throughout the rest of this guide. It can be very important to turn it on and off as needed. Notice that the Object Snap button on the Status bar is highlighted, meaning it is active. You may click the Object Snap button to toggle it on or off, similar to the Snap Mode and Grid buttons. Check your status bar to make sure that the Object Snap button is turned on (it appears highlighted).

Now you are ready to start creating arcs at accurate locations in the drawing. When you are prompted to select, look for the marker box on the crosshairs. When it's there, you know that Snap to Node is being used to select the points that were set previously in the drawing.

Using Arc

The Arc command is on the ribbon Home tab, Draw panel, or you can type ARC at the command prompt. There are eleven different ways to create arcs. To see the options, click on the small triangle next to show the Arc flyout as shown in Figure 2.20.

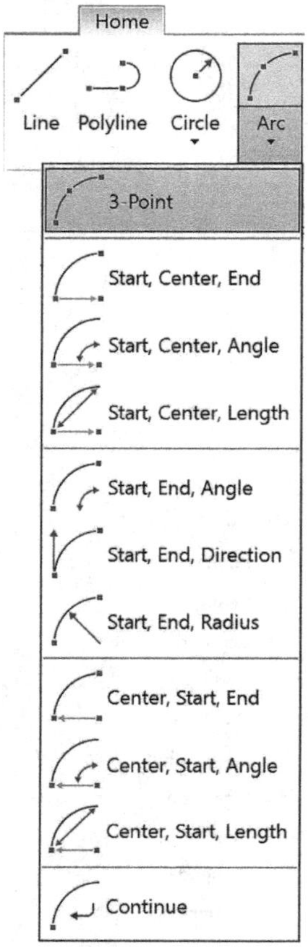

Figure 2.20

Each Arc command option requires that you input point locations. The icons on the buttons help show you which points that option expects for input. You can define those point locations by manually typing in the coordinate values or locating the points with the cursor and clicking your mouse. For the exercises presented in this tutorial, follow the directions carefully so that your drawing will turn out correctly. Keep in mind that if you were designing the subdivision, you might not use all the command options demonstrated in this tutorial. When you are using AutoCAD software later for design, select the command options that are appropriate for the geometry in your drawing.

Arc 3 Points

The 3 Points option of the Arc command draws an arc through three points that you specify. The dots located on the icon represent the three points of definition. This means that three point locations will be necessary for drawing that arc. Remember, to specify locations you can click them or type in absolute, relative, or polar coordinates. You will draw an arc using the 3 Points option. The Snap to Node running object snap will help you click the points drawn in the datafile.

 *Click: **3 Point** button*

Specify start point of arc or [Center]: ***select point 1**, using the AutoSnap marker as shown in Figure 2.21*

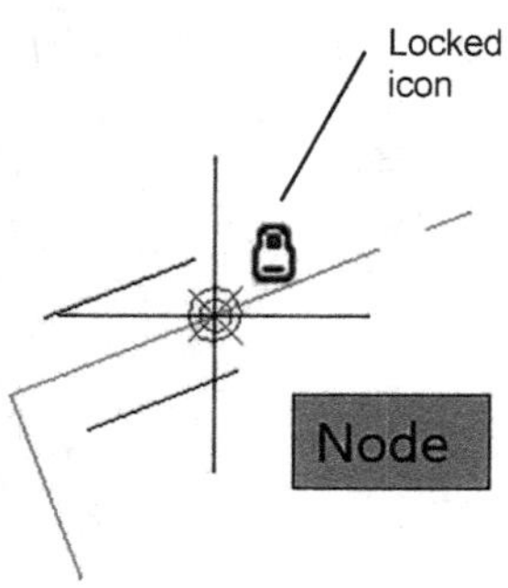

As can be seen in Figure 2.21, the AutoSnap marker for Node appears when the cursor is near a node point. Notice that when the cursor is right over the point, the locked icon appears to remind you the layer for the selected item is locked. You cannot make changes to locked layers but you can still select objects on them.

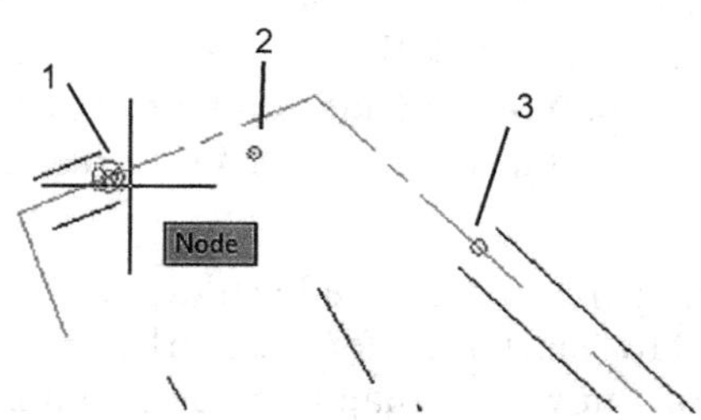

Figure 2.21

Now you will continue with selecting the points.

Specify second point of arc or [Center/End]: ***select point 2***

The cursor enters drag mode, whereby you can see the arc move on the screen as you move the cursor. Many AutoCAD commands permit dynamic specification, or dragging, of the image on the screen.

Move the cursor around the screen to see how it affects the way the arc would be drawn. Recall your use of this feature to draw circles in Tutorial 1.

Specify end point of arc: ***select point 3***

The third point defines the endpoint of the arc. The radius of the arc is calculated from the locations of the three points. Your drawing should now show the completed arc, as shown in the upper part of Figure 2.22.

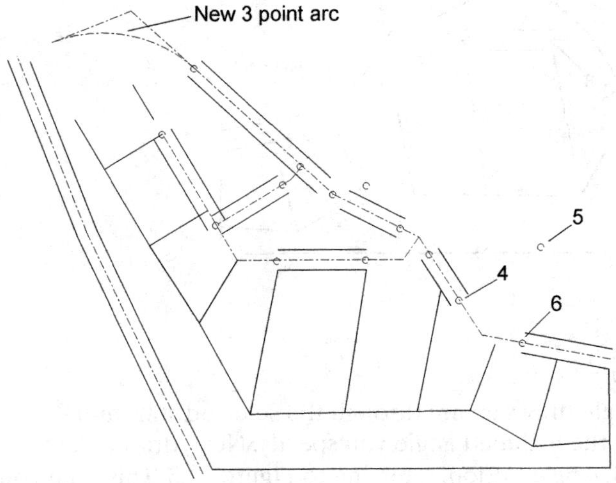

Figure 2.22

Arc Start, Center, End

Next, you will draw an arc by specifying the start, center, and endpoints. Figure 2.22 shows the points used to create this arc.

Tip: **Tip:** *Pressing the space bar or [Enter] key to restart the arc command uses Arc in a more general way, where you must select the command options by clicking on or typing in the option letter(s).*

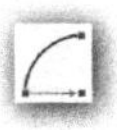

*Click: **Start, Center, End** button from the Arc flyout*

Specify start point of arc or [Center]: ***select point 4** as the start point*

Specify center point of arc: ***select point 5** to act as the arc's center*

Specify end point of arc or [Angle/chord Length]: ***select point 6** to end the arc*

The arc is drawn counterclockwise from the start point. Notice that now Start, Center, End is the top button on the Arc flyout. When you are using a flyout, the last item you clicked appears as the top flyout button, so options you use frequently take only one click.

Figure 2.22 shows the point locations needed to draw a *concave arc.* If the start point were located where the endpoint is, a *convex arc* outside the centerlines would have been drawn. When you have added the arc correctly, your arc should look like that in the lower part of Figure 2.23.

On your own, try drawing another arc with the Arc Start, Center, End option, this time clicking point 6 first, then the center, and then point 4.

Note that this arc is drawn counterclockwise, resulting in a convex arc.

Undo this backward arc by typing U [Enter] at the command prompt.

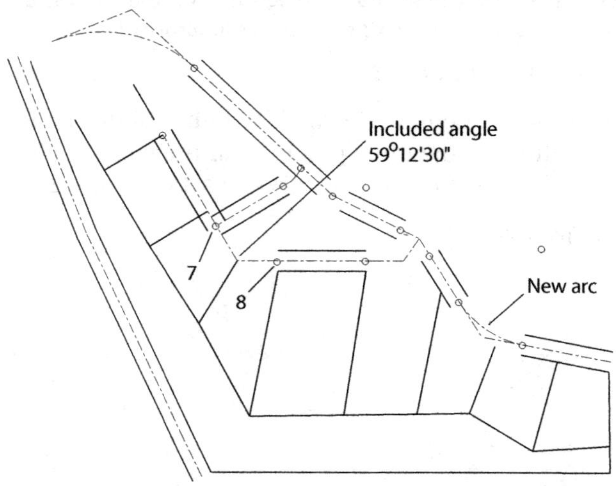

Figure 2.23

Arc Start, End, Angle

Arc Start, End, Angle draws an arc through the selected start and endpoints by using the included angle you specify. Next, draw an arc with the Start, End, Angle option, referring to Figure 2.23. This time you will use dynamic entry.

Click: ***to turn on Dynamic Input*** *from the Status Bar*

Click: ***Start, End, Angle button*** *from the Arc flyout*

Specify start point of arc or [Center]: ***select point 7***

Specify end point of arc: ***select point 8***

Specify included angle: ***59d12'30" [Enter]***

The arc is defined by the *included angular value* (often called the *delta angle* in survey drawings) from the start point to the end point. Positive angular values are measured counterclockwise. Negative angular values are measured clockwise. (Type d for the degree symbol when typing in surveyor angles. Use the single quote and double quote for minutes and seconds.)

Arc Start, Center, Length

Arc Start, Center, Length draws an arc specified by the start and center points of the arc and the chord length. The chord length is the straight-line distance from the start point of the arc to the endpoint of the arc. You can enter negative values for the chord length to draw an arc in the opposite direction. Figure 2.24 shows a diagram describing the geometry of this type of arc.

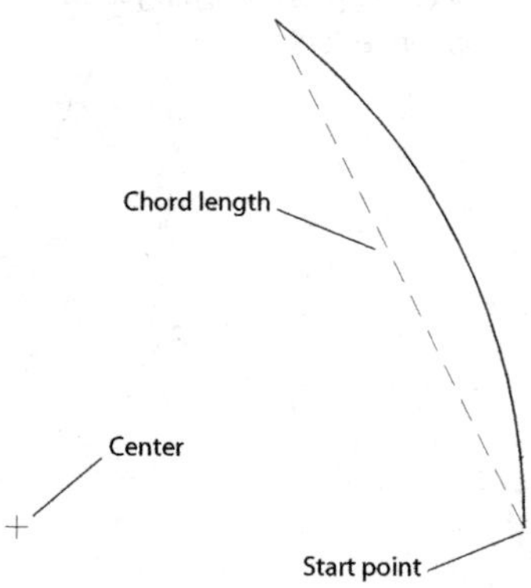

Figure 2.24

You will draw the next arc by using Arc Start, Center, Length. Figure 2.25 shows the dynamic entry to use for the chord length.

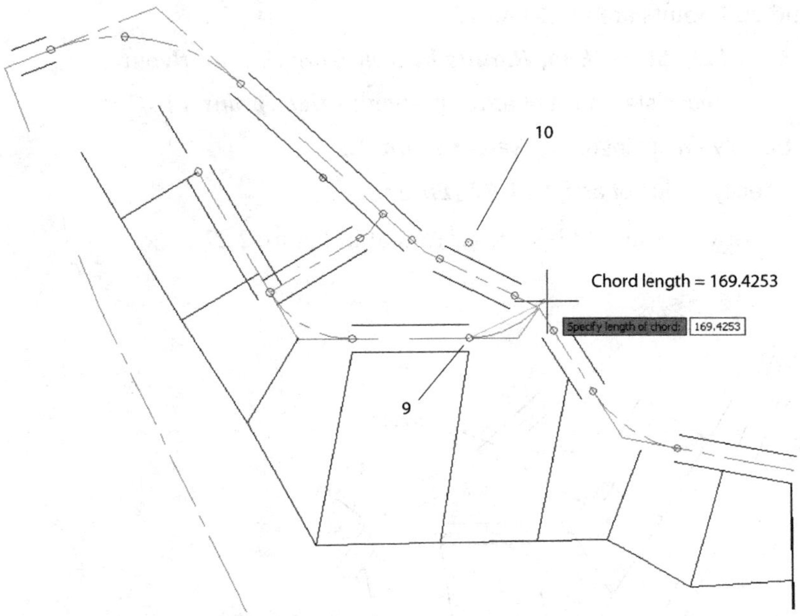

Figure 2.25

*Click:* ***Start, Center, Length button*** *from the Arc flyout*

Specify start point of arc or [Center]: ***select point 9***

Specify center point of arc: ***select point 10***

Specify length of chord: ***169.4253 [Enter]***

Your new arc should look like the one shown in Figure 2.26.

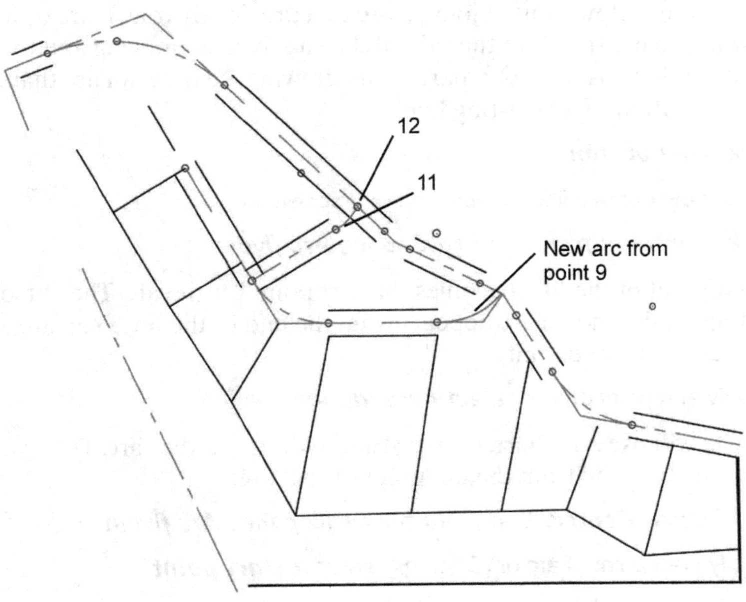

Figure 2.26

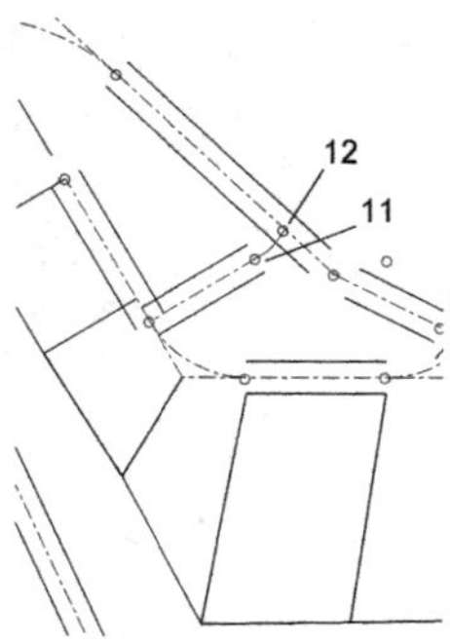

Arc Start, End, Radius

Draw the next arc using Start, End, Radius. The locations of the start and end points are at 11 and 12.

Click: ***Start, End, Radius button*** *from the Arc flyout*

Specify start point of arc or [Center]: ***select point 11***

Specify end point of arc: ***select point 12***

Specify radius of arc: ***154.87 [Enter]***

Your drawing should be similar to that in Figure 2.27.

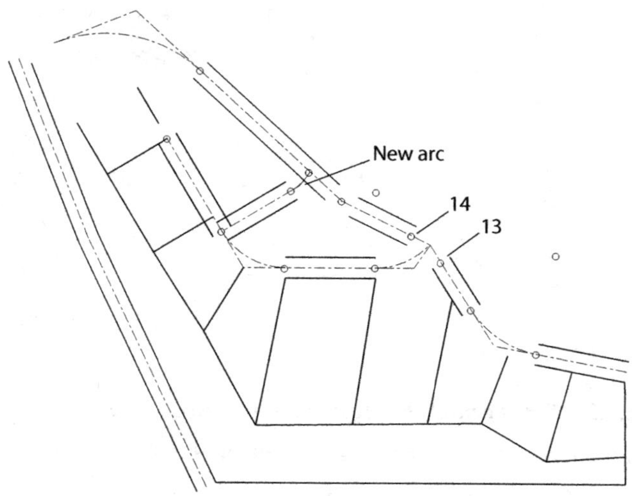

Figure 2.27

Continuing an Arc

Arc Continue allows you to join an arc to a previously drawn arc or line. You will give it a try off to the side of the subdivision drawing and then erase or undo it, as it is not a part of the drawing. To draw an arc that is the continuation of an existing line,

Click: ***Line button***

On your own, draw a line anywhere on your screen.

Click: ***Continue*** *from the Draw panel, Arc flyout*

The last point of the line becomes the first point for the arc. The cursor is in drag mode, and an arc appears from the end of the line. You are prompted for an endpoint.

Specify end point of arc: ***select an endpoint***

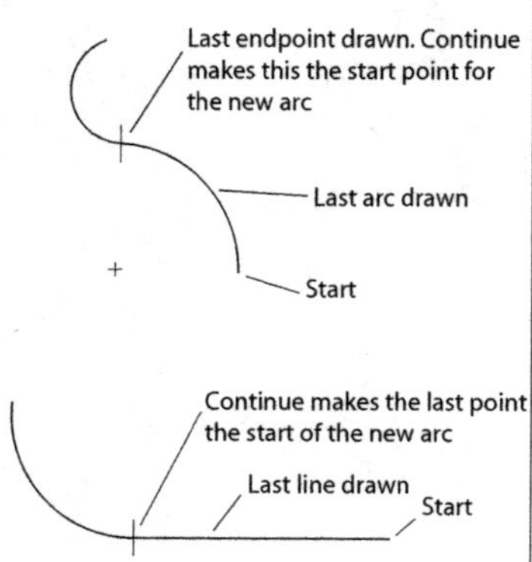

Figure 2.28

Next you will use Arc Start, Center, End to draw another arc. Then you will continue an arc from the endpoint of that arc.

Click: ***Start, Center, End*** *from the Draw panel, Arc flyout*

Specify start point of arc or [Center]: ***select a start point***

Specify center point of arc: ***select a center point***

Specify end point of arc or [Angle/chord Length]: ***select an endpoint***

***Click: Continue** from the Draw panel, Arc flyout*

Specify end point of arc: ***select an endpoint***

Your drawings should look similar to those in Figure 2.28.

On your own, erase or undo the extra continued arcs and lines that you created.

Using Arc at the Command Line

To select the Arc command, you can also type the command alias, A, at the command prompt. When you start the Arc command this way, the default is the 3 Points option you used earlier. If you want to use another option, you can type the command option letter at the prompt. You will start the Arc command by typing its alias. You will then specify the start, end, and angle of the arc by typing the command option at the prompt. Refer to Figure 2.27 for the points, 13 and 14, to select.

Tip: *After you draw an arc, restarting the command and then pressing the space bar or [Enter] also engages the Continue option. You can use this method to continue a line from the previously drawn arc or line.*

Command: ***A [Enter]***

The command Arc is echoed at the command prompt, followed by

Specify start point of arc or [Center]: ***click point 13***

Specify second point of arc or [Center/End]: ***E [Enter]***

Specify end point of arc: ***click point 14***

Specify center point of arc or [Angle/Direction/Radius]: ***A [Enter]***

Specify included angle: ***30d54'04" [Enter]***

*Click: **to turn Dynamic Input button off***

Tip: *You can click on the command option from the list instead of typing the letter. Try it both ways.*

The arc is added to your drawing. However, it may be hard to see because of the small size of the arc relative to the size of the screen and drawing.

Using Zoom

The Zoom commands change the size of the image on your display. The Zoom flyout is on the ribbon View tab, Navigate panel (Figure 2.29). If it does not, use Show panels to turn it on.

Right-click in the gray space at the left of the View tab

*Click: **Show panels** from the context menu, Click **Navigate***

The Navigate panel now appears on the ribbon View tab (Figure 2.30).

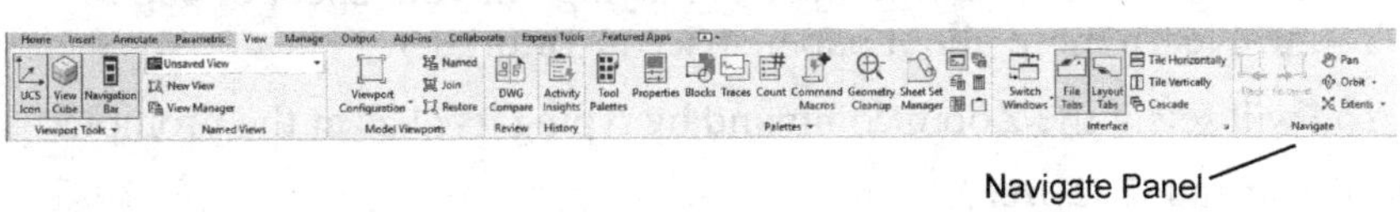

Figure 2.30 Navigate Panel on View Tab

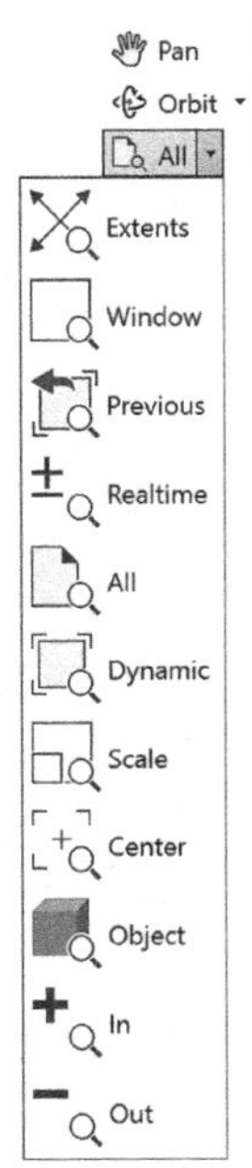

Figure 2.29

To zoom in on an area of the drawing, you can select Zoom In from the Zoom flyout.

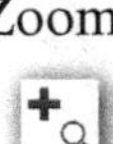

*Click: **Zoom In button***

Your drawing is enlarged to twice its previous size (Figure 2.31).

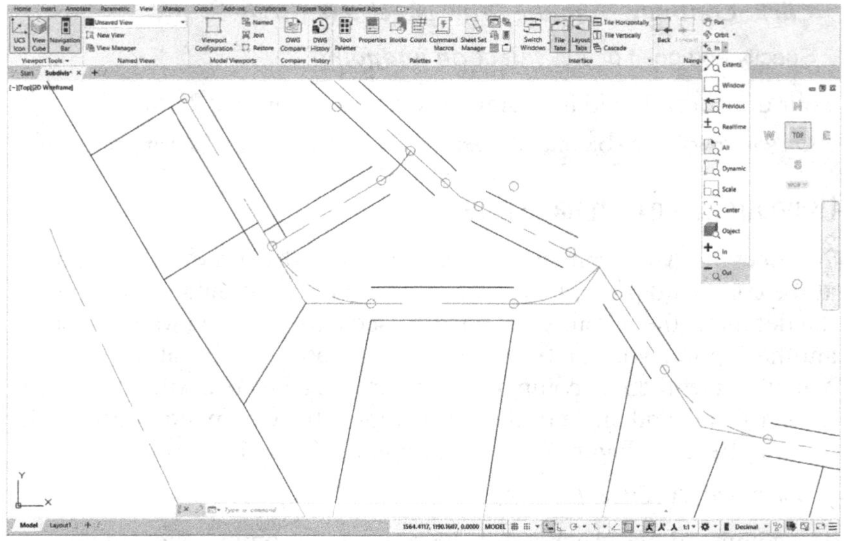

Figure 2.31

Next you will zoom out, using the Zoom Out button from the flyout.

Click: Zoom Out button

Your drawing should return to its original size on the screen. Zoom In and Zoom Out use the Scale feature of the Zoom command to zoom to a scale of 2X (twice the previous size) and 0.5X (half the previous size).

Zooming Using Scale Factors

You can also use *scale factors* to zoom when you click the Scale option of the Zoom command. Scale factor 1.00 shows the drawing limits (where the grid is shown). Scale factor 0.5 shows the drawing limits half-size on the screen. Typing X after the scale factor makes the zoom scale relative to the previous view. For example, entering 2X causes the new view to be shown twice as big as the view established previously, as you saw when using Zoom In. A scale factor of 0.5X reduces the view to half the previous size, as you saw when using Zoom Out. Zoom Scale uses the current left corner or (0,0) coordinates as the base location for the zoom. Typing XP after the scale factor makes the new zoom scale relative to paper space. A scale factor of 0.5XP means that the object will be shown half-size when you are laying out your sheet of paper. You will learn more about paper space in Tutorial 5.

You will select the Zoom command by typing its alias at the prompt.

Command: ***Z [Enter]***

Specify corner of window, enter a scale factor (nX or nXP), or [All/Center/Dynamic/Extents/Previous/Scale/Window/Object] <real time>: ***2X [Enter]***

The view is enlarged to twice the previous size.

Repeat the Zoom command.

Command: ***[Enter]*** *(to restart the last command)*

Specify corner of window, enter a scale factor (nX or nXP), or [All/Center/Dynamic/Extents/Previous/Scale/Window/Object] <real time>: ***.5 [Enter]***

The drawing limits appear on the screen at half their original size. The area shown on the screen is twice as big as the drawing limits. Now, restore the original view.

Command: ***[Enter]*** *(to restart the Zoom command)*

Specify corner of window, enter a scale factor (nX or nXP), or [All/Center/Dynamic/Extents/Previous/Scale/Window/Object] <real time>: ***1 [Enter]***

Zoom Window

To use Zoom Window, create a window around the area that you want to enlarge to fill the screen. This lets you quickly enlarge the portion of the drawing that you are interested in. You can select this command using the Zoom flyout. The Zoom command is "transparent." This means you can select it during another command. You will zoom in on the area shown in Figure 2.32.

Tip: *When typing transparent commands, use an apostrophe in front of the command name.*

Click: ***Zoom Window icon***
Specify first corner: ***select point A***
Specify opposite corner: ***select point B***

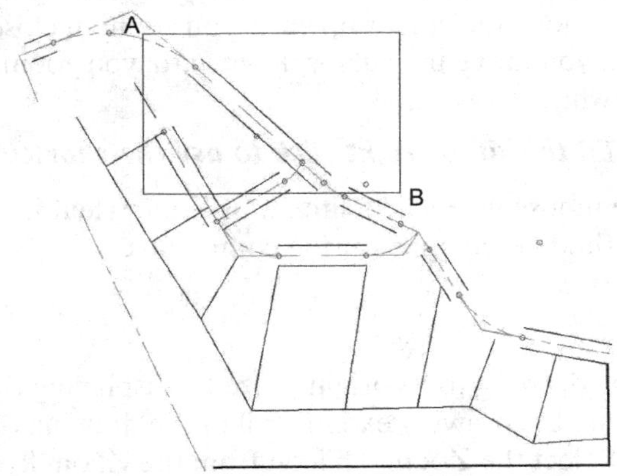

Figure 2.32

The defined area is enlarged to fill the screen as shown in Figure 2.33.

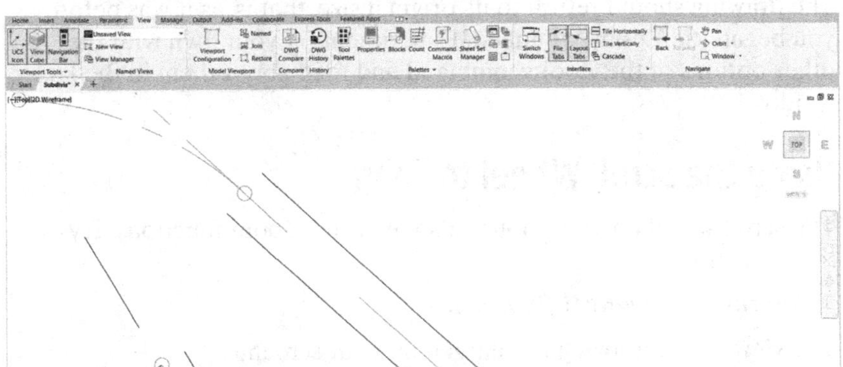

Figure 2.33

Zoom Previous

To return an area to its previous size, you will click Zoom Previous from the Standard toolbar.

Click: ***Zoom Previous button***

Your drawing is returned to its original size. Areas can be repeatedly zoomed, that is, you can zoom in on a zoomed area; in fact, you can continue to zoom until the portion shown on the display is ten trillion times the size of the original.

Zoom Realtime

An easy way to zoom your drawing to the desired size is to use the Zoom Realtime feature on the Standard toolbar.

Click: ***Zoom Realtime button***

Select an arbitrary point in the middle of your drawing and hold down the click button of your pointing device while dragging the cursor up and down. When you move the cursor upward, you zoom in closer to the drawing; when you move the cursor downward, you zoom out farther from the drawing.

Press ESC or ENTER to exit, or right-click to use the shortcut menu.

Scrolling the middle mouse wheel acts similar to Zoom Realtime. It is quick to use this method at any time during commands.

Zoom All

Zoom All returns the drawing to its original size by displaying the drawing limits, or displaying the drawing extents (all of the drawing objects), whichever is larger. Select the Zoom All icon from the Zoom flyout.

Click: ***Zoom All button***

The drawing should return to its original size, that is, as it was before you began the Zoom command. Experiment on your own with the other options of the Zoom command and read about them in the Help window.

Using the Scroll Wheel to Zoom

The scroll wheel on your mouse also provides Zoom functions. Try these out now.

Roll the scroll wheel forward.

The view of the drawing is enlarged on your screen.

Roll the scroll wheel towards yourself.

The view zooms out and appears smaller.

Double-click the scroll wheel.

The drawing fills the screen.

Tip: *If you open a drawing that you've saved with the view zoomed in, you can use Zoom All or double-click the scroll wheel to show the full drawing.*

Zoom Dynamic

Another way to zoom in and move around in a large drawing quickly is to use the Zoom Dynamic.

Click: ***Zoom Dynamic***

The *view box* appears on your screen, as shown in Figure 2.34.

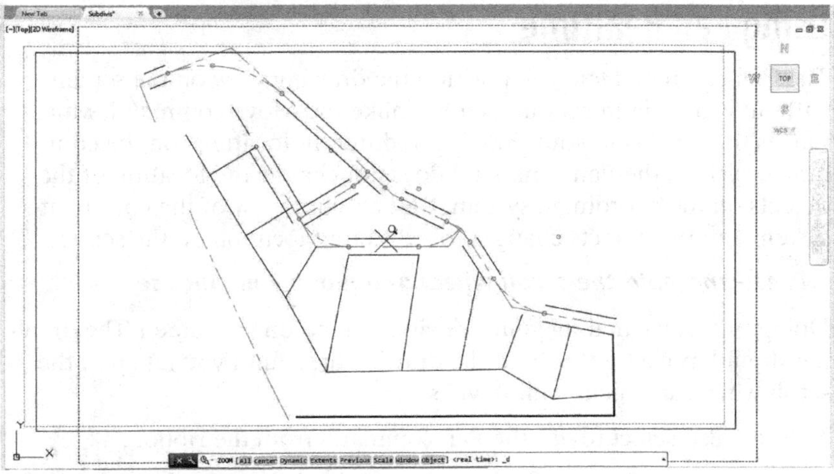

Figure 2.34

Move your mouse to position the view box.

The box shows an X in the center, indicating it is in position mode. As you move your mouse around, the view box moves with your mouse movements.

Position the view box at the location you desire and click the mouse.

Now an arrow appears at the right edge of the box and as you move your mouse, the size of the box is enlarged or reduced as shown in Figure 2.35.

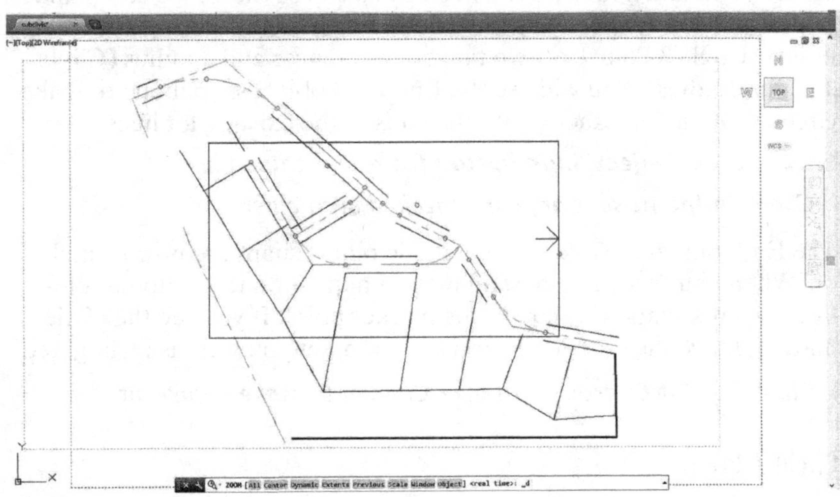

Figure 2.35

Try reducing the box and then click the mouse button.

You return to the position mode, so that you can move the box again.

When you are satisfied with the location of the box, right-click the mouse and select Enter.

The area enclosed in the box fills the graphics window.

Using Pan Realtime

The Pan command lets you position the drawing view on the screen without changing the zoom factor. Unlike the Move command, which moves the objects in your drawing to different locations on the coordinate system, the Pan command does not change the location of the objects on the coordinate system. Rather, your view of the coordinate system and the objects changes to a different location on the screen.

Press and hold the scroll wheel and move your mouse.

Doing this, you can drag your drawing around on the screen. The drawing should move freely about the drawing area until you let go of the scroll wheel, at which point it will stop.

You can also select to use the Pan command from the ribbon,

Click: ***Pan button*** *from the View tab, Navigate panel*

Press and hold the left mouse button to position the drawing on the screen.

Press: ***[Esc] or [Enter]*** *to exit the command*

Double-click the scroll wheel to Zoom to the drawing extents.

Your drawing should now fill the drawing window.

Using Circle Options

In Tutorial 1 you learned to use the Circle command by specifying a center point and a radius value. You can also use the Circle command to draw circles by specifying any two points (Circle 2 Point), any three points (Circle 3 Point), or two tangent references and a radius (Circle Tan Tan Radius). You will use the Endpoint object snap mode to make circles that line up exactly with the ends of the existing lot lines.

Right-click: ***Object Snap button*** *from the status bar*

Click: ***Endpoint*** *so it appears checked on the list*

The Endpoint and Node running mode object snaps are now turned on. When you see the AutoSnap marker appear on the endpoint of a line, the crosshairs will snap to the marker point. If you see the Node marker, move the crosshairs until the endpoint you want is highlighted.

Click: ***LOTLINES*** *from the Layer Control to make it current*

Circle 2-Point

You will draw a circle using Circle 2-Point. Points 1 and 2 will be endpoints of the circle's diameter, as shown in Figure 2.36.

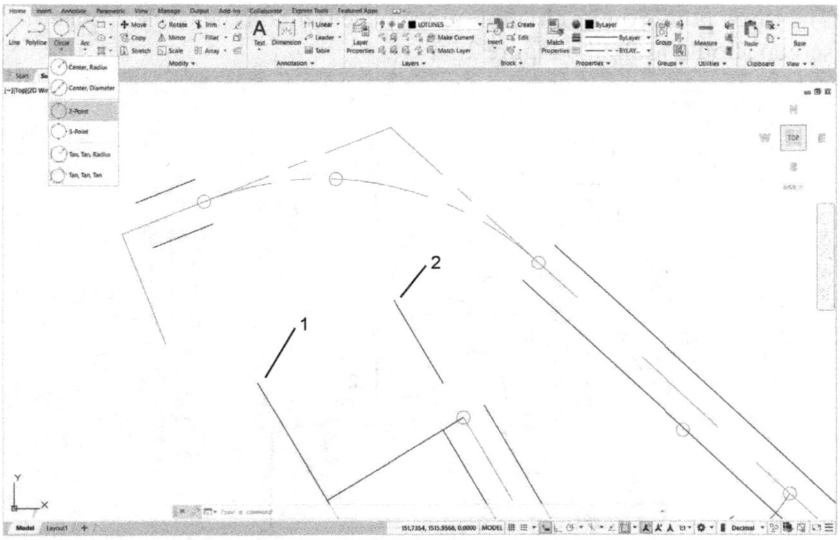

Figure 2.36

Click: ***2-Point button*** *from the Circle flyout*

Specify first end point of circle's diameter: ***select point 1***

Specify second endpoint of circle's diameter: ***select point 2***

The circle has been defined by the two selected endpoints defining its diameter. Your screen should look like Figure 2.37.

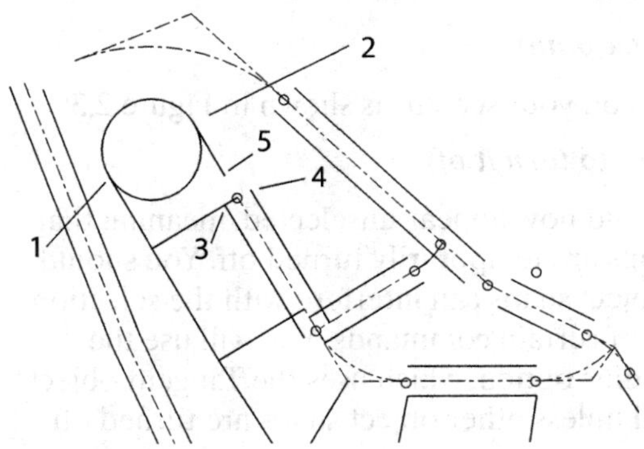

Figure 2.37

Tip: *Zoom as needed to see the features clearly.*

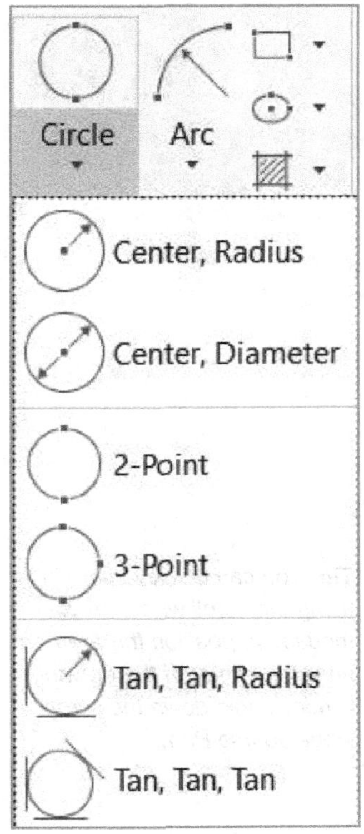

Circle 3-Point

To draw a circle using Circle 3-Point, specify any three points on the circle's circumference. Refer to Figure 2.36 for the points to select.

Click: ***3-Point*** *from the Circle flyout, Home tab Draw panel*

Specify first point on circle: ***select point 3***

Specify second point on circle: ***select point 4***

Because you are in drag mode, you see the circle being created on your screen as you move the cursor.

Specify third point on circle: ***select point 5***

The three points on its circumference have defined the circle. Your screen should look like Figure 2.37.

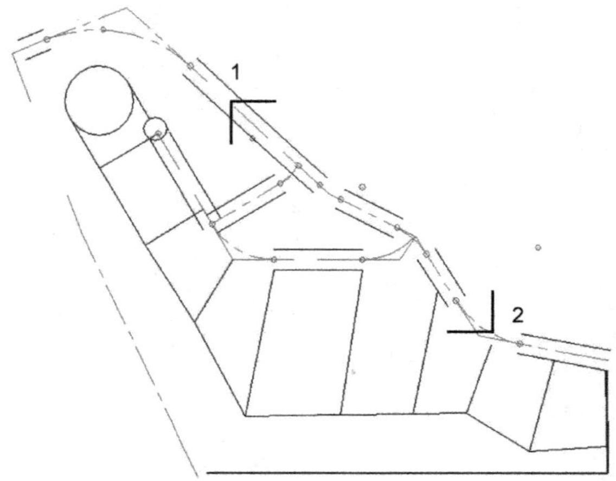

Figure 2.38

Next you will draw a circle tangent to two angled centerlines. First, you will change the current layer and zoom in on points 1 and 2, shown in Figure 2.37.

Tip: *You can quickly zoom in using the scroll wheel on your mouse. To position the area near the center of the drawing window, hold down the scroll wheel to use Pan.*

*Click: **CENTERLINE** from the Layer Control list to make it current*

*Click: **Zoom Window button***

Specify first corner: ***click point 1***

Specify opposite corner: ***click point 2***

The area should be enlarged on your screen, as shown in Figure 2.39.

*Click: **Object Snap button** to turn it off*

The Object Snap button should now appear unselected, meaning that all running mode object snaps are temporarily turned off. You should do so because sometimes object snaps can interfere with the selection of points and the operation of certain commands. You will use the Circle Tangent, Tangent, Radius option, which uses the Tangent object snap. This will not work well unless other object snaps are turned off.

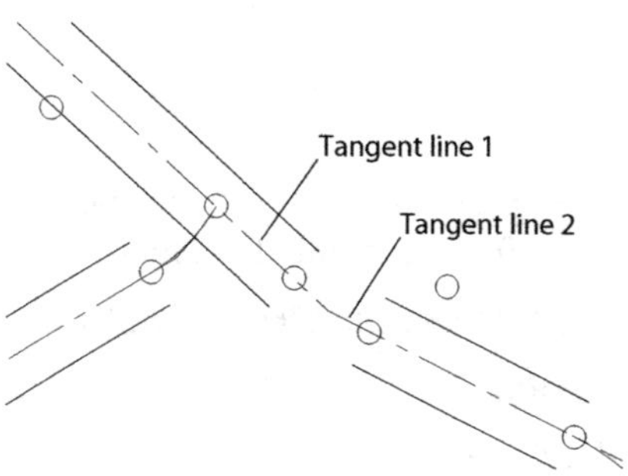

Figure 2.39

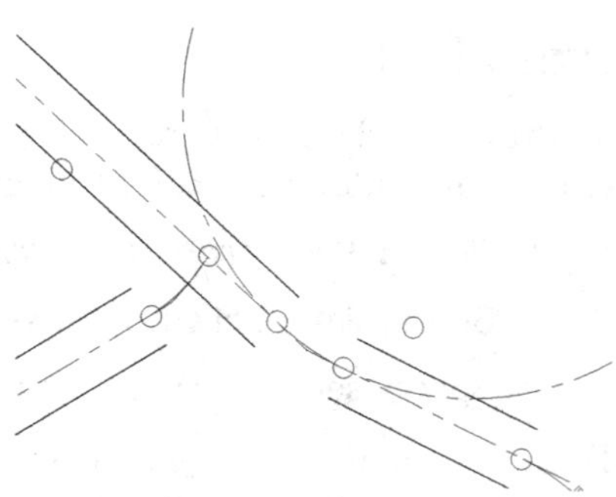

Figure 2.40

Circle Tangent, Tangent, Radius

Circle Tangent, Tangent, Radius requires that you specify two objects to which the resulting circle will be *tangent*. Then give the radius of the resulting circle. This method is frequently used in laying out road centerlines. It involves selecting the two straight sections of the road centerline to which the curve is tangent and then specifying the radius.

Click: ***Tan, Tan, Radius*** *from the Circle flyout on the Draw panel*

Note that the AutoSnap marker appears any time the cursor is near a line. Refer to Figure 2.39 for the lines to select. You can select either line first.

Specify point on object for first tangent of circle: ***click tangent line 1***

Specify point on object for second tangent of circle: ***click tangent line 2***

Specify radius of circle <34.0000>: ***267.3098 [Enter]***

A circle with a radius of 267.3098 is drawn tangent to both original lines, as shown in Figure 2.39.

You can also use Circle Tangent, Tangent, Radius to draw a circle tangent to two circles. You will try this next by drawing two circles off to the side of the drawing and then adding a circle that is tangent to both of them.

On your own, draw two circles off to the side of your subdivision drawing.

Click: ***Tan, Tan, Radius*** *from the Circle flyout*

Specify point on object for first tangent of circle: ***select one of the circles you just drew***

Specify point on object for second tangent of circle: ***select the other circle***

Specify radius of circle <267.3098>: ***150 [Enter]***

A circle with a radius of 150 is drawn tangent to both circles.

Tip: *If you get the message, Circle does not exist, the radius you specified may be too small or too large to be tangent to both lines.*

Tip: *The value shown as the default radius for the circle depends on the size of the last circle you drew.*

Circle Tangent, Tangent, Tangent

The Circle Tangent, Tangent, Tangent command lets you quickly define a circle that is tangent to three entities in the drawing.

Try it on your own by selecting the Tan, Tan, Tan button from the Circle flyout and then selecting three lot lines to draw a circle tangent to.

Now erase the extra circles on your own.

Using Ellipse

The command options for specifying an ellipse can be selected from the Ellipse flyout on the Home tab Draw panel.

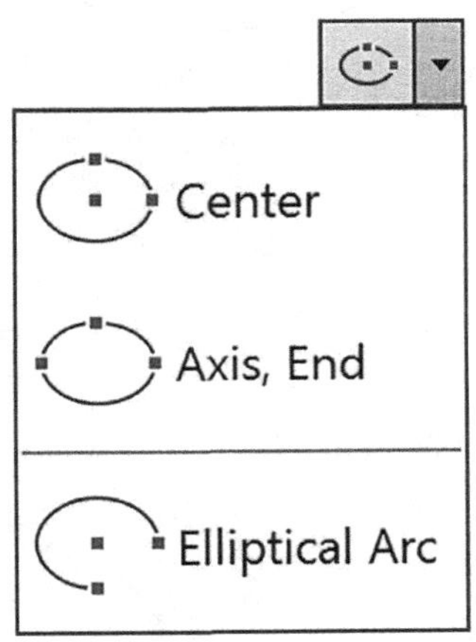

Next, you will practice using the Ellipse command by drawing some ellipses off to the side of the drawing. You will erase them when you are through. To draw an ellipse by specifying three points,

Click: ***Axis, End button from the Ellipse flyout***

Specify axis endpoint of ellipse or [Arc/Center]: ***select a point***

Specify other endpoint of axis: ***select a point***

Specify distance to other axis or [Rotation]: ***select a point***

An ellipse is created on your screen, using the three points that you selected. The ellipse has a *major axis* (the longest distance between two points on the ellipse) and a *minor axis* (the shorter distance across the ellipse). The AutoCAD program determines which axis is major and which is minor by examining the distance between the first pair of endpoints and comparing it to the distance specified by the third point.

One way to describe an ellipse is to create a circle and then tip the circle away from your viewing direction by a rotation angle. This method requires you to specify the angle of rotation instead of the endpoint of the second axis.

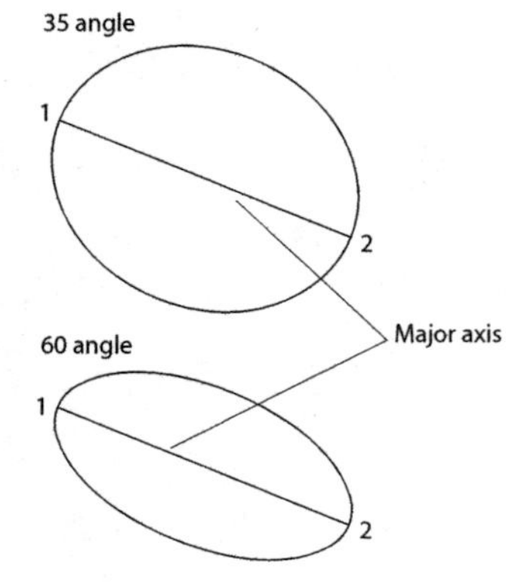

Figure 2.41

You will draw an ellipse using two endpoints and an angle of rotation. See Figure 2.41 to determine the location of the points.

Click: ***Axis, End button*** *from the Ellipse flyout*

Specify axis endpoint of ellipse or [Arc/Center]: ***select point 1***

Specify other endpoint of axis: ***select point 2***

This defined the distance between points 1 and 2 as the major axis (diameter) of the ellipse. This time at the command prompt, use the options to specify the rotation angle, as though tipping a circle.

Specify distance to other axis or [Rotation]: ***R [Enter]***

Specify rotation around major axis: ***35 [Enter]***

On your own, **erase** the ellipses that you created.

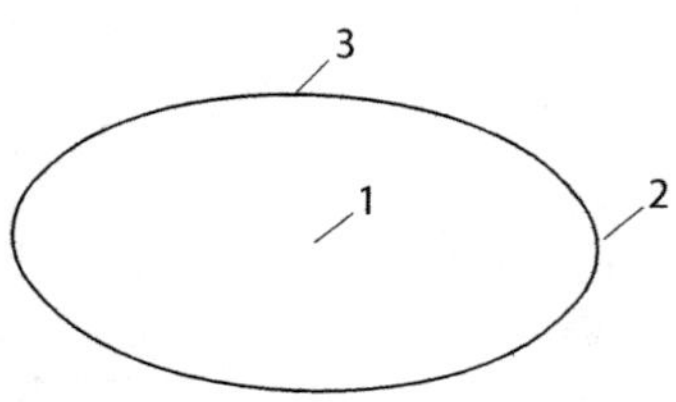

Figure 2.42

The remaining construction methods for ellipses are similar to specifying the axes, but use radius values rather than diameter values. This way, when the center point of the ellipse is known, you can use it as a starting point. Refer to Figure 2.42 for the locations of the points in the next steps. This time type the command.

Command: ***ELLIPSE [Enter]***

Specify axis endpoint of ellipse or [Arc/Center]: ***C [Enter]***

The center of the ellipse is the intersection of the major and minor axes. You can enter a coordinate or use the cursor to select a point on the screen.

Specify center of ellipse: ***select point 1***

Next, you provide the endpoint of the first axis. The angle of the ellipse is determined by the angle from the center point to this endpoint.

Specify endpoint of axis: ***select point 2***

Now specify the distance measured from the center of the ellipse to the endpoint of the second axis, measured perpendicular to the first axis (or a rotation angle can be used).

Specify distance to other axis or [Rotation]: ***select point 3***

The point that you selected determined whether the first axis is a major or minor axis. The ellipse is drawn on your screen.

Next, draw an ellipse by specifying a center point, one axis point, and an angle of rotation. Refer to Figure 2.43.

Click: ***Center from the Ellipse flyout***

Specify center of ellipse: ***click point 1***

Specify endpoint of axis: ***click point 2***

Specify distance to other axis or [Rotation]: ***R [Enter]***

Specify rotation around major axis: ***30 [Enter]***

Before you go on, **erase** the ellipses you drew for practice.

Use Zoom All to return to the original view.

Save your drawing at this time.

When you have successfully saved your drawing,

Click: ***Application button, Exit AutoCAD***

You are now back at the Windows desktop.

You will finish the subdivision drawing in Tutorial 3.

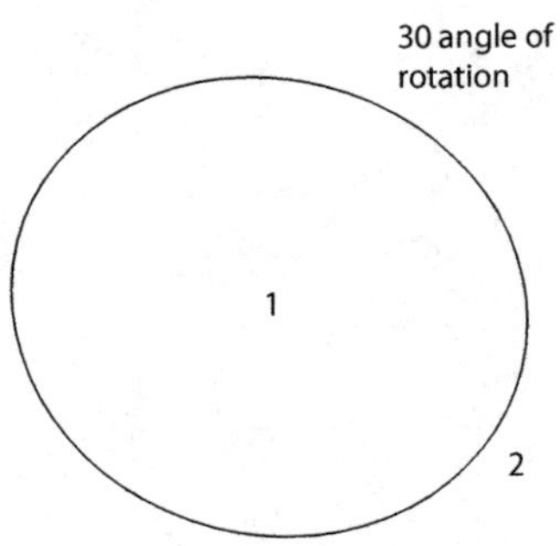

Figure 2.43

Tip: *Recall that AutoCAD keyboard entry is not case-sensitive. You can type uppercase, lowercase, or mixed-case letters. In this book your keyboard entry is shown uppercase to help you identify easily what you are supposed to type, but the program does not require uppercase letters.*

Tip: *Notice that when you pick the Center button from the Ellipse flyout, the "C" option is automatically selected at the command prompt :* Specify axis endpoint of ellipse or [Arc/Center]: **C**

Tip: *If you have older AutoCAD versions you can use the Save As command to save your drawing to the 2010, R14 or other formats. In the Save Drawing As dialog box, scroll through the Save Drawing Type list for the various options.*

Key Terms

chord length
concave arc
convex arc
current layer
delta angle
freeze
included angular value
layer
locked layer
major axis
minor axis
object snap
override mode
primitives
regenerate
running object snap
scale factor
tangent
target
virtual screen

Key Commands (keyboard shortcut)

Arc (A)
Arc, 3 Points
Arc, Continue
Arc Start, Center, End
Arc Start, Center, Length
Arc Start, End, Angle
Arc Start, End, Radius
Circle 2-Point
Circle 3-Point
Circle Tan, Tan Radius
Circle Tan, Tan, Tan
Color Control (COL)
DTEXT
Ellipse (EL)
Layer (LA)
Layer Control
MTEXT
Object Snap (F3)
Open Drawing (CTRL+O)
Pan Realtime (P)
SAVEAS
Snap to Endpoint
Snap to Node
Text
Zoom (Z)
Zoom Dynamic
Zoom In
Zoom Out
Zoom Previous
Zoom Realtime
Zoom Scale
Zoom Window

Exercises

Redraw the following shapes. If dimensions are given, create your drawing geometry exactly to the specified dimensions. The letter M after an exercise number means that the dimensions are in millimeters (metric units). If no letter follows the exercise number, the dimensions are in inches. Do not include dimensions on the drawings. The Ø symbol means diameter; R indicates a radius.

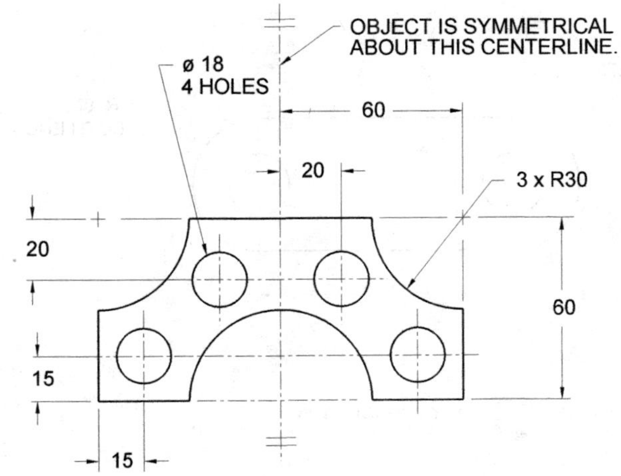

Exercise 2.1M Bracket

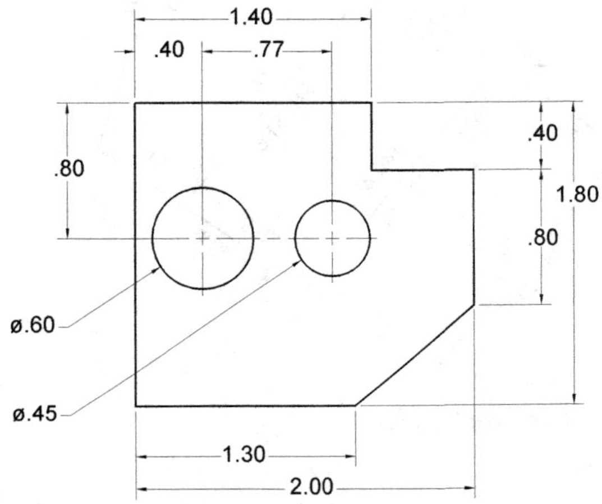

Exercise 2.2 Gasket

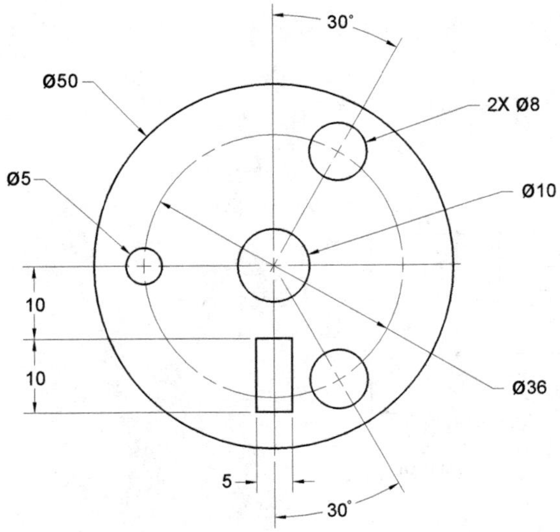

Exercise 2.3M Flange

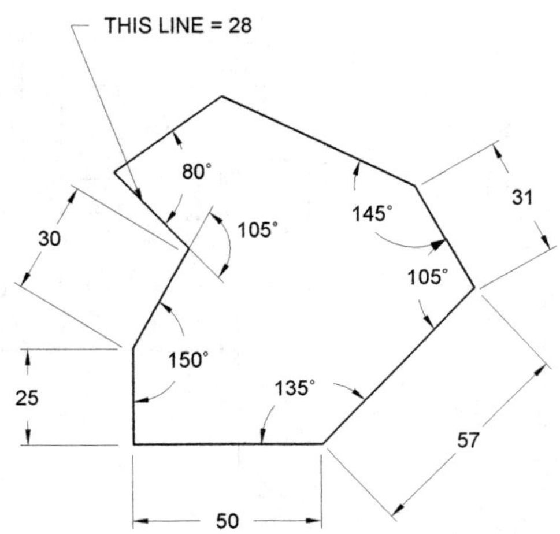

Exercise 2.4M Puzzle

Draw the figure shown according to the dimensions provided. From your drawing determine what the missing distances must be (Hint: use DIST).

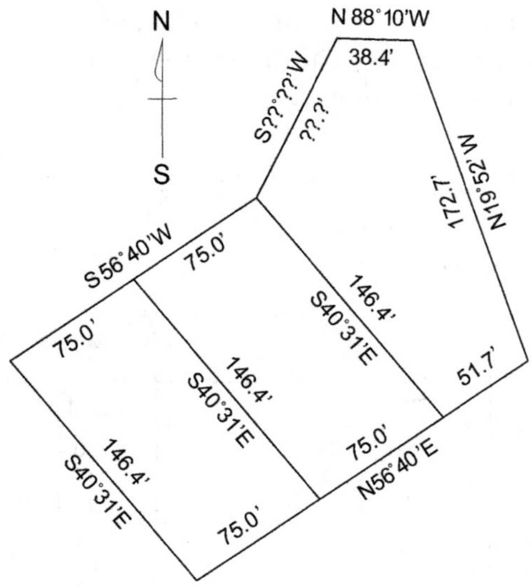

Exercise 2.5 Plot Plan

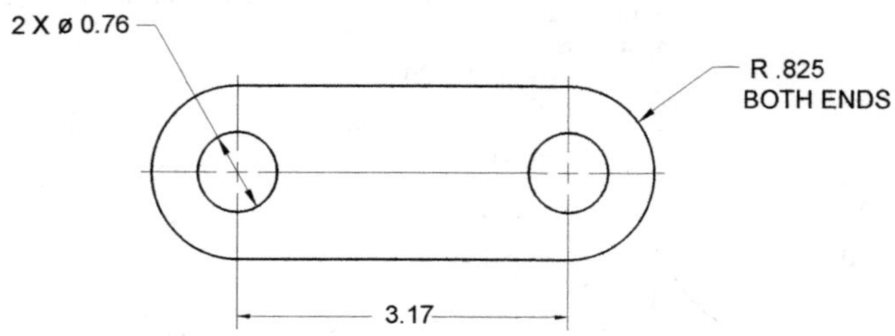

Exercise 2.6 Link

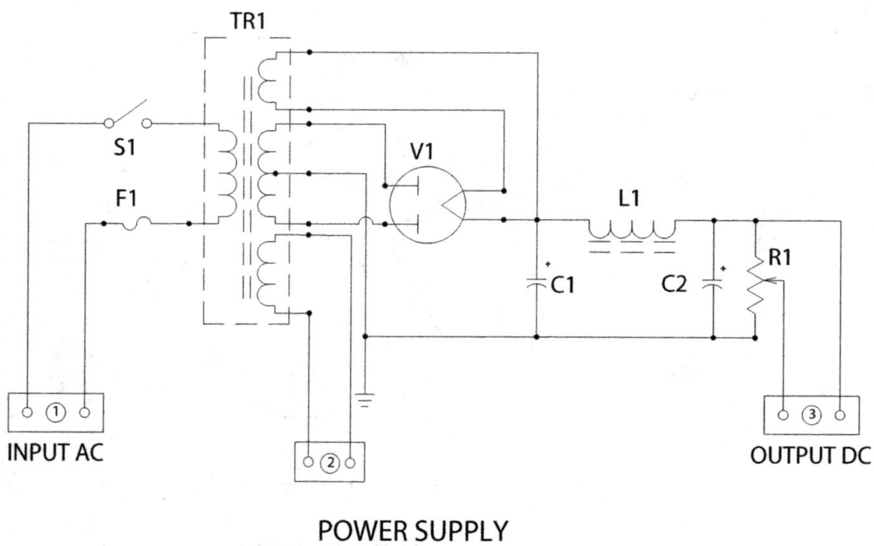

Exercise 2.7 Power Supply

Draw this circuit, using the techniques you have learned.

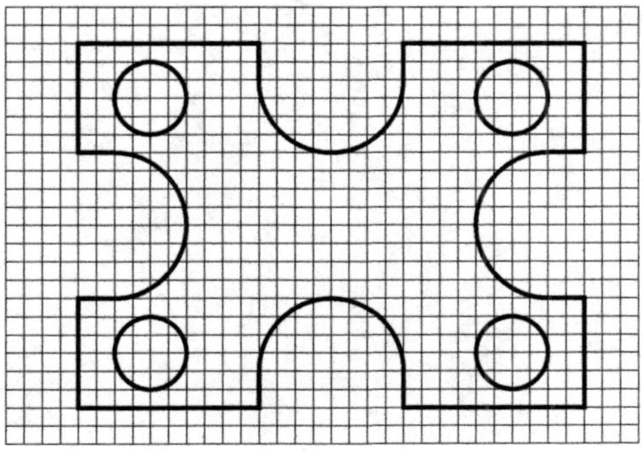

Exercise 2.8 Gasket

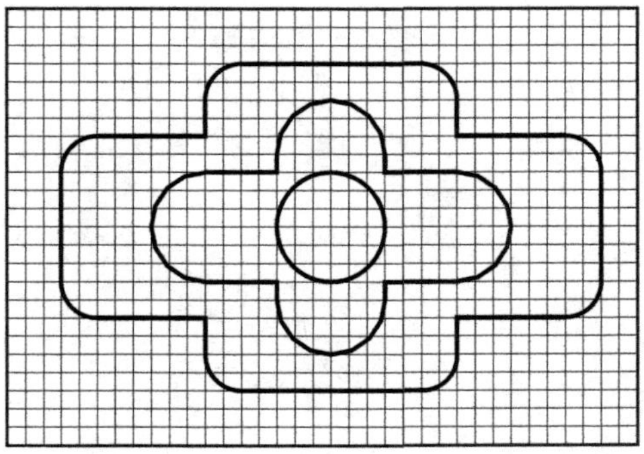

Exercise 2.9 Shape

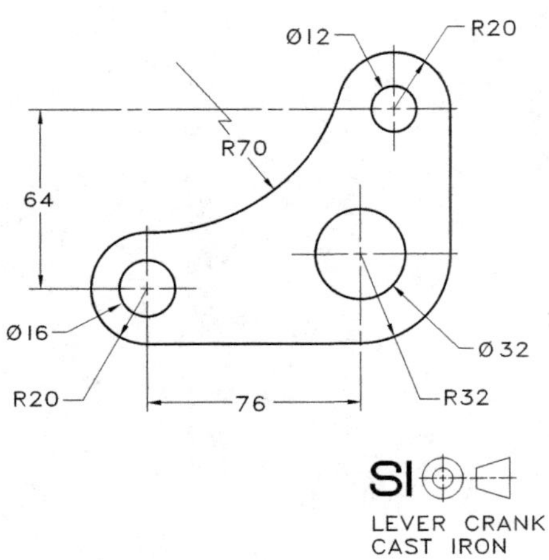

Exercise 2.10M Lever Crank

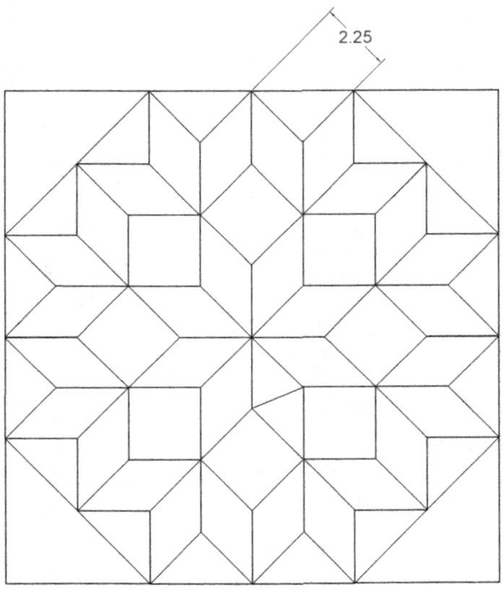

Exercise 2.11 Star Quilt Block

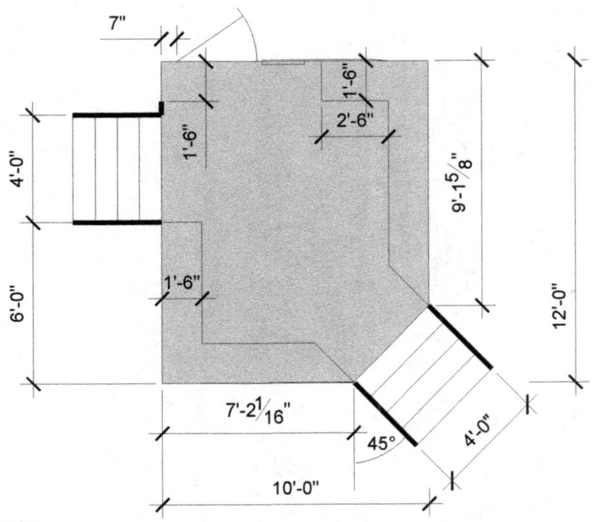

Exercise 2.12 Deck Plan

BASIC EDITING AND PLOTTING TECHNIQUES

3

Introduction

Next you will learn how to modify some basic shapes to create a wider variety of shapes needed in technical drawings. You will also see how to use the drawing to find areas, lengths, and other information.

In this tutorial you will finish drawing the subdivision that you started in Tutorial 2. A drawing has been provided with the datafiles that accompany this guide. You will start from it, in case the drawing that you created in Tutorial 2 has some settings that are different from the datafile. You will trim lines and arcs, and add fillets, multilines, and text to finish the subdivision drawing. When you've finished the drawing, you will plot your final result.

Starting

Launch AutoCAD 2027.

Starting from a Template Drawing

A template drawing is one designed to be used as the basis for new drawings. AutoCAD settings, preferences, and drawn objects in the template become part of the new drawing, while the original template remains unchanged. Files that can be used as templates have the extension *.dwt*. There is really no difference between them and regular drawings except for the file extension. Any drawing can be saved as a template file using Save As and selecting the file type as Drawing Template File (*.dwt*).

To continue with the subdivision drawing, you will start a new file, using the data file *subdiv2.dwt* as a template.

Click: ***New button from the Quick Access toolbar***

The Select Template dialog box should be showing, similar to Figure 3.1. You should see a list of premade templates to choose from; these are stored in the *Template* folder that was created when the software was installed.

Click: ***to pull down the selections in the Look in box***

The Look in area lists the storage devices connected to your computer.

Choose the location of the *datafiles* folder so you can see the files in it as shown in Figure 3.1.

Objectives

When you have completed this tutorial, you will be able to

1. Modify your drawing, using the Fillet, Chamfer, Offset, and Trim commands.
2. Create and edit polylines and splines.
3. List graphical objects, locate points, and find areas from your drawing database.
4. Change properties of drawing objects.
5. Create multilines and multiline styles.
6. Print or plot your drawing.

Tip: *If you have not downloaded and installed the datafiles, do so at this time! Open www.sdcpublications.com in your browser and download the datafiles. It is easy. For detailed instructions, see page GS1-5.*

Tip: *You can pick Application icon, Options and use the File tab of the Options dialog box to set a different default directory location for the template files.*

Tip: *If you do not see the file extensions listed when you are browsing, you may have Hide Extensions for Know Types selected in your Windows Explorer. You can change this using the Explorer Tools, Folder Options, View tab selection.*

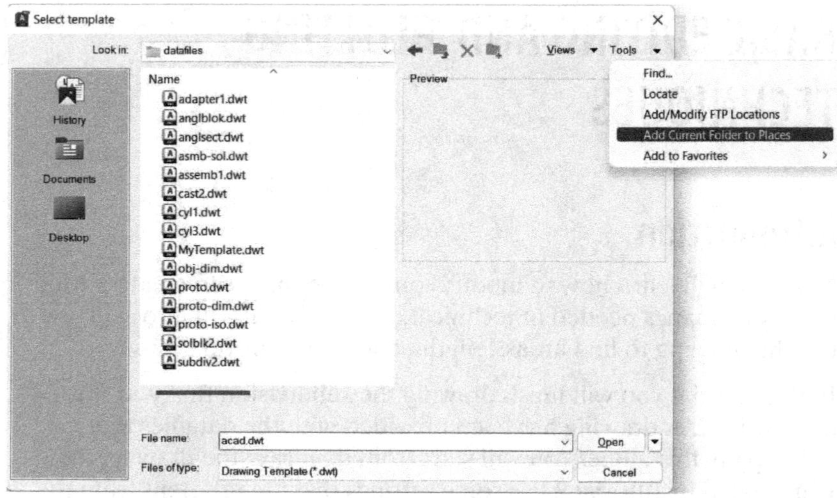

Figure 3.1

Click: ***Tools** to show the menu as shown in Figure 3.1*

Click: ***Add Current Folder to Places***

Tip: *If you have already added the datafiles to your places, the Add Current Folder to Places selection will be "grayed out."*

The *datafiles* folder is added to the list of places at the left of the dialog box as shown in Figure 3.2. This gives you a quick way to access the folder the next time you need it.

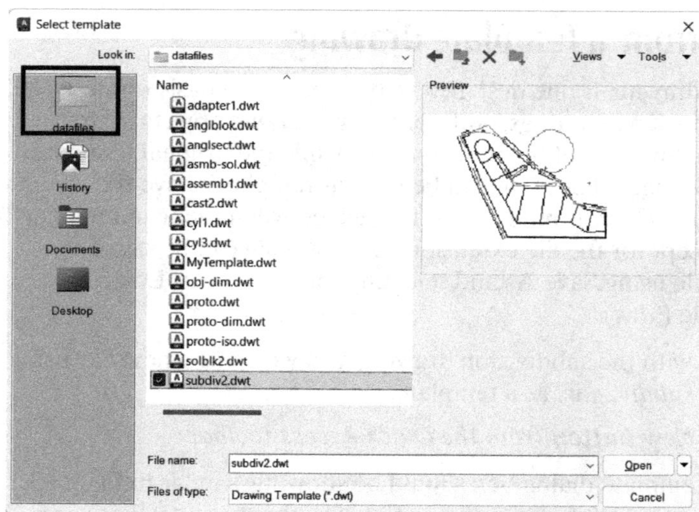

Figure 3.2

Select: ***subdiv2.dwt***

Click: ***Open (or double-click on the file name)***

You should see the drawing on your screen with the AutoCAD default name "*Drawing#*." The *.dwt* file extension signals the software to create a copy of the drawing so that the actual *subdiv2.dwt* datafile will not be changed.

Tip: *You will see Drawing followed by a different number depending on how many new drawings you have started in this AutoCAD session.*

Click: ***Save As button** from the Quick Access toolbar*

Change to the work folder.

Click: ***Tools,*** *Click:* ***Add Current Folder to Places*** *to add the Work folder to the places at the left of the dialog box.*

For the file name,

Type: ***MYSUBDIV [Enter]***

Now the drawing is saved with the new name MYSUBDIV in your *work* folder. The drawing on your screen should be similar to Figure 3.3.

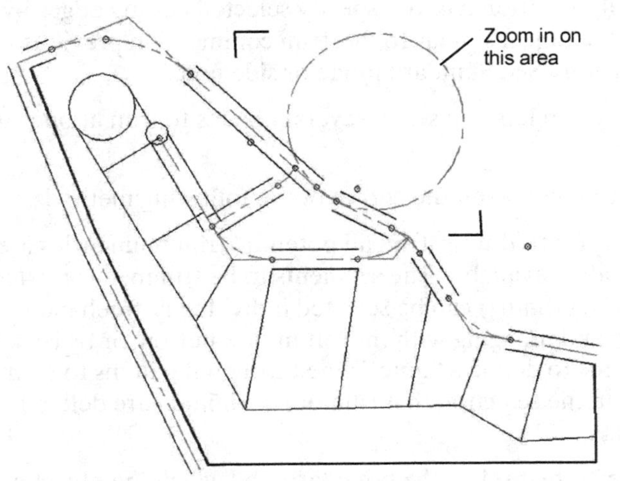

Figure 3.3

Zoom to enlarge the area with the large circle

When you have finished zooming, your screen will look like Figure 3.4.

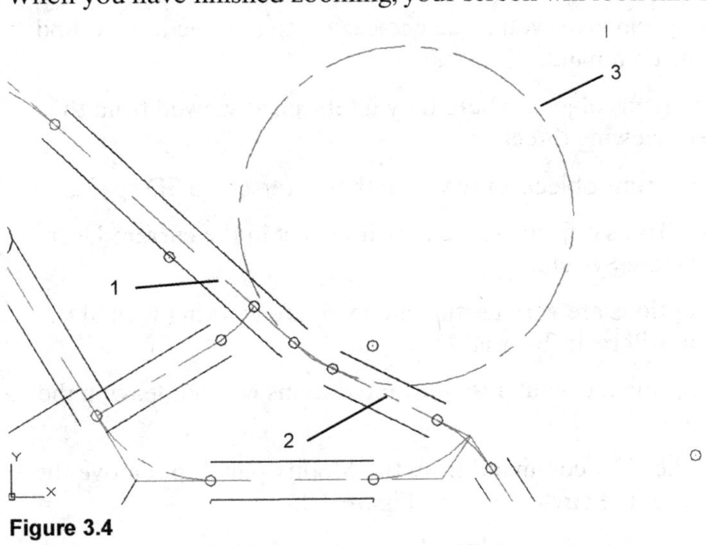

Figure 3.4

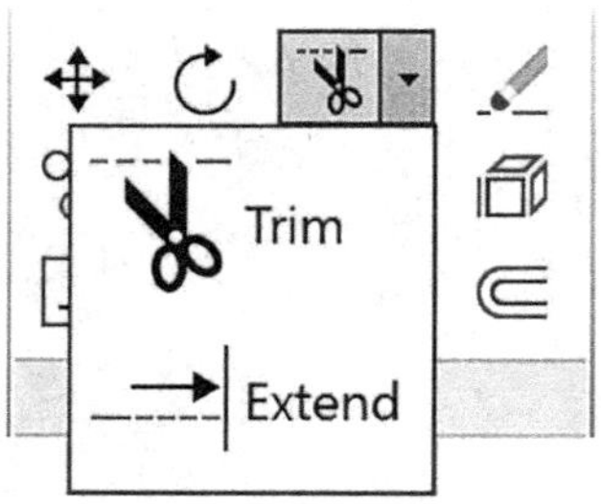

Note: *In previous versions of AutoCAD, to trim, you would first select the objects to use as cutting edges, which are drawing objects that will cut off the portions to trim. After the cutting edges are selected, pressing [Enter] indicates that you have finished selecting cutting edges and want to begin the second step of selecting the portions of the objects to remove. Now using the default Quick mode, you just select the portions to remove. You can still choose the previous command behavior by setting Mode to Standard, or setting the TRIMEXTENDMODE system variable to 0.*

Using Trim

The Trim button is located on the ribbon Home tab, Modify panel. Trim removes part of an object where it meets or crosses other objects. You can also hold down the shift key while selecting an object to extend an object to meet another edge or object. This Quick mode is the default for the Trim command. For many users it may seem more intuitive.

The Trim command has several options.

The **cuTting edges** option lets you specify selected cutting edges by which to trim the object similar to the Trim command in previous AutoCAD versions. See Standard mode or side note.

The **Crossing** option lets you select several objects to trim at once using a crossing box.

The **mOde** option gives you the choice of the following methods:

> **Quick** (default) during Trim all potential trim boundaries are immediately available. The segments to be trimmed (or extended by pressing [Shift]) can be selected individually, freehand by holding and dragging with the left mouse button, or by clicking two points to define a "fence" line through the items to trim. Object in the selection that cannot be trimmed are deleted instead.
>
> **Standard** first select the boundaries by which the object will be cut and then press Enter. Then select on the portions of the objects to be trimmed off. To use all objects as boundaries, press [Enter] at the first Select Objects prompt.

The **Project** option gives you three choices for the projection method used by the command.

> **View** Trims objects where they intersect, as viewed from the current viewing direction.
>
> **None** Trims objects only where they intersect in 3D space.
>
> **UCS** Trims objects where they intersect in the current User Coordinate System.

The Project options are very useful when you are working with 3D models as you will be in Tutorial 11.

The **eRrase** option lets you erase unwanted items without leaving the Trim command.

You will use the Trim command from the Modify panel to remove the excess portion of the circle. Refer to Figure 3.4.

In the next steps you will trim by selecting two points to draw a fence.

Click: ***Trim button***

Current settings: Projection=UCS, Edge=None, Mode=Quick

Select object to trim or shift-select to extend or

[cuTting edges/Crossing/mOde/Project/eRase]: ***click near points 1 and point 2*** *as shown in Figure 3.5*

As you are drawing the fence line across objects, the portions that will be trimmed are lighter color. As soon as you click the second fence point, the objects are trimmed (Figure 3.6).

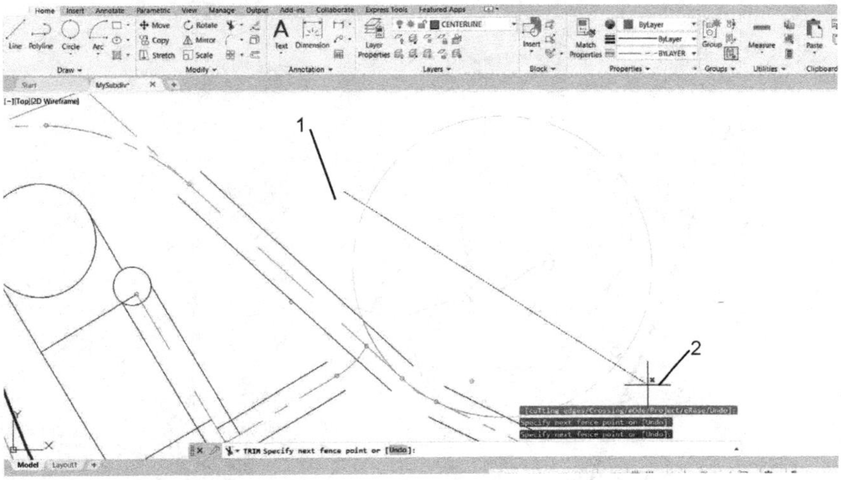

Figure 3.5

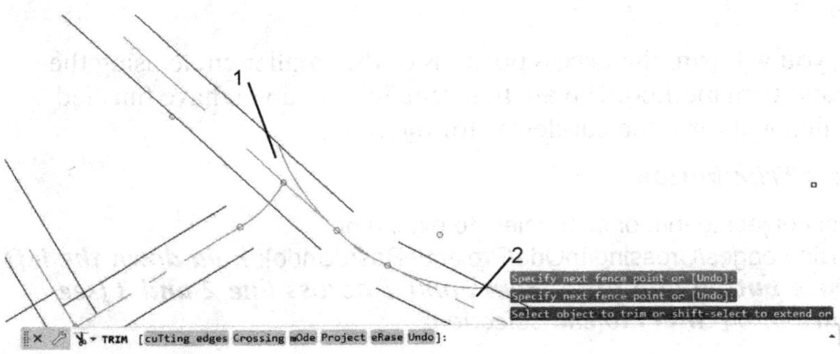

Figure 3.6

The command stays active so that you can continue trimming.

Select object to trim or shift-select to extend or
[cuTting edges/Crossing/mOde/Project/eRase]: ***click near points 3 and point 4*** *as shown in Figure 3.6 (zoom in as needed)*
[Enter] *to end the command*

When you are done, your figure should be similar to Figure 3.7.

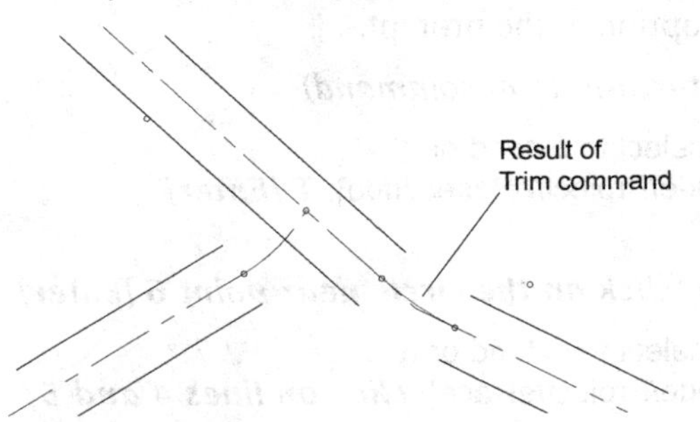

Figure 3.7

Tip: *When you zoom in on an area, circles may not be shown correctly. On the screen, circles are approximated with a number of straight-line segments. Type REGEN [Enter] at the command prompt, or the alias, RE, to cause the display to be recalculated from the drawing database to show the circular shapes correctly.*

Next restore the previous zoom factor and zoom in on the other circles to show them clearly.

Click: ***Zoom All button*** *(or double-click the scroll wheel)*

On your own, enlarge the area shown in Figure 3.8.

Tip: *Lines that do not cross the cutting edge cannot be trimmed. They will be erased instead when you are using the freehand or fence methods.*

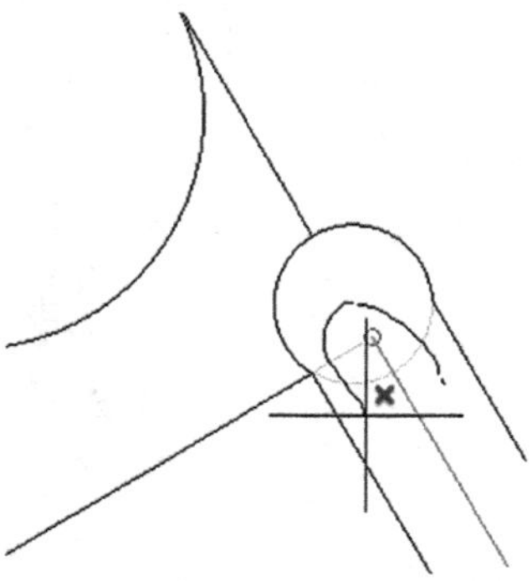

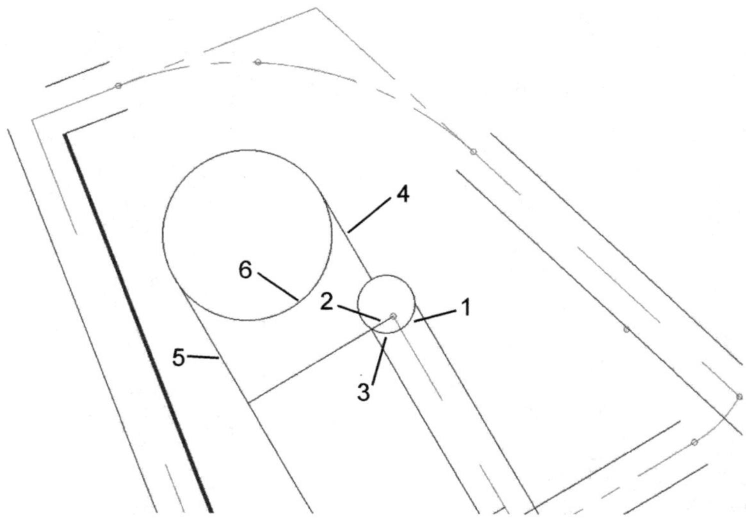

Figure 3.8

Next, you will trim the excess portions of the smaller circle using the freehand trim method. The arc that remains when you have finished trimming will form the cul-de-sac for the road.

Click: ***Trim button***

Select object to trim or shift-select to extend or
[cuTting edges/Crossing/mOde/Project/eRase/Undo]: ***hold down the left mouse button and drag from point 1 across line 2 and 3*** *(see Figure 3.8)* ***[Enter]*** *to end selection.*

The cul-de-sac should look similar to Figure 3.10. Next you will try the method of selecting the cutting edges first similar to that used in the previous versions of AutoCAD to trim the larger circle.

Refer to Figure 3.9 to understand how the cutting edge works in relation to the object to be trimmed. When lines come together, as at a corner, you can select one or both of the lines as cutting lines, as shown in Figure 3.9, parts 1 and 3. The cursor location determines which portion of the line is removed.

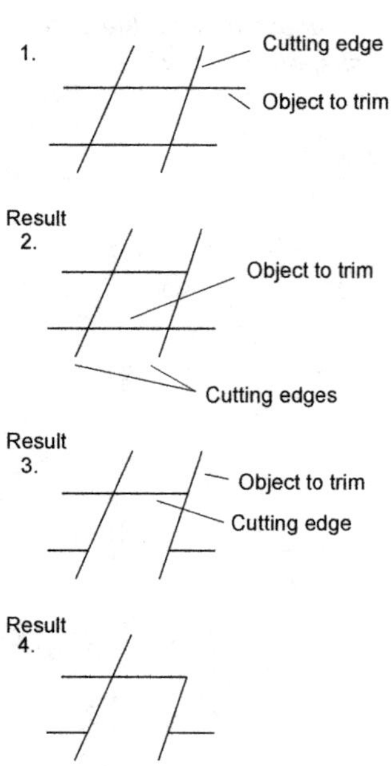

Figure 3.9

You will type the command option at the prompt.

Command: ***[Enter]*** *(to restart the Trim command)*

Select object to trim or shift-select to extend or
[cuTting edges/Crossing/mOde/Project/eRase/Undo]: ***T [Enter]***

Select cutting edges ...
Select objects or <select all>: ***click on the circle near point 6 [Enter]***

Select object to trim or shift-select to extend or
[cuTting edges/Crossing/mOde/Project/eRase]: ***click on lines 4 and 5 and press [Enter]***

Select object to trim or shift-select to extend or [cuTting edges/Crossing/mOde/Project/eRase]: ***Click on line 6 [Enter]***

When you have finished trimming the circles, your screen should look like Figure 3.10. If it doesn't, change the drawing on your own so that it looks like the picture. You can use Undo and start fresh if needed. You may decide to use the cutting edge method, freehand, or fence method depending on your needs.

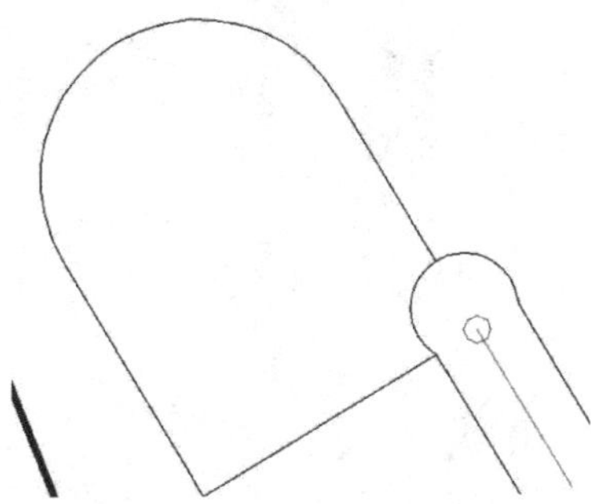

Figure 3.10

Using Offset

The Offset command creates a new object parallel to a given object. The Offset command is on the ribbon Home tab, Modify panel. You will use Offset to create parallel curves 30 units from either side of the curved centerlines that you drew in Tutorial 2.

Double-click the scroll wheel to Zoom out to the extents of the drawing.

Click: Offset button

To offset an object, you need to determine the *offset distance* (the distance away from the original object) or the *through point* (the point through which the offset object is to be drawn). The *layer* option lets you set whether offset objects are created on the current layer or on the layer of the source object. The default is to create the offset object on the same layer as the source object.

Refer to Figure 3.11 for the points to select,

Specify offset distance or [Through/Erase/Layer] <Through>: ***30 [Enter]***

Select object to offset or [Exit/Undo] <Exit>: ***select curve 1***

Specify point on side to offset [Exit/Multiple/Undo]: ***click below the curve, like location A***

Select object to offset or [Exit/Undo] <Exit>: ***select curve 1***

Specify point on side to offset [Exit/Multiple/Undo]: ***click above the curve, like location B***

Once you have defined the offset distance, the prompt *Select object to offset:* is repeated, allowing you to create additional parallel lines that have the same spacing.

Tip: *You can use most typical Windows shortcuts within AutoCAD. Try some of these:*

Ctrl+C	*Copy to clipboard*
Ctrl+N	*New*
Ctrl+O	*Open*
Ctrl+P	*Print*
Ctrl+S	*Save*
Ctrl+V	*Paste*
Ctrl+X	*Cut to clipboard*
Ctrl+Y	*Redo*
Ctrl+Z	*Undo*

On your own, repeat the steps just described to create lines offset 30 units from either side of the remaining curved centerlines so that your drawing looks like that shown in Figure 3.11. Use the scroll wheel to Zoom and Pan as necessary so that you can better see the smaller curves when making selections. You can Zoom and Pan during other commands.

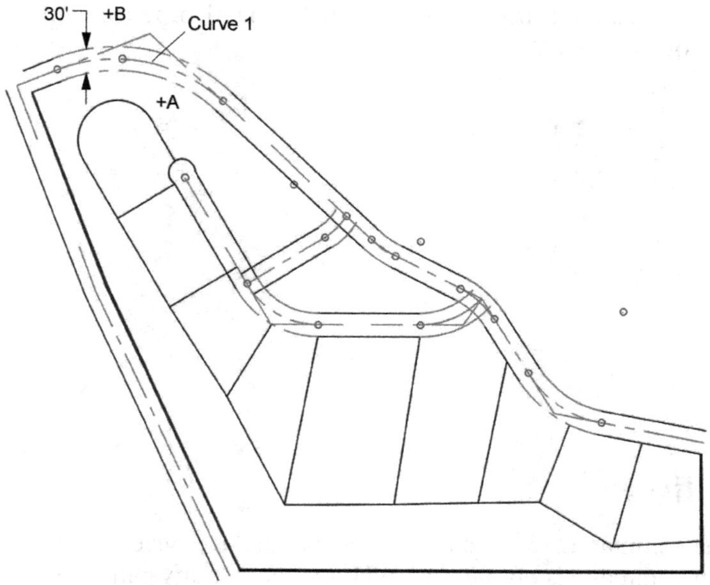

Figure 3.11

If you select the wrong item to offset, either erase the incorrect lines when you have finished or press [Esc] to cancel the command and then start again. When you have finished using the Offset command, press [Enter] to end the command.

Trimming the Remainder

Try the freehand and fence methods for some quick results.

Zoom in on the center area of the drawing.

The center portion of the drawing will be enlarged on your screen. Refer to Figure 3.12 to make your selections.

Click: ***Trim button***

Select object to trim or shift-select to extend or [cuTting edges/Crossing/mOde/Project/eRase/Undo]: ***select the extreme ends of the lines you want to remove and continue until all the excess lines are trimmed***

Hold down the Shift key *during some of the trims so that you can see how the extend feature works.*

When you are finished,

Select object to trim or shift-select to extend or [cuTting edges/Crossing/mOde/Project/eRase/Undo]: ***[Enter]***

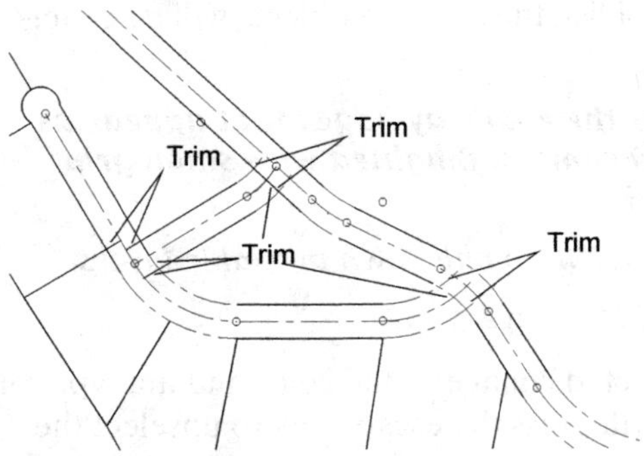

Figure 3.12

When you have finished trimming,

Zoom out to show the entire drawing on the screen.

If you have some short line segments left that no longer cross the cutting edges, use Trim, Erase or click them and press the Delete key to remove them on your own. Your drawing should now look like that shown in Figure 3.13.

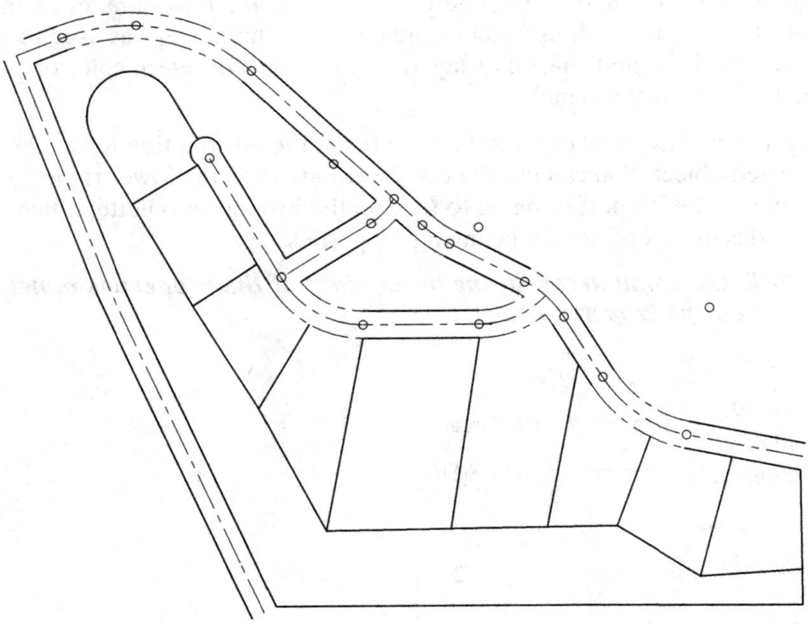

Figure 3.13

Changing Object Properties

Once you've drawn an object, changing the properties of the object or a group of objects may be useful. You will change the properties of the centerlines that you offset so that they are on the layer LOTLINES. The new offset lines are the edges of the road and should be on the same layer as the other lot lines.

A quick way to change objects to another layer is to use the Layer Control pull-down list. When you have objects selected and then choose

Tip: *If you set LOTLINES as the current layer and then use the Offset command Layer option for Current, you will not have to change the layer of the offset lines as on page 101. If so, you will still want to practice the commands for changing layers and other properties.*

a layer from the Layer Control list, the selected objects will be changed to the selected layer.

Click: ***some, but not all, of the roadway edges that appear as centerlines so that they become highlighted with small grip boxes***

Click: ***on the layer CENTERLINE*** *to pull down available layers*

Click: ***LOTLINES*** *from the list of layers*

You will see the lines you selected change to the color and linetype for layer LOTLINES. Next you will press the escape key to unselect the lines.

Press: ***[Esc]***

Notice that CENTERLINE once again shows as the current layer name in the Layer Control.

Using the Properties Panel

The Properties panel on the ribbon Home tab provides quick ways to change the color, lineweight, linetype, plot style, and transparency of an object. To do these things, you would perform similar steps as used to select an object and change its layer, only choose a different color or linetype Properties panel.

The Properties panel can also be used to list the information for a selected object. You can use the downward arrow in the lower right corner of the Properties panel to turn on the Properties palette, which provides more options for changing properties.

Click: ***the small arrow in the lower right of the Properties panel to show the Properties palette***

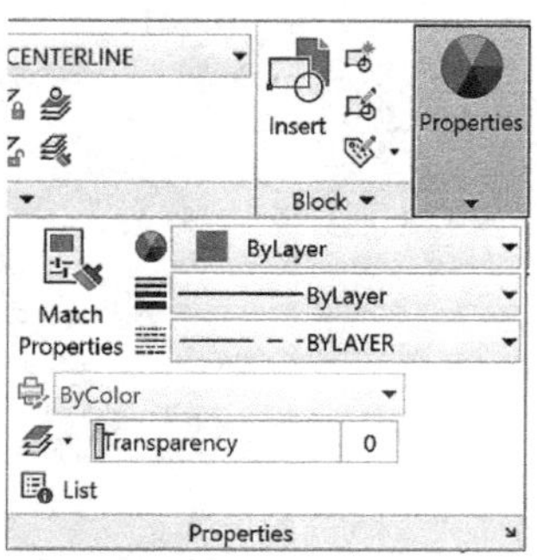

Tip: *You may have to click the Properties button to expand the Properties panel.*

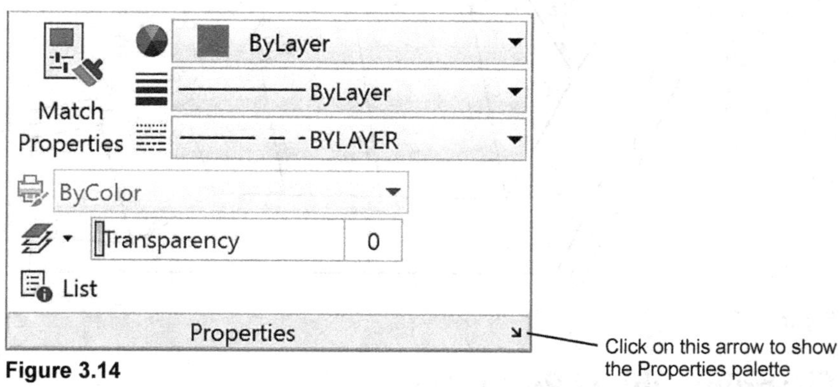

Figure 3.14

The Properties palette appears on your screen as shown in Figure 3.13. It can dock to the edge of the screen or be floating, so you can position it anywhere on the screen. To move it around, click on the gray band at its left. You can leave it open for continued use.

The Properties Palette

The Properties palette lets you change the linetype, layer, lineweight, color, transparency and geometric and other properties of the objects you select.

Currently there is no object selected, so the palette only reports general properties of the drawing.

Click: ***the roadway edges that have not been changed yet*** *(they are green and have a centerline pattern)*

The grip boxes for the objects you select appear when they are selected. The information reported in the Properties palette changes to show the information for the selected objects.

You will use the palette to change the objects you selected from layer CENTERLINE to layer LOTLINES.

Click: ***on layer CENTERLINE*** *to the right of the word Layer*

The list of layers appears, as in Figure 3.16.

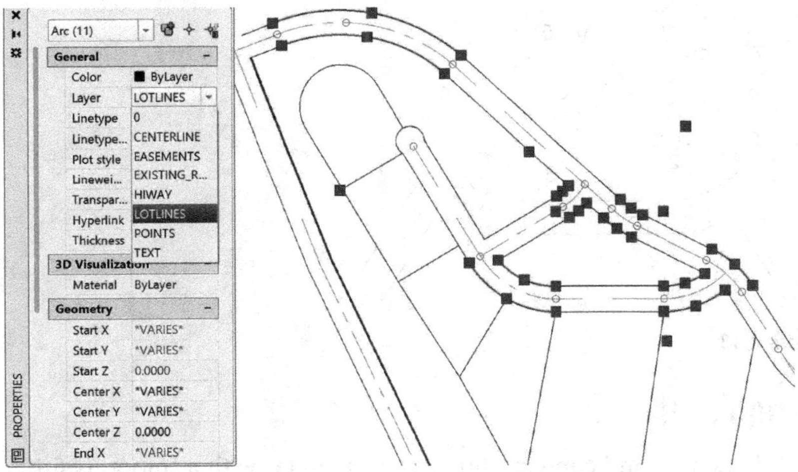

Figure 3.16

Click: ***LOTLINES*** *from the list*

Press: ***[Esc] [Esc]*** *to unselect the arcs*

On your own, select any of the remaining offset lines still on layer Centerline and change them to layer Lotlines.

Click: ***the Close button [X]*** *in the upper left corner to close the Properties palette*

In your drawing, the lines you selected change to black (or white, depending on your configuration) and linetype CONTINUOUS, as set by layer LOTLINES's properties.

Click: ***to preselect one of the drawing lines on layer LOTLINES***

Click: ***Make Current button***

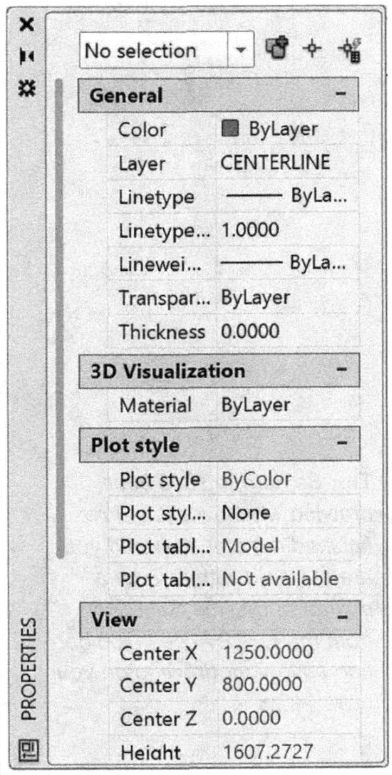

Figure 3.15

Tip: *You can double-click on an object to quickly bring up its properties.*

Tip: *You can right-click the title bar on the Properties palette and select Auto-hide. This will cause the Properties palette to only show the narrow toolbar title unless you hover your mouse over it, which causes it to expand. This only works when the palette is not docked. You can also make the Properties palette transparent, in a similar way.*

Tip: *You can resize the width of the Properties palette by moving your cursor over its vertical edges and then clicking and dragging when you see the cursor change to a double headed arrow symbol.*

The layer name LOTLINES now appears as the current layer (with no objects selected) as shown in Figure 3.17.

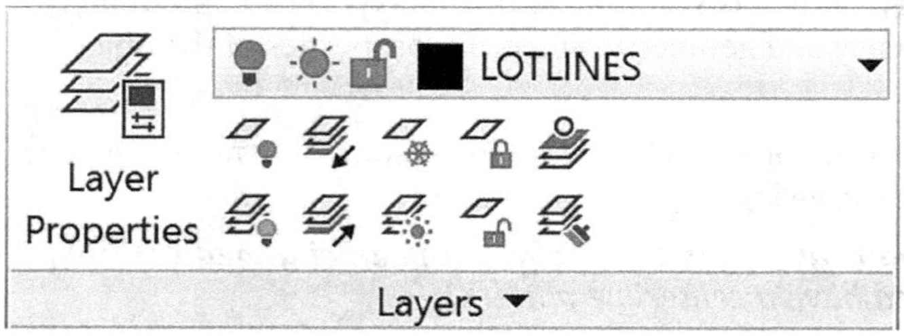

Figure 3.17

On your own, **Zoom** to enlarge the center area of the drawing, as shown in Figure 3.18.

Tip: Be sure to save your drawing whenever you have finished a major step and you are satisfied with it. Take a minute to use the Save icon from the Quick Access toolbar and save your drawing on your own.

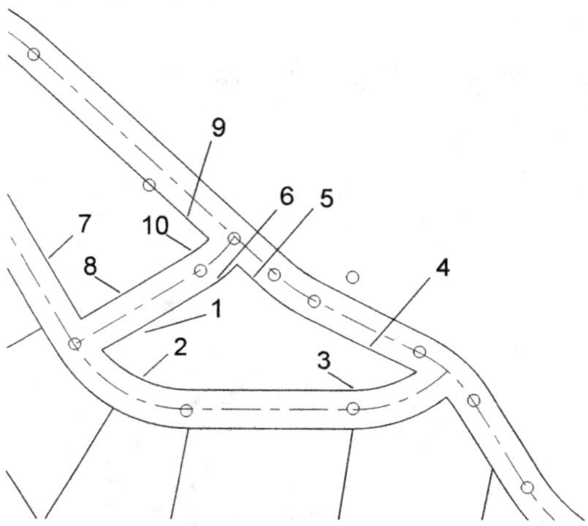

Figure 3.18

Using Fillet

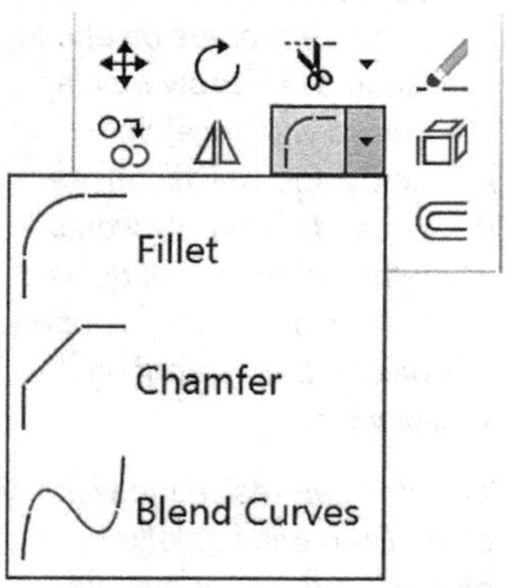

The Fillet command connects lines, arcs, or circles with a smoothly fitted arc, or *fillet*. The Fillet command is on the Modify panel.

Click: ***Fillet button***

Select first object or [Undo/Polyline/Radius/Trim/Multiple]: ***R [Enter]***

Clicking on the Radius option or typing R indicates that you want to enter a radius.

Specify fillet radius <0.0000>: ***10 [Enter]***

You are prompted to select the two objects. Refer to Figure 3.18 to select the lines.

Select first object or [Undo/Polyline/Radius/Trim/Multiple]: ***select line 1***

Select second object or shift-select to apply corner: ***select line 2***

A fillet should appear between the two lines, as shown in Figure 3.19.

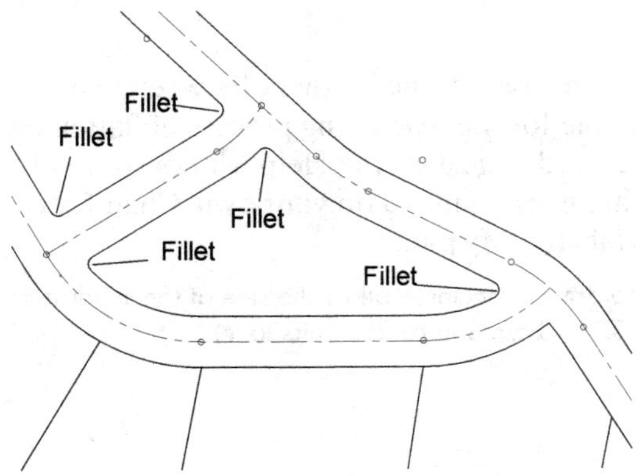

Figure 3.19

Command: ***[Enter]***

The previous command restarts when you press [Enter] or the spacebar at the blank command prompt. In this case, it returns to the original Fillet prompt, which allows you to repeat the selection process, drawing additional fillets of the same radius, or to type a command letter to select other fillet options. You will use the Multiple option to create multiple fillets of the same radius without having to restart the command. Create fillets between the lines shown in Figure 3.18.

Select first object or [Undo/Polyline/Radius/Trim/Multiple]: ***M [Enter]***

Select first object or [Undo/Polyline/Radius/Trim/Multiple]: ***select line 3***

Select second object or shift-select to apply corner: ***select line 4***

Select first object or [Undo/Polyline/Radius/Trim/Multiple]: ***continue to fillet lines 5 through 10 on your own and end the command***

Zoom out to the drawing extents. Erase any extra line segments left from using Fillet.

You can use the Fillet command to fit a smooth arc between any combination of lines, arcs, or circles. Once you have defined the radius value, the direction of the fillet is determined by the cursor location used to identify the two objects.

Figure 3.20 shows some examples of how you can create fillets of different shapes by choosing different point locations. Each example starts with a line located directly above an arc, as shown in the column on the left. Clicking the objects where indicated yields the results shown in the column on the right.

You can also set the Fillet command so that it does not automatically trim the lines to join neatly with the fillet, which is the default. You do so by selecting the command option Trim (typing the letter T at the command prompt) and then typing N to choose the option No trim. Experiment with this method on your own.

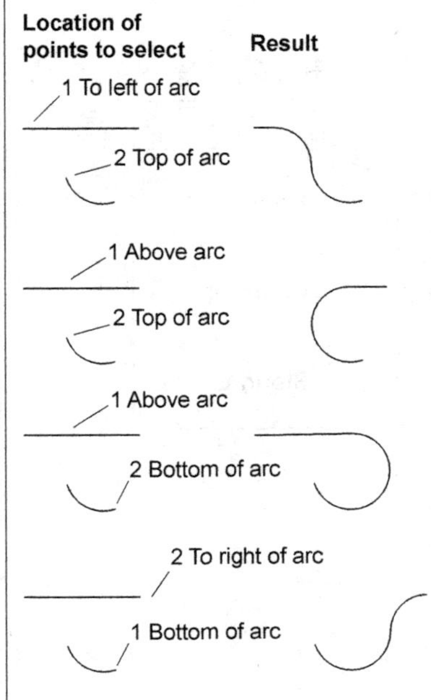

Figure 3.20

Tip: *Holding down shift while selecting lines during the fillet command creates a sharp corner between the two lines instead of making the rounded fillet.*

Tip: *If you use a radius value of 0 with the Fillet command, you can use the command to make lines intersect that do not meet neatly at a corner. This method also works to make a neat intersection from lines that extend past a corner. You can also do so with the Chamfer command (which you will learn next) by setting both chamfer distances to 0.*

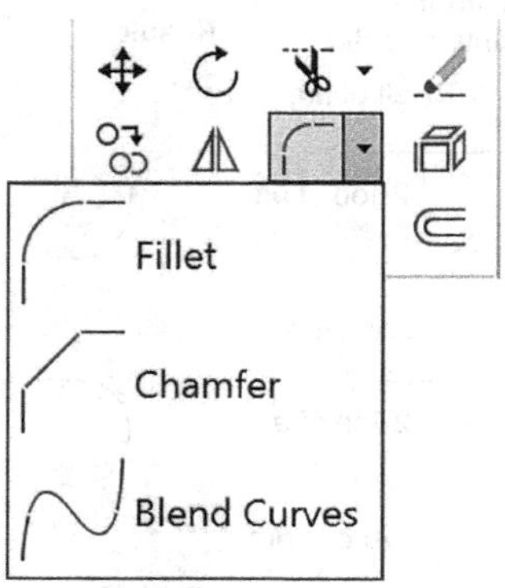

Using Chamfer

The Chamfer command draws a straight-line segment between two given lines. *Chamfer* is the name for the machining process of flattening a sharp corner to create a beveled edge. Use the Help window to read about the options for the Chamfer command on your own. Chamfer is found on the ribbon Home tab, Modify panel.

Use the Rectangle command to draw a rectangle, off to the side of the subdivision drawing, as shown in Figure 3.21 (about 500 by 250 units long).

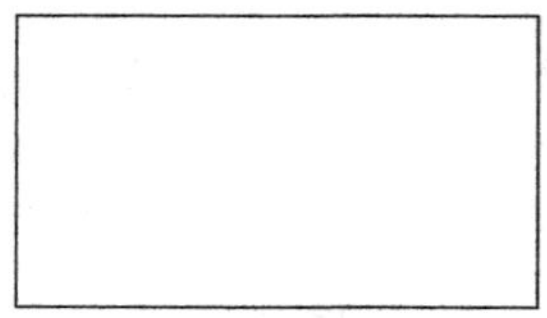

Figure 3.21

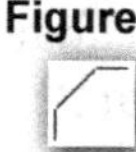 *Click:* ***Chamfer button***

Select first line or [Undo/Polyline/Distance/Angle/Trim/mEthod/Multiple]: ***D [Enter]***

Typing D indicates that you want to enter distance values.

Specify first chamfer distance <0.0000>: ***50 [Enter]***

Specify second chamfer distance <50.0000>: ***75 [Enter]***

The Chamfer command prompts you for selection of the first and second lines between which the chamfer is to be added. Refer to the upper part of Figure 3.22 to select the lines.

Select first line or [Undo/Polyline/Distance/Angle/Trim/mEthod/Multiple]: ***select the first line***

Select second line or shift-select to apply corner: ***select the second line***

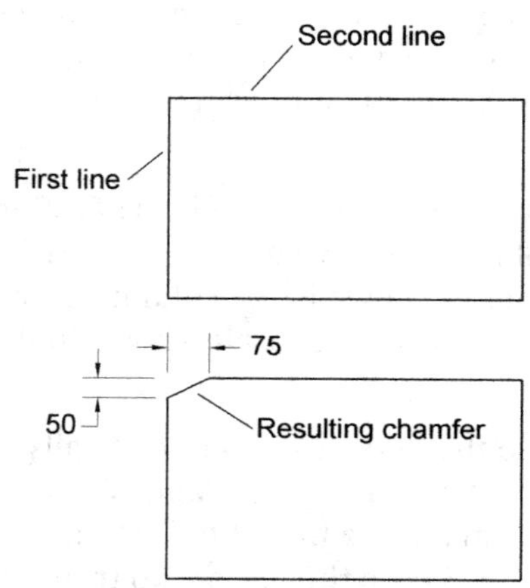

Figure 3.22

A chamfer should appear on your screen that looks like the one shown in the lower part of Figure 3.22. The distance that each end of the chamfer is from the corner defines the size of the chamfer. As with the Fillet command, once you have entered these distances, you can draw additional chamfers of the same size by typing the M option for

Multiple and pressing [Enter] to enter the option. The command will then repeat until you press [Enter] to end the command.

On your own, use the commands that you have learned to erase the chamfered rectangle from your drawing. Use Zoom All to restore the original appearance and then save the drawing.

In Tutorial 1 you learned how to draw a rectangle with the Rectangle icon, which had the options Fillet and Chamfer. The same Fillet and Chamfer principles that you just learned apply to using the Rectangle icon. At this point you may find it useful to practice with the Rectangle icon and changing the Chamfer and Fillet dimensions offered in the command prompt. When you have finished practicing drawing rectangles, erase them before moving on to the next section.

Using Polyline

The Polyline command draws a series of connected lines or arcs that AutoCAD treats as a single graphic object called a *polyline.* The Polyline command is also used to draw irregular curves and lines that have a width. The Polyline command is on the ribbon Home tab, Draw panel.

You will use the Polyline command to create the shape for a pond to add to the subdivision drawing. Before continuing, check to see that LOTLINES is the current layer.

 *Click:* ***Polyline button***

Specify start point: ***select any point to the right of the subdivision where you want to locate the pond***

Specify next point or [Arc/Halfwidth/Length/Undo/Width]: ***select 9 more points***

To use the Close option similar to that of the Line command,

Specify next point or [Arc/Close/Halfwidth/Length/Undo/Width]: ***C [Enter]***

Your screen should show a line made of multiple segments, similar to the one in Figure 3.22.

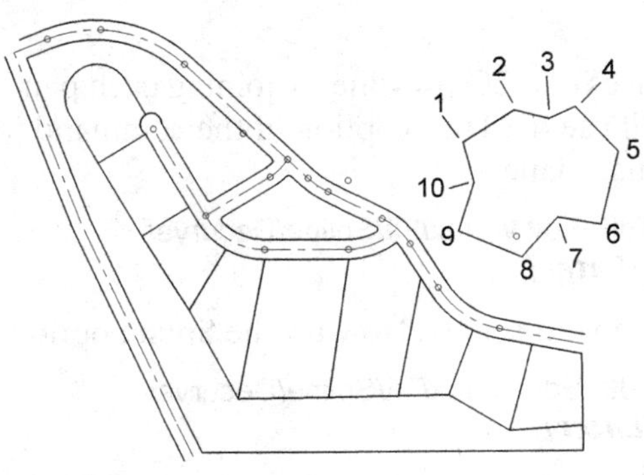

Figure 3.23

A shape drawn by using Polyline is different from a shape created by using the Line command because the polyline is treated as one object. You cannot erase one of the polyline segments. If you try, the entire polyline is erased.

Other Polyline options allow you to draw an arc as a polyline segment (Arc), specify the starting and ending width (or half-width) of a given segment (Width, Half-width), specify the length of a segment (Length), and remove segments already drawn (Undo).

Edit Polyline (PEDIT)

Once you have created a polyline, you can change it and its individual segments with Edit Polyline. The Edit Polyline (Pedit) command is on the Modify panel. You will use it to change the segmented line you just created to a smooth curve.

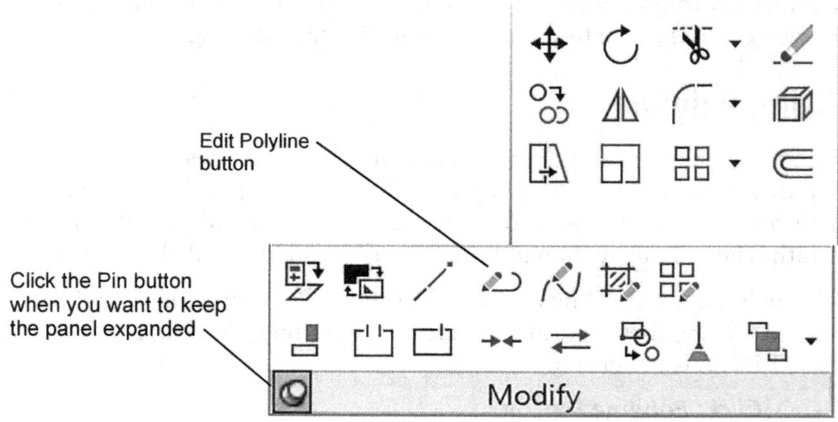

The Edit Polyline command provides two different methods of fitting curves: Fit and Spline. The **Fit** option joins every point you select on the polyline with an arc.

 *Click:* ***Edit Polyline button***

Select polyline or [Multiple]: ***select any part of the polyline***

Enter an option [Open/Join/Width/Edit vertex/Fit/Spline/Decurve/ Ltype gen/Reverse/Undo]: ***F [Enter]***

The straight-line segments change to a continuous curved line, as shown in Figure 3.24.

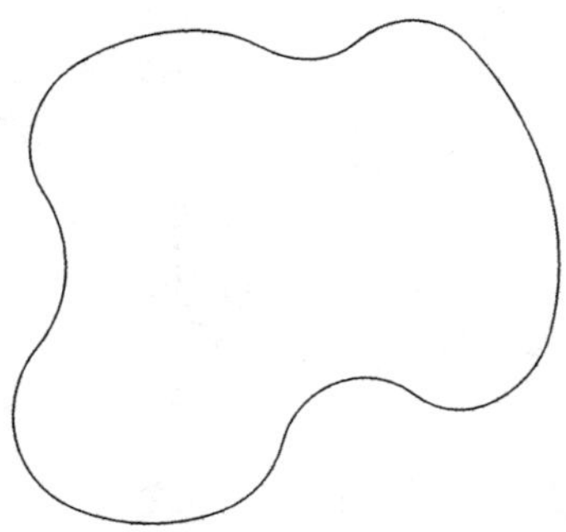

Figure 3.24

Fit curve connects all the vertices of a 2D polyline by joining each pair of vertices with an arc. You will use the Undo option of the command to return the polyline to its original shape.

Enter an option [Close/Join/Width/Edit vertex/Fit/Spline/Decurve/ Ltype gen/ Reverse/Undo]: ***U [Enter]***

The original polyline returns on your screen. Now try the Spline option.

Enter an option [Close/Join/Width/Edit vertex/Fit/Spline/Decurve/ Ltype gen/Reverse/Undo]: ***S [Enter]***

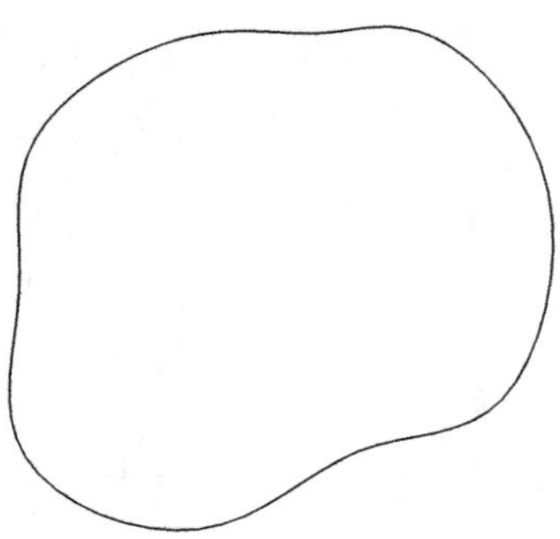

Figure 3.25

A somewhat flatter shape replaces the original polyline (Figure 3.25). The **Spline** option produces a smoother curve by using either a cubic or a quadratic B-spline approximation (depending on how the system variable Splinetype is set). Splines work like a string stretched between the first and last points of your polyline.

The vertices on your polyline act to pull the string in their direction, but the resulting spline does not necessarily reach those points. Among other things, splined polylines are useful for creating contour lines on maps.

Now try the **Width** option.

Enter an option [Close/Join/Width/Edit vertex/Fit/Spline/Decurve/ Ltype gen/Reverse/Undo]: ***W [Enter]***

Specify new width for all segments: ***5 [Enter]***

The splined polyline is replaced with one with a 5 unit width. To exit the Edit Polyline command,

Enter an option [Close/Join/Width/Edit vertex/Fit/Spline/Decurve/ Ltype gen/Reverse/Undo]: ***[Enter]***

Your drawing should look similar to Figure 3.26.

Tip: *You can use Edit Polyline to convert objects into polylines. At the Select polyline: prompt, pick the line or arc that you want to convert to a polyline. You will see the message Object selected is not a polyline. Do you want to turn it into one? <Y>:. Press [Enter] to accept the yes response to convert the selected object into a polyline and continue with the prompts for the Edit Polyline command. (You can use Explode to change a polyline back into individual objects.)*

Tip: *The Edit Polyline, Join option allows you to join arcs, lines, and polylines to an existing polyline.*

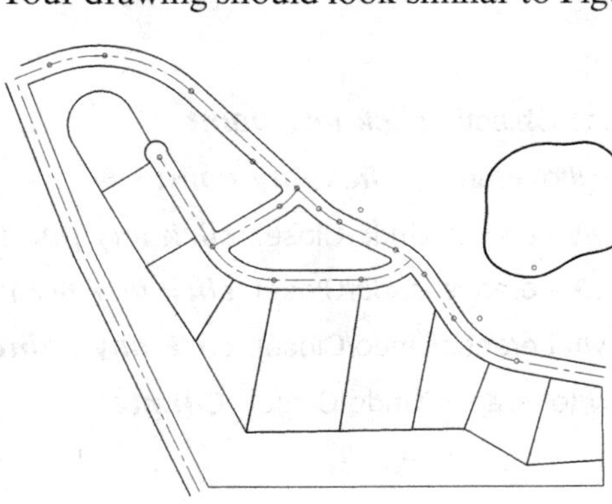

Figure 3.26

Editing Polylines using Grips

You can quickly edit polylines using grips. The [Ctrl] key is used to cycle between the editing options.

Click: ***on the Polyline to show its grips***

Click: ***on one of the grips to activate it as the base grip,*** *as shown in Figure 3.27*

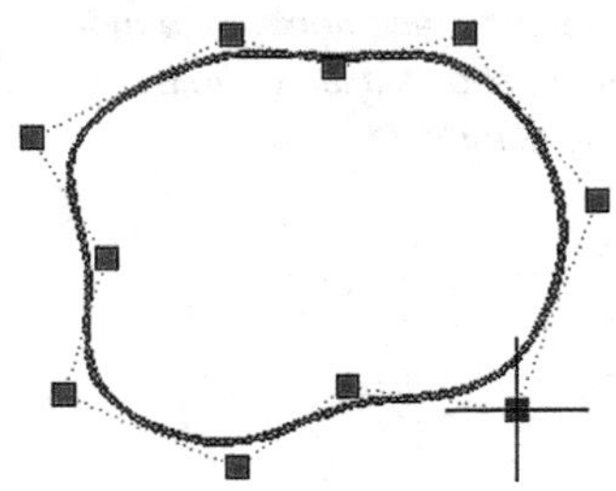

Figure 3.27

The stretch options is the default. Notice you can drag the grip around to change the shape of your polyline.

Specify stretch point or [Base point/Copy/Undo/eXit]: ***[Ctrl]***

After you press [Ctrl], the prompt ** REMOVE VERTEX ** appears in the Command line. This lets you change your polyline shape by deleting one of the defining points. (You can also just keep your mouse pointer over the selected vertex and a context menu will appear near the cursor with these options.)

Pick to remove vertex: ***click the mouse, removing the vertex***

The polyline changes so that it is not being pulled toward the deleted point.

Command: ***U [Enter]***

The grip editing is undone and the polyline returns to its previous shape.

Tip: *If you have a polyline that has already been curved with Fit or Spline, Decurve returns the original polyline.*

Using Spline

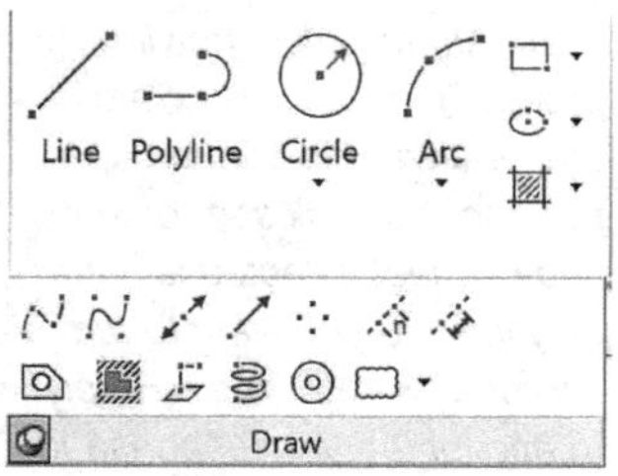

The Spline command lets you create spline using different methods. Among these are quadratic or cubic (*NURBS*) curves. The acronym NURBS stands for nonuniform rational B-spline, which is the method used to draw the curves. These curves can be more accurate than spline-fitted polylines because you control the tolerance to which the spline curve is fit. Splines also take less space in your drawing file than spline-fitted polylines.

The Object option of the Spline command converts spline-fitted polylines to splines. (The variable Delobj controls whether the original polyline is deleted after it is converted.) The Spline command is on the Draw panel. You will draw a spline off to the side of the subdivision and then later erase it.

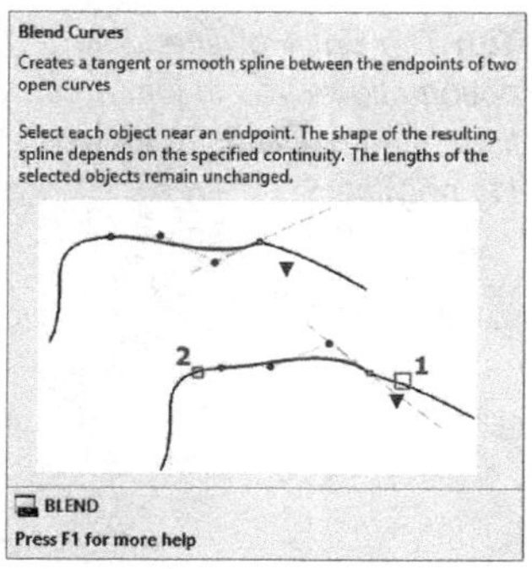

Tip: *Hovering your cursor over the command name for a moment shows a larger tip box for the command.*

*Click: **Spline Fit button***

Specify first point or [Method/Knots/Object] : ***click any point***

Enter next point or [start Tangency/toLerance]: ***click any point***

Enter next point or [end Tangency/toLerance/Undo/Close]: ***click any point***

Enter next point or [end Tangency/toLerance/Undo/Close]: ***click any point***

Enter next point or [end Tangency/toLerance/Undo/Close]: ***click any point***

Enter next point or [end Tangency/toLerance/Undo/Close]: ***C [Enter]***

The spline appears on your screen.

*Click: **Help button***

The Help window opens on your screen.

On your own, type **Spline** into the search box and select to view the help for the Spline command. Scroll as needed and select **About Spline** from the list that appears. Scroll down and study the information as shown (Figure 3.28) from the help screen and close it when you are finished.

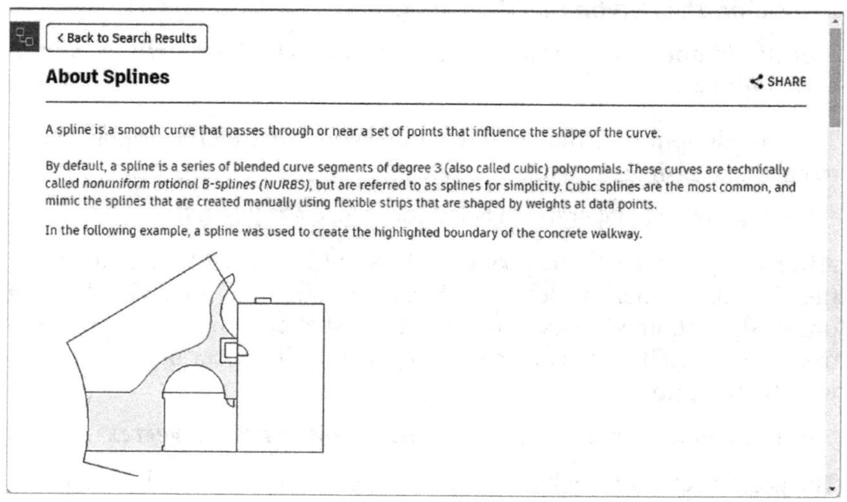
< Back to Search Results

About Splines

SHARE

A spline is a smooth curve that passes through or near a set of points that influence the shape of the curve.

By default, a spline is a series of blended curve segments of degree 3 (also called cubic) polynomials. These curves are technically called *nonuniform rational B-splines (NURBS)*, but are referred to as splines for simplicity. Cubic splines are the most common, and mimic the splines that are created manually using flexible strips that are shaped by weights at data points.

In the following example, a spline was used to create the highlighted boundary of the concrete walkway.

Figure 3.28

Splines are very useful in creating freeform surfaces on 3D models. Experiment by drawing splines on your own. You can edit Splines by using the Splinedit command on the Modify tab, similar to how polylines are edited. You can also edit Splines using their grips.

Using Blend

The Blend command creates a spline to connect two existing lines or curves. You can find it on the ribbon Modify tab on the drop down where the Fillet and Chamfer commands are located.

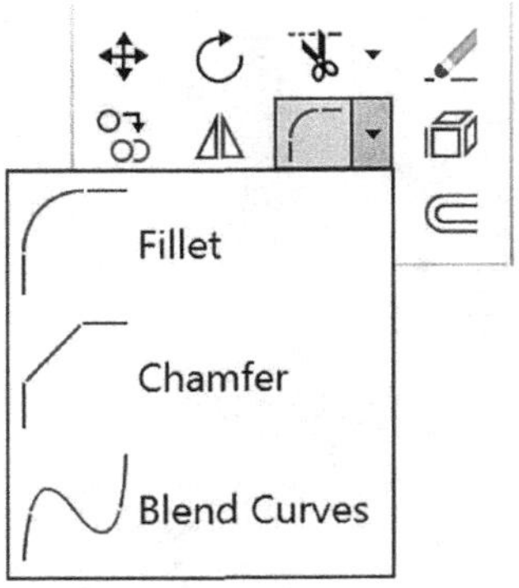

On your own, draw a line and an arc similar to those shown in Figure 3.27A off to the side of your current drawing.

Click: ***Blend Curve*** *button*

Select first object or [CONtinuity]: ***click on the line***

Select second object: ***click on the arc***

A spline is created forming a blend between the line and the arc, as shown in Figure 3.27B.

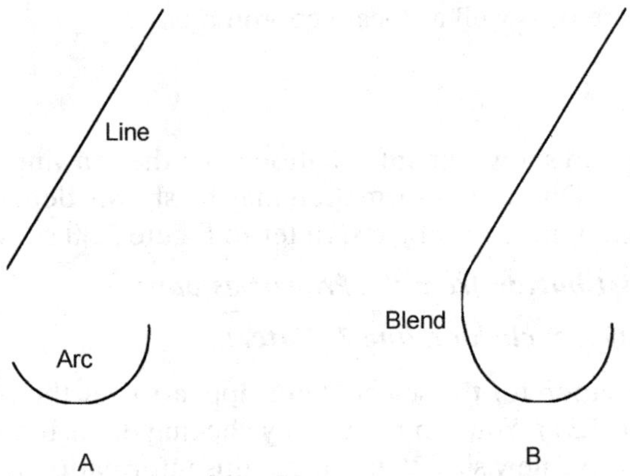

Figure 3.29

When you have finished experimenting,

Erase all the splines and extra lines and arcs that you created.

Click: ***to thaw layer TEXT***

Click: ***TEXT to set it as the current layer***

Use the Text command (Single Line Text) to add the label POND to the pond. Use a text height of 30.

Save your drawing.

When you have finished, your drawing should look like Figure 3.30.

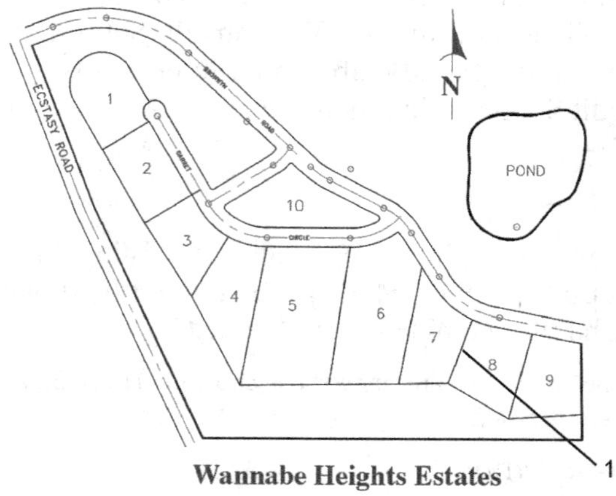

Figure 3.30

Getting Information about Your Drawing

Because your drawing contains accurate geometry and has been created as a model of real-world objects, you can find information about distances and areas, as well as locate coordinates.

Using List

The List command shows the information from the drawing database for the selection. Different information may be shown, depending on the types of and number of objects. Refer to Figure 3.30 as you select.

Click: ***List button*** *from the Properties panel*

Select objects: ***click on line 1 [Enter]***

The text information for the selected line appears near the command prompt (Figure 3.31). You can resize it by clicking on its top or sides and dragging it to a new size. You can use this information to make calculations or to label the lot lines of this subdivision.

```
Command: _list
Select objects: 1 found
Select objects:
                  LINE      Layer: "LOTLINES"
                            Space: Model space
                   Handle = a9
              from point, X=1560.6244  Y= 343.5051  Z=   0.0000
                to point, X=1634.9420  Y= 540.6647  Z=   0.0000
          Length = 210.7013,  Angle in XY Plane = N 20d39'13" E
                  Delta X =  74.3176, Delta Y =  197.1597, Delta Z =   0.0000
Type a command
```

Figure 3.31

This time try typing the command alias (LI).

Command: ***LI [Enter]***

Select objects: ***click on the polyline for the pond [Enter] [Enter] [Enter] [Esc]***

Tip: *You can get the same information by opening the Properties palette.*
You can press ***[F2]*** *to show or hide the command window history.*

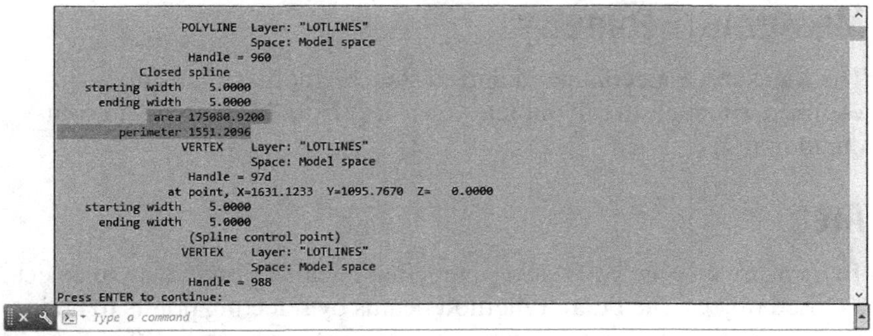

Figure 3.32

The command history appears on your screen as shown in Figure 3.32. It contains information about the vertices of the polyline. Use your keyboard Up arrow, or the scroll bar that appears when you mouse over the right area of the command line to scroll through the history. Near the beginning of the information listed, you will see the area and perimeter of the polyline. This information can be very useful for calculating the area of irregular shapes like the pond.

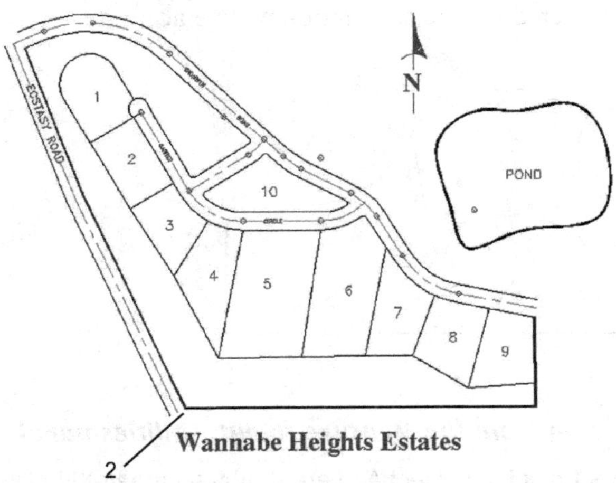

Figure 3.33

Locating Points

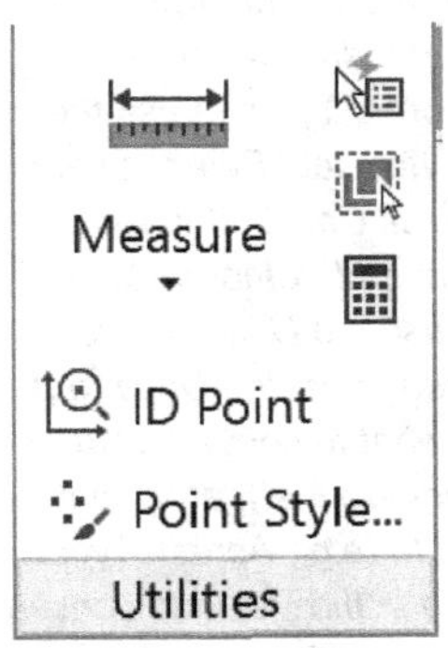

ID Point shows the coordinates of the location that you select. When you use this command in conjunction with object snaps, you can find the exact coordinates of an object's endpoint, center, midpoint, and other points. ID Point is located on the Utilities panel.

Right-click: ***Object Snap button and select Endpoint*** *(turn other modes off if they are on)*

Click: ***to turn on Object Snap*** *(if it is not already on)*

Click: ***to expand the Utilities panel, choose ID Point***

Specify point: ***click on the left end of line 2*** *(Figure 3.33)*

The command window displays the coordinates of the point,
X = 800.0000 Y = 169.5122 Z = 0.0000

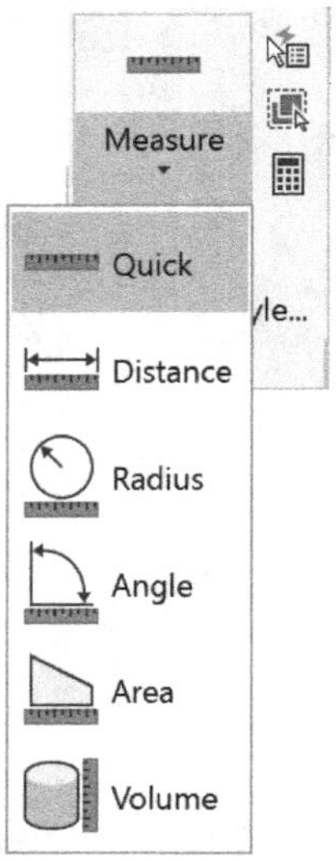

Tip: *When the Dynamic Input button on the status bar is on, you will also see these values in the dynamic cursor.*

Tip: *The area listed is in square units. If the drawing is in feet, the area will be in square feet. You can use the ribbon View tab, Palettes panel, Quick Calc button to convert to other units. To do so, use the Units Conversion area to set the Units (e.g., Area), what to convert from (e.g., square feet), and what to convert to (e.g., Acres). Type the area in the Value to convert box or cut and paste it from your Command area. The converted area will display in acres.*

Measuring Geometry

The Measuregeom command finds distances, radius, angles, areas, or volumes. The measure flyout lets you select from Measuregeom command options.

Area

To measure an area you select points that enclose a boundary, or select a closed object. The default method begins by selecting points to define straight-line boundaries for the area you want to measure. When you are done selecting, press [Enter] to select Total. As you select locations you will see the area being shaded to provide feedback on what area you are defining. The area inside the boundary that you specify is reported. The Object option reports the area of a closed object, such as a polyline, circle, ellipse, spline, region, or a solid object. You could use this method to find the area of the pond instead of using List as you did previously. The Add and Subtract options let you define more complex boundaries by adding and subtracting from the first boundary selected. Next, you will find the area of lot 5. Using the Endpoint object snap will ensure the area selected for the calculation will be accurate.

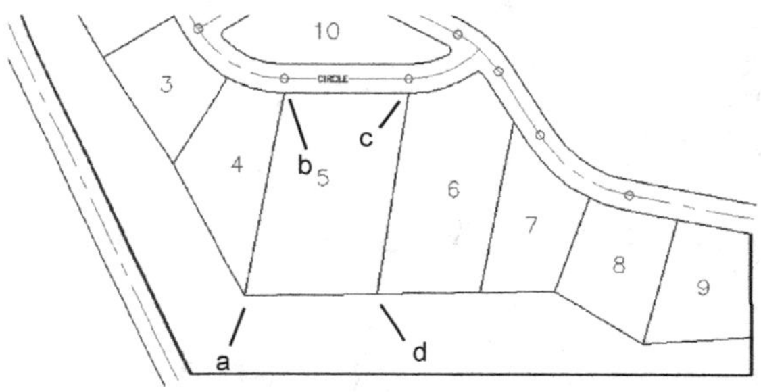

Figure 3.34

Click: ***Area button from the Measure flyout, Utilities panel***

Specify first corner point or [Object/Add area/Subtract area/eXit] <Object>: ***click point a***

Specify next point or [Arc/Length/Undo]: ***click b***

Specify next point or [Arc/Length/Undo/Total] <Total>: ***click c***

Specify next point or [Arc/Length/Undo/Total] <Total>: ***click d***

Specify next point or [Arc/Length/Undo/Total] <Total>: ***[Enter]***

The area and perimeter values of lot 5 are listed in the command window: Area = 113884.6680, Perimeter = 1398.9121. The command stays active at the prompt so that you can make other measurements.

Enter an option [Distance/Radius/Angle/ARea/Volume/eXit] <ARea>: ***D [Enter]***

Specify first point: ***click point a***

Specify second point or [Multiple points]: ***click point d***

Distance = 278.0000, Angle in XY Plane = N 89d13'56" E, Angle from XY Plane = E, Delta X = 277.9750, Delta Y = 3.7252, Delta Z = 0.0000 is reported at the command prompt.

Typing Q at the prompt deploys the quick measurement feature. (You can also select the Quick option from the Measure drop down.)

Enter an option [Distance/Radius/Angle/ARea/Volume/Quick/Mode/eXit] <Distance>: ***Q [Enter]***

Move your cursor in to the middle of lot 5 in your drawing.

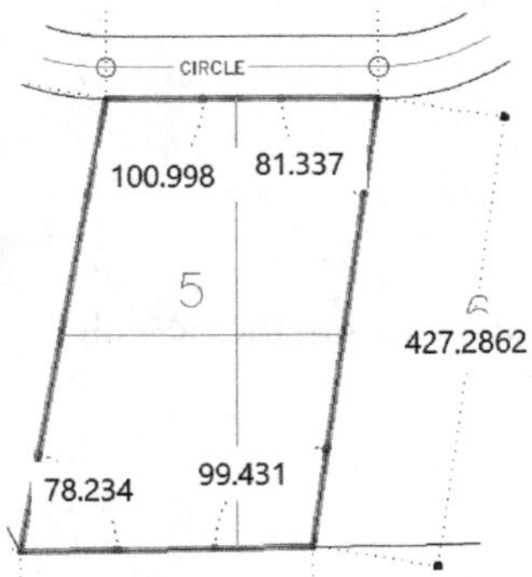

Figure 3.35

Notice the dimensions that appear as you move your cursor into different areas. This is handy for inspecting the sizes in drawings and checking to see if your drawing is correct.

Click inside the rectangular lot 5.

Now the shape becomes shaded and the area and perimeter are displayed as shown in Figure 3.36.

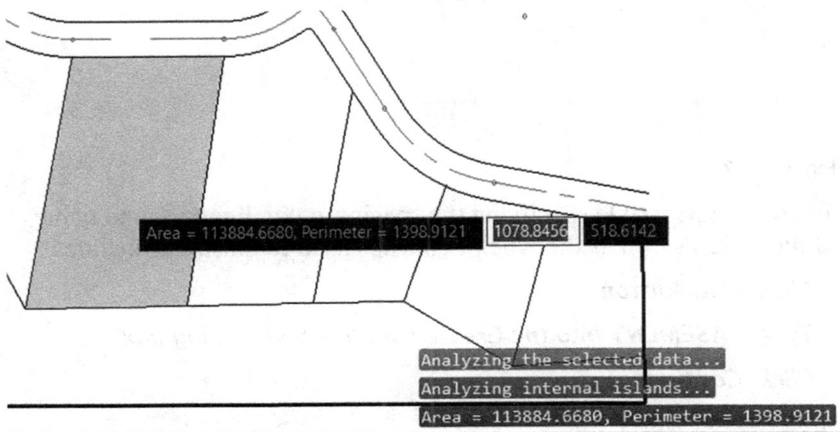

Figure 3.36

To exit the Measuregeom command,

Enter an option [Distance/Radius/Angle/ARea/Volume/eXit] <Distance>: ***X [Enter]***

Using Multilines

Next, you will create a Multiline style so you can add multiple lines in one step. This feature is especially useful in architectural drawings (for creating walls) and in civil engineering drawings. For example, you can draw the centerline of a road and automatically add the edge of pavement and right-of-way lines a defined distance away. Multiline also allows you to fill the area between two lines with a color. The Multiline Style command lets you define up to 16 *elements*. You can save multiline styles with different names so that you can easily reuse them. Set the Justification option of the Multiline command to specify the top, middle, or bottom for locating the multiple pattern. You can also directly set the variable Cmljust to 0, 1, or 2, respectively.

Creating a Multiline Style

You will type the command name,

Command: ***MLSTYLE [Enter]***

The Multiline Style dialog (Figure 3.37) appears showing the default style name, STANDARD. It is the current style.

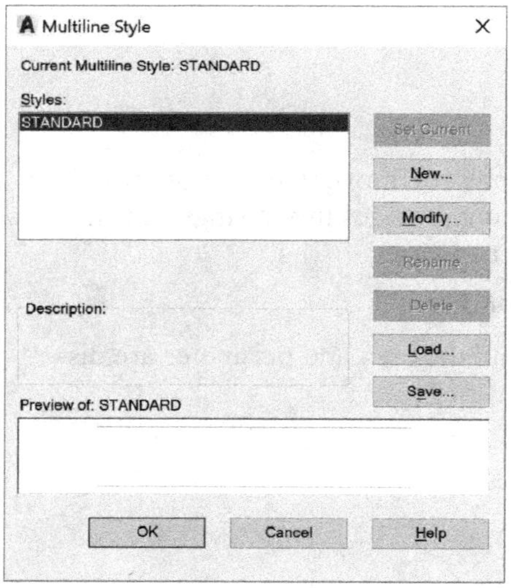

Figure 3.37

To create a new style specifying the spacing, color, linetype, and name of the style, as well as the type of endcaps used to finish off the lines,

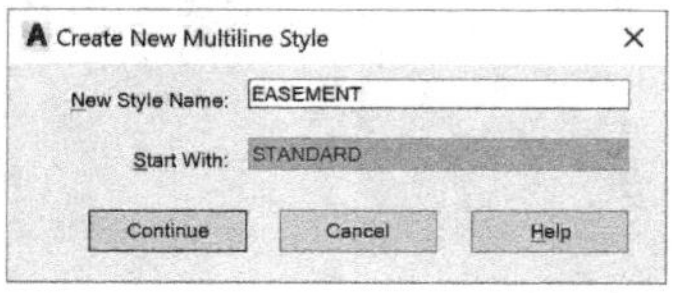

Click: ***New button***

Type: ***EASEMENT*** *into the Create Multiline Style dialog box*

Click: ***Continue***

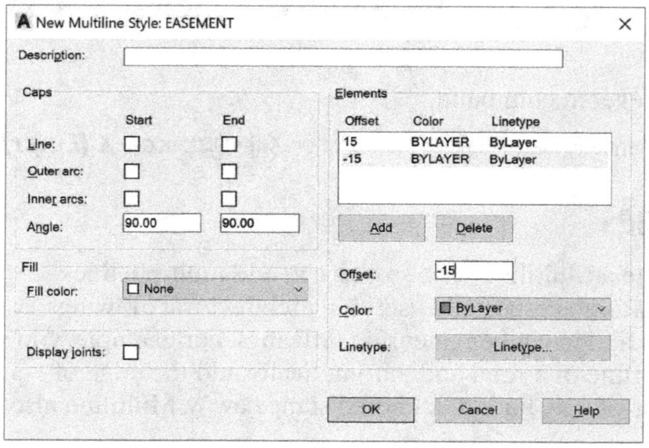

Figure 3.38

Use the New Multiline Style dialog box to set the spacing of the elements, as shown in Figure 3.38. The dialog box has two areas. You can use the Caps area to select different types of endcaps, including angled lines or arcs, to finish the multilines you create. You can also use this area to turn on Fill if you want the area between multiline elements to be shaded.

The Elements area is used to set the spacing, number, linestyle and color for the elements which make up the multiline. You will set the positive offset spacing to 15. To change the spacing for an element,

Click: ***on the top element shown in the list so that it becomes highlighted***

Click: ***in the input box to the right of the word Offset***

Type: ***15***

You should notice the offset value for the top element change to 15. Next, set the offset spacing for the second element to –15.

Click: ***on the second element in the list***

Click: ***to highlight the text in the box to the right of the word Offset***

Type: ***-15***

When you have set the element spacing, your dialog box should look like Figure 3.38. Leave the color and linetype set to BYLAYER, as layer EASEMENTS is already set to cyan color and the DASHED linetype. When you have finished,

Click: ***OK*** *to return to the Multiline Styles dialog box*

The Save button saves a style to the library of multiline styles. When you click the Save button, the Save Multiline Styles dialog box appears on your screen. Multiline styles are saved to *acad.mln* by default in your support path. You can create your own file for your multiline styles, if you want, by typing in a different name. The Load button loads saved multiline styles from a library of saved styles. Rename lets you rename the various styles you have created. You can't rename the STANDARD style.

When you have finished examining the dialog box,

Click: ***Save***

Click: ***Set Current***

Click: ***OK*** *to exit the Multiline Styles dialog box*

On your own, use [Ctrl]+S to quickly save your drawing file with the current name and folder location.

Drawing Multilines

You will add some multilines to represent easements along the lot lines of the subdivision drawing. You will start the command by typing its name, MLine, at the command prompt. The style, EASEMENT, that you created should be the current multiline style.

Click: ***EASEMENTS*** *as the current layer before continuing*

Command: ***MLINE [Enter]***

Now you are almost ready to draw some multilines. Before you do, decide on the justification to use. You can choose to have the multilines you draw align so that the points you select align with the top element, with the zero offset, or with the bottom element. You will set the justification so that the points you pick are the zero offset of the multiline, in this case the middle of the multiline.

Justification = Top, Scale = 1.00, Style = EASEMENT

Specify start point or [Justification/Scale/STyle]: ***J [Enter]***

Enter justification type [Top/Zero/Bottom] <top>: ***Z [Enter]***

You will see the message Justification = Zero, Scale = 1.00, Style = EASEMENT. Now, you are ready to start drawing the easement lines. Refer to Figure 3.34 for the points to select.

Tip: *Remember that the Endpoint running object snap should still be on.*

Specify start point or [Justification/Scale/STyle]: ***click point 1***

Specify next point: ***click 2***

Specify next point or [Undo]: ***click 3***

Specify next point or [Close/Undo]: ***click 4***

Specify next point or [Close/Undo]: ***click 5***

Specify next point or [Close/Undo]: ***click 6***

Specify next point or [Close/Undo]: ***click 7***

Specify next point or [Close/Undo]: ***pick 8***

Specify next point or [Close/Undo]: ***[Enter]***

Tip: *Double-clicking on a multiline shows the Multiline Edit dialog box for some handy features for making multilines join neatly.*

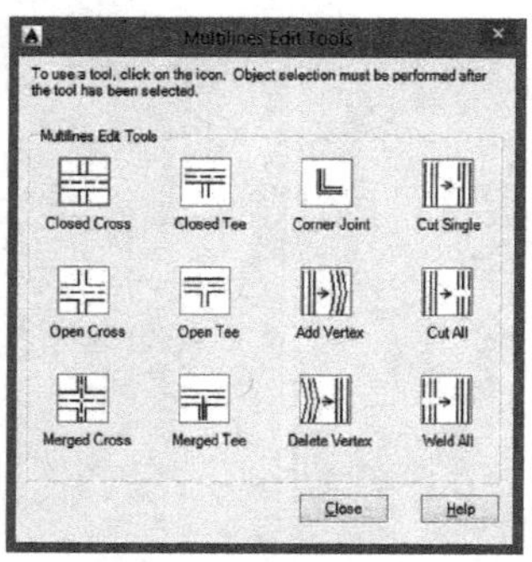

Your drawing should look like Figure 3.39.

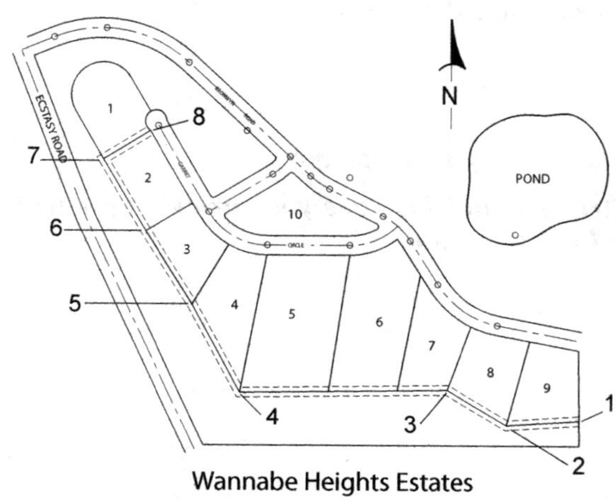

Figure 3.39

On your own, set TEXT as the current layer and use the Mtext (Multiline Text) command to add the following 15 unit tall text describing the location of the subdivision and the easements:

A SUBDIVISION LOCATED IN THE NE 1/4 OF THE SE 1/4 T.15, R.5E, SEC. 14, MPM

A 15′ UTILITY EASEMENT IS RESERVED ALONG ALL EXTERIOR LOTLINES.

The completed drawing is shown in Figure 3.40.

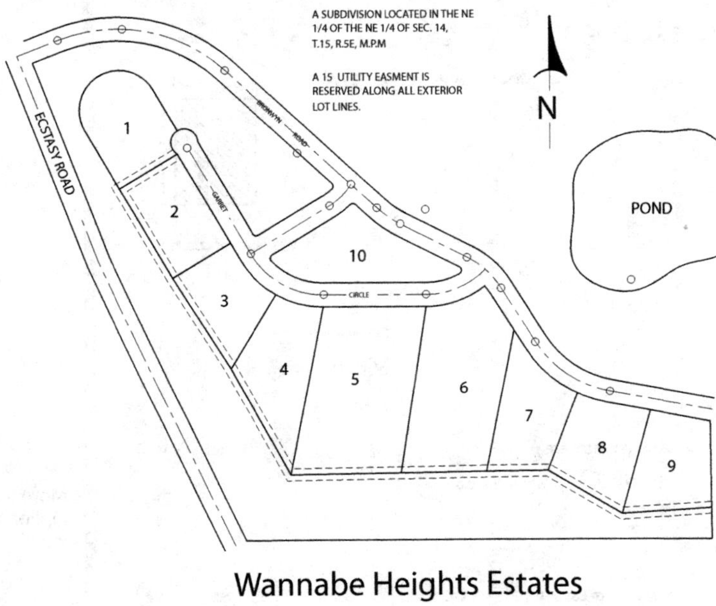

Figure 3.40

Save your drawing now.

The Plot Dialog Box

Depending on the types of printers or plotters you have configured with your computer system, the Plot command causes your drawing to be printed on the device that you configured for AutoCAD use. The same command is used for printing and for plotting. Selecting Plot causes the Plot dialog box (Figure 3.41) to appear on your screen. Among the things that the Plot dialog box lets you choose are:

- The plotter or printer where you will send the drawing (Printer/plotter);
- The portion of your drawing to plot or print (Plot area);
- The scale at which the finished drawing will be plotted (Plot scale);
- Where your plot starts on the sheet (Plot offset);
- Whether to use inches or millimeters as the plotter units;
- The pen or color, line weight, line fill, screening, dithering selections for the plotter or printer (Plot style);
- Whether the plot is portrait or landscape orientation.

Tip: *Right-clicking on the MText window brings up a shortcut menu that you can use to select many useful MText symbols that you can insert by picking Symbol from the shortcut menu.*

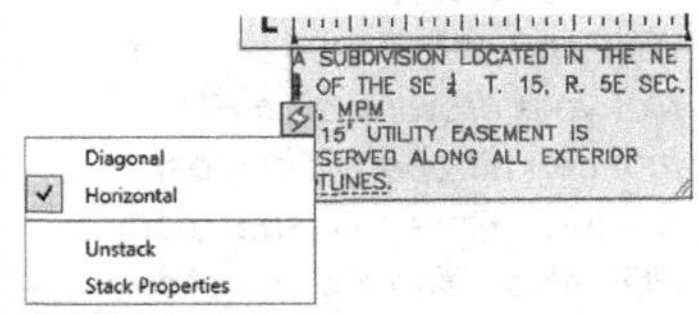

Tip: *You can set how fractions are stacked in the multiline text, either with a diagonal slash or horizontal bar. If autostacking is turned on, your fractions will stack automatically using whichever method you selected. To change the settings, highlight stacked text and click the icon to show the options.*

Tip: *You should save your drawing before you plot in case there is some problem with your printer.*

Tip: *To use the Plot command directly from the command prompt, type a hyphen (-) in front of the command (-plot). This also works for other commands.*

Tip: *Selecting Adobe PDF as your printer makes it easy to plot your drawing as a PDF that can be opened in most readers. You can also export PDF files using the selections from the application icon.*

Click: ***Plot button*** *from the Quick Access toolbar*

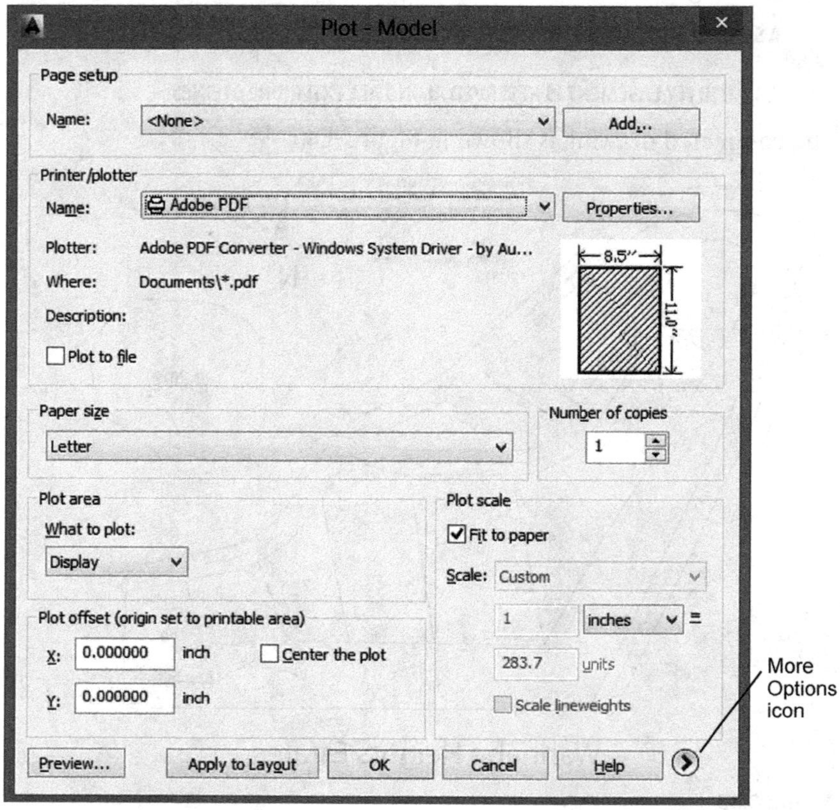

Figure 3.41

Because there are so many factors, some of them are not always displayed. If not already shown, to see the additional options,

Click: ***More Options icon*** *from the lower right of the dialog box*

The dialog box switches to show more options as shown in Figure 3.38.

When you are using the Plot dialog box, be careful not to change too many things about the plotter at once. That way you can see the effect that each option has on your plot.

Plot Device

Use the printer/plotter area to select from the plotters that you have configured. If no printers or plotters are listed, you must use the Plot and Publish tab from the Options dialog box to add a new printer or plotter configuration, or use the Windows operating system to install a printer. Refer to Getting Started 1 and 2 for details about configuring your output device.

To select a listed device, pull down the list of printers and click to highlight the name of the device you will use for your print. The options displayed for paper size and other items depend on your particular output device.

If an item in the Plot dialog box appears grayed instead of black, it is not available for selection. You may not be able to choose certain items, depending on the limitations of your printer or plotter.

Check that your plotter or printer name is selected in the Printer/Plotter Name area of the dialog box.

Plot Style Table (Pen Assignments)

A plot style table lets you assign properties such as color, line weight, line fill, screening, and dithering for your printer or other output device. There are two main methods used to assign the plotting properties: color dependent plot styles (*.ctb*), and named plot styles (*.stb*).

As you might guess, a color dependent plot style uses object color to determine the plot properties. A named plot style assigns a plot style property to objects or layers similar to the way the object color can be assigned.

Plot style tables are independent of the output device selected. If a particular device does not have that property, say screening for example, that property is just skipped. This way a single plot style (or set of styles) can be used with a variety of printers or plotters. Plot styles are saved separately from the drawing.

Changing the plot style changes how any drawing that uses that style will be output. For this example, you will use the default style named *acad.ctb*, which is a color dependent plot style. Refer to Figure 3.42.

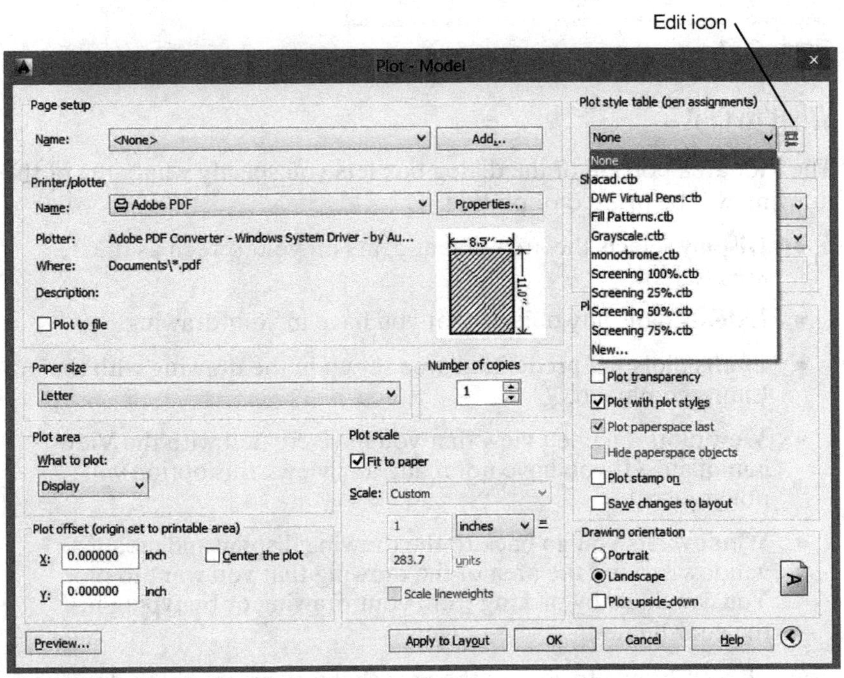

Figure 3.42

Click: ***to expand the menu in the Plot style table area***

Click: ***acad.ctb***

Assign this plot table to all layouts?

Click: ***Yes***

Click: ***Edit icon** (see Figure 3.42)*

The Plot Style Table Editor appears as shown in Figure 3.43. You can use it to set the parameters for the appearance of the plotted lines in the drawing. You will not change any of these settings at this time. You will learn more about plotting in Tutorial 5.

Click: ***Cancel***

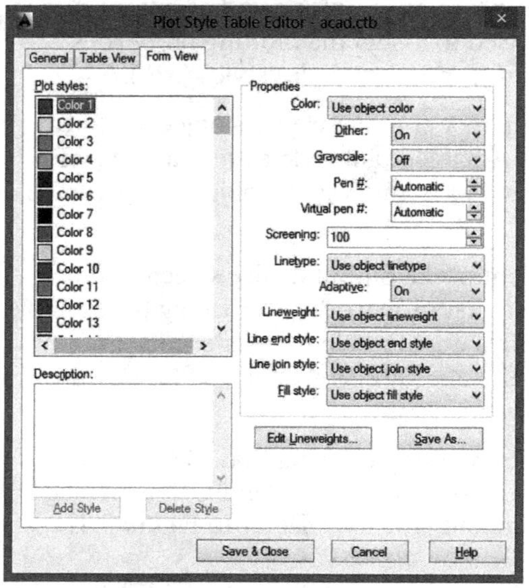

Figure 3.43

What to Plot

The Plot area portion of the dialog box lets you specify what area of the drawing will be printed or plotted:

- **Display** selects the area that appears on your screen as the area to plot.
- **Extents** plots any objects that you have in your drawing.
- **Limits** plots the predefined area set up in the drawing with the Limits command.
- **View** plots a named view that you have created with the View command. (If you have not made any views, this option will not appear.)
- **Window** lets you go back to the drawing display and create a window around the area of the drawing that you want to plot. You can do so by picking from your drawing or by typing in the coordinates.

You will pick Limits to choose the area that was preset in the drawing (where the grid showed in model space). If you have not set up the size with Limits, then Extents is often useful as it selects the largest area filled with drawing objects as the area to print. The What to Plot selections are shown in Figure 3.44.

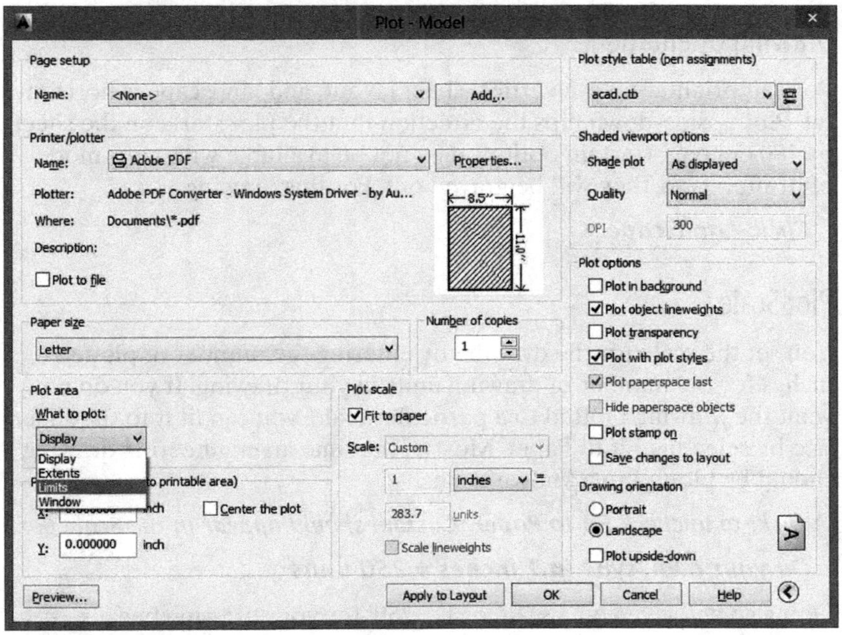

Figure 3.44

Click: ***Limits***

Paper Size

Click: ***the pull-down list under Paper Size*** *(Figure 3.45)*

Your paper sizes depend on your printer. US Standard 8.5 x 11 paper is size A; 11 x 17 paper is size B. (Smaller values indicate the image area that your printer can print on the sheet.) Max is the maximum size of paper for your printer.

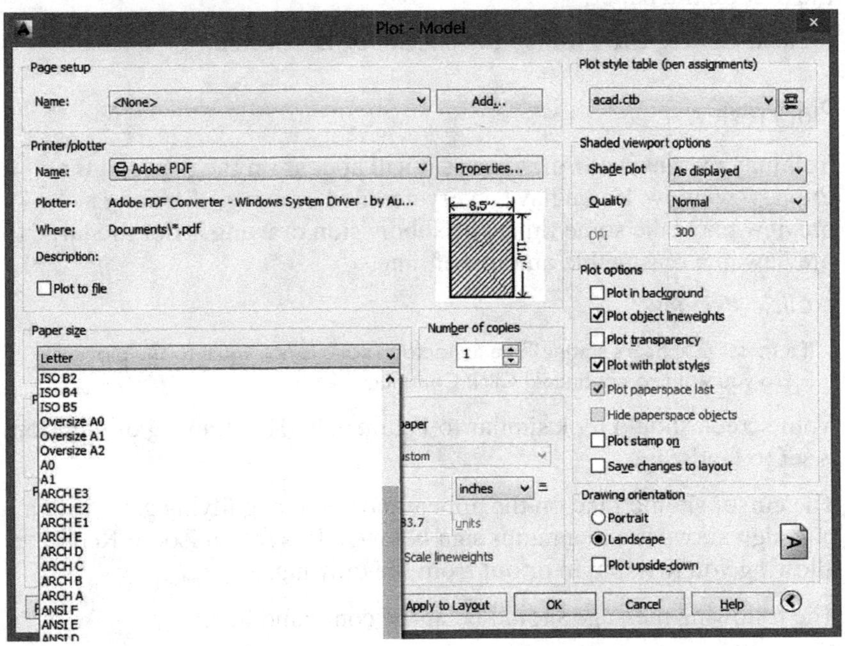

Figure 3.45

Click: ***A size sheet (8.5 x 11) or your printer's closest size***

Drawing Orientation

Portrait orientation is a vertical sheet layout, and landscape is horizontal. Plot upside-down flips the direction that the plot starts on the sheet by 180 degrees. Certain options may not be available with your model of printer. If so, they will be grayed out. For this drawing,

Click: ***Landscape***

Plot Scale

You set the scale for the drawing by entering the number of plotted inches for the number of drawing units in your drawing. If you do not want the drawing plotted to a particular scale, you can fit it to the sheet size by selecting Fit to Paper. Most of the time an engineering drawing should be plotted to a known scale.

Click: to uncheck ***Fit to Paper****. Custom should appear in the Scale box.*

On your own, type in 1 inches = 250 units

Doing so will give you a scale of 1"=250' for your drawing because the default units in the drawing represent decimal feet.

Plot Offset

You can use the Plot offset area of the dialog box to move the drawing to the right on the paper by using a positive value for X, and to move the drawing up on the paper by specifying a positive value for Y. You should be aware that moving the origin for the paper may cause the top and right lines of the drawing not to print if they are outside the printer limits. Center the plot automatically calculates X and Y values to center the plot on the paper.

Click: ***Center the plot*** *(so the check box is selected)*

Plot Preview

You may preview your drawing as it will appear on the paper in the Preview window. If you have a very detailed drawing, obtaining a preview may take some time. The subdivision drawing is not too large to preview in a reasonable amount of time.

Click: ***Preview***

If a message appears stating "The annotation scale is not equal to the plot scale. Do you want to continue?" Click Continue.

Your screen should look similar to Figure 3.46. The drawing orientation is set to landscape.

The cursor should take on the appearance of a magnifying glass with a plus sign above it and a minus sign below it. It is set on Zoom Realtime, allowing you to zoom in or out from the drawing.

The following message should be at the command line:

Press pick button and drag vertically to zoom, ESC or ENTER to exit, or right-click to display shortcut menu.

The toolbar across the top of the Preview window offers different Zoom options, Pan, and Close.

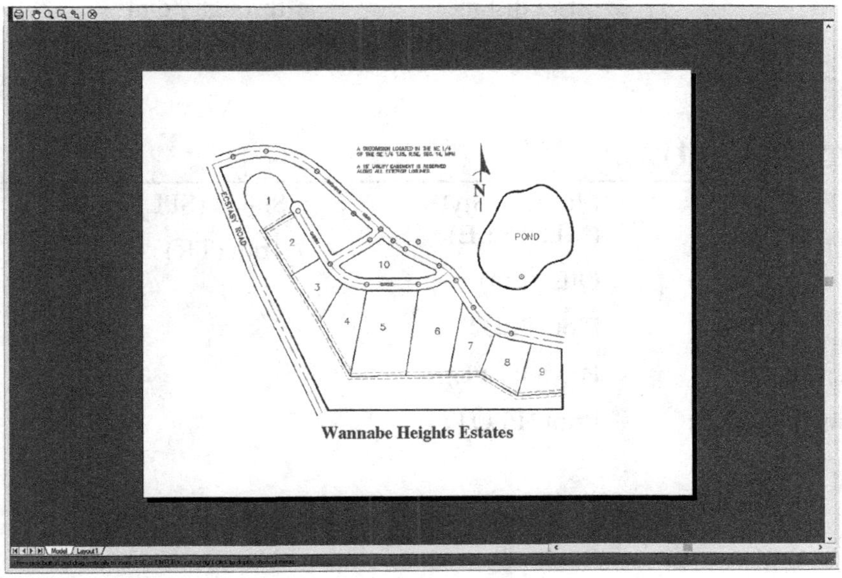

Figure 3.46

On your own, select different commands to familiarize yourself with them. If the drawing appears to fit the sheet correctly, click Close Preview Window from the toolbar or press [Esc].

When you have returned to the Plot dialog box, click OK to plot your drawing.

You will learn more about annotation scale in Tutorial 5.

You will see a prompt similar to the following, depending on your hardware configuration: Effective plotting area: 10.50 wide by 8.00 high. Plotting viewport 1.

If the drawing does not fit the sheet correctly, review this section and determine which setting in the Plot dialog box you need to change. You should have a print or plot of your drawing that is scaled exactly so that 1" on the paper equals 250' in the drawing.

When you have a successful plot of your drawing, you have completed this tutorial. To exit this session,

Click: ***Application icon, Exit***

Key Terms

chamfer	elements	offset distance	through point
cutting edges	fillet	polyline	

Key Commands (keyboard shortcut)

Area (AA)	Fillet (F)	Multiline Style (MLSTYLE)	Spline (SPL)
Blend Curve (BLEND)	List (LI)	Offset (O)	Trim (TR)
Chamfer (CHA)	Locate Point (ID)	Plot (PLOT)	
Change Properties (CTRL+1)	Measure Geometry (MEA)	Polyline (PL)	
Edit Polyline (PE)	Multiline (MLINE)	Print (PLOT)	

Exercises

Redraw the following shapes. If dimensions are given, create your drawing geometry exactly to the specified dimensions. The letter M after an exercise number means that the given dimensions are in millimeters (metric units). If no letter follows the exercise number, the dimensions are in inches. Don't include dimensions on the drawings.

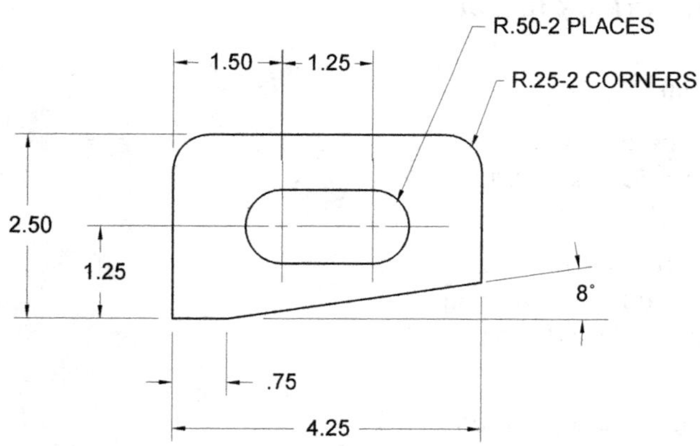

Exercise 3.1 Clearance Plate

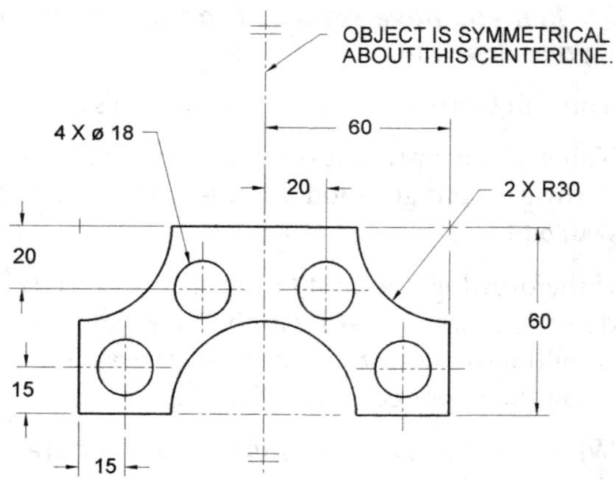

Exercise 3.2M Bracket

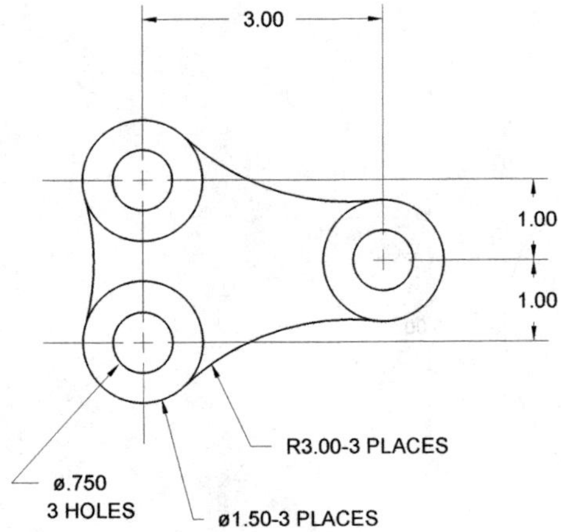

Exercise 3.3 Roller Arm

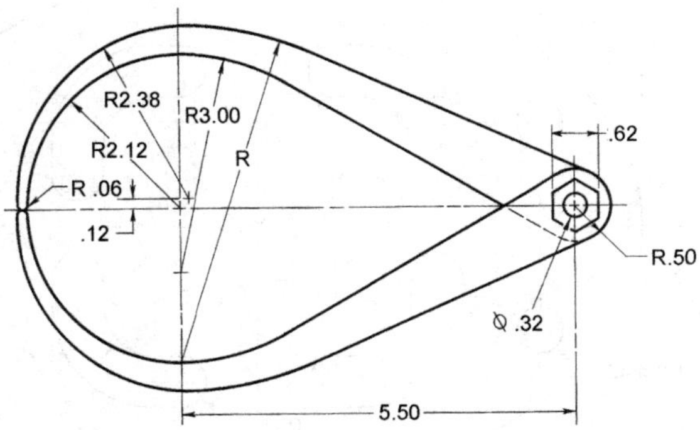

Exercise 3.4 Outside Caliper

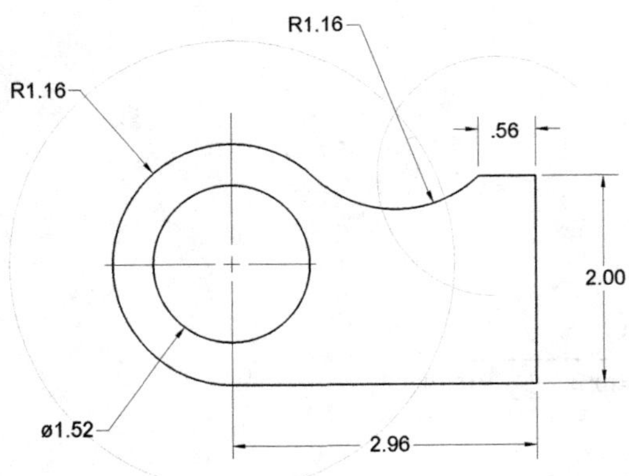

Exercise 3.5 Roller Support

Hint: *Create construction geometry to locate the center of the upper arc of radius 1.16. Offset the outer left-hand arc a distance of 1.16 to the outside. Turn on the Object Snap modes for Endpoint and Intersection. Draw a circle with radius 1.16 and its center at the left endpoint of the .56 horizontal line. Where the offset arc and the new 1.16 circle intersect will be the center of the tangent arc.*

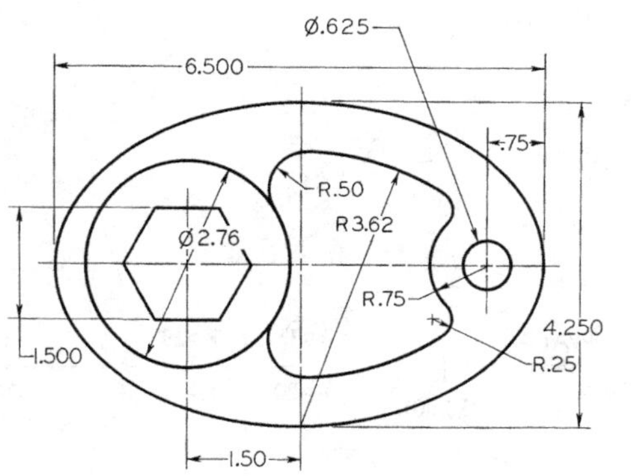

Exercise 3.6 Special Cam

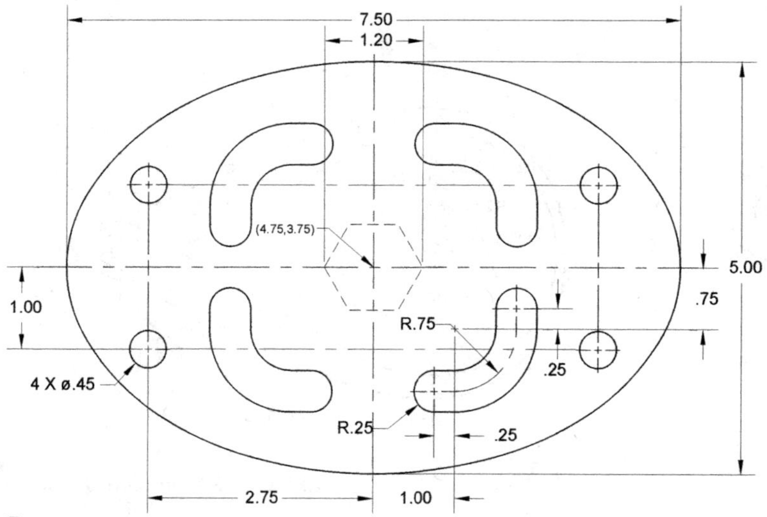

Exercise 3.7 Slotted Ellipse

Draw the figure shown (note the symmetry). Do not show dimensions.

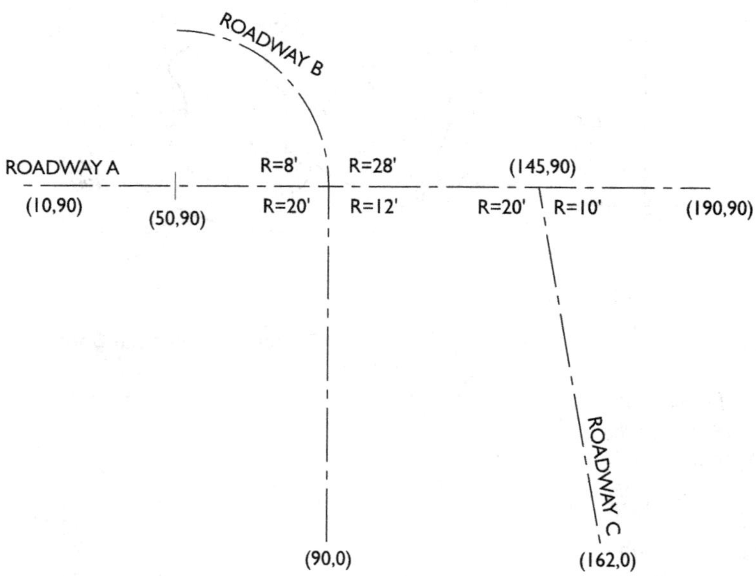

Exercise 3.8 Roadway

Shown is a centerline for a two-lane road (total width is 20 feet). At each intersection is a specified turning radius for the edge of pavement. Construct the centerline and edge of pavement. Add text only if requested by your instructor.

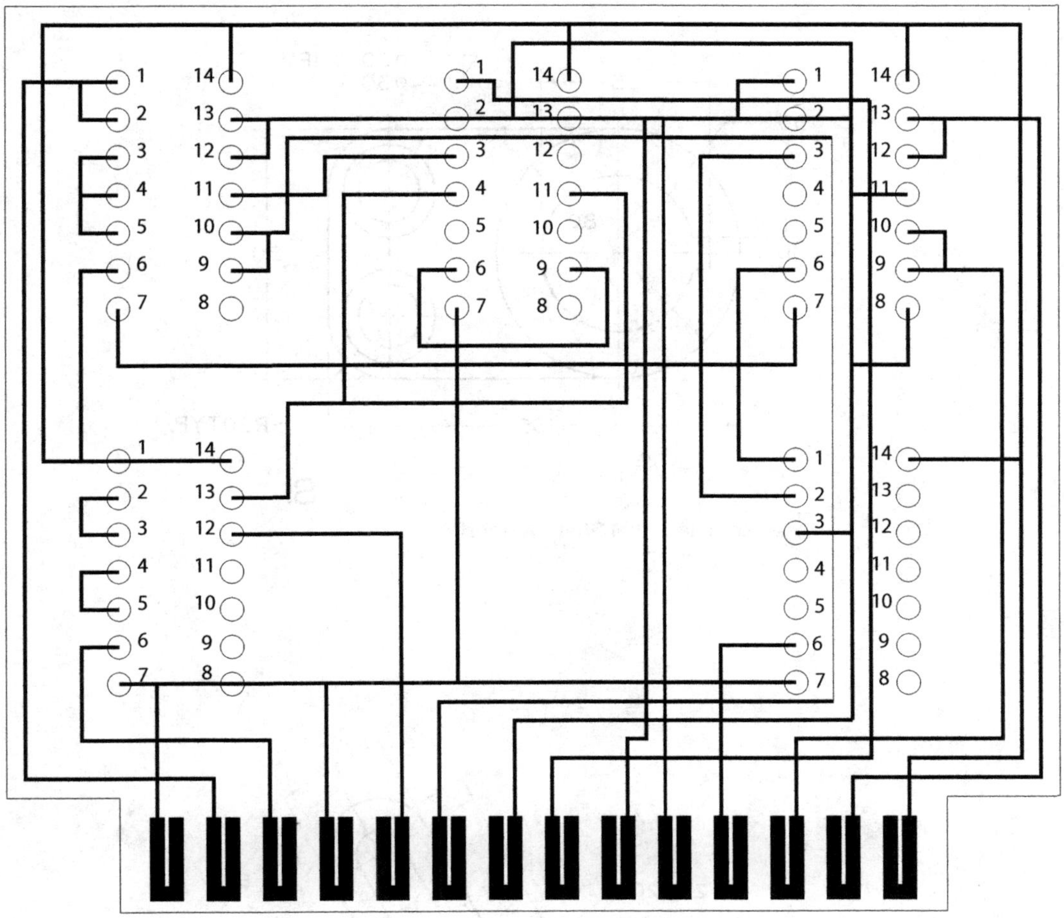

Exercise 3.9 Circuit Board

Draw the following circuit board, using Polylines with the width option to create wide paths.

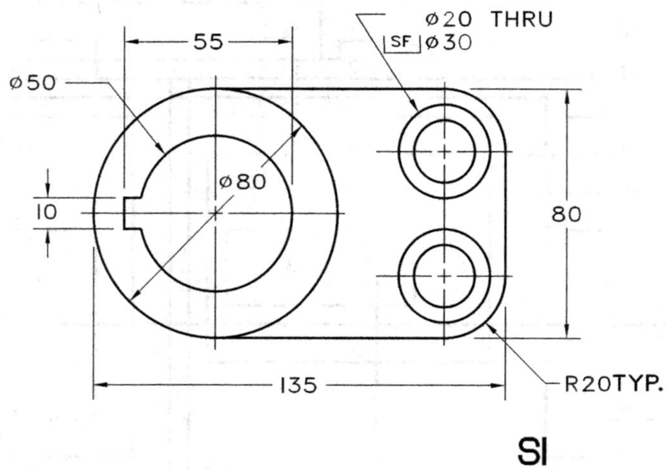

Exercise 3.10M Shaft Support

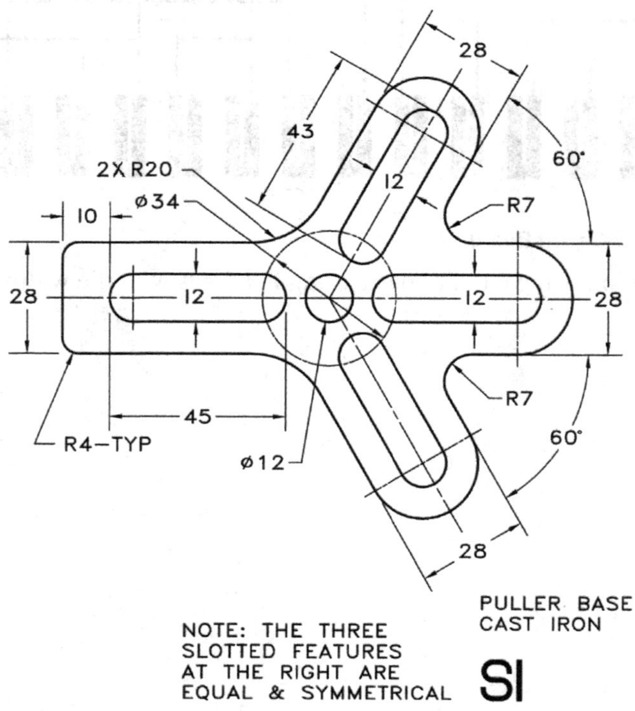

Exercise 3.11M Puller Base

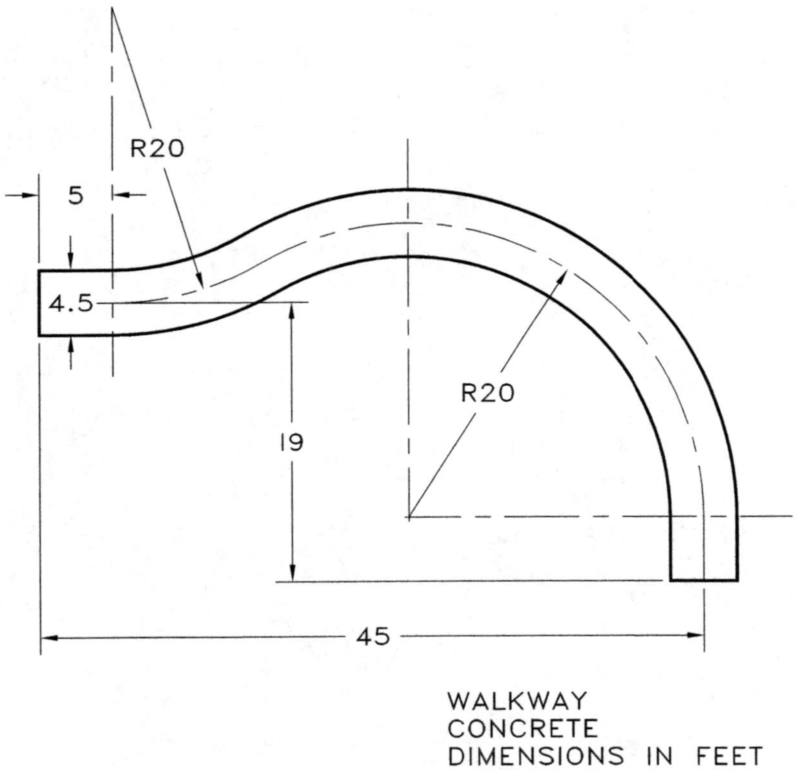

Exercise 3.12 Concrete Walkway

Hint: *Construct the straight centerlines first. Then use a circle to construct the top R20 arc. Use Circle, TTR to construct the right-hand arc, tangent to the upper arc and a vertical line 45' from the left end. Trim the lines and offset them to finish.*

GEOMETRIC CONSTRUCTIONS

4

Introduction

This tutorial will help you expand your skills by introducing several techniques used to construct accurate geometry. You will use object snaps to select locations, such as intersections, endpoints, and midpoints of lines, from your existing drawing geometry. You will also use object snap tracking to draw objects at specific angles or in geometric relationships to existing drawing objects. This tutorial shows how to apply the drawing commands to create shapes for technical drawings. You will create four drawings: a wrench, a coupler, a geneva cam and a gasket and use editing commands to create the drawing geometry quickly.

You will do many of the steps on your own, using the commands you have learned in the previous tutorials. Pay careful attention to the directions, being sure that you complete each step before going on.

Objectives

When you have completed this tutorial, you will be able to

1. Draw polygons and rays.
2. Use object snaps to pick geometric locations.
3. Load linetypes and set their scaling factors.
4. Use the Copy, Extend, Rotate, Move, Mirror, Array, and Break commands.
5. Build selection sets.
6. Edit an Array.
7. Use grips to modify your drawing.
8. Count instances of drawing objects.
9. Use 2D drawing constraints to define the geometry of a shape.

Starting

Launch AutoCAD® 2027.

Click: ***New button***

Double-click: ***acad.dwt*** *template*

Setting the Units and Limits

You will create the wrench drawing using decimal inch measurements. For example, 4.5 units in your drawing will represent 4.5 inches on the real object. Although the AutoCAD software's decimal units can stand for any measurement system, here you will have them stand for inches. When you create drawing geometry, make the objects in your drawing the actual size. Do not scale them down as you would when drawing on paper. Keep in mind that one advantage of the accurate CAD drawing database is that you can use it directly to control machine tools to create parts. You would not want your actual part to turn out half-size because you created a half-size drawing of the part. When you plot the final drawing, you specify the ratio of plotted inches or millimeters to drawing units to produce scaled plots.

On your own, use the Limits command to set up a larger drawing area whenever necessary and then Zoom All so that you see this larger drawing area on your screen.

Decimal units should be the default. If they are not, use the Units command and set them to decimal now.

Check to make sure that the limits for the drawing area are set to at least 12.0000 X 9.0000.

Use Zoom All to fit the drawing limits to your screen.

Turn on Grid display and Snap mode (both should be set to 0.5 inches).

Turn off all other modes on the Status bar, except for Grid and Snap.

Save your drawing in your ***work*** folder as ***wrench.dwg***.

Drawing the Wrench

You will start the wrench drawing by making some lines to use for construction. Later, you will change them into centerlines. Refer to Figure 4.1.

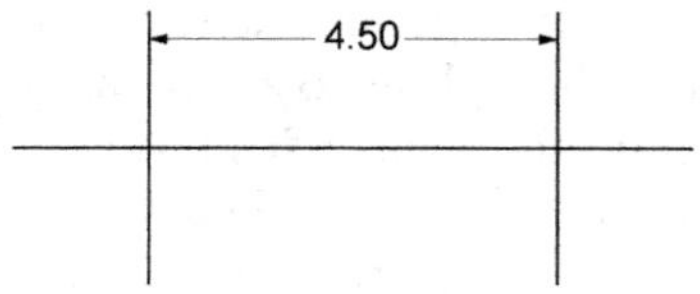

Figure 4.1

Tip: *Draw one line and then use the Offset command you learned in Tutorial 3, with an offset distance of 4.5, to create the other line.*

On your own, use **Line** to draw a horizontal line **7.5** units long near the middle of your graphics window. You may want to turn on Dynamic Input and use it to specify the line lengths.

The line does not have to be at the exact center because you can easily move your drawing objects later if they do not appear centered. You will learn how to move objects in this tutorial.

Draw two vertical lines that are **3.00** units long and **4.5** units apart, as shown in Figure 4.1. The exact location of the vertical lines on the horizontal construction line is not critical, as long as they are 4.5 units apart.

Remember, you cannot select accurately just by clicking from the screen, so use Snap, an object snap, offset or type exact values.

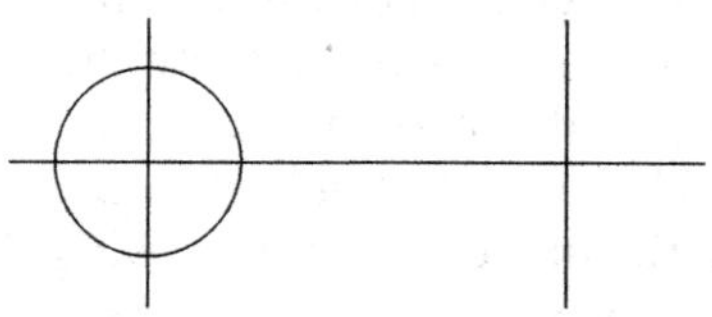

Figure 4.2

Click: ***Circle button***

Use Snap to draw a **1-inch radius circle** with its center at the intersection of the horizontal line and the left vertical line.

Tip: *Getting the cursor to select the circle with Snap on might be difficult. Using implied Windowing or Crossing would allow you to easily select the circle. You might also find that turning Snap off makes selecting the circle easier. Be sure to turn it back on again before selecting the base point or displacement, or you may not pick the exact center point.*

Using Copy Object

Just like it sounds, Copy makes copies of an object or group of objects within the same drawing. The original objects remain in place, and during the command you can move the copies to a new location. You can click Copy quickly from the ribbon, Home tab, Modify panel. Next, copy the circle to create a second one in your drawing.

Click: ***Copy button***

Select objects: ***select the circle***

Select objects: ***[Enter]***

Pressing [Enter] indicates that you have finished selecting objects and want to continue with the command. Be sure that Snap is on again so you can accurately select the center point of the circle, which you created on the snap increment.

Current settings: Copy mode = Multiple

Specify base point or [Displacement/mOde] <Displacement>: ***select the center point of the circle***

The cursor switches to drag mode so that you can see the object move about the screen as you are prompted for the second point of displacement. You can define the new location by typing new absolute or relative coordinate values or by clicking on a location from the screen.

The second circle must be centered at the intersection of the horizontal and right vertical lines, which should be a snap location.

Specify second point or [Array] <use first point as displacement>: ***click on the right intersection***

Specify second point or [Exit/Undo] <Exit>: ***[Enter]***

You will work with the mOde options and Array options of the copy command later in the tutorial. Don't forget that it is easy to use Help to look up information on all of the command options. Your drawing should now look like Figure 4.3.

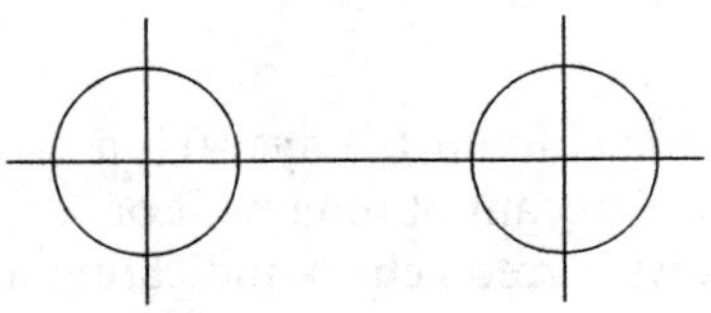

Figure 4.3

Next, use the Offset command on your own to offset the horizontal construction line a distance of 0.5 units to either side of itself to create the body of the wrench.

Your resulting drawing should look like Figure 4.4.

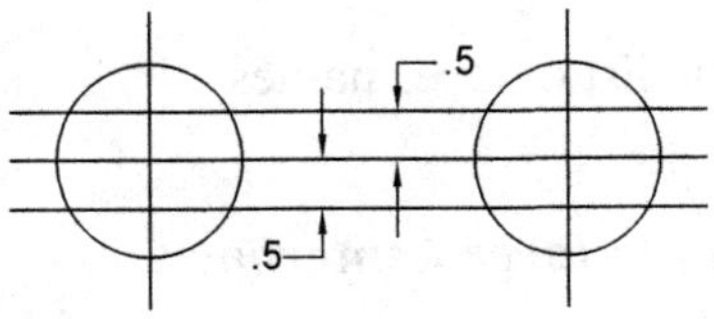

Figure 4.4

Now use the Trim command to trim the lines that you created with the Offset command so that they intersect neatly with the circles.

When you have finished, your drawing should look like Figure 4.5.

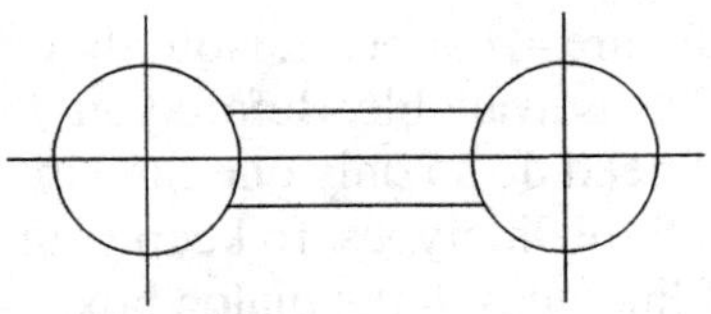

Figure 4.5

Effective Use of Layers

Recall that layers behave like clear overlay sheets in your drawing. To use layers effectively, choose layer names that make sense and separate the objects you draw into logical groups. You will create a centerline layer and then use it to change the middle lines of the wrench onto that layer so that they take on its color and linetype properties.

Click: ***Layer Properties button***

The Layer Properties Manager appears on the screen, as in Figure 4.6.

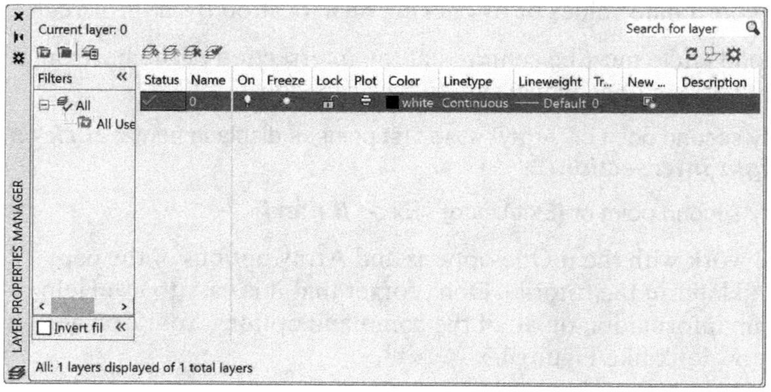

Figure 4.6

One layer name should be listed in the Name column, 0. Layer 0 is a special layer that is provided in AutoCAD. You cannot rename it or delete it from the list of layers. Layer 0 shows a green check indicating it is the current layer.

You will create a layer named, appropriately enough, Centerlines, for drawing the centerlines and set its color to green and linetype to center and make it the current layer.

Click: ***New Layer button*** *located near the top middle of the dialog box*

A new Layer1 should be highlighted in the list of layer names.

Tip: *Draw one line and then use the Offset command you learned in Tutorial 3, with an offset distance of 4.5, to create the other line.*

Type: ***Centerlines [Enter]***

Click: ***on the Color box corresponding to layer Centerlines***

Click: ***Green*** *(Color 3 from the list of standard colors)*

Click: ***OK***

Now the color for layer Centerlines is set to green.

Click: ***on Continuous*** *in the Linetype column for layer Centerlines*

The Select Linetype dialog box shown in Figure 4.7 appears. Note that only one choice of linetype, CONTINUOUS, is available. Before you can select a linetype, you must load it. You need do so only one time in the drawing, and you do not need to load all the linetypes. To keep your drawing size small and get a shorter list of linetypes in the dialog box, load only the linetypes that you use frequently in your drawing. You can always load other linetypes as needed during the drawing process. You will select Load, the second button from the right at the bottom of the dialog box, to load the linetypes you want to use.

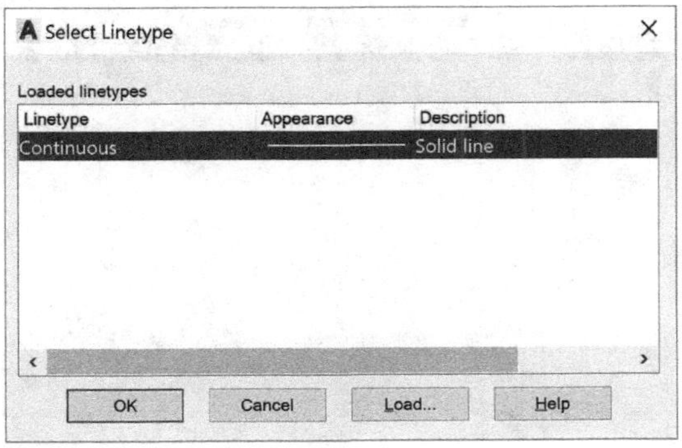

Figure 4.7

Click: ***Load***

Loading the Linetypes

The Load or Reload Linetypes dialog box appears, as shown in Figure 4.8. To the right of the File button is the name of the default file, *acad.lin*, in which the predefined linetypes are stored. You can also create your own linetypes, using the Linetype command. You can store your custom linetypes in the *acad.lin* file or in another file that ends with the extension **.lin.* Below the file name is the list of available linetypes and a picture of each.

Tip: *Objects that have had their color or linetype set to something other than BYLAYER will not be affected by changing the color or linetype of the layer they are on. In general, using layers to set the color and linetype is better.*

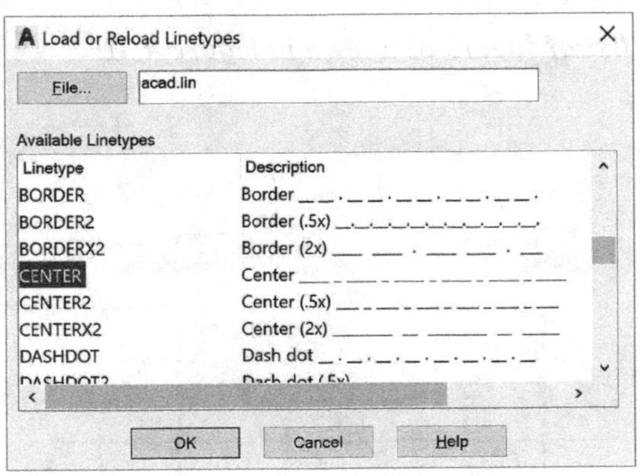

Figure 4.8

Use the scroll bar at the right of the list to move down the items until you see the selection CENTER.

Click: ***CENTER*** *so that the name becomes highlighted*

Click: ***OK*** *to exit the Load or Reload Linetypes dialog box*

Click: ***Center*** *so that it is the highlighted selection in the Select Linetype dialog box*

Click: ***OK*** *to exit the Select Linetype dialog box*

The centerline pattern is selected for the layer and is ready for use as shown in Figure 4.9.

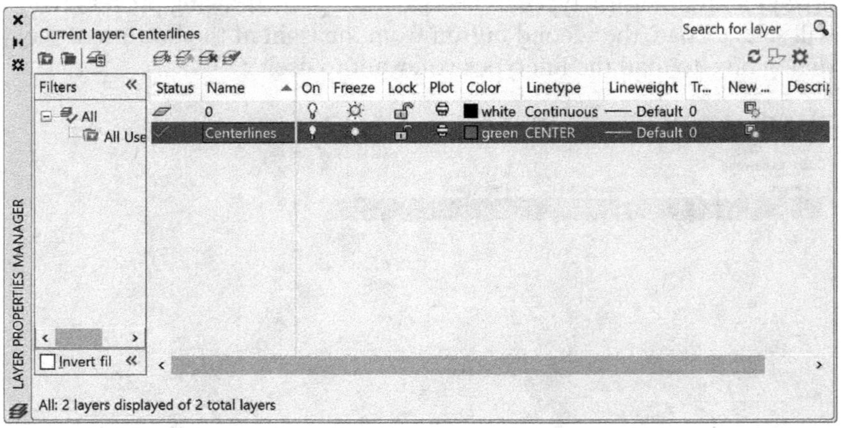

Figure 4.9

Double-click: ***Centerlines*** *so that it appears with a green check mark indicating that it is the current layer*

Click: ***X*** *to close the Layer Properties Manager*

Changing Properties

You will use the new layer you created to control the linetype and color of the centerlines.

Click: ***the middle horizontal line and the two vertical lines***

Small squares, called grips, show on the endpoints and midpoints of each line as shown in Figure 4.10.

Click: ***to pull down the list of layers*** *as shown in Figure 4.10*

Click: ***Centerlines***

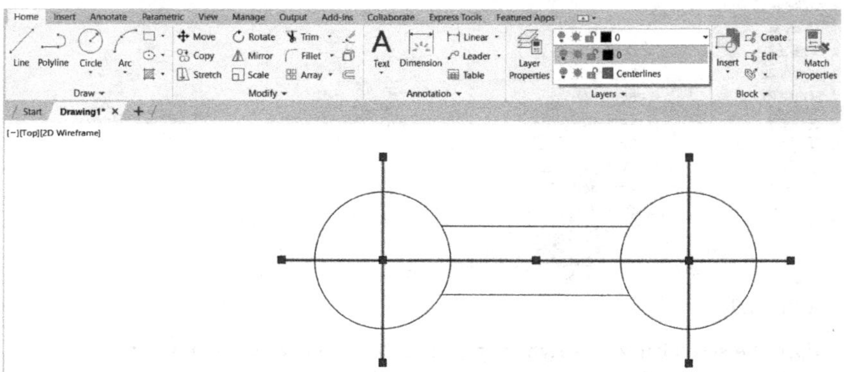

Figure 4.10

The lines change to have the properties of that layer—the color green and linetype center.

To unselect the lines,

Press: ***[Esc]***

Tip: *The grid is off in this image to make it easier to see the drawing lines. You can quickly toggle the grid using the icon on the status bar or the [F7] function key.*

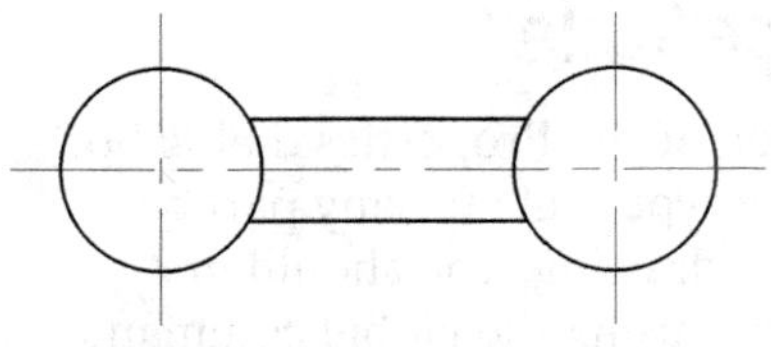

Figure 4.11

Your drawing looks like Figure 4.11

Setting the Global Linetype Scaling Factor

The *global linetype scaling factor* (LTScale command) is a value that you set to adjust the lengths of the lines and dashes used to make up various linetypes. This is important for giving your drawings the correct appearance. Linetype patterns are stored in a file with the *.lin* file extension, which is external to your drawing. The lengths of the lines and dashes are set in that external file. But when you are working on large-scale drawings and the distances are in hundreds of units, a linetype with the dash length of 1/8 unit will not appear correctly. To adjust the linetypes, you specify a factor by which the length of the dashes in the *.lin* file should be multiplied. The global linetype scaling factor adjusts the scaling of all the linetypes in your drawing as a group.

When you are working on a large drawing such as the subdivision plat that you created in Tutorials 2 and 3, increase the scale for the dashed lines of the linetype to make the dashes visible. When you are working on a drawing that you will plot full scale, generally you should set the global linetype scaling factor to 1.00, which is the default. Setting the global linetype scaling factor to a decimal less than one (e.g., 0.75) results in a drawing with smaller dashes making up the linetypes. In general, the linetype scaling factor you set in your drawing should be the reciprocal of the scale at which you will plot your drawing. When you learn about paper space in Tutorial 5, you will see that you can set the linetype scaling factor both in model space, where you are working now, and for the paper space layout. (When using multiple viewports, you can also set the linetype scale differently in each viewport.)

Tip: *If you have trouble with the lines returning to their previous LTscale property, press [Enter] after you type the value in the Properties palette before you close it.*

Next type the command to set the global linetype scale.

Command: ***LTSCALE [Enter]***

New scale factor <1.0000>: ***.75 [Enter]***

The centerlines should now cross in the center of each circle, as shown in Figure 4.12.

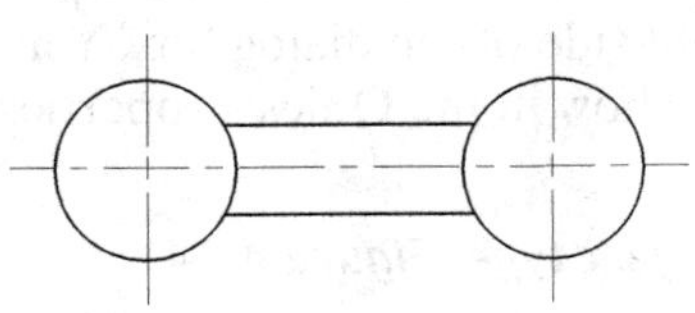

Figure 4.12

Changing an Object's Linetype Scale

You can also use the Linetype Scale area of the Properties dialog box (CELTSCALE command) to set the linetype scale for any particular object, independent of the rest of the drawing. You should first adjust the general appearance of the lines using the global command LTSCALE and then use the next method if some lines still need further adjustment. The object linetype scale factor is multiplied by the global LTSCALE to determine the object's linetype scaling.

Next, you will set the linetype scale for the two vertical lines to 1.5, giving them a different linetype scale than the horizontal line. You will click the Properties button from the Standard toolbar in order to use the Properties palette.

Click: ***the two vertical lines*** *to select them (their grips show)*

Double-click: ***one of the selected lines*** *to show the Properties palette*

The Quick Properties palette appears on your screen as shown in Figure 4.13. You will customize this palette to show the LTSCALE property.

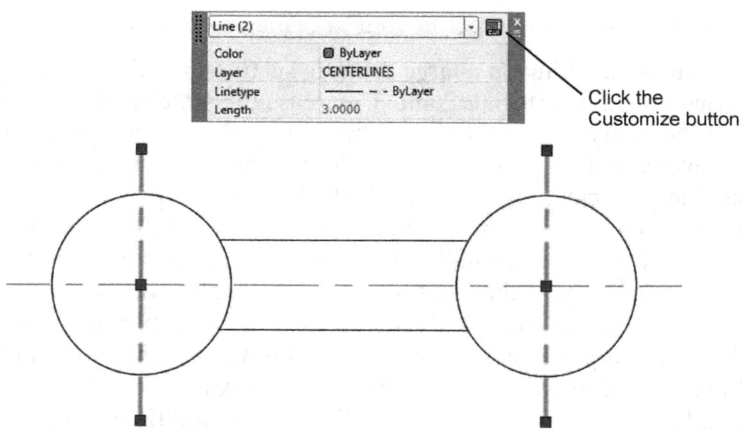

Figure 4.13

Click: ***the Customize button*** *near the upper right of the Properties palette*

The Customize User Interface dialog box appears as shown in Figure 4.14. The AutoCAD software is easy to customize to show the tools that you prefer. You will learn more about customization in Tutorial 10.

Notice that Color, Layer and Linetype appear checked, while Linetype scale and others are not selected in the right side of the dialog box. You can quickly turn on and off which items to show in the Quick Properties dialog box.

Ensure that Line is highlighted as the object type (Figure 4.14)

Click: ***to check the box to the left of Linetype scale***

Click: ***Apply***

Click: ***OK***

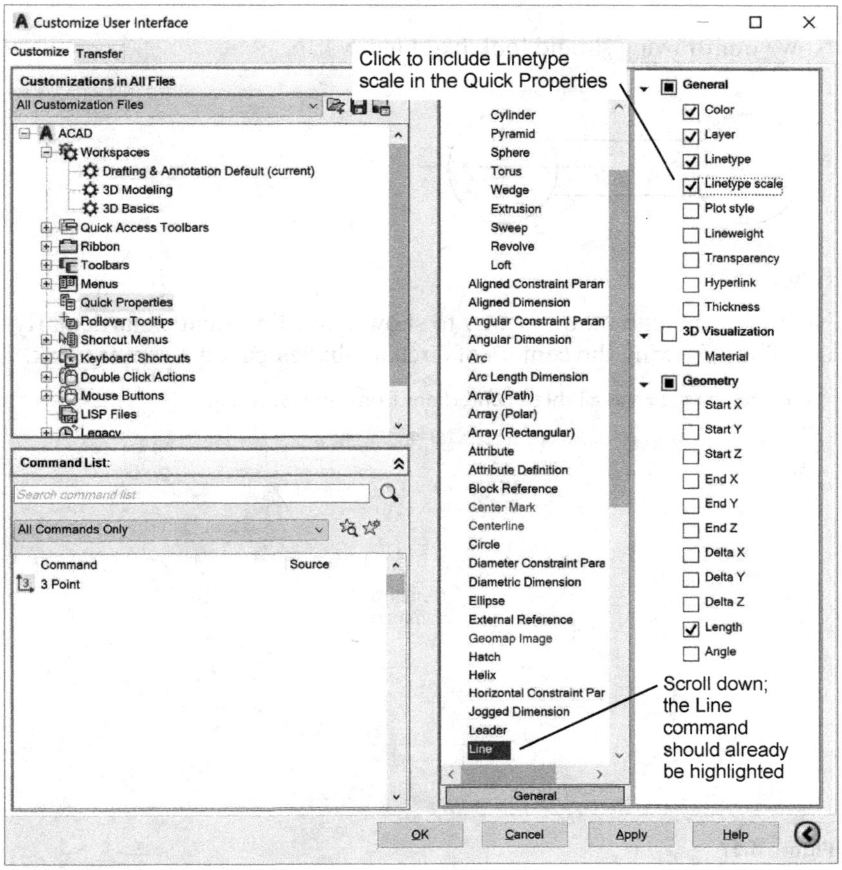

Figure 4.14

You will use the next steps to set the linetype scaling factor for the vertical lines you pre-selected to 1.5.

*Click: **the two vertical lines** to select them if they are no longer selected*

*Double-click: **one of the selected lines** to show the Properties palette. (Notice it now has Linetype scale listed.)*

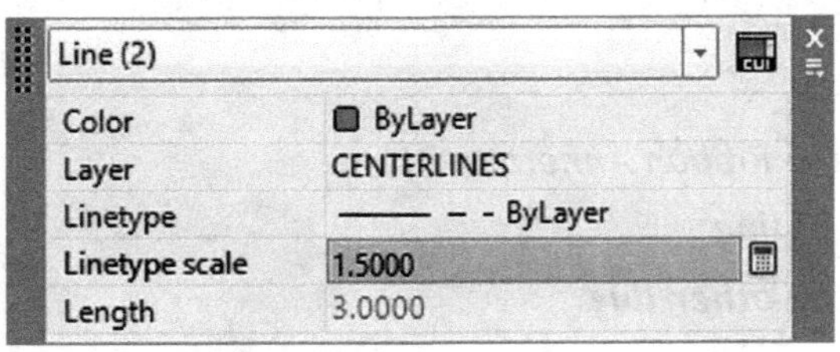

Figure 4.15

Highlight the text in the box to the right of Linetype Scale and overtype the new value.

*Type: **1.5 [Enter]***

*Click: **the Close button [X]** in the upper right of the Properties palette to close it*

*Press: **[Esc]** to unselect the object grips*

*Press: **[Ctrl]+S** to save your drawing*

Now your drawing should look like Figure 4.16.

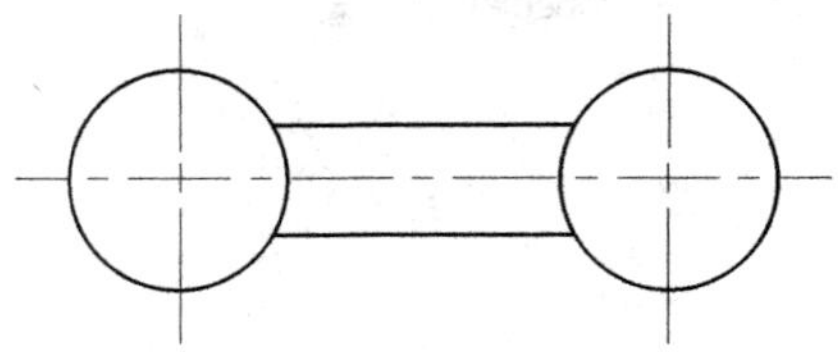

Figure 4.16

Next you will learn another way to show centerlines that is particularly useful for showing the centers of circular shapes, called a center mark.

On your own, **erase** all three centerlines from your drawing.

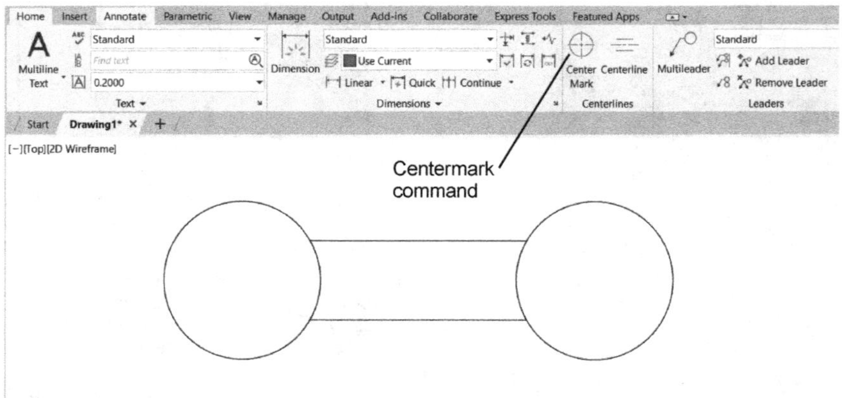

Figure 4.17

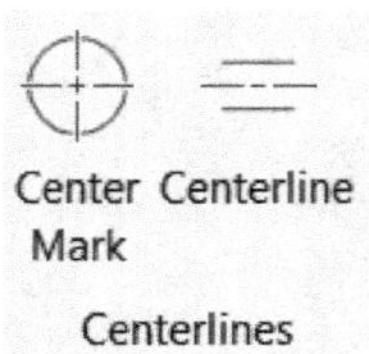

*Click: **Center Mark** from the Ribbon Annotate tab*

Select circle or arc to add center mark: ***Pick the two circles [Enter]***

The center marks are added to the drawing as shown in Figure 4.18.

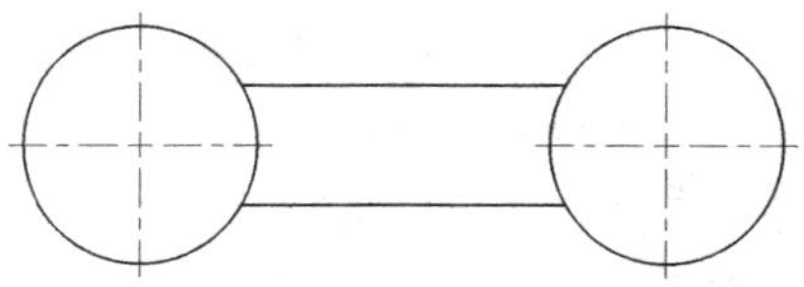

Figure 4.18

*Click: **Centerline** from the Ribbon Annotate tab*

Select first line: ***Pick either line***

Select second line: ***Pick the other line***

The centerline is added midway between the two drawing lines as shown in Figure 4.19.

Tip: *You can click the centermarks and use the handles to drag and resize them if needed.*

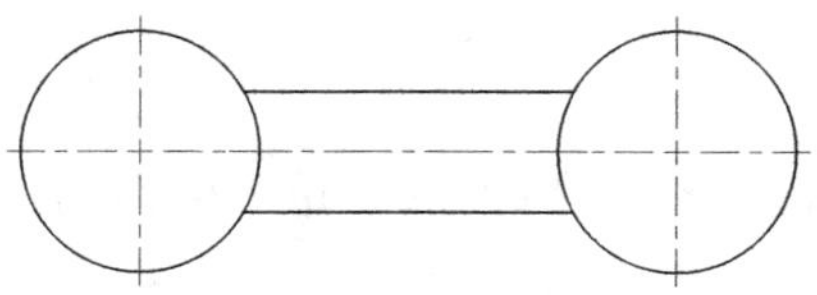

Figure 4.19

Now you are ready to add the fillets to your drawing, as shown in Figure 4.20. Refer to Tutorial 3 if you need to review Fillet.

Use the **Fillet** command, with a radius of **0.5**, to add the fillets on your own.

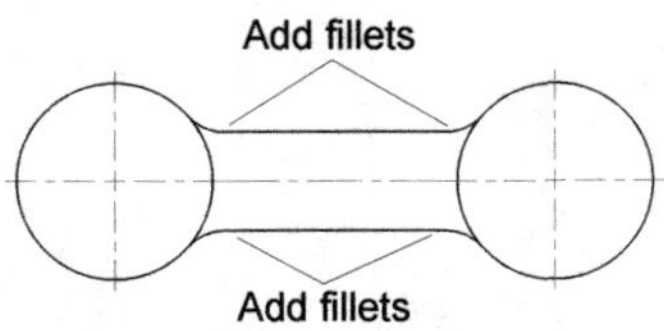

Figure 4.20

Using Polygon

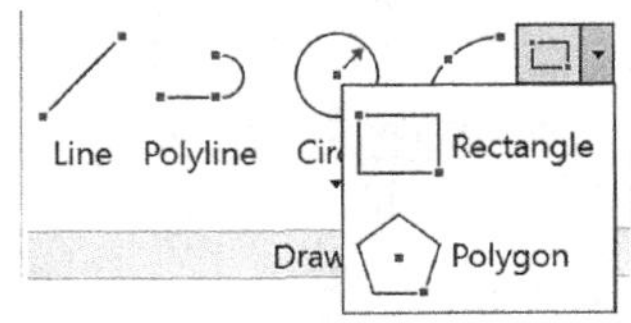

The Polygon command draws regular polygons with 3 to 1024 sides. Polygons act as a single object because they are created as a connected polyline. A regular *polygon* is one in which the lengths of all sides are equal. The size of a polygon is usually expressed in terms of a related circle. Polygons are either *inscribed* in or *circumscribed* about a circle. A pentagon is a five-sided polygon. Figure 4.21 shows a pentagon inscribed within a circle and a pentagon circumscribed about a circle.

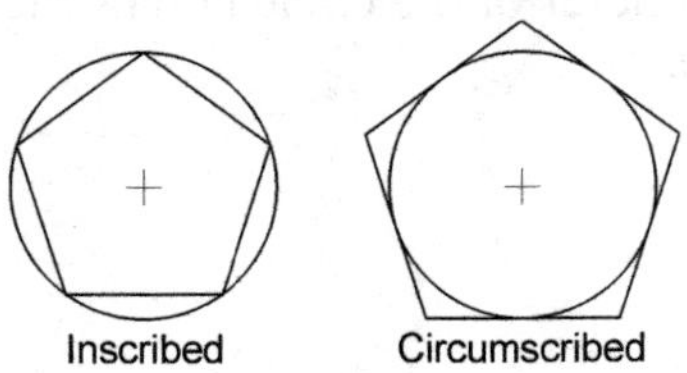

Figure 4.21 Examples

Next you will add a pentagon circumscribed about a circle to the right side of the wrench:

Make Layer 0 the current layer.

Expand the Home tab, Draw panel, (Rectangle flyout) to show the Polygon button.

Click: ***Polygon button***

Enter number of sides <4>: ***5 [Enter]***

Specify center of polygon or [Edge]: ***select the center point of the circle at the right end of the wrench drawing***

Enter an option [Inscribed in circle/Circumscribed about circle]<I>: ***C [Enter]***

You are now in drag mode; move your cursor around and notice how the pentagon changes size as you do so. You may specify the radius of the circle, either by clicking with the pointing device or by typing in the coordinates. For this object you will specify a radius of one-half inch.

Specify radius of circle: ***.5 [Enter]***

A five-sided regular polygon (a pentagon) is drawn on your screen. Your drawing should be similar to Figure 4.22.

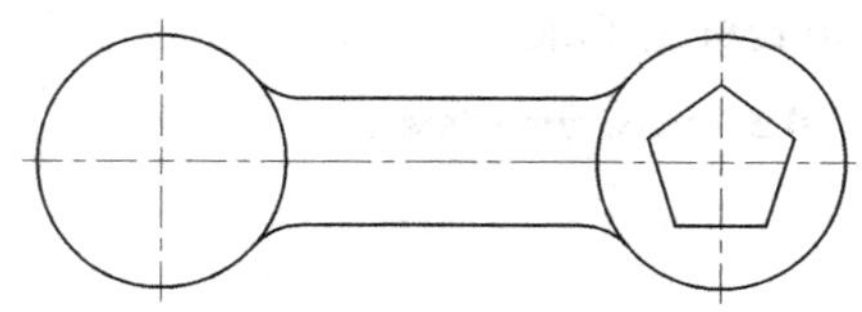

Figure 4.22

Drawing Hexagons

Hexagons are six-sided polygons and are common in technical drawings. The heads of bolts, screws, and nuts often have a hexagonal shape. The size of a hexagon is sometimes referred to by its *distance across the flats.* The reason is that the sizes of screws, bolts, and nuts are defined by the distance across their flat sides. For example, a 16-mm hexhead screw would measure 16 mm across its head's flats and would fit a 16-mm wrench. The distance across the flats of a hexagon is not the same as the length of an edge of the hexagon. Figure 4.23 illustrates the difference between the two distances. If a hexagon is circumscribed about a circle, the diameter of the circle equals the distance across the hexagon's flats. If a hexagon is inscribed in a circle, the diameter of the circle equals the distance across the corners of the hexagon.

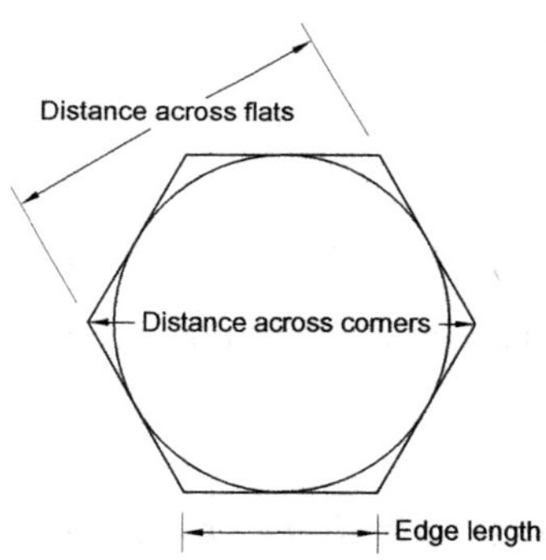

Figure 4.23

The Polygon command's Edge option draws regular polygons by specifying the length of the edge. This is helpful when you are creating side-by-side honeycomb patterns. Note that the software draws polygons counterclockwise. With the Edge option, the sequence in which you select points affects the position of the polygon (Figure 4.24).

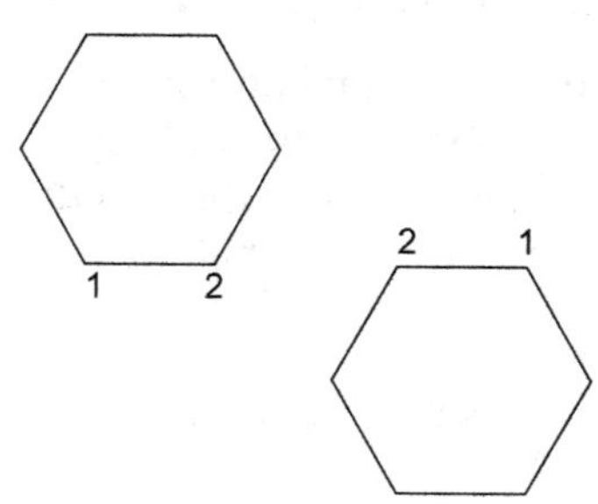

Figure 4.24

Next, you add the hexagon to the other side of the wrench.

Command: ***[Enter]*** *or right-click and select Repeat Polygon*

Enter number of sides <5>: ***6 [Enter]***

Specify center of polygon or [Edge]: ***click the center point of the left circle***

Enter an option [Inscribed in circle/Circumscribed about circle]<C>: ***[Enter]***

Radius of circle: ***.5 [Enter]***

A hexagon measuring 1.00 across the flats appears in your wrench. The final drawing should be similar to Figure 4.25.

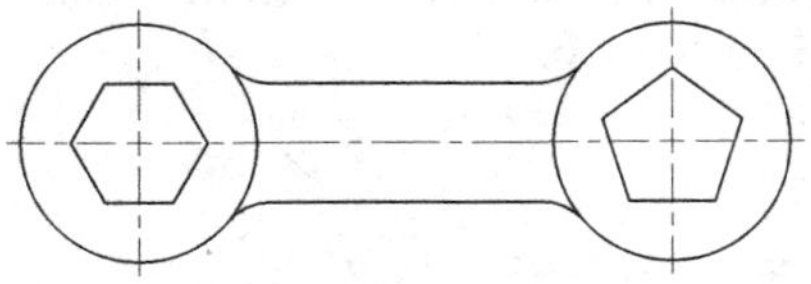

Figure 4.25

You have now completed your wrench. You will save this drawing and begin a new drawing for a coupler. You will close drawing Wrench so that it does not stay available on your screen.

Click: ***Save button***

Click: ***X on the*** *Wrench drawing tab to close it*

In this next section, you will practice with additional drawing commands and with object snaps. You will start a new drawing and name it *coupler.dwg.*

Click: ***New button***

Double-click: ***acad.dwt as the template to use and open***

You return to the drawing editor.

On your own, turn on the **Grid** display if it is not already. Set **Snap** Mode to **.25** and turn it on.

Use **Zoom All** *so that the limits area fills the graphics window.*

Click: ***Save button***

Choose: ***work*** *folder*

Type: ***coupler.dwg*** *as the name of the new drawing*

Using Polar Tracking

When you are in a command (such as Line or Circle) that prompts for a location such as From or To, you can use polar tracking to align the cursor along a path defined by a polar angle from the previous point. Polar tracking works along preset angle increments of 90° by default or you can specify other angles. The angles can be measured relative to the previous line segment or absolutely from the default of zero degrees being horizontal to the right.

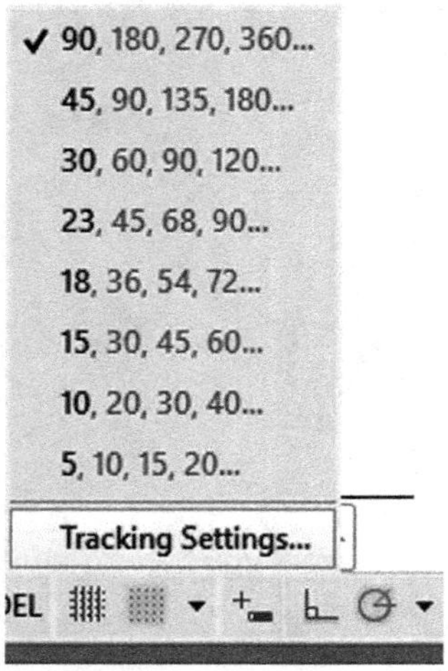

Next turn on polar tracking,

Click: ***Polar tracking button*** *from the status bar or press [F10]*

Like object snap, you will not notice any result until you select a command, such as Line or Circle, that prompts you to specify a location.

Next you will set the angle increment for polar tracking.

Right-click: ***Polar tracking button*** *from the Status bar*

Click: ***Tracking Settings*** *from the short-cut menu that appears near the cursor*

The Drafting Settings dialog box appears on your screen with the Polar Tracking tab uppermost, as shown in Figure 4.26.

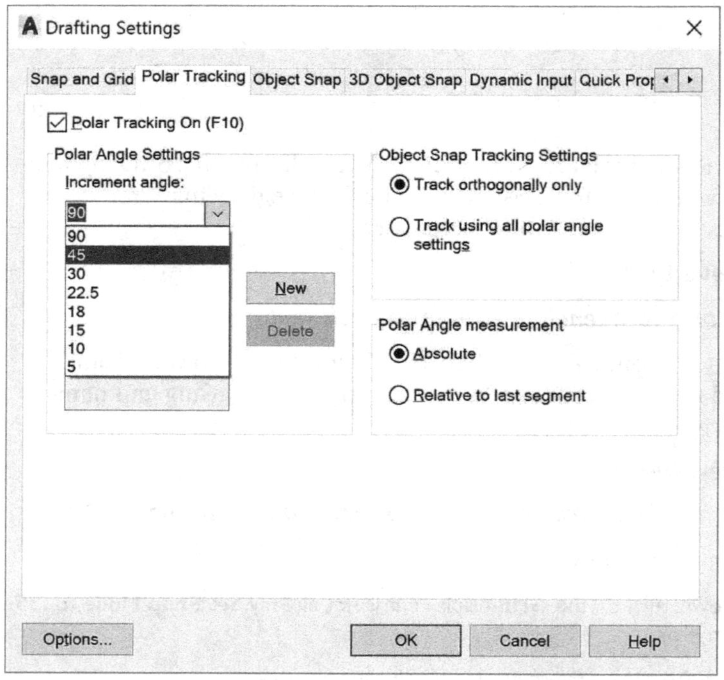

Figure 4.26

Notice that you can use the New button to add new angular measurements to the quick list.

Next, set the angle to use for polar tracking.

Click: ***45*** *from the Increment angle pull-down list*

Click: ***Relative to last segment*** *button (if not already selected)*

Click: ***Options button*** *from the bottom left of the dialog box*

The Options dialog box shows on your screen as in Figure 4.27.

Make sure that Display AutoTrack tooltip and Display polar tracking vector are checked.

Click: ***OK***

Click: ***OK***

Tip: *Polar tracking measures distances from the last point selected, so it is considered relative. An absolute measurement would be from the 0,0 point of the World Coordinate System. You can right-click on the Polar tracking button and use the Drafting Settings dialog box to control whether angles are measured relative to the last point or absolutely. This is also true for Dynamic Input.*

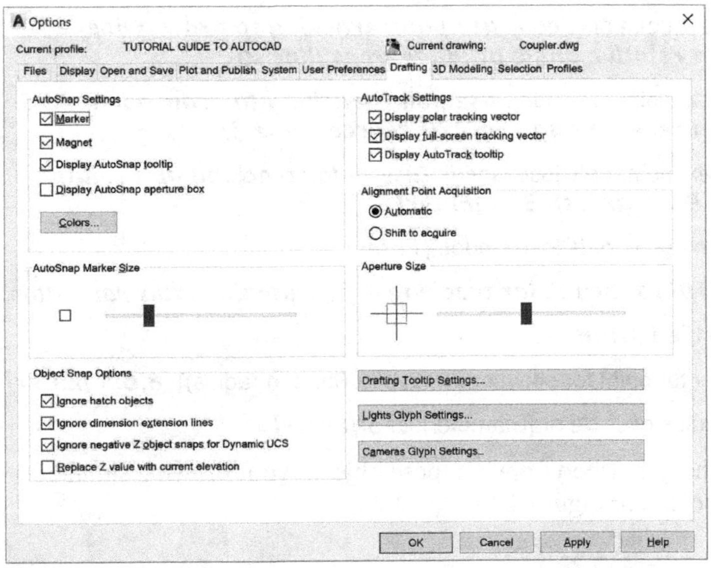

Figure 4.27

You will use polar tracking along with the Line and Circle commands to create lines 1–4 for the coupler shown in Figure 4.28.

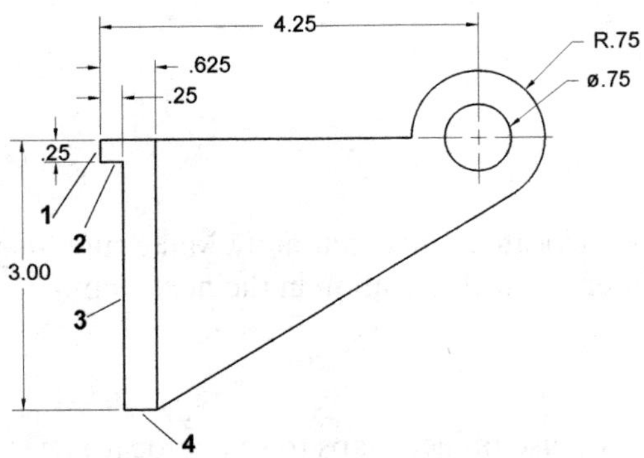

Figure 4.28

Check that the Polar tracking button on the status bar is turned on. *Make sure that* Dynamic Input button *is off.*

In the next steps, use your mouse scroll wheel to zoom in or out as necessary so you can see the lines easily.

Click: ***Line button***

Specify first point: ***3.75,6.5 [Enter]***

Press: ***[F7]*** *to turn off the grid so you can see the tracking line clearly*

Press: ***[F9]*** *to turn off the snap so cursor movement is not restricted*

A line will rubberband from coordinate point (3.75, 6.5) on your screen. Move the crosshairs around so that you see the rubberband line. As you get near 0 degrees, 45 degrees, and any other angle increments of 45 degrees, you will notice a tracking line appear on your screen.

Position your cursor below the previous point, as shown in Figure 4.29, to draw a line .25 units long along the angle of 270 degrees. When you see the tooltip appear in the correct orientation **type .25 to draw line 1** or use Snap and click.

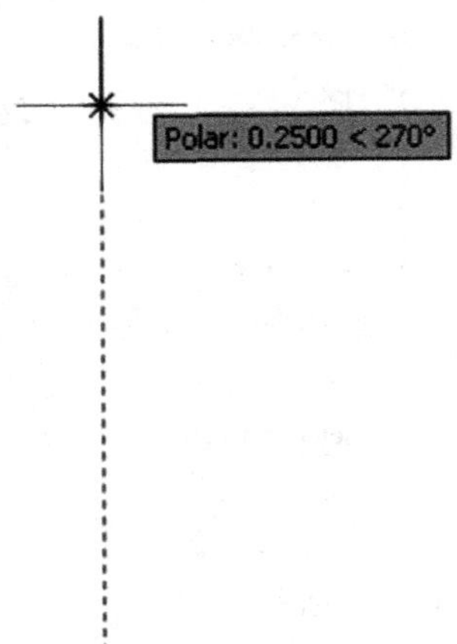

Figure 4.29

Specify next point or [Undo]: ***use polar tracking to draw a line .25 units at a relative angle of 90 degrees (line 2)***

Specify next point or [Undo]: ***use polar tracking to draw a line 2.75 units at a relative angle of 270 degrees (line 3)***

Specify next point or [Close/Undo]: ***(use polar tracking at a relative angle of 90 degrees) .375 [Enter]***

Specify next point or [Close/Undo]: ***[Enter]***

Press: ***[F10] to turn Polar tracking off*** *(or use the status bar button)*

Click: ***Circle button***

Specify center point for circle or [3P/2P/Ttr (tan tan radius)]: ***8,6.5 [Enter]***

Specify radius of circle or [Diameter]: ***.75 [Enter]***

Tip: *Ortho mode restricts the cursor to horizontal or vertical movement. Ortho mode and polar tracking cannot be turned on at the same time. When you select Ortho mode, polar tracking is automatically turned off and vice versa, so that only one mode is available at any time*

When you have finished drawing these objects, your drawing should look like the one in Figure 4.30.

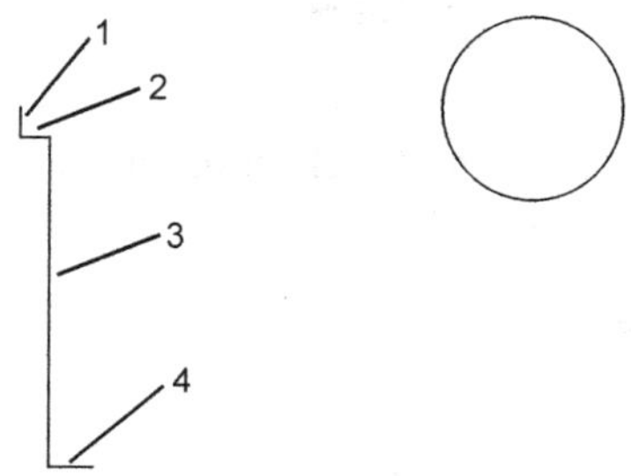

Figure 4.30

Next you will use object snaps to locate points accurately. Make sure Snap is off. Leaving Snap on may interfere with selection in the next steps.

Using Object Snaps

As you learned in Tutorial 2, you use object snaps to select locations accurately in relation to other objects in your drawing. Object snaps can operate in two different ways: override mode and running mode.

Remember, when an object snap is active, the AutoSnap™ marker box appears whenever the cursor is near a snap point. When you select a point, it will select the object snap point if the marker box is present, *whether or not the cursor is within the marker box.*

Showing a Floating Toolbar

You will show the floating Object Snap toolbar to make selecting object snaps easy. Recall that the object snaps are also on the Status bar. You can turn toolbars on by right-clicking any toolbar.

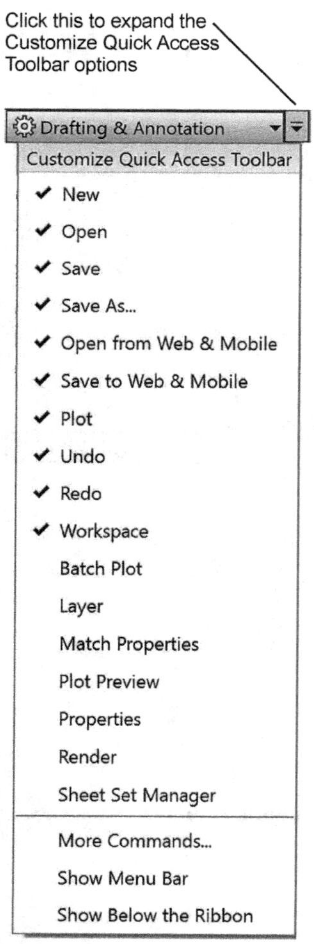

Figure 4.31

Click: ***to expand Customize Quick Access Toolbar*** *(Figure 4.31)*

Click: ***Show Menu Bar***

Click: ***Tools, Toolbars, AutoCAD*** *from the menu bar that appears above the ribbon (Figure 4.32).*

Click: ***Object Snap*** *from the list of toolbars as shown in Figure 4.33.*

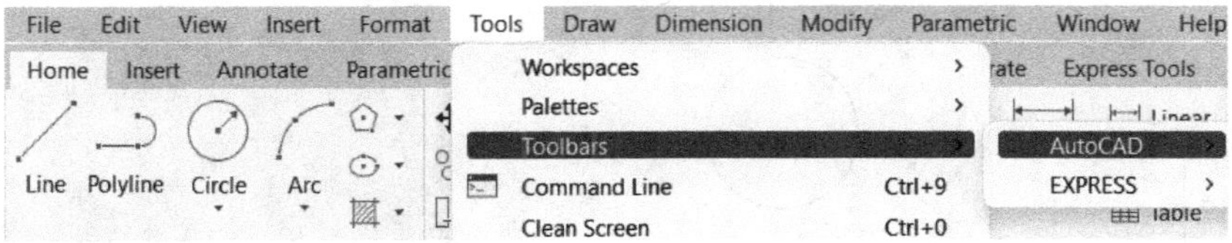

Figure 4.32

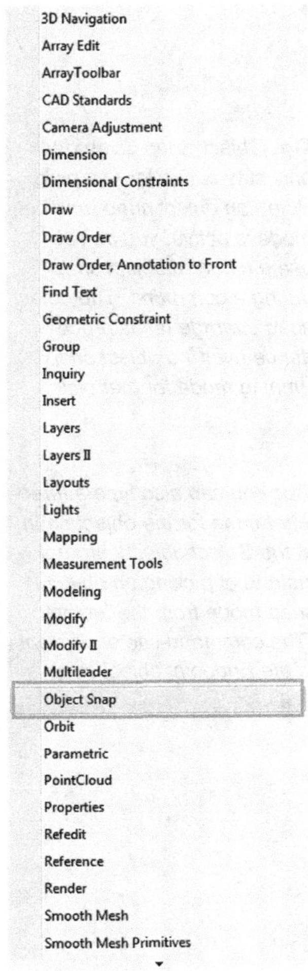

Figure 4.33

Click: ***to expand Customize Quick Access Toolbar***

Click: ***Hide Menu Bar***

The Object Snap toolbar appears on your screen (Figure 4.34). You can position it anywhere on the screen or dock it to the edge of the graphics window. You can also select object snaps from the Status bar, but this takes one extra click. Each mouse click takes seconds and in a complex drawing showing the toolbar may save hundreds of clicks. You can right-click on any toolbar to show the list of toolbars.

Figure 4.34

Note: *You can no longer switch to the AutoCAD Classic workspace, if you really preferred the old style menus and toolbars. But you can still show the menu bar. But* ***don't*** *do it during these tutorials unless directed or you may have trouble following the instructions.*

Object Snap Overrides

You will finish drawing the coupler, using object snap overrides to position the new lines and circles. (You may see other ways that you could use editing commands to create parts of this figure, but in this example object snaps will be used as much as possible. When you are working on your own drawings, use the methods that work best for you.)

Snap to Endpoint

The Endpoint object snap (END) locates the closest endpoint of an arc, line, or polyline vertex. You will draw a line from the endpoint of line 1, shown in Figure 4.26, to touch the circle at the quadrant point.

The *quadrant points* are at 0°, 90°, 180°, and 270° of a circle or an arc. You will use the Endpoint and Quadrant object snaps to locate the exact points. You will use the Object Snap toolbar to select the object snaps as overrides. This means they only stay active for one click.

Click: ***Line button***

Specify first point: ***click Snap to Endpoint button*** 

Move your mouse near the endpoint of a line. Notice the AutoSnap marker that appears.

Endp of: ***place the cursor on the upper end of line 1 shown in Figure 4.35 and click the mouse when the AutoSnap Endpoint marker shows***

The new line starting point should have jumped to the exact endpoint of line 1. Next you will specify the second endpoint of the new line.

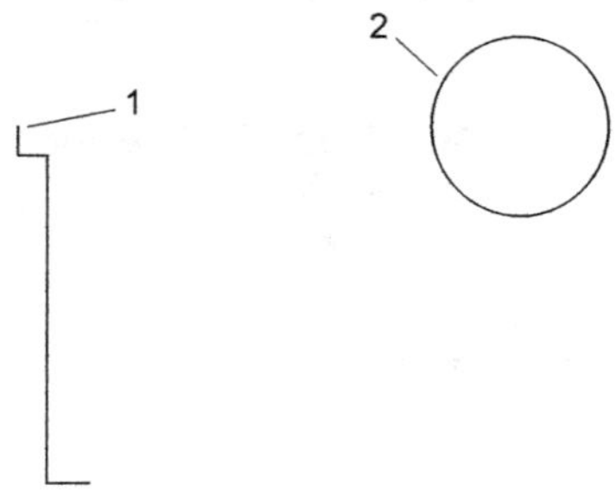

Figure 4.35

Tip: *Object Snap Overrides only stay active for one pick. When an object snap running mode is active, you can still use a different object snap during a command. The object snap override takes precedence over the object snap running mode for that pick.*

Tip: *You can also type a three-letter code for the object snap at the Select objects prompt instead of picking an object snap mode from the toolbar. (The command-line equivalent of the Endpoint object snap is END.)*

Snap to Quadrant

The Quadrant object snap attaches to the quadrant point on a circle nearest the position of the crosshairs. The command-line equivalent of Snap to Quadrant is QUA. The quadrant points are the four points on the circle that are tangent to a square that encloses it. They are also the four points where the centerlines intersect the circle. Next you will finish the line, using the Quadrant object snap to pick the quadrant point of the circle as the second endpoint for your line. You should still see the prompt for the next point of the Line command.

Specify next point or [Undo]: ***click Snap to Quadrant button*** 

Qua of: ***click on the circle near point 2*** *(Figure 4.35)*

Specify next point or [Undo]: ***[Enter]***

Your drawing should be similar to Figure 4.36

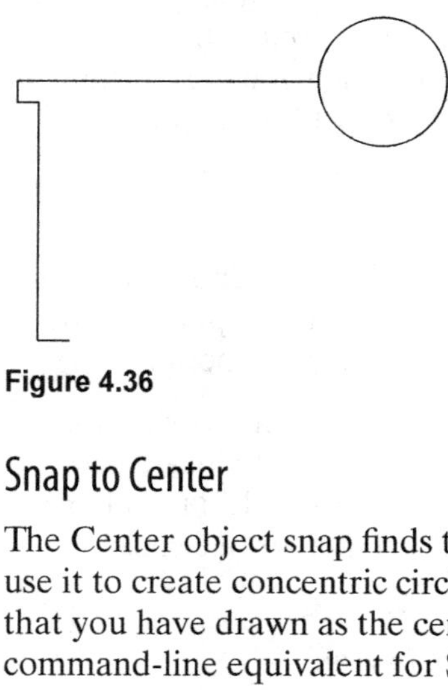

Figure 4.36

Snap to Center

The Center object snap finds the center of a circle or an arc. You will use it to create concentric circles by selecting the center of the circle that you have drawn as the center for the new circle you will add. The command-line equivalent for Snap to Center is CEN.

Click: ***Circle button***

Specify center point for circle or [3P/2P/Ttr (tan tan radius)]: ***click Snap to Center button*** 

Cen of: ***click on the edge of the circle***

The software finds the exact center of the circle and a circle rubberbands from the center to the location of the crosshairs. Note the marker that appeared when your cursor was on the circle. Remember, Object snap overrides stay active for only one pick. You are now prompted to specify the radius.

Specify radius of circle or [Diameter]<0.7500<: ***.375 [Enter]***

The circle should be drawn concentric to the original circle in the drawing, as shown in Figure 4.37.

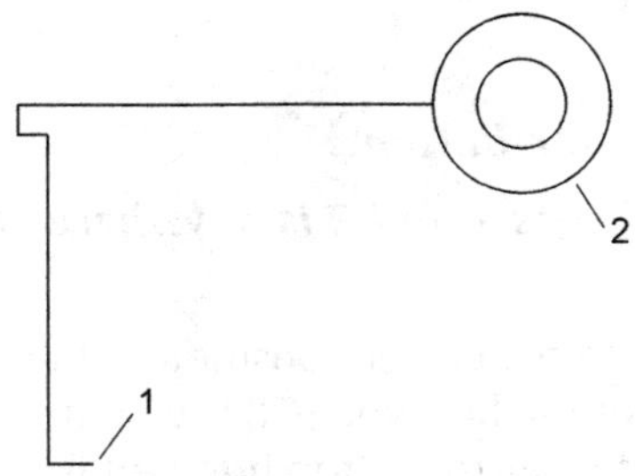

Figure 4.37

To position the next line from the endpoint labeled 1 in Figure 4.37 and tangent to the outer circle labeled 2, you will use the Endpoint object snap and then the Tangent object snap.

Click: ***Line button***

Specify first point: ***click Snap to Endpoint button***

Endp of: ***click near the right endpoint labeled 1***

A line rubberbands from the endpoint of line 1 to the location of the crosshairs. Next, you will locate the second point of the line to be tangent to the circle.

Snap to Tangent

The Tangent object snap attaches to a point on a circle or an arc; a line drawn from the last point to the referenced object is drawn tangent to the referenced object. The command-line equivalent is TAN.

Specify next point or [Undo]: ***click Snap to Tangent button***

Tan to: ***click the lower right side of the circle when you see the AutoSnap Tangent marker near point 2***

Specify next point or [Undo]: ***[Enter]***

Your drawing should be similar to Figure 4.38.

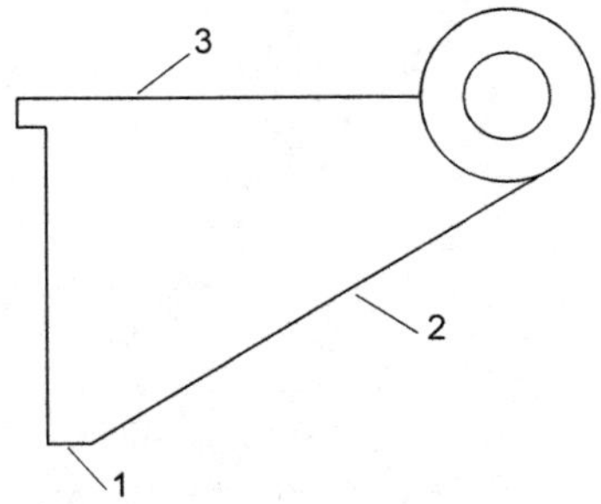

Figure 4.38

Tip: *To draw a line tangent to two circles, pick Line. At the Specify first point prompt, pick Snap to Tangent and pick on one of the circles in the general vicinity of the tangent line you want to draw. You will not see a line rubberband. At the Specify next point prompt, pick Snap to Tangent again and pick the other circle. When you select the second object, the tangent is defined and will be drawn on your screen.*

Again, using object snap, you will draw a line from the intersection of the short horizontal line and the angled line, perpendicular to the upper line of the object.

Snap to Intersection

Tip: *Note that when Snap to Intersection is on and the cursor passes over any object, the AutoSnap marker for intersection (an X) shows up with three dots to its right. These dots mean that if you select the line, you will be prompted for a second line or object that intersects with the first.*

Snap to Intersection finds the intersection of two graphical objects. The command-line equivalent for Snap to Intersection is INT.

Refer to Figure 4.38 when selecting your points.

Click: ***Line button***

Specify first point: ***click Snap to Intersection button***

Int of: ***click so that the intersection of lines 1 and 2 is anywhere inside the target area***

A line rubberbands from the intersection to the current position of the crosshairs. To select the second endpoint of the line, you will use Snap to Perpendicular to draw the line perpendicular to the top horizontal line.

Tip: *When you use 3D solid modeling in Tutorial 11, remember that when you are finding the intersection of two objects with Snap to Intersection, the objects must actually intersect in 3D space, not just apparently intersect on the screen. (One line may be behind the other in the 3D model.) To select lines that do not intersect in space, use the Apparent Intersection object snap. It finds the intersection of lines that would intersect if extended and also the apparent intersection of two lines (where they appear to intersect in a view).*

Snap to Perpendicular

The Perpendicular object snap attaches to a point on an arc, a circle, or a line; a line drawn from the last point to the referenced object forms a right angle with that object.

This time, use the Perpendicular object snap by typing its command-line equivalent, PER.

Specify next point or [Undo]: ***PER [Enter]***

Per to: ***click on line 3***

Specify next point or [Undo]: [Enter]

Tip: *Remember, in order to draw a perpendicular line, you must define two points. When you are defining a perpendicular from a line, no line is drawn until you define the second point. The reason is that infinitely many lines are perpendicular to a given line, but only one line is perpendicular to a line through a given point. Your perpendicular line will be drawn after you have selected the second point.*

The line is drawn at a 90° angle, perpendicular to the line, regardless of where on the line you clicked. The drawing on your screen should be similar to Figure 4.39. Although this example draws a perpendicular line that touches the target line, it need not touch it. If you choose to draw perpendicular to a line that does not intersect at an angle of 90°, the perpendicular line is drawn to a point that would be perpendicular if the target line were extended.

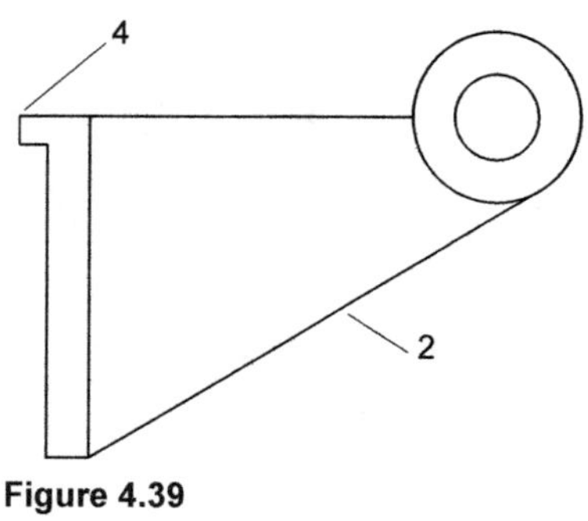

Figure 4.39

Snap to Parallel

To use the Parallel object snap you identify an object that your choice will be parallel to. Its command-line equivalent is PAR.

Click: ***Line button***

Specify first point: ***click Snap to Intersection button***

Int of: ***click point 4 shown in Figure 4.39***

Specify next point or [Undo]: ***click Snap to Parallel button***

Par to: ***hold your cursor over line 2 until you see the AutoSnap marker Parallel appear but do not click the mouse button***

Specify next point or [Undo]: ***move your cursor so that the line rubberbanding from point 4 is roughly parallel to line 2.***

You should see a parallel tracking line appear as shown in Figure 4.40.

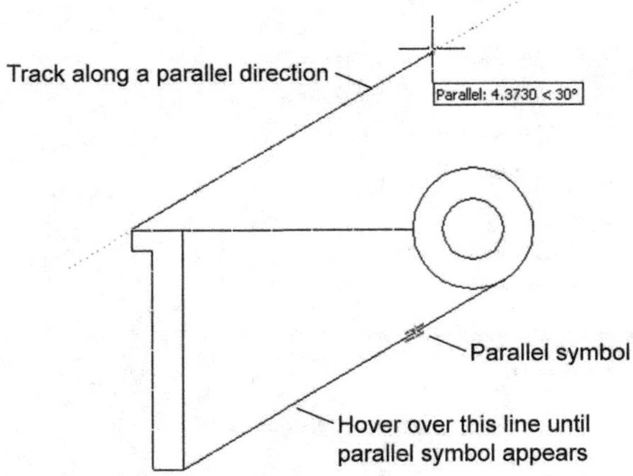

Figure 4.40

When it does,

Click: ***a point along the tracking line parallel to line 2 [Enter]***

Next you will undo the parallel line.

Command: U [Enter]

Use the techniques that you have learned to save your drawing now.

Practicing with Running Mode Object Snaps

You can also use object snap in the running mode, as you did in Tutorial 2 with Snap to Node. When you use object snaps this way, you turn the mode on and leave it on. Any time that a command calls for the input of a point or selection, the current object snap is used when you click. The running mode object snaps are very useful, as they reduce the number of times you must select from the menu to achieve the desired drawing results. You can use any of the object snaps in either the running mode or the override mode.

Tip: *The override object snaps are available by right-clicking and selecting Snap Overrides from the short-cut menu that appears on screen. OSnap Settings is also available this way.*

Warning: *When you are finished using running mode object snaps, be sure to turn them off. (You can do so by either deselecting them in the Object Snap Settings dialog box or toggling off the OSNAP button on the Status bar.) If you forget, you may have trouble with certain other commands. For example, if you turn on the running object snap for Perpendicular and leave it on and later try to erase something, you may have trouble selecting objects because the program will try to find a point perpendicular to every object you pick.*

Tip: *You can press [F3] to toggle on and off the running object snap mode.*

Tip: *You can quickly turn on and off running object snaps by expanding the list from the Status bar and clicking to select an object snap mode.*

*Right-click: **Object Snap button** and use the short-cut menu to choose **Settings***

The Drafting Settings dialog box appears on the screen with the Object Snap tab uppermost.

*Click: **Clear All** to remove any current selections*

*Click: **Intersection***

*Click: **Object Snap On (F3) check box** so that it is selected*

A check appears in the box to indicate that you have selected Intersection. The Drafting Settings dialog box should appear as shown in Figure 4.41.

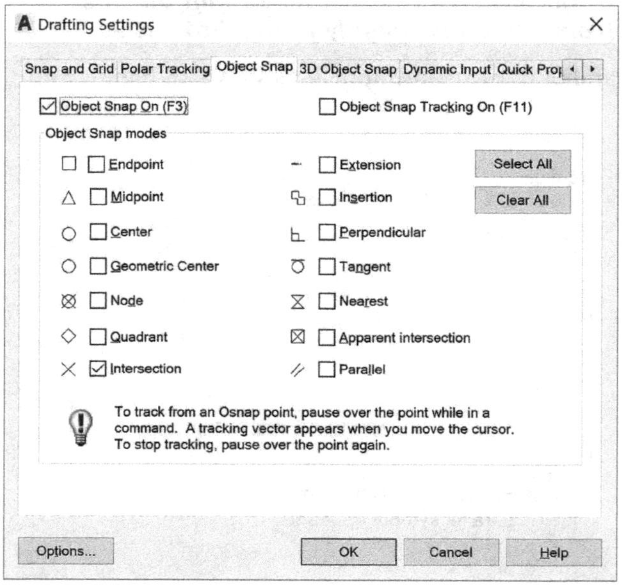

Figure 4.41

*Click: **OK** to exit the Drafting Settings dialog box*

Now Intersection is turned on. Anytime you are prompted to select, an AutoSnap marker box will appear when the cursor is near the intersection of two drawing objects.

More Object Snaps

The other object snaps are described next. Try them on your own until you are familiar with how they work.

Snap to Apparent Intersection (APPINT)

The Apparent Intersection object snap finds two different types of intersections that the regular Intersection object snap wouldn't find. One type is the point at which two objects would intersect if they were extended. The other type is the point at which two 3D lines appear to intersect on the screen, when they do not in fact intersect in space. The command-line equivalents for Snap to Apparent Intersection are APPINT and APP.

Snap to Nearest (NEA)

The Nearest object snap attaches to the point on an arc, circle, or line closest to the middle of the target area of your cursor. It will also find point objects that are within the target area.

A line drawn with the Nearest function may look like a line that could have been drawn simply using the Line command, but there is a difference. Many AutoCAD operations, such as hatching, require an enclosed area: All lines that define the area must intersect (touch). When you draw lines by clicking two points on the screen, sometimes the lines don't actually touch. They appear to touch on the screen, but when you zoom in on them sufficiently, you will see that they don't touch. They may only be a hundredth of an inch apart, but they don't touch. When creating an AutoCAD drawing, you should always strive to create the drawing geometry accurately. The Nearest function ensures that the nearest object is selected. The command-line equivalent is NEA.

Warning: *When you have finished experimenting, return to the Drafting Settings dialog box and turn off any object snaps you may have left on.*

Snap to Node (NOD)

The Node object snap finds the exact location of a point object in your drawing. You used it in Tutorial 2 to locate exact points that had already been placed in the drawing with the Point command. The command-line equivalent is NOD.

Tip: *The Locate Point (ID) command that you learned in Tutorial 3 lists the coordinates of a selected point. To find the exact insertion point of text or a block, pick Locate Point and then use the Insertion object snap and pick on the text or block. Similarly, you can find the coordinates of an endpoint or intersection by combining those object snaps with the Locate Point command.*

Snap to Insertion (INS)

The Insertion object snap finds the insertion point of text or of a block. (You will learn about blocks in Tutorial 10.) This method is useful when you want to determine the exact point at which existing text or blocks are located in your drawing. The command-line equivalent is INS.

Snap to Midpoint (MID)

The Snap to Midpoint object snap finds the midpoint of the selected object.

Tip: *You can turn on more than one object snap at the same time. For instance, you could select both Intersection and Nearest from the Drafting Settings dialog box. AutoSnap will show different marker boxes for each snap setting chosen.*

Snap to Midpoint Between Two Points (MTP)

The Midpoint between Two Points snap finds the midpoint between two points you select.

Tip: *You can right-click during selection operations to show the shortcut menu for object snap modes, including Midpoint between Two Points.*

Snap From (FROM)

The From object snap is a special object snap tool. It establishes a temporary reference point from which you can specify the point to be selected. Usually it is used in combination with other object snap tools. For example, you would use it if you were going to draw a new line that you want to start a certain distance from an existing intersection. To do so, click the Line command; when prompted for the starting point of your line, click the Snap From button. You will then be prompted for a base point. It is the location of the reference point from which you want to locate your next input. At the base point prompt, click Snap to Intersection. You will be prompted to select the intersection of two lines. Click on the intersection. As the result of your using Snap From, you will see the additional prompt of <Offset>. At this prompt, use relative coordinates to enter the distance you want the next point to be from the base point you selected.

Snap to Extension (EXT)

The Extension object snap also establishes a temporary reference. It displays a temporary extension line when you move the cursor over an object's endpoint, so that you can draw to an extension of the same line.

Snap to Geometric Center (EXT)

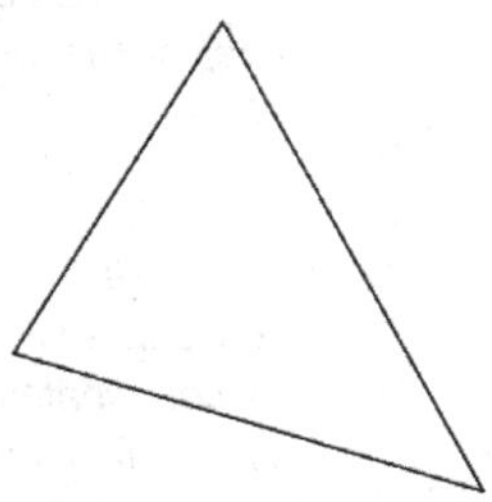

The Geometric Center object snap allows you to snap to the center of a closed polyline shape.

Click: ***Polyline button***

Specify start point: ***pick a point off to the side of your drawing***

Specify next point or [Arc/Halfwidth/Length/Undo/Width]: ***pick a second point***

Specify next point or [Arc/Close/Halfwidth/Length/Undo/Width]: ***pick a third point***

Specify next point or [Arc/Close/Halfwidth/Length/Undo/Width]: ***C [Enter}*** *to form a closed polyline in the shape of a triangle.*

Click: ***Line button***

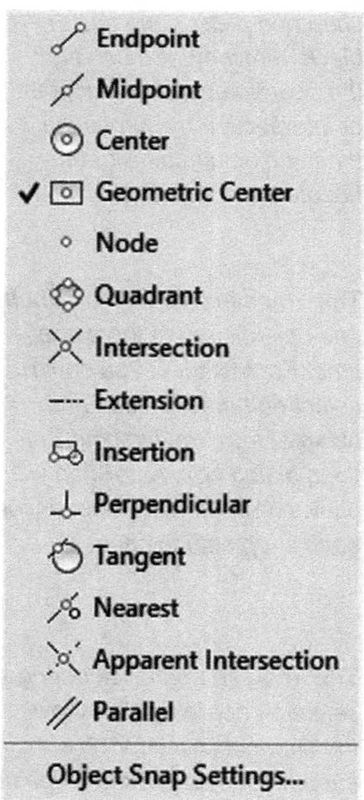

Specify start point: ***click to expand the object snap options*** *from the status bar and* ***select Geometric Center, then click the triangle.***

The starting point for the new line will be from the geometric center of the triangle.

Press: ***[Esc]*** *to cancel the Line command*

Erase the triangle on your own.

Turn off the object snap for Geometric Center.

Object Tracking

Object Tracking is a unique snap tool allowing you to start a line with reference to other locations. For instance, if you have drawn a rectangle and want to draw a line from the middle of the rectangle, there is no snap for that point. With Tracking, you can start the line with reference to as many points as you select. Tracking will be covered in Tutorial 6.

Practice on your own with each of the object snaps. Hover the cursor over each of the remaining object snaps from the toolbar and read the tooltips explaining their functions. Undo any changes you make while practicing until your drawing appears as shown in Figure 4.43.

Using Break

The Break command erases part of an object (for example, a line, arc, or circle). The Break button is on the Modify panel. When using the Break command, you can specify a single point at which to break the object or specify two points on the object and the Break command will automatically remove the portion between the points selected. You also can select the object and then specify the two points at which to break it.

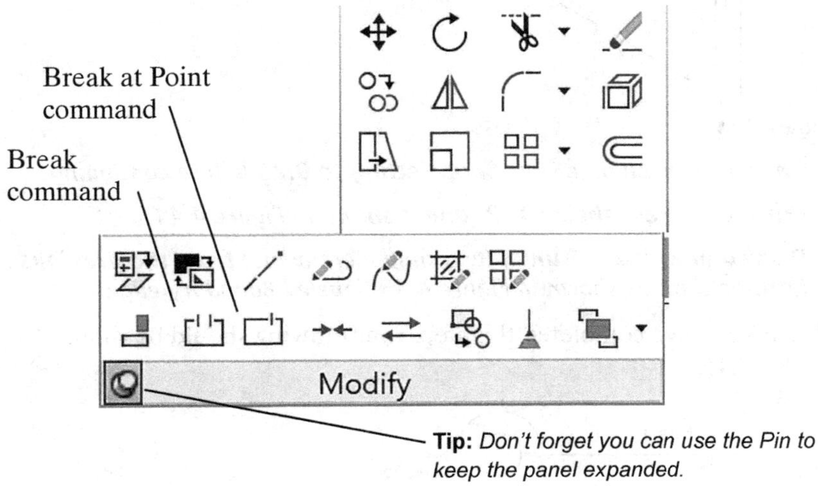

Figure 4.42

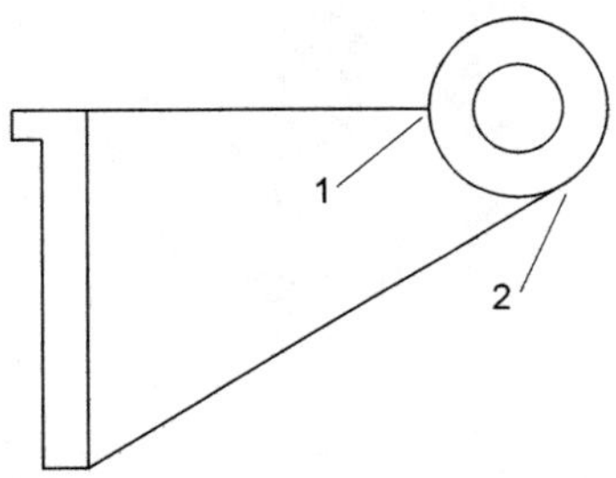

Figure 4.43

Tip: *Zoom in if necessary to see the intersections clearly.*

Tip: *The Break at Point icon allows you to break a selected object at a specified point without erasing any portion of it.*

You will break the circle between intersection 1 and intersection 2. (Note that you could also accomplish the same thing by using Trim.)

You will use the First point option after selecting the Break button. Refer to **Figure 4.43** for the points to select.

Turn off the running mode Object Snap for **Geometric Center** on your own.

Turn on the running mode Object Snap for **Intersection**.

Click: ***Break button*** *from the expanded Modify panel*

Select object: ***click the large circle***

Specify second break point (or First point): ***F [Enter]***

Specify first break point: ***click intersection 1***

Enter second point: ***click intersection 2***

Notice that as you are selecting, the portion of the object that will be removed is highlighted. When you select the second break point, the portion of the circle between the two selected points is removed. Your drawing should look like Figure 4.44. Save your coupler drawing.

Click: ***Save button***

Tip: *You can use the Snap isometric feature to create 2D pictorial drawings.*

Command: ***SNAP [Enter]***

Specify snap spacing or [ON/OFF/Aspect/Legacy/Style/Type] <0.2500>: ***S [Enter]***

Enter snap grid style [Standard/Isometric] <S>: ***I [Enter]***

Specify vertical spacing <0.2500>: ***.5 [Enter]***

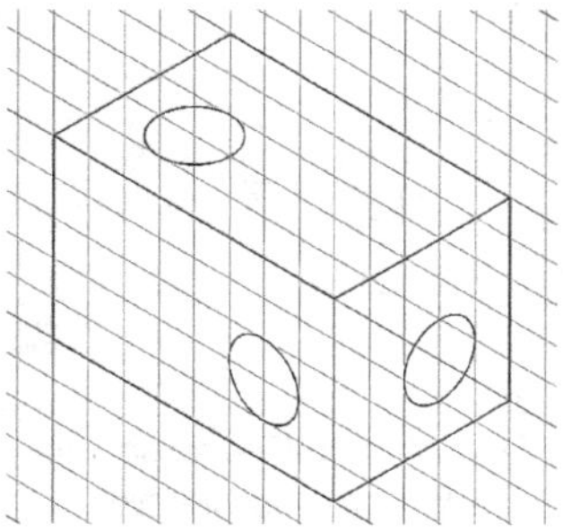

Press [CTRL] + E to toggle to a different "isoplane" orientation. To draw an ellipse with the correct appearance for a hole in the isometric view, use the Ellipse command, Isocircle option. Use [CTRL] + E to toggle the ellipse orientation.

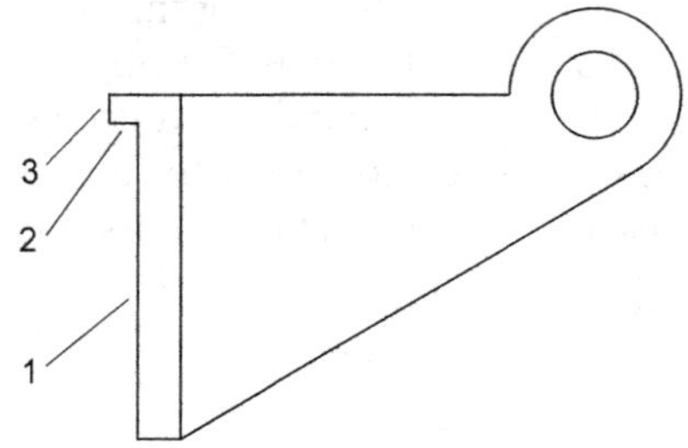

Figure 4.44

On your own, change your ***Snap setting to 0.25*** *before continuing.*

Erase the lines labeled 1, 2, and 3 *shown in Figure 4.44.*

Draw a new line 0.5 units *(two snap increments)* ***from the previous leftmost line*** *as shown in Figure 4.45 (labeled Boundary edge).*

When you have completed this step, your drawing should be similar to Figure 4.45.

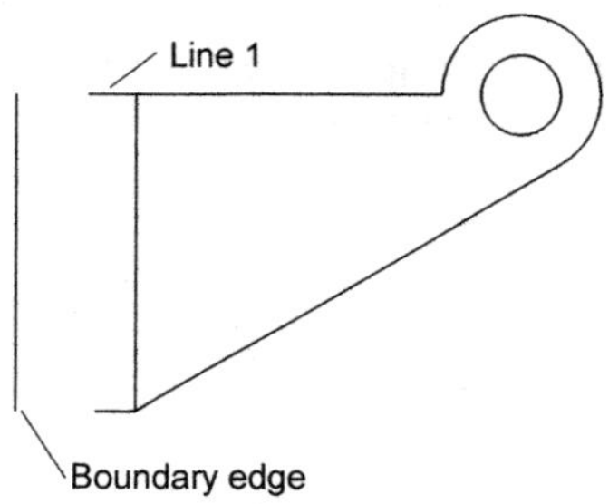

Figure 4.45

Using Extend

The Extend command extends the lengths of existing lines and arcs to end where it would meet another object. Its function is similar to the Trim command. Like Trim, you can directly select the item to extend and if the result shown in preview is what you want, just click to have it happen. You can also use the Boundary option for Extend and use the command in two parts: First you select the object to act as the boundary, press [Enter] and then select the objects you want to extend. Extend is on the ribbon Home tab, Modify panel.

The command-line options for the Extend command are similar to those you learned for Trim. The default option is just to select the objects to be extended.

The Project option allows you to specify the plane of projection to be used for extending. This option is useful when you're working in 3D drawings because it allows you to extend objects to a boundary selected from the current viewing direction or User Coordinate System.

Often 3D objects may not actually intersect the boundary edge but just appear to do so in the view. You can use the Project option to extend them as they appear in the view. The Undo option lets you undo the last object extended, while remaining in the Extend command.

Now you will use the Extend command to extend the existing lines to meet the new boundary. Refer to Figure 4.45.

Click: ***Extend button***

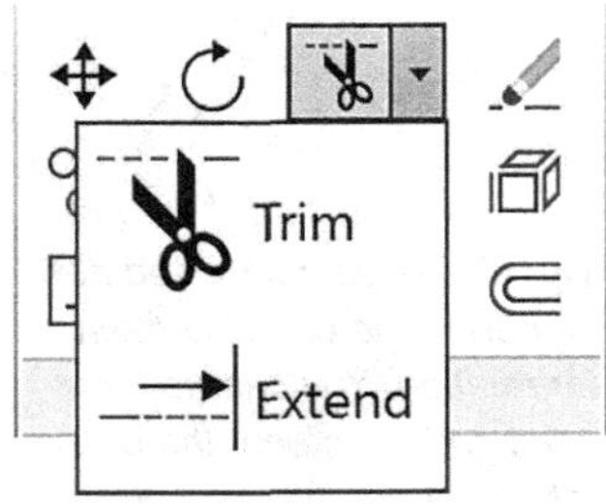

Current settings: Projection=UCS, Edge=None, Mode=Quick

Select object to extend or shift-select to trim or

[Boundary edges/Crossing/mOde/Project]: ***Hover over then click line 1***

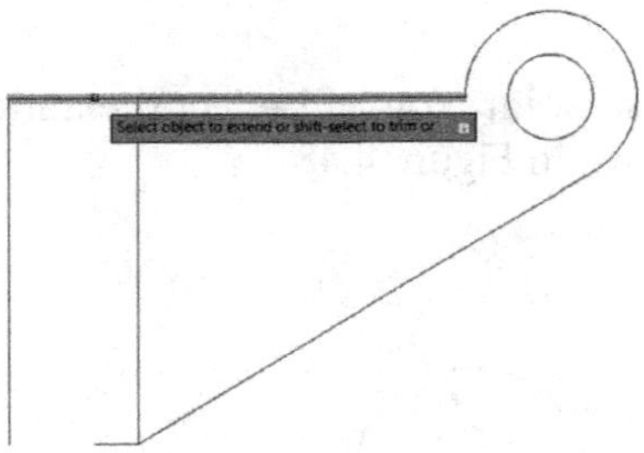

Figure 4.46

As you hover the cursor over the selected line it is highlighted as shown in Figure 4.46. If this is the correct result, all you have to do is click. The command continues. Try the boundary option next.

Select object to extend or shift-select to trim or
[Boundary edges/Crossing/mOde/Project/Undo]: ***B [Enter]***

Current settings: Projection=UCS, Edge=None, Mode=Quick
Select boundary edges ...
Select objects or <select all>: ***select boundary edge [Enter]***

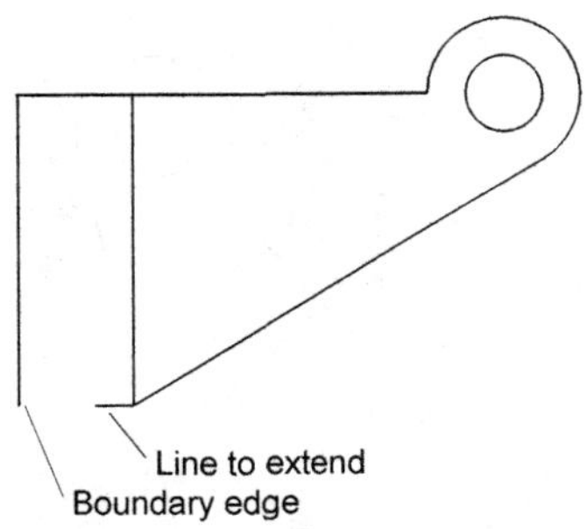

You have finished selecting boundary edges. To extend the horizontal line, select them by clicking points on them near the end closer to the boundary edge. (If you click closer to the other end, you will get the message "No edge in that direction," and the lines won't be extended.)

Select object to extend or shift-select to trim or
[Boundary edges/Crossing/mOde/Project]: ***select line to extend***

Select object to extend or shift-select to trim or
[Boundary edges/Crossing/mOde/Project]: ***[Enter]***

The drawing will look like Figure 4.47 once the lines have been extended.

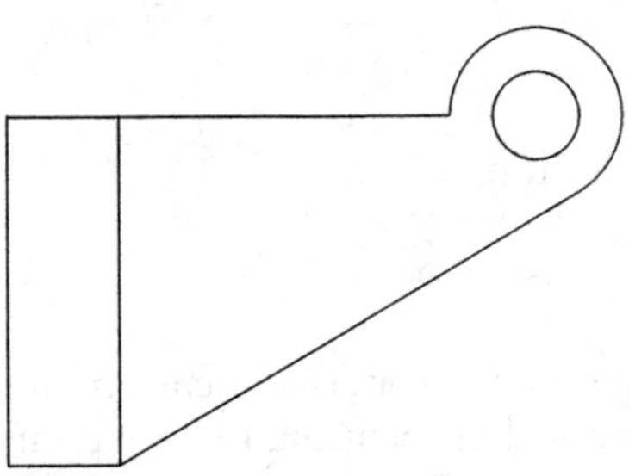

Figure 4.47

Using Rotate

The Rotate command allows you to rotate a drawing object or group of objects to a new orientation in the drawing. Rotate is on the ribbon Home tab, Modify panel.

Tip: The base point need not be part of the object chosen for rotation. You can use any point on the screen; the object rotates about the point you select. You may often find it useful to select a base point in the center of the object you want to rotate. As the object rotates, it stays in relatively the same position on the screen.

Click: ***Rotate button***

Select objects: ***select the entire coupler using a Crossing window***
7 found
Select objects: ***[Enter]***

Next, you are prompted for the base point. You will select the middle of the object as the base point, as shown in Figure 4.48.

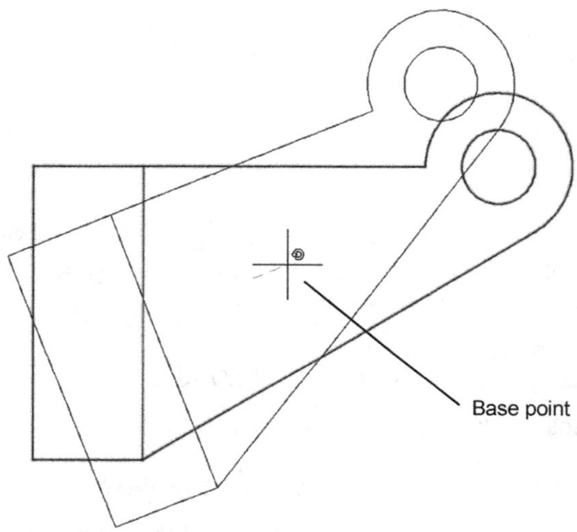

Figure 4.48

Specify base point: click in the middle of the coupler

Specify rotation angle or [Copy/Reference]: ***45 [Enter]***

Your coupler should be rotated 45 degrees, as shown in Figure 4.49. Positive angles are measured counterclockwise. A horizontal line to the right of the base point is defined as 0 degrees. You can also enter negative values.

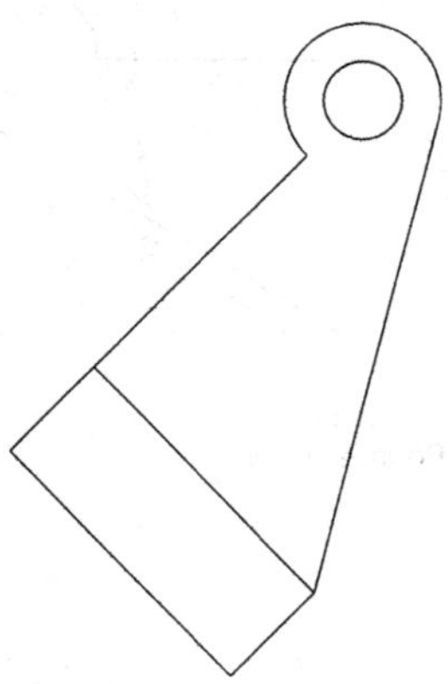

Figure 4.49

Next you will restore the object to its original position before you continue.

Click: ***Undo button***

The coupler returns to its original rotation.

Using Move

The Move command moves existing objects from one location on the coordinate system in the drawing to another location. Do not confuse the Move command and the Pan command. Pan moves your view and leaves the objects where they were. Move actually moves the objects on the coordinate system. Move is on the Modify toolbar.

 *Click:* ***Move button***

Select objects: ***use Crossing or Window to select all of the coupler drawing***

Select objects: ***[Enter]***

Specify base point or [Displacement] <Displacement>: ***click the Snap to Endpoint button***

Endpoint of: select the upper left corner of the coupler

The cursor switches to drag mode so that you can see the object move about the screen, as shown in Figure 4.50.

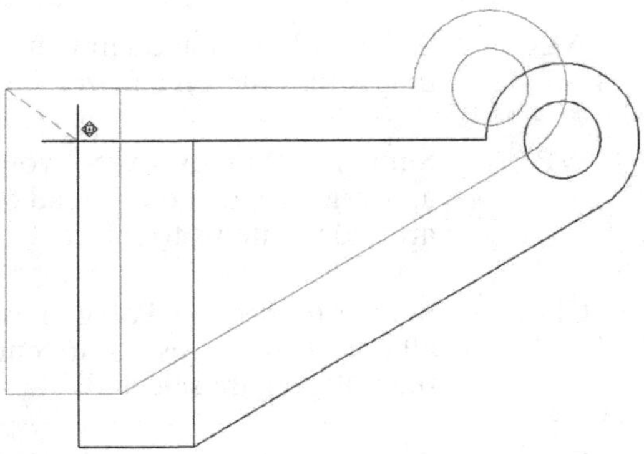

Figure 4.50

Specify second point or <use first point as displacement>: ***select a point so the coupler is to the lower right of its old location***

Methods of Selecting Objects

There are many ways that you can select graphical objects for use with commands. For example, Window and Crossing. You can save lots of time when creating and editing drawings by the clever use of the selection methods. Generally, whenever you are asked to select objects, you can continue selecting until you have all the objects that you want highlighted in one selection set. You can combine the various selection modes to select the objects you want. The command then operates on the selection set you have built.

At any *Select objects:* prompt, you can type option letters for the method to use. You may continue selecting, using any of the methods in the following table, until you indicate that you have finished building the selection set by pressing [Enter] or right-clicking. Then the command takes effect on the objects that you have selected.

Name	Option Letter(s)	Method
Clicking	none	Selects objects by positioning cursor and clicking the left mouse button
Select Window	W	Specifies diagonal corners of a box that only selects objects that are entirely enclosed

Select Crossing	C	Specifies diagonal corners of a box that selects all objects that cross or are enclosed in the box
Select Group	G	Selects all objects within a named group, prompts to enter group name
Select Previous	P	Reselects the previous selection set
Select Last	L	Selects the last object created
Select All	ALL	Selects all the objects in your drawing unless they are on a frozen layer
Select Window Polygon	WP	Similar to Window except you draw an irregular polygon instead of a box around the items to select
Select Crossing Polygon	CP	Similar to Window Polygon except that all objects that cross or are enclosed in the polygon are selected
Select Fence	F	Similar to Crossing except that you draw line segments through all the objects you want to select
Select Add	A	Use after Remove to add more objects to the selection set. Can continue with any of the other selection modes once Add has been chosen
Select Remove	R or Shift Click	Selects objects to remove from the current selection set; removal continues until Add or [Enter] is used; you can use Window, Crossing, etc., while selecting items to remove. Pressing shift and clicking on a selected object removes it from the current selection. (Do not select on a grip handle.)
Undo	U	During object selection, deselects the last item or group of items you selected
Control	[Ctrl]	After you click as close to the object as you can, press [Ctrl] to cycle through objects that are close together or directly on top of one another. Continue to press [Ctrl] until the object you want is selected.

You can also use Auto, Box, Subobject, Object, Single, and Multiple. Consult AutoCAD Help for the Select command for definitions of their use.

You can begin a selection window in one part of your drawing and pan and zoom to a different area of the drawing while the initial selection of objects off-screen remain. Off-screen selection is controlled using the SELECTIONOFFSCREEN system variable.

Select Similar

Select similar allows you to quickly select objects that are similar to one you have already selected. To see how this works,

Click: ***to select one of the straight lines*** *(its grips appear)*

Right-click: ***to show the short-cut menu*** *(Figure 4.51)*

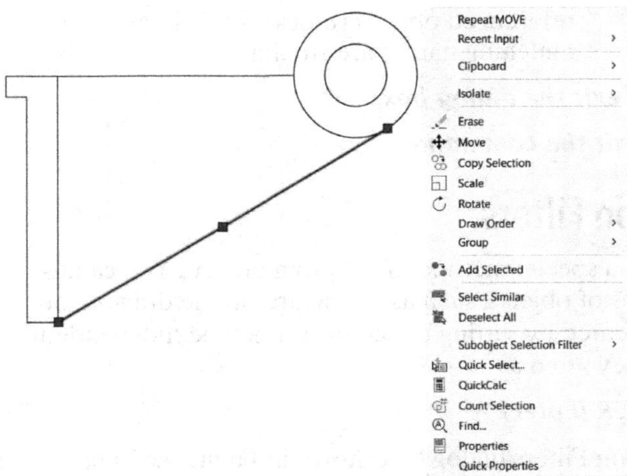

Figure 4.51

Click: ***Select Similar***

All of the straight line segments become selected and their grips appear.

Press: ***[Esc]*** *to deselect the lines*

You can set which properties of an object determine whether it is similar to the selected one, using the Select Similar Setting dialog box (Figure 4.52).

Command: ***[Enter]*** *to restart the command*

SELECTSIMILAR Select objects or [SEttings]: ***SE [Enter]***

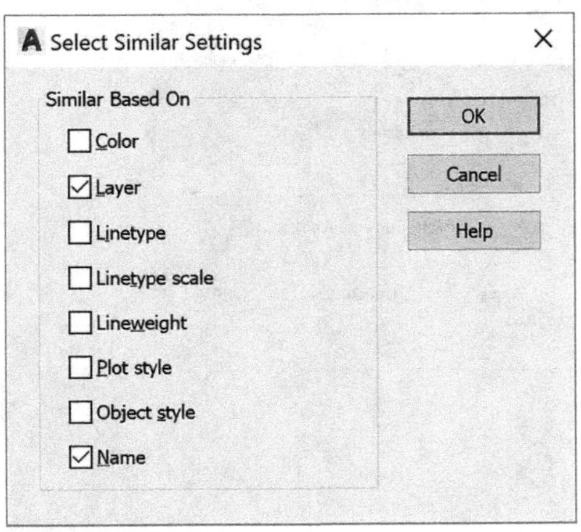

Figure 4.52

The properties which you can select to determine similarity from are:

Color	objects with matching colors are similar.
Layer	objects on matching layers are similar.
Linetype	objects with matching linetypes are similar.
Linetype scale	objects with matching linetype scales are similar.
Lineweight	objects with matching lineweights are similar.
Plot style	objects with matching plot styles are similar.
Object style	objects with matching styles (text styles, dimension styles, table styles) are similar.
Name	referenced objects (blocks, xrefs, images) with matching names are similar.

Click: ***Cancel to exit the dialog box***

Press: ***[Esc] to exit the command***

Using Selection Filters

Selection filters are a special method of selecting objects. You can use them to select types of objects, such as all the arcs in the drawing or objects that you created by setting the color or linetype independently of the layer that they are on.

Command: ***FILTER [Enter]***

The Object Selection Filters dialog box shown in Figure 4.53 appears on your screen. You can use this dialog box to filter the types of objects to select. You can save named filter groups for reuse.

Click: ***in the Select Filter area*** *to show the list, then click* ***Arc***

Click: ***Add to List***

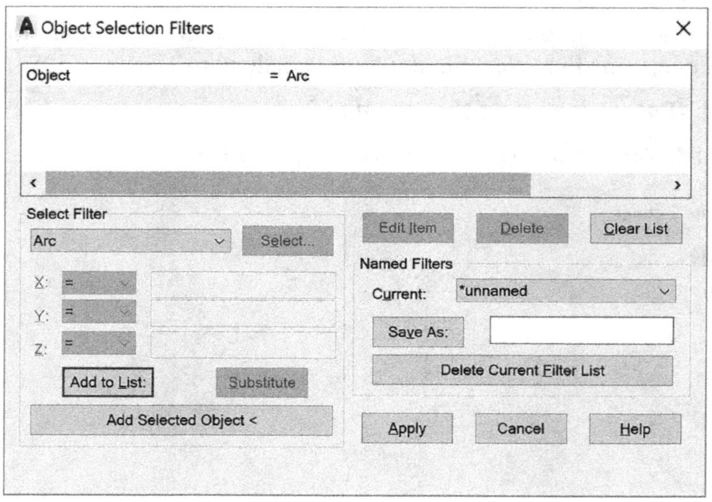

Figure 4.53

Click: ***Apply***

After choosing Apply, you return to the command prompt to select the objects in your drawing. Note the message,

Applying filter to selection.

Select objects: ***use Crossing to select all of the objects***

You should see the message "Applying filter to selection. 1 found." Only the arc object matched the filter list. The lines of the drawing were filtered out.

Select objects: ***[Esc]*** *to cancel*

Command: ***[Enter]*** *to restart the FILTER command*

You should see the Object Selection Filters dialog box on your screen.

Click: ***Clear List***

Click: ***[X] Windows Close button*** *to close the dialog box*

Using Quick Select

Use Quick Select (Qselect) to create a selection set which includes or excludes matching objects and properties. You can apply Quick Select to your entire drawing or to a previously created selection set. You can also append the Quick Select objects to the current selection set or replace the current selection. Quick Select is on the ribbon Home tab, Utilities panel and also the Properties palette. You can also right-click and choose Quick Select from the short-cut menu.

Click: ***Quick Select button*** *from the Utilities panel*

You should see the Quick Select dialog box as shown in Figure 4.54.

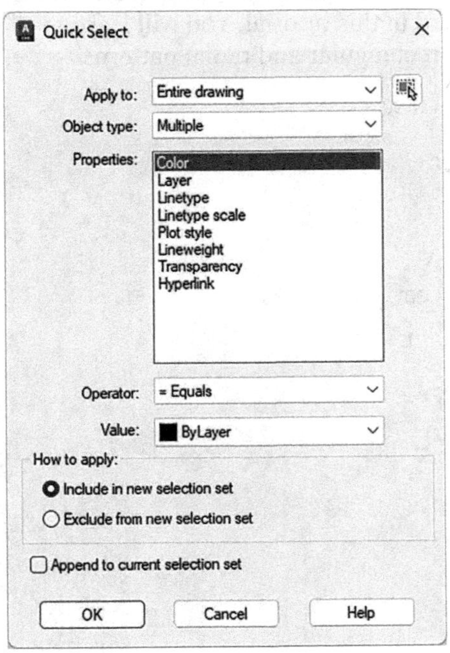

Figure 4.54

You will use Quick Select to select the entire drawing except for the top arc.

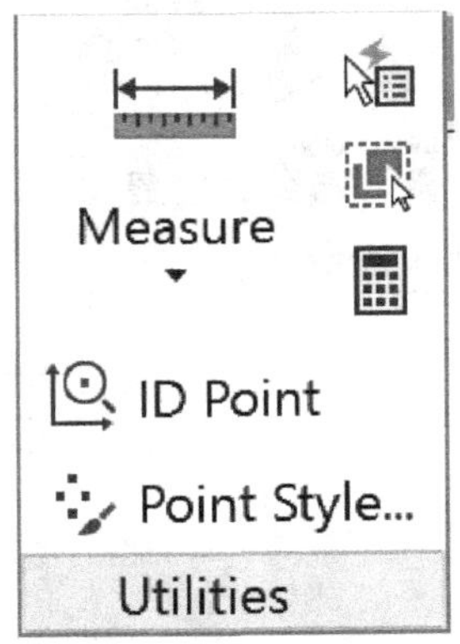

Tip: *The Quick Select icon appears at the top of the Properties palette to provide quick selection functions when changing properties.*

Verify that the Apply to area shows Entire drawing.

Click: ***Arc*** *from the pull-down list to the right of Object type*

The Properties area now displays properties of the arc which you could select for further filtering. In the How to apply area you can choose "Include in new selection set" which creates a new selection set of only objects that match the filtering criteria. Selecting "Exclude from new selection set" creates a new selection set composed only of objects that do not match the filtering criteria. In the How to apply area,

Click: ***Exclude from new selection set***

Make sure that Append to current selection set is not selected.

Click: ***OK*** *to exit the dialog box*

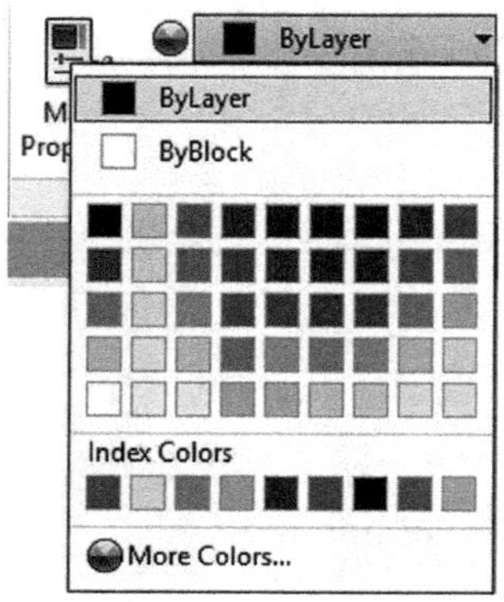

All of the objects, with the exception of the top arc, should now be selected. Next you will use the color control to set the color for the selected objects to red.

Click: ***Red*** *from the Color Control on the Properties panel*

Press: ***[Esc]***

All but the arc should now appear in red on your screen.

Closing the Coupler Drawing

On your own, **close** the coupler drawing. **Discard** the changes to *coupler.dwg*.

Creating the Geneva Cam

You will create the geneva cam shown in Figure 4.55, using many of the editing commands you have learned in this tutorial. You will learn to use the Array command to create rectangular and radial patterns.

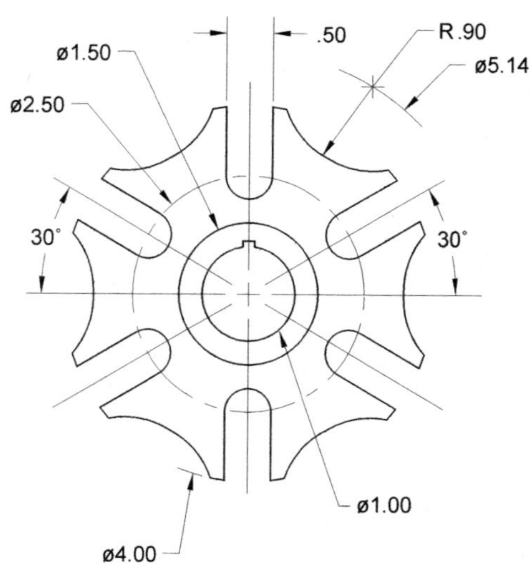

Figure 4.55

On your own, start a new drawing from the ***acad.dwt*** template.

Save the drawing to your **work** folder with the name ***geneva.dwg***.

Continuing on your own, set the **Snap** to **0.25.**

Check the status bar to be sure that **Snap** and **Grid** are turned on.

Use **Zoom All** if needed so that the grid area fills the graphics window.

Next you will use the Circle command to create the innermost circle of diameter 1.00. Locate the center of the circle at (5.5, 4.5).

Click: ***Circle button***

3P/2P/TTR/<Center point>: ***5.5,4.5 [Enter]***

Diameter/<Radius>: ***D [Enter]***

Diameter: ***1 [Enter]***

Use Offset or the Circle command to draw a **1.5-diameter** circle and a **4-diameter** circle **concentric** to the circle you just drew.

Tip: *If you use Offset, remember to calculate the offset distance based on the diameters given. You will need to subtract the diameter of the inner circle from the diameter of the outer circle and then divide the result by 2 to find the value to use for the offset distance.*

Your drawing should look like Figure 4.56.

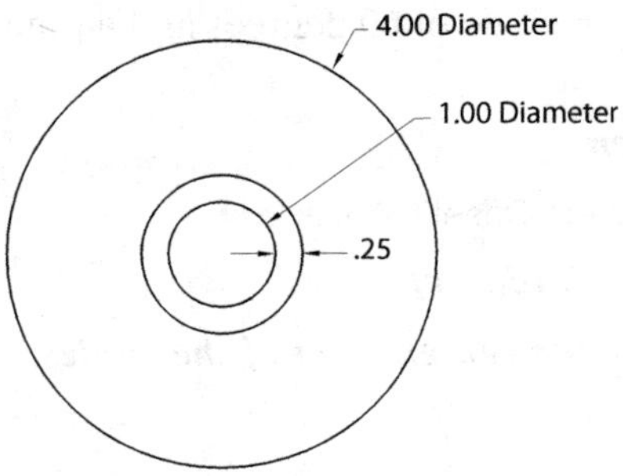

Figure 4.56

Tip: *You can keep a panel expanded by selecting to "pin" it, using the icon that looks like a push pin.*

Use Line to draw vertical and horizontal lines through the center of the circles.

Your drawing should look like Figure 4.57.

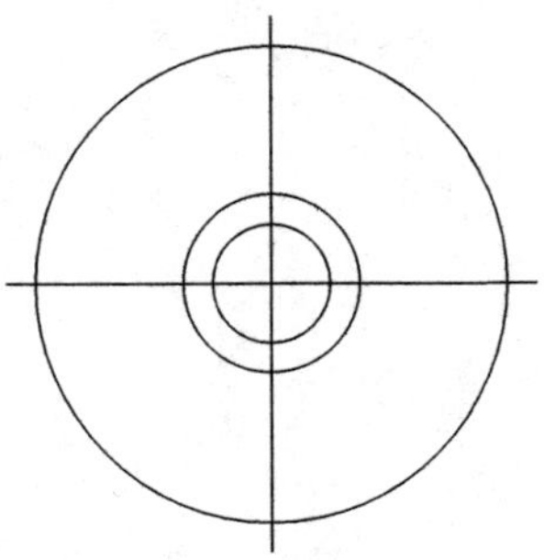

Figure 4.57

Next create lines parallel to the vertical centerline.

Click: ***Offset button***

Specify offset distance or [Through/Erase/Layer] <2.50000>: ***.25 [Enter]***

Select object to offset or [Exit/Undo] <Exit>: ***click the vertical centerline***

Specify point on side to offset or [Exit/Multiple/Undo] <Exit>: ***click on the right side of the line***

Select object to offset or [Exit/Undo] <Exit>: ***click the same vertical centerline***

Specify point on side to offset or [Exit/Multiple/Undo] <Exit>: ***click on the left side of the line***

Select object to offset or [Exit/Undo] <Exit>: ***[Enter]***

Using Construction Line (Xline)

Construction Line, on the ribbon Home tab, Draw panel, creates a line (through a point that you select) that extends infinitely in both directions from the first point selected. The Ray command, on the Draw panel, draws a line which extends infinitely in only one direction.

Using the XLINE command, you can select options to draw a horizontal or vertical line, to bisect a specified angle, or to offset the construction line by a distance from the object. You will use the Angle option from the command prompt to specify an angle of 60 degrees and a point for the line to pass through.

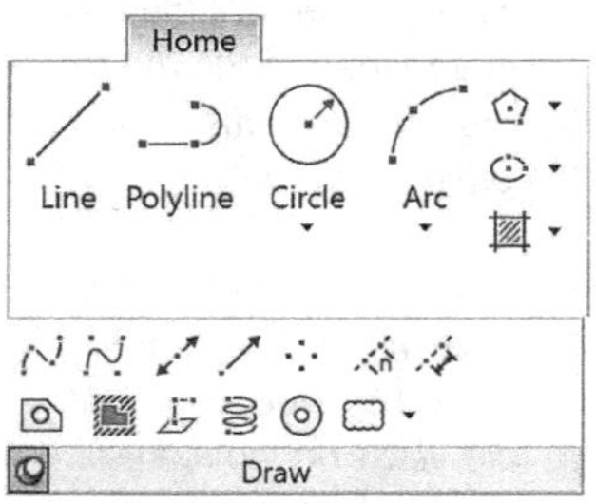

Click: ***Construction Line button***

Specify a point or [Hor/Ver/Ang/Bisect/Offset]: ***A [Enter]***

Enter angle of xline (0) or [Reference]: ***60 [Enter]***

Specify through point: ***5.5,4.5*** *or click the center point of the circles using Snap*

Specify through point: ***[Enter]***

Zoom to enlarge your view as needed.

The construction line appears in your drawing, as shown in Figure 4.58.

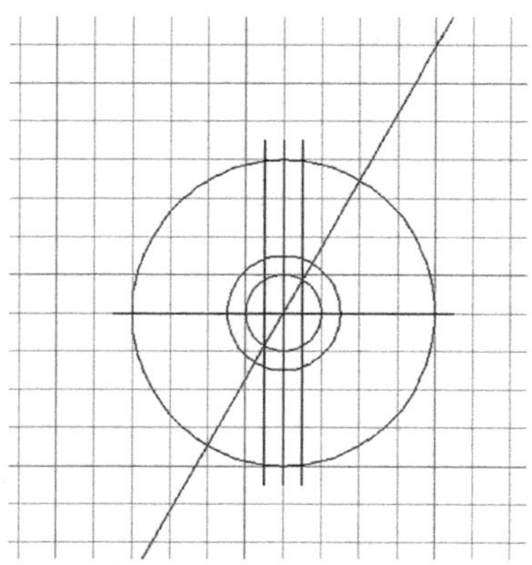

Figure 4.58

The construction line will extend as far as you pan your view in both directions of extension. If you trim a construction line at one end, it becomes a ray, extending infinitely in only one direction. If you trim it at both ends, it becomes a line.

Use Trim to remove the lower portion of the construction line where it passes the horizontal construction line. When you are finished, the construction line only extends upward from the center point.

Next you will use the Circle command to add the construction circles to your drawing. The first two circles to add are concentric with the existing circles in the drawing, in other words, they have the same centerpoint.

On your own, turn on **running object snap** for **Center** and **Intersection**.

*Click: **Circle button***

Specify center point for circle or [3P/2P/Ttr (tan tan radius)]: ***select the center of the circles using object snap***

Specify radius of circle or [Diameter] <2.0000>: ***2.57 [Enter]***

Command: ***[Enter]** or right-click and select to restart the command*

Specify center point for circle or [3P/2P/Ttr (tan tan radius)]: ***select the center of the circles using the object snap Center to select the same center point as before***

Specify radius of circle or [Diameter] <2.5700>: ***1.25 [Enter]***

Next you will add two construction circles which you will later trim to form arcs.

Command: ***[Enter]** to restart the Circle command*

Specify center point for circle or [3P/2P/Ttr (tan tan radius)]: ***Use object snap Intersection to select where the vertical centerline crosses the 1.25 radius construction circle identified as point A***

Specify radius of circle or [Diameter] <1.2500>: ***.25 [Enter]***

The small circle is added to your drawing between the two lines you offset. Your drawing should look like that in Figure 4.59.

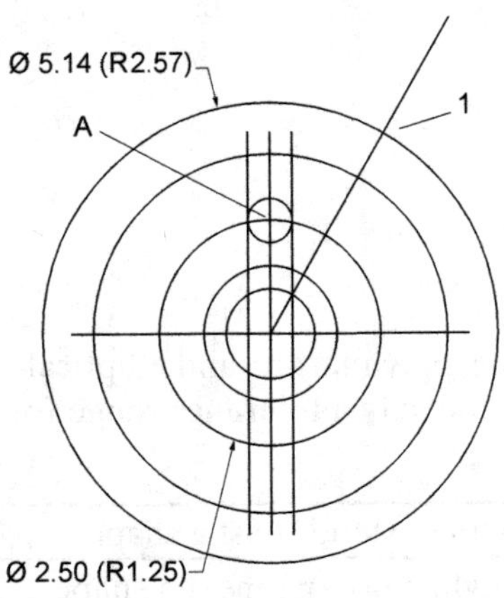

Figure 4.59

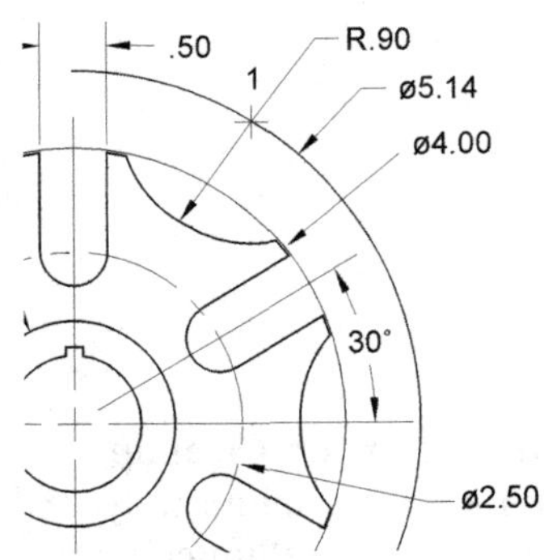

Tip: *Think back on the shape of the geneva cam. The R.90 circle has its center at point 1.*

Use the next steps to draw the final construction circle where the 60-degree ray and the outer circle intersect.

Command: ***[Enter]** to restart the Circle command*

Specify center point for circle or [3P/2P/Ttr (tan tan radius)]: ***click point 1** (Figure 4.59) using object snap Intersection*

Specify radius of circle or [Diameter]<.2500>: ***.90 [Enter]***

Your drawing should now look like Figure 4.60.

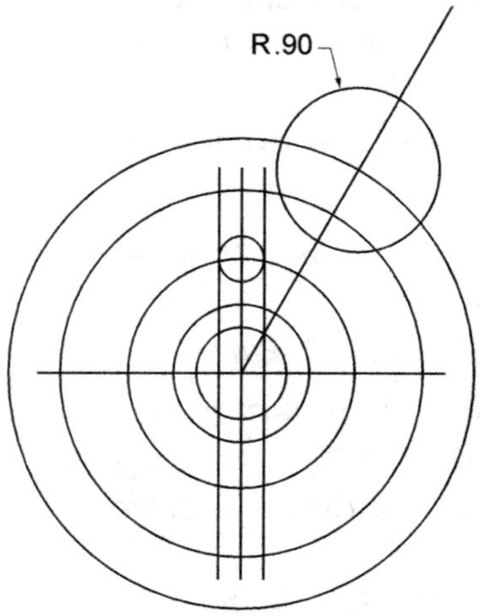

Figure 4.60

> **Tip:** *Try using Crossing to select several objects to trim at one time. Use the Erase option of the Trim command to remove any objects that no longer cross a cutting edge*

On your own, use Trim to remove the unwanted portions of the figure until your drawing looks like Figure 4.61.

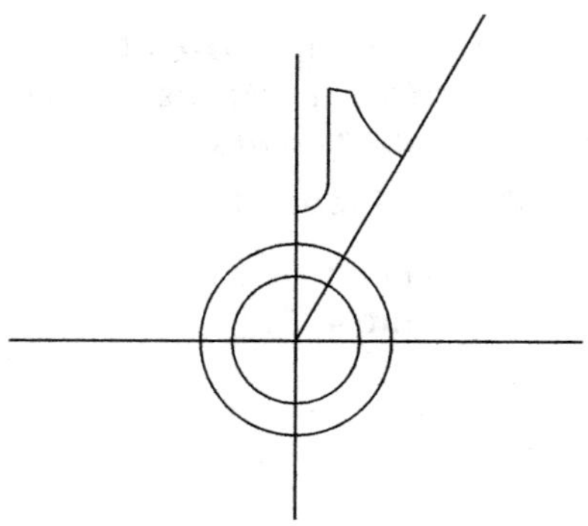

Figure 4.61

Using Geometry Cleanup

> **Tip:** Geometry Cleanup only works on line, polyline, arc, and elliptical arcs in the XY plane of the current UCS.

Geometry Cleanup works to connect line, polyline, arc, and elliptical arc objects in the drawing by letting you specify a tolerance range for the following conditions:

Overshoot	Endpoint of line or polyline extends past a shape.
Undershoot	Endpoint of a line or polyline doesn't meet a shape.
Gap	Endpoint of lines or polylines don't coincide.
Absolute Angle	Line or polyline is off from desired angle in the UCS (For example 0°, 45°, or 90°, or any value you specify.)
Relative Angle	Two intersecting lines or polylines do not meet at the intended angle relative to one another (not the UCS).

This is a good time to try it. If your shapes for the geneva aren't perfectly connected, you can use this to fix them before mirroring the shapes in later steps. You may not have errors in your drawing, so use the datafile, *GenevaCleanMe.dwg* which has some intentional errors.

On your own, open datafile GenevaCleanMe.dwg. Zoom in to view the arcs at the upper right. Notice they do not connect.

Click: ***Geometry Cleanup button from the panel***

The Geometry Cleanup panel appears on your screen when you finish selecting objects, similar to Figure 4.62.

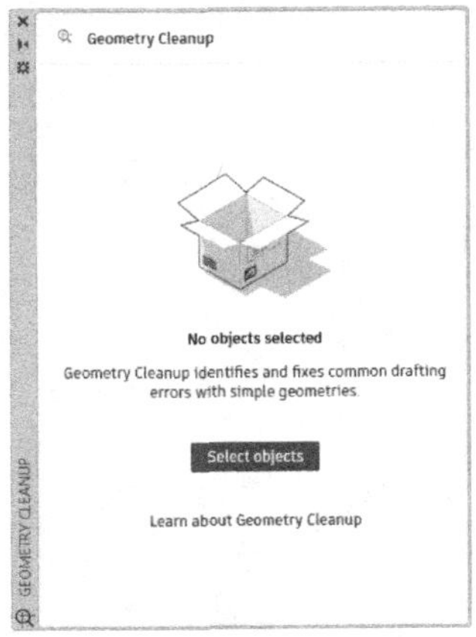

Click: ***Select Objects button*** *from the panel*

On your own, select the right arc and top arc segment.

Click: ***Scan*** *from the Geometry Cleanup Settings panel.*

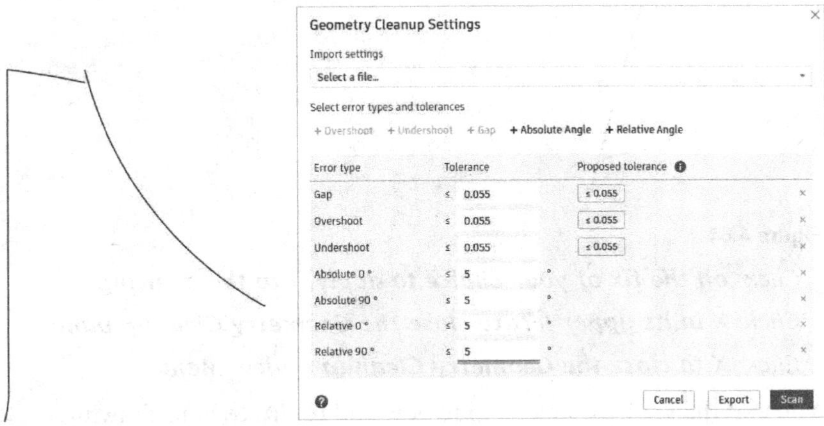

Figure 4.62

The Geometry Cleanup panel now lists areas that do not meet the tolerances specified in the Geometry Cleanup Settings. See Figure 4.63. Now you can review and fix the errors.

Click: ***to expand the selection under Gap*** (*Figure 4.63*)

Click: ***on the values of the gap error to show it in the drawing.***

Right-click: ***on the identified error to show the fixes menu.***

On your own, hover your mouse over each of the fix options.

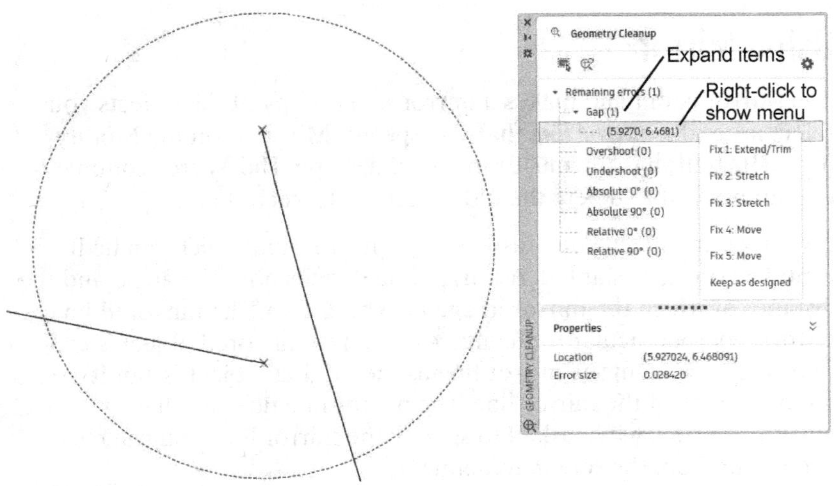

Figure 4.63

Hovering over a fix option shows you a preview of the fix as it would appear in your drawing. Clicking on a fix will apply it to your drawing. Use Keep as designed when the gap or other item is intended.

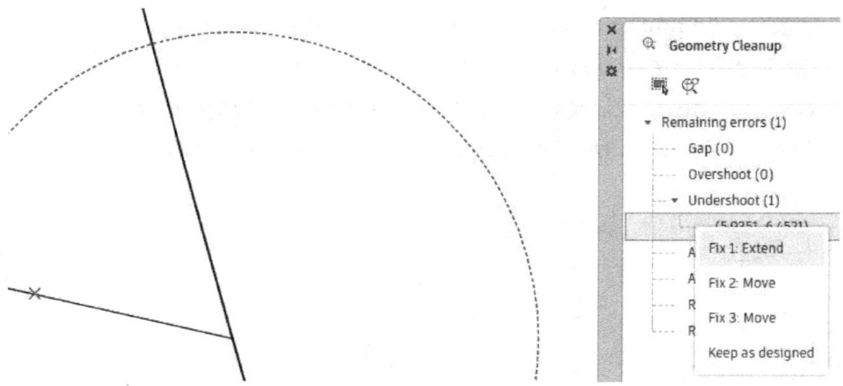

Figure 4.64

Click: ***on the fix of your choice to apply it to the drawing***

Click: ***X in its upper left to close the Geometry Cleanup panel***

Click: ***X to close the Geometry Cleanup review menu***

You exit the geometry cleanup review and return to your drawing.

Geometry Cleanup is a very handy tool. Keep in mind that it is usually quickest and best to create the drawing geometry accurately in the first place. You have to have a good understanding of the shape you are creat-ing in order to know which of the fix options is right for your particular use. Sometimes very small gaps or wrong angles can cause big problems later on. This is a great way to find and fix them.

On your own, close *GenevaCleanMe.dwg* without saving the changes. Saving the changes would overwrite the datafle .

Return to **geneva.dwg.** ***Try Geometry Cleanup to fix any errors you may have in your drawing.***

Using Mirror

The Mirror command makes a mirror-image copy of the objects you select around a *mirror line* that you specify. Mirror is on the Modify panel. Its button is the mirror image of a shape. The Mirror command also allows you to delete the old objects or to keep them.

To mirror an object, you must specify a mirror line, which can be hori-zontal, vertical, or slanted. A mirror line defines both the angle and the distance at which the mirror image is to be drawn. The mirrored image is drawn perpendicular to the mirror line. The mirrored object is the same distance from the mirror line as the original object is, but it's on the other side of the mirror line. The mirror line does not have to exist in your drawing; when asked to specify the mirror line, you can click two points from the screen to define it.

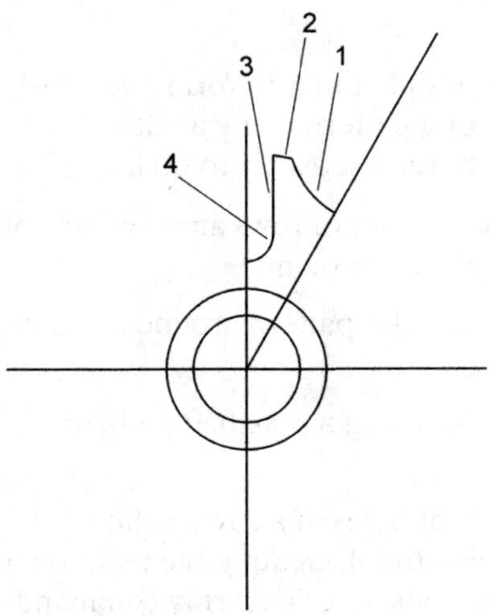

Figure 4.65

The vertical centerline will serve as the mirror line as you mirror the lines and arcs of the geneva cam. Refer to Figure 4.65 as you click on points. Be sure that Snap is turned on or use object snaps before clicking on the mirror line.

Click: ***Mirror button***

Select objects: ***click objects 1, 2, 3, and 4***

Select objects: ***[Enter]***

Specify first point of mirror line: ***select the exact center of the concentric circles***

Your cursor is now dragging a mirrored copy of the objects.

Specify second point of mirror line: ***select a point straight below the center point***

Erase source objects? [Yes/No] <N> ***[Enter]***

Your drawing should look like Figure 4.66.

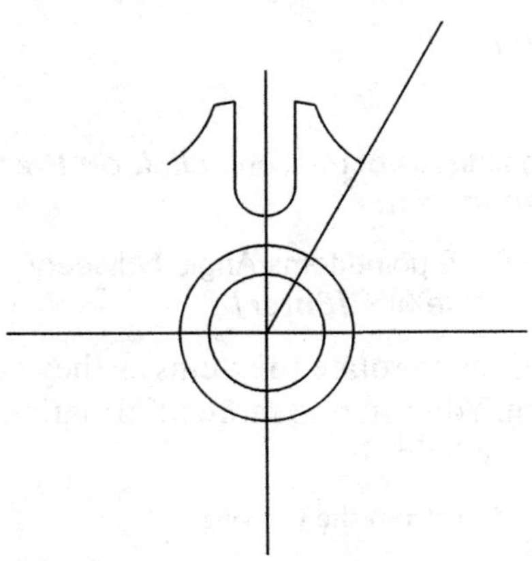

Figure 4.66

Using Array

The Array commands copy an object multiple times to form a regularly spaced rectangular or circular pattern, or a pattern along a path. When you need to create regularly spaced patterns, use Array to do it quickly.

A *rectangular array* has a specified number of rows and columns of the items with a specified distance between them.

A *polar array* copies the items in a circular pattern around a center point that you specify.

A *path array* evenly distributes copies along a specified path, or portion of the path.

Examples are creating a circular pattern of holes in a circular hub, creating rows of desks in laying out a classroom, creating the teeth on a gear, or setting lamposts along a curved walkway. The Array command is on the ribbon Home tab, Modify panel shown in Figure 4.67.

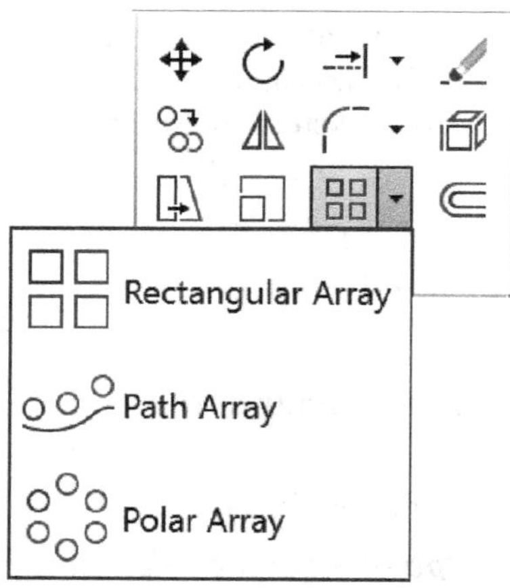

Figure 4.67

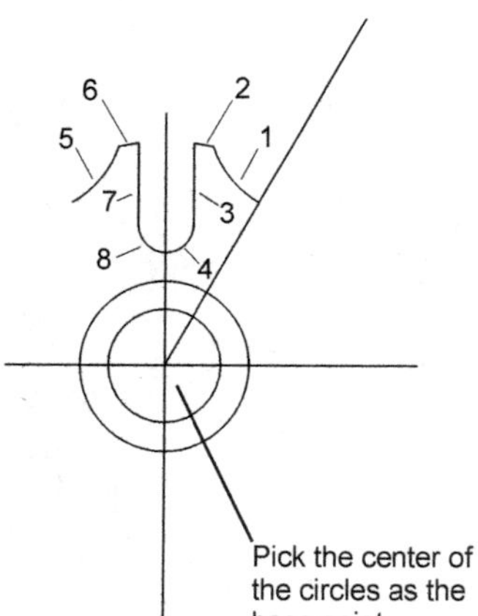

Click: ***Polar Array button***

The command prompt shows the options for a polar array.

Select objects: ***select lines 1-8 [Enter]***

Type = Polar Associative = Yes

Specify center point of array or [Base point/Axis of rotation]: ***click on the center of the circles*** *using object snap center*

Select grip to edit array or [ASsociative/Base point/Items/Angle between/Fill angle/ROWs/Levels/ROTate items/eXit]<eXit>: ***[Enter]***

You can use the command prompt options to rotate the items as they are copied to preserve their orientation. You can find more information about the Array commands in the on-line help.

On your own, use **Erase** to erase the angled ray from the drawing.

The geneva cam is now complete; **save** it on your own.

Your drawing should look like that in Figure 4.68.

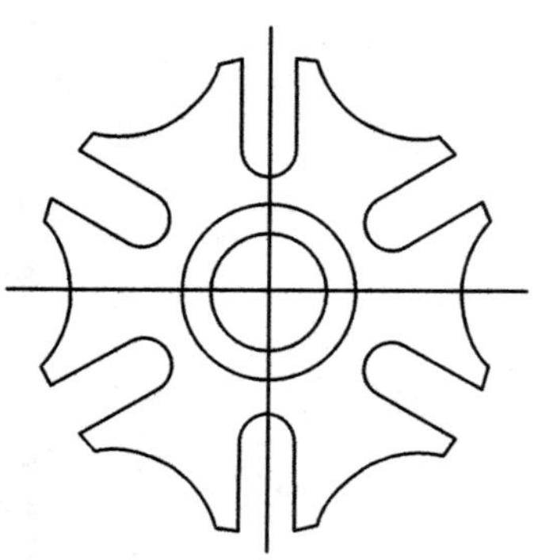

Figure 4.68

Editing Associative Arrays

When an associative array is created, its elements are linked to the arrayed object and can be easily accessed for later editing and updates. Associative arrays are the default. You can double-click on any part of the arrayed object to edit it.

Double-click: ***on one of the arcs or lines of the array***

Notice that all of the arcs and lines are grouped together as one object. After you double-click on an arrayed object, the Array Editor contextual tab appears on the screen as shown in Figure 4.69. You can also edit associative arrays using Quick Properties.

The left-most item on the contextual tab shows the type of array, in this case, Polar. Additional items are Items Panel, Item Count, where you can change the number of items in the array, Angle between Items, and the Angle to Fill (between 0° and 360°).

The Base Point area on the Properties panel lets you redefine the base point of the array. If you did not select the center of the circles as your base point, you could correct it here.

Rotate Items is used to control how objects rotate as they are arrayed.

Using Edit Source and Replace Item you activate an editing state in which you can change or replace the source objects you selected to array.

Reset Array restores erased items and removes any item overrides.

Row Count lets you specify the number of rows in your array, while Row Spacing and Total Row Distance provide spacing options for the rows. This is more commonly used in rectangular arrays, but you can create a second "row" of items in your polar array. This will appear like a second ring in the geneva cam.

Try this on your own: set Row Count to 2. When you are finished set it back to 1.

Remaining options let you set the spacing and number for 3D arrays or arrays along a path. For now leave those items unchanged.

Click: ✓ ***Close Array*** *to exit the Array Editor*

Tip: *If you did not select the correct objects and your drawing does not look like the figure, you can edit the source objects you selected to array or replace selected objects. Live previewing helps you see what the results will look like and then you can accept or change the selections as needed.*

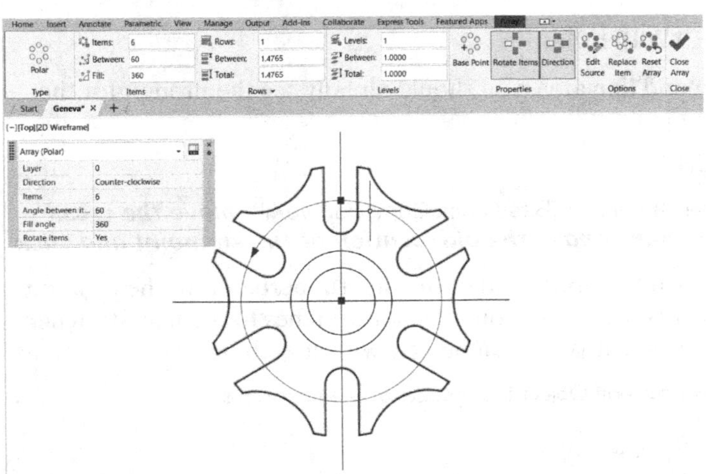

Figure 4.69

Making Changes using Grips

A quick way to make changes to your drawing is by using the object's grips. Grips let you grab an object already drawn on your screen and use editing commands directly using your mouse.

Tip: *Grips work best with a two- or three-button mouse. Use the Options dialog box to check that you have grips enabled. Pick on the Selection tab so that it becomes the uppermost tab in the dialog box. Select the box to the left of Enable Grips at this time if it is not already selected. You can also turn grips on or off and change their color and size using the Grip Size slider box.*

Activating an Object's Grips

Move the crosshairs over the upper vertical centerline of the geneva cam and click to select the line.

The line becomes dashed and small boxes, called grips, appear at the endpoints, as shown in Figure 4.70. You can use them to stretch, move, rotate, scale, and mirror the object.

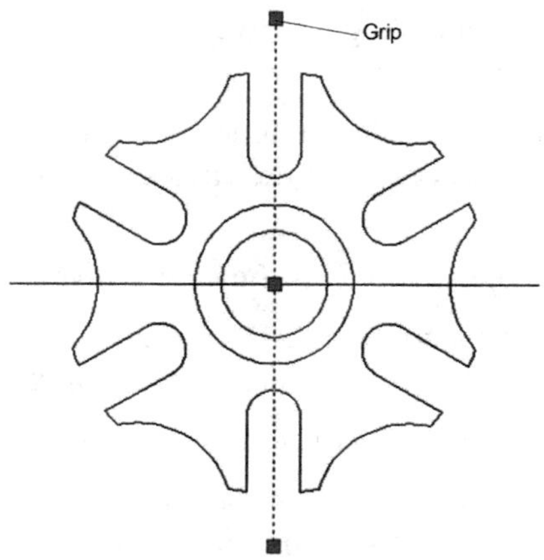

Figure 4.70

Selecting the Base Grip

Click the grip at the upper end of the line.

The selected grip changes to the highlighting color. This *base grip* will act as the base point for the command you will select using your mouse.

Using Stretch with Hot Grips

In the command line area, you should already see the prompt for the Stretch command.

STRETCH

Specify stretch point or [Base point/Copy/Undo/eXit]: ***move the crosshairs to a point above the old location of the endpoint and click***

The base grip at the upper end of the line rubberbands to the position of the crosshairs. The point you selected stretches to the new stretched location. (You can also shorten objects with stretching.)

On your own, turn off Object Snap mode for the next steps.

Using Move with Grips

On your own make a crossing box that crosses the entire geneva cam.

The grips appear as small boxes on all the selected objects.

Click on the grip at the circle's center to select it as the base grip.

The base grip becomes highlighted. You will see the prompt for the Stretch command in the command line area.

Right-click: ***to activate the Grips short-cut menu***

Click: ***Move*** *from the short-cut menu*

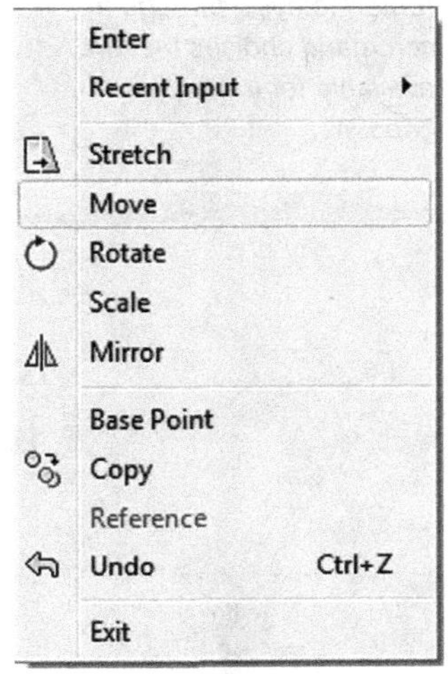

The command prompt shows the following options for the Move command. Next, move the geneva cam down and to the left. The objects seem attached to the crosshairs during the move as shown in Figure 4.71.

MOVE

Specify move point or [Base point/Copy/Undo/eXit]: ***click a new location for the center grip down and to the left of the previous location***

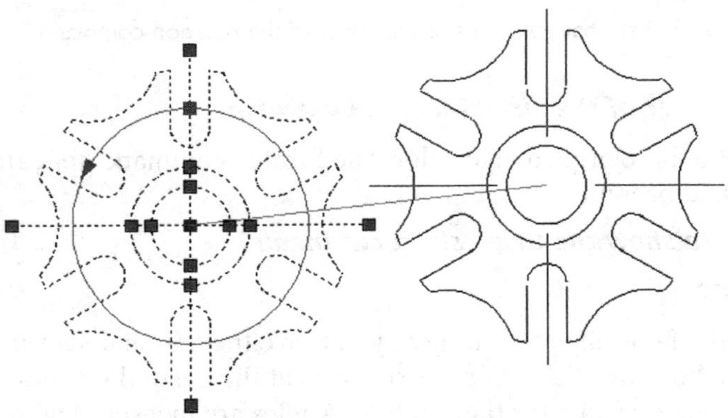

Figure 4.71

Using Move with the Copy Option

The grips should still be visible.

Click: ***the grip at the center of the circles as the base grip***

Right-click: ***to show the Grips short-cut menu***

Click: ***Move***

Specify move point or [Base point/Copy/Undo/eXit]: ***C [Enter]***

A new prompt, similar to the previous one, appears.

MOVE (multiple)

Specify move point or [Base point/Copy/Undo/eXit]:

On your own, move the crosshairs to a location where you would like to make a copy of the object and click; repeat this procedure to make several copies.

When you are finished, press [Enter] or the return button and click Exit to end the command.

If you were to choose Copy from the short-cut menu instead of selecting Move, only the object that shares the Grips box that you selected would be copied.

Tip: *If you want to cancel using the hot grips, press [Esc] twice.*

Tip: *You can also press [Enter] to cycle through the command choices that are available for use with hot grips.*

On your own, use the grips and select **Copy** from the short-cut menu (without selecting Move first).

Use the **Erase** command to erase some of the copies if your screen is too crowded.

Press **[Esc]** to unselect any object grips you may have on.

Using Rotate with Grips

Next you will use Crossing to select an entire geneva cam and activate its grips.

Click: ***above and to the left of one of the geneva cam copies***

Click: ***a point below and to the right of that geneva cam so that all of the drawing is selected***

The grips will appear on the objects in the drawing.

Turn Snap off [F9] so that you can see the effect of the rotation command clearly.

Click: ***the center of the circles as the base grip***

You will see the base grip change color. The Stretch command appears at the command prompt.

Right-click: ***to show the Grips short-cut menu***

Click: ***Rotate***

You will see the faint object rotating as you move the crosshairs around on the screen. You can click when the object is at the desired rotation or type in a numeric value for the rotation. Angles are measured with 0-degrees to the right and positive values counterclockwise, unless you change the default.

ROTATE

Specify rotation angle or [Base point/Copy/Undo/Reference/eXit]: ***45 [Enter]***

Now the object rotated 45°.

Using Scale with Grips

The Scale command changes the size of the object in your drawing database. Be sure that you use Scale only when you want to make the actual object larger. Use Zoom Window when you just want it to appear larger on the screen in order to see more detail.

On your own, activate the grips for the geneva cam, using implied Crossing.

When you have done this successfully, the grips will appear at the corners and midpoints of the lines, circles and arcs.

Click: ***the grip at the center of the circles as the base grip***

The grip becomes filled with the highlighting color. You will see the Stretch command in the command prompt area.

Right-click: ***to show the Grips short-cut menu***

Click: ***Scale***

SCALE

Specify scale factor or [Base point/Copy/Undo/Reference/eXit]:

As you move the crosshairs away from the base point, the faint image of the object becomes larger; as you get closer to the base point, it appears smaller. You can also type a scaling factor, similar to typing the rotation angle in the last steps. When you are happy with the new size of the object,

Click the left mouse ***button to accept the new size***

Tip: *To change the scale to known proportions, you can type in a scale factor. A value of 2 makes the object twice as large; a value of 0.5 makes it half its present size.*

Using Mirror with Grips

On your own, activate the **grips** with implied Windowing again.

Select the **center grip** as the base grip.

Right-click: to pop-up the menu and select **Mirror**

The Mirror command uses a mirror line and forms a symmetrical image of the selected objects on the other side of the line. You can think of this line as rubberbanding from the base grip to the current location of the crosshairs. Note that, as you move the crosshairs to different positions on the screen, the faint mirror image of the object appears on the other side of the mirror line. You will see the prompt

MIRROR

Specify second point or [Base point/Copy/Undo/eXit]: ***B [Enter]***

The Base point option lets you specify some other point besides the grip that you picked as the first point of the mirror line for the object.

Specify base point: ***click on a point to the left of the geneva shape***

Move the crosshairs on the screen and note the object being mirrored around the line that would form between the base point and the location of the crosshairs. When you are happy with the location of the mirrored object, click to select it. The old object disappears from the screen and the new mirrored object remains. End the command by pressing [Enter] or the return button.

Noun/Verb Selection

You can also use grips with other commands for noun/verb selection. *Noun/verb selection* is a method of selecting the objects that will be affected by a command first, instead of first selecting the command and then the group of objects. Think of the drawing objects as nouns, or things, and the commands as verbs, or actions. You will use this method with the Erase command to clear your screen.

Click: ***a point below and to the right of all your drawing objects***

Other corner: ***click a point above and to the left of the drawing objects***

You will see the grips for the objects that were crossed by the implied

Crossing box appear in your drawing. The objects are now preselected and their grips show on the screen.

Click: ***Erase button***

As soon as you clicked the Erase button, the items that you had selected were erased.

On your own, save the now empty drawing as **gasket.dwg.** Leave it open as you will return to it after the next section. Close geneva.dwg without saving the changes.

Using the Path Array

The command Arraypath lets you quickly arrange copies of a set of objects along a chosen path.

To see this command in action, you will open your subdivision drawing and add a row of trees along the roadway edge.

On your own, open your drawing named ***MySubdiv.dwg*** that you finished in Tutorial 3.

If needed, click the Model tab to show only model space.

Create a new layer named TREES and assign it color 94, a dark green, and linetype Continuous. Make this the current layer.

The subdivision drawing should appear on your screen similar to Figure 4.72. Next you will use the Tool Palettes to add a premade tree to your drawing. You will learn more about the Tool Palettes in Tutorial 10.

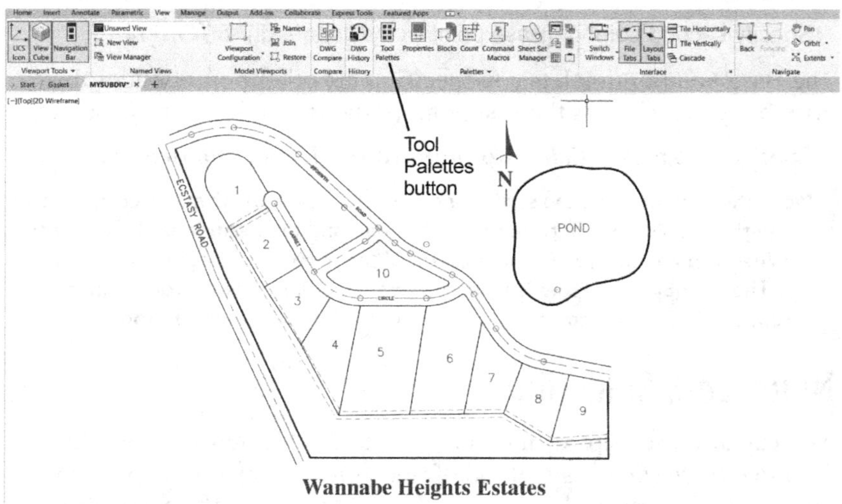

Figure 4.72

Click: ***Tool Palettes*** *from the View tab, Palettes panel*

Click: ***Architectural*** *to show it as the top tab on the palette*

Click and drag: ***Trees - Imperial*** *to add a tree to your drawing*

As you click on the tree symbol and drag it into your drawing, the top view of a tree moves with your cursor until you release the mouse button to place it. See Figure 4.73.

If the tree is larger than it should be for the scale of the drawing, you can use the grip editing Scale command to resize it. It will be shown larger here to make it easy to see the effects of the Path Array command.

Tip: *Try some of the other items from the Tool Palettes off the side in your drawing. Right-clicking on many of the items provides a menu that you can use to select different views, or different styles of the object. For example, by right clicking on a tree once it is in your drawing, you can select a deciduous tree or the side view instead of a top view.*

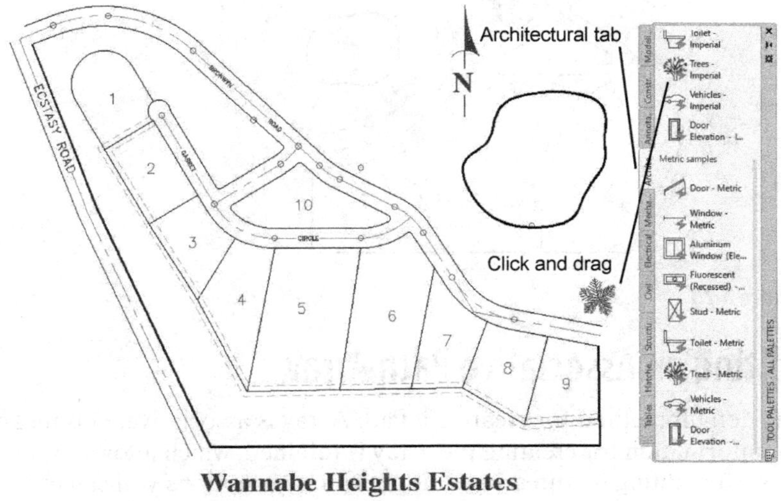

Figure 4.73

On your own, use the **Spline** command to draw a curve that follows along the edge of the road as shown in Figure 4.74.

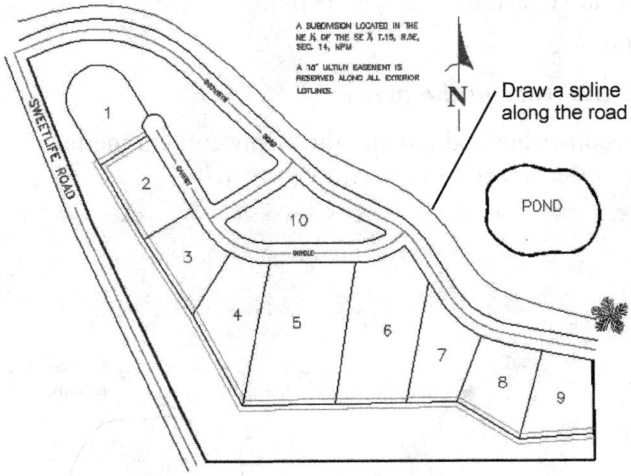

Figure 4.74

Click: ***Path Array*** *from the Home tab, Modify panel*

Select objects: ***click on the tree [Enter]***

Select path curve: ***click on the spline you drew***

Select grip to edit array or [ASsociative/Method/Base point/Tangent direction/Items/Rows/Levels/Align items/Z direction/eXit]<eXit>: ***[Enter]***

The tree is copied along the path curve as shown in Figure 4.75.

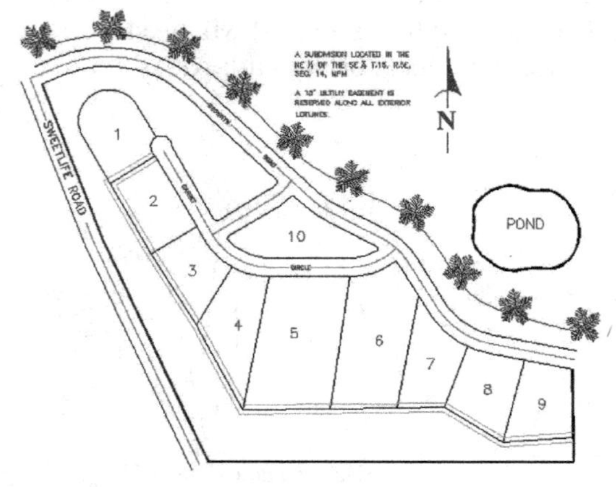

Figure 4.75

Editing an Associative Path Array

The default method for creating a Path Array is associative. This means the information for creating the array is retained, which allows for powerful editing features. In addition to similar options you can use while creating the array, after it is created you can change:

- the starting direction of the path.
- how the array objects are aligned to the path.
- the distance between items.
- how the objects are distributed along the path.
- the number of items.

Click: ***on any of the trees in the array***

The entire array becomes highlighted and the Array context menu appears at the top of the screen as shown in Figure 4.76.

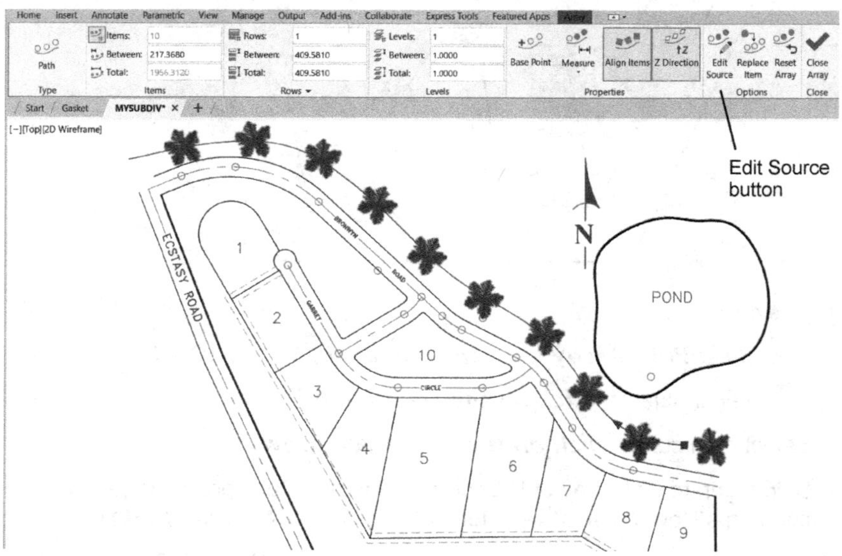

Figure 4.76

The trees are too large in proportion to the path. The scale of the original tree can be changed during array editing using Edit Source without losing the associativity of the array.

Click: ***Edit Source button***

Click: ***on one of the trees***

A message appears on your screen.

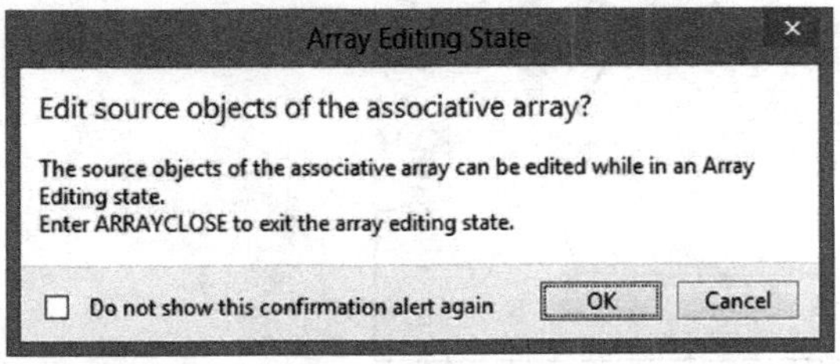

Figure 4.77

Click: ***OK***

You return to your drawing. Now you can edit the original tree.

Click: ***the tree** to show its grips*

Click: ***the central grip** to use as the base grip*

Right-click: ***to show the short-cut menu***

Click: ***Scale***

Specify scale factor or [Base point/Copy/Undo/Reference/eXit]: ***.5 [Enter]***

The trees become half the previous size. To close the array editing state,

Click: ***Edit Array, Save Changes***

Click: ***on any of the trees in the array***

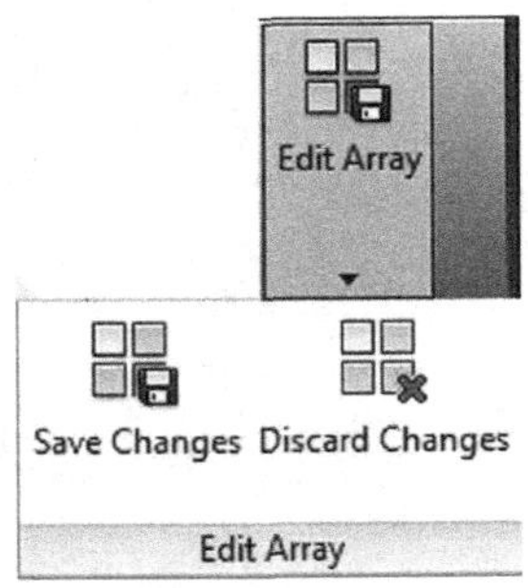

The array becomes highlighted and the Array context menu returns to the screen. Next you will change the method used for determining the item spacing and increase the number of items.

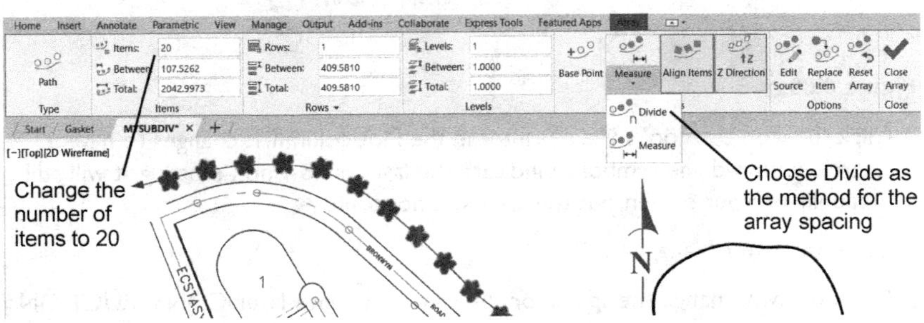

Figure 4.78

Click: ***Divide** as the method for the array spacing*

Type: ***20** into the Items input box (if needed click the icon to its left)*

Click: ***Close Array** from the right of the Array context menu*

The number of items updates to show 20 trees as shown in Figure 4.79.

Tip: *Objects in the array can be aligned tangent to the path. Try the effect of the Align Items button on your own.*

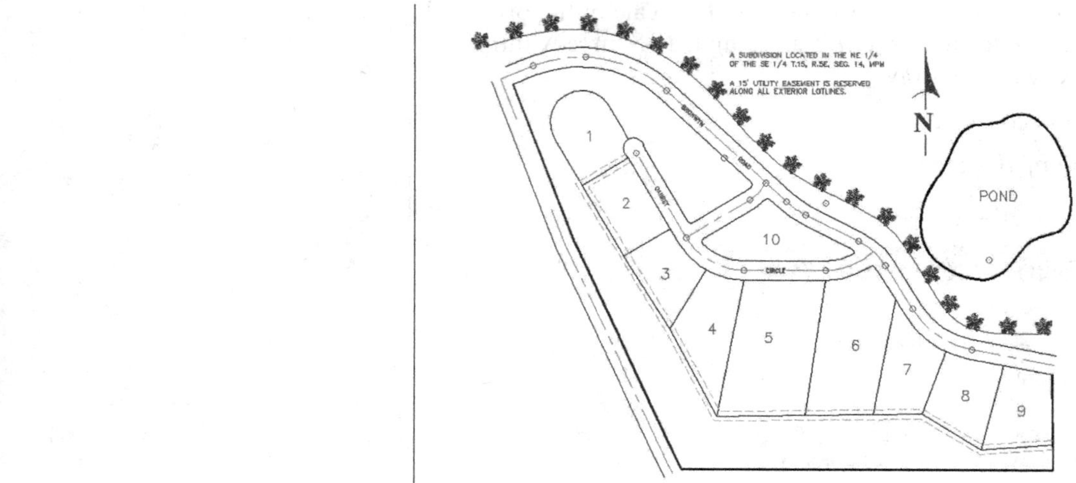

Figure 4.79

You can move the path curve to a separate layer and freeze that layer, or make a non-plotting layer for the path, so that the path doesn't show in the finished drawing. To do this,

Create a new layer named CONSTRUCTION and assign it color magenta–a purplish pink color, and linetype Continuous as shown in Figure 4.80.

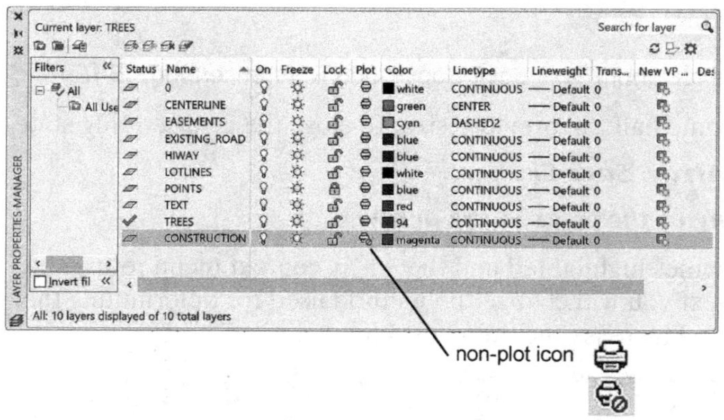

Figure 4.80

Click the icon that looks like a printer in the Plot column. It changes to have a circle with red line symbol to indicate the layer is now non-plotting. It will still appear on your screen, but the layer will not print.

Close the Layer Manager.

On your own, change the spline for the tree array onto layer CONSTRUCTION.

Close the Tool Palette.

Using the Count Command

The Count command quickly counts the instances of drawing, for example the trees in our current drawing. You can also use it to insert a table with the count data into the current drawing.

*Click: **Count** icon from the View tab, Palettes toolbar*

The Count palette appears on your screen as shown in Figure 4.81. You can select from objects in model space or click items listed in the Count palette to count the identified objects in the current drawing. The only objects which have multiple instances in the open drawing are the trees, so notice they are already listed. If they were not, you could enter "*tree*" in the search box or click on one.

*Click: **Tree - Imperial** from the Count palette*

Notice that the Count toolbar now shows at the top of the drawing area as shown in Figure 4.82. The Count toolbar includes the number of objects, in this case 20 (no surprise since that is how many you put in). Other controls let you step through the items or insert the counted number into the drawing. This command can be very handy when you must order the number of items based on the information in a complex drawing.

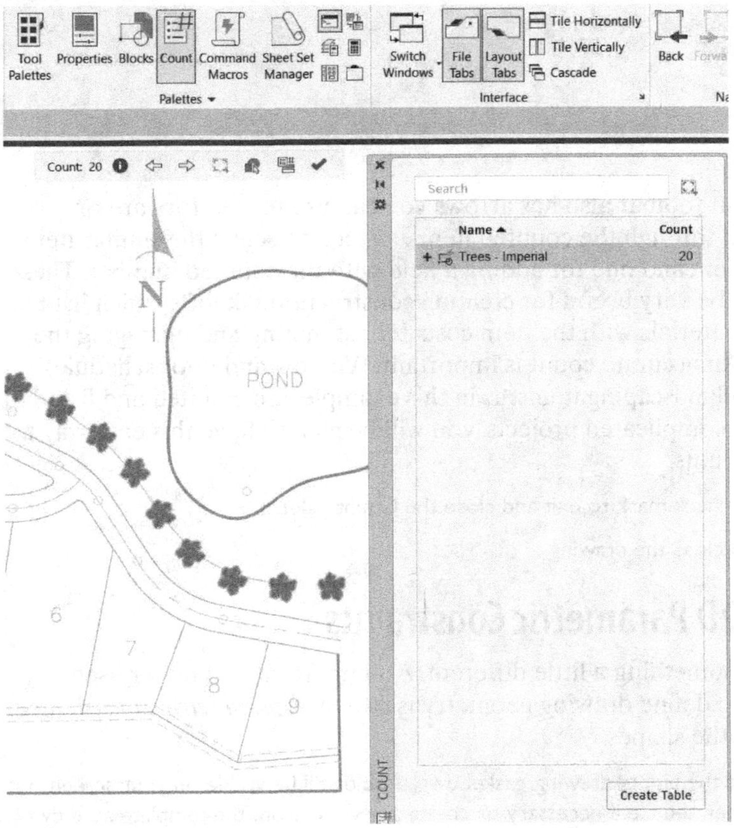

Figure 4.81

Figure 4.82

The *Countarea* command prompts you to box in an area in which to count the items. You can select if from the icon to the right of the count search bar, or from the Count toolbar.

*Click: **Countarea** icon from the Count toolbar*

Specify first corner point of the count area or [Current area/Entire model space/Object/Polygonal] <Current area>: ***click 2 points to define the corners of a box enclosing some of the trees***

The count updates to show the number of items in the selection, in this case 7. You can close the count area using the check mark at the end of the count toolbar, which closes the toolbar and exits the countarea, or you can enter the comment *Countareaclose.*

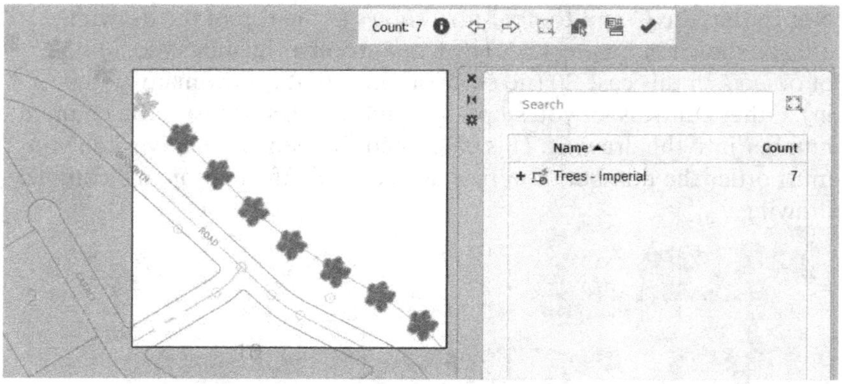

Figure 4.83

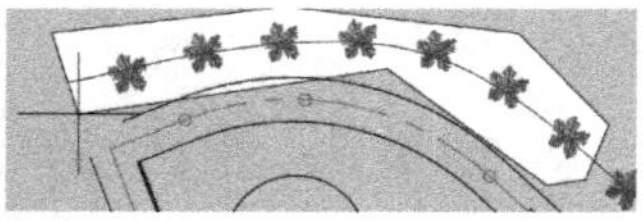

Tip: *Countarea also has a Polygonal option that lets you specify an irregular shape. Select it from the prompt, Specify first corner point of the count area or [Current area/ Entire model space/Object/ Polygonal] <Current area>: by typing* ***P*** *[Enter] This will show Specify start point: where you can start enclosing the shape to count within.*

The Count toolbar also has arrows you can use to step forward or backward through the counted items, an icon to select the similar items in the count, and one for adding a field with the counted number. These tools can be very useful for creating construction takeoffs which list the project materials with the item costs for estimating and managing the project. An accurate count is important. Window and door schedules, and even landscaping items, as in this example, are counted and listed in detail. In complicated projects, you will be glad to have this easy way to get the counts.

Use the check mark to exit and close the Count palette.

Save and close the drawing.

Using 2D Parametric Constraints

Now for something a little different. An important and under used method to define drawing geometry is to assign *parametric constraints* to define the shapes.

The tab for the empty drawing, gasket.dwg, should still be visible on your screen. If it is not, reopen the file if necessary or create a new file from the template acad.dwt and name it gasket.dwg.

Figure 4.84

Next you will draw the gasket shown in Figure 4.85 and use parametric constraints to define its geometry.

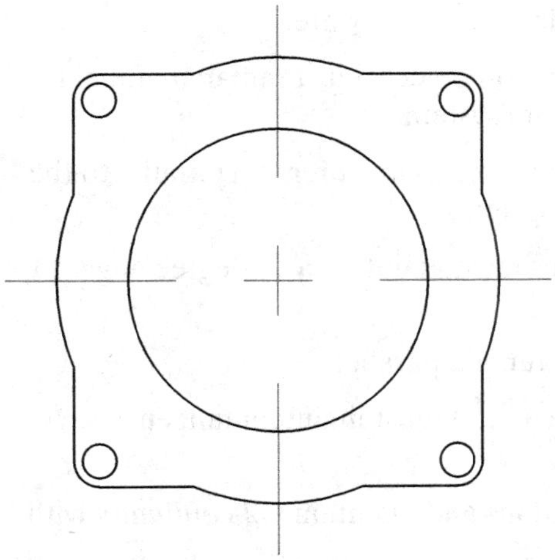

Figure 4.85

First, draw the general shapes for the gasket. The lines do not have to be perfectly straight, in fact, it is easier to see the effects of adding constraints if the drawing is not perfect.

On your own, use a **polyline** to draw the four connecting lines, making sure to use the **Close** option to connect the final segment to form a closed polyline. Add the circles and two lines that will become the centerlines. Something like Figure 4.86 will work just fine.

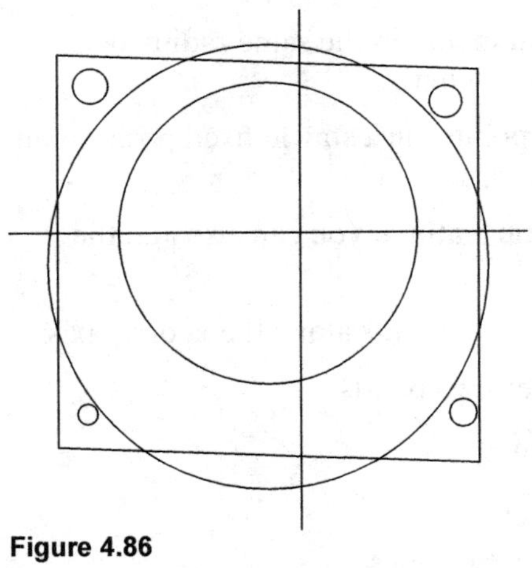

Figure 4.86

Click: ***Parametric tab***

The ribbon changes to show the parametric tools as shown in Figure 4.87

The Parametric tab is located on the ribbon. You can click and drag to reorder the tabs. Don't change them for now or your screen will not match the instructions. If a tab is not shown, you can right-click: in the ribbon, and choose Show tabs, then check the ones to show.

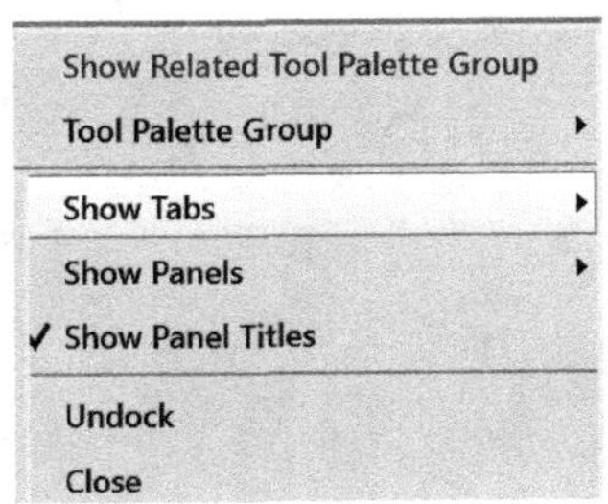

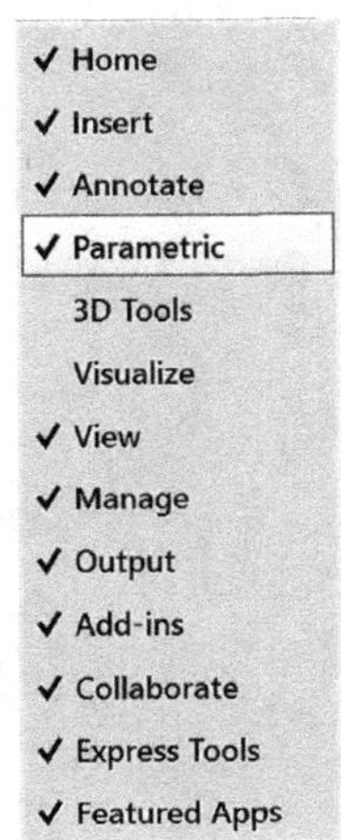

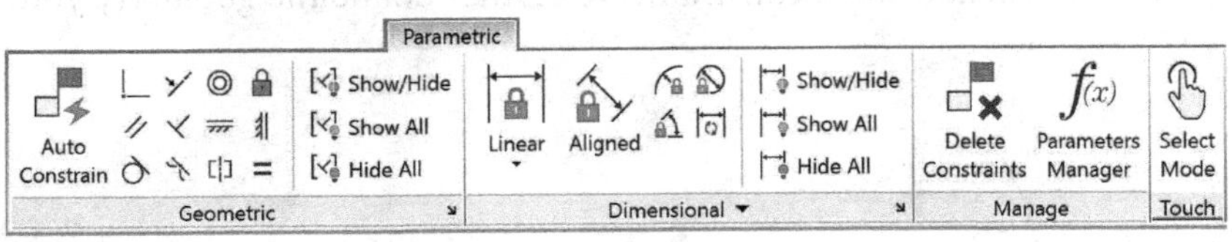

Figure 4.87

The constraints available for defining geometry are:

Horizontal: lines or pairs of points on objects must remain parallel to the X axis of the current coordinate system.

Vertical: lines or pairs of points on objects must remain parallel to the Y axis of the current coordinate system.

Perpendicular: two selected lines must maintain a 90 degree angle to one another.

Parallel: two selected lines must remain parallel.

Tangent: two curves (one can be a line) must maintain tangency to each other or their extensions.

Smooth: a spline must be contiguous and maintain *G2 continuity* with another spline, line, arc, or polyline.

Coincident: two points must stay connected or a point must stay connected to a curve or line (or its extension).

Concentric: two arcs, circles, or ellipses must maintain the same center point.

Collinear: two or more line segments must remain along the same line.

Symmetric: two selected objects or points must remain symmetric about a selected line.

Equal: selected arcs and circles must maintain the same radius, or selected lines must maintain the same length.

Fix: points, line endpoints or curve points must stay in fixed position on the coordinate system.

In addition to constraining geometric features, you can also add the following size constraints.

Linear: specifies a distance between two points along the x- or y- axis.

Aligned: specifies a distance between two points.

Radius: specifies the radius for a curve.

Diameter: specifies the diameter of a circle.

Angular: specifies the angle between two lines.

Convert: You can also convert dimensions placed with the software's dimensioning commands (Tutorial 7) into dimensional constraints.

Check that your software is not automatically adding constraints. While this can be useful, first try adding them yourself so you can see the results.

Next, you will add some constraints to further define the geometry you have drawn.

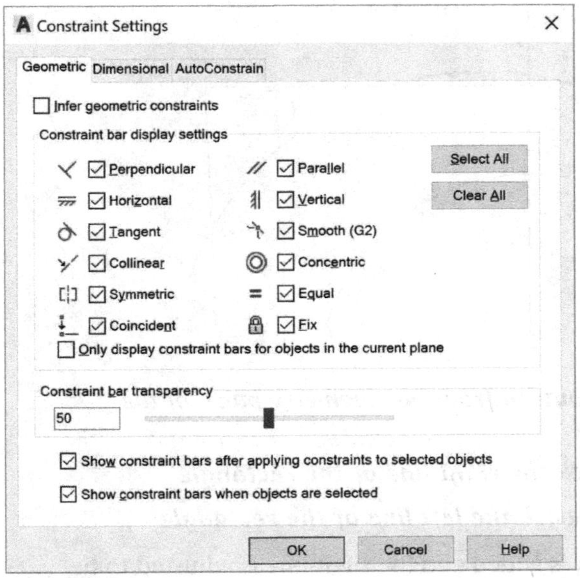

Figure 4.88

Click: ***downward arrow near the Geometric palette title to show the Constraint Settings dialog box.***

On your own, make sure that Infer geometric constraints is **not** selected. Then **close** the dialog box.

Next you will add some constraints to define the drawing geometry.

Click: ***Horizontal button*** *from the Geometric palette of the Parametric tab*

Select an object or [2Points] <2Points>: ***click the top line of the roughly rectangular shape*** *(see Figure 4.89)*

The line changes to be horizontal (if it was not already). The constraint marker for horizontal, which looks similar to the button appears along the line in the drawing as shown in Figure 4.89. Each segment of the polyline can be constrained individually.

Click: ***Perpendicular***

Select first object: ***click the left line*** *of the rectangular shape*

Select second object: ***click the top line*** *you constrained to horizontal*

The perpendicular constraint marker appears in the drawing and the lines adjust to become perpendicular.

On your own, select the polyline so that its grips appear. **Use grip editing** to move the vertices of the polyline. Notice that these lines now maintain the constrained relationships. When you are finished testing, press [Esc] to unselect the polyline. If you made any changes, use **Undo** to restore the original appearance.

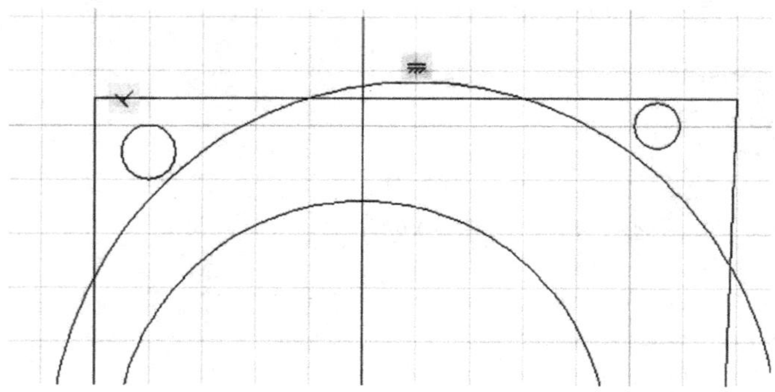

Figure 4.89

Tip: *If your lines do not stay connected like shown, you may not have created a closed polyline. If so, try adding a Coincident constraint to connect the endpoints of the lines.*

Click: ***Parallel button*** *from the Geometry panel of the Parameters tab*

Select first object: ***click the right line of the rectangle***

Select second object: ***click the left line of the rectangle***

The parallel constraint is added and the right line is adjusted to be parallel to the left one.

Tip: *If you do not get the result you are expecting, try selecting the items in the opposite order. When using constraints that create a relationship between two objects, the order of selection can make a difference. Generally the first object selected remains fixed and the second object selected adjusts to maintain the relationship. As more constraints are added, these relationships become more complex and the objects must satisfy a set of constraints.*

On your own, add a **perpendicular** constraint between the bottom line and the right line of the rectangle.

Add a **vertical** constraint to the line that will act as a vertical centerline.

Add a **horizontal** constraint to the line that will act as a horizontal centerline.

Your drawing should be similar to Figure 4.90. It may not be exactly the same depending on your first sketched shapes. Next you will make the rectangle symmetric about the centerlines you drew.

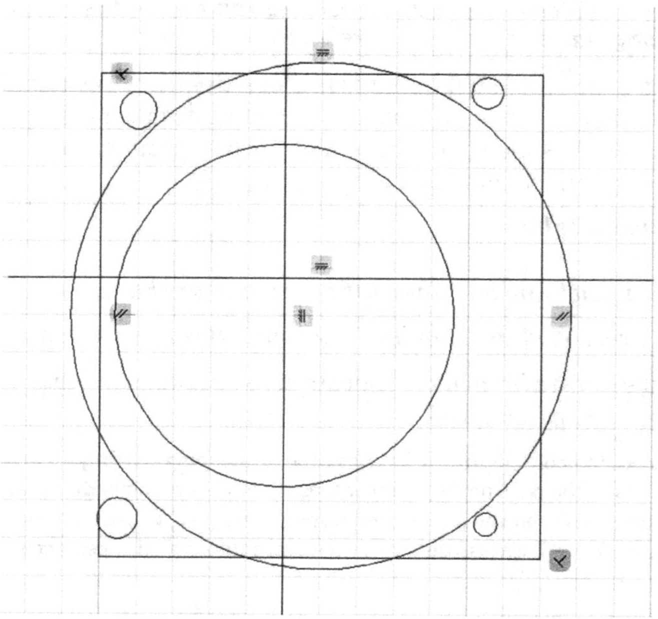

Figure 4.90

Click: ***Symmetric button*** *from the Geometry panel of the Parameters tab*

Select first object: ***click the right line of the rectangle***

Select second object: ***click the left line of the rectangle***

Select symmetry line: ***click the vertical centerline***

The drawing adjusts so that the lines are equal distance from the vertical centerline.

Click: ***Symmetric button*** *from the Geometry panel of the Parameters tab*

Select first object: ***click the upper line of the rectangle***

Select second object: ***click the lower line of the rectangle***

Select symmetry line: ***click the horizontal centerline***

The drawing adjusts again to satisfy this constraint condition. Next you will make the center of the smaller circle coincident with the vertical centerline.

Click: ***Coincident button*** *from the Geometry panel of the Parameters tab*

Select first point or [Object/Autoconstrain] <Object>: ***click the outer circle***

Select second point or [Object] <Object>: ***click the vertical centerline***

In the previous steps, selecting the circle automatically finds its center as the point to make coincident as shown in Figure 4.91.

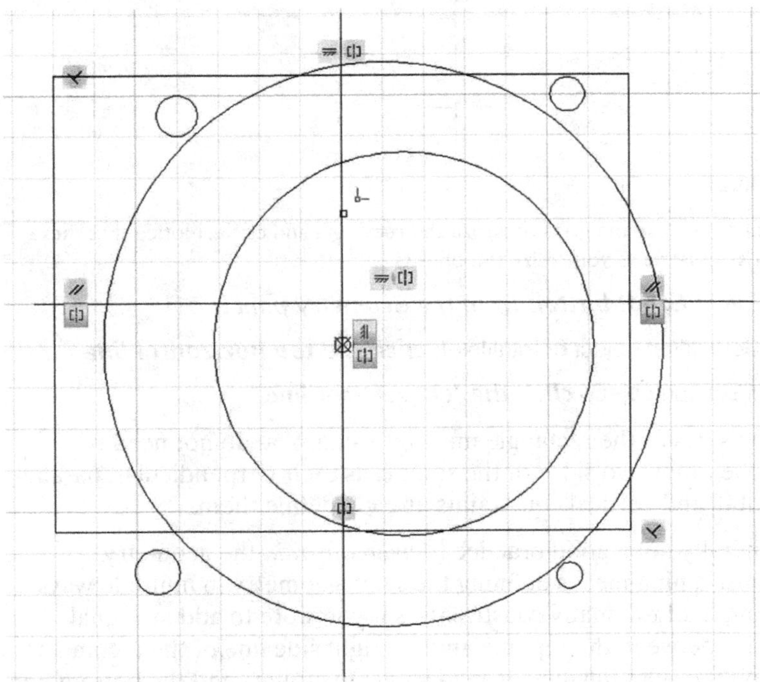

Figure 4.91

On your own, make the same circle center **coincident** with the horizontal centerline.

Tip: *You can drag the constraint markers to position them out of the way of your drawing objects.*

Tip: *Positioning the cursor over an object will highlight all of the constraint markers that apply to that object.*

Tip: *The Equal constraint provides an option that allows you to select multiple objects to make equal to the first. To use it, pick the Equal constraint button and enter M at the prompt.*

Click: ***Concentric button*** *from the Geometry panel*

Select first object: ***click the inner circle***

Select second object: ***click the outer circle***

Now your drawing should look similar to Figure 4.92. The smaller circles are still unconstrained, so they may be in different locations. Also the size of the rectangles and circles are not fixed.

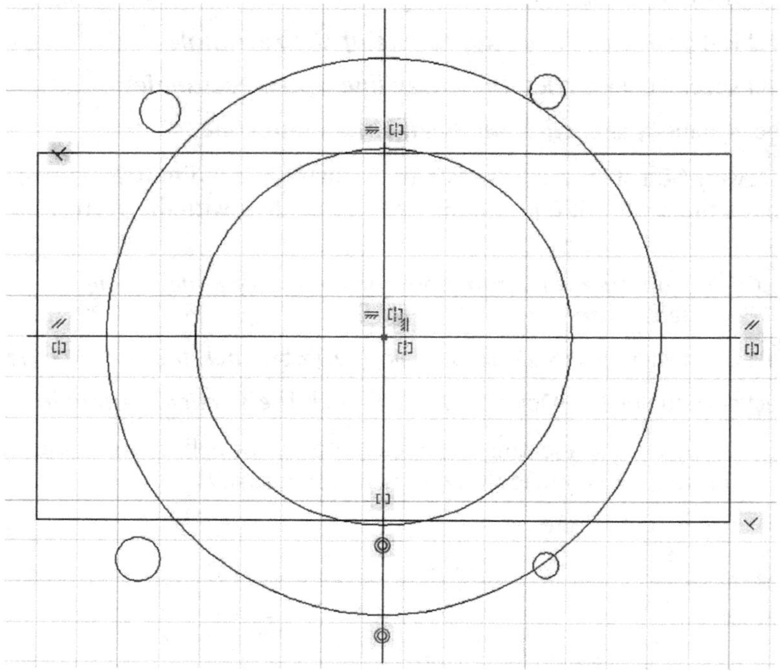

Figure 4.92

On your own, use the grips to resize the rectangle and circle. Notice that these stay symmetric as you resize the objects.

Click: ***Equal button*** *from the Geometry panel*

Select first object or [Multiple]: ***click the top horizontal line***

Select second object: ***click the left vertical line***

Now the sides of the rectangle must be equal. You do not need to define the other two sides of the square, as their perpendicular, parallel, horizontal, and vertical constraints already define them.

It is generally not a good practice to *overconstrain* the geometry. Overconstraining means defining the same geometry in multiple ways. An example of too many constraints is if you were to add an Equal constraint between the top line and the right side line of the rectangle. Based on the sides having perpendicular constraints and the bottom line being parallel to the top one, the left side length must be equal to the length of the right side, which has already been defined equal to the top.

Next you will constrain the size of the outer circle and the square.

Click: ***Linear*** *from the Dimensional panel of the ribbon Parametric tab*

Specify first constraint point or [Object] <Object>: ***click the left endpoint of the upper horizontal line***

Specify second constraint point: ***click the right endpoint of the upper horizontal line***

Specify dimension line location: ***click above the line to place the dimensional constraint [Enter]***

The value for the linear dimension constraint shows. In this example Dimension text = 6.8014. You may have a different value. Next add a diameter dimension for the circle.

Click: ***Diameter from the Dimensional panel of the ribbon Parametric tab***

Select arc or circle: ***click on the outer circle***

Specify dimension line location: ***click to place the dimension [Enter]***

Dimension text = 7.3891 *(You may see a different value)*

Figure 4.93 shows the drawing with these dimensional constraints added. Your values may be different.

Click: ***Parameters Manager button***

The Parameters Manager appears on your screen as shown in Figure 4.93. The two dimensional constraints you added are shown there.

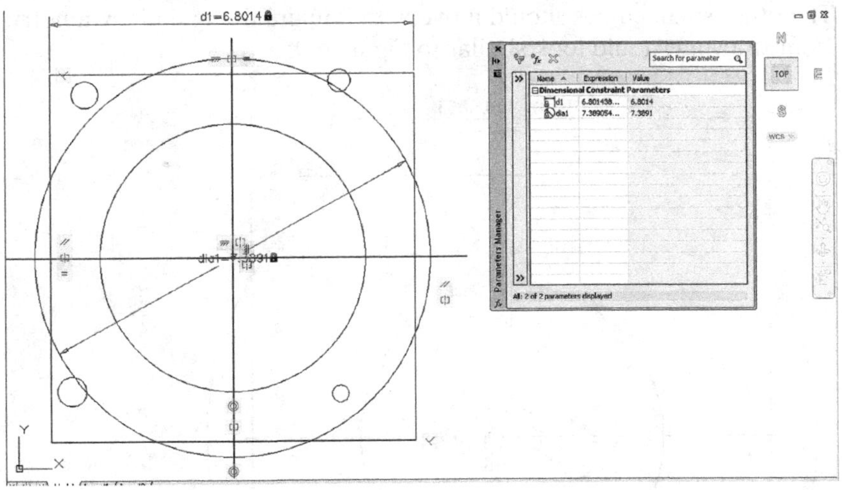

Figure 4.93

You can use mathematical expressions to define dimensional constraints. You can also type values and have the drawing geometry update to match the value.

Click: ***in the input box in the Expression column*** *across from the d1 linear dimension value*

Type: ***dia1*.85*** *as shown in Figure 4.94 (if your dimension parameters are identified differently use the ones for your drawing)*

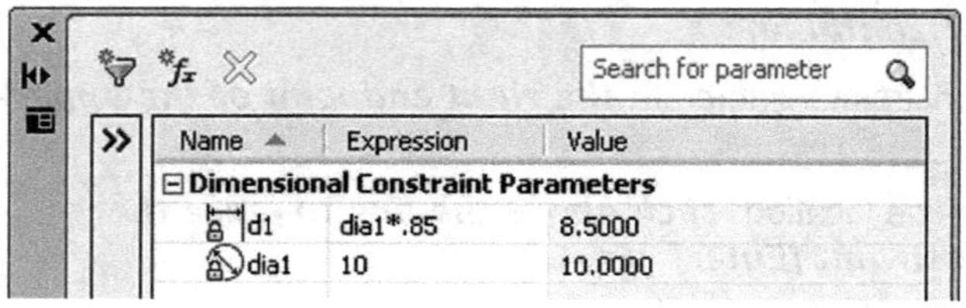

Figure 4.94

Now the size of the square is based on the size of the circle.

Double-click: ***on the diameter dimensional constraint in your drawing*** *(or you can type the value in the Parameters Manager)*

Type: ***10 [Enter]*** *for the circle diameter value*

The drawing automatically updates to the new size. Notice that the linear dimension for the square is now 8.5.

On your own, add **Equal** constraints to the four small circles.

Add a **Symmetry** constraint to the upper two circles using the vertical centerline as the symmetry line. Do the same for the two lower circles.

Next, add a **Symmetry** constraint to the two circles at the left using the horizontal line as the symmetry line. **Drag the upper left circle** into the upper left corner of the square, outside the circle. **Save** your drawing.

The other small circles should move with it maintaining their symmetry. Your drawing should look similar to Figure 4.95.

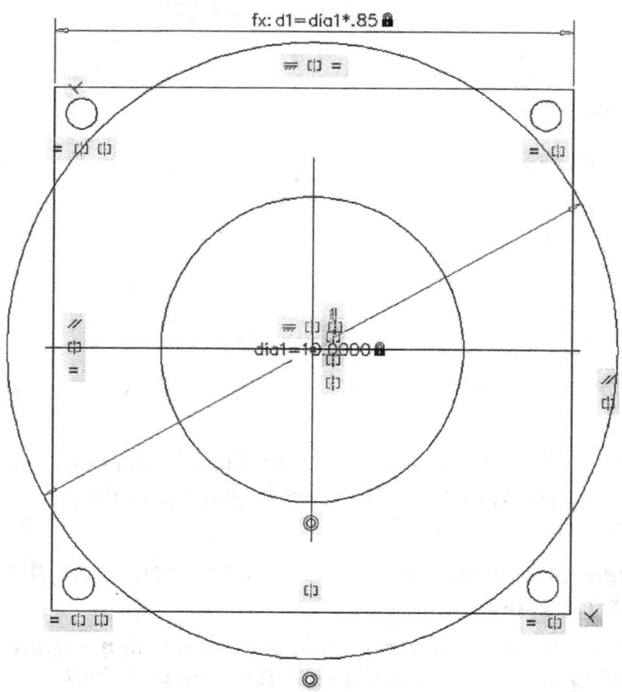

Figure 4.95

On your own, use the Fillet command, with a Radius of .5 and the Polyline option to add rounded corners to the square.

Trim the circle and square.

Notice that this changes the constraints. As the geometry changes, some of the constraints no longer apply and are deleted automatically.

Click: ***Autoconstrain*** *from the Geometry panel of the Parameters tab*

Select objects or [Settings]: ***use a window to select the entire drawing [Enter]***

The software has automatically applied constraints it infers might be useful for the shape you have drawn.

To delete a constraint you simply need to click on the constraint symbol and click the X that appears in its corner to eliminate it. If you are unsure which symbol is which, hovering your mouse over the symbol will show its tool tip (see Figure 4.96).

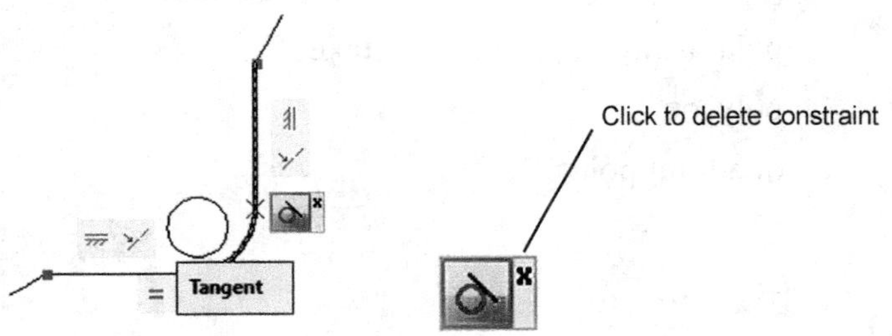

Figure 4.96

Experiment on your own. Use the grips to resize some of the drawing objects.

How does it behave differently than the version you constrained in the tutorial?

Add constraints and dimensions until the shape updates as you think best when you click and drag the top arc to reshape the gasket.

Save your drawings or exit without saving your changes if you do not want the most recent versions of the drawings saved.

Your final drawing should look similar to Figure 4.97.

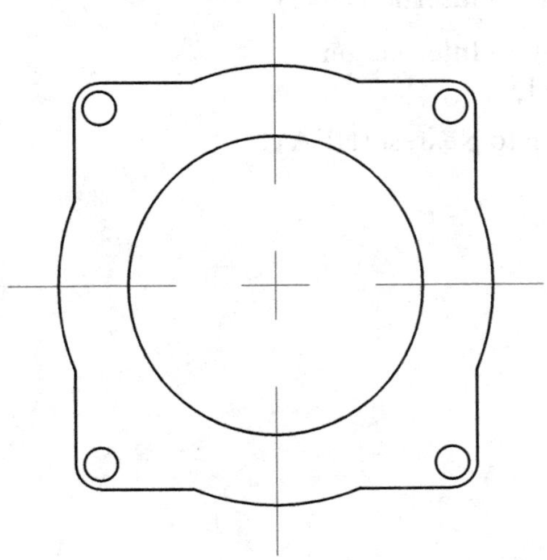

Figure 4.97

You have completed Tutorial 4.

Parametric constraints will not be used in the following tutorials. As you work through the tutorials, follow the directions so that you will get the results shown in the figures. Keep in mind geometric and dimensional constraints are very useful tools.

Close the tool palettes and toolbar and exit the AutoCAD software.

Key Terms

associative
base grip
circumscribed
distance across the flats
global linetype scaling
factor
G2 continuity
grips
inscribed
mirror line
noun/verb selection
parametric constraint
polar array
polygon
quadrant point
rectangular array
selection filters
takeoffs

Key Commands (keyboard shortcut)

Array (AR)
ARRAYPOLAR
Break (BR)
CELTScale
Construction Line (XL)
Copy Object (CP)
Count
Countarea
Countareaclose
Extend (EX)
FILEDIA
GRIPS
Linetype (LT)
Line Type Scale (LTS)
Mirror (MI)
Move (M)
Polygon (POL)
Quick Select (QSELECT)
RAY
Rotate (RO)
Scale (SC)
Snap From (FROM)
Snap to Apparent Intersection (APPINT)
Snap to Center (CEN)
Snap to Endpoint (ENDP)
Snap to Extension (EXT)
Snap to Insertion (INS)
Snap to Intersection (INT)
Snap to Nearest (NEA)
Snap to Node (NOD)
Snap to Parallel (PAR)
Snap to Perpendicular (PER)
Snap to Quadrant (QUA)
Snap to Tangent (TAN)
Stretch (S)

Exercises

The letter M after an exercise number means that the given dimensions are in millimeters (metric units). If no letter follows the exercise number, the dimensions are in inches. Don't include dimensions on the drawings.

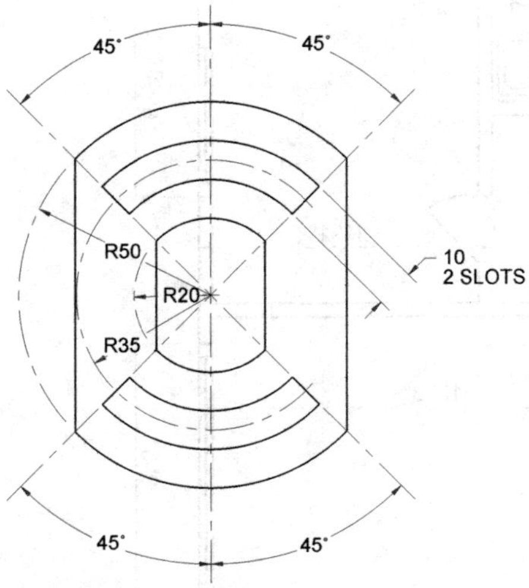

Exercise 4.1M Gasket

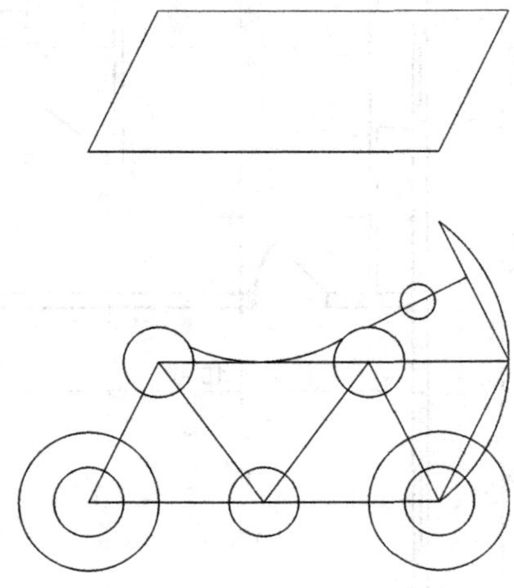

Exercise 4.2 The Cycle

Starting with the parallelogram shown, use Object snaps to draw the lines, arcs, and circles indicated in the drawing. Use parametric constraints if directed by your instructor.

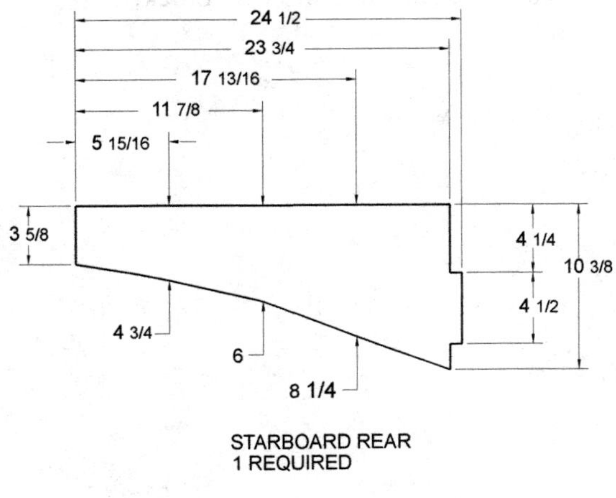

Exercise 4.3 Starboard Rear Rib

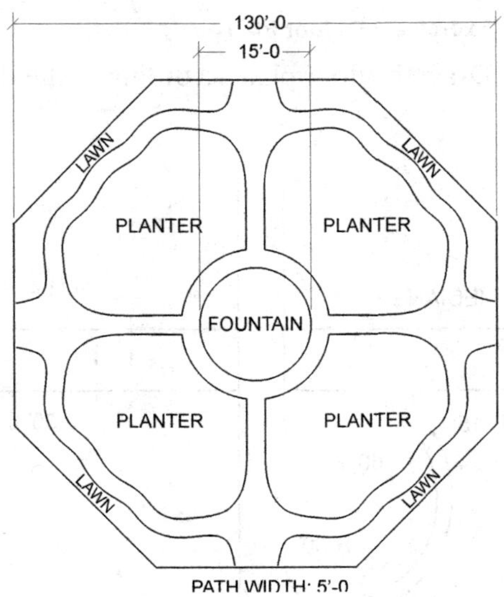

Exercise 4.4 Park Plan

Create a park plan similar to the one shown here. Use Polyline and Polyline Edit, Spline to create a curving path. Note the symmetry. Add labels with Single line text.

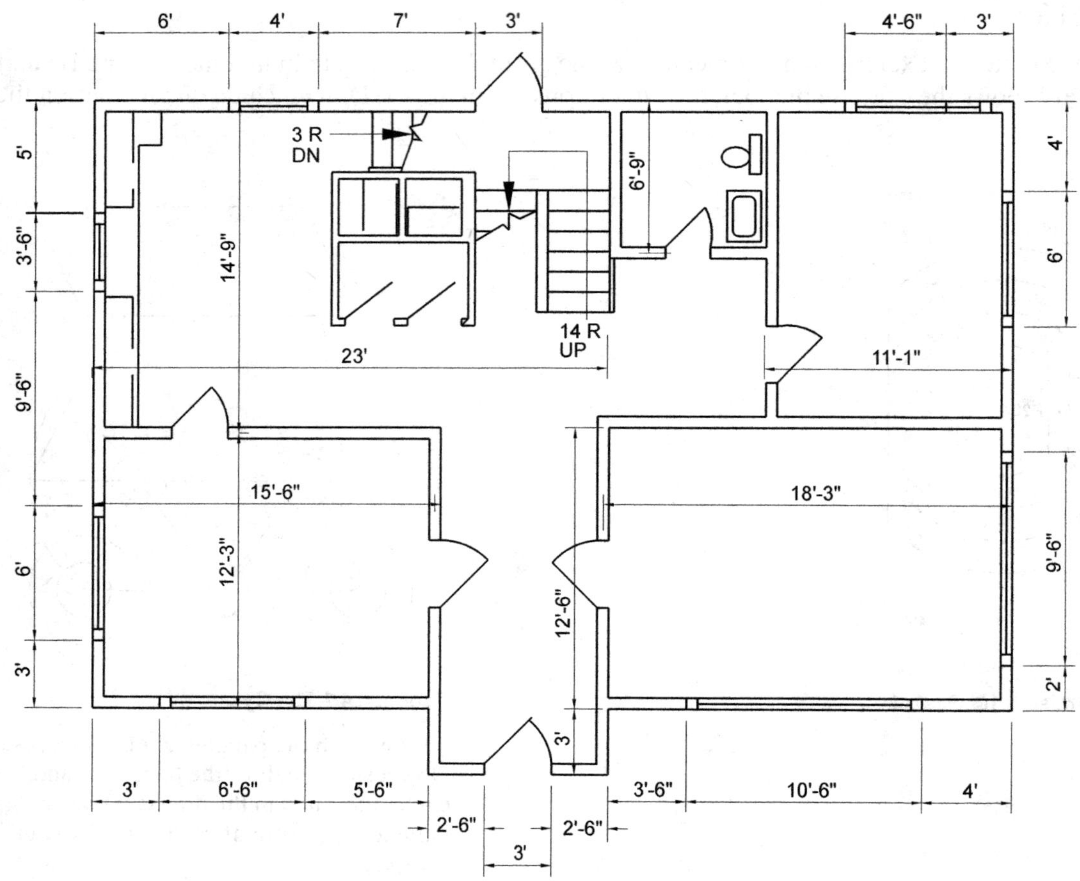

Exercise 4.5 Floor Plan

Draw the floor plan according to the dimensions shown. Add text, border, and title block.

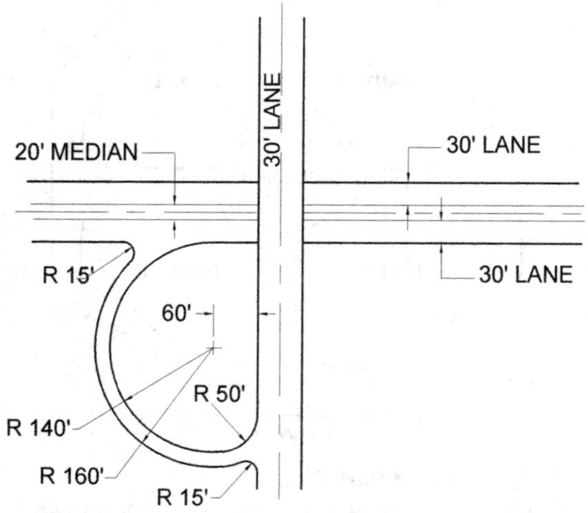

Exercise 4.6 Interchange

Draw this intersection, then mirror the circular interchange for all lanes to create a clover-leaf ramp pattern.

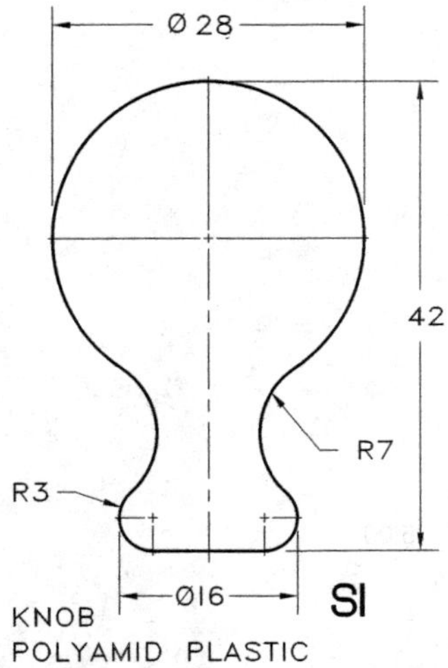

Exercise 4.7M Plastic Knob

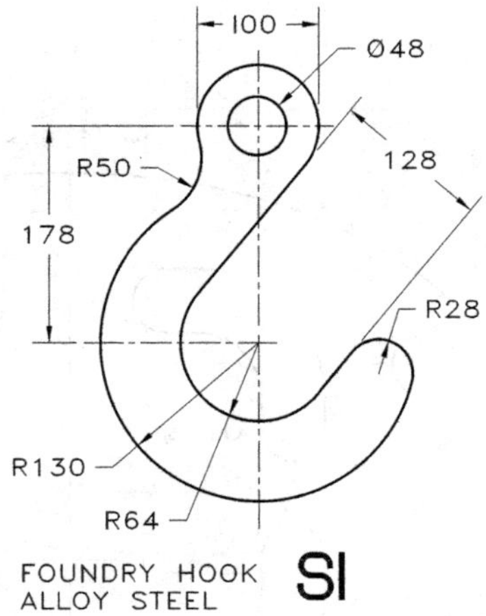

Exercise 4.8M Foundry Hook

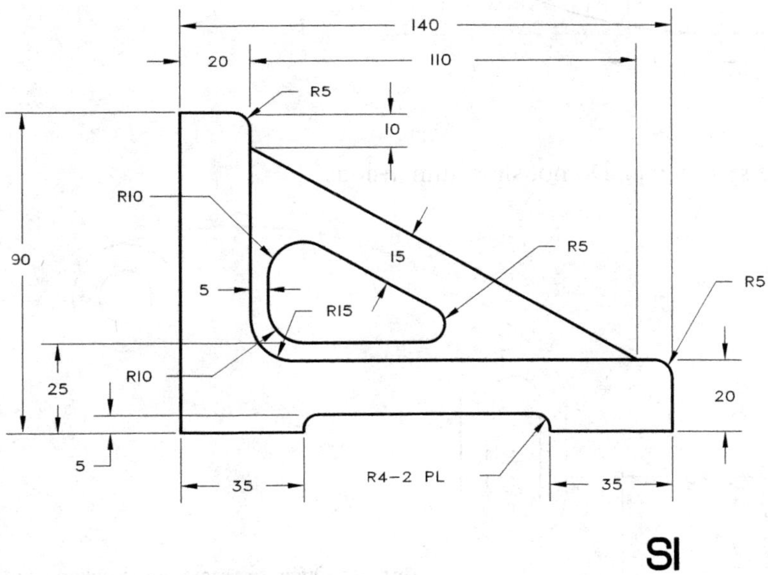

Exercise 4.9M Support

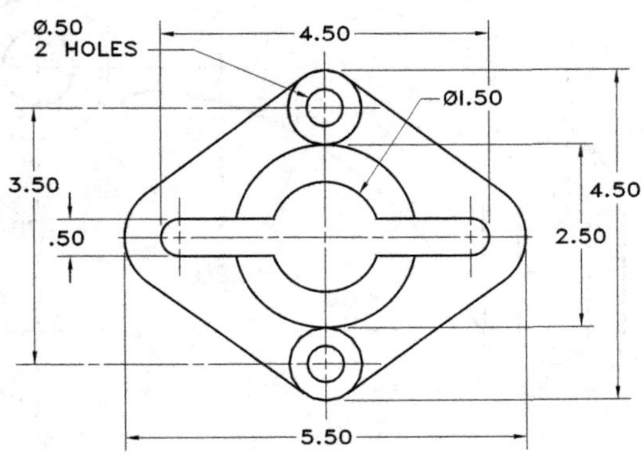

Exercise 4.10 Hanger

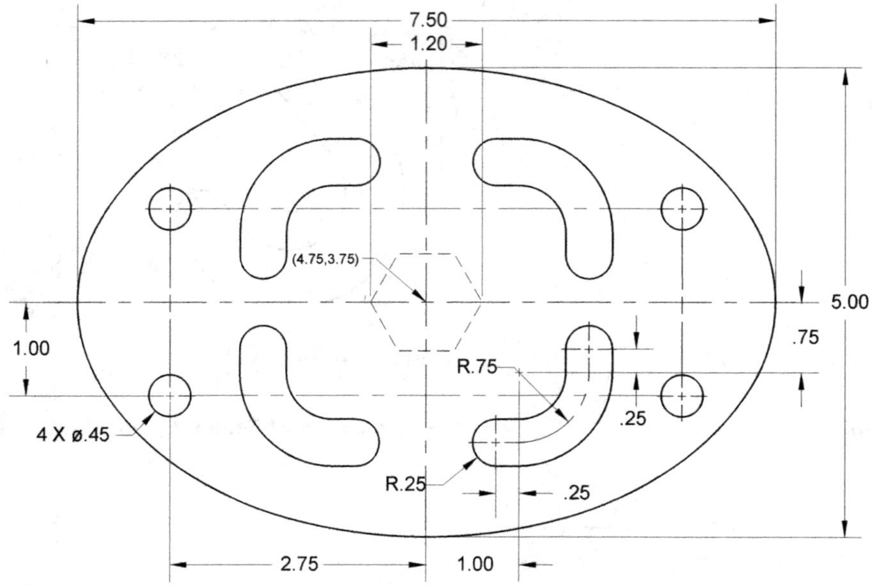

Exercise 4.11 Slotted Ellipse

Draw the figure shown (note the symmetry). Do not show dimensions.

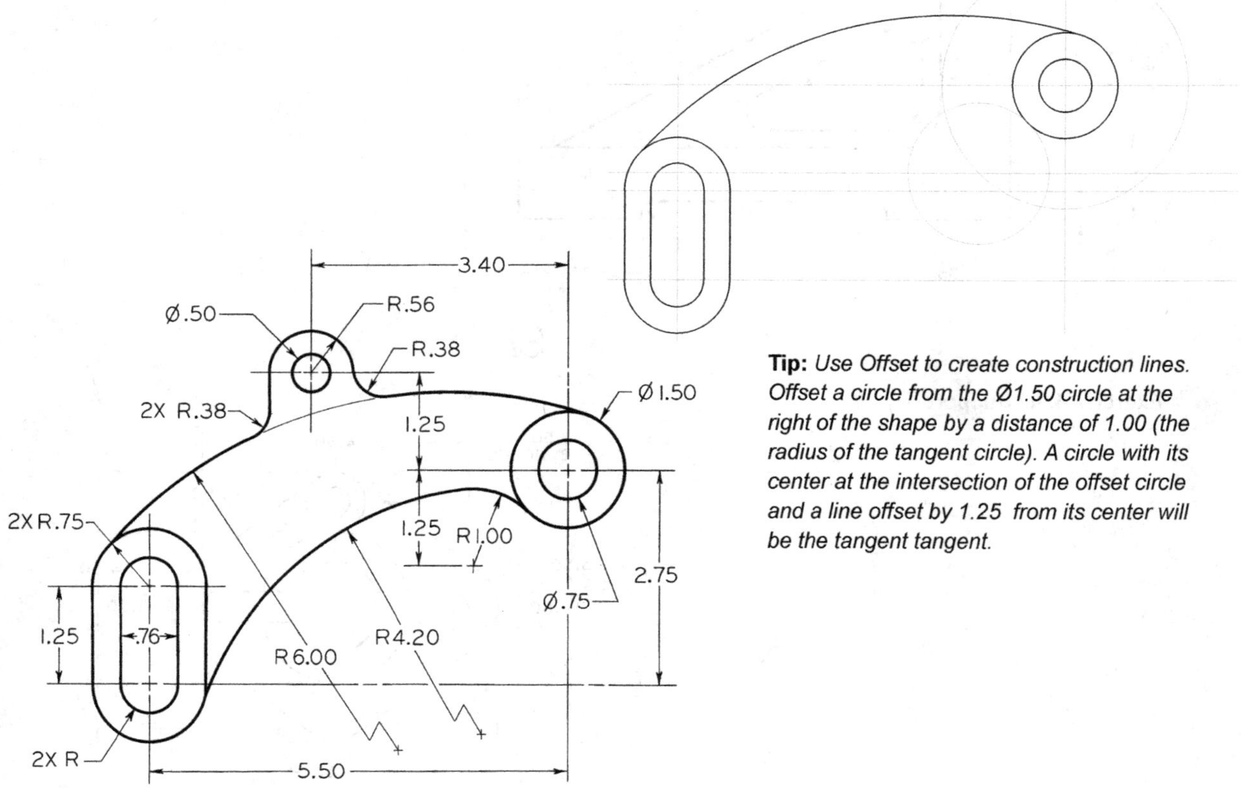

Tip: *Use Offset to create construction lines. Offset a circle from the Ø1.50 circle at the right of the shape by a distance of 1.00 (the radius of the tangent circle). A circle with its center at the intersection of the offset circle and a line offset by 1.25 from its center will be the tangent tangent.*

Exercise 4.12 Shift Lever

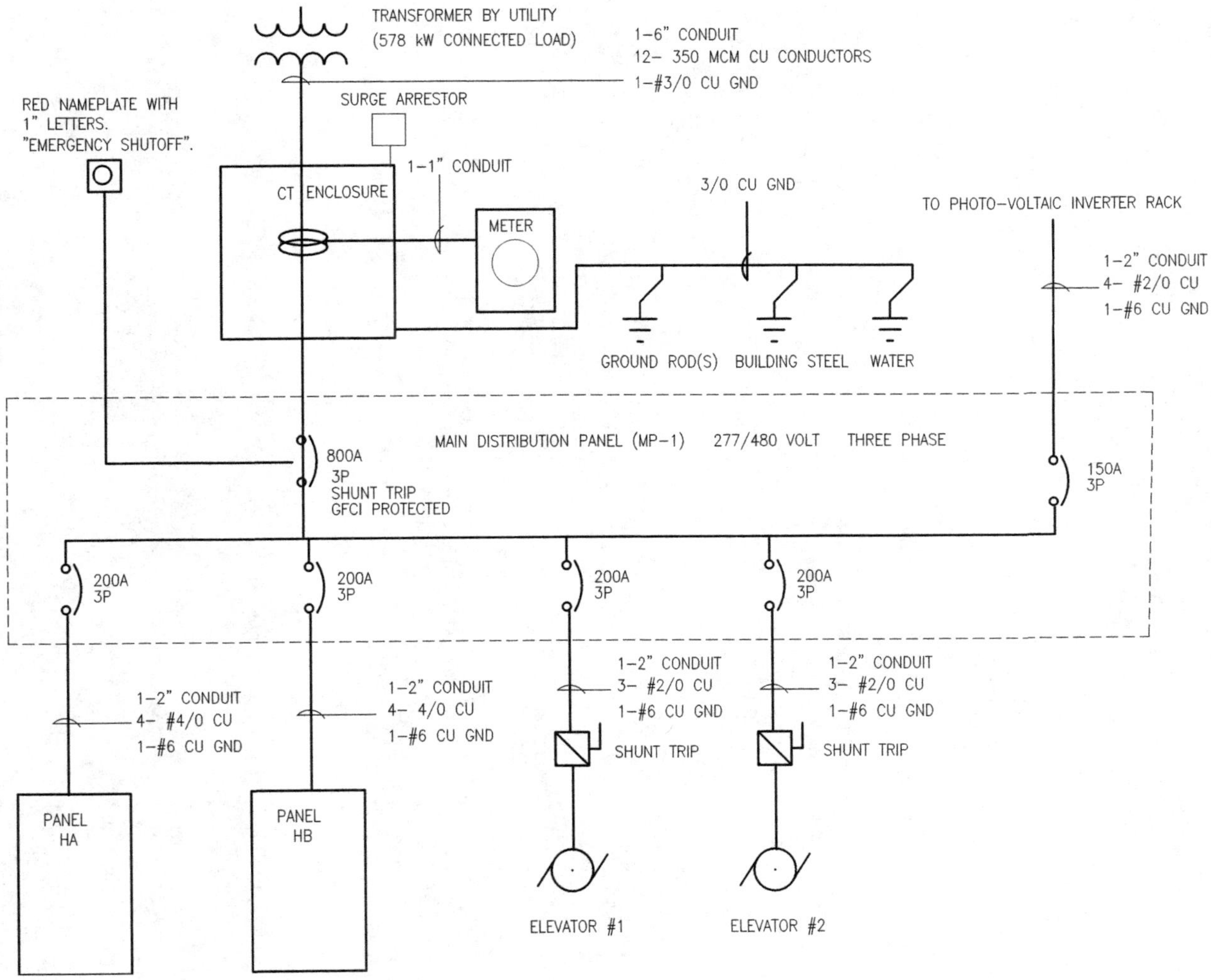

Exercise 4.13 Building Electrical Block Diagram

TEMPLATE DRAWINGS AND MORE PLOTTING

5

Introduction

One of the advantages of using AutoCAD is that you can easily rescale, change, copy, and reuse drawings. Up to this point, many drawings you created began from a drawing called *acad.dwt*. In *acad.dwt*, many variables are preset to help you begin drawing. A drawing in which specific default settings are saved for later use is called a *template*. You can save any drawing as a template from which to start a new drawing.

You may want to create different template drawings to use for different sheet sizes and types of drawings. In this tutorial you will use a template for a C-sized sheet (22" X 17") to arrange views of the subdivision drawing for easy plotting. You will also make a drawing template containing default settings of your own from which you will start 8.5" X 11" drawings in succeeding tutorials.

Using template drawings eliminates repetitive steps and helps you work efficiently. The amount of time you spend creating one template is roughly the amount of time you will save on each subsequent drawing you start from that template.

You will use paper space *layouts* to add views of your model space drawing as you want it to appear on the printed sheet. Using paper space layouts allows you to have more than one printed sheet format for a single model space drawing. You will also insert the *mysubdiv.dwg* into a new drawing as a *block* and use the settings there to plot it to scale.

Starting

Before you begin, launch the ***AutoCAD 2027*** *program.*

Using a Standard Template

Figure 5.1

You will create a new drawing using a standard AutoCAD template file: the ANSI-C template with color-dependent plot styles. This is set up to plot on a 22" X 17" sheet of paper following guidelines from the American National Standards Institute (ANSI/ASME). It will be used to demonstrate features you can use to lay out plotted sheets.

Click: ***small downward arrow to the right of New to expand options***

Click: ***Browse templates...***

Objectives

When you have completed this tutorial, you will be able to

1. Use a template drawing for standard sheet sizes.
2. Insert a drawing into another drawing as a block.
3. Zoom drawing views to scale for plotting.
4. Create and save a template drawing for later use.
5. Create a system of basic layers for mechanical drawings.
6. Use layer groups and filters.
7. Preset Viewres, Limits, and other defaults in a template drawing.
8. Set up paper space layouts in a template drawing.
9. Set the style for drawing points.
10. Use the Divide command.
11. Plot drawings using a layout.
12. Create a Sheet Set.

Note that the file extension from the pull-down at the bottom of the dialog box is set to *.dwt*. This is the template format.

The Select Template dialog box changes to show the template selections.

> *Use the Look in area to select the **SheetSets folder** as shown in Figure 5.1*

The templates stored in the SheetSets subfolder of the default template location (set using the Files Tab of the Options dialog box) are listed alphabetically. You should see a list similar to that shown in Figure 5.2.

Tip: *To change the default template directory pick Application icon, Options, select the Files tab, and change the setting under Drawing Template File Location. To see the setting, pick the + (plus sign) to expand the list under Drawing Template Settings and the items below it. You can use the Browse button at the right of the dialog box and click to select a new folder.*

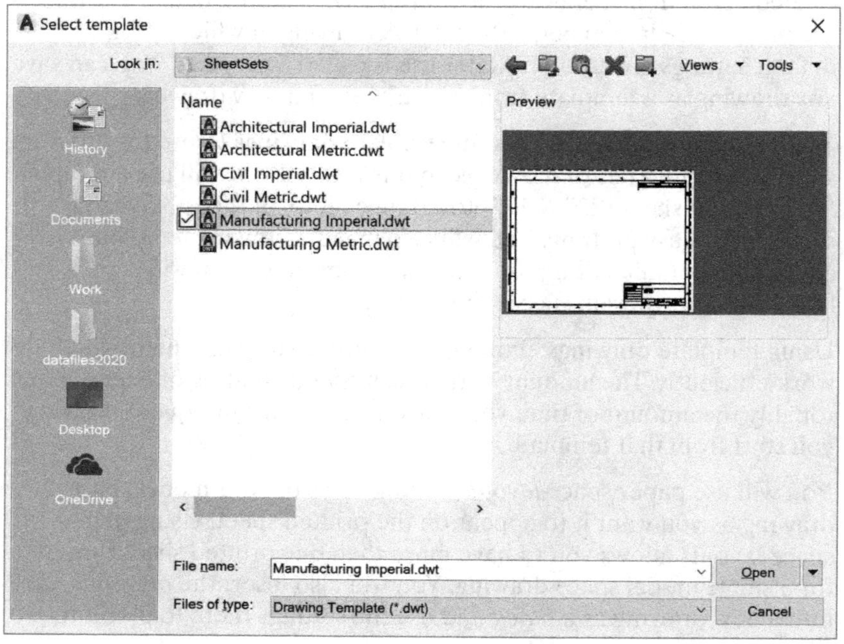

Figure 5.2

> *Click: **Manufacturing Imperial.dwt** from the list of available templates*
>
> *Click: **Open** (or double-click the file name)*
>
> *Double-click: the **mouse scroll wheel** to zoom to the extents of the drawing.*

A new drawing should appear on your screen with a border and standard title block for a C-sized sheet. You will save it with a new name to your *work* folder.

> *Click: **Save button***
>
> *Type: **Subd_Plot** as the file name to save*

The file name Subd_Plot should show in the AutoCAD title bar. Notice that when you save a drawing created from a template it does not overwrite the template file. You supply a new name. This way you will not accidentally change your template file. Your screen should look similar to Figure 5.3.

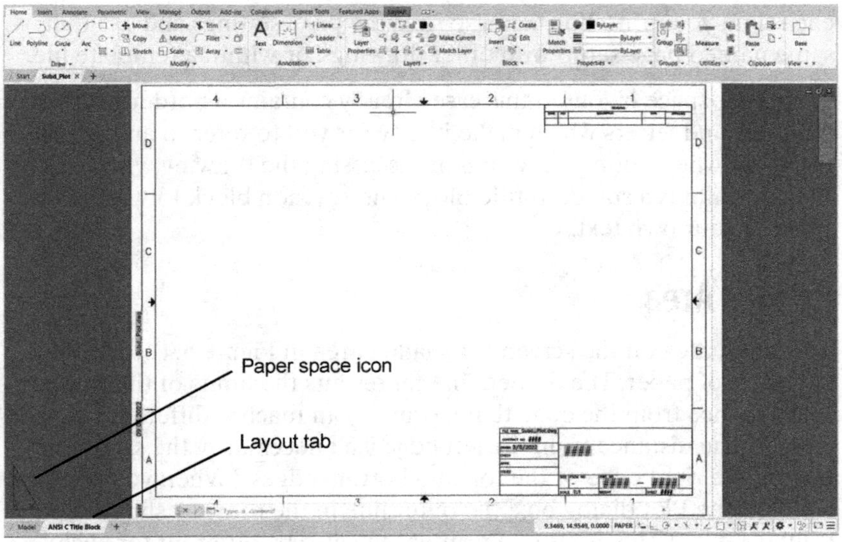

Figure 5.3

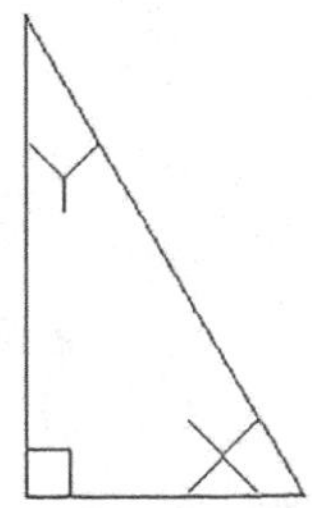

Paperspace icon

Paper Space Layouts

Using paper space layouts allows you to arrange views of your drawing as on a "sheet of paper." A *paper space layout* is used for things like borders, title blocks, text notes, and viewports. (A viewport is like a window that you can look through to see your model space drawing on the sheet of paper.)

Up to this point you have been working in *model space* to create your drawing geometry. As you have already seen in Tutorial 3, you can plot your drawing from model space if desired. A better method is to use paper space layouts to control the appearance of your plotted drawing.

The UCS icon now shows the paper space icon, which looks like a triangle. Also the ANSI C Title Block layout tab appears next to the Model tab on the status bar as shown in Figure 5.3.

Figure 5.4 illustrates the concept of using paper space layouts and model space drawings.

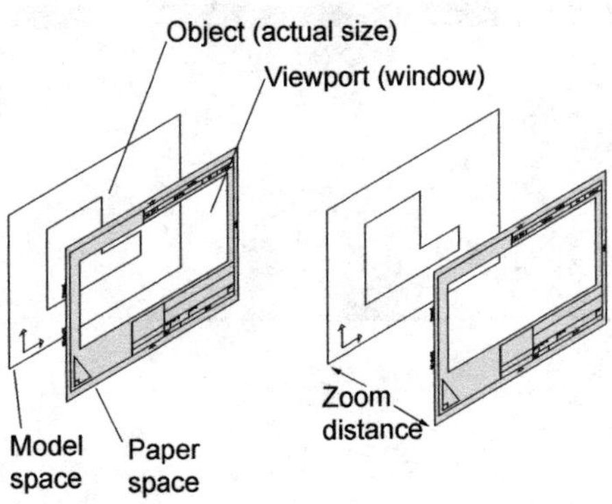

Figure 5.4

Page settings are used to control the plotter each time you plot the drawing. This way you do not have to reset the plotter requirements each time you print. You can also save the page settings and use that same named page setup with other drawings, or within a template file.

The paper space layout in this case already contains a border with zone numbers and letters which make it easy for you to refer to an area on the sheet when noting a revision or discussing the drawing with a client. It also contains a standard title block and revision block to which you can add your own text.

Printer Area

The white area on the screen (or shaded area in Figure 5.4) represents the sheet of paper. The dashed line represents the limits of the printer. The distance from the edge that a printer can reach is different for each printer. The distance from the left edge isn't necessarily the same as it is from the right edge or the top and bottom edges. (When you preview a plot in the Plot dialog box, the outer line in the preview shows the printer limits.) The limits of a printer may also be different for each sheet size.

Tip: *With the layout tab selected, the Layer Properties Manager shows the following additional columns:*
VP Freeze *freezes the selected layer only in the current layout viewport. (Layer frozen or turned off in the drawing can't be thawed in only the current layout viewport.)*
VP Color *overrides the color for the selected layer in the current layout viewport.*
VP Linetype *overrides the linetype for the selected layer in the current layout viewport.*
VP Lineweight *overrides the lineweight for the selected layer in the current layout viewport.*
VP Transparency *overrides the transparency for the selected layer in the current layout viewport.*
VP Plot Style *overrides the plot style for the selected layer for the current layout viewport (not used when the visual style is set to Conceptual or Realistic, which you will learn more about in the 3D tutorials).*

For now, just keep in mind that you can use viewport overrides for the layer color and other properties when in the layout. This can be handy for printing drawings where colors, like yellow, which are easy to see on a black screen aren't visible on white paper.

Viewport

The template you selected does not contain any viewports. A viewport is like a hole through the paper that you can look through to see model space.

Next, you will create a viewport on a new layer named Viewport. You will set the color for the layer to magenta, so that it stands out on your screen.

Click: ***Layer Properties icon***

The Layer Properties Manager appears on your screen. You will use it to create a new layer named Viewport, with the color magenta, and give it a non-plotting status as shown in Figure 5.5.

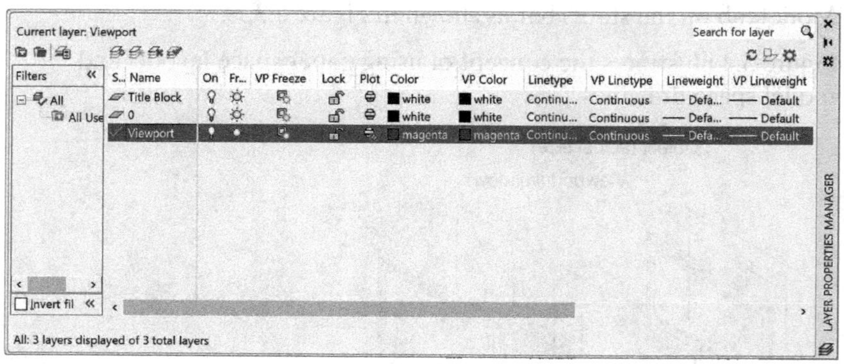

Figure 5.5

Click: ***New button***

Type: ***Viewport***

Click: ***the color box corresponding to layer Viewport***

Click: ***magenta*** *from the top row of standard colors*

*Click: **the icon in the Plot column row** associated with layer Viewport, so that the icon changes to a printer with a red crossed-circle to set it to non-plotting*

*Double-click: **Viewport** layer to set it current*

*Click: **[X]** from the upper left of the dialog box to close the Layer Properties Manager*

Tip: *Often you do not want to plot the actual viewport objects as they would appear as a box around the view. To do this, you can make the Viewport layer non-plotting. On your screen you will still see the objects, but you will notice later that this layer will not plot. This can also be useful for notes, construction lines and other information you want to show, but would not want to plot.*

Creating a Viewport

Next you will use the Vports command from the ribbon Layout tab, Layout Viewports panel to create a polygonal viewport (Figure 5.6). Paper space viewports can be irregular shapes. You will draw this one to match the inside border of the C-sized title block.

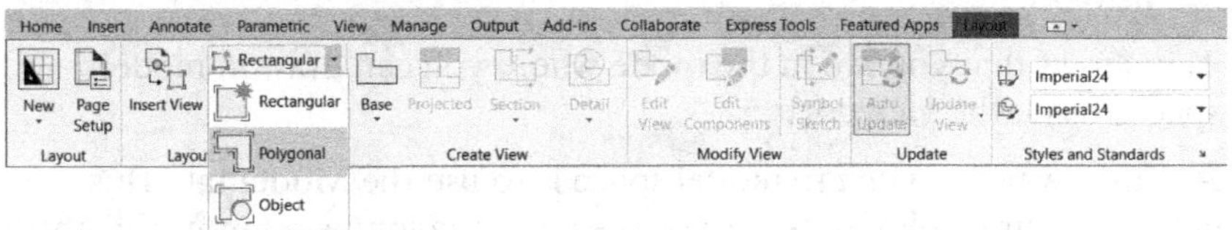

Figure 5.6

On your own, turn on **Object Snap Endpoint** for the next steps.

*Click: **Polygonal** from the Layout tab, Layout Viewports panel*

Specify start point: ***click point 1 as shown in Figure 5.7***

Specify next point or [Arc/Length/Undo]: ***click points 2-8 in order***

Specify next point or [Arc/Close/Length/Undo]: ***C [Enter]***

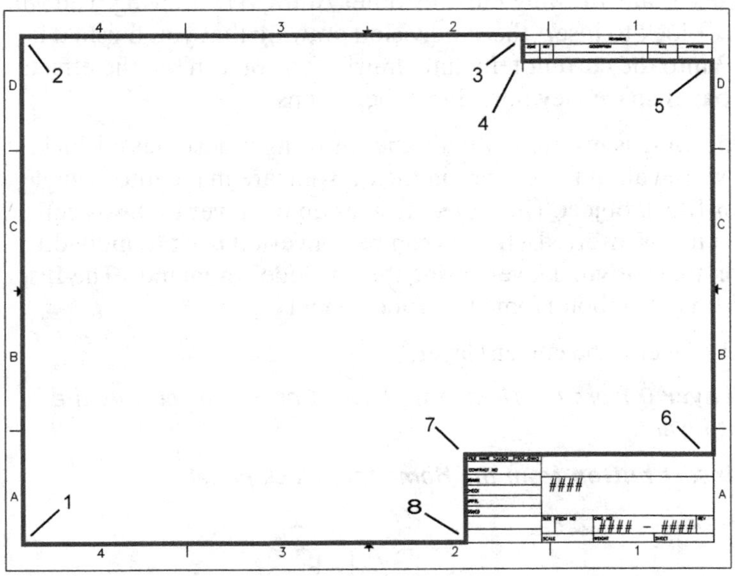

Figure 5.7 **Drawing the Viewport**

You should now see the magenta lines that make up the viewport. This viewport allows you to access your model space drawing from paper space.

Switching to Model Space

To access model space inside a viewport, you can double-click inside the viewport. To return to the paper space layout, double-click outside of the viewport area. You can also type the alias MS at the command prompt to switch to model space. Type PS to switch back to paper space. Next, switch to model space,

Double-click: ***anywhere inside the viewport***

The viewport border becomes highlighted. The paper space icon no longer shows on the screen.

Move your cursor around on the screen to notice that the crosshairs display while inside the viewport, but the pointer shows when you move outside the viewport.

This shows that you are in the mode where you can draw in model space, inside the viewport.

The Model tab

Another way to switch to model space is to use the Model tab. This changes your display so that the paper space layout is temporarily not visible. Often this is a useful way to work on your drawing.

Click: ***the Model tab*** *from below the drawing area*

The screen appears blank as you do not have a drawing created yet. You no longer see the title block and border.

Inserting an Existing Drawing

You can insert any drawing into any other AutoCAD drawing. You will use Insert Block to insert the subdivision drawing that you finished in Tutorial 3 into the current template drawing so you can see the effects of using paper space viewports in the next steps.

When a drawing is inserted into another drawing it becomes a Block. In other words, all of the objects in the drawing are made into a single symbol or Block object. This object resides on the layer that was current when it was inserted. (Blocks can be converted back to individual objects on their original layers using the Explode command.) The Insert button is on the ribbon Home tab, Block panel.

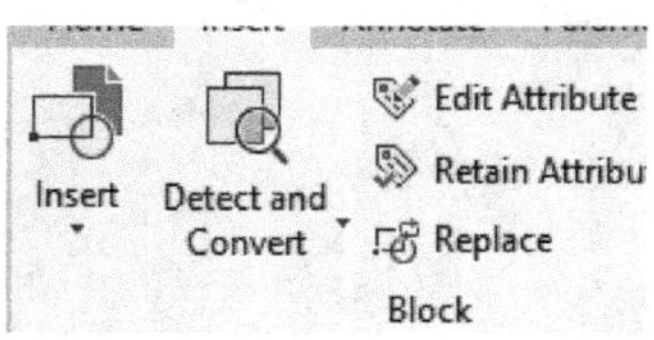

First, make layer 0 the current layer.

Click: ***Layer 0*** *from the Home tab, Layer Control to set it as the current layer*

Click: ***Insert button*** *from the Home tab, Block panel*

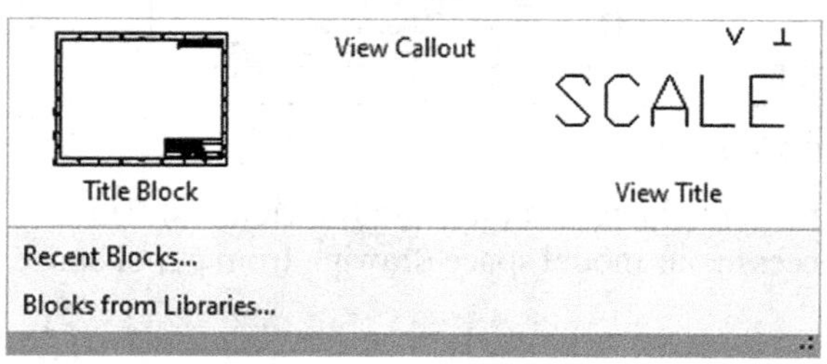

Figure 5.8

Click: ***Blocks from Libraries*** *from the bottom of the panel*

The Select Drawing File dialog box appears on your screen as shown in Figure 5.9. You will use *mysubdiv.dwg* you created in Tutorial 3.

Change to the folder where *mysubdiv.dwg* ***is saved.***

Click: ***Views*** *to expand the drop down list. On your own, try the various choices and return the selection to Thumbnails.*

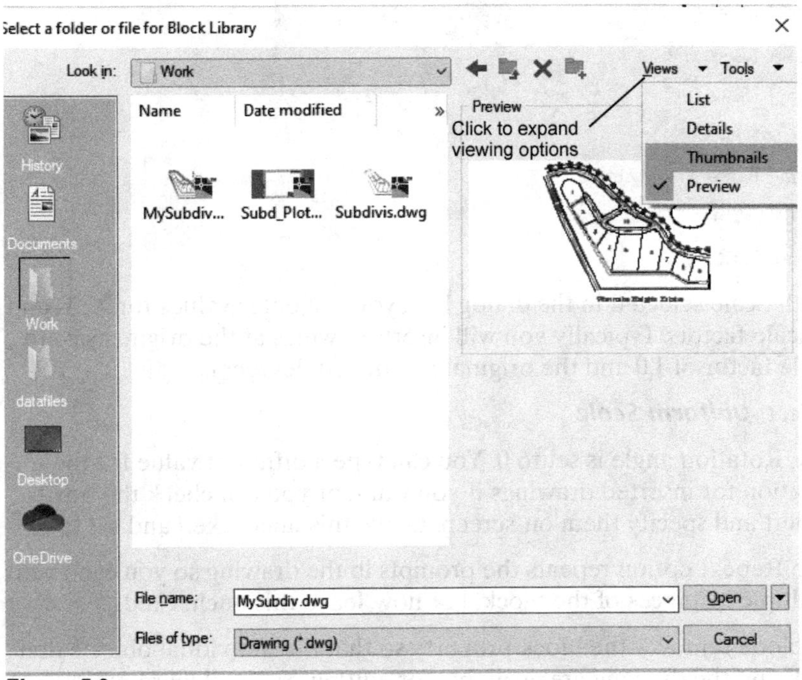

Figure 5.9

Click: ***mysubdiv.dwg***

Click: ***Open***

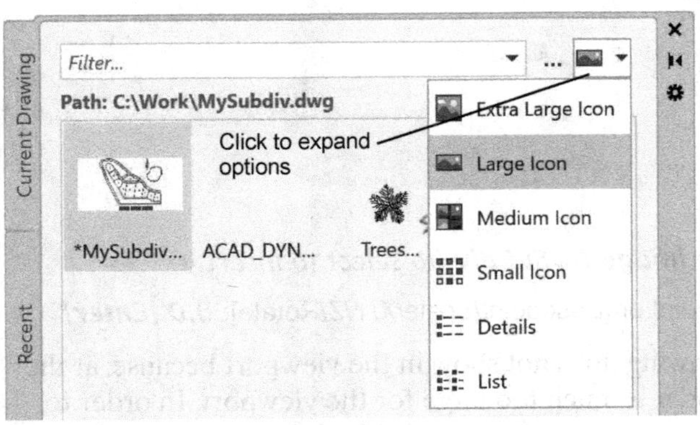

Figure 5.11

Click: ***to expand the list options***

On your own, try the various choices and then return the selection to Large icon.

Tip: *If you have not completed mysubdiv.dwg from Tutorial 3, use the datafile subdiv2.dwg instead. It will not be complete, but you will be able to see the effect of the commands.*

Note: *The Select Drawing File dialog box only opens the first time you select the Insert button. After that, the Blocks panel will already be open on your screen as shown in Figure 5.10. To show the Select Drawing File dialog box from the Block panel, use the drop down menu and choose Browse Block Libraries.*

Click: ***Browse Block Libraries*** *from the drop down list*

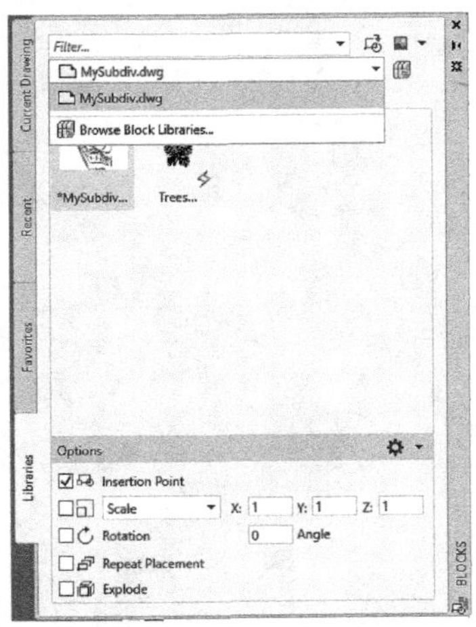

Figure 5.10

Note the check to the left of the Insertion Point under the Insert Options at the bottom of the Blocks panel. If there is no check, click the box now. This means you will return to your drawing to select the point where the subdivision drawing will be inserted.

The Scale option is set to Uniform Scale of 1. To show more options,

Select: ***Scale** by clicking to expand the choices below Uniform Scale*

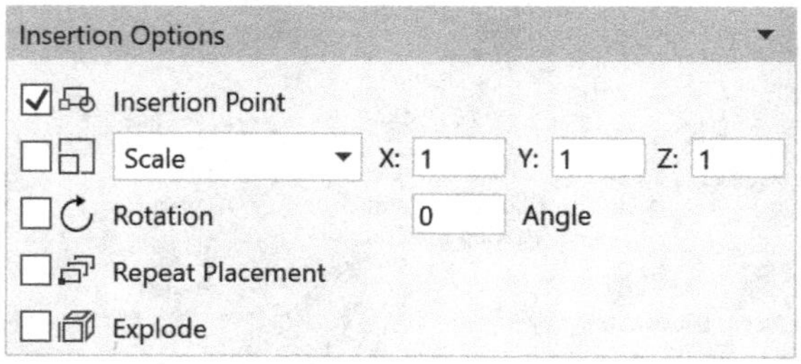

Figure 5.12

With Scale selected in the dialog box, you can enter values for X, Y, and Z scale factors. Typically you will insert drawings at the original size (a scale factor of 1.0 and the original rotation, 0-degrees).

Select: ***Uniform Scale***

The Rotation angle is set to 0. You can type a different value for the rotation for inserted drawings if you want, or you can check the box to its left and specify them on-screen. Leave this unchecked and set to 0.

The Repeat option repeats the prompts in the drawing so you can insert multiple instances of the block. For now, leave this unchecked.

Explode removes the block property so that the individual objects that make up the drawing are available for editing. You will learn more about exploding later. For now, leave this unchecked.

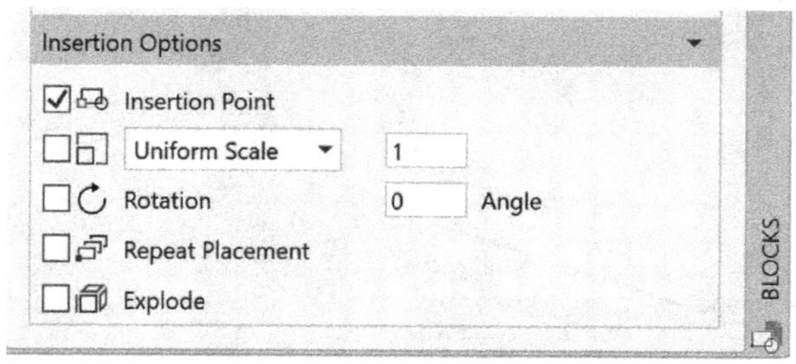

Figure 5.13

Double-click: ***the image MySubdiv** (to select to insert it)*

Specify insertion point or [Basepoint/Scale/X/Y/Z/Rotate]: ***0,0 [Enter]***

The subdivision drawing does not show in the viewport because, at the current zoom factor, it is much too large for the viewport. In order to see the subdivision, you must zoom out within the viewport. To make the subdivision fit inside the drawing window,

Click: ***Zoom All button** (or try typing Z [Enter] A [Enter])*

Click: ***X** (from the upper right corner of the Blocks panel to close it.)*

Now the entire subdivision drawing should appear in the drawing area, as shown in Figure 5.14.

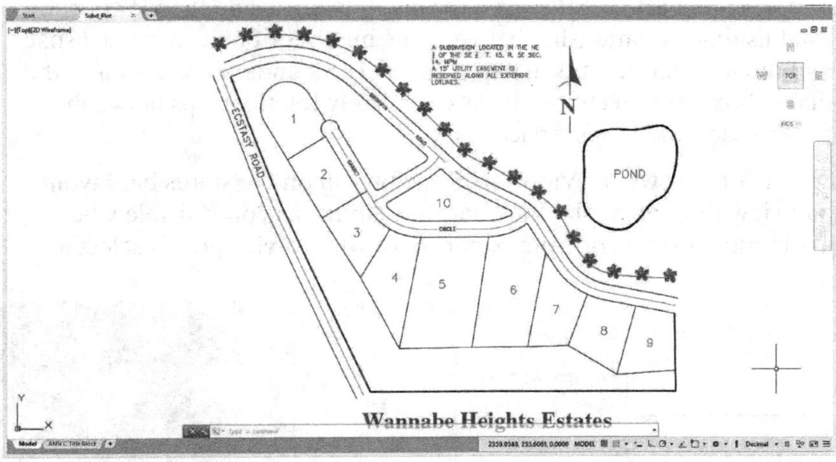

Figure 5.14

Tip: *You can also click and drag on the image tiles from the Block panel to insert them into the drawing, but this does not prompt for the insertion point. It uses the cursor position as the insertion point. This is a quick way to insert blocks.*

Showing the Drawing in the Layout

Next switch back to the layout tab to show the subdivision drawing in the layout containing the border and title block.

Click: ***ANSI C Title Block layout tab***

The view switches back to the layout. Now you still do not see the subdivision drawing. Why? Because once again the view is zoomed in a way that only shows a blank portion of the drawing. To change this, first make sure you are inside the model space viewport,

Double-click: ***inside the viewport area*** *to switch to model space*

Double-click: ***the mouse scroll wheel*** *to zoom to drawing extents*

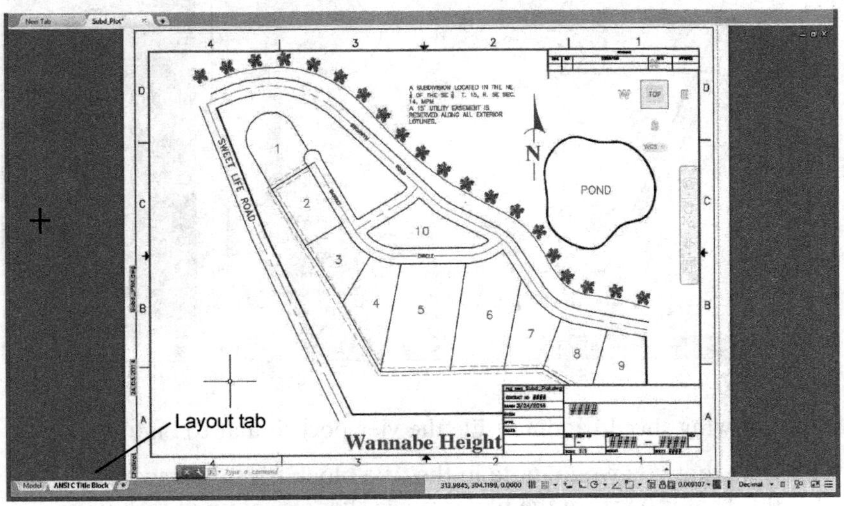

Figure 5.15

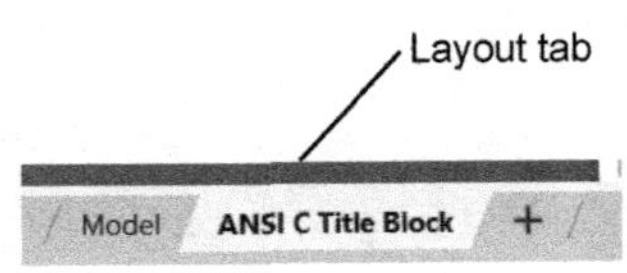

Setting the Viewport Zoom Scale

The next step is to set the scale for the drawing inside the viewport by establishing a relationship between the number of units in model space and the number of units in paper space. The standard scale area of the dialog box lets you choose from some likely relationships between paper space and model space.

Figure 5.16 shows the Viewport Scale button on the status bar layout and view tools area. The Viewport Scale button is only visible when you are in model space, or from paper space when a viewport is selected.

Tip: Use the Customization button from the right of the Status bar and verify you have the Viewport options showing on the status bar. You can also use this to show a Model/Paper button on the Status bar.

✔ Viewport Lock
✔ Viewport Scale
✔ Viewport Scale Sync

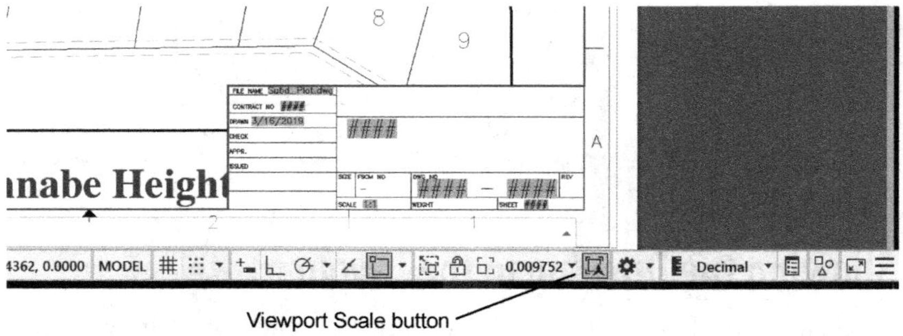

Figure 5.16 Status Bar Layout and View tools

*Click: **to expand the Viewport Scale list** as shown in Figure 5.17*

*Click: **1:100***

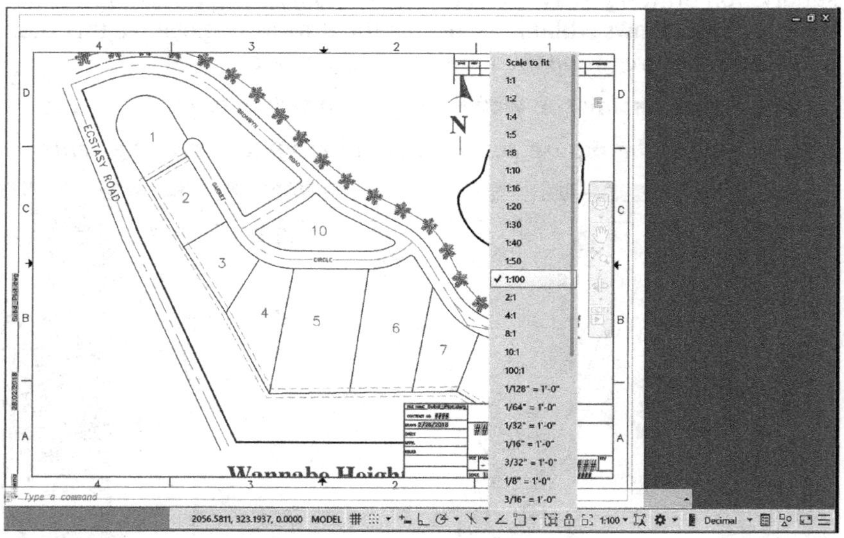

Figure 5.17

Your drawing should zoom inside the viewport similar to Figure 5.18.

The scale that you would note in the title block for this drawing is 1"=100'. That is because the paper space sheet is set up in inch units. The model space subdivision was drawn with decimal units where 1 unit equals 1 foot. The drawing is now zoomed so that when it plots, one paper space unit will equal 100 model space units, or a scale of 1"=100'.

Tip: *Viewports are drawing objects in paper space. Try selecting the viewport and using the Properties dialog box to quickly set its scale.*

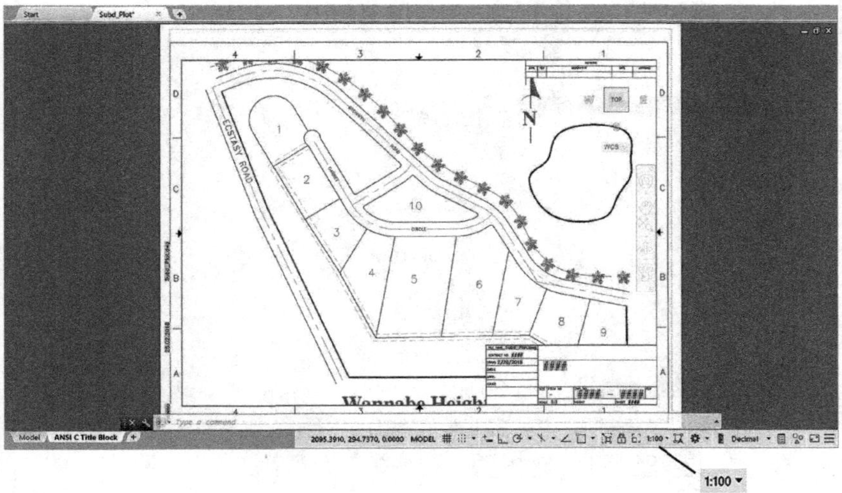

Figure 5.18

At scale 1:100, the entire subdivision does not fit inside the viewport, so next you will create a custom scale to fit the entire subdivision in the viewport.

It is preferred to plot drawings at typical scales such as the ones available on the standard scales selection. Custom scales should be used only when necessary to show the drawing clearly.

The Custom selection from the Viewport Scale list lets you add new scales to the list that you can select later. The viewport scale actually specifies the zoom XP scale factor. From model space, you can type the Zoom command and set this scale factor from the command prompt.

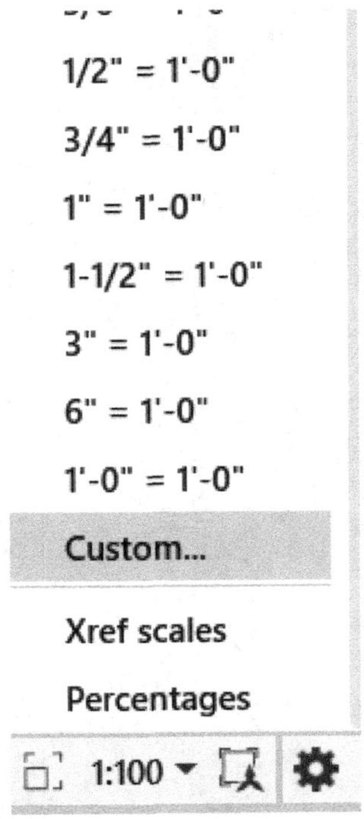

The zoom XP scale factor is a ratio. It is the number of units from the object in paper space divided by the number of units in model space. For example, if you want the model space object to appear twice its size on the paper, specify 2XP as the scale factor (2 paper space units/1 model space unit). You can also think of the zoom XP factor as the value or size of one model space unit when shown in paper space.

To specify a scale of 1"=150' for the subdivision, you would set the XP scaling factor to 0.006667 (1 unit in paper space/150 units in model space).

You will create a scale of one unit in paper space equal to 150 units in model space (a scale of 1"=150').

You will use the status bar Viewport Scale selection to zoom the model space drawing so that one paper space unit equals 150 model space units.

> *Click:* ***to expand the Viewport Scale list*** *from the status bar*
>
> *Click:* ***Custom*** *from near the bottom of the list (you may need to scroll to see it near the bottom of the list)*

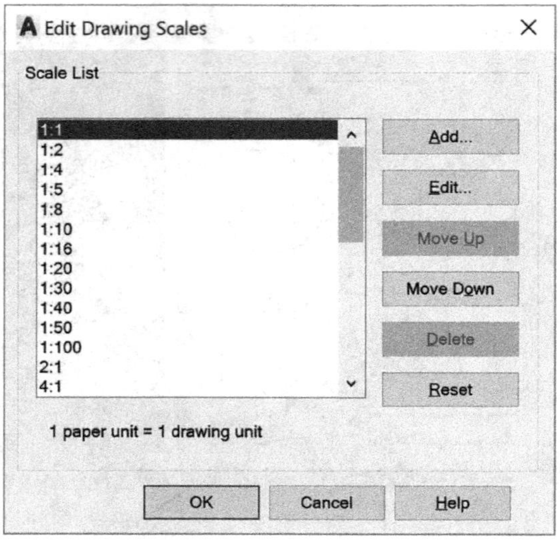

Figure 5.19

The Edit Drawing Scales dialog box appears as shown in Figure 5.19. The scale you would like to choose 1: 150 is not listed, so you will add a new scale.

Click: ***Add button*** *from the upper right of the dialog box*

Type the following settings into the dialog box as shown in Figure 5.20:

Name appearing in scale list: ***1"=150'***

Paper units: ***1***

Drawing units: ***150***

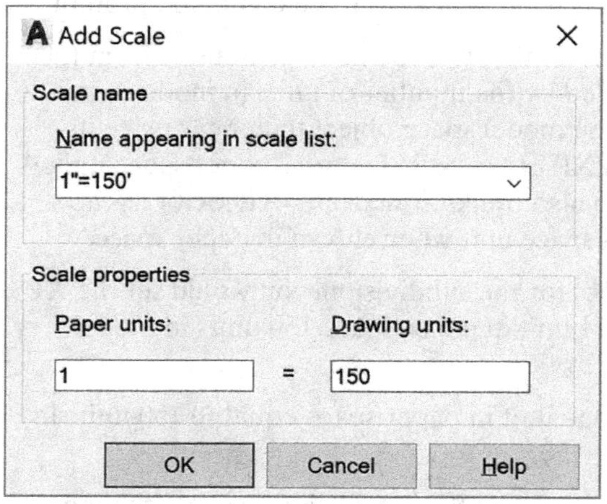

Figure 5.20

Click: ***OK*** *to exit Add Scale*

Click: ***OK*** *to exit Edit Drawing Scales*

Now the new scale name 1"=150' is added to the list.

Double-click: ***inside the viewport*** *to make it active*

Click: ***to expand the Viewport Scale list***

*Click: **1"=150'** from the list (it may be near the top of the list)*

Note the image is now smaller. The scale you would note for the drawing is now 1"=150'

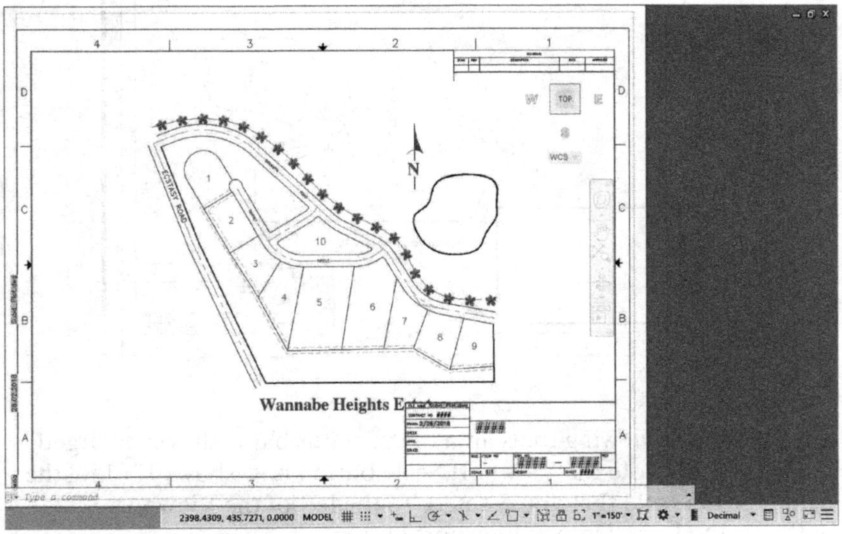

Figure 5.21

You have set up the zoom scale for the viewport so that if you plot paper space at a scale of 1=1, the model space object is shown at a scale of 1"=150' on the paper. Remember, in the original subdivision drawing, each unit represented one foot.

Using Pan to Position the Drawing

Use the Pan command to drag the model space drawing around in the paper space viewport without changing the scale or the location of the drawing on the model space coordinate system. Once you have selected the Pan command, the cursor changes to look like a hand.

Check that you are in model space inside the viewport, before using pan to position the view.

Command: ***MS [Enter]***

The viewport should be highlighted and the paper space icon does not show.

*Click: **Pan Realtime icon** (or press and hold the scroll wheel)*

Click a point near the top center of the subdivision and drag the image until it is centered in the viewport as shown in Figure 5.22.

Tip: *You will learn more about the relationship between viewport and annotation scale in Tutorial 7.*

Tip: *You can right=click to show the context menu with the Pan command.*

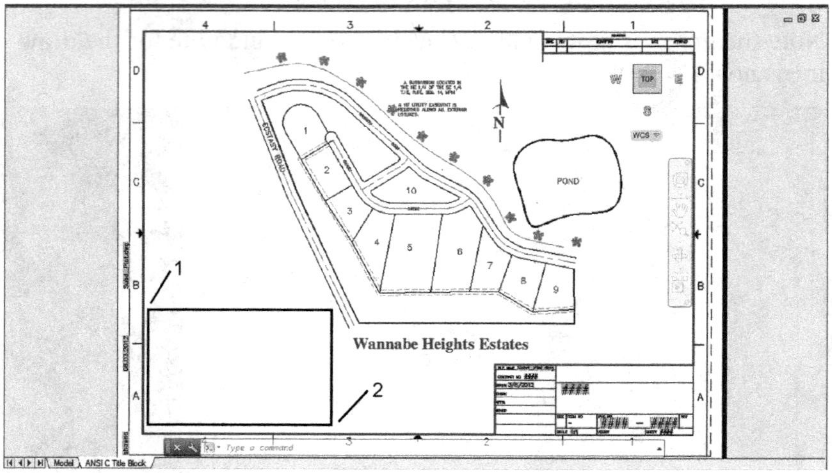

Figure 5.22

The layout and viewing tools area of the status bar is shown enlarged in Figure 5.23. Note the Viewport Scale button now shows 1"=150', the name for the scale that you created. To the left of the Viewport Scale button is the Lock/Unlock Viewport button.

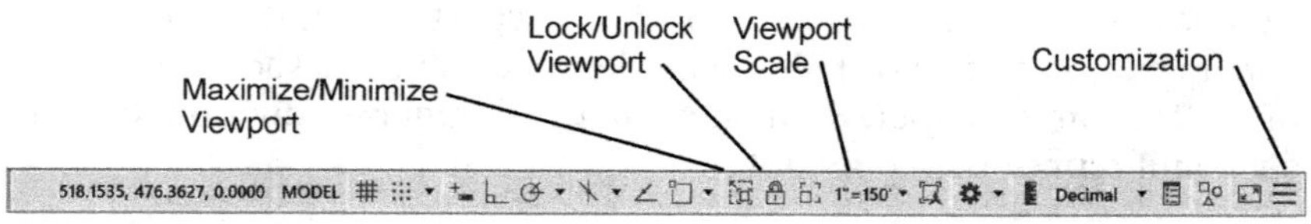

Figure 5.23

Locking the Viewport Scale

In order to preserve the relationship between model space and paper space, be sure that if you use Zoom Window to enlarge your drawing, you use Zoom Previous, not Zoom All, to return to this Zoom XP size before you plot. Additionally, you can always return to this list and specify the scale factor again if needed. Develop a habit of checking the viewport scale before you plot a drawing.

You can use the layout and view tools area of the status bar to lock the viewport, so that its scale cannot be inadvertently changed by zooming.

Click: ***Lock/Unlock Viewport button*** *so that it appears locked*

Creating a Second Floating Viewport

Viewports can be created in model space or in paper space. Model space viewports are called *tiled viewports* because their edges line up next to each other like floor tiles. Paper space viewports are called *floating viewports* because they can overlap each other or "float" on top of one another. Multiple paper space viewports can be printed on one layout sheet.

You can use floating viewports to create enlarged details, location drawings, or additional views of the same object. (You will learn more about this method when you create solid models in Tutorial 11.)

Next switch to paper space and set the layer before creating the new viewport.

Double-click: ***outside the viewport border*** *to switch to paper space*

Click: ***to make the Viewport layer current*** *using the Layer Control*

Click: ***to turn off running Object Snap*** *from the status bar*

Click: ***small arrow to the right of Layout Viewports*** *from the Layout tab, Layout Viewports panel*

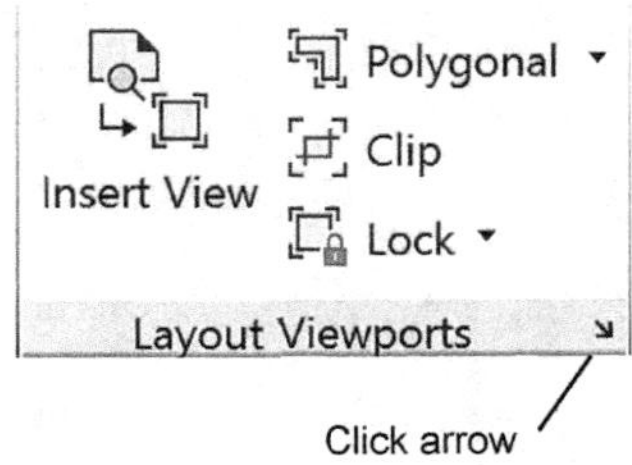

Click: ***New Viewports tab***

The Viewports dialog box appears as shown in Figure 5.24.

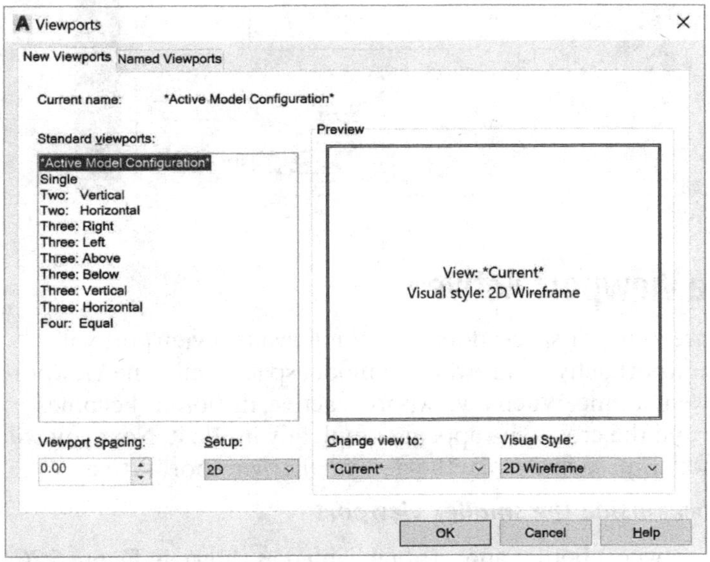

Figure 5.24

The left side of the dialog box shows options for standard viewport configurations you can select. Click an item from the Standard viewports list to see that arrangement in the preview pane. In later tutorials you will work with 3D drawings. For now, leave 2D selected in the Setup area and 2D Wireframe in the Visual Style area.

Click: ***Single*** *from the Standard viewports area*

Leave Setup set to ***2D***

Leave Change view to: set to ****Current****

Leave Visual Style set to ***2D Wireframe***

Click: ***OK***

At the next prompts, you click a location for corners of the viewport.

Specify first corner or [Fit] <Fit>: ***click near point 1*** *(Figure 5.22) as the upper left corner for the viewport*

Specify opposite corner: ***click near point 2** for the lower right corner*

A second viewport is added to the drawing as shown in Figure 5.25. It shows the entire subdivision drawing, zoomed so that all of the drawing limits fit inside the viewport.

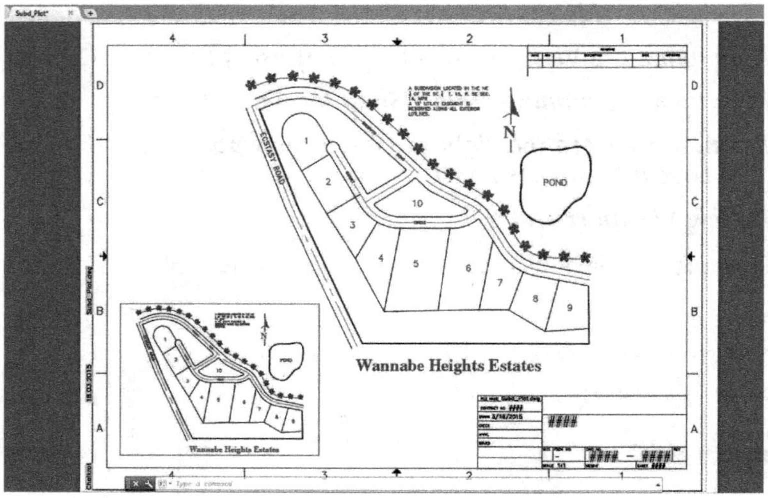

Figure 5.25

Tip: *If you have trouble, make sure that object snaps are turned off when you draw the viewport. You can click the viewport and resize it by dragging its corners.*

Making a Viewport Active

When you are in paper space, double-clicking inside a viewport will make the viewport active and switch to model space. Only one viewport can be active at a time. When a viewport is active, its border becomes highlighted and the crosshairs appear completely inside it. Next you will switch to model space and make the new smaller viewport active.

Double-click: ***inside the smaller viewport***

The smaller viewport border appears highlighted as shown in Figure 5.26. The crosshairs should be inside the viewport. If you move past the viewport border, the crosshairs change to a pointer.

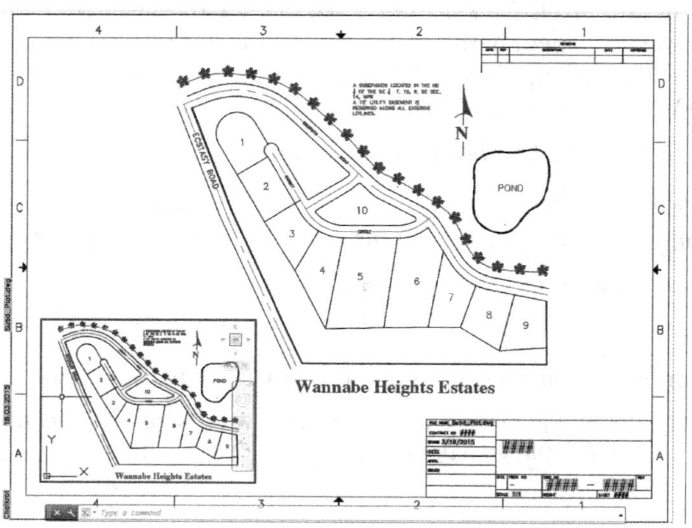

Figure 5.26

Once you are already in model space, to make a different viewport active, move the arrow cursor into that viewport and click.

Next, you will use the Zoom Window command to enlarge an area inside the smaller viewport you created. (You could use the scroll wheel, but that can be more difficult to position exactly.)

*Command: **Z [Enter]***

Specify corner of window, enter a scale factor (nX or nXP), or [All/Center/Dynamic/Extents/Previous/Scale/Window/Object] <real time>: ***click to set the first corner***

Specify opposite corner: ***click to create a window around lot 1***

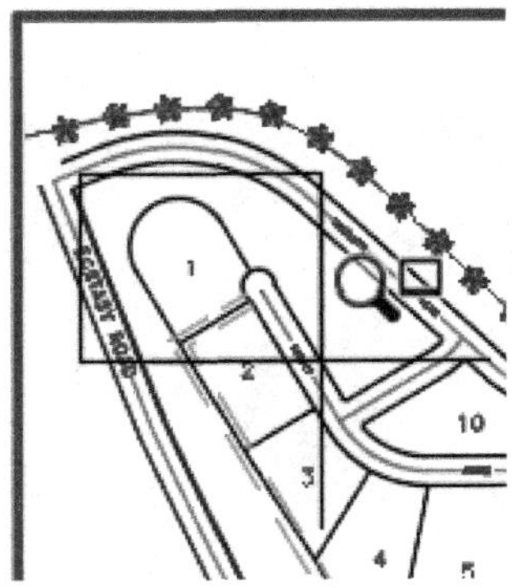

The area inside the window you selected is enlarged inside the viewport, as shown in Figure 5.27.

*Use **Pan Realtime** if needed to position the objects inside the viewport.*

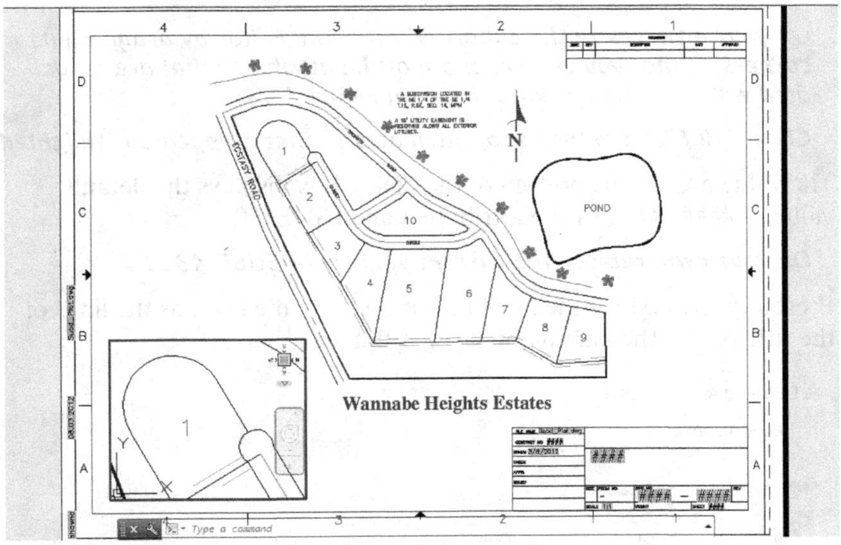

Figure 5.27

Tip: *To avoid inadvertently changing the zoom scale for the viewport, you can lock the viewport scale. Doing so will manage zooming so that the zoom XP factor does not change.*

Tip: *If you have trouble picking a viewport to make it active, press **[Ctrl]-R** to select it.*

Tip: *You cannot edit a viewport when its layer is turned off. You can still edit the contents of the viewport, that is, the objects that are in model space. If at some time you are trying to change or erase a viewport while in paper space and you cannot get it to work, check to see if the layer where the viewport border was created is turned off, locked, or frozen. Making the layer non-plotting allows you to still see the layer so it is always available for editing but it will not plot. You can also use non-plotting layers to add notes to your drawing, such as reminders, that you do not want to print.*

Attributes and Fields

Attributes are a way of attaching data to items in your drawing. The Manufacturing Imperial title block from which you started your drawing uses attributes to store information such as the revision and sheet number. In addition the title block uses fields to store information such as the file name and date. *Fields* are used to display data that can be read from information which may change, such as the date. You probably noticed that the date and your drawing name were already displayed in the title block. You will learn more about defining attributes in Tutorial 13. Some of the attributes have default values set for them in this title block that appear as number signs (###). This helps you notice them and provide the information.

*On your own, **switch to paper space**.*

*Double-click: **on an attribute item (###)** to show the Enhanced Attribute Editor as shown in Figure 5.28.*

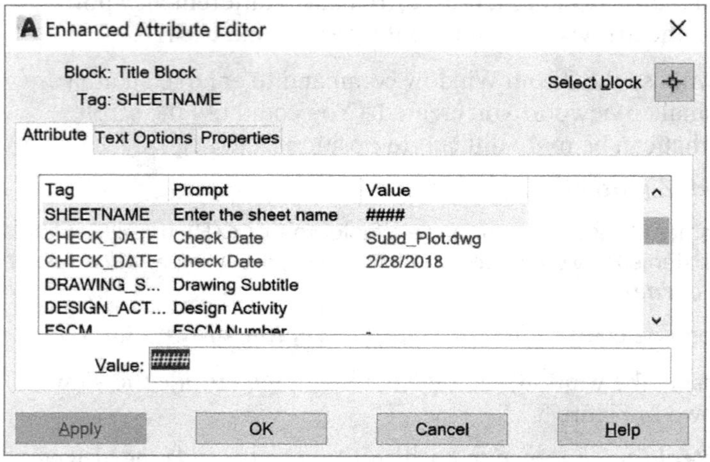

Figure 5.28

On your own, resize the Enhanced Attribute Editor by dragging its corners so that you can see more of the attributes that are associated with the title block as shown in Figure 5.29.

*Click: **SHEET** from the list of attributes so that it appears highlighted*

The value area at the bottom of the dialog box displays the default value of #### - #### or the attribute named SHEET.

*On your own, replace the current value with **SUBD-4321**.*

Presently, the text for the attributes is on the same layer as the lines of the title block. They are all on layer, Titleblock.

Figure 5.29

On your own, ***fill in the remaining values*** *to complete the title block.*

Click: ***Properties tab*** *from the dialog box*

Change the layer for each attribute to TEXT (see Figure 5.30).

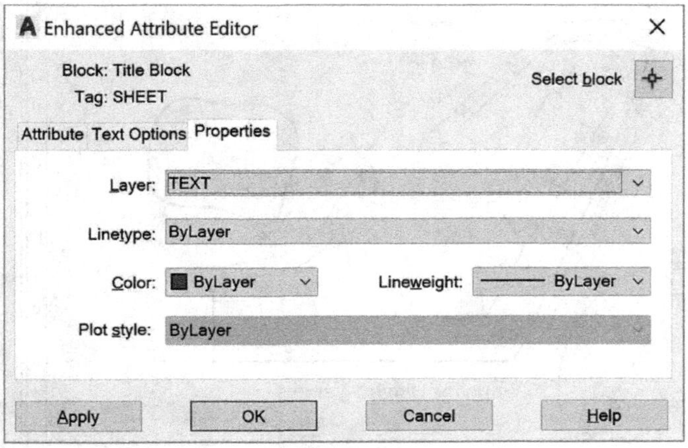

Figure 5.30

Click: ***Apply***

Click: ***OK***

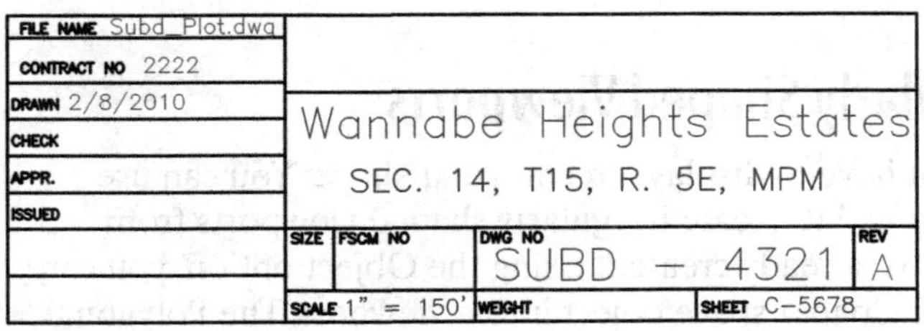

Figure 5.31

Next you will use the Circle command to draw a circle around the area shown in the second viewport, which is going to serve as a detail of lot 1. This circle will be drawn in paper space. Lines added to model space will show up in every viewport (unless you control the visibility of the viewport). Paper space represents a virtual sheet of paper on which you are laying out the drawing.

On your own, check that you are in ***paper space****. You should see the paper space icon.*

Click: ***Zoom All button***

On your own, ***add a dashed circle*** *on layer* ***Titleblock****. Fit it around the area that is zoomed in the detail. Use the circle's hot grips to stretch or move it as necessary so that it fits around the area in the main drawing that is zoomed up in the detail.*

Add text SEE DETAIL A *below the circle.*

Add a ***second circle*** *around the area in the small viewport. Below it,* ***add text DETAIL A*** *as shown in Figure 5.21.*

Click: ***Save button*** *to save your drawing*

When these steps are complete, your drawing should look like Figure 5.32.

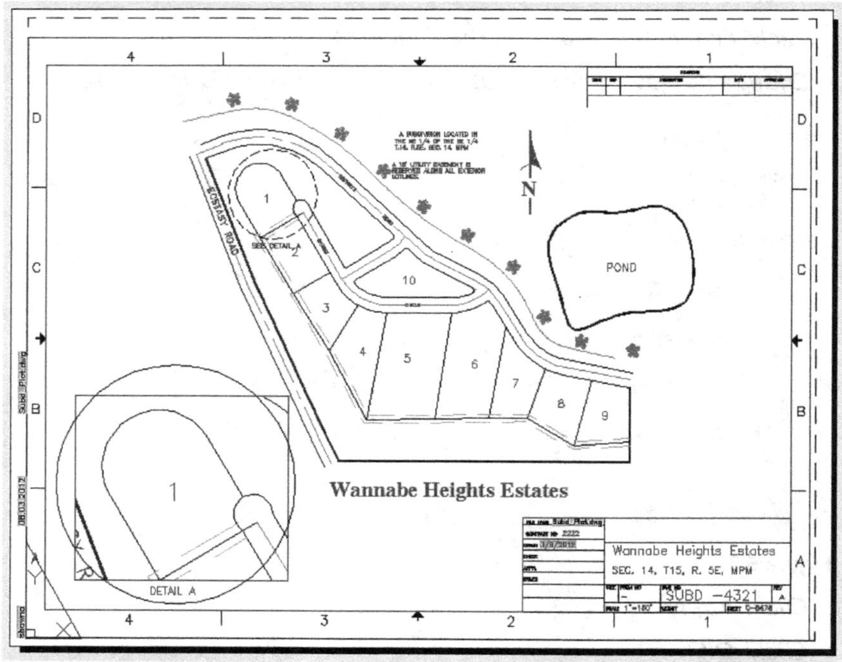

Figure 5.32

Using Irregularly Shaped Viewports

Viewports do not have to display a rectangular shape. You can use the VPClip command to create irregularly shaped viewports from viewports you have already created. Using the Object option, you can convert an existing paper space object into a viewport. The Polygonal option allows you to select points to define an irregular boundary.

The boundary for a viewport must have at least three points and must be closed. The software locates a viewport object using the points you specify and then clips the content of the viewport to the specified boundary. You will try each of the viewport clipping methods next.

On your own, make the ***VIEWPORT layer current****.*

Turn ***off object snap****.*

Select: ***the small magenta rectangular viewport*** *so that its grips appear*

Right-click: ***in the drawing area*** *to show the short-cut menu*

Click: ***Viewport Clip***

Select clipping object or [Polygonal] <Polygonal>: ***[Enter]***

Specify start point: ***click a point near A*** *in Figure 5.33*

Specify next point or [Arc/Close/Length/Undo]: ***click points B through J*** *to form an irregular boundary inside the circle*

Specify next point or [Arc/Close/Length/Undo]: ***C [Enter]***

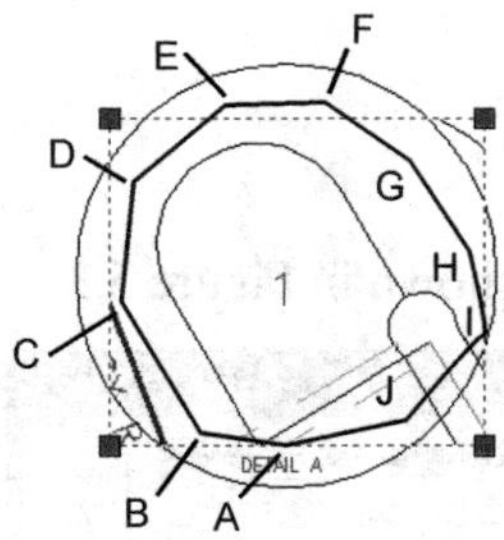

Figure 5.33

The contents of the viewport are clipped to the irregular polygon boundary. Next you will use the option to clip the viewport to the circle drawn around the detail shape.

Command: ***VPClip [Enter]***

Select viewport to clip: ***click the irregular viewport boundary***

Select clipping object or [Polygonal/Delete] <Polygonal>: ***click the circle around the irregular shaped small viewport***

The contents of the viewport are clipped to the shape of the circle as shown in Figure 5.34.

Save your drawing at this time.

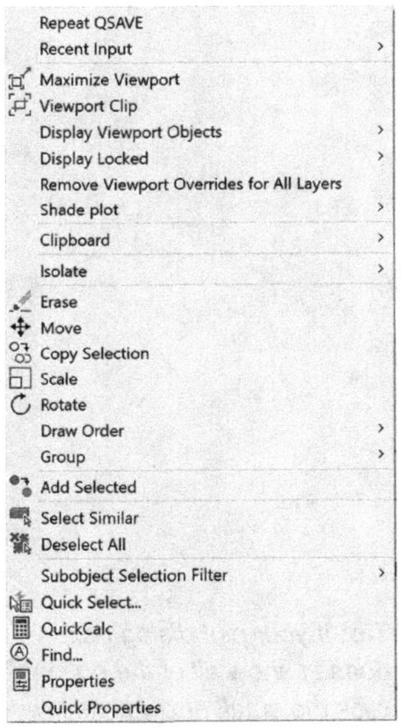

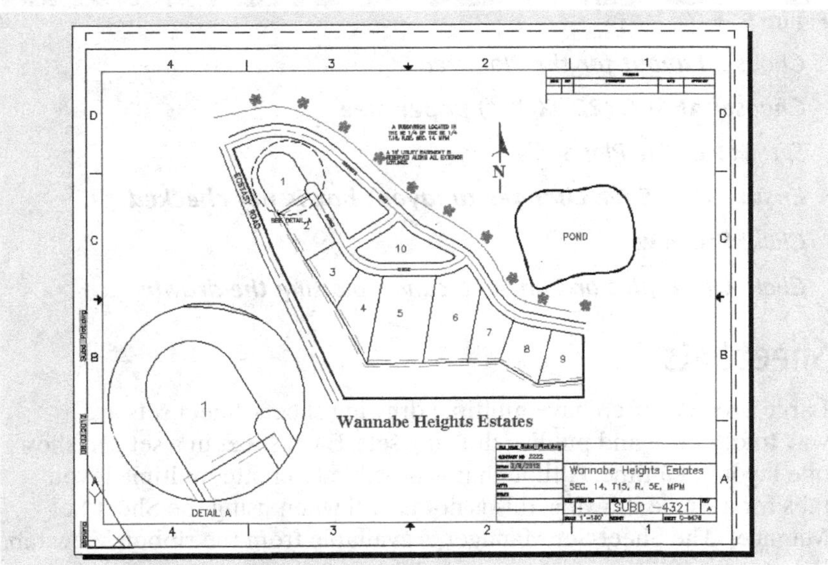

Figure 5.34

Plotting from Paper Space

You set up your drawing in paper space and set a scaling factor for the number of units in model space that equal one unit in paper space. Because you used a template for a C-sized sheet, you will use 1=1 for the plot scale when choosing that sheet size. You will choose to plot the layout in order to show the title block.

Check that you are in ***paper space****.*

Click: ***Plot button***

The Plot dialog box will appear on your screen as shown in Figure 5.35.

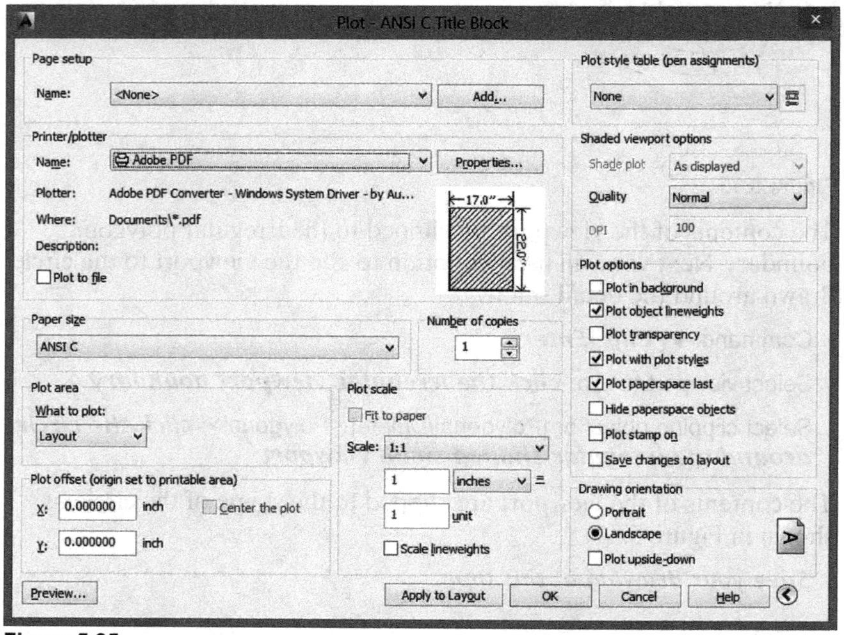

Figure 5.35

Choose: ***Layout*** *for the Plot area*

Choose: ***ANSI C (22" X 17") paper size***

Set: ***1:1*** *as the Plot Scale*

Tip: *If your plot dialog box doesn't show all of the options, click the small arrow in its lower right to expand more options.*

Ensure that Save changes to layout box is not checked

Click: ***Preview***

Click: ***OK to plot*** *or Cancel to cancel plotting the drawing*

Tip: *If you do not have a plotter capable of using the C-sized sheet, you can plot a check print to a standard 8.5" X 11" printer or plotter. To do this, select this sheet and choose Fit to paper in the Plot scale area. The entire drawing border and contents will be scaled to fit on the smaller sheet size. Of course this means that the drawing scale of 1"=150' no longer applies. Make sure that the Save changes to layout box near the top of the Plot dialog box is not selected before you change your paper size.*

Sheet Sets

Large projects often have multiple drawing sheets. Sheet sets are a way to organize and publish drawing sets. Each sheet in a set can show one layout at a time. Although it is possible to create multiple layout tabs for a single drawing, this is not useful when using the Sheet Set Manager. The Sheet Set Manager is available from the ribbon View tab, Palettes panel.

Next you will create a sheet set that contains the layout for the subdivision drawing you just created along with other drawings.

Here are some things to consider before creating a sheet set:

- Only one layout can function as a sheet within a sheet set. It is best to create your drawings with only one layout tab per drawing file. Using multiple layouts from a single drawing as separate sheets within a set makes it impossible for multiple users to access that sheet or layout at the same time. It also makes your sheet sets more complicated and harder to keep organized.

Tip: *If you do not have a printer or plotter that is capable of printing a C-sized sheet, try creating a PDF file of the drawing instead.*

- Organize your drawing files. Generally you will want all of the drawings for a project to be in the same folder (or subfolders of one folder). The sheet set aids you in locating the files and publishing them but it will not overcome disorganized files.
- Think about which template file will be used to add new sheets to the set. You will specify this in the Sheet Set Properties dialog box.
- Consider the page setup file you will use to store page setups for plotting the entire set of sheets. (Often PDF files are saved to a shared location to serve as the final result.)
- A version of the Sheet Set Manager for the web lets you create and manage drawings stored in Autodesk Docs. A system variable, SSMDetectmode lets you set which version of the sheet set manager is used when a *.dst* file is opened.

Tip: *This text shows using the original Sheet Set Manager. These sets can still be opened in the new web version. You will be creating a .dst sheet set file in the next steps.*

Wannabe Estates.dst

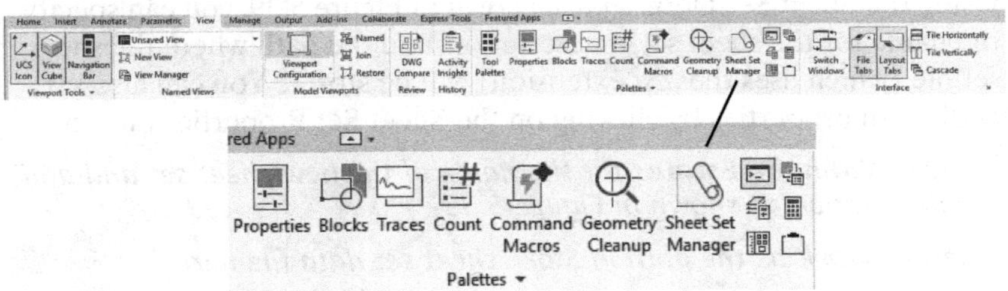

Figure 5.36

Click: ***Sheet Set Manager button*** *from the ribbon View tab, Palettes panel (as shown in Figure 5.36)*

The Sheet Set Manager appears on your screen as shown in Figure 5.37.

Tip: *You can drag on the corners of the Sheet Set Manager to resize it.*

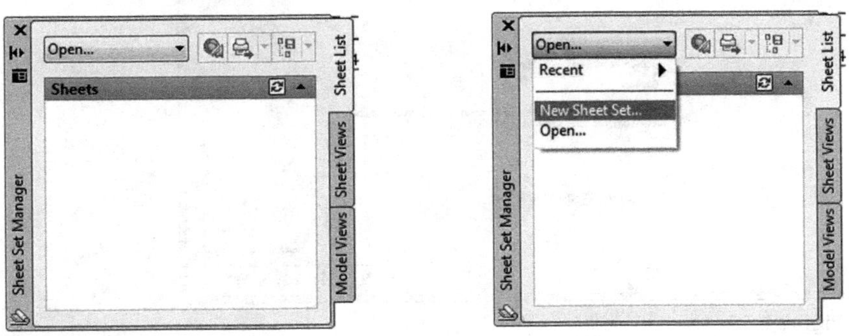

Figure 5.37

Click: ***New Sheet Set*** *from the pull-down list near the top of the dialog box as shown in the left Figure 5.37*

The Create Sheet Set wizard appears on your screen. You can begin a new sheet set from an example showing sheet organization or by adding your existing drawings.

Click: ***Existing Drawings*** *as shown in Figure 5.38*

Click: ***Next***

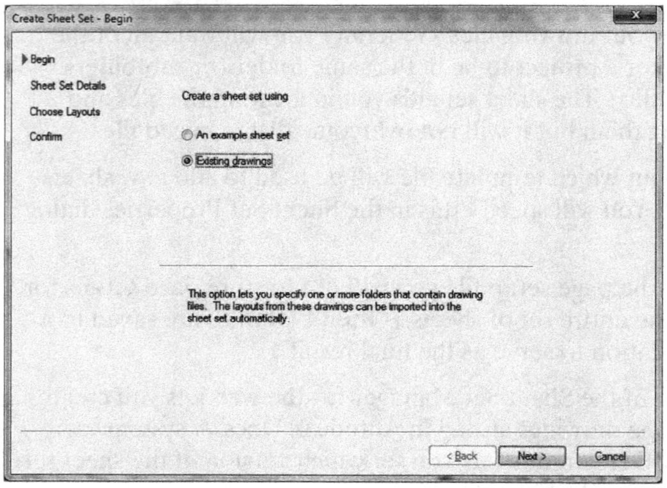

Figure 5.38

Using the Sheet Set Details page shown in Figure 5.39, you can specify the name for the sheet set, a description, and the path where the sheet set file (which uses the *.dst* extension) will be stored. You can also set additional properties by clicking on the Sheet Set Properties button.

Type: ***Wannabe Estates*** *for the name of the new sheet set and add a description as shown in Figure 5.39*

Set: ***c:\work*** *as the path in Store sheet set data file here*

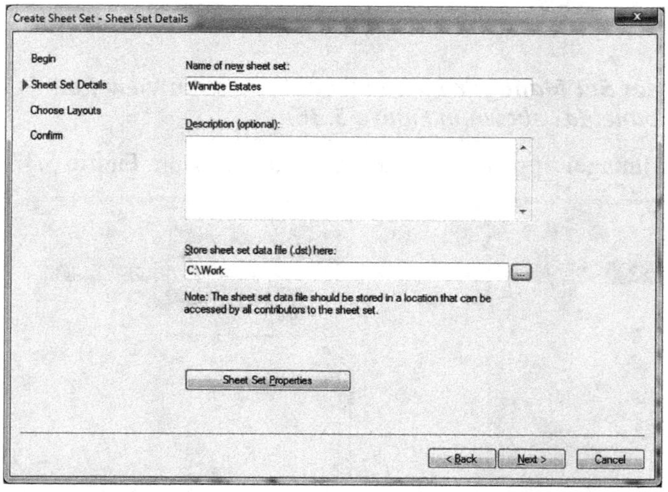

Figure 5.39

Click: Sheet Set Properties button

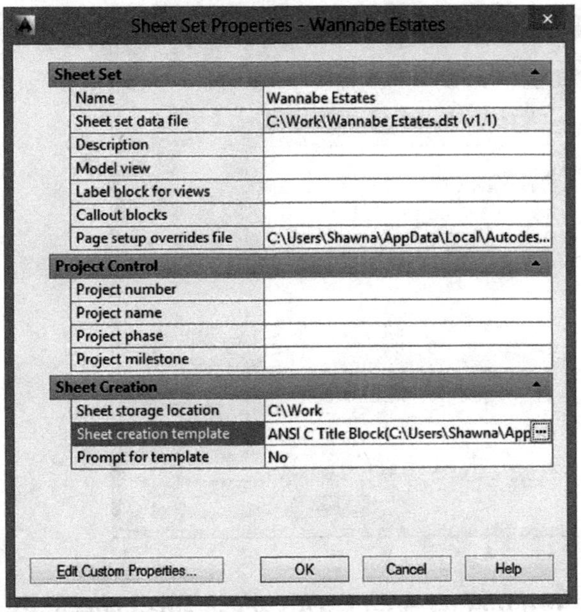

Figure 5.40

The Page Setup Overrides files area displays the path for the page setup file (containing the page size and other necessary printing information) that will override any different user settings when the sheet set is plotted as a batch.

Use your default location for your page setup files.

The Sheet Creation Template area displays the path for the template that will be used by default when a new sheet is added to the sheet set. This makes creating additional sheets that have the same sheet size and format quick and easy. Most drawing sets standardize on one sheet size and title block style for an organized appearance and ease of handling the printed sheets.

Use your default location (shown in the dialog box) and browse to select a C-sized template.

Click: ***OK*** *to exit the Sheet Set Properties dialog box*

Click: ***Next***

The Choose Layouts page is used to select layouts from existing drawings to add as sheets in your organized sheet set.

Click: ***Browse and select: c:\work***

Click: ***OK***

You should see a list of the drawings inside the folder *c:\work* that contain layouts that can be used as sheets as shown in Figure 5.41.

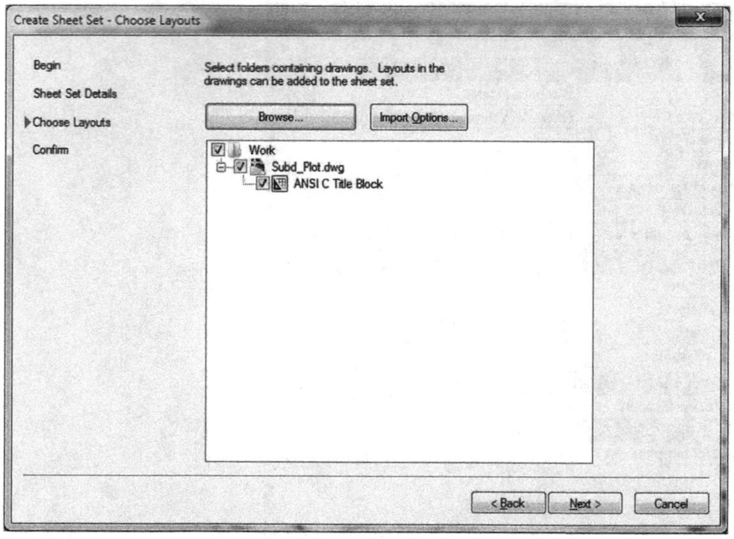

Figure 5.41

*Leave the **subd_plot.dwg and its ANSI C Title Block sheet checked***

Click: ***Next***

The Sheet Set Preview as shown in Figure 5.42 shows the drawings you selected and the default paths you set for the sheet set to be defined.

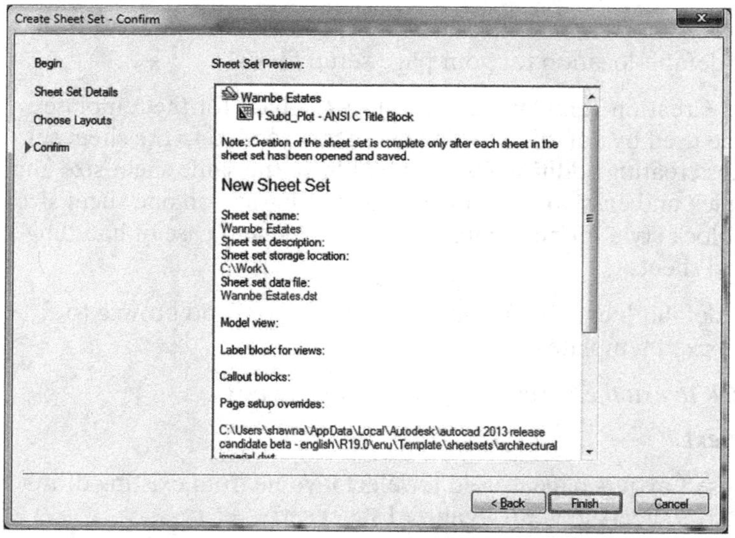

Figure 5.42

Click: ***Finish***

You return to the drawing editor where the Sheet Set Manager shows the drawing layouts you have selected listed. Figure 5.43 shows the appearance of the Sheet Set Manager.

Hover your mouse over the sheet name to show the sheet details

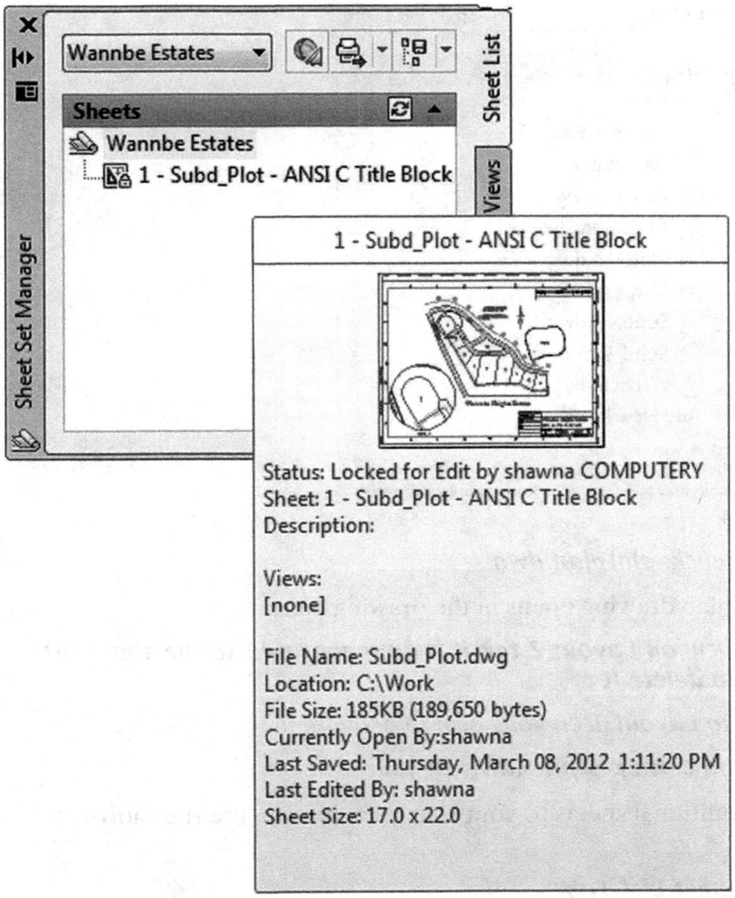

Figure 5.43

To open a sheet, you only need to double-click on its name in the Sheet Set Manager. To open a drawing from the sheet set you only need to double click on its file name.

Click: ***Model Views tab***

Click: ***the Add New Location button***

Browse to your \work folder and click Open to add it.

You should see the drawings listed that are in your *c:\work* folder as shown in Figure 5.34.

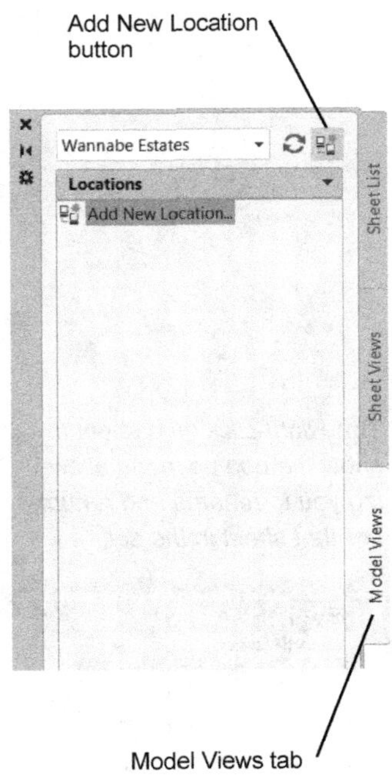

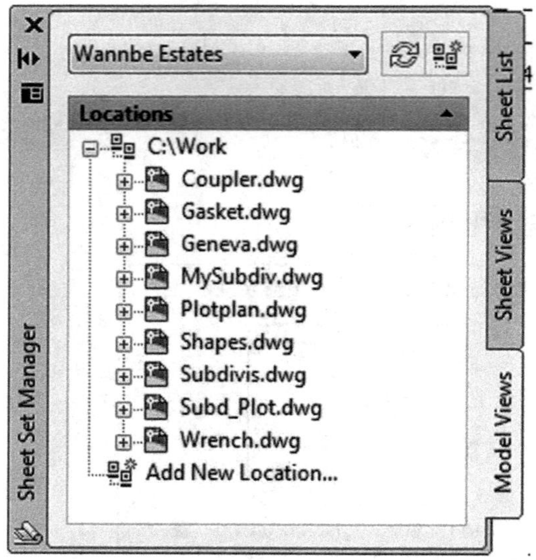

Figure 5.44

Double-click: ***plotplan.dwg***

The plot plan drawing opens in the drawing editor.

Right-click: ***on Layout 2 tab if it appears and use the short-cut menu to delete it***

Switch to ***Layout 1*** *on your own to activate it.*

Save *and* ***close plotplan.dwg*** *on your own.*

To add additional sheets to your sheet set, you can use the short-cut menu.

Click: ***Sheet List Tab***

Right-click: ***Wannabe Estates sheet set name***

The short-cut menu pops up on your screen as shown in Figure 5.45.

Tip: *Right-click on a sheet to show the pop up menu allowing you to rename and renumber that sheet in the set.*

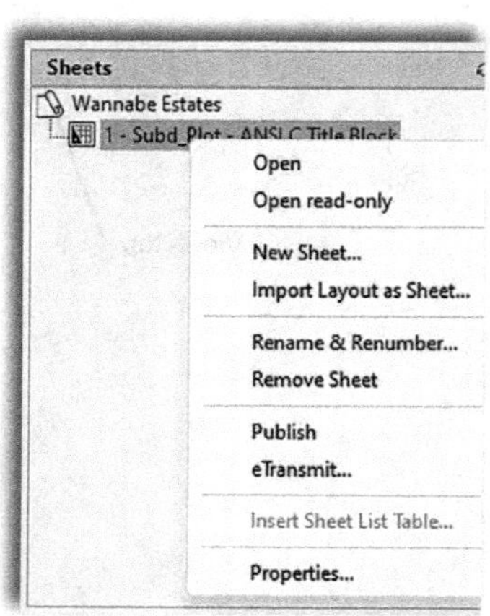

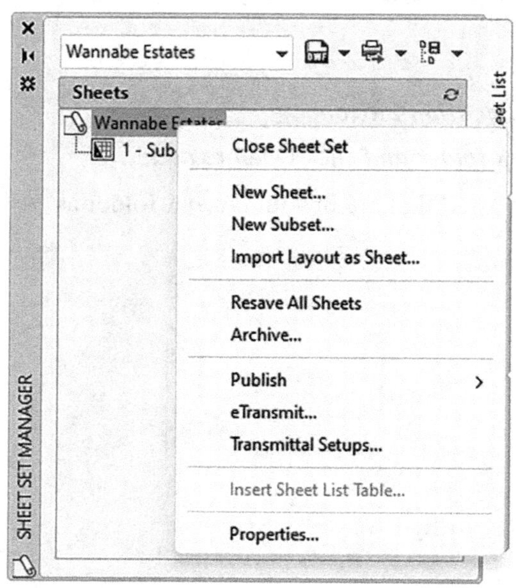

Figure 5.45

Notice that you can use this menu to create new sheets, new subsets or categories of sheets, and to publish a sheet set.

Sheet sets can be a very important productivity and organization tool when you are working on large projects. You can explore sheet sets more using Help.

You are finished with this portion of the tutorial.

Click: ***[X] to close the Sheet Set Manager***

Click: ***[X] to close any drawings that remain open***

Creating a Template Drawing

Next you will create a template drawing that you will use for most of the remaining tutorials in this book. The file you will create is also provided as a template named *proto.dwt* in the datafiles for this book (in case you do not complete this portion of the tutorial).

Click: ***small arrow at right of New selections***

Click: ***acad.dwt** as the template to use*

You should be in the drawing editor with a blank drawing showing.

Click: ***Save button***

The Save Drawing As dialog box appears. Located at the bottom of the dialog box is a Files of type: option as shown in Figure 5.37 used to save the drawing in various formats.

You will save your drawing as an AutoCAD template (*.*dwt*) file. The only difference between a drawing file (*.*dwg*) and a template file (*.*dwt*) is the file extension. The default is Release 2018 (*.*dwg*) format.

Tip: *You can use the operating system to rename template files to drawing files and vice versa.*

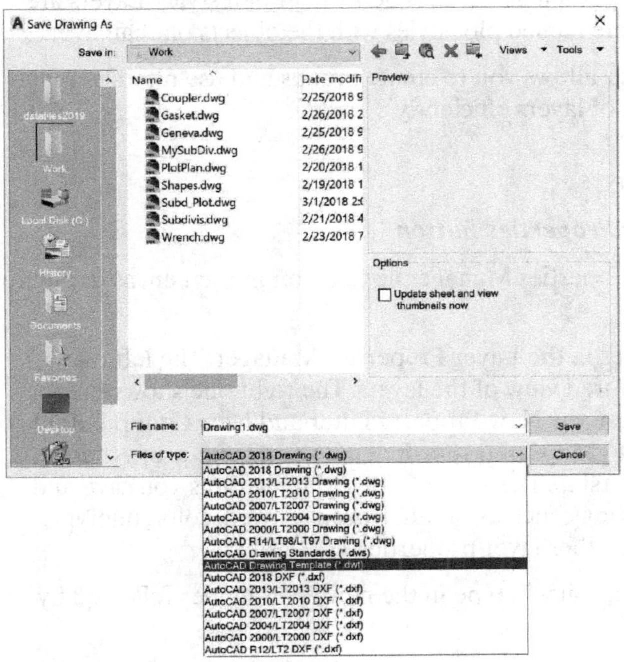

Figure 5.46

Click: ***AutoCAD Drawing Template (*.dwt)***

Type: ***MYTEMPLATE*** *as the File name*

*Navigate to c:**work**, if necessary.*

Click: ***Save***

Click: ***OK*** *to accept the defaults in the Template Options dialog box*

The main AutoCAD drawing editor appears on your display screen, with Mytemplate in the title bar.

You will set the limits, grid, snap, layers, text size, and text style in this drawing, as well as set up the paper space limits, viewport, and linetype scale. This approach will save time, make plotting and printing easier, and provide a system of layers to help you keep future drawings neatly organized.

Creating Default Layers

Using a template drawing helps you maintain a consistent standard for layer names. Using consistent and descriptive layer names allows more than one person to work on the same drawing without puzzling over the purpose of various layers. A template drawing is an easy way to standardize layer names and other basic settings, such as linetype.

Tip: *Using "reconciled" layers, you can be notified automatically when new layers are added to a drawing. This is useful for maintaining drawing standards especially if you work with other contributors who may add layers to your drawing instead of using the standard.*

Using different layers helps standardize the colors of groups of objects in the drawing, which in turn helps standardize plotting the drawing. Object color in the drawing helps you quickly recognize the type of information shown. Color can also be used to control line thickness on printers. The AutoCAD default is to set color by layer. You should use different colors for different types of objects in order to plot more than one color or line thickness effectively when using color dependent plot styles. Layers are also used to associate named plot styles with the objects on that layer.

The Layer Manager allows you to create groups and use filters to manage large numbers of layers efficiently.

Defining the Layers

Click: ***Layer Properties button***

The Layer Properties Manager appears on the screen, as in Figure 5.47.

There are two panes in the Layer Properties Manager. The left one shows a tree-structured view of the layers. The right one shows the list view. You can use the New Property Filter and New Group Filter to display different groups of layers depending on layer properties or layer group membership. The Layer States Manager lets you save and restore various settings, such as on/off, frozen/thawed, color, linetype, lineweight, and the other layer properties.

From the keyboard, you will type in the new layer names followed by commas.

Click: ***New Layer button*** *near the top of the dialog box*

Type: ***HIDDEN_LINES,TEXT,VISIBLE,THIN,CENTERLINE, CUTTING_PLANE,HATCH,PROJECTION, DIM,BORDER, VPORT [Enter]***

Each time you type a comma (,) a new "Layer1" pops up on the list of layer names. Then the name you type replaces the name Layer1.

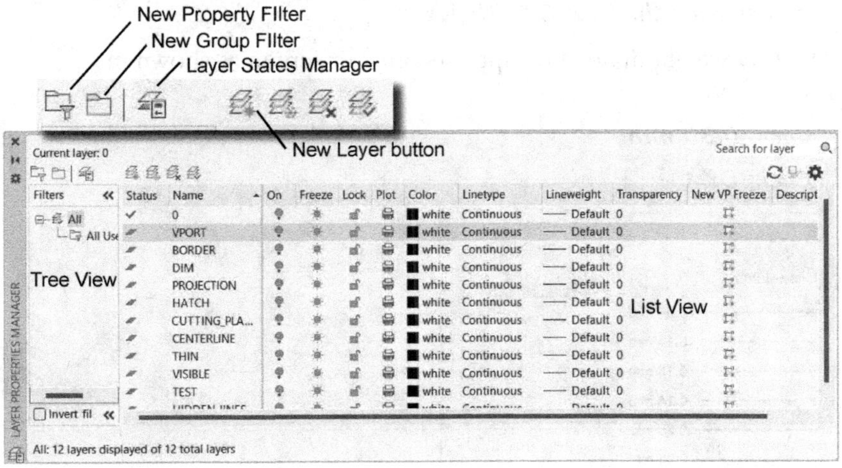

Figure 5.47

Note that the layers you have created are turned on. The color for all the layers is white (or black depending on your system configuration). In addition to the color and linetype, you can also set a lineweight value in the default units of millimeters (mm) or inches. Lineweights in the drawing only show on the screen when paper space is enabled and when the LWT button on the status bar is turned on. You will set the lineweight for the HIDDEN_LINES layer to 0.30 mm, the standard for plotting or sketching hidden lines. Lineweights should be used only to control the plotted appearance, not to represent the actual thickness of an object. Next you will set the color, linetype, and then lineweight for the hidden line layer.

Click: ***the color box in the Color column across from the HIDDEN_LINES layer***

Click: ***Blue*** *from the Standard Colors boxes*

Click: ***OK***

Click: ***Continuous*** *in the Linetype area to the right of layer Hidden_Lines*

The Select Linetype dialog box appears on your screen.

Click: ***Load***

Click: ***HIDDEN***

Click: ***OK*** *to exit the Load or Reload Linetypes dialog box*

You will see the linetypes HIDDEN and CONTINUOUS.

Click: ***HIDDEN***

Click: ***OK*** *to close the Select Linetype dialog box*

Now you should see that the linetype for layer HIDDEN_LINES is set

Tip: *You can right-click on a heading in the Layer Properties Manager, and select Maximize Column Headings from the pop-up menu that appears.*

Tip: *If you selected dark lines on a light background when configuring your video display, white lines will be black on your monitor and color boxes indicating white will be black.*

Tip: *Many Windows programs identify typing shortcuts by use of an underlined letter. Note the underlined letter N on the tooltip for the New Layer icon. This indicates that you can quickly select this operation by typing the key combination [Alt]-N. Look for the quick key combinations in other dialog boxes.*

Tip: *If the list of layer names is long, you may need to use the scroll bars located on the right-hand side of the dialog box.*

to linetype HIDDEN. Its color should be set to blue.

Click: ***HIDDEN_LINES*** *from the layer name list if it is not already highlighted*

Click: ***the thin line with the word Default*** *from the Lineweight area across from the HIDDEN-LINE layer*

The Lineweight dialog box appears on your screen as shown in Figure 5.48.

Click: ***0.30 mm***

Click: ***OK***

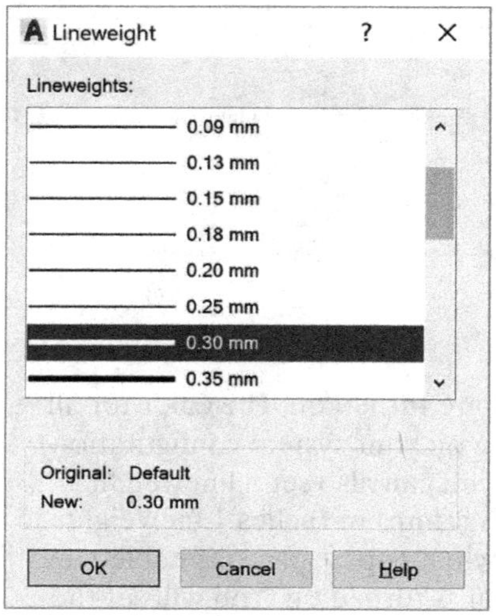

Figure 5.48

The 0.30 lineweight is displayed as the setting for layer HIDDEN. The list of layer names should now show layer HIDDEN_LINES having color blue, linetype HIDDEN, and a lineweight of 0.30.

Setting Up the Remaining Layers

Next, you will set the colors and linetypes for the remaining layers that you have created. You can select more than one Layer name at the same time by using the [Ctrl] or [Shift] keys in conjunction with the mouse (as you would to select multiple files in other Windows programs).

Use the arrow cursor to move to the desired layer name.

Click: ***Thin***

Press: ***[Ctrl]*** *(keep it depressed) and then*

Click: ***Hatch*** *(keeping [Ctrl] depressed)*

Click: ***Text*** *(keeping [Ctrl] depressed)*

You should now have three layers selected.

Click: ***the Color box across from one of the selected layers***

The Select Color dialog box, which you used earlier in this tutorial, pops up on the screen. Use the standard colors as before.

Click: ***Red*** *from the Standard Colors boxes*

Click: ***OK***

Click: ***the thin line with the word Default*** *in the Lineweight area across from one of the selected layers*

Click: ***0.30 mm***

Click: ***OK***

Layers Thin, Hatch, and Text should now have their color set to red and lineweight set to 0.30 mm. Next, you will set the color, linetype, and lineweight for layer Centerline.

Select: ***Centerline*** *so that its name is highlighted*

Click: ***the Color box*** *across from the Centerline layer*

Click: ***Green*** *from the Standard Colors boxes*

Click: ***OK***

Click: ***Continuous*** *from the Linetype column associated with layer Centerline*

The Select Linetype dialog box appears on your screen. You will need to load linetype CENTER before it can be used.

Click: ***Load***

On your own use the Load or Reload Linetypes dialog box and select the line pattern CENTER to use for layer Centerlines.

Click: ***the thin line with the word Default*** *in the Lineweight area associated with layer Centerline*

Click: ***0.30 mm***

Click: ***OK***

When you have finished, the Centerline layer should be green, linetype CENTER, and lineweight 0.30 mm.

On your own, set the colors and linetypes in the following table for the other layers. Magenta is a purplish pink color (number 6 in the row of standard colors). Color white appears as black if you have chosen to draw on a light background.

Layer	Color	Linetype	Lineweight
0	WHITE	CONTINUOUS	default
HIDDEN LINES	BLUE	HIDDEN	0.30 mm
TEXT	RED	CONTINUOUS	0.30 mm
VISIBLE	WHITE	CONTINUOUS	0.60 mm
THIN	RED	CONTINUOUS	0.30 mm
CENTERLINE	GREEN	CENTER	0.30 mm
PROJECTION	MAGENTA	CONTINUOUS	default
HATCH	RED	CONTINUOUS	0.30 mm
CUTTING_PLANE	WHITE	DASHED	0.60 mm
DIM	BLUE	CONTINUOUS	0.30 mm
BORDER	WHITE	CONTINUOUS	0.60 mm
VPORT	MAGENTA	CONTINUOUS	default

Before you exit the dialog box, you will set the current layer to VPORT.

Tip: *When you are selecting the color and linetype, be sure to highlight only the names of the layers you want to set.*

Tip: *You can click on the Name heading in the Layer Properties Manager to switch the list of layer names to reverse alphabetical order. Pick it again to restore it to A-Z order.*

Tip: *The variable Maxsort controls the number of layers that will be sorted in the Layer Control dialog box. It is set at 200 as the default. If you do not want your layer list to be sorted, you can type MAXSORT at the command prompt and then follow the prompts to set its value to 0.*

Double-click: ***Vport to set it as the current layer****—it will show a green check mark*

Click: ***the Plot button across from layer Vport*** *so that the layer becomes non-plotting*

Click: ***Name*** *from the column headings to sort the layer names alphabetically. (Click it a second time to reverse the order.)*

When you have finished creating the layers and setting the colors and linetypes, the dialog box should be similar to Figure 5.49.

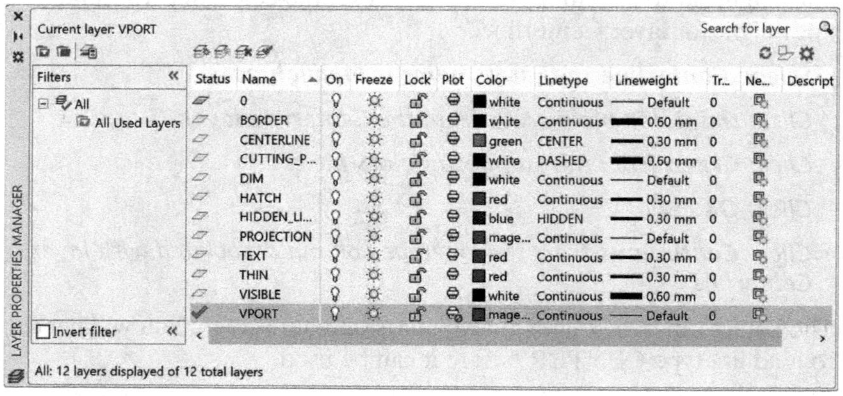

Figure 5.49

Remember that lineweights do not display unless selected and paper space has been enabled. You will see the effect of the lineweight later in this tutorial.

Using layers to control the color and linetype of new objects that you create will work only if BYLAYER is active as the method for establishing object color, object linetype, and lineweight. It is the default, so you should not have to change anything. To check,

Examine the Color Control, Linetype Control, and the Lineweight Control on the Properties panel. All three should be set to BYLAYER.

You have now created a basic set of layers for use in future drawings. Next you will explore the New Property Filter and New Group Filter.

Click: ***New Property Filter button*** *from the dialog box upper left*

The Layer Filter Properties dialog box appears as in Figure 5.50.

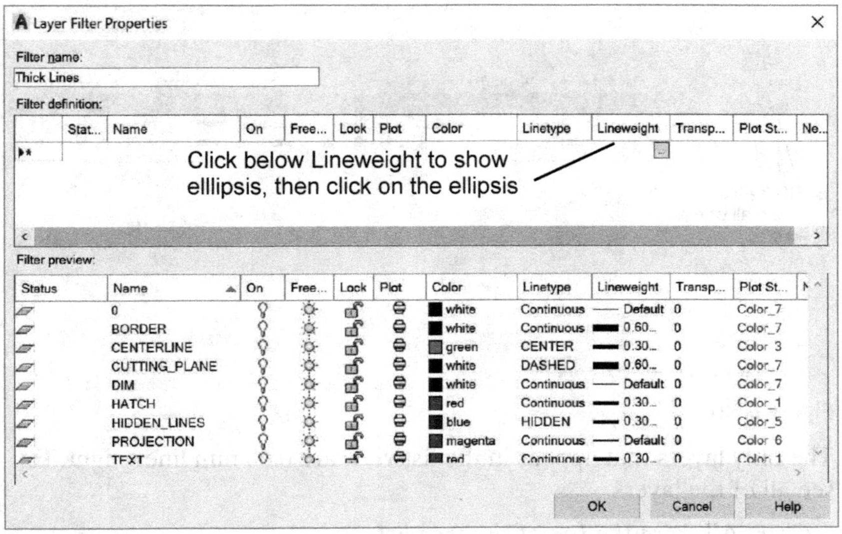

Figure 5.50

Type: ***Thick Lines in the Filter Name area*** *at the upper left of the dialog box*

Click: ***below the Lineweight area*** *of the top part of the dialog box*

Click: ***the ellipsis box that appears***

Click: ***0.60 mm*** *from the Lineweight dialog box that appears*

Click: ***OK***

The Layer Filter Properties dialog box changes as in Figure 5.51 to show a preview list that includes only the layers that have a 0.60 mm lineweight.

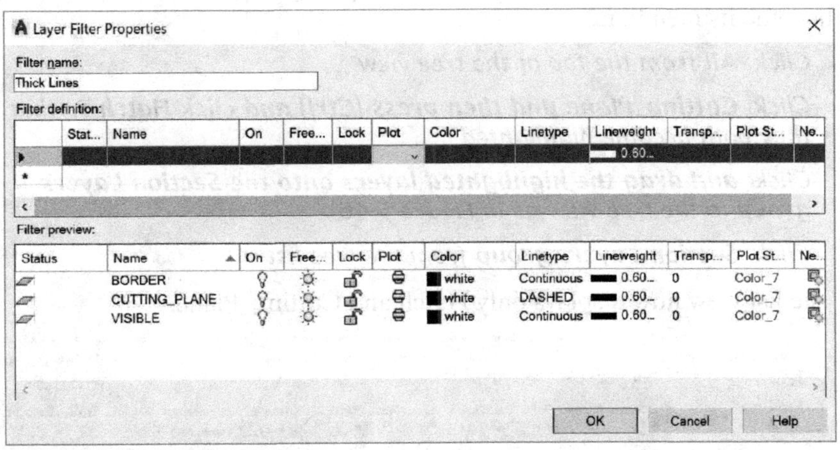

Figure 5.51

Click: ***OK***

You return to the Layer Properties Manager with the Thick Lines properties filter showing in the tree view as shown in Figure 5.52.

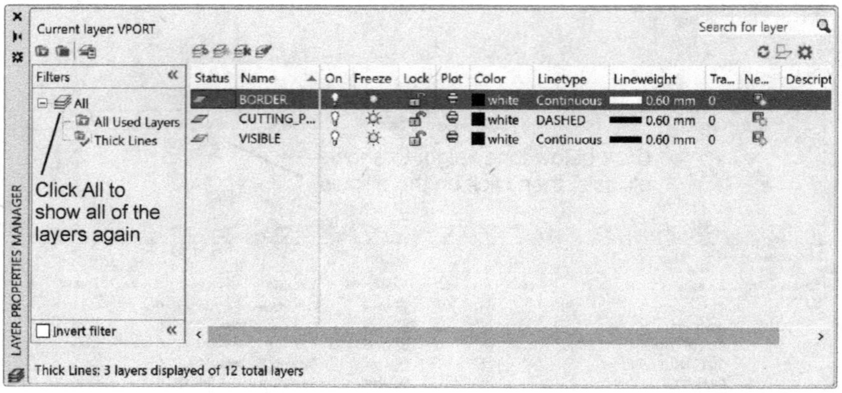

Figure 5.52

The only layers that appear in the list view are 0.60 mm lineweight. To see all of the layers,

Click: ***All*** *from the top of the tree list*

All of the layers display in the list area now. You can select the Thick Lines filter whenever you want to display just the 0.60 mm lines.

Click: ***New Group Filter***

Group Filter1 is added as a group to the tree list as shown in Figure 5.53. It is highlighted so that you can overtype it with a descriptive name.

Type: ***SECTION LAYERS*** *as the Group name*

The group Section Layers appears in the tree view. Currently no layers are a member of this group, so nothing is displayed in the list view. Next you will display all of the layers and then drag the Hatch and Cutting_Plane layers onto the Section Layers group so that they will become its members.

Click: ***All*** *from the top of the tree view*

Click: ***Cutting_Plane and then press [Ctrl] and click Hatch*** *so that they both become highlighted*

Click: ***and drag the highlighted layers onto the Section Layers group*** *in the tree view as in Figure 5.46*

Click: ***Section Layers group*** *from the tree list*

The list view now displays only Hatch and Cutting_Plane.

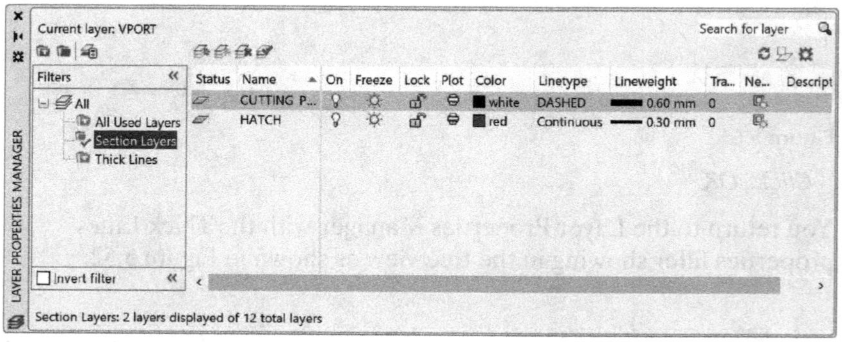

Figure 5.53

Click: ***All***

All of the layers now return to the list view.

Click: ***to Freeze layers 0 and Projection***

Click: ***Layer States Manager button***

Click: ***New***

Type: ***Frozen*** *in the Layer State to Save dialog box*

Click: ***OK*** *to return to the Layer States Manager*

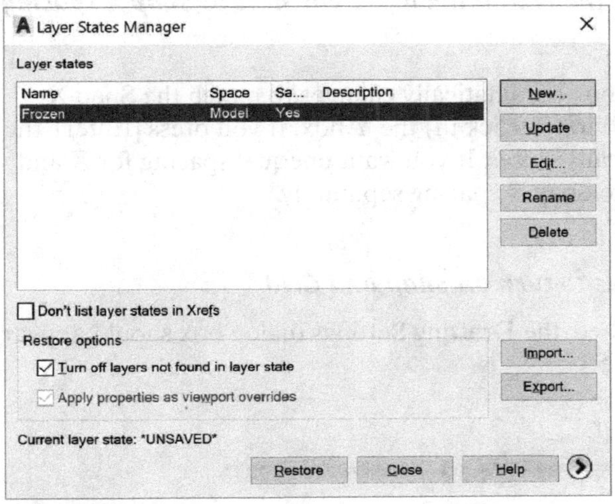

Figure 5.54

Click: ***Save***

"Do you want to overwrite Frozen?" *Click:* ***Yes***

Click: ***Close***

You return to the Layer Properties Manager.

On your own, ***thaw the frozen layers*** *and* ***set layer 0 current****.*

Click: ***Layer States Manager button***

The layer state you created named Frozen should already be highlighted as the selection. If it is not, select it.

Click: ***Restore***

Click: ***[X]*** *to close the Layer States Manager*

You return to the Layer Properties Manager.

The thawed layers return to the frozen state. The current layer returns to Vport. Now you will close the Layer Properties Manager and continue setting up your template file.

On your own, ***thaw the frozen layers****. Check that layer* ***Vport is set as current****.*

Click: ***[X]*** *to close the Layer Properties Manager*

Save your drawing before continuing.

Using the Drafting Settings Dialog Box

Next you will select the Drafting Settings dialog box and use it to set the Snap and Grid.

Right-click: ***on the Snap button*** *to show the short-cut menu*

Click: ***Snap Settings***

The Snap and Grid tab should be active.

Click: ***to highlight the text in the input box next to Snap X spacing***

Type: .25 [Tab]

The Snap Y spacing box automatically changes to match the Snap X spacing when you tab to (or click in) the Y box. If you press [Enter], the dialog box automatically closes. If you want unequal spacing for X and Y, you can change the Snap Y spacing separately.

Leave the ***Grid*** *set to* ***0.5****.*

Use the check boxes to ***turn on Snap and Grid****.*

When you have finished, the Drafting Settings dialog box should appear as shown in Figure 5.55.

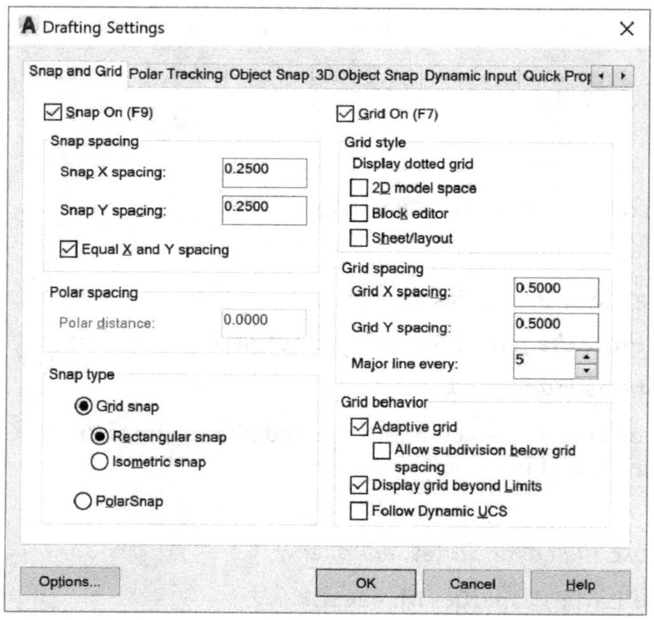

Figure 5.55

Click: ***OK*** *to exit the dialog box*

You should see the grid on your screen. You will use Zoom All to show your drawing limits (12" X 9") in the drawing area. When you start a drawing from your template, you will set the drawing limits at that time to a value large enough for the particular part you will draw. Then you can use the Zoom command to view the new drawing limits.

For now,

On your own, ***Zoom All****.*

Selecting the Default Text Font

The software offers various fonts for different uses. One of the best fonts that ships with the software for lettering engineering drawings is called *romans*, for Roman Simplex. The *.shx* fonts are provided, so all other AutoCAD users will also have this font. True Type fonts and other system fonts may look great in your drawing, but may not be available on someone else's system, causing them to have to substitute another font which may make the lettering not fit correctly in the drawing.

Click: ***Text Style button*** *from the Home tab, Annotation panel*

The Text Style dialog box, which you used in Tutorial 1, appears, showing the Style name, Font, and Effects choices.

Click: ***New***

Type: ***MYTEXT***

Click: ***OK*** *(or press [Enter])*

Click: ***romans.shx*** *from the Font Name pull-down*

You will use the defaults in all other areas of the dialog box. Remember, accepting the defaults now means you will be prompted for these values when you create the text; this method offers you a lot of flexibility when drawing. Do not become confused between style names and font names. A font is a set of characters with a particular shape. When you create a *style*, you can assign it any name you want, but you must specify the name of a font that already exists for the style to use. Your dialog box should look like Figure 5.56.

Tip: *If you are using a slower computer system, you may notice that performance on your computer slows down. It may be because of this setting. If you need to, you can reset Viewres to a lower number. Type REGEN at the command prompt to regenerate circles that do not appear round.*

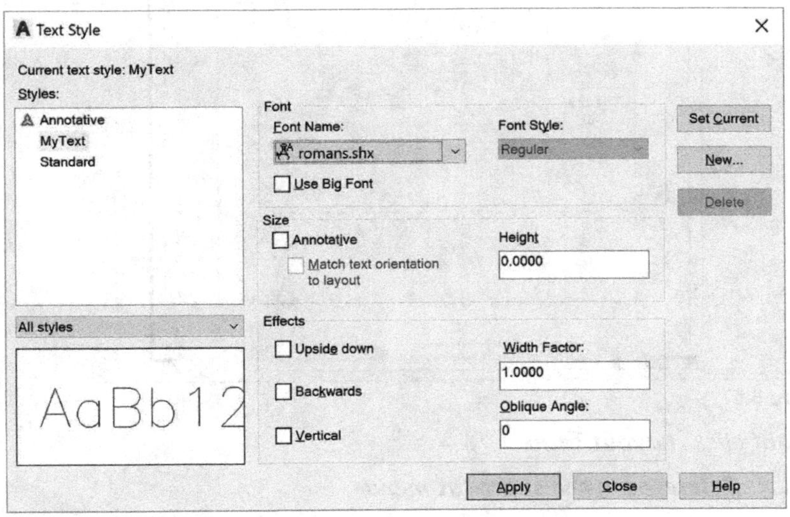

Figure 5.56

Click: ***Apply***

Click: ***Close***

Setting the Viewres Default

The *Viewres* command controls the number of line segments used to draw a circle on your monitor. It does not affect the way that circles are plotted—just how they appear on the screen. Have you noticed that when you use Zoom Window to enlarge a portion of the drawing, circles may appear as octagons? The reason is that Viewres is set to a low number. The default setting is low to save time when you draw circles on the screen. With faster processors and high-resolution graphics optimization, you may never need this setting. You will type VIEWRES at the command prompt.

Command: ***VIEWRES [Enter]***

Do you want fast zooms? [Yes/No] <Y>: ***[Enter]***

Enter circle zoom percent (1-20000)<1000>: ***5000 [Enter]***

Click: ***Save button*** *to save your template thus far*

Tip: *When the grid is turned on in both model space and paper space, two patterns of grid dots, which don't necessarily align, are produced, which can be confusing. Generally, you will want to turn off the paper space grid before you return to model space.*

Switching to a Paper Space Layout

Next you will create a drawing layout to use for plotting.

Click: ***Layout1 tab***

Figure 5.57 shows the paper space layout as it appears on your screen.

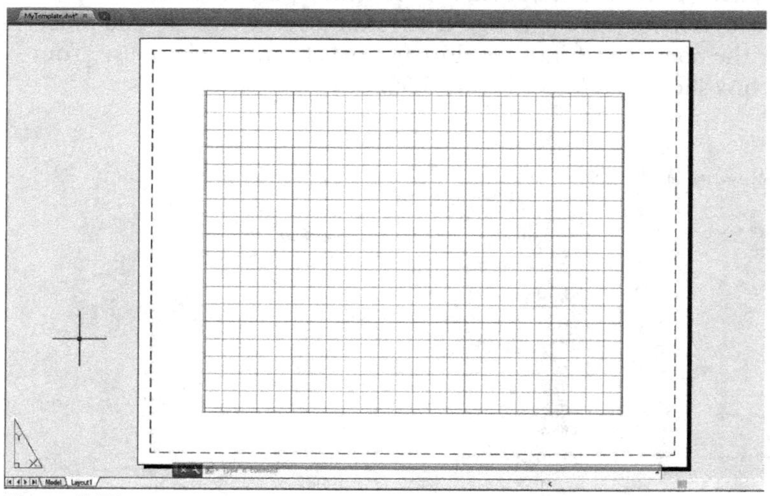

Figure 5.57

Right-click: ***Layout2 tab***

Click: ***Delete*** *from the short-cut menu*

At the message "The selected layouts will be permanently deleted ...";

Click: ***OK***

Layout 2 is deleted. Keep in mind that multiple layouts in a single drawing are not recommended for use with the Sheet Set Manager.

The magenta box around the drawing view is the AutoCAD paper space viewport. It is like a hole or window that you can use to look through the paper and see your model space drawing. Figure 5.58 shows another illustration of the concept of model space and paper space. The viewport border is a drawing object in paper space that defines the shape of the window to model space. The zoom factor determines the size at which the model space objects appear in the paper space viewport.

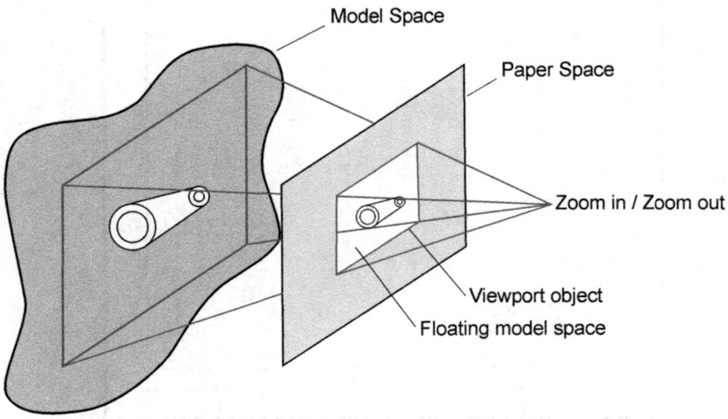

Figure 5.58

Tip: Turn off Object snaps before entering values, otherwise objects within the snap cursor will be selected. Turning off dynamic input can be helpful when entering a list of values.

Adding a Title Block and Text to Paper Space

You can easily add a title block to your drawing using lines and text in paper space. The advantage of adding the title block, notes, and border to paper space is that the measurements there are the same as you would make them on a regular sheet of paper.

You will draw the border on a separate layer so that you can turn on the display of lineweights to their effect in paper space.

Select layer **BORDER** as the current layer.

Click: ***Show/Hide Lineweight button*** *from the status bar* ***to show lineweights***

Draw the lines for the border of the drawing shown in Figure 5.59.

Click: ***Line button***

Specify first point: ***.5,.25 [Enter]***

Specify next point or [Undo]: ***10,.25 [Enter]***

Specify next point or [Undo]: ***10,7.75 [Enter]***

Specify next point or [Close/Undo]: ***.5,7.75 [Enter]***

Specify next point or [Close/Undo]: ***C [Enter]***

Now you will use the Offset command to offset a line across the bottom of the viewport.

Click: ***Offset button***

Specify offset distance or [Through/Erase/Layer] <Through>: ***.375 [Enter]***

Select object to offset or [Exit/Undo] <Exit>: ***click the bottom border line***

Specify point on side to offset or [Exit/Multiple/Undo] <Exit>: ***click above the bottom border line***

Select object to offset or [Exit/Undo] <Exit>: ***[Enter]***

The border lines and title strip should appear in your drawing as shown in Figure 5.59.

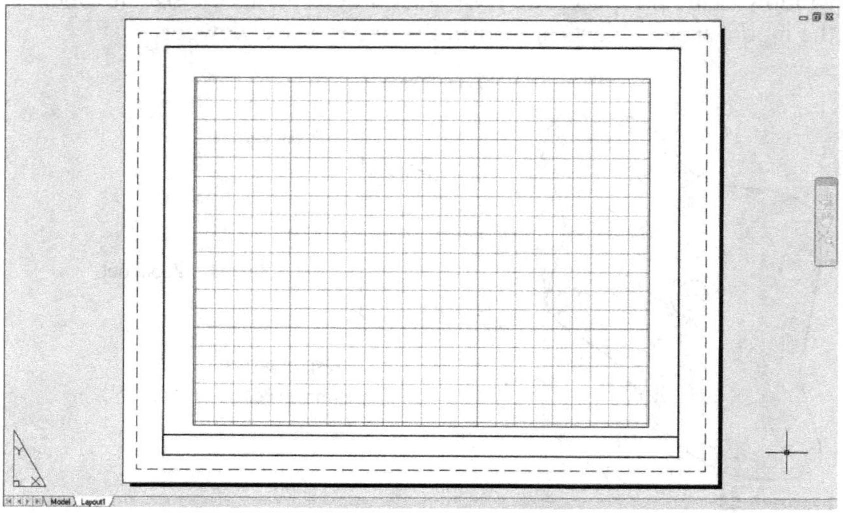

Figure 5.59

Hide/Show Lineweight on Status Bar

It is often convenient to turn on and off the display of lineweights using a button on the status bar. You can show the button using the Customization selection from the right of the status bar.

Click: ***Customization*** *from the right of the status bar*

Select: ***Lineweight*** *from the list so it appears checked*

Click: ***Lineweight*** *button from the status bar to turn it on*

On your own, ***enlarge the lower left corner of the drawing*** *as in Figure 5.60 so that you can see the lineweight used to represent the border.*

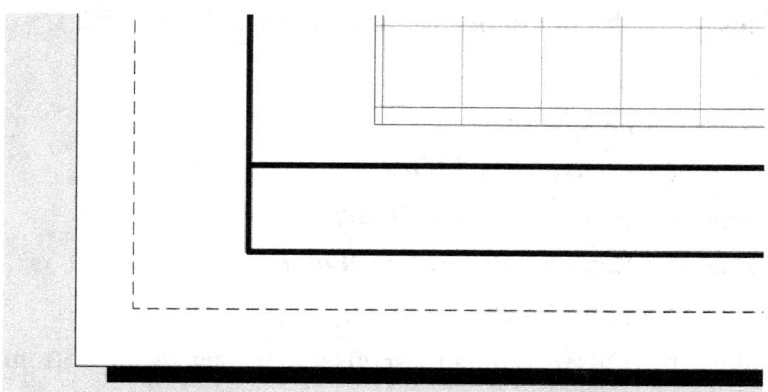

Figure 5.60

Click: ***Zoom Previous button***

Your view returns to show the entire drawing area.

Using Divide

The *Divide* command places points along the object that you select, dividing it into the number of segments you specify. You can also choose to have a block of grouped objects placed in the drawing instead of points. You will use the Divide command to place points along the line that you created using Offset, dividing it into three equal segments. Divide is on the Home tab, Draw panel drop-down.

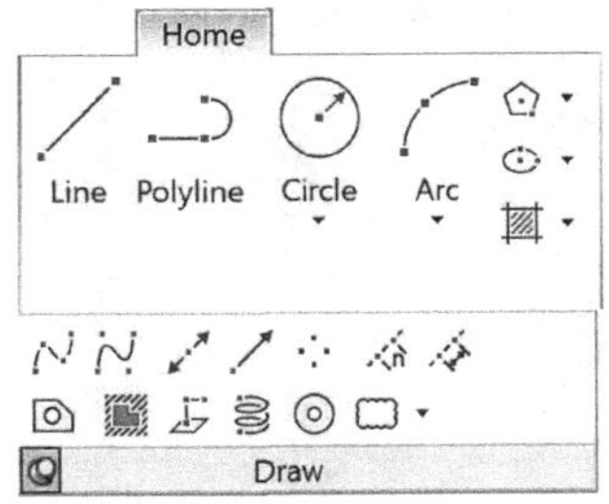

Click: ***Divide button** from the Home tab, Draw panel*

Select object to divide: ***click the line above the bottom border line***

Enter the number of segments or [Block]: ***3 [Enter]***

Setting Point Style

Because the Point Style is set at just a dot, you probably won't be able to see the points that mark the equal segment lengths. You will use the Point Style dialog box to change the display of points in the drawing to a larger style so you can see them easily.

Click: ***Point Style button from the Home tab, Utilities panel***

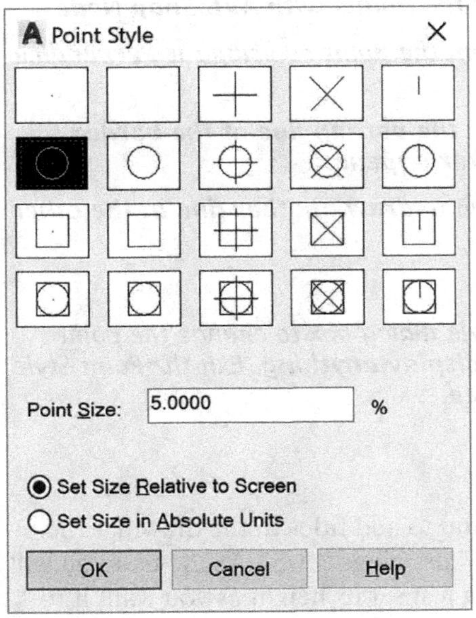

Figure 5.61

The Point Style dialog box shown in Figure 5.61 appears. On your own, select one of the point styles that has a circle or target around the point so that it is easily seen. To exit the dialog box,

Click: OK

The points appear larger on the screen now, similar to Figure 5.62.

Tip: *The Measure command is similar to the Divide command. However, instead of specifying the number of segments into which you want to have an object divided, with Measure you specify the length of the segment you would like to have. Like Divide, Measure puts points or groups of objects called blocks (which you will learn about in Tutorial 10) at specified distances along the line. Don't get it confused with the Measuregeom command used to find the area and distances.*

Tip: *When the points are sized relative to the screen, they may appear large when you zoom in. To recalculate the display file for your drawing in order to resize them, use the Regen command on the View menu.*

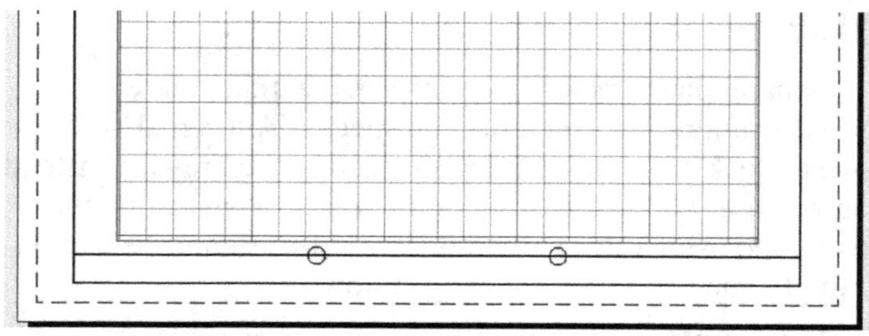

Figure 5.62

You can use the Node object snap to find point objects in your drawing. To draw lines dividing the title area exactly into thirds,

Right-click: ***Object Snap button*** *to show the short-cut menu*

Click: ***Settings***

Click: ***to turn on the Node and Perpendicular snap modes***

Click: ***OK***

Click: ***Object Snap button*** *from the status bar to turn it on*

Click: ***Line button***

Specify first point: ***target one of the points with AutoSnap Node***

Draw a line straight down from the point *by using the* ***Perpendicular*** *object snap.*

Specify next point or [Undo]: ***click the bottom line of the border when the Perpendicular marker appears***

Repeat this process on your own to ***draw another line at the other point****.*

Click: ***Point Style button***

On your own, use the ***Point Style*** *dialog box to change the point style to a mode that* ***does not display anything****. Exit the Point Style dialog box when you are finished.*

Tip: *The default justification for Dtext is Bottom Left, so you do not need to specifically select that option. If you want text to be justified bottom left, just select the start point and no other justification options. You can also use the Properties dialog box to change the justification of existing text.*

Adding the Titles

Next you will use the Text command to add titles to the drawing. The standard size for text on 8.5" X 11" drawings is 1/8". As the text you will add here is in paper space, you can just set its height as you want it to print.

Tip: *A field storing information can be inserted into any text area except for tolerances. Fields store information that will update automatically, such as the date or sheet number. Pick Insert, Field from the pull-down menu and use the dialog box that appears to select the type of information to insert. From there follow the prompts similar to inserting text.*

Set TEXT as the ***current layer****.*

Make sure you are in ***paper space****.*

Click: ***Single line text*** *from the Annotation panel*

Specify start point of text or [Justify/Style]: ***C [Enter]***

Specify center point of text: ***5.25, .375 [Enter]***

Specify height <0.2000>: ***.125 [Enter]***

Specify rotation angle of text: ***0 [Enter]***

Type: ***DRAWING TITLE [Enter] [Enter]***

The words DRAWING TITLE appear, centered on the point you selected. The centering is horizontal only; otherwise the letters would appear above the point selected for the center. If you want both horizontal and vertical centering, choose the Justify option and then Middle.

Now, repeat this process using the Justify, BL (Bottom Left) option of the Dtext command to position the words DRAWN BY: YOUR NAME in the left part of the title block. You are prompted for the bottom left starting point for the text that you will enter. Use the Justify, BR (Bottom Right) option to right justify the words SCALE: 1=1 in the area to the right.

The Justify BR option prompts you for the lowest, rightmost point for the text that you will enter.

Now you have completed a simple title block for your template. Next, switch to model space and set the viewport scale to 1:1 using the zoom XP option.

On your own, set the current layer to **VISIBLE**.

Command: ***MS [Enter]***

Command: ***Z [Enter]***

Specify corner of window, enter a scale factor (nX or nXP), or [All/Center/Dynamic/Extents/Previous/Scale/Window/Object] <real time>: ***1XP [Enter]***

You will save this drawing in floating model space so that you can see the paper space border, but still create your new drawing objects in model space. You will leave the drawing zoomed to a scale of 1=1 and with VISIBLE set as the current layer. Then, when you begin a new drawing from this template, you will be ready to start drawing on the layer for VISIBLE lines.

Your drawing should look like Figure 5.63.

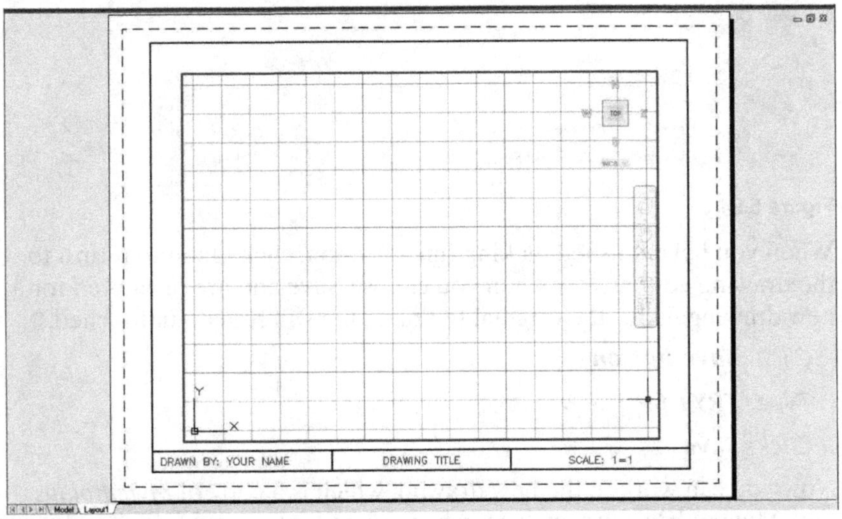

Figure 5.63

Click: ***Save button***

Click: ***to close mytemplate.dwt***

Tip: *You can set your drawing limits by zooming to show the area of the coordinate system you want to use and then picking from the screen to set the lower left corner and then the upper right corner.*

Now you have completed *mytemplate.dwt.* Be sure to keep a copy of the drawing on your own disk. You also should keep a second copy of your drawings on a backup disk, in case the first copy becomes damaged.

You can easily edit the text by double-clicking on it to make changes to the standard information you provide in the title block. Refer to Tutorial 1 if you need to review the Edit Text (Ddedit) command.

Tip: *If you have access to several different printers or work with different sheet sizes, having several different template drawings is very useful. Or use a standard AutoCAD template and modify it for your uses. Then save it with a new template name.*

Beginning a New Drawing from a Template Drawing

You can use any AutoCAD drawing as a starting point for a new drawing. The settings that you have made in drawing *mytemplate.dwt* will be used to start future drawings. An identical template drawing, called *proto.dwt*, is in your datafiles. If you want to use the template you just created, substitute *mytemplate.dwt* whenever you are asked to use *proto.dwt.* Next, you will start a new drawing from your template.

Tip: *You can rename a layout tab by right-clicking on it and picking Rename from the short cut menu.*

Click: ***New***

Use the dialog box shown in Figure 5.64 to select the correct drive and folder and select *mytemplate.dwt.* (If you have not created the template in the previous steps, you may substitute the datafile *proto.dwt.*)

Tip: *You can change the style of text that has already been added to your drawing using the Text Style selection. Select a text object. Use the Text Style pull down to view the list of available styles and make a new selection. Remember that you must create styles with the Style command before you can use them. You can also use the Properties palette to change the style, height, width factor, rotation, and location of the text entry.*

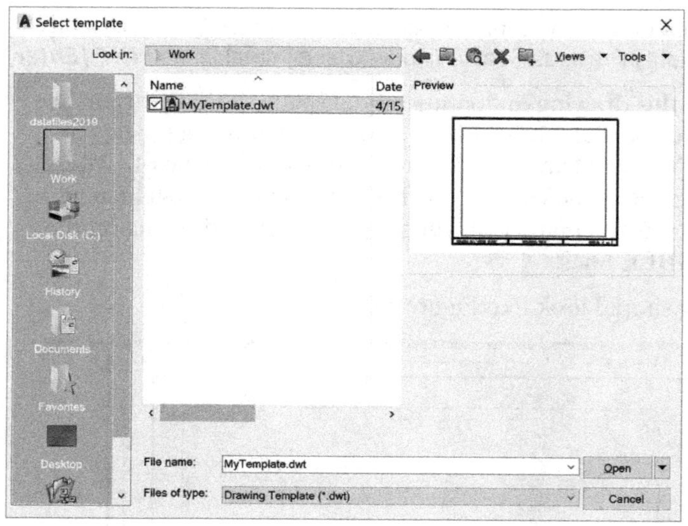

Figure 5.64

When you have finished making this selection, click Open to return to the drawing editor. Now when you choose Save and are prompted for a new drawing name, the original template file will remain untouched.

Click: ***Save button***

Type: ***TRY1*** *for File Name*

Click: ***Save***

Now you can work in the new drawing which is a copy of *mytemplate.dwt.* *Mytemplate.dwt* remains unchanged, so that you can use it to start other drawings. Your current drawing name is *try1.dwg.* For future drawings in this book, use *proto.dwt* or *mytemplate.dwt* as a template drawing unless you are directed to do otherwise.

Changing the Title Block Text

You created the border, text, and lines of the title block in paper space. To make a change to any of them, you must first return to paper space. Then, you will double-click on the text or use the Edit Text selection (Ddedit command) to change the title block text so that it is correct for the new drawing that you are starting.

Command: ***PS [Enter] or double-click outside the viewports***

Double-click: on the text ***Drawing Title***

The Edit Text box appears in place containing the text you selected.

Use the [Backspace] and/or [Delete] keys to remove the words "Drawing Title." Change the entry to "Try1."

When you have finished editing the text,

Select an annotation object or [Undo]: ***[Enter]*** *to end the command*

When using a template, remember to make sure that you are in model space before creating drawing objects. Only items like the border, titleblock, and general notes and keys should be placed in paper space.

Exit *the AutoCAD program and* ***discard the changes*** *to drawing try1.dwg.*

Using company standards for layer naming, title blocks, reuseable blocks, etc. saves time, helps with accuracy, improves useability, and provides a professional appearance for your drawings. Autodesk's Forma Data Management subscription allows project members to standardize plot styles and drawing templates and many other things for working and managing a group of CAD users. Whether you are using Forma, another system, or doing it yourself, plan to save time, and improve your drawing appearance and accuracy by following standards.

You have completed Tutorial 5.

Key Terms

aspect ratio	paper space	template drawing
floating viewports	paper space layouts	text style
model space	pin-registry	tiled viewports

Key Commands (keyboard shortcut)

Divide (DIV)	MEASURE	Paper Space (PS)	(VPCLIP)
Insert Block (INS)	Model Space (MS)	REGEN	VIEWRES
Layer (LA)	Mview (MV)	Viewport Clip	

Exercises

Draw the following objects. The letter M after an exercise number means that the given dimensions are in millimeters (metric units).

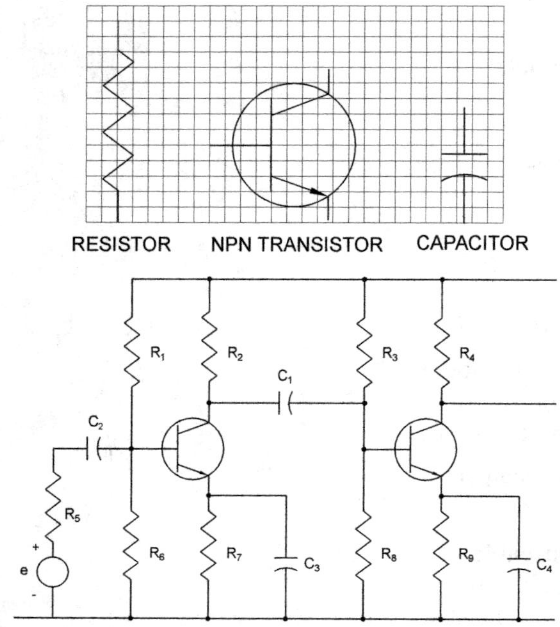

Exercise 5.1 Amplifier Circuit

Draw the amplifier circuit. Use the grid at the top to determine the sizes of the components. Each square = 0.0625.

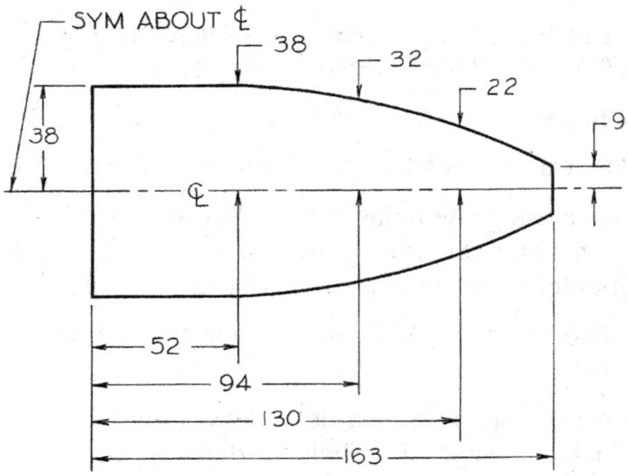

Exercise 5.2 Support

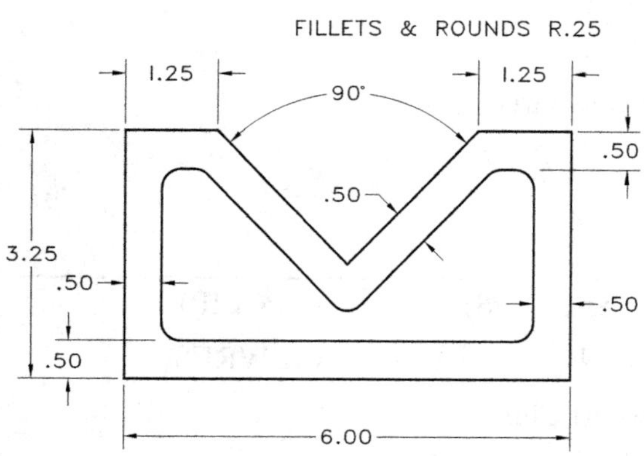

Exercise 5.3 Vee Block

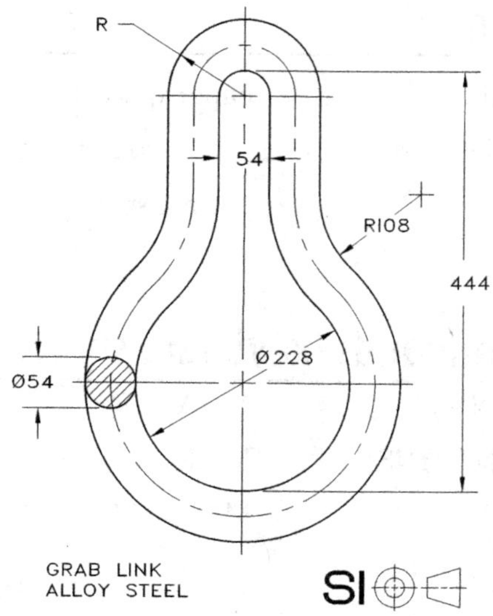

Exercise 5.4M Grab Link

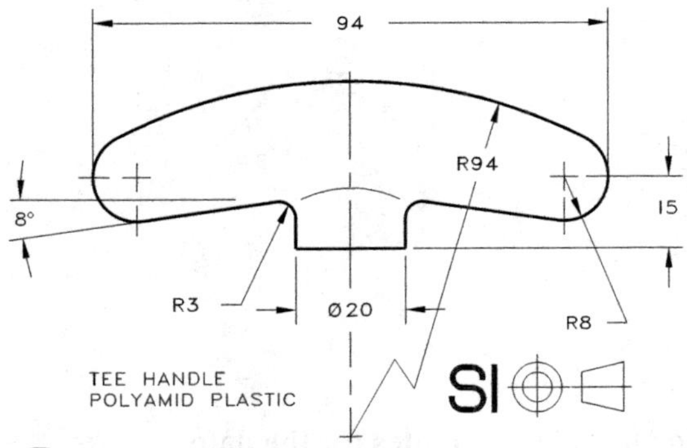

Exercise 5.5M Tee Handle

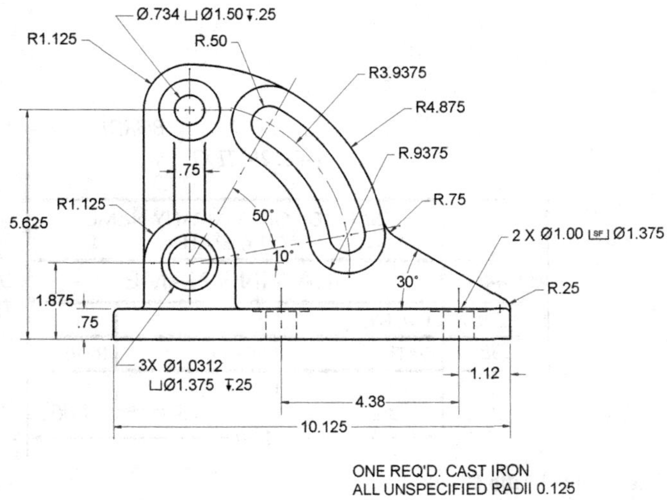

Exercise 5.6 Idler Pulley Bracket

Create the drawing of the front view of the object as shown.

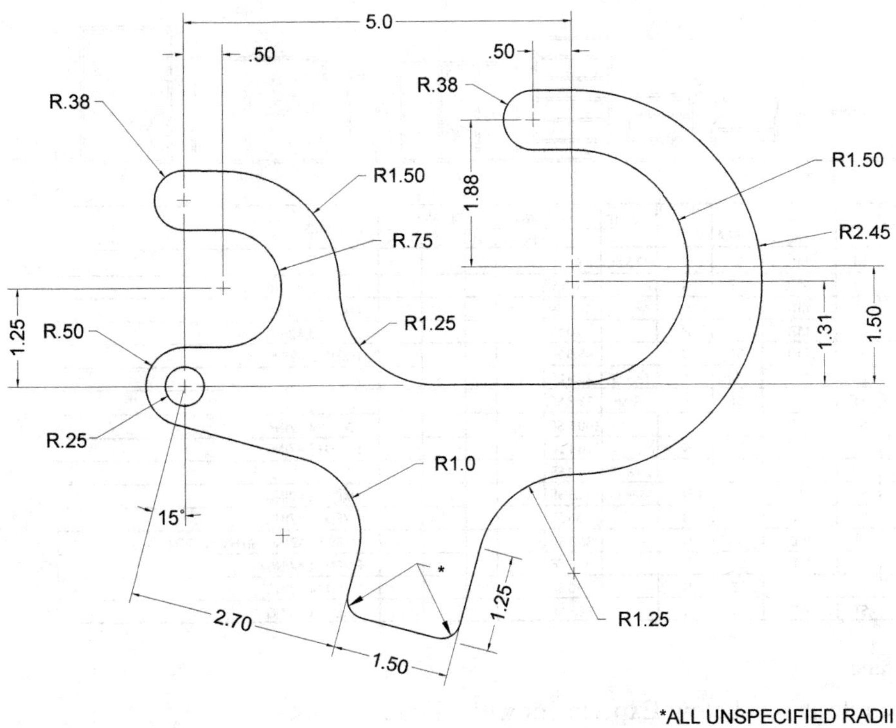

Exercise 5.7 Hanger

Draw the object shown. Set Limits to (–4, –4) and (8, 5). Set Snap to 0.25 and Grid to 0.5. The origin (0, 0) is to be the center of the left circle. Do not include the dimensions.

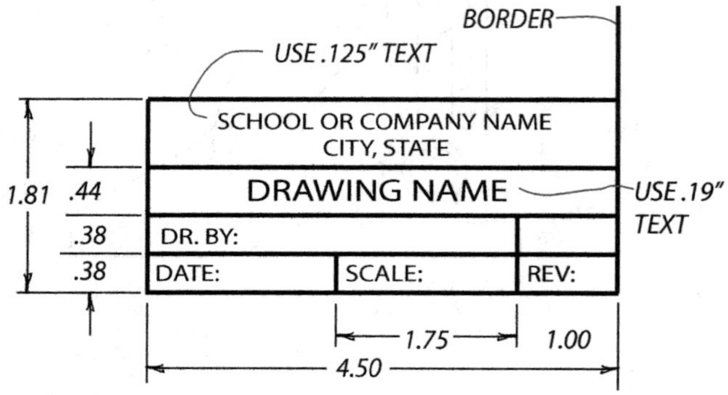

Exercise 5.8 Title Block

Create this title block as a model space drawing. Explore using fields or attributes for the date, scale, and other changeable information. Use the Insert command to add this title block in paper space to other drawings.

WINDOW SCHEDULE

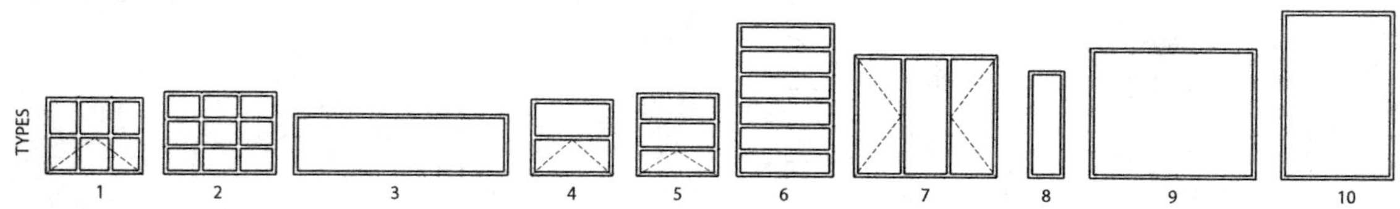

SYM	TYPE	SIZE		MATL FIN	FRAME	FIN SCRN AREA	AREA		VENT	GLAZING		DETAILS			REMARKS
		H	W								MAT'L	H	J	S	
A	1	5'-0"	6'-4"	MTL	ST	MTL	ST	Y	32.5 SF	65 SF					
B	2	5'-5"	7'-4"	MTL	ST	MTL	ST	N		40.5 SF					FIXED GLAZING
C	3	4'-0"	14'-8"	MTL	ST	MTL	ST	N		58.8 SF					FIXED GLAZING
D	4	7'-0"	5'-0"	MTL	ST	MTL	ST	N		70 SF					FIXED GLAZING
E	5	5'-5"	4'-6"	MTL	ST	MTL	ST	N		48.6 SF					FIXED GLAZING
F	6	5'-0"	5'-4"	MTL	ST	MTL	ST	Y	13.3 SF	26.5 SF					
G	7	5'-5"	5'-4"	MTL	ST	MTL	ST	Y	9.9 SF	29.7 SF					
H	8	8'-0"	6'-4"	MTL	ST	MTL	ST	N		100.8 SF					FIXED GLAZING
I	9	5'-6"	6'-4"	MTL	ST	MTL	ST	N		126.1 SF					FIXED GLAZING
J	10	8'-0"	9'-4"	MTL	ST	MTL	ST	Y	24.8 SF	74.4 SF					
K	11	5'-6"	4'-8"	MTL	ST	MTL	ST	N		25.3 SF					FIXED GLAZING
L	12	6'-0"	3'-0"	WD	ST	WD	ST	N		36 SF					FIXED GLAZING
M	13	7'-6"	11'-6"	WD	ST	WD	ST	N		86.3 SF					FIXED GLAZING WITH CURVED GLASS
N	14	10'-0"	8'-0"	MTL	ST	MTL	ST	N		160 SF					FIXED GLAZING
O	15	10'-0"	14'-0'	MTL	ST	MTL	ST	N		140 SF					FIXED GLAZING
P	16	6'-0"	6'-6"	WD	ST	WD	ST	N		32.5 SF					FIXED GLAZING

Exercise 5.9 Window Schedule

Redraw the window schedule shown below. Experiment with different fonts.

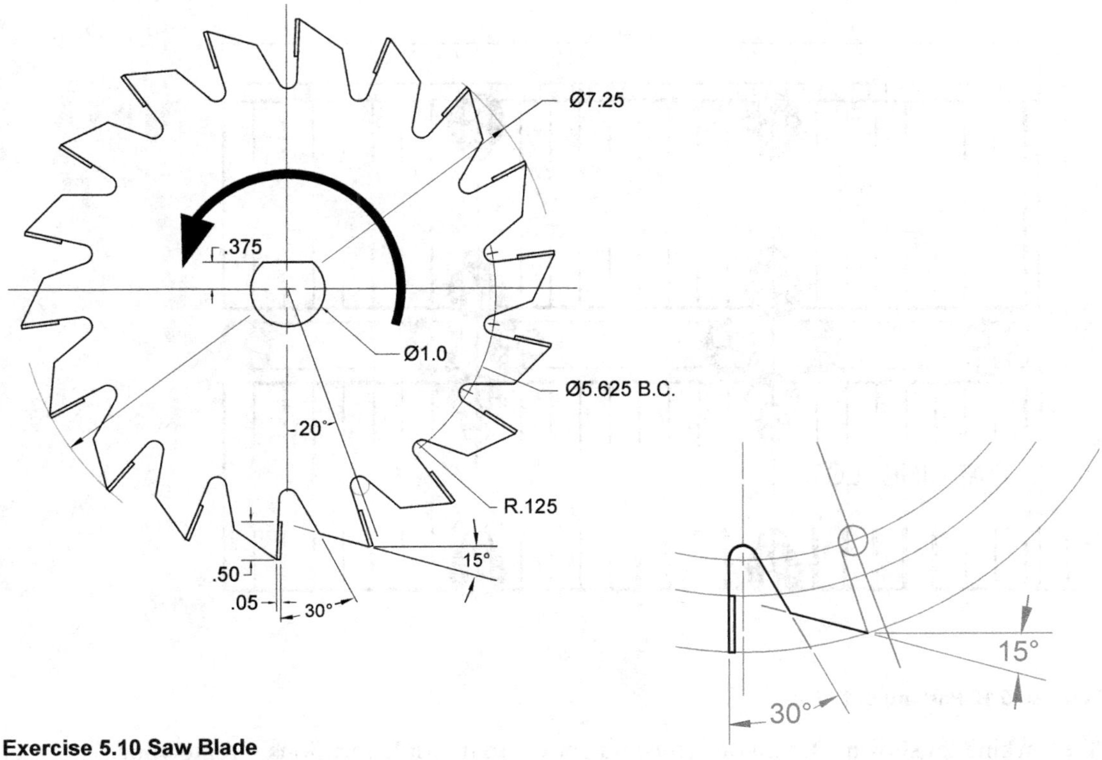

Exercise 5.10 Saw Blade

Draw the saw blade shown. Use Array and Polyline. Do not include dimensions. Use the Arc option of the Polyline command to create the thick arc. Add the arrow to the arc by making a Polyline with a beginning width of 0 and a thicker ending width to show the blade's rotation.

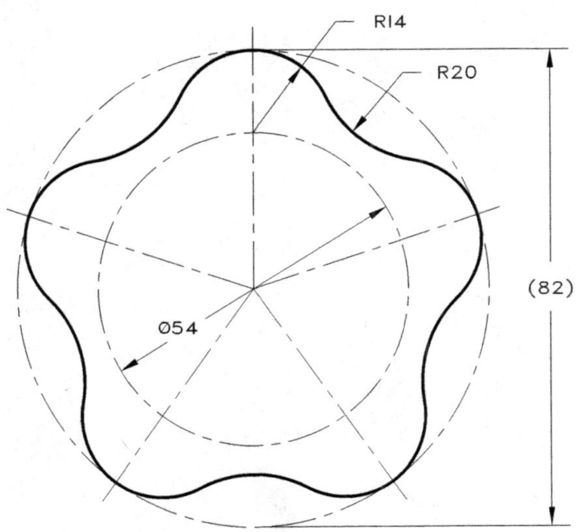

Exercise 5.11M Five Lobe Knob

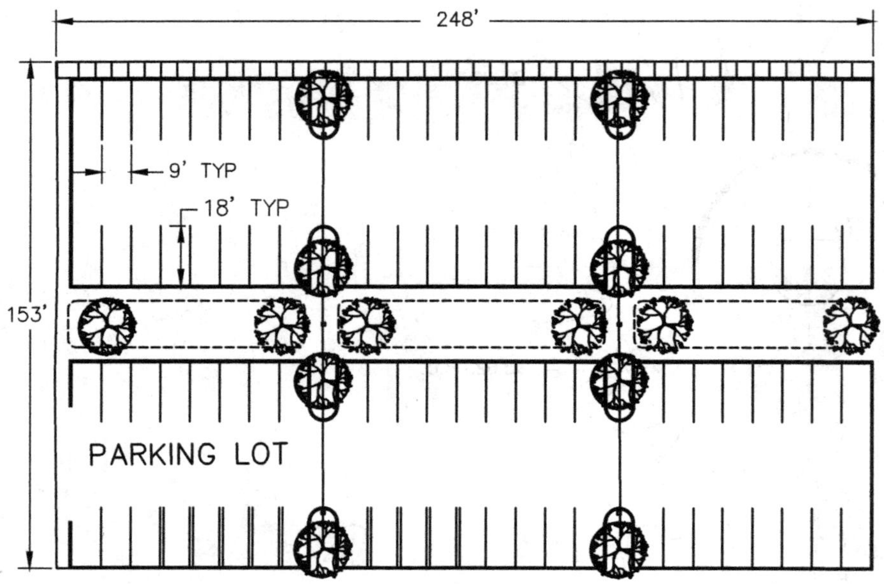

Exercise 5.12 Parking Lot Plan

Draw the parking lot shown. Design one tree and copy it to multiple locations. Create your drawing using architectural units. Make the plan full size in model space and then plot it to a reduced scale on a standard sheet with a title block.

2D ORTHOGRAPHIC DRAWINGS

6

Introduction

Orthographic views are two-dimensional (2D) drawings that depict the shape of a three-dimensional (3D) object. In this tutorial, you will draw orthographic views that define the shape of a 3D object. You will apply many commands you have already learned. In Tutorial 11 you will learn to create a 3D solid model of an object and later generate orthographic views from the model.

The Front, Top, and Right-Side Orthographic Views

Technical drawings usually require front, top, and right-side orthographic views to define the shape of an object. Some objects require fewer views and others require more. Each orthographic view is a 2D drawing showing only two of the three dimensions (height, width, and depth). So, you must look at all three views together to understand the shape being represented. For this reason it is important that the views be shown in the correct relationship to each other.

Figure 6.1 left shows a pictorial drawing of a part. At the right are the front, top, and right-side orthographic views of the part.

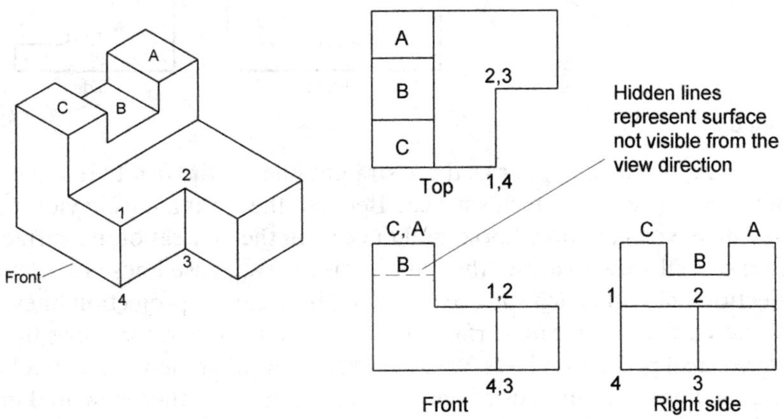

Figure 6.1

Three rectangular surfaces, labeled A, B, and C, are located on the left side of the top view. Which surface is the highest? The top view alone is not sufficient to answer this question. You must locate the three surfaces in the other views to determine the relationships between them. The right-side view (often just referred to as the side or profile view) shows that surfaces A and C are the same height and that surface B is lower.

Objectives

When you have completed this tutorial, you will be able to

1. Create 2D orthographic drawings.
2. Use Ortho for horizontal and vertical lines.
3. Create construction lines.
4. Draw hidden, projection, center, and miter lines.
5. Set the global linetype scaling factor.
6. Add correctly drawn centermarks to circular shapes.

The side view shows the relative locations of surfaces A, B, and C, but the surfaces appear as straight lines. You need all three views to determine the shape of the surfaces.

All surfaces should be drawn in all views or the view should be clearly labeled as a partial view. Surface C is shown in the front view of Figure 6.2 with a hidden line. A *hidden line* represents a surface not directly visible, that is, hidden from view by some other surface of the object.

View Location

The locations of the front, top, and side views on a drawing are critical. In Third Angle Projection (used in USA) the top view must be located directly above the front view. The side view should be located directly to the right of the front view. An alternative position for the side view is to rotate it 90° and align it with the top view. By aligning the views precisely with each other, you can interpret them together to understand the 3D object they represent. Because views are shown in alignment, you can project information from one view to another (Figure 6.2).

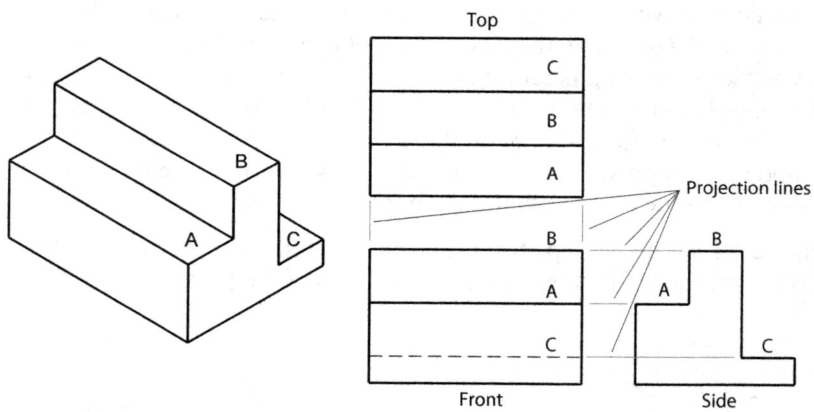

Figure 6.2

Surfaces A, B, and C appear as three straight lines in the front view. Which line represents which surface? Because the front and side views are aligned, you can draw horizontal lines from the *vertices* of the surfaces in the front view to locate them in the side view. These lines are called projection lines and each surface is located between its projection lines in both views. You can locate surfaces between the front and top views by using vertical projection lines. Without exact view alignment, you couldn't relate the lines and surfaces of one view to those of another view, making it difficult or impossible to interpret the object shown in the drawing.

Starting

Launch **AutoCAD® 2022.**

You will start your new drawing from the template file *proto.dwt* that is provided with the datafiles. This way you will be sure you are using the same settings as those in the tutorial.

Click: ***New button***

Use the dialog box that appears on your screen to select the file ***proto.dwt*** from the datafiles that accompany this text in the ***datafiles*** folder.

Click: ***Save button***

Type: ***ADAPTORT*** *for the file name and use* ***work*** *for the folder*

Click: ***Save***

Adaptort.dwg should appear on your screen, similar to Figure 6.3.

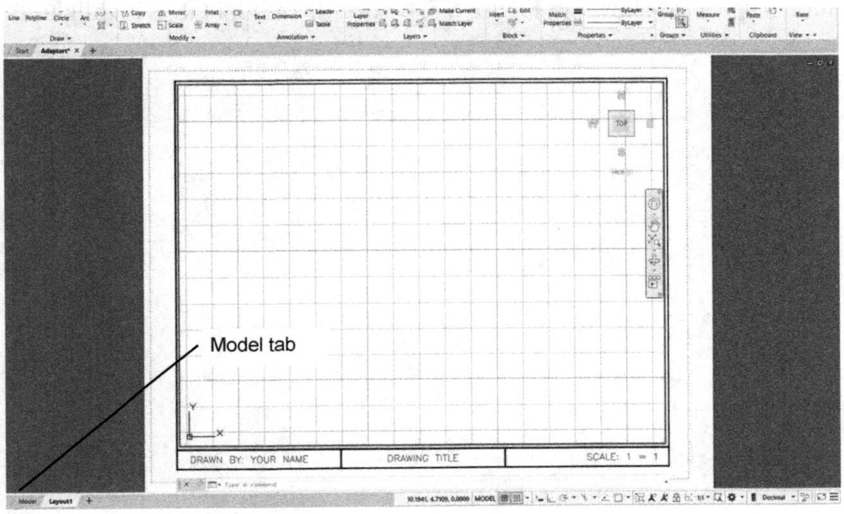

Figure 6.3

On your own, check that the grid is set to **0.5** spacing and the snap to **0.25** and that grid and snap are turned on. You should be in floating **model space**. Make sure that **VISIBLE** is the current layer. Check that the **Polar Tracking**, **Object Snap**, **Object Snap Tracking**, and **Dynamic Input** buttons on your status bar are turned **off**.

Figure 6.4 shows the adapter you will draw next. All dimensions are in decimal inches.

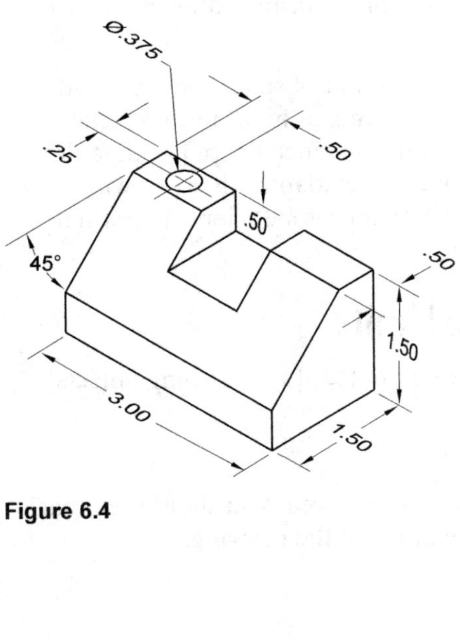

Figure 6.4

Tip: *You can substitute your drawing mytemplate.dwt if you have finished it correctly.*

Switching to Model Space

You can view and edit model space from a layout in the area inside a viewport (floating model space) as you see on your screen. You can also choose to work in model space alone. You will work in model space during this tutorial and then switch back to the layout for plotting.

*Click: **Model tab** (shown in Figure 6.3)*

The border and text should disappear from your screen leaving only model space, as shown in Figure 6.5. Notice the model tab is highlighted.

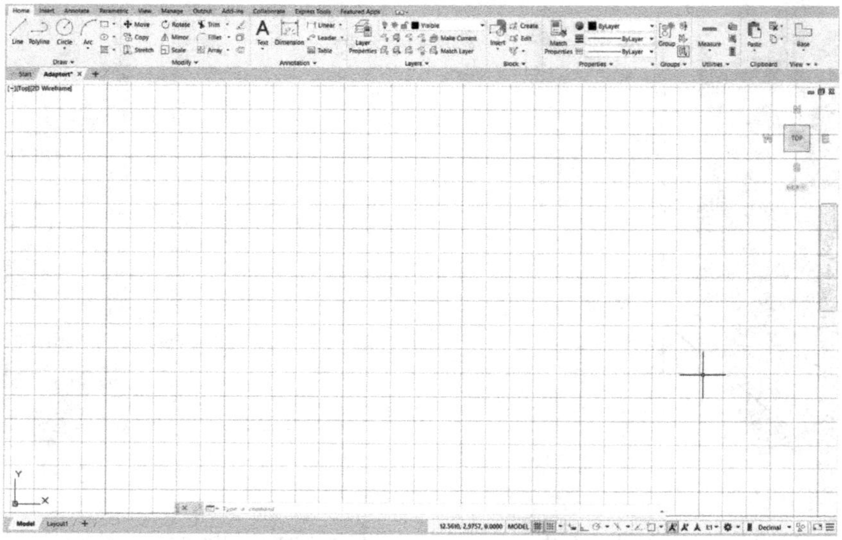

Figure 6.5

Deciding the Model Space Limits

Use the Limits command in model space to set the limits to the size necessary to fit the views of the real-world object that you are creating. The limits set in paper space and in model space do not have to be the same. You can change the limits at any time during a drawing session using the Limits command.

Examine the size of the part and the amount of space the views will require. The adapter is 3 inches wide, 1.5 inches high, and 1.5 inches deep. The slot in the top of the adapter is 0.5 inch deep. The default limits for model space are 12 X 9 units. The adapter that you will draw does not require much space, so 12 X 9 units is sufficient. You will not need to reset the limits at this time.

Viewing the Model Space Limits

Zoom to show the drawing limits or extents (of the drawing objects), whichever is larger.

Double-click the mouse scroll wheel

Move the cursor around inside the drawing area. You should see that the coordinates and grid match the limits of the drawing.

Using Ortho

You can use the Ortho command to restrict Line and other commands to operate only horizontally and vertically. This feature is very handy when you are drawing orthographic views and projecting information between the views. You toggle the Ortho mode on and off by clicking the Ortho Mode button on the status bar or by pressing the [F8] function key to easily activate it when you are in a different command.

Click: ***Ortho Mode button***

The Ortho Mode button on the status bar should now be highlighted to show that it is active.

Next, you will draw the horizontal and vertical construction lines, as shown in Figure 6.6. These lines represent the leftmost and bottom edges of your orthogonal views. The coordinates are given for the lines you will create to ensure that your results look the same as in the tutorial. In general, you can create the construction lines at any location and then move the views if necessary. Don't worry if the group of views are not perfectly centered when you begin your drawing. You will center the views after they are drawn and you can see how much room is needed.

Drawing Construction Lines

Construction lines extend infinitely. The default method for drawing a construction line is to specify two points it passes through. When using the Horizontal option, the line drawn is parallel to the X-axis through the point you select. The Vertical option is the same, but creates a line parallel to the Y-axis. Using the Angle option, you specify the construction line by entering the desired angle and a point the line will go through. The Bisect option lets you define an angle by three points and create a construction line that bisects it. Finally, the Offset option allows you to specify the offset distance or through point, as when you use the Offset command, to create an infinite construction line.

Click: ***Construction Line button*** *from the Home tab, Draw panel*

Specify a point or [Hor/Ver/Ang/Bisect/Offset]: ***2,1.5 [Enter]***

Specify through point: ***click to the right to define a horizontal line***

Specify through point: ***click above to define a vertical line***

Specify through point: ***[Enter]***

Two infinite construction lines appear in your drawing similar to Figure 6.8: One is vertical through point (2,1.5), and the other is horizontal through the same point. They are on layer VISIBLE.

You should have the Show/Hide Lineweight button turned off, which often makes it easier to work on the drawing. If you do not see the Lineweight button on your status bar, use the Customization button from the status bar to show the Lineweight button, then turn off the display of the lineweights.

If the grid makes it hard to see your lines, turn the grid off.

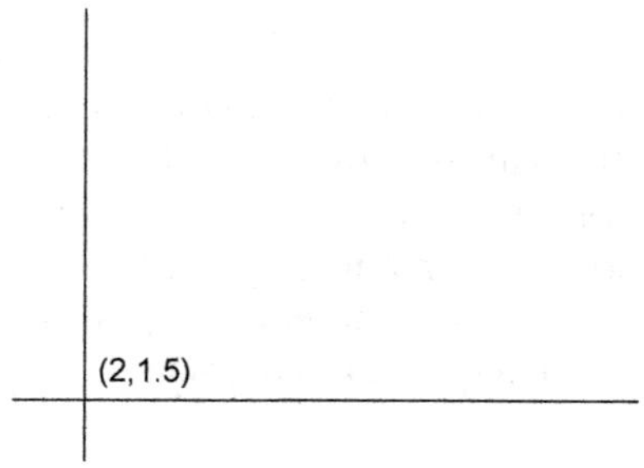

Figure 6.6

Next, you will offset a series of parallel horizontal and vertical lines to define the overall dimensions of each view, as shown in Figure 6.7. Then, you will trim the lines to remove the excess portions. If you need to, review the Offset command in Tutorial 3.

For the first horizontal line,

Click: ***Offset button***

Specify offset distance or [Through/Erase/Layer] <Through>: ***1.5 [Enter]***

Select object to offset or [Exit/Undo] <Exit>: ***click the horizontal line***

Specify point on side to offset? ***click any point above the horizontal line***

A new line is created, parallel to the bottom line and exactly 1.5 units away. You will end the command with the [Enter] key because the next line will be a different distance away.

Select object to offset or [Exit/Undo] <Exit>: ***[Enter]***

You will restart the Offset command by pressing [Enter] so that you are prompted again for the offset distance.

Command: ***[Enter]***

Specify offset distance or [Through/Erase/Layer] <1.5000>: ***1 [Enter]***

Select object to offset or [Exit/Undo] <Exit>: ***click the newly offset line***

Specify point on side to offset? ***click any point above the line***

A line appears 1.00 unit away from the line you selected.

Select object to offset or [Exit/Undo] <Exit>: ***[Enter]***

Now repeat this process on your own until you have created all the horizontal and vertical construction lines according to the dimensions shown in Figure 6.7.

The lines are parallel to the bottom horizontal line at distances of 1.5 (the given height of the object), 2.5 (the 1.5-inch height and an arbitrary 1-inch spacing between the front and top views), and 4 (the 1.5-inch height plus 1 plus the 1.5-inch depth of the object).

Your drawing should look like Figure 6.7.

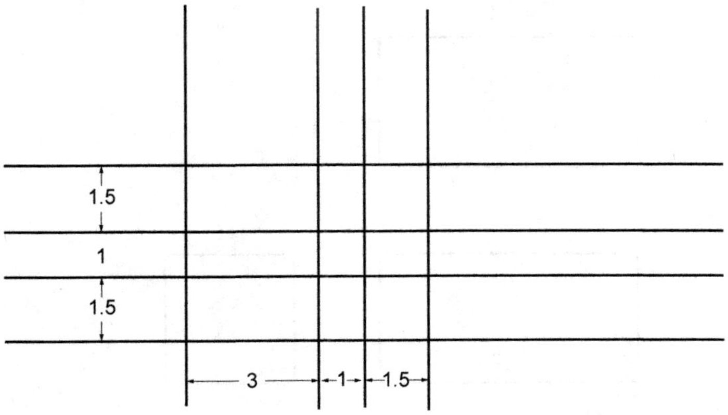

Figure 6.7

Next, trim to remove excess lines that define the areas for the front, top, and side views. When construction lines have one end trimmed, they become rays. When rays are trimmed, they become lines. Refer to Figure 6.8 for the portions to remove.

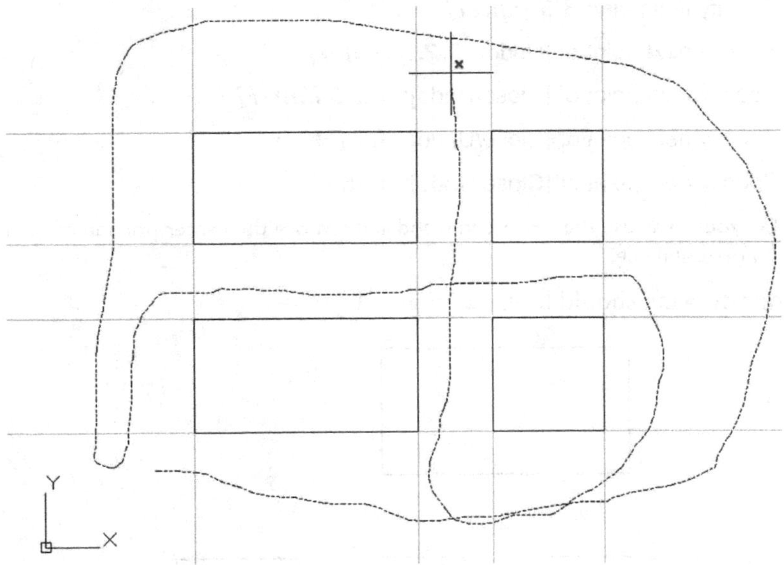

Figure 6.8

Tip: *Turn Snap off while trimming to make it easier to select lines.*

Click: ***Trim button*** *from the Modify panel*

Use the freehand method to specify the portions to remove. *Press* ***[Enter]*** *when finished.*

On your own, **zoom** to enlarge the drawing so that it fills the screen.

Your drawing should be similar to Figure 6.9. The overall dimensions of the views are established and aligned correctly.

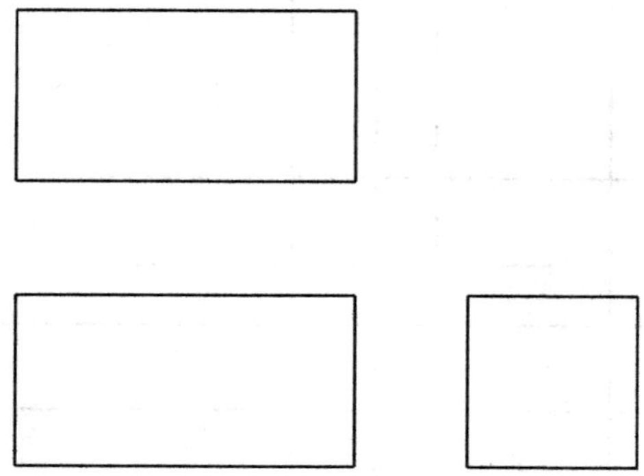

Figure 6.9

Next, draw the slot in the front view. Use the following points or create the lines on your own by looking at the dimensions specified on the object in Figure 6.4.

Click: ***Line button***

Specify first point: ***3,3 [Enter]***

Specify next point or [Undo]: ***3,2.5 [Enter]***

Specify next point or [Close/Undo]: ***4,2.5 [Enter]***

Specify next point or [Close/Undo]: ***4,3 [Enter]***

Specify next point or [Close/Undo]: ***[Enter]***

On your own, use the **Trim** command and remove the center portion of the top horizontal line.

Your drawing should look like Figure 6.10.

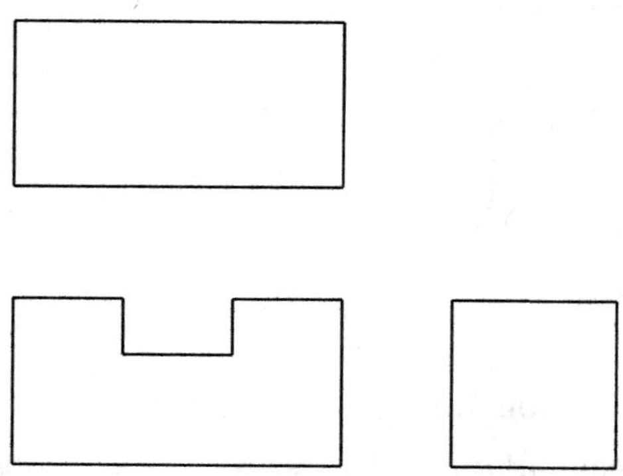

Figure 6.10

Hidden Lines

You will use hidden lines to represent the lines that are not visible in the side view. Remember, each view is a view of the entire object drawn from that line of sight. All surfaces are shown in every view.

A hidden line in the drawing represents one of three things:

1. An intersection of two surfaces that is behind another surface and therefore not visible;
2. The edge view of a hidden surface; or
3. The hidden outer limit of a curved surface, also called the limiting element of a contour.

You should follow at least three general practices when drawing hidden lines to help prevent confusion and to make the drawing easier to read. See Figure 6.11.

- Clearly show intersections, using intersecting line segments.
- Clearly show corners, using intersecting line segments.
- Leave a noticeable gap (about 1/16") between colinear continuous lines and hidden lines.

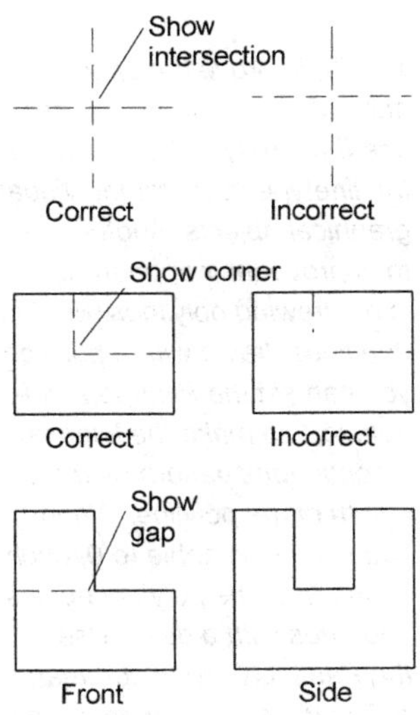

Figure 6.11

Traditional hidden line practices are sometimes difficult to implement using CAD. If you change one hidden line using the global linetype scale command, so that it looks better, all the other hidden lines take on the same characteristics and may be adversely affected. As you saw in Tutorial 4, you can change individual lines to have different linetype scales than the general pattern. However, hidden line practices are not followed as strictly as they once were, partly because with CAD drawings plotted on a good-quality plotter, the thick visible lines can easily be distinguished from the thinner hidden lines. The results of a reasonable attempt to conform to the standard are acceptable.

Hidden lines are usually drawn in a different color than the continuous object lines in the drawing. This helps you distinguish the different types of lines and makes them easier to interpret. Also, you may control your printers by using different colors in the drawing to represent different thicknesses or patterns of lines on the plot. You can use any color, but be consistent. A good approach is to set the color and linetype by layer and draw the hidden lines on that separate layer with the correct properties. That's why BYLAYER is the AutoCAD default choice for color, lineweight, and linetype. A separate layer for hidden lines already exists in the *proto.dwt* template drawing from which you started *adaptort.dwg*.

Drawing Hidden Lines

Now you will create a hidden line in the side view of your drawing to represent the bottom surface of the slot. You will use the Layer Control to set the current layer.

*Click: **HIDDEN_LINES** to make it current using the Layer Control*

Next you will add a horizontal line from the bottom edge of the slot in the front view into the side view. This line will be used to *project* the depth of the slot to the side view.

For drawing the following lines, the running object snap Intersection will be quite helpful.

Right-click: ***Object Snap button***

Click: ***Settings***

Click: ***Clear All*** *(from the Object Snap tab of the dialog box)*

Click: ***Intersection***

Click: ***OK*** *to exit the dialog box*

Click: ***Object Snap button*** *to turn it on*

Verify that the ORTHO button from the status bar is ON.

Click: ***Line button***

Specify first point: ***click the lower right corner (A) of the slot*** *in the front view then the object snap Intersection marker appears*

Specify next point or [Undo]: ***click any point to the right of the side view***

Specify next point or [Undo]: ***[Enter]***

Your drawing should look like Figure 6.12.

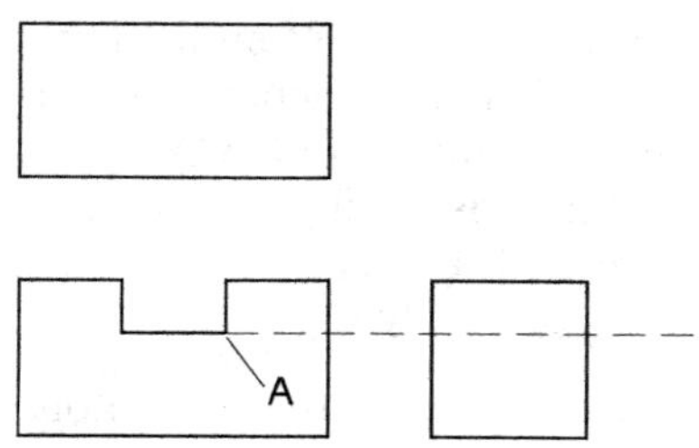

Figure 6.12

On your own, **trim** the projection line so that only the portion within the side view remains.

Your drawing should look like Figure 6.13.

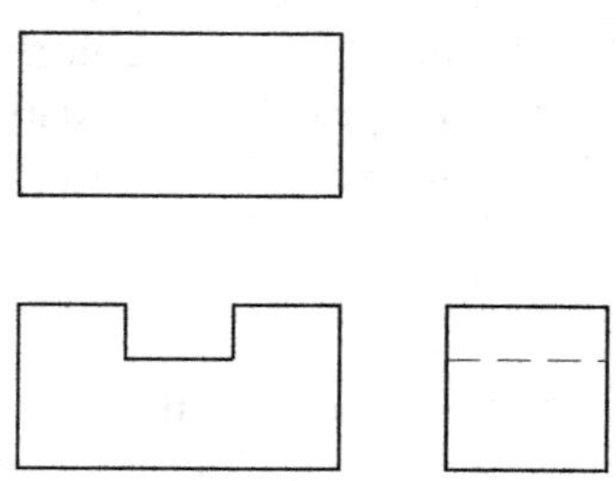

Figure 6.13

Next, you project the width of the slot from the front view into the top view using vertical lines on layer VISIBLE. Use the running object snap Perpendicular.

Click: ***VISIBLE*** *to set it current using the Layer Control*

Click: to expand ***Object Snaps*** *(small downward arrow)*

Click: ***Perpendicular*** *from the list so it appears checked*

Tip: *To improve the appearance of hidden lines, you can use the Linetype Control to set the linetype scale for individual graphical objects. Another way to improve their appearance is by drawing polylines. For hidden lines drawn with a polyline, you can set the Plinegen variable to 1 to make the linetype a continuous pattern over the length of the polyline. When you set this variable to 0, each segment of the polyline begins and ends with a dash. Use the Pedit, Ltypegen command option to set this variable. This method can improve the appearance of intersecting hidden lines.*

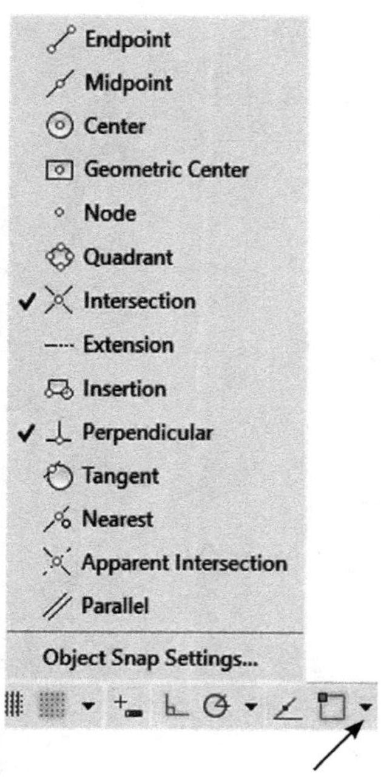

*Check that **Ortho is on**, so that your projection lines will be straight.*

Now you are ready to draw the lines for the slot.

*Click: **Line button***

Specify first point: ***click the upper left corner of the slot** in the front view, labeled 1 in Figure 6.14**[Enter]***

Specify next point or [Undo]: ***target the upper line of the top view, labeled 2,** using snap to Perpendicular*

Specify next point or [Undo]: ***[Enter]***

Command: ***[Enter]** to restart the Line command*

Specify first point: ***click the upper right corner labeled 3** of the slot in the front view*

Specify next point or [Undo]: ***target the upper line of the top view, labeled 2, using snap to Perpendicular***

Specify next point or [Undo]: ***[Enter]***

*On your own, use the **Trim** command to remove the excess lines.*

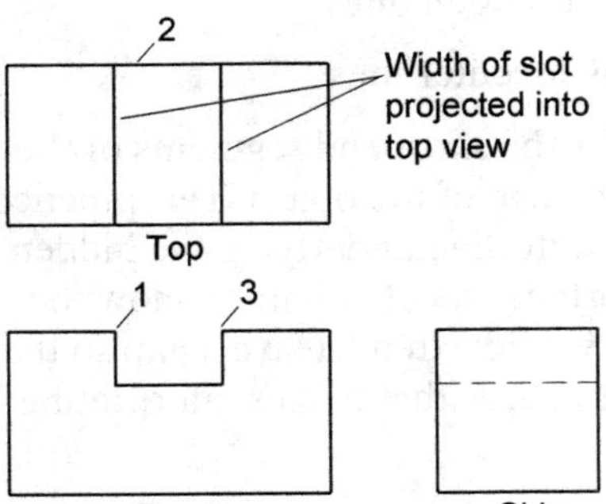

Figure 6.14

Your drawing should be similar to Figure 6.15.

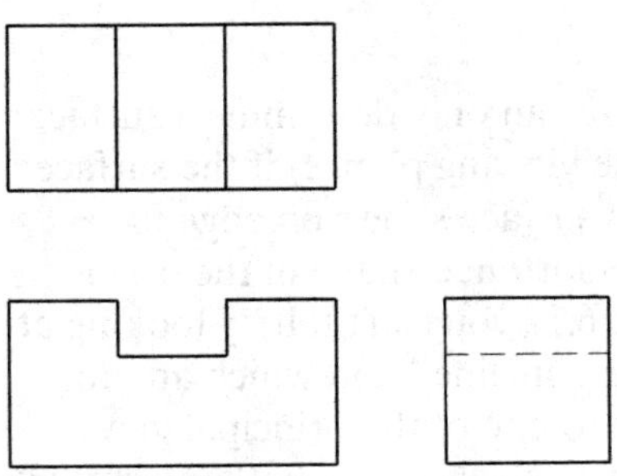

Figure 6.15

Save *adaptort.dwg* before you continue.

Line Precedence

Different types of lines often align with each other within the same view, as illustrated in Figure 6.16.

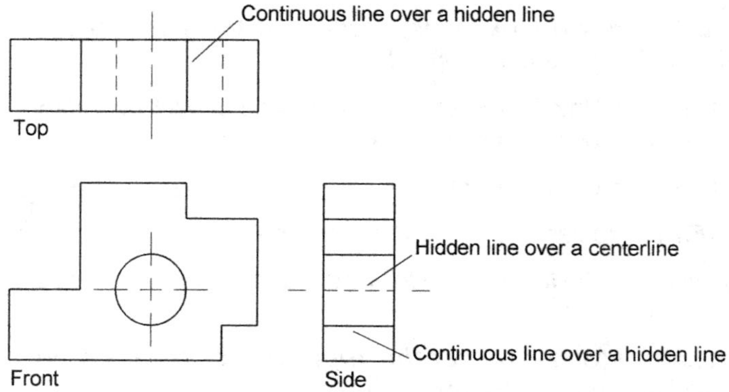

Figure 6.16

Which line should you draw when two overlap? The rule is:

- visible lines take *precedence* over hidden lines
- hidden lines take precedence over centerlines.

Note that in the side view of Figure 6.16, the short end segments of the covered-up centerline show beyond the edge of the object. This practice has sometimes been used to show the centerline underlying the hidden line. It is best to leave off the less important line. If you must show the short end segments where a centerline would extend, leave a gap so that the centerline does not touch the other line, as that makes interpreting the lines difficult.

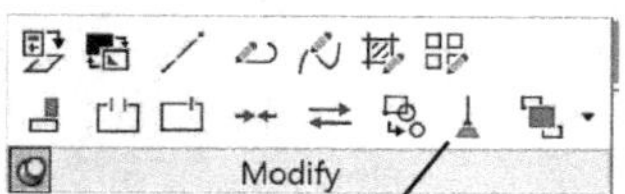

Delete Duplicate Objects (OVERKILL)

Tip: *You can use the OVERKILL command to delete duplicate objects. This is particularly useful for making a perfectly closed boundary needed for 3D modeling and hatch boundaries.*

The AutoCAD software doesn't determine line precedence for you. You must decide which lines to show in your 2D orthographic views. If you draw a line on top of another line, both lines will be in your AutoCAD drawing. Both lines will print, which may not show correctly. On your screen you may not notice that there are two lines because one line will be exactly over the other.

Slanted Surfaces

When reading an orthographic view, you can only determine a surface is *inclined* (tipped away from one of the viewing planes) if the surface is shown on edge in a view. An inclined surface shows on edge in one principal view and shows as a foreshortened shape in the other principal views. As illustrated in Figure 6.17, you can't tell by looking at the top and side views which surfaces are inclined and which are not. A *normal* surface is one that is parallel to one of the principal views. When looking at a single view you cannot always tell whether a surface is inclined or normal.

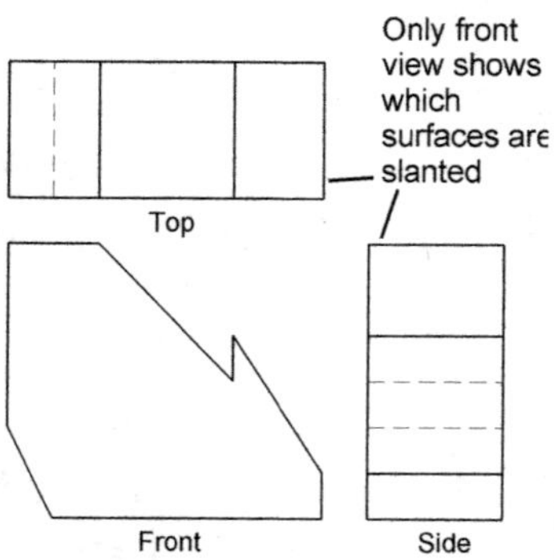

Figure 6.17

For the adapter, the front view is required, along with the other two views, to define the object's size and shape completely. In the next steps you will add the slanted surface to the adapter as shown in Figure 6.18.

You will use relative coordinates to add the 45-degree line starting 0.5"to the left of the top right corner in the right-side view.

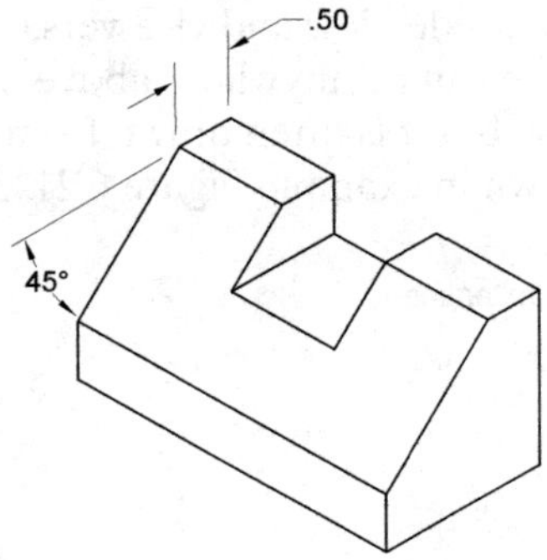

Figure 6.18

Click: ***Line button***

Specify first point: ***7,3 [Enter]***

Specify next point or [Undo]: ***@3<225 [Enter]***

Specify next point or [Undo]: ***[Enter]***

The distance 3 was chosen because the exact distance is not known and 3 is obviously longer than needed, as the entire object is only 1.5 inches high. Your screen should look like Figure 6.19.

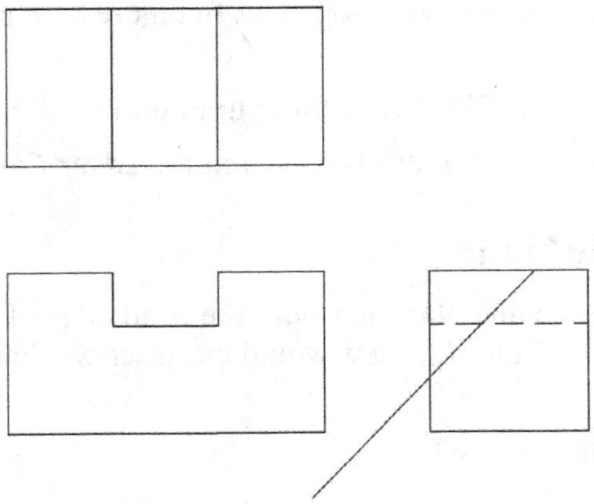

Figure 6.19

On your own, use the **Trim** command to remove the lines above the slanted surface. When you have finished, your drawing should look like Figure 6.20.

Tip: *Use Zoom Window to zoom the side view to help you locate the points to trim. Return to your drawing with Zoom Previous when all the excess lines are removed. You may want to turn Snap and Ortho off to trim the lines.*

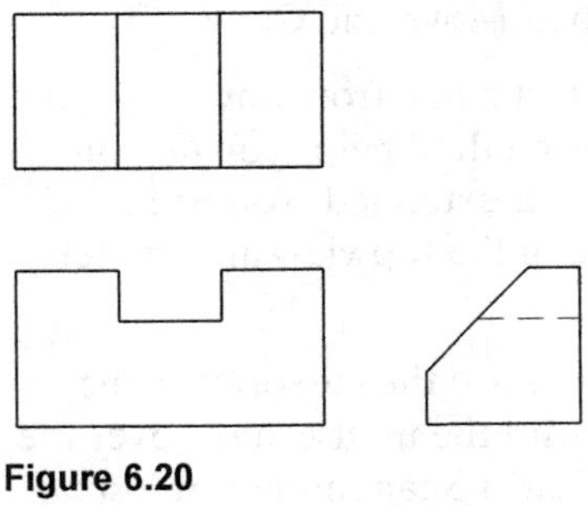

Figure 6.20

Top-View to Side-View Projection

You can *project* locations from a top view to a side view and vice versa by using a 45-degree *miter line.* The miter line can be anywhere above the side view and to the right of the top view, but it is often drawn from the top right corner of the front view as shown in example Figure 6.21.

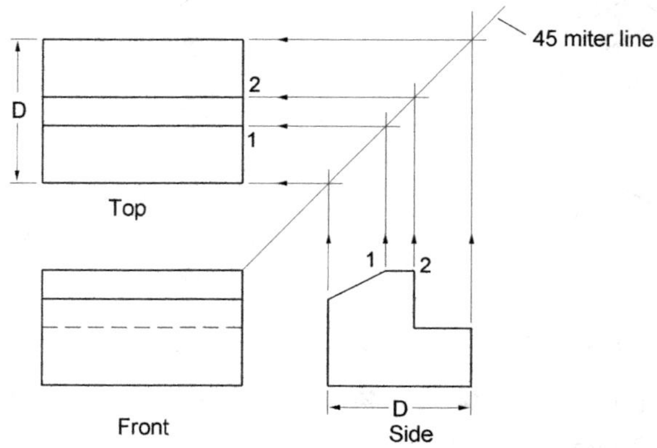

Figure 6.21

To project information from the side view to the top view, draw vertical projection lines from the points in the side view so that they intersect the miter line. From the miter line, project horizontal lines where the vertical lines intersect it, across to the top view. In Figure 6.21, points 1 and 2 are projected.

Next, you will use layer PROJECTION for your miter line.

*Click: **PROJECTION** as the current layer using the Layer Control*

Drawing the Miter Line

You will draw a 45-degree line, starting where the front edge of the top view and the front edge of the side view would intersect. So that you can draw angled lines,

On your own, turn **Ortho** mode **off**.

Using Object Snap Tracking

Object Snap Tracking constrains your selections to line up with the X-, Y-, or Z-coordinates of an acquired tracking point. Object Snap Tracking also works with other commands such as Move and Copy.

You can use the Tracking object snap to start a line from any point on the screen, based on reference points. This method helps you find an intersection where two objects would meet if extended. You will use it to find the point where the bottom edge of the top view and the left edge of the side view would intersect.

To acquire an Object Snap Tracking point, move the cursor over the object location temporarily. Do not click with the mouse, just hover the mouse over the object until you see the Object Snap marker or a small plus sign (+) appear.

Refer to Figure 6.22 for the objects you will use to acquire tracking points. Once the tracking points are acquired you will start to draw the line.

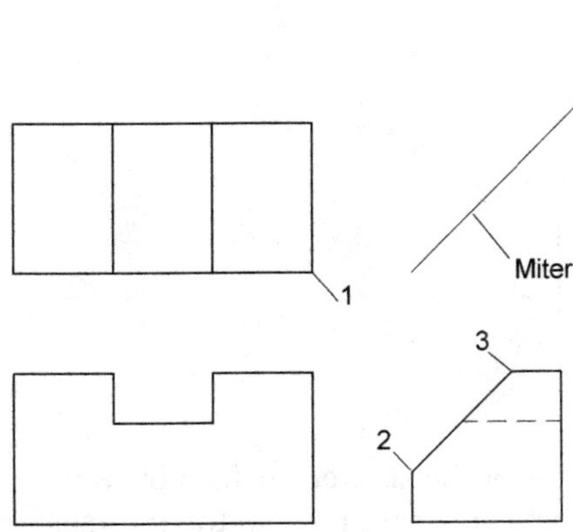

Figure 6.22

On your own, make sure that **Object Snap Intersection** is turned on.

*Click: **Object Snap Tracking** button from status bar to turn it on*

*Click: **Line button***

Specify first point: ***move the cursor over intersection 1 until it is acquired as an Object Snap Tracking point, then move the cursor over point 2 until it is acquired***

Tip: *If the Object snap tracking button does not show on your status bar, pick Customize and select it to show on the status bar.*

Tip: *To clear an Object Snap Tracking point once it has been acquired, move the cursor back over the point until the marker is gone. Starting a new command will also clear the Object Snap Tracking points, as will toggling the Object Snap Tracking button on the status bar.*

You should see the tracking points acquired as in Figure 6.23.

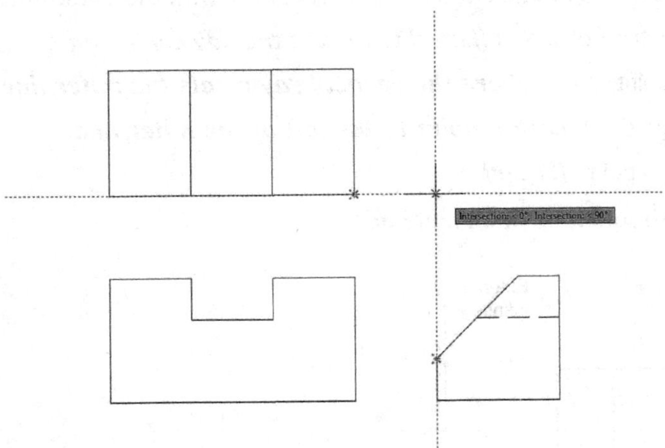

Figure 6.23

Specify next point or [Undo]: ***click where the tracking lines intersect,** as shown in Figure 6.25, to begin drawing the miter line*

Specify next point or [Undo]: ***@3<45 [Enter]***

Specify next point or [Undo]: ***[Enter]***

*Click: **Object Snap Tracking** button to turn it off*

The line that you will use for the miter line is added to the drawing, as shown in Figure 6.24.

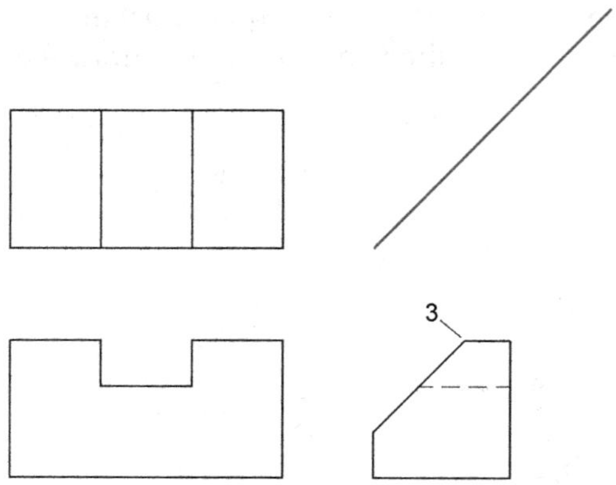

Figure 6.24

Next, you will project the corner point of the slanted surface from the side view to the miter line by drawing a vertical ray from the intersection. The Ray command is on the Draw panel.

Click: ***Ortho mode button*** *to turn it on before you click any points*

Click: ***Ray button***

Specify start point: ***click point 3*** *using Object Snap Intersection*

Specify through point: ***click anywhere above point 3***

Specify through point: ***[Enter]***

The ray is added to your drawing, extending up from point 3. Next, project a ray from the intersection of the vertical ray with the miter line.

Click: ***Ray button*** *or press [Enter] to restart the Ray command*

Specify start point: ***click where the vertical ray meets the miter line***

Specify through point: ***click a point to the left of the miter line***

Specify through point: ***[Enter]***

Your drawing should look like Figure 6.25.

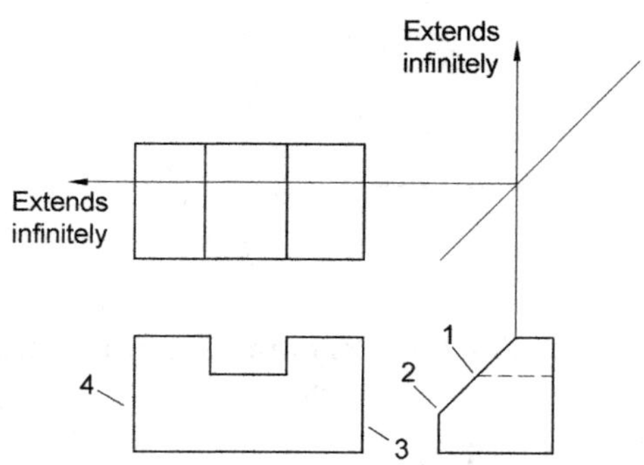

Figure 6.25

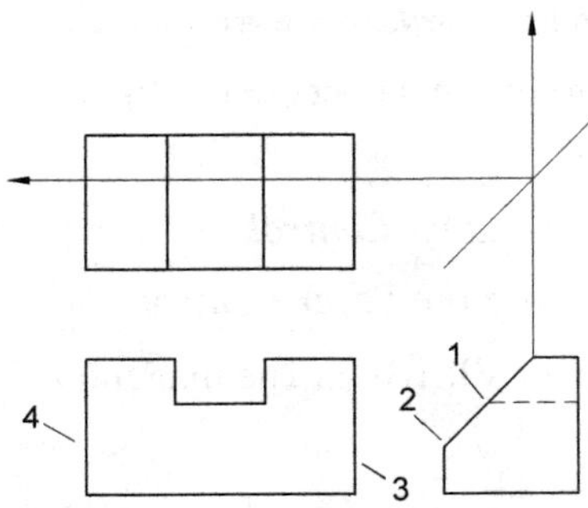

Figure 6.26

On your own, **project point 1** to the top view using the same method as you used for the previous projection lines.

Next you project point 2, shown in Figure 6.26, into the front view.

Make sure that **Object Snap** is **on** with **Perpendicular** selected.

Make sure that **SNAP** and **Ortho mode** are toggled **off**, and **Object Snap Tracking** is on.

*Click: **Line button***

Specify first point: acquire tracking point 2 and click on line 3 *using the AutoSnap Intersection marker to start the line*

Specify next point or [Undo]: click on line 4 *using the AutoSnap Perpendicular marker*

Specify next point or [Undo]: [Enter]

The front view should now have a solid line representing the lower part of the block's sloping surface. Now you only have to trim the Rays used in projecting the surface depths to the top view. Remember, when rays are trimmed they become regular lines.

On your own, **trim** the lines so that your screen looks like Figure 6.27.

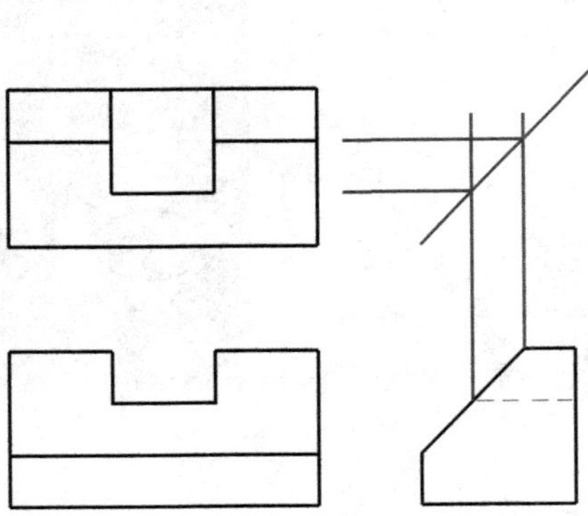

Figure 6.27

Now, you will change the new lines in the top and front views to the layer VISIBLE. Then you will set layer VISIBLE as the current layer and freeze layer PROJECTION. Leaving the projection lines frozen in the drawing is useful because, if you need to change something, you can just thaw the layer instead of having to re-create the projection lines.

Tip: *For a quick pop-up menu of Object Snaps, you can press the Shift key in combination with the right mouse button.*

On your own, select the new lines in top and front views so the grips appear.

Select layer VISIBLE from the Layer Control to change the lines to that layer.

*Press: **[Esc]** to remove the hot grips*

*Click: **VISIBLE** to set it current using the Layer Control*

*Click: **to Freeze layer PROJECTION** using the Layer Control*

The selected lines change to reside on layer VISIBLE. The magenta projection lines disappear from your screen.

Sizing and Positioning the Drawing

Next you will switch to the paper space layout and verify the scaling factor for the drawing view, as you learned in Tutorial 5. When you used Zoom All in model space, the entire drawing or the limits area is fit on the screen, which does not give you any particular scale for the end drawing. You will check the viewing scale to make sure that the drawing will print so that 1 unit in paper space is equal to 1 unit in model space.

*Click: **Layout1 tab***

*Double-click: **inside the viewport to** ensure that you are in floating model space inside the viewport*

Tip: *If your paper space layout does not fill the screen, switch to paper space and then use Zoom All. Make sure to return to model space.*

Next, use pan to position the views you drew inside the viewport.

Press and hold the mouse scroll wheel and pan the views so that they appear centered in the viewport.

Check that the Viewport Scale is still set to 1:1 as shown in Figure 6.28.

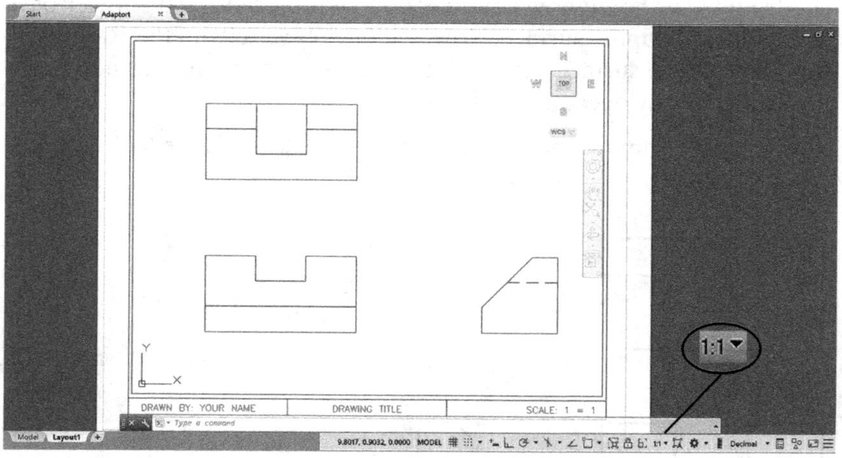

Figure 6.28

Locking the Viewport Scale

You can lock the scaling for the viewport so that zooming inside the floating viewport does not change the scale relationship between paper space and model space.

*Click: **Lock/Unlock Viewport button** so that it appears locked*

Now that the viewport display is locked, when you zoom in or pan, it will not change the relationship between the model space drawing and its position or scale inside the viewport.

Make sure you are in **model space** inside the viewport.

On your own, try using Zoom and Pan.

Did you notice that your view enlarges with the viewport staying at the same size relationship? And when you pan, the entire drawing moves on the screen? When the display is locked, the zoom and pan works by switching to paper space and performing the zoom or pan and then switching back to model space.

Tip: *It is good practice to frequently save your drawings on your disk. If your system experiences a power failure and you lose the drawing in memory, you can always retrieve a recent version from your disk.*

*Click: **Object Snap** on the status bar to turn it off*

*Click: **Object Snap Tracking** to turn it off*

*Click: **Save***

Showing Holes

Figure 6.29 shows an object with two holes and the ways in which they are represented in front and top views. The *diameter symbol* (Ø) indicates a diameter value. If no depth is specified for a hole, the assumption is that the hole goes completely through the object. As no depth is specified for these holes, the hidden lines in the front view go from the top surface to the bottom surface.

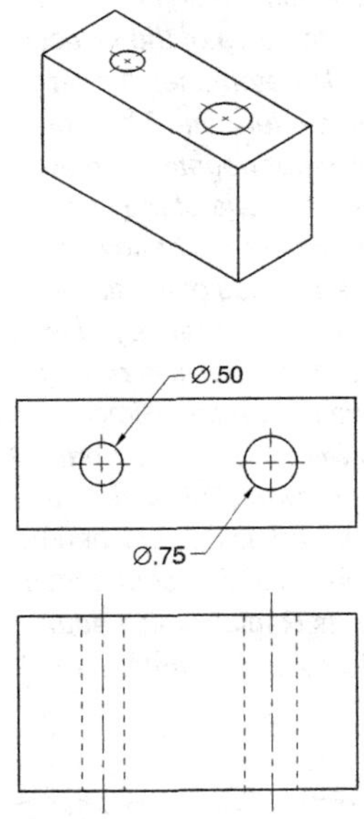

Figure 6.29

A centermark and four lines extending beyond the four quadrant points are used to define the center point of a hole in its *circular view* (the view in which the hole appears as a circle). A single centerline, parallel to the two hidden lines, is used in the other views, called *rectangular views* because the hole appears as a rectangle. Centerlines should extend beyond the edge of the symmetrical feature by a distance of about 3/16" on the plotted drawing.

You will add a hole to the adapter, as shown in Figure 6.30.

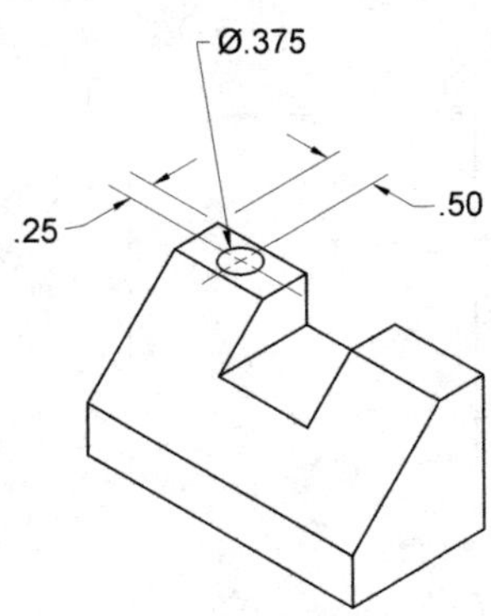

Figure 6.30

Next, switch back so that you are working in model space.

*Click: **Model tab***

The layout disappears from your screen as you are showing only model space. Next you will draw the 0.375 diameter circle for the top view of the hole. The hole's center is 0.5 from the left surface of the view and 0.25 from the back surface.

Click: ***to turn Snap on***

Click: ***Circle button***

Specify center point for circle or [3P/2P/Ttr (tan tan radius)]: ***2.5,5.25 [Enter]*** *or pick using snap*

Specify radius of circle or [Diameter]: ***D [Enter]***

Diameter: ***.375 [Enter]***

Tip: *The new Centermark command makes it easier to draw centermarks. In older versions of AutoCAD the Dimcen variable was used to control the size and appearance of the centermark added with the Dim Center command. The absolute value of the Dimcen variable determines the size of the centermark. The sign (positive or negative) determines the style of the centermark. Figure 6.31 shows the different styles of centermarks that you can create by setting Dimcen to a positive or negative value. Setting Dimcen to zero will cause no centermark to be drawn. (This lack of a centermark is useful when using dimensioning commands such as Radial, which automatically add a centermark.)*

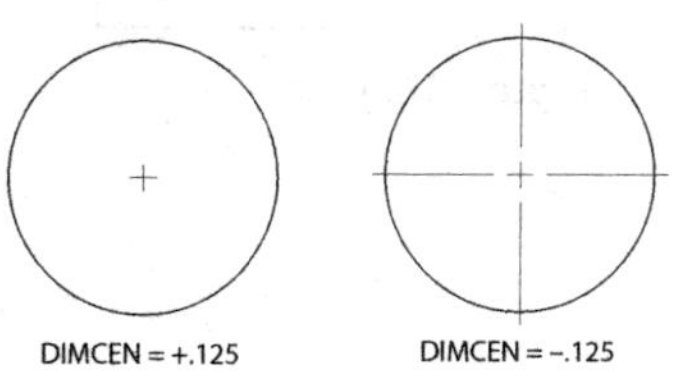

Figure 6.31

Drawing Centerlines and Centermarks

Next, you will draw the centerlines for the circle. Engineering drawings use two different thicknesses of lines:

- thick lines for visible lines, cutting plane lines, and short break lines
- thin lines for hidden lines, centerlines, dimension lines, section lines, long break lines, and phantom lines.

Centerlines should be thin drawing lines. Improvements to the Centermark command make it even easier to add nice looking centerlines to your drawings. You can set the layer to use for the centermarks.

You will learn more about dimensioning and adding centermarks in Tutorial 7.

On your own **zoom in** on the top view.

Click: ***to turn Snap off*** *to make selection easier*

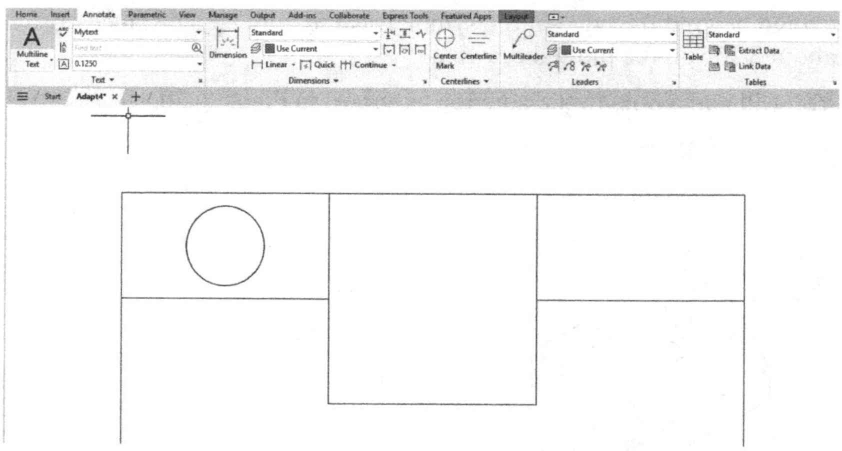

Figure 6.32

Click: ***to expand the layer options*** *from the Annotate tab, Centerlines panel* ***as shown in Figure 6.33***

Click: to chose ***Centerline*** *as the layer for the centermarks*

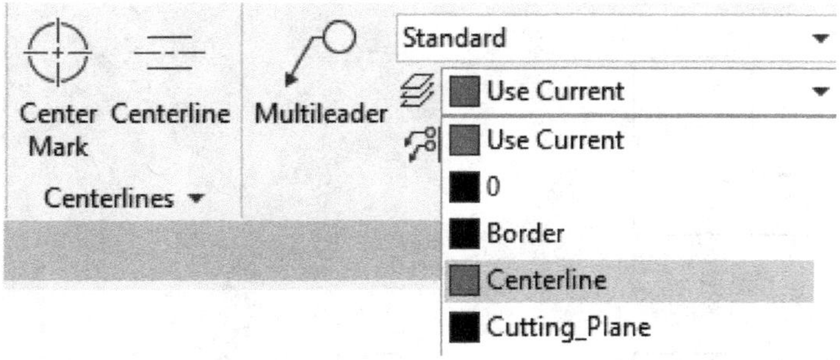

Figure 6.33

Click: ***Centermark***

Select circle or arc to add centermark: ***click on the outer edge of the circle [Enter]***

The circular view centerlines appear as shown in Figure 6.34. You may not see them clearly unless the view is enlarged using zoom.

Tip: *You can use the Properties button to change the linetype for your centermarks.*

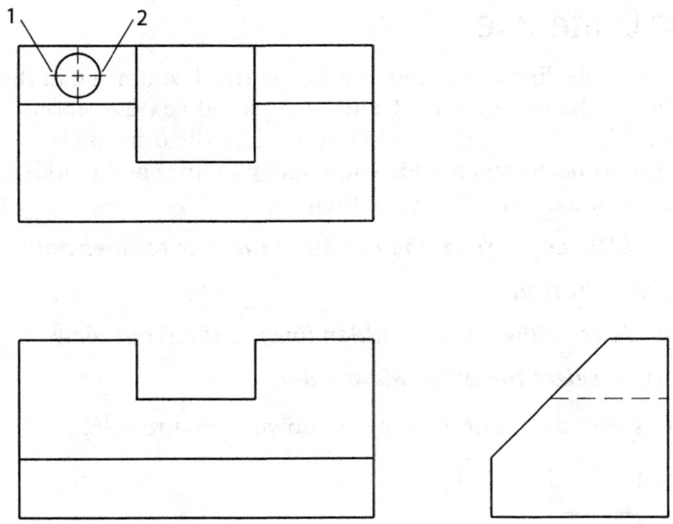

Figure 6.34

Tip: *Use Zoom Window if you need to make targeting the objects and intersections easier.*

Next, project the hole into the front view.

On your own, set **HIDDEN_LINES** as the current layer. Turn on **Object Snap** for **Intersection.** Turn on **Ortho** mode.

Click: ***Line button***

Specify first point: ***click the intersection of the circle's horizontal centerline with the left edge of the circle identified as point 1***

Specify next point or [Undo]: ***click Snap to Perpendicular button***

Per to: ***click on the bottom line in the front view***

Specify next point or [Undo]: ***[Enter]***

On your own, repeat this procedure to draw the hidden line for the right side of the hole (point 2). Trim the lines on your own. Save your drawing.

The hidden lines for the hole should appear like those in Figure 6.35.

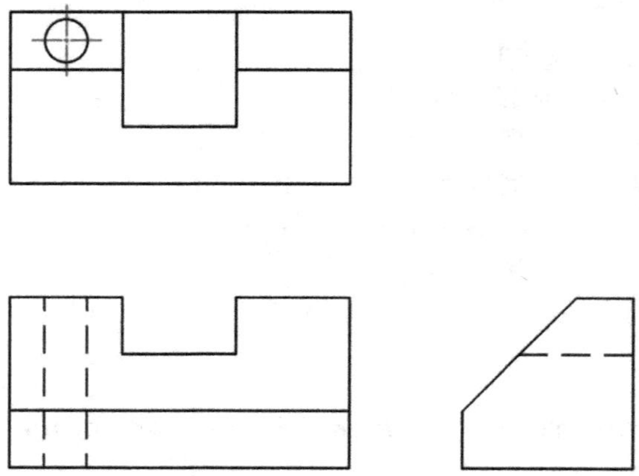

Figure 6.35

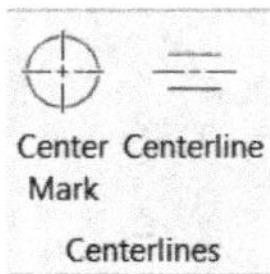

Tip: *Be sure that Snap is off to make selecting easier.*

Adding the Centerline

Tip: *You can use grips and stretch a line to lengthen it. You can also use the Lengthen command and select the DElta option to lengthen a line by a specified amount.*

You will use the Centerline command to add a vertical centerline in the front view between the hidden lines. Centerlines should extend about 0.1875" past the edge of the cylindrical feature when the drawing is plotted. The Centerline command lets you select two lines and it adds a centerline pattern line midway between them.

Click: ***CENTERLINE** Layer from the Annotate tab, Centerlines panel*

Click: ***Centerline button***

Select first line: ***Select either of the hidden lines in the front view***

Select second line: ***select the other hidden line***

The centerline is added to your drawing as shown in Figure 6.36.

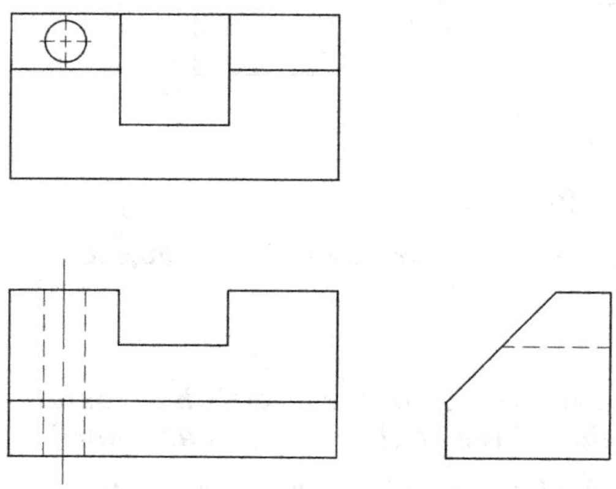

Figure 6.36

Next, project the location for the hole into the side view.

Click: ***to thaw layer PROJECTION and make it current.***

On your own, draw a projection line from the top view where the vertical centerline intersects the circle to a point past the miter line. Refer to Figure 6.37. Use the Object Snap (Intersection) mode and Ortho to help you.

Now project that line from the miter line into the side view, creating a vertical projection line locating the center of the hole in the side view.

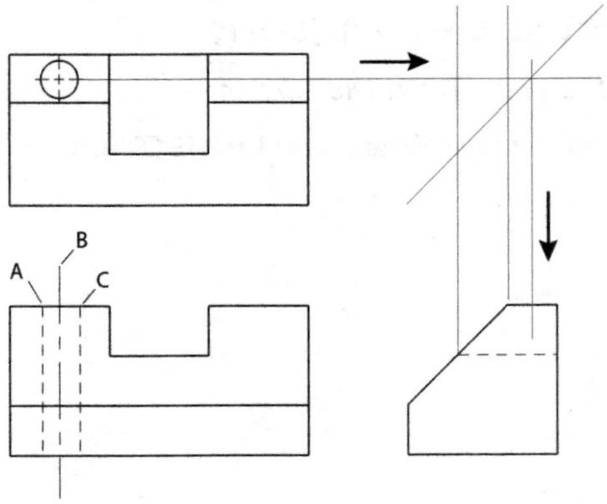

Figure 6.37

Because holes are symmetrical, the side view of the hole appears the same as the front view, except for the location. You will use hot grips with the Move, Copy option to copy the two hidden lines and the centerline from the front view to the side view. You will also change the Basepoint to the intersection of the centerline with the top line.

Check that you have Object Snap active, with Intersection selected.

Select: ***the hidden lines and centerline*** *(A, B, and C in Figure 6.37)*

Click: ***any grip as the base grip***

Specify stretch point or [Base point/Copy/Undo/eXit]: ***right-click*** *to show the menu and click* ***Move***

Specify move point or [Base point/Copy/Undo/eXit]: ***right-click*** *to show the menu and click* ***Copy***

Specify move point or [Base point/Copy/Undo/eXit]: ***right-click*** *to show the menu and click* ***Base point***

Specify base point: ***click the intersection of the centerline and top line of the front view*** *identified as Basepoint in Figure 6.38*

Specify move point or [Base point/Copy/Undo/eXit]: ***click the intersection of the top line and the projection line*** *(D in Figure 6.38)*

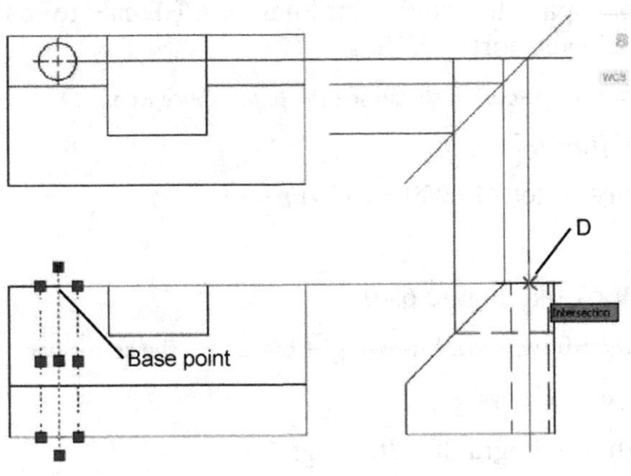

Figure 6.38

You see faint lines attached to your cursor as they are copied to this location. To exit the command,

Specify move point or [Base point/Copy/Undo/eXit]: ***[Enter]***

*Press: **[Esc] twice** to remove the grips from the screen*

On your own set **VISIBLE** as the current layer. Freeze layer **PROJECTION**.

Your drawing will look like Figure 6.39.

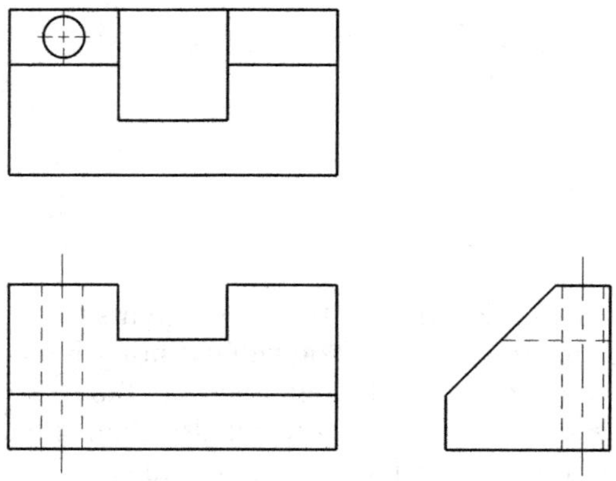

Figure 6.39

Tip: *Use Zoom Previous or Zoom All, if necessary, to return your screen to full size.*

Setting the Global Linetype Scaling Factor

You can change the linetype scale factor for all linetypes at once by setting the global linetype scaling factor.

Each linetype is defined by the distance that each dash, gap, and dot is to be drawn. Because linetypes are defined by specific distances, you may need to adjust the lengths of the dashes and gaps for use in your drawing. The LTscale command lets you adjust all the linetype lengths by the scaling factor you specify.

As you will be plotting from a paper space layout, that is the best place to adjust the appearance of the line patterns, first using the LTscale command and then adjusting individual lines as needed.

You will switch to paper space to adjust your lines with LTscale to make the HIDDEN linetype have shorter dashes.

Tip: *The variable PSLTscale controls whether the Ltscale command in paper space controls the appearance of the linetypes over the same command in model space. By default PSLTscale is set to 1, so that the paper space LTscale has control.*

On your own, switch to **Paper space**. *You should see the paper space icon.*

Command: ***LTSCALE [Enter]***

Enter new linetype scale factor <1.0000>: ***.65 [Enter]***

Regenerating Layout

Your drawing should look like Figure 6.40.

On your own, turn on the **Show/Hide Lineweight** button on the status bar.

Save and close drawing *adaptort.dwg*.

You have completed this orthographic drawing.

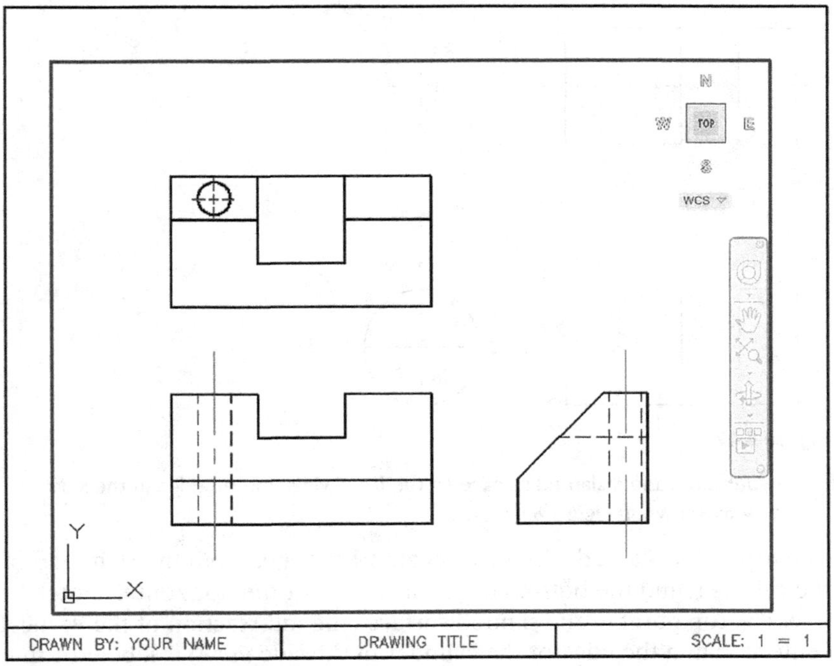

Figure 6.40

Tip: *Especially when you are working in metric units, the linetypes may not always appear correctly. Using a standard AutoCAD template for a metric drawing can help provide the proper settings. Sometimes a line may appear to be the correct color for the layer but not the correct pattern. The reason is that the lengths defined in the linetype file are defined in terms of inches. Incorrectly shown metric lines may have changed pattern, but the spacing is so small that you can't see it. Use LTscale to adjust the spacing. For metric units, try a value of 25.4 when in model space.*

Projecting Slanted Surfaces on Cylinders

Next, you will start a drawing from the datafile *cyl1.dwt* and use it to practice projecting slanted surfaces on cylinders.

> On your own, begin a new drawing called ***cyl1orth.dwg*** from the datafile template drawing ***cyl1.dwt***. Zoom and pan as necessary to position the views near the center of the screen.

Your screen should be similar to Figure 6.41.

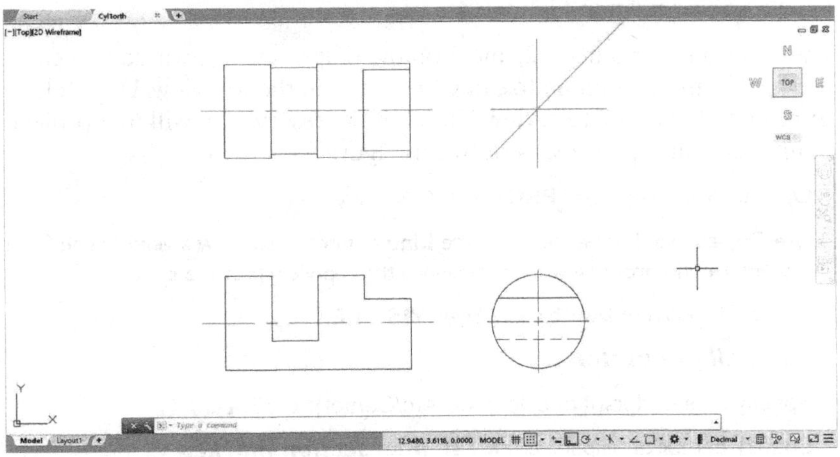

Figure 6.41

Tip: *If possible, install your datafiles on the hard drive. If you are opening a file from a USB drive, pick New and then use the file you want to open as a template. You should specify the new drawing file name so that it is created on the hard drive. These actions will prevent many problems and the likelihood of corrupted drawing files. Copy the completed files to your USB drive. Make sure to close the software before removing your drive.*

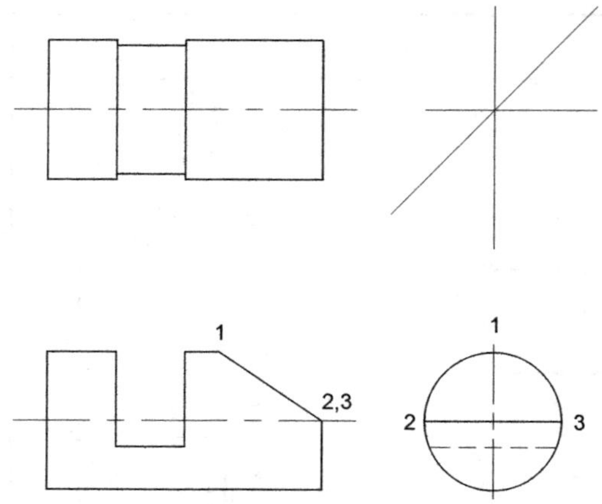

Figure 6.42

On your own, add a slanted surface to the front view and on edge in the side view, as shown in Figure 6.42.

The top of the slanted surface is located 1.5 inches from the right end of the cylinder, and the bottom of the surface is at the horizontal centerline. The top point of the slanted surface (the intersection of the vertical centerline and the edge of the cylinder in the side view) is labeled 1 in Figure 6.43. The bottom edge of the slanted surface is labeled 2, 3 and is located directly on the horizontal centerline in the side view.

On your own, remove the excess lines from the shallow surface in the front view.

Remove the same surface from the top and side views; you will be creating a different surface in its place.

Your drawing should look like Figure 6.42.

What is the shape of the slanted surface in the top view? The front view of the surface appears as a straight slanted line. The side view of the surface is a semicircle. In the top view the slanted surface is a portion of an ellipse, as shown in Figure 6.45.

The locations of points 1, 2, and 3 on the ellipse are known, so you can use the Ellipse command to draw the shape in the top view. Use Help or refer to Tutorial 2 to review Ellipse if necessary. You will first project point 1 into the top view, as shown in Figure 6.43.

On your own, make layer **PROJECTION** current.

Use Object Snap Intersection and the **Line** command to draw a vertical line from point I in the front view extending into the top view past the center.

Change the current layer back to layer **VISIBLE**.

Click: ***Ellipse button***

Specify axis endpoint of ellipse or [Arc/Center]: ***C [Enter]***

Specify center of ellipse: ***click the intersection marked C***

Specify endpoint of axis: ***click on point 1 in the top view,*** *where your projection line crosses the centerline*

Specify distance to other axis or [Rotation]: ***click point 2***

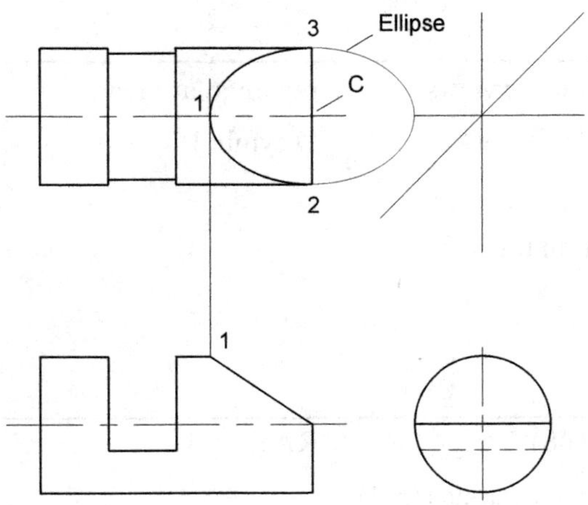

Figure 6.43

Your ellipse should look like the one shown in Figure 6.43.

On your own, **Trim** to remove the unnecessary portion of the ellipse.

Freeze layer **PROJECTION**.

Your drawing should be similar to Figure 6.44.

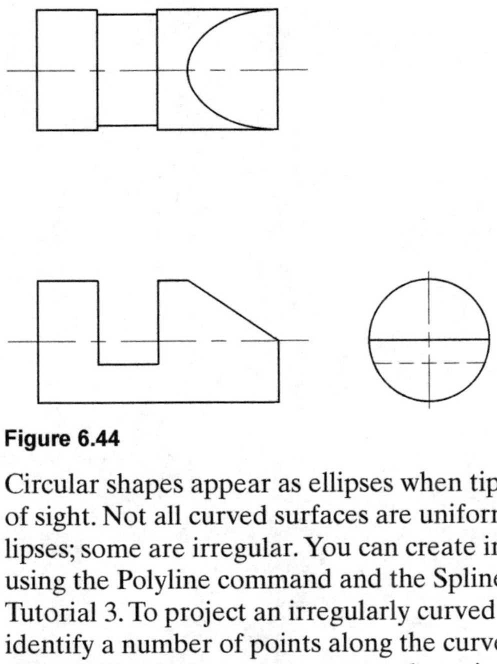

Figure 6.44

Circular shapes appear as ellipses when tipped away from the direction of sight. Not all curved surfaces are uniform shapes like circles and ellipses; some are irregular. You can create irregularly curved surfaces by using the Polyline command and the Spline option that you learned in Tutorial 3. To project an irregularly curved surface to the adjacent view, identify a number of points along the curve and project each point. Use the Polyline command to connect the points. Then use the Pedit, Spline option to create a smooth curve through the points.

You have now completed Tutorial 6.

Save the drawing as *cyl1orth.dwg* and **print** the drawing from the paper space layout. Exit the AutoCAD software.

Key Terms

circular view
diameter symbol
edge view
hidden line
inclined surface
limiting element
miter line
normal surface
orthographic views
precedence
project
projection lines
rectangular view
Ø symbol

Key Commands (keyboard shortcut)

Center Mark (DIM CEN)
DIMCEN
Ellipse (EL)
Ortho (F8)
Object Snap Tracking (F11)
RAY

Exercises

Draw front, top, and right-side orthographic views of the following objects. The letter M after an exercise number means that the problem's dimensional values are in millimeters (metric units). If no letter follows the exercise number, the dimensions are in inches.

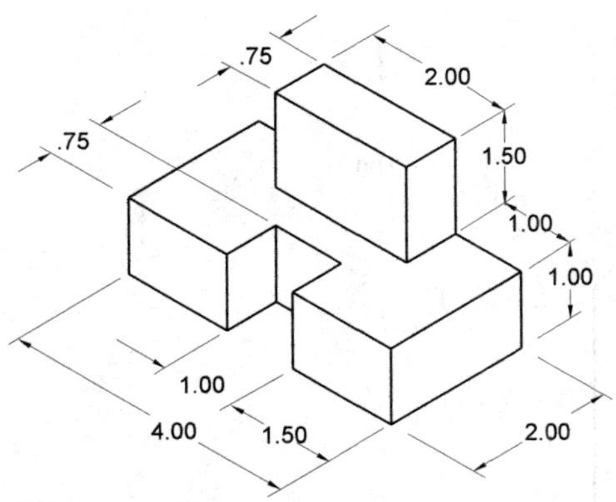

Exercise 6.1 Base Block

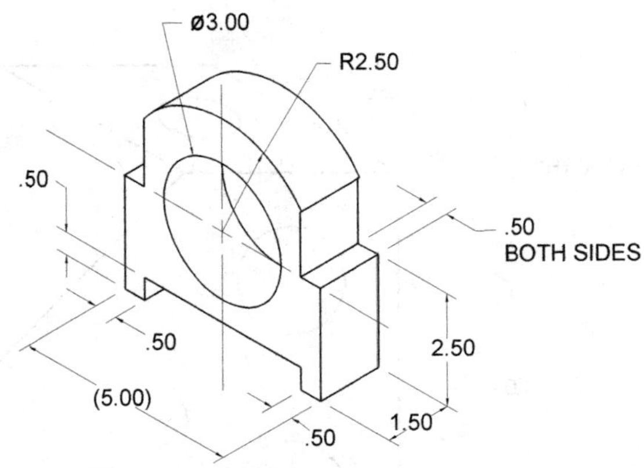

Exercise 6.2 Piston Guide

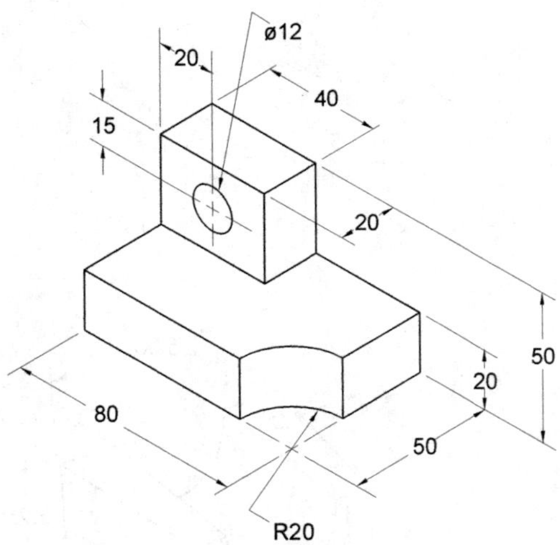

Exercise 6.3M Shaft Guide

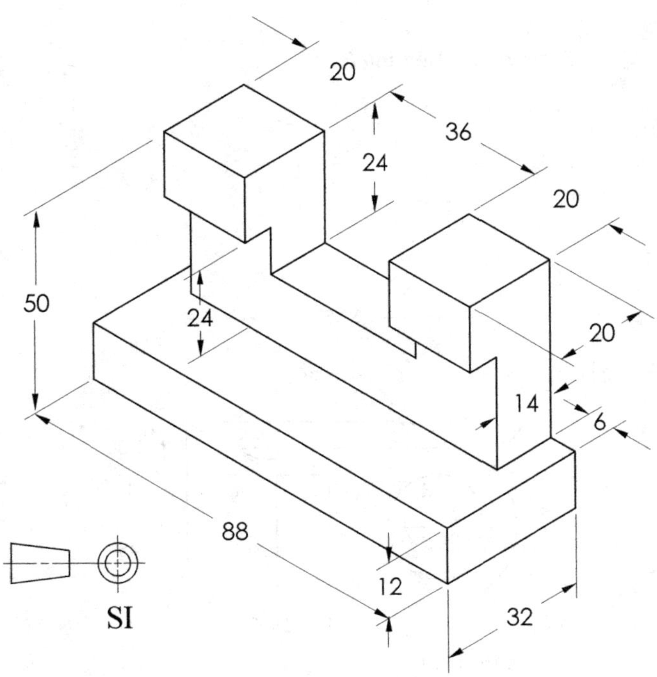

Exercise 6.4M Lock Catch

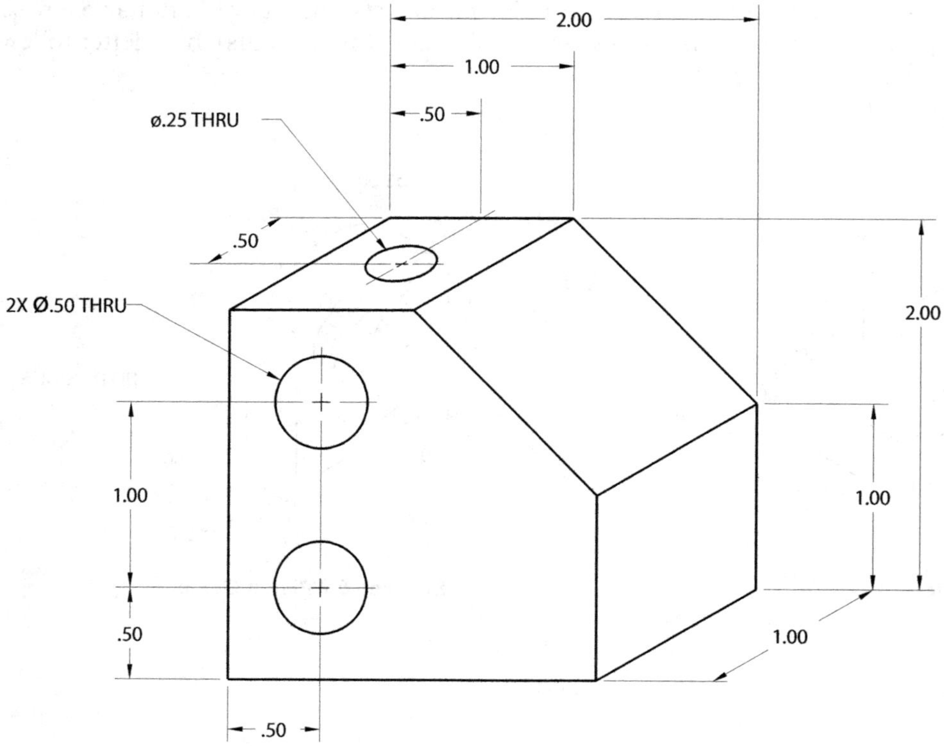

Exercise 6.5 Bearing Box

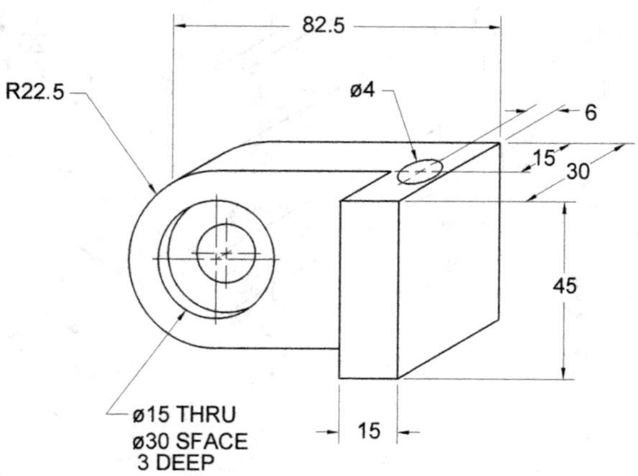

Exercise 6.6M Bushing Holder

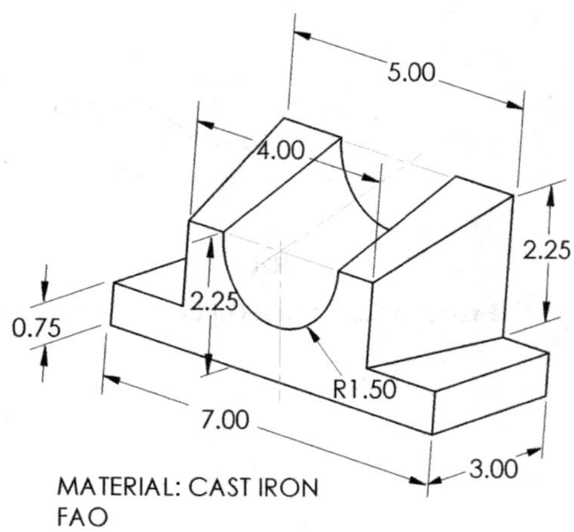

Exercise 6.7 Lift Guide

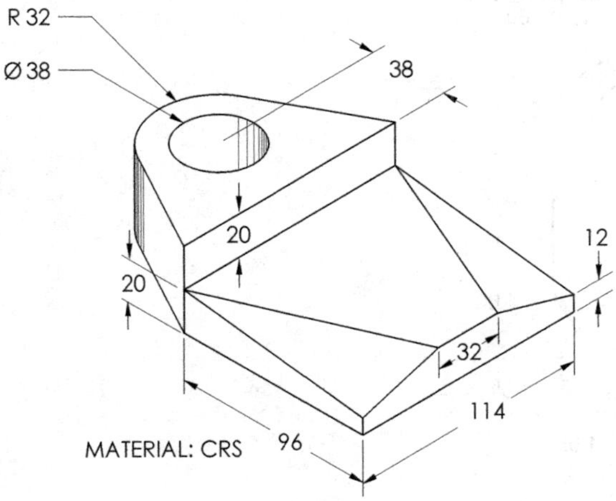

Exercise 6.8M Stop Plate

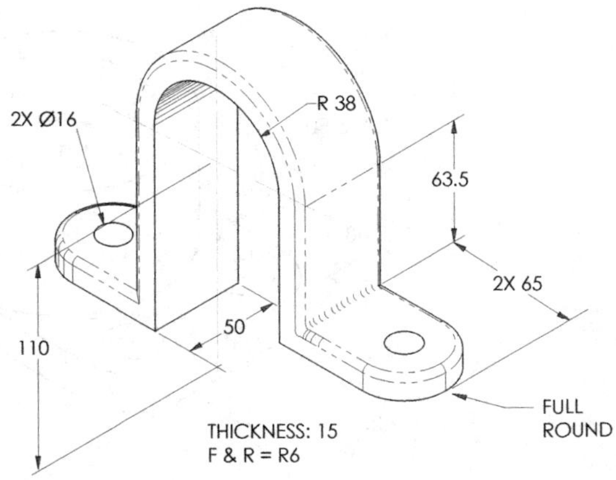

Exercise 6.9M Clamp

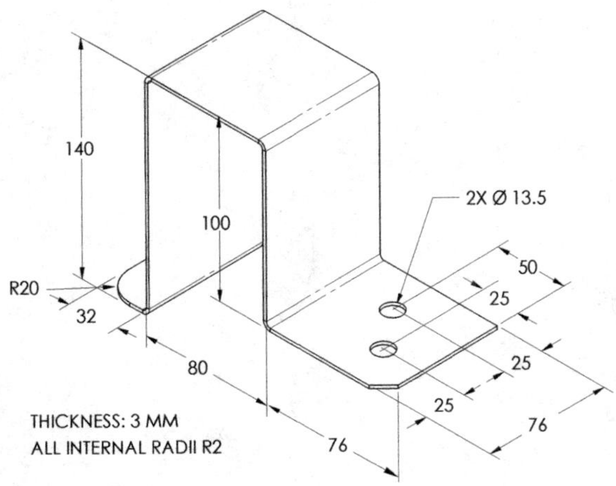

Exercise 6.10M Holder Clip

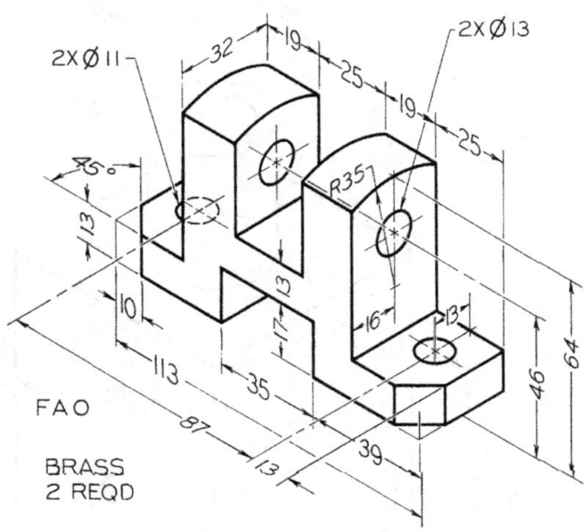

Exercise 6.11M Rod Support

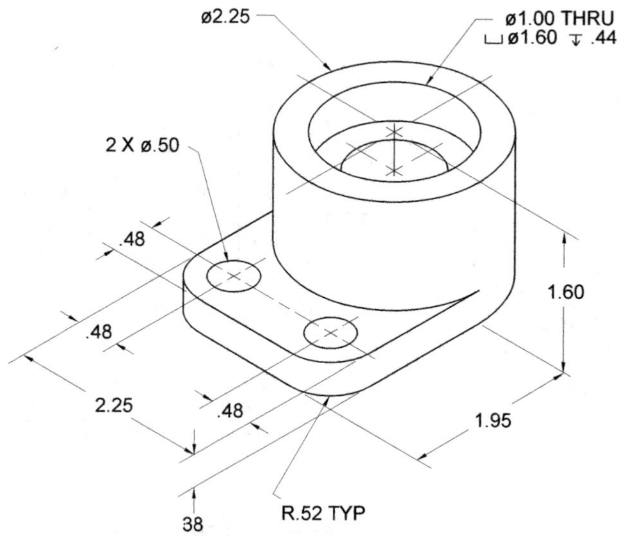

Exercise 6.12 Shaft Support

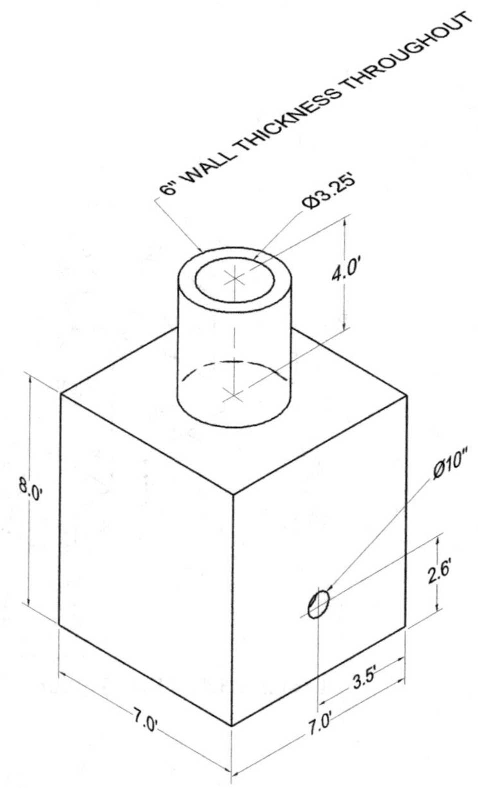

Exercise 6.13 Manhole Junction

Draw standard orthographic views. Wall thickness is 6 inches throughout. The 10-inch hole is through the entire manhole junction (exits opposite side).

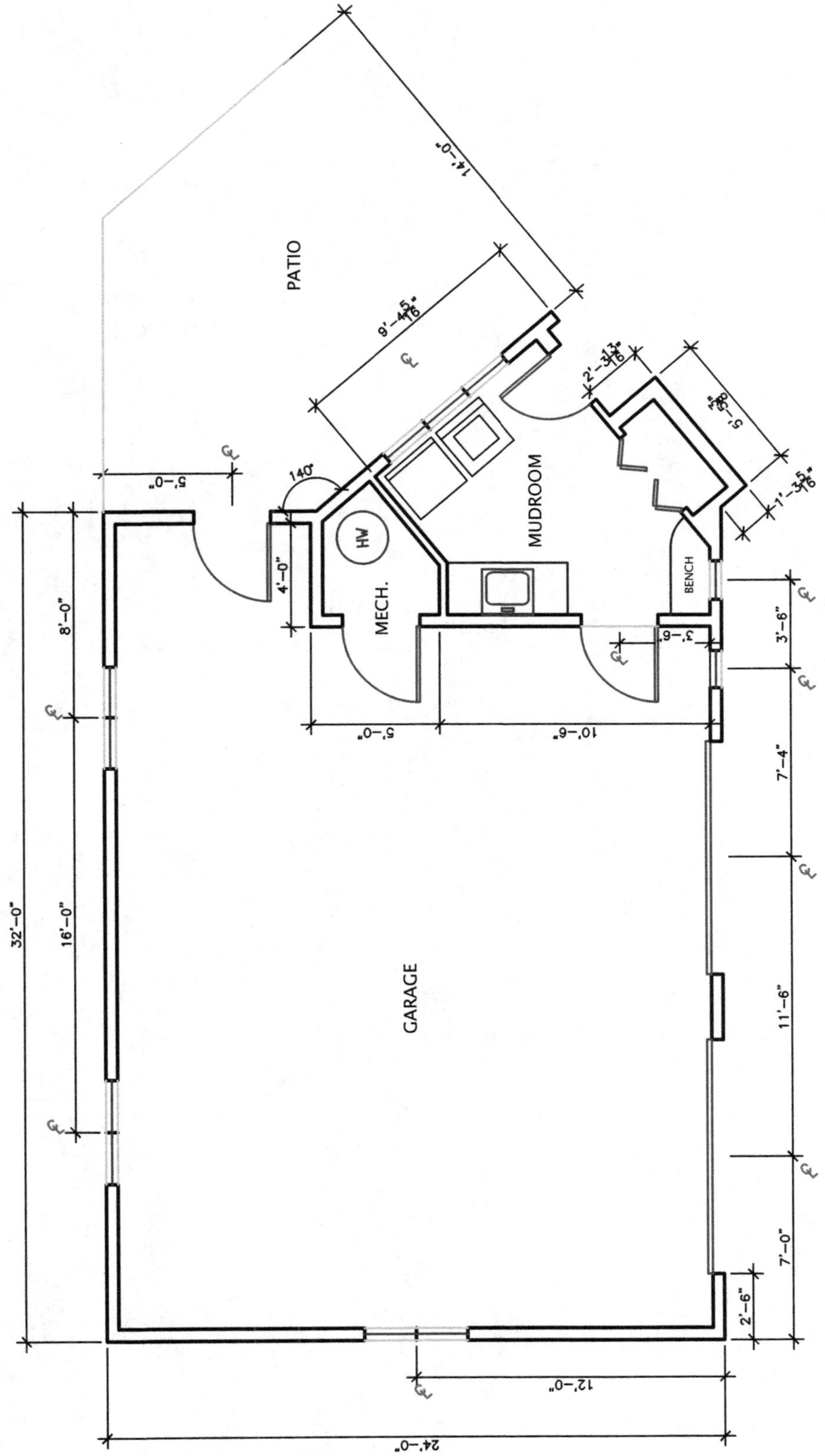

Exercise 6.14 Garage Floor Plan

Draw the garage floor plan shown according to the dimensions given here. Do not dimension your drawing at this time.

DIMENSIONING

7

Introduction

In the preceding tutorials you learned to define the shape of an object. Dimensioning is used to show the size of the object in your drawing. The *dimensions* you specify will be used in the *manufacture* and *inspection* of the object. Figure 7.1 shows a dimensioned drawing.

For the purpose of inspecting the object, a *tolerance* must be stated to define to what extent the actual part may vary from the given dimensions and still be acceptable. In this tutorial you will use a general tolerance note to give the allowable variation for all dimensions. Later, in Tutorial 8, you will learn how to specify tolerances for specific dimensions and geometric tolerances.

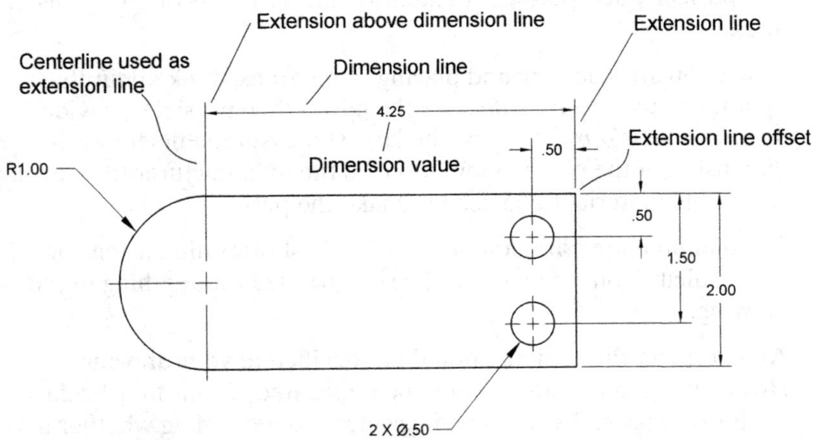

Figure 7.1

Terminology and Conventions

Dimensions are used to accurately describe the details of a part or object so that it can be manufactured. In engineering drawings, dimensions are placed outside the object outline, unless placing the dimension on the object would result in a drawing that is easier to interpret.

Extension lines relate the dimension to the feature on the part. On the plotted drawing, there should be a gap between the feature and the beginning of the extension line, called the *extension line offset*, as shown in Figure 7.1.

Centerlines can be extended across the object outline and used as extension lines without leaving a gap where they cross object lines.

Dimension lines are drawn between extension lines and have arrowheads at each end to indicate how the dimension relates to the feature on the object.

Objectives

When you have completed this tutorial, you will be able to

1. Understand dimensioning nomenclature and conventions.
2. Control the appearance of dimensions.
3. Set the dimension scaling factor.
4. Locate dimensions on drawings.
5. Set the precision for dimension values.
6. Dimension a shape.
7. Use baseline and continued dimensions.
8. Use quick dimension.
9. Save a dimension style and add it to the template drawing.
10. Use associative dimensioning to create dimensions that can update.
11. Use associative styles.

Keep these general rules in mind when you are dimensioning:

- Dimensions should be grouped around a view and evenly spaced to give the drawing a neat appearance.
- The *dimension values* should never touch the outline of the object.
- Dimension values are usually placed near the midpoint of the dimension line, except when it is necessary to stagger the numbers from one dimension line to the next so that all the values do not line up in a row. Staggering the numbers makes the drawing easier to read.
- Because dimension lines should not cross extension lines or other dimension lines, begin by placing the shortest dimensions closest to the object outline. Place the longest dimensions farthest out. In this way, you avoid dimension lines that cross extension and other dimension lines.
- It is perfectly acceptable for extension lines to cross other extension lines.
- When you are selecting and placing dimensions, think about the operations used to manufacture the part. When possible, provide *overall dimensions* that show the largest measurements for each dimension of the object. Doing so tells the manufacturer the starting size of the material to be used to make the part.
- The manufacturer should not have to add shorter dimensions or make calculations to arrive at the sizes needed for anything in the drawing.
- All necessary dimensions should be specified in your drawing. However, no dimensions should be duplicated, as this may lead to confusion, especially when an inspector is determining whether a part meets the specified tolerance.

Semiautomatic Dimensioning

The semiautomatic dimensioning feature does much of the work for you. You can create the extension lines, arrowheads, dimension lines, and dimension values automatically. To get the most benefit from the dimensioning feature, use *associative dimensioning.* Associative dimensions are linked to their locations in the drawing by information stored on the DEFPOINTS layers that the program creates. As a result, associative dimensions automatically update when you modify the drawing. Although you can also use non-associative dimensions, it isn't good practice because these dimensions are created from separate line, polyline, and text objects and do not update when the drawing changes.

Associative dimensioning is the default. This allows for trans-spatial dimensioning, which makes it possible to add dimensions in paper space for an object that is in model space. When dimensions are associative, if the model space object is moved, the paper space dimension will update to the new location.

Starting

Start by launching the AutoCAD software.

Click: ***New button***

Use the file **proto.dwt** located in the datafiles as a template.

Click: ***Application icon, SaveAs***

Save your drawing as ***obj-dim.dwg***.

You return to the drawing editor with the border and settings you created in the template drawing on your screen.

Dimensioning a Shape

Review the object in Figure 7.2. You will draw this shape and then dimension it.

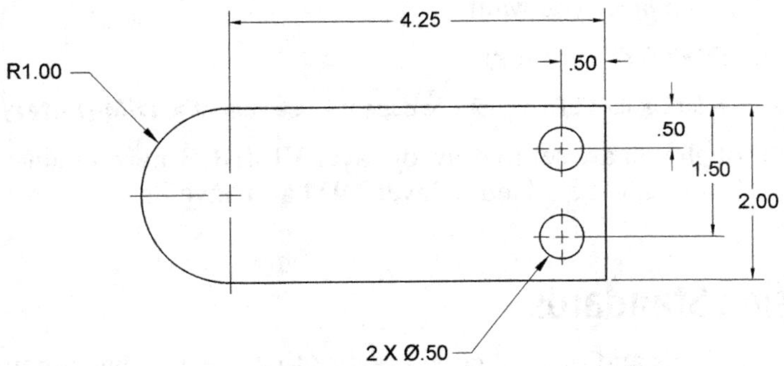

Figure 7.2

Layer **VISIBLE** should be the current layer in the drawing. If it is not, set layer VISIBLE as the current layer. Set **Grid** to **0.25** and **Snap** to **0.25**. Be sure that both are turned on.

Make sure that you are drawing in **model space**.

On your own, use the commands that you learned in the preceding tutorials to **draw the object** according to the specified dimensions.

You don't have to draw the centerlines now. Create the drawing geometry exactly, in order to derive the most benefit from the AutoCAD software's semiautomatic dimensioning capabilities. When you have finished, your drawing should look like Figure 7.3.

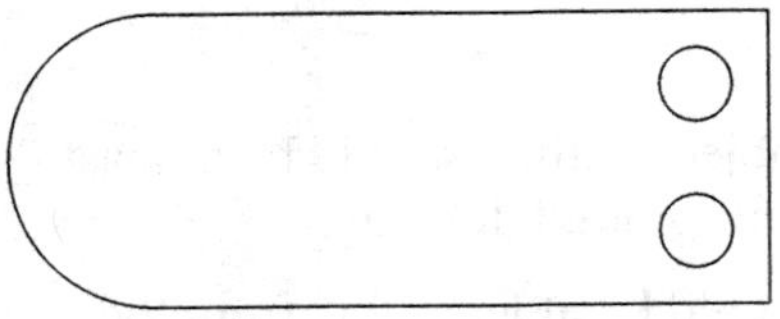

Figure 7.3

Tip: *If your paper doesn't fill the drawing window, switch to paper space and use Zoom All to enlarge the paper area to fill the view. Then make sure to switch back to model space to create the drawing.*

Tip: *Screen display of lineweights is controlled by the LWDISPLAY command. You can type it at the command prompt to turn on or off the diplay of lineweights. You can use the Customization button from the status bar to show the Lineweight button. Once it is shown, you can use it to turn on and off lineweight display.*

Setting the Dimension Layer

In order to produce a clear drawing of a subject, the outline and visible lines of the object are printed with a thick line. The dimension, hidden, center, and hatch lines are printed with a thin line. This way your eye is drawn first to the bold shape of the object and then to the details of its size and other features. The color of the object or a lineweight setting (usually set by layer) can be used to set a thin width for the dimension lines when plotting.

You will frequently want to turn off all of the dimensions in the drawing to make it easy to work on the drawing lines. Having dimensions on a separate layer makes this easy.

The DIMLAYER system variable allows you to set which layer will be used when dimensions are created. The default is Use Current, but any layer may be set. This way when a dimension is created it is automatically placed on the layer you want.

Command: ***DIMLAYER [Enter]***

Enter new value for DIMLAYER, or . for use current <"use current">: ***DIM [Enter]***

Now even though you are set to draw on layer VISIBLE, new dimensions will automatically be added to layer DIM and have its layer properties.

Dimension Standards

There are standards and rules of good practice that specify how dimension lines, extension lines, arrowheads, text size, and various aspects of dimensioning should appear in the finished drawing. Mechanical, electrical, civil, architectural, and weldment drawings, among others, each have their own standards. Professional societies and standards organizations publish drawing standards for various disciplines. The American Society of Mechanical Engineers (ASME/ANSI) publishes a widely used standard for mechanical drawings to help you create clear drawings that others can easily interpret.

Typical spacings for an 8.5" X 11" drawing are:

- A .0625" space is used between the extension lines and the feature from which they are extended.
- Extension lines should extend .125" past the last dimension line.
- Arrowheads and text should be approximately .125" tall.
- Titles should be .20" tall.
- The dimension line closest to the object outline should be at least .375" from the object outline on your plotted drawing.
- Each succeeding dimension line should be at least .25" from the previous dimension line.

Associating Dimensions

AutoCAD's dimensions are fully associated with the drawing objects. Versions of the program prior to Release 2004 created points in the non-printing layer, DEFPOINTS, with which to associate the dimension. The defpoints that were created coincided with the locations on the object that you selected for the dimension endpoints. Updating dimensions was accomplished by changing the location of these defpoints if they were selected when the object was moved or scaled, which did not fully associate the dimension. Now the dimensions are associated with the object geometry, but still use layer defpoints.

When adding dimensions to your drawing, it is important to have already determined the scale at which you will plot your drawing on the sheet of paper and established the zoom scaling factor. That way you can place the dimensions where they will show clearly on the layout for the final plot.

If you are going to plot using a layout (paper space), you should set the scaling factor for the view before you dimension your drawing. Setting the scaling factor first allows you to place the dimensions around the drawing views where they will show clearly. If you change the scale, you will generally have to spend some time cleaning up the dimension placement.

For this drawing the scale should be set to 1=1, as you started your drawing from *proto.dwt*, which had that setting. Check it using the Viewports Scaling button on the status bar, or by showing the viewport properties and verifying that the standard scaling is set to 1=1.

Annotation Scaling

Annotation is the general term for any type of notes and labels that are added to a drawing. For example, a parts list, dimensions, notes, callouts, and other items.

Text information needs to be visible in the drawing. Consider the subdivision plot that you created in Tutorials 2 and 3. The final drawing was planned to plot on a C-sized (17"X 22") sheet at a scale of 1"= 150'. What if you decided to plot it at a scale of 1"= 300'? This might make the text too small to read. One advantage of CAD is the ability to easily plot the drawing to a different scale, without having to redraw it. If the text is set to a specific size, plotting to a smaller scale will result in smaller text, at some point too small to be legible.

AutoCAD provides a method to flexibly scale the text and other annotation items based on the viewport scale for the plotted drawing. Annotation items that use this special annotative scale feature are able to automatically update to a new size when the scale of the drawing changes.

The types of objects that can have the annotative scale feature include:

- Text (single-line and multiline)
- Dimensions
- Leaders and multileaders
- Tolerances
- Hatches
- Tables
- Blocks
- Attributes

You will learn more about tolerances, hatches, tables, blocks and attributes in later tutorials.

The Dimension Panel

You can quickly select the dimensioning commands from the Dimension panel on the ribbon Annotate tab.

On your own, expand and pin the Dimension panel as shown in Figure 7.4.

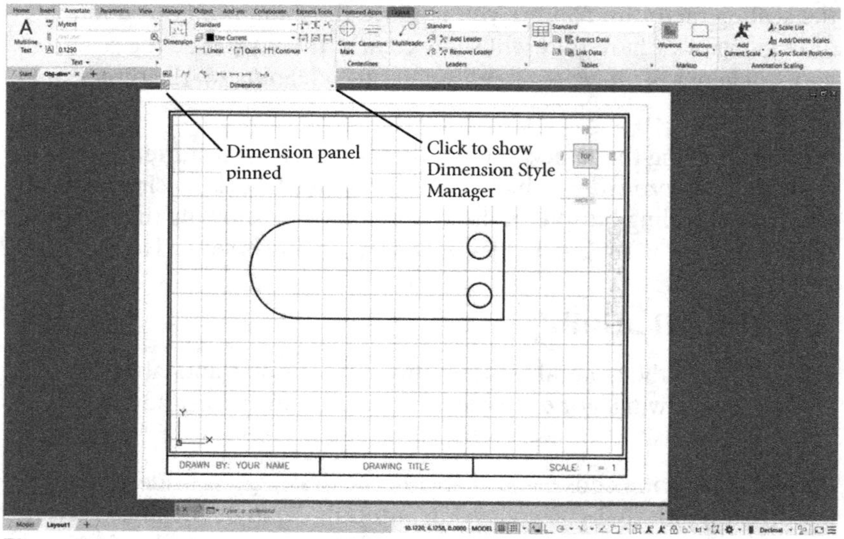

Figure 7.4

Tip: *You can quickly display the Properties dialog box for an object by double-clicking on it or selecting it and then pressing [Ctrl]+1.*

Using Dimension Styles

Many features controlling the appearance of the dimensions are set by *dimension variables (dim vars)*, which you can set using the Dimension Style Manager. Dimension variables all have names, and you can set each one by typing its name at the command prompt. However, the dialog box allows you to set many dimension variables at the same time.

Tip: *Dimensions take a lot of drawing space, especially between the views of a multiview drawing. Often you may need to zoom your drawing to half-size (.5XP) (standard scale of 2:1) or some other smaller scale to have room for dimensions. Keep this possibility in mind for future drawings. Do not change your XP scale factor for this tutorial unless directed to do so.*

You start this dialog box from the ribbon Annotation tab, Dimension panel as shown in Figure 7.4, or by typing Dimstyle or DDIM at the command prompt.

Click: ***the small arrow in the lower right corner of the dimension panel to show the Dimension Style manager***

The Dimension Style Manager appears as shown in Figure 7.5.

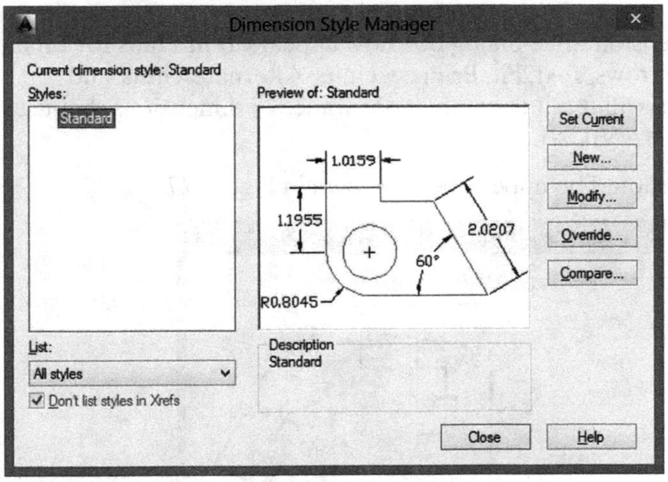

Figure 7.5

Creating a Named Dimension Style

You use the Dimension Style Manager to change the dimension variables that control the appearance of the dimensions. The current style name is STANDARD. It is displayed on the dimension panel. This basic set of features is provided as the default.

You can create your own *dimension style* with a name that you specify. This way you can save different sets of dimension features that will be useful for different types of drawings—such as mechanical or architectural. You will create a new dimension style named MECHANICAL.

Click: ***New from the right side of the dialog box***

The Create New Dimension Style dialog box appears on your screen. In the New Style Name area, highlight the existing text, Copy of Standard,

Type: ***MECHANICAL***

Mechanical now appears as the new style name. See Figure 7.6. In the Start With area, Standard is listed as the style to use as the basis for the new Mechanical style.

Leave the Annotative box unchecked. *You will learn more about this feature later in the tutorial.*

Near the bottom of the dialog box you will see the Use for area. This style will be used for all dimension types: linear, angular, radial, etc.

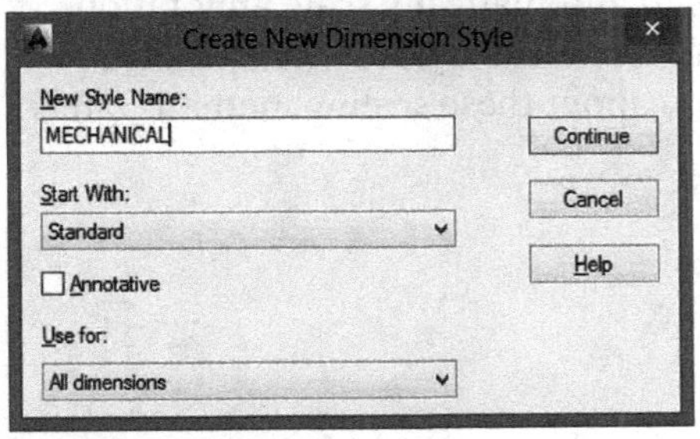

Figure 7.6

Click: ***Continue***

The New Dimension Style dialog box now appears. It has tabs for Lines, Symbols and Arrows, Text, Fit, Primary Units, Alternate Units, and Tolerances. You will use it to set the appearance of dimensions that use the style MECHANICAL.

The Lines tab should be uppermost as shown in Figure 7.7.

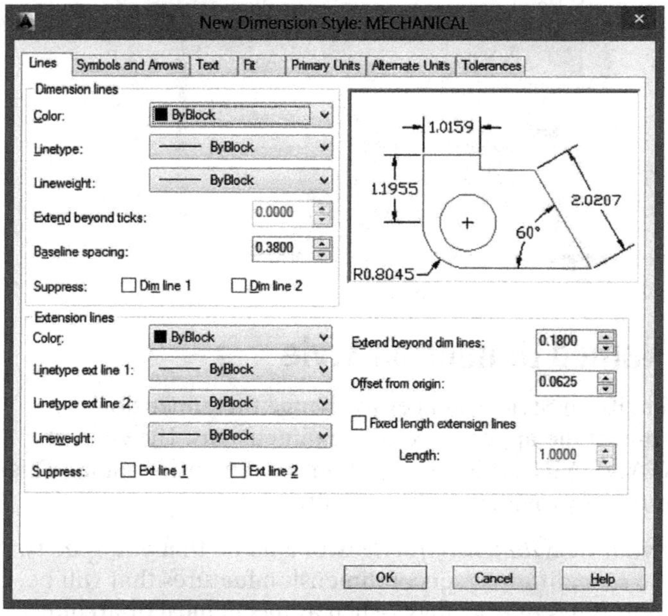

Figure 7.7

Scaling Dimension Features

As you go through the next steps of setting up the sizes and appearance of the dimensions using the dialog box, keep in mind that there are at least three different ways to control the sizes of the dimensions as a group. These are accomplished using an important dimensioning variable called the *dimension scaling factor* (Dimscale). It can be set from the Fit tab.

You will see later that using Dimscale, you can rescale as a group all of the values that control dimension appearance, either by calculating a value to multiply times all the dimension size settings or automatically determining that value based on the viewport scale factor.

You can also use annotative styles to automatically scale annotation items like dimensions. (The use of annotative styles automatically sets Dimscale to 0.) You will learn more about these scaling methods later in the tutorial.

Lines tab

The lines tab of the New Dimension Style dialog box is used to set the appearances of the dimension lines and extension lines. You will set the sizes of dimension features to the size that should be plotted on a standard 8.5" X 11" mechanical drawing.

You will use the Fit tab in a moment to tell the program that the sizes you have specified for dimensions are the sizes on the plotted layout, and not the size in model space. The settings that you will make are based on an 8.5" X 11" sheet size. Larger drawing sheets often use larger sizes.

Dimension Lines

Use the Dimension Lines area at the upper left of the dialog box to control the appearance of the dimension lines. You can set the color, linetype, lineweight, and the distance for the baseline spacing.

The value entered in the box to the right of baseline spacing controls the distance between successive dimensions added using *baseline dimensioning.* The default value, 0.38, will work for now. (The ASME/ANSI standard states that successive dimensions should be at least 1/4" [0.25"] apart, so 0.38 will meet this criterion.)

You can choose to suppress the first or second dimension line when the dimension value divides the dimension line into two parts by checking the boxes near the bottom of this area.

On your own make sure that none of the suppress dimension line boxes are checked. You will set the color, linetype, and lineweight for dimension lines so that they are controlled by the dimension's layer.

*Click: **ByLayer** from the pull-down adjacent to **Color***

*Click: **ByLayer** from the **Linetype** pull-down*

*Click: **ByLayer** from the **Lineweight** pull-down*

Extension Lines

The Extension lines area lets you control the color, linetype and lineweight for extension lines. In addition, you can set the distance that extension lines extend beyond the dimension line drawn, and the distance from the selected dimension placement that the extension line will begin (offset from origin).

Tip: *You can set the lineweight for extension and dimension lines so that it is controlled by layer or to a specified width using the Lineweight area of the Lines tab.*

You can also suppress either extension line. Make sure that neither box is checked to suppress the extension lines.

You will use this area to control the color by layer, and then set the distance to extend beyond dimension lines to .125 (the ANSI standard for this size drawing).

Click: ***ByLayer*** *from the* ***Color*** *pull-down*

Click: ***ByLayer*** *from the* ***Linetype ext line 1*** *pull-down*

Click: ***ByLayer*** *from the* ***Linetype ext line 2*** *pull-down*

Click: ***ByLayer*** *from the* ***Lineweight*** *pull-down*

Select: ***the text in the input box to the right of Extend beyond dim lines*** *so that it appears highlighted*

Type: ***.125***

When you have made the settings the dialog box should look like Figure 7.8.

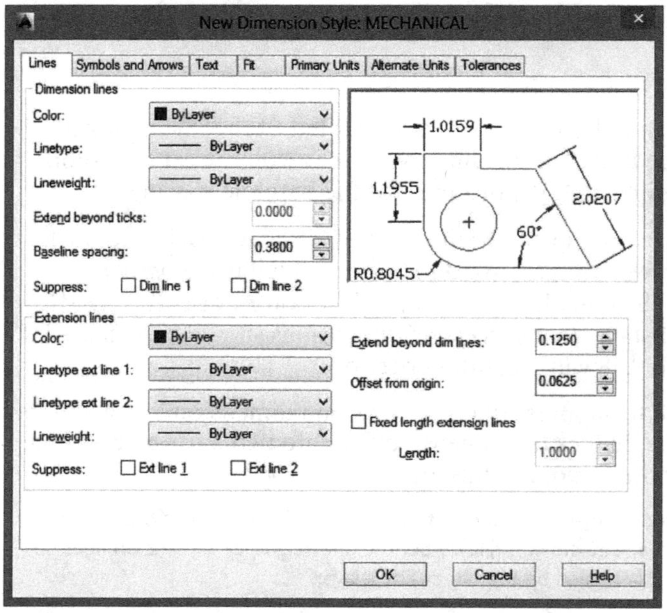

Figure 7.8

Symbols and Arrows tab

Use the Symbols and Arrows tab of the dialog box to set the arrow size, centermark size and style, arc length style, and jogged radius dimension angle.

Tip: *You can also use the downward arrow to set the value to .125.*

Click: ***the Symbols and Arrows tab***

Click: ***to pull down the list of available arrow styles*** *adjacent to the First Arrowhead box as shown in Figure 7.9*

When you select an arrowhead style from the list, the arrows shown in the *image tile*, or active picture near the top right, change. Scroll through the available styles.

Return the setting to **Closed filled** when you are finished.

Notice that when you select a style for the first arrowhead, the second arrowhead box automatically changes to reflect that. You can select a different style for the second arrowhead by choosing it last.

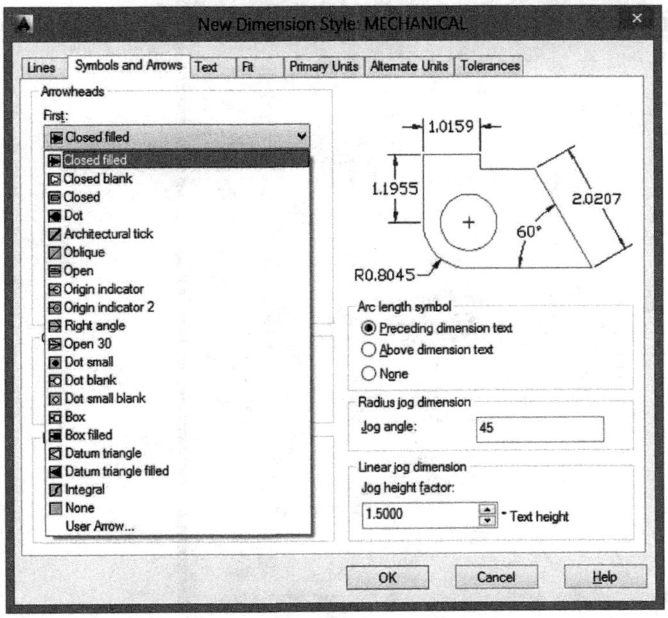

Figure 7.9

Next set the size for the arrowhead.

Click: ***to highlight the value in the box below Arrow size***

Type: ***0.125 to replace the value***

Centermark Size and Style

The Center Marks area controls the size and style of the centermark which is added when you create radius or diameter dimensions. Selecting Line draws a full set of centermarks. Selecting Mark draws just a tick at the center of the circle. Selecting None will cause no centermarks to be drawn.

Click: ***Line from the Centermark area***

Set the size of the centermark using the box below the word Size. The value for Size sets the distance from the center to the end of one side of the center cross of the centermark. To make a smaller center cross, set it to a smaller value; for a larger center cross, set the size larger.

Tip: *If the value for the centermark size is too large, full centermarks will not be drawn even when the style is set to Line; instead, just the mark will appear in the center of the circle.*

Leave the value for your centermarks set to the default value, 0.09, for now. You can type Dimcen at the command prompt, as you did in Tutorial 6.

Notice the Arc length symbol and Radial dimension jog areas at the right of the dialog box. These are used to set the placement for the arc length symbol used for arc length dimensions and for specifying the angle used for jogged radial dimension lines. For now, leave these areas set at the defaults.

When you have finished selecting, the Symbols and Arrows tab should look like Figure 7.10.

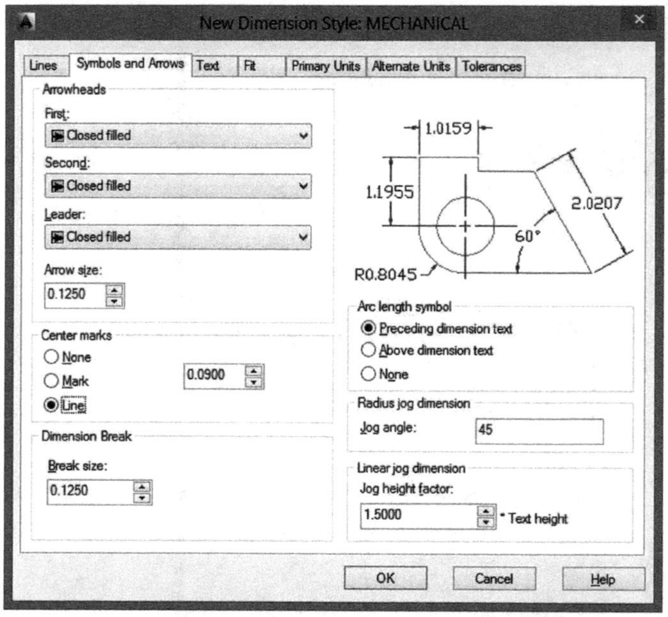

Figure 7.10

Text tab

The Text tab allows you to control the text style, height, color, background fill, and the gap between the end of the dimension line and the start of the dimension text.

*Click: **the Text tab** so that it appears uppermost*

Tip: *Using a text style with the text height set to 0 for dimensioning allows the dimension settings to control the text appearance.*

The Text Alignment area (bottom right) controls whether text always reads horizontally (i.e., is unidirectional text) or whether it will be aligned with the dimension line. The image tile changes to display the appearance for the selected setting.

On your own, choose Aligned with dimension line. Then choose ISO Standard. When you have finished experimenting, return the setting to **Horizontal** alignment.

The Text Placement area has a control for horizontal or vertical text placement. Use the pull-down menu adjacent to Horizontal to center text, place it near the first or second extension line, or place it over the first or second extension line. Usually, the default choice, Centered, is used for mechanical drawings.

On your own, try each setting and notice the effect of the selection on the image tile. When you are finished, return the setting to the default choice, **Centered**.

The pull-down menu adjacent to Vertical sets the placement of text relative to the dimension line. The options for vertical justification are Centered, Above, Outside, and JIS (Japanese Industrial Standard).

For ANSI standard mechanical drawings, select Centered to create dimension values that are centered vertically, breaking the dimension line. The ISO (International Standards Organization) standard usually uses the options for text above or outside the dimension line. The JIS option orients the text parallel to the dimension line and to its left. The

Above selection is often used on architectural drawings.

When you are finished examining this portion of the dialog box, return its setting to **Centered** on your own.

The Text style selection is used to select text styles you have predefined in the drawing with the Style command. Style MYTEXT was previously created in the template drawing you started from. MYTEXT was created with a text height of 0 (zero) which allows you to set the text height at the time the text is placed. This is important for correct looking dimension text. Clicking the ellipsis (...) next to the style name opens the Text Style dialog box, so that you can create new styles if needed.

*Click: **MYTEXT** from the pull-down for Text Style*

Next you will set the text height to 0.125, the standard height for 8.5" X 11" drawings.

Replace the Text height value with .125

Now you will set the color for the dimension text to BYLAYER.

*Click: **ByLayer** from the pull-down adjacent to Color*

On your own, try a color from the Fill color selection and then return it to **None**. Notice the image tile shows the fill color shading behind the dimension value.

The Text tab should now appear as shown in Figure 7.11.

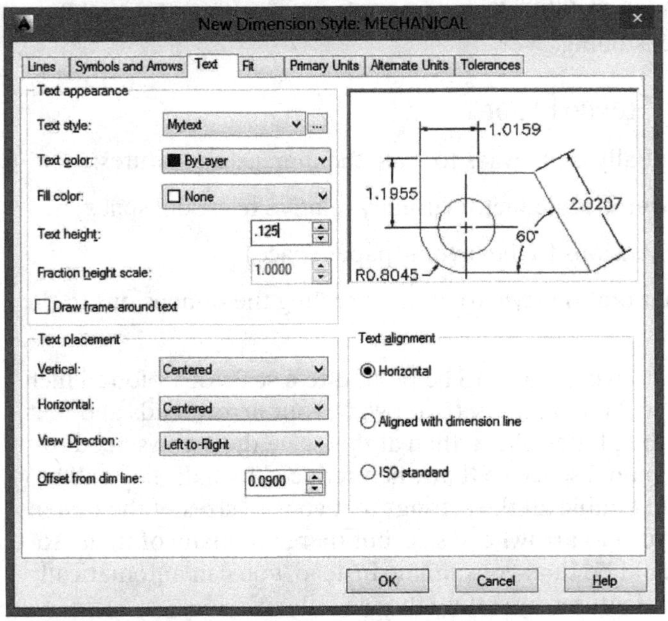

Figure 7.11

Fit Tab

The Fit tab lets you set the options for how the dimensions will be placed in the drawing. These settings are especially helpful when there is not enough room to place both the dimension value and dimension lines and arrowheads inside the extension lines.

Click: ***the Fit tab***

The setting "Either text or arrows (best fit)" places both the text and arrows inside the extension lines, if possible. If that is not possible, either the text or the arrows will be placed inside the extension lines. If neither will fit, both the arrows and text are placed outside the extension lines. Generally, these are all accepted practices, as long as the dimension can be correctly interpreted. You can also set which will be moved outside first: the text, the arrows, or both text and arrows; or to always keep the text between the extension lines. You can also specify to suppress the arrows if they don't fit inside the extension lines.

Tip: *To make radial dimensions that look like those shown in the exercises, choose the Place text manually selection in the Fine Tuning area of the Fit tab. Then you can drag the radial and diameter dimension value to place it around the outside of the object.*

On your own, choose **Either text or arrows (best fit)**.

The Text placement area of this dialog box allows you to control how text is placed when it is not in the default location (between the extension lines). You can select to place it beside the dimension line, or over the dimension line, either with or without a leader.

The Fine Tuning area in the lower right of the dialog box lets you select either to place text manually or to force a line to be drawn between the extension lines, even when text and arrows are placed outside the extension lines. If you select Place text manually, when you click or type the location for the dimension line, the dimension value will appear at that position. This can be important for creating radial and diameter dimensions that are placed outside the drawing outline. You will learn more about specific "child" dimension styles to do this in Tutorial 8 on advanced dimensioning.

The Dimension Scaling Factor

There are essentially three ways to scale the dimension features:

1. use an overall scale factor (usually relative to model space)
2. scale dimensions to the layout (paper space)
3. use an annotation style to manage scaling the dimensions to the layout

Think about a drawing that is to be plotted to a scale of 1 plotted inch in paper space to 2 model units. If you want your arrowheads and text to be .125" on the plotted sheet, then at this scale the arrows need to be .25" high in model space so that when reduced by half they will be .125". You could double all the settings that control sizes of the dimension elements, such as arrowhead size, but there are many of them, so this method would be time-consuming. Instead, you can automatically scale all the size features by setting the overall scale.

Overall scale sets a scaling factor to use for all of the dimension variables that control the sizes of dimension elements. Its value appears in the box to the right of "Use overall scale of:." Setting the overall scale to 2 doubles the size of all the dimension elements in the drawing so that, when plotted half-size, your arrowheads, text, and other elements will maintain the correct proportions on the final plot. (You can also type Dimscale at the command prompt and enter the value by which the dimension elements are multiplied.)

Clicking Scale dimensions to layout uses the viewport scale (zoom XP) factor to set the scaling for dimension elements so that the values you enter in the dialog box are the sizes on the drawing when paper space is plotted at a scale of 1=1.

For this portion of the tutorial,

Click: ***Scale dimensions to layout button***

Leave the Annotative box unchecked

Your Fit tab should appear as shown in Figure 7.12.

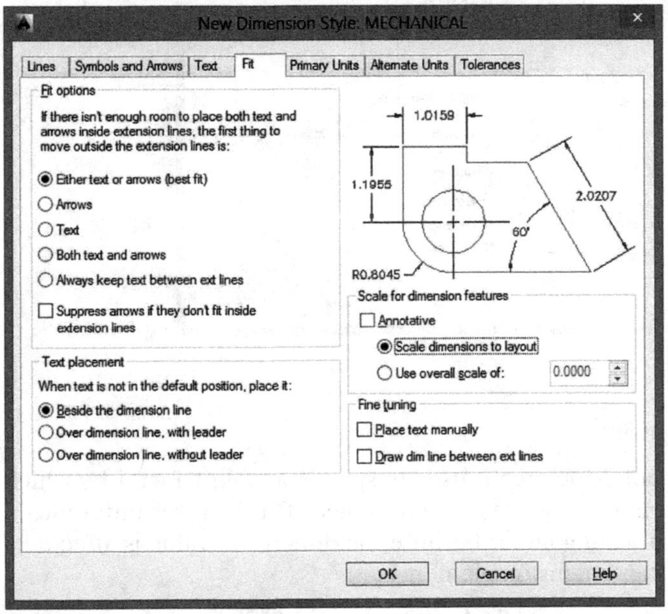

Figure 7.12

Primary Units

You use the Primary Units tab to set up the number of decimal places, the prefix, and the suffix for dimensions. When dimensioning a drawing, you must consider the precision of the values to be used in the dimensions. Specifying a dimension to four decimal places, which is the AutoCAD default, implies that accuracies of 1/10,000th of an inch are appropriate tolerances for this part. Standard practice is to specify decimal inch dimensions to two decimal places (an accuracy of 1/100th of an inch) unless the function of the part makes a tighter tolerance desirable.

You can select the type of units and set the number of decimal places displayed for linear and angular dimension values. For this tutorial you will leave the linear dimension units set to Decimal.

Click: ***Primary Units tab*** *so that it appears uppermost*

Set the precision for the dimension values using the pull-down as shown in Figure 7.13.

Click: ***0.00 from the pull-down for Precision***

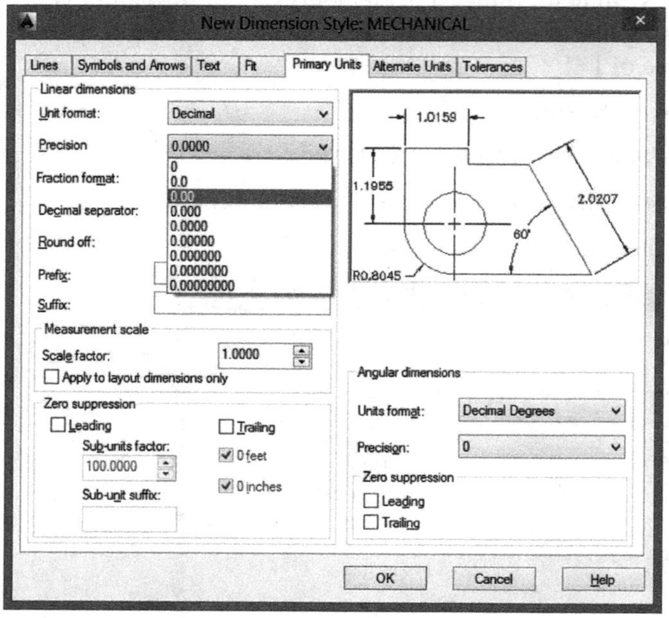

Figure 7.13

Measurement Scale

The Measurement Scale area is used to specify a scaling factor by which all the actual dimension values are multiplied. This factor is different from the overall scaling factor because the dimension value is affected, not the size of the dimension elements.

Leave the value to the right of **Scale factor** set to **1.0000**.

You can use this area to scale only layout (paper space) dimensions by clicking the check box.

Zero Suppression for Linear Dimensions

The Zero Suppression area allows you to suppress leading or trailing zeros in the dimension value. You can also suppress dimensions of 0 feet or 0 inches. In decimal dimensioning, common practice is to show leading zeros in metric dimensions and to suppress them in inch dimensions when dimensions are less than 1 unit. Zero Suppression is available for both linear dimensions and angular dimensions, in four categories: leading zeros, trailing zeros, 0 feet, and 0 inches. Selecting the box to the left of any of these items suppresses those zeros; a check appears in the box when you select it. In the Linear Dimensions area under Zero Suppression,

Click: ***to suppress Leading zeros***

Angular Dimensions

The type of units used to dimension angles can be set using the Angular Dimensions area of the Primary Units tab. To select, pull down the list and choose from the types of units shown. (You can further control the appearance of angular dimensions by selecting the Angular in the Dimension Styles dialog box.)

Zero Suppression for Angular Dimensions

You will suppress the leading zeros for angular dimensions as you did for linear dimensions. In the Angular Dimensions area under Zero Suppression,

Click: ***to suppress Leading zeros***

When you have finished setting this tab of the dialog box, it should appear as shown in Figure 7.14.

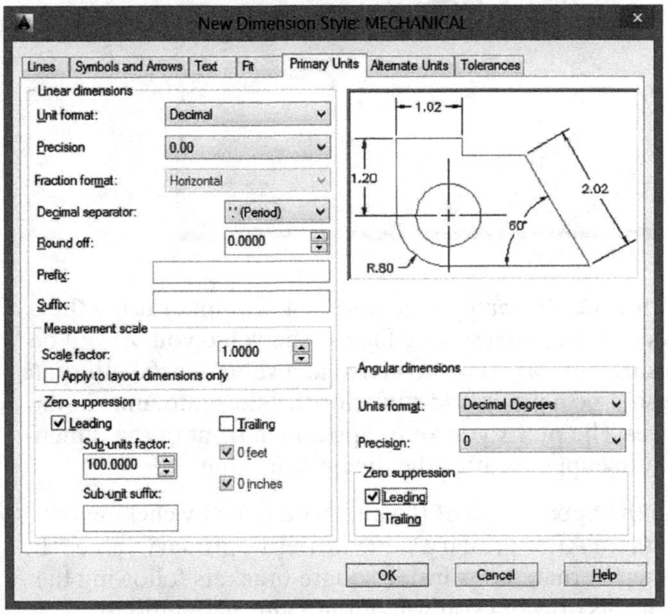

Figure 7.14

Alternate Units

Alternate units are useful when you want to dimension a drawing with more than one system of measurement. For example, dimensioning drawings with both metric and inch values is fairly common. When you use alternate units, the AutoCAD program automatically converts your drawing units to the alternate units, using the scaling factor you provide. You can enable alternate units by clicking the box to the left of "Display alternate units" in the upper left of the Alternate Units tab. Until you select the box to display the alternate units, the remaining selections are grayed out.

Next you will look at the settings that can be controlled using the Alternate Units tab.

Click: ***Alternate Units tab***

Click: ***Display alternate units*** *so that it is checked*

The Alternate Units tab appears on your screen as shown in Figure 7.15.

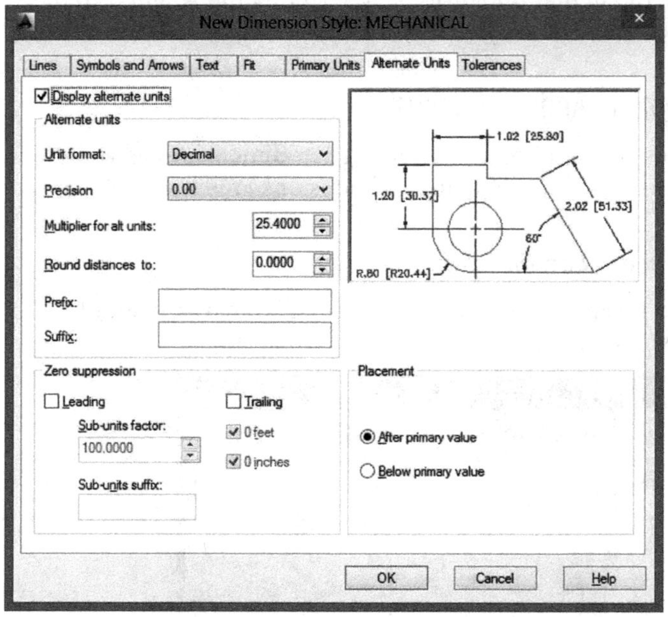

Figure 7.15

To set the scale for the alternate units, you set a Multiplier using the up/down arrows or typing in a scaling factor. The value you set will be multiplied times the primary units to arrive at a value for the alternate unit. You can also type a prefix and suffix for the alternate units in the appropriate boxes. The prefix you enter appears in front of the dimension value; the suffix appears after the dimension value.

You can control the appearance of the alternate units by clicking the button to place them After primary value or Below primary value. The default places the alternate units inside square brackets following the normal units. For this drawing you will not use alternate units, so

Click: ***to unselect Display alternate units*** *so that it is not checked*

Tolerances

You can use the Tolerances tab to specify limit or variance tolerances with the dimension value. You can set the tolerance method to Symmetrical, Deviation, Limits, Basic, or None. You will learn more about setting tolerances in Tutorial 8.

Click: ***Tolerances tab***

Click: ***Deviation*** *from the pull-down for Method*

The image tile shown in Figure 7.16 reflects the choices you have made thus far in setting up the Dimension style. Notice that now the tolerance is shown after the dimension values.

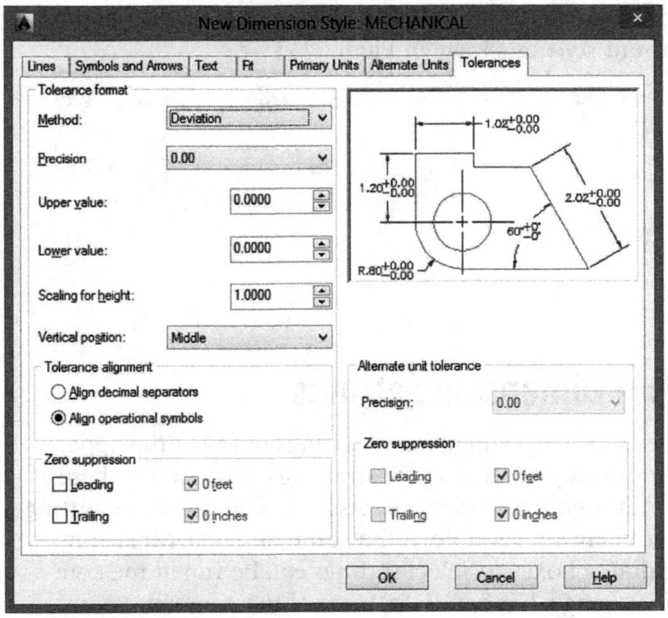

Figure 7.16

On your own, click on the other tolerance methods to view the effect of these settings in the image tile.

Click: ***None** from the pull-down for Method so that tolerances are not used*

Now you have set up your basic style for the dimensions.

Click: ***OK***

You are returned to the Dimension Style Manager dialog box.

Setting the Current Style

In order to apply your dimension style MECHANICAL so that new dimensions use this style, click the Set Current button near the top of the Dimension Style Manager.

Click: ***Set Current***

The selections you have made apply to dimension style MECHANICAL only. As you dimension your drawing, you can return to this dialog box and create a new style if you need to create dimensions with a different appearance.

When you change a style and click OK, the changes are applied to all existing dimensions in the drawing that you created with that style. If you want to make changes to a style and not have them take effect on existing dimensions, you can click the Override button to allow changes to take effect on newly created dimensions, but not on existing dimensions having that style. The Compare button lets you compare two different styles to view their differences.

Click: ***Close** to exit the Dimension Style Manager*

Notice that the name MECHANICAL now appears in the Dimension panel as the current style as shown in Figure 7.17.

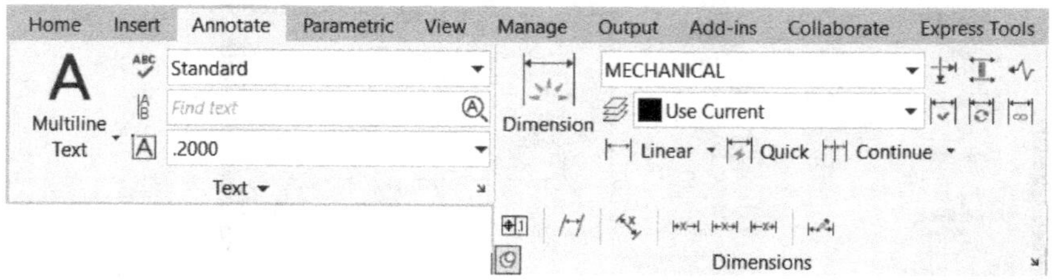

Figure 7.17

Checking Your Dimension Settings

As you have seen, you can change many settings to affect the appearance of the dimensions you add to your drawings. You can set these variables either through the Dimension Styles dialog box or by setting each individual dimension variable at the command line. Most commands that use dialog boxes to select settings can be run at the command prompt by typing a hyphen (-) in front of the command name.

You can use the —Dimstyle command to list and set dimension styles and variables at the command line. If any dimension variable overrides are set, they will be listed after the name of the dimension style. There should not be any overrides set for style MECHANICAL because you have saved your settings to the parent style.

Command: ***—DIMSTYLE [Enter]***

Current dimension style: Mechanical

Enter a dimension style option [Save/Restore/STatus/Variables/Apply/?]<Restore>: ***ST [Enter]***

Press: ***[Ctrl]+[F2]*** *to show the text window*

The dimension variables and their current settings are listed as shown in Figure 7.18. On your own, scroll to see all the entries.

```
DIMTFILL     0              Text background enabled
DIMTFILLCLR BYBLOCK         Text background color
DIMTIH       On             Text inside extensions is horizontal
DIMTIX       Off            Place text inside extensions
DIMTM        0.0000         Minus tolerance
DIMTMOVE     0              Text movement
DIMTOFL      Off            Force line inside extension lines
DIMTOH       On             Text outside horizontal
DIMTOL       Off            Tolerance dimensioning
DIMTOLJ      1              Tolerance vertical justification
DIMTP        0.0000         Plus tolerance
DIMTSZ       0.0000         Tick size
DIMTVP       0.0000         Text vertical position
DIMTXSTY     Mytext         Text style
DIMTXT       0.1250         Text height
DIMTXTDIRECTIONOff             Dimension text direction
DIMTZIN      0              Tolerance zero suppression
DIMUPT       Off            User positioned text
DIMZIN       4              Zero suppression
```

Figure 7.18

Click: ***the Windows Close button [X]*** *to exit the Text window*

Associative Dimensioning

The Dimassoc variable controls whether associative dimensioning is turned on or off. Associative dimensioning inserts each dimension as a block or group of drawing objects relative to the points selected in the drawing. If the drawing is scaled or stretched, the dimension values automatically update. The Dimassoc variable has three settings for the associativity between dimensions and drawing objects. A setting of 2 causes dimensions to automatically adjust their locations, orientations, and measurement values when the geometric objects associated with them are modified. A setting of 1 causes dimensions to be nonassociative. This means that the dimension does not change when the geometric object it measures is modified. Finally, a setting of 0 causes the dimension to be a collection of separate objects (exploded) rather than a single dimension object. Dimensions created with Dimassoc set to 0 cannot be updated, but their individual parts, such as arrowheads or extension lines, can be erased or moved.

Note: *Dimassoc was a new variable in AutoCAD 2004, Replacing the old Dimaso variable from prior releases.*

Dimensions created with Dimassoc set to 0 also do not automatically update when you change their dimension styles. When Dimassoc is set to 2 or 1, the entire dimension acts as one object in the drawing.

Make sure that Dimassoc is set to the default value of 2,

Command: ***DIMASSOC [Enter]***

Enter new value for DIMASSOC <2>: ***2 [Enter]***

Now you are ready to start adding dimensions to your drawing. Look at the status bar. You will see that the coordinates still display the cursor position with four decimal places of accuracy, even though you selected to display only two decimal places in your dimensions. AutoCAD keeps track of your drawing and the settings you have made in the drawing database to a precision of at least fourteen decimal places. However, the dimensions will be shown only to two decimal places, as set in the current style. The display of decimal places on the status bar is set independently of the dimension precision (using the Units command you learned in Tutorial 1). This feature is useful because you can still create and display an accurate drawing database while working on the design, yet dimension according to the often lower precision required to manufacture acceptable parts.

Note: *Prior to Release 2005, placing dimensions in the layout was not preferred because these were not associated to the objects in a way that let them move as the model was panned inside the viewport.*

Adding Dimensions to the Layout or the Model

Dimensions are usually added in model space, where your geometric objects reside. They may also be added to the paper space layout, where notes, borders, and other such information are placed. Many factors influence the decision whether to add the dimensions to model space or to paper space. Adding the dimensions to the layout is not common, but can be useful for layout dimensions or showing a dimension between two separate viewports. Generally, you will add the dimensions for most shapes in model space.

Tip: *Adding dimensions to the Layout or to Model Space are both acceptable, but only one method is generally used within a drawing to make it easier to manage the dimensions. For future drawings, decide whether you prefer dimensions in model or paper space.*

All in all it depends on your particular drawing application, company practices, and downstream uses for the drawing which one you should ultimately choose. You will try each method in this tutorial. For this drawing you will add the dimensions to model space, working inside the viewport.

Grid and Snap can be set differently for model space and for paper space. It can look confusing when both grids are turned on at the same time.

Tip: *If you see two grids that don't align with one another, check to see that you have the grid turned off in model space before you turn the grid on in paper space.*

On your own, double-click inside the viewport to ensure you are in model space.

Set the Grid and **Snap** to **.25.**

Press F7 to turn the **Grid on. Leave Snap turned off.**

Tip: *Use the grid as a visual reference to help you position the dimension text 0.5 unit away from the object outline.*

You will use the grid to help visually locate the dimensions 0.5 unit away from the object outline. This way the dimension placement will meet the criterion of being at least 3/8" (.375) from the object outline. Once you are accustomed to placing dimensions, you can just do this by eye. Keep in mind this measurement is relative to the paper units; in this drawing it will be at scale 1"=1" so the units are the same in the model and on the paper.

Adding Dimensions

The Dimension command measures and annotates a feature with a dimension line. The value inserted into the dimension line is the perpendicular distance between the extension lines. With the Dimension command (DIM) the dimension is adjusted depending on the type of objects selected and the location of the cursor when you are placing the dimension.

Tip: *When dimensioning a full circle of 360 degrees (as opposed to an arc), use the diameter command rather than the radius. This is important because equipment used to manufacture and inspect holes and cylinders is designed to measure diameter, not radius. The machinist making the part should never have to calculate any dimensions, including not having to double the radius to arrive at the diameter. Measuring the radius of a hole is difficult because the center has already been drilled out.*

You will use the intersection and quadrant modes to select the exact intersections in the drawing for the extension lines so that the dimensions will be drawn accurately. You will dimension the horizontal distance from the end of the block to the center of the upper hole. Refer to Figure 7.19 for your selections.

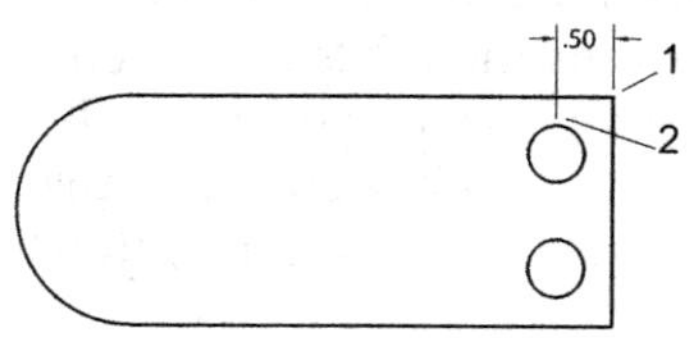

Figure 7.19

On your own, turn the **Intersection** and **Quadrant** running mode object snaps on and all other object snaps and tracking off.

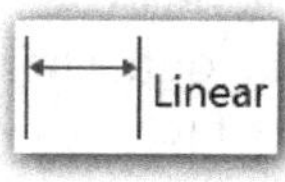

Click: ***Linear dimension button***

Specify first extension line origin or <select object>: ***click point 1*** *at the top right-hand corner*

Specify second extension line origin: ***click on the upper small hole, using snap to Quadrant to locate point 2***

Specify dimension line location or [Mtext/Text/Angle/Horizontal/Vertical/Rotated]: ***Press [F9] to toggle Snap to on and click a point two snap***

increments above the top line of the object

The dimension should appear in your drawing, as shown in Figure 7.19. Next you will add the diameter dimensions for the two small holes.

Creating a Diameter Dimension

A diameter dimension shows a centermark and draws the *leader line* from the point you select on the circle to the location you select for the dimension value. The leader line produced is a radial line, which, if extended, would pass through the center of the circle. You can make changes to the appearances by setting the dimension style.

You will use the DIM command. Depending on the type of object you select, different options for the dimension automatically appear. You will use the Mtext option to add additional text to the left of the dimension value. Refer to Figure 7.21 for the placement of the dimension.

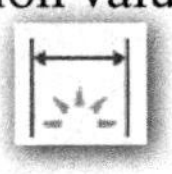

Click: ***Dimension button***

Select objects or specify first extension line origin or [Angular/Baseline/Continue/Ordinate/aliGn/Distribute/Layer/Undo]: ***Press [F3]to turn off Object Snap and then click on the lower left of the lower small circles***

Specify diameter dimension location or [Radius/Mtext/Text/text aNgle/Undo]: ***M [Enter]***

The Text Editor similar to Figure 7.20 appears on your screen. You will use the dialog box to add the text 2X in front of the dimension value.

The cursor should be positioned in front of the .50 value.

Type: ***2X***

Click: ***anywhere outside the Text Editing box***

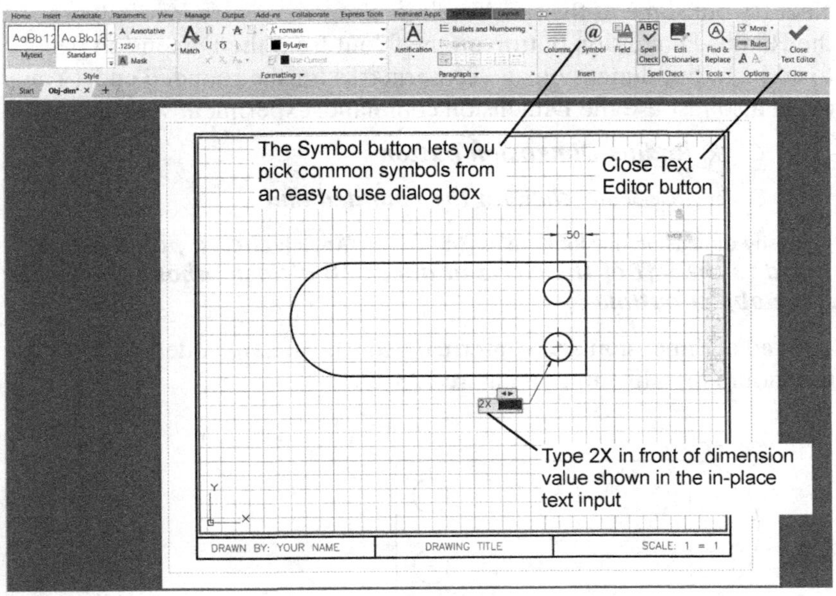

Figure 7.20

Tip: *When dimensioning a full circle of 360 degrees (as opposed to an arc), use the diameter command rather than the radius. This is important because equipment used to manufacture and inspect holes and cylinders is designed to measure diameter, not radius.*

Tip: *Be sure that Snap and Ortho are off to make selecting the circles and drawing angled leader lines easier.*

Tip: *Take care that the text is not highlighted; you want to insert text, not replace the dimension value.*

Tip: *You can replace the default value for the dimension with a different value. If you do so, however, your dimension values won't automatically update when you change your drawing. A better practice is to create your drawing geometry accurately and accept the default value provided.*

Specify diameter dimension location or [Radius/Mtext/Text/text aNgle/Undo]: ***click a point below and to the left of the circle at about 7 o'clock, about .5 outside the object outline;*** *see Figure 7.21* ***[Enter]***

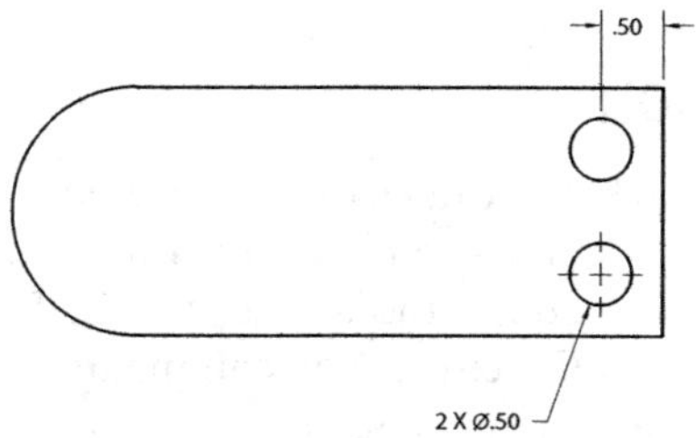

Figure 7.21

Next, you will add a centermark for the upper of the two small holes. You will use the DIMCENTER command, which uses the dimension style to determine the centermark size.

On your own, set **DIM as the current layer.**

TYpe: ***DIMCENTER [Enter]***

Select arc or circle: ***click on the edge of the top circle***

The centermark is added to the drawing, as shown in Figure 7.22.

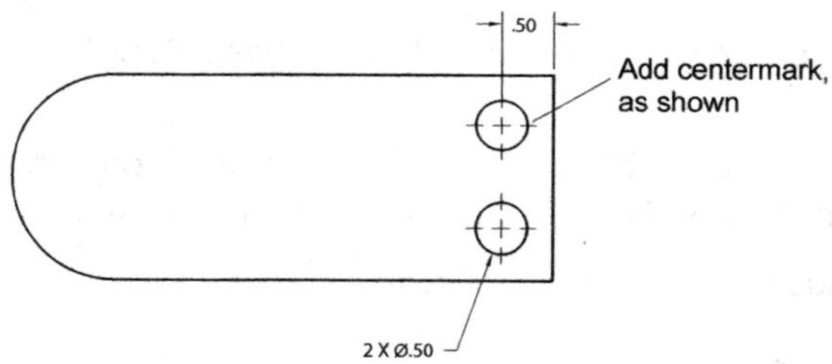

Figure 7.22

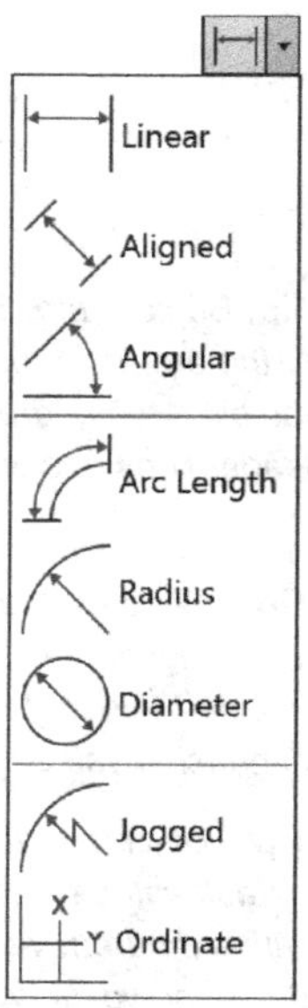

Next try out some of the specific dimension commands. You will use the Radius Dimension button on the flyout from the Dimension panel to add a radius dimension and centermarks for the rounded end. (You could also just use the Dimension command; experiment with this also.)

 *Click:* ***Radius Dimension button***

Select circle or arc: ***click on the rounded end***

Specify dimension line location or [Mtext/Text/Angle]: ***click a point above and to the left of the circle at about 10 o'clock, about .5 outside the object outline***

The radial dimension and centermark for the arc are added. Your drawing should look like that in Figure 7.23.

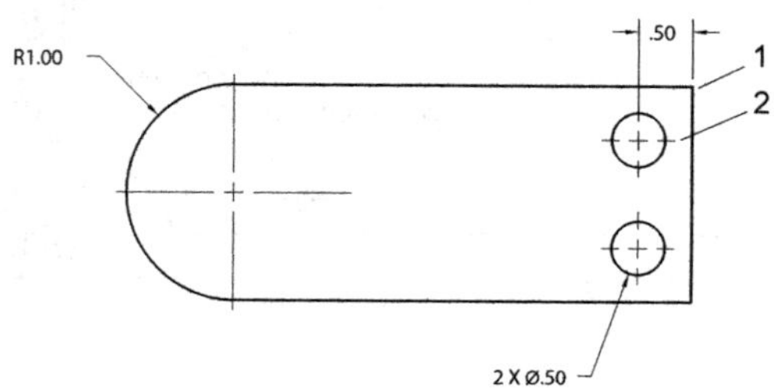

Figure 7.23

Next, you will add a linear dimension for the vertical distance from the upper edge of the part to the center of the top hole.

On your own, turn on **Object Snap Intersection and Endpoint.**

Click: ***Linear Dimension button***

Specify first extension line origin or <select>: ***click intersection 1 at the top right-hand corner*** *(refer to Figure 7.23)*

Specify second extension line origin: ***target quadrant point 2***

Specify dimension line location or [Mtext/Text/Angle/Horizontal/Vertical/Rotated]: ***click to the right of the object***

The dimension added to your drawing should look like that in Figure 7.24.

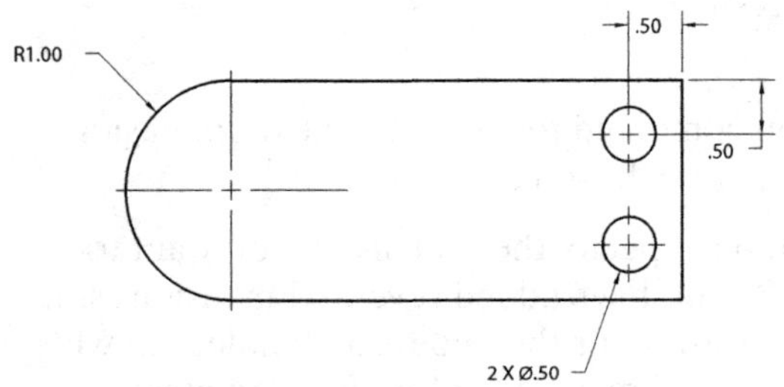

Figure 7.24

When you use the best fit method for placing text, the text value is automatically placed outside the extension lines in instances where there is not enough space to fit the text cleanly. You can click on a dimension and use its grips to fine tune the placement if needed.

On your own, turn Snap and Object Snap off to make it easier to reposition the value. Click on the linear dimension. Click the grip centered in the dimension value to make it active. Use it to drag the text inside the extension lines.

Next, you will use baseline dimensioning to add the horizontal dimension between the edge of the part and the rounded end.

Baseline Dimensioning

Baseline and *chained dimensioning* are two different methods of relating one dimension to the next. In baseline dimensioning, as the name suggests, each succeeding dimension is measured from one extension line or baseline. In chained or *continued dimensioning*, each succeeding dimension is measured from the last extension line of the previous dimension. Baseline dimensioning can be the more accurate method because the tolerance allowance is not added to the tolerance allowance of the preceding dimension, as it is in chained dimensioning. However, chained dimensioning often may be preferred because the greater the tolerances allowed, the cheaper the part should be to manufacture. The more difficult the tolerance is to achieve, the more parts will not pass inspection. Figure 7.25 depicts the two different dimensioning methods. Note that, if a tolerance of ±.01 is allowed, the baseline dimensioned portion can be as large as 4.26 or as small as 4.24. However, with chained dimensions, an acceptable part could be as large as 4.27 or as small as 4.23.

Tip: *To add the linear dimension for the location of the hole and have the centermark appear correctly, pick the quadrant point of the circle, not the center. If you select the center, the extension line will extend into the circle and obscure the centermark.*

Turn *Snap on and off as needed to make selecting easier.*

Tip: *If you have difficulty selecting the dimensions when editing, check that you are in paperspace, where you created them.*

Tip: *The Dimension command now has many features that make use of special dimensioning options, like Linear, Radial, unnecessary. As you make a selection and hover the mouse over items, a preview of the likely dimension desired appears. Clicking to place it selects those features.*

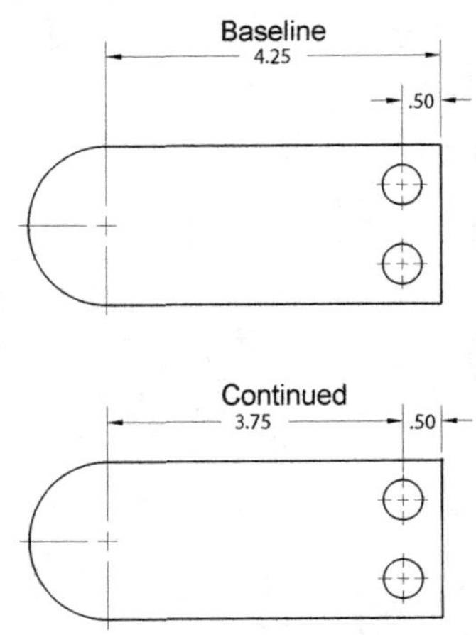

Figure 7.25

Adding dimensions with Baseline or Continue is preferable because adding a second dimension with the Linear Dimension command will draw the extension line a second time, which may give a poor appearance to your drawing when it is printed or plotted.

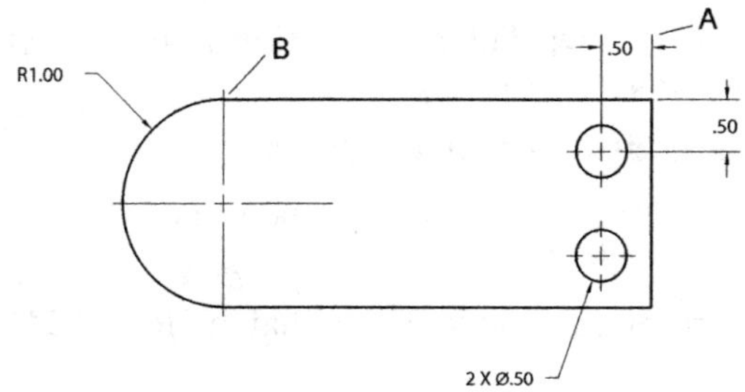

Figure 7.26

Use the Baseline Dimension command to create the next dimension. Refer to Figure 7.26 as you make selections.

You will use the Select option to specify the dimension you want to use as the base dimension. As you have added several dimensions since determining the horizontal location for the upper small hole, you will need to specify that it is the base dimension before you can create the baseline dimension.

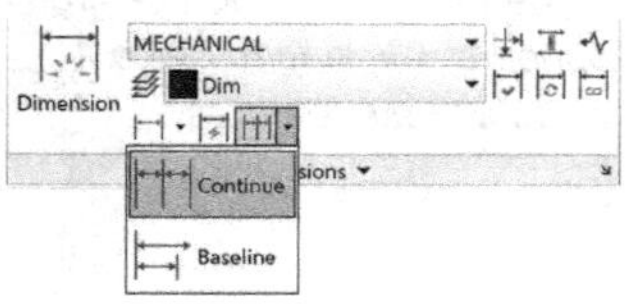

Click: ***Baseline Dimension button from the flyout***

Specify second extension line origin or [Select/Undo] <Select>: ***[Enter]***

Select base dimension: ***click A for the base dimension***

Specify second extension line origin or [Select/Undo] <Select>: ***click intersection B***

Specify second extension line origin or [Select/Undo] <Select>: ***[Enter]***

Select base dimension: ***[Enter]***

The new dimension appears, as in Figure 7.27. Note that the program located the dimensions automatically based on your dimension style settings.

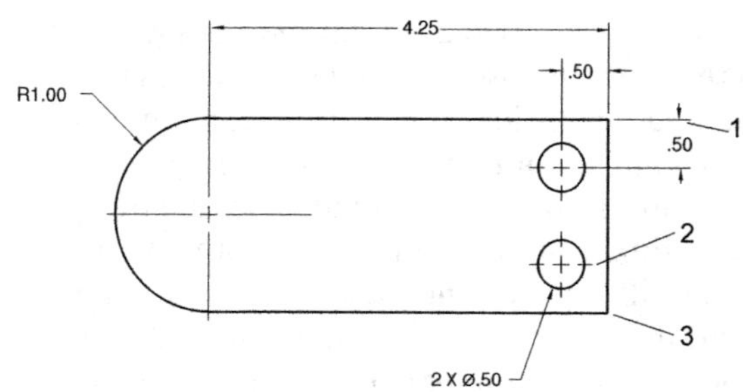

Figure 7.27

Next you will see the contrast of using the Dimension command to add baseline dimensions for the vertical location of the lower hole and for the overall height. Refer to Figure 7.27 for the points to select.

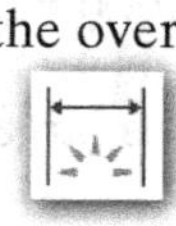

Click: ***Dimension button***

Select objects or specify first extension line origin or [Angular/Baseline/Continue/Ordinate/aliGn/Distribute/Layer/Undo]: ***hover the cursor over the upper right extension line***

The prompt automatically switches to options for continued or baseline dimension while the extension line is highlighted (see Figure 7.28).

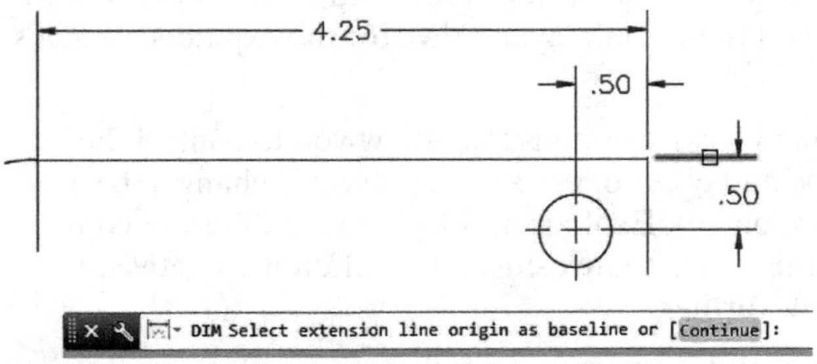

Figure 7.28

Select extension line origin to continue or [Baseline] ***B [Enter]***

Select extension line origin as baseline or [Continue]: ***click 1 for the base dimension***

Specify second extension line origin or [Select/Offset/Undo] <Select>: ***click the centerline endpoint 2***

Specify second extension line origin or [Select/Offset/Undo] <Select>: ***click intersection 3***

Specify first extension line origin as baseline or [Offset]: <Select>: ***[Enter]***

Turn off grid and snap to make viewing and selection easier.

Use **Pan** to center the view in the viewport.

Save your drawing now.

Tip: The default option switches between Baseline and Continued, depending on which you used last. If the Baseline option is already selected, you do not need to type B and press [Enter].

Your drawing should now look like that in Figure 7.29.

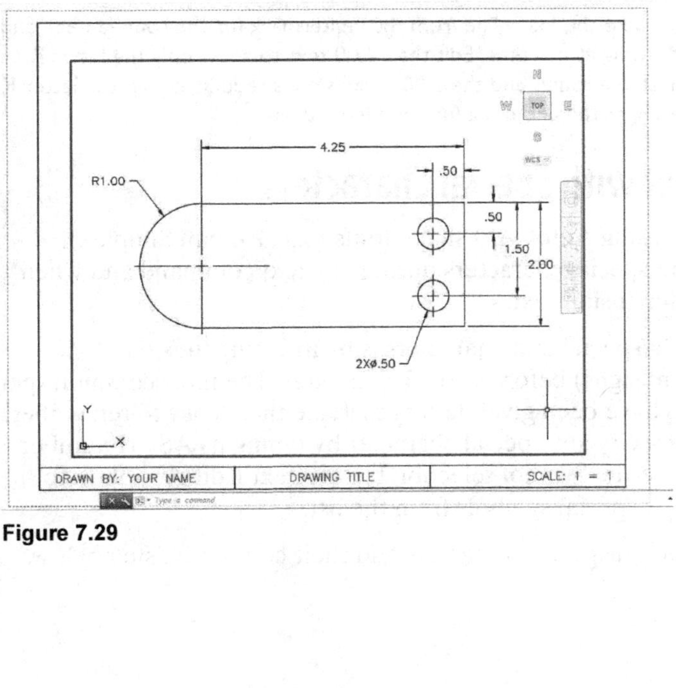

Figure 7.29

Note: *There is also a command named Explode that doesn't have any options. Explode simply changes the grouped objects back to individual objects, regardless of the X-, Y-, and Z-scaling factors. (In early AutoCAD releases, the X-, Y-, and Z-scaling factors of a block had to be the same or it could not be exploded.)*

Using Xplode

The Xplode command lets you change dimensions, blocks, polylines, and other grouped objects back to their individual components; at the same time, you can control the color, layer, and linetype of the components. You will use Xplode to erase just the single right line of the centermark for the rounded end. You will select the Layer option of the Xplode command and the default layer, DIM, for the exploded object's layer.

The Xplode command has suboptions that allow you to control the color, layer, linetype and other options as the object is changed back into its original components. Explode and Xplode are different commands. Refer to on-line help to investigate the differences between these two commands further.

Because the rounded end is an arc, not a full circle, its centermark should extend only for the half-circle shown. Because associative dimensions are created as blocks, they are all one object: No part can be erased singly. To eliminate the extra portion of the centermark on the rounded end, you will type the Xplode command.

Command: ***XPLODE [Enter]***

Select objects to XPlode.

Select objects: ***click on the dimension for the rounded end***

Select objects: ***[Enter]***

[All/Color/LAyer/LType/LWeight/Inherit from parent block/Explode] <Explode>: ***LA [Enter]***

Enter new layer name for exploded objects <DIM>: ***[Enter]***

The message "Object exploded onto layer DIM" appears. The drawing doesn't look any different, but now the dimension is made up of individual pieces that you can select.

On your own, **erase** the extra line from the centermark for the rounded end and **save** your drawing at this time. Edit the R1.00 text to show only the letter R. To specify both the radius and the 2.00 dimension is redundant, but the letter R makes it clear that the end has a full rounded radius.

Adding Text with Special Characters

When you are using AutoCAD shape fonts (e.g., Roman Simplex), you can type in special characters during any text command and when entering the dimension text.

One way to add special text characters is by inserting the code %% (double percent signs) before special characters. The most common special characters have been given letters to make them easy to remember. You can also specify any special character by typing its ASCII number. You can also use the Symbol selection for the Text Editing ribbon to quickly click the special symbols from the list.

The most common special characters and their codes are listed below.

Code	Character	Symbol
%%C	Diameter symbol	Ø
%%D	Degree symbol	°
%%P	Plus/minus sign	±
%%O	Toggles on and off the overscore mode	On
%%U	Toggles on and off the underscore mode	On
%%%	Draws a single percent sign	%
%%N	Draws special character number n	n

Next use MultilineText to add a block of notes.

On your own, make layer **TEXT** current.

Switch to **Paperspace**.

Start the **Multiline Text** command and define an area near the lower right of the drawing to add the notes. Notes in engineering drawings are often in uppercase letters, so you may want to use Caps Lock.

Add the note "ALL TOLERANCES ± .01 UNLESS OTHERWISE NOTED." Use the Symbol selection from the Text editor to enter %%P to make the ± sign as shown in Figure 7.30.

Below the tolerance note add notes indicating the material from which the part is to be made, such as "MATERIAL: SAE 1020" and a note stating "ALL MEASUREMENTS IN INCHES."

Use the Edit Text command to change the text in your title block, noting the name of the part, your name, and the scale, to complete the drawing.

Save your drawing.

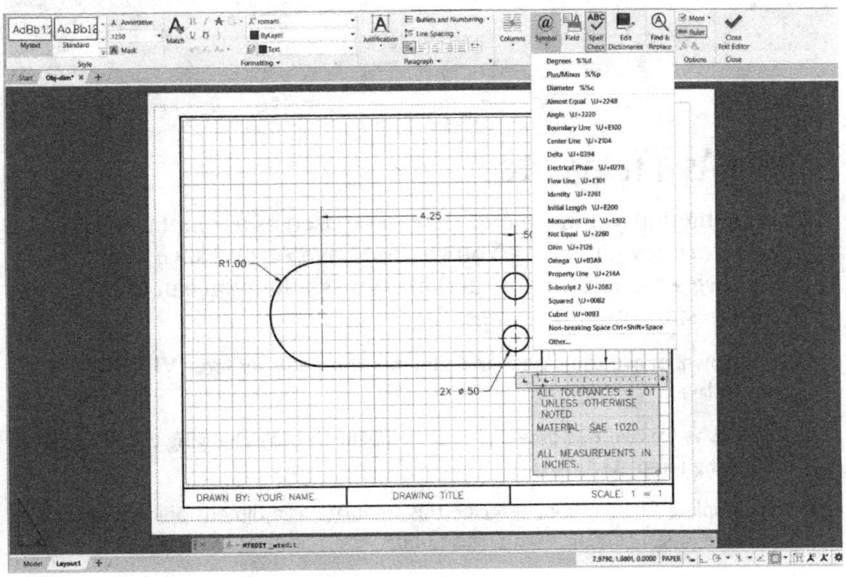

Figure 7.30

Tip: *You can double-click on text to edit it in place.*

Using Quick Dimension

Next you will erase the dimensions that you added and try using the Quick Dimension command to add them.

Switch to **Model** space inside the viewport by double-clicking inside the viewport.

On your own, **erase** the dimensions that you added.

Make layer **DIM** current.

*Click: **Quick Dimension button** from the Annotate tab, Dimension panel*

Select geometry to dimension: ***use Window to select all of the drawing lines and press [Enter]***

Specify dimension line position, or [Continuous/Staggered/Baseline/Ordinate/Radius/Diameter/datumPoint/Edit/seTtings: ***click two snap increments above the object***

Two dimensions are added to the drawing as shown in Figure 7.31.

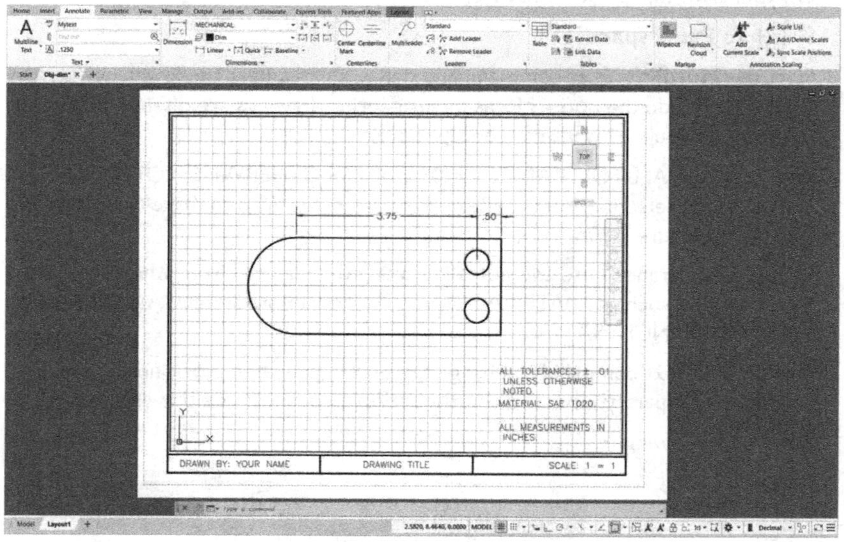

Figure 7.31

Tip: You can use the AutoCAD DesignCenterTM to import dimension styles from an existing drawing into your current drawing. You will learn more about the DesignCenter in Tutorial 10.

Saving As a Template

Any drawing that you have created can be used as a template from which to start new drawings. You will use Save As and save your *obj-dim.dwg* with a new name and file type so that you can use it as a template to start other drawings.

Tip: Drawings started from dimtemplate.dwt will have the dimension styles that you created earlier in this tutorial available for use.

On your own, **erase** the object and all dimensions and set layer **VISIBLE** as the current layer.

Use **Save As** to save this drawing as *dimtemplate.dwt* (by changing the file type to a Drawing Template *.dwt).

In the Template Description, describe this template as a dimensioning template and leave measurement with English units.

Close the file when you have finished saving it.

Dimensioning the Adapter

Next, you will add dimensions to a drawing similar to the adapter you created in Tutorial 6. Here, the hole has not been added and the views have been moved apart to make room for dimensions. You will be adding the dimensions to model space for this drawing.

On your own, use the **New** button to start a drawing from the datafile template, *adapter1.dwt* **Save** your drawing as *adapt-dim.dwg*.

Check that you are in **Model space.**

Check that **Intersection** running object snap mode is turned on.

Check the Layer Control to see that you are on layer **DIM** or set Dimlayer to DIM.

Next, set the dimension style using the Annotate tab, Dimension panel.

*Click: **on the dimension style name STANDARD** to show the pull down list as shown in Figure 7.32*

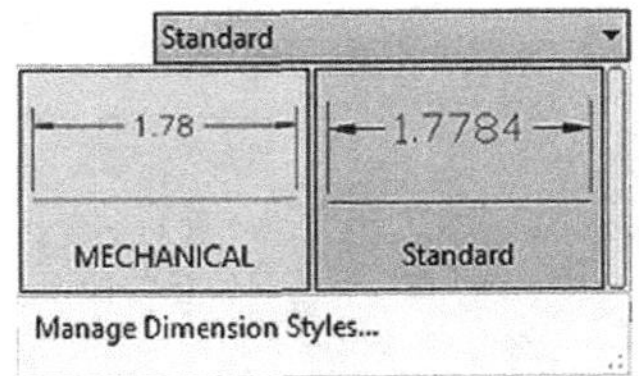

*Select: **MECHANICAL** from the pull-down list*

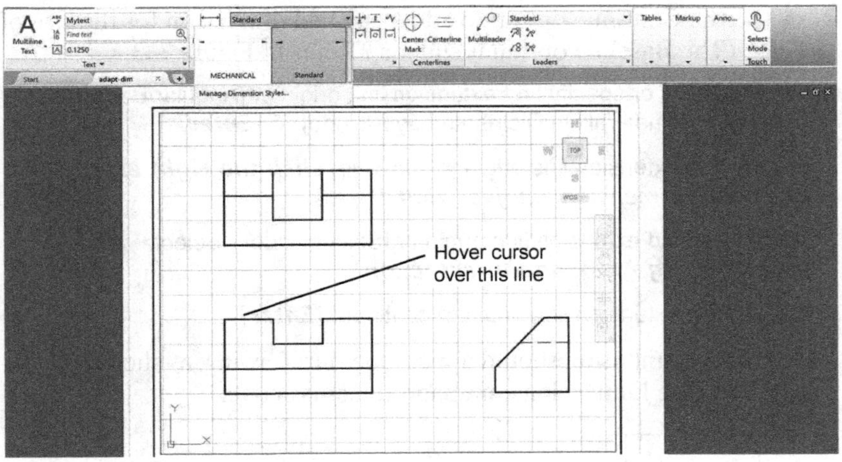

Figure 7.32

Dimensions are placed between views when possible, except for the overall dimensions, which are often placed around the outside.

Next you will add the horizontal dimension that shows the width of the left portion of the block. The shape of this feature shows clearly in the front view, so add the dimension to the front view between the views. You will use the Select object option, which allows you to click an object instead of specifying the two extension line locations. The software will automatically locate the extension lines at the extreme ends of the object you select.

*Click: **Dimension button***

Select objects or specify first extension line origin or [Angular/Baseline/Continue/Ordinate/aliGn/Distribute/Layer/Undo]: ***hover the cursor over the top left line in the front view***

Select line to specify extension lines origin: ***click the top left line in the front view***

Specify dimension line location or second line for angle [Mtext/Text/text aNgle/Undo]: ***click about 0.5 unit above the object outline***

Your drawing should be similar to Figure 7.33.

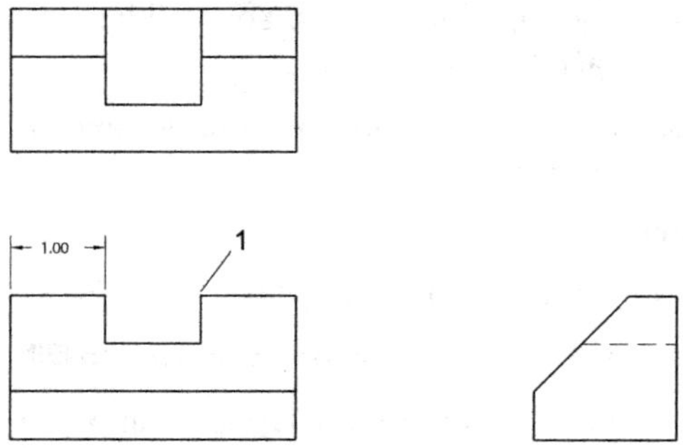

Figure 7.33

Using the Continue Option

Now use the Continue option to add a chained dimension for the size of the slot. (The Baseline option is similar.) Refer to Figure 7.33.

Select objects or specify first extension line origin or [Angular/Baseline/Continue/Ordinate/aliGn/Distribute/Layer/Undo]: ***C [Enter]***

Specify first extension line origin to continue: ***click the right extension line of the dimension you just added***

Specify second extension line origin or [Select/Undo] <Select>: ***click point 1 using AutoSnap Intersection***

Specify first extension line origin to continue: ***[Enter]***

The chained dimension should appear in your drawing, as shown in Figure 7.34. The Dimension command remains active.

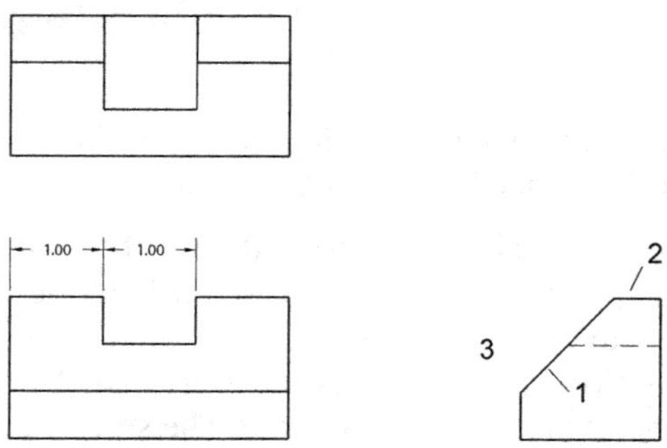

Figure 7.34

Tip: *If the dimension continues from the wrong side of the existing dimension, use the Select option and click the right extension line.*

When using the Continue Dimension command, you can press [Enter] to select a different dimension to continue from.

Angular Dimensions

You can also add angular dimensions using the Dimension command by selecting two angled lines and then clicking the location for the angle dimension. Depending on where you select, you will define the major angle or the minor angle between the lines. You also have the option during the command of selecting other options from the command line. If you do so, you will be prompted for three points to define the angle.

You do not have to use the %%D special character to make the degree sign; it is inserted automatically unless you override the default text.

Next, add the angular dimension for the angled surface to the side view,

Select objects or specify first extension line origin or [Angular/Baseline/Continue/Ordinate/aliGn/Distribute/Layer/Undo]: ***hover over line 1***

Select line to specify extension lines origin: ***click line 1***

Select line to specify second side of angle: ***click line 2***

Specify angular dimension location or [Mtext/Text/text aNgle/Undo]: ***click near point 3***

The angular dimension is added to the side view, as in Figure 7.35. Notice that since the precision for angular dimensions was set to zero (0) decimal places in the MECHANICAL style, the angle value is shown to a whole number of degrees. The Dimension command remains active.

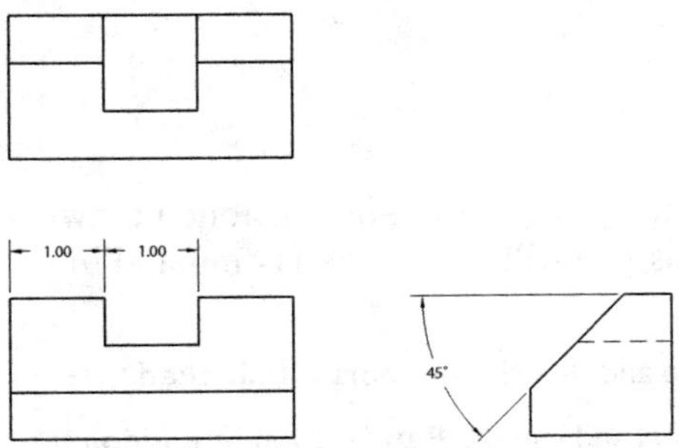

Figure 7.35

Next, add the dimension for the height of the slot in the front view.

Click: ***Dimension button***

Select line to specify extension lines origin: ***hover the cursor over the right line of the slot***

Select line to specify extension lines origin: ***click the right line of the slot***

Specify dimension line location or second line for angle [Mtext/Text/text aNgle/Undo]: ***click to the right of the front view***

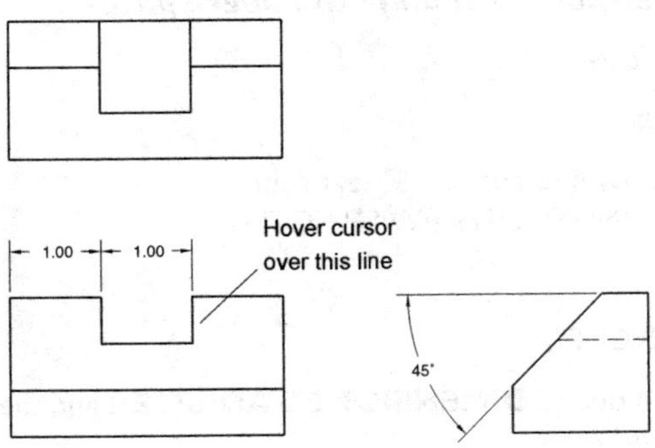

Figure 7.36

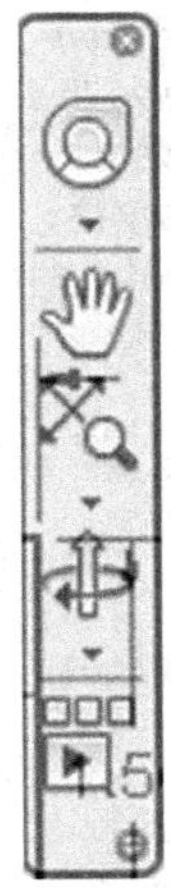

Tip: *Use the [X] in its upper right corner to close the Navigation Bar if it is in the way.*

Select objects or specify first extension line origin or [Angular/Baseline/Continue/Ordinate/aliGn/Distribute/Layer/Undo]:

On your own, **add the dimension for the top line in the side view and the overall dimensions** to the outsides of the views so that your drawing looks like Figure 7.37. When you are finished, press [Enter] to end the command.

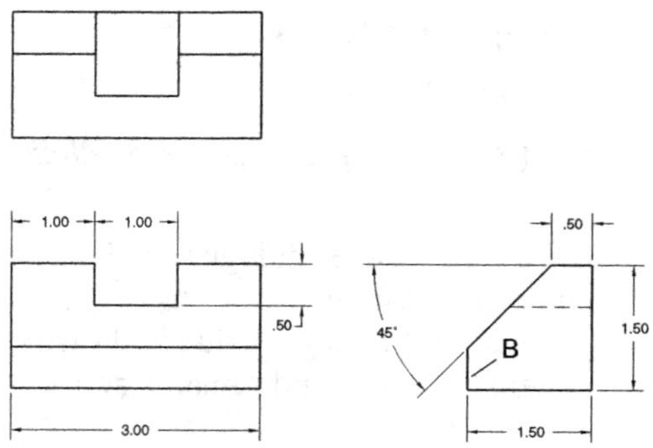

Figure 7.37

Tip: *Note that you do not need dimensions for the short vertical line (B) in the side view. Its length is already defined by the overall dimension for the height of the part, the 0.50 distance across the top surface, and the 45° angle. To include this dimension would be overdimensioning. If you want to give this dimension, include the value in brackets, or followed by the word REF, to indicate that it is a reference dimension only.*

Centering the Views

Now you will use the Pan command to center the dimensioned drawing views inside the border. To do this you will use the Pan command in model space.

Check that you are in **model space** and that the viewport is **unlocked**.

Press and hold the mouse scroll wheel and use the **Pan** function to position the view upward to center the dimensioned views inside the border.

Dimensions that are located in paper space sometimes do not pan with the drawing objects even with fully associated dimensions. You can use the Dimension Update button to help if that is the case. Generally, it is often better to place the dimensions in model space.

Adding the Tolerance Note

Next you will add notes and titles in paper space.

*Double-click **outside the viewport to change to Paper space***

*Click: **TEXT** as the current layer*

*Click: **Multiline Text button***

Use the Mtext command on your own to add 0.125" text stating ALL TOLERANCES ARE ± .01 UNLESS OTHERWISE NOTED.

MATERIAL: SAE 1020.

ALL MEASUREMENTS ARE IN INCHES.

On your own, change the drawing title to **DIMENSIONED ADAPTER** and the YOUR NAME text to your actual name.

If you want, plot your drawing from paper space using the drawing limits at the scale of 1=1.

Save your drawing *adapt-dm.dwg* before you continue.

Your finished drawing should be similar to Figure 7.38.

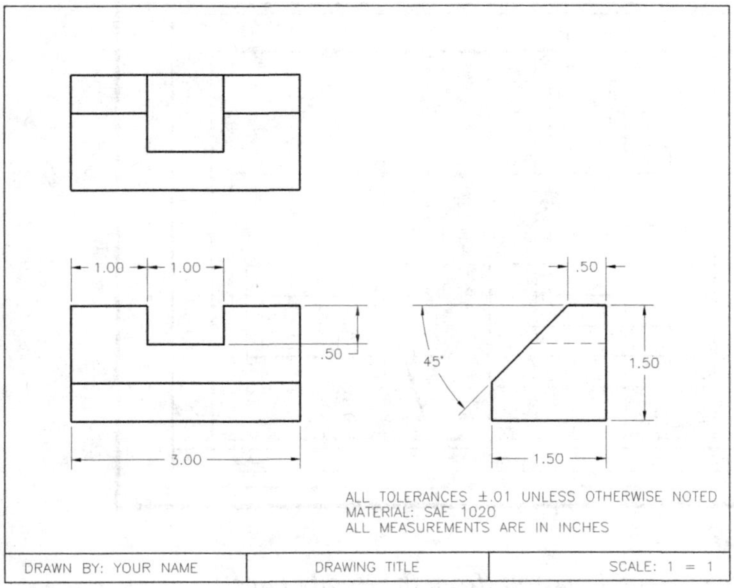

Figure 7.38

Updating Associative Dimensions

Dimensions created using associative dimensioning are AutoCAD block objects. Blocks are a group of objects that behave as a single object. If you try to erase an associative dimension, the entire dimension is erased, including the extension lines and arrowheads. Because these dimensions have the special properties of a block, you can also cause them to be updated automatically.

As the geometric objects that you are going to change are in model space, you must return to model space in order to change them.

Double-click ***inside the viewport to change to Model space***

Using Stretch

The Stretch command is used to stretch and relocate objects. It is similar to stretching with hot grips, which you did in Tutorial 4. You must use implied Crossing, Crossing, or Crossing Polygon methods to select the objects for use with the Stretch command. As you select, objects entirely enclosed in the crossing window specified will be moved to the new location rather than stretched. Keep this in mind and draw the crossing box only around the portion of the object you want to stretch, leaving the other portion unselected to act as an anchor.

Next, make the front and top views of the adapter wider. The starting width of the front view is currently 3.00. Refer to Figure 7.39.

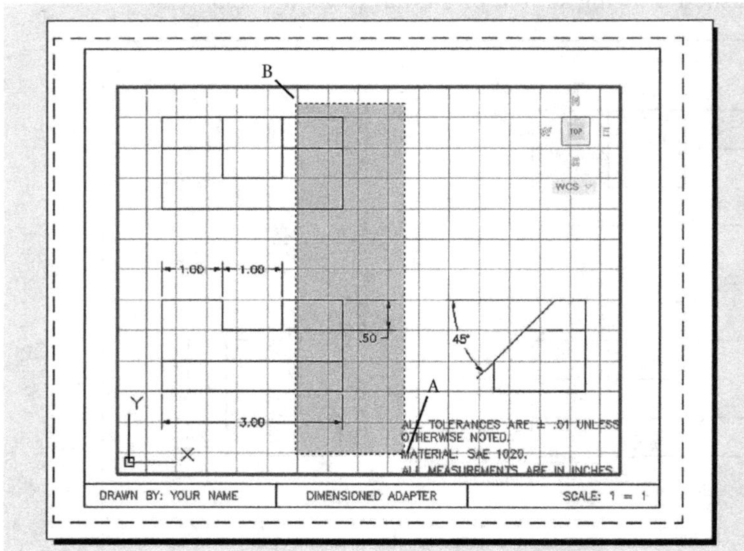

Figure 7.39

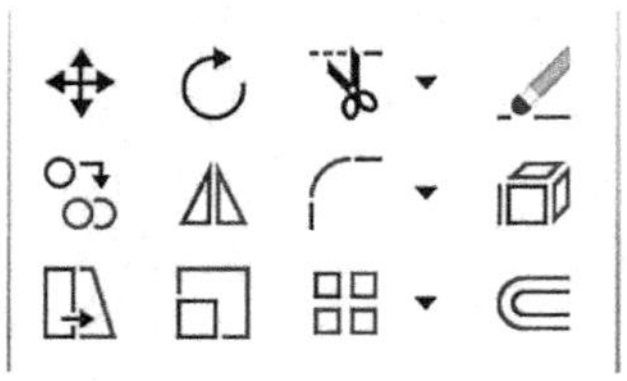

 *Click:* ***Stretch button*** *(from the Modify panel)*

Select objects to stretch by crossing-window or crossing-polygon

Select objects: ***use Crossing and select point A***

Specify opposite corner: ***select point B***

Select objects: ***[Enter]***

Specify base point or [Displacement] <Displacement>: ***target the lower right-hand corner of the front view***

Specify second point or <use first point as displacement>: ***move the cursor .5 units to the right and click***

Note that the overall dimension now reads 3.50 and that it has updated automatically. The result is shown in Figure 7.40.

Tip: *When a Crossing selection box is being drawn, it appears green or with a dashed outline depending on your settings. When a Window selection box is being drawn, it appears blue or has a solid outline. Use this visual cue. Crossing boxes are drawn from right to left.*

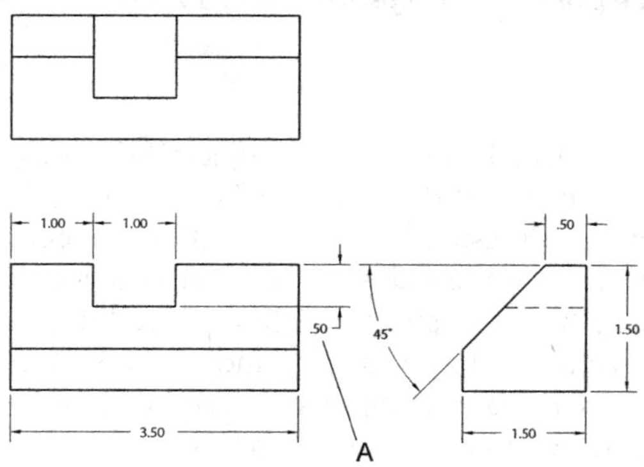

Figure 7.40

Tip: *If you have trouble stretching, double-check to be sure that you are in model space. Also, the Stretch command works only when you use the Crossing option. If you type the command, you must be sure to select Crossing or type C and press [Enter] afterward, or use implied Crossing (by drawing the window box from right to left), as you did in the previous step.*

Modifying Dimensions

You can modify individual dimensions and override their dimension styles using the Properties palette. To edit a dimension's properties, you must be in the same space (model/paper space) where that dimension resides.

Click: ***on the vertical dimension labeled A*** *to select it (grips show)*

Right-click: ***to show the shortcut menu***

Click: ***Properties*** *to show the Properties palette*

As with other objects, you can modify the dimension's layer, color, linetype, lineweight, linetype scale. Near the bottom of the palette are selections for Misc, Lines & Arrows, Text, Fit, Primary Units, Alternate Units, and Tolerances (like in the Modify Dimension Style dialog box). You can click on the arrows (v) to the right of the name to expand the list for the related feature.

Tip: *If the Text inside align option is grayed out, that may be because you have already dragged the dimension value to a new location. If so, try erasing the dimension and adding it again so you can see how this property works.*

You will change the text orientation to be parallel to the dimension line.

Click: ***to expand Text selections (using the down arrow)***

The Text area should appear expanded as shown in Figure 7.41.

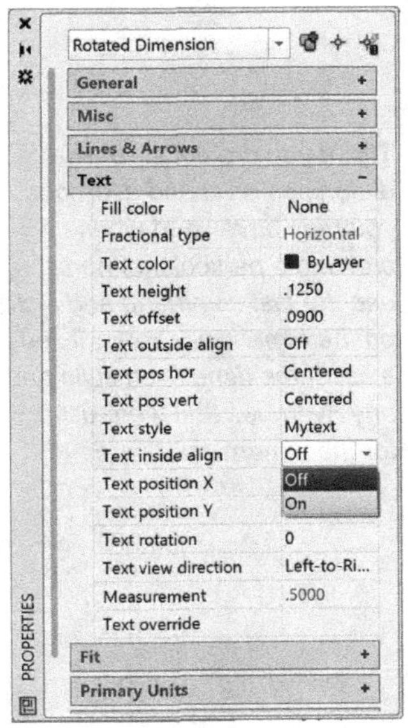

Figure 7.41

Click: ***the text box to the right of Text inside align to expand it***

Click: ***On*** *to align the dimension text inside the extension lines with the dimension line*

Click: ***Windows Close button*** *to close the Properties palette*

Press: ***[Esc]*** *to remove the grips from vertical dimension*

The 0.50 dimension value changes to be parallel to the dimension line, as shown in Figure 7.42. The dimension style for MECHANICAL has not changed; only that single dimension was overridden to produce a new appearance.

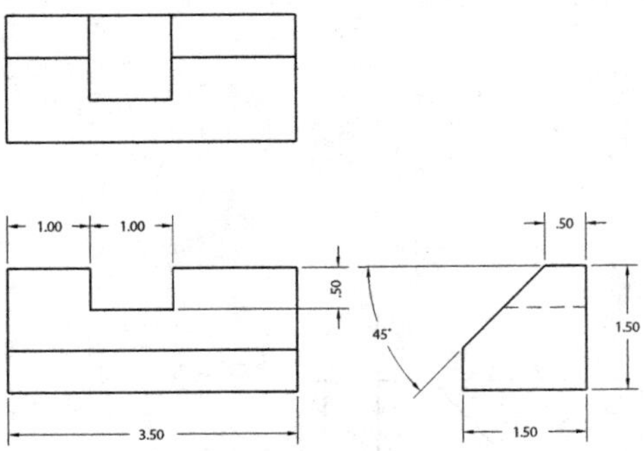

Figure 7.42

Tip: *You can trim and extend linear and ordinate dimensions with the Trim and Extend commands. When trimmed or extended, the dimension acts as though there were a line between the endpoints of the extension line origins. Trimming and extending takes effect on the dimension at that location.*

Updating a Dimension Style

When you change a dimension style, all the dimensions using that style automatically take on the new appearance (when using associative dimensioning.) Next you will use the Dimension Styles Manager to update the arrow style used for the dimensions in your drawing.

Click: ***to Show the Dimension Style Manager***

Make sure that MECHANICAL is the style name highlighted.

Click: ***Modify***

Click: ***Symbols and Arrows tab*** *as shown in Figure 7.43*

Click: ***Right Angle*** *for the First and Second Arrowhead*

Click: ***OK***

Click: ***Close*** *to exit the Dimension Style Manager*

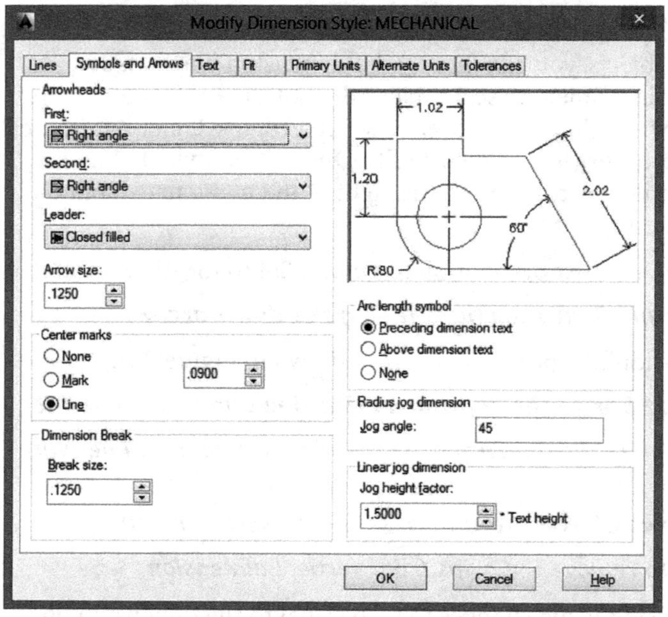

Figure 7.43

The dimensions in the drawing update automatically to reflect this change. The arrows are now right-angled arrows instead of filled arrows. Your drawing should be similar to Figure 7.44.

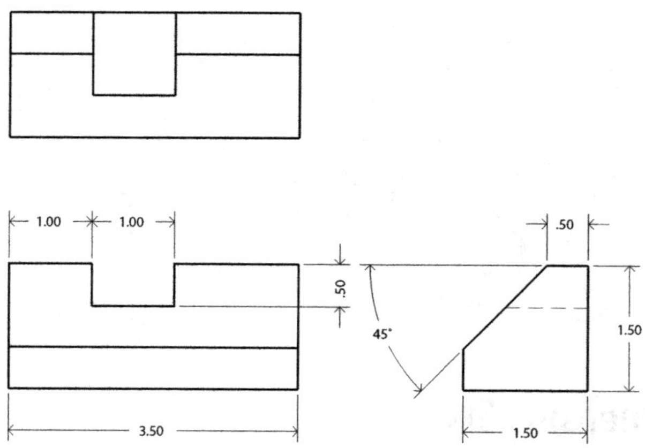

Figure 7.44

Tip: *If you are not sure what dimension style and overrides you may have used when creating a particular dimension, use the List command and pick on the dimension. You will see a list of the dimension style and any overrides that were used for the dimension.*

Changing the Drawing Scale

You have been working in the drawing with the drawing zoomed so that the viewport scale is at 1:1. Since the paper units are inches and the drawing units are inches, this drawing is full scale. If you plot the drawing from paper space at a scale of 1=1, you should be able to measure the lines and have them be equal to the dimension value.

Next you will change the drawing viewport scale.

On your own, make sure you are in **Model** space.

If locked, use the status bar button to **Unlock the viewport scale.**

At the command prompt, you will type the alias for the Zoom command,

Command: ***Z [Enter]***

Specify corner of window, enter a scale factor (nX or nXP), or [All/Center/Dynamic/Extents/Previous/Scale/Window/Object] <real time>: ***.5XP [Enter]***

The zoom factor changes as shown in Figure 7.45. Now the viewport shows the drawing with each .5 model space unit equals 1 paper space unit. In other words, half size. The viewport scaling displays 6"=1'.

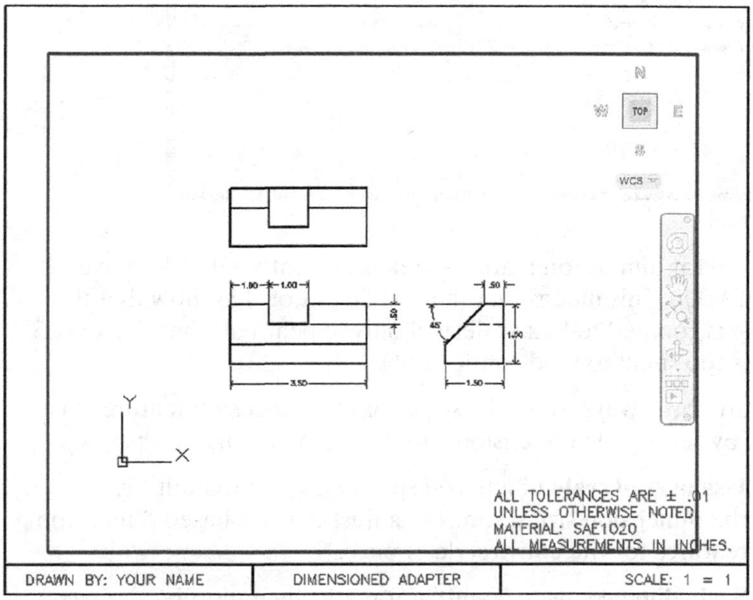

Figure 7.45

Notice the appearance of the dimensions. They are almost too small to read. The size set for the height of the dimension value text is too small at this scale.

The Fit tab of the Dimension Style Manager is used to manage the scaling of the dimensions for the entire style as a group.

Click: ***to Show the Dimension Style Manager***

Make sure that MECHANICAL is the style name highlighted.

Click: ***Modify***

Click: ***Fit tab*** *as shown in Figure 7.46*

Tip: *If you find the magenta colored viewport border distracting, you can freeze its layer so that it doesn't appear.*

By switching to paperspace, you can click and drag the viewport grips to the size of the outer border.

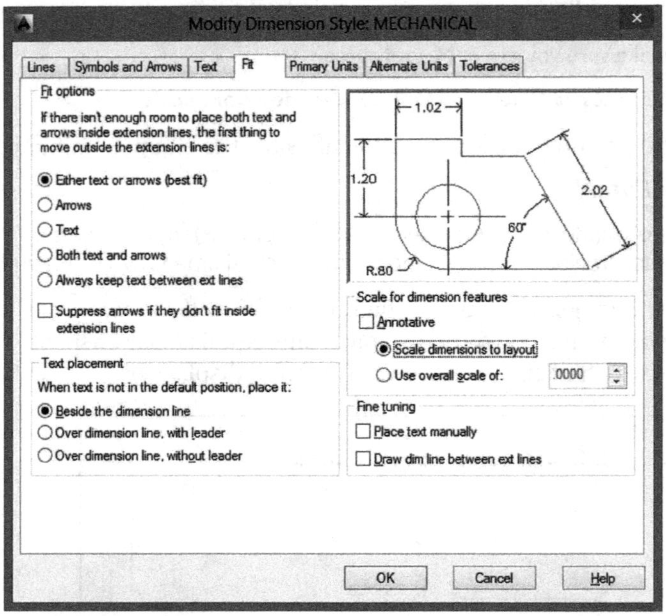

Figure 7.46

The Scale for dimension features area is currently set to Use overall scale of 1.000. This means that the text height of .125", now that the drawing is zoomed to half scale, will only appear half that size (.0625") which is too small to read comfortably.

There are three ways to set the scale for the dimension features as a group (by setting the dimension variable named Dimscale):

1. **Use overall scale of** lets you specify a value to multiply times the dimension size settings to adjust the size based dimension features for the entire style at once.
2. **Scale dimensions to layout** automatically multiplies the size dimension features based on the viewport scale factor.
3. **Annotative** uses the annotative styles to automatically scale annotation items like dimensions. (The use of annotative styles automatically sets Dimscale to 0.)

Click: ***Scale Dimensions to layout***

Click: ***OK***

Click: ***Close***

The drawing automatically updates to show the dimensions with the dimension feature sizes scaled to the layout as shown in Figure 7.47. Now the heights of the dimension values, arrow sizes, etc. are .125". You can click the dimensions and use their grips to reposition the values for better visibility and to eliminate overlap.

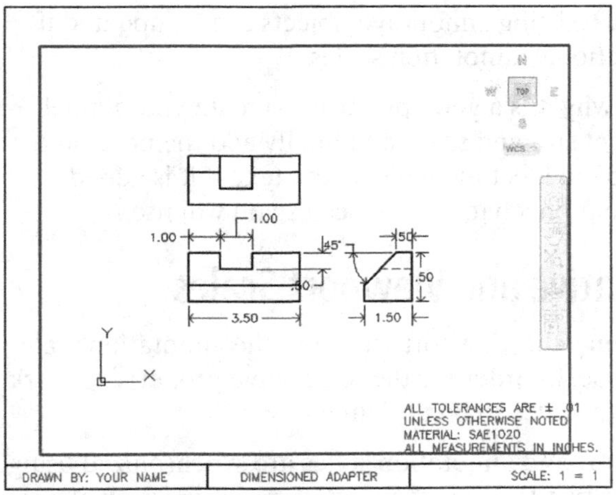

Figure 7.47

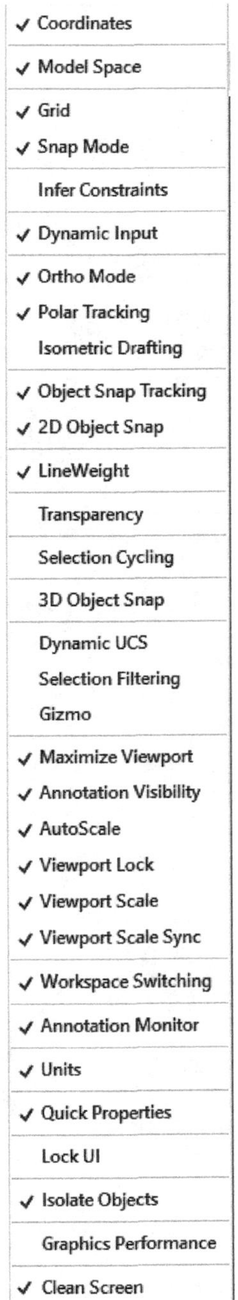

The Annotation Property

The scale at which you plot your drawing directly affects the size and placement required for drawing notes and dimensions. You can see in Figure 7.47 that the dimension values need to be repositioned now that the scale of the drawing has changed.

In the past, CAD designers had to create copies of dimensions and local notes on multiple layers, which they would turn on and off for different plot scales. This was time consuming and hard to maintain as note changes had to be made in multiple places. Errors would creep in when a copy was neglected.

Annotation scale is a property for objects like text, dimensions, and hatching. The annotation property is similar to the other object properties like color, linetype, and layer, except that it is used to scale the object. The annotation property for each object can set its size, placement, and appearance based on the scale set for the viewport.

You can show special annotation tools on the status bar. Figure 7.48 shows the right side of the status bar with the buttons labeled. You can also find similar selections on the Annotation Scaling panel of the Annotate tab.

On your own, use the Customize button from the status bar to turn on Annotation Visibility, AutoScale, Annotation Monitor, Viewport Scale Sync.

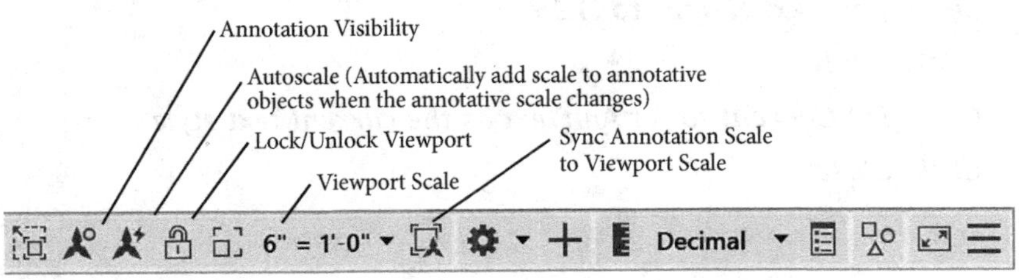

Figure 7.48

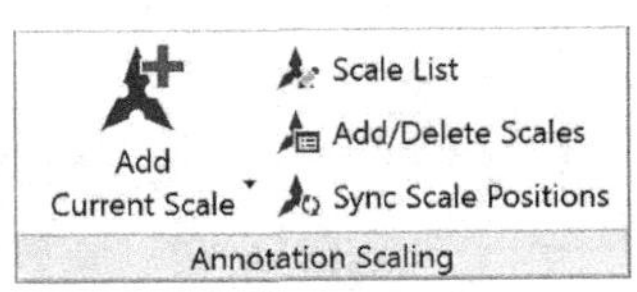

Annotative objects support one annotation scale: the one that is current when you create the object. So, you want to set the annotation scale and then create the objects. Existing annotative objects can be updated if necessary to allow additional annotation scales.

This is another reason why it is a good practice to create your model, then determine the sheet size and scale, and finally add the notes and dimensions. You will spend less time revising the text, if it is added when you are pretty clear on what scale or scales you will use.

Synch the Annotative and Viewport Scales

In drawing *adapt-dim.dwg* the viewport scale and the annotation scale may now not be the same. In order for the annotative property to work well, you need these two scales to be the same.

Check that your viewport and annotation styles are synchronized using the button on the status bar. If it is grayed out, they are in synch, if not you will see the message "Annotation scale is not equal to viewport scale: Click to synchronize," when your cursor is over the Sync Annotation Scale button as shown in Figure 7.49. If needed,

Click: ***to synchronize the viewport and annotation scales***

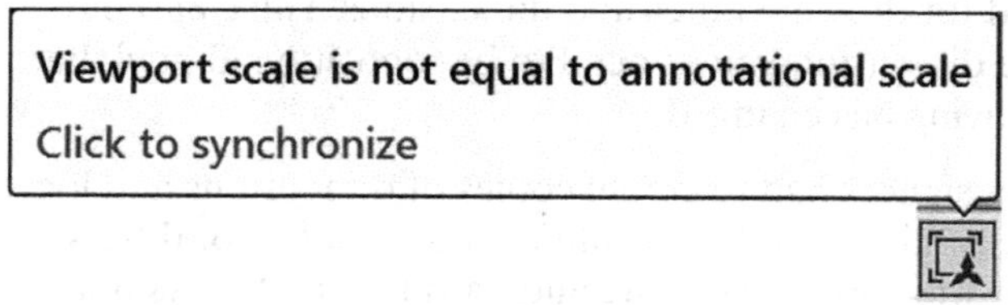

Figure 7.49

Creating an Annotative Text Style

Next, create a new annotative text style,

Click: ***to show the Text Style Manager***

Click: ***New***

The New Text Style dialog box appears on your screen.

Type: ***AnnText*** *for the new style name*

Click: ***OK***

Select the Annotative check box *from the Size area, so it appears checked as shown in Figure 7.50*

Set Paper Text Height to .125

Click: ***Apply***

Click: ***Set Current*** *to set AnnText as the current text style*

Click: ***Close***

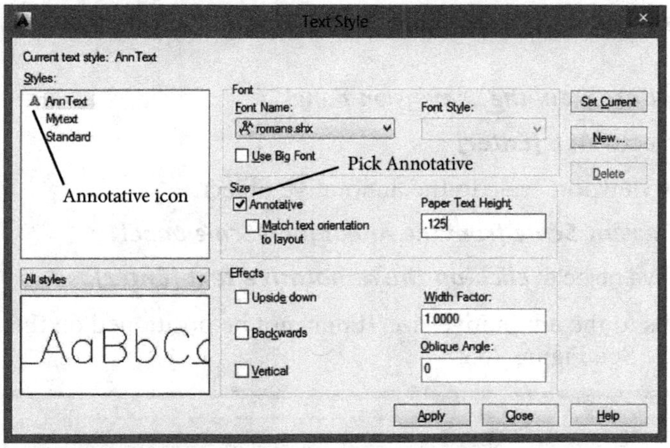

Figure 7.50

Notice AnnText has the special annotative icon next to it where it shows as the current style in the Text panel. See Figure 7.51.

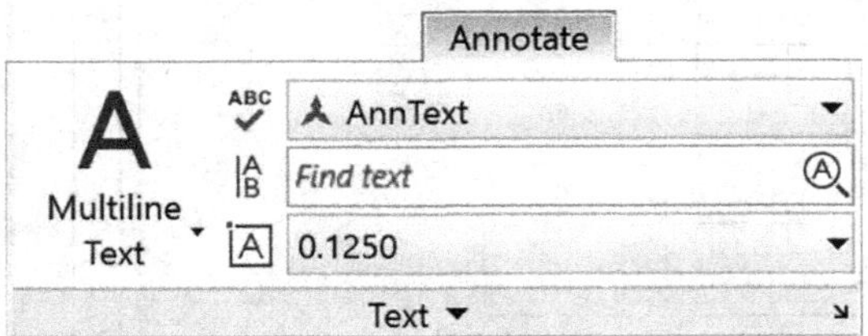

Figure 7.51

Next add some local notes to model space.

On your own, set the viewport scale to 1=1 if it is not already. Then add the text "PAINT THIS SURFACE" to the top view, as shown in Figure 7.52.

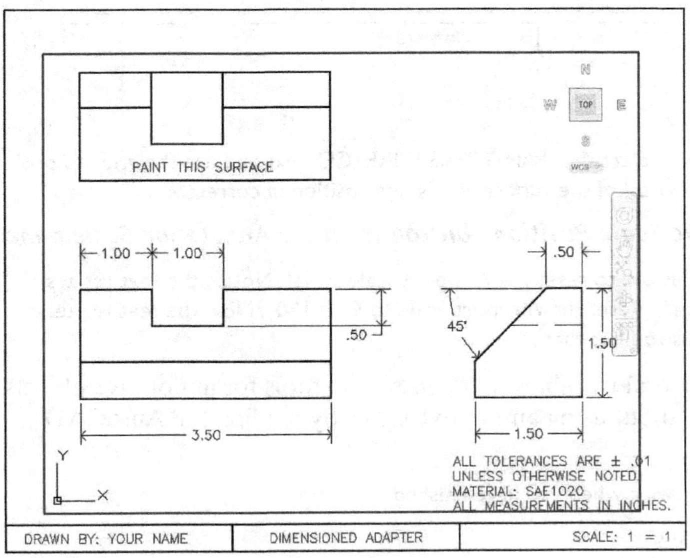

Figure 7.52

On your own, use the status bar to change the viewport scale to **6" = 1'**.

The view is resized.

Tip: *If your annotative text does not show up, check that the Annotation Visibility button on the status bar is set to show annotative objects for all scales.*

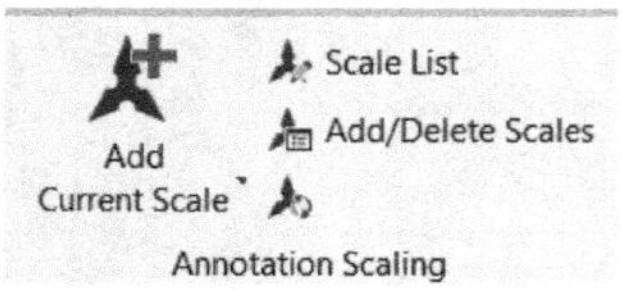

If the text doesn't show up, use Dimension Update to show the text in the new scale.

Click: ***Update*** *from the Dimension panel*

Select objects: ***ALL [Enter]***

To add the new viewport scale to the annotative object,

Click: ***Add Current Scale*** *from the Annotation Scale panel*

Select annotative objects: ***click on the annotative text [Enter]***

The text updates to the annotative size. It may not be positioned on the surface correctly. See Figure 7.53.

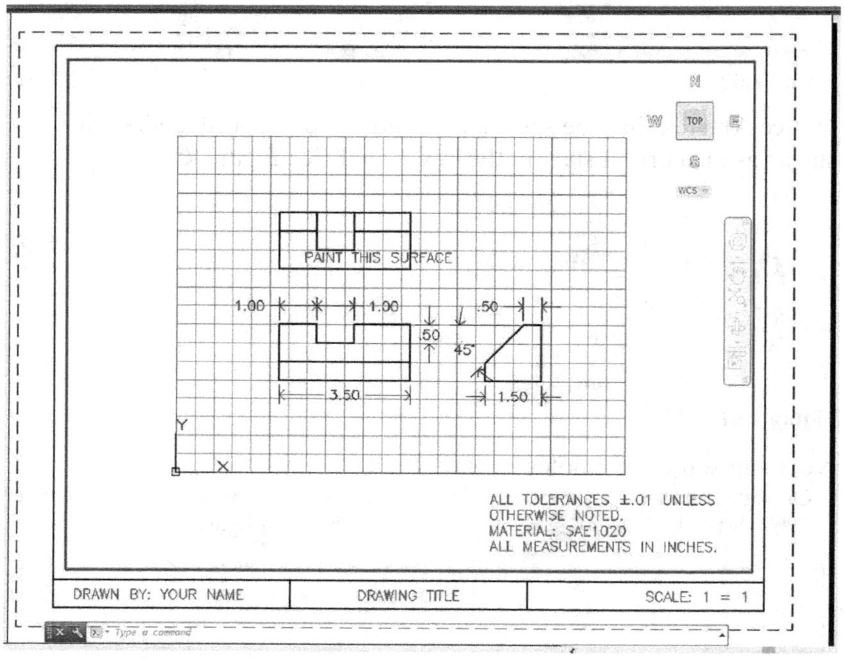

Figure 7.53

On your own, select the "PAINT THIS SURFACE" text and use the grips to position the text off of the surface, if it is not positioned correctly.

Click: ***Sync Scale Positions button*** *from the Annotation Scale panel*

Use the status bar to reset the Viewport scale to 1:1. Notice the text resizes automatically. Reset the Viewport Scale to 6" = 1'-0". Now the text resizes and repositions to fit at that scale.

There are several variables that control the tools for annotative objects. Learn more about using annotative styles by reading the AutoCAD Help files.

Save the drawing when you have finished.

Exit AutoCAD.

You have completed Tutorial 7.

Key Terms

- associative dimensioning
- baseline dimensioning
- chained (continued) dimensioning
- dimension line
- dimension style
- dimension value
- dimension variables (dim vars)
- dimensions
- extension line
- extension line offset
- image tile
- inspection
- leader line
- manufacture
- overall dimensions
- tolerance

Key Commands (keyboard shortcut)

- Angular Dimension
- Baseline Dimension
- Continue Dimension
- Diameter Dimension
- DIMASSOC
- Dimension Status
- Dimension Style
- Linear Dimension
- Radius Dimension
- Stretch (STR)
- Xplode (XP)
- Annotation Scale
- Annotation Property

Exercises

Draw and dimension the following shapes. The letter M after an exercise number means that the units are metric. Add a note to the drawing saying, "METRIC: All dimensions are in millimeters for metric drawings." Specify a general tolerance for the drawing.

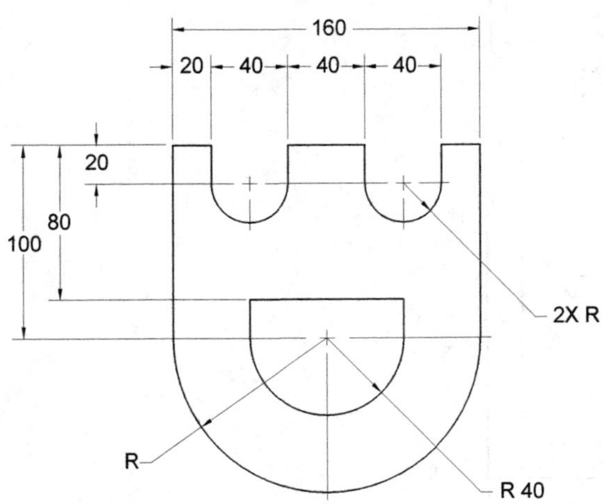

Exercise 7.1M Stop Plate

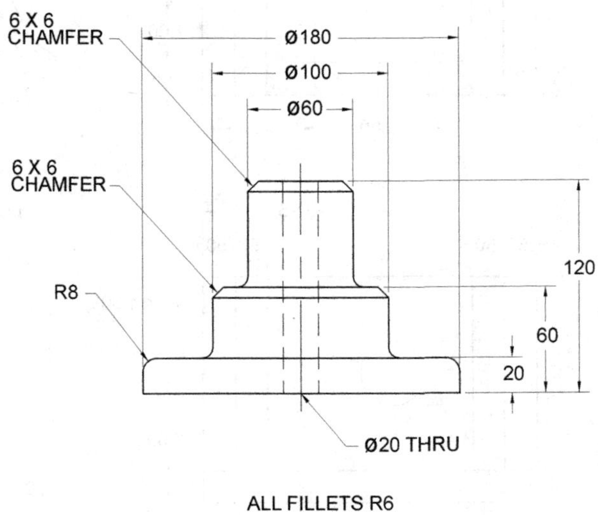

Exercise 7.2M Hub

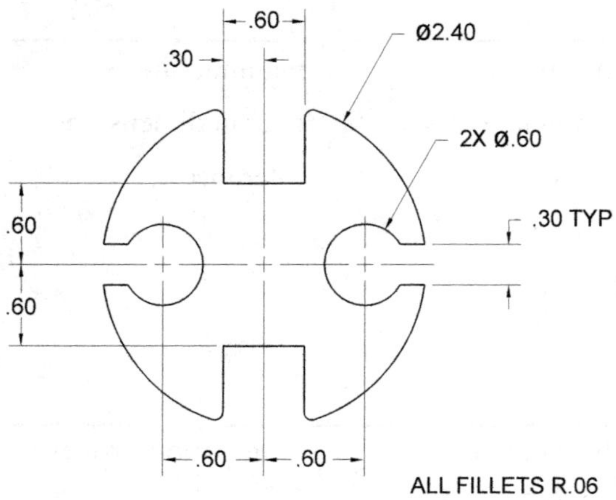

Exercise 7.3 Guide Block

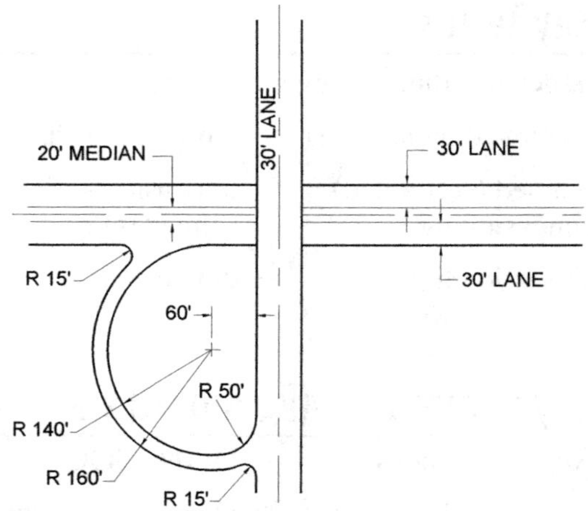

Exercise 7.4 Interchange

Draw and dimension this intersection, then mirror the circular interchange for all lanes.

***Hint*:** *To make radial dimensions with placements as shown, you may need to use the Dimension Style, Fit tab and then select Place text manually in the Fine Tuning area of the dialog box.*

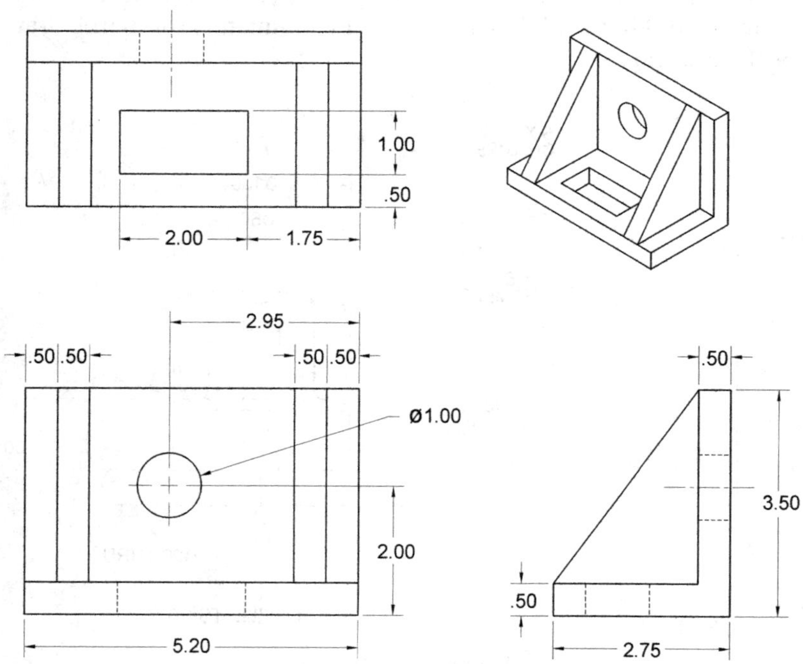

Exercise 7.5 Angle Bracket

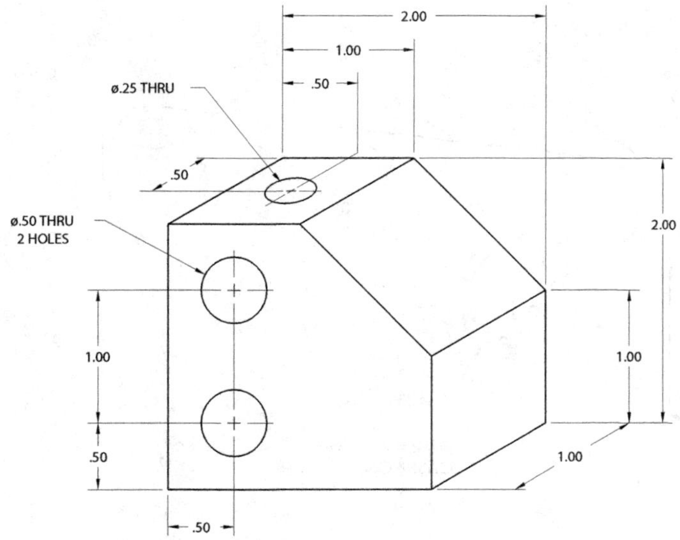

Exercise 7.6 Bearing Box

Draw and dimension the orthographics views for the bearing box.

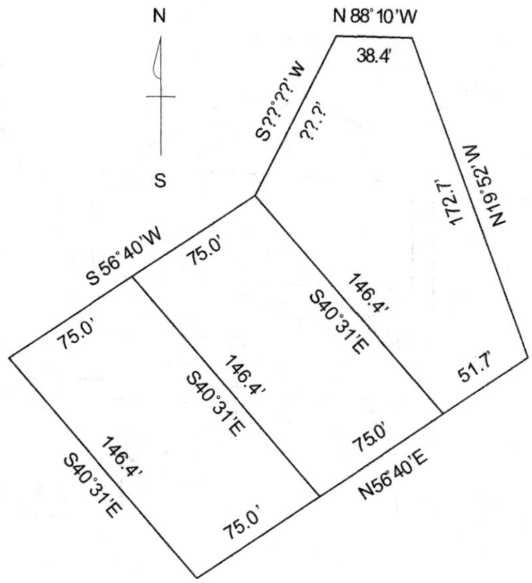

Exercise 7.7 Plot Plan

Draw and dimension using the civil engineering dimensioning style shown. Find the missing dimensions.

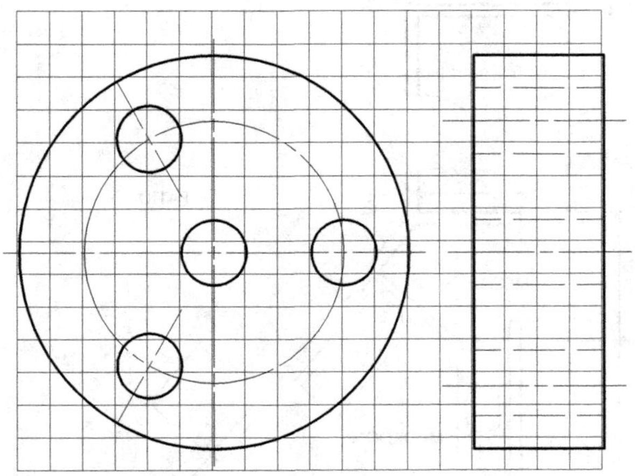

Exercise 7.8 Hub

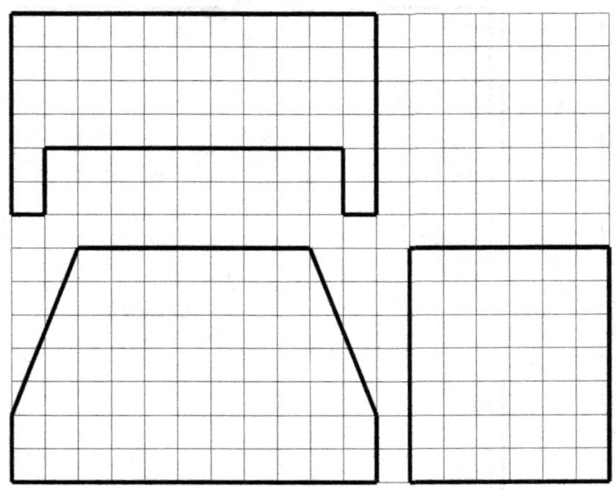

Exercise 7.9 Support

Draw and dimension the drawings above. Use 1 grid unit = .0125 " for a decimal inch drawing or 25 mm for a metric drawing.

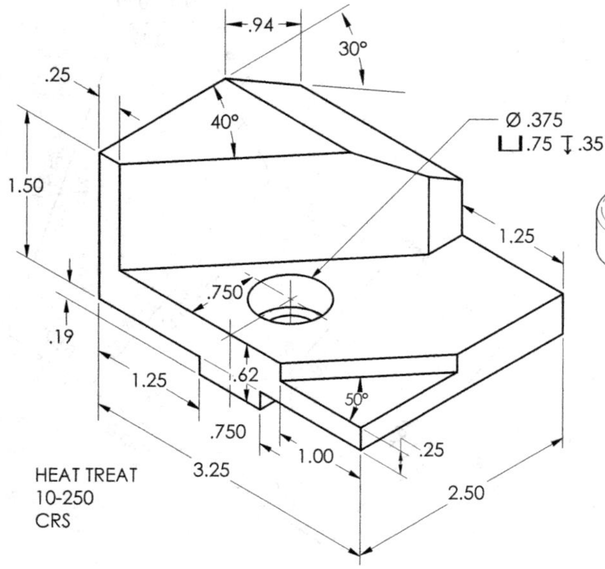

Exercise 7.10 Index Feed

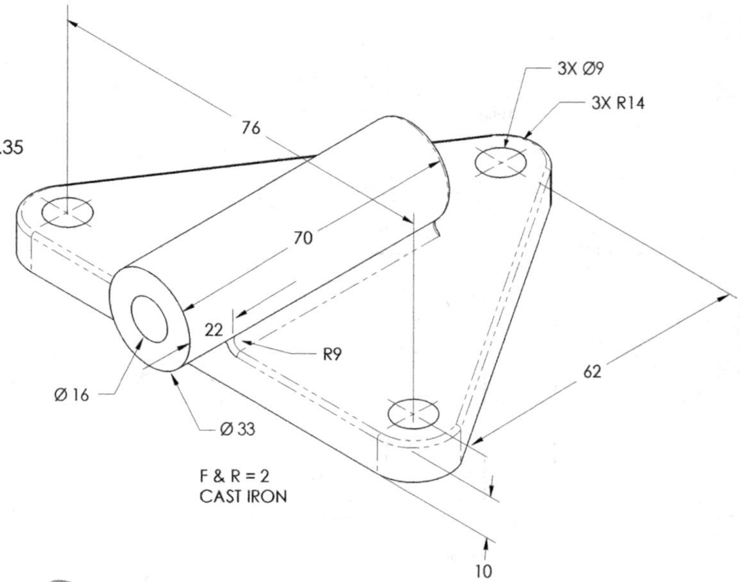

Exercise 7.11M Socket Bearing

Draw dimensioned orthographic views of the parts shown above. Show only the necessary views.

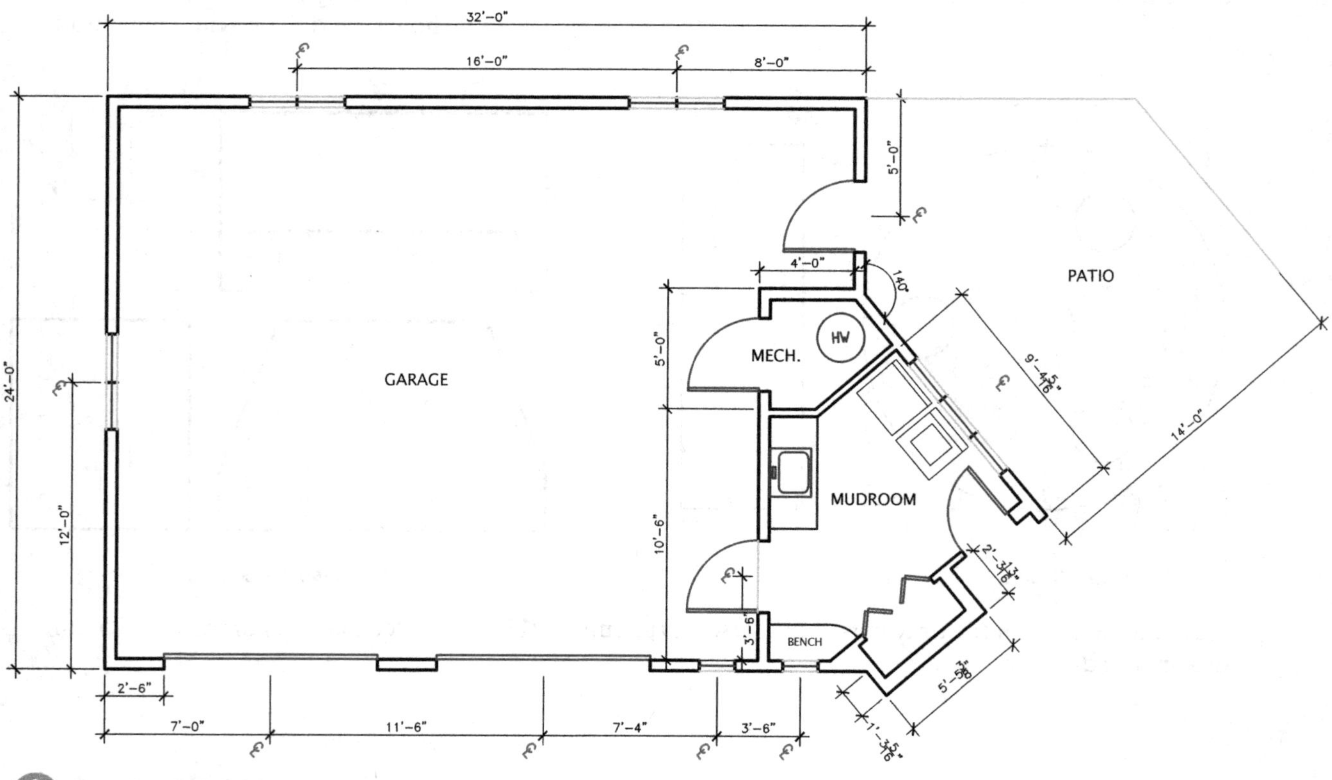

Exercise 7.12 Garage Floor Plan

Create a new dimension style for architectural dimensions. Dimension the garage floor plan drawing. It is shown larger in the exercise section of the previous chapter.

ADVANCED DIMENSIONING

8

Tolerance

No part can be manufactured to exact dimensions. There is always some amount of variation between the size of the actual object when it is measured and an exact dimension specified in the drawing. To take this variation into consideration, tolerances are specified along with dimensions. A *tolerance* is the amount of variation that an acceptable part is allowed to have from the specified dimension. Tolerances are assigned so that parts in an assembly will fit together.

Dimensions given in the drawing are used to make and inspect the part. In order to determine whether a part is acceptable, the measurements of the actual part are compared to the toleranced dimensions specified in the drawing. If the part feature falls within the tolerance range specified, it is acceptable.

To better understand the role that tolerances play in dimensioning, consider Figure 8.1.

Surface A on the actual object is longest when the 5.00 overall dimension shown for surface B is at its largest acceptable value and when the 2.00 dimension shown for surface C is at its shortest acceptable value.

$A_{max} = 5.04 - 1.95 = 3.09$

Surface A is shortest when surface B is at its smallest acceptable value and surface C is at its largest acceptable value.

$A_{min} = 4.96 - 2.05 = 2.91$

In other words, the given dimensions with the added tolerances permit surface A to vary between 3.09 and 2.91 units.

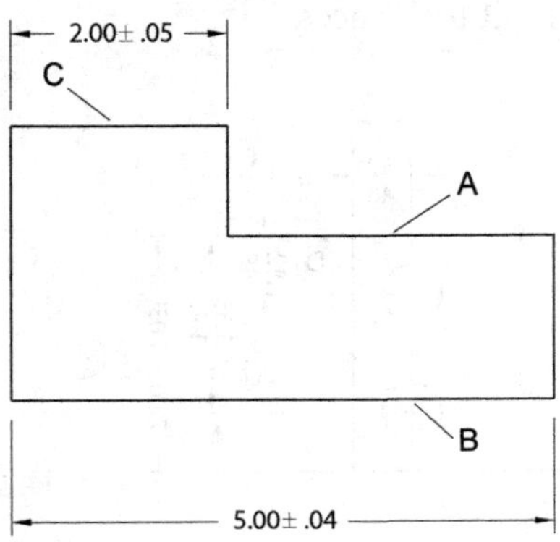

Figure 8.1

Objectives

When you have completed this tutorial, you will be able to

1. Use tolerances in a drawing.
2. Set up the dimension variables to use limit tolerances and variance (plus/minus) tolerances.
3. Add geometric tolerances to your drawing.
4. Use dimension overrides.
5. Create an Annotative Dimension Style.

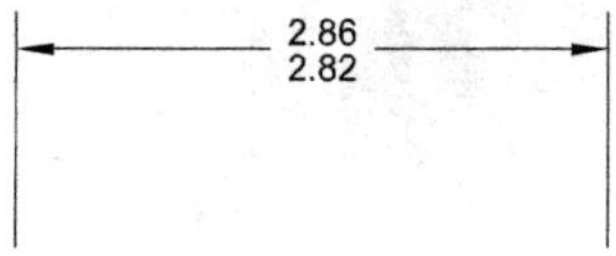

Limit tolerance

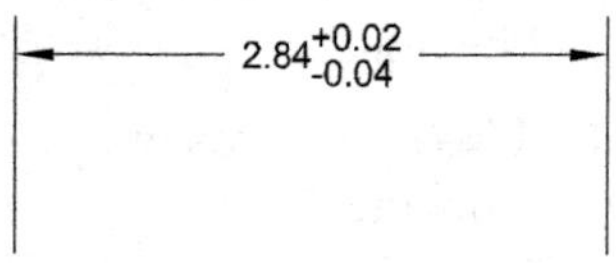

Deviation tolerance

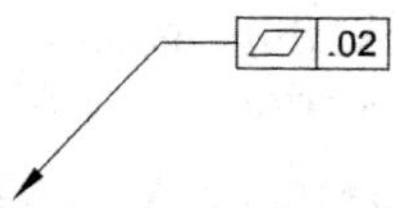

Geometric tolerance

Tip: *There are some setting differences between the datafile and the similar file you created in Tutorial 7, so make sure to use the datafile.*

Tolerance Formats

In Tutorial 7, you learned how to add a general tolerance note to your drawing to specify this allowable variation. AutoCAD provides three ways to add a tolerance to a dimension value:

- limit tolerances
- variance tolerances
- geometric tolerances.

Limit tolerances specify the upper and lower allowable measurements for the part. A part measuring between the two limits is acceptable.

Deviation (variance) tolerances or *plus/minus tolerances* specify the *nominal dimension* and the allowable range that is added to it. From this information you can determine the upper and lower limits. Add the plus tolerance to the nominal size to get the upper limit; subtract the minus tolerance from the nominal size to get the lower limit. (Or you can think of it as always adding the tolerance, but when the sign of the tolerance is negative, it has the effect of subtracting the value.) The plus and minus values do not always have to be the same.

There are two types of variance tolerances: bilateral and unilateral. *Bilateral tolerances* specify a nominal size and both a plus and minus tolerance. *Unilateral tolerances* are a special case where either the plus or the minus value specified for the tolerance is zero. You can create both bilateral and unilateral tolerances.

Geometric tolerances use special symbols inside feature control frames that describe *tolerance zones* that relate to the type of feature being controlled. The Tolerance command allows you to create feature control frames quickly and select geometric tolerance symbols for them. You will learn to create these frames later in this tutorial.

Figure 8.2 shows the drawing from Tutorial 7 with tolerances added to the dimensions. Tolerances A, B, F, and G are examples of bilateral tolerances. Tolerances C, D, and E are limit tolerances.

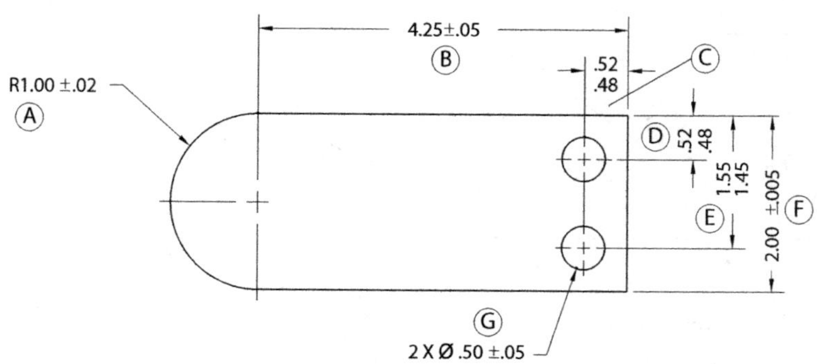

Figure 8.2

Starting

Start the AutoCAD program.

On your own, use the datafile ***obj-dim.dwt*** as the template for a new drawing.

Name your new drawing ***tolernc.dwg***.

Your screen should be similar to Figure 8.3. Be sure that layer DIM is the current layer. Next, set the dimension variables to use tolerances.

Tip: *If the full drawing does not show on your screen, switch to paperspace and zoom out to the drawing extents. Then switch back to model space.*

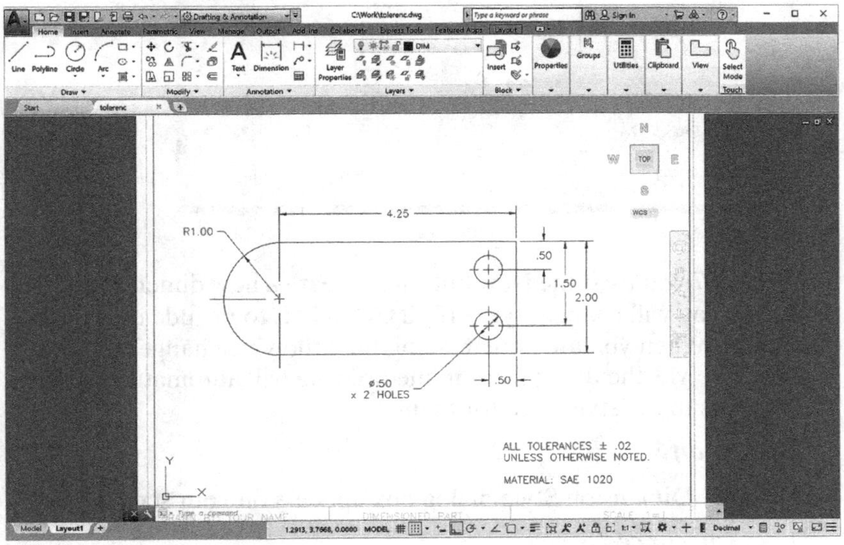

Figure 8.3

Automatic Bilateral Tolerances

You can have the program automatically add bilateral tolerances by setting the dimensioning variables with the Dimension Styles dialog box. The small arrow in the lower right corner of the ribbon Annotate tab, Dimension panel launches the Dimension Style Manager (Figure 8.4).

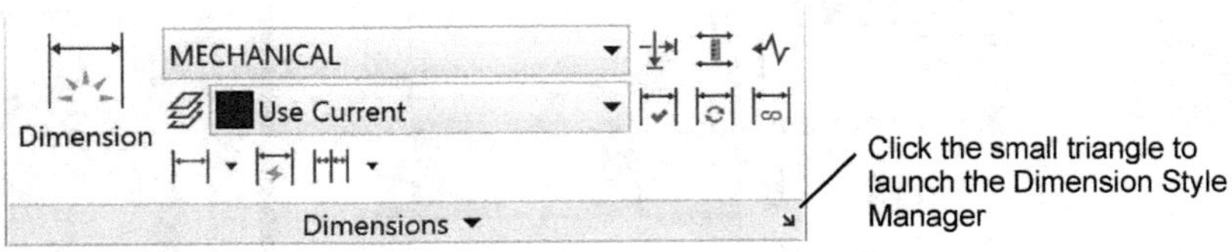

Figure 8.4

Click: ***to show the Dimension Style Manager***

The Dimension Style Manager appears on your screen, as shown in Figure 8.5. You will use it to set up the appearance of the tolerances to be added to the dimensions.

The dimension style MECHANICAL is current. It is like the style you created in Tutorial 7. You will make changes to it so that the dimensions in the drawing created with that style will show a variance, or deviation tolerance.

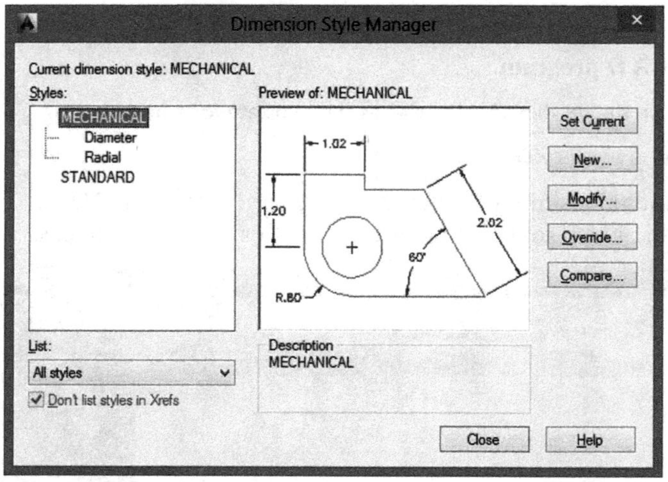

Figure 8.5

In Tutorial 7 you used the New button to create a new dimension style. This time you will change style MECHANICAL to include deviation tolerances. When you are done making the following changes to the dimension style, the dimensions in the drawing will automatically reflect the changes to the style used for them.

Click: ***Modify***

The Modify Dimension Style dialog box appears on your screen.

Click: ***Tolerances tab***

The Tolerances tab appears uppermost.

Click: ***to pull down the Method list*** *in the Tolerance Format area as shown in Figure 8.6*

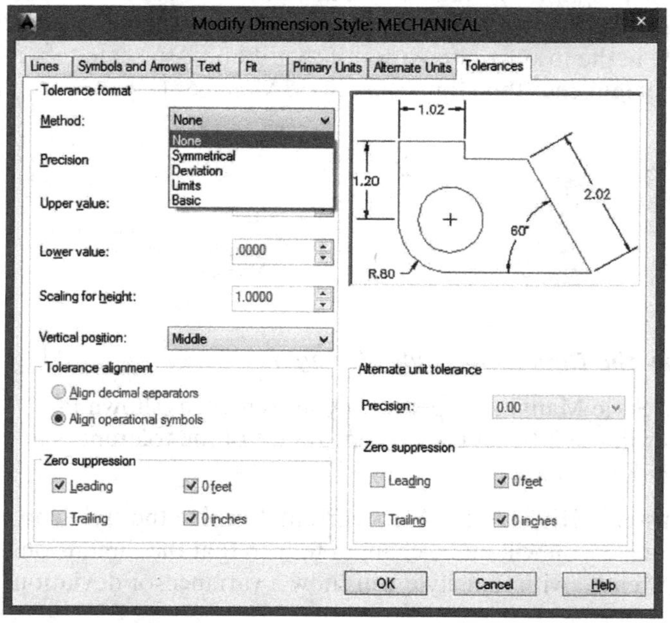

Figure 8.6

The choices of tolerance methods are None, Symmetrical, Deviation, Limits, and Basic.

- *None* uses just the dimension and does not add a tolerance, as your current dimensions reflect.
- *Symmetrical tolerances* are lateral tolerances with the same upper and lower values; these tolerances generally specify the dimension plus or minus a single value.
- *Deviation tolerances* are lateral tolerances that have a different upper and lower deviation.
- *Limit tolerances* show the maximum value for the dimension and the minimum value for the dimension.
- *Basic dimension* is a term used in geometric dimensioning and tolerancing to specify a theoretically exact dimension without a tolerance. Basic dimensions appear in your drawing with a box drawn around them.

If you choose any of the tolerance methods, you can preview what your dimensions will look like in the image tile.

Click: ***Deviation***

Note the image tile at the right of the dialog box; it shows a dimension with a deviation style tolerance added.

Click: ***Limits*** *(as the tolerance Method)*

Notice the change to the image tile. Continue clicking the tolerance methods on your own until you cycle through all the options.

On your own, return to Deviation tolerance, as shown in Figure 8.7.

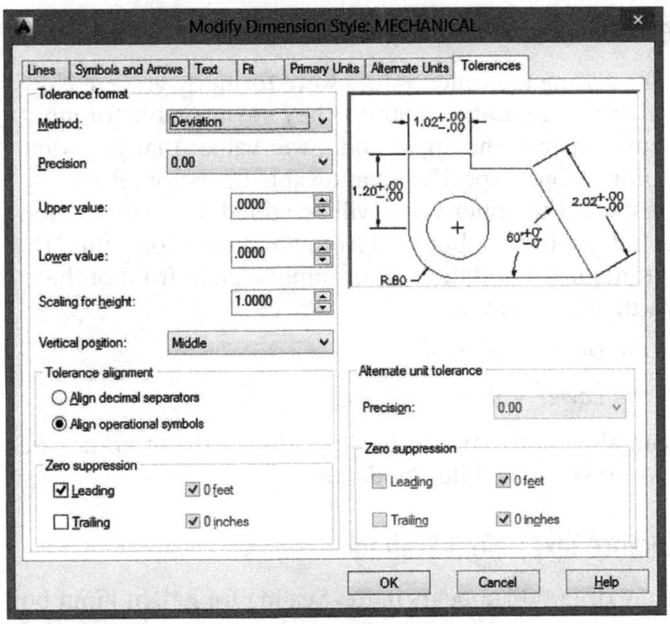

Figure 8.7

Setting the Tolerance Precision

The tolerance values can have a different precision from the dimension values. You control the precision by using the Precision pull-down near the top left of the dialog box.

Click: ***to show the Precision list*** *as shown in Figure 8.8.*

Click: ***0.00***

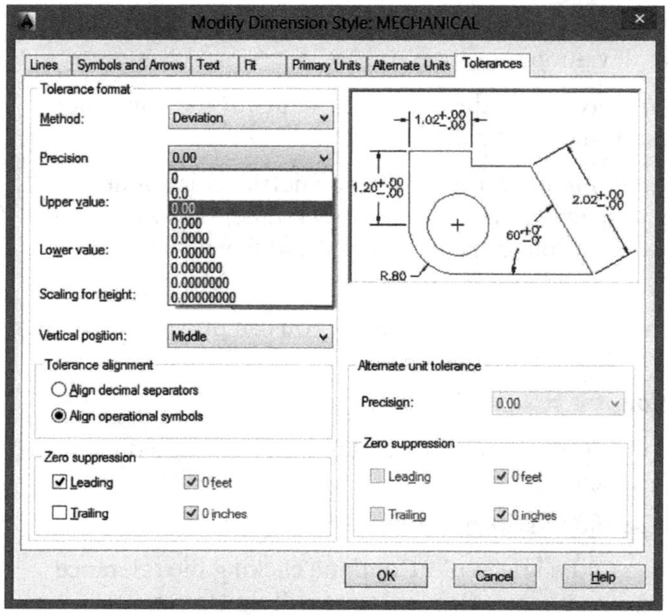

Figure 8.8

Specifying Tolerance Values

The text boxes for setting tolerance values were formerly grayed. Now that you have selected a tolerance method, they are available for input. You will use them to specify the upper and lower values that you want to use with the dimension to specify the allowable deviation. Both values will be positive. The upper value will be added to the dimension value; the lower value will be subtracted from the dimension value. The program will automatically add the plus or minus sign in front of the value when showing the tolerance.

Tip: *You can press [Tab] to move to the next text entry box. Doing so will also highlight the text in that box.*

Type: ***.05*** *for the Upper Value*

Type: ***.03*** *for the Lower Value*

Note that you can also control the vertical position of the tolerance. For now you will leave it set to Middle, the default.

Setting the Tolerance Text Height Scaling

The default setting of 1.0000 appears in the Scaling for height input box in the Tolerance Format area. This value is a scaling factor. A setting of 1.0000 makes the tolerance values the same height as the standard dimension text. For this tutorial you will set tolerance height to 0.8 (so that the height of the tolerance values will be 8/10 the height of the dimension values).

*Type: **.8** in the Scaling for height input box*

The same text style used for the dimension text, MYTEXT, will also be used for the tolerance text. You can control the text style and the dimension text height, color, and gap using the Text tab of the dialog box. You will leave these features set as they are. The Tolerances tab should now appear as shown in Figure 8.9.

*Click: **OK** to exit the Modify Dimension Style dialog box*

*Click: **Close** to exit the Dimension Style Manager*

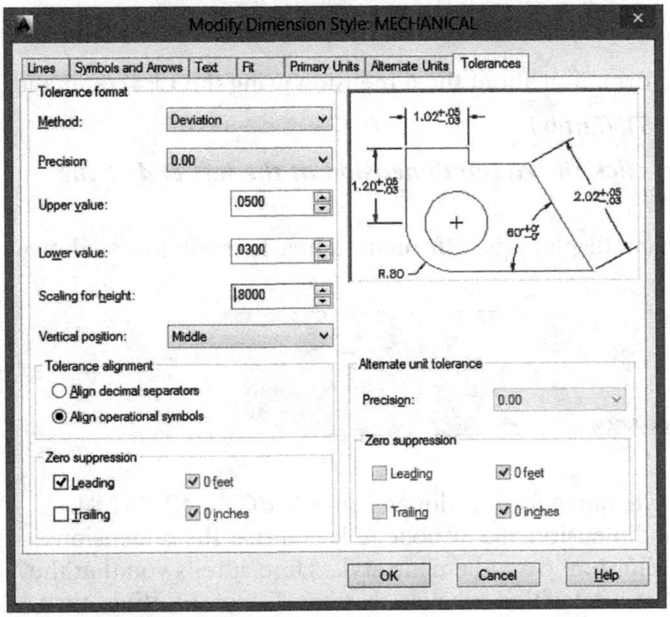

Figure 8.9

You return to your drawing. The dimensions created with style MECHANICAL automatically update to show the deviation tolerance. Your drawing should look like that in Figure 8.10.

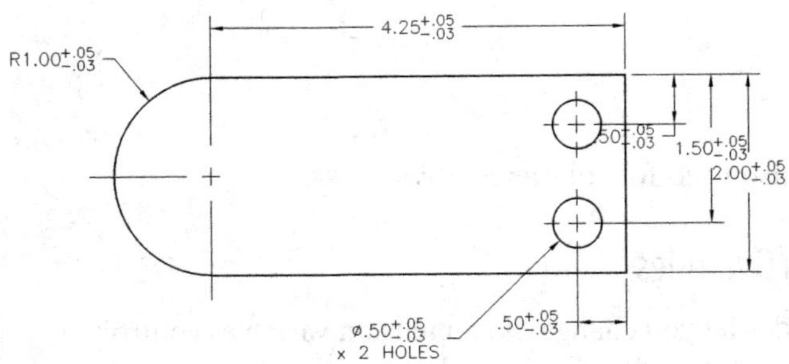

Figure 8.10

On your own, turn off Snap, Ortho, Object snap and other modes. Use the grips to edit the dimensions and move the dimension values so that the text is not crossing drawing lines as shown in Figure 8.11.

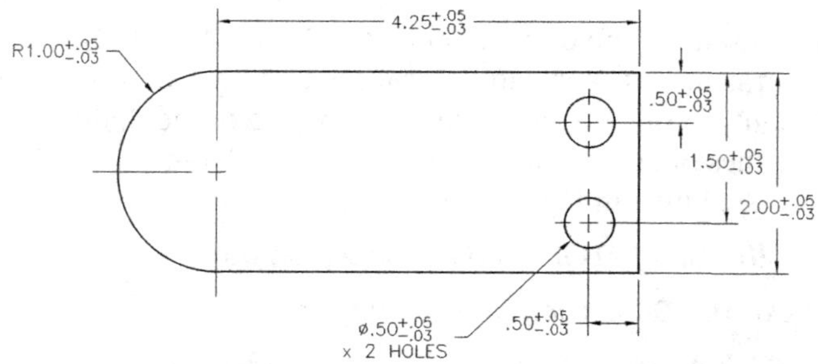

Figure 8.11

You can find information about the dimension using the List command.

Command: ***LIST [Enter]***

Select objects: ***click the radial dimension at the left end of the object [Enter]***

The List command displays the information in a Text window as shown in Figure 8.12.

Tip: *Press [F2] to toggle the text window on if you do not see it. You may have to scroll down to see the full text.*

```
type: radial
center defining point: X=   3.5000  Y=   5.0000  Z=   0.0000
defining point:        X=   2.8658  Y=   5.7732  Z=   0.0000
user specified text position: X=   2.5139  Y=   6.2023  Z=   0.0000
default text
dimension style: "MECHANICAL$4"
```

Figure 8.12

Note that the style name for this dimension is MECHANICAL$4. When you list a dimension, the $# code tells you that the dimension uses a substyle different from the main style. Here, it tells you that the dimension was created with a substyle that has different settings than the parent style, MECHANICAL. The codes for the substyles are:

$0	Linear
$2	Angular
$3	Diameter
$4	Radial
$6	Ordinate
$7	Leader (also used for tolerance objects)

Using Dimension Overrides

Dimension overrides let you change the dimension variables controlling a dimension and leave its style as is. A good approach is to change the general appearance of the dimensions by changing the dimension style and to change individual dimensions that need to vary from the overall group of dimensions (to suppress an extension line, for instance) by using overrides.

You can change dimension variables by typing DIMOVERRIDE at the command prompt. Dimoverride has the alias Dimover. When you use Dimoverride at the command prompt, the program prompts you for the exact name of the dimension variable you want to control and its new value. Then you select the dimensions to which you will apply the override. The Clear option of the Dimoverride command lets you remove overrides from the dimensions you select. You can also use the Dimension Style command, and select the Override button from the Dimension Style Manager.

You can also use the Properties palette to do the same thing.

Click: ***the radial dimension for the rounded end*** *to select it*

Right-click: ***to show the short-cut menu***

Click: ***Properties*** *to show the Properties palette*

The Properties palette appears on your screen. You will use it to override the dimension style for the radial dimension. Because the 2.00 vertical dimension at the right side of the part controls the part's height, providing the radial dimension is an example of overdimensioning.

When you want to call attention to the full rounded end, which is tangent to the horizontal surfaces at the top and bottom of the object, you can show the 1.00 radius value as a *reference dimension.* Or you can simply identify it with the letter R, indicating the radius but leaving its value to be determined by the other surfaces.

Click: ***to expand the Tolerances area***

Click: ***None*** *as the selection in the Tolerance display area*

When you have finished making these selections, your palette should look like Figure 8.13.

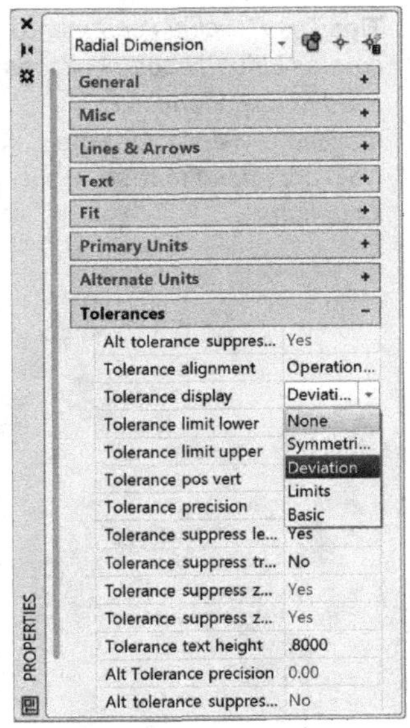

Figure 8.13

Click: ***to Close the Properties palette***

Press: ***[Esc] twice*** *to unselect the radial dimension*

Overriding/Adding Text to Dimensions

Next you will add the text, REF, after the radial dimension value to indicate that it is provided as a reference dimension only. It is also acceptable to note reference dimensions by including the dimension value in parentheses ( ).

Double-click: ***the radial dimension for the rounded end*** *to show the* ***text input box***

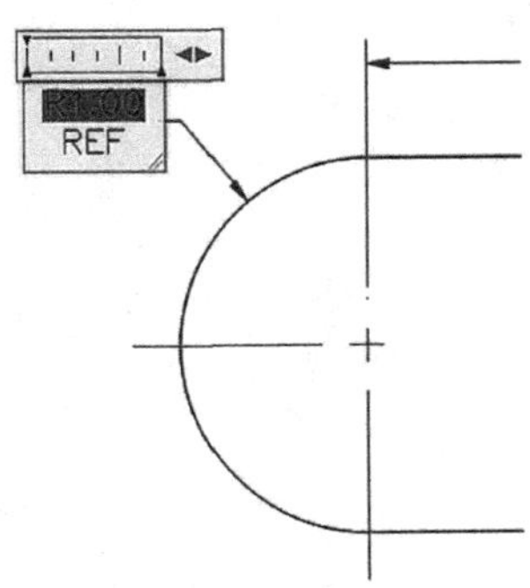

Figure 8.14

You can use the input box (Figure 8.14) to add text before or after the value, or overtype the value. You can also click and drag to expand the Text area, select a different font, font size, or other properties from the Text Editor ribbon tab that appears when the input box is visible.

After you have overridden the text, your dimension values no longer update if you stretch or change the object. Your drawing should look like the one in Figure 8.15. To fit the text to one line, stretch the corners of the input box larger to keep the text from wrapping.

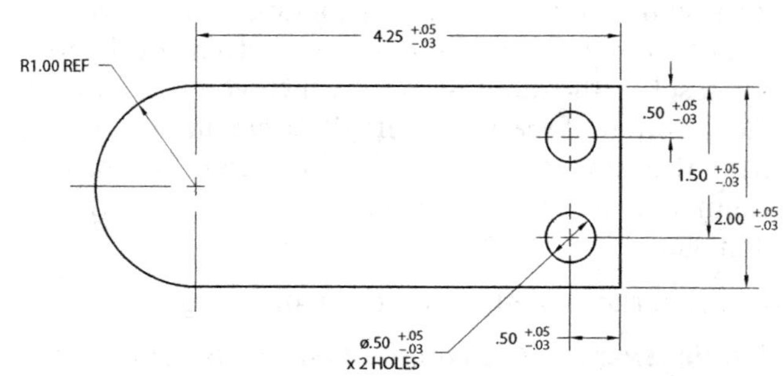

Figure 8.15

Next, use List again to list the radial dimension.

Command: ***LIST [Enter]***

Select objects: ***click the radial dimension [Enter]***

Tip: The Revcloud command creates cloud-shaped balloons used to call attention to drawing revisions. Use the Help command to read about its options.

A Text window appears, as shown in Figure 8.16, listing the information about the radial dimension. Note that overrides for the dimension variable Dimpost displays the dimension suffix, which is set to REF. Dimlim is set to Off, so that no deviation tolerance is applied to the dimension.

When dimensioning, keep your dimension styles organized by creating new dimension styles and controlling the substyles as needed. Use dimension overrides when certain dimensions need a different appearance than the general case for that type of dimension.

Press [Enter] if needed to show additional text in the text window.

You can now close the Text window.

```
associative: no
type: radial
center defining point: X=   3.5000  Y=   5.0000  Z=   0.0000
defining point:         X=   2.8658  Y=   5.7732  Z=   0.0000
user specified text position: X=   2.5139  Y=   6.2023  Z=   0.0000
dimension text modifier: <> REF
dimension style: "MECHANICAL$4"
Press ENTER to continue:
dimension style overrides:
 DIMGAP      0.0900
 DIMLIM      Off
 DIMTOL      Off
Annotative: No
```

Figure 8.16

Using Limit Tolerances

Next you will create a new style for dimensions using limit tolerances, and then you will change the object's overall dimension to use that style.

Open ***the Dimension Style Manager***

The Dimension Style Manager appears; you will create a new style.

Click: ***New***

The Create New Dimension Style dialog box appears. For the New Style Name,

Type: ***LIMITTOL***

Check that the Start With selection says MECHANICAL, and the Use for area says All dimensions. Leave Annotative unchecked.

Click: ***Continue***

Click: ***Tolerances tab***

Click: ***Limits as the tolerance method***

The dialog box should now look like Figure 8.17.

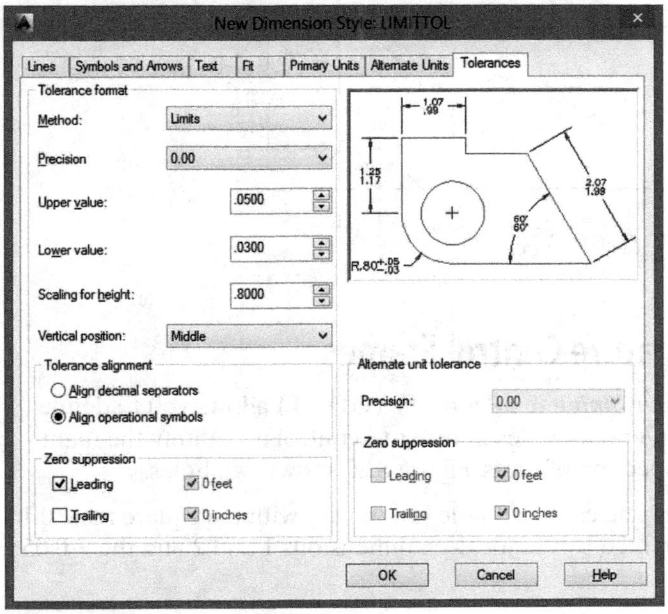

Figure 8.17

You can leave the upper and lower values and text height set as you did for deviation tolerances.

Click: ***OK*** *to exit the dialog box*

Click: ***Close*** *to exit the Dimension Style Manager*

Next, you will change the overall dimension of the object to use the new style, LIMITTOL. To do so, you will use the Styles toolbar.

Select: ***the 4.25 overall dimension*** *so that its grips appear*

To change the dimension to style LIMITTOL,

Click: ***to expand the dimension styles*** *as shown in Figure 8.18*

Click: ***LIMITTOL*** *from the list of dimension styles*

Press: ***[Esc]*** *to release the grips*

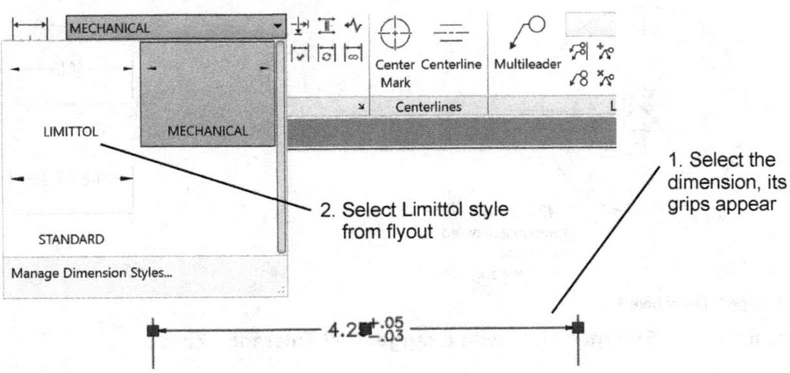

Figure 8.18

Tip: *You can also use the Properties palette to change the selected dimension. Expand the MISC heading and select the desired style.*

The limit tolerance appears, as shown in Figure 8.19.

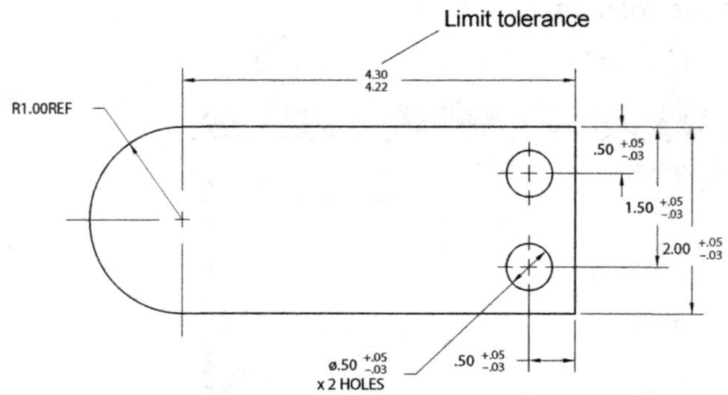

Figure 8.19

Creating Feature Control Frames

Geometric dimensioning & tolerancing (GD&T) allows you to define the shapes of tolerance zones in order to control accurately the manufacture and inspection of parts. Figure 8.20 shows two holes.

The location for the center of hole A can vary within a square zone 0.1 unit wide, as defined by the location dimensions 1 and 2 and the ± 0.05 tolerance.

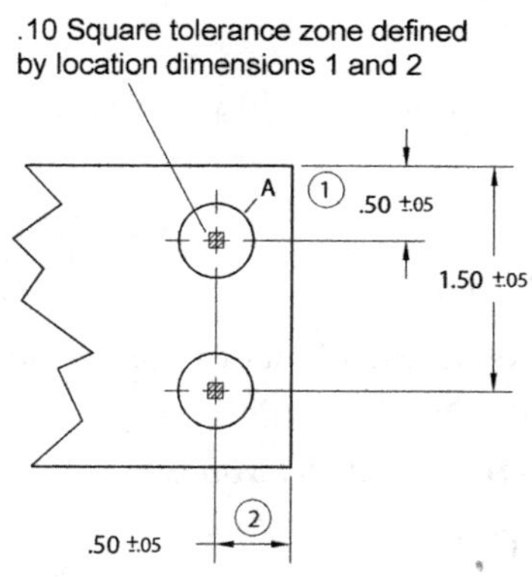

Figure 8.20

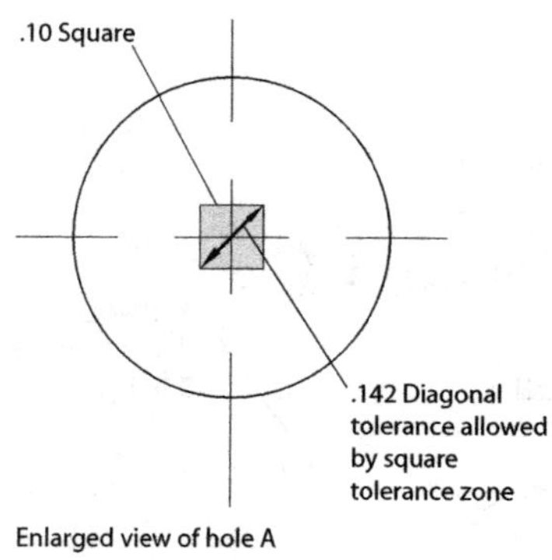

Figure 8.21 **Enlarged Hole with Exaggerated Tolerance Zone**

This tolerance zone is not the same length in all directions from the true center of the hole. The stated tolerances allow the location for the center of the actual hole to be off by a larger amount diagonally.

Figure 8.21 shows hole A and the square zone where the location of its center may still pass inspection according to the dimensions given. Its size is exaggerated in the picture.

The realization that this method did not sufficiently meet the need for specifying tolerances led to the development of specific tolerance symbols for controlling the geometric tolerance characteristics for position, flatness, straightness, circularity, concentricity, runout, total runout, angularity, parallelism, and perpendicularity.

Geometric tolerances allow you to define a *feature control frame* that specifies a tolerance zone shaped appropriately for the feature being controlled (sometimes this method is called feature-based tolerancing). A feature control frame is shown in Figure 8.22.

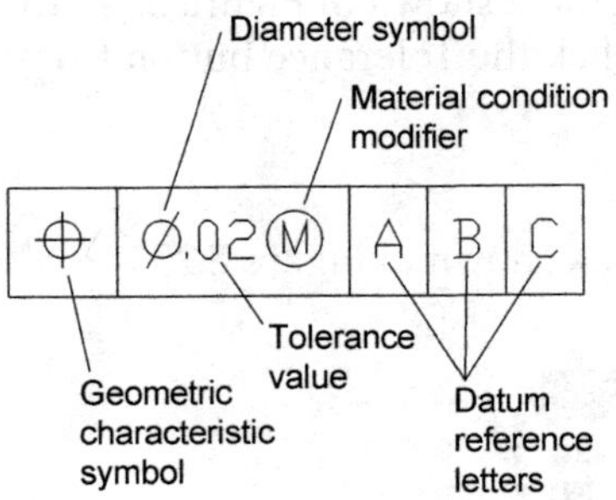

Figure 8.22

The feature control frame begins with the *geometric characteristic symbol*, which tells the type of geometry being controlled.

Figure 8.22 first shows a geometric characteristic symbol for positional tolerance. It next specifies the total allowable tolerance zone; in this case a diametral-shaped zone 0.02 wide around the perfect position for the feature. These two symbols are followed by any modifiers, for instance those for material condition or projected tolerance zone. The circled M shown is the modifier for maximum material condition, meaning that at maximum material, in this case the smallest hole, the tolerance must apply, but when the hole is larger a greater tolerance zone may be calculated, based on the size of the actual hole measured.

The remaining boxes indicate that the position is measured from datum surfaces A, B, and C. Not every geometric tolerance feature control frame requires a datum; for example, flatness can just point to the feature and control it, without respect to another surface.

Features such as perpendicularity that are relationships between two different surfaces require a datum.

Among other things, proper application of geometric tolerancing symbols requires that you understand:

- design intent for the part
- shapes of the tolerance zones specified with particular geometric characteristic symbols
- selection and indication of datum surfaces on the object
- placement of feature control frames in the drawing

Next, you will use the Tolerance command to add a feature control frame specifying a geometric tolerance to the drawing. To understand the topic of geometric tolerancing fully, refer to your engineering design graphics textbook or a specific text on geometric tolerancing. Merely adding feature control frames to the drawing will not result in a drawing that clearly communicates your design intent for the part to the manufacturer.

Next you will create the feature control frame shown in Figure 8.22. To create a feature control frame, you will click the Tolerance button from the Dimension panel.

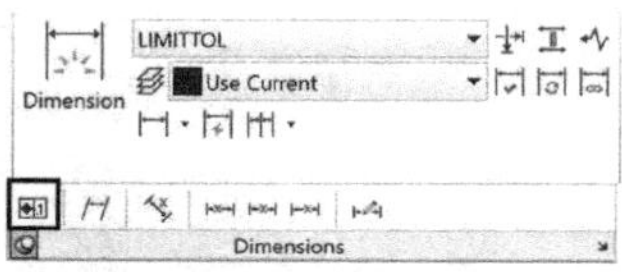

 *Click:* ***Tolerance button***

The Geometric Tolerance dialog box shown in Figure 8.23 appears on your screen.

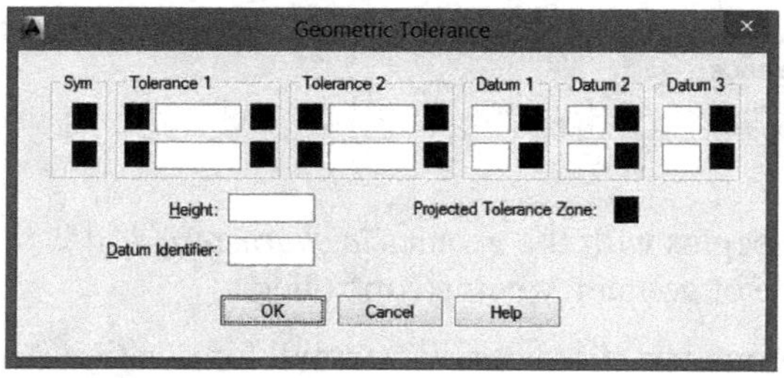

Figure 8.23

You will use it to create the geometric tolerance feature control frame by filling in tolerance values and selecting symbols.

Click: ***on the blank symbol area at the top left of the dialog box***

The Symbol palette appears on your screen as shown in Figure 8.24.

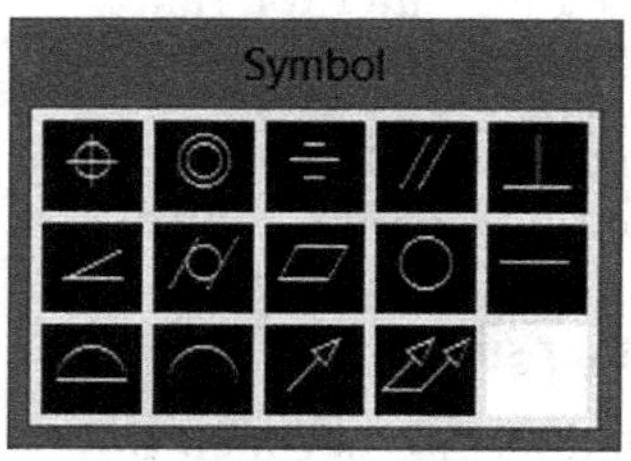

Figure 8.24

Click: ***the positional tolerance symbol*** *from the upper left corner of the tolerance symbol palette*

The symbol you selected appears in the box you clicked. You will make selections so that the dialog box appears as shown in Figure 8.25. The positional tolerance symbol should already be shown at the left.

The box to the right of the positional tolerance symbol is a toggle.

Click: ***in the empty box to turn on the diameter symbol***

When you click in the empty box, the symbol should appear.

Click: ***in the empty input box and type 0.02.***

To add a modifier,

Click: ***the blank symbol tile to the right of the value you typed***

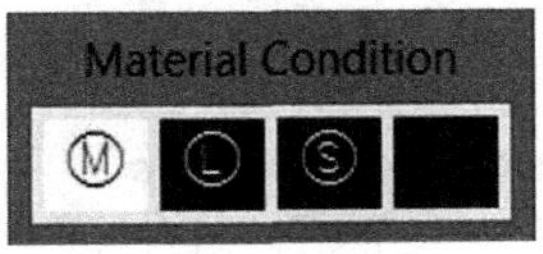

The Material Condition dialog box appears as shown. To select the modifier for maximum material condition,

Click: ***on the circled M***

You return to the Geometric Tolerance dialog box. The modifier appears for the feature control frame. Next, specify datum surfaces A, B, and C.

Click: ***in the empty text box below Datum 1***

Type: ***A***

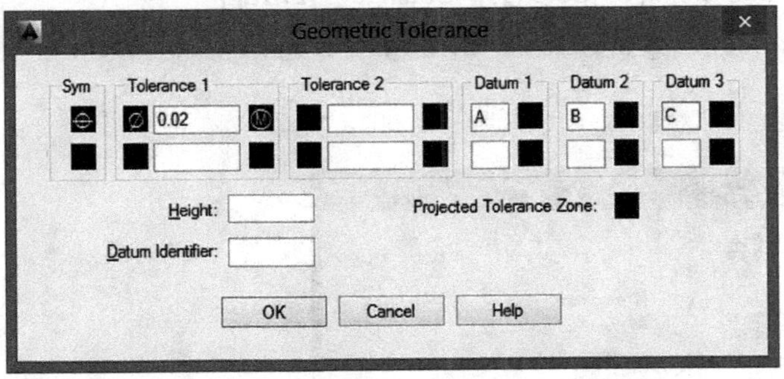

Figure 8.25

Repeat this process for **datum B** and **datum C** on your own.

Note that datums can also have modifiers. If you wanted to, you could click on the empty symbol tile to add a modifier for the datum.

Now you are ready to add the feature control frame to your drawing.

Click: ***OK*** *to exit the Geometric Tolerance dialog box*

Locate the feature control frame below the 0.50 diameter dimension.

Enter tolerance location: ***click below the diameter dimension for the holes as the location for the tolerance symbol***

Your drawing should look like that shown in Figure 8.26.

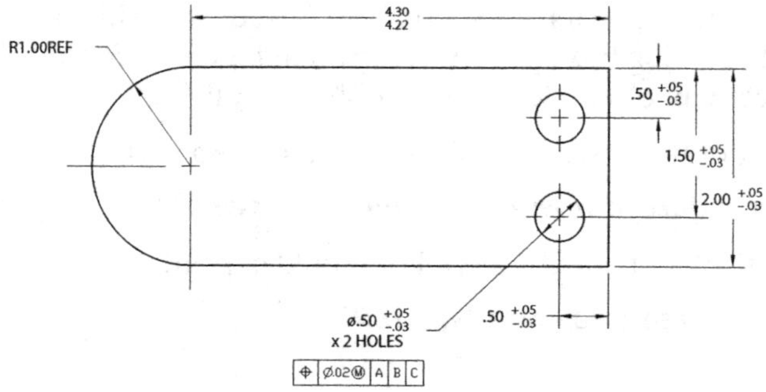

Figure 8.26

Using Leader with Tolerances

Tip: *AutoCAD also has a Multileader command (MLeader). This is useful for making stacked callouts in assembly drawings. You will learn more about it in Tutorial 12.*
Experiment with it on your own or check out the help for now.

You can also use the Quick Leader (QLeader) command to add a leader with an attached geometric tolerance symbol to your drawing. You will create the next feature control frame by starting with the Quick Leader command.

Turn on running Object Snap for **Nearest.**

Command: ***QLeader***

Specify first leader point, or [Settings] <Settings>: ***[Enter]***

*Click: **Tolerance** from the Leader Settings dialog box, as shown in Figure 8.27*

*Click: **OK***

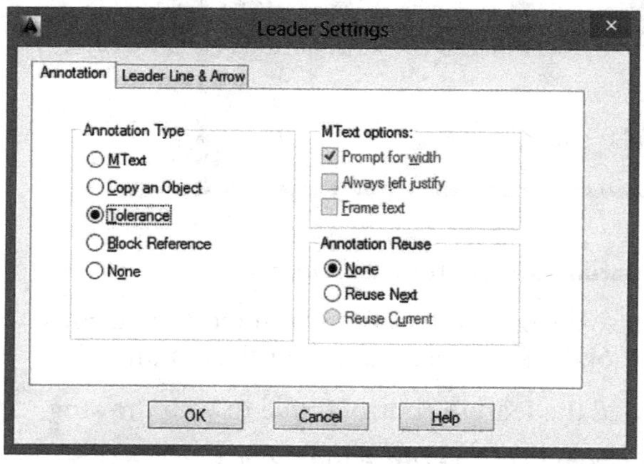

Figure 8.27

Specify first leader point, or [Settings] <Settings>: ***click at about 2 o'clock on the upper hole, using AutoSnap Nearest***

Specify next point: ***click above and to the right of the drawing***

Specify next point: ***[Enter]***

The Geometric Tolerance dialog box appears; from there you can start creating the feature control frame.

On your own, **create another feature control frame like the first one.**

*After you've finished making selections in the Geometric Tolerance dialog box, click **OK.***

The feature control frame is added to the end of the leader line, as shown in Figure 8.28.

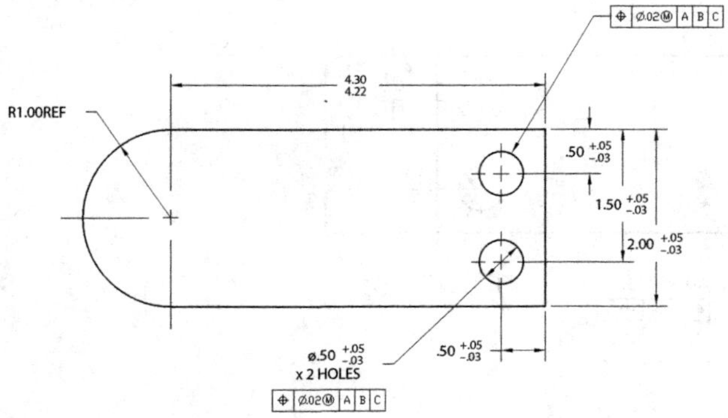

Figure 8.28

Next, you will override the location dimensions for the holes so that they appear as basic dimensions. When you specify a positional tolerance, the true position is usually located with basic dimensions, which are theoretically exact dimensions. The feature control frame for positional tolerance controls the zone in which the true position can vary. To create basic dimensions by overriding the dimension style,

*Click: **the 0.50 vertical dimension** at the upper right of the object to select it*

*Right-click: to show the **short-cut menu***

*Click: **Properties** to show the Properties palette*

The Properties palette appears on your screen.

*Click: **to expand the Tolerances area***

*Click: **Basic** as the tolerance display*

When you have finished

*Press: **[Esc] twice** to unselect the dimension*

Figure 8.29 shows the drawing with the 0.50 basic dimension.

On your own, override the dimension style for the 0.50 horizontal dimension below the object, and then for the 1.50 vertical dimension so they are basic dimensions.

Double-click on the text "Ø.50 X 2 HOLES" dimension and change it to read "2X Ø.50".

*Click: **to Close the Properties palette***

When you have finished, save your drawing on your own.

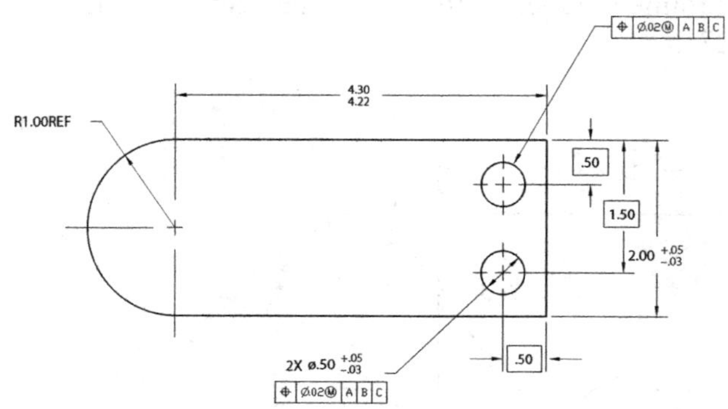

Figure 8.29

Creating Datum Flags

Datum flags are boxed letters identifying the feature on the object that is being used as a datum. Often they are attached to the extension line that is parallel to the surface being identified as the datum surface. Next, you will add datum flags to identify datum surfaces A and B, from which the position feature can vary. To create a datum flag, you will use the Quick Leader command and then select to add the tolerance.

Command: ***QLeader [Enter]***

Specify first leader point, or [Settings] <Settings>: ***[Enter]***

*Check to see that **Tolerance** is still selected on the Annotation tab.*

Click: ***Leader Line & Arrow tab***

Click: ***Datum triangle filled for the arrowhead style as shown in Figure 8.30***

Click: ***OK***

Tip: *If you have trouble making the straight leader segment for the datum flag, create the datum identifier separately using the Tolerance command. Use the leader command to draw the filled triangle and line or just use the Line command and add a filled triangle on your own.*

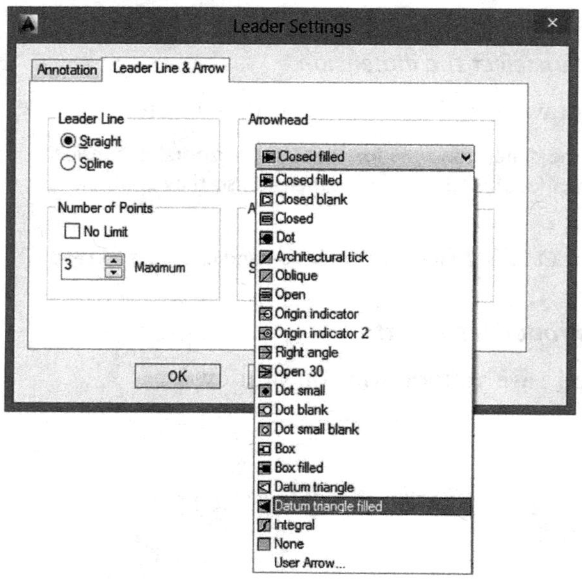

Figure 8.30

You will return to your drawing to select the location for the leader line that will attach the datum flag.

Turn on ***ORTHO Mode*** *from the status bar*

Specify first leader point, or [Settings] <Settings>: ***click on the upper right extension line***

Specify next point: ***click a point above the previous point***

Specify next point: ***click a point to the right of the previous point***

The Geometric Tolerance dialog box appears on your screen. You will leave the selections blank, except for the datum identifier.

Click: ***in the input box to the right of Datum Identifier***

Type: ***A***

Tip: *Datum plane C would be identified in another view if used.*

When you have finished, the dialog box should look like Figure 8.31.

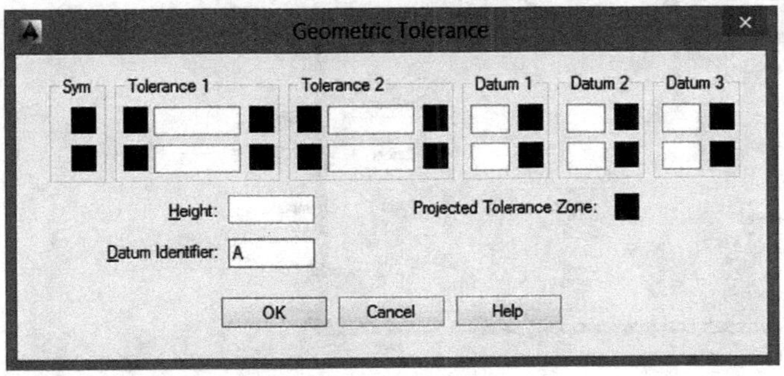

Figure 8.31

Click: ***OK***

The datum flag appears in your drawing as shown in Figure 8.32.

Add datum flag B to the drawing on your own.

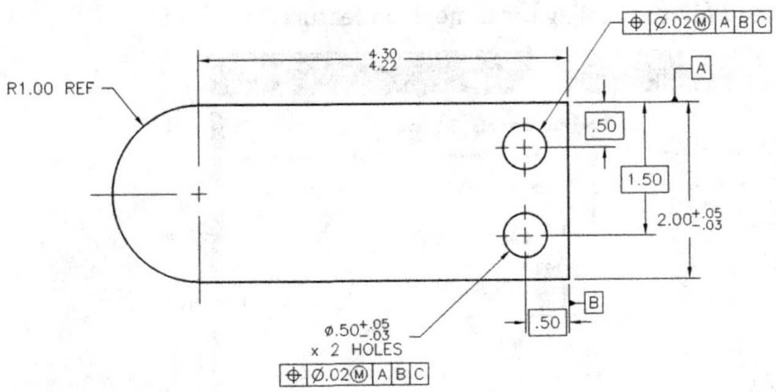

Figure 8.32

Creating an Annotative Dimension Style

In the previous chapter, you created an annotative text style. Dimensions, Multileaders, and hatches (which you will learn about in Tutorial 9) also can have annotative properties, so that their size is relative to the zoom scale. To create a new annotative dimension style:

Click: ***to show the Dimension Style Manager***

Click: ***New***

Type: ***AnnotDim*** *for the New Style Name*

Select: ***MECHANICAL*** *as the style to Start With*

Select: ***Annotative*** so it appears checked as shown in Figure 8.33

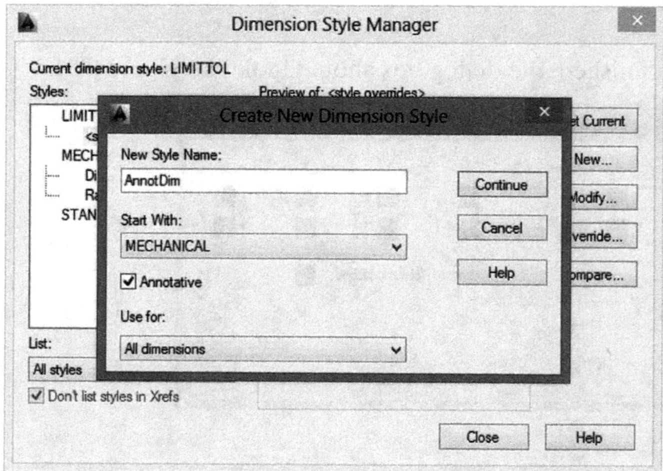

Figure 8.33

Click: ***Continue***

On your own, navigate to the **Fit tab** which should look like Figure 8.34. Notice Annotative is selected for the scaling for dimension features method.

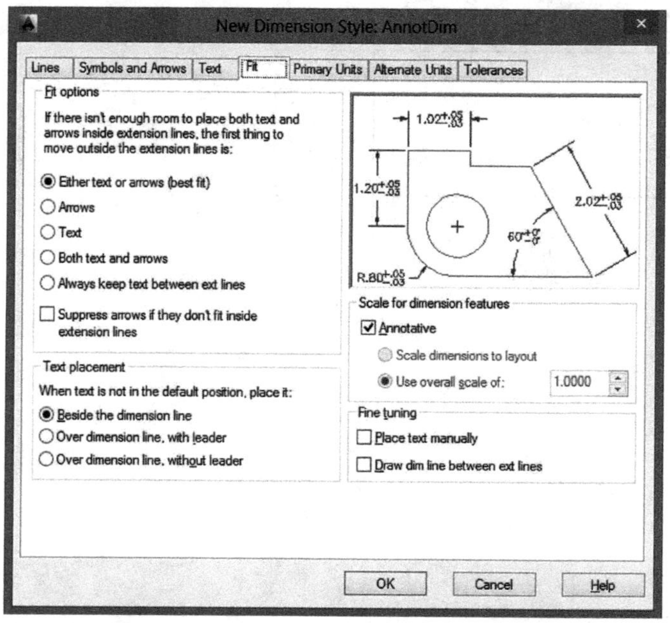

Figure 8.34

Click: ***OK***

Click: ***Set Current*** *to set AnnotDim as the current dimension style*

Click: ***Close*** *to exit the dialog box*

Using an Annotative Dimension Style

To use an annotation style, check that it shows as the current style on the Dimension panel.

Once you have created a paper space layout and set the viewport to the proper plot scale, the annotation scale will affect the scale of the associated annotative objects and their visibility. Recall that you will want the viewport scale and annotation scales to be synchronized. With normal visibility set for the annotative objects, only those with the same annotation scale will be visible. Objects with other annotation scales will not show. ANNOALLVISIBLE is the variable which controls this visibility.

Experiment on your own with adding some dimensions to layouts at different scales.

Save your drawing, and **exit** the AutoCAD program.

You have completed Tutorial 8.

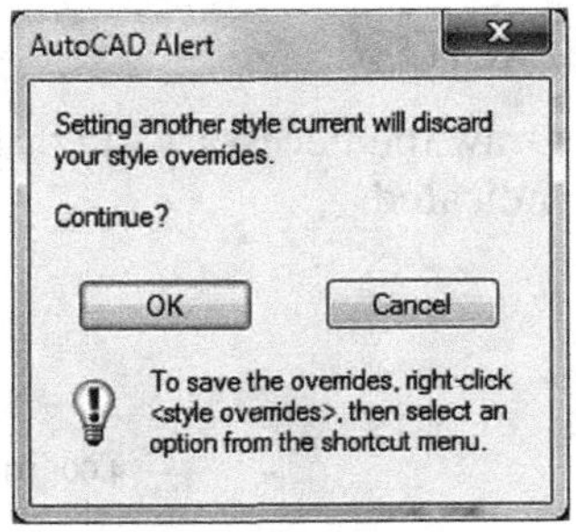

Note: *If you see the alert prompting whether to discard the style overrides, click* **OK** *for this tutorial. In general, deciding whether to save the overrides to a style depends on whether you would save time in the future by reusing that set of dimension appearances as a style.*

Key Terms

annotative style
basic dimension
bilateral tolerances
datum flags
deviation tolerances
feature control frame
geometric characteristic symbol
geometric tolerances
limit tolerances
nominal dimension
plus/minus tolerances
reference dimension
symmetrical tolerances
tolerance
tolerance zones
unilateral tolerances
variance tolerances

Key Commands

Annoallvisible
Dimgap
Dimlim
Dimoverride
Dimpost
Dimtol
QLeader
Tolerance

Exercises

Draw the necessary 2D orthographic views and dimension the following shapes. Include tolerances if indicated.

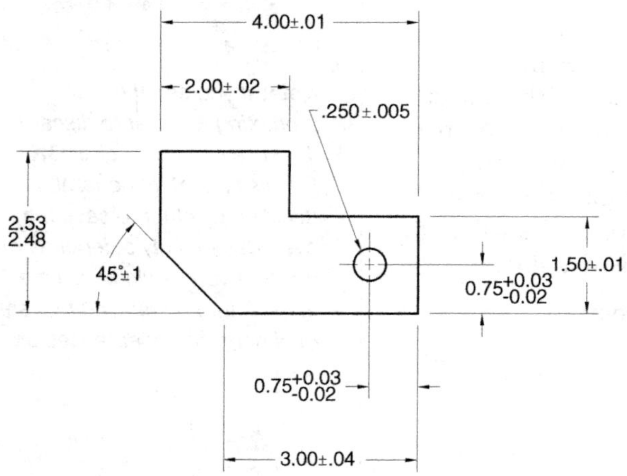

Exercise 8.1 Stop Base

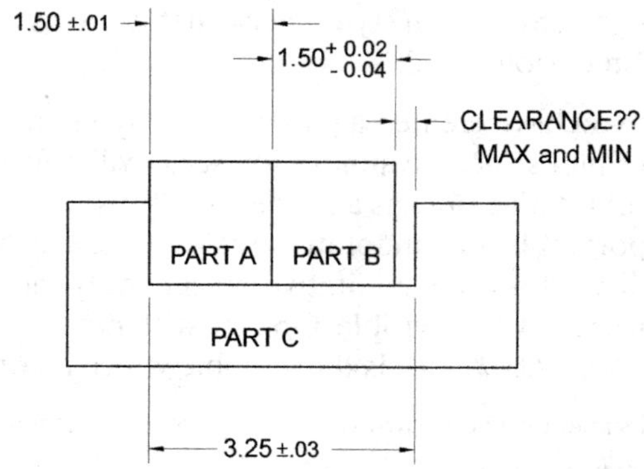

Exercise 8.2 Tolerance Problem

Calculate the maximum and minimum clearance between Parts A and B and Part C as shown.

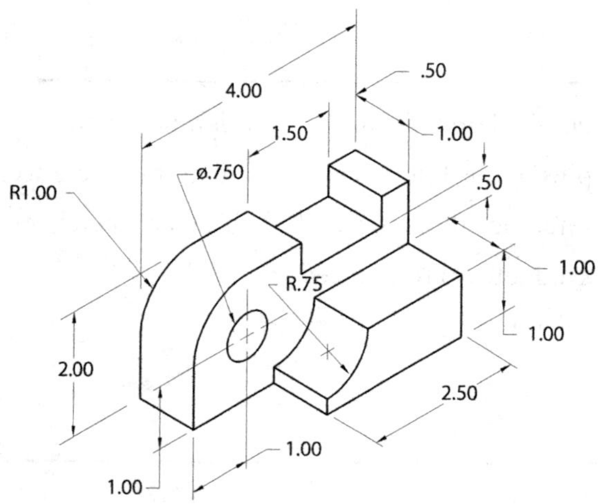

Exercise 8.3 Lathe Stop

Show bilateral tolerances of ±.02 for the Ø.75 hole and the 1.50 upper slot.

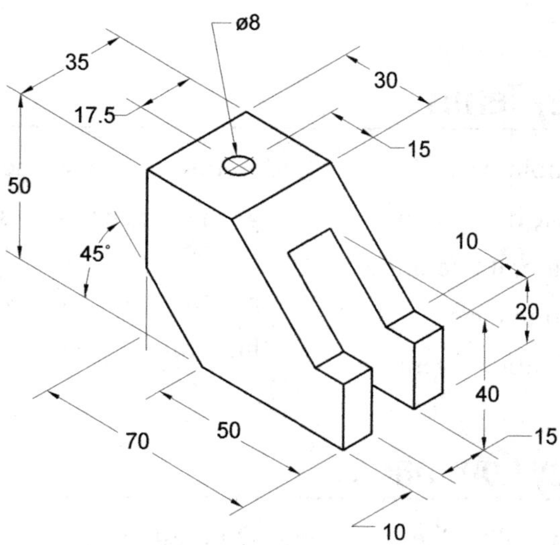

Exercise 8.4M Mill Tool

Consider the symmetry of this part as you dimension the orthographic views.

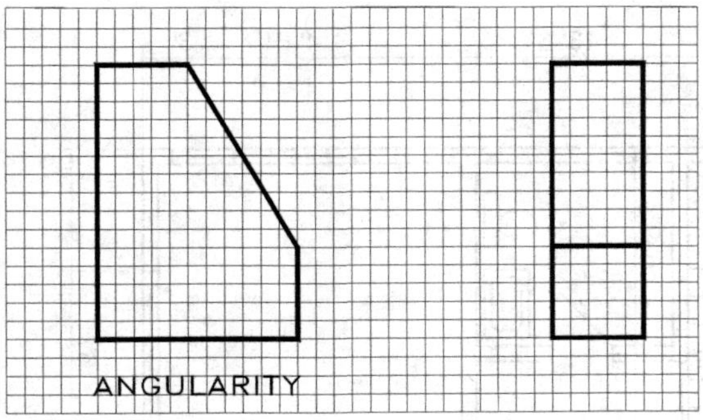

Exercise 8.5 Angular Tolerance

Using a feature control frame and the necessary dimensions, indicate that the allowable variation from the true angle specified for the inclined plane is 0.7 mm, using the bottom surface of the object as the datum.

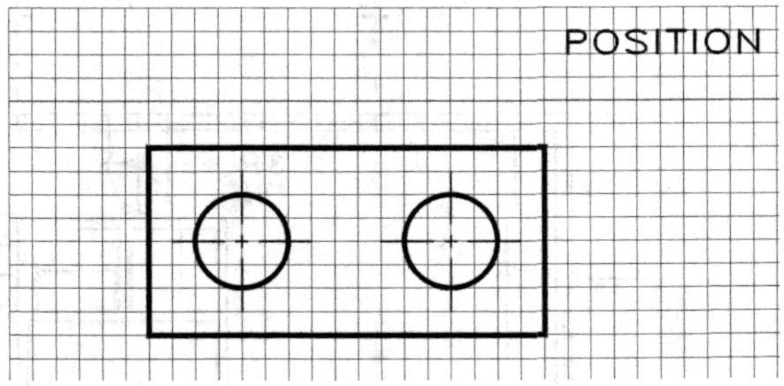

Exercise 8.6 Positional Tolerance

Locate the two holes with an allowable size tolerance of 0.05 inches and a position tolerance of Ø.02 inches. Use the proper symbols and dimensions. Each square is .25 inches.

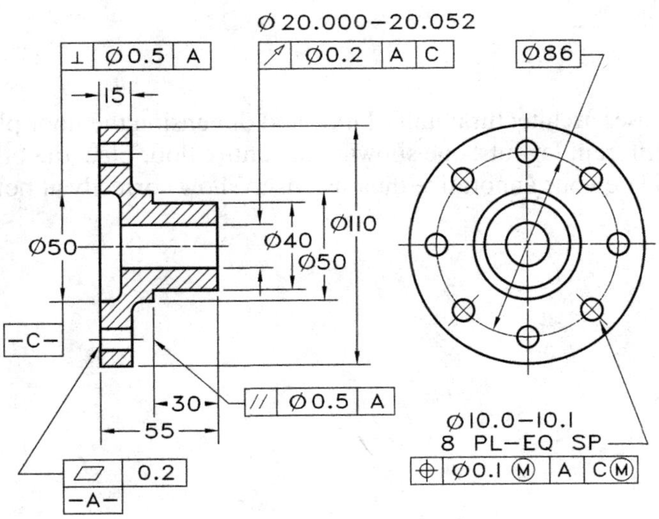

Exercise 8.7 Hub

Create the drawing shown.

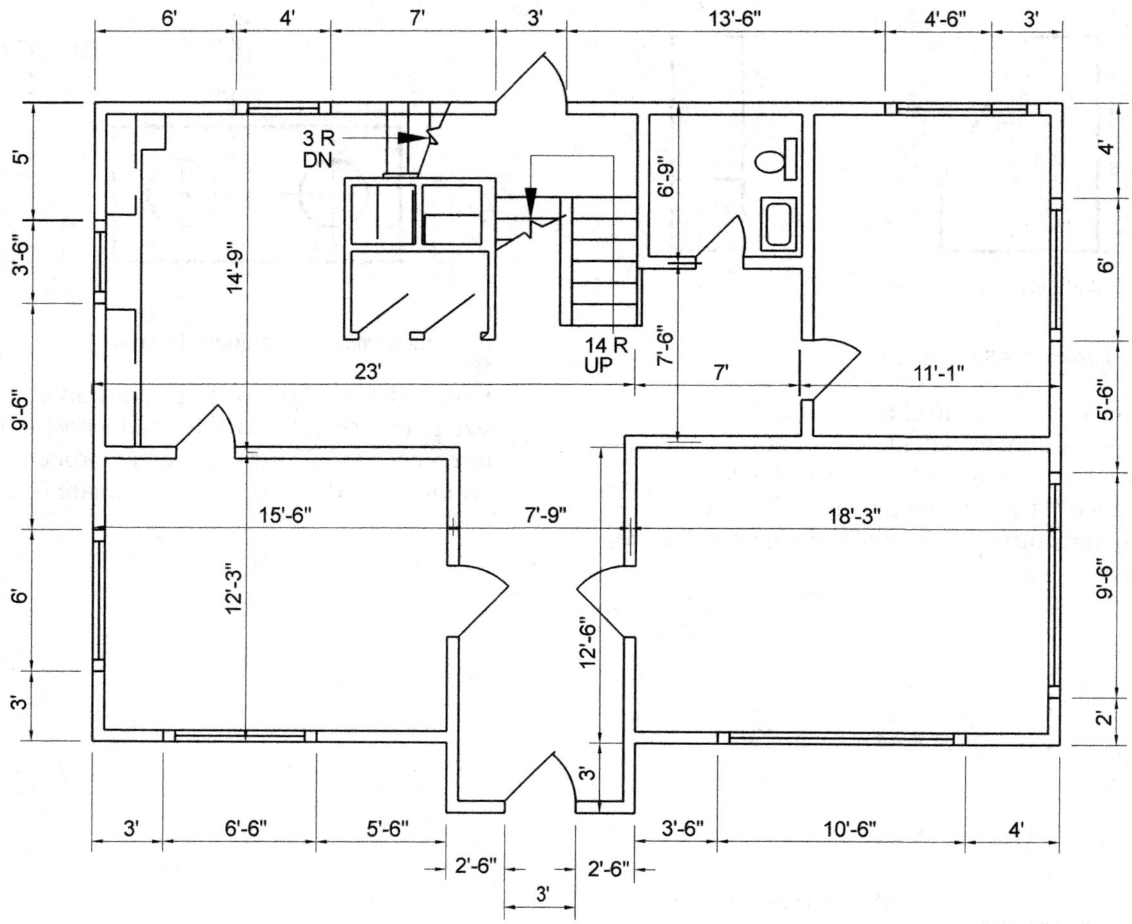

Exercise 8.8 Floor Plan

Create an annotative dimension style that uses architectural units. Draw and dimension the floor plan shown, making good use of layers. Create two different layouts: one showing the entire floor plan, the other showing an enlarged detail of the stair area. Update your annotative dimensions to show correctly at both viewport scales.

SECTION AND AUXILIARY VIEWS

9

Introduction

In this tutorial you will learn first how to draw section views and, in the second half of the tutorial, how to draw auxiliary views.

Section Views

A *section view* is a special view used to show the internal structure of an object. Essentially, it shows what you would see if a portion of the object were cut away and you were to look at the remaining part. Section views are often used when the normal orthographic views contain so many hidden lines that they are confusing and difficult to interpret. In this tutorial you will learn to use two-dimensional (2D) projection to create section views. In Tutorial 14 you will learn to use solid modeling to generate a section view directly from a solid model.

Section View Conventions

Figure 9.1 shows the front and side views of a cylindrical object. The side view contains many hidden lines and is hard to interpret. Figure 9.2 shows a *pictorial section* drawing of the same object.

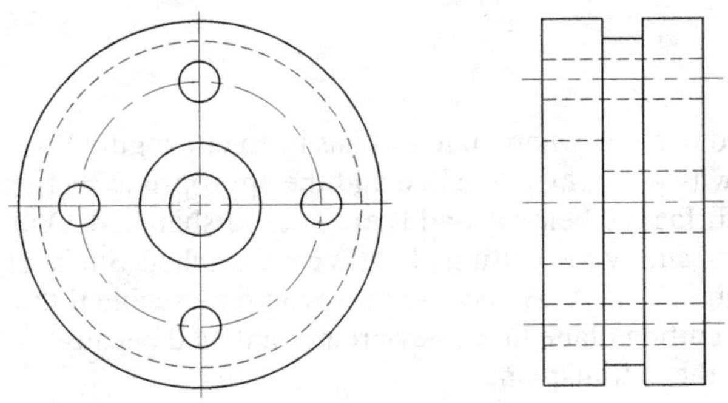

Figure 9.1

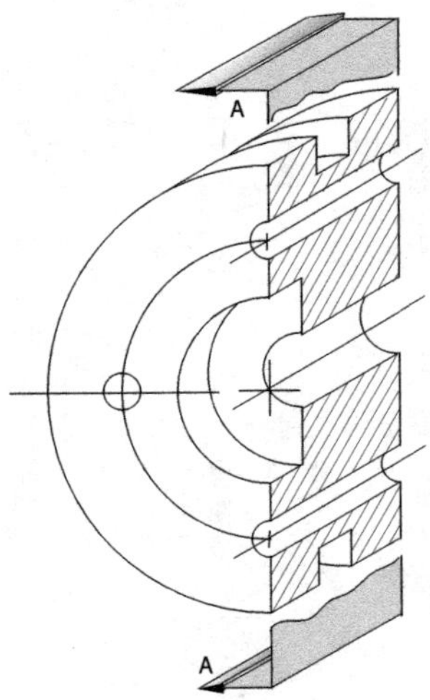

Figure 9.2

Objectives

When you have completed this tutorial, you will be able to

1. Show the internal surfaces of an object, using 2D section views.
2. Locate and draw cutting plane lines and section lines on appropriate layers.
3. Hatch an area with a pattern.
4. Edit associative hatching.
5. Draw auxiliary views using 2D projection.
6. Set up a UCS to help create a 2D auxiliary view.
7. Rotate the snap to help create a 2D auxiliary view.
8. Draw auxiliary views of curved surfaces.

In a section view, the portion of the object that has been cut is shown filled with a pattern to make the drawing easier to interpret. You can accomplish this *crosshatching* or pattern filling using the AutoCAD Hatch command.

Figure 9.3 shows front and section views of the same circular object. A *cutting plane line*, A–A, defines the location of the sectional cut and shows arrows to indicate the viewing direction for the section view.

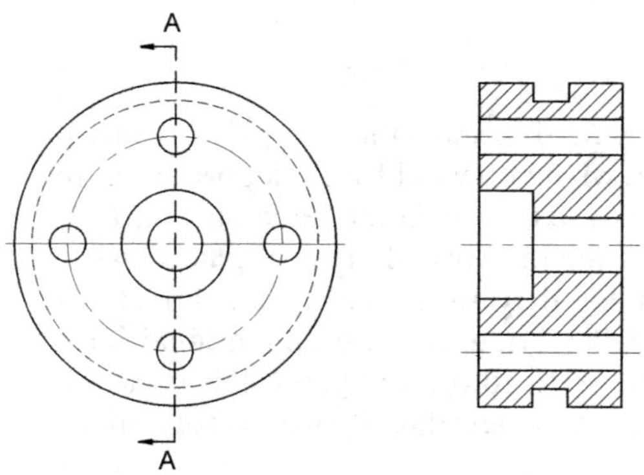

Figure 9.3

Compare the side view in Figure 9.1 with the section view in Figure 9.3 and the pictorial section view shown in Figure 9.2. The sectional views are easier to interpret than drawings that just show the front and side views.

Crosshatching

Crosshatching is used to show where material has been cut. Figure 9.4 shows a new object with a cutting plane line and the appropriate section view. Note that the surfaces labeled A and B are not crosshatched. Only material that has been cut by the cutting plane is crosshatched. Surfaces A and B are shown in section A–A because they would be visible if the part were cut on the cutting plane line. They are not hatched because they were not cut by the cutting plane.

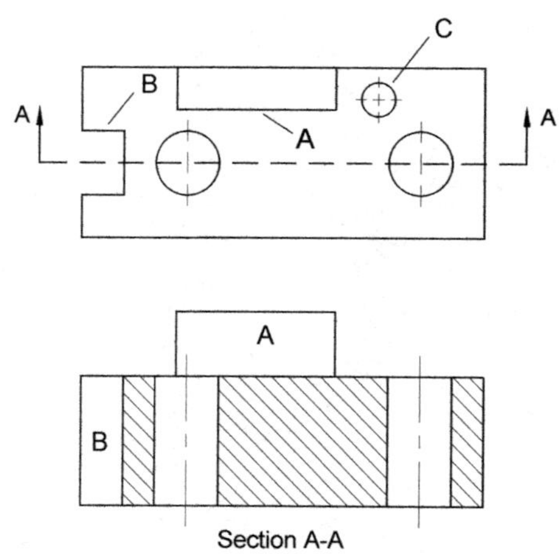

Figure 9.4

A section view shows what you would see if the object were cut along the cutting plane line and you looked at the remaining portion of the object in the direction the arrows point. For the view shown in section, ignore the portion of the object that would be cut off. Draw the view to show the remaining portion. Some features that were previously hidden will be visible and should be shown.

The hole labeled C in Figure 9.4 is in the remaining portion of the object, but is not visible in the section view, so it is not shown. The purpose of a section view is to show the internal structure without the confusion of hidden lines. You should use hidden lines only if the object would be misunderstood if the lines were not included. (To show hole C in the section view, you could use an *offset cutting plane* line—which bends 90° to pass through features that are not all in the same plane. Refer to any standard engineering graphics text to review conventions for cutting plane lines and types of section views.)

Starting

Start AutoCAD.

Use the datafile ***cast2.dwt*** *as a template file to begin a new drawing. Save the drawing as* ***bossect.dwg****.*

Adjust the position of the drawing on your screen using ***zoom*** *and* ***pan*** *from paperspace.*

Return to model space *when you are finished.*

Creating 2D Section Views

The top, front, and side orthographic views of a casting are displayed on your screen. Your screen should look like Figure 9.5.

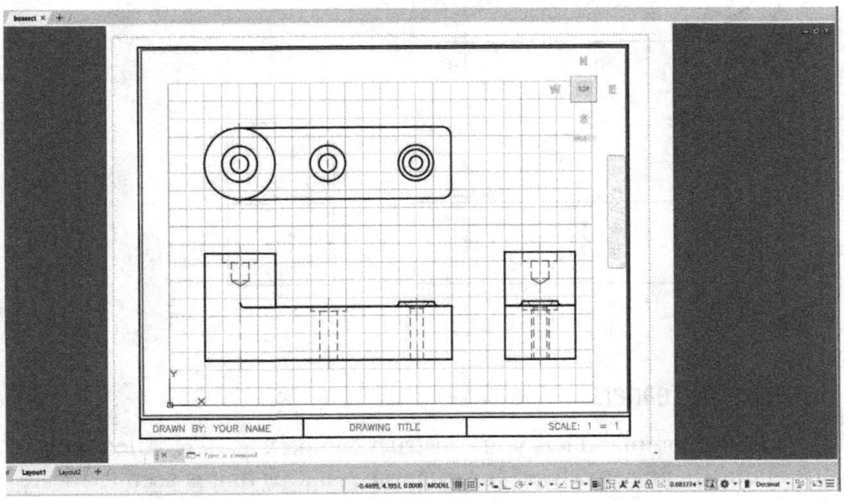

Figure 9.5

Often one or more of the orthographic views are replaced with section views. You will change the front orthographic view to be a front section view. You will change the side view to be a side section view.

Cutting Plane Lines

The cutting plane line uses one of two different linetypes: either long dashes (DASHED) or long lines with two short dashes followed by another long line (PHANTOM). You should use only one type of cutting plane line in any one drawing. You will make dashed cutting plane lines using the Cutting_Plane layer that was created in the template. Linetype DASHED has longer dashes than linetype HIDDEN. The Cutting_Plane layer has a different color than the Hidden_Line layer to help distinguish it. Also, cutting plane lines are printed as thick lines, so the lineweight for the layer is set to 0.6 mm.

Creating Dashed Lines

*Set layer **Cutting_Plane** as the current layer.*

*Be sure that **Snap** is turned **on** and set to **0.25**.*

*On your own, use the **Line** command to add a horizontal dashed cutting plane line in the top view of the boss that passes through the center of the holes in the top view between points A-A in Figure 9.6.*

Now add a vertical dashed cutting plane line through the center of the top view of the boss between points B-B.

***Save** your drawing at this time.*

The lines on layer Cutting_Plane should extend beyond the edges of the object by about 0.5 units as shown in Figure 9.6.

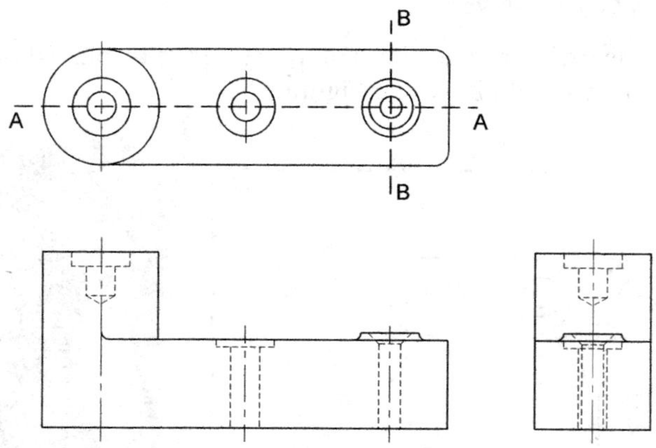

Figure 9.6

Drawing the Leaders

The Leader command lets you construct complex leaders. A leader is a line ending in an arrowhead (or sometimes a dot) that is used to locate specific notes and drawing information for an item. Leaders should generally be drawn at some angle other than horizontal or vertical.

AutoCAD provides three different commands for creating leaders:

Leader- starts with an arrowhead or dot and creates the leader line and a short ending segment (called the landing line) which you can connect to text, tolerance, block or other drawing objects.

QLeader- quick leader starts with an arrowhead or dot and creates the leader line and a short landing line segment and text, tolerance or a block object.

MLeader- multileader consists of an arrowhead, a horizontal landing, a leader line or curve, and either a multiline text object or a block. Unlike Leaders and Qleaders, multileaders may start arrowhead first, leader landing first, or content first. The settings for a multileader can be saved as a named style to make it easy to reuse the settings. The Content First option also allows you to select existing multiline text from which to draw the leader. (You will learn more about multileaders in Tutorial 13.)

Leaders can have annotative properties, so that they update as the zoom scale for the viewport changes.

Next you will make a new MLeader style and use MLeader as a quick way to add line segments ending in arrows for the cutting plane lines.

Making a Multileader Style (MLEADERSTYLE command)

Similar to creating a dimension style, the Multileader Style Manager lets you set and save the appearance of the leader. Use the ribbon Annotate tab, Leaders panel.

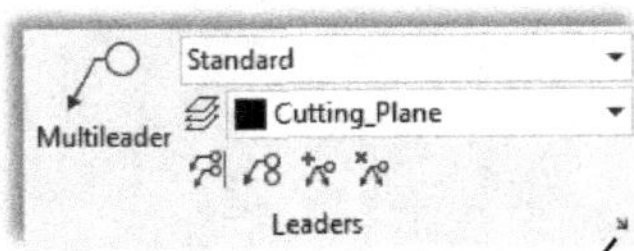

Click to show Multileader Style Manager

Click: ***the small arrow from the right corner of the Leaders panel*** *to show the Multileader Style Manager*

The Multileader Style manager appears on your screen as shown in Figure 9.7.

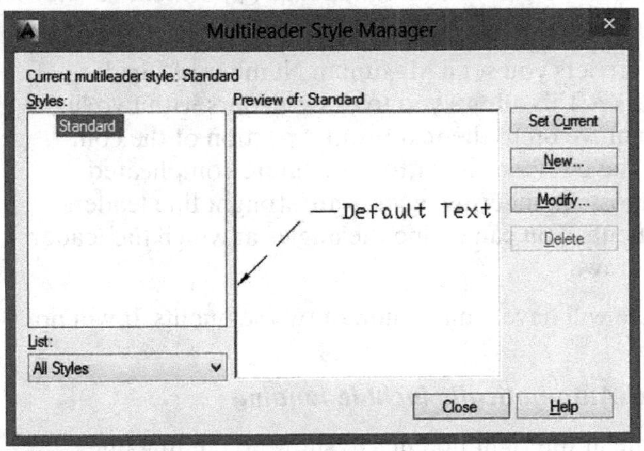

Figure 9.7

Click: ***New***

Type: ***CuttingPlaneArrows*** *as the name of your new style*

Do not select Annotative

Click: ***Continue***

Tip: *Notice that you can also set the layer from the pulldown options in the Leaders panel.*

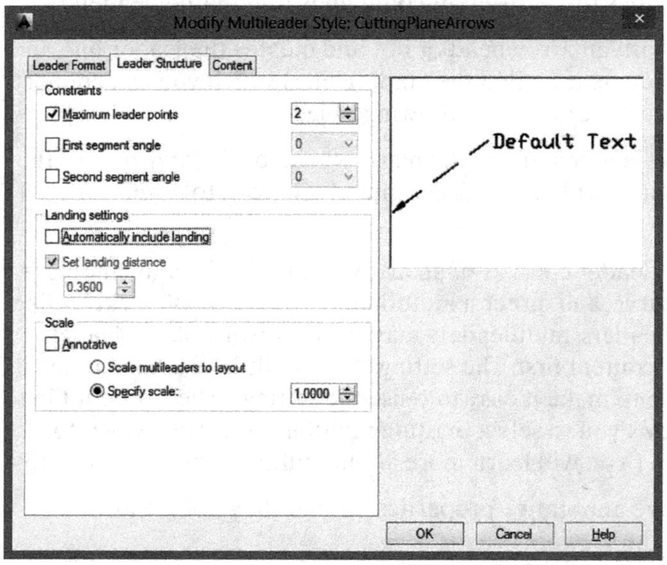

Figure 9.8

Use the Modify Multileader Style dialog box to set up the appearance for your special cutting plane line leader.

The Leader Format tab lets you select the shape for the leader line: Splined or Straight, so that you can make a curved leader or straight lines (like the leaders you have drawn so far). You will leave this set to straight. The Arrowhead pull-down lets you select the style of arrowhead, including none. You can also specify a user arrow style from a file you select, which is useful for Architectural drawings that use stylish arrows and labels for their cutting plane lines. Leave the settings for color, arrow size, etc. set to the defaults.

Click: ***Leader Structure tab*** *so that it appears uppermost as shown in Figure 9.8.*

The Leader Structure lets you set a Maximum Number of Leader Points. The default is 3. This allows you to draw leaders with two line segments and then move on to the text prompt portion of the command. You can set the number higher to make more complicated leaders; however, most engineering leaders are straight line leaders with only two segments. You can define the angles at which the leader segments must be drawn.

The new leader style will have a maximum of two segments. It will not use a landing line.

Click: ***to unselect Automatically include landing***

Notice the image tile at the right updates to show no landing line.

Click: ***Content tab***

The Content tab appears on top, as shown in Figure 9.9. The pull down list for Multileader type allows you to select from Mtext, Block and None. The default option is Mtext; you have a similar option to create text with QLeader. It lets you create multiple lines of text. Choosing

Block lets you select a block to be added to the end of the leader, as you will in Tutorial 13. The None option lets you draw a leader line with no text added to the end. You will use the None option to end the Leader command when you draw the leaders for cutting plane lines.

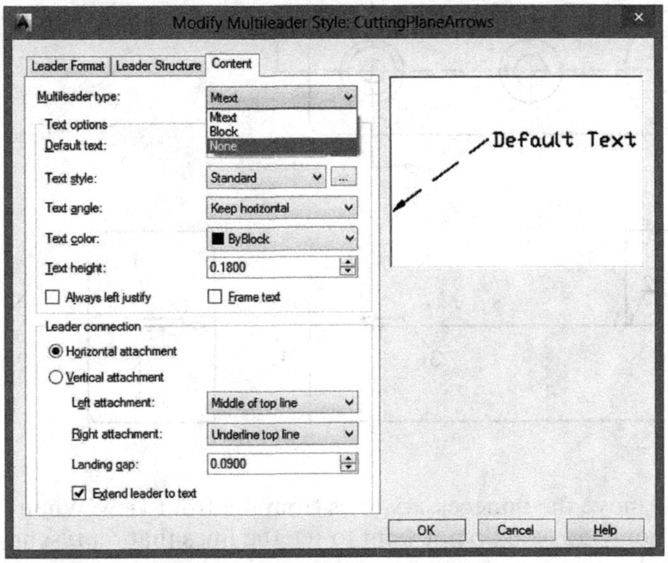

Figure 9.9

*Click: **None** from the pull down list for Multileader type*

The choices disappear and the image tile updates show a line and arrow.

*Click: **OK** to exit the Modify Multileader Style dialog box*

*Click: **Set Current** to make this the current style*

*Click: **Close** to exit the Multileader Style Manager dialog box*

Now you are ready to draw some arrow and line segments on to the ends of the cutting plane lines. Draw the lines on layer Cutting_Plane. After drawing the leaders, you add text labeling the cutting plane lines, using the Text command. You will start the leader with the landing line on the cutting plane and pick second the end with the arrow.

*On your own, turn **Ortho on**.*

*Click: **Multileader button***

Specify leader arrowhead location or [pre enter Text/leader Landing first/Content first/Options] <Content first>: ***L [Enter]***

Specify leader landing location or [pre enter Text/leader arrowHead first/Content first/Options] <Options>: ***use Snap and select the end of line A-A***

Specify leader arrowhead location: ***click past the end of line A-A***

The line ending in an arrow appears in your drawing; see Figure 9.10.

Repeat these steps to create a leader for the other end of cutting plane line A-A and for the ends of line B-B.

*Use the **Text** command to add the label A to both ends of cutting plane line A-A. Add the label B to both ends of cutting plane line B-B.*

Tip: *MLEADER has a handy option where you can select an existing mtext object from which the leader will extend. At the MLEADER command prompt, choose **Content** first: and then choose the select **M**text option and pick the text.*

Tip: *If you see the option Specify leader arrowhead location or [pre enter Text/**leader Landing first**/Content first/Options], you will need to type **L** [Enter] to select to start with the landing line first. Otherwise the arrow will be first.*

Tip: *The Leader command will not draw the arrow if the first line segment of the leader is too short. The first line segment must be longer than the current arrowhead size. You can set the arrowhead size with the dimensioning variables that you learned to use in Tutorial 7.*

Tip: *You can easily insert arrowheads at the end of a cutting plane line by making your own arrowhead block. A quick way to make a block for arrowheads is to explode a leader line and make a block from its arrowhead. You can also use a Polyline with a zero starting width and larger ending width to create an arrowhead from scratch*

Tip: *Use a crossing box to make selecting the hidden lines in the front view easier.*

When completed, your leader lines should look like the ones shown in Figure 9.10.

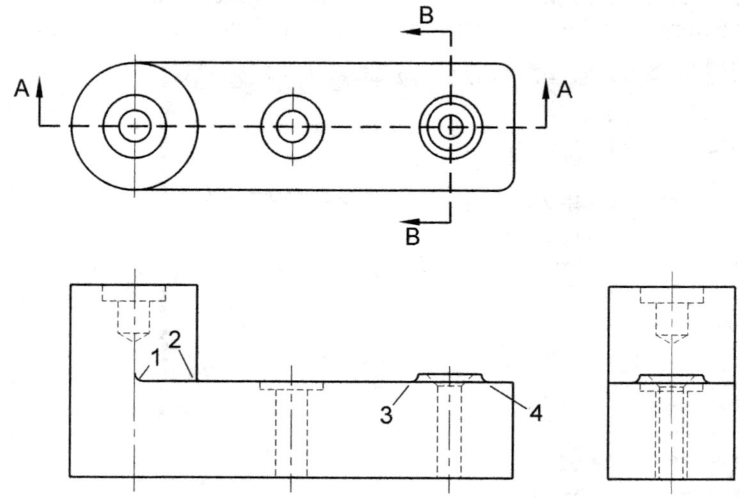

Figure 9.10

Next, you will remove the unnecessary lines from the front view. When you draw a section view, you do not want to see the lines that represent intersections and surfaces on the outside of the object.

*Turn **off** the **Grid** for easier viewing.*

*Use **Zoom to enlarge** the view to help select the points.*

*Use **Trim** to remove the following:*

the runout (or curve that represents the blending of two surfaces) labeled 1 in Figure 9.10

the portion of the line to the left of point 2

the solid line from point 3 to point 4, which defines the surface in front of the boss.

Your drawing should be similar to that in Figure 9.11.

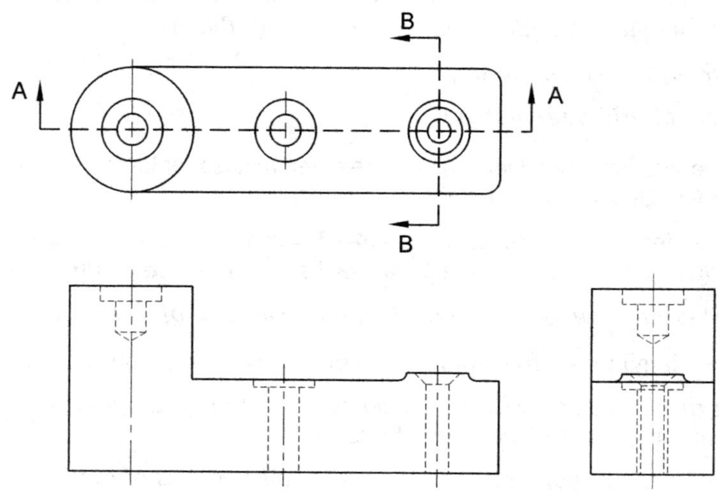

Figure 9.11

Changing Hidden Lines to Visible

In the section view, the interior details become visible. You will use the Layer Control to change the layer of the hidden lines to VISIBLE.

Select: ***all the hidden lines in the front view*** *(their grips appear)*

Click: ***to pull down the Layer Control***

Click: ***on Layer VISIBLE*** *to move the selected lines to that layer*

Press: ***[Esc]*** *to unselect the objects*

Now all the hidden lines in the front view have been changed to layer VISIBLE. Your drawing should now be similar to Figure 9.12.

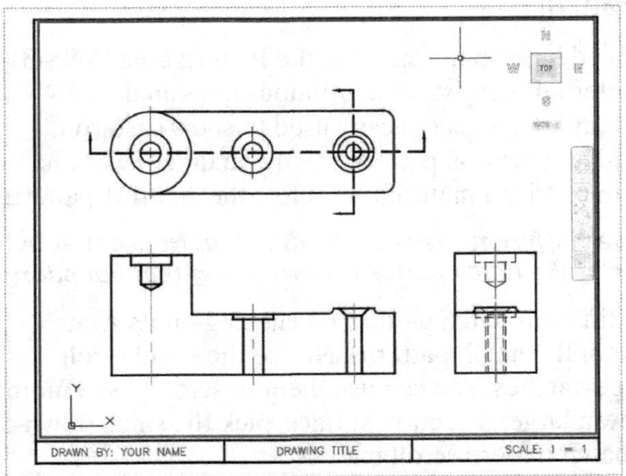

Figure 9.12

If you have zoomed your drawing, use Zoom Previous to return to the original size.

Hatching for sections should be on its own layer and should be plotted with a thin line. Having the hatch on its own layer is useful so that you can freeze it if you do not want it displayed while you are working on the drawing. In the drawing you started from, a separate layer for the hatching has already been created. Its color is red, and its linetype is CONTINUOUS.

Click: ***HATCH*** *to set it current using the Layer Control*

Using Hatch

Hatching uses a series of lines, dashes, or dots to form a pattern. The Hatch command fills an area with a pattern or solid fill. It creates *associative hatching*, which means that, if the area selected as the hatch boundary is changed, the hatching updates to fill the new area. Associative hatching is the default for the Hatch command. If you update the selected boundary so that it no longer forms a closed area, the hatching will no longer be associative. Hatch helps you choose the boundary for the pattern by selecting from its various boundary selection options.

Click: ***Hatch button*** *from the Draw toolbar*

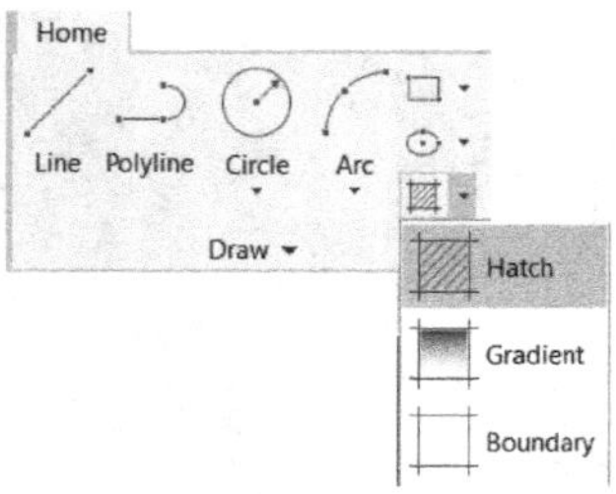

The Hatch Contextual tab appears across the top of your screen as shown in Figure 9.13. The Associative check box in the Options area at the right of the dialog box should indicate that associative hatching is turned on.

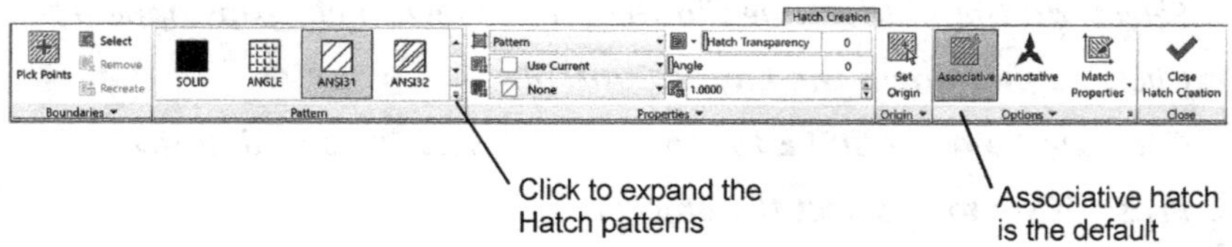

Figure 9.13

Selecting the Hatch Pattern

You can select predefined hatch patterns from the Pattern area. ANSI31 is the default hatch pattern. It consists of continuous lines angled at 45° and spaced about 1/16" apart, and is typically used to show cast iron materials. It is also used as a general pattern when you do not want to use the hatch pattern to specify a material. To select the ANSI31 pattern,

Move your cursor over different areas of the drawing. Notice that as you do so, a preview of the hatch pattern shows filling that boundary.

You can also select a different hatch pattern by clicking on its swatch tile (showing a picture of the hatch pattern). Notice the small scroll bars to the right of the swatches. You can use them to scroll to see more hatch patterns. To show a larger selection at once, pick the small downward arrow near the hatch pattern scroll bar.

Click: ***to expand Hatch Pattern***

The expanded hatch patterns, shown in Figure 9.14, appears on your screen. You can use it to preview hatch patterns by looking at a sample of their appearance.

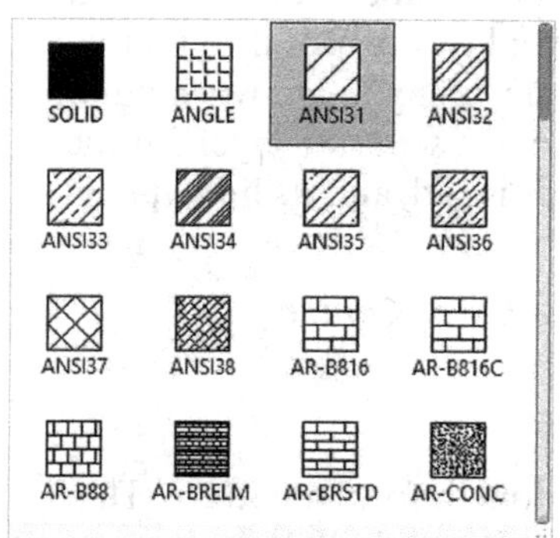

Figure 9.14

There are many standard hatch patterns available. In addition to predefined hatch patterns, you can use *custom hatch patterns* that you previously created and stored in the file *acad.pat* or another *.pat* file of your own making. You can make *user-defined hatch patterns* more complex by setting the linetype for the layer on which you will create the hatch. Remember to refer to the AutoCAD online help for more information about any of the commands described in these tutorials.

After you have looked at some of the hatch patterns,

Click: ***ANSI31*** *as the hatch pattern*

Angling the Hatch Pattern

The Angle input allows you to specify a rotation angle for the hatch pattern. You can do so by typing a value, or dragging the slider to change the angle. The default is 0 degrees, or no rotation of the pattern. In the hatch pattern you selected, ANSI31, the lines are already at an angle of 45°. Any angle you choose in the Angle area will be added to the chosen pattern; for example, if you added a rotation angle of 10 degrees to your current pattern, the lines would be drawn at an angle of 55 degrees.

Try some values and test the appearance by moving your cursor over the drawing to show the effect on the previewing hatch. Leave the default value of **0** ° for now.

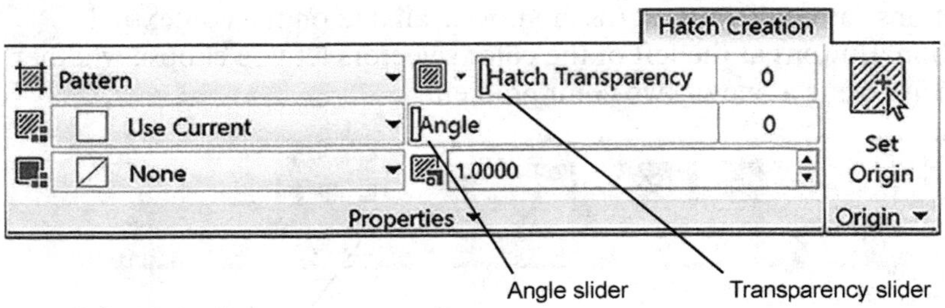

Figure 9.15

Hatch Transparency

You can use the slider to make the hatching more or less transparent. If you will be hatching over the top of other drawing entities, changing the transparency can be helpful. For now, leave it set to 0.

Scaling the Hatch Pattern

The Scale input increases or decreases the sizing of the hatched pattern. The hatch pattern is similar in some ways to a linetype. Hatch patterns are stored in an external file, with the spacing set at some default value. Usually the default scale of 1.0000 is the correct size for drawings that will be plotted full scale, resulting in hatched lines that are about 1/16" apart. If the views will be plotted at a smaller scale, half-size for instance, you will need to increase the spacing for the hatch by setting the scale to a larger value so that the lines of the hatch are not as close together. For this drawing, you will not need to change the scale of the hatch pattern. Hatch patterns can also be annotative, so that multiple scales versions of the pattern are stored.

Change the value to 2 and inspect the previewed appearance in your drawing.

When you are done ***return the scale to 1****.*

Tip: *Hatch can have an annotative property so that its scale is based on the Viewport Scaling Factor.*

Note: *In early versions of AutoCAD, it was possible to space the hatch lines too closely together, causing performance problems. Now there is a limit to prevent creating a huge number of hatch lines in a single operation. You can change the maximum allowed number of hatch lines with the HPMAXLINES system variable.*

Warning: *Be cautious when specifying a smaller scale for the hatch pattern. If the hatch lines are very close together, the AutoCAD software will take a long time calculating them.*

Gradient Fills

A *gradient fill* fills an area with a smooth transition between darker and lighter shades of one color, or transitions between two colors. While gradients are not frequently used in engineering drawings, they can add the appearance of shading or interest to logos, maps, and other graphics.

*Click: **Gradient** from the Properties area of the Hatch contextual tab as shown in Figure 9.16*

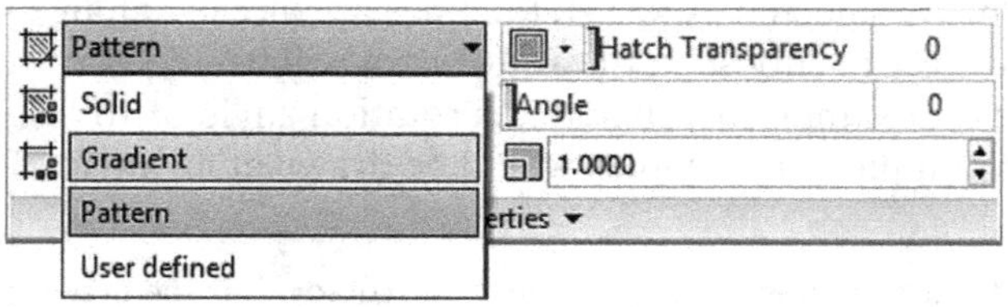

Figure 9.16

Options for gradient patterns are now available on the contextual ribbon. Buttons at the left of the color selectors let you choose whether you are using a one or two color gradient.

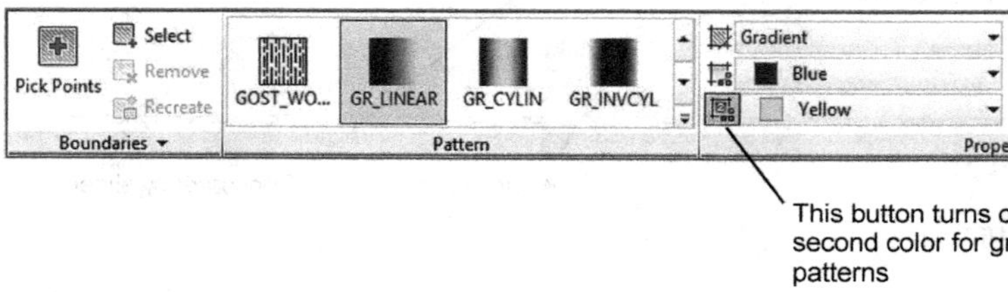

Figure 9.17

*Click: **to expand the gradient** patterns*

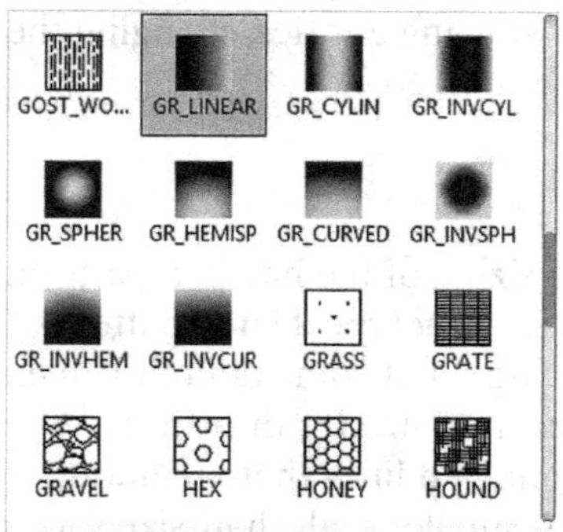

Figure 9.18

*On your own, experiment with the colors and styles of gradient. Preview them by moving your cursor over some areas inside the drawing. **Do not add any gradient fills to your drawing at this time**.*

*Return the selection to Pattern (as opposed to Gradient). Make sure that the **ANSI31 pattern** is still selected.*

You can also make hatches and gradients transparent. One useful application for gradient or solid colors is to make them transparent when filling large areas in color maps, charts, and architectural drawings.

Options for Hatch Boundaries

The Boundaries area at the right side of the Hatch Creation tab lets you select among the different methods used to specify the area to hatch. *Pick Points* allows you to click inside a closed area to be hatched. *Select Objects* lets you select drawing objects to form a closed boundary for the hatching. Clicking the small downward arrow to expand the Boundaries panel lets you select more options for the creation of the hatch boundary.

Click: ***to expand the Boundaries area***

Click: ***to expand the Retaining Boundary objects options** as shown in Figure 9.19*

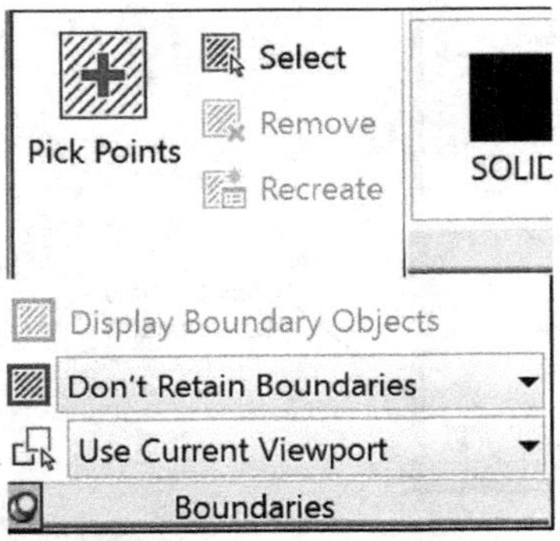

Figure 9.19

You have the option to retain the hatch boundary and have it created using a polyline, or to retain the boundary and have it be created as a region (you will learn more about regions in later tutorials). You can also choose not to retain the hatch boundary.

In order to easily update the hatch when you make changes to the drawing objects, you will retain the hatch boundary.

Click: ***Retain Boundaries - Polyline***

You also use the boundary area to choose whether to place the hatch in the drawing by directly clicking points inside the areas to hatch, or to select objects in the drawing.

When you clicked the Hatch button, in addition to the ribbon changing to show the contextual tab, the command prompt shows options. You should still see the command prompt line for the hatch command active. If not, select the command again, then use the settings option as follows:

Pick internal point or [Select objects/Draw/Undo/seTtings]: ***T [Enter]***

The Hatch dialog box which was available in previous versions of AutoCAD appears on your screen as shown in Figure 9.20. If you have the ribbon turned off you will see this dialog box instead of the Create Hatch contextual tab.

Tip: *The Hatch command shows different command line options based on which method was used last. You may see additional options, but they should still have* seTtings *as a choice. Remember type the capitalized letter(s) for the selection or use your mouse to click it. Restart the Hatch command if needed.*

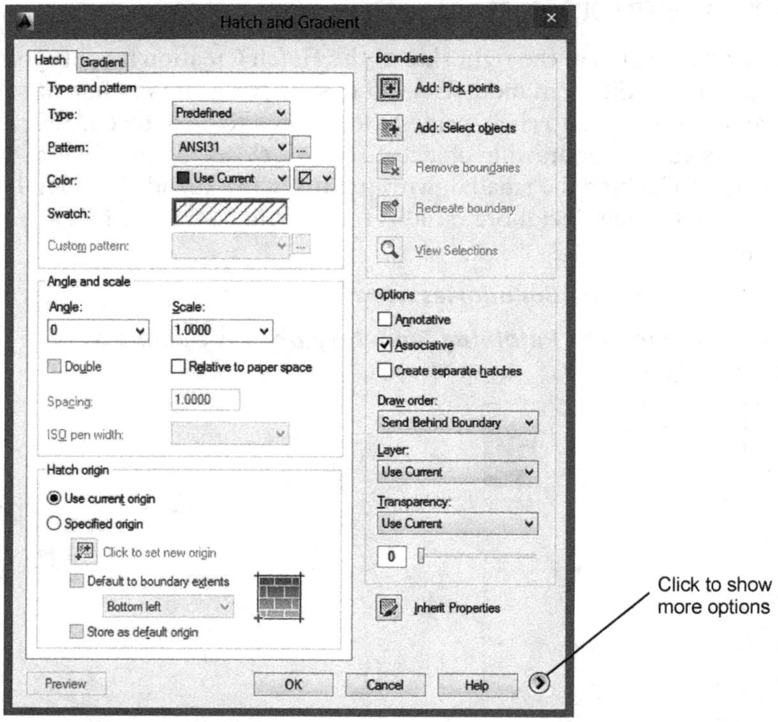

Figure 9.20

Click: ***the right facing arrow at the bottom right of the dialog box*** *to show more options*

Figure 9.21 shows additional options for creating hatch boundaries. Notice that these can be accessed from the contextual tab also. By clicking the Retain boundaries box, you can save the AutoCAD generated hatch boundaries as one of two different types of objects: a polyline or a region (a region is a 2D enclosed area). When determining the hatch boundary, the software analyzes all the objects on the screen. This step can be time-consuming if you have a large drawing database. To define a different area to be considered for the hatch boundary, you would click the New button in the Boundary set area. You would then return to your drawing, where you could select the objects to form the new set. Using implied Windowing works well for this procedure.

You can use the Islands area to change the way islands inside the hatch area are treated. Observe the pictures above the radio buttons that describe the options. The selection Normal causes islands inside the hatched area to be alternately hatched and skipped, starting at the outer area. Choosing Outer causes only the outer area to be hatched; any islands inside are left unhatched. You can also choose Ignore; then, the entire inside is hatched, regardless of the structure. Leave this area of the dialog box set to Normal.

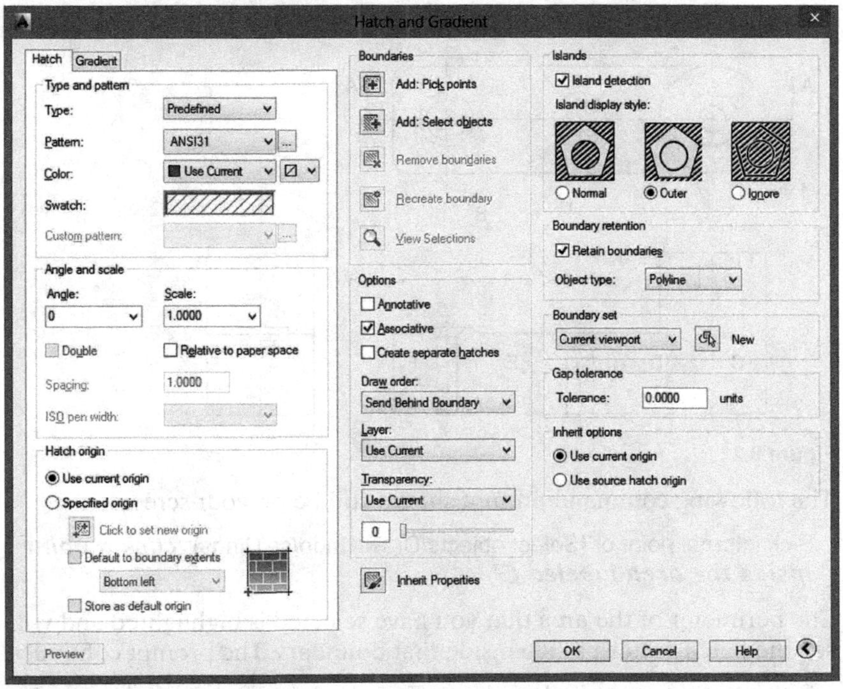

Figure 9.21

Click: ***Cancel*** *to exit the Hatch and Gradient dialog box*

The contextual tab for hatch should still be on your screen.

On your own, explore the Help for the Hatch command. Review the options for setting a Gap Tolerance and setting the Hatch Origin Points. ***Close the Help screen*** *to return to the command prompt.*

Adding the Hatch Pattern

You use the Pick Points method to specify the area to fill with the hatch pattern. (To use the Select Objects method, you would return to your drawing and click on the objects that form the boundary.) The program will determine the boundary around the areas you clicked. (If there are islands inside the area that you did not want hatched, you would use Remove Islands to choose them after you have clicked the area to be hatched.) When you are finished selecting, you will press [Enter] to indicate that you are finished selecting and want to continue with the Hatch command.

You can use any standard selection method to select the objects. Refer to Figure 9.22 as you make selections.

Tip: *Turn Grid off before previewing, as it can make reading the hatch pattern difficult*

Tip: *You can pick Create Separate Hatches from the Options area of the contextual tab if you would like each area you pick to be created as a separate hatch, so that they can be edited individually later.*

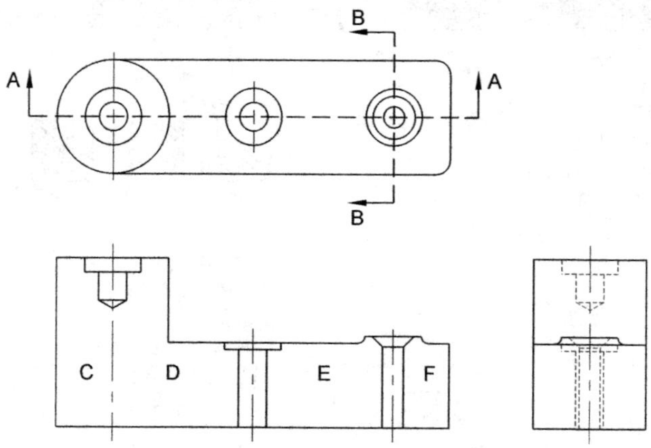

Figure 9.22

The following command prompt should still be on your screen.

Pick internal point or [Select objects/Draw/Undo/seTtings]: ***click a point inside the area labeled C***

The perimeter of the area that you have selected is highlighted and you see the hatch pattern filling inside that boundary. The prompt continues,

Pick internal point or [Select objects/Draw/Undo/seTtings]: ***click area D***

Pick internal point or [Select objects/Draw/Undo/seTtings]: ***click area E***

Pick internal point or [Select objects/Draw/Undo/seTtings]: ***click area F***

Pick internal point or [Select objects/Draw/Undo/seTtings]: ***[Enter]***

The areas that you selected become hatched in your drawing. Your drawing should now look like the one in Figure 9.23.

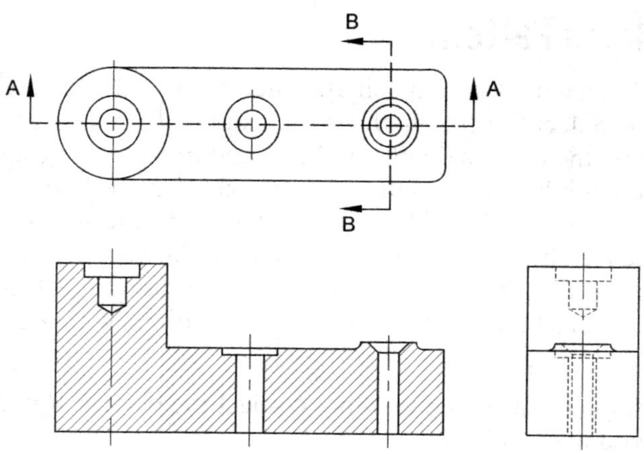

Figure 9.23

Creating the Side Section View

Make room to the right of the existing views to draw the side section view.

*Use **Pan Realtime** (you can press and hold the mouse scroll wheel to drag the view close to the left hand side of the viewport).*

Reorient the Side View

One of the alternative positions for a side view is rotated and lined up with the top view. You will use the Rotate button from the ribbon Home tab, Modify panel to reorient the side view so that you can align it with the top view, as shown in Figure 9.21.

*On your own, verify that **Snap is on**.*

Click: ***Rotate button***

Select objects: ***select all of the objects in the side view with implied Crossing***

Select objects: ***[Enter]***

Specify base point: ***click the top left corner of the side view***

Specify rotation angle or [Copy/Reference] <0>: ***90 [Enter]***

Now you will align the rotated side view with the top view. You will enter the selection option **P** to reselect the previous selection set.

Click: ***Move button***

Select objects: ***P [Enter]***

Select objects: ***[Enter]***

Specify base point or [Displacement] <Displacement>: ***click the upper left corner of the rotated object***

Specify second point or <use first point as displacement>: ***click a point on the snap that lines up with the top line in the top view***

Your drawing should now look like that in Figure 9.24.

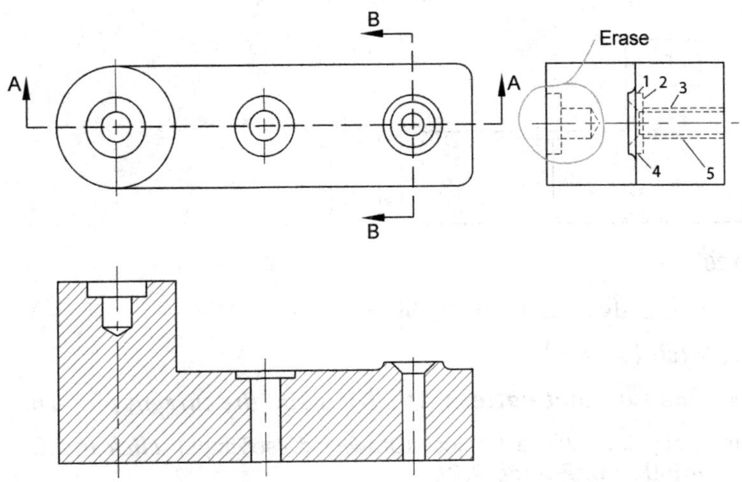

Figure 9.24

On your own, ***turn Snap off.***

Erase *the unnecessary hidden lines (those for the counterbored hole and lines 1 through 5.)*

Change the hidden lines for the countersunk hole in the rotated side view to ***layer VISIBLE.***

The countersunk hole is the only one that will show in the section view. Your drawing should now look like Figure 9.25.

Tip: *Although you won't always be instructed to do so, remember to save your work frequently while creating drawings. The AutoCAD autosave feature saves automatically to a file named auto.sv$. You set the time interval for the autosave feature with the system variable Savetime. The default is to save every 120 minutes. You would not want to lose two hours of work, so you should set Savetime to save automatically at shorter intervals. To make such a change, type SAVETIME at the command prompt and enter the new number in minutes. However, do not rely on automatic saves. Save your file whenever you have made a major change that you want to keep or about every 10 minutes otherwise.*

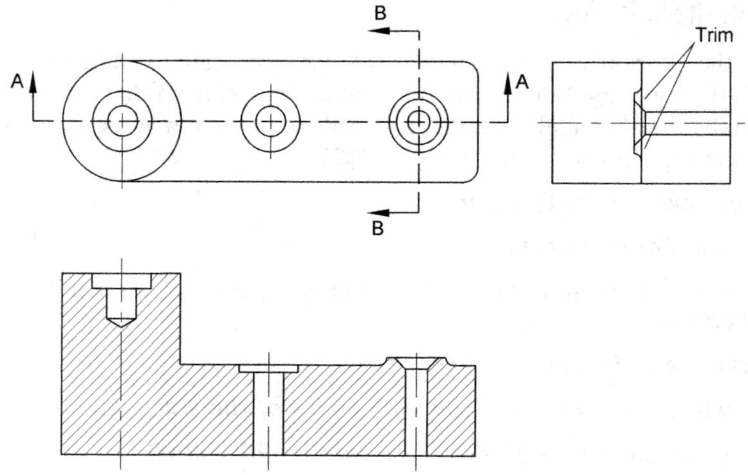

Figure 9.25

Tip: *You may need to use Zoom Window to enlarge the area on the screen. When you are finished erasing and changing the lines, use Zoom Previous to return the area to its original size.*

Use the ***Trim*** *command on your own to* ***remove the visible line*** *that crosses the outer edge of the boss.*

When you are finished trimming, your drawing should look like Figure 9.26.

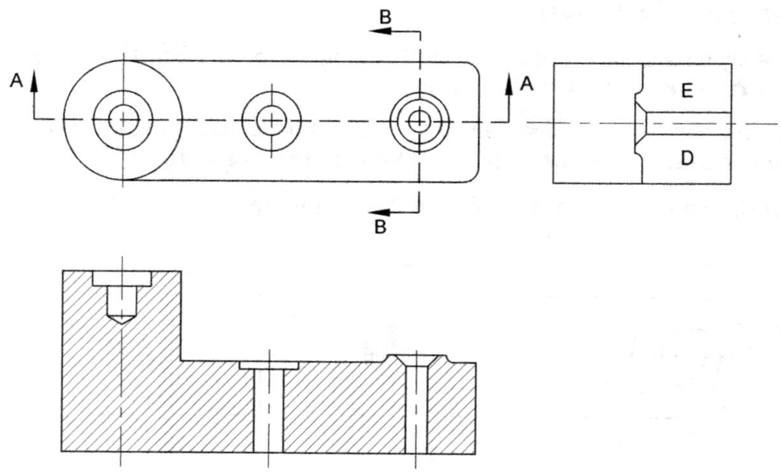

Figure 9.26

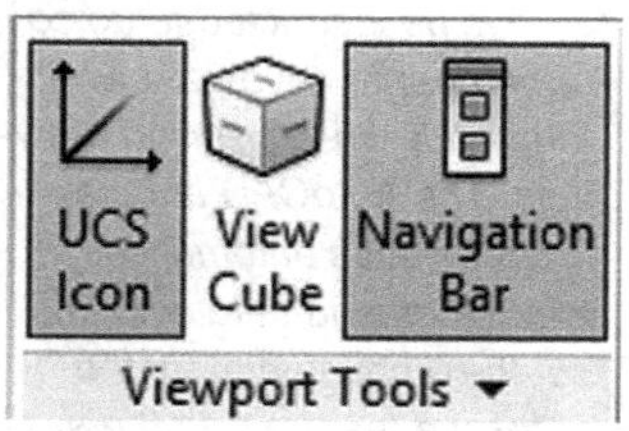

Tip: *If the View Cube is on, it may be in your way for creating the hatch. If so, use the ribbon View tab, Viewport Tools panel to click and turn it off as shown.*

Now you are ready to add the hatching.

Click: ***Hatch button***

Check to be sure that ***pattern ANSI31*** *is still the current pattern.*

Pick internal point or [Select objects/Draw/Undo/seTtings]: ***click inside area D labeled in Figure 9.26***

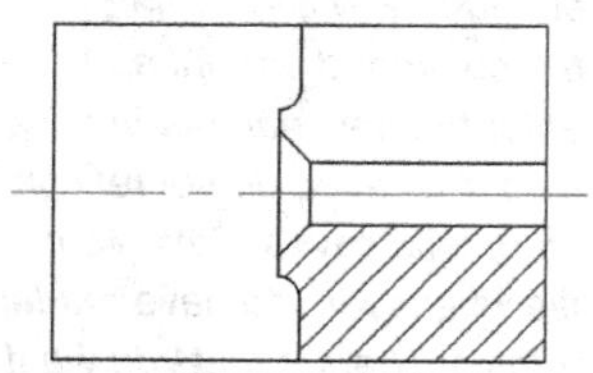

Figure 9.27

The hatching in your drawing should look like that in Figure 9.30.

Hatch Command, Draw Option

Tip: *The Draw option is useful for large areas where you do not want hatching to fill the entire area—for example, to represent earth around a foundation on an architectural drawing, or in mechanical drawings to hatch only the perimeter of a large shape.*

Next you will use the Hatch command Draw option to draw a boundary for the hatching. This is useful when you want to hatch a shape that is not inside a boundary, or is not bordered by other shapes. It makes it quick to put some hatching in a freeform area.

At the Hatch command prompt,

Pick internal point or [Select objects/Draw/Undo/seTtings]: ***D [Enter]***

Specify start point or [picK internal point/Select objects/Rectangle/Circle/Mode/seTtings]: ***Click a location a blank area of your drawing.***

Specify the next point or [Arc/Length/Undo/Exit] <Exit>: ***click another location from your drawing***

Specify the next point or [Arc/Close/Length/Undo/Exit] <Exit>: ***click another location from your drawing. You now see the hatch appearing in the shape you defined. Continue to choose a few more points.***

While still at the Draw option prompt of the Hatch command, try the Arc feature.

Specify the next point or [Arc/Length/Undo/Exit] <Exit>: ***A [Enter]***

Specify endpoint of arc (hold Ctrl to switch direction) or [Angle/CEnter/Close/Direction/Line/Radius/Second pt/Undo]: ***click a location and notice you are now drawing an arc.***

Next, use the Close option to join back to the starting point. It is **important to use Close**, do not click the first point again.

Specify endpoint of arc (hold Ctrl to switch direction) or [Angle/CEnter/CLose/Direction/Line/Radius/Second pt/Undo]: ***C [Enter]***

When the shape is completely defined, the lines drawing the perimeter are removed from the screen. Your hatch should look like Figure 9.28 in general, depending on your selections.

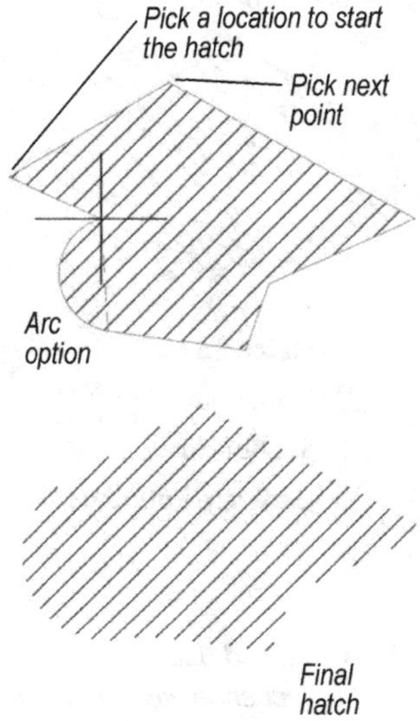

Figure 9.28

Click the Close Hatch Creation button from the Hatch Creation ribbon to end making hatches.

On your own restart the hatch command and notice the command prompt — It still shows the Hatch command Draw options.

When the Hatch command Draw option starts the command line shows important information including the Mode.

Current hatch mode: Area

Specify start point or [picK internal point/Select objects/Rectangle/Circle/Mode/seTtings]: ***M [Enter]***

Specify draw hatch mode [Area/Path] <Area>: ***P [Enter]***

Current hatch mode: Path, Width = 0.2500, Alignment = Center

Specify start point or [picK internal point/Select objects/Rectangle/Circle/ALignment/Width/Mode/seTtings]: ***Click a location from your screen.***

Specify the next point or [ALignment/Width/Arc/Length/Undo/Exit] <Exit>: ***Click more locations.***

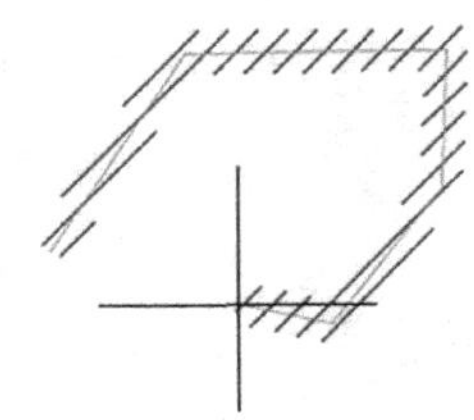

Figure 9.29

Notice that now the hatch is centered on both sides of the path you draw as in Figure 9.29.

Tip: *Click on a hatch to select it, then right-click to show the shortcut menu. You can use the Generate Boundary selection to create a polyline around your drawn hatch.*

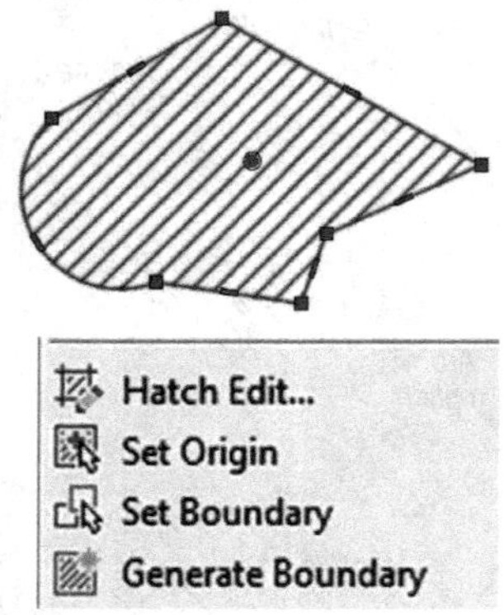

On your own, press [Enter] to exit drawing the hatch using a path.

Set the Mode back to Area.

To return to hatching areas by picking internal points as you used on the front and side views in the drawing you will type K at the prompt.

Specify start point or [picK internal point/Select objects/Rectangle/Circle/Mode/seTtings]: ***K [Enter]***

Pick internal point or [Select objects/Draw/Undo/seTtings]:

Erase your drawn hatches.

Use one of the hatch techniques you learned to complete the hatching in area E.

Save and Plot your drawing. Before you plot, be sure to switch to paper space.

If you need help plotting, refer to Tutorials 3 and 5.

If you zoomed your drawing and it isn't fitting inside the border, try using the Zoom command with the scale factor .75XP to set the scale. Update the scale noted for the drawing to .75:1.

You can also add a custom scale of .75 to 1 to the Viewport Scale items on the status bar and then use that to set the scale.

Tip: *You could use the Endpoint object snap with the draw option to hatch area E.*

Tip: *You can also create open, irregular hatch boundaries by typing the -Hatch command at the command prompt and selecting the W for the draW option. This is not the same as the Draw option you previously used.*

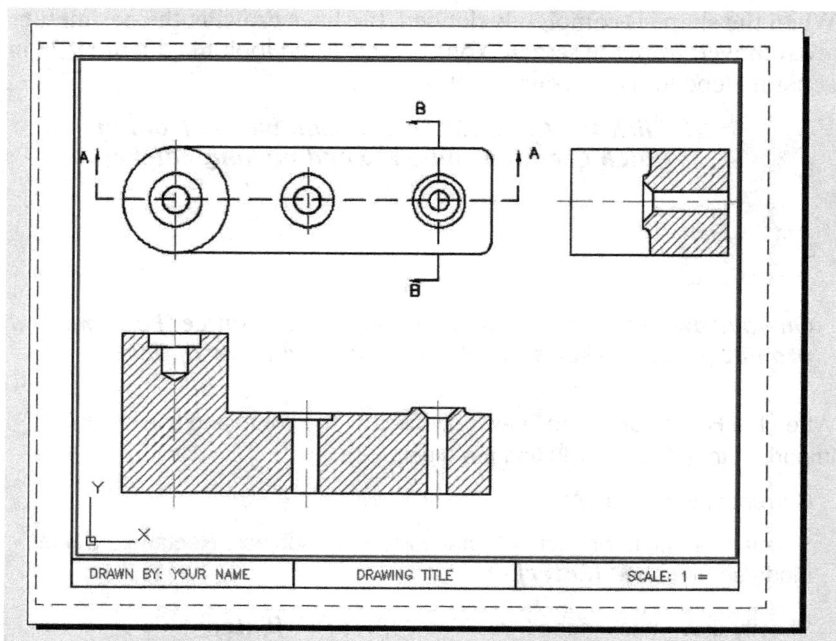

Figure 9.30

Solid Fill

Sometimes you want areas of the drawing to be filled in with a solid color instead of a hatch pattern or gradient. The Hatch command also lets you solidly fill an area. Use solid fill sparingly in your drawings because some printers and plotters do not show it correctly. Many large engineering drawings are still printed in one color, and large gray areas do not improve the drawing. You will add a rectangle on layer DIM and add solid hatch inside it.

*Return your drawing to **Model space** if it is not selected.*

*Make **DIM** the current layer.*

*Click: **Rectangle button***

Draw a small rectangle overlapping the lower right of the front section view as shown in Figure 9.31.

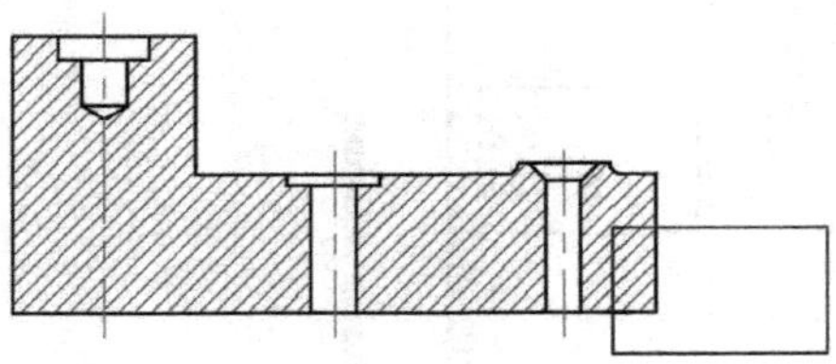

Figure 9.31

*Click: **Hatch button***

The contextual tab for hatch creation appears on your screen. This time instead of selecting inside the boundaries to hatch, you will use the option to Select Boundary objects.

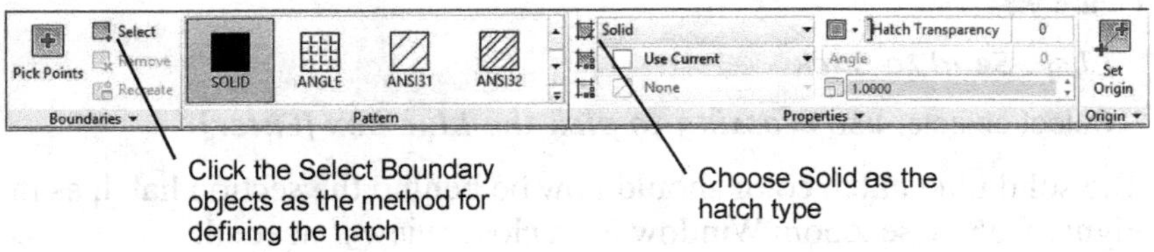

Figure 9.32

*Click: **Select button** from the Boundaries area (Figure 9.32)*

*Click: **Solid** from the Hatch type*

Click internal point or [Select objects/seTtings]: ***S [Enter]***

Select objects or [picK internal point/Undo/seTtings]: ***click on the edge of the new rectangle [Enter]***

The rectangle is filled with a solid color, similar to Figure 9.33. The rectangle is on layer DIM, so it is blue.

On your own, try the Hatch Transparency slider to adjust the transparency of the solid fill. Restore the transparency to 0 when you are finished.

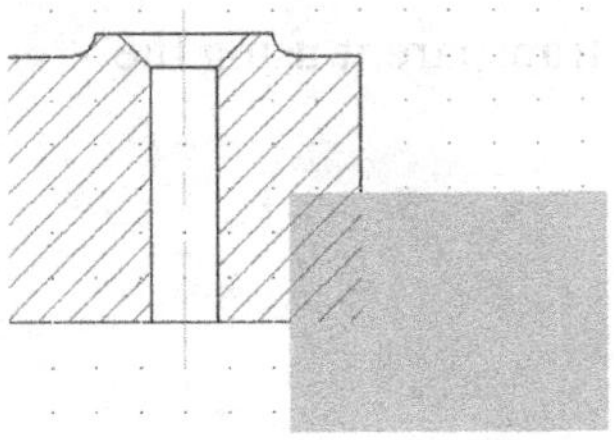

Figure 9.33

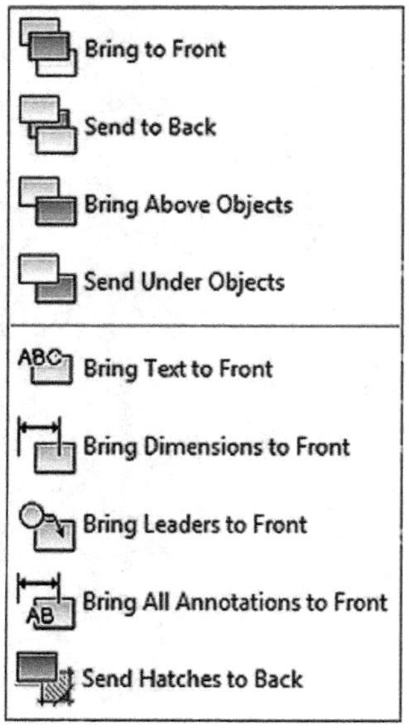

Using Draworder

The Draworder option can be used to specify which object is on top when objects overlap.

Click: ***to pin the Modify panel*** *so it stays expanded.*

Click: ***to expand the Draworder flyout*** *as shown in Figure 9.34*

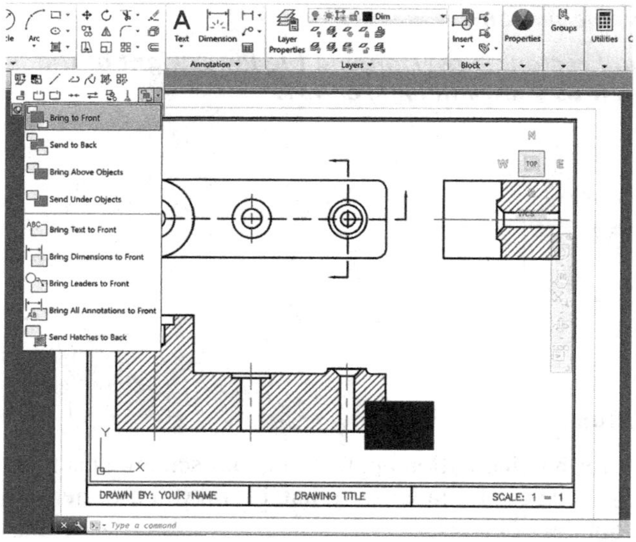

Figure 9.34

Click: ***Send to Back***

Select objects: ***use crossing to pick the blue box [Enter]***

The solid blue hatch color should now be behind the section hatch as in Figure 9.35. Use Zoom Window for a closer view if needed.

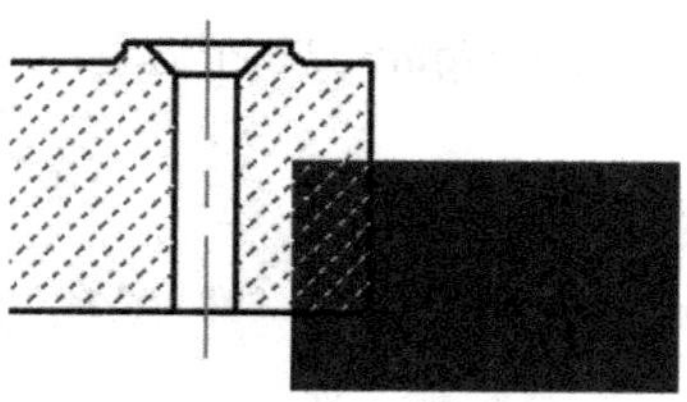

Figure 9.35

On your own, practice with the other draworder options: Send to Back, Bring to Front, Send Hatches to Back etc. When you are done, restore the previous Zoom if you changed it.

You can also click on hatches and make them transparent using the slider from the contextual tab.

Erase *the rectangle and solid hatch.*

Change the current layer back to ***HATCH.***

Tip: *You can also click on the Drawworder command from the Modify II toolbar, or by clicking Tools, Display Order from the Classic menu bar to change the draw order for objects that overlay.*

Tip: *If you have trouble selecting hatches and solid fills, try clicking on their edges, not in the middle of the area.*

Changing Associative Hatches

Hatching is associative. It automatically updates to continue to fill the boundary as it is stretched, moved, rotated, arrayed, scaled, or mirrored. You can also use grips to modify hatching in the drawing.

Next, you will stretch the top and front views to see how the hatching updates to fill the new area. Refer to Figure 9.36 for the points to select.

Check that you are in model space.

Click: ***Stretch button***

Select objects to stretch by crossing-window or crossing-polygon. . .

Select objects: ***click point 1***

Specify opposite corner: ***click point 2***

Select objects: ***[Enter]***

Specify base point or [Displacement] <Displacement>: ***use object snap to select the lower right corner of the front view (point 3)***

Specify second point or <use first point as displacement>: ***turn Snap off and turn Ortho on, then click to the right of the previous location***

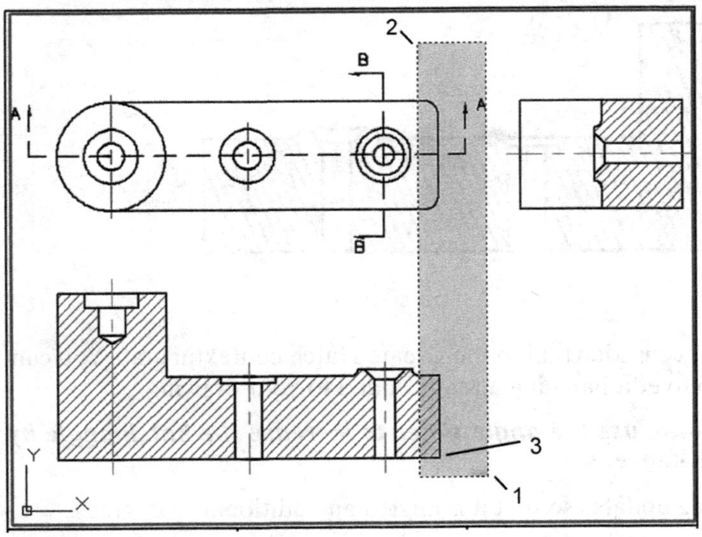

Figure 9.36

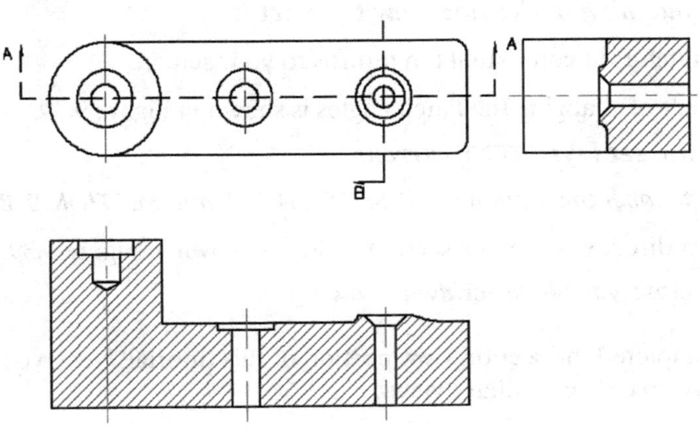

Figure 9.37

The objects selected by the crossing box are stretched, as shown in Figure 9.37. The hatching updates to fill the new boundary.

Hatchedit

You will now use the Hatchedit command to change the angle of the hatching. Because the angled edge of the countersunk hole is drawn at 45°, you will change the angle of the hatch pattern so that the hatch is not parallel to features in the drawing. (Having the hatch run parallel or perpendicular to a major drawing feature is not good technical drawing practice.) You will edit the hatch in the front view.

Click: ***the hatching in the front view*** *(it will appear highlighted)*

The Hatch Editor appears on your screen similar to Figure 9.38.

Tip: *You can double-click on an existing hatch to edit it quickly.*

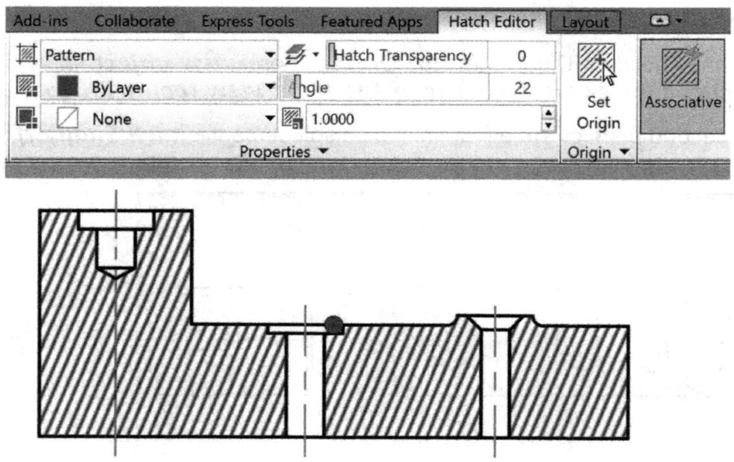

Figure 9.38

Its appearance is identical to the Create Hatch contextual tab. You can use this tab to edit hatching already added to your drawing.

On your own, ***use the angle slider to increase the hatch angle by about 15 degrees****.*

The hatching updates so that it is angled an additional 15 degrees.

Press: ***[Esc]*** *to deselect the hatch in the front view*

Click: ***the hatching in the side view to select it***

Again the Hatch Edit contextual tab returns to your screen.

The final result of changing the hatch angles is shown in Figure 9.39.

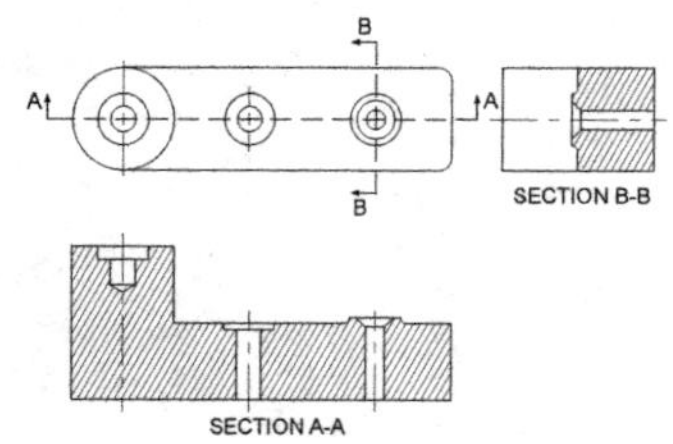

Figure 9.39

On your own, ***set layer TEXT current****.*

Use **Dtext** *to label the section views* ***SECTION A–A*** *and* ***SECTION B–B****.*

Place the text directly below the section views, as shown in Figure 9.39.

Save and close *your* ***bossect.dwg drawing.***

You have completed the section view portion of this tutorial. Next, you will learn how to create auxiliary views.

Auxiliary Views

An *auxiliary view* is an orthographic view of the object that has a line of sight different from the six *basic views* (front, top, right-side, rear, bottom, and left-side). Auxiliary views are most commonly used to show the true size of a slanted or oblique surface. Slanted and oblique surfaces are *foreshortened* in the basic views because they are tipped away from the viewing plane, causing their projected size in the view to be smaller than their actual size. An auxiliary view shows a surface true size when its line of sight is perpendicular to the surface.

You will learn to create auxiliary views first using 2D methods. You can easily project 2D auxiliary views from the basic orthographic views by rotating the snap or by aligning a new User Coordinate System.

Figure 9.40 shows three views of an object and an auxiliary view.

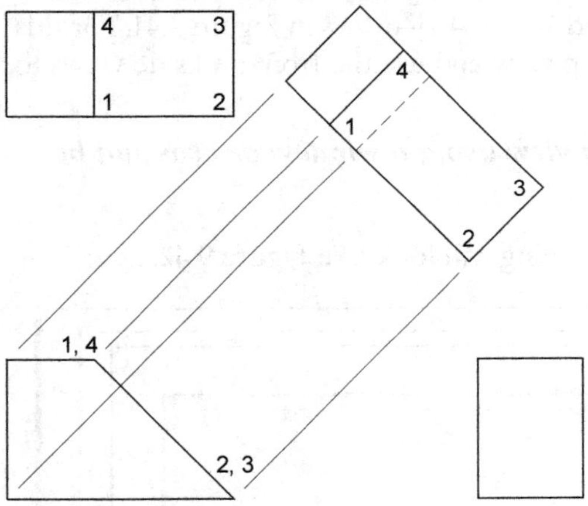

Figure 9.40

The surface defined by vertices 1–2–3–4 is inclined. It is perpendicular to the front viewing plane and shows on edge in the front view. Both the top and side views show foreshortened views of the surface.

The true size of surface 1–2–3–4 is projected in the auxiliary view by drawing projection lines perpendicular to the edge view of the surface, in this case the angled line in the front view. The width of the surface is measured from a *reference surface*, and transferred to the auxiliary view to complete the projection. Note that, as with the front, top, and side views, the auxiliary view shows the entire object as viewed from the line of sight perpendicular to that surface, causing the base of the object to show as a hidden line. Auxiliary views often use partial views that only show the surface of interest.

Drawing Auxiliary Views Using 2D

*Open the drawing **adapt4.dwg**, provided with the data files.*

*Save your drawing as **auxil1.dwg**.*

The orthographic views for the adapter appear similar to Figure 9.41.

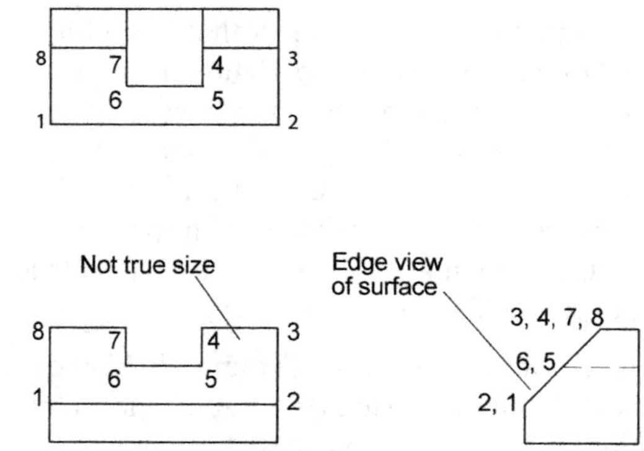

Figure 9.41

You will create an auxiliary view showing the true size of the inclined surface. The surface is labeled 1–2–3–4–5–6–7–8 in Figure 9.41. For this tutorial, you will erase the top view and use the front and side views to project the auxiliary view.

Select: ***all lines in the top view using a window or crossing box***

Press: ***[Delete]***

The lines are erased. Your drawing will look like Figure 9.42.

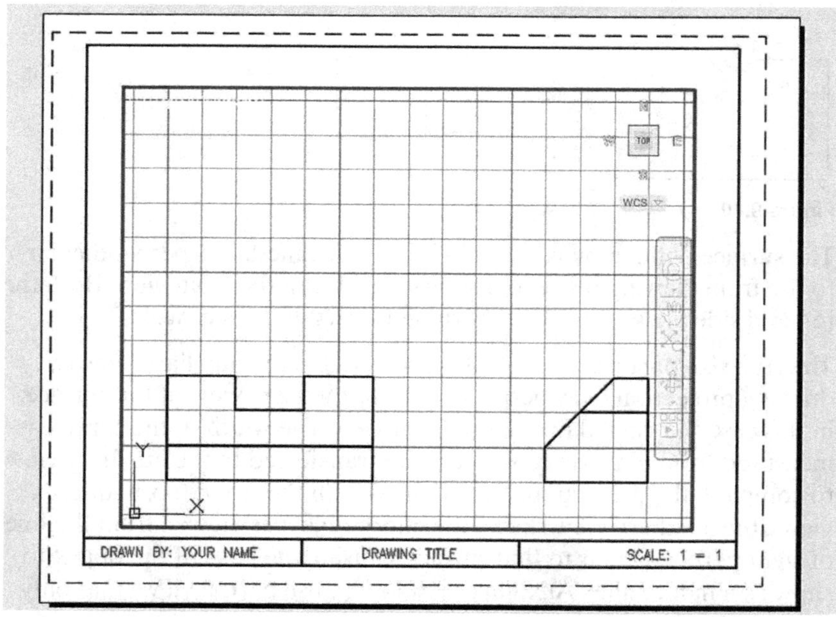

Figure 9.42

Click: ***Model tab*** *to show only model space*

Click: Show/Hide ***Lineweight button*** *from the status bar to hide the lineweights if they are shown.*

On your own, turn ***Snap off and turn Osnap Intersection on****.*

You will use object snaps to select the intersections in the next steps.

Aligning the UCS with the Angled Surface

Next, you will create a new UCS aligned with the angled surface to help you project lines perpendicular from the edge view of surface 1–2–3–4–5–6–7–8.

You can type the command UCS and use its options to create new user coordinate systems. You can *drag* the UCS icon to reorient the coordinate system. You will use the dragging method in the next steps.

Click: ***on the UCS icon in the lower right of the drawing area*** *so that its grips appear as shown in Figure 9.43*

Click the square grip at the origin to select it

Drag the UCS icon and click intersection A in Figure 9.42

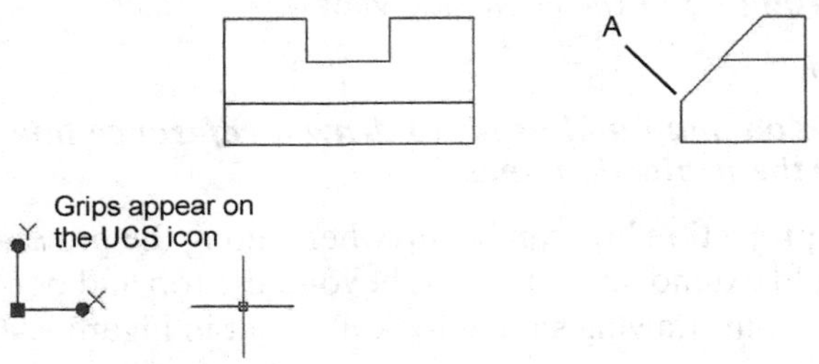

Figure 9.43

When you have finished moving the UCS, it should appear similar to Figure 9.44.

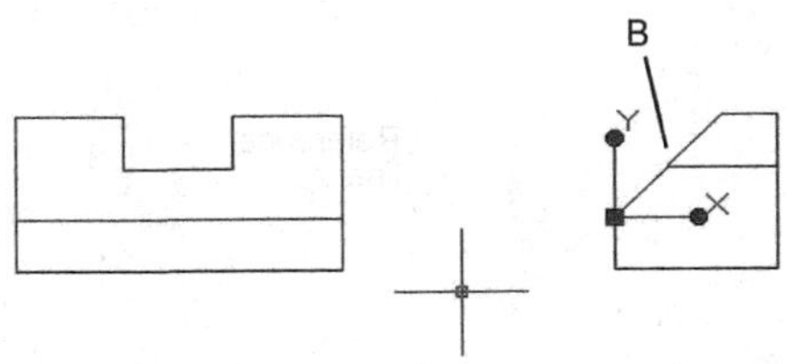

Figure 9.44

Next you will align the X axis with the angled surface. The grips should still be active on the UCS icon.

Click the circular grip at the end of the X axis to select it.

Drag the X-axis and click intersection B

The UCS icon should now be oriented as shown in Figure 9.45

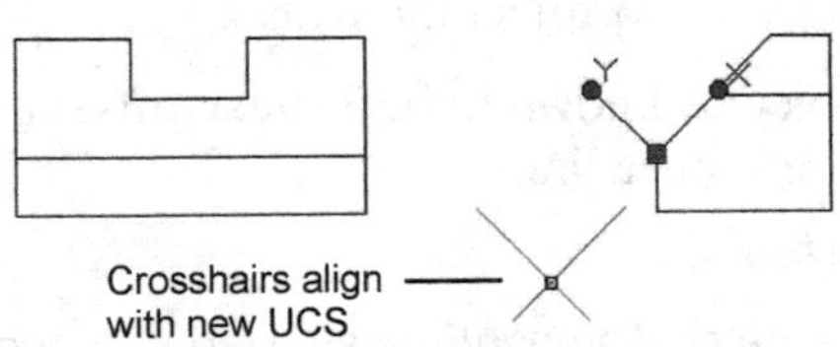

Figure 9.45

*Set **PROJECTION** as the **current** layer.*

*Turn **Ortho on**.*

*Make sure that **Snap is off**.*

Now you will draw rays from each intersection of the object in the side view into the open area of the drawing above the front view. You will click Ray from the Draw panel; if you need help creating rays, refer to Tutorial 4.

*Click: **Ray button** from the ribbon Home tab, Draw panel*

Specify start point: ***click intersection 1***

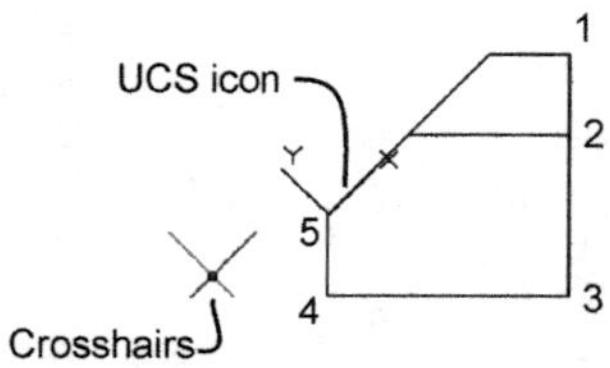

Specify through point: ***with Ortho on, click a point above and to the left of the side view***

Specify through point: ***[Enter]***

*On your own, restart the **Ray** command and **draw projection lines from points 2 through 5** in the right-side view.*

*Click: **Line button***

*On your own, **turn on Snap and use it to draw a reference line perpendicular to the projection lines**.*

The location of the projection line can be anywhere along the projection lines, but it should extend about 0.5 unit beyond the top and bottom projection lines. Your drawing should look like that in Figure 9.46.

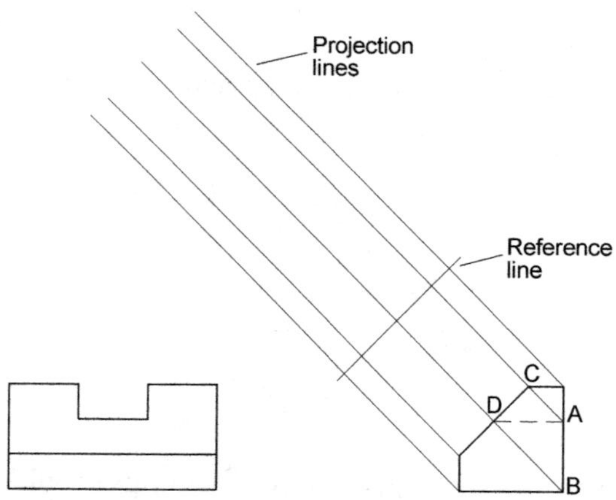

Figure 9.46

Note that the back edge of the slot (labeled A) and the lower right corner (labeled B) in the side view align with the projection lines through the corners of the angled surface (C and D) to produce a single projection line. If C and D did not align on the projection lines already created, you would need to project them also.

The width of the object is known to be 3. Next, offset a line 3 units from and parallel to the reference line.

*Click: **Offset button***

Specify offset distance or [Through/Erase/Layer] <Through>: ***3 [Enter]***

Select object to offset or [Exit/Undo] <Exit>: ***click the reference line,** as shown in Figure 9.46*

Specify point on side to offset or [Exit/Multiple/Undo] <Exit>: ***click a point anywhere to the left of the reference line***

Select object to offset or [Exit/Undo] <Exit>: ***[Enter]***

Your drawing should look like the one in Figure 9.47.

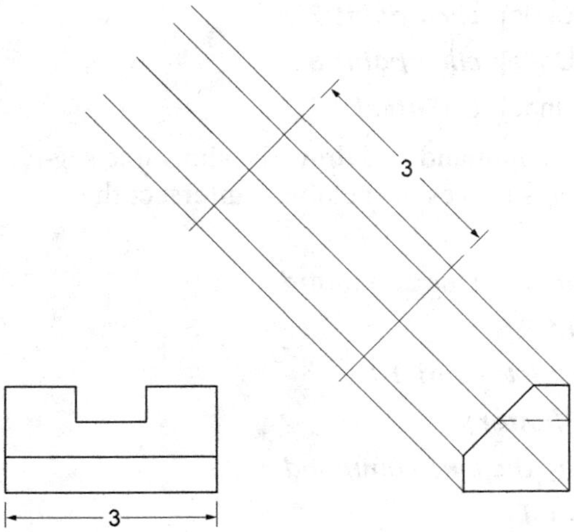

Figure 9.47

Add the width of the slot on your own by using **Offset** to create two more parallel lines, 1 unit apart.

Your drawing should look like that in Figure 9.48.

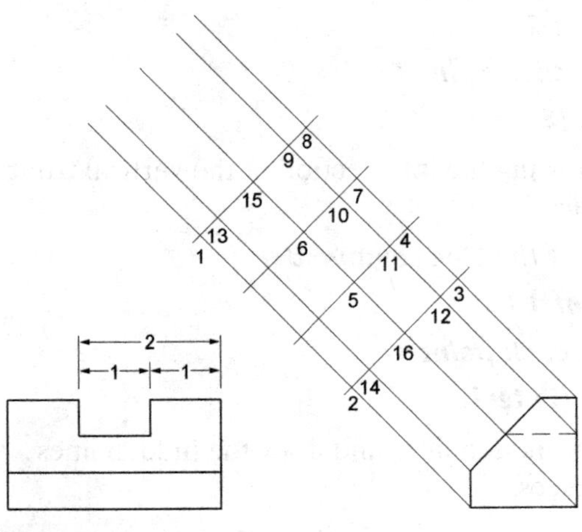

Figure 9.48

Next, you will draw the visible lines in the drawing over the top of the projection lines. Be sure to draw the correct shape of the object as it will appear in the auxiliary view. Refer to Figure 9.40 for your selections.

*Set **VISIBLE** as the **current layer**.*

Use Snap to Intersection *when selecting points in the following steps.*

Click: ***Line button***

Specify first point: ***click the intersection of the projection lines at point 1***

Specify next point or [Undo]: ***click point 2***

Tip: *If you did not know the dimensions, you could use the Distance command (available from the Tools menu under Inquiry) with the Intersection object snap in the front view to determine the distance.*

Specify next point or [Close/Undo]: ***click point 3***

Specify next point or [Close/Undo]: ***click point 4***

Specify next point or [Close/Undo]: ***click point 5***

Specify next point or [Close/Undo]: ***click point 6***

Specify next point or [Close/Undo]: ***click point 7***

Specify next point or [Close/Undo]: ***click point 8***

Specify next point or [Close/Undo]: ***C [Enter]***

Now you will restart the Line command and draw the short line segments where the two short top surfaces of the object intersect the slanted front surface:

Command: ***[Enter]*** *to restart the Line command*

Specify first point: ***click point 9***

Specify next point or [Undo]: ***click point 10***

Specify next point or [Undo]: ***[Enter]***

Command: ***[Enter]*** *to restart the Line command*

Specify first point: ***click point 11***

Specify next point or [Undo]: ***click point 12***

Specify next point or [Undo]: ***[Enter]***

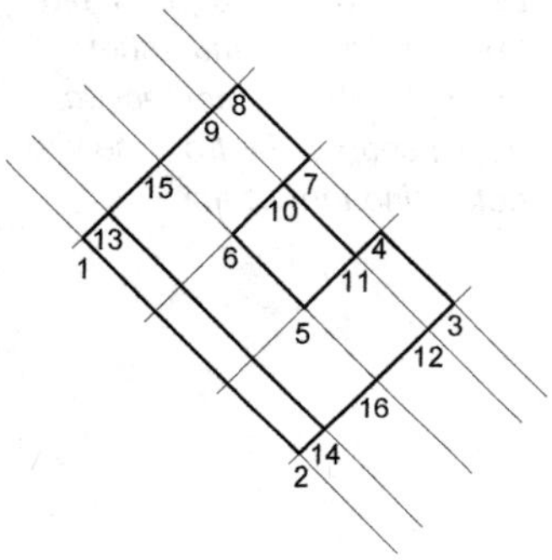

Next, you will add the line representing the back edge of the slot.

Command: ***[Enter]*** *to restart the Line command*

Specify first point: ***click point 10***

Specify next point or [Undo]: ***click point 11***

Specify next point or [Undo]: ***[Enter]***

Now you will add the line showing the intersection of the vertical front surface with the angled surface.

Command: ***[Enter]*** *to restart the Line command*

Specify first point: ***click point 13***

Specify next point or [Undo]: ***click point 14***

Specify next point or [Undo]: ***[Enter]***

Next you will set the layer for hidden lines and draw the hidden lines for the bottom and back surfaces.

Tip: *You could use Draworder and bring the visible lines to the front. The length of the hidden line is more accurate if it is not trimmed, but it is difficult to produce the gaps in the hidden line exactly where they are wanted without breaking it.*

Set **HIDDEN_LINES** as the current layer using the Layer Control

Command: ***L [Enter]*** *the alias for the Line command*

Specify first point: ***click point 15***

Specify next point or [Undo]: ***click point 16***

Specify next point or [Undo]: ***[Enter]***

Next freeze the projection layer so that those lines do not appear.

Click: ***Freeze icon adjacent to layer PROJECTION*** *(so that it looks like a snowflake)*

Click: ***Trim button***

On your own, trim the portion of the hidden line that coincides with the visible line from point **5** to point **6**.

When you have finished, your screen should look like Figure 9.49.

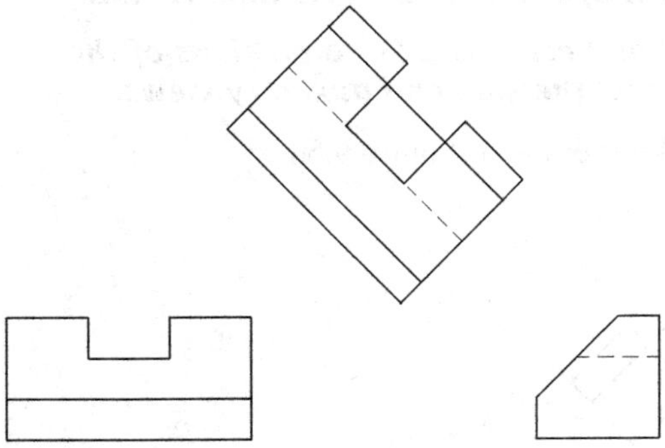

Figure 9.49

Adding Visual Reference Lines

Next, you will add two visual *reference lines* to your drawing from the extreme outside edges of the surface shown true size in the auxiliary view to the inclined surface in the side view. The lines will provide a visual reference for the angles in your drawing and help show how the auxiliary view aligns with the standard views. You can extend a centerline from the primary view to the auxiliary view or use one or two projection lines for the reference lines. In this case, as there are no centerlines, you will create two reference lines. Leave a gap of about 1/16" between the reference lines and the views.

Click: ***Thaw button for PROJECTION layer*** *(so that it looks like a sun)*

Select: ***the two rays that project from the ends of the angled surface*** *so that their grips appear*

Click: ***to pull-down the Layer Control list***

Click: ***THIN layer,*** *so that the selected lines change to that layer*

Refer to Figure 9.50 if you are unsure which lines to select.

The rays should change to layer THIN. You can verify this result visually because the lines will turn red, the color for layer THIN.

Linetype Conventions

Two lines of different linetypes should not meet to make one line. You must always leave a small gap on the linetype that has lesser precedence. In the case of the visible and the reference lines, the reference line should have a small gap (about 1/16" on the plotted drawing) where it meets the visible line. In the case of the visible and the hidden lines, the hidden line should have a small gap (about 1/16" on the plotted drawing) where it meets the visible line. You can use the Break command to do this.

Tip: *You could offset the edge of the object by 1/16 in each view and use Trim to create the gap between the lines, but it is probably fastest and accurate enough just to use the grips and make the gap by eye.*

Click: ***to freeze layer PROJECTION***

Click: ***Break button*** *from the ribbon Home tab, Modify toolbar*

On your own, create a gap of about 1/16" between each view and the reference lines.

Create a similar gap where the hidden line extends from the visible line, forming the front of the slot in the auxiliary view.

Thaw layer PROJECTION and erase the extra portions of the rays where they extend past the side and auxiliary views.

Your drawing should look like the one in Figure 9.50.

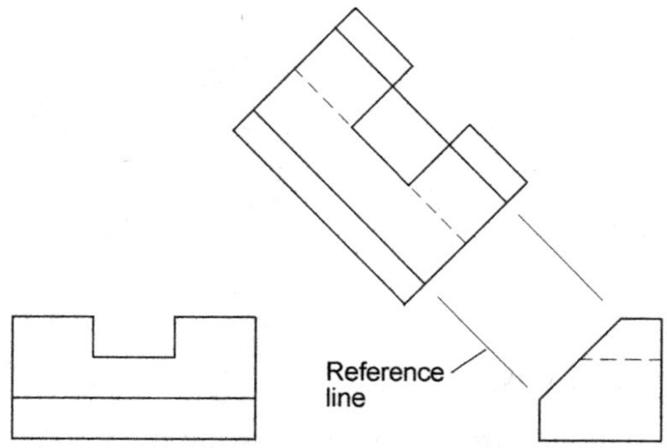

Figure 9.50

To restore the world coordinate system, the default where X is to the right and Y is upward, you will use the short-cut menu.

Hover the cursor over the UCS icon so that it becomes highlighted *(do not click on it).*

Right-click: ***to show the shortcut menu***

Click: ***World***

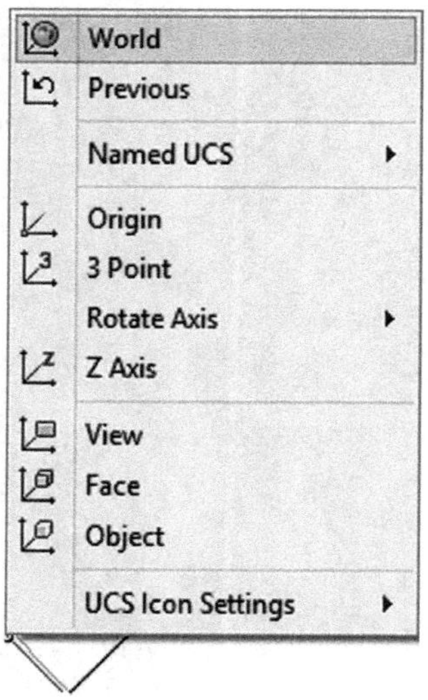

The UCS icon returns to its original location and the world coordinates are restored to use.

On your own, ***save and close your drawing.***

Curved Surfaces

Now you will create an auxiliary view of the slanted surface in a cylinder drawing like the one you created at the end of Tutorial 6. The drawing has been provided for you as *cyl3.dwt* in the data files that came with this book.

On your own, ***begin a new drawing.***

Use ***cyl3.dwt*** *as a* ***template.***

Name your new drawing ***auxil3.dwg.***

You return to the AutoCAD drawing editor, showing the orthographic views of the cylinder with the slanted surface (Figure 9.51).

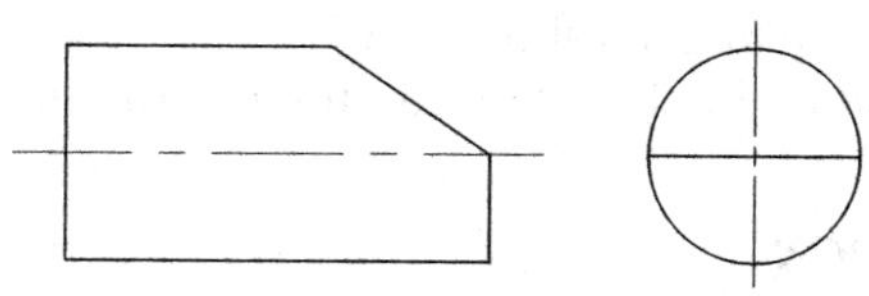

Figure 9.51

The drawing shows the front and side views of the slanted surface but not the true shape of the surface. You will draw a *partial auxiliary view* to show the true shape of the surface. Partial auxiliary views are often used because, in the auxiliary view, the inclined or oblique surface chosen is shown true size and shape, but other surfaces are foreshortened. As these other surfaces have already been defined in the basic orthographic views, there is no need to show them in the auxiliary view. A partial auxiliary saves time in projecting the view and gives a clearer appearance to your drawing.

Figure 9.52 shows an example. This drawing shows the front view of an object, along with two partial auxiliary views.

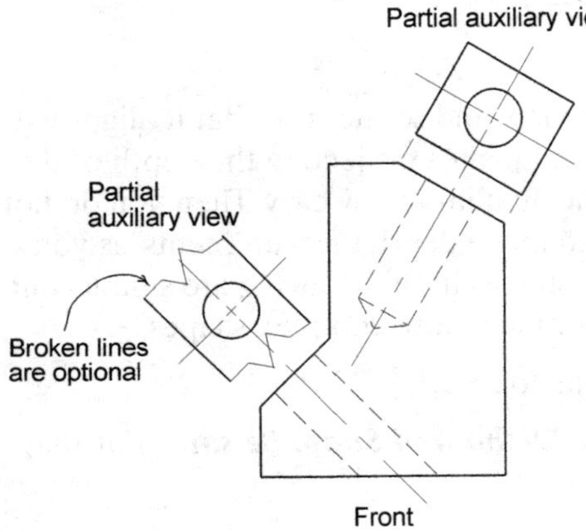

Figure 9.52 **Example**

Turn running Object Snap Intersection on.

Make sure the ***grid is on****.*

Turn ***Ortho off****.*

Make sure that ***PROJECTION is the current layer****.*

The UCS icon is not always set to show at the origin of the coordinate system. If it is not, you may drag it to a new location, but it will jump back to display in the set position. The UCSicon command lets you specify the location and appearance of the icon.

Command: ***UCSICON [Enter]***

Enter an option [ON/OFF/All/Noorigin/ORigin/Selectable/Properties] <ON>: ***OR [Enter]***

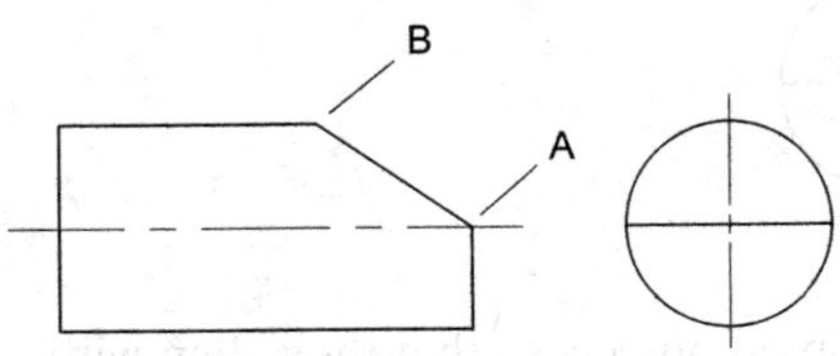

Figure 9.53

On your own, ***drag the UCS so that the origin is at point A****, and* ***the Y axis is aligned toward point B****.*

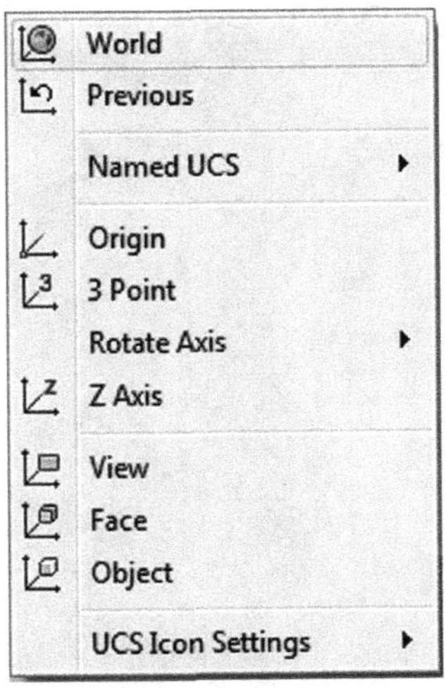

Tip: *If the UCS icon does not drag to the new location, right-click to show the context menu. Click UCSIcon Settings. Make sure that Show UCSicon at Origin is checked.*

Your screen should be similar to Figure 9.54. Note that the crosshairs align with the inclined surface.

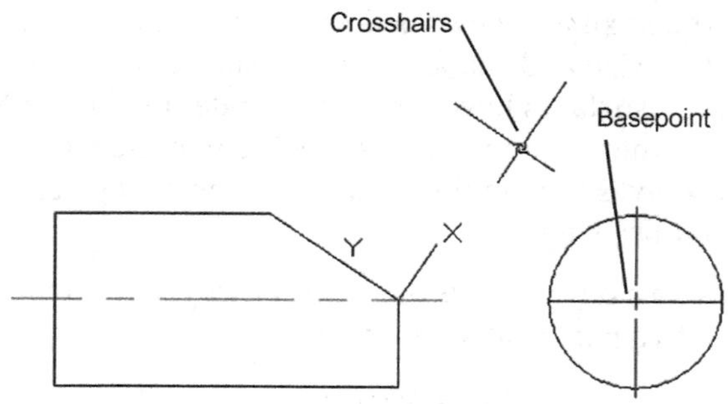

Figure 9.54

Next, copy the object in the side view and rotate it so that it aligns with the rotated grid and snap. Doing so makes projecting the depth of the object from the side view into the auxiliary view easy. Then you do not have to use a reference surface to make depth measurements, as you did in the previous drawing. The shapes in this drawing are simple, but these methods will also work for much more complex shapes.

Refer to Figure 9.45 for the points to select.

*For the next steps you will use **Ortho and Snap.** Be sure that they are turned **on.***

Click: ***Copy button***

Select objects: ***use a window to select the entire side view***

Select objects: ***[Enter]***

Specify base point or [Displacement] <Displacement>: ***click the intersection labeled Base point***

Specify second point of displacement or <use first point as displacement>: ***click a point above and to the right of the side view***

Specify base point or displacement: ***[Enter]***

A copy of the side view appears on your screen, as shown in Figure 9.55.

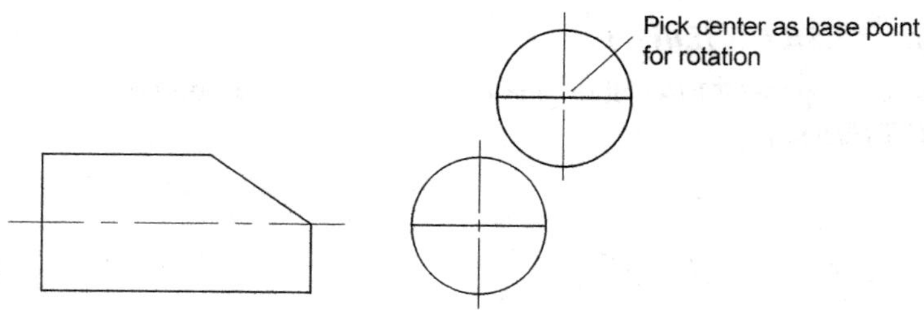

Figure 9.55

Now you are ready to rotate the copied objects so that they align with the snap and can be used to project the auxiliary view. You will use the Rotate button from the ribbon Home tab, Modify panel and type in the angle, which is 56°. If you were not given this information you can use the angular dimension command, or the Measuregeom command to determine it.

Click: ***Rotate button***

Select objects: ***use Window or Crossing to select the copied objects***

Select objects: ***[Enter]***

Specify base point: ***click the intersection of the centerlines of the copied objects***

Specify rotation angle or [Copy/Reference] <0>: ***56 [Enter]***

The objects that you copied previously should now be rotated into position so that they align with the snap and grid. Your drawing should look like that in Figure 9.56.

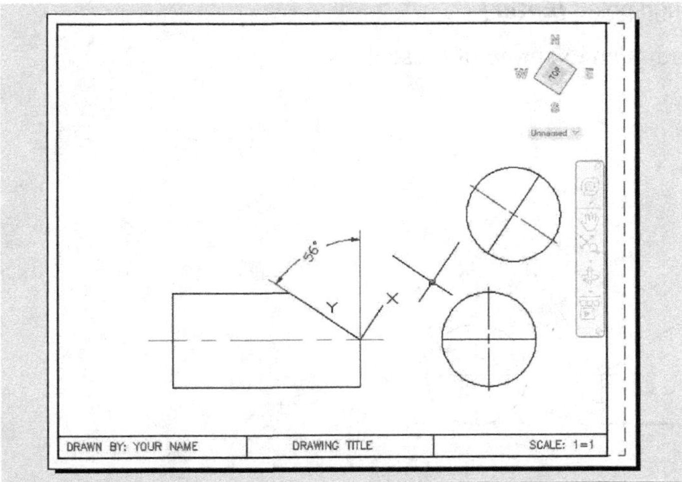

Figure 9.56

Now you will change the copy onto layer PROJECTION because it is part of the construction of the drawing, not something you will leave in the drawing when you are finished. You will freeze layer PROJECTION when you have finished the drawing.

On your own, change the copied objects to layer PROJECTION.

The objects that you selected are changed onto layer PROJECTION. Their color is now magenta, which is the color of layer PROJECTION. Next, you will draw projection lines from the front view to the empty area where the auxiliary view will be located.

Make sure that ***Ortho and the Intersection*** *running object snap are turned* ***on.***

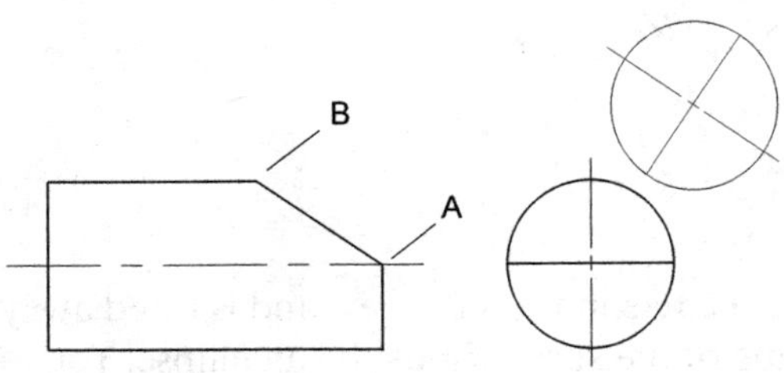

Figure 9.57

Refer to Figure 9.57 for the points to select.

Click: ***Ray button***

Specify start point: ***click the intersection labeled A***

Specify through point: ***click a point above the front view***

Specify through point: ***[Enter]***

Command: ***[Enter]*** *to restart the Ray command*

Specify start point: ***click the intersection labeled B***

Specify through point: ***click a point above the front view***

Specify through point: ***[Enter]***

Figure 9.58 shows an example of these lines.

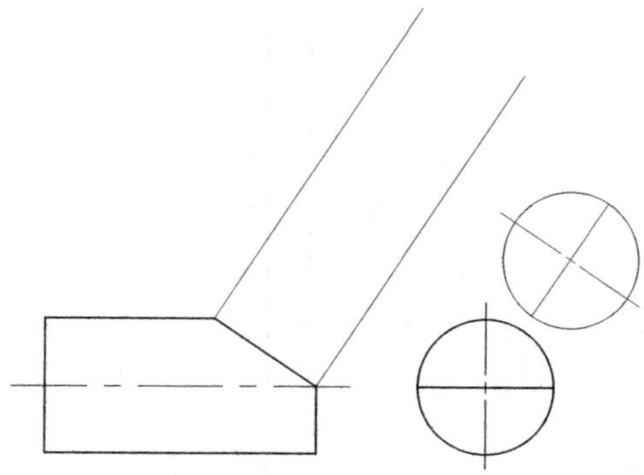

Figure 9.58

On your own, ***project rays from the intersections in the copied side view*** *so that your drawing looks like the one in Figure 9.59.*

Click: ***VISIBLE*** *as the current layer*

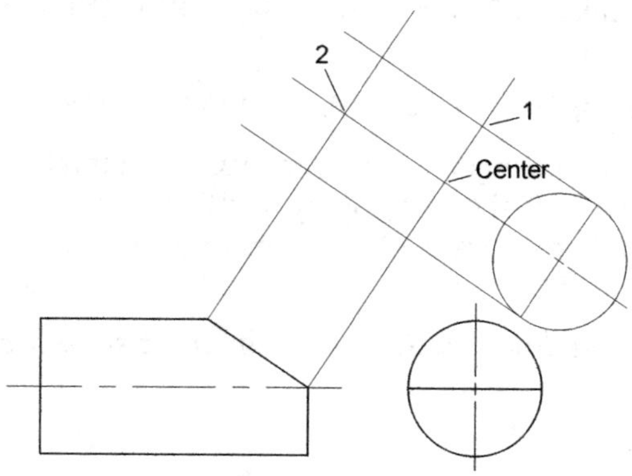

Figure 9.59

Drawing the Ellipse

Because the object appears as a circle in the side view and is tilted away in the front view, the true shape of the surface must be an ellipse. You will select the Ellipse button from the Draw toolbar to create the elliptical surface in the auxiliary view. Refer to Figure 9.59 for your selections.

Click: ***Ellipse button***

Specify axis endpoint of ellipse or [Arc/Center]: ***C [Enter]***

Specify center of ellipse: ***click the intersection labeled Center***

Specify endpoint of axis: ***click intersection 1***

Specify distance to other axis distance or [Rotation]: ***click intersection 2***

The ellipse in your drawing should look like the one in Figure 9.60. You will need to trim the lower portion of it to create the final surface.

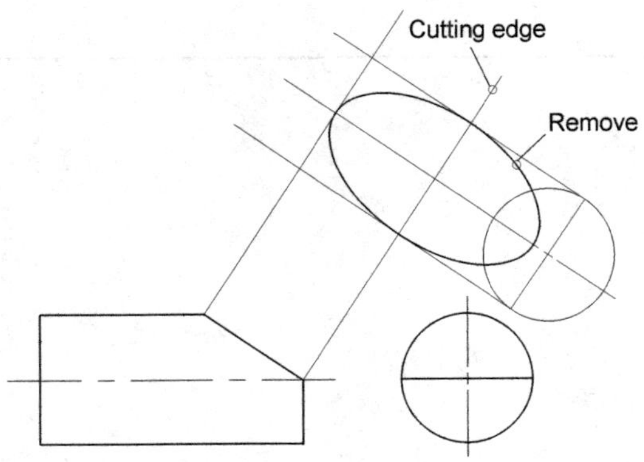

Figure 9.60

On your own, use the ***Trim*** *command to* ***eliminate the unnecessary portion of the ellipse*** *in the auxiliary view.*

Change the two projection lines *from the front view onto* ***layer THIN****. Then use the* ***Break*** *command to break them so that they do not touch the views.*

Draw in the final line across the bottom of the remaining portion of the ellipse on layer VISIBLE.

Freeze layer PROJECTION *to remove the construction and projection lines from your display.*

When you are finished, your screen should look like Figure 9.61.

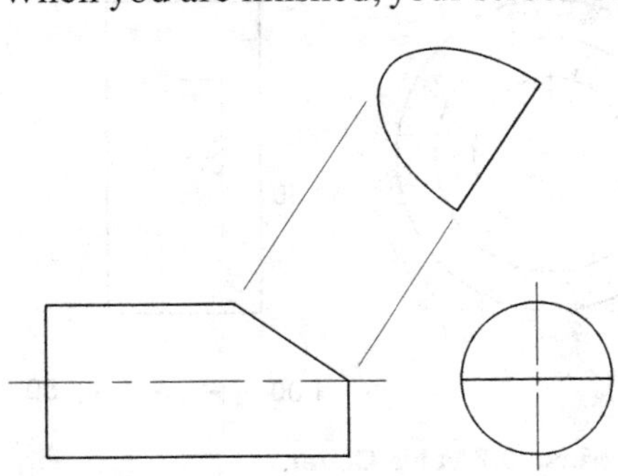

Figure 9.61

Save and **close** your drawing.

You have completed Tutorial 9.

Tip: *If the surface in the side view were an irregular curve, you could project a number of points to the auxiliary view and then connect them with a polyline. After connecting them, you could connect them in a smooth curve, using the Fit Curve or Spline option of the Edit Polyline command. Although this method would also produce an ellipse, the Ellipse command is quicker.*

Key Terms

- associative hatching
- auxiliary view
- basic view
- crosshatching
- custom hatch pattern
- cutting plane line
- foreshortened
- gradient fill
- partial auxiliary view
- pictorial full section
- reference line
- reference surface
- runout
- section view
- user-defined hatch pattern

Key Commands (keyboard shortcut)

- Distance (DI)
- Edit Hatch
- Ellipse Center
- Hatch (H)
- RAY
- Savetime
- UCS 3 Point
- UCSICON

Exercises

Redraw the given front view and replace the given right side view with a section view. Assume that the vertical centerline of the front view is the cutting plane line for the section view. The letter M after an exercise means that the given dimensions are in millimeters.

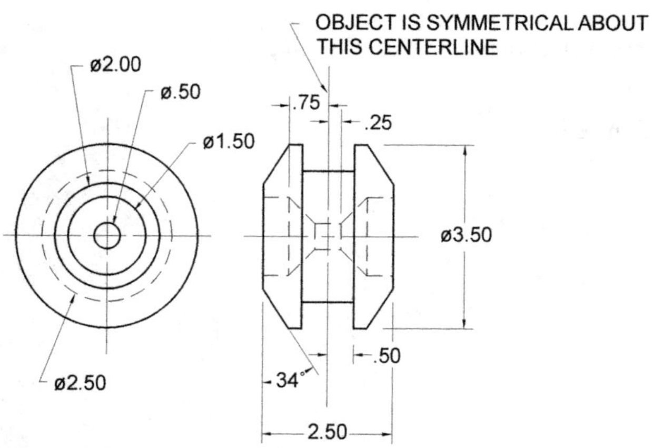

Exercise 9.1 High-Pressure Seal

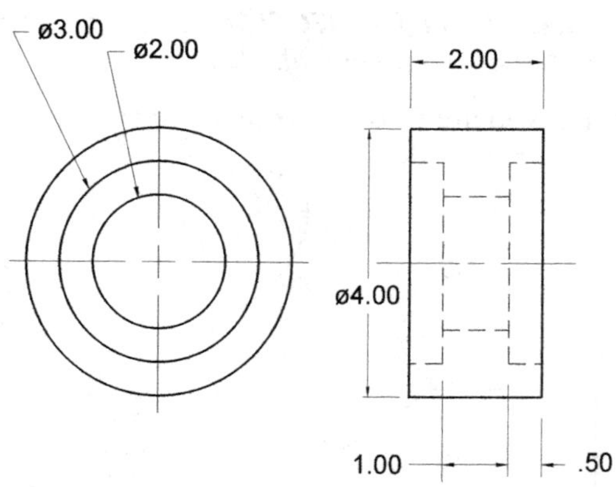

Exercise 9.2 Valve Cover

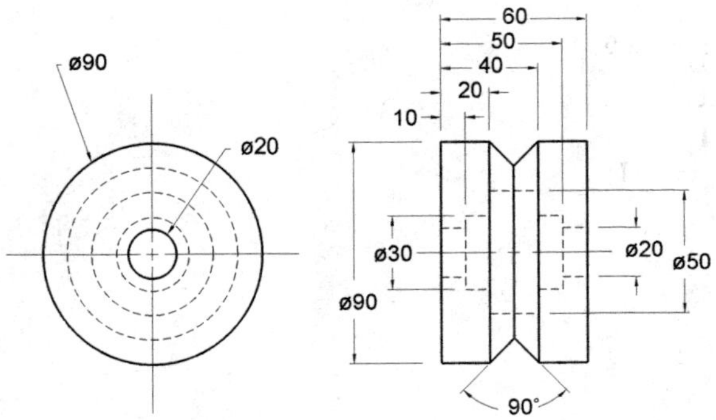

Exercise 9.3M Pulley

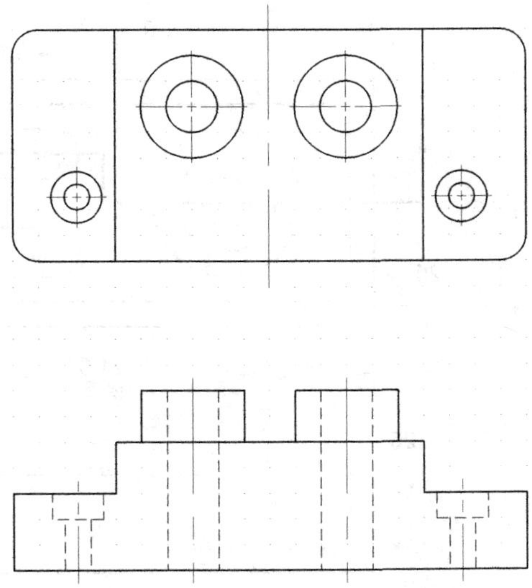

Exercise 9.4 Double Cylinder

Use 2D techniques to draw this object; the grid shown is 0.25 inch. Show the front view as a half section and show the corresponding cutting plane in the top view. On the same views, completely dimension the object to the nearest 0.01 inch. Include any necessary notes.

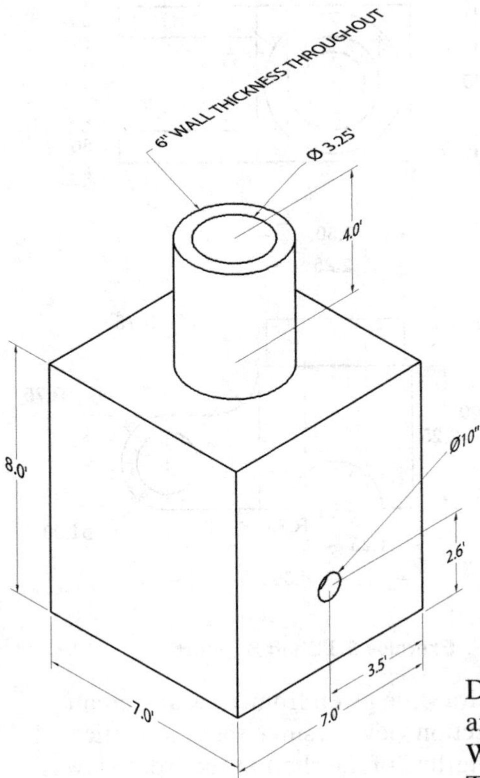

Exercise 9.5 Manhole Junction

Draw standard orthographic views and show the front view in section. Wall thickness is 6 inches throughout. The 10-inch hole is through the entire manhole junction (exits opposite side).

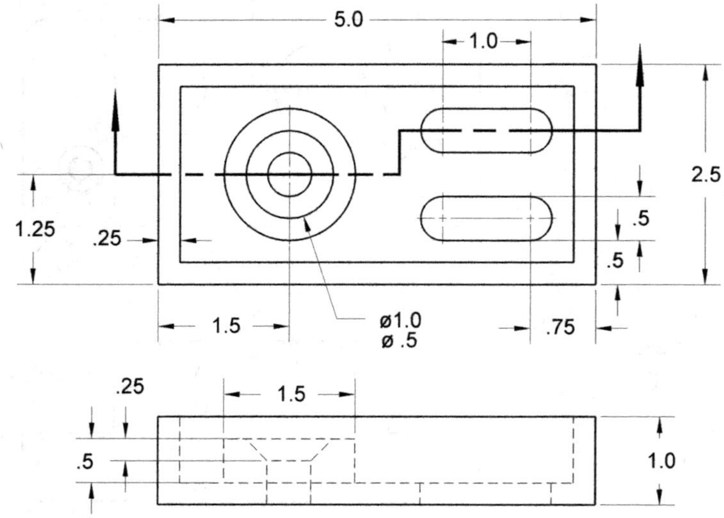

Exercise 9.6 Plate

Use 2D to construct the top view with the cutting plane shown and show the front view in section.

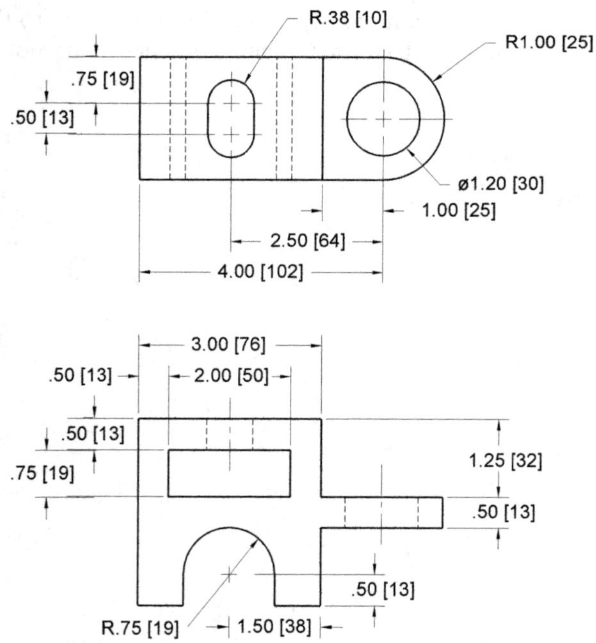

Exercise 9.7 Support Bracket

Create a drawing of the object shown with a plan view and full section front view. Note the alternate units in brackets; these are the dimensions in millimeters for the part.

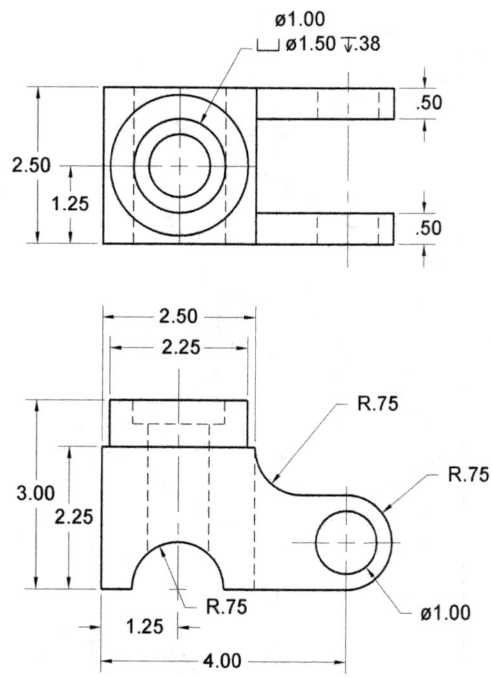

Exercise 9.8 Shaft Support

Redraw the given front view and create a section view. Assume that the vertical centerline of the shaft in the front view is the cutting plane line for the section view.

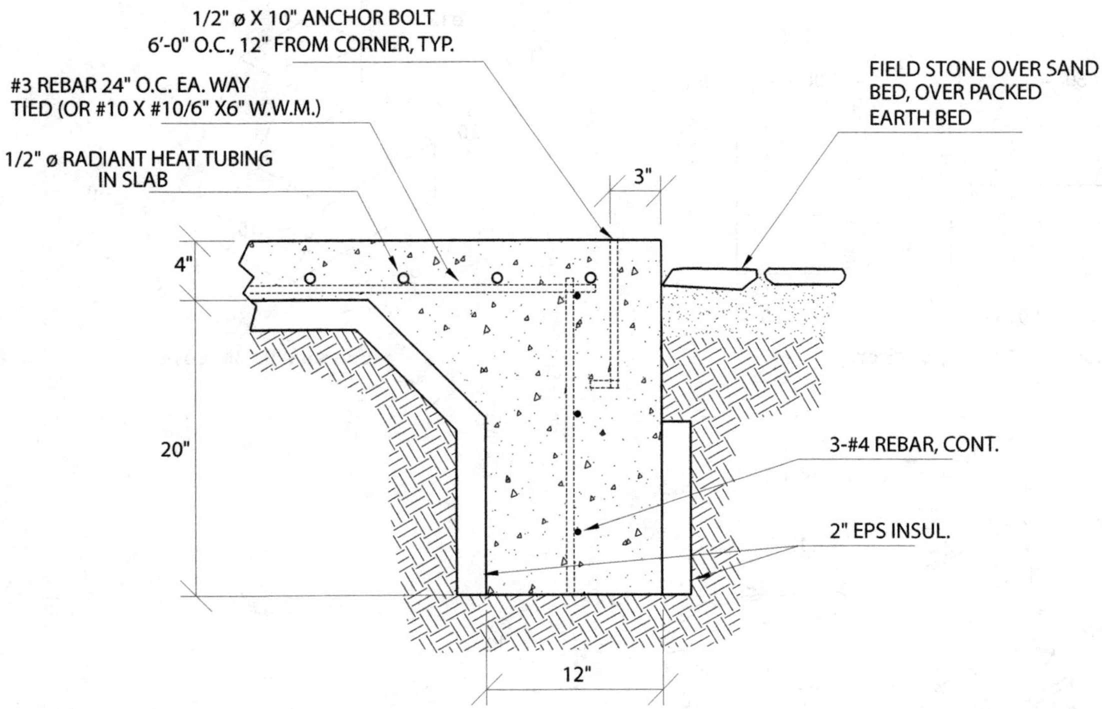

Exercise 9.9 Turned Down Slab Detail

Use 2D methods to create the drawing shown. Use Boundary Hatch to fill the area with the pattern for concrete. Use the Hatch command Draw option to make irregular areas to fill with patterns for sand and earth.

Use the 2D techniques you have learned in the tutorial to create an auxiliary view of the slanted surfaces for the objects that follow. The letter M after an exercise number means that the given dimensions are in millimeters.

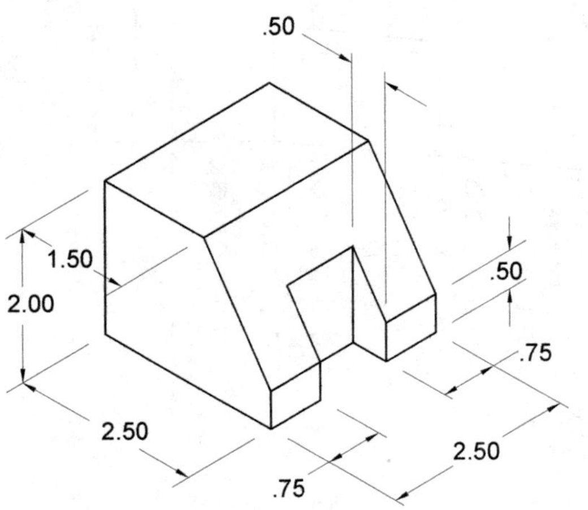

Exercise 9.10 Stop Block

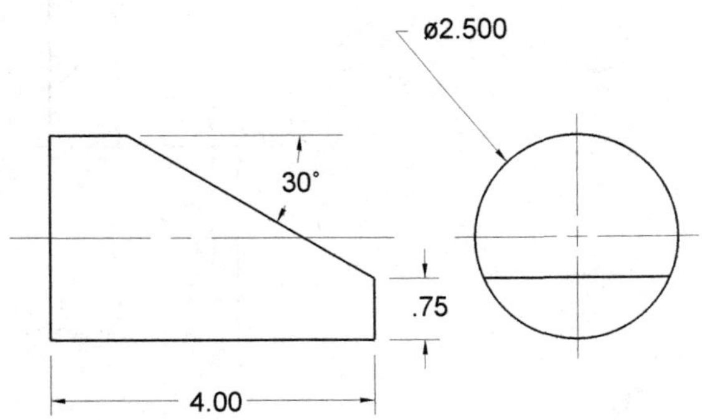

Exercise 9.11 Bearing

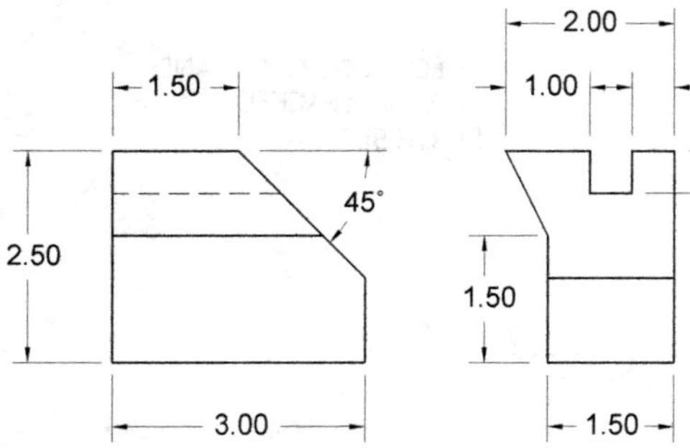

Exercise 9.12 Tooling Support

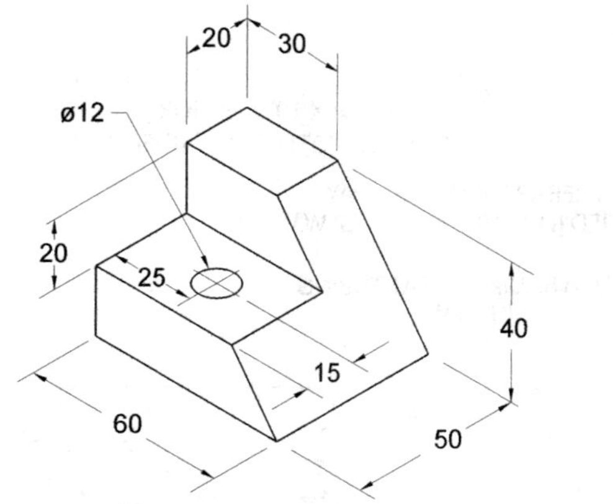

Exercise 9.13M Level

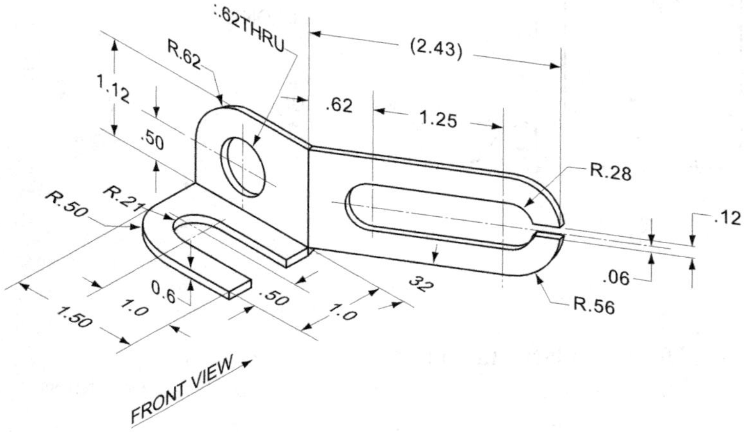

Exercise 9.14 Mounting Clip

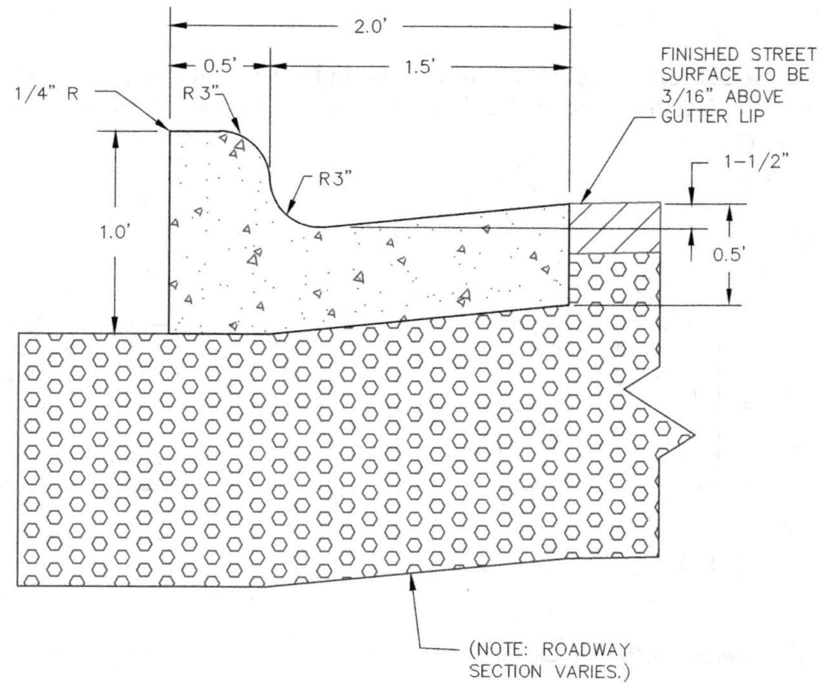

Exercise 9.15 Catch Curb Section

BLOCKS, DESIGNCENTER, AND TOOL PALETTES

10

Introduction

You can unify a collection of drawing objects into a single symbol using the Block command. Using blocks helps organize your drawing and makes updating symbols easy. Text objects called attributes can be associated with blocks. These attributes can be visible or invisible. You can extract attribute information to an external database or spreadsheet for analysis or record keeping. (You will learn more about attributes in Tutorial 13.)

The use of blocks has many advantages. You can construct a drawing by assembling blocks that consist of many small details. This way objects that appear often only need to be drawn once and inserted as needed. Inserting blocks rather than copying basic objects results in smaller drawing files, which saves time in loading and regenerating drawings. Blocks can also be nested, so that one block is a part of another block.

In this tutorial, you will learn to use the Block and Insert Block commands, while creating reusable symbols used in drawing electronic logic circuits. Using Write Block, you will make the symbols into separate drawings that you can add to any drawing. You will use the DesignCenter to access blocks, layers, and other named entities from your existing drawings. Finally, you will learn to create custom tool palettes and toolbars to which you can add your block symbols and to save your custom work space.

The AutoCAD *Group* command lets you group objects into named selection sets. You can also form *selectable groups*. When a group is selectable, clicking on one of its members selects all the members of the group that are in the current space and not on locked or frozen layers. An object can belong to more than one group. Groups are another powerful way of organizing the information in your drawing. In many ways groups are like blocks, but groups differ because of their special use for selecting objects as named sets.

An example where you might use both blocks and groups is in an architectural drawing. You could create each item of furniture—a table, chair, etc.—as a separate block and then insert it multiple times into the drawing. You could use several different layers to draw each block. You could then name all the tables as a group called TABLES and all the chairs as a group called CHAIRS. The TABLES and CHAIRS groups could belong to a group named FURNITURE. Unlike a block, which acts as a single object, you can still move or modify items in groups individually, but you can also quickly select the group and modify it as a unit.

Objectives

When you have completed this tutorial, you will be able to

1. Use the Block, Write Block, Insert Block, and Donut commands.
2. Use the DesignCenter™.
3. Add blocks and commands to a Tool Palette.
4. Add your block symbols to toolbar buttons.
5. Create a logic circuit diagram using blocks.
6. Create named groups.
7. Create your own toolbars.
8. Use a macro.
9. Customize your workspace.

Starting

Start AutoCAD and open the drawing file ***electr.dwg*** provided with the datafiles. Save the drawing and name it ***eblocks.dwg***. Switch to paperspace and zoom and pan to fit the drawing on your screen. Return to model space. When you have finished, it should appear as in Figure 10.1.

Figure 10.1 shows six symbols used in drawing electronic logic circuits: the *Buffer*, *Inverter*, *And*, *Nand*, *Or*, and *Nor gates.* You will make each symbol into a block.

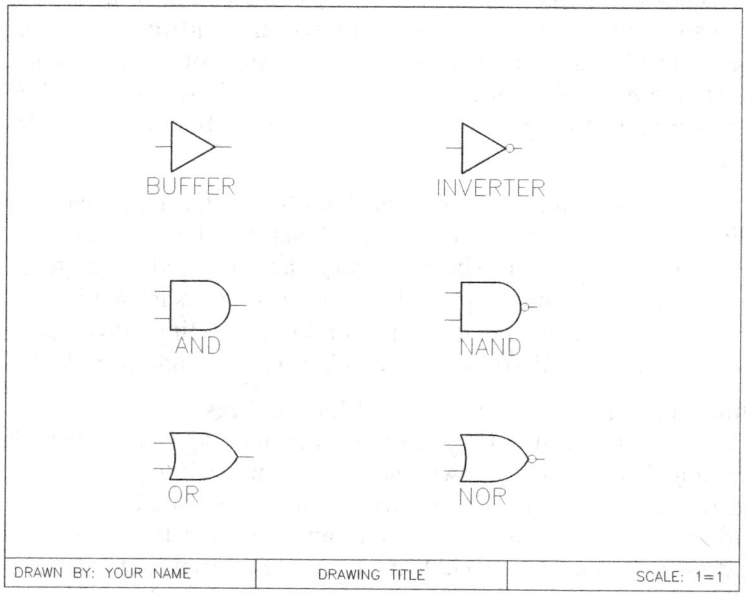

Figure 10.1

Using the Block Command

A *block* is a set of objects formed into a compound object. You define a block from a set of objects in your current drawing. You specify the *block name* and then select the objects that will be part of the block.

The block name is used whenever you insert the compound object (block) into the drawing. Each insertion of the block into the drawing, the *block reference*, can have its own scale factors and rotation. The software treats a block as a single object. Select a block for use with commands such as Move or Erase simply by clicking any part of the block, like you would any other drawing object.

You can take blocks apart into their individual objects by using the Explode or Xplode commands, but doing so removes the blocks' special properties.

A block can be composed of objects that were drawn on different layers with varying colors and linetypes. The layer, color, and linetype information of these objects is preserved in the block. Upon insertion, each object is drawn on its original layer with its original color and linetype, regardless of the current drawing layer, object color, and object linetype.

There are three exceptions to this rule.

1. Objects that were drawn on layer 0 are generated on the current layer when the block is inserted, and they take on the characteristics of that layer.
2. Objects that were drawn with color BYBLOCK inherit the color of the block (either the current drawing color when they are inserted or the color of the layer when color is set by layer).
3. Objects that were drawn with linetype BYBLOCK inherit the linetype of the block (either the current linetype or the layer linetype, as with color).

Blocks are stored only in the current drawing and you can use them only in the drawing in which they were created. To use a block in another drawing, you need to use the Write Block command or the Windows Clipboard. You can use blocks in other drawings by copying vectors (graphical objects) to the Windows Clipboard and pasting them into another drawing, which results in a block. In addition, you can insert the drawing containing a block into another drawing. When you insert a drawing as you did in Tutorial 4 with the subdivision drawing, *subdivis.dwg*, any blocks it contains are then defined in the drawing in which it is inserted.

Unlike using the Windows Clipboard to copy a block, or inserting a file containing a block, using the Write Block command saves the selected block or drawing objects as a separate drawing file. This file can then be inserted into any drawing.

Zoom up the area of the drawing showing the And gate so that your screen is similar to Figure 10.2.

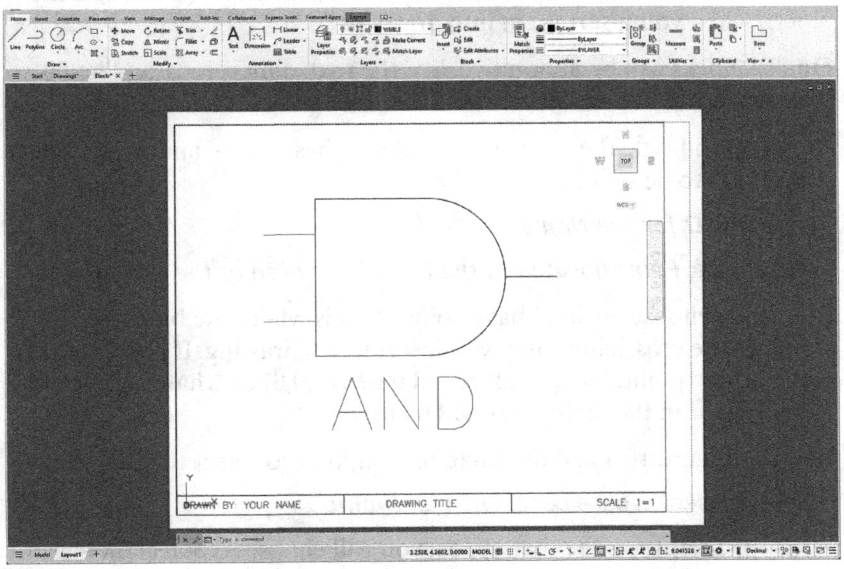

Figure 10.2

You will create a block from the objects making up the And gate on the screen. Be sure to select Create Block and not Insert Block from the same palette. When typing the command, enter BLOCK.

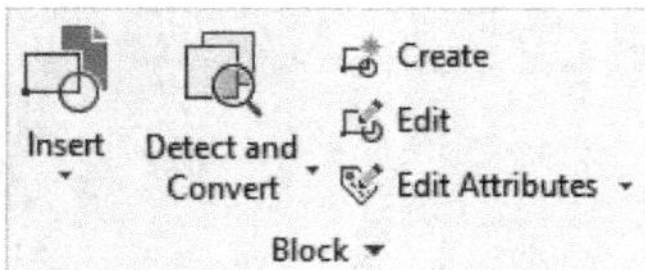

*Turn on running object snap **Endpoint**.*

*Turn **off any other modes** from the status bar.*

*Click: **Create button** from the Home tab, Block palette*

The Block Definition dialog box appears, similar to Figure 10.3.

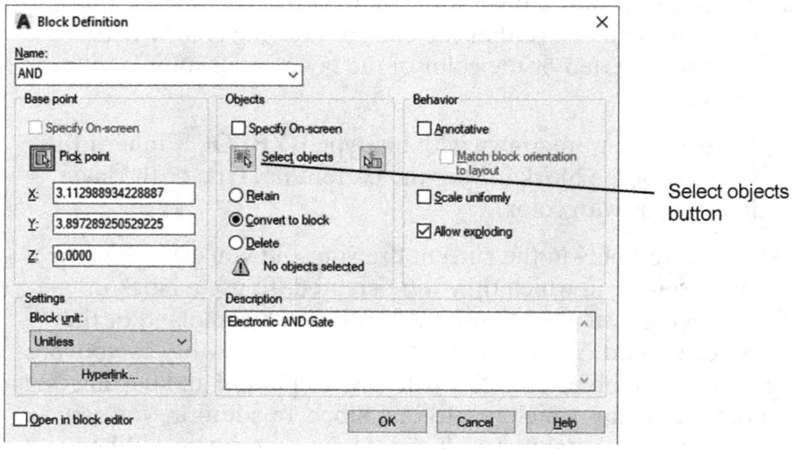

Figure 10.3

Tip: Block names can be as many as 255 characters long and can include spaces and any other characters that are not reserved for system use. The AutoCAD Release 14 software allowed for block names that were up to 31 characters long and which could contain letters, numbers, and the following special characters: $ (dollar sign), - (hyphen), and _ (underscore). If you will be saving back to older versions or converting information to other CAD software, it is a good idea to use simpler block names, especially ones that are different within the first 8 characters if possible. If a block with the name you choose already exists, the program tells you that it does. You can either exit without saving so that you do not lose the original block, or you can choose to redefine the block.

The dialog box lets you type in a block name, select a base point, select objects to be used in that group, and view existing blocks. The Objects area lets you choose whether items you select for the block will be retained in your drawing (as individual objects), converted to a block (as a single object), or deleted.

*Leave the Objects radio buttons set to **Convert to block**.*

You can also add a description, and specify the default units for size features in the block. These things will help you later find and size the blocks when you insert them into drawings.

Finally, blocks can be annotative, like the text, dimensions, and hatch you used in earlier drawings.

Next you will type the block name, select a base point, and finally select the objects to be used.

*Type: **AND** for the Name*

*Click: **Pick Point** (located in the Base Point area of the dialog box)*

Be sure to choose a useful base point. This is where the block will attach to the crosshairs when you insert it in a drawing. If you do not select a base point, the default coordinates (0,0,0) or whatever coordinates appear in the dialog box will be used.

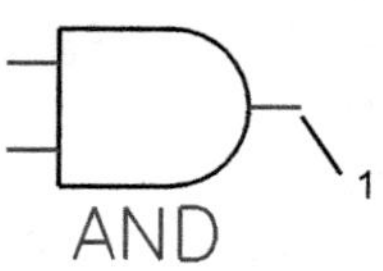

Figure 10.4

Refer to Figure 10.4 and use Snap to Endpoint to select the base point.

Specify insertion base point: ***click endpoint 1***

When you return to the dialog box, you will choose to Select objects.

*Click: **Select objects button***

Select objects: ***use implied Crossing to select all of the objects making up the And gate, including the name AND [Enter]***

*Click: **Unitless** as the Block Unit type under Settings*

*Type: **Electronic AND gate** as the description*

*Click: **OK***

You now have a block of the And gate to be used in later drawings. Next use the alias to zoom previous and show the entire drawing and finish creating the remaining blocks on your own.

Command: ***Z [Enter]***

Specify corner of window, enter a scale factor (nX or nXP), or [All/Center/Dynamic/Extents/Previous/Scale/Window/Object] <real time>: ***P [Enter]***

*Click: **Create block button***

*On your own, **create a block for each of the other electronic logic symbols**.*

*Name the blocks **NAND, OR,** NOR, **INVERTER,** and **BUFFER**.*

*Select the **right endpoint** of the line from each electronic logic gate as the **base point**.*

To see how you can use blocks within the current drawing, you will insert the And block you created.

Tip: *You may have to zoom previous more than once to show the entire drawing if you zoomed in multiple times.*

Inserting a Block

The Insert Block command inserts blocks or other drawings into your drawing. When inserting a block, you use a dialog box to specify the block name, the insertion point (the location for the base point you selected when you created the block), the scale, and the rotation for the block. A scale of 1 causes the block to remain the original size. The scaling factors for the X-, Y-, and Z-directions do not have to be the same. However, using the same size ensures that the inserted block has the same proportions, or aspect ratio, as the original. Blocks (even those with different X-, Y-, and Z-scaling factors) can be exploded back into their original objects with the Explode command. A rotation of 0° ensures the same orientation as the original. The REpeat option is handy when inserting multiple copies of the block. You can also use Insert Block by typing INSERT at the command prompt.

Tip: *You can use the Design-Center to import blocks from existing drawings into your current drawing.*

You will select Insert Block from the ribbon Home tab, Block panel and use the dialog box to insert the And gate into your drawing.

*Click: **Insert button** from the Block palette*

The options expand to show the blocks available in your drawing as shown in Figure 10.5.

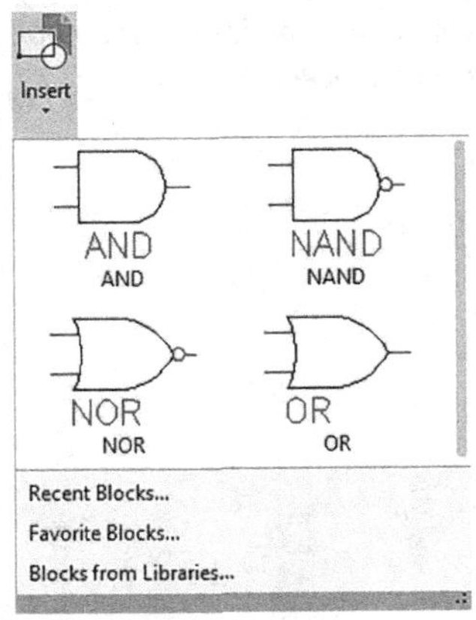

Figure 10.5

*Click: **AND** from the list of blocks*

The And block appears, attached to the crosshairs by its endpoint, the base point you specified. Continue with the Insert command.

Specify insertion point or [Basepoint/Scale/X/Y/Z/Rotate/Explode/REpeat]: ***click anywhere to the right of the logic symbols***

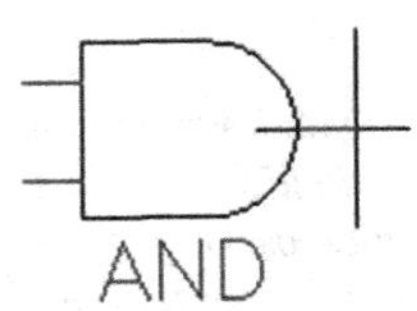

The And block is added to your drawing.

Tip: *You can reenter the Block Definition dialog box and update the selections for any of the blocks in the drawing. To do this, pick the Create block button and expand the list of names in the dialog box to select the block you want to redefine. Make any necessary changes to the dialog box and then pick OK.*

On your own, ***try to erase only one of the lines*** *of the newly added block.*

Press ***[Esc] to cancel the Erase*** *command without erasing anything.*

The entire block behaves as one object. In Tutorial 7, when you added associative dimensions to your drawing, they were also blocks. That's why they behave as a single object, even though they are a collection of lines, polylines, and text.

Click: ***Insert button*** *from the Block palette*

Click: ***Recent Blocks*** *from the list that pulls down*

Click: ***Current Drawing tab*** *from the left side of the panel*

The Blocks panel appears on your screen, as shown in Figure 10.6.

Coordinate entry boxes show only when item is not checked.

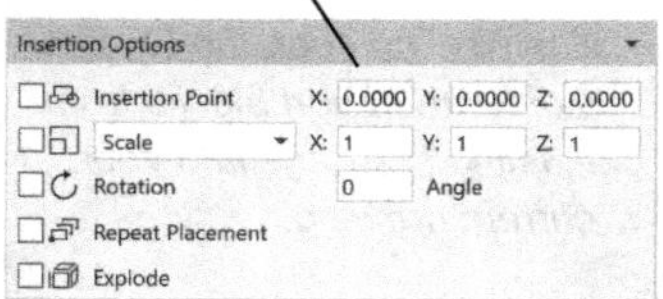

Tip: *The entry boxes show only when the specify on-screen box is not checked.*

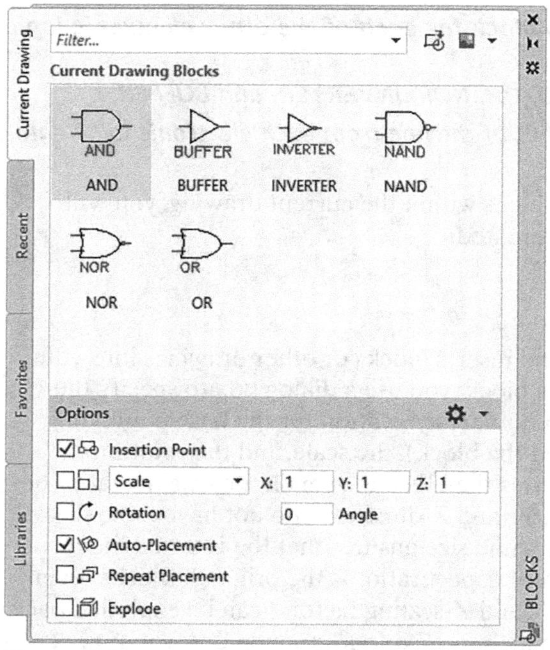

Figure 10.6

Click: ***AND*** *from the blocks in the upper area*

The Insertion Options area lets you select whether to return to your drawing to specify the Insertion point, Scale, and Rotation or to type a value for these (or use the defaults) into the input boxes.

Leave the ***Scale factor set to 1*** *for the X, Y, and Z coordinate directions.*

This way the block will retain the same size in the drawing as where it was created.

Leave the ***Rotation set to an angle of 0*** *degrees so that the block retains its original angle.*

The specify on-screen feature allows you to click the location for the block from your screen. Otherwise, you type the coordinates for its location in the Block panel. The entry boxes show only when the specify on-screen box is not checked.

Tip: *If you have trouble, try pressing [Esc] a couple of times and then clicking on the block from the upper part of the panel once again.*

Make sure ***Insertion Point*** *has a check in it.*

To begin specifying the insertion parameters on screen, simply move your cursor into the drawing area. Try that now.

Move your cursor into the drawing area.

Notice that the Insertion options of the Blocks panel are grayed out during the block insertion.

Specify insertion point or [Basepoint/Scale/X/Y/Z/Rotate]: ***click anywhere to the right of the logic symbols***

The And block is added to your drawing. To insert the block again, simply click it in the upper portion of the Blocks panel and move your cursor into the drawing area.

Tip: *With **Auto-placement** checked as you place blocks placement defaults show as you move the block on screen. You can click to accept the block placement suggestion or press [Ctrl] to switch to the next placement suggestion, or simply move the cursor. The auto-placement suggestions are generated using machine learning stored as you use blocks. The more you use the feature, the more likely it will produce useful suggested placements. You can turn it off using the Blocks-datacollection system variable. Pressing [Shift]+W toggles suggestions off temporarily while you place a block.*

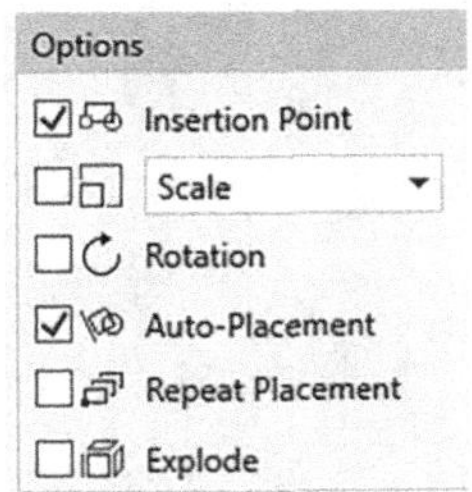

Using Explode

A block behaves as a single object. The Explode command replaces a block reference with the collection of simple objects the block comprises.

Explode also turns 2D and 3D polylines, associative dimensions, and 3D mesh back into individual objects. When a 3D solid object is exploded, it becomes a collection of surfaces.

When you explode a block, the resulting image on the screen is identical to the one you started with, except that the color and linetype of the objects may change. That can occur because properties such as the color and linetype of the block return to the settings determined by their original method of creation, either BYLAYER or the set color and linetype with which they were created. There will be no difference unless the objects were created in layer 0 or with the color and linetype set to BYBLOCK, as specified in the list at the beginning of this tutorial.

You will use the Explode command to break the newly inserted And block into individual objects for editing.

*Click: **Explode button** from the ribbon Home tab, Modify panel*

Select objects: ***click any portion of the inserted And block***

Select objects: ***[Enter]***

The block is now broken into its component objects. Notice that now you can erase one line at a time, rather than the whole block.

*On your own, **try to erase a line** from the block.*

Erase both of the newly added AND blocks.

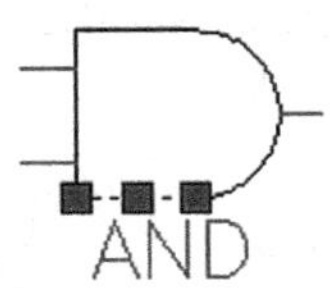

Notice that you can also check the Explode box from the Block panel during the original insertion of the block. This is useful if you know in advance that you want the objects making up the block to be individual elements. However, blocks are very useful. You should only explode them if that is needed, not as a general rule.

Using Write Block

The block you created is only defined within the current drawing. The Write Block command makes it into a separate drawing for use in other drawings. A drawing file made using Write Block is the same as any

Warning: *Do not give the write block the same name as an existing drawing. If you do, you will see the message "This file already exists. Replace existing file?" Select No unless you are certain that you no longer want the old drawing file.*

Tip: *Write Block does not save views, User Coordinate Systems, viewport configurations, unreferenced symbols (including block definitions), unused layers or linetypes, or text styles. This compresses your drawing file size by getting rid of unwanted overhead.*

other drawing file. You can open it and edit it like any other drawing. Any AutoCAD drawing can be inserted into any other drawing, as you did in Tutorial 5 when inserting the subdivision drawing. This is a great tool. Try to never draw anything twice!

You will use the Write Block command to make the AND block into a new AutoCAD drawing file called *and-gate.dwg.* The alias for the WBLOCK command is W.

Command: ***W [Enter]***

The Write Block dialog box similar to that shown in Figure 10.7 appears on the screen.

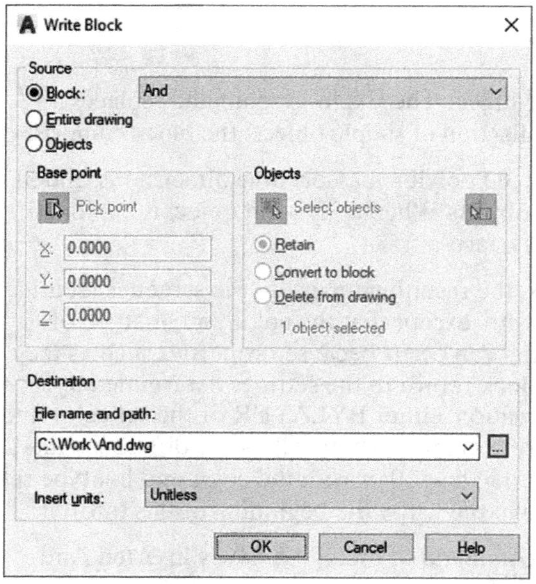

Figure 10.7

You can select the source information for the Wblock by clicking one of the following three radio buttons:

- **Block:** Click on the name of a block that already exists in the current drawing. The objects that make up the specified block are written to the drawing file being created.
- **Entire drawing:** This saves the entire current drawing to the name specified as the Destination file name (as the Save command does), except that unused named objects, layers, and other definitions are eliminated.
- **Objects:** Clicking this allows you to specify the objects and the base point, similar to the Make Block options. You can choose whether the items you select are retained, deleted, or converted to blocks in the current drawing. The selected objects are written to the drawing file name that you specify in the Destination area.

In the Source area,

Click: ***Block button***

Select: ***AND as the block name (from the pull-down list)***

Tip: *Detect and Convert uses AutoCAD's machine learning service to search your drawing for objects and let you quickly convert them to blocks. Use the mini-toolbar Convert button to name them as blocks. Search and Convert allows you to select drawing objects to convert to blocks.*

The middle area of the dialog box appears grayed out. Next set the destination file and default units for the block. You will name the new file *and-gate*. You do not need to include the file extension; the *.dwg* extension is automatically added. (Manage the directory for the new file to keep your files organized.)

Type: ***AND-GATE** for the File name*

*Click: **the ellipsis button** to the right of File name and path to navigate to your **work** directory as necessary*

*Click: **Unitless** for the Insert units*

*Click: **OK***

The block that you created, named AND, has been saved to the new AutoCAD drawing file *and-gate.dwg*.

*On your own, **use WBlock** to create separate drawing files for each of the other blocks that you created. Name them **or-gate, nor-gate, nand-gate, inverter,** and **buffer**.*

Tip: *You can use Write Block to export part of any drawing to a separate file. This action can speed up your computer's response time by keeping file sizes smaller. When you are working in an extremely large file, but just need to work on a certain part of it, use Write Block to export that area to a new file. Work on the new, smaller file that contains only the part of the drawing you need. When done, use Insert Block to reinsert the finished work in the larger drawing. You will have to explode it after inserting it before you can edit it.*

Using DesignCenter and Tool Palettes

Next you will use the DesignCenter and Tool Palettes to manage blocks so that you can add them easily to your drawings. The DesignCenter is an easy way to save time on drawings by copying and pasting layer definitions, layouts, and text and dimension styles between drawings. DesignCenter allows you to:

- Browse for drawings or symbol libraries on your computer, your network, or on web pages.
- View definitions for blocks and layers and insert, attach, copy or paste them into the current drawing.
- Update (redefine) a block definition.
- Make shortcuts to drawings, folders, and web pages that you use frequently.
- Add xrefs, blocks, and hatches to drawings.
- Open drawing files in a new window.
- Drag drawings, blocks, and hatches to a convenient tool palette.

*Start a **new** drawing from the **proto.dwt template** provided with the datafiles. Name it **hfadder.dwg**.*

The ribbon View tab, Palettes palette shown in Figure 10.8 provides access to the DesignCenter, and search tools to find information from external sources to quickly add to your drawing. Notice that at the middle of the palette, you can also access the Block commands.

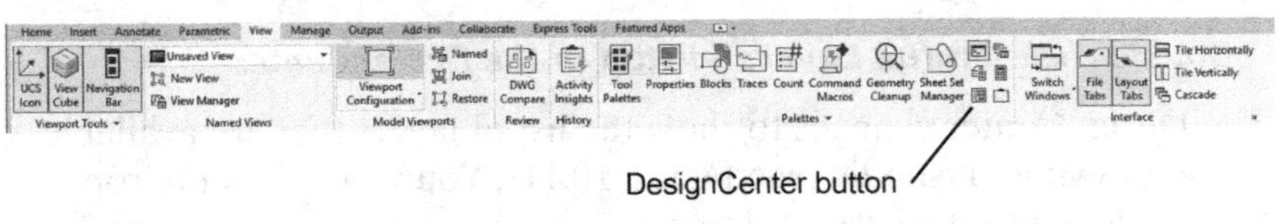

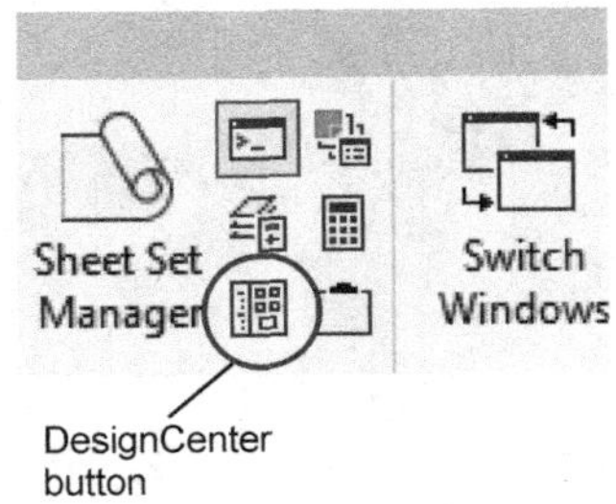

Figure 10.8

Click: ***DesignCenter button*** *from the ribbon View tab, Palettes palette*

On your own, use the ***Folder List area*** *to show your files.*

The DesignCenter appears on your screen similar to Figure 10.9.

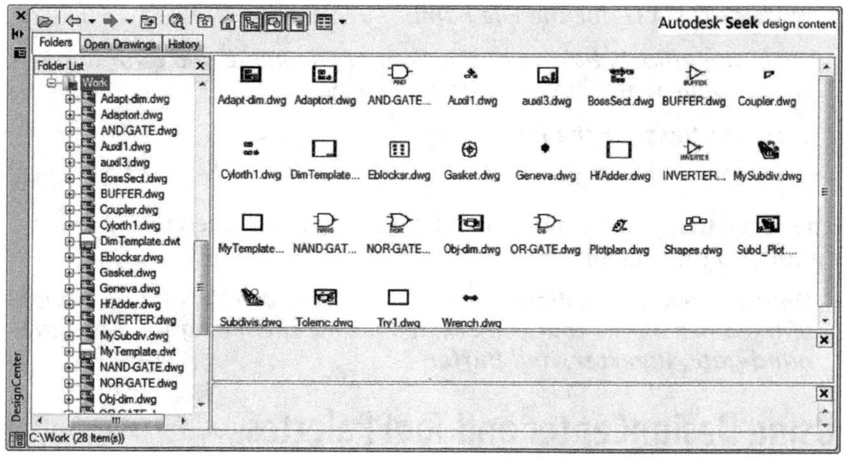

Figure 10.9

Tip: *You can click and drag on the corner of the dialog box to resize it.*

The DesignCenter shows a list of all of the files in the selected directory. You can drag and drop named drawing objects, such as layers, blocks, text and dimension styles, layouts, linetypes, and xrefs into your drawing.

Tip: *You can also show the contents of a drawing by double-clicking on its thumbnail pictured in the list at the right*

Double-click: ***mysubdiv.dwg*** *from tree list at left (if you don't have this drawing use the datafile named subdiv2.dwt)*

The types of named objects in that drawing show (Figure 10.10).

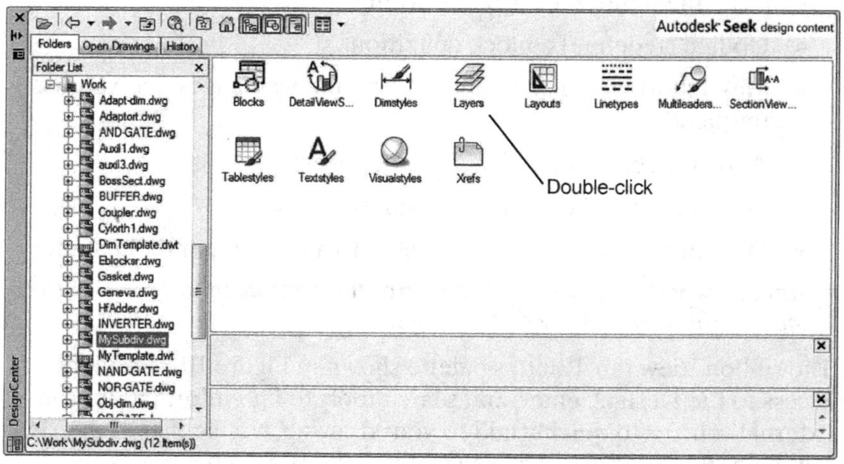

Figure 10.10

Double-click: ***on the Layers button*** *in the DesignCenter*

The DesignCenter changes to show the list of layers that are available inside drawing Mysubdiv (see Figure 10.11). You will drag and drop layer Points into the current drawing.

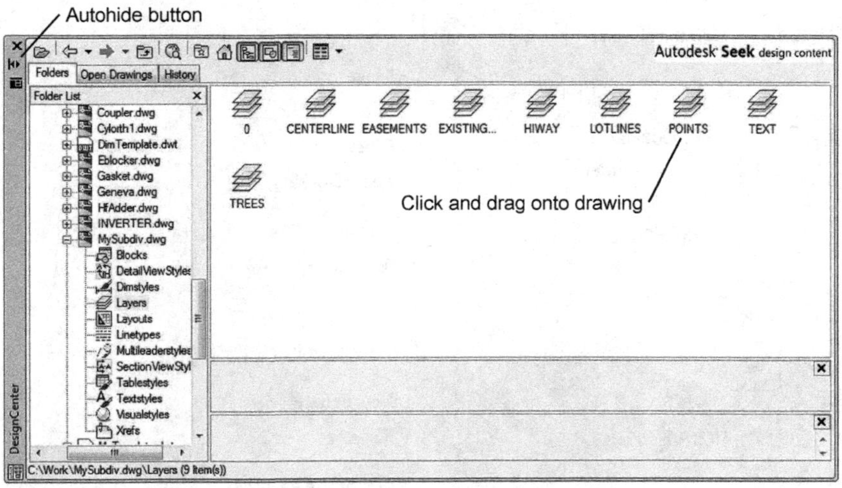

Figure 10.11

Drag layer Points to your current drawing.

Click: ***Layer Control***

Click: ***Autohide*** *from the upper left of the DesignCenter*

You should see that your current drawing now has a new layer named Points as shown in Figure 10.11. It has all the same properties as the layer Points from drawing Mysubdiv, is locked, and has color blue.

Tip: *You do not need to close the Design Center to view the layers. Autohiding leaves it open with only the title bar showing. You will need it in the next steps.*

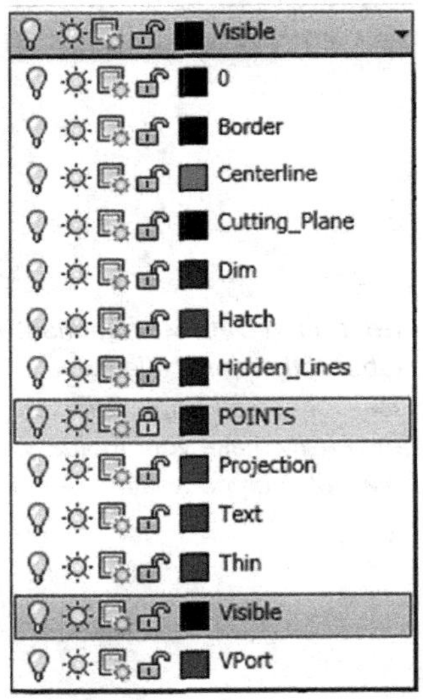

Figure 10.12

Next you will turn on the Tool Palettes and then add your electronic gates to a new tool palette. The Palettes panel is shown in Figure 10.13.

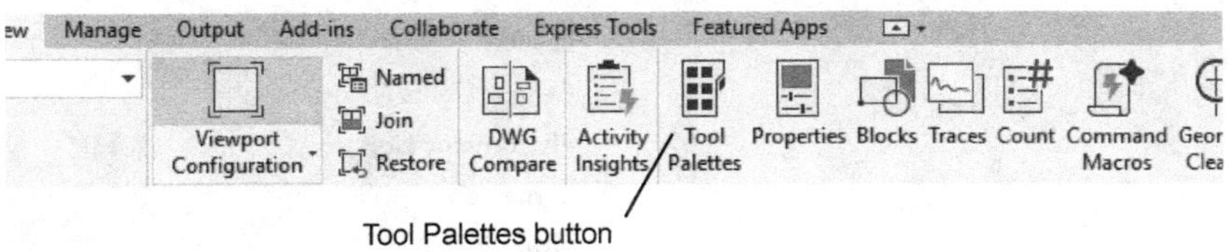

Figure 10.13

Click: ***Tool Palettes button*** *from the ribbon View tab, Palettes panel*

You should see the Tool Palettes appear on your screen as shown in Figure 10.14. The Tool Palettes are an easy way to quickly add hatches and blocks to your drawing without having the entire DesignCenter open. A tool palette is not backward compatible. A new tool palette cannot necessarily be used in an older version of AutoCAD.

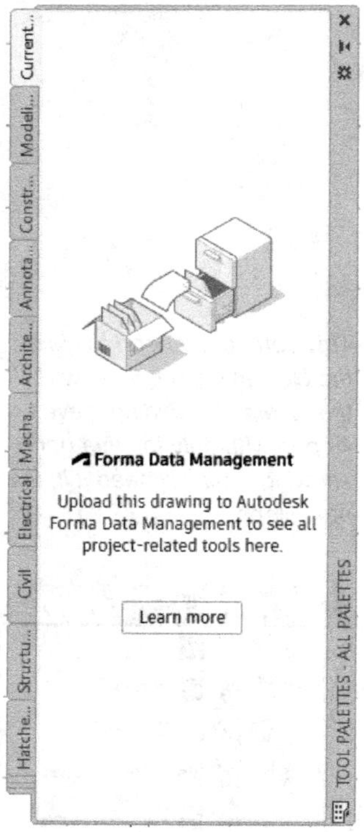

Tip: *Forma Data Management subscription service lets you use Connected Support Files and easily make your toolbars available company wide.*

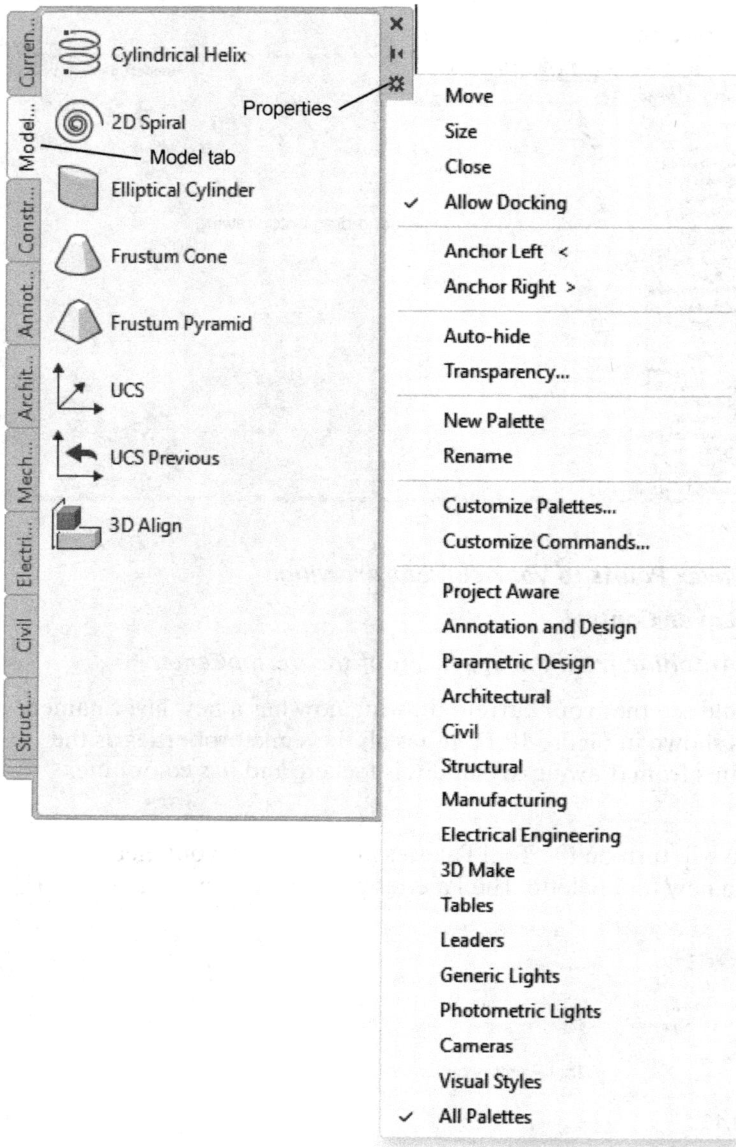

Figure 10.14

*Click: **Model tab** to show it uppermost*

*Click: **the Properties button** at the top right of the Tool Palettes to show the menu choices*

The pop-up menu appears as shown in Figure 10.14. You will use it to add a new tab to the Tool Palettes for your electronic blocks.

*Click: **New Palette***

*Type: **Electronic** when the text cursor appears and press [Enter]*

A new tab has been added to the Tool Palettes. It is shown in Figure 10.15. You will drag and drop your electronic gate drawings onto this new Tool Palette.

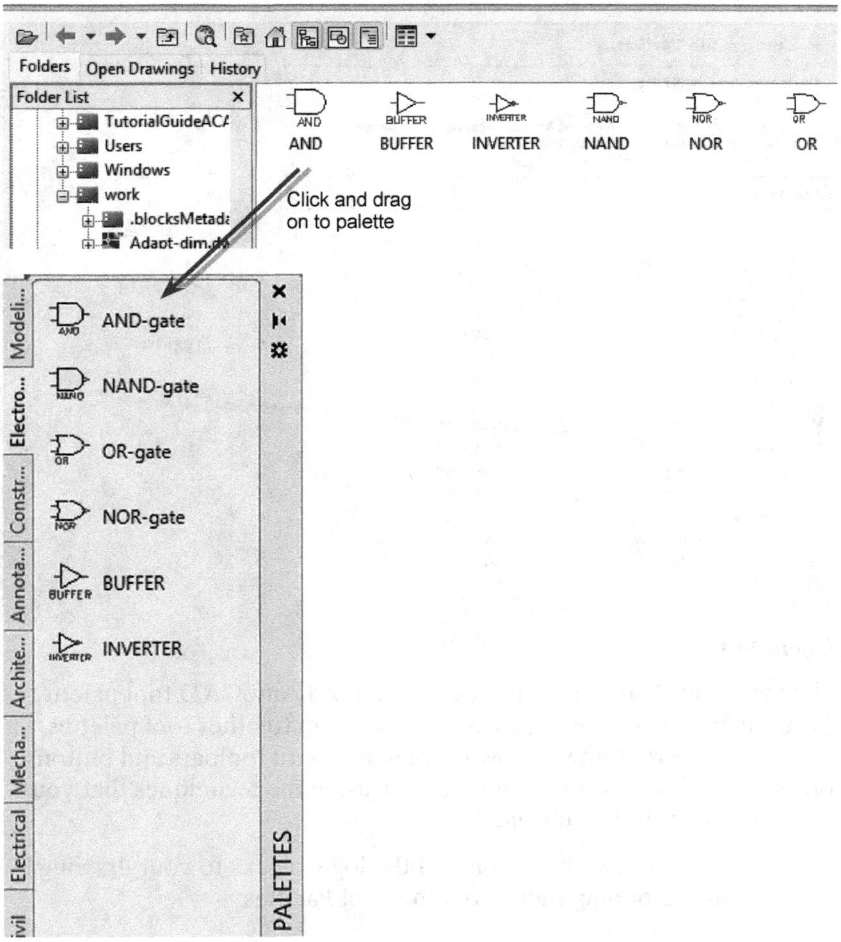

Figure 10.15

On your own, use the DesignCenter to show the drawings in your \work folder. ***Drag and drop the logic gate drawings onto the Tool Palette*** *as shown in Figure 10.13.*

Continue until you have added all 6 logic gates so that your Tool Palette is similar to Figure 10.15.

Close *the DesignCenter.*

Next you will add the Explode command to this tool palette. You can drag tools (command buttons) onto a palette when the Customize User Interface dialog box is open.

Right-click: ***on a blank area of the tool palette***

Click: ***Customize commands*** *from the menu that pops up*

The Customize dialog box appears on your screen.

On your own, drag a copy of the Explode command from the dialog box onto the tool palette as shown in Figure 10.16.

Close the Customize dialog box when you have finished.

The Explode command is added to the tool palette as in Figure 10.16.

Tip: *You can also drag blocks from your drawing directly onto a tool palette.*

Tip: *You can import PDF files into your AutoCAD drawings. The PDFimport command is located on the Insert tab. This can be very useful.*

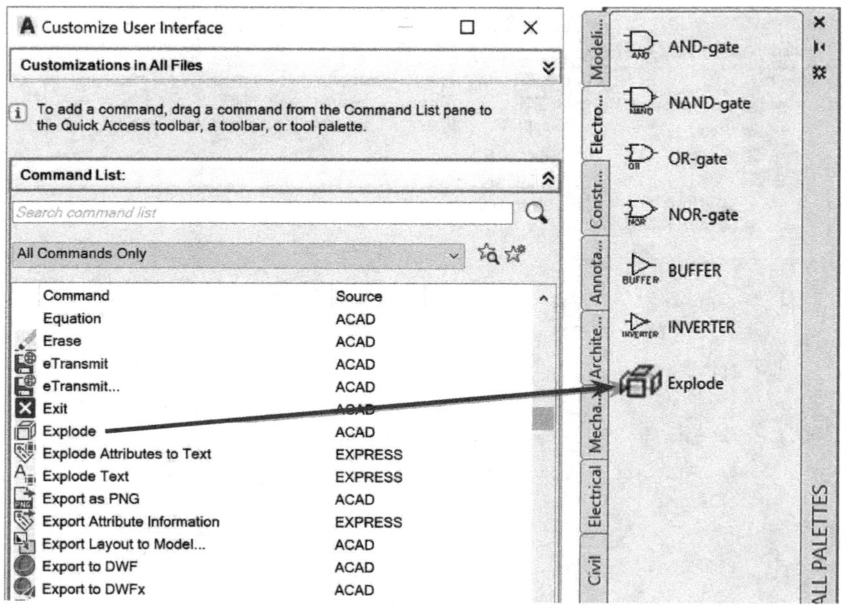

Figure 10.16

Now you have learned to create a customized AutoCAD tool palette. You can create your own blocks and add them to other tool palettes. You can also program your own commands onto toolbars and buttons or modify existing toolbars and buttons using the techniques that you will learn later in this tutorial.

Tip: *The Minsert command lets you insert a rectangular array of blocks. It can be useful when you're laying out drawings that have a pattern, such as rows of desks or rows of electronic components. Typing the command MULTIPLE and pressing enter allows you to make any command repeat multiple times without restarting it. The Divide and Measure commands also allow you to insert blocks. The Divide command divides an object that you select into the number of parts that you specify. You can either insert a point object where the divisions will be (as you did in Tutorial 5), or you can select the Block option and specify a block name. The Measure command works in much the same way, except that instead of specifying the number of divisions that you want to use, you specify the lengths of the divisions. Use the on-line Help facility to get more information about these commands.*

You are ready to try adding some of the logic blocks to your drawing by dragging and dropping them from the Tool Palettes.

Drawing the Half-Adder Circuit

You will use the new tool palette you created to draw a half-adder circuit with electronic logic symbols.

> ***Switch to paper space*** *and use the* ***Edit Text*** *command to* ***change the text in the title block to HALF-ADDER CIRCUIT.*** *Add your* ***name****. Specify* ***NONE for the scale,*** *as electronic diagrams usually aren't drawn to scale.*
>
> ***Switch back to model space*** *when you are finished.*
>
> *On your own, set the* ***current layer to THIN*** *and* ***Snap to 0.1042*** *so that it will align with the spacing between the leads on the logic symbols that you created.*
>
> ***Use the Electronic tool palette on your own to insert the logic symbols*** *as shown in Figure 10.17.*

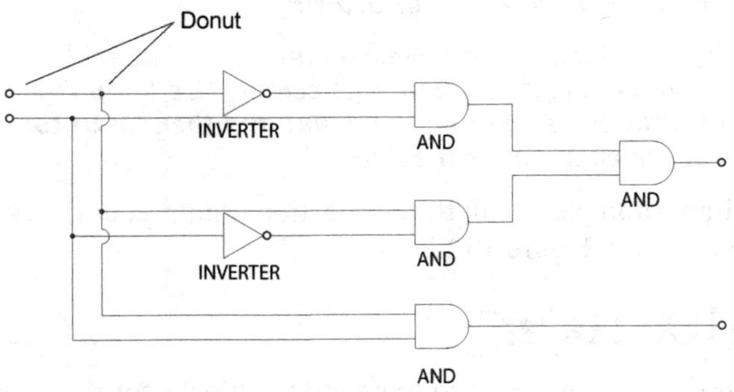

Figure 10.17

*Use the **Line and Arc** commands with **Snap to Endpoint** to connect the output from one logic circuit to the inputs of the next as shown.*

You will use the Donut command to make the filled and open circles for connection points.

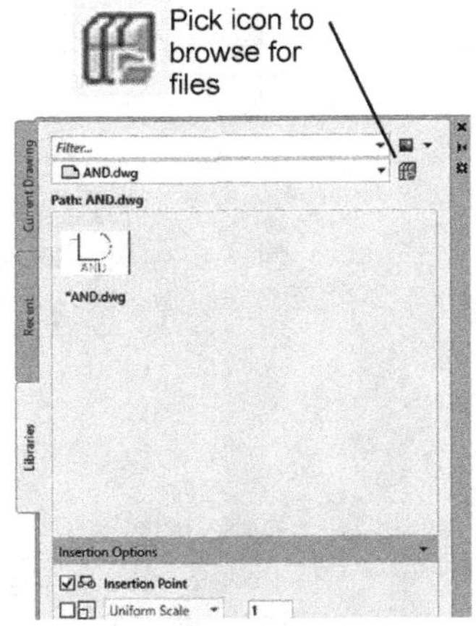

Tip: *You can use the Libraries tab from the Blocks panel to insert blocks easily. Group your blocks into libraries or keep similar blocks in a folder. You can store the libraries in the cloud so they are available to all your devices.*

Using Donut

The Donut command draws filled circles or concentric filled circles. See Figure 10.18. Donut is found on the ribbon Home tab, expanded Draw panel. The Donut command requires numerical values for the inside and outside diameters of the concentric circles, as well as a location for the center point. If you enter a zero value for the inside diameter, a solid dot appears on the screen. The diameter of the dot will equal the stated outside diameter value. Next, you will draw some donuts off to the side of your logic circuit drawing.

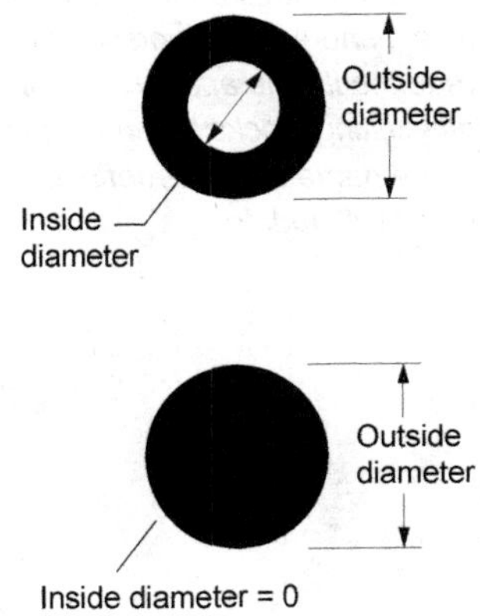

Figure 10.18

*Click: **Donut button,** from the ribbon Home tab, Draw panel*

Specify inside diameter of donut <0.5000>: ***[Enter]***

Specify outside diameter of donut <1.0000>: ***[Enter]***

Note that a doughnut-like shape is now moving with your cursor. The Center of donut prompt is repeated so that you can draw more than one donut. Select points on your screen.

Specify center of donut or <exit>: ***select a point off to the side of your drawing***

Specify center of donut or <exit>: ***select another point***

Specify center of donut or <exit>: [Enter] to exit the command

*On your own, **erase the donuts** that you drew to the side.*

***Restart Donut** and set the **inside diameter** for the donut to **0**.*

*Set the **outside diameter** to **0.075**.*

***Draw the solid connection points** for the logic circuit that you see in Figure 10.17.*

Next add the open donuts at the ends of the lines.

*Restart **Donut** and set the **inner diameter** to **0.0625** and the **outer diameter** to **0.075**.*

Create four donuts on the side of your drawing.

Place the four donuts by using the ***Move*** *command so that each donut is attached at its outside edge, not its center. Use* ***Snap to Quadrant*** *to select the base point on the donut and then* ***Snap to Endpoint*** *to select the endpoint of the line.*

When you have drawn and placed all the connection points, your drawing should look like that in Figure 10.17.

Freezing the TEXT2 Layer

The drawing *electr.dwg*, which you used to create the blocks for the logic gates, contained different layers for the text, lines, and shapes of the logic gates. You can freeze or turn off layers to control the visibility within parts of a block. You will freeze the text in the blocks because it is there to help identify the blocks while you are inserting them but would not ordinarily be shown on an electronic circuit diagram. The text in the blocks is on layer TEXT2. The text in the title block is on layer TEXT. You will use Layer Control to freeze the layer that holds the text showing the name of the type of gate.

Tip: *You can quickly change blocks by redefining them. If you redefine a block, the appearance of all the blocks with that name will update. To redefine a block, make the changes you want to the block. Then use the Block command to save it as a block again, retaining the same file name. You will be prompted that the block already exists and asked if you want to redefine it. The appearance of all existing blocks that have the same name as the redefined block will update.*

Use the **Layer Control** list that appears on your screen to **freeze layer TEXT2.** The names of the gates should disappear from the screen.

Save your drawing on your own before continuing.

Your drawing should look like Figure 10.19.

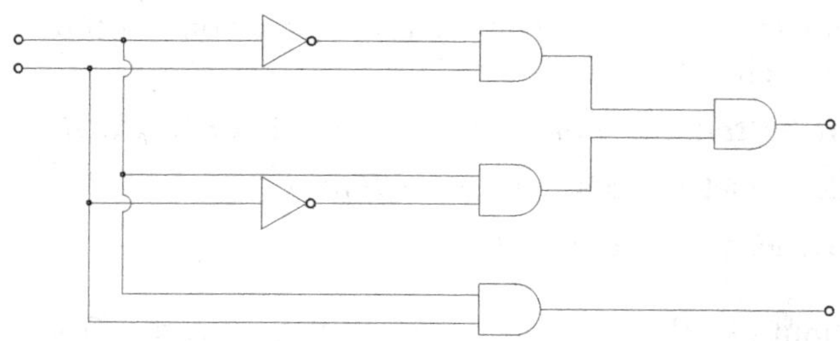

Figure 10.19

Creating Object Groups

Tip: *You can quickly create unnamed groups using the Group palette on the Home tab.*

Another powerful method of organizing objects is to use named groups. You can select these groups for use with other commands. You will select Group Manager from the Home tab Group panel (Figure 10.20).

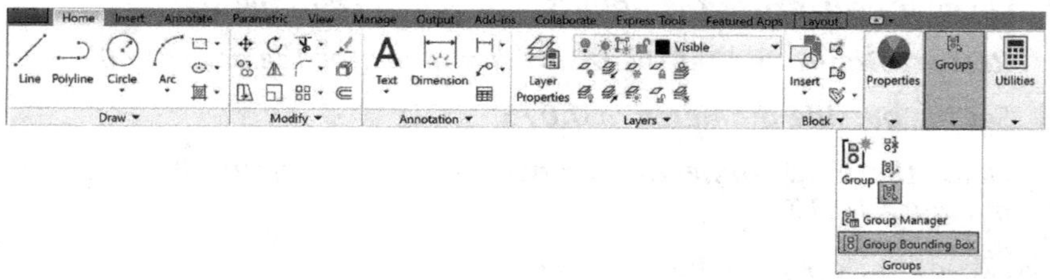

Figure 10.20

 *Click:* ***Group Manager button***

The Object Grouping dialog box appears on your screen, as shown in Figure 10.21.

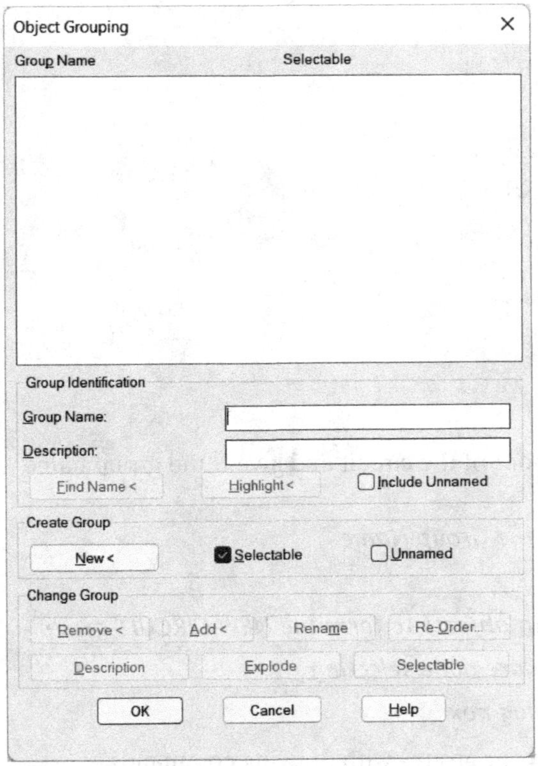

Figure 10.21

You will create a new group named EXISTING- CIRCUIT comprised of the upper Inverter and And gate and their leads. Groups can be selectable, not selectable, named, or unnamed. When a group is selectable, the entire group becomes selected if you click on a member of the group when selecting objects. You can return to the dialog box and turn Selectable off at any time.

Type the following information into the Group Identification area of the dialog box.

Group Name: ***EXISTING-CIRCUIT***

Description: ***Portions of the Existing Circuit***

Make sure Selectable is checked.

Click: ***New***

You return to your drawing for the next selections.

Select objects for grouping: ***click the upper Inverter and upper And gate and the two leads to the left of each of them***

Select objects: ***[Enter]***

The dialog box returns to your screen as shown in Figure 10.22 so that you can continue creating groups.

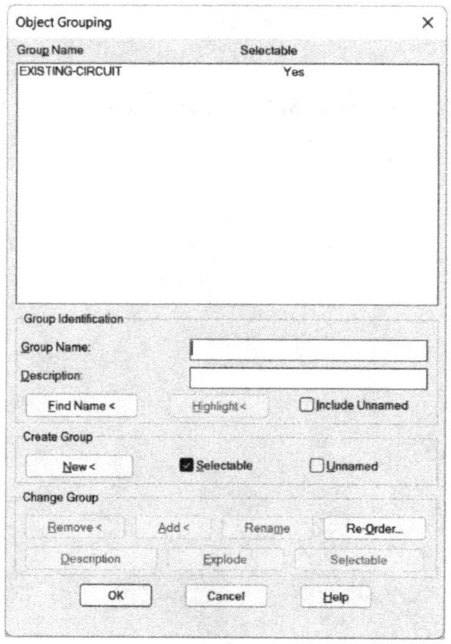

Figure 10.22

You will group the remainder of the circuit and give it the group name NEW-CIRCUIT.

Type: ***NEW-CIRCUIT*** *as the Group Name*

Click: ***New***

Select all the remaining objects *to form the NEW-CIRCUIT group.*

Press: ***[Enter]*** *when you are done selecting*

Click: ***OK*** *to exit the dialog box*

Now, you are ready to try your groups with drawing commands. Remember, you can click on any member of a selectable group to select the entire group. You will change the linetype property for the NEW-CIRCUIT group to a HIDDEN linetype. To cause the Properties palette to appear on your screen,

Press: ***[Ctrl]+1*** *to show the* ***Properties palette***

Click: ***on one of the symbols from the NEW-CIRCUIT group***

The entire group becomes selected similar to Figure 10.23.

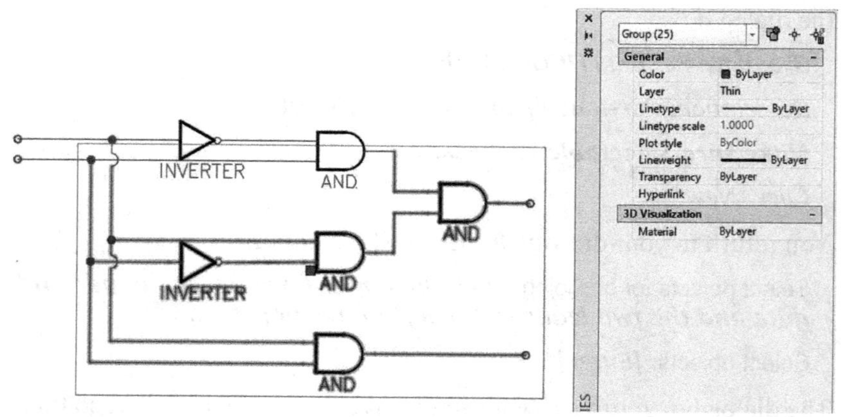

Figure 10.23

Click: ***Hidden*** *from the pull-down list for Linetype*

Click: ***Windows Close button*** *to remove the Properties dialog box from your screen*

Press: ***[Esc] twice*** *to unselect the objects*

The wiring diagram for the new portion of the circuit becomes dashed lines.

Click: ***Undo*** *from the Quick Access toolbar*

This will reverse this linetype change before you go on.

To be able to select each object individually, return to the Object Grouping dialog box on your own and turn Selectable off.

Your finished drawing should look like Figure 10.24.

Save and **plot** your drawing. Do not close the drawing yet.

Close the Tool Palettes if you have not already done so.

Warning: *You should avoid creating groups of a hundred or more items as this will degrade software performance.*

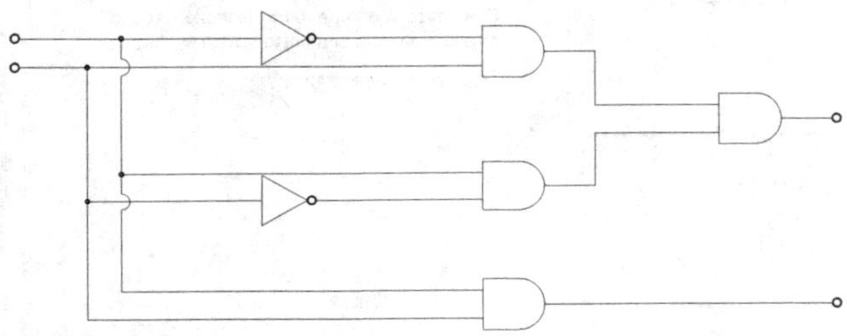

Figure 10.24

The DesignCenter and Tool Palettes are important tools for reusing your past work efficiently. Make the most of them! Reuse layers, blocks, dimension styles, and other named objects from your past drawings to create new drawings quickly.

Creating Custom Interfaces

Another way in which you can *customize* your AutoCAD software is by creating new toolbars and palettes and programming the existing toolbars and palettes to contain the commands you use most frequently. You can also reprogram existing buttons.

You can save customized user interfaces called workspaces which show the tools and palettes that you find useful. Using different workspaces for different tasks makes it quick to create the drawings you need. Follow the next steps to create a custom workspace.

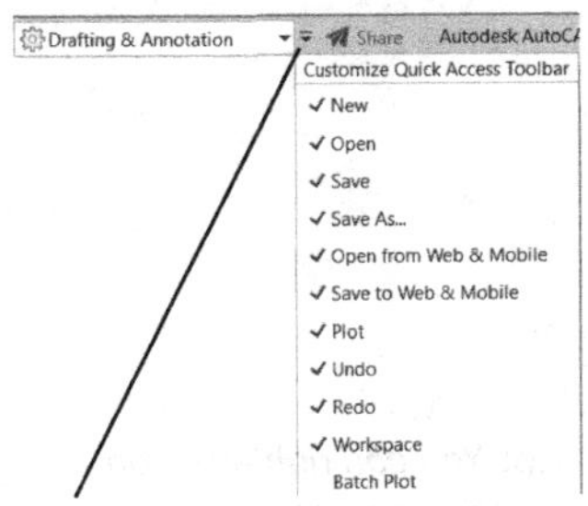

Tip: *If you do not see the Workspace selection on your Quick Access toolbar, expand the options using the right hand arrow and select it.*
You can also right-click the workspace icon from the status bar and use that menu.

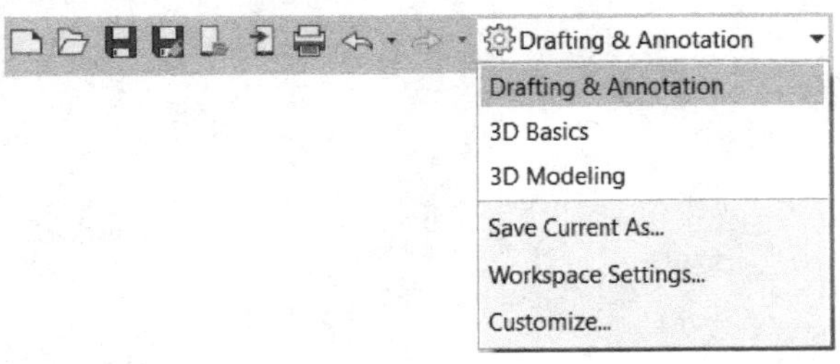

Figure 10.25

Expand the workspace selections *as shown in Figure 10.25.*

Click: ***Customize***

The Customize User Interface dialog box appears on your screen.

Right-click: ***Workspaces as shown in Figure 10.26***

Click: ***New, Workspace***

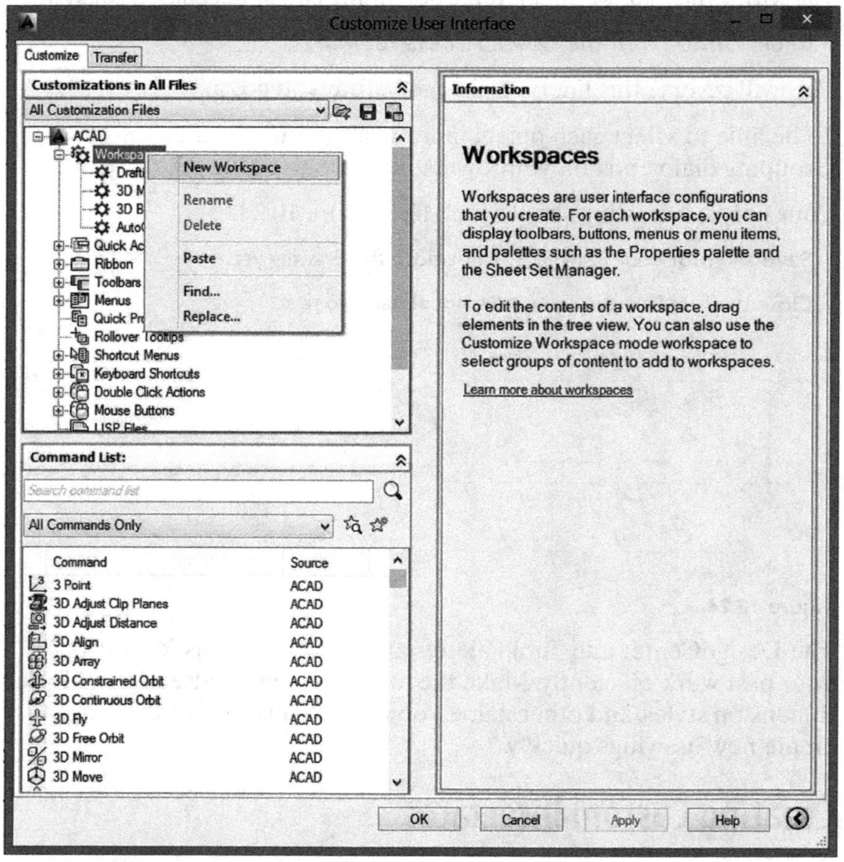

Figure 10.26

A new workspace named Workspace1 is added to the list below the AutoCAD Default workspace.

Type: MyWay *as the name for your workspace, overtyping the name Workspace1*

Tip: *You can right-click on a workspace name and use the pop-up menu to choose Rename to change the name if you missed overtyping it.*

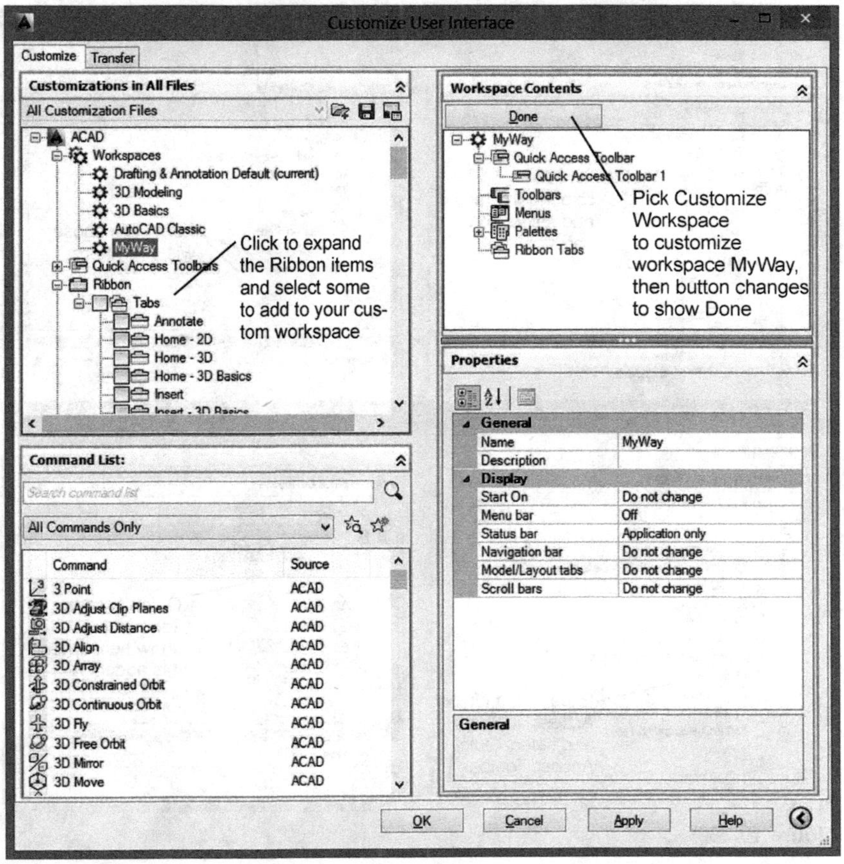

Figure 10.27

Figure 10.27 shows the dialog box as it appears after the new workspace is added. Next, customize your workspace, *MyWay*, by selecting which standard interface items are shown on it.

Click: ***Customize Workspace button*** *from the upper right of the dialog box in the Workspace Contents area similar to Figure 10.27.*

The items in the right side of the dialog box become active. Next, select items from the left side of the dialog box to add to your workspace.

On your own, **select some of the ribbon tabs** by clicking them so they appear checked as shown in Figure 10.28. You will notice them add to the Ribbon Tabs in the area at the right where your workspace is shown.

Scroll down in the upper left portion of the dialog box and expand the list of **Quick Access Toolbars**. Click to show the **Quick Access Toolbar 1** in your custom workspace. This is important or switching back to the normal workspace will be more difficult.

Warning: *Be sure to add the Workspaces toolbar or you will have trouble switching back to the default workspace quickly.*

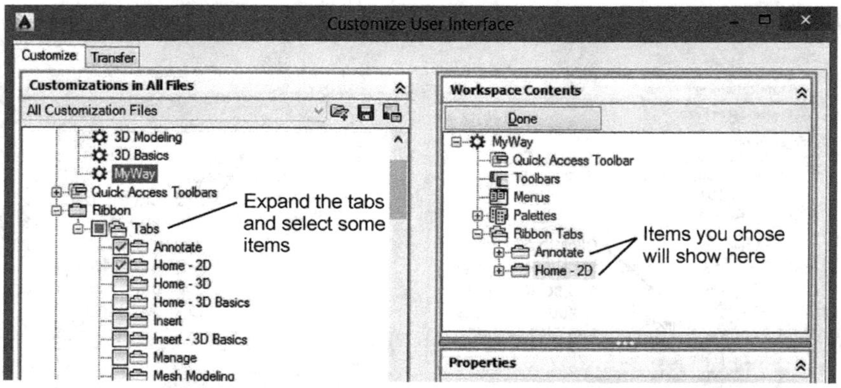

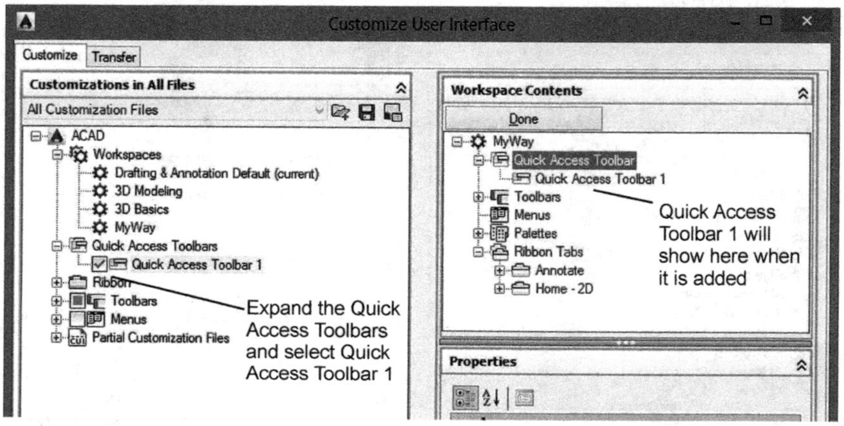

Figure 10.28

Click: ***Done*** *to finish customizing your new workspace*

Creating a Toolbar

Next, you will create your own toolbar for the logic symbols that you created. You will program the buttons on the new toolbar to insert the logic symbols. All workspaces use the same version of a toolbar. Any changes made to a toolbar are reflected in all workspaces that have that toolbar. By default, a new toolbar is displayed in all workspaces. To create a new toolbar,

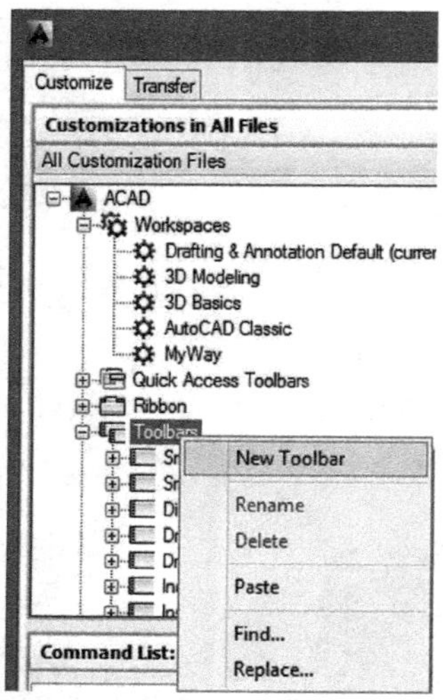

Right-click: ***on Toolbars*** *in the top left window to show the pop-up menu (you may have to collapse some of the times in the tree or scroll to see it)*

Click: ***New, Toolbar***

Toolbar1 is added to the end of the list of toolbars shown in the dialog box, as in Figure 10.29.

On your own, rename Toolbar1 to **Logic**.

Click: ***Apply***

You will see a small toolbar appear on your screen. (It does not have any buttons on it, so it may be very hard to notice. You may have to move the dialog box around as it may be behind it.) See Figure 10.30.

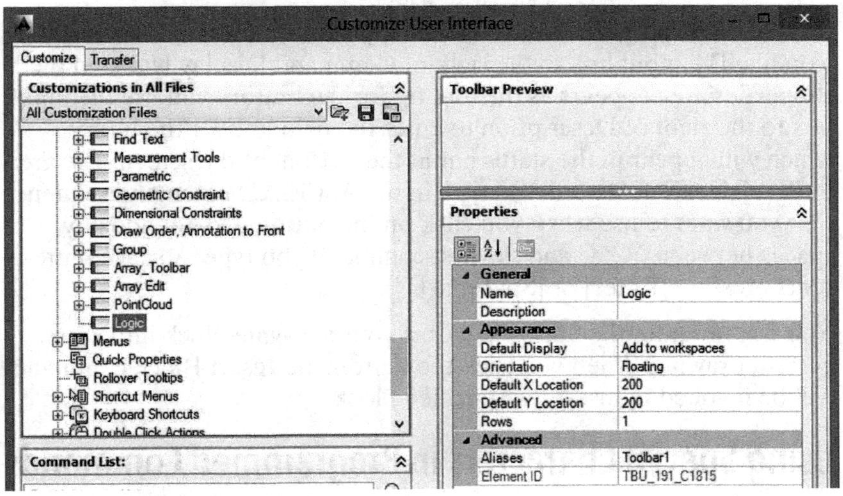

Figure 10.29

Next you will create a new command from the Command List area.

*Click: **New button to the right of the command categories***

Command1 is added to the list of commands that appear in the lower left of the dialog box.

On your own, rename Command1 in the list in the lower left to And-gate as shown in Figure 10.31.

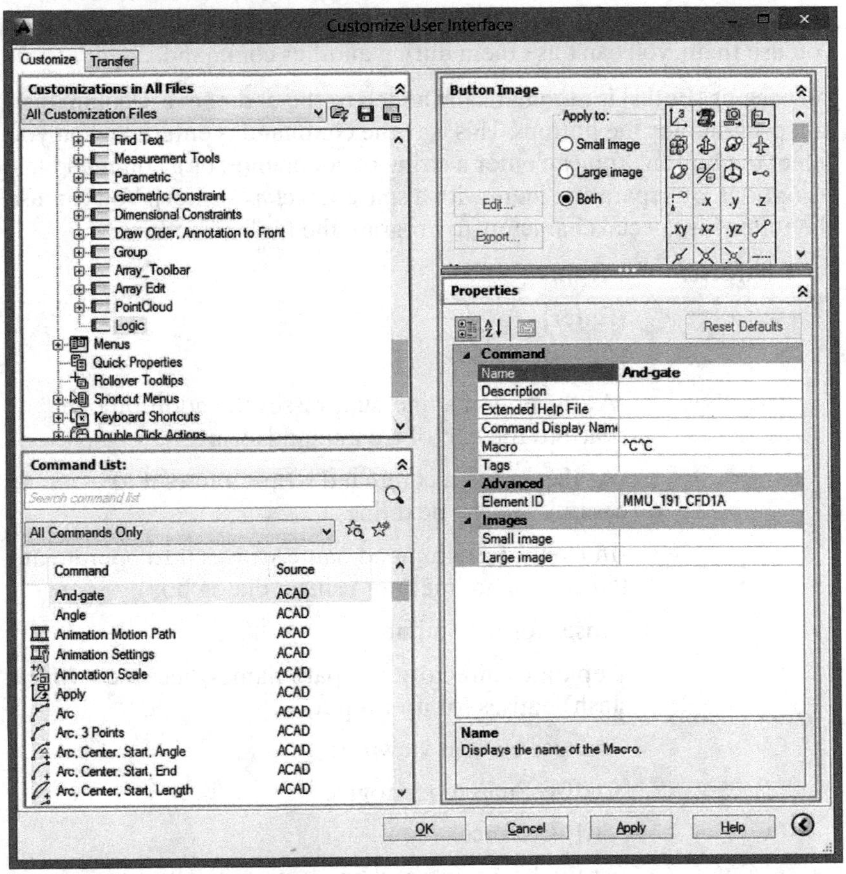

Figure 10.31

Tip: *When you create a toolbar, it is added by default to all workspaces. This is controlled by the On By Default item in the Properties window for the toolbar.*

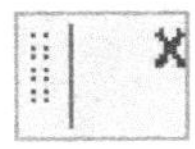

Figure 10.30

Next you will program the command appearance and select the button icon file. The input box to the right of Command Display Name in the Properties area appears as the tool tip for the button. You use the input box to the right of Description to enter the help line for the button, which will appear in the status bar at the bottom of the screen. The area to the right of Macro lets you type in the AutoCAD command sequence that you want to use when you click on the button. Do not add any spaces between ^C^C and the first command you type. A space represents pressing [Enter] or [Spacebar].

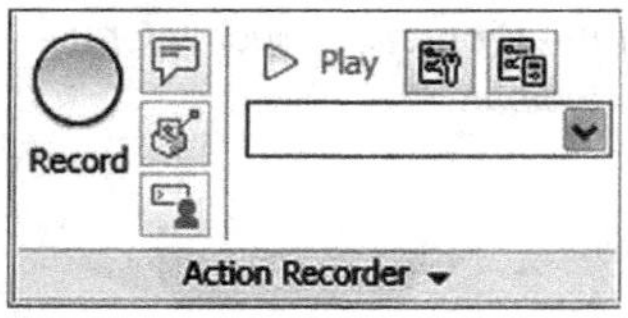

Tip: *You can use the Action recorder from the Manage tab to quickly save macros.*

You will program the button to insert your and-gate block into your current drawing. When you click the button, the Insert Block command will be invoked to insert the specified block.

Using Special Characters in Programmed Commands

There are some special characters that you can use in programming the toolbars. One of these is ^C. If you put ^C in front of the command name you are programming, it will cancel any unfinished command when you select its button from the toolbar. In programming menus and buttons, putting cancel twice before a command is often a good idea in case you have left a subprompt active (so that it would take two cancels to return to the command prompt). Putting cancel before the Insert Block command is useful because you cannot select this command during another command. Do not add cancel before the toggle modes or transparent commands (a ' must precede them) because, if you execute cancel before you use them, you can't use them during another command.

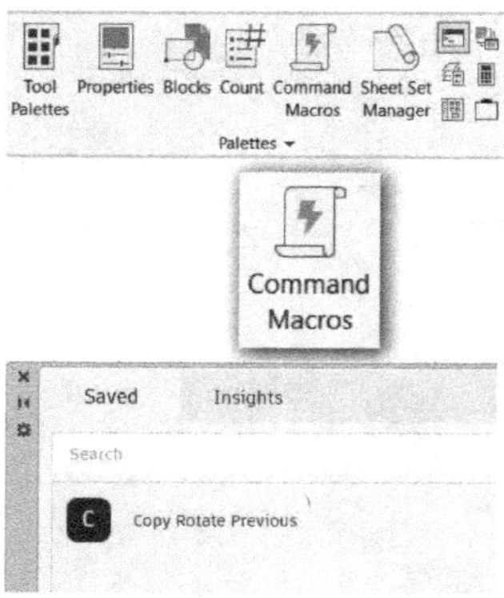

Tip: *The View tab, Palettes panel, Command Macros button opens the Command Macros palette.*
The Command Macros palette has two tabs; Saved and Insights. These provide helpful tools for creating macros. These work the same as the macro you will create using Customize User Interface. One handy feature is that from the Saved tab you can right-click a command macro and choose Add to Ribbon.
From the Command prompt, enter Commandmacros to open the Command Macros palette.

A space or [Enter] is automatically added to the end of every command you program for the buttons. This way the command is entered when you select the button. You can enter a string of commands, or a command and its options, by separating them with a space to act as [Enter]. You can use the following special characters to program the toolbar buttons:

Character	Meaning
space	[Enter]
;	[Enter]
^Z	-At the end of a line, suppresses the addition of a space to the end of a command string
+	-At the end of a command string, allows it to continue to the next line
–	-In front of a command name, causes it to operate at the command line (not using a dialog box)
\	Pauses for user input
/	-Separates directories in path names, because \ (backslash) pauses for user input
^V	Changes current viewport
^B	[Ctrl]-B Snap mode toggle
^C	[Ctrl]-C Cancel
*^C^C	-At the beginning of a line, automatically restarts command sequence (repeating)

^D	[Ctrl]-D Coordinates toggle
^E	[Ctrl]-E Isoplane toggle
^G	[Ctrl]-G Grid mode toggle
^O	[Ctrl]-O Ortho mode toggle

An __ (underscore) preceding a command or option automatically translates AutoCAD keywords and command options for use with foreign-language versions.

Click: ***in the input box to the right of Command Display Name***

Type: ***AND-GATE INSERT***

Click: ***in the input box to the right of Description***

Type: ***INSERTS AND-GATE SYMBOL***

Click: ***to the right of ^C^C, for Macro***

Type: ***-INSERT c:/work/AND-GATE.dwg***

Click: ***to the right of Small Image***

Type: ***c:\datafiles\And.bmp** (or click ... and browse for the file)*

Click: ***Both** (if needed in the upper right near the image tile)*

When you have finished making the selections, the dialog box appears as shown in Figure 10.32.

Tip: *The block or file that you are inserting must be in the current path or you must specify where the block is located by adding the path name ahead of the block name. (You can change the current path in the Preferences dialog box.) The back slash has a special meaning in this dialog box: pause for user input. Therefore, when you add a path to a macro, you use the forward slash instead of the backslash to separate the directories (e.g., c:/work/and-gate.dwg). Finally, you can create a block library drawing and insert it into the drawing so that all the blocks are available in the current drawing prior to using the Logic toolbar that you just created.*

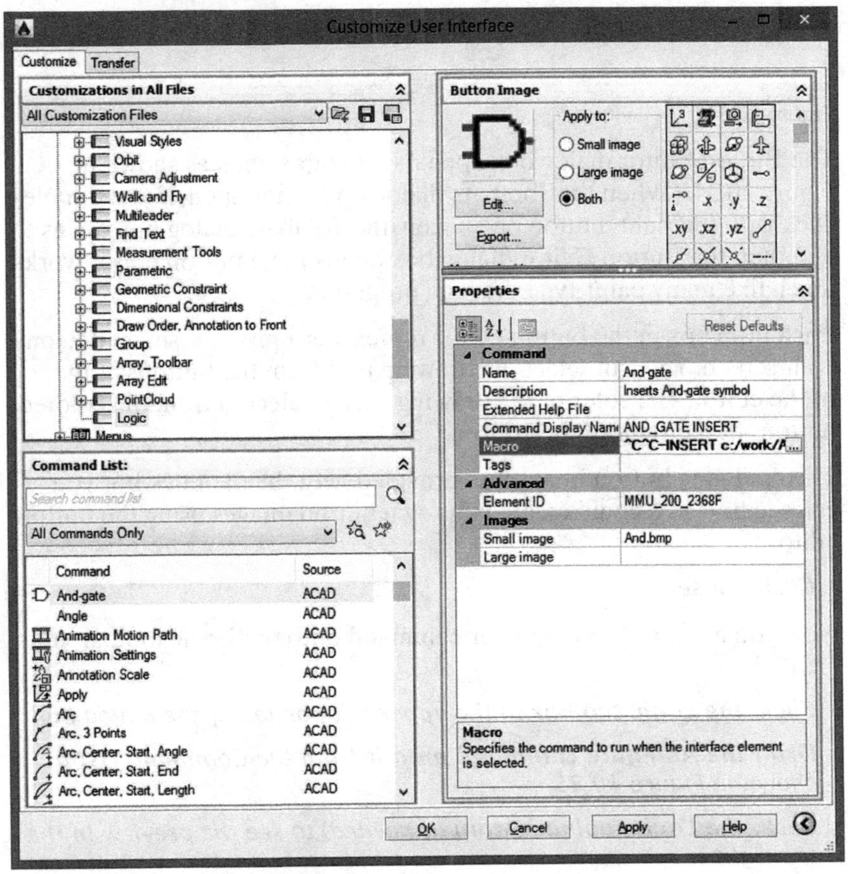

Figure 10.32

Tip: *You may need to add the path to where your and-gate drawing is stored (i.e., ^C^C-Insert c:/work/and-gate). You must use a forward slash in the path. Do not add spaces between the ^C^C and the Insert command. Do not forget to type the hyphen (-) in front of the insert command so the command will run at the command prompt.*

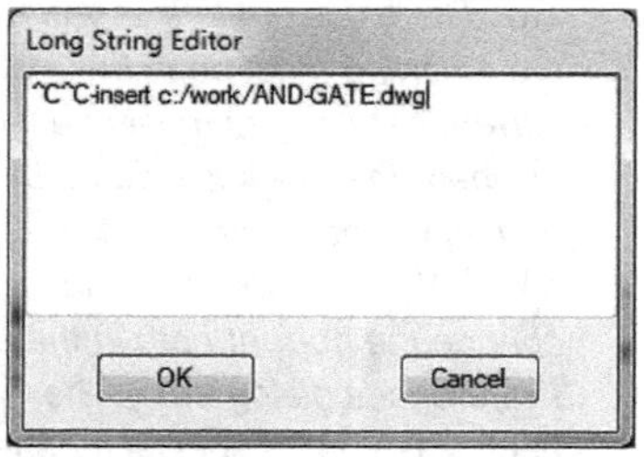

Figure 10.33

Click: ***in the text box next to Macro***

Click: ***... (the ellipsis to the right of the Macro area)***

The Long String editor appears on your screen as shown in Figure 10.33. You can use it to see and edit long macros for commands. Your command to insert the And-gate should look like the figure.

Click: ***OK** to exit the Long String Editor*

Scroll down in the image list in the Button Image area; if needed click the new *And.bmp* icon if it does not already appear as shown in Figure 10.32, then

Click: ***Edit** below the Button Image tile at the top right*

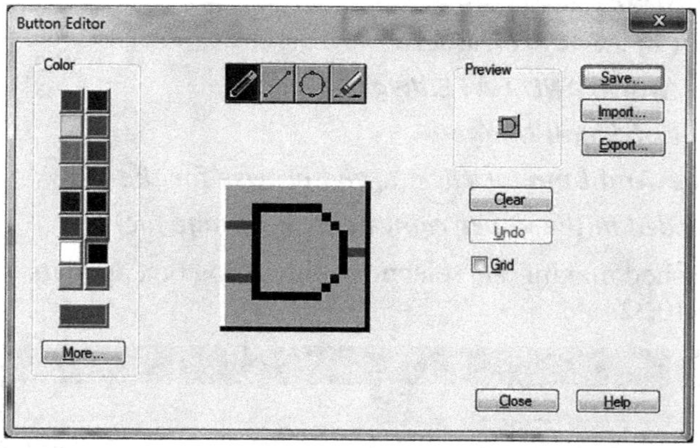

Figure 10.34

The Button Editor dialog box appears on your screen as shown in Figure 10.34. (When the Toolbars dialog box is not open, if you double-click with the right button on an icon, the Toolbars dialog box opens and then the Button Editor dialog box opens.) The button editor works much like many paint-type drawing programs.

Each little box in the button editor represents a pixel, or single dot, on your screen. You can select the drawing tool from the buttons at the top of the editor. The color of the drawing tool is selected from the colored buttons at the right of the editor.

The And-gate button image was provided with the datafiles, but you can see how you could create your own button images using the button editor.

Click: ***Close***

Now you are ready to drag your command onto the Logic toolbar you created.

Click: ***the Logic toolbar** in the upper left portion of the dialog box*

***Drag the And-gate command onto it** from the Command List as shown in Figure 10.35.*

Click: ***the Logic toolbar again** (if needed) to see the preview in the top right*

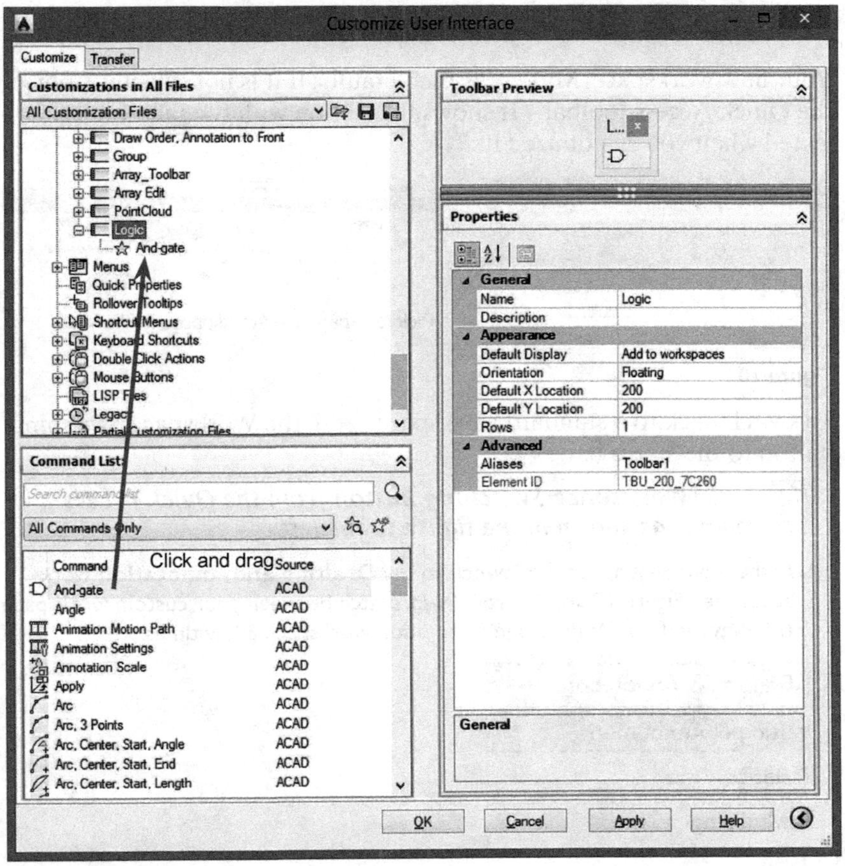

Figure 10.35

Click: ***Apply***

Click: ***OK*** *to close the Customize User Interface dialog box*

Close the Design Feed window if it appears.

When you click Apply, your selections are applied to the toolbar. You should now see the And-gate icon that you made appear on your Logic toolbar as shown in Figure 10.36.

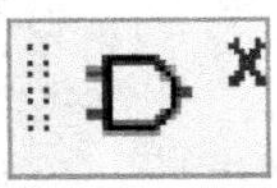

Figure 10.36

All the dialog boxes should now be closed. Close Tool Palettes if necessary to see the drawing editor.

Click: And-gate button *from your new toolbar*

The And gate appears attached to the crosshairs, ready for insertion into your drawing.

Position it as you like in your drawing and then click. Press [Enter] for the remaining prompts for scale and rotation.

The And-gate should appear in your drawing.

On your own, close all drawings.

Tip: *If the And gate doesn't move with the cross hairs, press the [Esc] key and try it again. If that doesn't fix the problem, return to the button properties dialog and check to see that you have the command entered with the correct syntax.*

Start a new drawing from the default template ***acad.dwt.***

Your new workspace, MyWay, is the default. (If it is not select it from the Quick Access toolbar.) It shows the ribbon with the tabs you selected when you customized it.

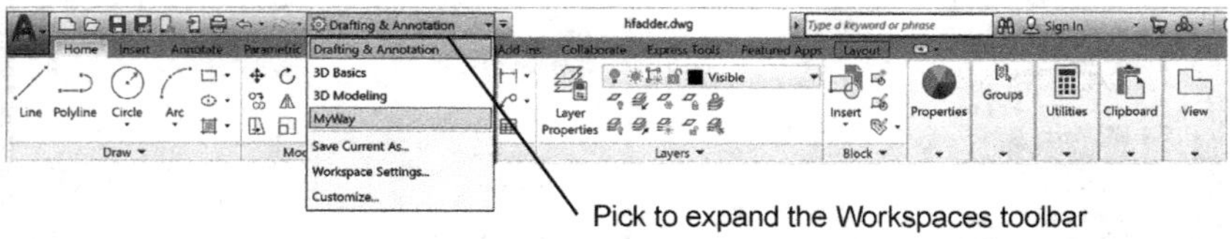

Figure 10.37

To switch back to a standard workspace, add the Workspace Switching button to the status bar.

 *Click: **Workspace Switching button** from the Quick Access toolbar as shown in the figure to the left.*

Use the menu that appears to switch to the **Drafting and Annotation** workspace (see Figure 10.38). On your own, switch between your custom workspace (MyWay) and the Drafting and Annotation workspace a few times.

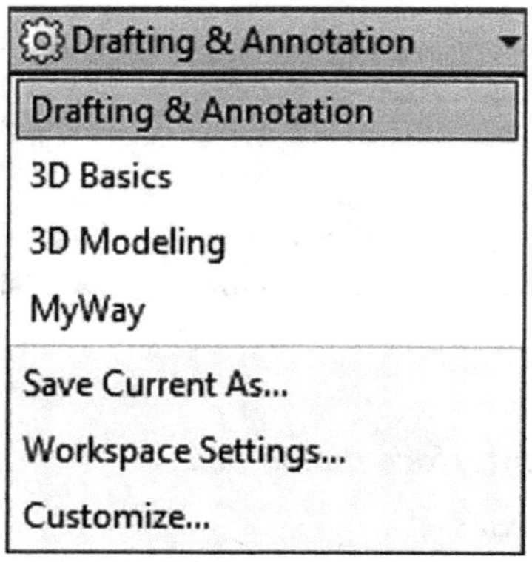

Figure 10.38

Click the [X] to close the Logic toolbar.

Exit the AutoCAD program.

You have completed Tutorial 10.

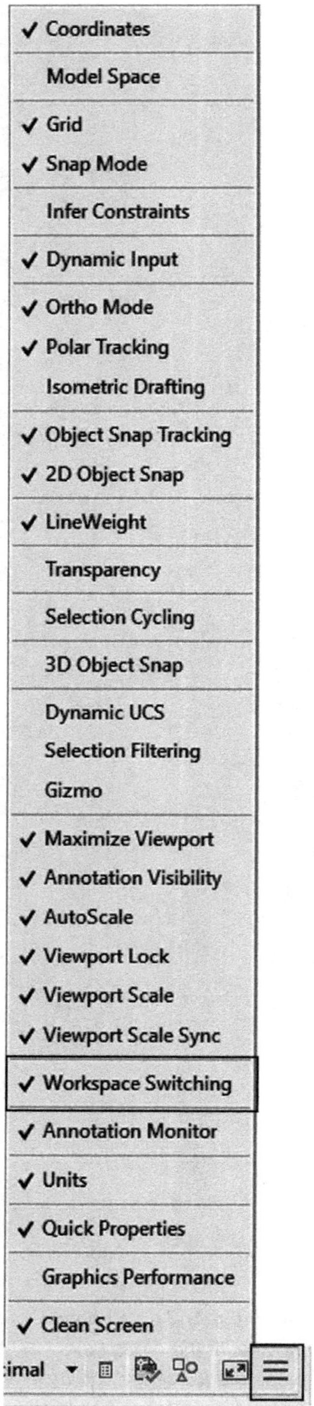

Tip: *You can select the Customization button and add the Workspace Switching button to the status bar.*

Key Terms

And gate	block reference	group	Nor gate
block	Buffer gate	Inverter gate	Or gate
block name	customize	Nand gate	selectable group

Key Commands (keyboard shortcut)

Block (B)	DesignCenter	Multiple Insert (MINSERT)	Write Block (W)
Commandmacros	Donut	Object Group (GROUP)	
Customize User Interface (CUI)	EXPLODE	Tool Palettes	
Customize Workspace	Insert Block (INS)		

Exercises

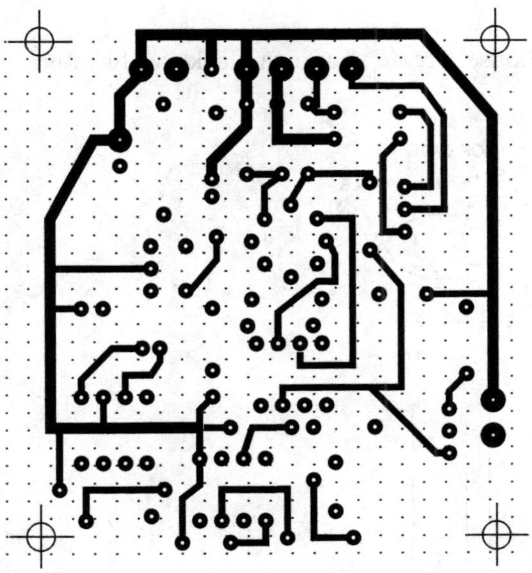

Exercise 10.1 Stress Test Circuit

Create this circuit board layout, using Grid and Snap set to 0.2. Use donuts and polylines of different widths to draw the circuit.

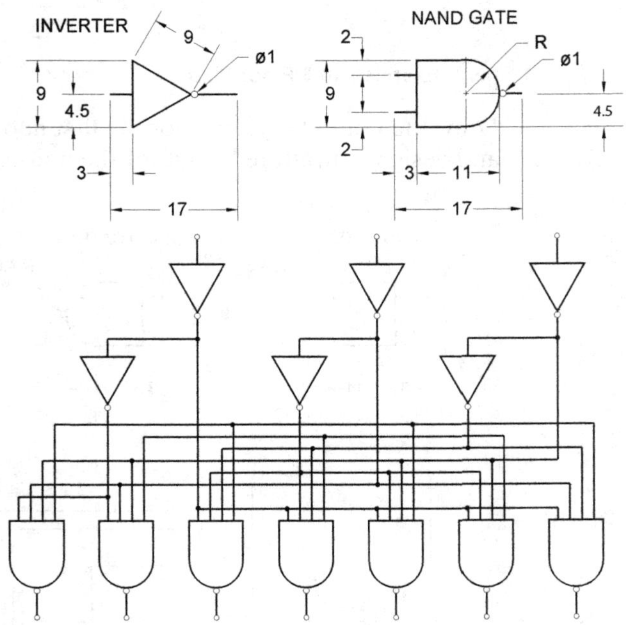

Exercise 10.2M Decoder Logic Unit

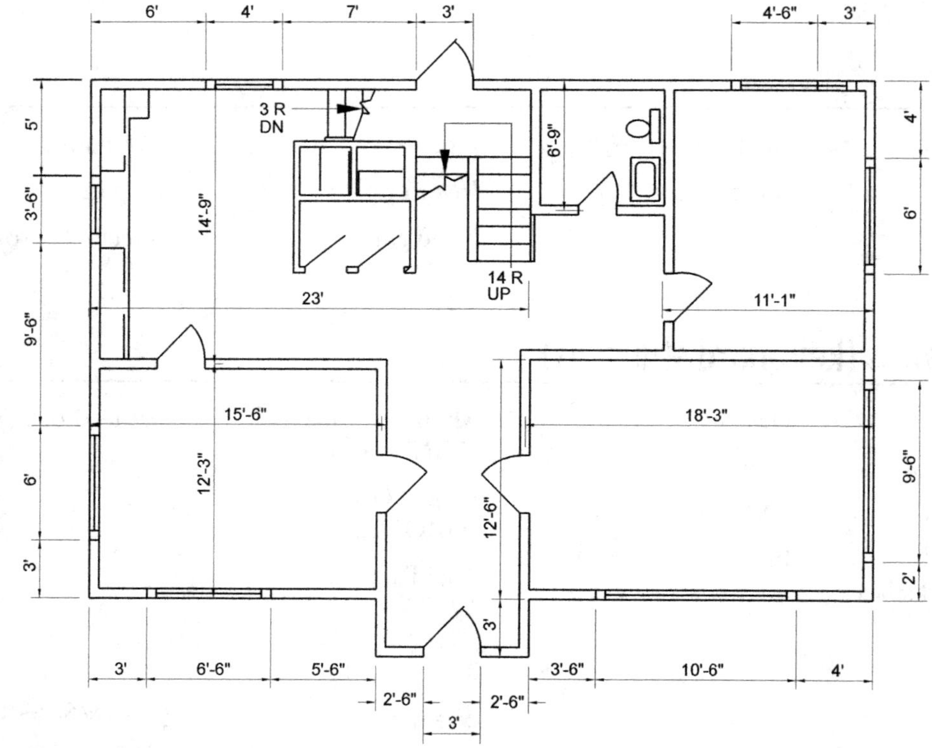

Exercise 10.3 Floor Plan

Draw the floor plan shown for the first floor of a house. Create your own blocks for furniture and design a furniture layout for the house.

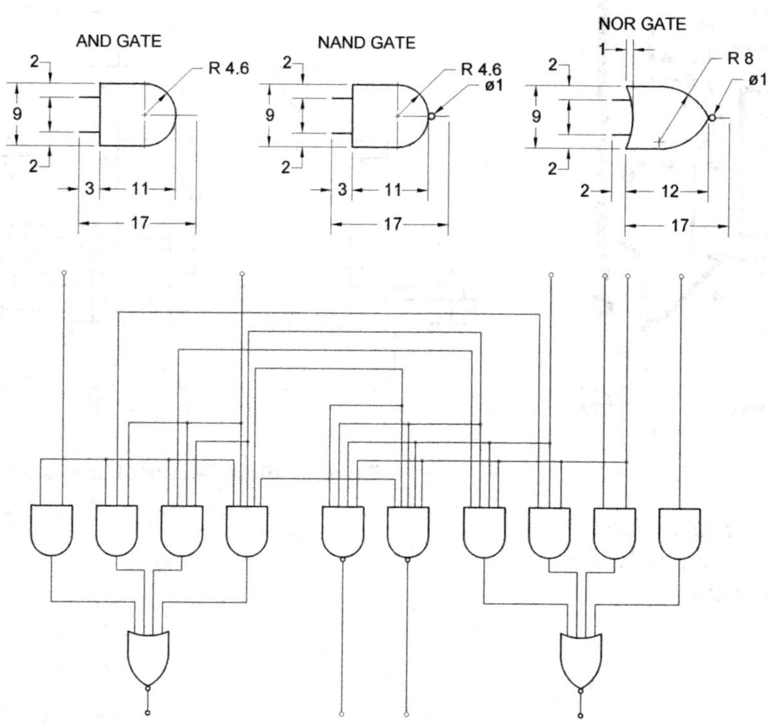

Exercise 10.4M Arithmetic Logic Unit

Create blocks for the components according to the metric sizes shown. Use the blocks that you create to draw the circuit shown.

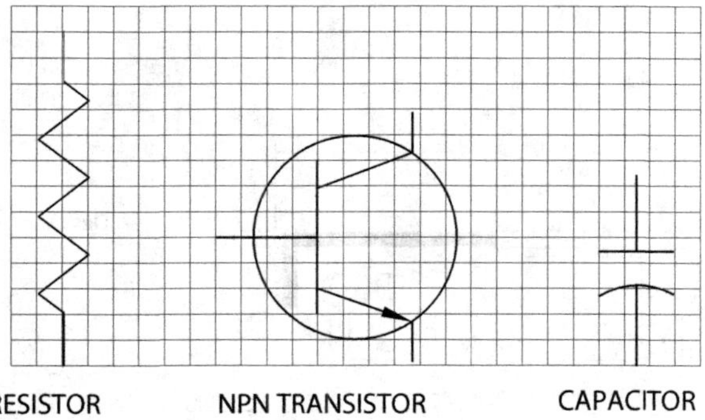

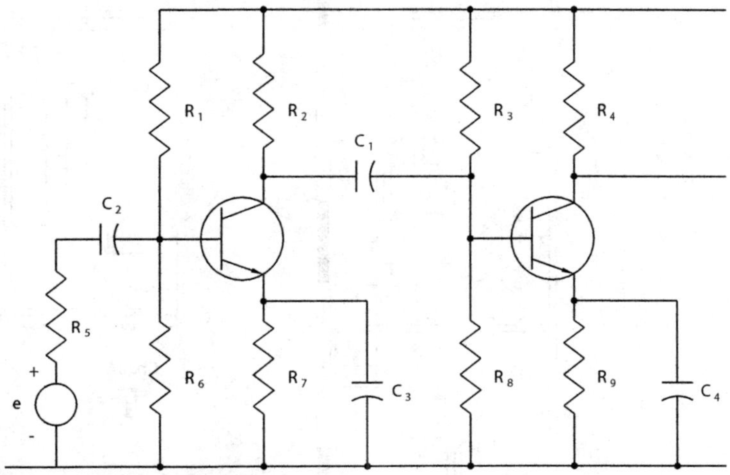

Exercise 10.5 Amplifier Circuit

Use the grid at left to draw and create blocks for the components shown. Each square equals 0.0625. Use the blocks that you create to draw the amplifier circuit.

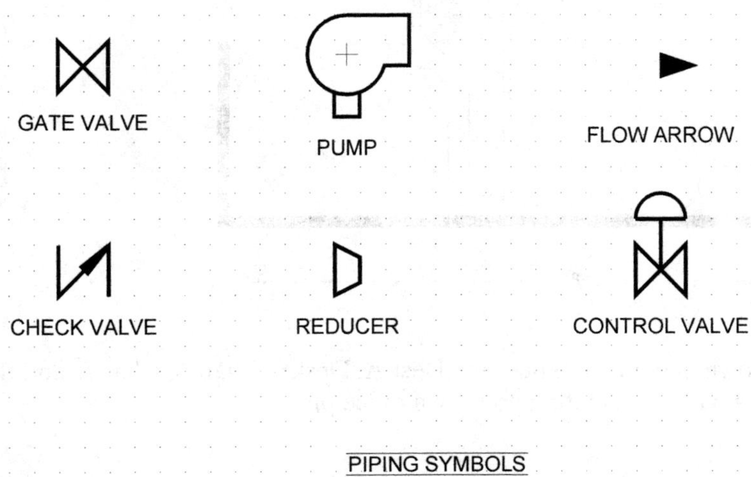

Exercise 10.6 Piping Symbols

Draw the piping symbols at right to scale; the grid shown is 0.2 inch (you do not need to show it on your drawing). Use polylines 0.03 wide. Make each symbol a separate block and label it. Insert all the blocks into a drawing named pipelib.dwg.

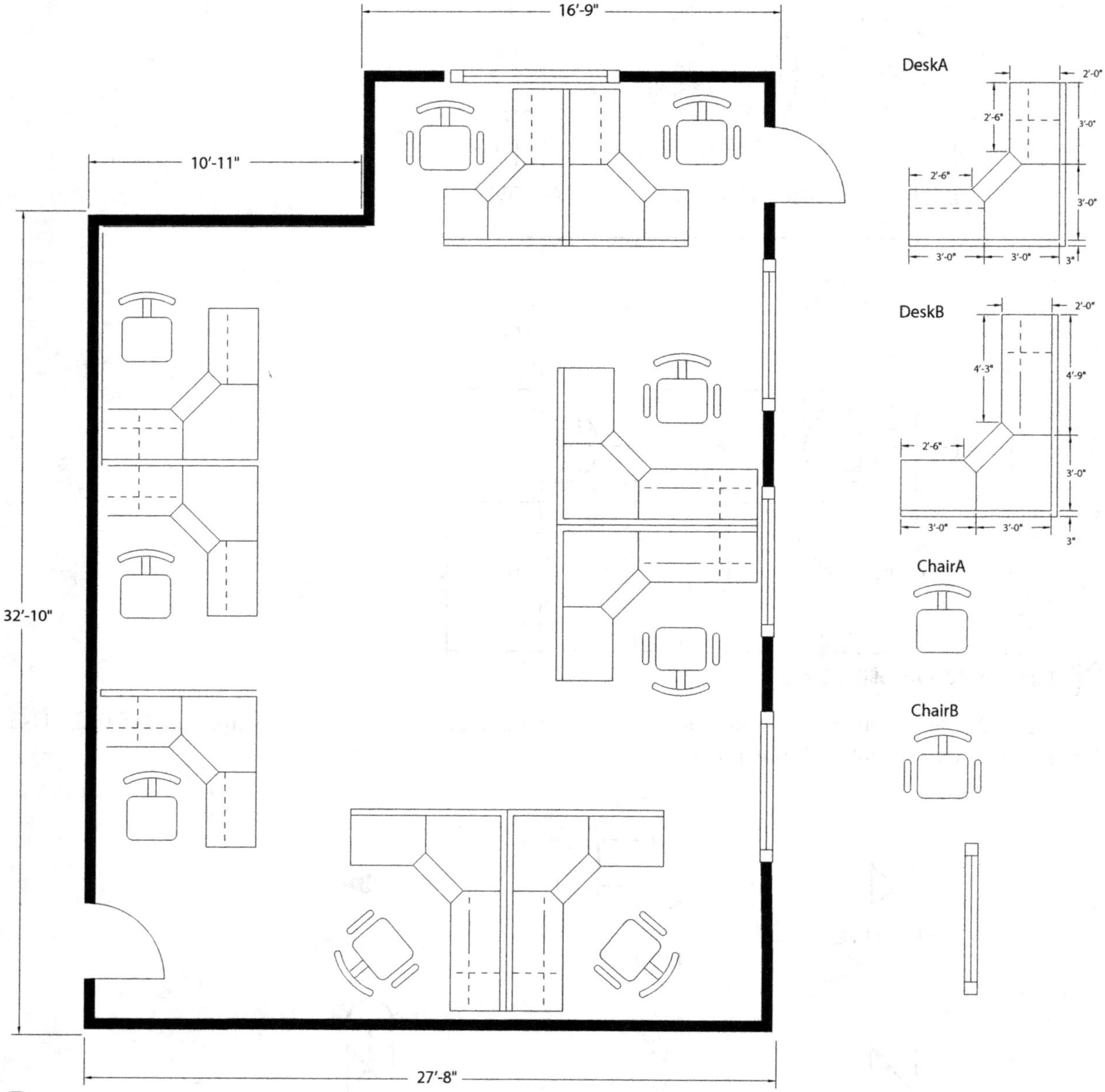

Exercise 10.7 Office Plan

Draw the office furniture shown and create blocks for DeskA, DeskB, ChairA, ChairB, and the window. Use the floor plan shown as a basis for creating your own office plan.

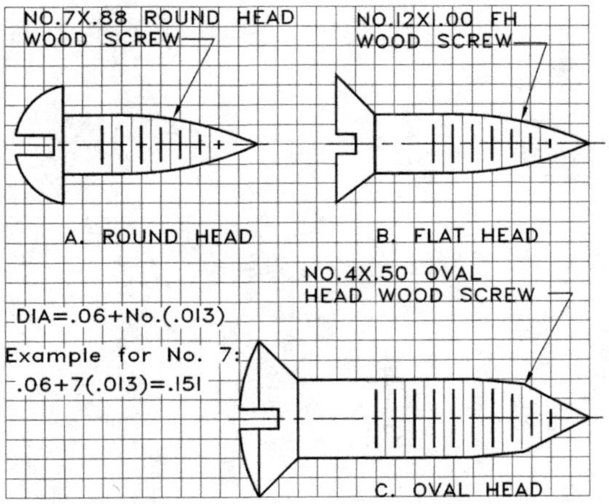

Exercise 10.8 Wood Screws

Create blocks for each of the wood screws shown. The grid gives their proportions. Make the diameter of each 1.00 so that you can easily determine the scale needed for inserting them at other sizes.

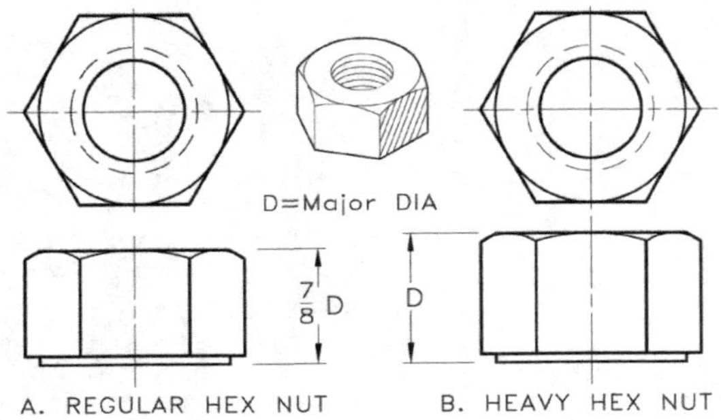

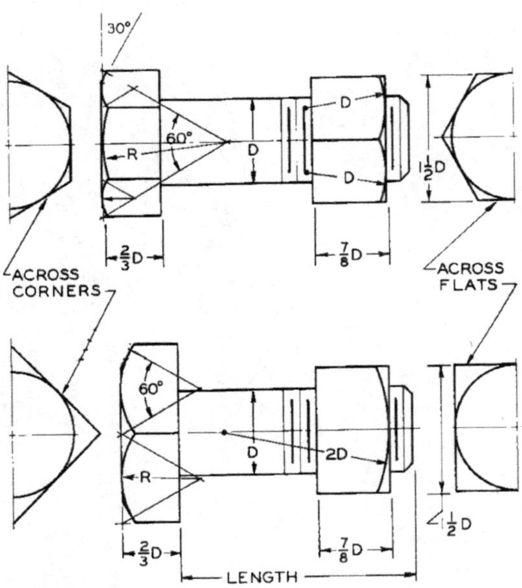

Exercise 10.9 Fasteners

Draw the hex head bolt, square head bolt, regular hex nut, and heavy hex nut according to the proportions shown. Make each into a block. Base the dimensions on a major diameter (D) of 1.00, so when you insert the block you can easily determine the scaling factor.

INTRODUCTION TO SOLID AND SURFACE MODELING

11

Introduction

In Tutorials 1 through 10 you learned how to use AutoCAD to draw objects in two dimensions. When you create a multiview drawing, it contains enough information within the views to give the person interpreting it an understanding of the complete 3D shape. Your drawings have been composed of multiple two-dimensional (2D) views, which convey the information. Using the computer, you can represent three dimensions in the drawing database using X-, Y-, and Z-coordinates. Next you will learn to use AutoCAD to create 3D models.

AutoCAD 3D models are of three types: wireframe, surface, and solid. *Wireframe modeling* uses 3D lines, arcs, circles, and other graphical objects to represent the edges and features of an object. It is called wireframe because it looks like a sculpture made from wires.

Surface modeling takes 3D modeling one step further, adding surfaces to the model so that it can be shaded and hidden lines can be removed. A surface model is like an empty shell: there is nothing to tell you how the inside behaves.

Solid modeling is the term for creating a 3D model that describes a volume contained by the surfaces and edges making up the object. A solid model is most like a real object because it represents not only the lines and surfaces, but also the volume contained within. In this tutorial you will first learn to create solid models and then how to create surface models.

Benefits of solid models include easier interpretation; rendering (shading) so that someone unfamiliar with engineering drawings can visualize the object easily; direct generation of 2D views from the model; and analysis of the solid's *mass properties*. The need to create a physical prototype of the object may even be eliminated.

Creating a solid model is somewhat like sculpting the part in clay. You can add and subtract material with *Boolean operators* and create features by *revolution* and *extrusion.* Of course, when modeling with AutoCAD, you can be much more precise than when modeling with clay.

At first, the software's solid modeling may look much like wireframe or surface modeling. The reason is that wireframe representation often is used in solid modeling and surface modeling to make many drawing operations and selections quicker. When you want to see a more realistic representation, you can shade or hide the back lines of solid models and surface models.

Objectives

When you have completed this tutorial, you will be able to

1. Change the 3D viewpoint.
2. Work with multiple viewports.
3. Set individual limits, grid, and snap for each viewport.
4. Create and save User Coordinate Systems.
5. Set Isolines to control model appearance.
6. Create model geometry using primitives, extrusion, and revolution.
7. Use Boolean operators to add, subtract, and intersect parts of your model.
8. Use region modeling.
9. Create basic surface models.

Starting

*Launch **AutoCAD**.*

*Begin a **new** drawing based on the AutoCAD default template drawing **acad.dwt**.*

*Save your new drawing as **block.dwg**.*

*Check to see that you are in **model space**. The limits should be set to **12 X 9**.*

*Set the **grid** to **2** and turn it **on**.*

*Use **Zoom All** so that the grid area fills the screen.*

The regularly spaced grid should appear every 2 units, filling your screen. When you are working in 3D, the grid can help you relate visually to the current viewing direction and coordinate system.

The 3D Modeling Workspace

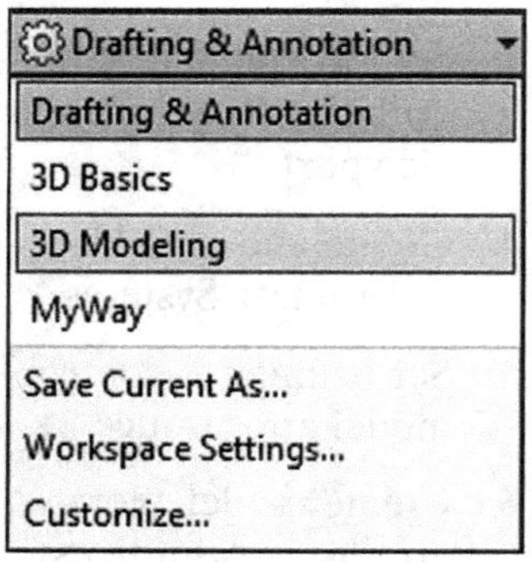

The 3D Modeling workspace customizes the ribbon with tabs and panels providing useful tools for 3D modeling. Since you will be creating 3D models, you will switch to this workspace. As you have seen in Tutorial 10, it is easy to customize the workspace should you want to add additional tools and commands.

*Click: **3D Modeling** workspace from the workspace pull-down list*

The ribbon changes to show the tabs and panels for the 3D Modeling workspace as shown in Figure 11.1.

Tip: *If the Materials Browser is turned on, you can set it to Autohide so that it takes up less space when you are not using it.*

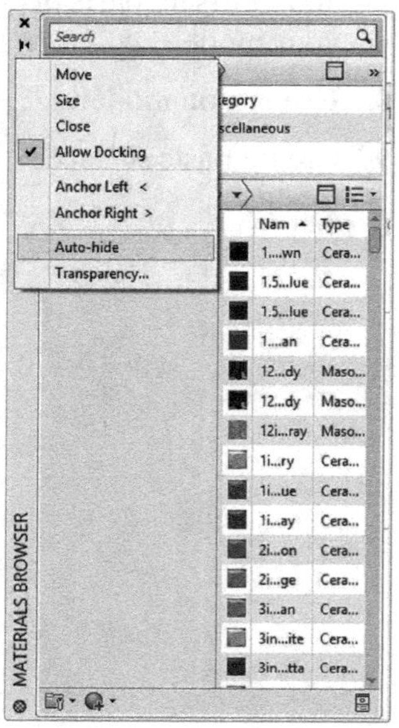

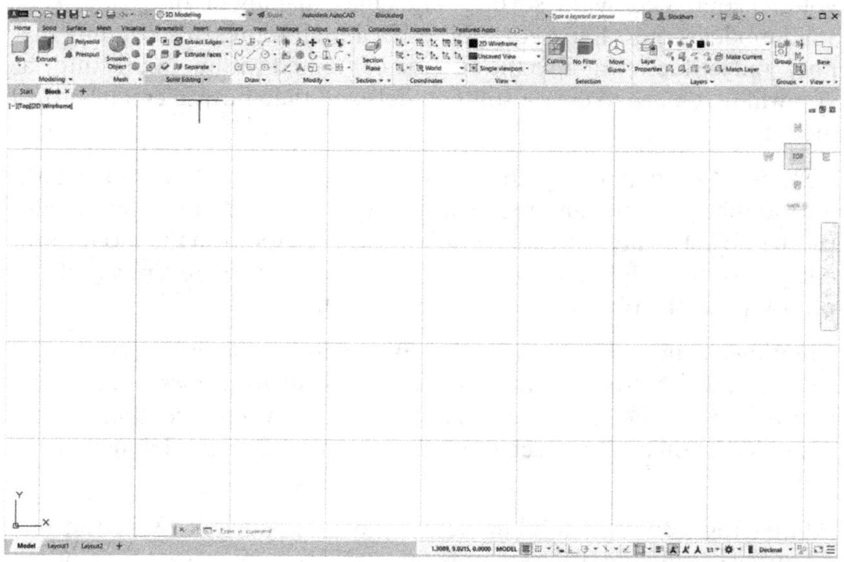

Figure 11.1

3D Coordinate Systems

AutoCAD defines model geometry using precise X-, Y-, and Z-coordinates in what is called the *World Coordinate System (WCS)*. The WCS is fixed and is used to store both 2D and 3D drawing geometry in the database. Its default orientation on the screen is a horizontal X-axis, with positive values to the right, and a vertical Y-axis, with positive values above the X-axis. The Z-axis is perpendicular to the computer screen, with positive values in front of the screen. The default orientation of the axes is shown in Figure 11.2.

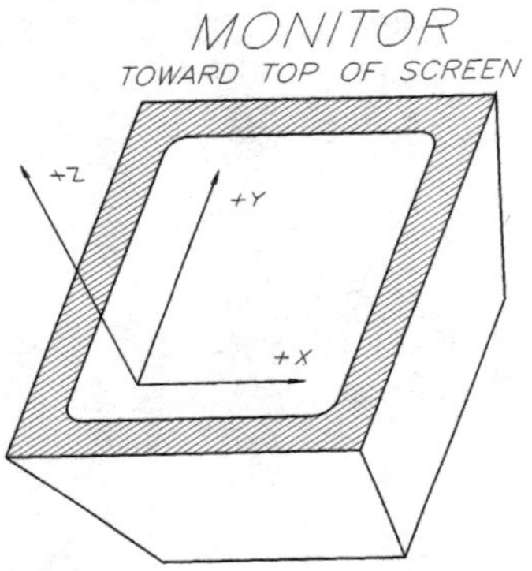

Figure 11.2

While creating 2D geometry, you have been using this default WCS. You have been looking straight down the Z-axis, so that a line in the Z-direction appears as a point. When you do not specify the Z-coordinate, the AutoCAD software uses the default elevation, which is zero. This method made creating and saving 2D drawings easy.

Creating 3D Objects

There are several methods for creating model geometry including *primitives*, extrusion, and revolution. First you will use primitives to create basic shapes (e.g., boxes, cylinders, and cones) that can be joined to form more complex shapes. Later in this tutorial you will learn how to join shapes by using Boolean operators and to create other shapes with extrusion and revolution.

The Box command enables you to draw a solid rectangular prism. You can draw a box by specifying the corners of its base and its height, its center, corner, and height, or its location and length, width, and height. Figure 11.3 shows the information you specify to draw a box using these methods. The default method of defining a box is to specify two corners across the diagonal in the XY-plane and the height in the Z-direction.

You will draw a solid box by specifying the corners of the base and then its height.

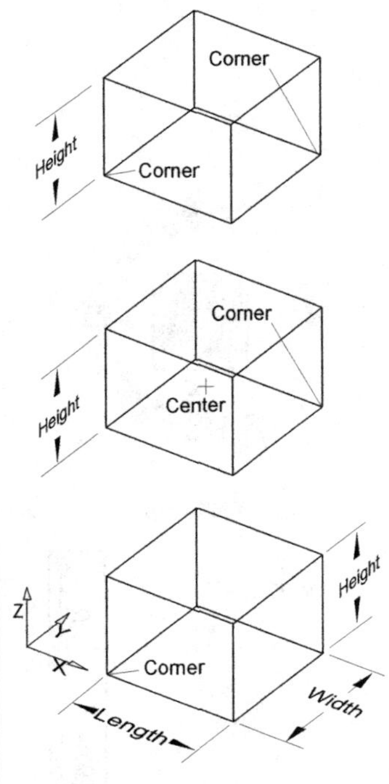

Figure 11.3

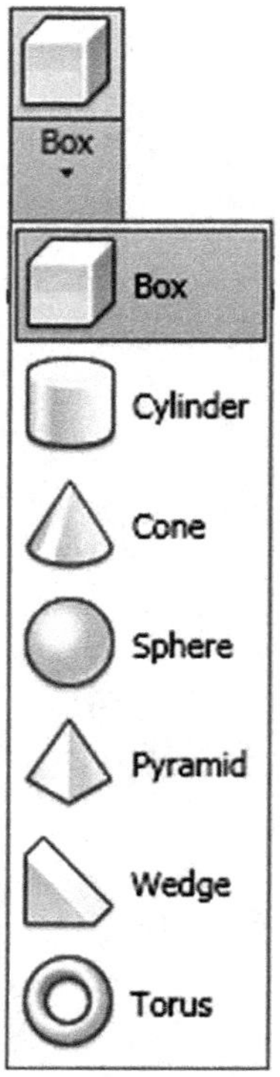

Click: ***Box button*** *from the Home tab, Modeling panel*

Specify corner of box or [CEnter] <0,0,0>: ***2,2,0 [Enter]***

Specify corner or [Cube/Length]: ***8,6,0 [Enter]***

Specify height or [2Point]: ***3 [Enter]***

On your own, turn off the grid.

Your screen should be similar to Figure 11.4. The box appears, but you are still looking straight down the z-axis at it, so it appears as a rectangle.

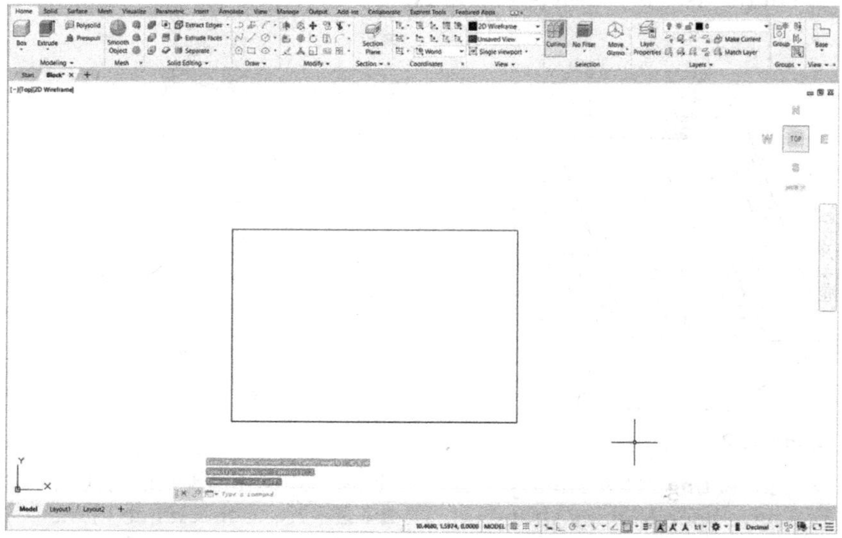

Figure 11.4

Setting the Viewpoint

When creating 3D geometry, it is useful to view the XY-plane from different directions, to see the object's height along the Z-axis. You can do so using the ViewCube. First make sure that it is turned on.

Click: ***View tab*** *from the ribbon*

Verify that **ViewCube, Navigation Bar,** and **UCS Icon** are on in the Viewport tools panel *(Figure 11.5)*

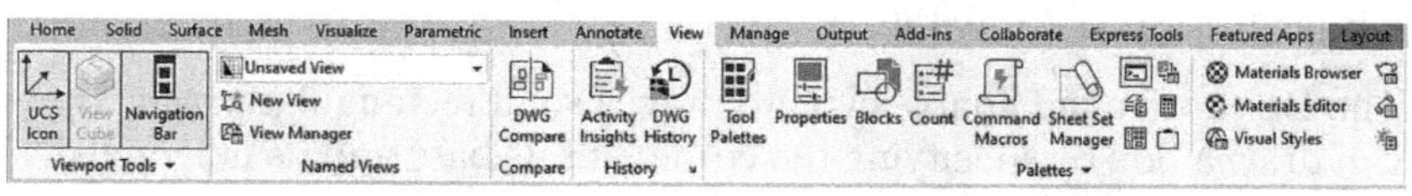

Figure 11.5

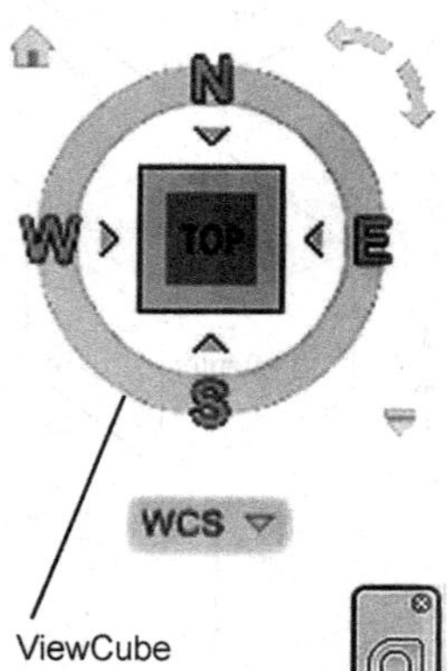

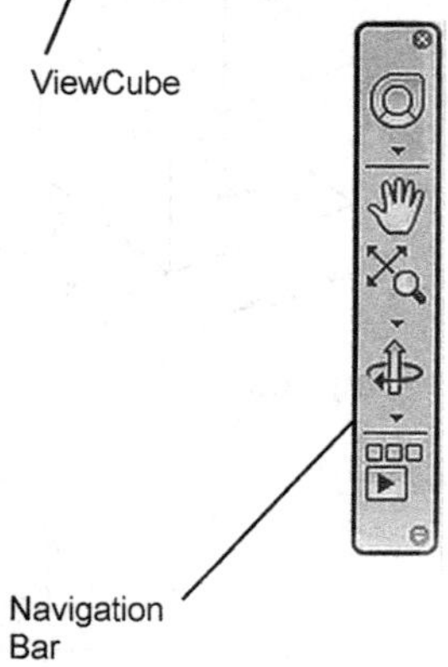

The ViewCube and Navigation Bar and UCS icon should be visible on your screen. The ViewCube is surrounded by a circle with N, E, S, W (North, East, South, West) labeled at its quadrants.

At the center of the ViewCube is a target cube which is shown from your view point. At present you should be looking straight down the z-axis, showing the center cube from the top, so that it appears as a square labeled "Top".

Figure 11.6 shows the ViewCube enlarged, with its features identified.

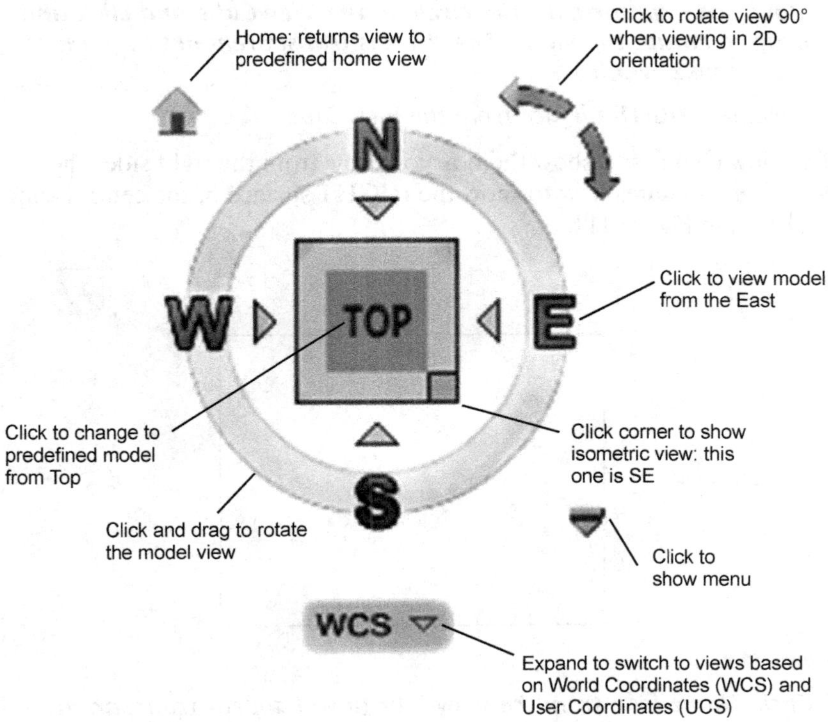

Figure 11.6

Click and drag your cursor inside the circle to rotate the view.

Notice the view rotate around the pivot point shown on the screen.

Click: ***TOP*** *from the ViewCube*

The view returns to show a top view with the x-axis aligned horizontally.

Click: ***the lower right (SE) corner of the ViewCube*** *(see Figure 11.6)*

The viewing direction changes as shown in Figure 11.7.

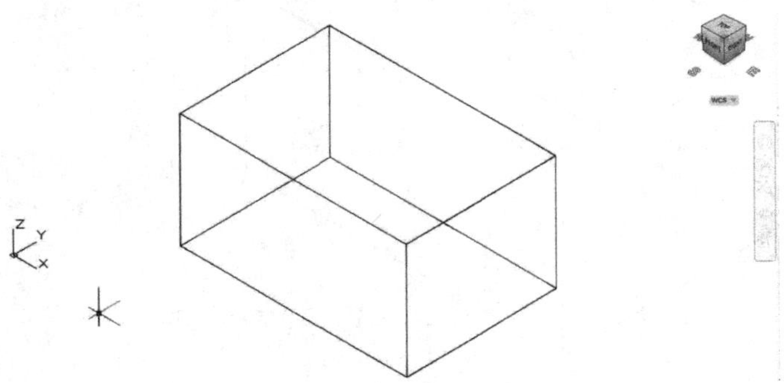

Figure 11.7

Note that your view has changed. You are no longer looking straight down on the XY-plane. Your view is now from an angle. The ViewCube updates to show the central cube as viewed from the direction you selected. Notice the changed appearance of the UCS icon. It updates to reflect the new viewing direction, still showing you the directions for the x, y, and z-axes. The cursor also updates to a 3D appearance.

Move your cursor over the circle in the ViewCube and click and drag to rotate the view. (The circle is transparent until you move your mouse over it.)

*Click: the **RIGHT** surface from the ViewCube*

The view changes to show the box you drew from the right side. The ViewCube updates now to show the RIGHT surface of the central cube as shown in Figure 11.8.

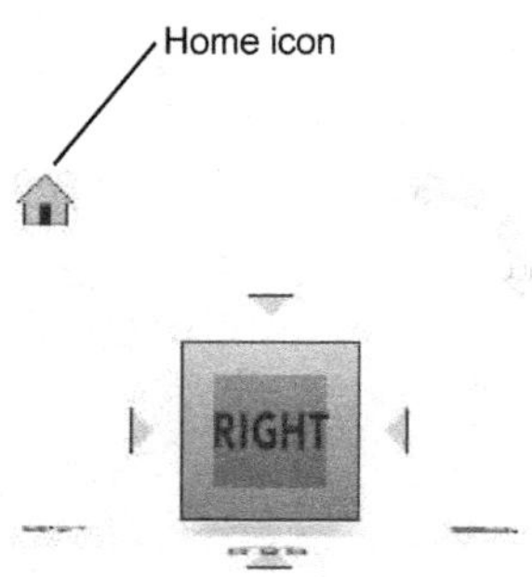

Figure 11.8

*Click: **Home icon** from the ViewCube (it will appear transparent, until your cursor passes over it)*

The view updates to a Southwest (SW) isometric view as shown in Figure 11.9.

*Experiment with the ViewCube. When you are done, reselect the **Home** view.*

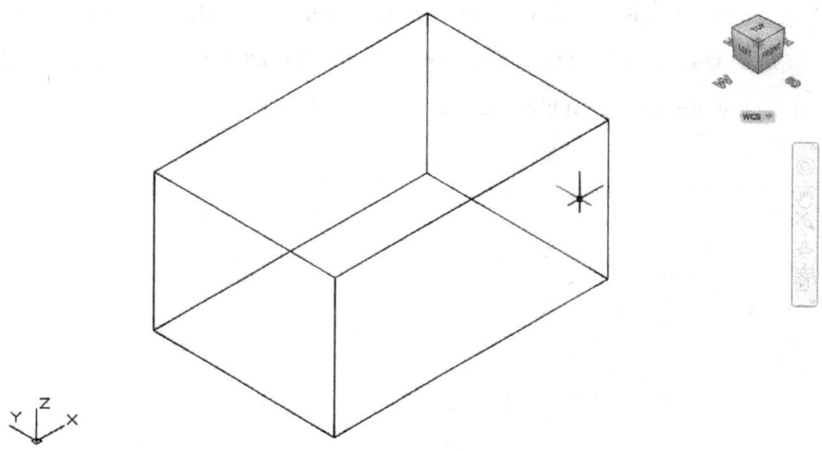

Figure 11.9

*Right-click: **on the ViewCube** (or click the small downward arrow) to show the menu*

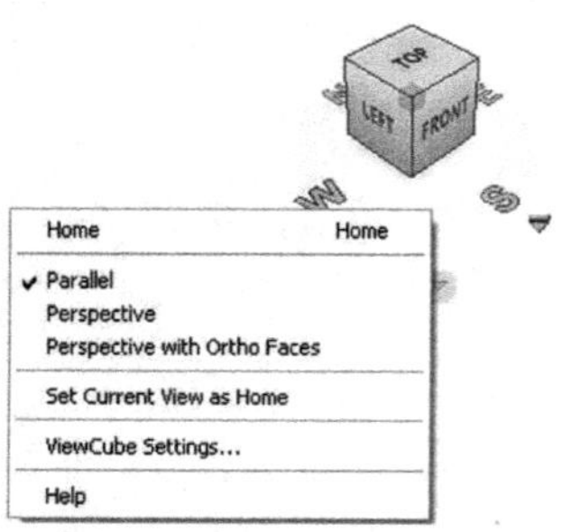

The pop-up menu appears. You can use it to quickly change from parallel to perspective projection, set the current view as Home, and change the settings for the ViewCube.

*Click: **ViewCube Settings***

The ViewCube Settings dialog box appears similar to Figure 11.10.

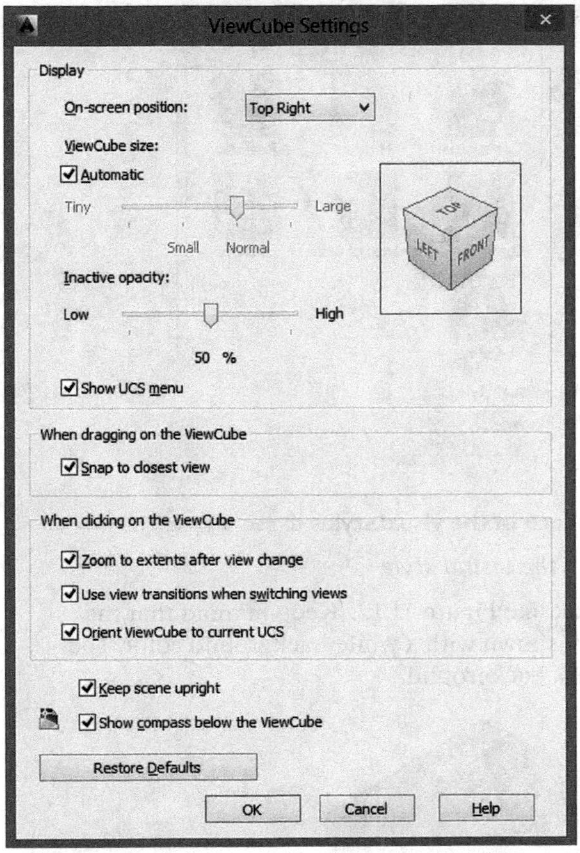

Figure 11.10

Notice that you can change the position, size, opacity, and the behavior of the ViewCube. You can also choose whether or not the view is automatically zoomed to the extents when using the ViewCube to change your viewing direction.

In addition, notice that by default, Keep Scene Upright is selected. This prevents confusion that you may have when the view is shown from below the object, looking from a negative z-direction toward the origin. For now, leave these settings at the defaults.

If you have changed anything, select ***Restore Defaults****.*

If desired, use the slider to increase the opacity for the ViewCube, so that it shows more clearly on your screen.

Close *the ViewCube Settings dialog box on your own.*

Click: ***on 2D Wireframe*** *from the Visualize tab, Visual Styles panel to expand the Visual Styles as shown in Figure 11.11*

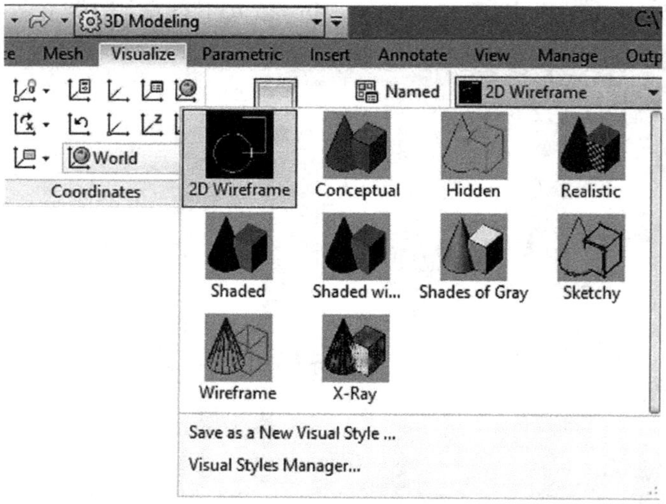

Tip: *You can use the Visual Styles Manager to create new appearance styles, or modify the existing ones.*

Figure 11.11

On your own, **click on each of the visual styles** to see their effect.

Click: ***Conceptual*** *as the visual style*

Tip: *To change the background color, pick the Application icon, then pick the Options button at the lower right to show the Options dialog box. Use the Display tab to select Colors... and select white as the background*

Your screen should look like Figure 11.12. Keep in mind that the screens in this book are shown with a white background color. The default is to show a dark background.

Figure 11.12

User Coordinate Systems

A *User Coordinate System (UCS)* is a set of X-, Y-, and Z-coordinates that you define to help you create your 3D models. You can define your own UCS, which may have a different origin and rotation from the WCS and may be tilted at any angle with respect to it. UCSs are helpful because your mouse moves in only two dimensions (unless you have a special 3D style one). Defining a UCS lets you orient the basic drawing coordinate system at a new angle in the 3D model space of the drawing, so you can continue using your mouse or other pointing device to draw easily. You can define any number of UCSs, give them names, and save them in a drawing, but only one can be active at a time.

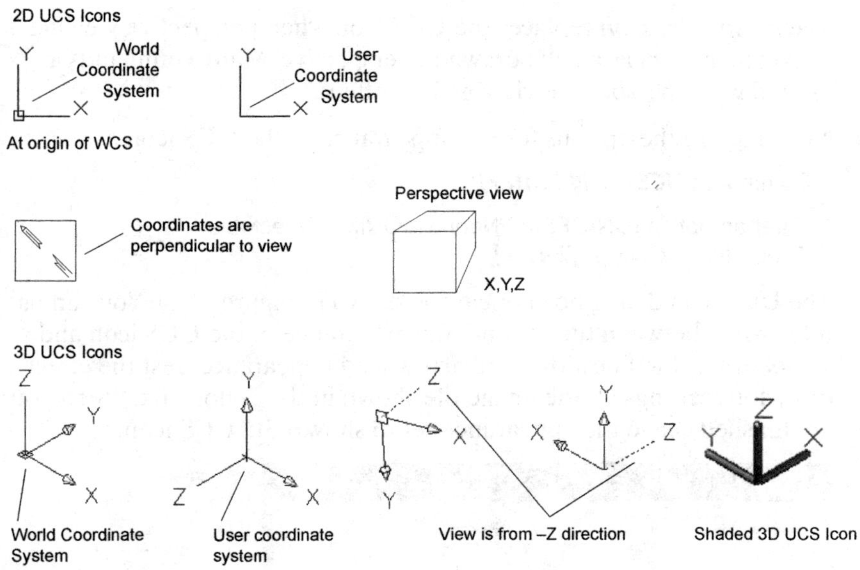

Figure 11.13

Tip: *Recall from Tutorial 9 that you can click and drag the UCS icon as a quick way of aligning a new user coordinate system.*

The UCS Icon

The UCS icon appears in the lower left of the screen to help you to orient yourself when looking at views of the object. The screen is essentially flat, so even if the object is a 3D model, only 2D views of it can be represented on the flat screen. Because unshaded models look the same from front and back or from any two opposing viewpoints, keeping track of which view you are seeing is especially important.

Figure 11.13 shows some of the appearances of the 2D and 3D UCS icons. When you are displaying the 2D UCS icon, it is shown in the XY-plane of the current UCS. The arrows at the X- and Y-ends always point in the positive direction of the X- and Y-axes of the current UCS.

A special symbol may appear instead of the UCS icon to indicate that the current viewing direction of the UCS is edgewise. (Think of the X- and Y-coordinate system of the UCS as a flat plane like a piece of paper; the viewing direction is set so that you are looking directly onto the edge of the paper.) In this case you can't use most of the drawing tools, so the icon appears as a box containing a broken pencil. Take special note of this icon.

The 3D UCS icon shows the X-, Y-, and Z-axis directions. When the Z-axis is viewed from the negative direction, it appears dashed. A box at the intersection of the X-, Y-, and Z-axes indicates the World Coordinate System is active.

A plus sign in the lower left of the icon indicates that the icon is positioned at the origin of the current UCS. When you start a drawing from the *acad.dwt* template, the origin (0,0,0) of the drawing is in the lower left of the screen. If the UCS were at the origin, it would be partially out of the view; thus the default for the 2D UCS icon is not at the origin. You can use the UCSICON command to reposition the icon so that it is at the origin of the X-, Y-, and Z-coordinate system.

The *perspective icon* replaces the UCS icon when perspective viewing is active; it appears as a cube drawn in perspective. Many commands are limited when perspective viewing is in effect.

Next explore the options for the appearance of the UCS icon.

Command: ***UCSICON [Enter]***

Enter an option [ON/OFF/All/Noorigin/ORigin/Selectable /Properties] <ON>: ***P [Enter]***

The UCS icon dialog box appears as shown in Figure 11.14. You can use it to switch between the 2D and 3D appearance of the UCS icon and set its size, color, linewidth, and arrowhead appearance. Test the effect of various settings on the image tile shown in the dialog box. When you are finished, leave the appearance set to show a 3D UCS icon.

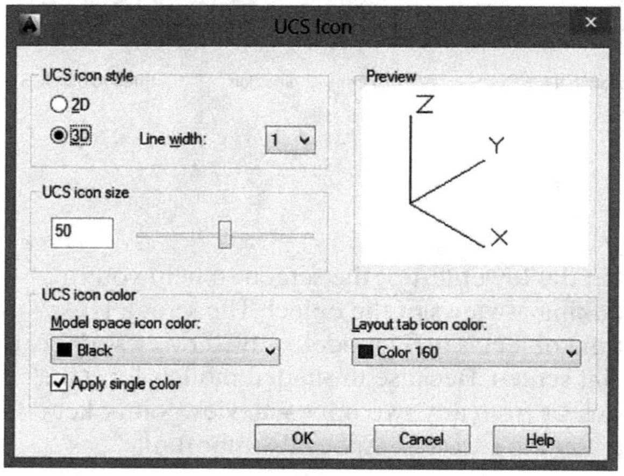

Figure 11.14

*Click: **Cancel** to exit the UCS icon dialog box*

Dynamic UCS System Variable

The system variable UCSDETECT controls whether temporary UCSs are created automatically during some 3D operations. You will start with this feature off. Though automatically created temporary coordinate systems can be handy, they can also produce confusing results. You will first learn to create your own UCSs as needed and then later experiment with this automatic mode.

Command: ***UCSDETECT [Enter]***

Enter new value for UCSDETECT <1>: ***0 [Enter]***

Using Layers

Next create new layers for the solid model, the viewports, and the drawing's border. Hint: try typing the shortcut LA [Enter].

*Use the **Layer Properties Manager** to create the following layers:*

• MYMODEL	Blue	Continuous	
• VPORT	Magenta	Continuous	Non-plotting
• BORDER	White	Continuous	

*Set layer **VPort** as the **current** layer.*

*Click on the **Box** you drew and **change** it onto **layer MYMODEL**. Its color changes to blue.*

*Turn the **Grid on**.*

Creating Multiple Viewports

Next, you will create viewports to show several views of the object at the same time. This way you can create a solid model and produce a drawing with the necessary 2D orthographic views directly from the 3D model. Having several views can make creating the model easier, as you can quickly switch between them to draw on different surfaces. You already used a paper space viewport for printing in Tutorial 5. Now you will create four viewports and change them so they contain four different views of the model; like watching four separate TV screens, each one of them showing the model. Each TV screen (viewport) can show a different view (similar to watching the same televised sports event on several different stations at once). When watching several televisions, each cameraperson is looking at the game from a different angle, producing a different view on each TV. Yet there is only one real event being televised. Multiple viewports work the same way. You can have many AutoCAD viewports, each with a different view of the model, but there is only one model space object and it only needs to be created once. You will create paperspace viewports in layer VPORT.

*Click: **Layout1 tab** (from near the status bar)*

When you switch to Layout1, note the triangular paper space icon in the lower left of your screen as shown in Figure 11.15.

If needed, use Zoom All so that the paper space layout fills the graphics area.

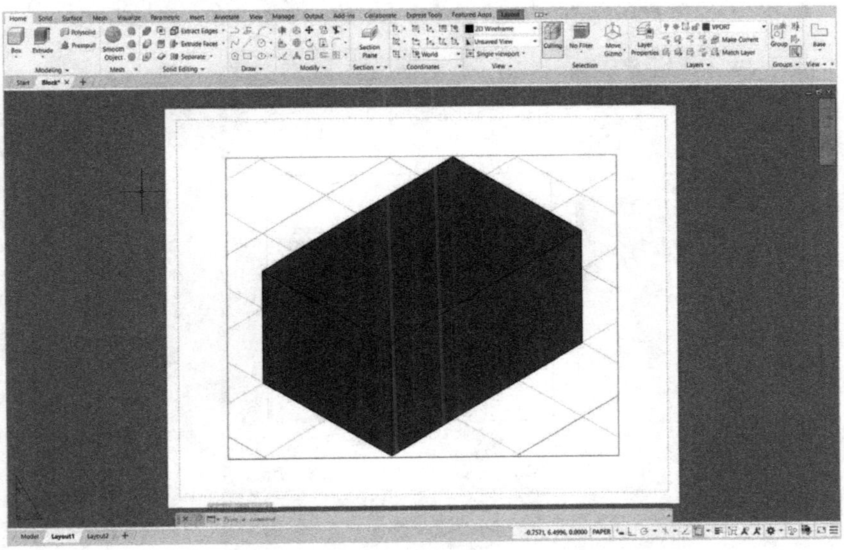

Figure 11.15

Next, you will erase the current viewport which was created automatically when you switched to the Layout1 tab. Then you will create four viewports in its place.

Tip: *The type of viewports created depends on whether you are in model space or paper space. Paper space (or layout) viewports are called floating viewports because they can be arranged on top of each other or with space between them. You can also create viewports in model space. These are called tiled viewports because they must always abut one another like floor tiles. In these tutorials you will use floating viewports. Tiled viewports can be a useful modeling tool. Experiment with them on your own.*

Check to make sure you are in paper space.

Type: ***E [Enter]***

Select objects: ***the magenta viewport border***

Select objects: ***[Enter]***

The viewport and objects showing in it disappear from your layout. The block you created is still there; you just cannot see it without a viewport to "look through." You will make four new viewports in which to show it. You use the VPort command to create viewports. You will use the New button from the Layout Viewports panel on the ribbon Layout tab.

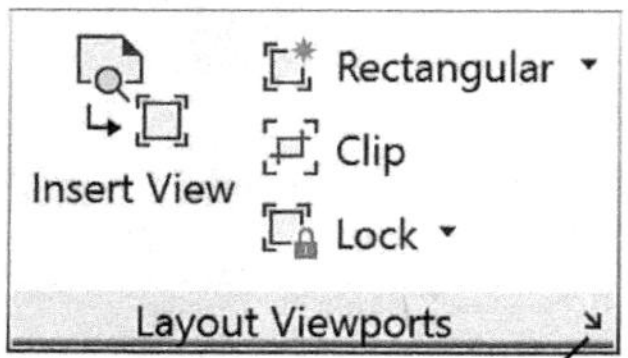

Click arrow to show Viewports dialog box.

Click: ***small downward arrow*** *from the Layout Viewports panel of the Layout tab*

The Viewports dialog box appears on the screen similar to Figure 11.16. You can use its New Viewports tab to select from preconfigured viewport arrangements, or use the Named Viewports tab to select from named viewport configurations you create ahead of time.

Click: ***New Viewports*** *tab*

Click: ***Four: Equal*** *from the Standard Viewports area*

Click: ***3D*** *from the Setup drop-down list*

Click the **upper left image** *tile and use the* **Change view to** *drop down to set the view to Top, then use the* **Visual Style** *drop down from the lower right of the dialog box to select* **Wireframe** *(if it is not already).*

Use the same process to set the **lower left** *viewport to* **Front** *view and Wireframe style. Set the* **lower right** *viewport to* **Right** *view and* **Wireframe** *visual style.*

Set the **upper right** *viewport to* **SE Isometric** *view and leave it set to the* **Conceptual** *visual style.*

Click: ***OK*** *to return to the drawing for the remaining selections*

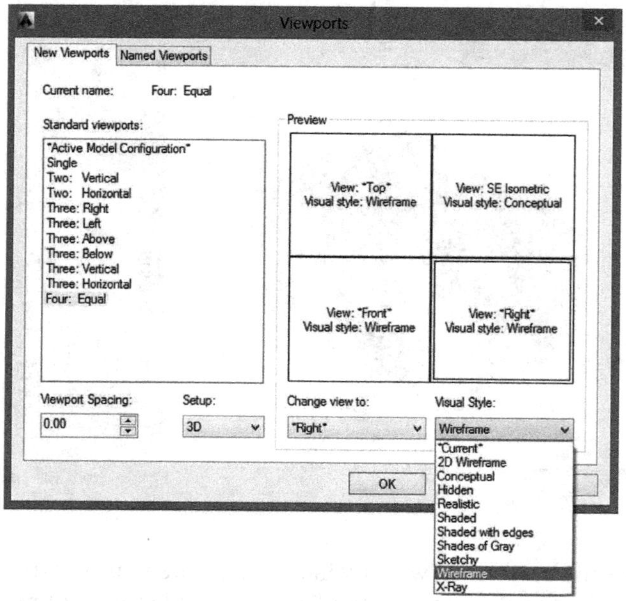

Figure 11.16

You will place the viewports inside the area that you want to plot full size, centered on your page, as you did in Tutorial 5. You may find that the following values work for your printer. If you used a different setting in Tutorial 5, apply the one that works for your printer.

Specify first corner or [Fit] <Fit>: ***.25,.25 [Enter]***

Specify opposite corner: ***10.25,7.75 [Enter]***

Four viewports appear on your screen, each containing a different view of the object. The upper right viewport shows the shaded conceptual style object and the other viewports show the top, front, and right side views with no shading. Your screen should be similar to Figure 11.17.

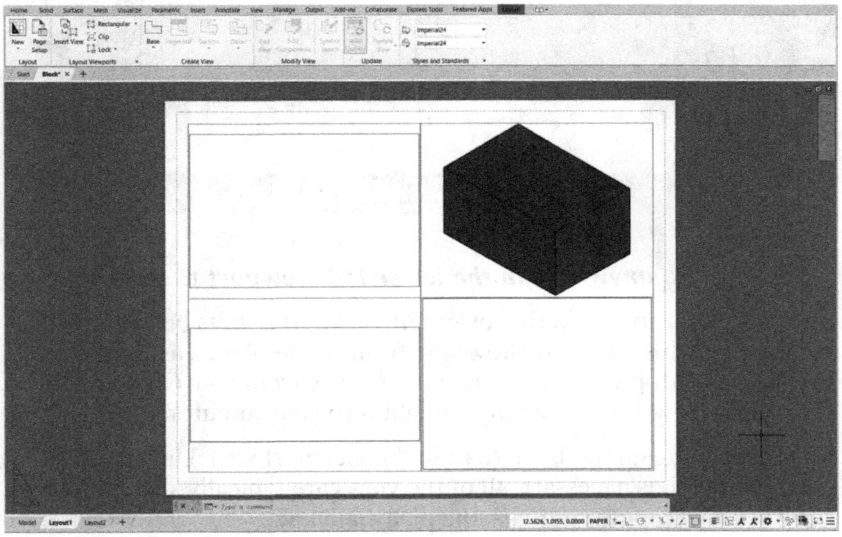

Figure 11.17

Tip: *You can press [Ctrl]-R to toggle the active viewport. This action is helpful when you are unable to pick in the viewport for some reason.*

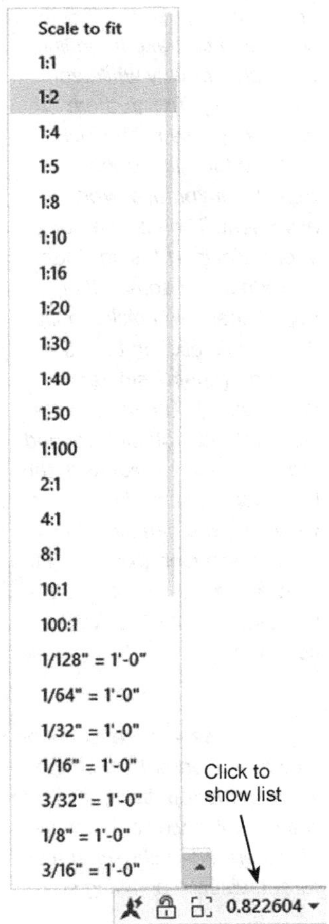

Selecting the Active Viewport

To make the upper left viewport active,

Double-click: ***anywhere in the upper left viewport***

The crosshairs will appear in the viewport and the viewport becomes highlighted. This indicates that it is now the active viewport.

You can only draw and click to select points in a viewport when it is active. After you create something, whatever you created is visible in all other viewports showing that area of the WCS, unless the layer that the object is on is frozen in another viewport. (You can freeze layers in specific viewports.) You can start drawing something in one viewport and finish drawing it in another. Keep in mind that you are using a certain viewport to access model space, but there is only one model space.

Each viewport can contain its own setting for Grid, Snap, and Zoom (or Viewport Scale). The status bar lists the Viewport Scale. Next, you will set the scale for the viewports so that the drawing views are at the same scale.

Click: ***1:2*** *from the list of Viewport Scales*

Tip: *Check whether the viewport is active by moving your cursor around. If the crosshairs will not move outside of that viewport boundary, it is the active viewport.*

Tip: *Turn the grid off to make it easier to see the shape.*

The top view of the box fits into the viewport at half scale (Figure 11.18).

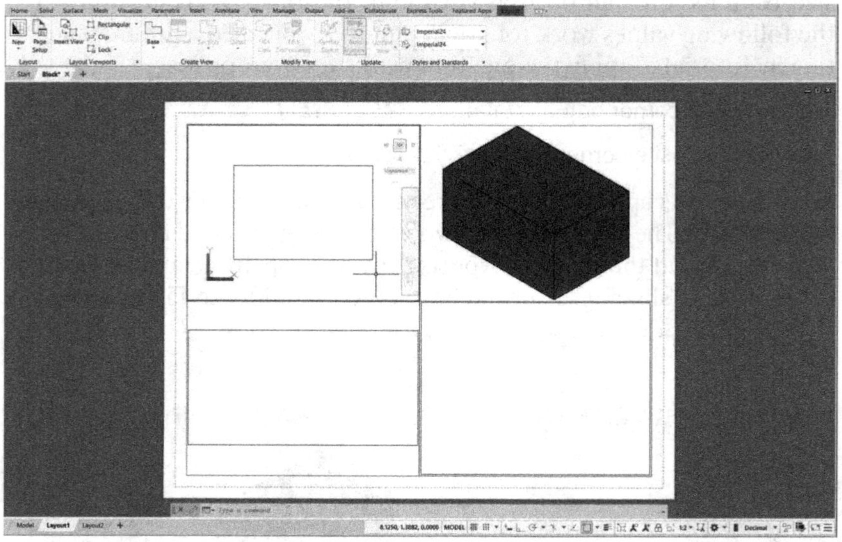

Figure 11.18

Double-click: ***anywhere in the lower left viewport*** *to make it active*

The crosshairs appear in the lower left viewport and its border becomes highlighted. This viewport shows the front of the object, as though you had taken the top view and tipped it 90° away from you. (Imagine that the original Y-axis is projecting straight into your monitor.)

Tip: *If you have trouble lining up the views, use the Pan command to make them line up approximately while you are working. To line them up exactly, use MVSETUP and use the Align option. Select Horizontal or Vertical alignment. Then pick a point in one viewport (using Snap to Endpoint or some other object snap) and pick a point that should align in the other viewport (again using an object snap). The view in the viewport that you pick second will be shifted to align with the point you selected in the first viewport. You can use Pan in the first viewport to position the view where you want it before you begin the MVSETUP command.*

The object is again too large to fit in the viewport well. Unless an enlarged detail is necessary, all of the views are typically shown to the same scale, except for perhaps the pictorial view.

Click: ***1:2*** *from the Viewport Scale on the status bar*

Now the front view of the object shows in the lower left viewport at half size related to the paper units (similar to Figure 11.19).

Notice that the XY coordinates of the UCS are aligned to be parallel to each of the top, front and side views. The world coordinate system (WCS) is parallel to the bottom surface of the block. You see the WCS in the upper right viewport. When you double-click to make a viewport active, your drawing's current XY-plane automatically changes to align with that viewing direction (not the WCS). This is a convenient feature to help you create 3D drawings. Think about what would happen if it did not. It would be like looking at a piece of paper edgewise at eye level and then trying to draw on it. If the user coordinates are "on edge" in your view, you can not easily click points to draw objects.

Double-click: inside the lower right viewport to make it active

Click: ***1:2*** *from the Viewport Scale on the status bar*

Save *your drawing block.dwg at this time.*

Tip: *The scale in the isometric viewport need not match the scale in the top, front, and side orthographic views. Isometric views are often shown at a different, visually pleasing scale.*

Viewports Using Different UCSs

The ability to display more than one UCS at a time in different viewports is controlled by system variable UCSVP. When UCSVP is set to

1 in a viewport, the UCS last used in that viewport is saved with the viewport and is restored when the viewport is made current again.

The Top, Front, and Right Side oriented viewports have the UCSVP variable preset to 1 during their creation.

When UCSVP is set to 0 in a viewport, its UCS is always the same as the UCS in the current viewport. The UCSVP variable for the upper right (isometric view) is set to 1 by default. You will set this variable to 0 in the upper right viewport only, so that it always displays the current UCS. This is useful so that you can use this isometric view to see how your current UCS (drawing plane) is aligned with the model.

Double-click: ***the upper right viewport*** *to make it active*

Command: ***UCSVP [Enter]***

Enter new value for UCSVP <1>: ***0 [Enter]***

Double-click: ***inside the lower left viewport to make it active***

Notice the UCS X-Y plane becomes parallel to the front surface of the object. Notice also that a small ViewCube shows in the active viewport.

Click: ***the small downward arrow*** *near the small ViewCube in the lower right viewport (near Unna...)*

Short-cut menu selections appear as shown in Figure 11.19. The UCS used in the viewport is unnamed.

Click: ***WCS*** *to choose the World Coordinate System*

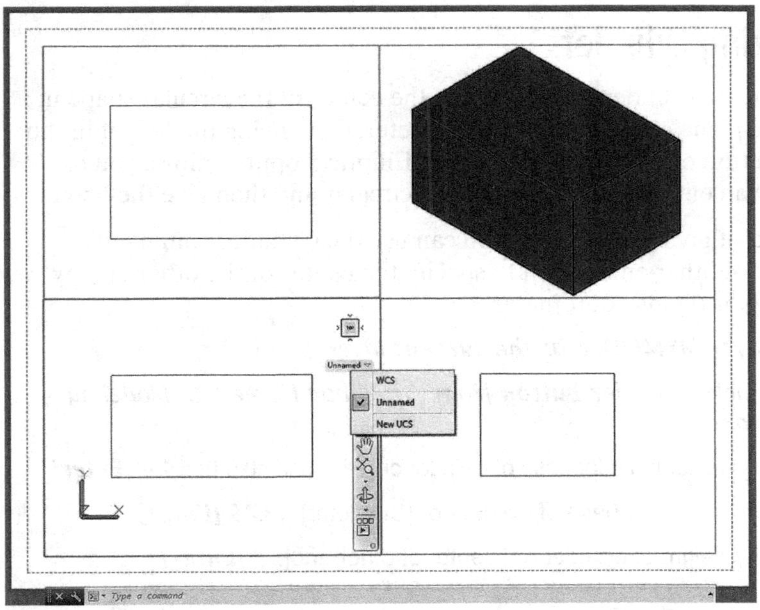

Figure 11.19

Double-click: ***to make the upper left viewport active***

Click: ***Customization button*** *from the status bar*

Click: ***Selection Cycling*** *to show the button on the status bar*

Your screen should look similar to Figure 11.20.

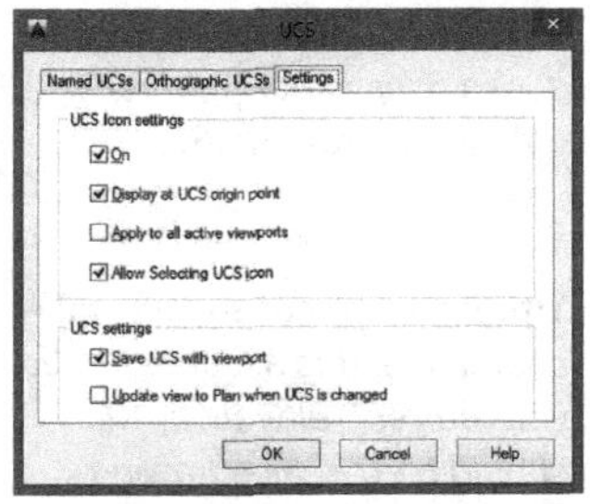

Tip: *You can use the UCSMAN command to show the dialog box. The Settings tab allows you to select whether the UCS is saved with the viewport. You can also directly set the UCSVP variable.*

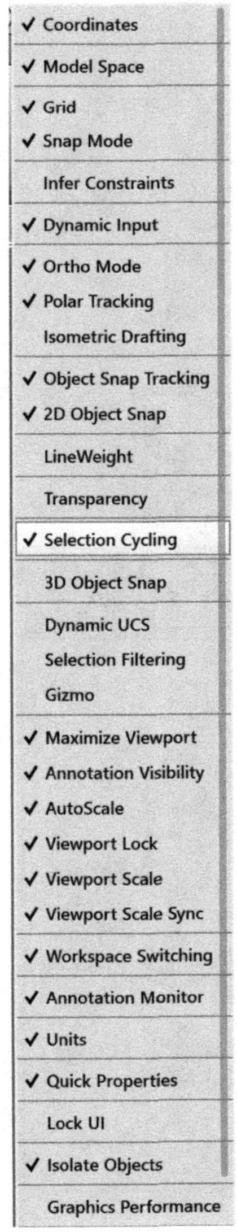

Tip: *The PLAN command produces a view looking directly onto the current UCS.*

Tip: *If you do not specify a Z-coordinate, it is assumed to be your current elevation, which should be 0 in this drawing.*

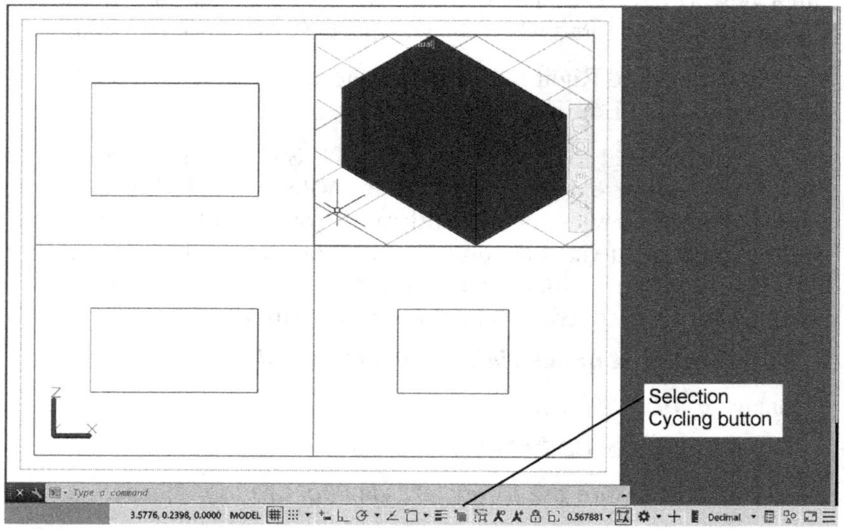

Figure 11.20

Now the current UCS X-Y plane is parallel to the top view in the upper left viewport. The default AutoCAD XY-plane is considered to be the *plan view* of the WCS. A plan view is basically a top view, which may sound familiar if you have worked with architectural drawings.

Next, you will add a cylinder to the drawing. Later, you will turn the cylinder into a hole using the Subtract command.

Creating Cylinders

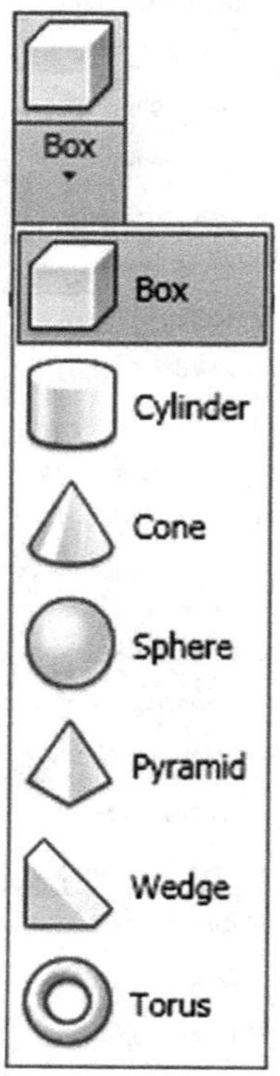

You create cylinders by specifying the center of the circular shape in the XY-plane and the radius or diameter, then giving the height in the Z-direction of the current UCS. The Elliptical option allows you to specify an elliptical shape instead of circular and then give the height.

Instead of giving the height, you can use the Cylinder command's Center of other end option to specify the center of the other end by clicking or typing coordinates.

*Set layer **MYMODEL** as the **current** layer.*

*Click: **Cylinder button** from the ribbon Home tab, Modeling panel*

Specify center point for base of cylinder or [Elliptical] <0,0,0>: ***4,4 [Enter]***

Specify radius for base of cylinder or [Diameter]: ***.375 [Enter]***

Specify height of cylinder or [Center of other end]: ***3 [Enter]***

Selection Cycling

When two solids overlap as the box and cylinder do, it can be difficult to select the internal one. Selection cycling is often useful when working in 3D as objects often overlap, which makes selecting difficult.

The Selection Cycling button located on the status bar makes it easy to click the object you want.

There are two ways that selection cycling operates. One way is to show a list of possible objects when an ambiguous area is clicked. The other way is to use a keyboard short-cut (Shift+spacebar+click) to toggle between the items on the screen when selecting in an area where there are multiple objects. Selection cycling can also be turned off.

One way to control the selection cycling mode used is the Drafting Settings dialog box.

Right-click: ***Selection Cycling button*** *on the status bar to show the short-cut menu*

Click: ***Selection Cycling Settings***

The Drafting Settings dialog box appears with the Selection Cycling tab uppermost as shown in Figure 11.21.

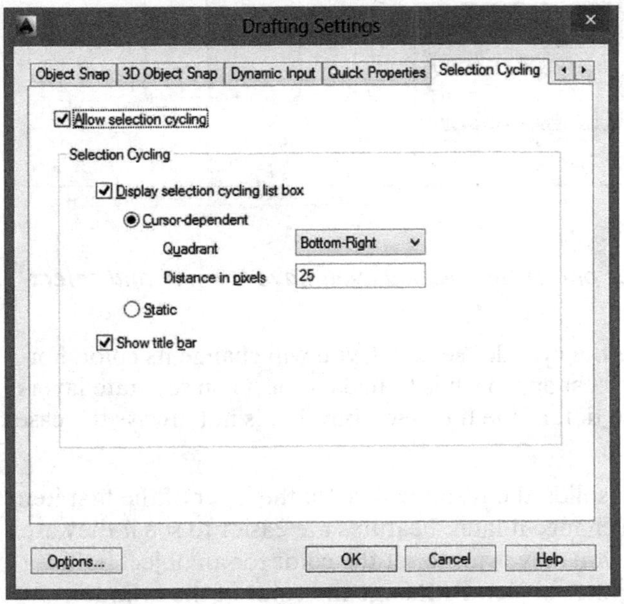

Figure 11.21

On your own, make sure that ***Allow selection cycling*** *is checked and that* ***Display selection cycling list box*** *is checked.*

You can set the list to either appear at the cursor or at a static location.

Leave these settings as you see in Figure 11.21.

Click: ***OK*** *(to close the Drafting Settings dialog box)*

Click: ***Selection Cycling button*** *from the status bar to turn it on*

Click: ***to make the lower left viewport active***

Click: ***on the top line of the box where the lines of the box and cylinder meet***

Move your cursor over items in the Selection list (Figure 11.22). Notice that an object becomes highlighted on the screen when it is the active item on the selection list.

Try the keyboard shortcut on your own. ***Press [Shift]+[spacebar]*** *to toggle between the different entities near your cursor location.*

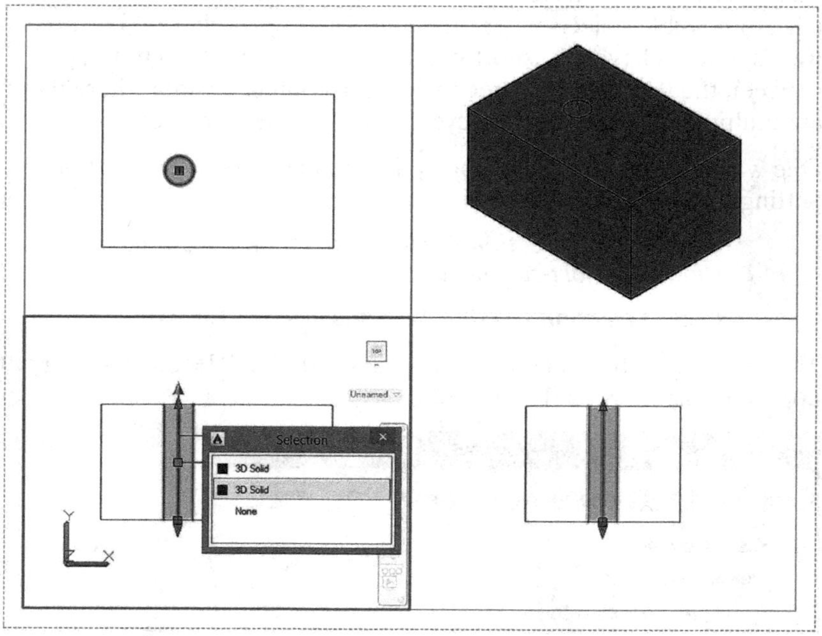

Figure 11.22

On your own, use one of the methods you have learned and ***select the cylinder****.*

Now that you have the cylinder selected, you will change its color. For many drawings the best approach is to make objects on separate layers and use the layer to determine the color, but that is not always the case with solid modeling.

When you join two solids, the result will be on the layer of the first item clicked, unless you change it later. Features are easier to see if they are different colors, so you may want to set the color for an object before you join it with another object. To change the color of the cylinder, which you will use to create a hole,

While the cylinder is still selected,

Press: ***[Ctrl]+1*** *to show the Properties dialog box*

Click: ***Red*** *from the Properties dialog box Color list*

Click: ***[X] to close*** *the Properties dialog box*

Press: ***[Esc]*** *to unselect the cylinder*

Click: ***to turn off Selection Cycling button*** *from the status bar*

The cylinder should be changed to the new color.

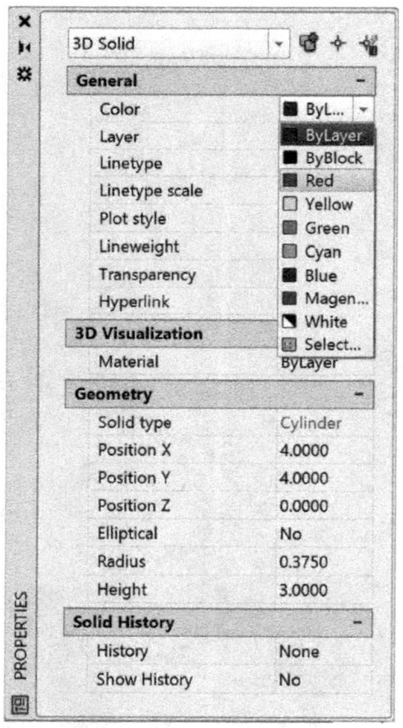

Tip: *You can press [Ctrl]-1 to pop up the Properties dialog box*

Tip: *You can change the color of a single face of a model by using the Solidedit command and then selecting the Face and Color options. You can use a similar method to recolor single edges.*

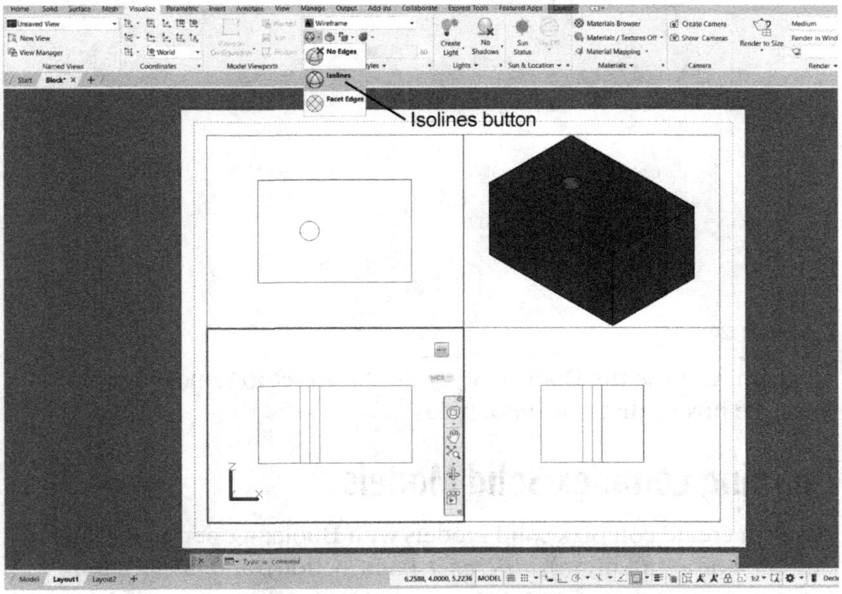

Figure 11.23

Tip: **Tip:** *The Facetres variable adjusts the smoothness of shaded objects and objects from which hidden lines have been removed. Its value can range from .01 to 10. Viewres controls the number of straight segments used to draw circles and arcs on your screen. Viewres can be set between 1 and 20000. You can type these commands at the command prompt and set their values higher to improve the appearance of rendered objects.*

Now you have a box and a cylinder, each occupying the same space. Although they could not do so in the real world, in the drawing data base these two objects are both occupying the volume inside the cylinder.

Setting Isolines

Before you continue, you will set the variable called Isolines. This variable controls the wireframe appearance of the cylinders, spheres, and tori (3D "donuts") on the screen. You can set the value for Isolines between 4 and 2047, to control the number of tessellation lines used to represent rounded surfaces. Displayed on a curved surface, tessellation lines help you better visualize the surface. The number of *tessellation lines* that you set will be shown on the screen, representing the contoured surface of the shape. The higher the value for Isolines, the better the screen appearance of rounded wireframe shapes will be. The default setting of 4 looks poor but saves time in drawing. The highest setting may look best, but more time is needed for the calculations, especially for a complex drawing.

You will set the value to 12. You can change the setting for Isolines and regenerate the drawing at any time. You can use the Isolines command from the Vizualize tab, Visual Styles panel. You will use the Regenall command to regenerate all of the viewports to show the new setting for Isolines.

Command: ***ISOLINES [Enter]***

Enter new value for ISOLINES <4>: ***12 [Enter]***

Command: ***REGENALL [Enter]***

Tip: *The new Regen3 command helps fix 3D display problems by rebuilding all 3D graphics in the displayed views.*

The cylinder should be redrawn with more tessellation lines, similar to Figure 11.23.

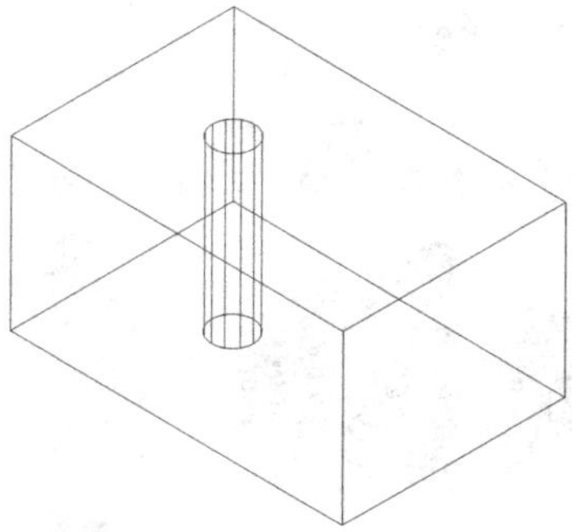

Figure 11.24

Next you will use the Boolean operator Subtract to remove the cylinder from the box so that it forms a hole.

Building Complex Solid Models

You can create complex solid models with Boolean operators, which find the *union* (addition), *difference* (subtraction), and *intersection* (common area) of two or more sets. These operations are named for Irish logician and mathematician George Boole, who formulated the basic principles of set theory. In the AutoCAD software the sets can be 2D areas (called regions), they can be surfaces (like an empty shell) or they can be 3D solid models. Often *Venn diagrams* are used to represent sets and Boolean operations. Figure 11.25 will help you understand how the Union, Subtract, and Intersection commands work. The order in which you select the objects is important only when you're subtracting (i.e., A subtract B is different from B subtract A). Keep in mind that when objects are on different layers, the solid resulting from a Boolean operation will reside on the layer of the first item clicked.

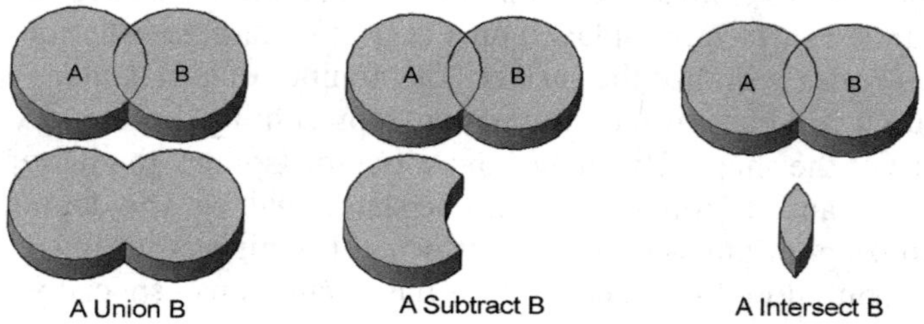

Figure 11.25

Next you will remove the volume of the cylinder from the box, thereby forming a solid model with a hole in it. You will use the Subtract command from the Home tab, Solid Editing panel.

*Click:* ***Subtract button***

Select solids, surfaces and regions to subtract from...

Select objects: ***click the 3D box and then press [Enter]***

Select solids, surfaces and regions to subtract...

Select objects: ***click the cylinder and then press [Enter]***

The resulting solid model is a rectangular prism with a hole through it.

If you selected the items in the wrong order (i.e., clicked the cylinder and subtracted the box from it) the result would be a null solid model or one that has no volume. If you clicked both the box and the cylinder and then pressed [Enter], the command would not work unless you selected something else to subtract. If you make a mistake, you can back up by typing U [Enter] at the command prompt to use the Undo command and then try again.

Note that you can now see that the cylinder has formed a hole in the block. The color inside the hole is red and the rest of the block is blue. Your drawing in the upper right viewport should look like Figure 11.26.

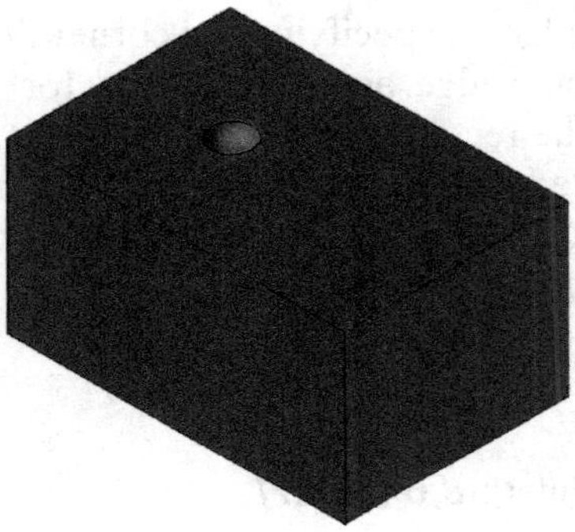

Figure 11.26

Tip: *If your hole formed by subtracting the cylinder does not go all of the way through the 3D box, this may be because the height of both parts is exactly the same. At times, this will leave a thin surface over the top of the hole. If this has happened, undo the Subtract operation. Click on the cylinder and use its grips to drag it to extend beyond the box. When the cylinder is subtracted, the excess portion will be removed during subtraction.*

You will make the isometric view in the upper right use the wireframe appearance. Objects are easier to select when they are not shaded. Also, overlapping solids are much easier to see when they are not shaded.

Using the Viewport Controls

By default, near the upper left of the active viewport is a series of labels called the Viewport control. These labels also act as menus used to maximize the viewport, set to a named view, or change the visual style.

*Make the **upper right viewport current** if it is not already.*

*Click: **on Conceptual** from the Viewport control to show the Visual Styles short-cut menu as shown in Figure 11.27*

*Click: **Wireframe***

The upper right viewport changes to wireframe display.

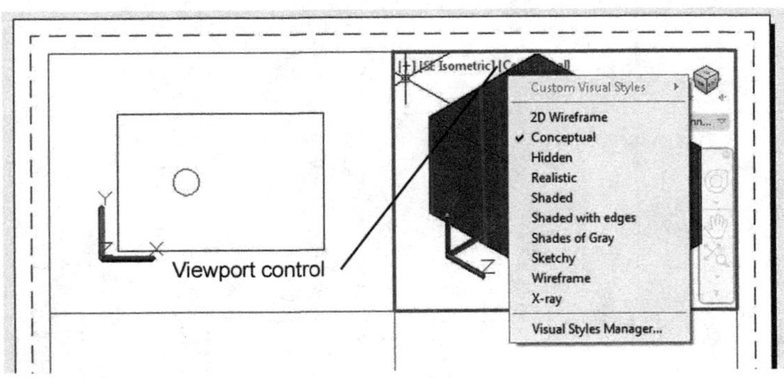

Figure 11.27

Tip: *The Viewport controls may be hard to see if you are using a white background and you have not set them to a darker color. Use the Options dialog box Display tab. Pick Colors... and select a medium color for the Viewport control.*

***Save** your drawing, block.dwg, before continuing.*

Saving your work after you've completed a major step and before you go on to the next step is useful. That way, if you want to return to the preceding step, you can open the previous version of the drawing, discarding the changes that you have made. This is useful when a sequence cannot easily be undone.

Creating Wedges

Now you will add a Wedge primitive to the drawing and then subtract it from the main block. The Wedge command has two options: Corner (the default) and Center. Drawing a wedge by specifying the corner first lets you draw the rectangular base of the wedge, and prompts you for two points that define the diagonal of the rectangular base. The height you enter starts at the first point specified for the base and gets smaller in the X direction toward the second point. The Center option asks you to specify the center point of the wedge you want to draw.

Double-click: ***Inside the top left viewport to make it active***

Click: ***Wedge button***

Specify first corner of wedge or [CEnter]: ***8,6 [Enter]***

Specify corner or [Cube/Length]: ***6,2 [Enter]***

Specify height or [2Point] <0.5000>: ***3 [Enter]***

Now you will use the Boolean operators to subtract the wedge from the object.

Click: ***Subtract button***

Select solids, surfaces and regions to subtract from...

Select objects: ***click the box with the hole and press [Enter]***

Select solids, surfaces and regions to subtract...

Select objects: ***click the wedge and press [Enter]***

With the wedge subtracted, your drawing should look like that in Figure 11.28.

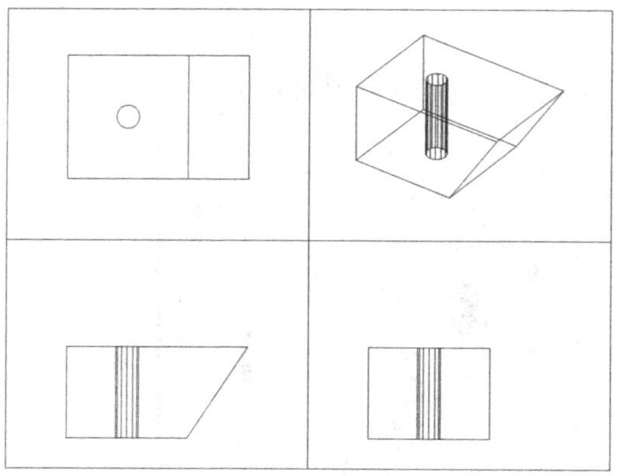

Figure 11.28

Next, switch to the Hidden visual style to remove hidden lines from the upper right view.

Be sure that the ***upper right viewport is active****.*

Click: ***Wireframe*** *from the View control to show the menu*

Click: ***Hidden*** *as shown in Figure 11.29.*

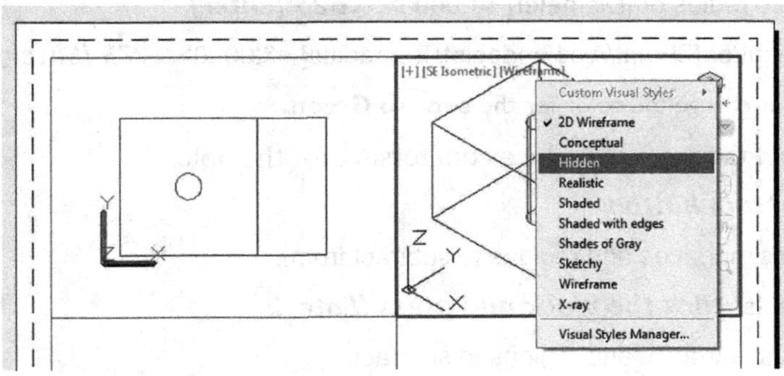

Figure 11.29

The 3D object will appear on your screen with the hidden lines removed. The shape in the upper right viewport should look like that in Figure 11.30.

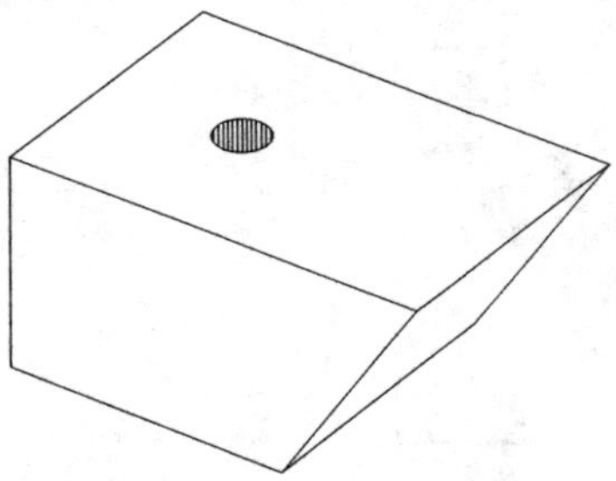

Figure 11.30

You will continue to work with wireframe representation for the isometric view.

Click: ***Hidden*** *from the View control to show the menu*

Click: ***Wireframe*** *to return to that representation*

Creating Cones

The cone primitive creates a solid cone, defined by a circular or elliptical base and tapering to a point perpendicular to the base. It is similar to the cylinder primitive that you have already used. The circular or elliptical base of the cone is always created in the XY-plane of the current UCS. The height is along the Z-axis of the current UCS.

Now you will create a cone using the cone primitive and then subtract it from the block to make a countersink for the hole. It will have a circular base and a negative height. Specifying a negative height causes the cone to be drawn in the opposite direction from a positive height (i.e., in the negative Z-direction).

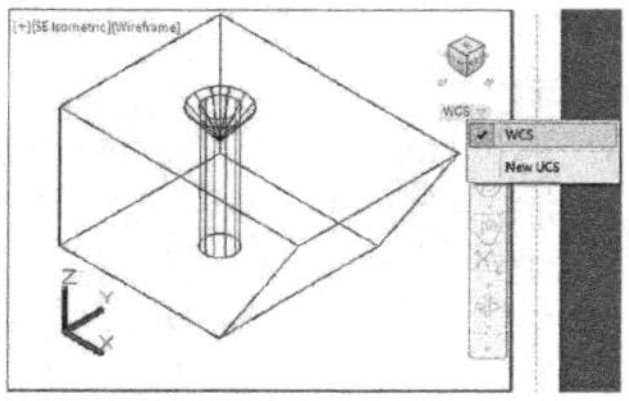

On your own, make the upper right viewport active.

Click to expand the coordinate systems and select WCS for that viewport.

Click: ***Cone button***

Specify center point of base or [3P/2P/Ttr/Elliptical]: ***4,4,3 [Enter]***

Specify base radius or [Diameter] <1.0000>: ***.625 [Enter]***

Specify height or [2Point/Axis endpoint/Top radius] <3.0000>: ***-.75 [Enter]***

On your own, change the color for the **cone** to **Green**.

Next, subtract the cone to make a countersink for the hole.

Click: ***Subtract button***

Select solids, surfaces and regions to subtract from...

Select objects: ***click the block and press [Enter]***

Select solids, surfaces and regions to subtract...

Select objects: ***click the cone and press [Enter]***

Click: ***Xray*** *from the Viewport control (or the Vizualize tab)*

The upper right viewport now displays a transparent view of the shaded object. Your screen should look like Figure 11.31.

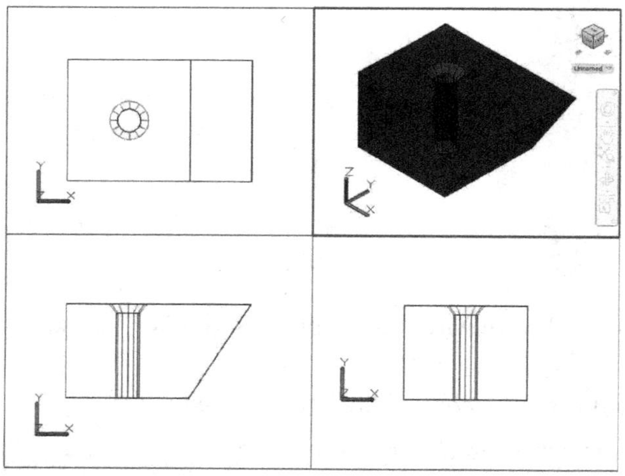

Figure 11.31

Next, you will use the cylinder primitive to add a rounded surface to the top of the block.

Creating User Coordinate Systems

As you have seen, you can have more than one coordinate system. The object is stored in the WCS, which stays fixed, but you can use the UCS command to create a User Coordinate System oriented any way you want. The UCS command allows you to position a User Coordinate System anywhere with respect to the WCS. You can also use it to change the origin point for the coordinate system and to save and restore named coordinate systems. You will create a new UCS that aligns with the left side of the block. This will make it easy to select back edges.

*Make sure the **upper right viewport is active**.*

*Cick: **to expand the Object Snaps** from the status bar*

*Select: **Endpoint** and **Midpoint** (unselect any other modes)*

*On your own, check that **object snap** is **ON***

*Click: **Wireframe** from the View control*

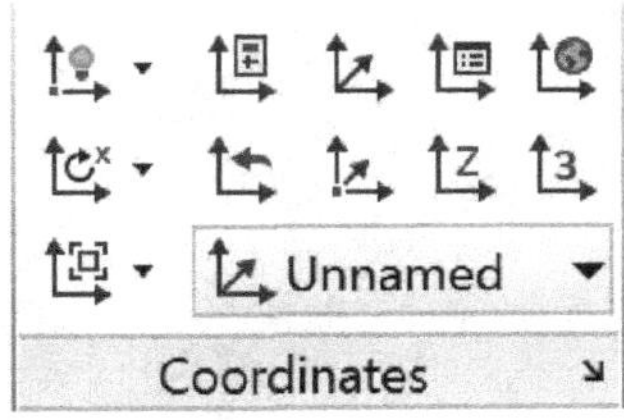

*Click: **3 Point button** from the Home tab, Coordinates panel*

Specify new origin point <0,0,0>: ***target endpoint 1*** *(Figure 11.32)*

Specify point on positive portion of X-axis <3.0000,2.0000,0.0000>: ***target endpoint 2*** *(the back corner)*

Specify point on positive-Y portion of the UCS XY plane <1.0000,2.0000,0.0000>: ***target endpoint 3***

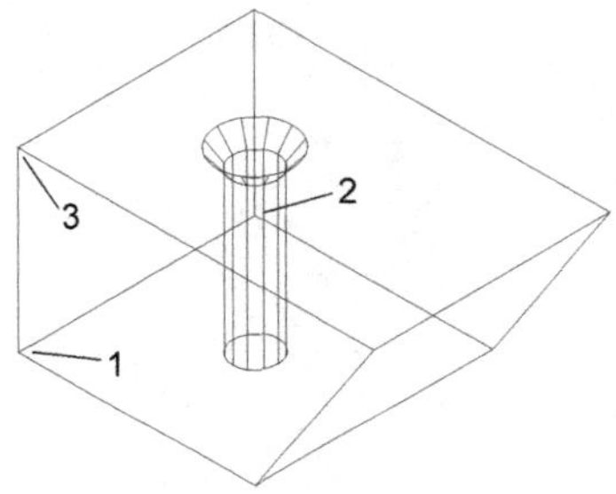

Figure 11.32

Now the UCS is aligned with the left surface of the object.

You will save the new UCS that you created parallel to the left side of the part and give it a name so that you can select it again later.

Command: ***UCS [Enter]***

Current ucs name: *NO NAME*

Specify origin of UCS or [Face/NAmed/OBject/Previous/View/World/X/Y/Z/ZAxis] <World>: ***NA [Enter]***

Enter an option [Restore/Save/Delete/?]: ***S [Enter]***

Enter name to save current UCS or [?]: ***LEFT [Enter]***

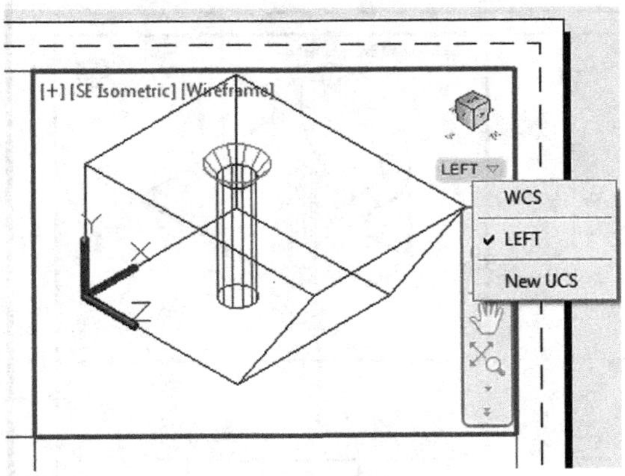

Figure 11.33

Notice the new UCS named LEFT appears on the Named UCS drop down list near the ViewCube. You can click on the named UCS (LEFT) to show the short-cut menu shown in Figure 11.33. In addition to typing the UCS command as you did above, you can also select New UCS from this menu.

Next, you will use the Cylinder button and choose to draw a cylinder by specifying its center. Refer to Figure 11.34 for the points to select. You will use the object snaps for Midpoint and Endpoint to aid in selecting locations from the object.

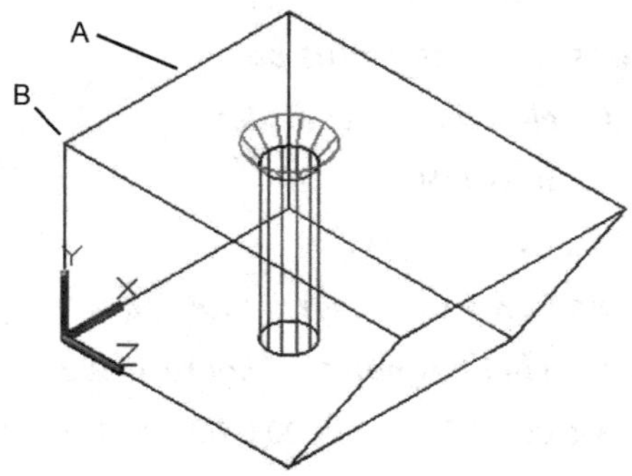

Figure 11.34

On your own, make sure that running object snap is turned on. Verify that the upper right viewport is active.

Click: ***Cylinder button***

Specify center point for base of cylinder or [Elliptical] <0,0,0>: ***click the midpoint of the back top line A***

Specify radius for base of cylinder or [Diameter]: ***click endpoint B***

Specify height or [2Point/Axis endpoint]: ***1 [Enter]***

On your own, use **pan** and **zoom** if necessary to fit the model in the upper right viewport.

Your drawing should look like the one shown in Figure 11.35.

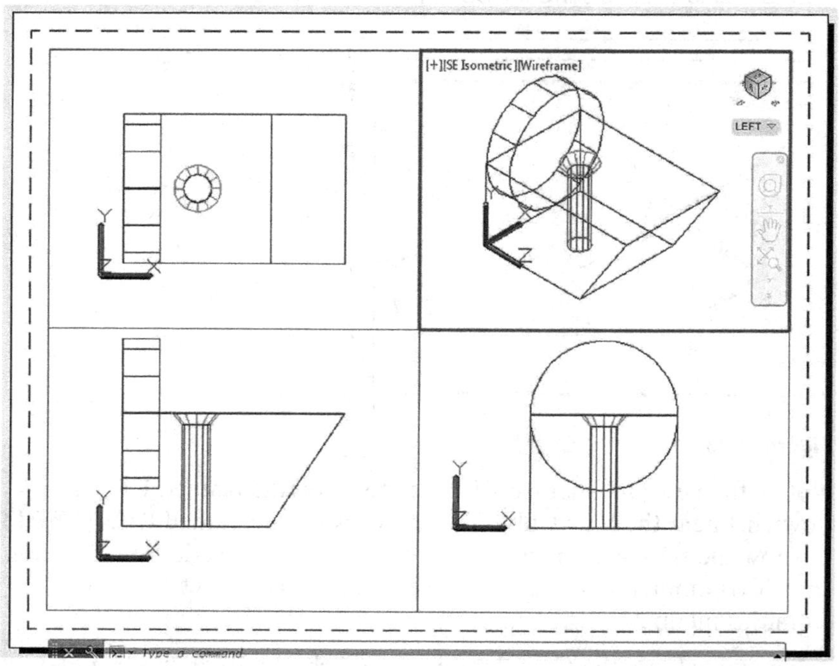

Figure 11.35

Next, use the Boolean operator Union to join the cylinder to the block.

Click: ***Union button***

Select objects: ***click the new cylinder and the block [Enter]***

Click: ***Conceptual*** *from the View control*

Save your completed *block.dwg* drawing.

The joined objects are shown in Figure 11.36.

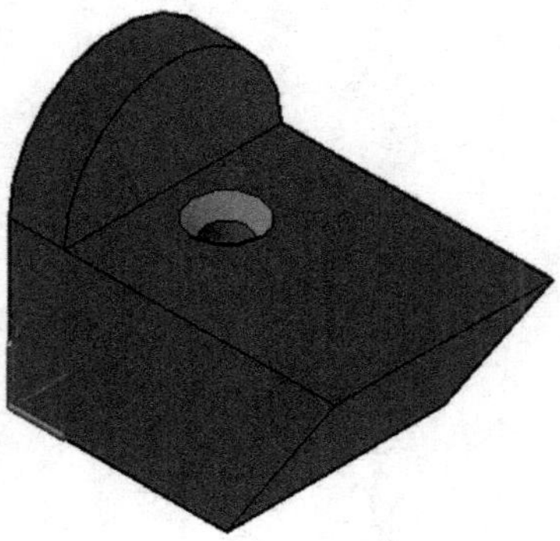

Figure 11.36

Warning: *Do NOT explode 3D models after you have created them, as it converts them back to 3D lines and surfaces. Once you've exploded a 3D solid, you can't easily rejoin the resulting objects to form the 3D object again.*

Plotting Solid Models from Paper Space

Change to **paper space** on your own by typing PS [Enter] at the command prompt or by double-clicking outside the viewport borders.

When you have done so, the paper space icon appears.

Next you will insert a simple title block like you created in Tutorial 5. *TitleBlockA.dwg* is provided with the datafiles for the book.

Click: ***Insert*** *from the Insert tab, Block panel*

Click: ***Blocks from Libraries***

Navigate to your ***datafiles*** *directory and select* ***TitleBlockA****.dwg.*

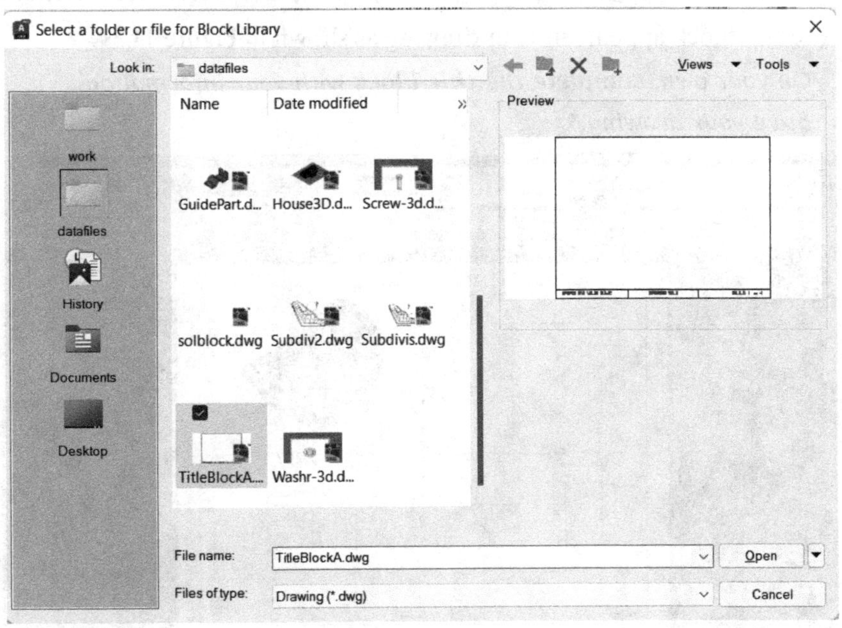

Figure 11.37

Insert Blocks opens with the Libraries tab uppermost.

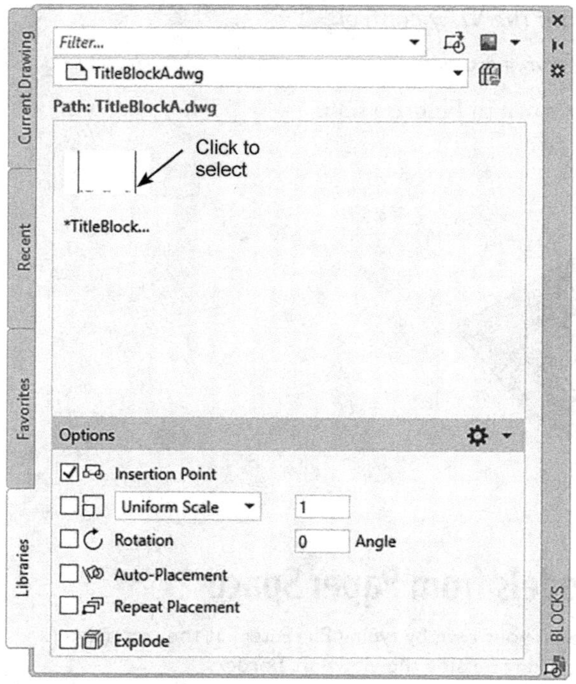

Figure 11.38

From the Insert dialog box, have Insertion Point checked. Use Uniform Scale of 1 and Angle 0 as shown in Figure 11.38.

Click: ***TitleBlock... to select it***

Return to your drawing for the remaining prompt.

Specify insertion point or [Basepoint/Scale/Rotate]: ***use Object Snap Endpoint to target the lower left corner of the lower left viewport***

The titleblock appears in your drawing as shown in Figure 11.39.

On your own, ***complete the title block*** *with your information.*

Save *your drawing.*

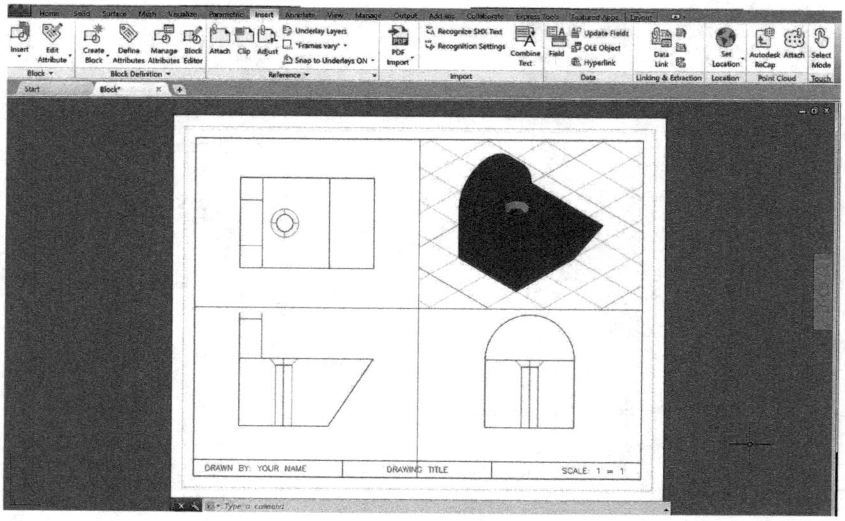

Figure 11.39

Next, set the top, front, and side views to the Hidden visual style.

Double-click: ***inside the top left viewport to make it active***

Click: ***Hidden from the View control***

On your own, change the two lower viewports to use the ***Hidden visual style****.*

Three viewports should now show views with the back lines removed. Use the techniques you learned in Tutorial 5 to plot your drawing.

On your own, switch to ***paper space****.* ***Plot*** *the drawing limits at a scale of 1=1.*

The orthographic views that you have drawn should be exactly half-size on the finished plot because the Viewport Scale was 1:2. Your plotted drawing should be similar to that in Figure 11.40.

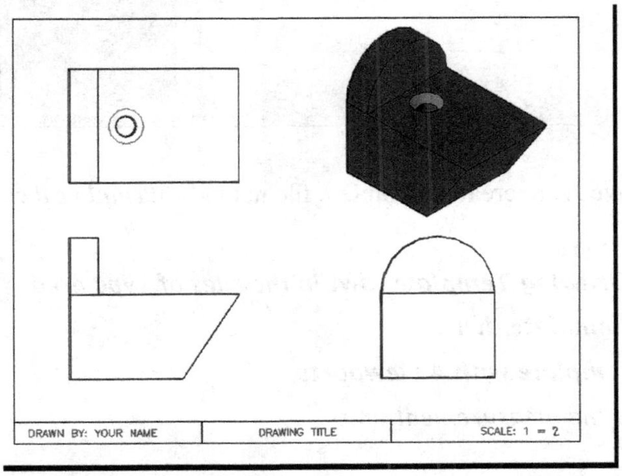

Figure 11.40

Saving Your Multiview Setup as a Template

Next you will switch back to model space, so that when the template is saved, the 3D model space will be active.

Double-click: ***inside the top right viewport*** *to switch to model space inside that viewport*

On your own, ***freeze layer VPort****.*

The magenta viewport borders no longer show, but you can still use the viewports and switch to them.

Next you erase the object and save the basic settings to use as a template for new 3D drawings. Type the alias for Erase.

Command: ***E [Enter]***

Select objects: ***click the solid block object you have drawn***

Select objects: ***[Enter]***

It is erased from all viewports.

*On your own, in the **upper right viewport, restore the World Coordinate System by clicking WCS** as shown in Figure 11.41.*

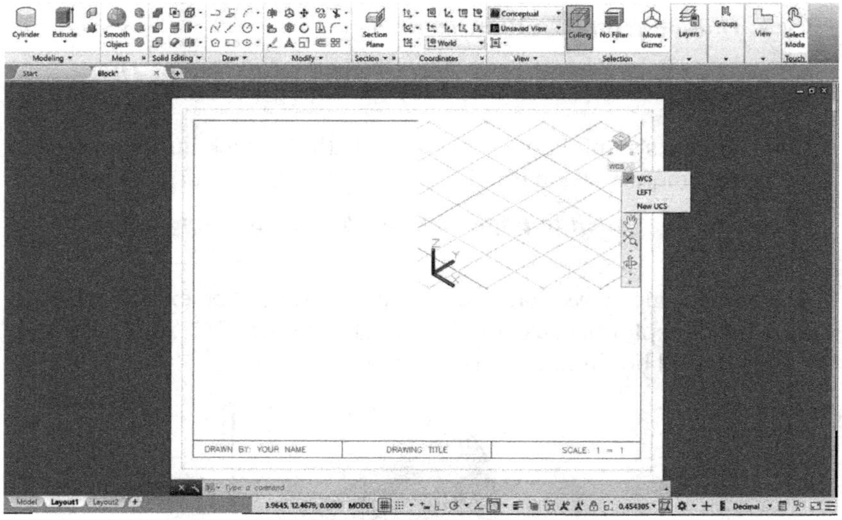

Figure 11.41

Tip: Switch to paper space and use Zoom All if necessary so that the paper area fills the graphics window. Be sure to switch back to model space.

Tip: If you want to see the viewports, you can thaw the layer VPORT and make it a non-plotting layer, so that it will not print.

Next you will use Save As to create a template file named *soltemplate.dwt.*

*Click: **Save As***

*Click: **AutoCAD Drawing Template .dwt** in the Files of Type area*

*Name the file **soltemplate.dwt.***

*Description: **3D template with 4 viewports***

*Select: **English** as the measurement units*

*Click: **OK***

*Click: **to close the current drawing***

Creating Solid Models with Extrude and Revolve

Next, you will learn how to create new solid objects using the extrusion and revolution methods.

*Click: **New button***

*Use the drawing **proto-3D.dwt** provided with your datafiles. It is similar to soltemplate.dwt that you just created.*

*Use **Save As** and name the new drawing **extrusn.dwg**.*

*Make sure layer **Mymodel is the current layer**.*

*Click: the **upper right viewport** to make it active. Select the **WCS** from the control for this viewport or from the ribbon Home tab, Coordinates panel.*

*Set **Grid and Snap to .5** each and turn them on.*

Your screen should be similar to Figure 11.42.

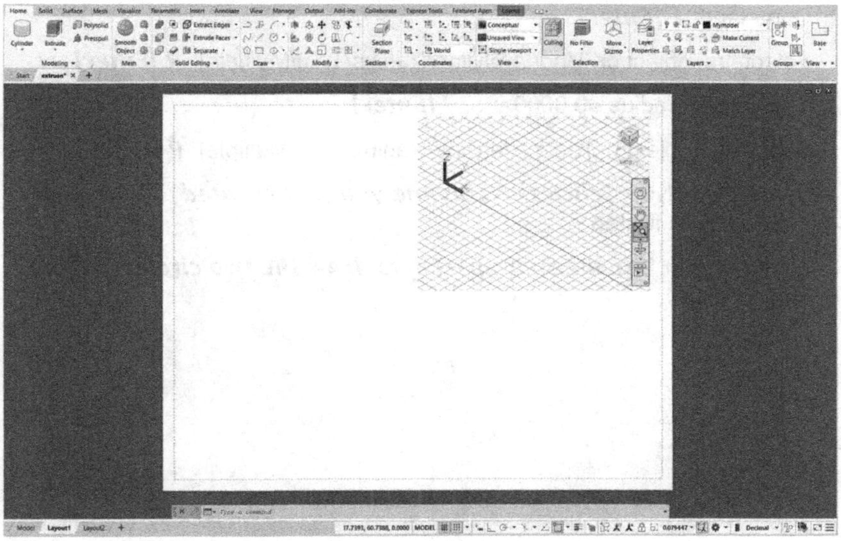

Figure 11.42

Because you started your new drawing from the solid modeling template, the viewports already exist. The viewports themselves are on layer VPORT, which is currently frozen. You can still make each viewport active by clicking inside it.

You will draw the H shape shown in Figure 11.43 using the 2D Polyline command. The coordinates have been provided to make selecting the points to match the tutorial easier for you.

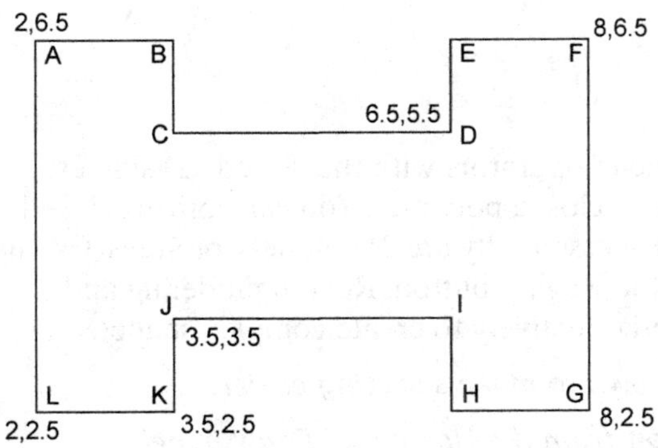

Figure 11.43

Click: ***Polyline button*** *from the Home tab, Draw panel*

Specify start point: ***click point A***

Current line-width is 0.0000

Specify next point or [Arc/Halfwidth/Length/Undo/Width]: ***click points B-L in order***

Specify next point or [Arc/Close/Halfwidth/Length/Undo/Width]: ***C [Enter]***

On your own, use ***Zoom and Pan*** *to position the shape in the viewport.*

You will set the fillet radius to 0.25 and then use the Fillet command's Polyline option to round all the corners of the polyline. Use the alias for the Fillet command.

Tip: *If you did not close your object by typing C, you will get the message 11 lines were filleted. In this case, undo the last two commands and redraw your H shape, closing the polyline with the Close option.*

Command: ***F [Enter]***

Select first object or [Undo/Polyline/Radius/Trim/Multiple]: ***R [Enter]***

Specify fillet radius <0.0000>: ***.25 [Enter]***

Tip: *Switch to paper space and use Zoom All if necessary so that the paper area fills the graphics window. Be sure to switch back to model space.*

Select first object or [Undo/Polyline/Radius/Trim/Multiple]: ***P [Enter]***

Select 2D polyline: ***click the polyline you just created***
12 lines were filleted

On your own, use the Snap spacing to ***draw the two circles*** *shown in Figure 11.44.*

Tip: *Using the Boundary or Pedit commands to join objects into a closed polyline is an effective way to create 2D shapes to extrude. You can also use the Join command to connect line segments.*

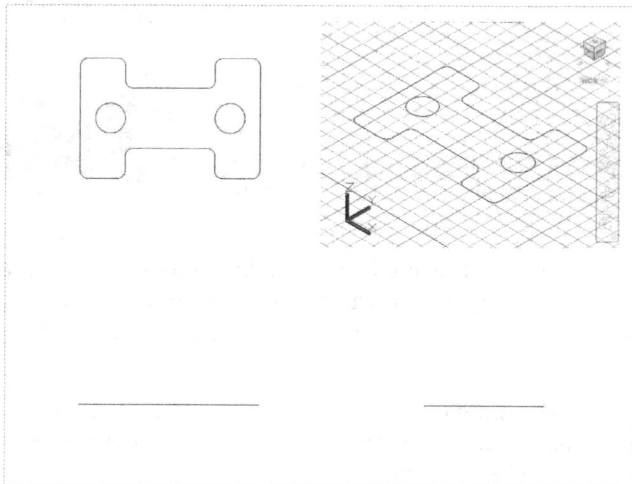

Figure 11.44

Region Modeling

You can also use the Boolean operators with the closed 2D shapes made by circles, ellipses, and closed polylines. You can convert closed 2D shapes to *regions*, which essentially are 2D models, or areas. Expand the Draw panel to select the Region button. Region modeling and extrusion can be combined effectively to create complex shapes.

Tip: *Now is a great time to try the Geometry Cleanup command. To create a region your shape must be completely closed. If you have a little gap you will see the message: "0 loops created". Try using Geometry Cleanup to find and repair any gaps or overshoots and then retry the region command. Experiment with it to fix and close 2D shapes that you will turn into 3D solids.*

Turn ***Snap off*** *on your own to make selecting easier.*

Click: ***Region button*** *from the Home tab, Draw panel*

Select objects: ***use implied Crossing to click the polyline and both circles; then press [Enter]***

3 loops extracted
3 regions created

Now you are ready to subtract the two circles from the polyline region to form holes in the area.

Click: ***Subtract button***

Select solids, surfaces and regions to subtract from...

Select objects: ***click the polyline region and press [Enter]***

Select solids, surfaces and regions to subtract...

Select objects: ***click the circles and press [Enter]***

Now there is only one region, which has two holes in it. Notice that in the shaded view in the upper right viewport, the circles now appear as holes in a shaded flat region, as shown in Figure 11.45.

Tip: *Each viewport can have a different grid setting. In later figures, the grid is turned off to make it easier to see.*

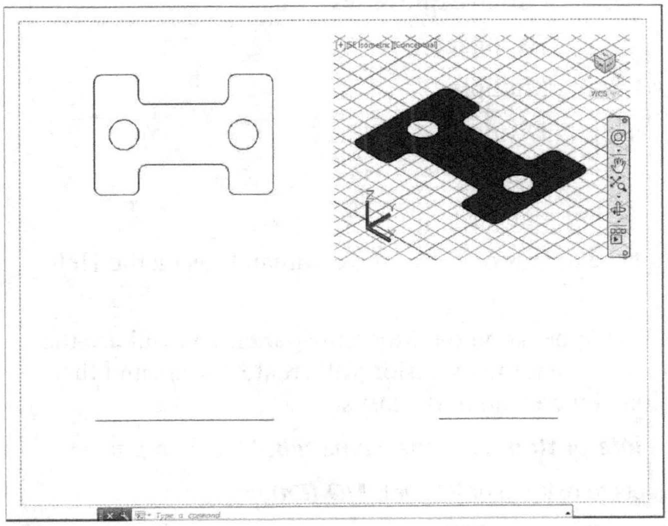

Figure 11.45

Extruding a Shape

Now you can extrude this shape to create a 3D object. Extrusion is the process of forcing material through a shaped opening to create a long strip that has the shape of the opening. The Extrude command works similarly to form a 3D shape. Closed 2D shapes such as splines, ellipses, circles, donuts, polygons, regions, and polylines can be given a height, or extruded to create solids. Polylines must have at least three vertices in order to be extruded.

The Mode option is used to control whether a solid or surface is created by the extrusion. The variable, Surfacemodelingmode, controls the type of surface created (either NURBS or procedural).

The Direction option lets you specify two points to give the length and direction of the extrusion with two specified points. The points cannot be in the same plane as the shape to be extruded.

The Path option lets you select an object to extrude the shape along a path you have previously drawn. When you select the path, it automatically locates to the centroid of the profile shape you selected to extrude. Path curves can be lines, splines, arcs, elliptical arcs, polylines, circles, or ellipses. (You may encounter problems when trying to extrude along path curves with a large amount of curvature and where the resulting solid would overlap itself.)

Taper angle lets you angle the extrusion inward or outward as it is formed. A positive number causes the taper to be inward; a negative number causes the taper to be outward.

The Expression option of the Extrude command allows you to enter an equation for the height of the extrusion.

Use the symbols below to enter expressions:

Operator	Function
( )	Group expressions
^	Exponent
*,	Multiply
/	Divide
+	Add
–	Subtract

Read more about the details of any of the commands using the Help feature.

The Extrude button appears on the Modeling panel. You will use the Mode option to check that the extrusion will create a solid, and then extrude the region you created in the last steps.

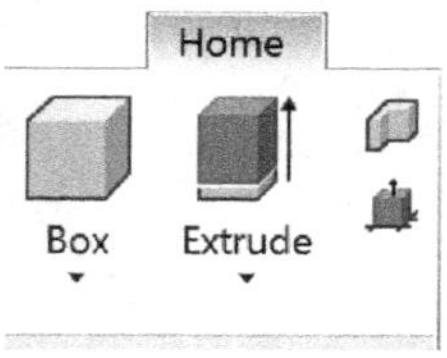

Click: ***Extrude button*** *from the Home tab, Modeling panel*

Select objects to extrude or [MOde]: ***MO [Enter]***

Closed profiles creation mode [SOlid/SUrface] <Solid>: ***SO [Enter]***

Select objects to extrude or [MOde]: ***click the region and press [Enter]***

Specify height of extrusion or
[Direction/Path/Taper angle/Expression] <0>: ***1 [Enter]***

The extruded solid should look like Figure 11.46.

On your own, ***save*** *your drawing, extrusn.dwg.*

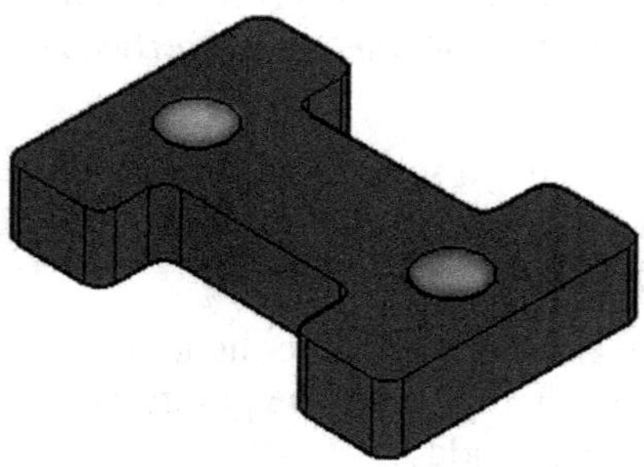

Figure 11.46

Next you will save the drawing with a new name and use it to create a solid using revolution techniques.

Click: ***SaveAs button***

Browse to your ***/Work*** *directory and save the new drawing with the name revolutn.dwg. Check that the name of the drawing shown in the title bar is revolutn.dwg.*

Erase *the previous solid created by extrusion.*

Make sure that ***Snap is on*** *and that* ***Object Snap is turned off****.*

Creating Solids by Revolution

Creating a solid model by revolution is similar in some ways to creating an extrusion. You can use it to sweep a closed 2D shape about a circular path to create a symmetrical solid model that is basically circular in cross section. You can revolve closed polylines, polygons, circles, ellipses, closed splines, donuts, and regions to form solid objects. You can also use revolution to create surfaces.

Use the 2D Polyline command on your own to draw a closed shape like that shown in Figure 11.47.

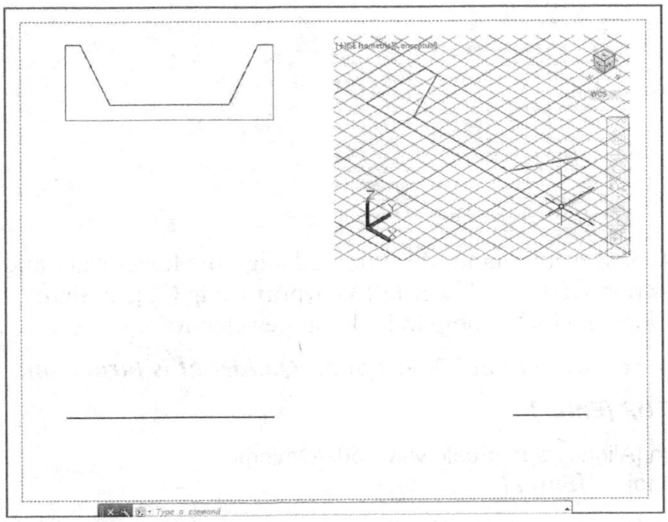

Figure 11.47

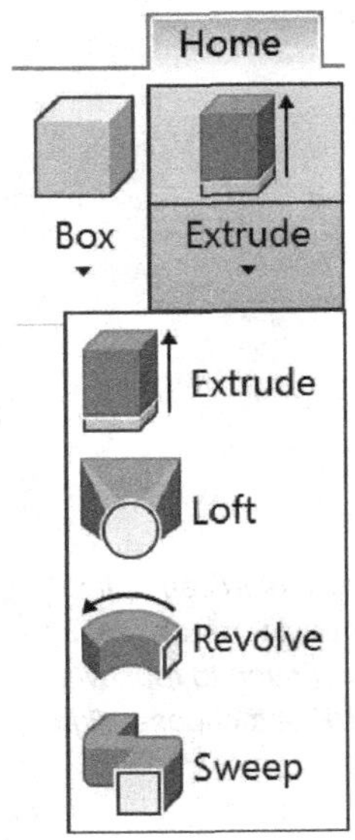

Now you will revolve the polyline about an axis to create a solid model. You don't need to draw the axis line; you can specify it by two points. The Revolve button is on the Home tab, Modeling panel.

Click: ***Revolve button***

Select objects to revolve or [MOde]: ***click the polyline***

Select objects to revolve or [MOde]:***[Enter]***

Specify axis start point or define axis by [Object/X/Y/Z] <Object>: ***click one endpoint of the bottom line***

Specify endpoint of axis: ***click the other endpoint***

Specify angle of revolution or [STart angle/Reverse/EXpression] <360>: ***[Enter]***

Aligning the Views

Next, you will use the Pan Realtime command and Mvsetup to help align the views in the lower left, lower right, and upper left viewports.

Click: ***the lower left viewport to make it active***

Click: ***Pan Realtime button or use the mouse scroll wheel to pan***

Pan so that the solid appears centered in the lower left viewport.

Press: ***[Esc]*** *if needed to exit the Pan command*

Your screen should now be similar to Figure 11.48.

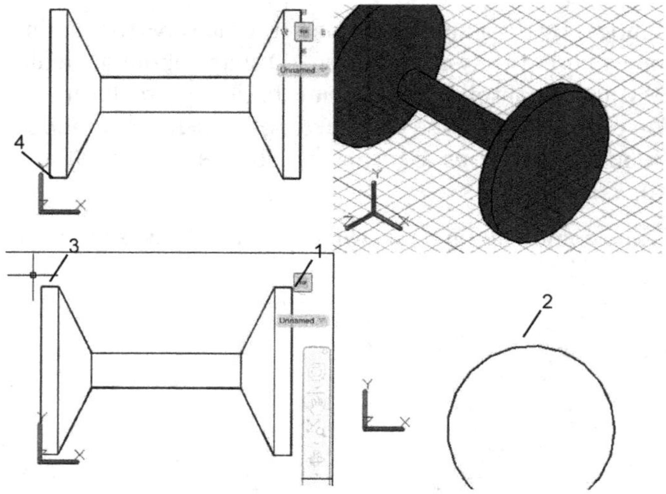

Figure 11.48

Next, you will type the command Mvsetup and align the lower right and upper left views relative to the lower left viewport using Object Snap Quadrant. Use Figure 11.48 to help in making the selections.

On your own, be sure that 2D Object ***Snap Quadrant*** *is turned* ***on****.*

Type: ***MVSETUP [Enter]***

Enter an option [Align/Create/Scale viewports/Options /Title block/Undo]: ***A [Enter]***

Enter an option [Angled/Horizontal/Vertical alignment /Rotate view/Undo]: ***H [Enter]***

Specify basepoint: ***select point 1, using the AutoSnap Quadrant marker to help***

Specify point in viewport to be panned: ***select the lower right viewport and point 2, using the AutoSnap Quadrant marker***

The view in the lower right viewport should align with the view in the lower left viewport relative to the points you selected. Continue with the command to align the upper left viewport vertically.

Tip: *If the V (vertical) option line is not active, then press the return button to reactivate MVSETUP and choose align again.*

Enter an option [Angled/Horizontal/Vertical alignment /Rotate view/Undo]: ***V [Enter]***

Specify basepoint: ***select point 3 using the AutoSnap Quadrant marker to help***

Specify point in viewport to be panned: ***select the upper left viewport and point 4, using the AutoSnap Quadrant marker to help***

On your own, use ***Zoom Extents*** *and* ***Pan Realtime*** *to fit the pictorial view in the upper right viewport.*

Save *your drawing.*

When you are done, your drawing should look similar to Figure 11.49.

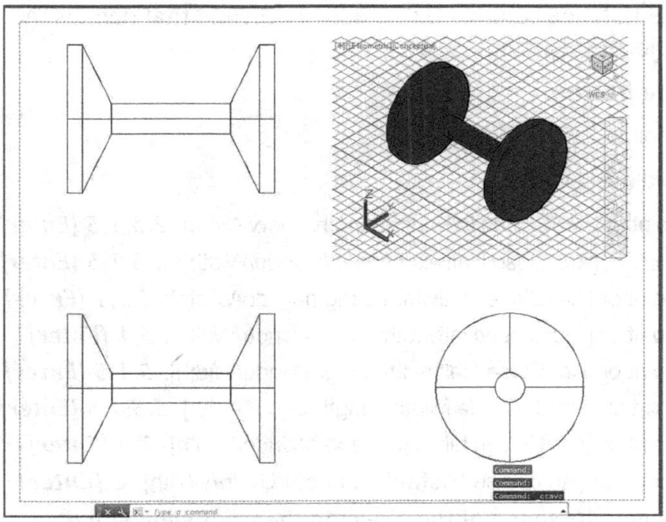

Figure 11.49

Click: ***Save As***

Name your new drawing ***intersect.dwg****.*

On your own, ***erase*** *the solid model that you just revolved.*

Using the Boolean Operator Intersection

Like the Union and Subtract Boolean operators, Intersection lets you create complex shapes from simpler shapes. Intersection finds only the area common to the two or more solid models or regions that you have selected. You will create the shape shown in Figure 11.50 by creating two solid models and finding their intersection.

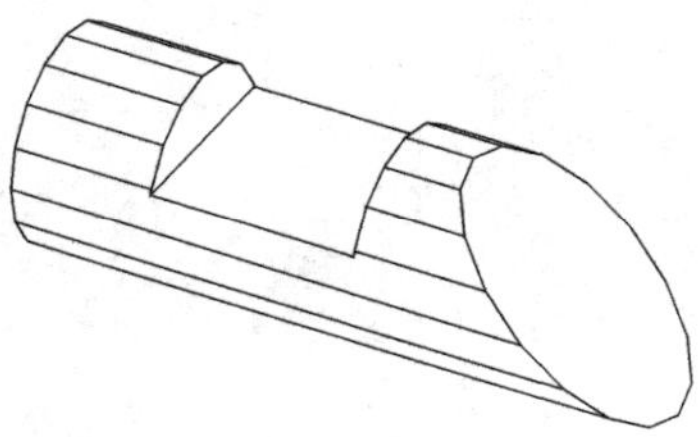

Figure 11.50

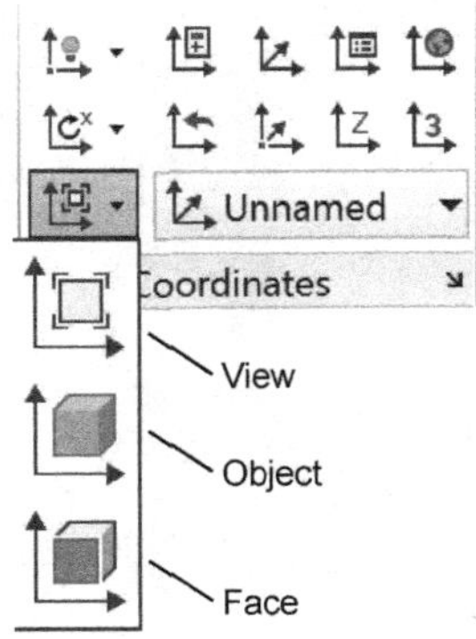

First, you will select to work in the lower left viewport and create a UCS parallel to this viewport.

Click: ***the lower left viewport to make it active***

 *Click:* ***View from the Home tab, Coordinates panel***

A UCS is created parallel to the view in the lower left viewport. Notice the X-Y plane is now parallel to the view.

Set the ***grid to .5*** *and turn it* ***on*** *in the* ***lower left viewport****.*

Check that ***Object Snap*** *is turned* ***off****.*

Next, you will create the shape of a surface in the front view that you will extrude to create the angled face and notch.

You will use the Polyline command to create a polyline that defines the shape of the object in the front view.

Click: ***Polyline button***

Specify start point: ***2.5, 0 [Enter]***

Current line-width is 0.0000

Specify next point or [Arc/Close/Halfwidth/Length/Undo/Width]: ***2.5,1.5 [Enter]***
Specify next point or [Arc/Close/Halfwidth/Length/Undo/Width]: ***3.5,1.5 [Enter]***
Specify next point or [Arc/Close/Halfwidth/Length/Undo/Width]: ***3.5,1 [Enter]***
Specify next point or [Arc/Close/Halfwidth/Length/Undo/Width]: ***5,1 [Enter]***
Specify next point or [Arc/Close/Halfwidth/Length/Undo/Width]: ***5,1.5 [Enter]***
Specify next point or [Arc/Close/Halfwidth/Length/Undo/Width]: ***5.5,1.5 [Enter]***
Specify next point or [Arc/Close/Halfwidth/Length/Undo/Width]: ***7,0 [Enter]***
Specify next point or [Arc/Close/Halfwidth/Length/Undo/Width]: ***C [Enter]***

After you've drawn the shape of the object in the front view, you may need to Pan so that you can see it in the top and side views.

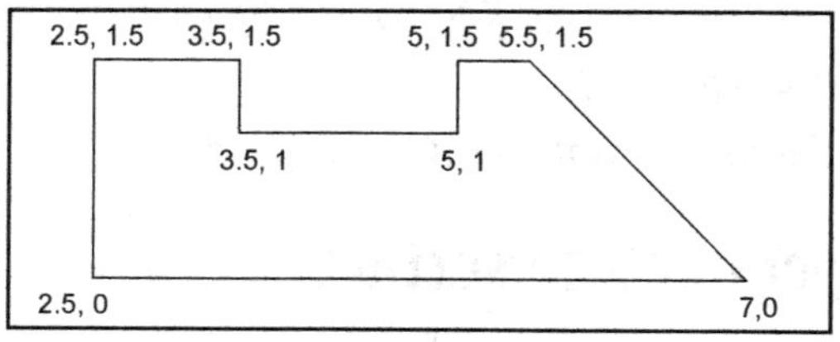

Figure 11.51

Tip: *The Delobj variable controls whether the 2D object is automatically deleted after being extruded or revolved. A value of 1 means delete the object that was used to create the other object (the circle that created the cylinder, for example); a value of 0 means do not delete the object. The default AutoCAD setting is 1 (delete).*

When you have finished, your drawing will look like Figure 11.52.

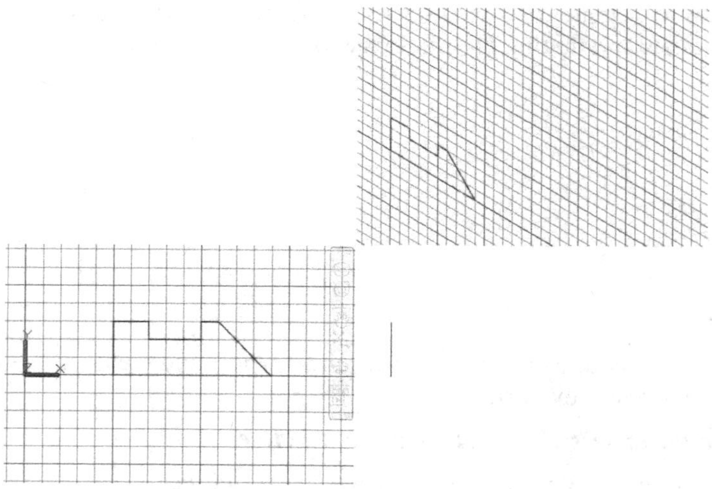

Figure 11.52

Now extrude this shape to form a solid model.

Click: ***Extrude button***

Select objects to extrude or [MOde]: ***click the polyline [Enter]***

Specify height of extrusion or [Direction/Path/Taper angle /Expression] <-4.5000>: ***-3 [Enter]***

The solid model shown in Figure 11.53 has been created. Next, you will make the upper right viewport active and enlarge that viewport to fill the drawing area. (Often when you are modeling it is useful to disable the paper space layouts temporarily and work only in the model view.)

Click: ***the upper right viewport*** *to make it active*

Click: ***to turn the Grid and Snap off*** *in the upper right viewport*

Click: ***Maximize viewport button*** *from the status bar*

Your screen should show a single view of the object.

Command: ***Z [Enter]***

Specify corner of window, enter a scale factor (nX or nXP), or [All/Center/Dynamic/Extents/Previous/Scale/Window/Object] <real time>: ***O [Enter]***

Select objects: ***click on the extruded shape***

The viewport and zoomed object fill the screen as in Figure 11.53.

Tip: *You can also use the [+]/[-] from the Viewport control to maximize and minimize the viewport.*

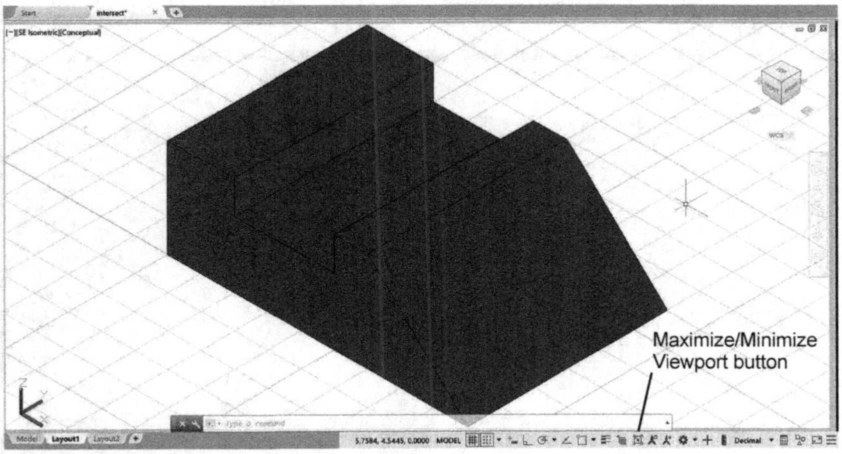

Figure 11.53

Command: [Enter] *to restart the Zoom command*

Specify corner of window, enter a scale factor (nX or nXP), or [All/Center/Dynamic/Extents/Previous/Scale/Window/Object] <real time>: ***.8X [Enter]***

The view is zoomed to 80% of the previous size. Next you will create a new unnamed UCS parallel to the vertical back face of the object.

Click: ***on the UCSicon*** *to activate its grips*

Use ***object snap Endpoint and drag the UCS icon*** *to the front corner of the shape; then drag the X axis and Y axis to align with the back surface as shown in Figure 11.54. Use* ***Wireframe*** *shading to make it easier to see the back edges.*

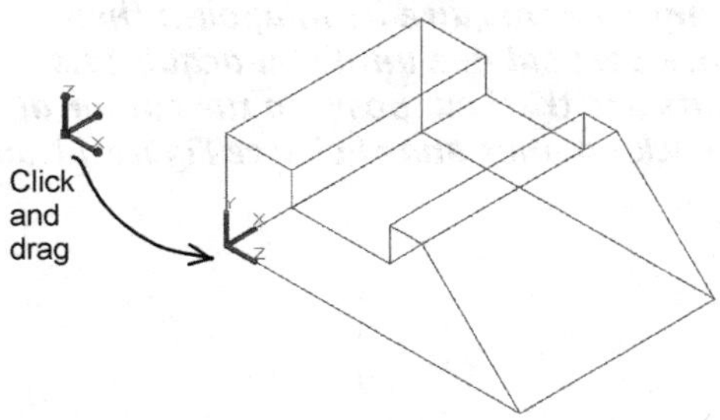

Figure 11.54

Dynamic UCS

Dynamic UCS automatically aligns the XY plane of the UCS with a plane on a 3D solid while you are creating an object. After you are done, it returns to the original UCS.

You may have noticed surfaces becoming highlighted and the cursor appearance changing to align with various surfaces of the model. This happens when dynamic UCS is active. For the next steps you will make sure it is turned off. If dynamic UCS is on, it will be very difficult to draw a shape on the back surface of the object. (Of course you could change your view, but for this example you are going to leave the view set as it is.) You will work with dynamic UCS later in the tutorial.

*Click: **Customization button** from the status bar to show the list*

*Click: **Dynamic UCS** to show the button on the status bar*

(see Figure 11.55)

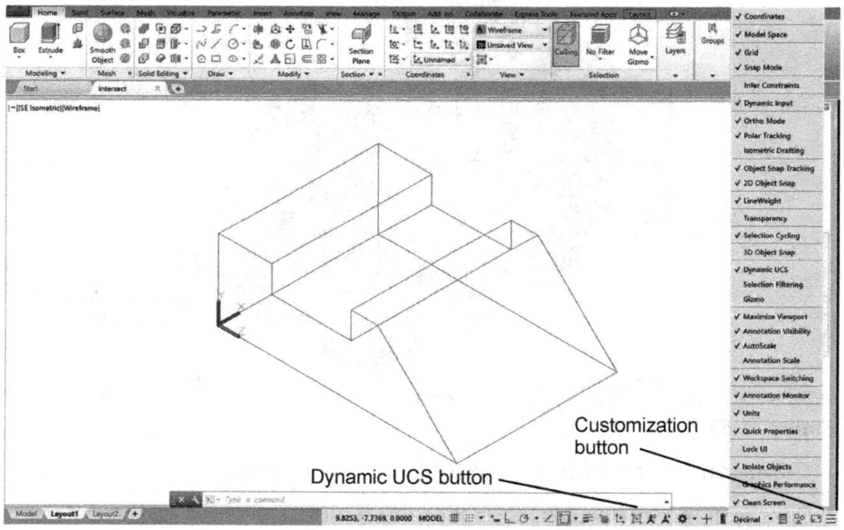

Figure 11.55

*Click: **Dynamic UCS** to turn it OFF*

Next you will create the circular shape of the object.

*Click: **Object Snap Tracking button** from the status bar to turn it on.*

Verify that object snap **midpoint** is turned on.

*Click: **Circle button***

Specify center point for circle or [3P/2P/TTR (tan tan radius)]: ***hover the cursor over the bottom line until you acquire its midpoint; then hover the cursor over the back vertical line until you acquire its midpoint. Once both midpoints are tracked, position the cursor at the intersection of the two tracking lines and click*** *(see Figure 11.56)*

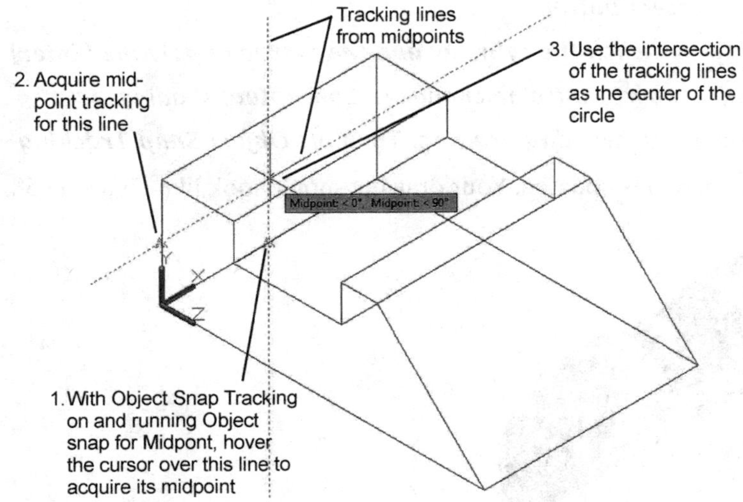

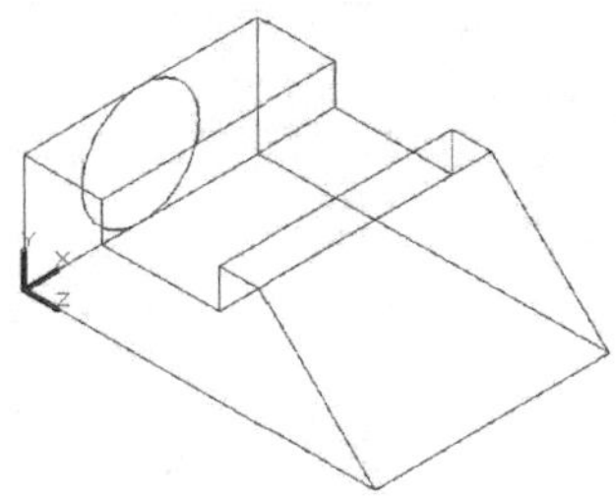

Figure 11.56

Specify radius of circle or [Diameter]: ***0.75 [Enter]***

The circle is drawn at the center of the back surface. You will use the Extrude command to elongate the circle into a cylinder.

Click: ***Extrude button***

Select objects to extrude or [MOde]: ***click the circle [Enter]***

Specify height of extrusion or [Direction/Path/Taper angle/Expression] <-3.0000>: ***7 [Enter]*** *(or use the mouse to drag the length past the right end of the solid)*

Your shapes should look like Figure 11.57.

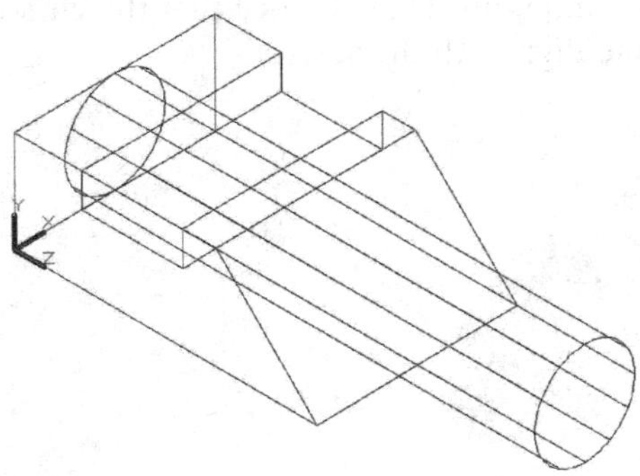

Figure 11.57

Experiment by typing DELOBJ at the command prompt and changing the setting to 0. Create a polyline and extrude it in one direction using a taper angle. The original polyline will remain. Select it again and extrude it in the other direction using the same taper angle. This way you can create a surface that tapers in both directions.

Now you are ready to use the Intersection command to create a new solid model from the overlapping portions of the two solid models that you have drawn.

Click: ***Intersect button***

Select objects: ***click the cylinder and the extruded polyline [Enter]***

Use the viewport control to change to ***Conceptual*** *shading.*

Save *your intersect.dwg drawing.* ***Turn off Object Snap Tracking.***

The solid model is updated. Your drawing should look like Figure 11.58.

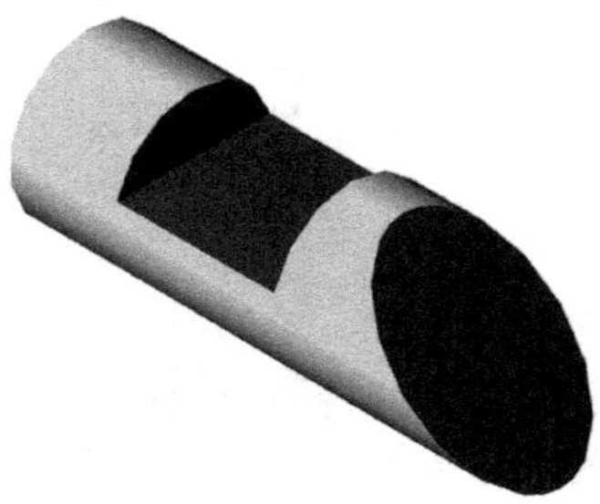

Figure 11.58

Next you will add an extruded cylinder to the slanted end of the shape. This time you will use dynamic UCS to automatically align the XY plane for the shape you will draw.

Click: ***Dynamic UCS*** *from the status bar to turn it ON*

Set ***Hidden as the display method.*** *Turn off Object Snap.*

Click: ***Circle button***

Move your cursor around on the shape until the slanted end surface is highlighted as shown in Figure 11.59. Notice that the cursor changes showing crosshairs that align with the surface.

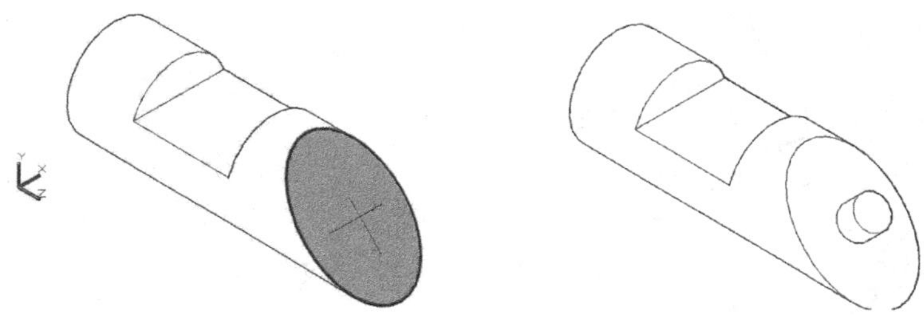

Figure 11.59

Finish drawing a ***.25 radius circle*** *roughly centered on the slanted face on your own.* ***Extrude it to a distance of .375. Save*** *and* ***close intersect.dwg.***

Creating Surface Models

Surfaces behave much like solids but are basically a shell, like a paper cup. Surface modeling tools are useful for irregularly shaped contours. You can convert the following objects into surfaces by using the CONVTOSURFACE command: 2D solids, regions, bodies, open polylines (with thickness and zero-width), lines with thickness, arcs with thickness, and planar 3D faces. To create a surface object from a solid you explode the solid.

Once you have created a surface you can use the editing commands such as union and subtract to create more complex surfaces. You can create a solid from a surface using the THICKEN command.

The AutoCAD software provides two types of surface modeling: procedural surfaces or NURBS. Which type is in use is controlled by the Surfacemodelingmode variable. Setting Surfacemodelingmode to 0 creates procedural surfaces during surface modeling commands. Setting it to 1 creates NURBS surfaces instead. (You can convert from procedural surfaces to NURBS surfaces using the CONVTONURBS command.) NURBS surfaces may allow you more control over individual vertices making it easier to reshape the surfaces you create.

*Start a **new drawing from contrdat.dwg**, which was provided with the datafiles.*

***Name your new drawing surf1.dwg**.*

The Viewport control shows the visual style Shaded with Edges.

*Click: **Surface tab** from the ribbon*

Zoom and pan your drawing to show the contours like Figure 11.60.

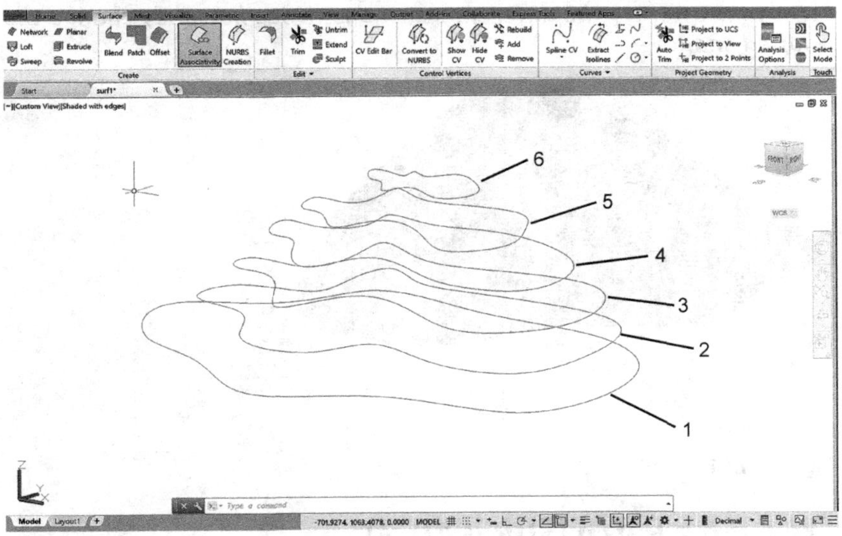

Figure 11.60

Tip: *You can use the Elevation command to set the Z height at which new drawing objects will be created as you draw.*

On the screen are 2D splines representing contours (lines of equal elevation on a contour map). The splines are at different heights along the Z-axis. The bottom line is at Z 200, the next at Z 220, the next at Z 240, and so on. You can create these contour lines on your own by drawing splines (or polylines) through your data points, joining points of equal elevation. Then use Move to relocate the resulting spline. Specify a base point of (0,0,0) and a displacement of (0,0,200) (or whatever your elevation may be).

Using Loft

Loft creates a surface or a solid between contours. These can also be the existing edges of a surface or solid. You must have at least two edges to create a loft. Next you will create a loft surface (often called "lofting") between the contour lines in the drawing.

Click: ***Loft button***

Current wire frame density: ISOLINES=4, Closed profiles creation mode = Surface

Select cross sections in lofting order or [POint/Join multiple edges/MOde]: ***click contour lines 1through 6 in order [Enter]***

6 cross sections selected

Enter an option [Guides/Path/Cross sections only/Settings] <Cross sections only>: ***[Enter]***

The lofted surface is created as shown in Figure 11.61.

Click: ***on your lofted shape***

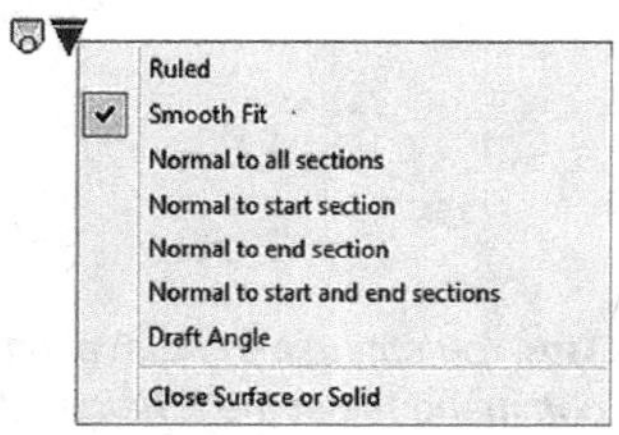

A small loft icon appears near the lofted shape.

Click: ***the arrow to show the options for generating the loft***

On your own, try the different selections to see how they change the lofted shape.

Figure 11.61

Creating a Patch (SURFPATCH)

The top surface is flat. Loft creates a surface between contours so it has no way to form a closed top. You can use the Surfpatch command to create a surface, like a cap, using a single closed loop, from a curve, or from contiguous edges of separate surfaces.

On your own, **freeze layer CONTOURS**.

Click: ***Patch button*** *from the Surface tab, Create panel*

Select surface edges to patch or [CHain/CUrves] <CUrves>: ***click the top edge [Enter]***

Press Enter to accept the patch surface or [CONtinuity/Bulge magnitude/Guides]: ***CON [Enter]***

Tip: *The Guides option lets you specify additional curves or points used to shape the patch surface.*

Patch surface continuity [G0/G1/G2] <G0>: ***G1 [Enter]***

Press Enter to accept the patch surface or [CONtinuity/Bulge magnitude/ Guides]: ***B [Enter]***

Patch surface bulge magnitude <0.5000>: ***.75 [Enter]***

Press Enter to accept the patch surface or [CONtinuity /Bulge magnitude/Guides]: ***[Enter]***

The patch appears as a surface over the top loop as shown in Figure 11.62.

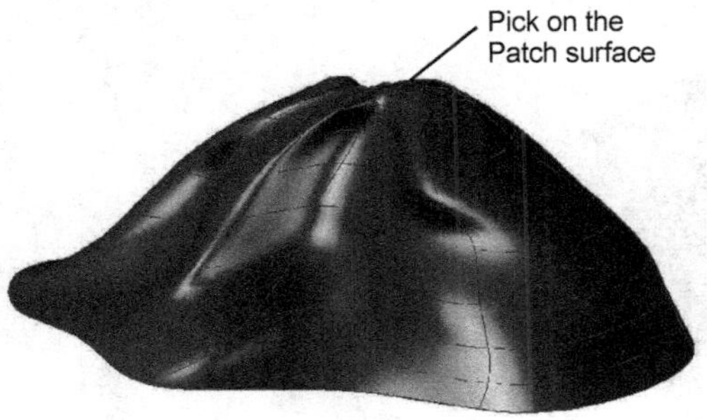

Figure 11.62

*Click: **the Patch surface** to show its editing features*

Figure 11.63

The *3D gizmo* as shown in Figure 11.64 provides quick editing for surfaces and solids similar in a way to using grips with 2D objects. Like using grips, you can right-click the 3D gizmo to show the context menu and make selections from it.

The 3D UCS icon uses red associated with the x-axis, green with the y-axis, and blue with the z-axis. The 3D gizmo uses the same colors to identify the x, y, and z directions. Click and drag on one of the colored features to use the gizmo.

Notice that if you use the gizmo to move the top surface patch, you will see a message "One or more surfaces are associated with a defining curve, surface, or parametric equation." You see the message because the patch was defined by the top edge of the lofted surface. You have the option to continue and break the associativity, or to cancel. If so, click Cancel.

***Click the small blue downward arrow** to show the Continuity options as shown in Figure 11.65*

*Click: **Tangent (G1)***

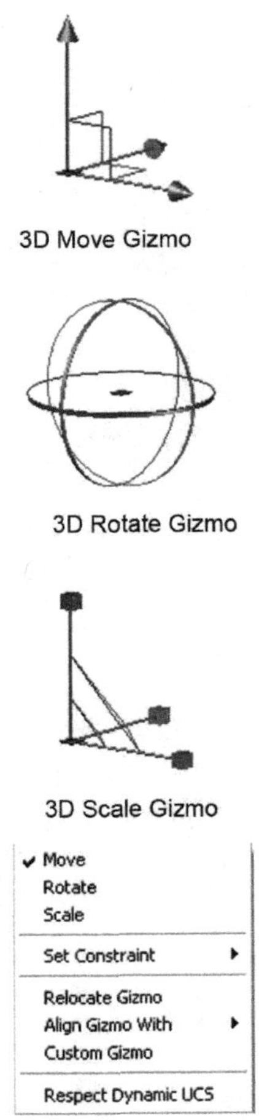

Figure 11.64

The patch surface curves are tangent to the lofted surface. These continuity options were available when you created the patch surface, but as you have just seen, you can still access them after the surface has been created. You can also use the Properties dialog box to access the bulge and contour settings.

Save and close your drawing.

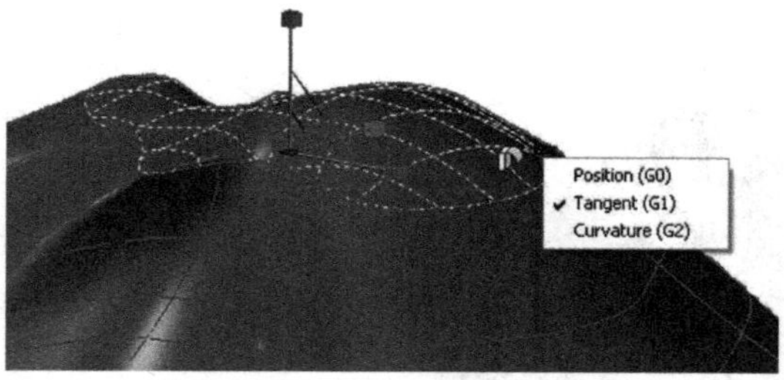

Figure 11.65

Creating Mesh Models

You can also use the AutoCAD software to create mesh models. Mesh models and surface models are different types of objects and have different editing features. Many 3D objects can be converted to mesh models using the Smooth Object (MESHSMOOTH) command.

AutoCAD mesh models are composed of a faceted polygonal mesh that approximates curved surfaces. Mesh modeling can be more difficult to use than solid modeling and provides less information about the object. The reason is that only the surfaces and not the interior volumes of the object are described in the drawing database. You must edit the mesh that creates surface models differently. However, mesh modeling is well suited to applications such as modeling 3D terrain for civil engineering applications.

In general you should not mix solid modeling, surface modeling, and wireframe modeling for the same model, as you can't edit them in the same ways to create a cohesive single structure. Select the single method that is best for your application.

Because using Box, Wedge, Pyramid, Cone, Sphere, Dome, Dish, Torus, Revolved Mesh, and Tabulated Mesh is basically similar to the method you used earlier in the tutorial to create solid models, these tools are not covered here. Instead, on your own, refer to AutoCAD Help for further information about creating these shapes.

Next, you will learn to create an Edge Mesh and a 3D Mesh. Understanding how to create these objects will allow you to create a wider variety of shapes. Surface modeling is especially useful for creating 3D terrain, such as mountainous topography or 3D roadway models.

The commands to create meshes can be selected from the ribbon Mesh tab.

Start a new drawing on your own from the datafile edgsurf.dwg.

Name your new drawing surf2.dwg.

On your own, make MESH the current layer.

Turn the grid off.

Your drawing should look like Figure 11.66.

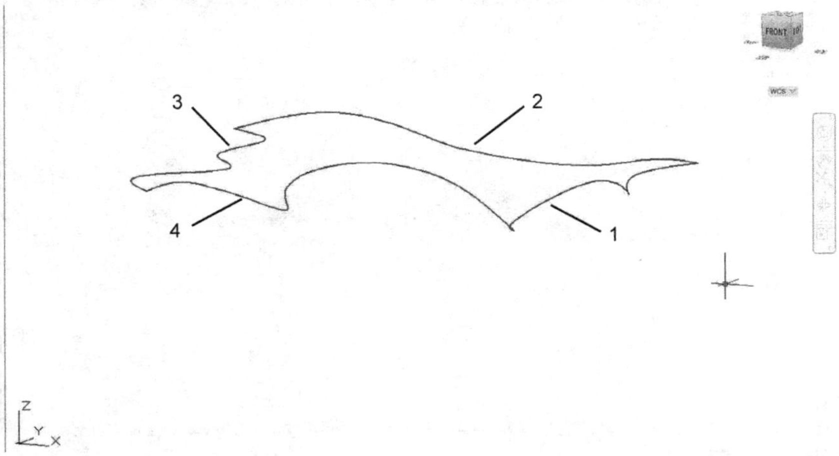

Figure 11.66

You will use the four 3D splines shown to define an edge surface.

Creating an Edge Mesh

The Edge Mesh selection from the Mesh tab, Primitives panel creates a mesh defined by four edges. The mesh density for an edge surface is controlled by the Surftab1 and Surftab2 variables. The Edge Surface selection creates a *Coons patch mesh.* A Coons patch mesh is a *bicubic surface* interpolated between the four edges. Refer to Figure 11.66 for the splines to select.

Command: ***SURFTAB1 [Enter]***

New value for SURFTAB1 <6>: ***20 [Enter]***

Command: ***SURFTAB2 [Enter]***

New value for SURFTAB2 <6>: ***20 [Enter]***

Click: ***Edge Surface*** *from the Mesh tab, Primitives panel*

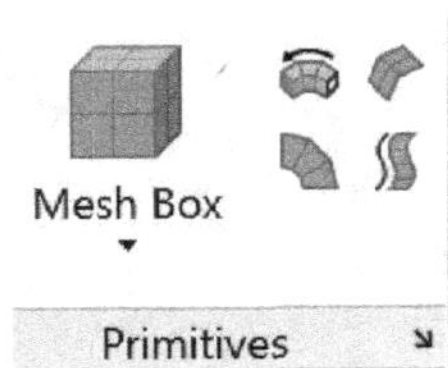

Select object 1 for surface edge: ***click curve 1***

Select object 2 for surface edge: ***click curve 2***

Select object 3 for surface edge: ***click curve 3***

Select object 4 for surface edge: ***click curve 4***

The edge surface appears in your drawing.

On your own, change the visual style for the view to **Shaded with Edges**.

Using the Steering Wheel

The Steering Wheel feature lets you quickly adjust your 3D view. It can be selected from the Viewport control as shown in Figure 11.67.

Click: [-] from the Viewport control in the upper left

Click: ***Steering Wheel***

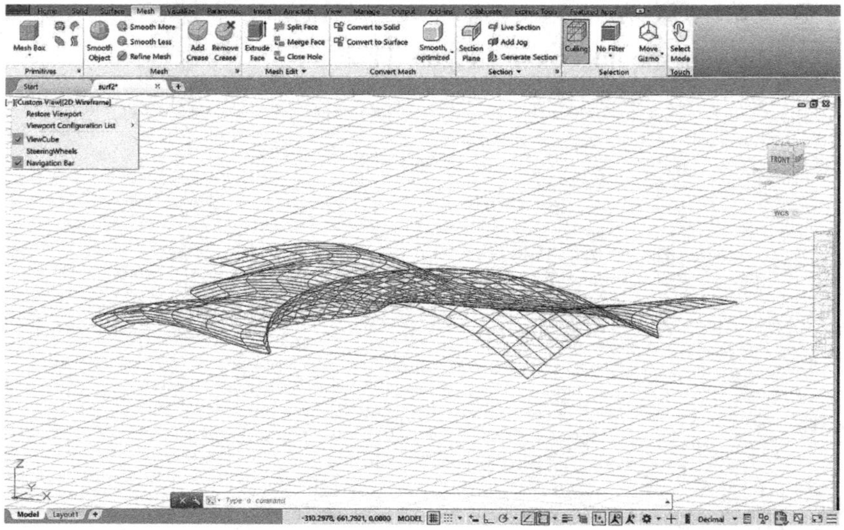

Figure 11.67

The Steering Wheel appears attached to your cursor as shown in Figure 11.68.

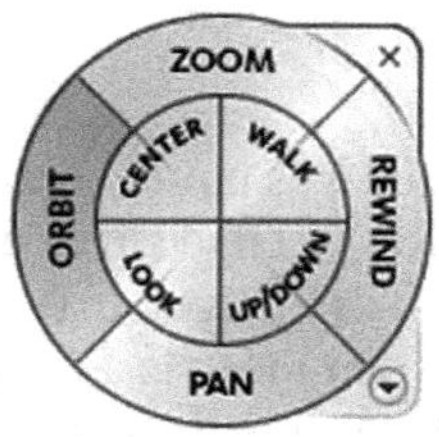

Figure 11.68

To use the steering wheel, move your cursor to highlight the steering tool you want to use and then press the mouse button while dragging to use the tool.

Try the Orbit feature on your own now.

As you press and drag with your mouse, while the orbit area is highlighted, the pivot point shows at the center of the object and dragging revolves the 3D viewpoint (Figure 11.69).

Figure 11.69

Experiment with the other modes on your own. When you are done, press [Esc] or click the small x in the upper right corner of the steering wheel to close it. Note that if you have the navigation bar turned on you can quickly access the steering wheel from it.

Save and close your drawing.

Creating a Network Surface

A network surface is similar to the edge mesh that you just created and similar to the lofted surface you created earlier. The network surface forms a surface between splines, 2D and 3D curves, and edge subobjects. A subobject is just that: a portion of an existing object, such as the edge of a model. To define a network surface, you first select the curves to define one direction (u or v) and then the curves defining the other direction.

Unlike the edge mesh and the lofted surface, the network surface does not have to be made from a closed boundary (although of course the boundary can also be closed). First you will use the 3D gizmo to move the lines apart and adjust their shapes.

On your own, use **edgesurf2.dwg** to start a new drawing with the new name *surfnetwork.dwg*. Four lines should appear on your screen similar to Figure 11.70.

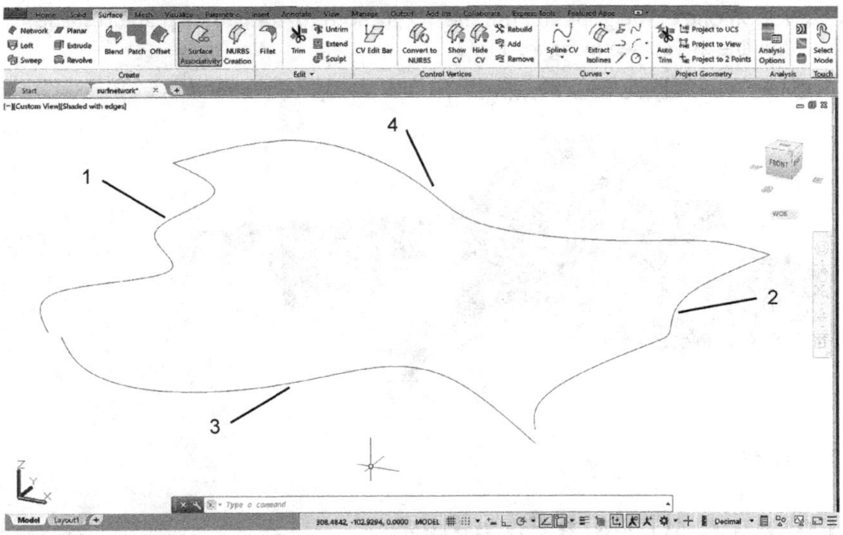

Figure 11.70

Click: ***Network*** *from the Surface tab, Create panel*

Select curves or surface edges in first direction: ***click lines 1 and 2 [Enter]***

Select curves or surface edges in second direction: ***click lines 3 and 4 [Enter]***

The network surface appears on your screen similar to Figure 11.71.

When the lines selected have too much curvature in different directions or are too far apart, you may see the message, "Can't create a network from the selected curves". If this happens, modify the curves and try again.

Because the surface is created to be associated with the lines, you can modify the lines to change the shape of the surface. This is easy to do using the 3D gizmo.

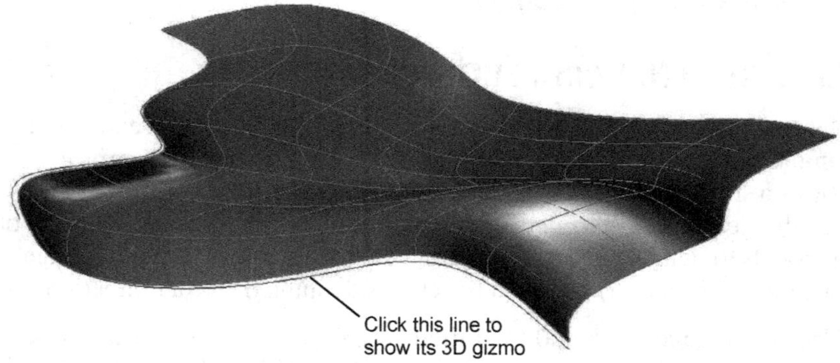

Figure 11.71

Click on the **front line** so that its grips show and you see the 3D gizmo.

Use the 3D Move gizmo to move the line a slight distance away from the other three lines. Notice how the surface updates.

Click on one of the grips and use the 3D gizmo to **drag the grip** and reshape the line as you see in Figure 11.72.

On your own, **save** your drawing.

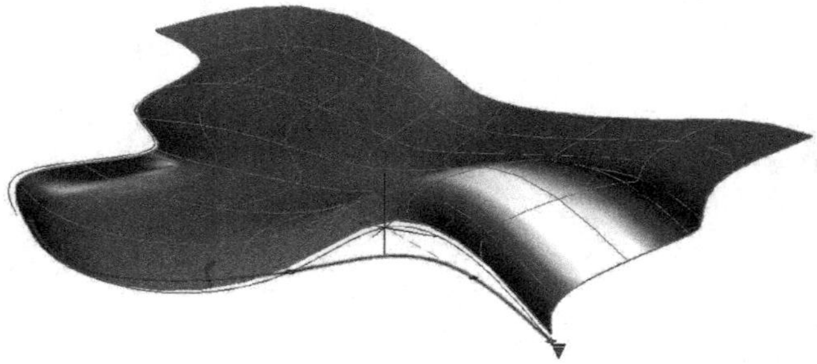

Figure 11.72

Creating 3D Mesh Primitives

The 3D Mesh command lets you construct mesh primitives, similar to the solid features for box, cylinder, wedge, you used earlier in the tutorial.

Click: ***Erase button***

Select objects: ***ALL [Enter]***

Select objects: ***[Enter]***

Use **Save As** to save the empty drawing with the name *mesh.dwg*. On your own, experiment with the Mesh Primitives similar to those shown in Figure 11.73. Use the Orbiter and shade and spin the view on your own.

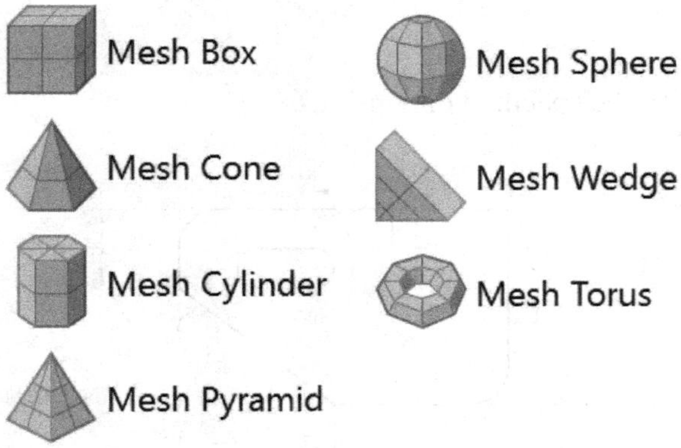

Figure 11.73

Now you know how to establish viewports and viewing directions and create and join the basic shapes used in solid modeling. With these tools you can create a variety of complicated shapes. In Tutorial 12, you will learn how to change solid models further, as well as to plot them. Practice creating shapes and working with the User Coordinate Systems on your own. You have now completed Tutorial 11.

Save and **close** all drawings before exiting the software.

Key Terms

3D gizmo
arcball
bicubic surface
Boolean operators
Coons patch mesh
difference
extrusion
intersection
mass properties
matrix
perspective icon
plan view
primitives
regions
revolution
solid modeling
surface modeling
tessellation lines
union
User Coordinate System (UCS)
vector
Venn diagrams
viewpoint
wireframe modeling
World Coordinate System (WCS)

Key Commands

3DMesh
3DWireframe
Box
Cone
CONVTONURBS
CONVTOSURFACE
Cylinder
Delobj
Edge Surface
Extrude
Facetres
Front View
Hide
Intersection
Isolines
Loft
Mview
Mvsetup
Named UCS
Network Surface
Plan
Regenerate All
Region
Revolve
Right View
Ruled Surface
SE Isometric View
Shademode
Subtract
Surfacemodelingmode
Surfpatch
Surftab1
Surftab2
Top View
UCS
Union
Viewres
View UCS
Vpoint
Wedge Center
Wedge Corner
World UCS

Exercises

Use solid modeling to create the parts shown according to the specified dimensions.

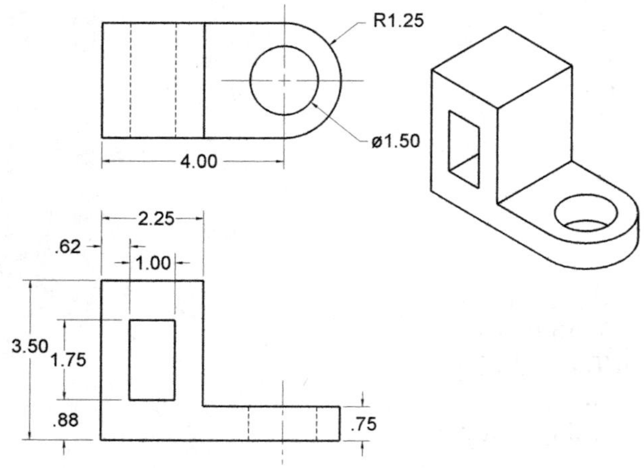

Exercise 11.1 Connector

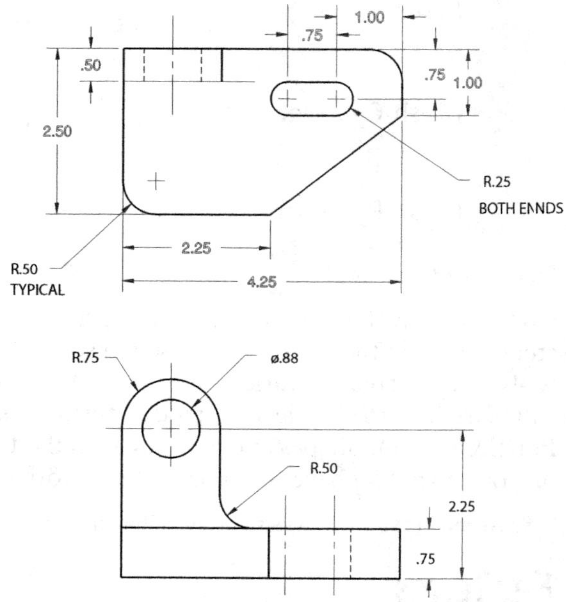

Exercise 11.2 Support Base

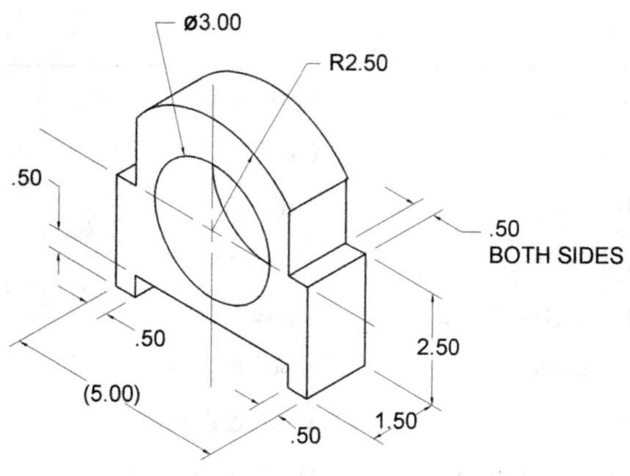

Exercise 11.3 Shaft Support

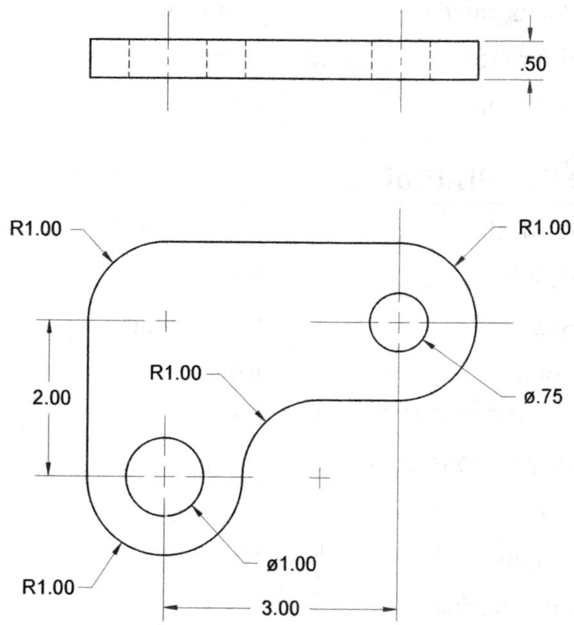

Exercise 11.4 Angle Link

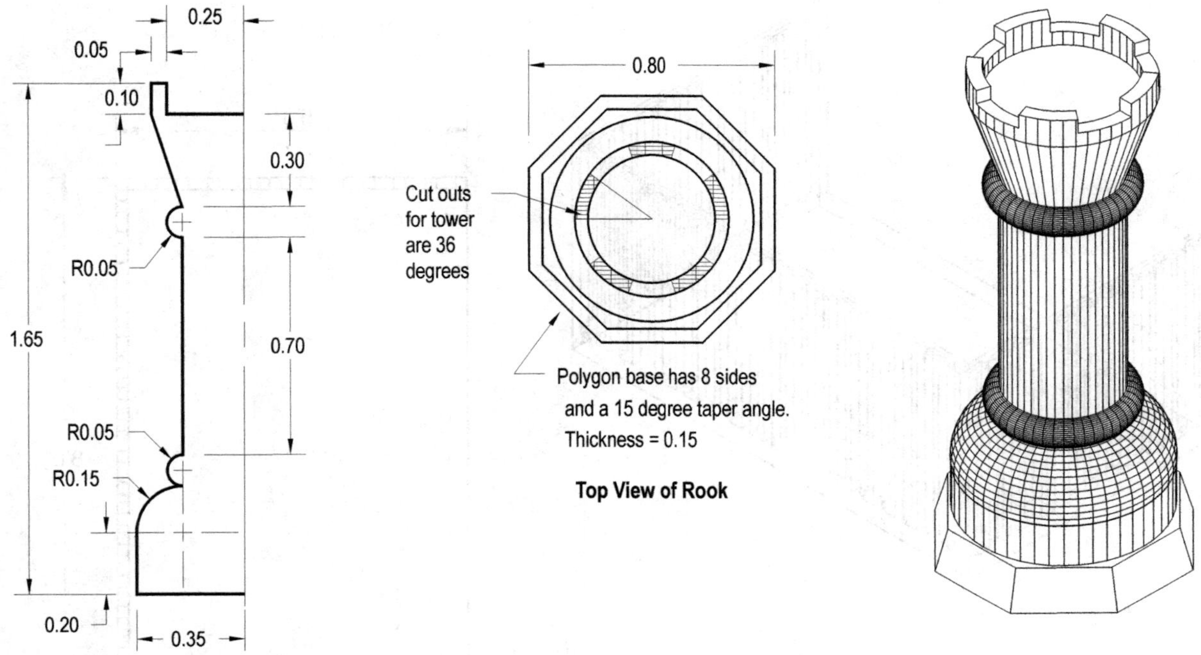

11.5 Exercise Chess Piece

Create the rook chess piece body by revolving a polyline. Use Subtract to remove box primitives to form the cutouts in the tower. Add an octagon for the base. Extrude it to a height of 0.15 and use a taper angle of 15°. (Use your soltemplate.dwt as the template from which you start the rook.) Draw the following shapes by using solid modeling techniques. The letter M after an exercise number means that the units are in millimeters.

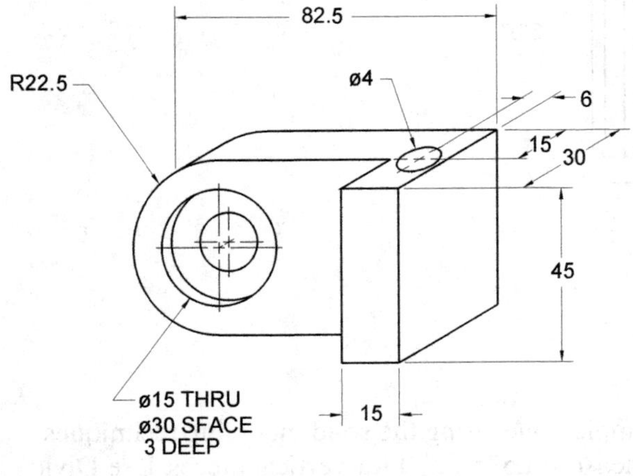

Exercise 11.6M Bushing Holder

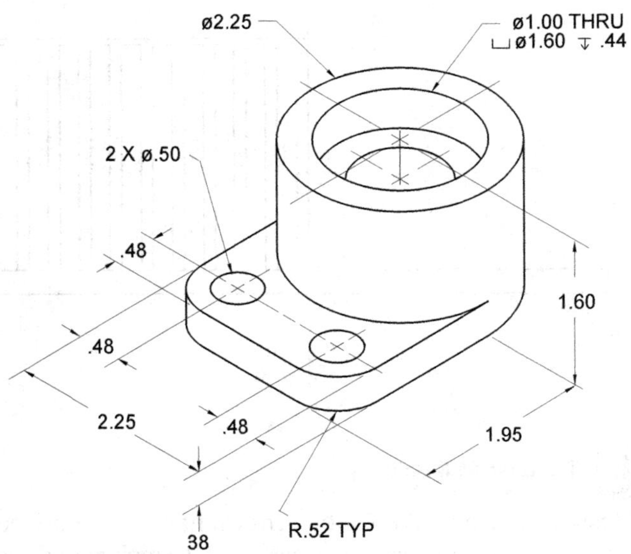

Exercise 11.7 Shaft Support

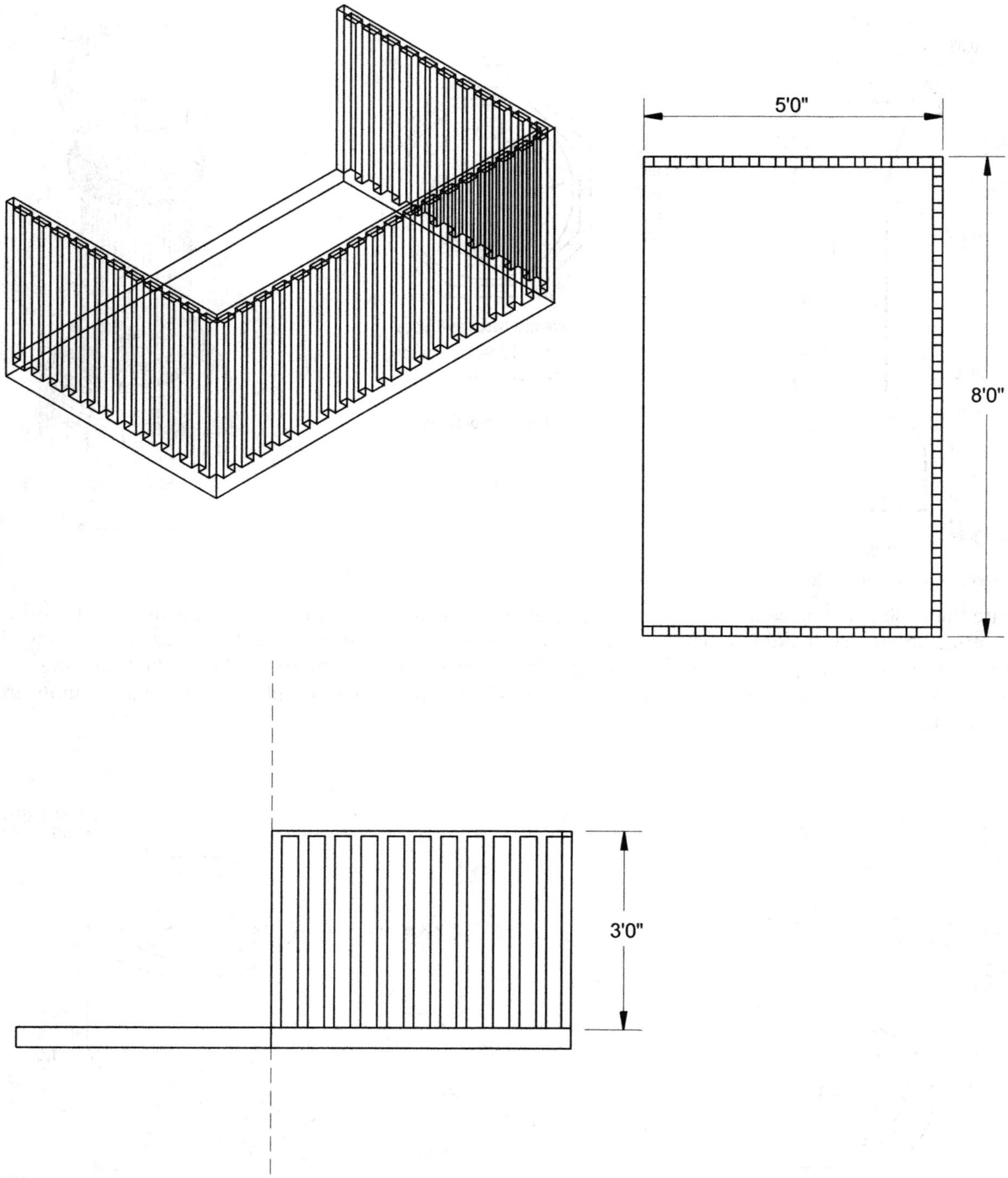

Exercise 11.8 Balcony

Design a balcony like the one shown here, or a more complex one, using the solid modeling techniques you have learned. Use "two-by-fours" (which actually measure 1.5" x 3.5") for vertical pieces. Use Divide to ensure equal spacing.

Exercise 11.9 Bridge

Create the bridge shown. First, determine the size of the bridge that you want and the area to be left open with the arc. Use extrusion to create the arc. Add the structure of the bridge, making sure that the supports are evenly spaced and of sufficient height.
(You can create one-half of the supports and then use Mirror.)

CHANGING AND PLOTTING SOLID MODELS

12

Introduction

You have learned how to create solid models and use multiple viewports. In this tutorial you will learn to use the solid modeling editing commands to make changes and create a larger variety of shapes.

From 3D models you can directly generate two-dimensional (2D) orthographic views that correctly show hidden lines. You will learn a method for controlling layer visibility that allows you to add centerlines so that they appear in a single view. You can also use this method for adding dimensions that appear only in a single viewport.

In later tutorials you will learn how to apply solid modeling to create many different standard types of engineering drawings.

Objectives

When you have completed this tutorial, you will be able to

1. Add a rounded fillet between two surfaces.
2. Add an angled surface or chamfer to your model.
3. Remove a portion from a solid.
4. List the solid information and tree structure.
5. Plot 2D views of the model with hidden lines shown correctly.
6. Control visibility of layers within each viewport.

Starting

Launch AutoCAD.

Open your drawing block.dwg that you created in Tutorial 11 or the ***datafile solblock.dwg****.*

Save *it with the name* ***soledit.dwg****.*

Make the ***upper right viewport active****.*

Make the ***WCS current*** *if it is not already.*

Verify that you are using the ***3D Modeling Workspace****.*

Verify that ***UCSDETECT (dynamic UCS) is OFF (0)****.*

Your screen should be similar to Figure 12.1.

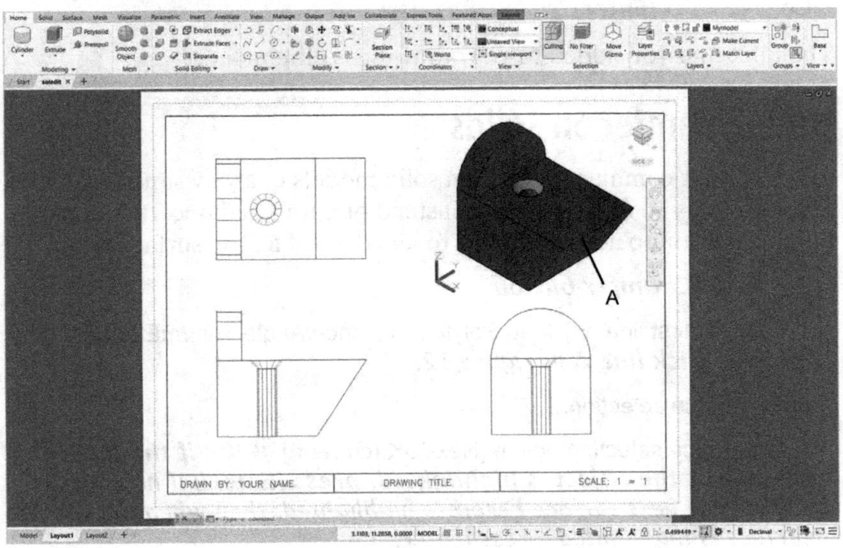

Figure 12.1

Tip: *As you work through this tutorial, you may need to redraw or regenerate the drawing to eliminate partially shown lines or shading. Use Redraw to eliminate partially shown lines in a single viewport. Use RedrawAll to redraw all the viewports at the same time. The Redraw commands refresh the screen from the current display file. The Regen commands recalculate the display file from the drawing database and refresh the screen. Use Regen to regenerate the current view port or RegenAll to regenerate all the viewports at once.*

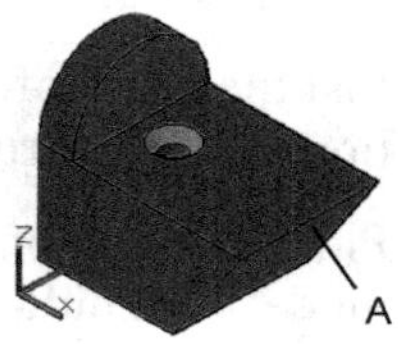

Using Fillet on Solids

The Fillet command lets you add concave or convex rounded surfaces between plane or cylindrical surfaces on an existing solid model. You have already used it to create rounded corners between 2D objects. Now you will use it to create a rounded edge for the front, angled surface of the object. Refer to Figure 12.1 for your selection of line A.

Click: ***Fillet button***

Select first object or [Undo/Polyline/Radius/Trim/Multiple]: ***click on line A***

Enter fillet radius: ***.5 [Enter]***

Select an edge or [Chain/Loop/Radius]: ***[Enter]***

Your drawing with the rounded edge should look like Figure 12.2.

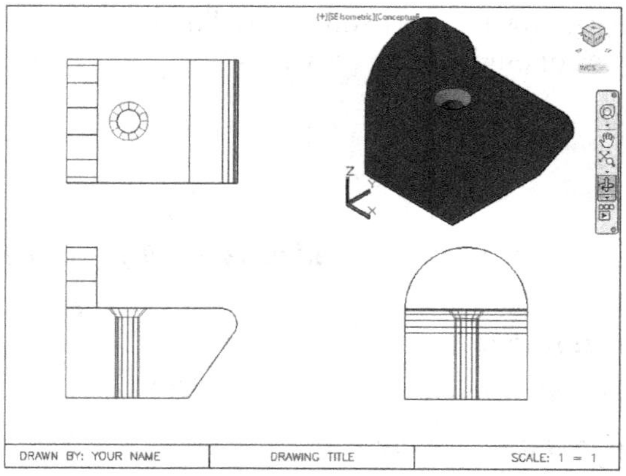

Figure 12.2

Next, you will undo the fillet and then use the Chamfer command to add an angled surface.

Command: ***U [Enter]***

The fillet that you added to your drawing is eliminated.

Using Chamfer on Solids

The Chamfer command works on solid models in a way similar to Fillet, except it adds an angled surface instead of a rounded one. Its Loop option allows you to add a chamfer to all edges of a base surface at once.

Tip: *To make selecting easier, remember the 'Zoom Window command. Transparent zooming allows you to zoom a view during another command. You can use it to enlarge an area to make selecting easier. To return the area to the original size, always use 'Zoom Previous, not 'Zoom All. To use the transparent version of Zoom, don't forget to add the apostrophe in front of the command (or select it from the View tab).*

Click: ***Chamfer button***

Select first line or [Undo/Polyline/Distance/Angle/Trim/mEthod/Multiple]: ***click line A*** *in Figure 12.1*

Base surface selection...

Enter surface selection option [Next/OK (current)] <OK>: ***if the top surface of the object is highlighted, press [Enter];*** *if not, type N so that the next surface becomes highlighted; then when the top surface is highlighted, press [Enter]*

Specify base surface chamfer distance or [Expression]: ***.75 [Enter]***

Specify other surface chamfer distance or [Expression] <0.7500>: ***[Enter]***

Select an edge or [Loop]: ***click line A** in Figure 12.1* ***[Enter]***

Your screen should look like Figure 12.3.

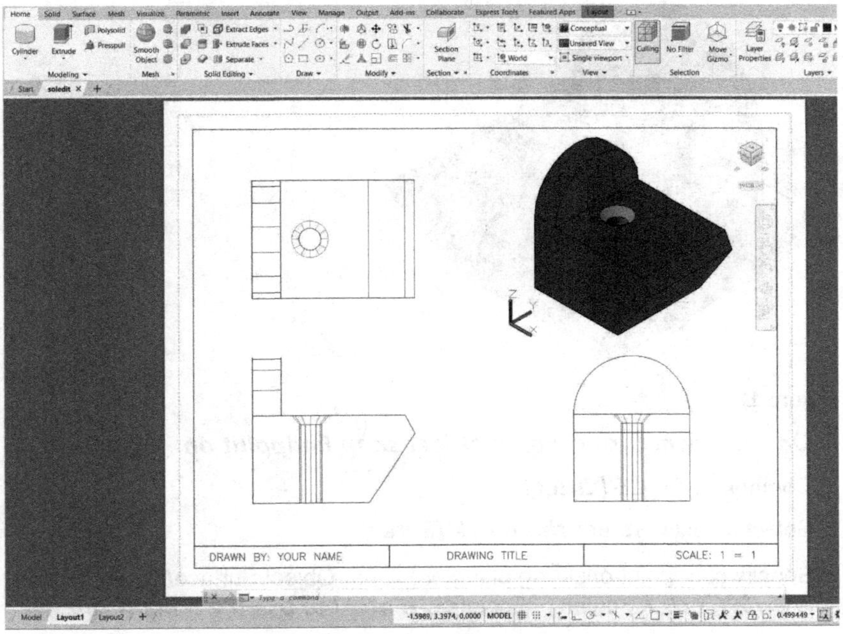

Figure 12.3

Command: ***U [Enter]***

The chamfer that you added to your drawing is eliminated.

Using Slice

Using the Slice command, you can cut a solid using a specified *cutting plane,* also called the *slicing plane.* The cutting plane does not have to be an existing drawing entity. You can specify the cutting plane in several ways.

Option	Function
Object	Select an existing planar entity
Zaxis	Specify a point for the origin and a point that gives the direction of the Z-axis of the cutting plane
View	Align a plane parallel to the current view and through a point
XY, YZ, ZX	Choose a plane parallel to the XY-, YZ-, or ZX-coordinate planes and through a point
3points	Choose three points to define a plane

When you have specified the cutting plane, you are prompted to click a point on the side of the plane where you want the object to remain. The portion of the object on the other side is then deleted. You can choose the Both sides option so that neither side is deleted.

Tip: *When you are clicking on the solid model, you may have trouble at first deciding which surface to select because each wire of the wireframe represents not one surface, but the intersection of two surfaces. Many commands have the Next option to allow you to move surface by surface until the one you want to select is highlighted. If the surface you want to select is not highlighted, use the Next option until it is. When the surface you want to select is highlighted, press [Enter]. You can also cycle through surfaces by pressing the [Ctrl] key when selecting.*

In this example you will use the 3points option of the Slice Command to separate the rounded top surface from the block itself. Refer to Figure 12.4 for your selections.

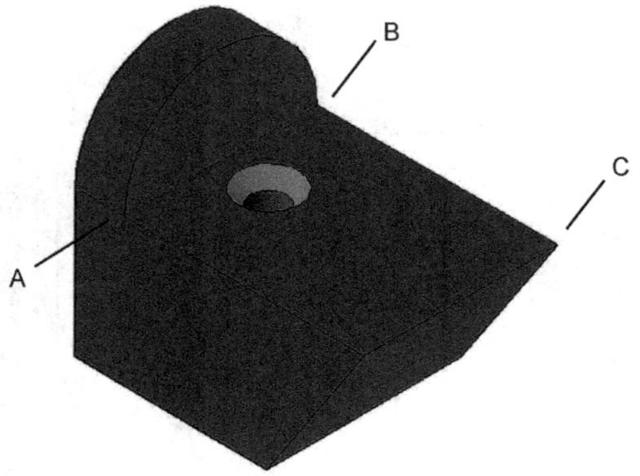

Figure 12.4

On your own, turn running ***object snap Endpoint on.***

Command: ***SLICE [Enter]***

Select objects: ***select the block [Enter]***

Specify start point of slicing plane or [planar Object/Surface/Zaxis /View/XY/YZ/ZX/3points] <3points>: ***[Enter]*** *to use the 3 points option*

Specify first point on plane: ***use object snap and click endpoint A***

Specify second point on plane: ***use object snap and click endpoint B***

Specify third point on plane: ***use object snap and click endpoint C***

Specify a point on the desired side of the plane or [keep Both sides]: ***B[Enter]***

Select the **half-cylinder** that used to be the top surface of the block.

Tip: *To keep both sides of the sliced object, press [Enter] to accept the default value (keep Both sides). You can also type B [enter].*

It is now separate from the block. The grips and 3D gizmo appear as shown in Figure 12.5.

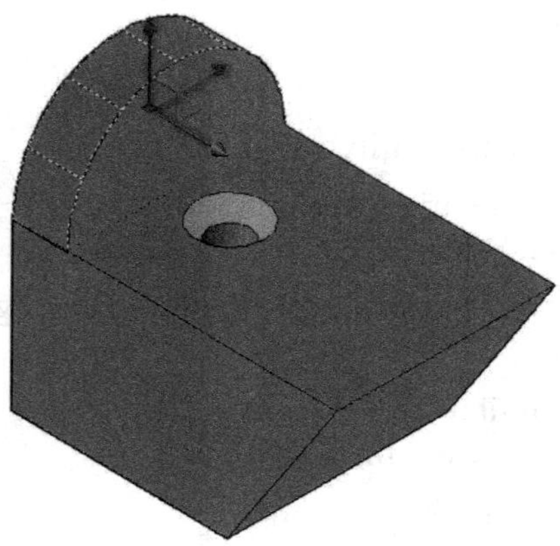

Figure 12.5

Next, you will move the half-cylinder up one unit in the Z-direction and then create a new rectangular piece beneath it.

Check that WCS is current. Turn off object snap mode.

Click: ***Move button***

Select objects: ***click on the half-cylinder*** *that you separated from the block, unless it is already selected*

Select objects: ***[Enter]***

Specify base point or Displacement <Displacement>: ***0,0,1 [Enter]***

Specify second point of displacement or <use first point as displacement>: ***[Enter]***

The cylinder is moved upward 1 unit in the Z direction, as shown in Figure 12.6.

Tip: *If the half-cylinder does not move upward, check that you have the WCS active and that object snap is off.*

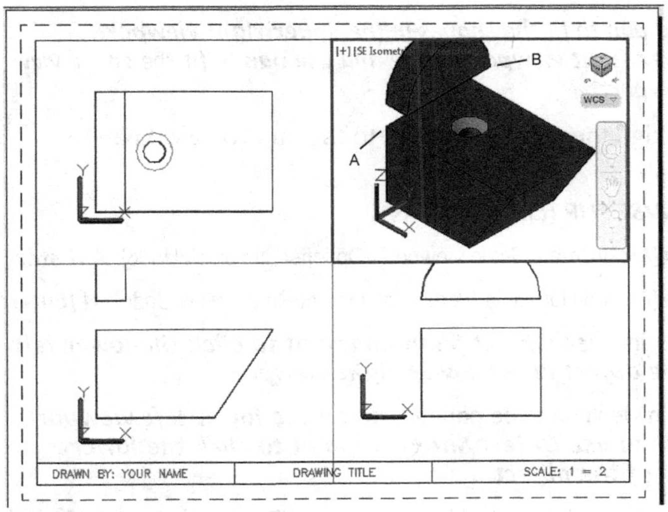

Figure 12.6

Next you will create two boxes. For the first one, you will use object snaps and *point filters* to draw the box. Point filters allow you to target a point and select only the x, y, z, or xy, zy, or yz portion of its coordinates. The WCS should still be active. Use Figure 12.6 for your selections.

On your own, turn ***running object snap Endpoint on.***

Click: ***Box button***

Specify corner of box or [CEnter] <0,0,0>: ***click corner A using Object Snap Endpoint***

Specify other corner or [Cube/Length]: ***right-click to show the short-cut menu and use it to select Snap Overrides, Point Filters, XY***

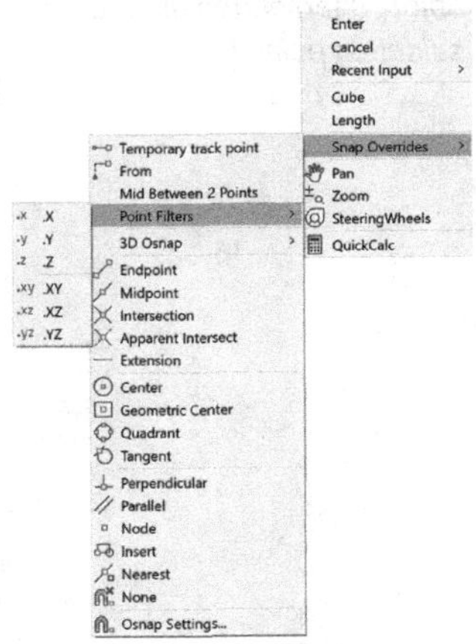

.XY of: ***click corner B*** *from the upper block*

Specify other corner or [Cube/Length]: .XY of (need Z): ***.Z [Enter]***

.Z of: ***click corner B again,*** *this time to select the z-coordinate*

The box appears between the top surface of the block and the half cylinder as shown in Figure 12.7. Your object will appear shaded. The second box will be where you subtracted a wedge in Tutorial 11.

Double-click inside the ***active upper right viewport to zoom extents*** *so that the entire object is visible inside the viewport.*

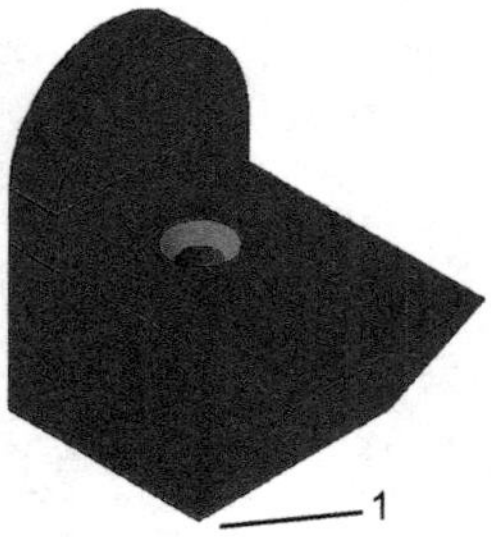

Figure 12.7

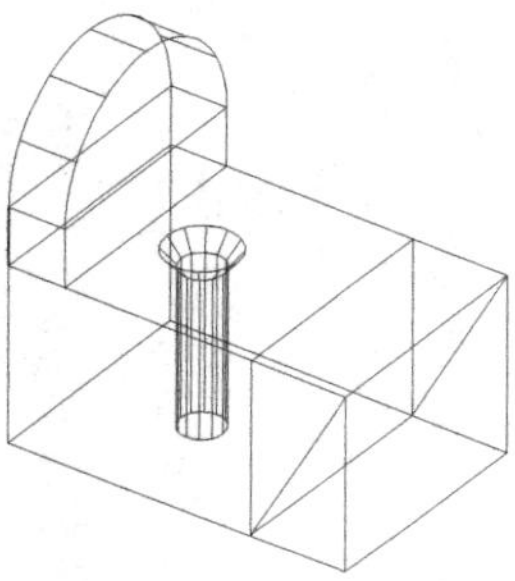

Figure 12.8

Tip: *If your box does not align as shown, make sure you have the WCS active in the top left viewport. Also, try toggling object snap endpoint off after selecting point 1.*

Tip: *Many of the editing commands that you learned in the 2D tutorials are still effective in solid modeling. Try them when they seem useful.*

Command: ***BOX [Enter]***

Specify corner of box or [CEnter] <0,0,0>: ***click corner 1 in Figure 12.7, using Object Snap Endpoint then turns osnap off.***

Specify corner or [Cube/Length]: ***L [Enter]***

Specify length: ***2 [Enter]***

Specify width: ***4 [Enter]***

Specify height: ***3 [Enter]***

Your objects will appear similar to Figure 12.8 except that they will be shaded. Note that the object is not centered well in all viewports. You will pan the view in the lower right viewport.

*Use zoom and pan to fit the shapes in the **upper right viewport**. Make the **lower right viewport** active and use **pan** to fit the entire view inside the viewport.*

Next you will align the other viewports to the one you used pan to position.

Command: ***MVSETUP [Enter]***

Enter an option [Align/Create/Scale viewports/Options/Title block/Undo]: ***A [Enter]***

Enter an option [Angled/Horizontal/Vertical alignment/Rotate view/Undo]: ***H [Enter]***

Specify basepoint: ***use Object Snap Endpoint to click the lower left corner of the object in the lower right viewport***

Specify point in viewport to be panned: ***make the lower left viewport active and then use Object Snap Endpoint to click the lower right corner of the object***

Enter an option [Angled/Horizontal/Vertical alignment/Rotate view/Undo]: ***[Enter]***

Enter an option [Angle/Create/Scale viewports/Options/Title block/Undo]: ***[Enter]***

Your screen should be similar to Figure 12.9.

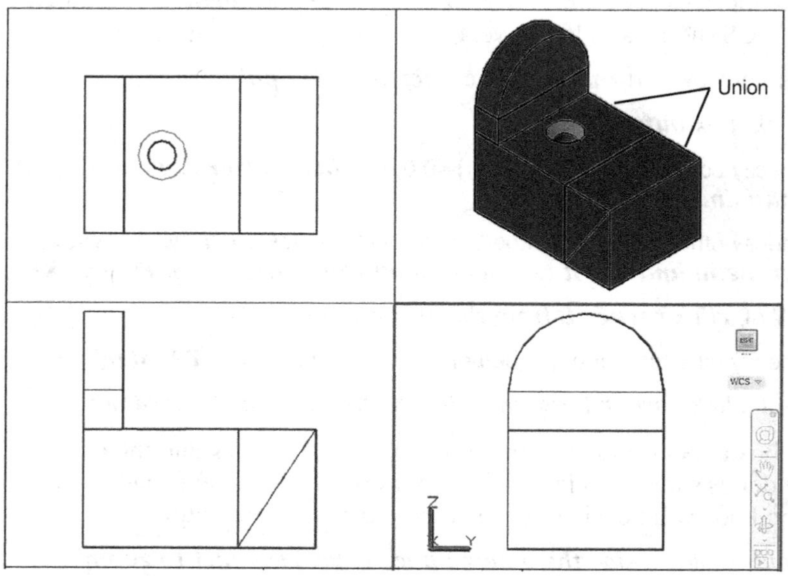

Figure 12.9

Now you will use Union to join the block and the new second box.

Click: ***Union button***

Select objects: ***use Crossing to select ONLY the block and the second box,*** *using Figure 12.8 for reference*

Select objects: ***[Enter]***

The two objects should now be joined, forming one object similar to that in Figure 12.10.

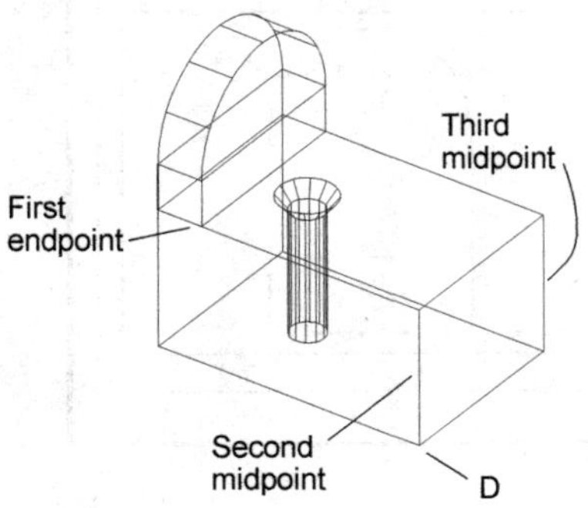

Figure 12.10

Now you will use the 3points Slice option again to slice an angled portion from the block. Select the Slice command from the Home tab, Solids Editing panel. Refer to Figure 12.10 for the three points.

 *Click:* ***Slice button***

Select objects: ***select the block object***

Select objects: ***[Enter]***

Specify start point of slicing plane or [planar Object/Surface/Zaxis/ View/ XY/YZ/ZX/3points] <3points>: ***[Enter]*** *to select 3points*

Specify first point on slicing plane by [Object/Zaxis/View/XY/ YZ/ ZX/3points] <3points>: ***use Object Snap Endpoint and click the end-point labeled First endpoint,***

Specify second point on plane: ***use Object Snap Midpoint to select the midpoint of the front vertical edge labeled Second midpoint***

Specify third point on plane: ***use Object Snap Midpoint and click the midpoint of the front vertical edge labeled Third midpoint***

Specify point on the desired side of the plane or [keep Both sides]: ***click the bottom left corner, labeled D***

The upper portion of the block is cut off, leaving an angled surface, as shown in Figure 12.11.

Now use the Union command to join the three parts.

Click: ***Union button***

Select objects: ***use implied Crossing to select all three objects***

Select objects: ***[Enter]***

Your drawing should look like that in Figure 12.12.

Tip: *The AutoCAD software has a handy Quick Calculator (QUICKCALC) function that can be very useful in specifying points that would be impossible to specify by other drawing means. Whenever you see a prompt requesting input of a point, real number, integer, or vector, you can use the Quick Calculator or the transparent command 'CAL. 'CAL lets you write an expression in infix notation, such as 112*sin(30), at the prompt and the resultant value is used. You can also use Object Snap functions and acquire points from your drawing in combination with the Quick Calculator. This is very useful in creating complex models.*

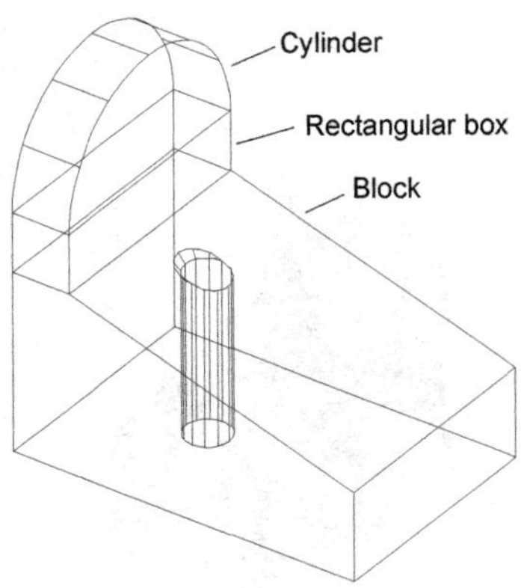

Figure 12.11

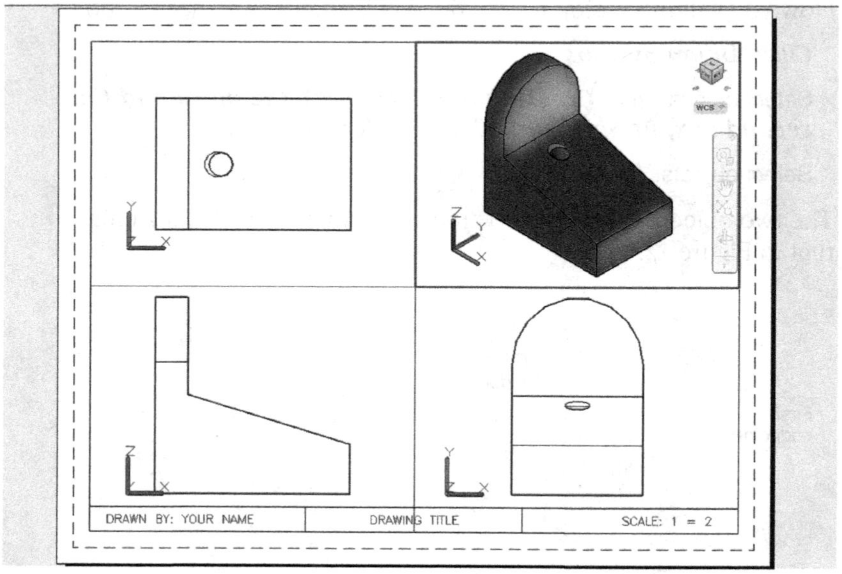

Figure 12.12

Next, you will add a 0.375 deep hole of diameter 0.5, perpendicular to the angled surface.

To create a hole perpendicular to the angled surface, you will align the UCS icon with the angled surface, creating a new user coordinate system. Refer to Figure 12.13.

*Make the **upper right viewport active**.*

***Turn on running Object Snap for Endpoint**.*

Click: ***on the UCS icon***

Use object snap Endpoint while clicking and dragging the UCS icon to the lower left corner of the angled surface

Then, click the end of the Y axis and drag it to align the Y axis with the slanted surface as shown. Use object snap Endpoint and target the upper left vertex of the slanted line.

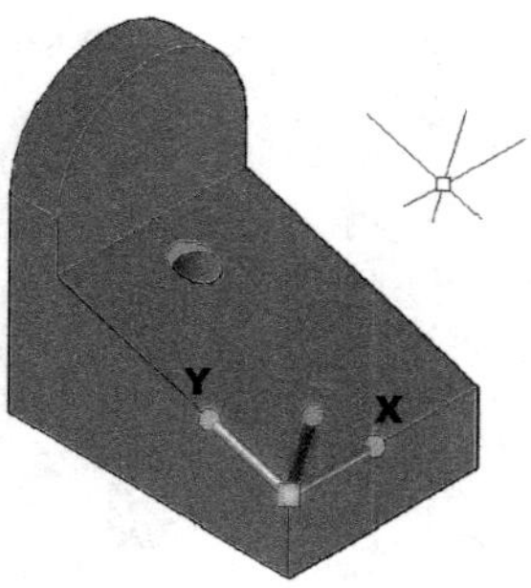

Figure 12.13

The UCS changes so that it now aligns with the angled surface.

Next you will turn the shading off in the top right viewport so that you can see the back surfaces of the object, then use the Plan command to align your view so that you are looking straight down the Z-axis. The resulting view shows the XY-plane of the new UCS that you created in the previous step. The Plan command will fit the drawing extents to the viewport.

Click: ***Wireframe*** *from the View control for the upper right viewport*

Command: ***PLAN [Enter]***

Enter an option [Current ucs/Ucs/World] <Current>: ***[Enter]***

*Turn the **Grid on**. **Pan** the view to position it in the viewport.*

The view in the upper right viewport should now be directly perpendicular to the angled surface of the object. Your drawing should look like that in Figure 12.14.

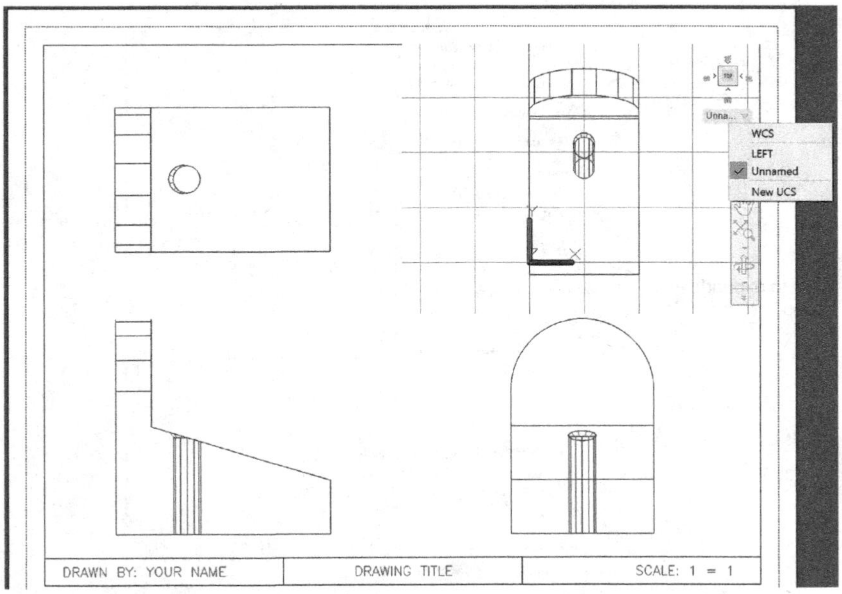

Figure 12.14

Next, save the UCS and the view so you can restore them later.

Click: ***on the small arrow by Unnamed*** *below the ViewCube to show the menu as seen in Figure 12.14*

Click: ***New UCS***

Specify origin of UCS or [Face/NAmed/OBject/Previous/View/World/X/Y/Z/ZAxis] <World>: ***NA [Enter]***

Enter an option [Restore/Save/Delete/?]: ***S [Enter]***

Enter name to save current UCS or [?]: ***ANGLE [Enter]***

Command: ***VIEW [Enter]***

The View Manager appears as shown in Figure 12.15. You will use it to create a new named view.

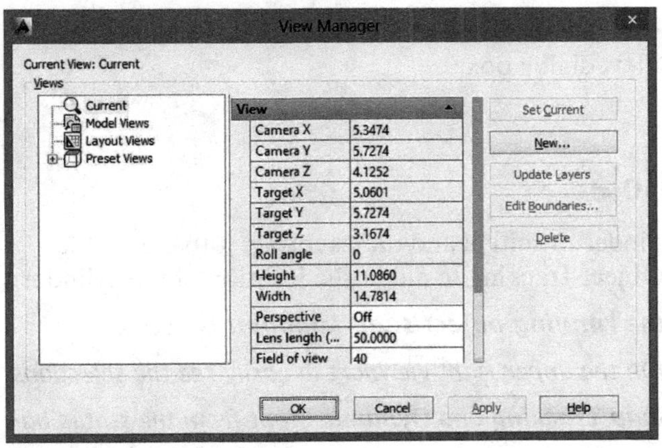

Figure 12.15

Click: ***New*** *from the View dialog box*

The New View dialog box appears on your screen. Use it to make the settings shown in Figure 12.16.

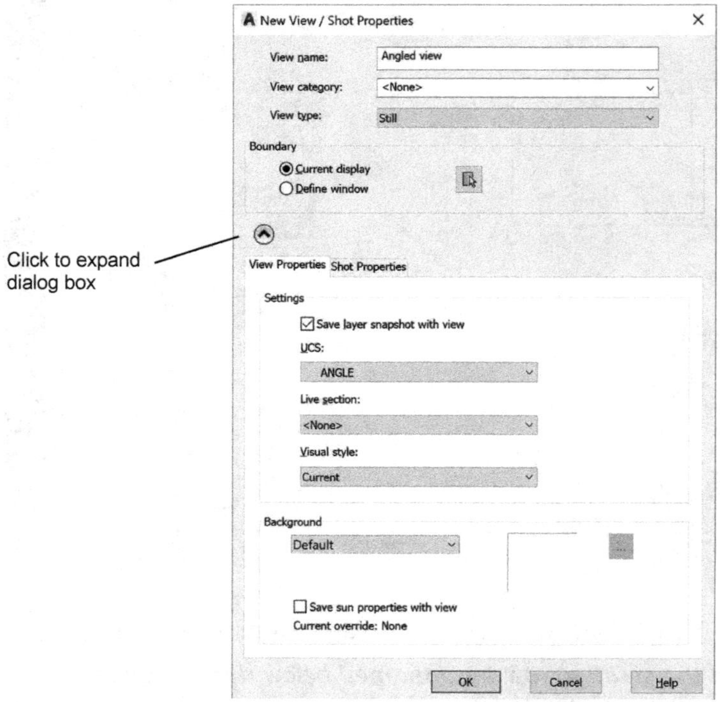

Figure 12.16

*Type: **Angled View** for the View name*

*Select: **Still** for the View type*

*Click: **Current Display** in the Boundary area*

*Select: **ANGLE** for **UCS** in the Settings area*

Notice that you can also set the visual style for the view as well as the background color. You can use this also to make walkthrough and cinematic as well as still views.

*Click: **OK***

You return to the View dialog box.

*Click: **OK***

Creating the Hole

You will use the cylinder primitive and then subtract it to create the hole. You will use Object Tracking to aid in the location of the cylinder.

*Make sure that the **running object snap Midpoint** is active.*

*Turn the **Grid off** in the upper right viewport to easily see the selections.*

*Turn on **Object Snap Tracking** and **Dynamic Input** from the status bar.*

*Click: **Cylinder button***

Specify center point for base of cylinder or [Elliptical] <0,0,0>: ***Hover the cursor over line 1, using Object Snap Midpoint as shown in Figure 12.17 to acquire the tracking point.***

Specify center point for base of cylinder or [Elliptical] <0,0,0>: ***positioning cursor along temporary tracking line that appears, type 1 [Enter] to specify a distance of 1 along the tracking line***

Specify radius for base of cylinder or [Diameter]: ***D [Enter]***

Specify diameter for base of cylinder: ***.5 [Enter]***

Specify height of cylinder or [Center of other end]: ***–.375 [Enter]***

On your own, change the small cylinder you just created to color ***Red****.*

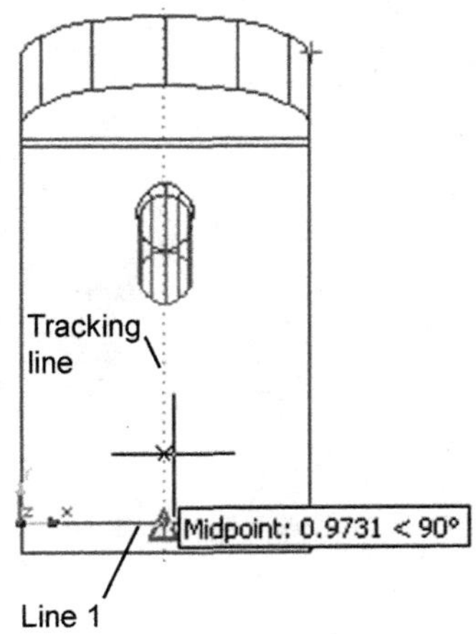

Figure 12.17

Next, subtract the cylinder to form a hole in the object.

Click: ***Subtract button***

Select objects: ***click the large block***

Select objects: ***[Enter]***

Select solids and regions to subtract...

Select objects: ***click the short cylinder you just created [Enter]***

Next return to World Coordinates in the upper right viewport..

Click: to expand the menu and choose ***WCS*** *(near the ViewCube)*

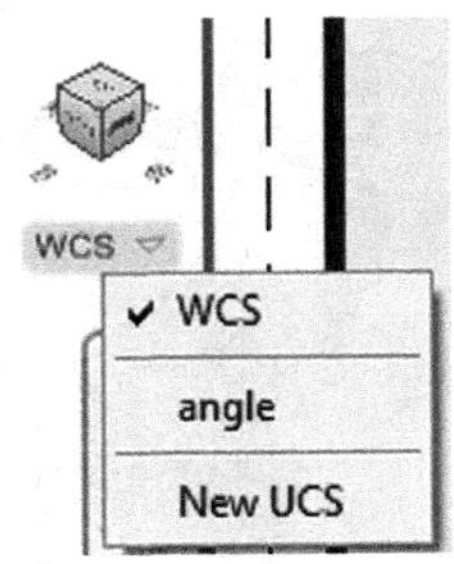

Next, reset the viewpoint for the upper right viewport,

Click: ***on Custom View*** *from the Viewport control to show the menu and choose* ***SE Isometric.***

Set ***Conceptual for the upper right*** *viewport visual style. Set the other three views to* ***Wireframe****.*

Turn ***off Object Snap Tracking*** *and* ***Dynamic Input****.*

Use ***Save As*** *to name your drawing* ***anglblok.dwg****.*

Your drawing should now look like Figure 12.18.

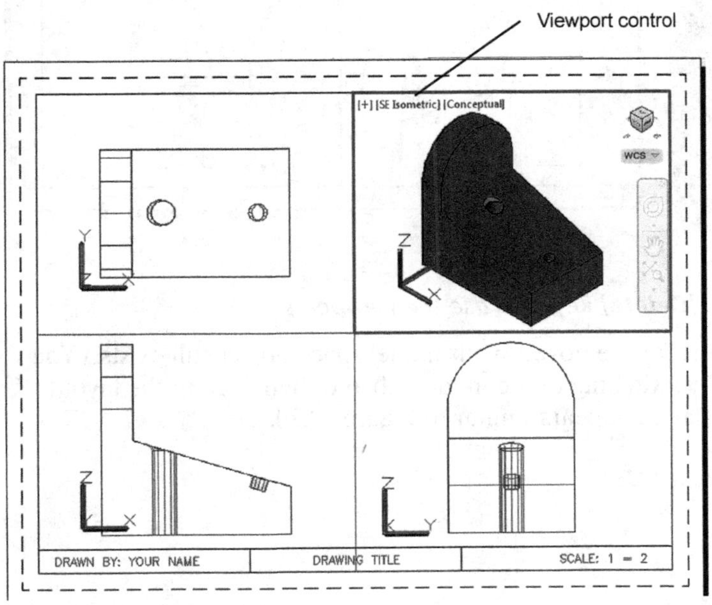

Figure 12.18

Placing Views to Create a Drawing

AutoCAD commands make it easy to create orthographic drawing views from your model. In the past you may have used the Setup Profile, SOLPROF command to create a 2D projection, or *profile*, of each view–now that is no longer necessary. Next, you will learn to use the Viewbase command to place drawing views to quickly and easily create multiview drawings from the 3D model.

First you will erase the existing viewports from the layout. Then you will start by placing the base view, which is typically the front view in technical drawings.

On your own, switch to paperspace.

Thaw layer Vport *(if it is frozen).*

The magenta borders of the viewports return to your screen.

Make a small crossing box that crosses the intersection of the four viewports near the center of your screen.

The viewport borders are selected and their grips appear as shown in Figure 12.19.

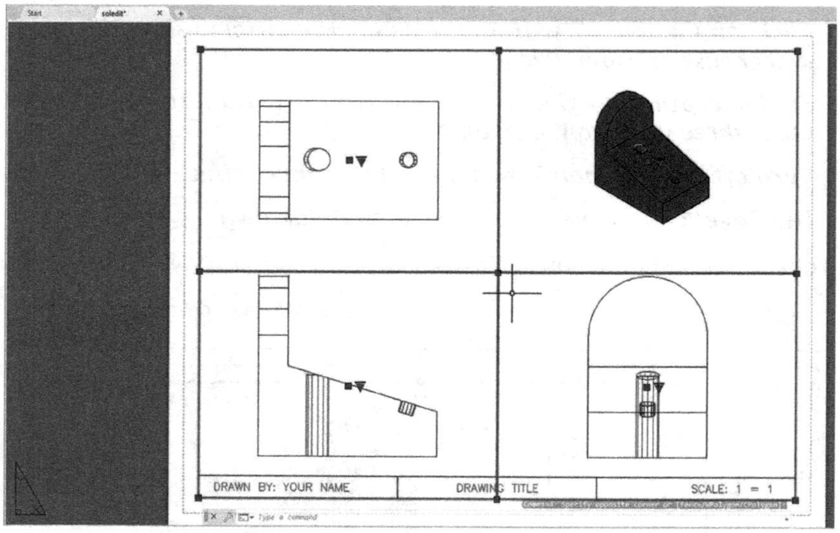

Figure 12.19

Press the ***[Delete]*** *key to erase the viewports.*

The viewports are removed. Your model space object still exists. (You can check by switching to the model tab and then back to the layout tab.) Your screen appears similar to Figure 12.20.

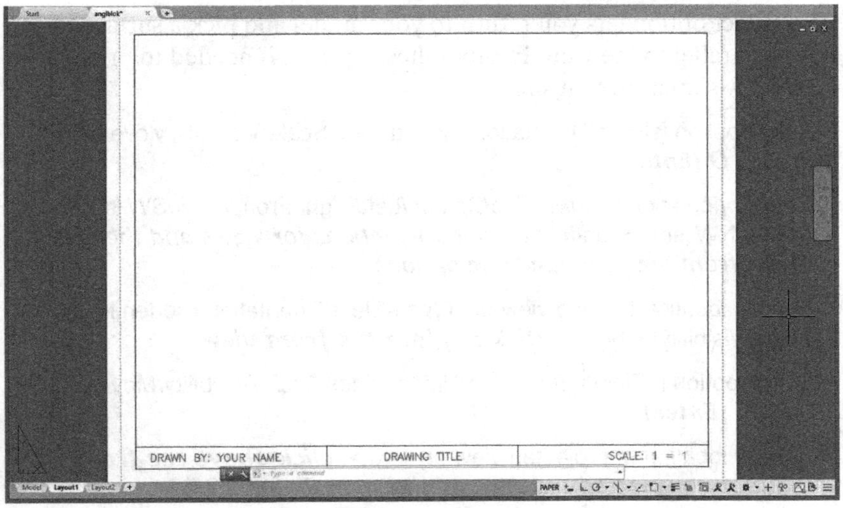

Figure 12.20

Next you will use the Viewbase command to place the base view of the model to start your drawing. The view base command is located on the ribbon Layout tab, Create View panel. You have options to create a base view from model space or from an Autodesk Inventor model.

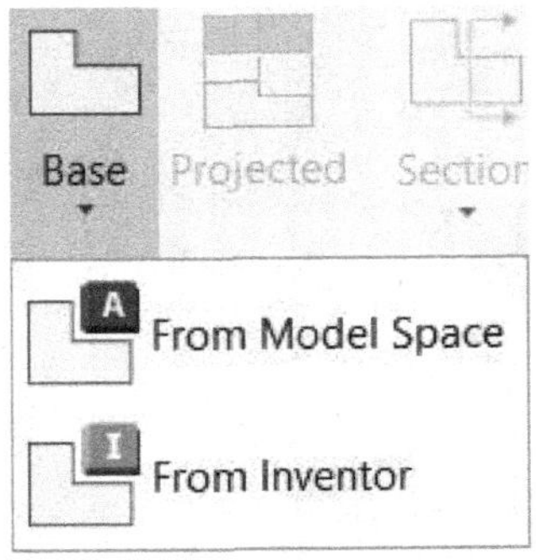

Click: ***Base View from Model Space button*** *from the Layout tab, Create View panel*

Specify location of base view or [Type/sElect/Orientation/Hidden lines/Scale/Visibility] <Type>:

The front view of the model appears at your cursor location as shown in Figure 12.21.

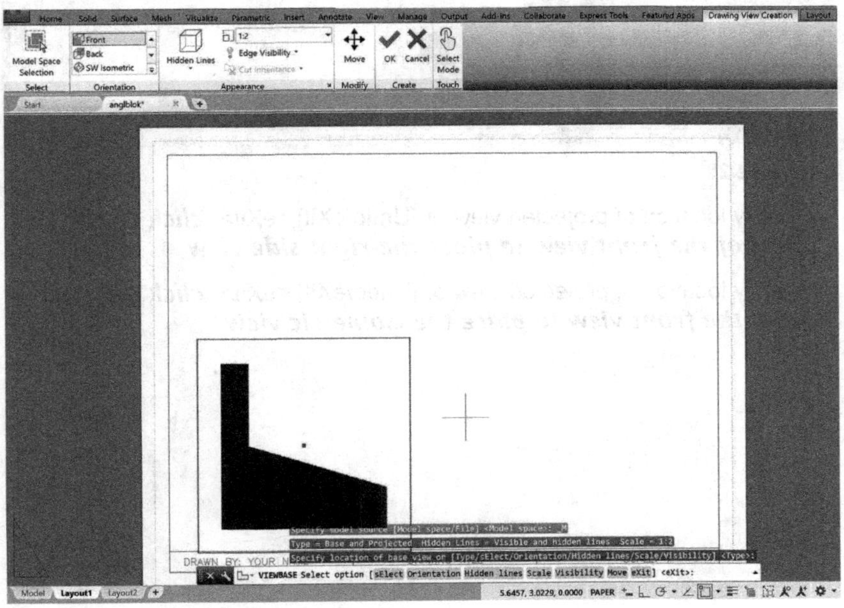

Figure 12.21

You can select the Orientation option from the command prompt to select a different model view as the starting base view if needed.

The sElect option lets you return to your model and pick a surface to orient parallel to the view. Explore these options if needed to orient a base view similar to that shown.

Select option [sElect/Orientation/Hidden lines/Scale/Visibility/Move/eXit] <eXit>: ***O [Enter]***

Select orientation [Current/Top/Bottom/Left/Right/Front/BAck/SW iso/SE iso/NE iso/NW iso] <Front>: *examine the options for views and then click* ***Front*** *from the command line options*

Specify location of base view or [Type/sElect/Orientation/Hidden lines/Scale/Visibility] <Type>: ***click to place the front view***

Select option [sElect/Orientation/Hidden lines/Scale/Visibility/Move/eXit] <eXit>: ***[Enter]***

Specify location of projected view or <eXit>: ***click above the front view*** *to place a projected top view as shown in Figure 12.22.*

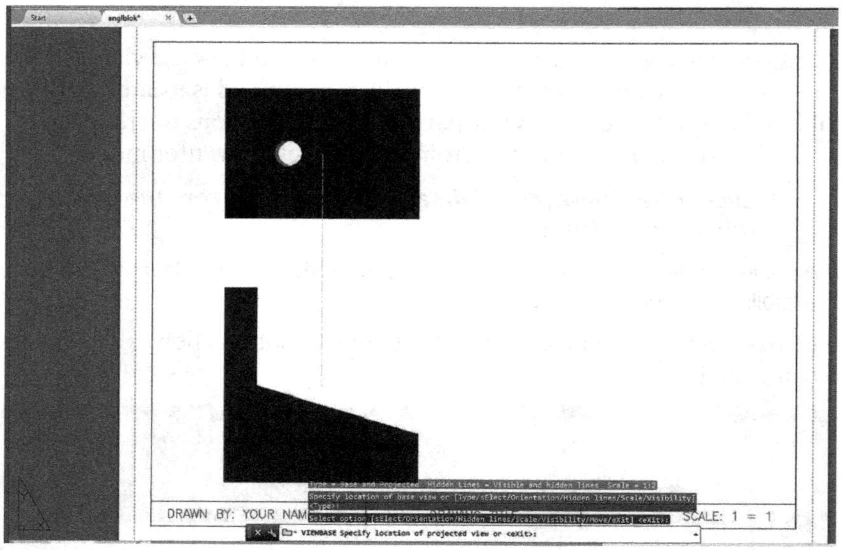

Figure 12.22

Specify location of projected view or [Undo/eXit] <eXit>: ***click to the right of the front view to place the right side view***

Specify location of projected view or [Undo/eXit] <eXit>: ***click diagonally from the front view to place the isometric view***

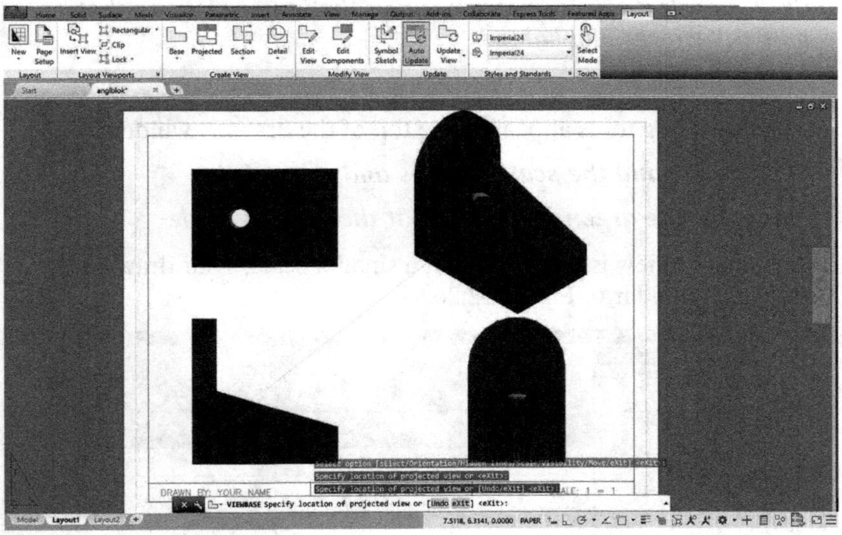

Figure 12.23

Specify location of projected view or [Undo/eXit] <eXit>: ***[Enter]***

Base and 3 projected view(s) created successfully.

The drawing lines change to show hidden as visible lines as shown in Figure 12.24.

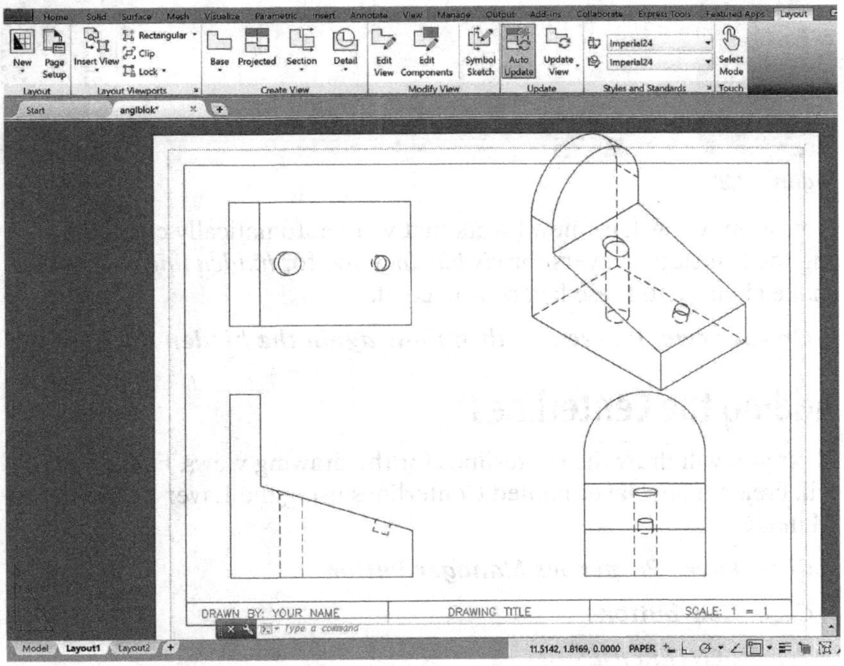

Figure 12.24

Next you will edit the isometric view in the upper right of the drawing to show it to a smaller scale. Because the object is tipped and therefore foreshortened in the isometric view, it would appear about 80% of the size of the standard views. It is often useful to make the isometric view even smaller, as it is used for visualization and not for dimensioning.

*Click: **to select the isometric view in the upper right** so that its border becomes highlighted*

Tip: *You can double-click the view to show the editing menu in one step.*

*Click: **Edit View***

The view editing tools appear at the top of the drawing window.

*Click: **to expand the scale choices and select 1:4***

*Click: **OK (the green arrow) to exit the editing mode***

The isometric view is now shown at a smaller scale. Your drawing should look similar to Figure 12.26.

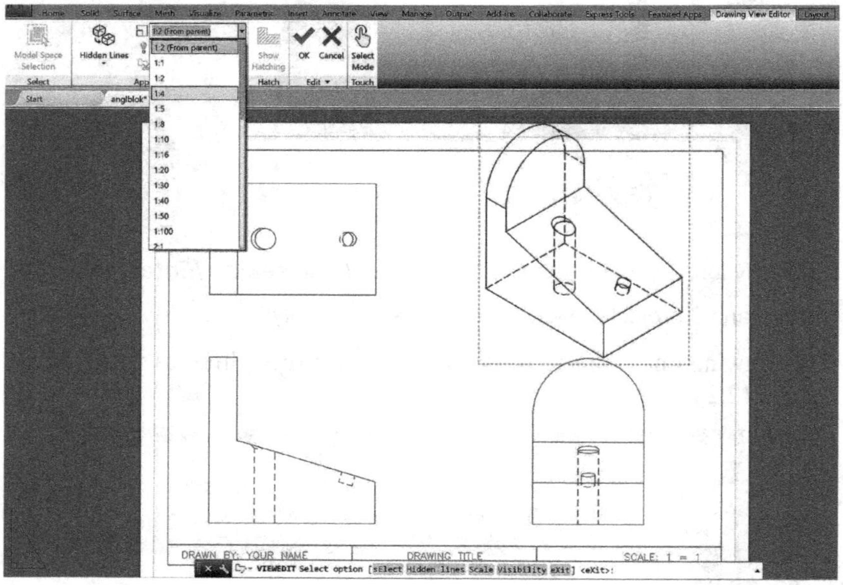

Figure 12.25

You should now have new layers that were automatically created during the last step —layers for *visible lines* and for *hidden lines*. You can make changes to these layers as needed.

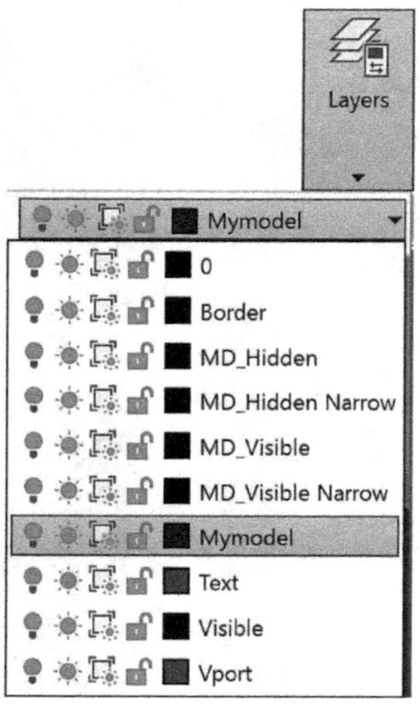

*On your own, **freeze** and then **thaw again the hidden lines**.*

Adding the Centerlines

Next you will draw the centerlines for the drawing views. First you will create a new layer named Centerlines using the Layer Properties Manager.

*Click: **Layer Properties Manager button***

*Click: **New button***

*Type: **CENTERLINES***

*Click: **the Color box** to the right of the new layer*

*Click: **Green** from within the Select Color dialog box*

*Click: **OK** to exit the Select Color dialog box*

*Click: **to show the lineweight list** for the new layer*

*Click: **0.30 mm***

Click: ***OK*** *to exit the Lineweight dialog box*

Double-click: ***on CENTERLINES*** *to set it as the current layer*

Click: ***[X]*** *to exit the Layer Properties Manager dialog box*

Click: ***Centerline*** *from the Annotate tab, Centerlines panel*

On your own, select the two hidden lines in the front view to ***draw the centerline for the hole*** *using the techniques you have already learned. Add a centerline for the smaller hole. Use the Centermark command to* ***add centermarks*** *for the top arc and the holes in the top view.*

Set ***LTSCALE to .85*** *to adjust the hidden line pattern.*

Tip: *Try various values for LTScale until you are pleased with the results.*

Double-Click: ***the upper right pictorial view*** *to show the Drawing View Editor*

Click: ***Visible and Hidden Lines*** *to expand the choices*

Select: ***Visible Lines***

Click: ***Edge Visibility*** *to expand the choices*

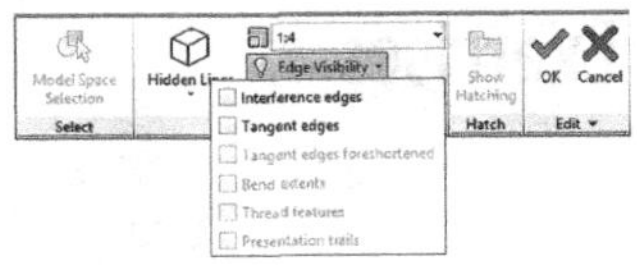

On your own ***unselect tangent edges*** *and* ***click the green check mark to exit*** *editing mode.*

When you have finished, your drawing should be similar to Figure 12.26.

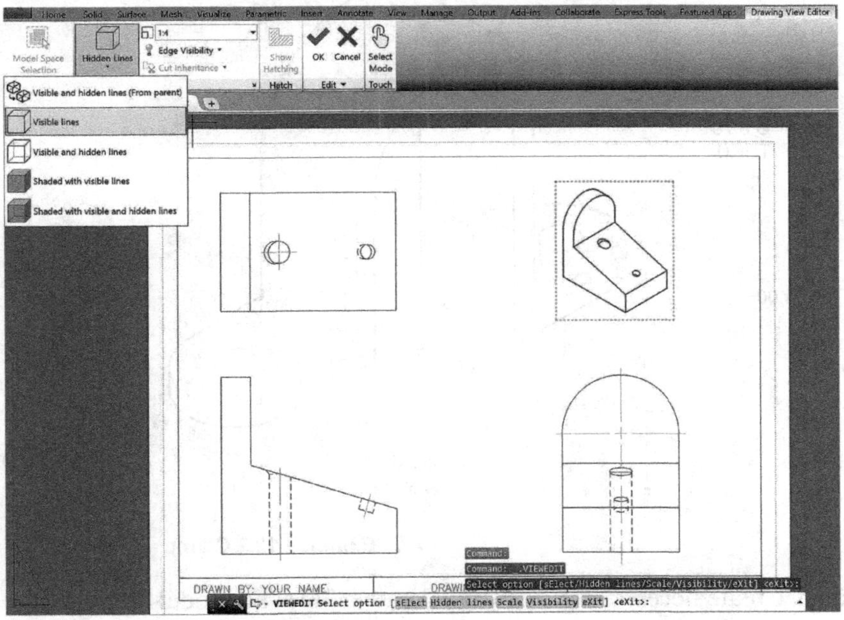

Figure 12.26

On your own, ***save*** *your drawing.*

Use the techniques you have learned to plot the drawing.

Close *all drawings and exit the AutoCAD software.*

You have now completed Tutorial 12.

Key Terms

cutting plane
handles
hidden profile line
profile
slicing plane
visible profile line

Key Commands

Calculator ('CAL)
Chamfer (CHA)
Fillet (F)
List (LI)
Setup Profile (SOLPROF)
SLICE

Exercises

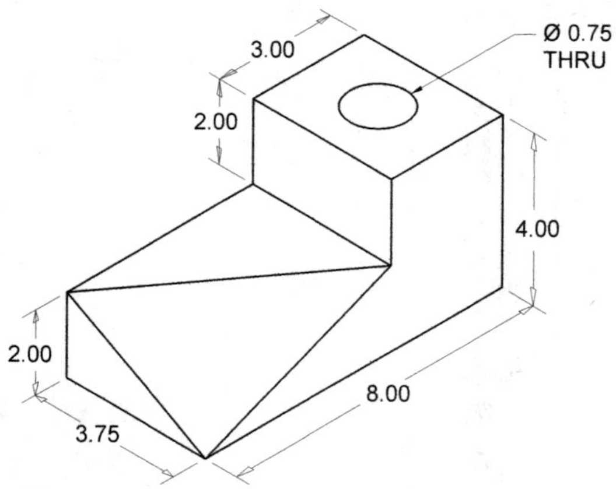

Exercise 12.1 Angled Support

Create this figure as a 3D solid model. Create necessary views and plot with correct hidden lines and centerlines.

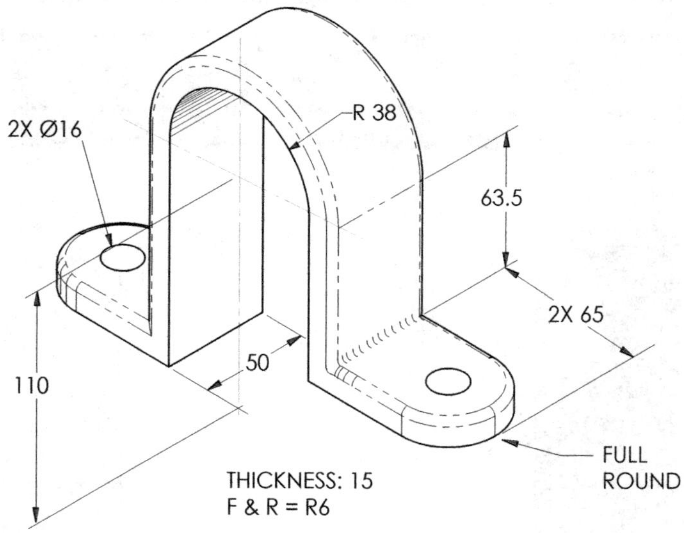

Exercise 12.2 Clamp

Create a 3D solid model of the part shown. Make a multiview drawing from the model.

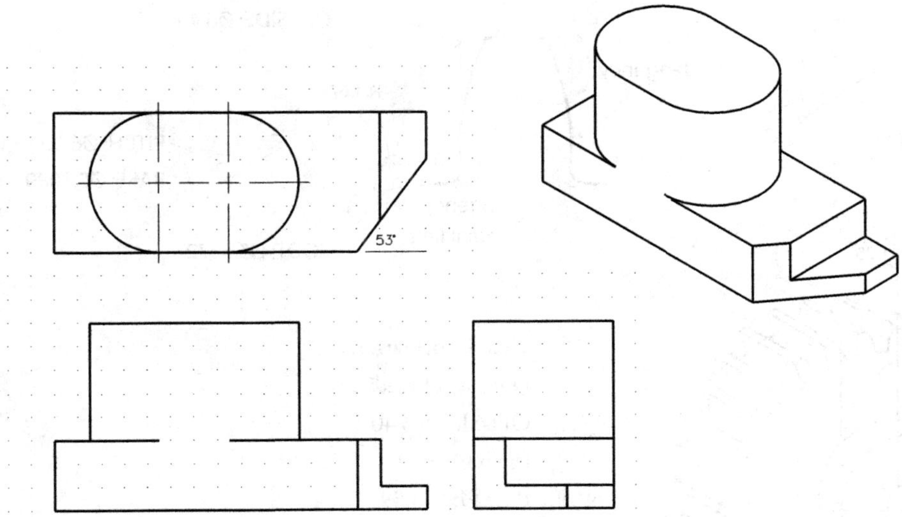

Exercise 12.3 Step Model

Construct a solid model of this object. Grid spacing is 0.25 inch. Use a viewpoint of (3,–3,1) in the upper right viewport.

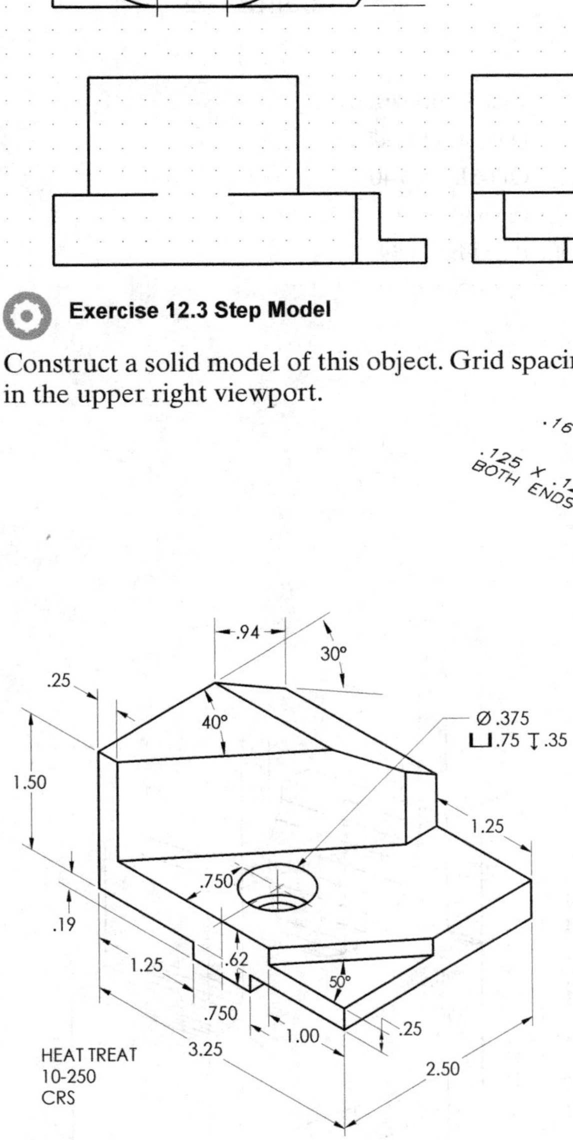

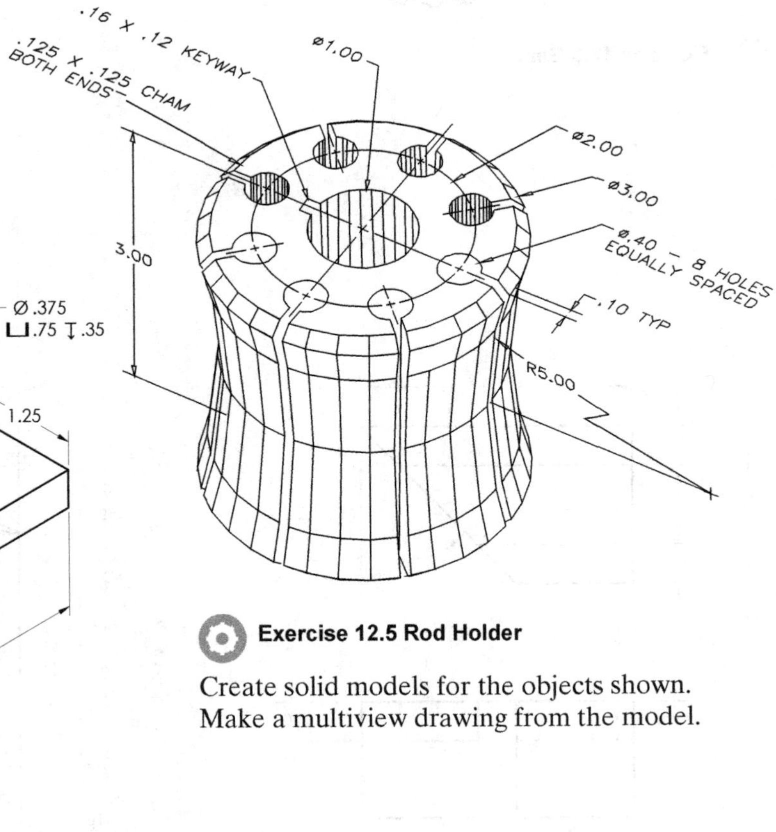

Exercise 12.5 Rod Holder

Create solid models for the objects shown. Make a multiview drawing from the model.

Exercise 12.4M Index Feed

Create a 3D solid model of this metric part. Create solid models for the objects shown. Make a multiview drawing from the model.

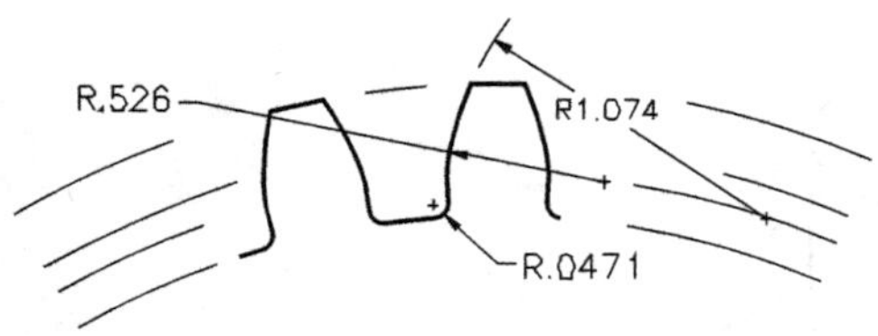

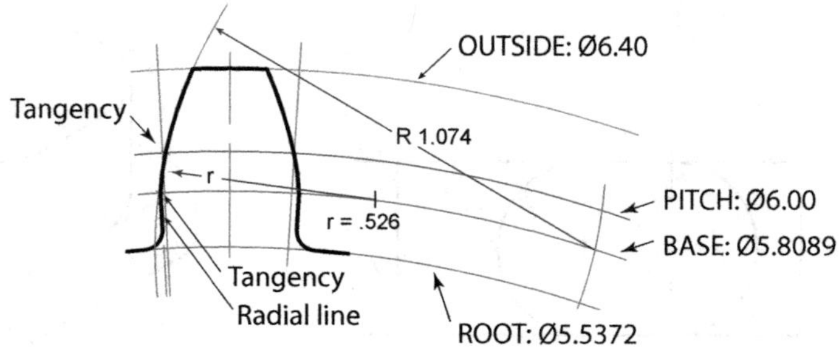

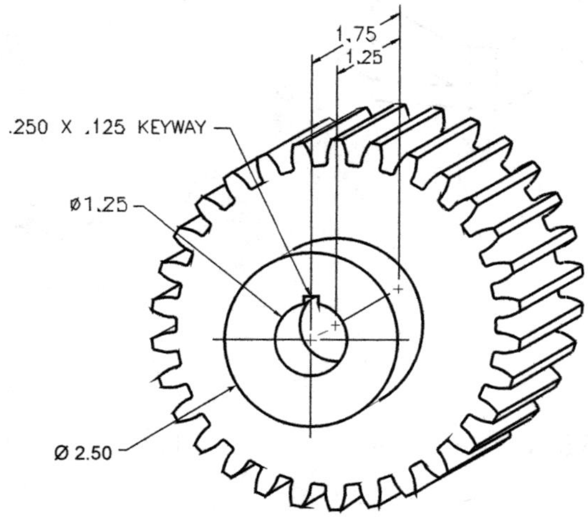

Gear information:

Number of teeth: 30

Outside Ø: 6.40

Pitch Ø: 6.00

Base Ø: 5.8089

Root Ø: 5.5372

Exercise 12.6 Gear

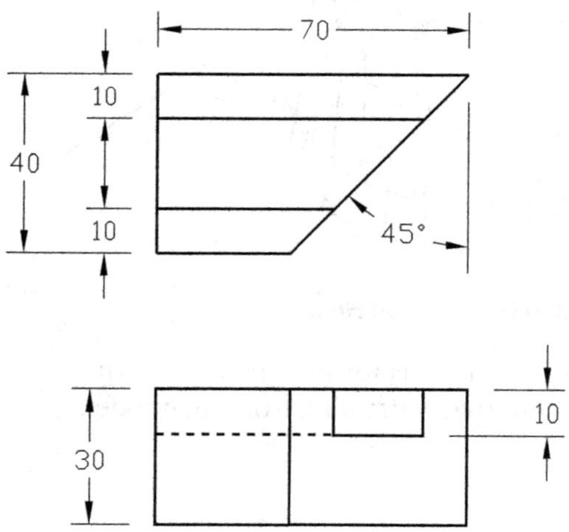

Exercise 12.7 Router Guide

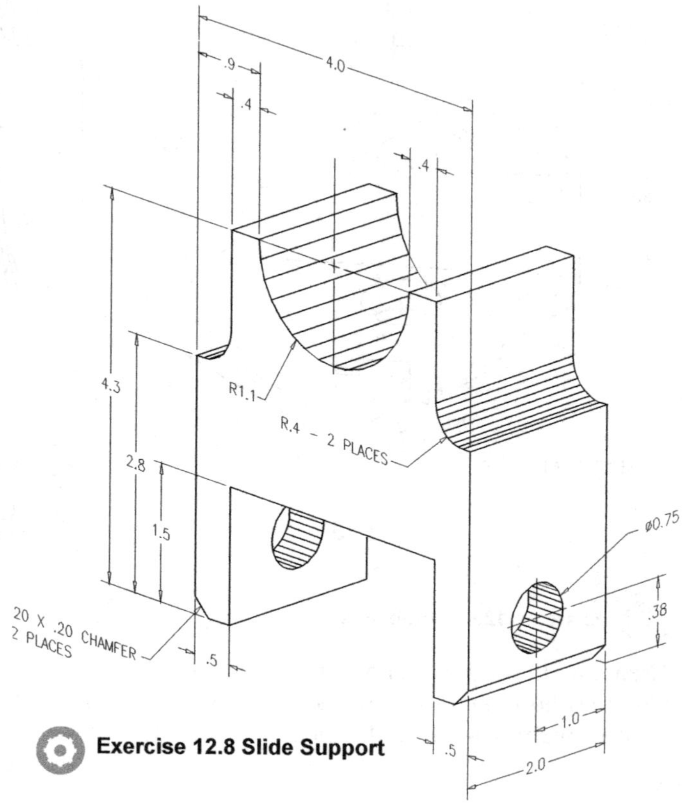

Exercise 12.8 Slide Support

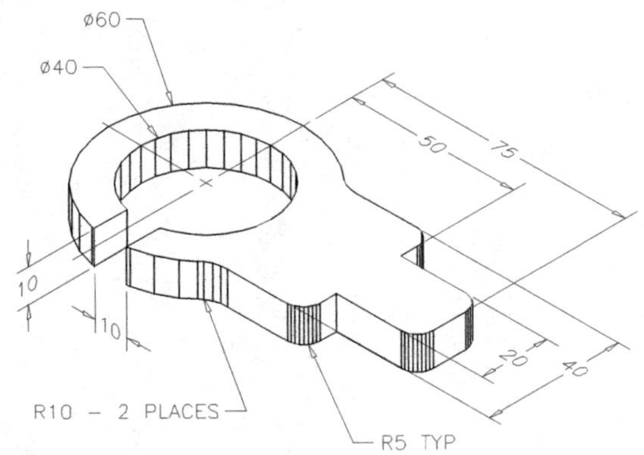

Exercise 12.9 Spacer

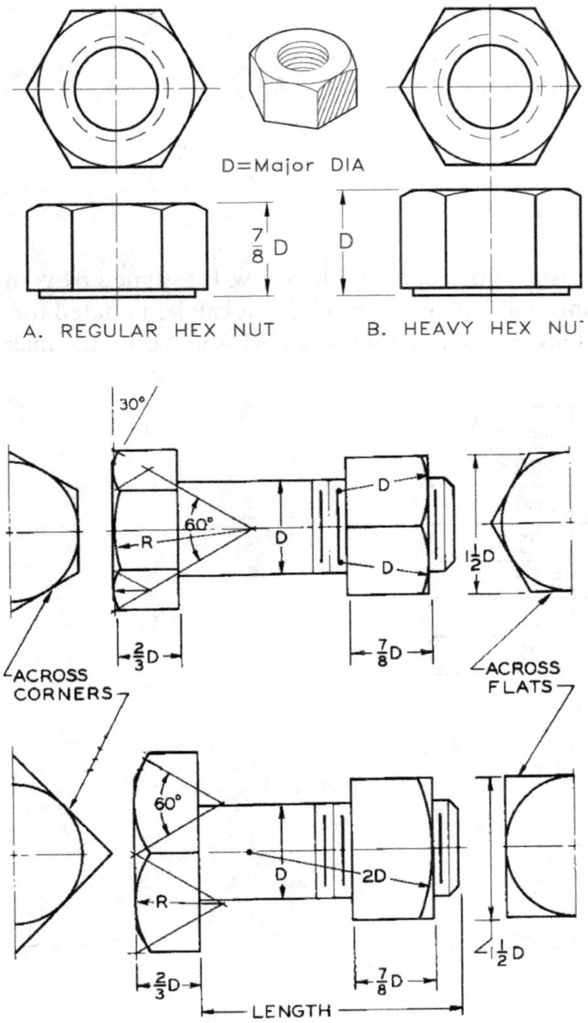

Exercise 12.10 Fasteners

Create solid models for the hex head bolt, square head bolt, regular hex nut, and heavy hex nut according to the proportions shown. Make each into a block. Base the dimensions on a major diameter (D) of 1.00, so when you insert the block you can easily determine the scaling factor.

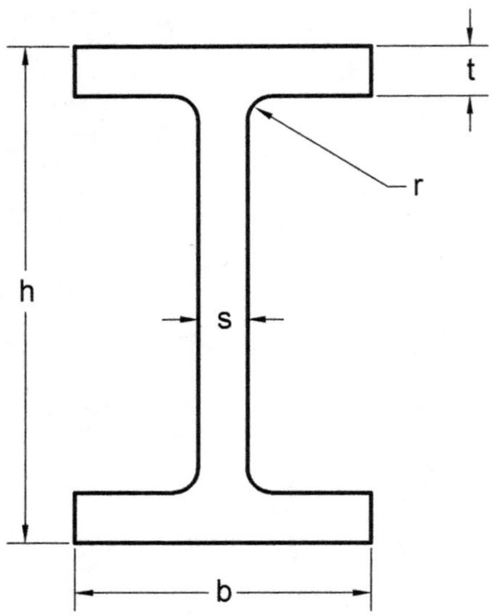

Exercise 12.11M I-Beam

Create a solid model for the I-Beam according to the proportions in the table below. If assigned by your instructor, review parametric dimensions and constraints and create one model that can be updated for all of the sizes in the table. Extrude the shape to 200mm length. The material is ASTM A36. Verify the mass given in the table using the MASSPROP command.

Name	h (mm)	b (mm)	s (mm)	t (mm)	r (mm)	mass (kg/m)
IPE 80	80	46	3.8	5.2	5	6.00
IPEA 80	78	46	3.3	4.2	5	5.00
IPEAA 80	78	46	3.2	4.2	5	4.95
IPE 100	100	55	4.1	5.7	7	8.10
IPEA 100	98	55	3.6	4.7	7	6.90
IPEAA 100	97.6	55	3.6	4.5	7	6.72

CREATING ASSEMBLY DRAWINGS FROM SOLID MODELS

13

Introduction

In this tutorial you will create an assembly drawing of a clamp, similar to the one shown in Figure 13.1. The parts for the assembly drawing have been created as solid models and are included with the datafiles. The purpose of an assembly drawing is to show how the parts go together, not to describe completely the shape and size of each part. (That information is shown on individual part drawings.) Assembly drawings usually do not show dimensions or hidden lines.

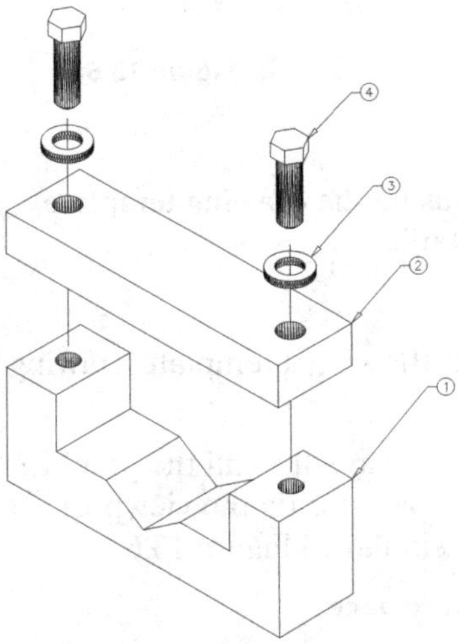

Figure 13.1

Attaching Solid Models

Next you will learn how to use the external reference (XREF) commands to attach part drawings to create an assembly drawing. When you use external references to attach a part drawing to the assembly drawing, AutoCAD automatically updates the assembly drawing whenever you make a change to the original part drawing. You can use this same method to attach any drawing information into any other drawing, for example, to include the outline of a floor plan of a house in a site plan drawing.

You will also learn more about the Insert command and Tool Palettes, which you used to insert the electronic logic symbols. Objects added to a drawing with the Insert command or dragged from a Tool Palette are included in the new drawing, but if you update the original drawing, AutoCAD doesn't automatically update the drawing from which the copy was inserted.

The parts in Figures 13.2 through 13.5 are provided with the datafiles.

Objectives

When you have completed this tutorial, you will be able to

1. Create an assembly drawing from solid models.
2. Use external references.
3. Check for interference.
4. Analyze the mass properties of solid models.
5. Create an exploded isometric view.
6. Create leaders with part identification numbers.
7. Create and extract attributes.
8. Create a parts list.

The basepoints points are identified as 0,0 in the figures.

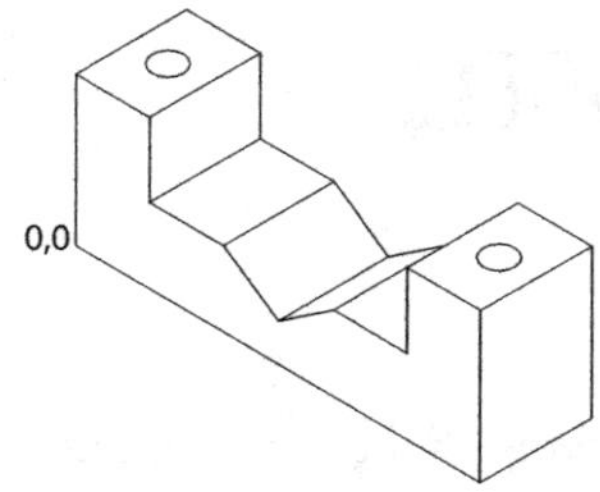

Figure 13.2

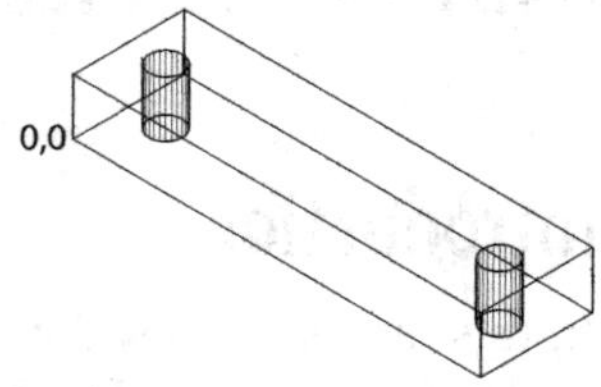

Figure 13.3

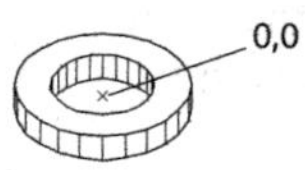

Figure 13.4

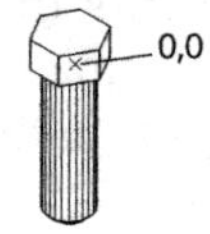

Figure 13.5

Starting

Start AutoCAD and begin a new drawing using the drawing template called *proto-iso.dwt* (provided with the datafiles).

Name the drawing *asmb-sol.dwg*.

The drawing editor appears on your screen showing a template drawing for 3D isometric views.

If necessary, switch to paper space and use Zoom All to fill the graphics area with the layout. Switch back to model space inside the viewport when you are done. Your screen should be similar to Figure 13.6.

Check that you are using the **3D Modeling workspace**.

*Click: **the Insert tab** so that it appears uppermost on the ribbon*

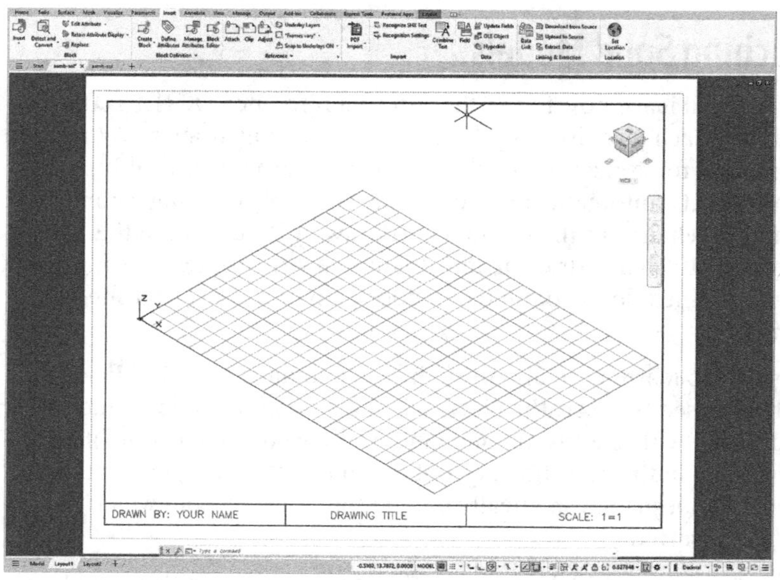

Figure 13.6

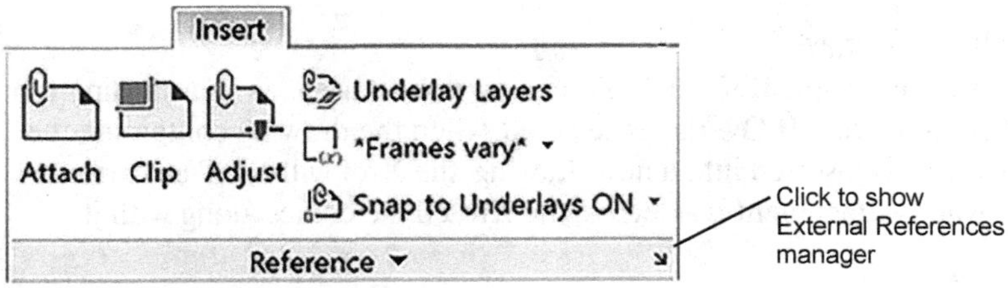

Figure 13.7

Using External References

The external reference (XREF) command lets you show another drawing, without adding all of its data to your current drawing. The advantage of this is that if you make a change to the referenced (original) drawing, any other drawing to which it is attached updates automatically the next time you open that drawing. You can also select to Synchronize the drawing. As with blocks, you can attach external references anywhere in the drawing; you can also scale and rotate them. You can quickly select the External Reference command options from the Reference panel of the ribbon Insert tab. You can also type the command name, -XREF, and select the option you want. Next, you will attach the clamp base to your drawing as an external reference.

Click: ***the small downward arrow at the lower right of the References panel*** *to show the Xref Manager as shown in Figure 13.7*

The External Reference Manager appears, as shown in Figure 13.8.

Click: ***the small downward arrow at the lower right Attach icon*** *near the top left of the External Reference Manager to expand the options as shown in Figure 13.9.*

Click: ***Attach DWG...***

The Select Reference File dialog box appears on your screen.

Click: ***base-3d.dwg,*** *which is in the datafile folder*

Click: ***Open***

The Attach External Reference dialog box appears, similar to Figure 13.10.

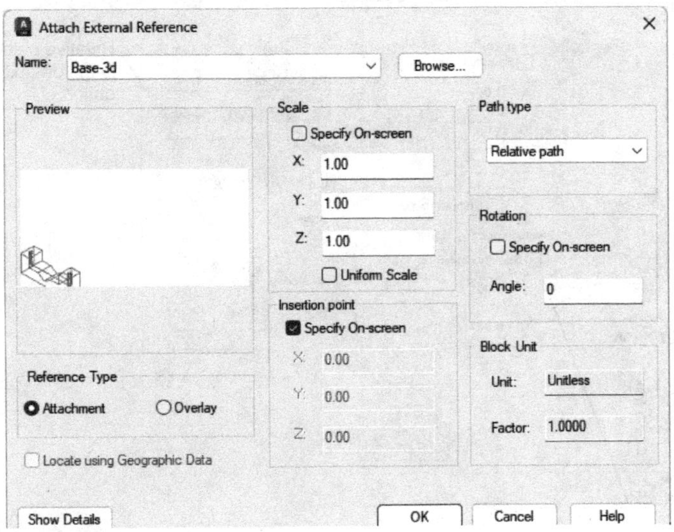

Figure 13.10

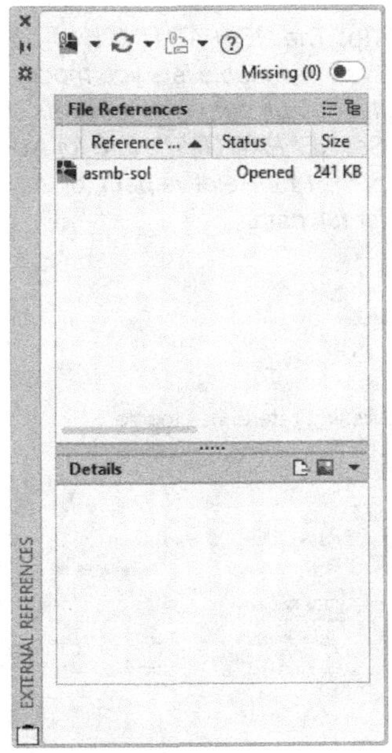

Figure 13.8

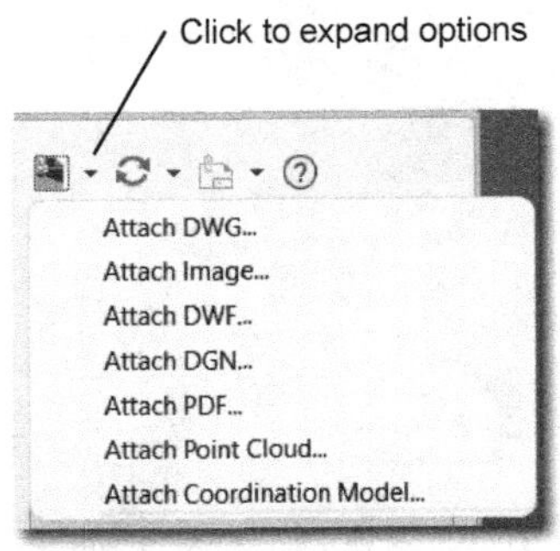

Figure 13.9

Attachment/Overlay

Options available for Reference Type allow you to use it as an attachment or use it as an overlay. If Overlay is selected, when the drawing containing the Xref overlay is inserted into a new drawing, the Xref will NOT be carried along; when Attachment is selected, the Xrefed file comes along with it.

Path Type

Tip: *The REFPATHTYPE system variable lets you modify the default path type for Xrefs. Set REFPATHTYPE to 0 for No path, 1 for Relative path, or 2 for full path.*

Relative path is now the default type. The path is the location to the file that has been referenced or placed into the drawing. A *full path* includes the drive and folder names to the file using designators like c:\myfolder\mydrawing.dwg or \myfolder\mydrawing.dwg. The relative path gives the location related to the current folder using designators like \\mynetworkdrive\mydrawing.dwg or ..\myotherfolder\mydrawing.dwg. A selection of *No path* provides none of this location information with the placed Xref drawing, but in that case, the Xref and the drawing it is being inserted into must be in the same folder.

Why does all this path information matter? When you send a drawing to someone with Xref'd drawings that are included within it, they must be located on that new computer. The path information tells AutoCAD how to find the referenced files. Relative is the default choice because as you move or send a copy of the drawing to another system, it is most likely to locate the needed files. You can use the Missing toggle to aid you in finding missing references.

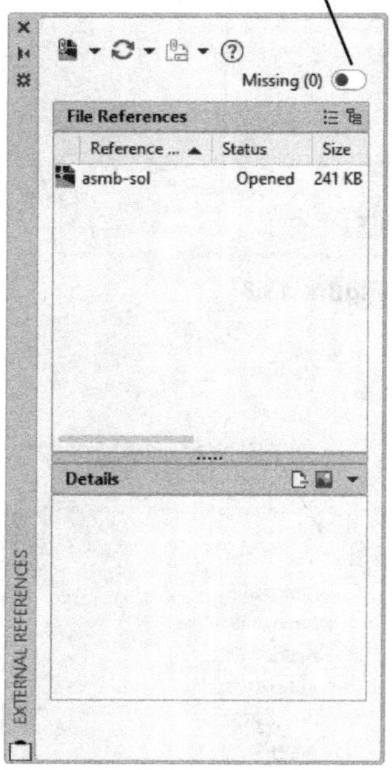

Tip: *Turn the Missing toggle on to display all of the missing references. Turn it off to show only the attached references. Click Resolve Selected to update the paths of the missing references based and load the files.*

Specify On-screen/Scale/Insertion point/Rotation

Choosing specify on-screen returns you to the drawing where you can select or enter the options for scale, insertion point, and rotation. To use the input boxes, unselect Specify On-screen, then enter the values in the input boxes. With Specify On-screen selected, they are "grayed-out."

In the Insertion point area of the dialog box,

Deselect: ***Specify On-screen*** *(remove the checks from all)*

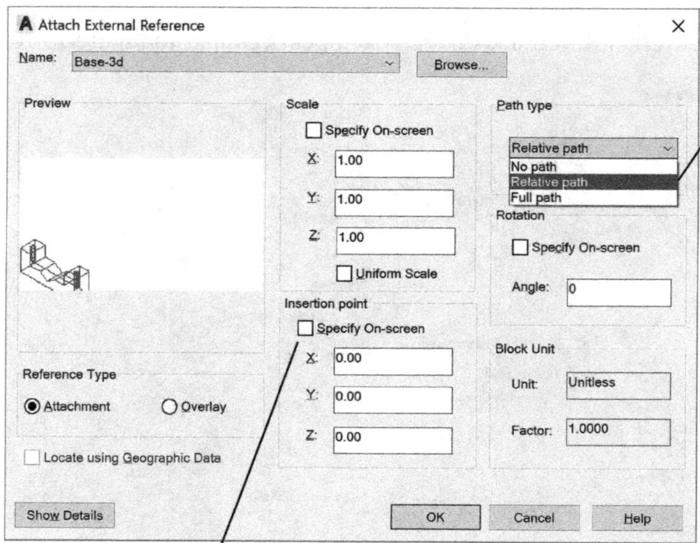

Figure 13.11

The Insertion point should be 0,0,0. It is possible to overtype these with new values (leave them as is for now). The scale will remain at 1 for X, Y, and Z, and the Rotation will remain at angle 0 (Figure 13.11).

Click: ***OK***

The base part appears in your drawing with its corner at 0,0,0. You see a message stating that there are "Unreconciled New Layers."

A special xref icon shows on the status bar to alert you there are xrefs in the drawing (Figure 13.12). When an xref is missing an exclamation point is added to that icon. You can click the Xref icon to quickly show the External References palette.

Figure 13.12

When a new layer is added to a drawing, often through the Xref process, AutoCAD alerts you. You can review the new layer to make sure it will print correctly and conform to your drawing standards. Once you accept the layer (reconcile it) it is cleared from the unreconciled layer filter.

Click: ***Unreconciled layer*** *icon to open the Layer Manager (or click the link in the message window).*

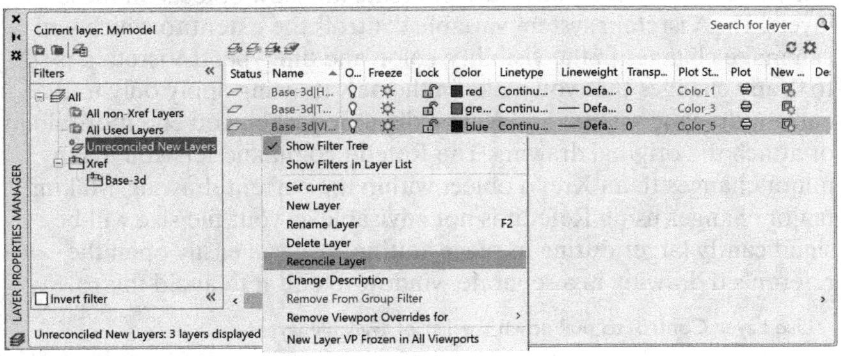

Figure 13.13

Right-click: ***on an unreconciled layer*** *to show the menu (Figure 13.13)*

Click: ***Reconcile Layer***

Reconcile any remaining layers. Close the Layer Manager. Close ***the External Reference manager.***

Next you will set the Isolines variable to a larger value to produce more tessellation lines and improve the appearance of the rounded surfaces.

Command: ***ISOLINES [Enter]***

Enter new value for ISOLINES <4>: ***12 [Enter]***

Command: ***REGEN [Enter]***

On your own, set the visual style to **Shaded with Edges.** Use **pan** to position the base near the bottom center of the drawing area.

Your screen should be similar to Figure 13.14.

Tip: *You can choose whether you want notification of "unreconciled layers" and many other properties of the imported layers using the Layer Settings dialog box.*

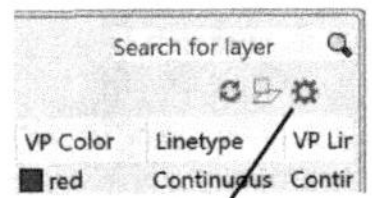

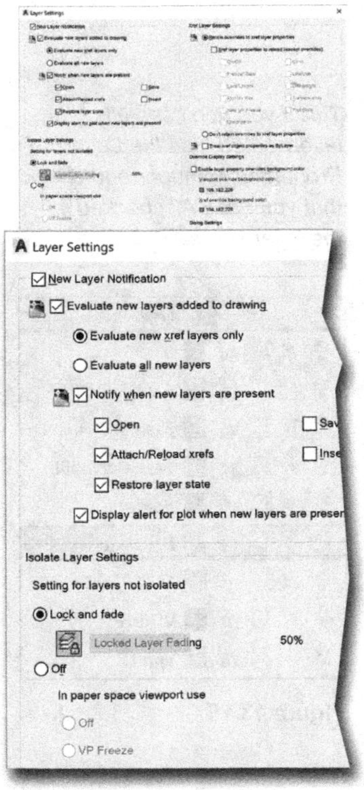

Tip: *The command alias for Regen is RE. You can type this shortcut instead of typing REGEN.*

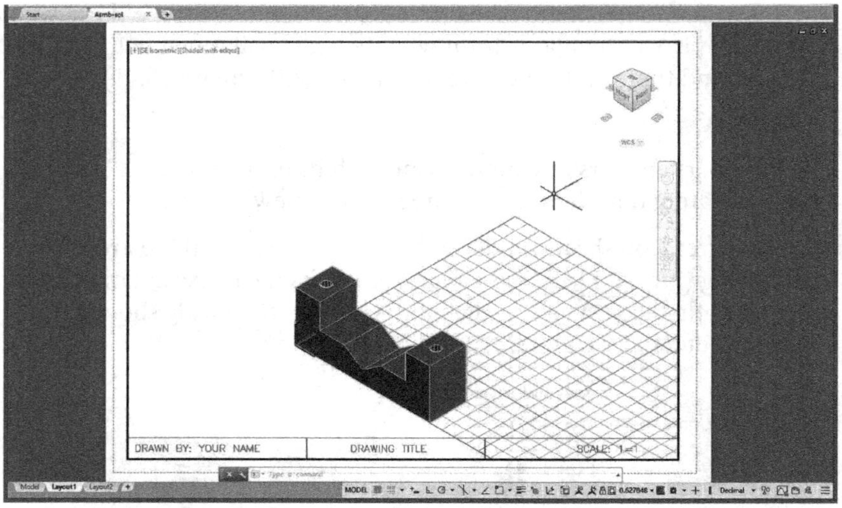

Figure 13.14

Layers and External References

Tip: *if you don't see all of the layers listed, use the Layer Properties Manager and check that you have All checked in the layer filters.*

When you attach a drawing to another drawing by using External Reference Attach, all its subordinate features (e.g., layers, linetypes, colors, blocks, and dimensioning styles) are attached with it. You can control the visibility of the layers attached with the referenced drawing, but you cannot modify anything or create any new objects on these layers. The Visretain system variable controls the extent to which you can make changes in the visibility, color, and linetype. If Visretain is set to 0, any changes that you make in the new drawing apply only to the current drawing session and will be discarded when you end it or reload or attach the original drawing. The Refedit command lets you make minor changes to an Xref'd object within the current drawing. Making major changes using Refedit is not advisable as your file size will be significantly larger during in-place editing. You can easily open the referenced drawing in a separate window to edit it to avoid this.

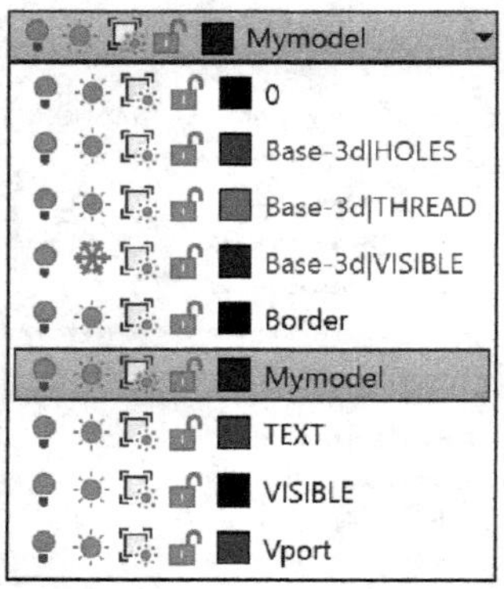

Figure 13.15

Use Layer Control to pull down the list of available layers.

Scroll to the top of the list, if necessary, to see the result of attaching the base as an external reference.

The list should be similar to that in Figure 13.15.

Note that the layer names attached with the external reference have the name of the external reference drawing in front of them.

Click: ***to freeze layer BASE-3D|VISIBLE***

The base externally referenced to the drawing disappears from the screen.

Click: ***to thaw layer BASE-3D|VISIBLE***

You can also control which portions of an external reference are visible by using the External Reference Clip command. This command creates a paper space viewport that you can use as a window to select the portion of the external reference that you want to be visible in the drawing.

On your own, use Help for more information about Xrefclip.

Inserting the Solid Part Drawings

Next, you will insert the solid model drawing *cover-3d.dwg* into the assembly drawing as a block using the Insert command.

> ***Turn on** running mode Object Snap for **Endpoint** and **Center**.*
>
> ***Turn on 3D Object Snap** for **3D Object Snap** for **Vertex** and **Center of Face**.*
>
> *Click: **Insert Block icon** from the Insert tab, Block panel*
>
> *Click: **Blocks from Libraries** to show the dialog box*
>
> *Select: **cover-3d.dwg** from the datafiles folder*
>
> *Click: image tile for **cover-3d.dwg***
>
> *Leave the **Scale unchecked** and **set to the default values of 1** for X, Y, and Z, and the **Rotation unchecked** and set to the default of **angle 0**.*
>
> *Check the box for **Insertion Point** from the Insertion Options*
>
> *Move the cursor into the drawing area.*

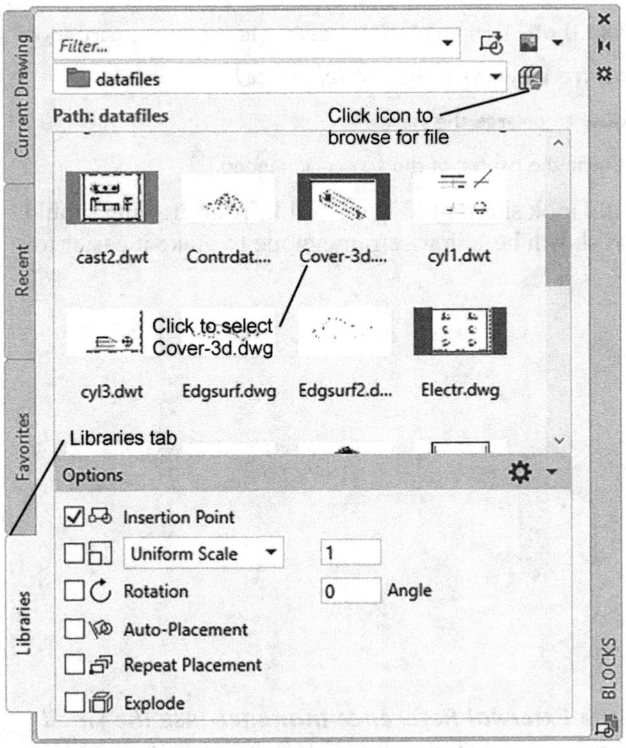

Figure 13.16

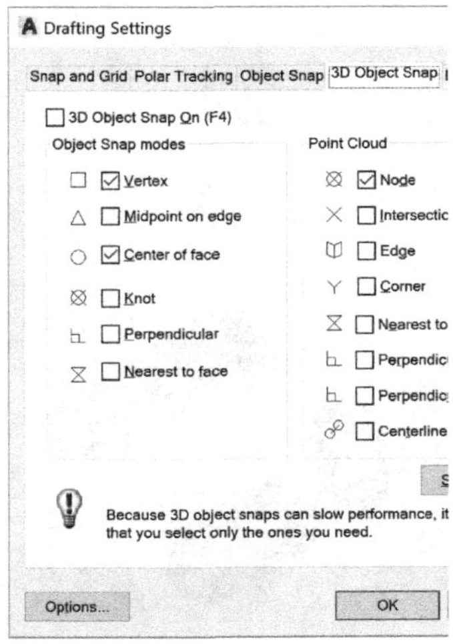

> Specify insertion point or [Basepoint/Scale/X/Y/Z/Rotate/PScale/PX/PY/PZ/PRotate]: ***click anywhere in the drawing editor, away from the base part***

The solid model of the clamp cover appears in your drawing, similar to Figure 13.17.

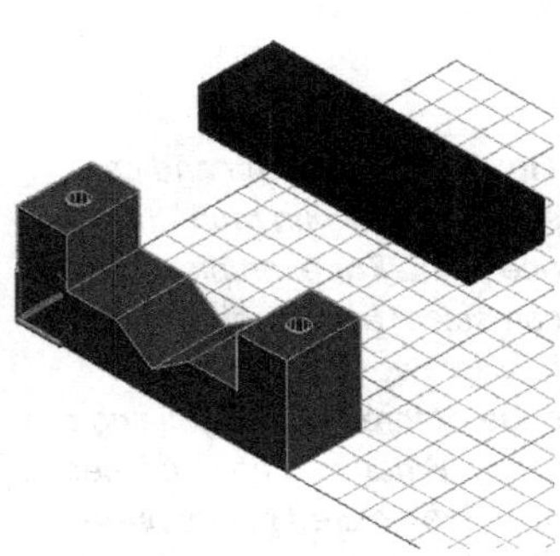

Figure 13.17

You will now use the Align command to align the edge of the cover with the edge of the base. Refer to Figure 13.17 for the points to select.

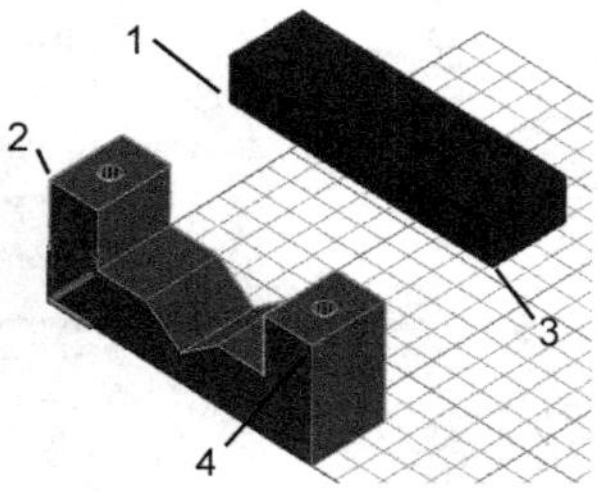

Command: ***ALIGN [Enter]***

Select objects: ***select the cover that you just inserted***

Select objects: ***[Enter]***

Specify first source point: ***use Object Snap Endpoint to select point 1***

Specify first destination point: ***use Object Snap Endpoint to select point 2***

Specify second source point: ***use Object Snap Endpoint to select point 3***

Specify second destination point: ***use Object Snap Endpoint to select point 4***

Specify third source point or <continue>: ***[Enter]***

Scale objects based on alignment points? [Yes/No] <N>: ***[Enter]***

Save your drawing.

The solid model of the clamp cover moves to align with the base.

Next you will insert the washers and screws into the assembly. You will select the Attach button from the External Reference dialog box.

Make sure that **Snap** is **off**. Turn **Grid off** for easier viewing of the part edges.

Click: ***Model tab*** *(to view only the model space)*

Use **Zoom Window** to enlarge the view.

Pan to position it near the center of the screen, if needed.

Your drawing should look similar to Figure 13.13. Your drawing should still be shaded. It is shown here in wireframe mode to make it easier to see.

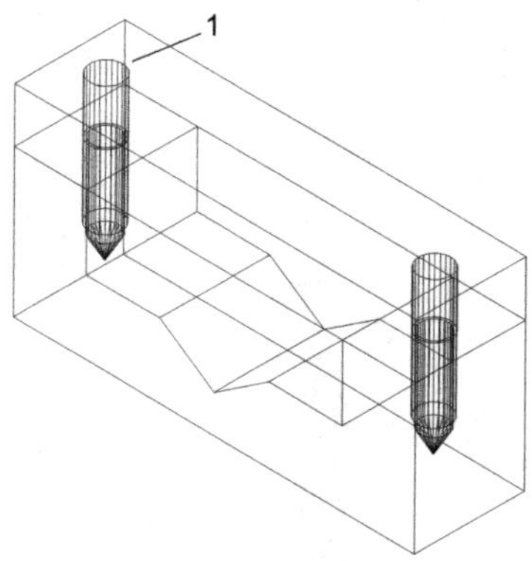

Figure 13.18

Tip: *The Align command can also be used with more than one point. For example, you can select additional points to align two points along an edge or three points defining a plane. When you have aligned all of the desired points press [Enter] to have the command take effect.*

Click: ***to show the External Reference manager*** *(use the small downward arrow from the ribbon Insert tab, Reference panel)*

Click: ***Attach icon***

Click: ***washr-3d.dwg*** *(being sure to select the drive and folder for your datafiles)*

Click: ***Open***

The Attach External Reference dialog box appears on your screen. You will use Specify On-screen for the Insertion point selection.

Leave the Scale and Rotation set to the defaults of 1 for scale and 0 for rotation angle.

Refer to Figure 13.18 for the points to select.

Click: ***Specify On-screen*** *so it is checked in the Insertion point area*

Click: ***OK*** *to exit the dialog box*

Specify insertion point or [Scale/X/Y/Z/Rotate/PScale/PX/PY/PZ/PRotate]: ***use Object Snap Center and target the top edge of hole 1***

The washer appears as shown in Figure 13.19.

To insert the second washer,

Right-click: ***on washr-3d*** *from the file references list to show the short cut menu*

Click: ***Attach***

Click: ***Specify On-screen*** *so it is checked in the Insertion point area*

Click: ***OK*** *to exit the dialog box*

Specify insertion point or [Scale/X/Y/Z/Rotate/PScale/PX/PY/PZ/PRotate]: ***use Object Snap Center and target the top edge of the remaining hole***

Close the External References manager.

The second washer appears in the drawing.

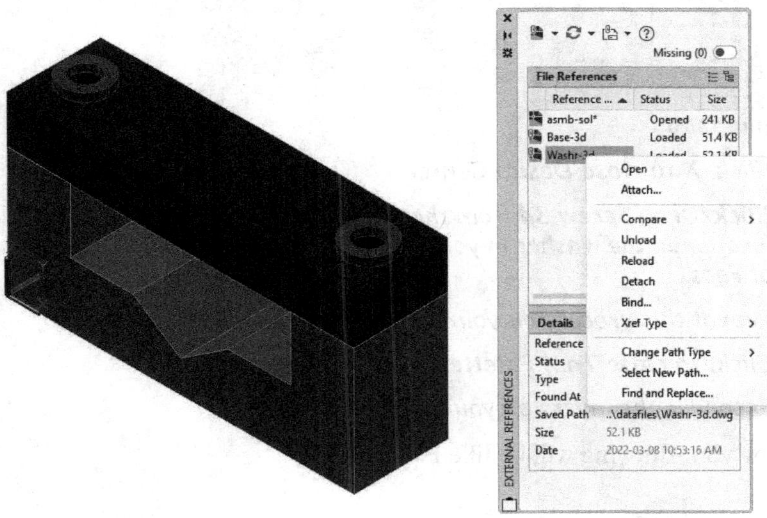

Figure 13.19

If you knew that drawing *washr-3d.dwg* had changed and you wanted to update it without having to exit the drawing, you could use the Reload option of the Xref command.

Reload is especially useful if you are working on a networked system and sharing files with other members of a design team. At any point you can use the Reload option to update the definition of the referenced objects in your drawing.

In this case, you inserted another copy of the same drawing. (You could also use the Copy command to create the other washer.)

Tip: *You can right-click on the DesignCenter to pop up a context menu of useful options, including changing how the items are viewed. You can right-click the DesignCenter title bar and choose to Auto-hide it.*

Next, you will add the two screws to finish the assembly. To do this, you will make a new Tool Palette that has the screw and washer. This is another way that you can insert parts.

Click: ***Tool Palettes button*** *from the View tab, Palettes panel*

Right-click: ***on the Tool Palettes***

Click: ***New Palette*** *from the pop-up menu*

Type: ***3D Parts*** *for the name of the new Tool Palette* ***[Enter]***

Click: ***DesignCenter™ button*** *from the View tab, Palettes panel*

Use the Folders list in the DesignCenter on your own to select the datafile folder and ***drag and drop Screw-3d*** *and* ***Washr-3d*** *onto the* ***Tool Palettes*** *as shown in Figure 13.20.*

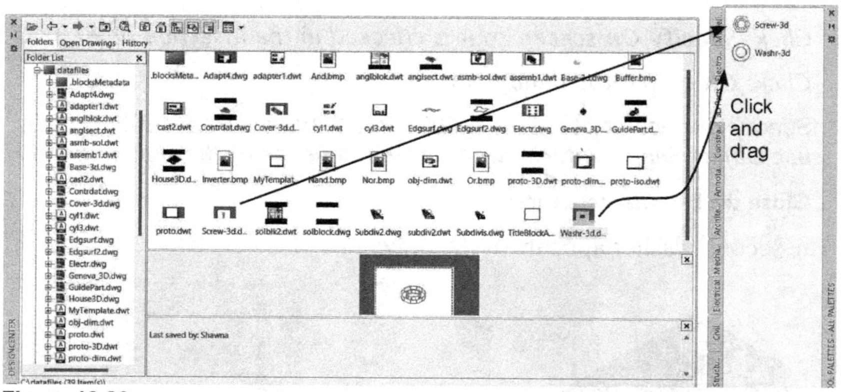

Figure 13.20

Click: ***X to close DesignCenter***

Click/Drag Screw-3d *from the Tool Palettes and drop it into the hole location in the washer in your drawing using 3D Object Snap Center of Face.*

Repeat this process on your own for the second screw.

Click: ***to close Tool Palettes***

Reconcile the layers on your own as needed.

Now your drawing will be like Figure 13.21.

Figure 13.21

Checking for Interference

When you are designing a device, you often want to know whether the parts will fit correctly. You can use the Interfere command to determine whether two parts overlap. If they do, Interfere creates a new solid showing where they do. You can measure this solid and use the information to correct your parts so they fit together as intended.

Next determine whether the screws in the assembly will fit the holes in the cover. The Interfere command only analyzes solids, but objects that you've inserted in the drawing are now blocks. To return the cover and screws to solids, you will explode them.

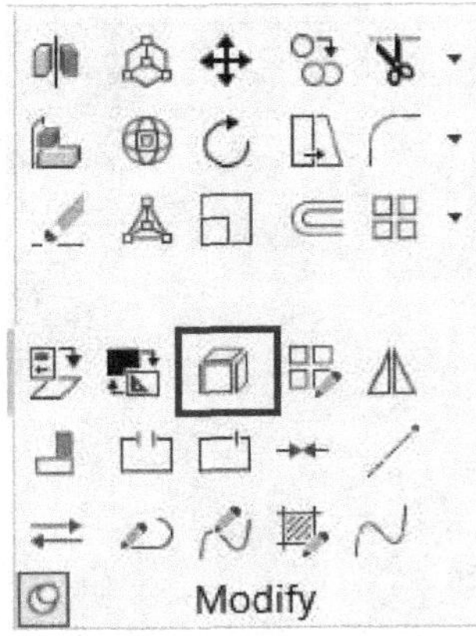

When you explode an object, doing so removes one level of grouping at a time, so exploding the block will return it to a solid. If you explode the solid, it will become a region or surface model.

First, you will check to see what type of objects they are.

On your own, ***List the cover and two screws*** *(they should show as block references).*

Click: ***Explode button*** *from the Home tab, Modify panel*

Select objects: ***click the cover and the two screws***

Select objects: ***[Enter]***

The cover and two screws are now exploded.

List the cover and two screws again on your own (they should now be listed as 3DSOLID objects).

Tip: *Only explode the objects one time. Exploding them more will turn them into surfaces or just 3D lines & arcs, which you cannot check for solid interference.*

Next you will determine whether the screws interfere with the cover. You can type INTERFERE to run the command or select it from the ribbon Solid tab, Solid Editing panel.

Tip: *You may need to use Zoom Window to select the screw. If you list the cover and screws and they are regions, not solids, use Undo to undo the Explode command.*

Click: ***Interfere button***

Select first set of solids:

Select first set of objects or [Nested selection/Settings]: ***click on the cover [Enter]***

Select second set of objects or [Nested selection/checK first set] <checK>: ***click on the two screws***

Select objects: ***[Enter]***

Solids do not interfere.

Because the solids do not interfere, you know that the screws fit through the cover. If the solids do interfere, you see a dialog box with information about the interference. You will test this next by inserting another screw so that it overlaps the left screw and then use Interfere again.

Tip: *If your solids do interfere, your screws may not be assembled properly. If so, erase the screws and use the Insert command to add them. Make sure to use Object Snap Center to place them accurately.*

On your own, ***drag another screw into the drawing so that it overlaps the left screw.***

Use ***Interfere to compare the two overlapping screws.***

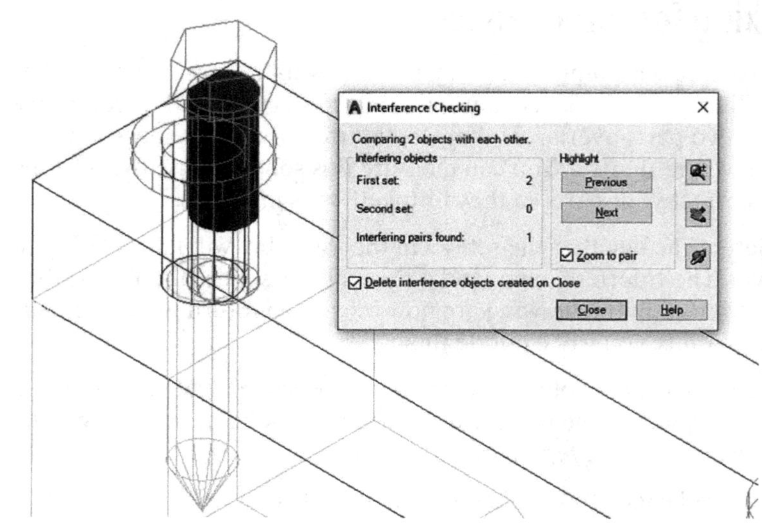

Figure 13.22

When 3D solids overlap so that there is interference, a solid is created from the overlap area. The view temporarily changes to wireframe so that you can see the interference area clearly.

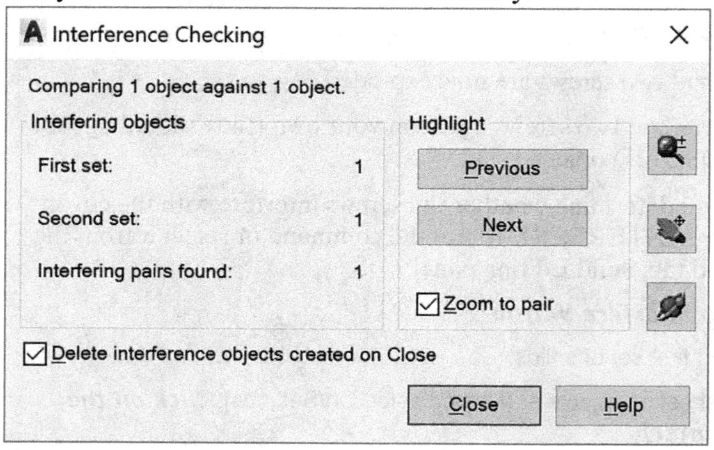

Figure 13.23

If you have multiple interferences you can step through them. With Deleter interference object created on close checked, the object is not retained, but you can uncheck this box if you want to keep this solid on exiting the dialog box. Controls at the right let you return to the drawing to zoom, pan, and rotate the view. If you use those, pressing [Esc] returns you to the dialog box.

Leave ***Delete interference objects created on Close*** *checked*

Click: ***Close***

Use Zoom Previous to restore your original view. Delete the extra screw on your own. Set the display to Shaded with Edges.

Save your drawing.

Determining Mass Properties (MASSPROP)

The software enables you to determine mass properties of solids. One of the advantages of the solid modeler is the accuracy with which volumes and mass properties are calculated. Like Interfere, the Mass Properties command works only on solids, not on external references.

To make it easy to select the Region/Mass Properties command, you will turn on the Inquiry toolbar.

Command: ***-TOOLBAR [Enter]***

Enter toolbar name or [ALL]: ***INQUIRY [Enter]***

Enter an option [Show/Hide/Left/Right/Top/Bottom/Float] <Show>: *L* ***[Enter]***

Enter new position (horizontal,vertical) <0,0>: ***[Enter]***

The small inquiry toolbar appears at the upper left of your screen as shown in Figure 13.24. On your own, drag it to a convenient location.

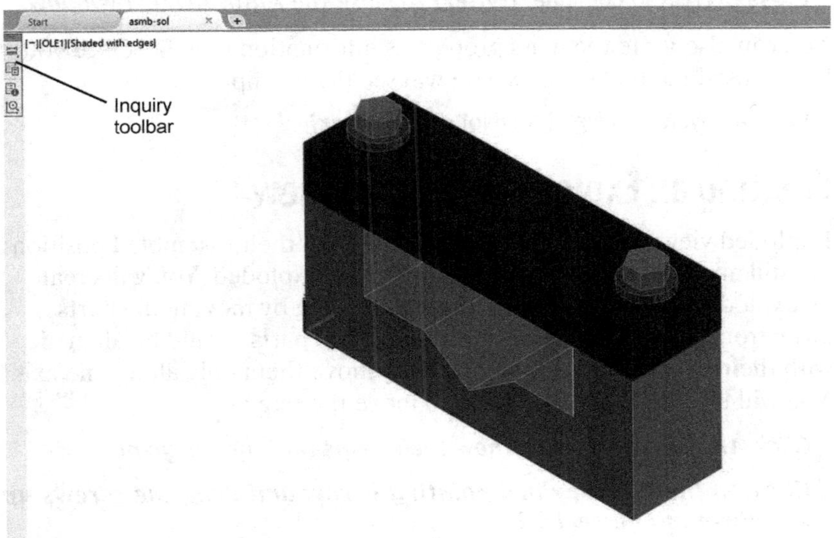

Figure 13.24

Click: ***Region/Mass Properties button*** *from the Inquiry toolbar*

Select objects: ***click the clamp cover***

Select objects: ***[Enter]***

The text window opens displaying the mass property information, as shown in Figure 13.25. Scroll through the information if necessary.

Tip: *If you see the message: "No solids or regions selected." check that you exploded the cover in the previous steps.*

```
Bounding box:          X: 0.0000  --  5.5000
                       Y: 0.0000  --  1.5000
                       Z: 2.0000  --  2.7500
Centroid:              X: 2.7500
                       Y: 0.7500
                       Z: 2.3750
Moments of inertia:    X: 38.4038
                       Y: 93.4026
                       Z: 64.0179
Products of inertia: XY: -12.2913
                     YZ: -10.6152
                     ZX: -38.9225
Radii of gyration:     X: 2.5385
                       Y: 3.9589
                       Z: 3.2775
Principal moments and X-Y-Z directions about centroid:
                       I: 1.4367 along [1.0000 0.0000 0.0000]
                       J: 14.7196 along [0.0000 1.0000 0.0000]
                       K: 15.5976 along [0.0000 0.0000 1.0000]
MASSPROP Write analysis to a file? [Yes No] <N>:
```

Figure 13.25

Press ENTER to continue: ***[Enter]*** *to close the AutoCAD text window*

You can also write the mass properties information to a file. Once you have closed the text window, you will see the prompt,

Write analysis to a file? [Yes/No] <N>: ***[Enter]***

Creating an Exploded Isometric View

Exploded views show the parts removed from their assembled positions yet still aligned, as though the assembly had exploded. You will create an exploded view from your assembly drawing by moving the parts away from each other. Because the exploded parts should be aligned with their assembled positions, you will move them only along one axis. You will use the Move 3D gizmo to move the screws.

Click: ***the two screws*** *to show their grips and the 3D gizmo*

Click on the blue upward pointing arrow and drag the screws up as shown in Figure 13.26.

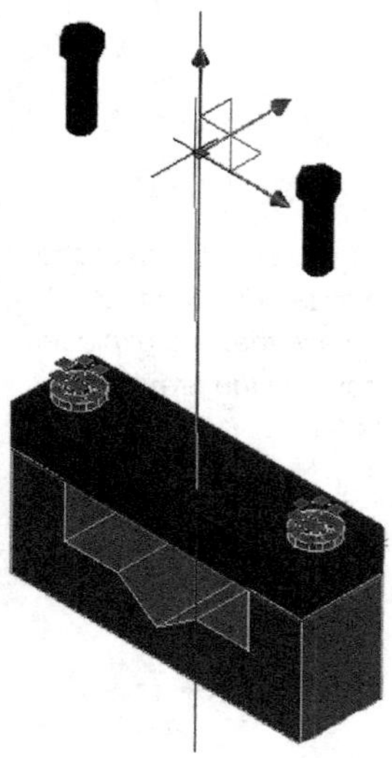

Figure 13.26

You will continue to use the 3D gizmo to relocate the washers and the clamp cover, keeping them aligned with their present position but three units above, along the Z-axis.

On your own, ***restore the Layout*** *view.*

Double-click inside the viewport to make it active.

Turn the ***grid off****.*

Zoom out *so that the parts fit on your screen as needed.*

Move the washers to align below the screws.

Move the clamp cover up *as shown in Figure 13.27.*

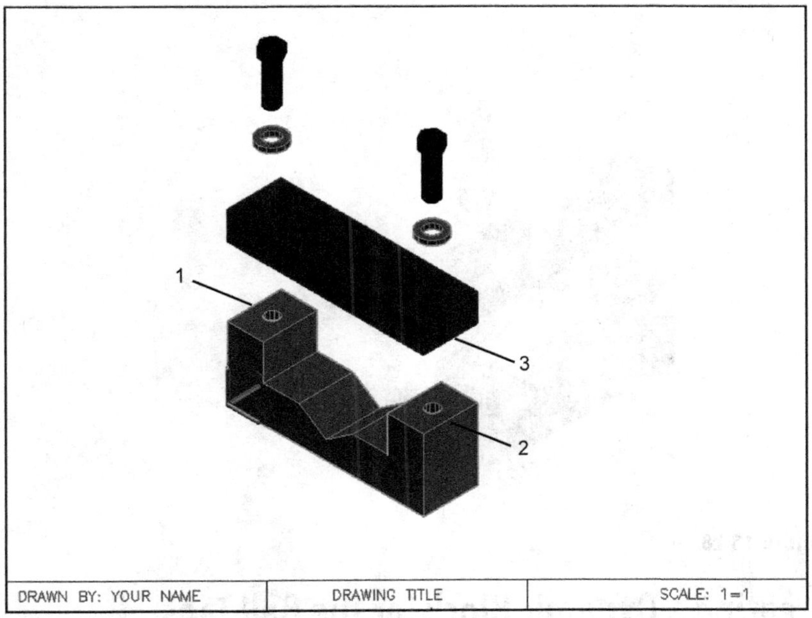

Figure 13.27

When you create an exploded view, you should add thin lines to show how the parts assemble. To create lines in the same plane as the objects' centers, you need to define a UCS that aligns through the middle of the objects. You will make a new layer for the lines. As usual, zoom in if necessary to click the correct locations on the part.

Turn on *Object Snap for* ***Midpoint.***

Create a new layer called **ALIGN** that has color cyan and linetype CONTINUOUS. Set ALIGN as the current layer.

Click: ***3 Point*** *from the Home tab, Coordinates panel*

Specify new origin point <0,0,0>: ***click the middle of line 1 in Figure 13.27***

Specify point on positive portion of X-axis <1.0000,0.7500,0.0000>: ***click the middle of line 2***

Specify point on positive-Y portion of the UCS XY plane <1.0000,0.7500,0.0000>: ***click the middle of line 3***

The UCS icon and grid change to align with the plane through the middle of the parts. If they do not, repeat the command and try again.

Draw the lines, *showing how the parts align, by clicking points on the Snap or using Object Snap.*

Save *your drawing before you continue.*

When you have finished, your drawing should look like Figure 13.28.

Tip: *Another useful technique in aligning 3D objects in an assembly drawing is to use the Tracking command. You can Attach or move the solids with reference to locations on other solids.*

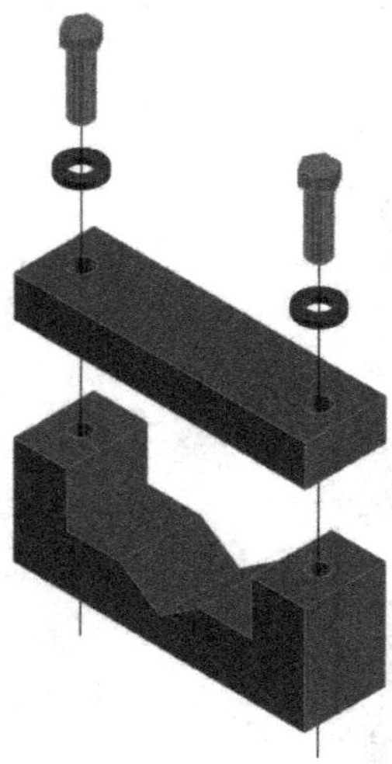

Figure 13.28

Creating a Dynamic Block for the Ball Tags

Ball tags identify the parts in the assembly. They are made up of the item number in the assembly enclosed in a circle, hence the name ball tags. You can easily add ball tags to the drawing by making a block. You will make a block that has one visible attribute and several invisible attributes. An *attribute* is basically text information that you can associate with a block. It is an effective method of adding information to the drawing. You can also extract attribute information from the drawing and import it into a database or word processing program for other uses.

Dynamic Blocks

Dynamic blocks have custom properties that allow you to adjust inserted blocks within your drawing instead of having to redefine them or insert another block. Dynamic blocks must have at least one parameter and one action associated with the parameter. The types of parameters that can be associated with the block are:

Parameter	Control Location	Associated Actions
Point	Defines an X and Y location	Move, Stretch
Linear	Defines a distance between two anchor points	Move, Scale, Stretch, Array
Polar	Defines a distance between two anchor points and an angle value	Move, Scale, Stretch, Polar Stretch, Array
XY	Defines X and Y distances from a base point	Move, Scale, Stretch, Array
Rotation	Defines an angle	Rotate
Flip	Defines a reflection line about which objects can be flipped	Flip

Parameter	Control Location	Associated Actions
Alignment	Defines an X and Y location and an angle which applies to the entire block	No action needs to be associated with this parameter. The alignment parameter allows the block reference to automatically rotate around a point to align with another object in the drawing. An alignment parameter affects the rotation property of the block reference.
Visibility	Controls visibility of objects in the block	No action is assigned, but a list of visibility states for the block is created which can be controlled.
Lookup	Defines a custom property used to look up or evaluate a value from a defined list or table	Lookup
Base	Defines a base point for the dynamic block	Cannot be associated with any actions, but can belong to an action's selection set.

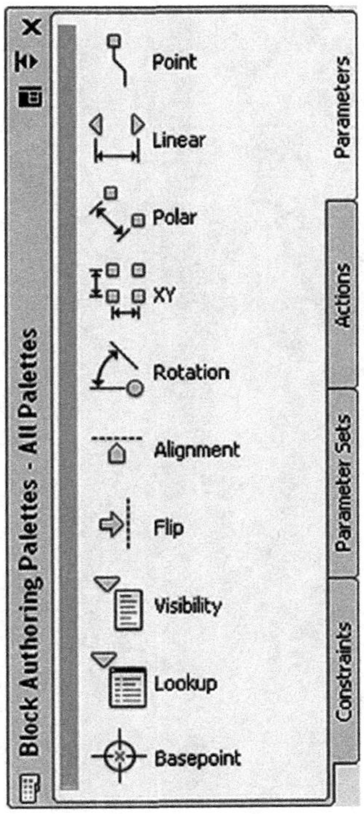

You will add dynamic properties to your ball tag block so that you can flip the leader to the opposite side of the block and stretch the leader extending from it wherever the block has been inserted. You can create the dynamic block and add its attribute using the Block Editor.

Tip: *You can also use the Block Editor to add dynamic properties and attributes to blocks you have previously created with the block command. Attributes can also be added to blocks using the Attdef command and then selecting the attribute you have defined when you create a block.*

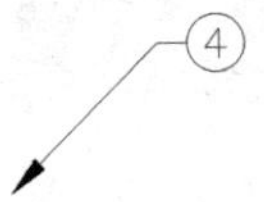

Figure 13.29

Figure 13.29 shows ball tags like the ones you will create. You will use the Block Editor to create the “smart” block for the ball tag.

Click: ***TEXT*** *as the current drawing layer*

Click: ***Block Editor button*** *from the Insert tab, Block Definition panel*

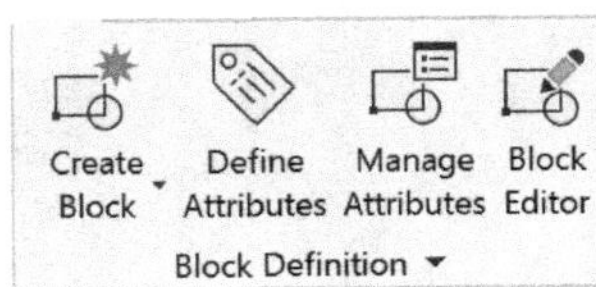

The Block Editor Definition dialog box appears on your screen similar to Figure 13.30.

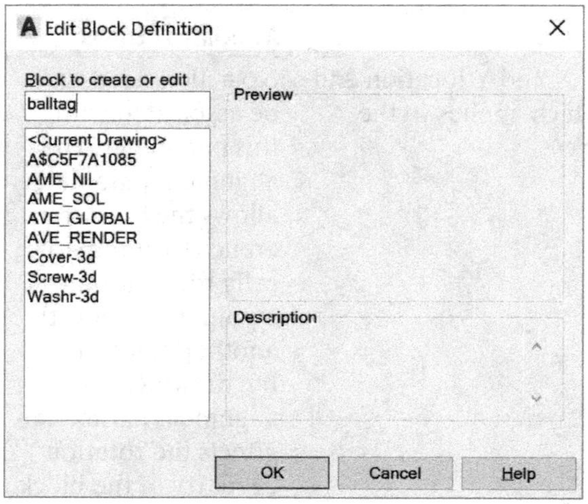

Figure 13.30

Type: ***BALLTAG*** *in the input box for Block to create or edit, as shown in Figure 13.30*

Click: ***OK***

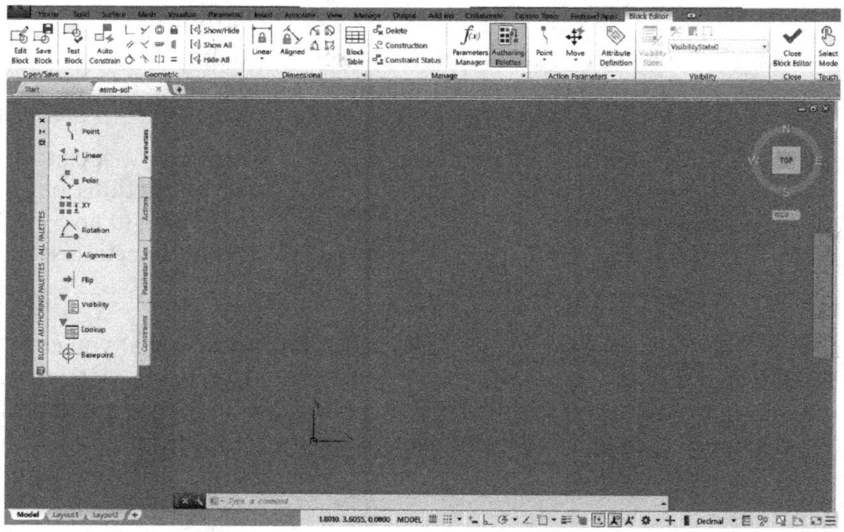

Figure 13.31

Your screen appearance changes to look like Figure 13.31 showing the ribbon and tools for the Block Editor. A new toolbar appears at the top of the screen and the Block Authoring palette is open.

Click: ***Parameters tab*** *to show it uppermost on the Block Authoring palette*

Click: ***Circle button***

On your own, draw a **circle** of diameter 0.25 to the side of the Block Authoring Palettes in the blank area of the drawing editor as shown in Figure 13.32.

Command: ***QLEADER [Enter]***

Use the Quick Leader command to draw a leader with the arrow pointing to the left and connected to the left quadrant of the circle as shown in Figure 13.32. Do not add any text at this time.

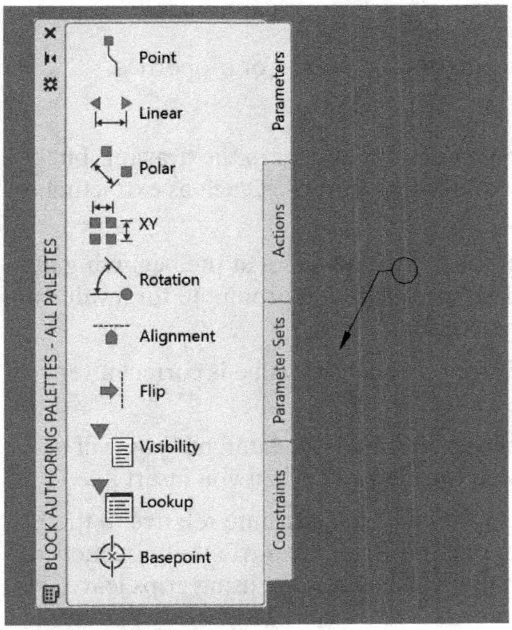

Figure 13.32

Defining Attributes

The Define Attributes command is on the Insert tab, Attributes panel. You can use Define Attributes to create special attribute text objects.

> *Click:* ***Define Attributes button*** *from the ribbon Insert tab, Block Definition panel*

The Attribute Definition dialog box appears on your screen. You will use it to make the selections shown in Figure 13.33.

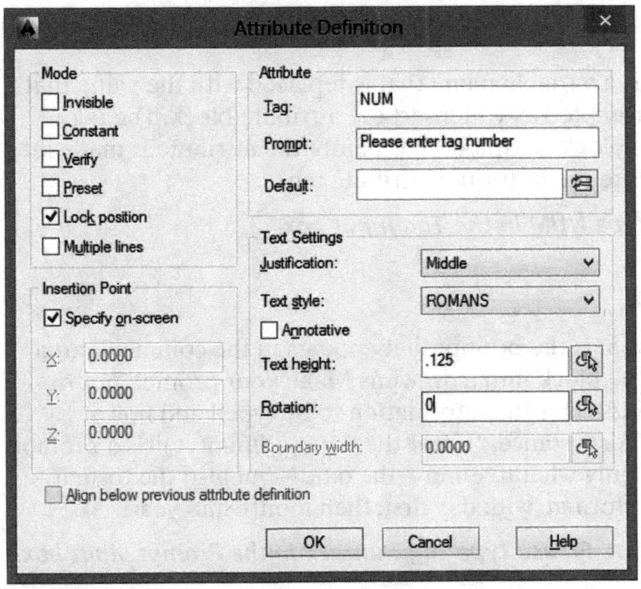

Figure 13.33

Attribute Modes

Attributes can have the following special modes, or properties.

Mode	Definition
Invisible	The attribute does not appear in the drawing, but can still be used for other purposes, such as extracting to a database.
Constant	The value of the attribute is set at the beginning of its definition, so you are not prompted for a value on insertion of the block.
Verified	You can make sure that the value is correct after typing the value.
Preset	You can change the attribute later, but you will not be prompted for the value when you insert it.
Lock position	Locks the position of the attribute relative to the block reference. To allow the attribute to be moved relative to the rest of the block using grips leave this unchecked.
Multiple lines	Allows the attribute value to contain multiple text lines. You specify a boundary width for the attribute.

You will now use the Attribute Definition dialog box to add the number in the center of the ball tag as a visible attribute. You will also create attributes for the other information commonly shown in the parts list (such as the part name, part number, material, and quantity) as invisible attributes.

Leave each of the Mode boxes unchecked to indicate that you want this attribute to be visible, variable, not verified, and typed in, not preset.

Attribute Tag

The *attribute tag* is a variable name that is replaced with the value that you type when prompted as you insert the attribute block. The tag appears when the block is exploded or before the attribute is made into a block. You will use NUM for the attribute tag.

*On your own, type **NUM** in the Tag input box.*

Attribute Prompt

Tip: *The prompt appears with a colon (:) after it to indicate that some entry is expected. The colon is included automatically; you do not need to type a colon in the dialog box.*

The *attribute prompt* is the prompt that appears in the command area when you insert the block into a drawing. Make your prompt descriptive, so it clearly identifies the information to be typed and how it should be typed. For instance, "Enter the date (dd/mm/yy)" is a prompt that specifies not only what to enter—the date—but also the format—numeric two-digit format, with day first, then month and year.

*On your own, type **Please type tag number** in the Prompt input box.*

Default Attribute Value

Default defines a default value for the attribute. Leaving the box to the right of Value empty results in no default value for the tag. As every tag number will be different, there is no advantage to having a default value for the ball tag attribute. If the prompt would often be answered with a particular response, that response would be a good choice for the default value.

Attribute Text Options

Attributes and regular text use the same types of options. You can center, fit, and align attributes just like any other text.

*Select the **Middle Center** option from the Justification pull-down menu.*

Selecting Middle will cause the middle of the text to appear in the center of the ball tag when you type it.

*Set the text style to **ROMANS**.*

You do not need to change the Text Style setting.

*Set the text height to **0.125**.*
*Leave the rotation set at **0 degrees** for this attribute. You do not want the attribute rotated at an angle in the drawing.*

Attribute Insertion Point

You can select Specify On-screen in the Insertion Point section to select the insertion point on your screen, or you can type the X-, Y-, and Z-coordinates into the appropriate boxes.

*Make sure that **Specify On-screen** is checked.*

*Click: **OK***

*Verify that **Object Snap** is on with **Center** selected.*

Your drawing returns to the screen. The Block Editor should still be present.

Specify start point: ***use Object Snap to click the center of the circle***

The tag NUM is centered in the circle. The circle and the attribute tag should look like Figure 13.34. If the attribute is not in the center of the circle, use the Move command to center it in the circle on your own.

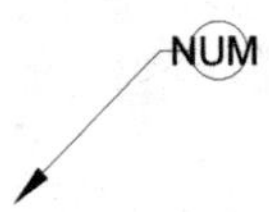

Figure 13.34

Next you will make the attributes for part name (description), part number, material, and quantity. These attributes will be invisible, to avoid making the drawing look crowded, but they can still be extracted for use in a spreadsheet or database.

Command: ***[Enter]*** *to restart the ATTDEF command*

Tip: *You can create a title block for your drawings that uses attributes. For the drafter's name, you make the attribute prompt "Enter drafter's name."*
In the Value text box, you put your own name as the default value.
When you insert the block into a drawing, the default value after the prompt within the AutoCAD default angle brackets will be your own name. To accept the default values press [Enter] instead of having to type in your name each time.

You can also use Fields to display information, such as the current date in the title block.

Tip: *Clicking on the Height or Rotation buttons lets you set the height or rotation, either by clicking from the screen or by typing at the command prompt.*

Tip: *The Block Attribute Manager command (Battman) lets you edit a block definition's attributes.*

The Attribute Definition dialog box appears on your screen. Continue to use it to create an invisible attribute with the following settings.

Select: **Invisible mode** so that a check appears in the box to its left

Tag: **PART**

Prompt: **Please type part description**

Default: (leave the input box empty so that there is no default value)

Justification: **Left**

Text Style: **ROMANS**

Height: **.125**

Rotation: **0**

Make sure that **Specify On-screen** is checked.

When you have entered this information into the dialog box, you are ready to select the location in the drawing for your invisible attribute.

*Click: **OK***

Your drawing returns to the screen.

*Specify start point: **click a point to the right of the ball tag circle***

Command: ***[Enter]***

The tag PART should appear at the location you selected.

On your own, use this method to create the following three invisible attributes. Choose the box to the left of **Align below previous attribute** to locate each new attribute below the previous attributes.

Select: **Invisible**

Tag: **MATL**

Prompt: **Please type material**

Default: **Cast Iron**

Justification: **Left**

Text Style: **ROMANS**

Height: **.125**

Rotation: **0**

Select: **Invisible**

Tag: **QTY**

Prompt: **Please type quantity required**

Default: (leave blank)

Justification: **Left**

Text Style: **ROMANS**

Height: **.125**

Rotation: **0**

Select: **Invisible**

Tag: **PARTNO**

Prompt: **Please type part number, if any**

Default: (leave blank)

Justification: **Left**

Text Style: **ROMANS**

Height: **.125**

Rotation: **0**

When you have finished, each of the tags should appear in the drawing below the Part tag as shown in Figure 13.35.

Figure 13.35

Defining the Parameters

Now you will add the parameters for the block for the features you will control dynamically.

Click: ***Point Parameter*** *from the Block Authoring Palette*

Specify parameter location or [Name/Label/Chain/Description/Palette]: ***click the endpoint of the leader arrow***

Specify label location: ***click a location near the leader arrow*** *as shown in Figure 13.36*

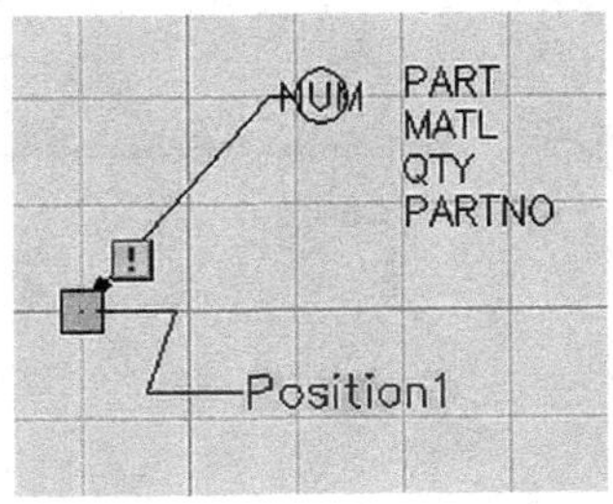

Figure 13.36

The parameter is added to the block definition as in Figure 13.36.

Click: ***Flip Parameter*** *from the Block Authoring Palette*

Specify base point of reflection line or [Name/Label/Description/Palette]: ***use Object Snap to click the center of the circle***

Specify endpoint of reflection line: ***use Ortho or Object Tracking to specify a point directly above the center point you clicked***

Specify label location: ***click a point above and to the right of the circle*** *as shown in Figure 13.37*

The Flip parameter should appear on screen as in Figure 13.37.

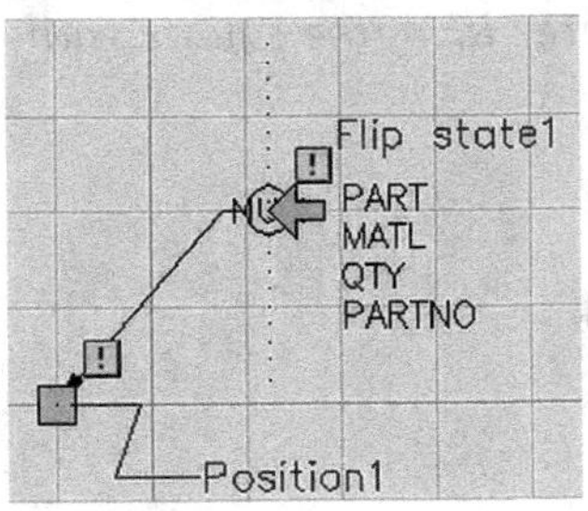

Figure 13.37

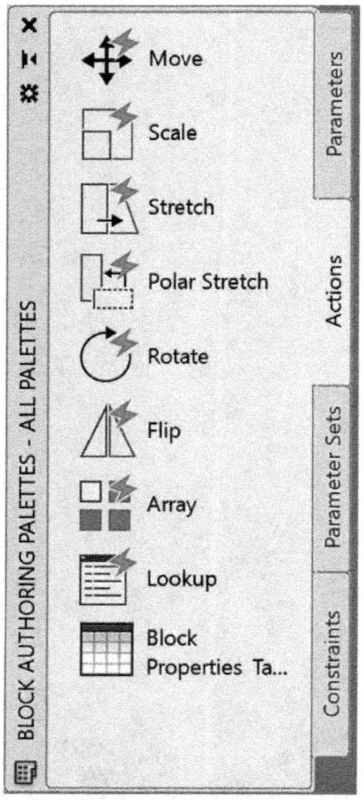

Figure 13.38

Defining the Actions

Now that you have the parameters defined, you are ready to add actions to them.

Click: ***Actions Tab** of the Block Authoring palette*

The Actions tab should appear uppermost on the Block Authoring palette as shown in Figure 13.38.

The Actions tab shows the actions that you can add to control blocks dynamically. You will add the stretch action to the point parameter at the end of the leader and the flip action to the flip parameter to allow the leader to flip to the opposite side of the block.

Click: ***Stretch Action***

Select parameter: ***click on the Point parameter icon that appears as a small square near the end of the leader***

Specify first corner of stretch frame or [CPolygon]: ***click below and to the right of the leader***

Specify opposite corner: ***click toward the left of the leader at about its midpoint as shown in Figure 13.39*** *(you only want to stretch this portion)*

Specify objects: ***click the leader line***

Select objects: ***[Enter]***

When you have finished, the Stretch action icon will appear on your screen. Moving your cursor over the Stretch action icon shows its features as in Figure 13.39.

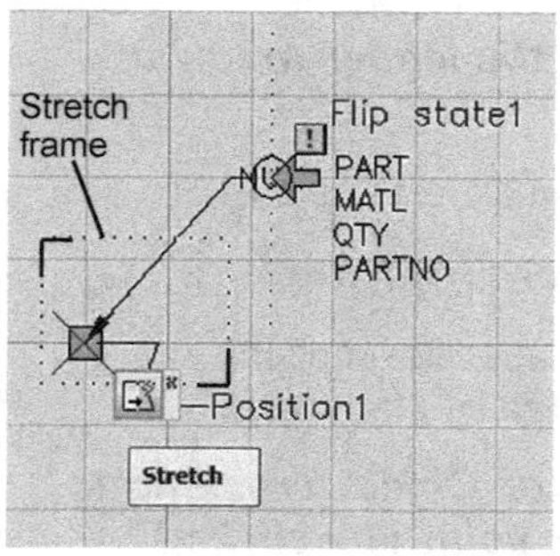

Figure 13.39

To add the Flip action,

Click: ***Flip Action***

Select parameter: ***click on the Flip parameter icon*** *(the square with the arrow)*

Specify selection set for action: ***[Enter]***
Select objects: ***click the leader [Enter]***

The Flip action icon appears as in Figure 13.40.

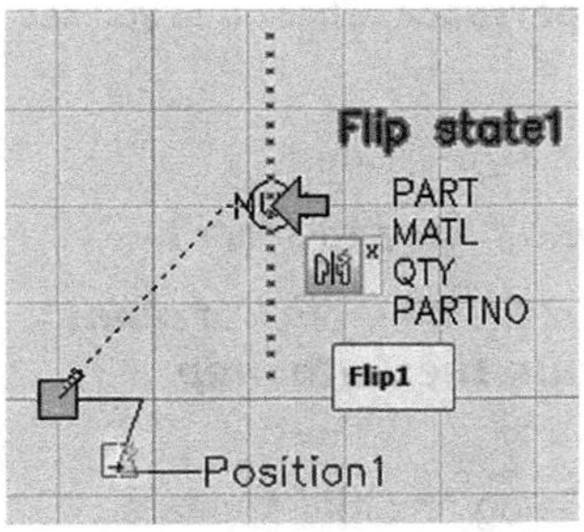

Figure 13.40

Click: ***Parameters tab (from the Block Authoring palette)***

Click: ***Base Point Parameter***

Specify parameter location: ***click the endpoint of the leader arrow***

A small icon will be added to the dynamic block indicating the base point for the block.

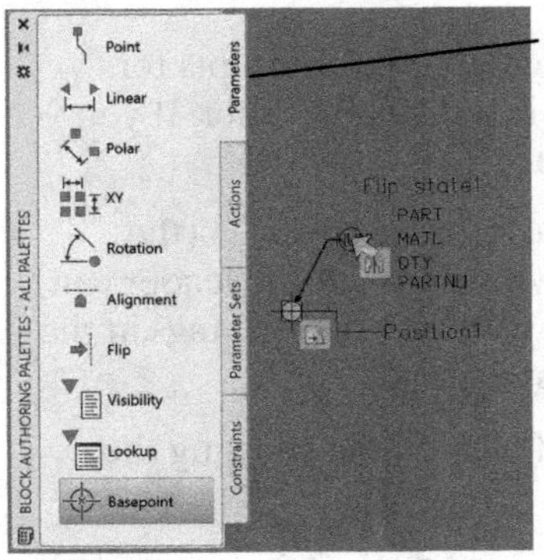

Figure 13.41

Click: ***Close Block Editor***

Click: ***Save the changes to Balltag*** *from the Warning message as shown in Figure 13.41*

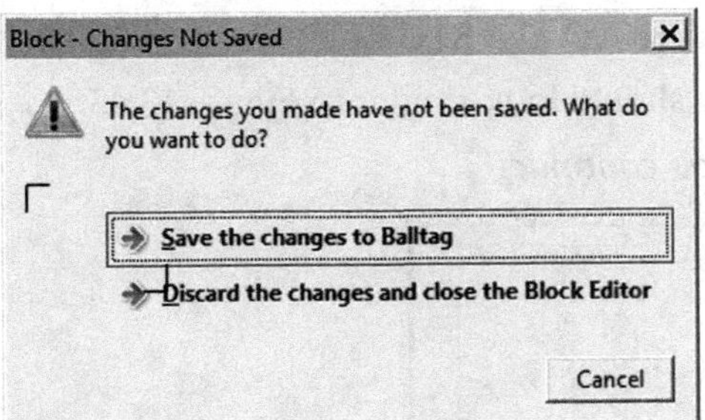

Figure 13.42

Tip: *You may want to use the Write Block command (Wblock) so that the block is available for other drawings. Remember, without Write Block, the block is defined only in the current drawing.*

Inserting the Ball Tags

You will insert the BALLTAG block in paper space. Use Figure 13.43 as your guide as you insert the ball tags.

Turn Object Snap Nearest on*.*

Make sure ***Ortho*** *is* ***off****.*

Double-click outside the viewport to switch to **Paperspace**. Check that you see the paperspace icon.

Click: ***Insert Block button***

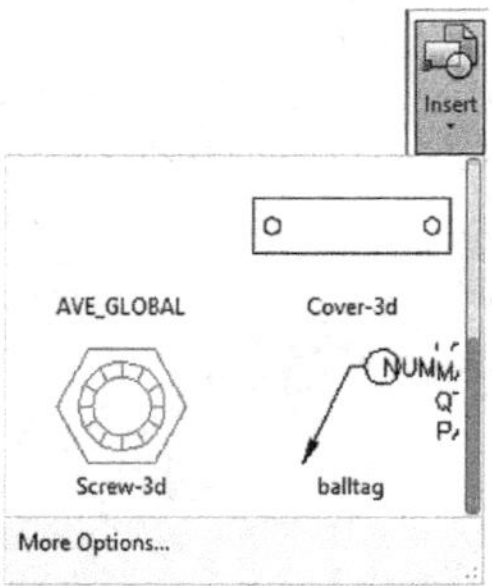

Click: ***Balltag*** *from the pulldown list (you may have to scroll)*

Specify insertion point or [Basepoint/Scale/X/Y/Z/Rotate]: ***click a point on the right edge of part 1, the base, using the AutoSnap Nearest marker***

On your own, enter the attribute values in the dialog box that appears.

Please type tag number: ***1***

Please type part description: ***BASE***

Please type material <Cast Iron>: ***STEEL***

Please type quantity required: ***1***

Please type part number, if any: ***ADD1***

Click: ***OK***

The circle and number 1 appear on your screen. Your prompts for attribute information may have appeared in a different order. If you made a mistake, you can correct it in the next section.

Continue to insert the balltag block for parts 2 (the cover), 3 (the washers), and 4 (the hex head) on your own. The tip of the leader can start anywhere on the edge of the part. Try to place the ball tags in the drawing where they are accessible and easy to read.

Tip: *Remember, the space bar does not act as [Enter] when you are entering text. Because text may include spaces, when you are entering text commands, press [Enter] to end the command.*

When adding the ball tags, refer to the following table showing the information for each part.

Item	Name	Mat'l	Q'ty	Number
1	BASE	STEEL	1	ADD1
2	CLAMP TOP	1020ST	1	ADD2
3	.438 X .750 X .125 FLAT WASHER	STOCK	2	ADD3
4	.375-16 UNC X .50 HEX HEAD	STOCK	2	ADD4

Tip: *If the attribute values are not replaced with the text that you typed and do not become invisible, try opening the Block Editor and then resaving the block and closing the Block Editor.*

When completed, your drawing should look similar to Figure 13.43.

Save *your drawing before you continue.*

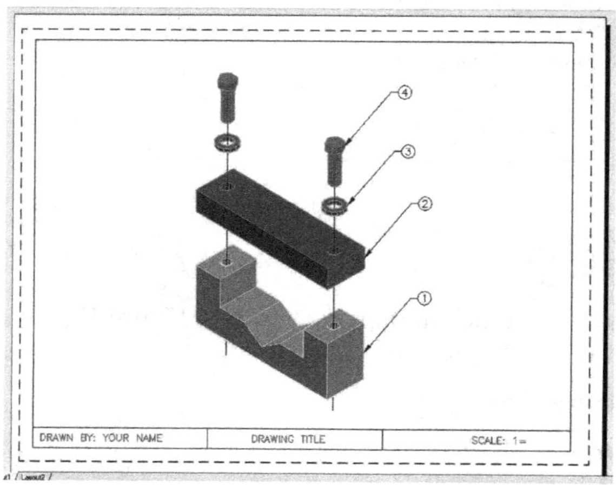

Figure 13.43

Use Zoom Window to enlarge ball tag 1 attached to the base part so that it appears larger on your screen.

Click: on the ball tag

The ball tag block becomes highlighted and icons appear indicating its dynamic properties as shown in Figure 13.44.

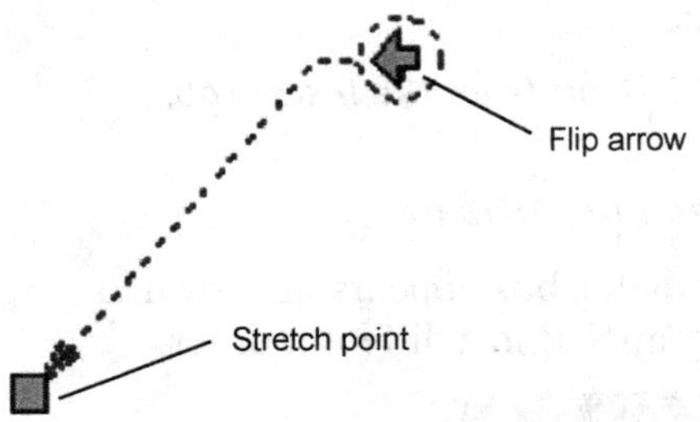

Figure 13.44

Now it is time to check out your smart block!

Click: on the Flip arrow

The leader on the ball tag flips to the right side of the block as shown in Figure 13.45.

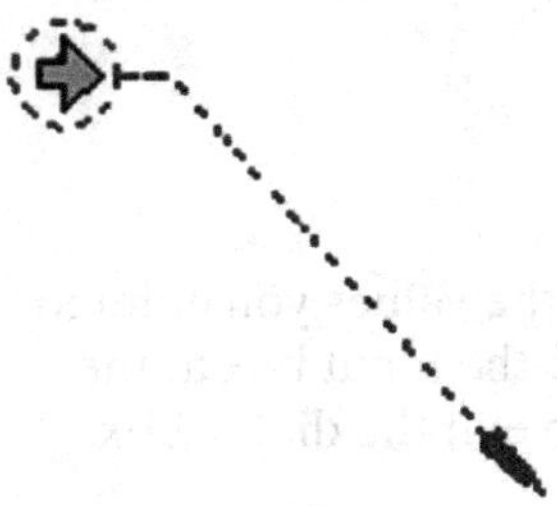

Figure 13.45

*Click: **on the Flip arrow again to return it to the right side***

*Click: **on the Stretch point on the tip of the arrow and stretch it to a new location** as shown in Figure 13.46*

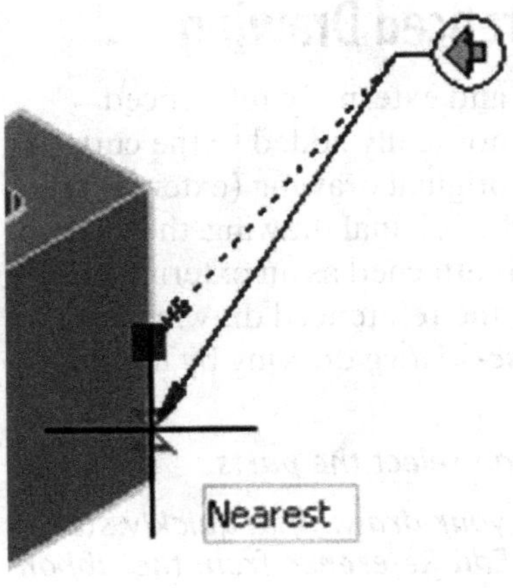

Figure 13.46

Using these and the other features of dynamic blocks you can make some very useful and sophisticated blocks for use with your drawings.

Changing an Attribute Value

Tip: *You can start the Enhanced Attribute Editor by double-clicking on a block that has attributes if you have Noun Verb selection turned on in the Options dialog box.*

Tip: *If you have added the datafile base-3d.dwg from a directory where it is "read only" on your network, you will not be able to edit it. Use the Windows Explorer to copy the base-3d.dwg file from the datafile2021 directory to work. Use the XREF command and select the reference for base-3d. Browse to select the file from work (where you should have permission to change files). Select Reload to reload the external reference from this location*

The Edit Attribute command (EATTEDIT) is very useful for changing an attribute value, especially if you mistyped a value or you want to change an existing attribute value.

*Click: **Edit Attribute (Single) button** from the Insert tab, Attribute panel*

*Click: **on balltag 1 block** to edit its attributes*

The Enhanced Attribute Editor dialog box appears, as shown in Figure 13.47. Your attributes may appear in a different order.

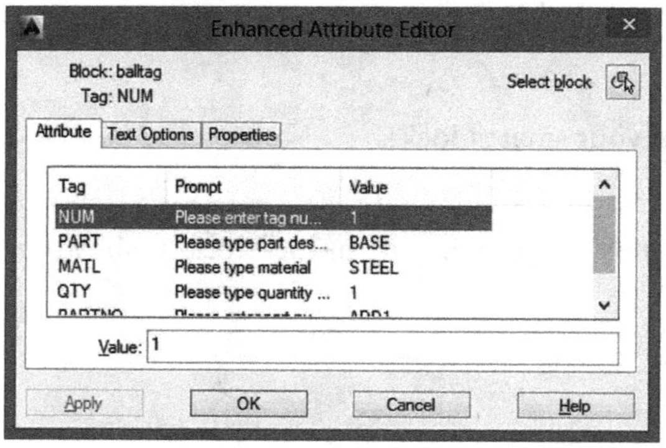

Figure 13.47

Shown are the block's attributes, prompts, and the values you entered. To change a value, click on an attribute and use the input box at the bottom of the dialog box to change its value. To exit the dialog box,

*Click: **OK** or click Cancel*

You can also edit multiple attributes at the same time. You might use this if you had created the attribute incorrectly and wanted to change an entire group at once. To do so use Edit Attributes (Multiple) to start the command, –ATTEDIT.

Changing an Externally Referenced Drawing

The primary difference between blocks and externally referenced drawings is that external references are not really added to the current drawing. A pointer is established to the original drawing (external reference) that you attached. If you change the original drawing, the change is also made in any drawing to which it is attached as an external reference. You will try this feature by editing the referenced drawing *base-3d.dwg* in place. You will change the *base-3d.dwg* drawing by filleting its exterior corners.

***Switch to model space** so that you can select the parts.*

*Double-click: **on the Base-3d part** in your drawing to quickly start the Reference Edit command or click Edit Reference from the ribbon Insert tab, Reference panel*

The Reference Edit dialog box appears as shown in Figure 13.48.

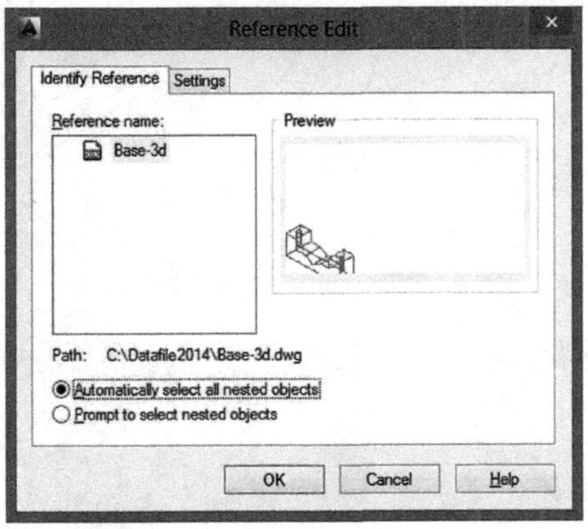

Figure 13.48

If the base part is selected as shown,

Click: ***OK***

The Edit Reference panel appears on the ribbon. You may see the message, "Use REFCLOSE or the Refedit toolbar to end reference editing session."

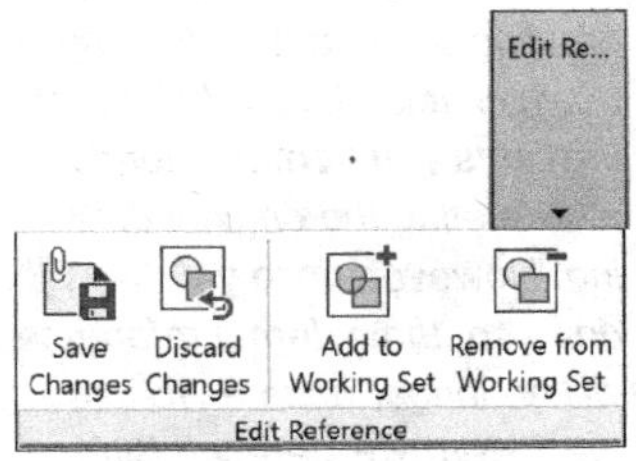

Now the base part is open for editing in place.

Use the commands that you have learned to ***add a fillet of radius 0.25*** *to all four exterior corners of the base so that it looks like Figure 13.49. You may find it helpful to switch to a wireframe view.*

Tip: *You must carefully keep track of your drawings when using external references. If you did not intend to change the assembly but made a change to its externally referenced drawing, the assembly will change. If you want to change an externally referenced drawing but not the assembly, use Save As and save the changed drawing to a new file name. If you move an externally referenced drawing to a different directory, you will have to Reload the external reference and supply the new path in order for the AutoCAD program to find it.*

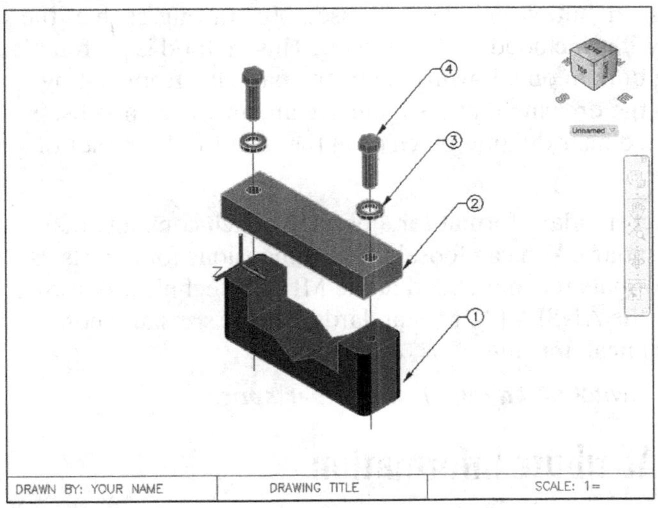

Figure 13.49

Click: ***Save Changes from the Edit Reference panel***

Click: ***OK*** *at the message* "All reference edits will be saved."

Open the ***base-3d*** *part you attached as a reference.*

Tip: *If you cannot open base-3D, check to see that your file is not "read-only." Also be sure that the file is not open in another AutoCAD window or session. If it is, you may need to Refclose to close it.*

Observe that the changes you made in the assembly also have been made to the referenced drawing *base-3d.dwg*. That part now has rounded corners as shown in Figure 13.50.

Tip: *If you are going to send a drawing to someone on a disk, you must be sure to send any externally referenced drawings too. Otherwise the recipient will not be able to open the referenced portions of the drawing. A good way to avoid this problem is to use the External Reference command with the Bind option at the command prompt to link the two drawings. Doing so makes the referenced drawing a part of the drawing to which it is attached. Also, it prevents you from unintentionally deleting the original drawing. However, once you have done so, the external reference will no longer update. To use the External Reference Bind option, after you have attached the drawing, pick the External Reference icon, select the referenced objects you want to bind, select the Bind option, and then choose the Bind type (Bind or Insert). One drawback to binding the files is that the file size for the assembly drawing will be larger.*

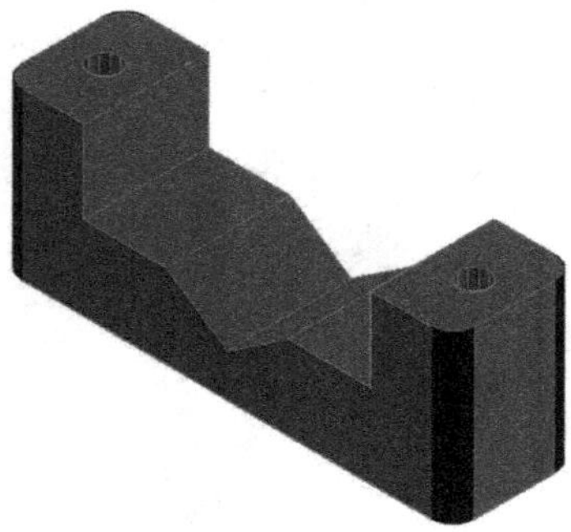

Figure 13.50

Close base-3d.dwg.

*Verify that **asmb-sol.dwg** is your current drawing before continuing.*

Its name should appear in the title bar near the top of the screen.

Creating the Parts List

The next task is to create a parts list for your drawing. The required headings for the *parts list* are Item, Description, Material, Quantity, and Part No. The item number is the number that appears in the ball tag for the part on your assembly drawing. Sometimes a parts list is created on a separate sheet; but often in a small assembly drawing, such as the clamp assembly, it is included in the drawing. This method is preferable because having both in one drawing keeps the parts list from getting separated from the drawing that it should accompany. The parts list is usually positioned near the title block or in the upper right corner of the drawing.

There is no exact standard format for a parts list; each company may have its own standard. You can loosely base dimensions for a parts list on one of the formats recommended in the MIL-15 Technical Drawing Standards or in the ANSI Y14-2M Standards for text sizes and note locations in technical drawings.

*On your own, switch to **Layout 1** and **paper space**.*

Extracting Attribute Information

You will extract the attribute information that you created to generate the parts list. This data can also be saved to an external file, imported into a spreadsheet or word processing program, and reinserted into your drawing. For this tutorial, you will create a table in the drawing.

*Click: **Extract Data button** from the ribbon Insert tab, Linking & Extraction panel*

The Data Extraction wizard appears. You can start from scratch or use a template previously created using this wizard. Templates allow you to extract data using a format previously established.

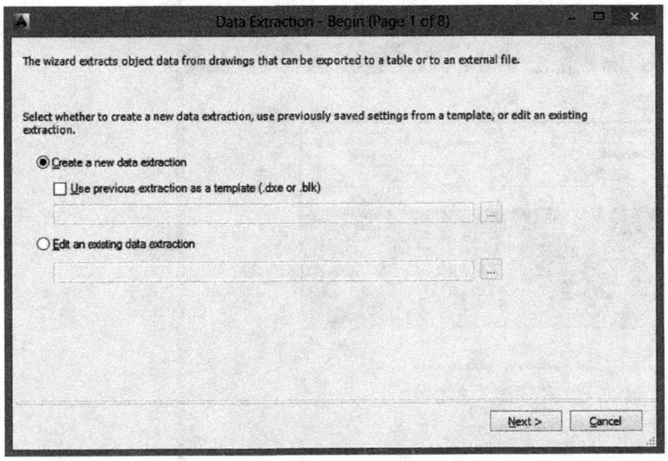

Figure 13.51

Click: ***the Create a new data extraction*** *as shown in Figure 13.51*

Click: ***Next***

Use the Save Data Extraction page to name your file ***DataOut.dxe****.*

The next page of the wizard appears.

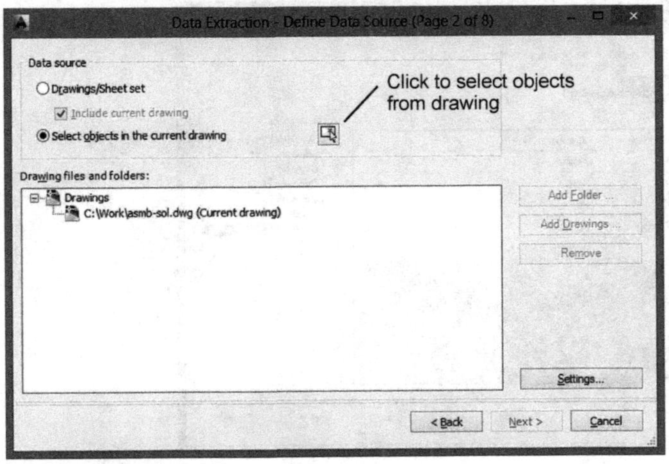

Figure 13.52

Click: ***Select objects in the current drawing*** *as shown in* ***Figure 13.52.***

Click: ***the Select icon from near the center of the dialog box***

Select objects: ***click the four ball tag blocks and press [Enter]***

Click: ***Next***

The Select objects page appears as shown in Figure 13.53.

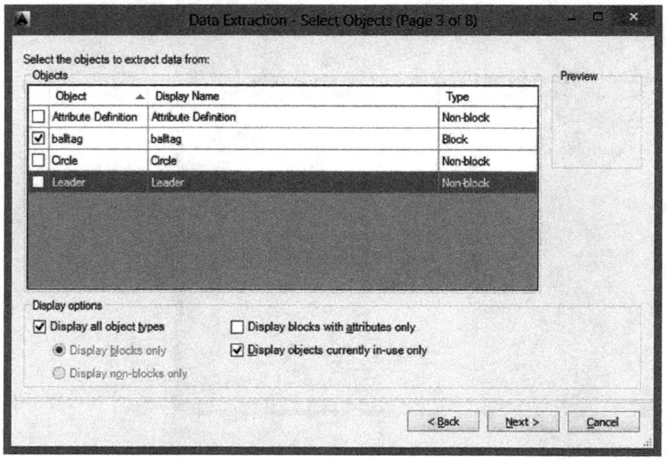

Figure 13.53

Click: ***so that only balltag is checked from the left column***

Click: ***Next***

The Select Properties page appears as shown in Figure 13.54.

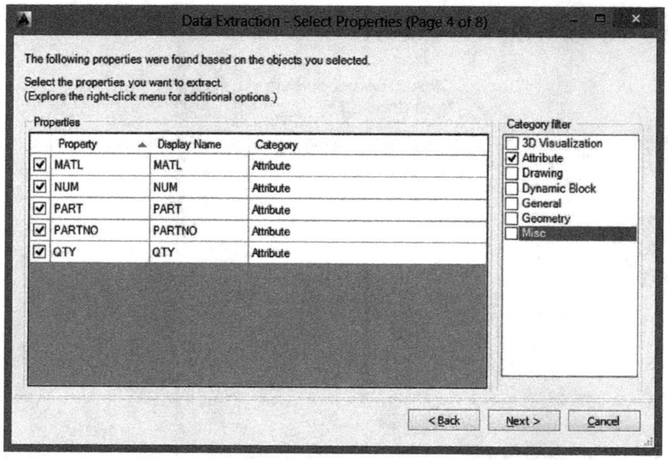

Figure 13.54

Select: ***Attribute*** *from the Category filter list at the right of the dialog box. It should appear checked. All others should be unchecked.*

Select: ***MATL, NUM, PART, PARTNO,*** *and* ***QTY*** *so that they appear checked in the Properties column at the left of the dialog box*

Click: ***Next***

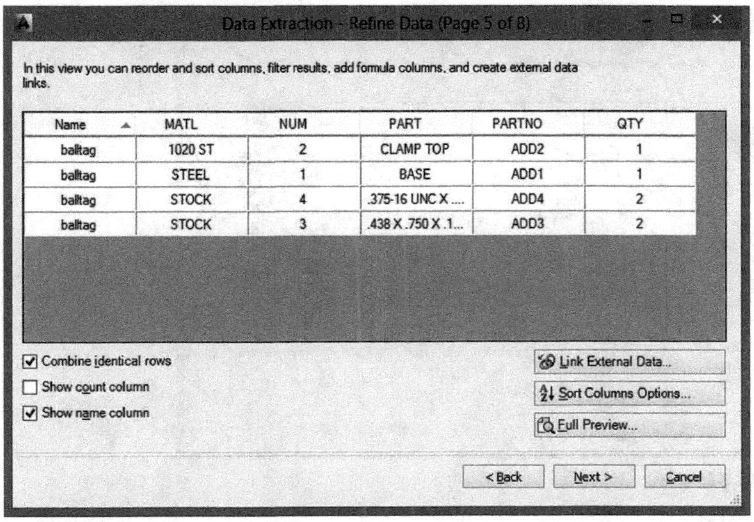

Figure 13.55

Click: ***to unselect Show count column*** *from the lower left of the dialog box, so it appears unchecked*

Right-click: ***the Name column*** *to show the short-cut menu as shown in* ***Figure 13.56***

Click: ***Hide Column***

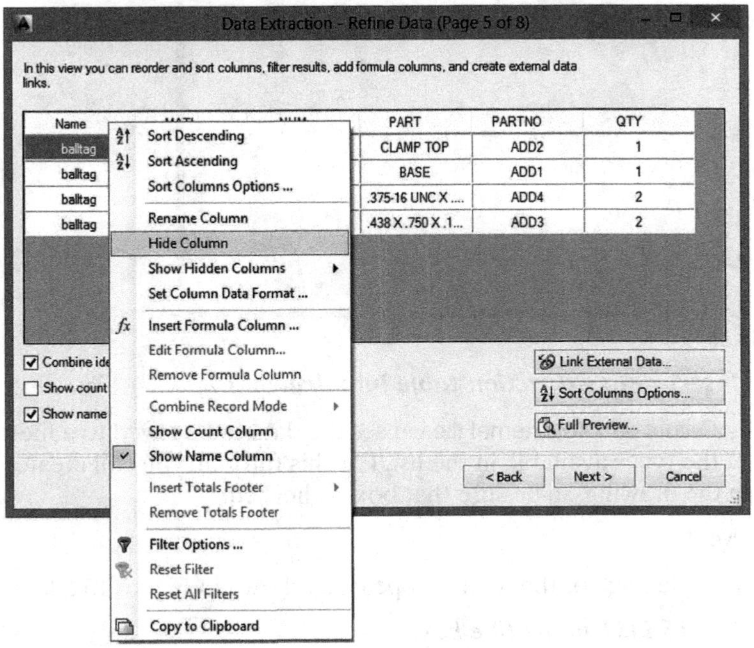

Figure 13.56

On your own, ***drag and drop the columns*** *so that they appear as in Figure 13.57.*

Click on the Item column heading *to sort the column in ascending order. (Clicking it a second time sorts to descending order.)*

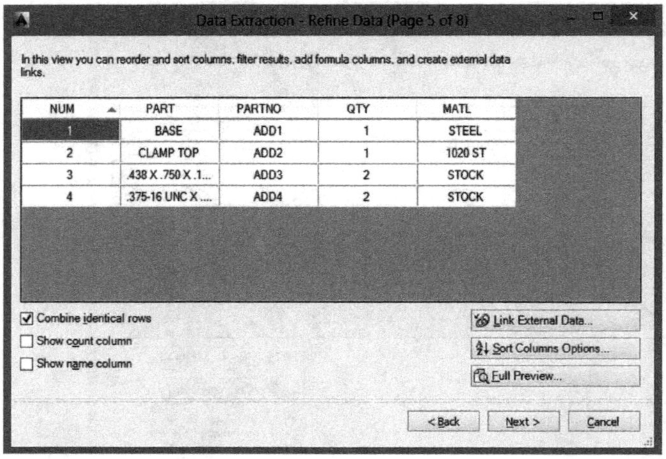

Figure 13.57

Click: ***Next***

The Choose Output page of the wizard appears as shown in Figure 13.58.

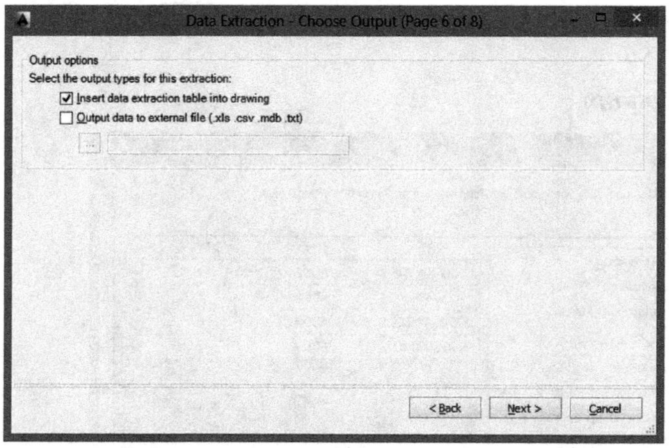

Figure 13.58

Click: ***Insert data extraction table into drawing***

Checking Output data to external file causes the data to be saved to a file format of the types available in the list. For this tutorial, you will create a table in the drawing, so be sure that box is checked.

Click: ***Next***

The Table Style page of the wizard appears as shown in Figure 13.59.

Type: ***PARTS LIST*** *in the title box*

Select: ***Use property names as additional column headers***

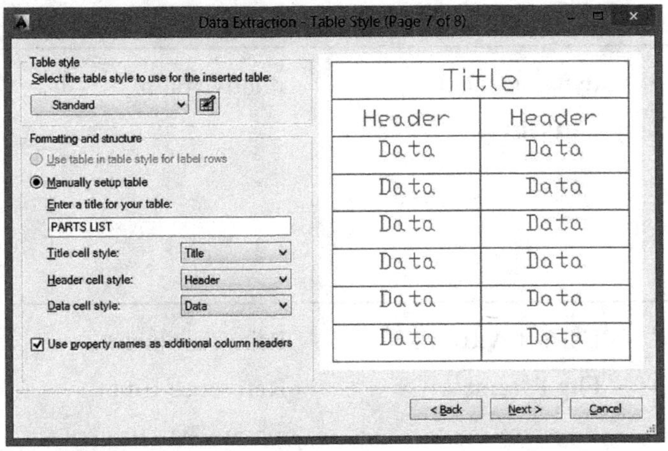

Figure 13.59

Click: ***Next***

Click: ***Finish to extract the data***

The table appears in your drawing attached to the crosshairs.

On your own, ***position the table near the top of the drawing and click to insert it****. Then* ***use the Scale command*** *with a scaling factor of* ***.5*** *to resize the table. Use* ***Move*** *and locate the parts list in the upper right corner of the drawing. If necessary, switch to model space and pan the parts to a new position on the screen. Switch back to paperspace and move the balltags.*

Your drawing should look similar to Figure 13.60.

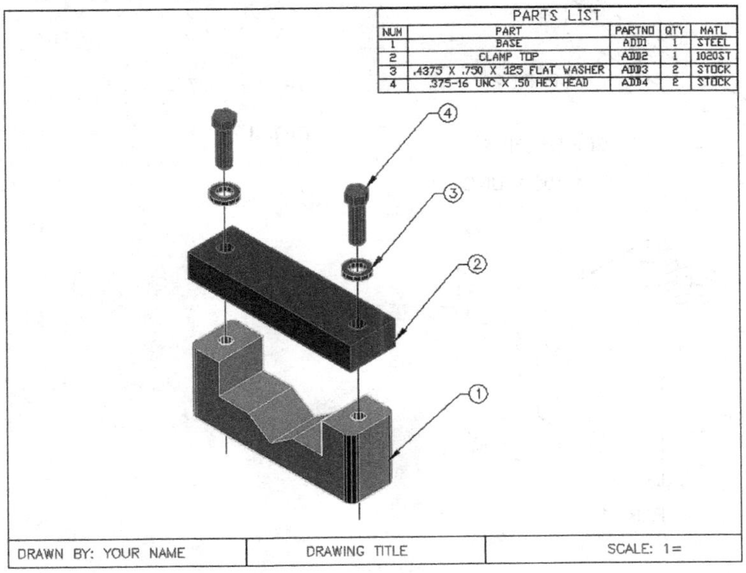

Figure 13.60

Save *your drawing.*

Exit *the AutoCAD program.*

You have completed Tutorial 13.

Tip: *The Count command found on the View tab Palettes area opens the Count palette. You can use it to insert a table with the selected objects and their count into your drawing. This is a quick way to determine the number of instances of a block in the drawing. You can use it to make quick parts lists.*

Tip: *You will usually insert parts lists, notes, and other similar items into the paper space layout, depending on how your drawing is organized.*

Key Terms

attribute
attribute prompt
attribute tag
ball tag
dynamic block
parts list
relative path

Key Commands

Data Extraction
Define Attribute
Edit Attribute
Edit Block Definition
External Reference
External Reference Attach
External Reference Clip
Extract Attributes
Flip Parameter
Interfere
Mass Properties
Point Parameter
Reference Edit
Zoom Extents

Exercises

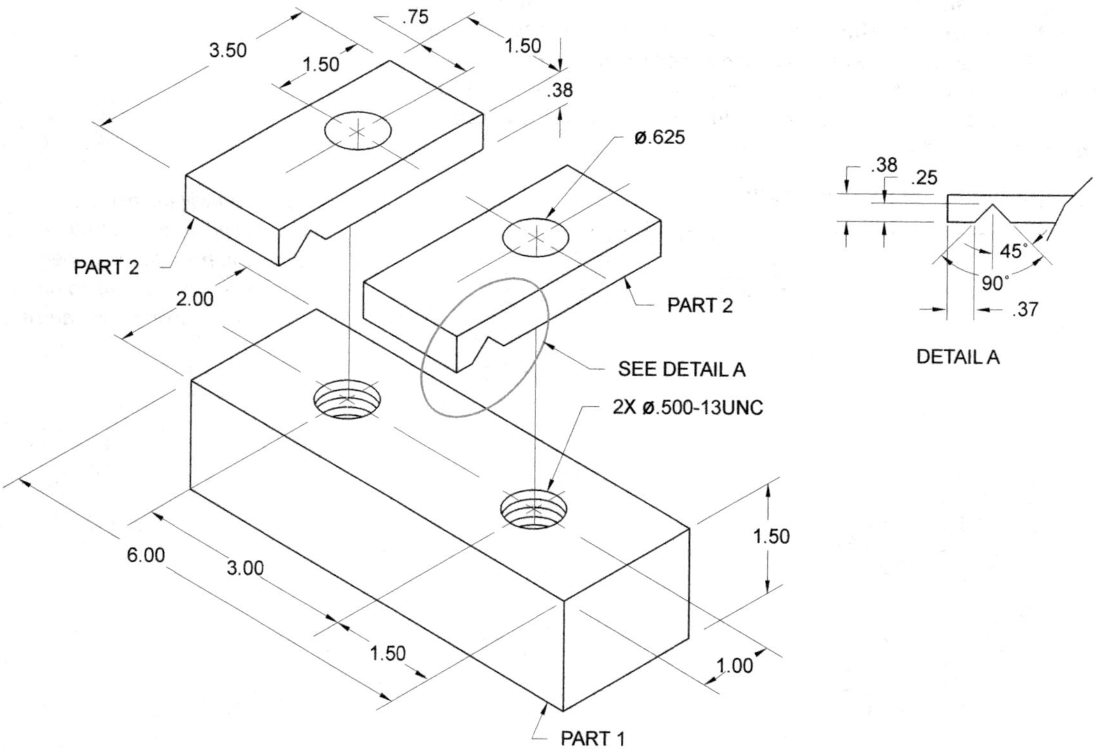

Exercise 13.1 Clamping Block

Prepare assembly and detail drawings and a parts list based on the following information, using solid modeling techniques. Create solid models of Parts 1 and 2. Join Part 2 to Part 1, using two .500-13UNC 3 2.50 LONG HEX-HEAD BOLTS. Include .500-13UNC NUTS on each bolt. Locate a .625 3 1.250 3 .125 WASHER under the head of each bolt between Parts 1 and 2 and between Part 1 and the NUT. (Each bolt will have three washers and a nut.)

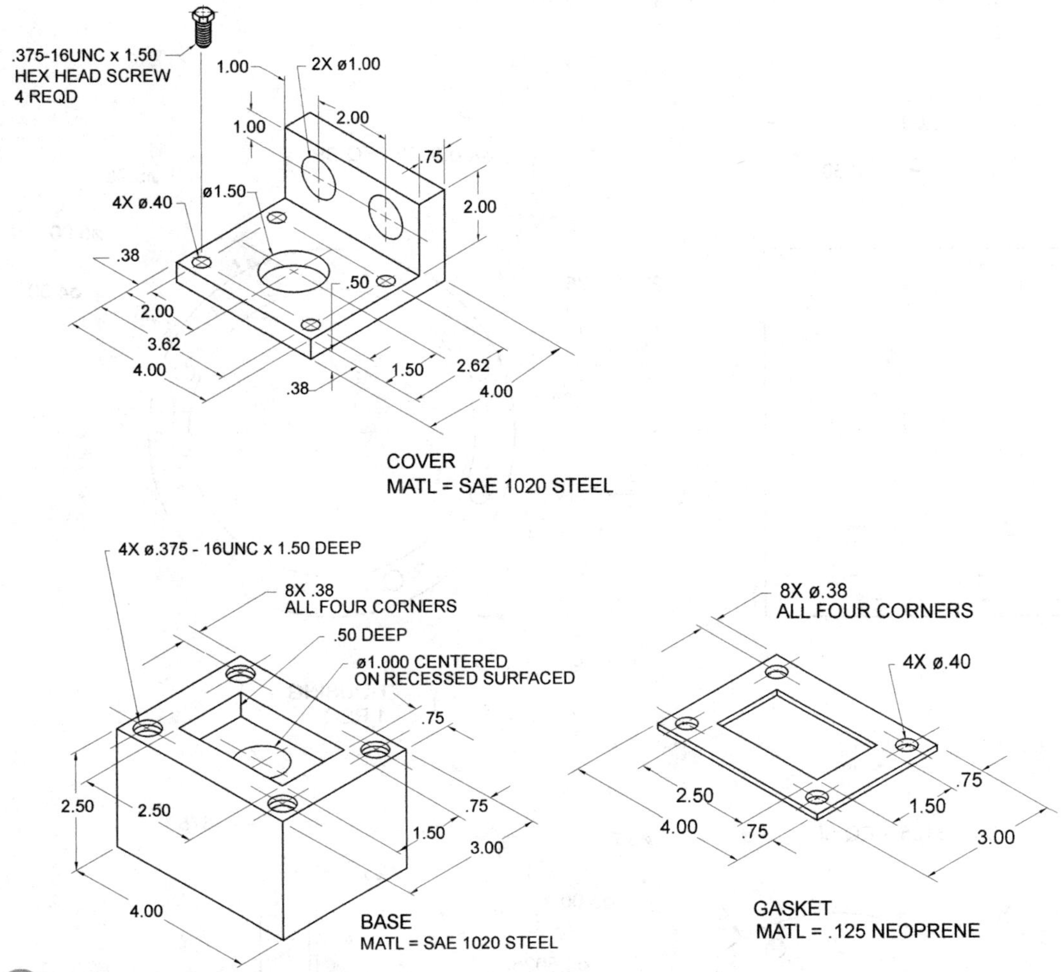

Exercise 13.2 Pressure Assembly

Prepare assembly and detail drawings and a parts list of the pressure assembly. Create solid models of the BASE, GASKET, and COVER shown. Use four .375-16UNC 3 1.50 HEX-HEAD SCREWS to join the COVER, GASKET, and BASE. The GASKET assembles between the BASE and COVER.

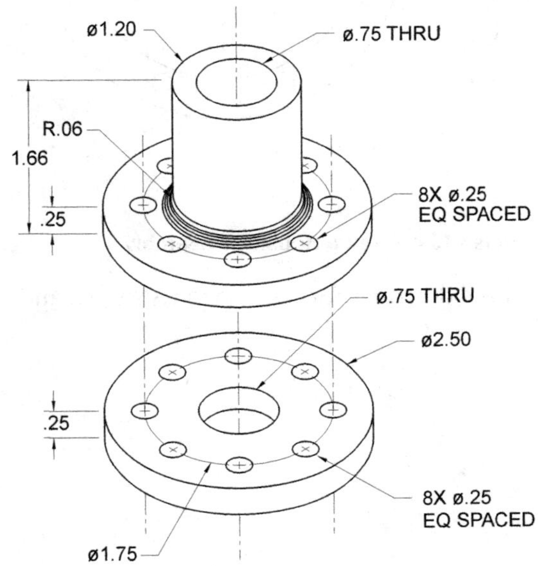

Exercise 13.3 Hub Assembly

Create an assembly drawing for the parts shown. Use eight bolts with nuts to assemble the parts.

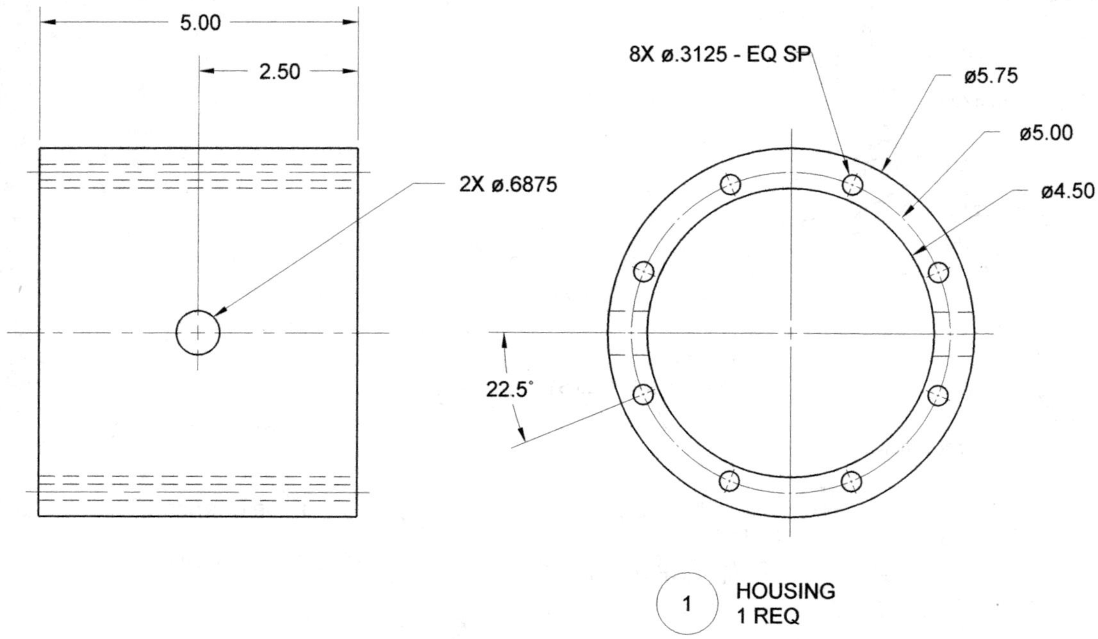

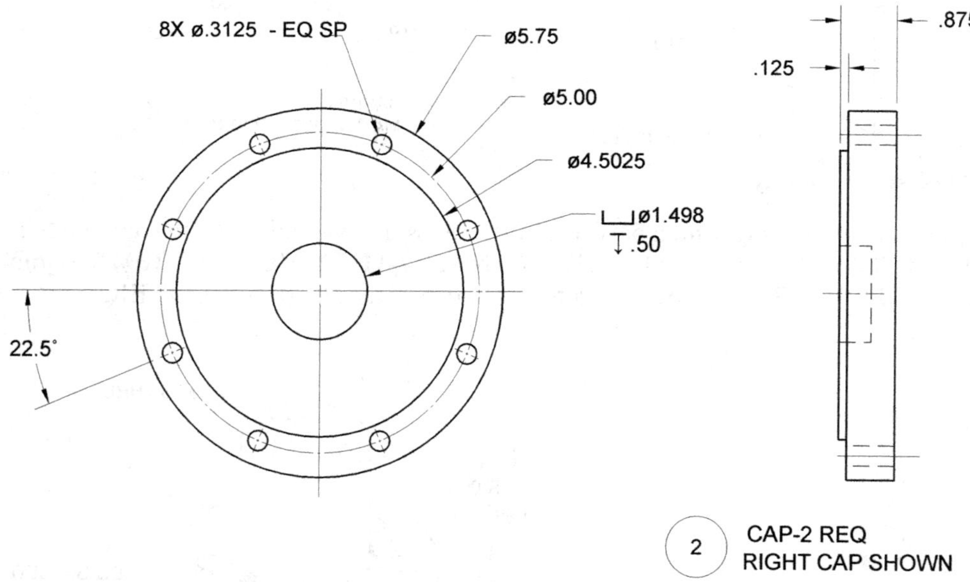

Exercise 13.4 Turbine Housing Assembly

Create detail drawings for the two parts shown and save each as a Wblock. Insert each block to form an assembly.

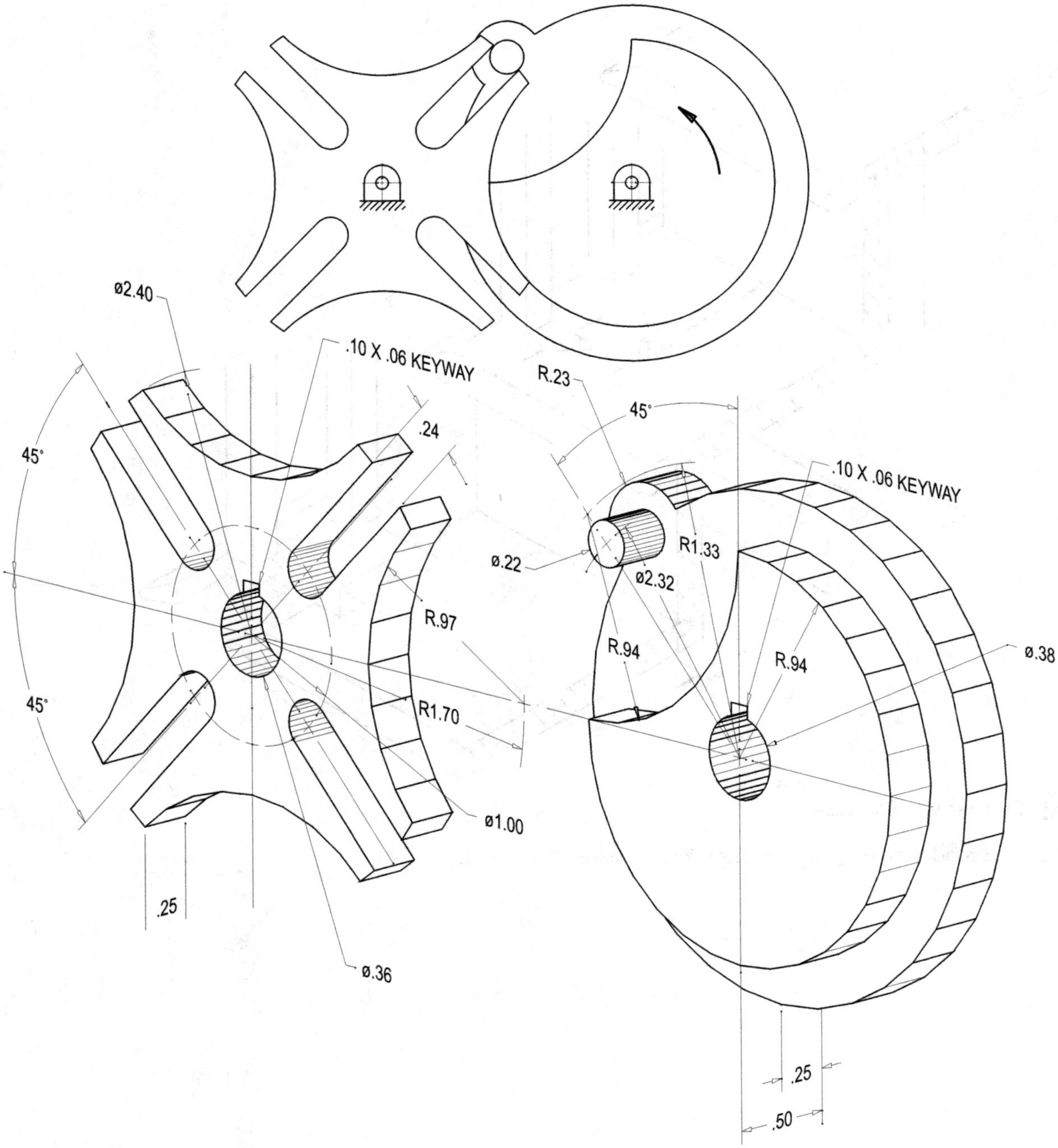

Exercise 13.5 Geneva Wheel Assembly

Create an assembly drawing for the parts shown, using solid modeling techniques. Experiment with different materials and analyze mass properties.

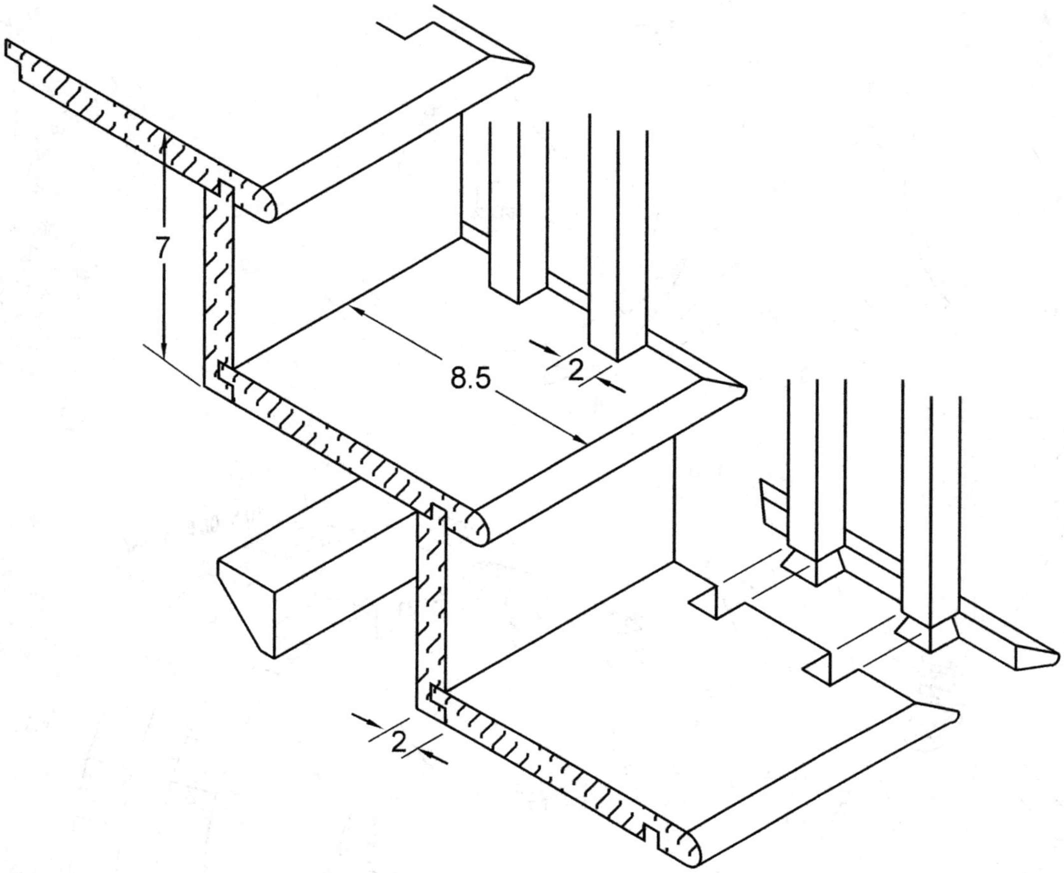

Exercise 13.6 Staircase

Use solid modeling to generate this staircase assembly detail.

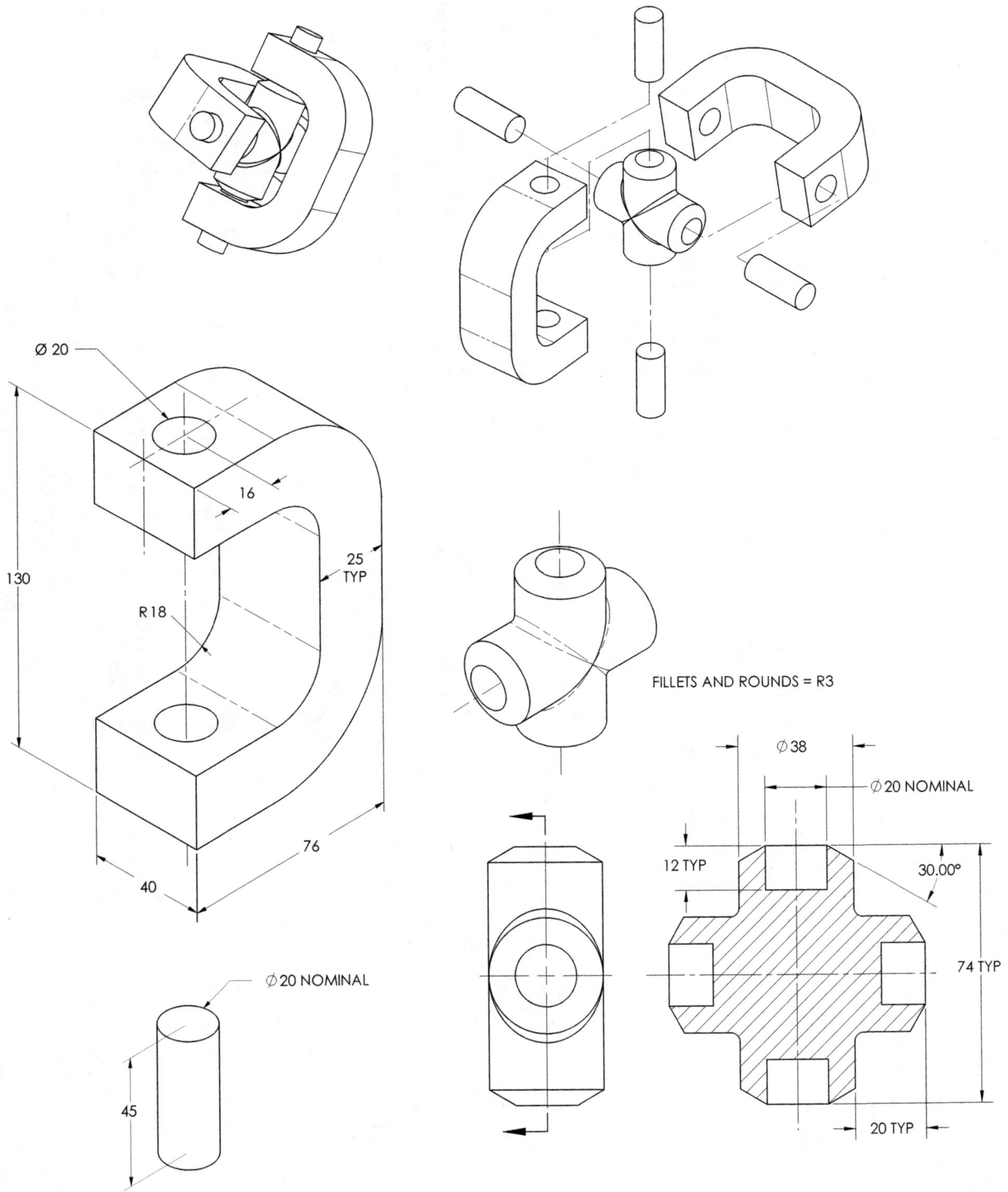

Exercise 13.7M Universal Joint

Create an assembly drawing for the parts shown, using solid modeling techniques. Analyze the mass properties of the parts.

SOLID MODELING FOR SECTION AND AUXILIARY VIEWS

14

Introduction

In this tutorial you will learn how to draw section and auxiliary views from 3D solid models. You can generate section and auxiliary views directly from solid models. Refer to Tutorial 9 for review.

Creating Sections from a Solid Model

This time you will start your drawing from a solid model template provided with the datafiles. It is similar to the object that you created in Tutorial 11.

Launch the AutoCAD software.

*Click: **New button***

*Use the **datafile anglsect.dwt** as a template for your new drawing.*

*Save it as **solsect.dwg**.*

*Select the **3D Modeling workspace**.*

*Set layer MYMODEL as the **current** layer.*

A drawing showing an angled mounting block appears on your screen, as shown in Figure 14.1.

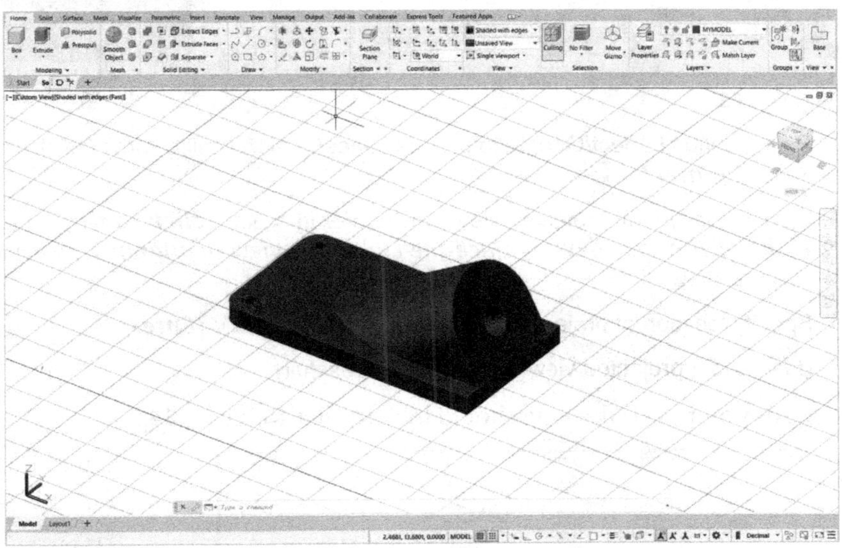

Figure 14.1

You will use layout command to create a drawing with a baseview and section view.

*On your own, switch to **Layout 1** showing **paperspace**.*

Objectives

When you have completed this tutorial, you will be able to

1. Show the internal surfaces of an object, using 3D section views.
2. Section a solid model.
3. Create an auxiliary view from a 3D model.

Tip: *If necessary, zoom and pan to enlarge the model inside the graphics area.*

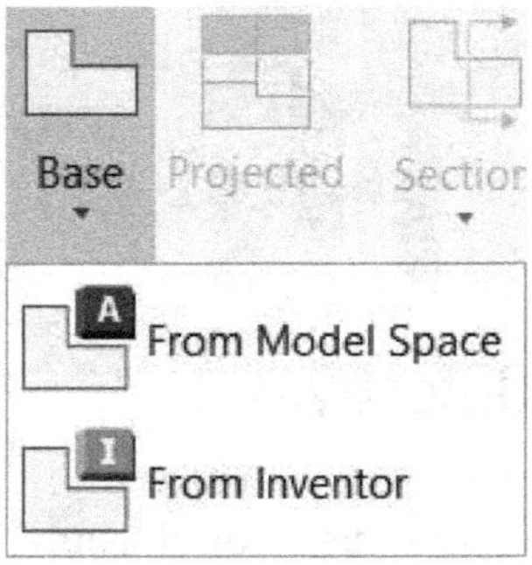

Tip: *This feature uses interoperability between AutoCAD and Inventor. If not already installed, you may have a wait time while it installs.*

The layout appears blank. You will use the Viewbase command to add the front view as the starting point for the drawing as in Figure 14.2.

 *Click:* ***Base View from Model Space*** *button from the Layout tab*

Specify location of base view or [Type/sElect/Orientation/Hidden lines/Scale/Visibility] <Type>: ***O [Enter]***

Select orientation [Current/Top/Bottom/Left/Right/Front/BAck/SW iso/SE iso/NE iso/NW iso] <Front>: ***T [Enter]***

The top view of the angled block appears at your cursor location similar to Figure 14.2.

Specify location of base view or [Type/sElect/Orientation/Hidden lines/Scale/Visibility] <Type>: ***click to place the top view***

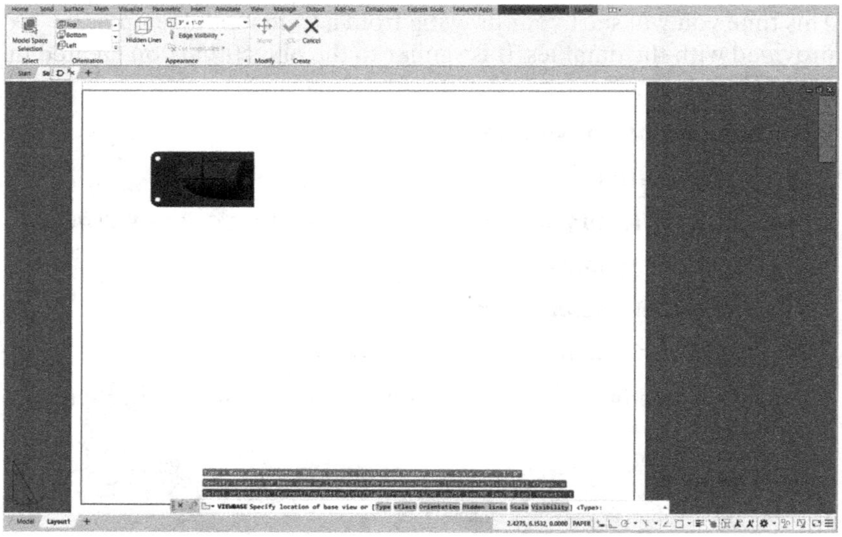

Figure 14.2

Select option [sElect/Orientation/Hidden lines/Scale/Visibility/Move/eXit] <eXit>: ***[Enter]***

Specify location of projected view or [Undo/eXit] <eXit>: ***click to the right of the top view*** *to place the right side view in alignment with the top view*

Specify location of projected view or [Undo/eXit] <eXit>: ***[Enter]***

Base and 2 projected view(s) created successfully.

At this point, your drawing should look similar to Figure 14.3.

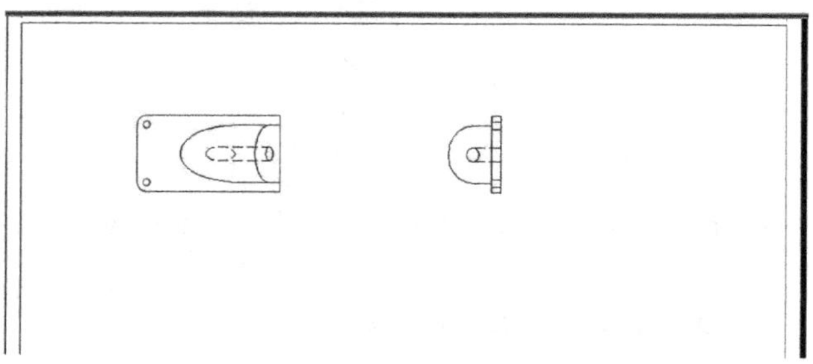

Figure 14.3

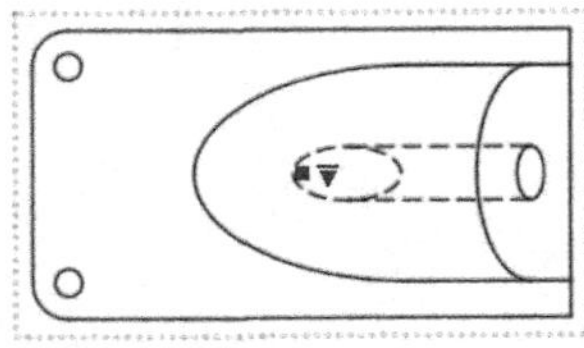

Click: ***on the top view*** *(the upper left view) to select it*

Click: ***Edit View***

Select view: ***click on the top view***

Select option [sElect/Hidden lines/Scale/Visibility/eXit] <eXit>: ***S [Enter}***

Enter scale <0.5000>: ***.5 [Enter]***

Select option [sElect/Hidden lines/Scale/Visibility/eXit] <eXit>: ***[Enter]***

On your own, click the side view and use the grip to reposition the view as needed.

The scale for the group of views changes to half-scale as compared to the model. Your drawing should be similar to Figure 14.4.

Tip: *You can change the scale from the drop-down list by picking 6"=1'.*

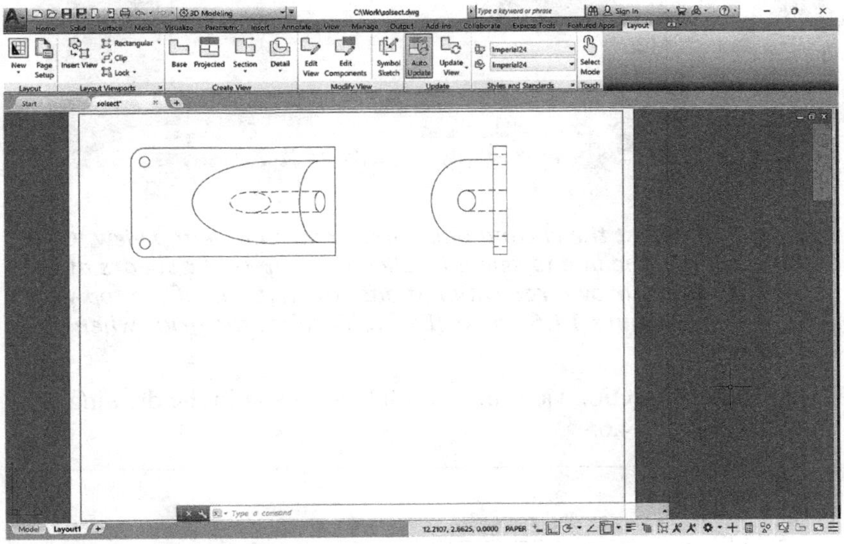

Figure 14.4

Adding a Section View

Next, you will add a section view to the drawing.

On your own, turn on object snap ***Midpoint*** *and* ***Object Snap Tracking****.*

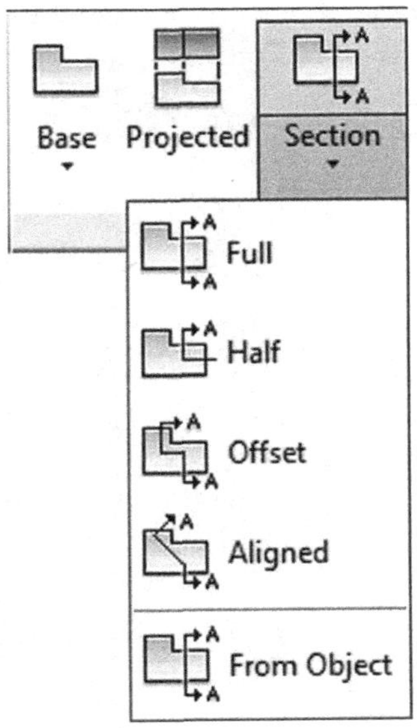

Click: ***Full*** *from the Section View list*

Select parent view: ***click on the top view***

Specify start point: ***use object snap Midpoint to target the left line in the top view*** *as shown in Figure 14.5; use the tracking line to select the endpoint for the cutting plane line*

Specify end point or [Undo]: ***with Ortho on, click past the right end of the top view***

Specify next point or [Undo/Done] <Done>: ***D [Enter]***

Specify location of section view or: ***click below the top view***

Select option [Hidden lines/Scale/Visibility/Projection/Depth/Annotation/hatCh/Move/eXit] <eXit>: ***[Enter]***

Notice that as you are positioning the view, the arrows on the cutting plane line adjust to point in the viewing direction for the section.

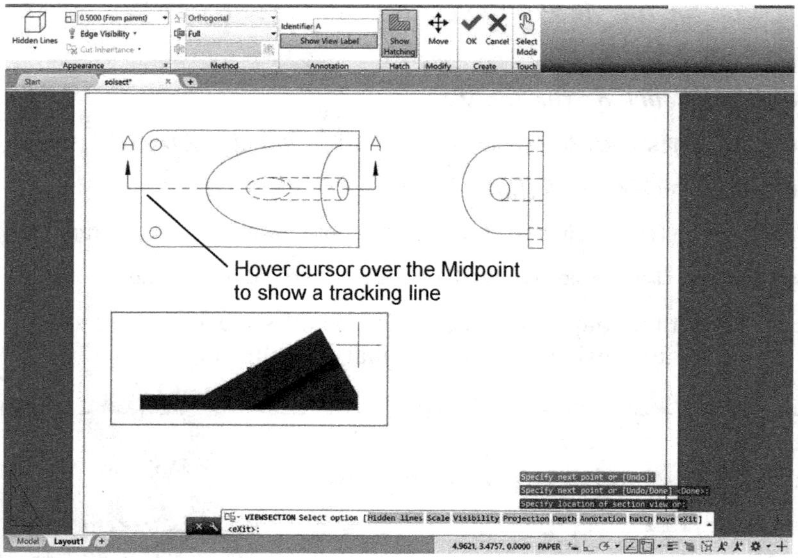

Figure 14.5

If needed, adjust the cutting plane line shown in the top view. Click the cutting plane line to select it. Click the grip that appears at the left end. On your own reposition it past the left end of the top view as shown in Figure 14.6. Press [Esc] to deselect the grips when you are finished.

The completed section view and view labels appear in the drawing as shown in Figure 14.6.

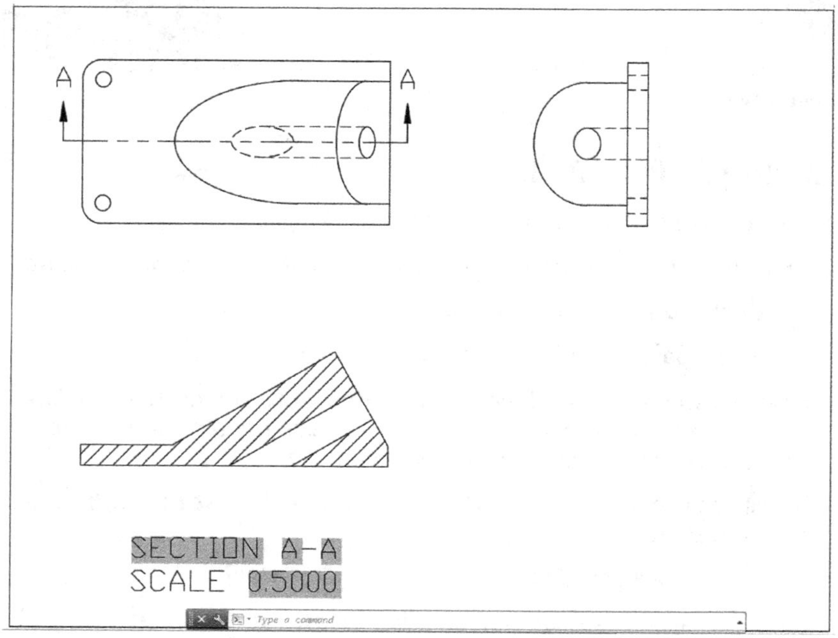

Figure 14.6

*On your own, use the **Layer Properties** from the Home tab to make the following changes. Leave the other layers as they were. When you are finished, close the Layer Properties Manager.*

Layer	**Color**	**Linetype**	**Lineweight**
MD_Annotation	RED	CONTINUOUS	0.25 mm
MD_Hatching	RED	CONTINUOUS	0.30 mm
MD_Hidden	BLUE	HIDDEN2	0.30 mm
MD_Visible	WHITE	CONTINUOUS	0.60 mm

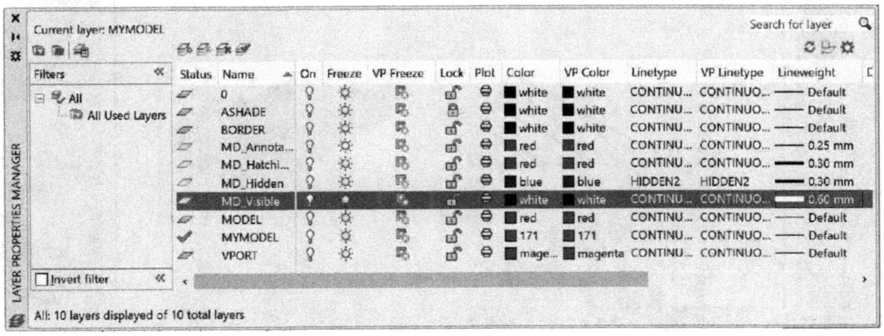

Figure 14.7

Click to Show ***Lineweight*** *using the button on the status bar.*

Use the Properties dialog to set the ***text height*** *for the view label to* ***.125****.*

Tip: Remember that you can use Draworder to locate the hatch behind or in front of the object outline.

Add centerlines *on your own.*

Save *your drawing before continuing.*

Adding a Shaded Isometric View

Next you will use add a small view port in the lower right to show a shaded isometric view.

On your own, ***set layer VPORT current****.*

Click: ***Rectangular*** *button from the Layout tab, Layout Viewports panel*

Specify corner of viewport or [ON/OFF/Fit/Shadeplot/Lock/Object/Polygonal/Restore/LAyer/2/3/4] <Fit>: ***click to set the first corner of the new viewport***

Specify opposite corner:]: ***click to set the diagonal corner***

The new viewport appears with a view of the model.

Double-click: ***inside the small viewport*** *to switch to model space inside that viewport*

On your own, use the view controls to set the view to use ***Shaded with Edges*** *and show a* ***SE Isometric*** *view.* ***Zoom*** *and* ***pan*** *to position the view inside the viewport.*

Tip: If the view is too small for you to work in, switch to paperspace and zoom to enlarge the viewport area on your screen. Then switch back to model space inside the viewport.

The isometric view appears as shown in Figure 14.8.

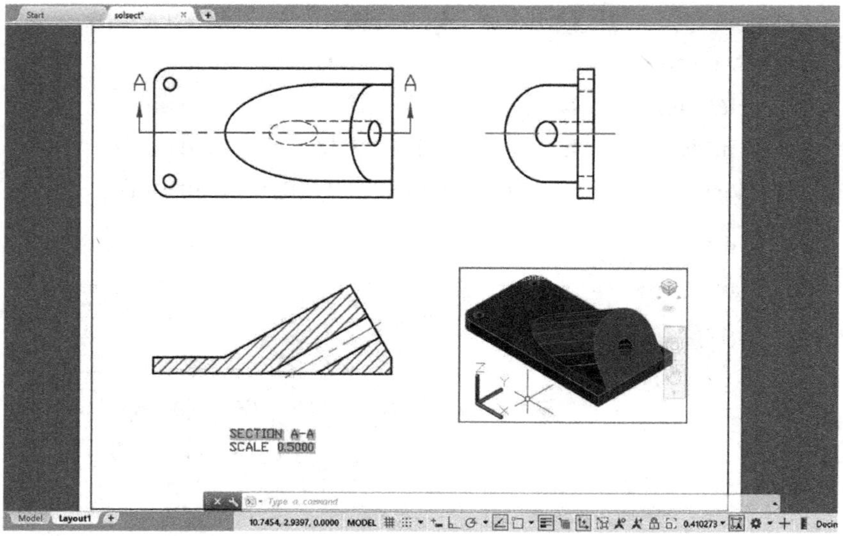

Figure 14.8

Using Section Plane

The Sectionplane command is used to create a section plane object, which represents a cutting plane. The section plane object can be used with the Livesection command to slice the part for visualization or with the Sectionplanetoblock command to generate blocks which can be placed to use as drawing views. Sectionplane can be used with 3D solids, surfaces, and meshes. When you are in the 3D Modeling workspace, Section Plane is available both from the ribbon Home tab, Section panel and from the Solid tab, Section panel. You will use the Solid tab to select it.

You will use the Midpoint running object snap to create a UCS through the center of the part. You will type the UCS command at the prompt. Refer to Figure 14.6 to make your selections.

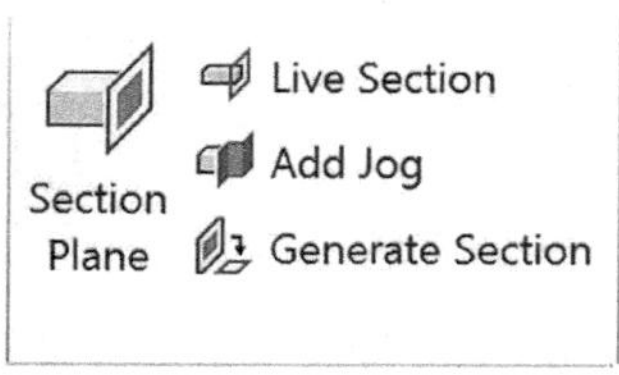

*Turn on running Object Snap for **Midpoint**.*

*Restore the **WCS** in the lower right viewport you just created.*

Click: in the small viewport to make it active

*Click: **Section Plane button** from the ribbon Solid tab, Section panel*

Select face or any point to locate section line or [Draw section/Orthographic]: ***O [Enter]***

Align section to: [Front/bAck/Top/Bottom/Left/Right] <Top>: ***F [Enter]***

The cutting plane object appears parallel to the front view.

In addition to the aligning to an Orthographic orientation relative to a UCS as you just did, you can also specify the cutting plane by choosing:

a *face* -aligns the cutting plane with any surface you select.

a *point* -select any point that is not on a face, then give a through point to define the plane of the section object.

Draw -prompts you for points through which the cutting plane passes. You can draw more than two points that are not in a line to create aligned and offset cutting planes.

Click: ***Generate Section button*** *from the ribbon Solid tab, Section panel*

Click: ***Select section plane button*** *from the dialog box*

Select section object: ***Click on the gray cutting plane***

Click: ***Create button*** *from the dialog box*

Specify insertion point or [Basepoint/Scale/X/Y/Z/Rotate/Explode/REpeat]: ***[Esc]***

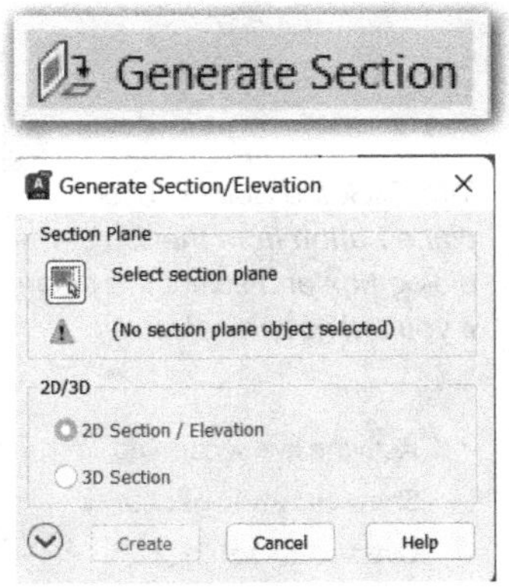

The model appears cut by the section plane as shown in Figure 14.9.

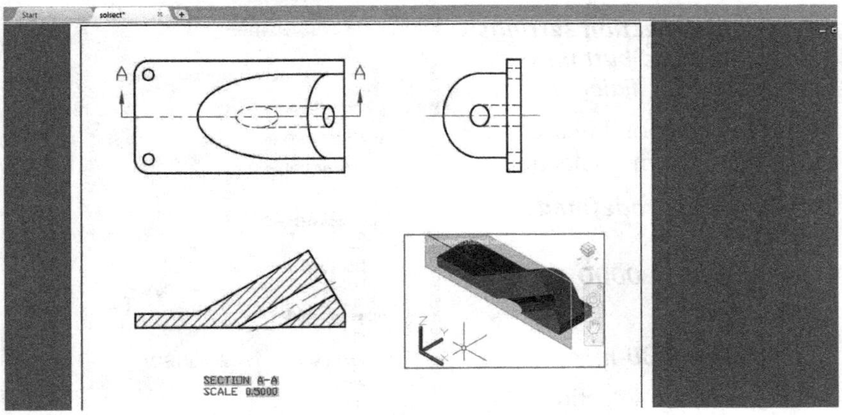

Figure 14.9

Using Live Section

Live section generates cross sections of 3D objects intersected by a section plane object. In the last step, the live section was generated in the same step as the Sectionplane. Next you will use Live Section to return the normal appearance of the object. This command also works the other way, to show the cut view.

Click: ***Live Section button***

Select section object: ***click on the gray section plane object***

Drag handles for the live section appear as shown in Figure 14.10.

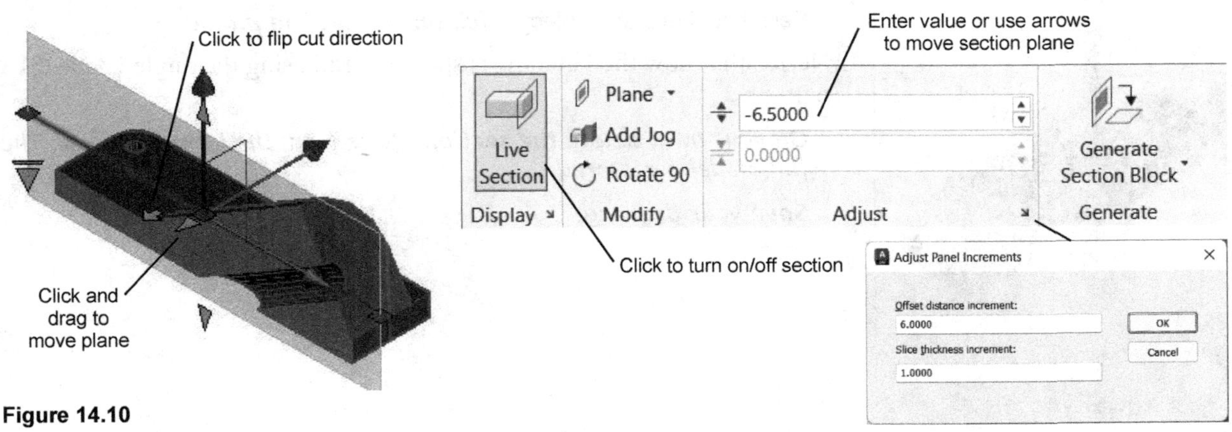

Figure 14.10

Section Settings

The Section Settings dialog box lets you control the appearance of 2D section blocks, 3D section blocks, and Live Sections.

To show the Section Settings dialog box,

Click: ***the gray section plane object*** *to select it*

Right-click: ***to show the menu***

Click: ***Live sections settings***

Tip: Click the Select section plane button from the top of the dialog box and select the plane if you did not preselect it.

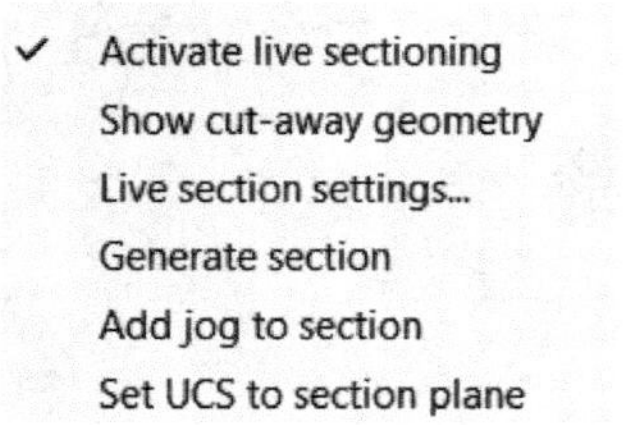

The dialog box appears on your screen.

Select: ***Live Section settings from the radio buttons near the top of the dialog box***

In the Intersection Fill area, make the following selections:

Face Hatch: ***Predefined ANSI31***

Hatch Scale: ***2.0000***

Color: ***Red***

Lineweight: ***0.30 mm***

Leave the other selections set to the defaults.

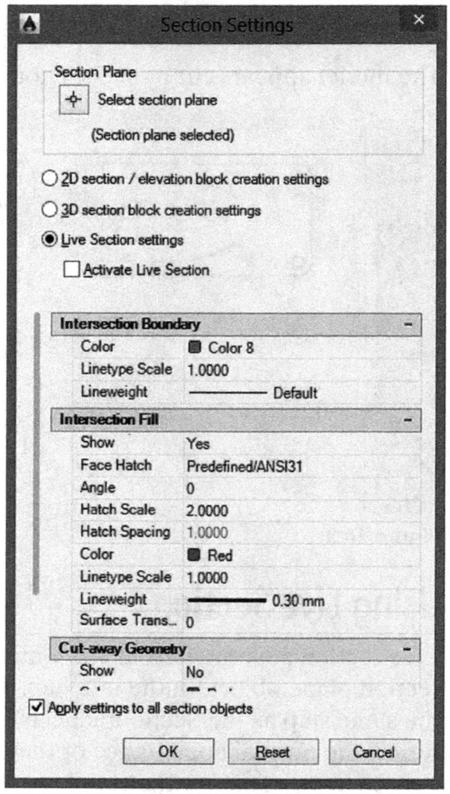

From the bottom of the dialog box,

Select: ***Apply settings to all section objects, so that it appears checked***

Click: ***OK to exit the dialog box.***

The settings are applied to the section in your drawing. To see them,

Click: ***Live Section button***

Select cutting plane object: ***click on the cutting plane***

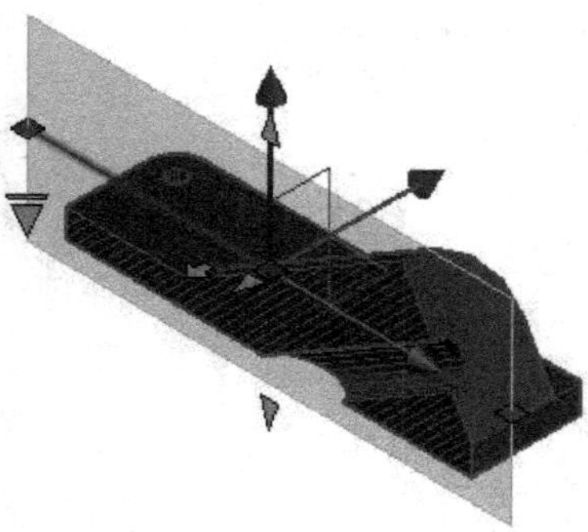

Notice that now the hatching is shown in red using the angled ANSI31 pattern.

On your own, ***delete the section plane*** *from the isometric view. The full model is restored.*

Save *your drawing.*

Creating an Auxiliary View from a 3D Model

You can easily create auxiliary views of 3D solid models by changing the viewpoint in any viewport to show the desired view. You can view the model from any direction inside any viewport. However, good engineering drawing practice requires that adjacent views align; otherwise, interpreting the drawing can be difficult or impossible. In general, you should show at least two principal orthographic views of the object. Additional views are sometimes placed in other locations on the drawing sheet or on a separate sheet. If you use a separate sheet, you should clearly label on the original sheet the view that is located elsewhere. When placing auxiliary views in other locations, you should show a viewing plane line, similar to a cutting plane line, that indicates the direction of sight for the auxiliary view. A viewing direction arrow can also be used to specify the viewing direction. You should clearly label the auxiliary view and preserve its correct orientation, rather than rotate it to a different alignment.

You will continue working with this drawing, creating an auxiliary view that shows the true size of the inclined surface.

You will add another viewport to show the auxiliary view. Layer VPORT should be current.

Viewports are paper space objects. Like any other object, you can modify them using Scale, Rotate, Stretch, and Copy, among other commands. To do so, you must be in paper space.

Verify that you are in paperspace.

Click: ***on the right side view at the upper right of the drawing*** *to select it (its grips show)*

Press: ***[Delete]***

That view is now deleted. Next you will move the isometric view into the upper right of the drawing.

Click: ***on the viewport border for the isometric view*** *to select it*

Right-click: ***pick Move*** *from the context menu*

Specify destination point or [Base point/eXit]: ***click near the center of the isometric view*** *and* ***click in the upper right*** *of the drawing area to reposition the view*

Click: ***Rectangular*** *from the Layout tab, Layout Viewports panel*

Specify corner of viewport or [ON/OFF/Fit/Shadeplot/Lock/Object/Polygonal/Restore/2/3/4] <Fit>: ***click point A***

Specify opposite corner: ***click point B***

The new viewport appears, as shown in Figure 14.11. The new view is the same as the isometric view. This is okay. You will create the auxiliary view in the viewport after a few more steps.

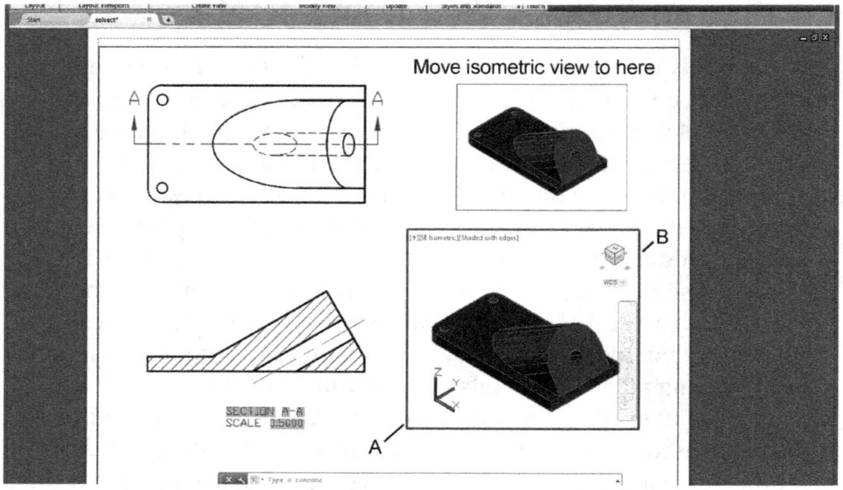

Figure 14.11

Orienting the View

You will reorient the view in the new viewport so that you can see the angled face clearly.

*Switch to **model space** inside the new viewport. If the viewport is difficult to select, click in any viewport and press **[CTRL]+R** until the center viewport is selected.*

*If necessary, **use the Steering wheel** to rotate the view of the angled face so that it is clearly visible.*

Next you will align the UCS with the angled surface and then use the Plan command inside the new viewport to show the view looking straight toward the UCS. The points you will select are shown in Figure 14.12.

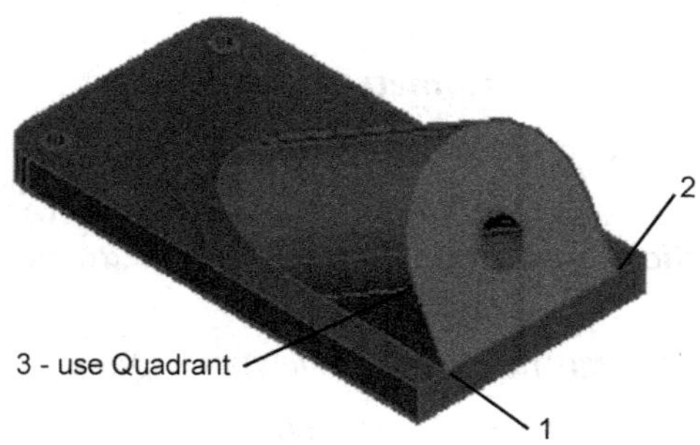

Figure 14.12

3 Point UCS

The 3 Point option of the UCS command creates a User Coordinate System that aligns with the three points you specify. You are prompted to click the origin, a point in the positive X-direction, and a point in the positive Y-direction. Refer to Figure 14.17 for the points to select.

First make sure the UCS icon is displayed at the origin of the coordinate system.

Command: ***UCSICON [Enter]***

Enter an option [ON/OFF/All/Noorigin/ORigin/Properties] <ON>: ***OR [Enter]***

On your own, be sure that Object Snap is active with **Endpoint** and **Quadrant** selected.

*Click: **3 Point UCS button** from the Vizualize tab, Coordinates panel*

Specify new origin point <0,0,0>: ***click Endpoint 1***

Specify point on positive portion of the X-axis <14.000,4.5000,0.5000>: ***click Endpoint 2***

Specify point on positive-Y portion of the UCS XY plane <12.0000,4.5000,0.5000>: ***click on the upper curved line at point 3, using Object Snap to Quadrant***

Tip: *You can click and drag the UCSicon to align it to the angled face.*

The UCS icon should appear aligned with the angled face. This is important because it tells you that the User Coordinate System is correctly aligned with the angled surface. Make sure that the coordinate system appears parallel to the angled face as shown in Figure 14.13.

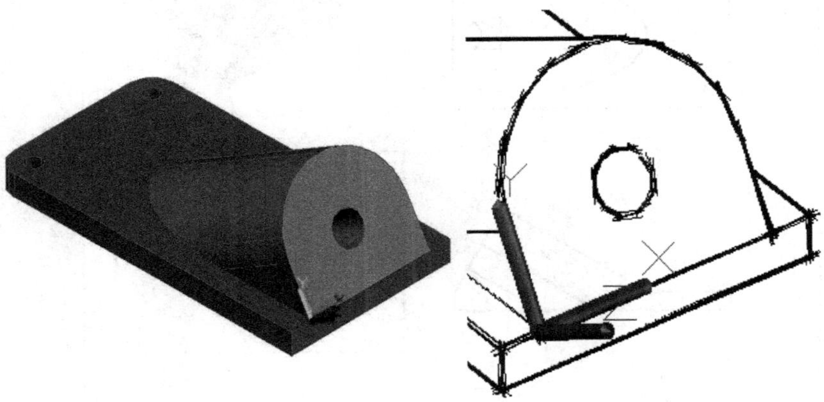

Figure 14.13

Using Plan

The Plan command aligns the viewpoint in the active viewport so that you are viewing the current UCS, a named UCS, or the WCS straight on. You will accept the default, the current UCS, to show the true size view of the angled surface, with which you have already aligned the coordinate system. You will type the Plan command at the command prompt.

*On your own, change the visual style for the viewport to **Wireframe**.*

Command: ***PLAN [Enter]***

Enter an option [Current ucs/Ucs/World] <Current>: ***[Enter]***

The view in the center viewport changes so that you are looking straight at the angled surface as shown in Figure 14.14. Next you will name and save this view so it can easily be restored.

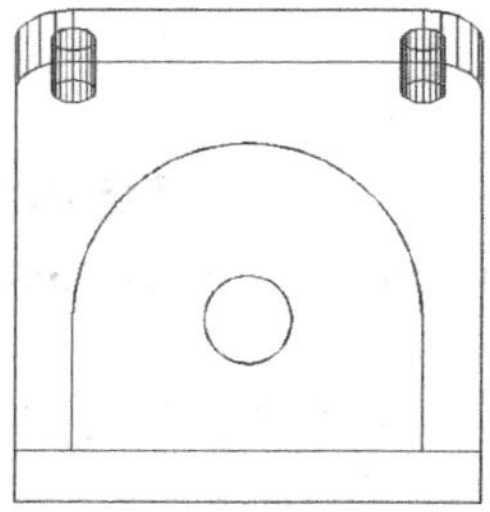

Figure 14.14

Command: ***VIEW [Enter]***

*Select **New** and name the new view **PlaneTrueSize**. When you have finished, **exit** the dialog box. Use the Viewport control to select the Custom view. Pan the view to fit inside the viewport.*

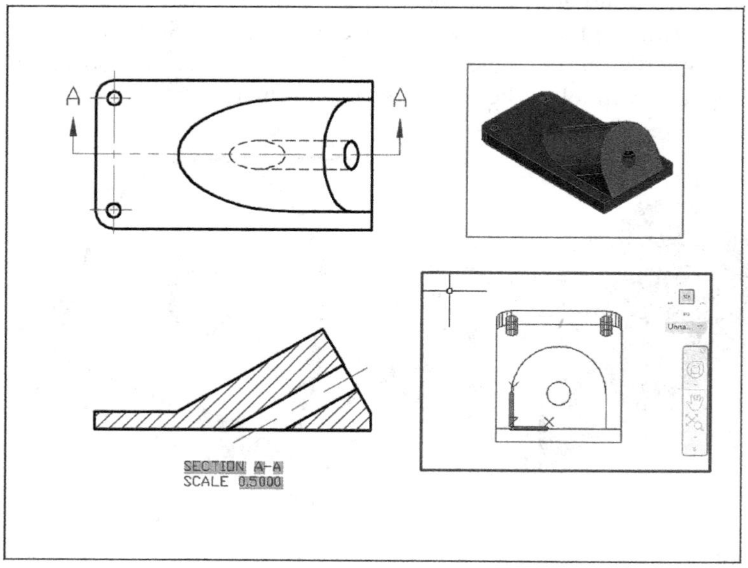

Figure 14.15

Next set the Viewport Scale to half size for the new view. The original views were at half size in the data file.

*On your own, switch to **paper space**.*

*Click: **the new viewport** to select it*

*Click: **6"=1'** from the Viewport Scale list on the status bar*

*Switch to **model space** inside the center viewport. Use the Pan to center the view inside the viewport on your own.*

Using 3D Dynamic View

The 3D Dynamic View command uses the metaphor of a camera and a target, where your viewing direction is the line between the camera and the target. It is called 3D Dynamic View because while you are in the command, you can see the view of the selected objects change dynamically on the screen when you move your pointing device. If you do not select any objects for use with the command, you see a special block shaped like a 3D house instead. Use AutoCAD Help to discover more information about the options of the 3D Dynamic View command.

In the next steps you will use the 3D Dynamic View command with the Twist option to twist the viewing angle. You will type DVIEW at the command prompt. The angled surface is at 60° in the front view. You will type 30 for the twist angle, which will produce a view that is aligned 90° to the front view.

*On your own, switch to **model space** inside the new viewport.*

Command: ***DVIEW [Enter]***

Select objects or <use DVIEWBLOCK>: ***click the 3D model [Enter]***

Enter option [CAmera/TArget/Distance/POints/PAn/Zoom/TWist/CLip/Hide/Off/Undo]: ***TW [Enter]***

Specify view twist angle <0.00>: ***30 [Enter]***

CAmera/TArget/Distance/POints/PAn/Zoom/TWist/CLip/Hide/Off/Undo/<exit>: ***[Enter]***

The view is twisted 30° to align with the edge view of the angled surface. Your screen should look like Figure 14.16.

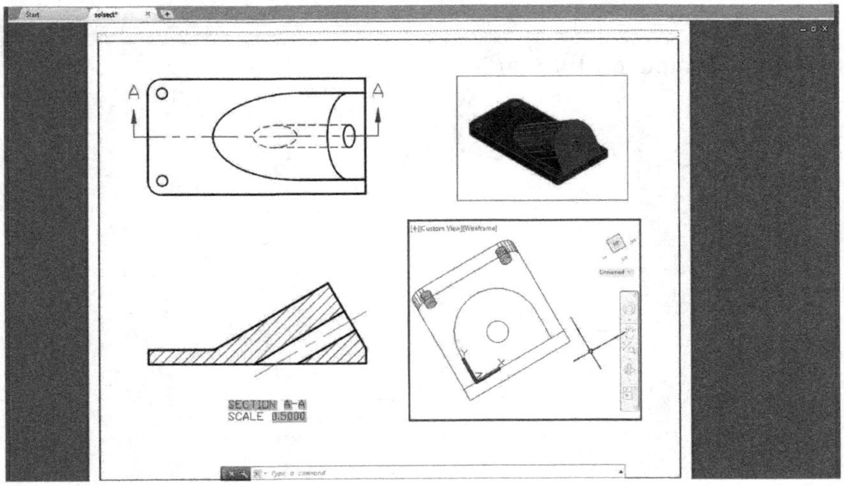

Figure 14.16

*On your own, switch to **paper space** and use the hot grips to **stretch the viewport** so that it is large enough to show the entire object. You may need to move the upper right viewport showing the pictorial view further up to make room.*

*Use the grips and **lengthen the centerline** from the front section view to extend it into the true size auxiliary view in the lower right viewport.*

***Pan** the auxiliary view so that the center of the hole lines up with the centerline.*

*When you have it sized as you want, set layer **MYMODEL** as the **current layer**.*

*Freeze layer VPORT. **Save** your drawing.*

When you have finished, your screen should be similar to Figure 14.17. Dimensions can be added in paper space to complete the drawing.

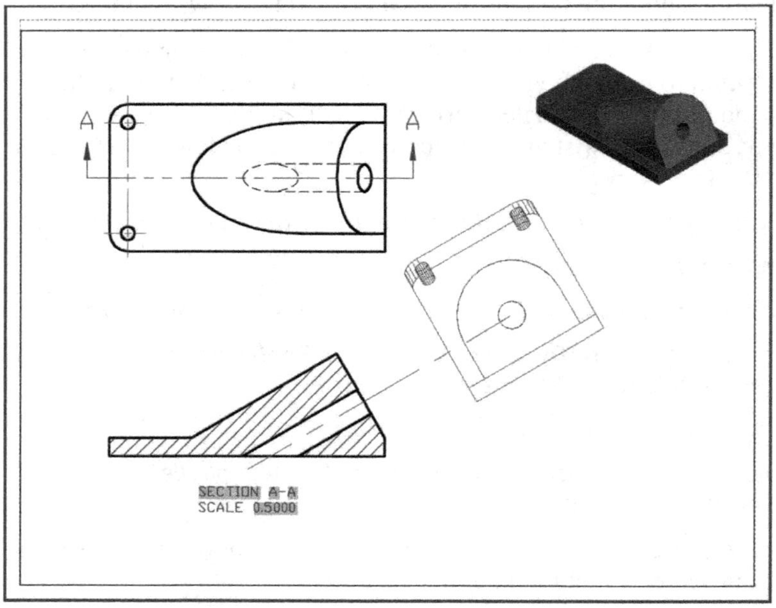

Figure 14.17

You have completed Tutorial 14.

Tip: *If you have trouble clicking inside a viewport because it overlaps other viewports, type [Ctrl]-R to toggle the viewport.*

Tip: *When viewports overlap you may notice some viewing issues in the software.*

Tip: *You can set the Ucsfollow variable to generate the plan view of the current UCS automatically. Pick in a viewport to make it active and then set Ucsfollow to 1. The AutoCAD software automatically generates a plan view of the current UCS in that viewport whenever you change the UCS.*

Tip: *You can use generate hidden and visible lines for the auxiliary view as follows:*

Command: **SOLPROF** *[Enter]*

Select objects: *pick the solid object in the auxiliary viewport and press [Enter].*

Display hidden profile lines on a separate layer? <Y>: *[Enter]*

Project profile lines onto a plane? <Y>: *[Enter]*

Delete tangential edges? <Y>: *[Enter]*

Change *the linetype and color of the PH- layers to hidden and blue with lineweight 0.30 mm. Set the lineweight for the PV- layers to 0.60 mm. Freeze layer MYMODEL in this viewport only (using the Current VP Freeze selection from the Layer Control).*

Key Terms

cutting plane line

pictorial full section

section view

Key Commands

3 Point UCS

3D Dynamic View (DVIEW)

Hide

Livesection

Object UCS

Sectionplane

Sectionplanetoblock

Setup Drawing

Soldraw

Solview

Setup View (Solview)

Viewbase

Exercises

Use solid modeling to create the parts shown. Section the part along the vertical centerline in the front view. The letter M after an exercise means that the given dimensions are in millimeters.

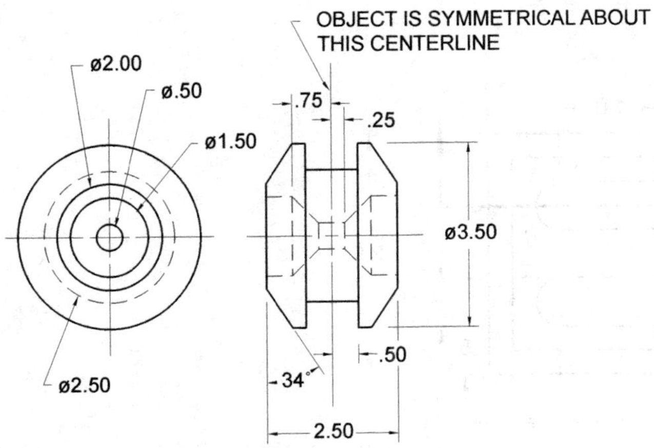

Exercise 14.1 High-Pressure Seal

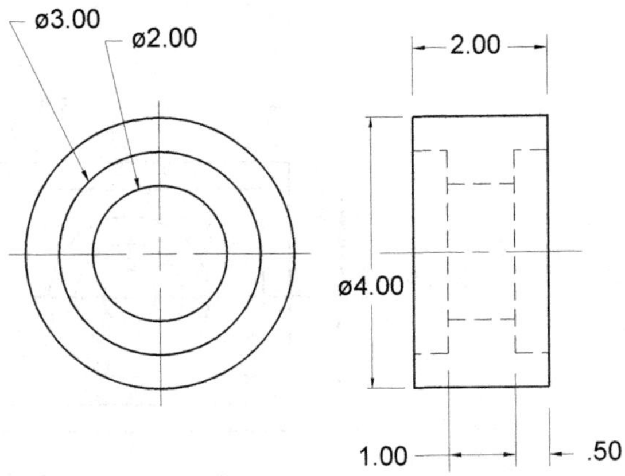

Exercise 14.2 Valve Cover

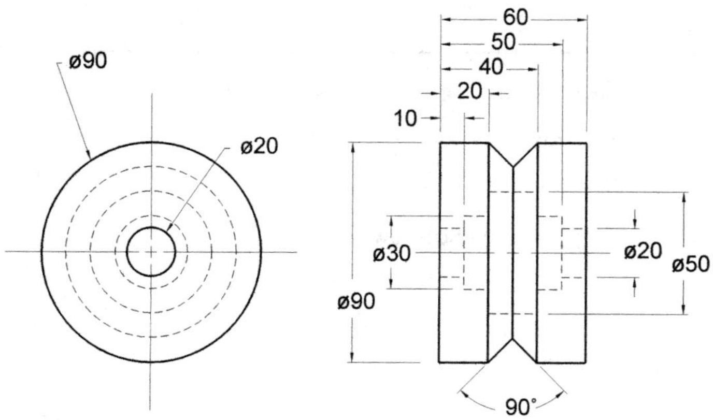

Exercise 14.3M Pulley

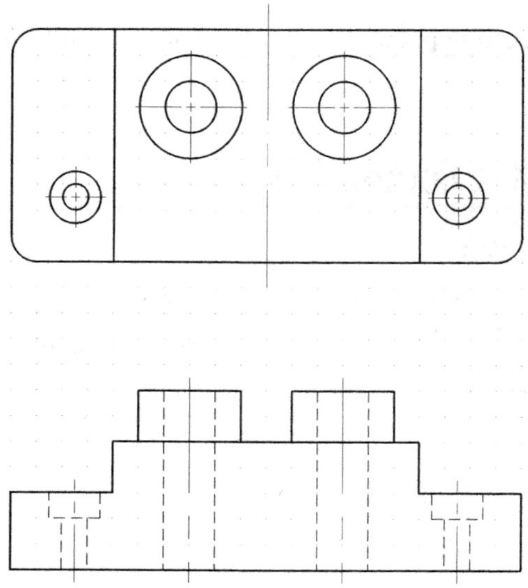

Exercise 14.4 Double Cylinder

Use solid modeling to draw this object; the grid shown is 0.25 inch. Show the front view as a half section and show the corresponding cutting plane in the top view. On the same views, completely dimension the object to the nearest 0.01 inch. Include any notes that are necessary.

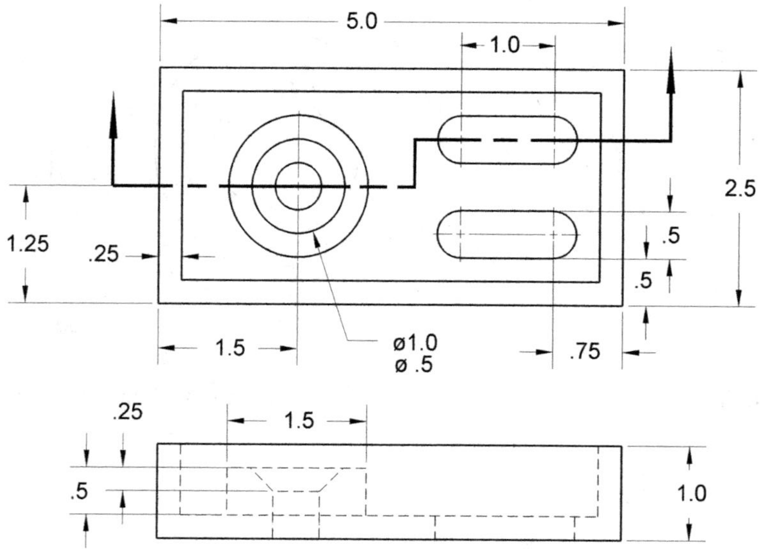

Exercise 14.5 Plate

Use solid modeling to construct the part. Make a drawing with the top view showing the cutting plane and show the front view in section.

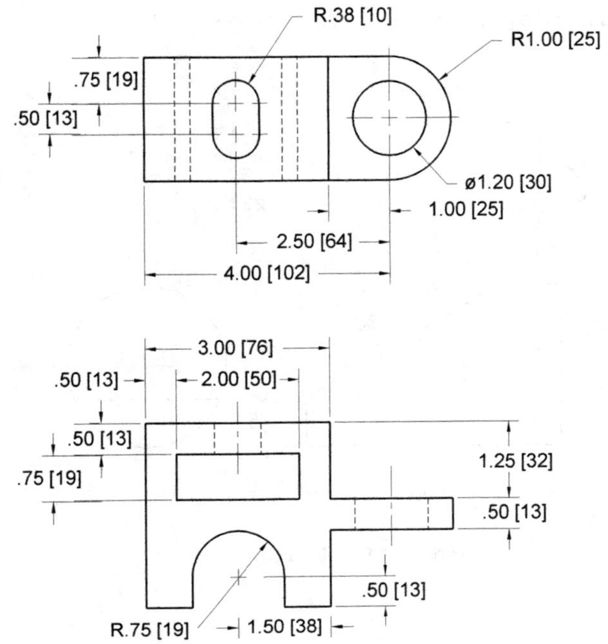

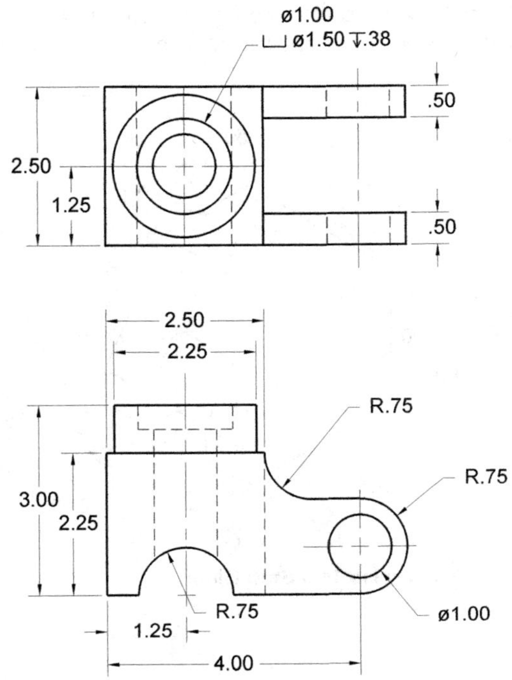

Exercise 14.6 Support Bracket

Create a solid model of the object shown, then produce a plan view and full section front view. Note the alternate units in brackets; these are the dimensions in millimeters for the part.

Exercise 14.7 Shaft Support

Generate the given front view from your solid model and create a section view. Assume that the vertical centerline of the shaft in the front view is the cutting plane line for the section view.

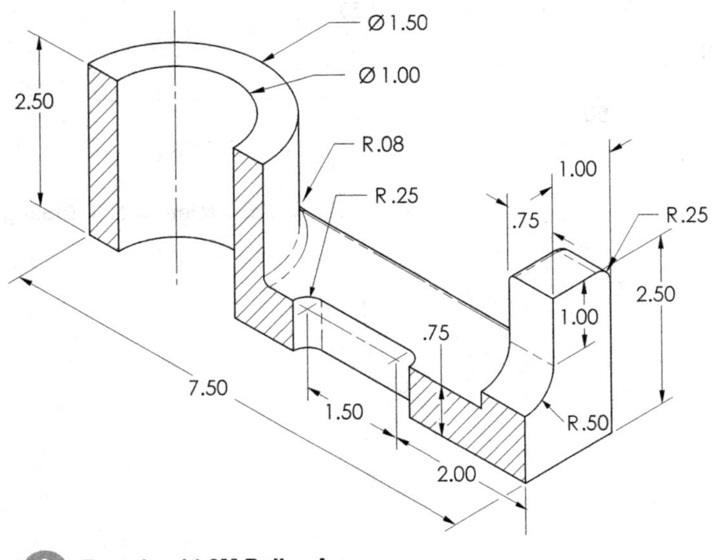

Exercise 14.8M Pulley Arm

Use solid modeling to create a pictorial view like the one shown.

Use the 2D or solid modeling techniques you have learned in the tutorial to create an auxiliary view of the slanted surfaces for the objects below. The letter M after an exercise number means that the given dimensions are in millimeters.

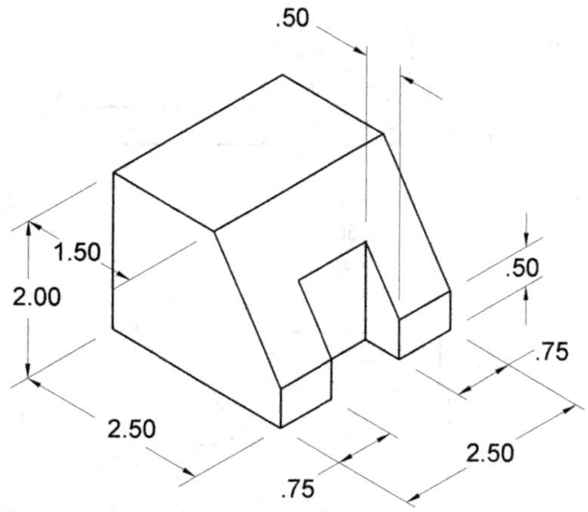

Exercise 14.9 Stop Block

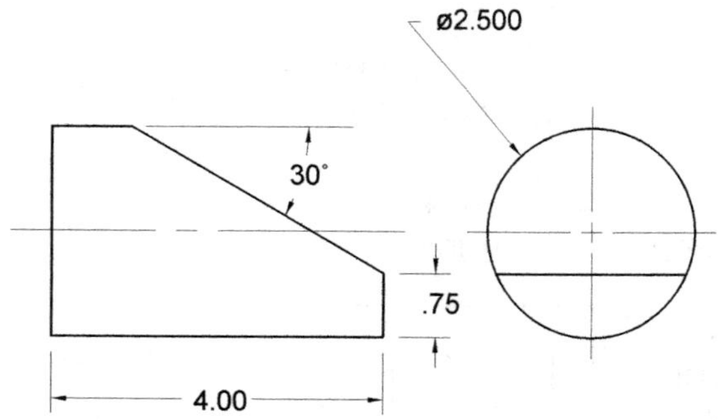

Exercise 14.10 Bearing

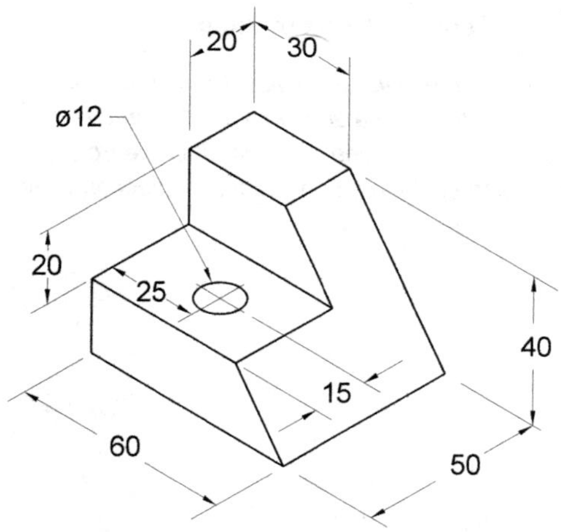

Exercise 14.11 Level

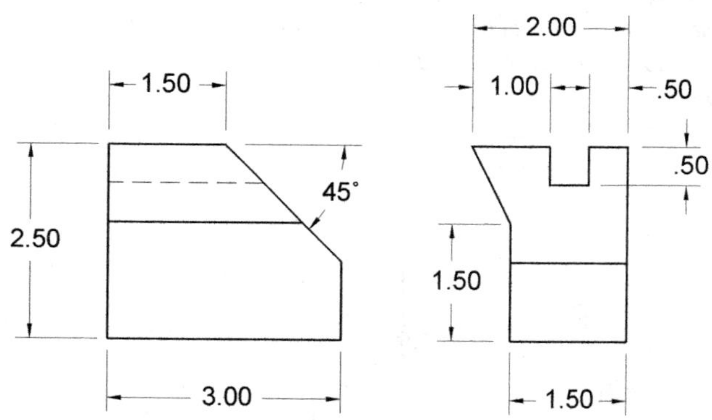

Exercise 14.12M Tooling Support

RENDERING

15

Introduction

The *Render* command allows the creation of rendered images of AutoCAD objects that have surfaces. Rendering is the process of calculating the lighting effects, color, and shape of an object to produce a single view. A rendered view adds greatly to the appearance of the drawing. It makes the object appear more real and aids in interpretation of the object's shape, especially for those unfamiliar with engineering drawings. Rendered drawings can be used very effectively in creating presentations.

AutoCAD objects that have surfaces can be rendered. Objects that have surfaces include solid models, regions, and objects created with the AutoCAD surface modeling commands.

Rendering is a mathematically complex process. When you are rendering, the capabilities of your hardware, such as speed, amount of memory, and the resolution of the display, are particularly noticeable. The complex calculations demand more of your hardware, so you may notice that your system seems slower. Resolution affects not only the speed with which objects are rendered,but also the quality of the rendered appearance. Better appearance can be gained by rendering to a higher resolution and more colors; however, increased resolution and more colors take longer to render.

In this tutorial you will apply materials, surface maps, and lighting to your drawing and to render realistic views of it. Applying a material to a surface in your drawing gives the surface its color and shininess, similar to painting the surface. Materials can also reflect light like a mirror or be transparent like glass. Adding a surface map is similar to adding wallpaper; surface maps are patterns or pictures that you can apply to the surface of an object. Lighting illuminates the surfaces. Lighting is very important in creating the desired effect in your rendered drawing.

In addition to single views, views can be rendered sequentially to produce the sense of motion, similar to the way a flip book works. You can use this to create animations for presentations and snapshot views for navigating through a complex drawing.

Starting

In this tutorial you will use Render to shade a solid model.

Launch AutoCAD.

*Start a **new** drawing **from** the **GuidePart.dwg** provided with the datafiles.*

*Save your drawing as **GuideRender.dwg**.*

The drawing appears on your screen, as shown in Figure 15.1.

Objectives

When you have completed this tutorial, you will be able to

1. Realistically shade a solid model or surface mesh-modeled drawing.
2. Set up and use lighting effects.
3. Apply materials.
4. Save rendered files for use with other programs.

The Render palette is found on the Visualize tab of the 3D Modeling workspace. Check that you have this workspace active.

Click: ***Visualize tab***

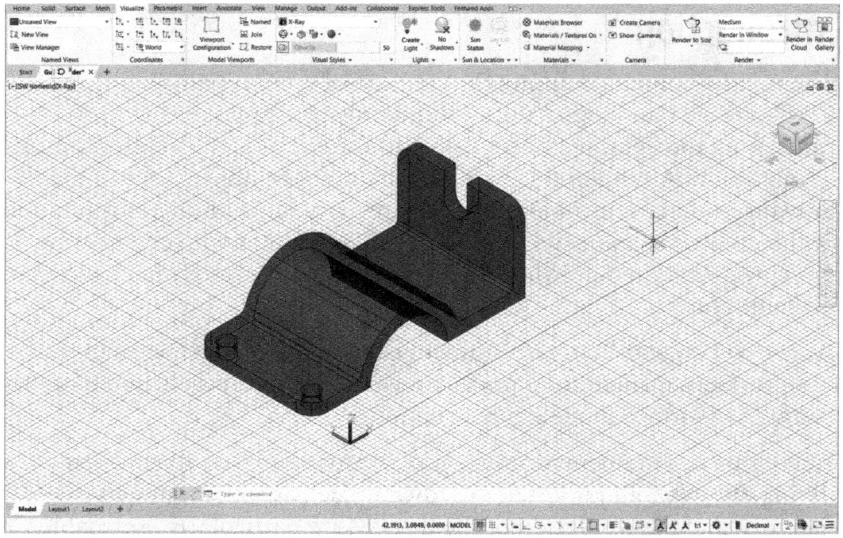

Tip: *Turn off the grid if you do not like its appearance.*

Figure 15.1

The Visualize tab has the following default panels: Named Views, Coordinates, Model Viewports, Visual Styles, Lights, Sun and Location, Materials, Camera, and Render. Each of these panels provides settings that control the resulting image when you render your model. For the beginner many of the settings can be left set at the defaults. In general, when you have a number of settings, it is best to make small changes and view the result, rather than making a number of changes at once.

The Render Panel

Render Preset List/Select Render Preset

At the top of the Render panel (Figure 15.2) is a list of standard render presets ranging from lowest to highest quality. It also allows access to the Render Presets Manager.

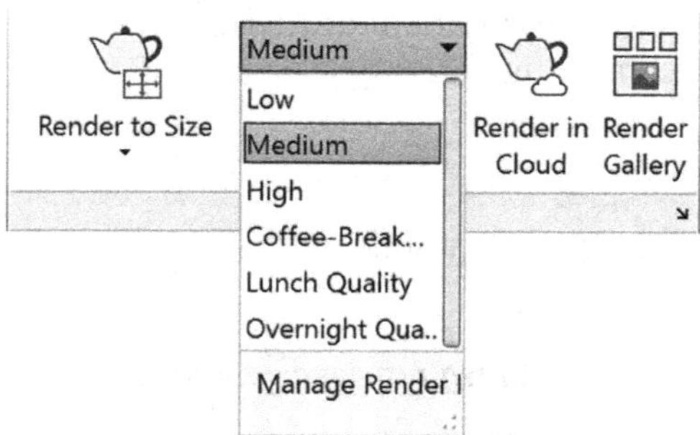

Figure 15.2

Click: to expand the Render Preset list

The rendering presets that control the quality of the output image are low, medium, high, coffee break quality, lunch quality, and overnight quality.

Low - This preset is best used for test renders that do not require much detail. It uses just 1 rendering level and therefore is quicker.

Medium - The Medium preset offers a good balance between quality and render speed. It uses 5 rendering levels to provide a better quality image.

High - The Height preset takes longer to process, but the image quality is much better. It uses 10 rendering levels.

Coffee Break - This method renders the image for as many levels as it takes during 10 minutes of rendering. The quality is improved and you have time to go get coffee before you see results.

Lunch Quality - This is used for high-quality, photo-realistic rendered images. This method renders for 60 minutes.

Overnight Quality - This method renders for 12 hours and produces the best results.

When you are rendering, the best approach is to start with the least time consuming method and progress to more detailed renderings. This way, while you are working out the details of how to set up the lighting and surfaces for a realistic appearance, you do not have to wait a long time for a complex rendering. For this tutorial, you will use the Medium preset setting.

Click: ***Manage Render Presets***

The Render Presets Manager appears on your screen as shown in Figure 15.3. You can add your own custom presets or review and change the standard ones.

On your own, explore the various presets. Close the Render Presets Manager dialog box when you are done reviewing.

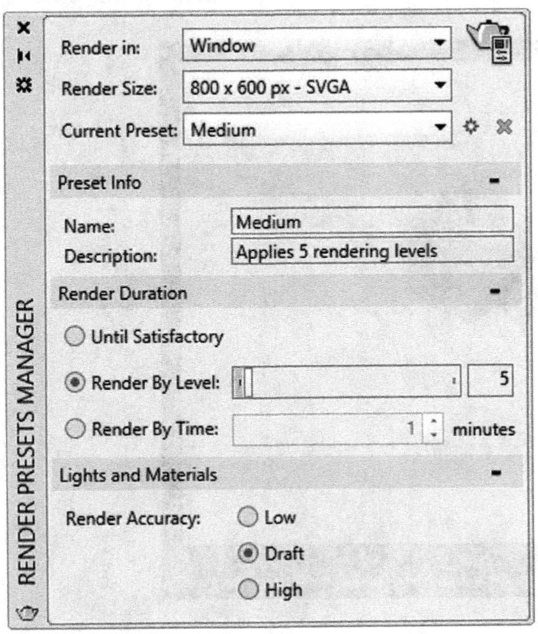

Figure 15.3

Render

Tip: *If prompted whether to install the medium images library, do so.*

Rendering generates a realistically shaded image of the model. Use low settings to start out so you may see the results quickly when you are testing your rendering choices. Producing the best appearance often takes a sequence of changing settings, lighting, and materials a bit at a time.

Several options for rendering to different sizes are available from the drop down selection.

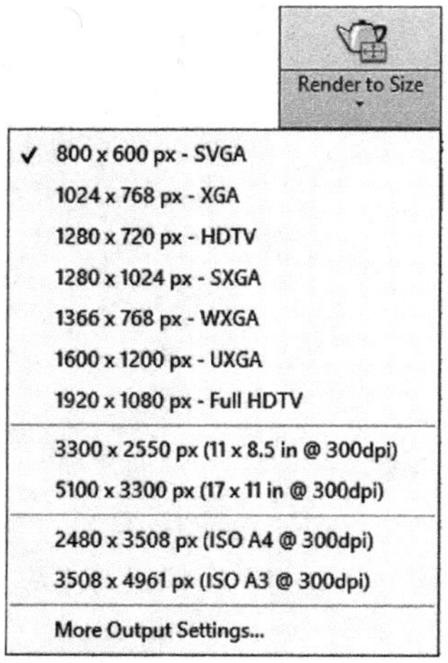

Click: to expand the choices below Render to Size

Click: ***800 x 600 px - SVGA***

The selections are the number of pixels in the image that is generated during rendering. You can use the More Output Settings selection to define your own custom size and pixels per inch (dpi). 300 dpi is typically used for printed images, 72 to 96 dpi is typical for images on the web. You can calculate the size of your image by dividing the total pixels by the number of pixels per inch that will be used. For example, a 4" × 6" photo (1/4 page) for a magazine or report needs to be at least 1200 x 1800 pixels to print at 300 dpi.

Click: ***X to close the Render Presets Manager***

Click: ***Render to Size***

The Render Window

The render window appears on your screen with the generated rendering of the object similar to Figure 15.4. The rendered image looks very similar to your original drawing. This is because there are no lights or material added. You will add those later in this tutorial. The more complex the calculations, the more time it will take to render.

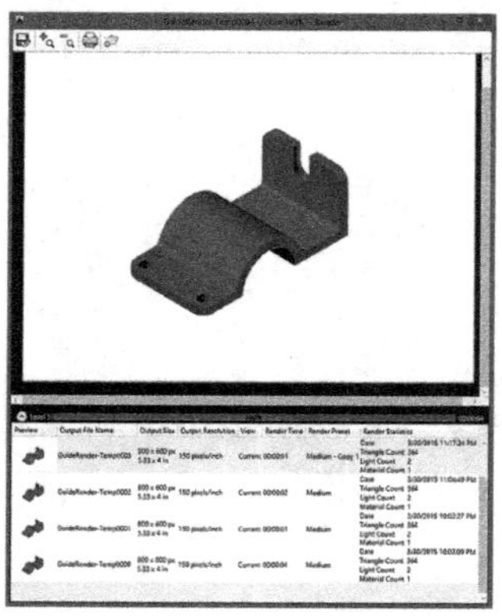

Tip: *Click the down arrow to the left of the progress bar to expand the render information.*

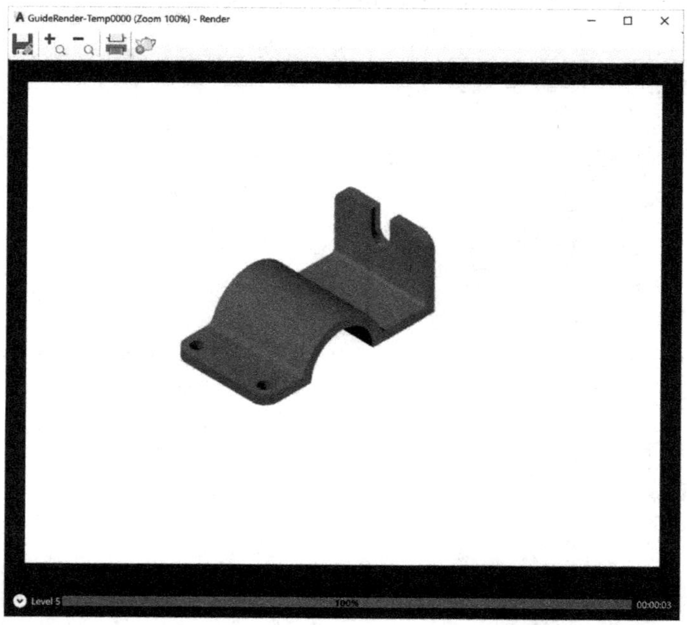

Figure 15.4

Render Progress Shows a visual bar representing the percentage complete for the rendering. This allows you to estimate how much longer the rendering will take.

Render Window Buttons The render window has buttons at its upper left for Save, Zoom In, Zoom Out, Print, and Cancel. When saving from the render window, you have options for the following file types.

- **BMP (*.bmp)** Still-image bitmap file in the Windows bitmap (*.bmp*) format.
- **TGA (*.tga)** File format that supports 32-bit true color; (24-bit color plus an alpha channel). It is typically used as a true color format.
- **TIF (*.tif)** Multiplatform bitmap format.
- **JPEG (*.jpg)** Popular format for posting image files on the Internet for minimum file size and minimum download time.
- **PNG (*.png)** Still-image file format developed for use with the Internet and World Wide Web.

*Click: **Saves the rendered image to a file button***

The File dialog box appears on the screen as shown in Figure 15.5.

*On your own, **expand the options for Files of type**. Select one and save your rendered image.*

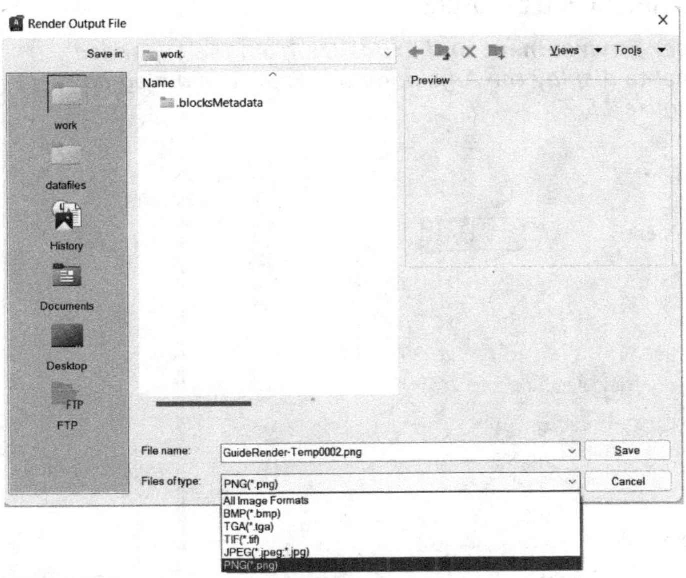

Figure 15.5

Close the Render window.

Render Output Settings

You can use features available from the Render Size Output Settings dialog box to select that the rendered image be written to a file in the location and filename you specify in the input box area. You can browse to select using the ellipsis (...) selection at the right, when the Automatically save rendered image check box is selected.

Click: ***More Output Settings*** *from the Render to Size drop down list*

Tip: *For good print quality you will generally want to use a resolution of 300 pixels/inch. For images to be shown on the web 96 pixels/inch may be plenty.*

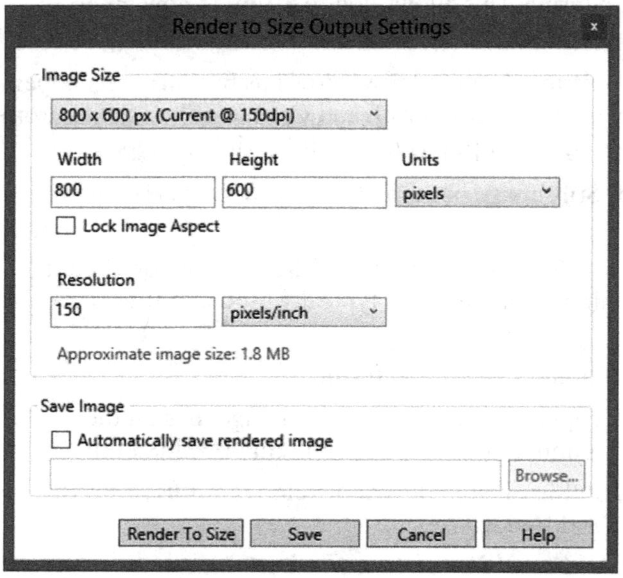

Figure 15.6

Close the Render to Size Output Settings dialog box

Render Environment and Exposure

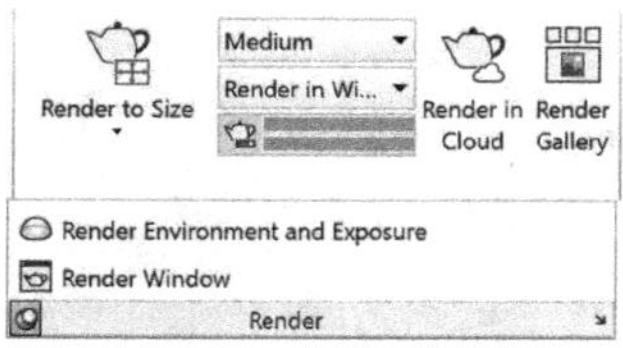

Click: ***Render Environment and Exposure*** *from the expanded Render panel to display the Adjust Render Exposure dialog box shown in Figure 15.7*

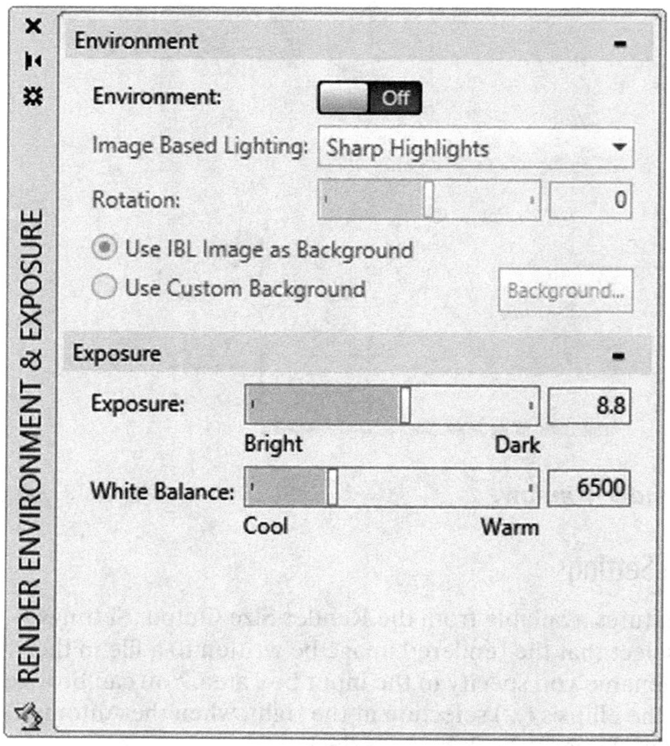

Figure 15.7

Environment Turns on and off the use of Image Based Lighting (IBL) effects, which provide a number of background images with preset lighting effects for easy use.

Note: The viewport must be in perspective view to use IBL. You will not see the background until you render the image.

Click: ***Environment button to On** (click on the word Off to change to On)*

Click: ***to expand the Image Based Lighting options***

The choices for image based lighting backgrounds are shown in Figure 15.8.

Click: ***Gypsum Crater***

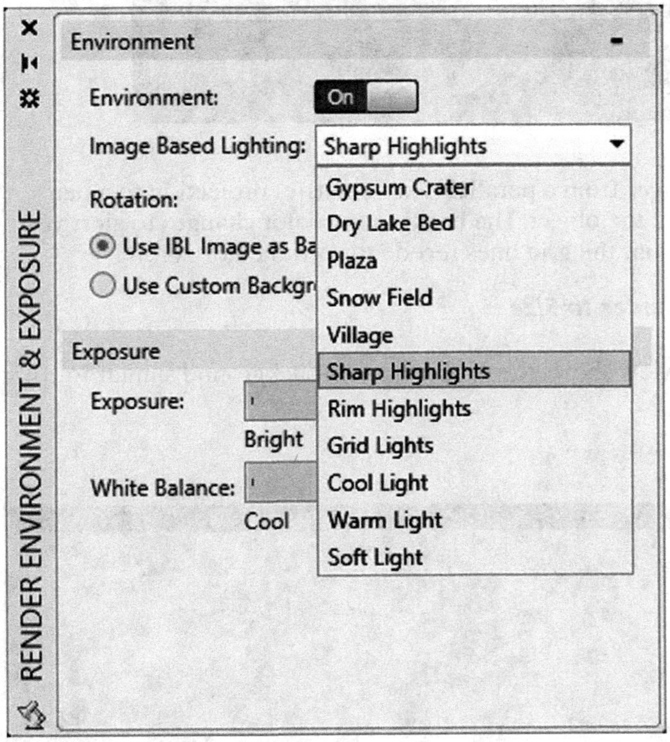

Figure 15.8

Use Custom Background allows you to select your own background image.

Rotation slider allows you to adjust how your model appears oriented to the background image.

Exposure provides a slider for adjusting between brightness or darkness of the rendered image.

White Balance controls whether the lighting appears cool (toward blue) or warm (toward yellow).

Click: ***X to close the dialog box***

Click: ***Realistic*** *from the viewport visual styles*

Click: ***Perspective View*** *from the viewport view controls*

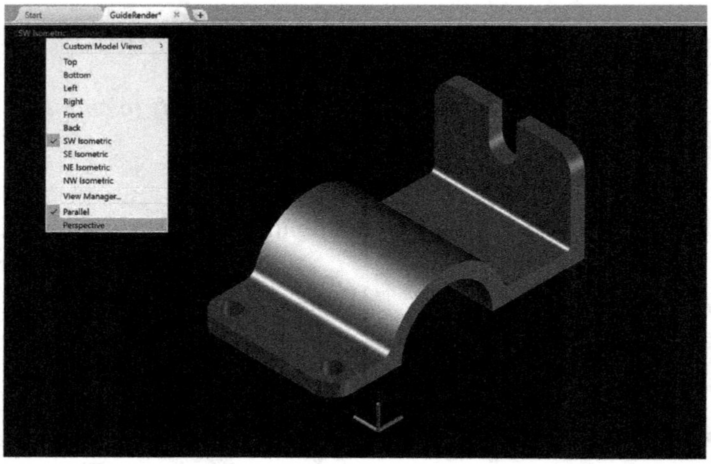

Figure 15.9

The view changes from a parallel (axonometric) projection to a perspective view of the object. The background color changes to alert you to this. Notice that the grid lines recede toward the horizon.

Click: ***Render to Size***

The rendered view shows the gypsum crater background similar to Figure 15.10.

Figure 15.10

*Click: **Zoom In** from the left of the rendered window and use the middle mouse button to pan and center the image.*

Experiment on your own with the other backgrounds and the rotation slider.

Next, turn the render environment back off while you work with the lighting features so you can better see their effect.

*Click: **Render Environment and Exposure** from the expanded Render panel to display the Adjust Render Exposure dialog box*

*Click: **Environment button to Off***

On your own, close the dialog box using the X.

Change the viewport back to **Parallel** *projection. (It is possible to continue in Perspective view if you desire.)*

Adding Lights

When there are no lights in a scene, the scene is shaded or rendered with default lighting. Default lighting is derived from two distant sources that follow the viewpoint as you move around the model. All faces in the model are illuminated so that they are discernible. To turn the default lighting on or off use the DEFAULTLIGHTING system variable or click the button from the Lights panel.

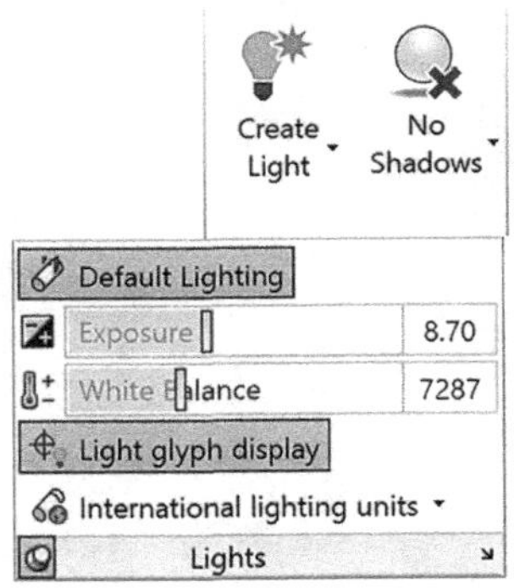

You can control the overall brightness of the rendering by adjusting the render exposure, which is used to simulate ambient light. To adjust the exposure/ambient light, use the Render slider or enter RENDEREXPOSURE on the command line.

The White Balance slider lets you adjust the lighting appearance in the rendered image to be cooler (more blue) or warmer (more orange/red).

Ambient lighting illuminates every surface equally, so distinguishing one surface on the object from the next may be difficult. The best use for ambient lighting is to add some light to back surfaces of the object so that they do not appear entirely dark. You can improve the look of your rendered drawing by adding additional lights. Lighting is very important in achieving good-looking rendering results.

In addition to ambient light, three different types of lights are available.

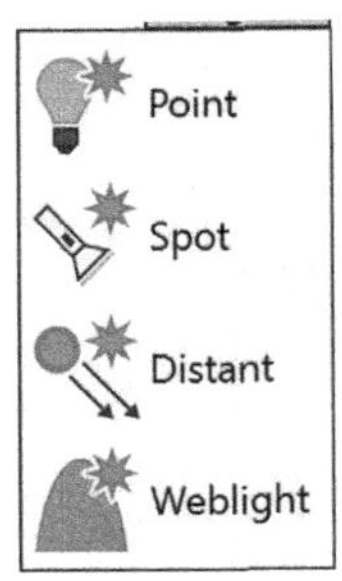

- A *point light* is like a bare lightbulb that casts light in every direction (i.e., it is omnidirectional).
- A *spotlight* highlights certain key areas and casts light only toward the selected target.
- A *distant light* is like sunlight. It illuminates with equal brightness all the surfaces on which it shines.
- A *web light* is similar to a point light, but it represents the nonuniform light intensity distribution of a light source from data provided by manufacturer data of the actual light. This gives a more accurate representation of the lighting effect. This light data is stored in an IES LM-63-1991 standard file format for photometric data.

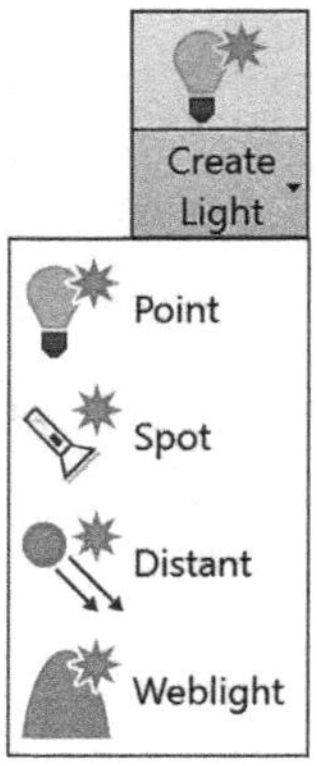

Click: ***Create Lights button*** *to expand the lighting choices*

Click: ***Point*** *from the list*

A warning may display as shown in Figure 15.11 with choices to turn off or leave on the default lighting when you use custom lighting.

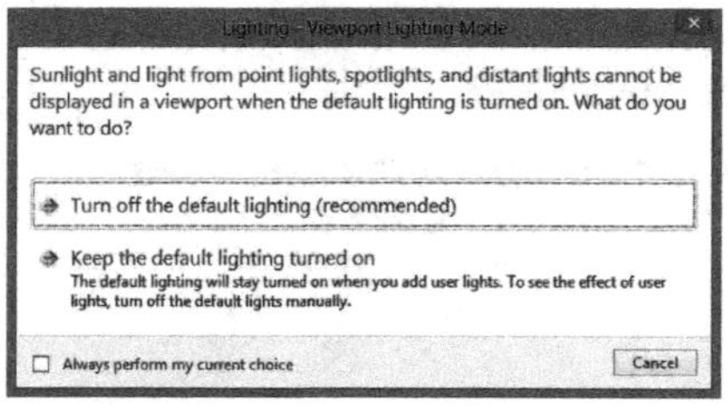

Figure 15.11

Click: ***Turn off the default lighting (recommended)***

You are now prompted to enter the location of the light source. You can position the light by clicking a location from the screen; however, for this example you will type in the coordinates for the light. When specifying the coordinates for the light position, do not position it too close to the object. (You can click from the screen to position the light, but this selects in the current UCS plane, which isn't always convenient.)

Specify source location <0,0,0>: ***0,-2,5 [Enter]***

Next, you will enter a name and appearances such as intensity (brightness).

Enter an option to change [Name/Intensity/Status/shadoW/Attenuation/Color/eXit] <eXit>: ***N [Enter]***

Enter light name <Pointlight1>: ***FILL [Enter]***

Enter an option to change [Name/Intensity/Status/shadoW/Attenuation/Color/eXit] <eXit>: ***I [Enter]***

Enter intensity (0.00 - max float) <1.0000>: ***.5 [Enter]***

Enter an option to change [Name/Intensity/Status/shadoW/Attenuation/Color/eXit] <eXit>: ***[Enter]***

The light is represented with a symbol called a glyph. It appears like a circle with a cross at the center as shown in Figure 15.12.

On your own, use **Zoom** to see the point light *glyph*. Set the view style to **Xray**.

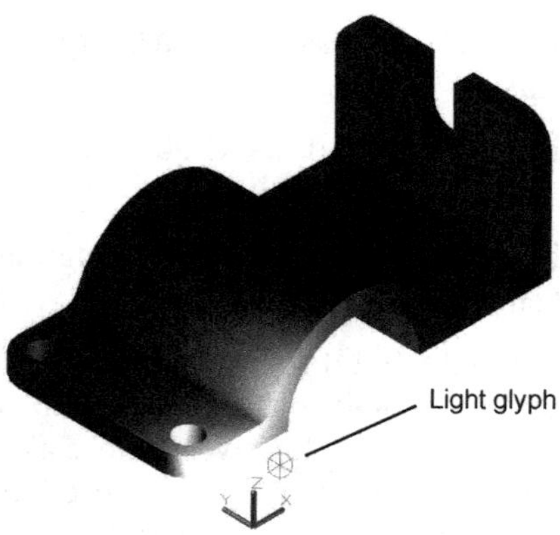

Figure 15.12

Whenever you make changes that affect the rendered appearance of your object, check the result by rendering your drawing.

Click: ***Render to Size button***

Use your task bar to show the Render Window if it is behind another window. You may have to use the Render Window Zoom + to get a closer look at the rendering. Notice the image now has directed light and the addition of shadows. Close the Render Window on your own.

The new light is too close to the object, causing it to appear washed out near the light. Next you will move it up using the 3D gizmo.

Click: ***on the point light glyph*** *to show the 3D gizmo (Figure 15.13).*

Tip: *Your view may look different depending on the visual style you have set. Here it is easier to see the light glyph with the X-Ray style selected. The rendered result will be the same regardless of the visual style selected for the screen display.*

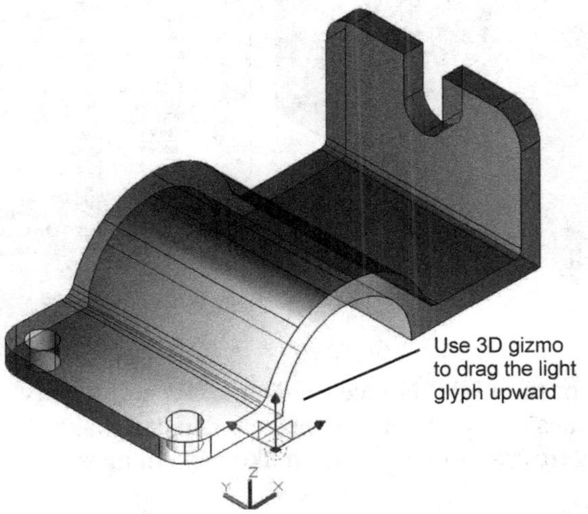

Figure 15.13

Click: ***the blue arrow and drag the light glyph upward*** *in the z-direction to a location of about 0,-2,22*

When you quit dragging, you will notice the lighting on the screen view of the object changing to reflect the new position of the light.

Click: ***Render to Size button***

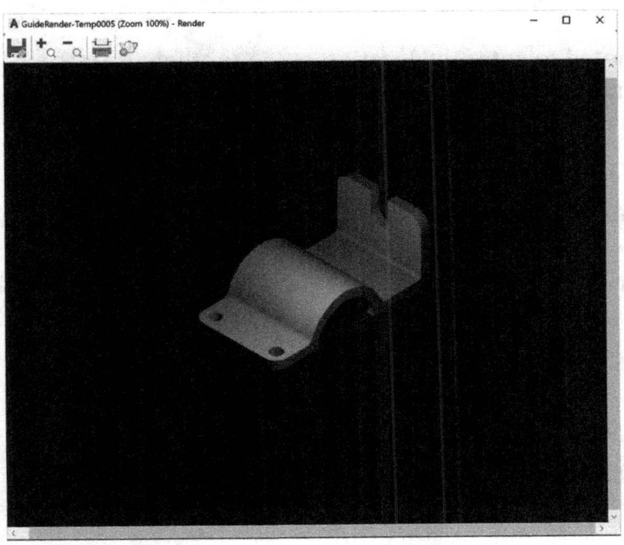

Figure 15.14

Click: ***to close the Render Window***

Click: ***the light glyph***

Press: ***[Ctrl]+1 to show the Properties palette***

The Properties palette appears as shown in Figure 15.15.

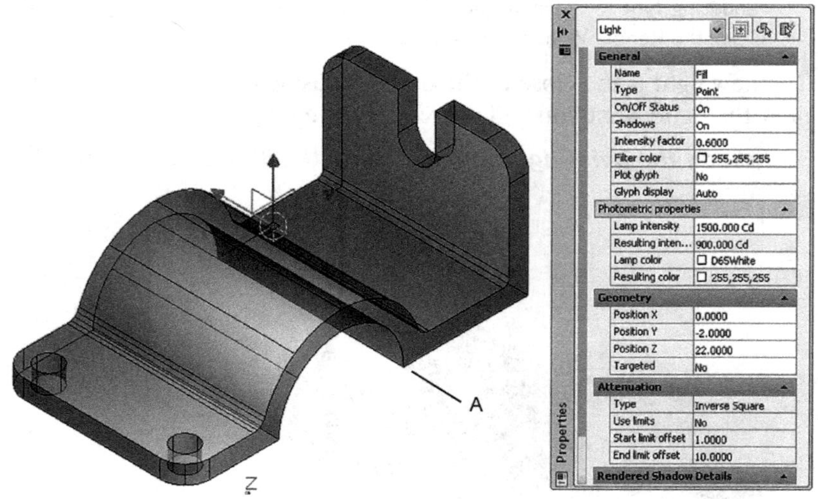

Figure 15.15

Review the properties of the Light. Notice the Name, Type, Intensity factor, and position values that you entered earlier. You can make changes to these at any time. For now, do not make any changes.

Close the Properties palette.

Press [ESC] twice to unselect the light glyph.

Change the Visual Style to Realistic on your own.

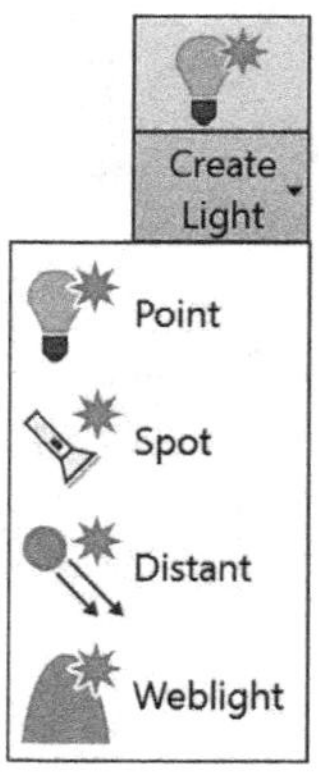

Next, you will add a spotlight behind the object to light the right surface and provide highlights in the drawing.

Click: ***the Create Lights button to expand the lighting choices***

Click: ***Spot***

You are now prompted to enter the location of the spotlight source followed by the target that the light will point at. You will also name the light "Accent" and set the intensity.

Specify source location <0,0,0>: ***0,-60,50 [Enter]***

Specify target location <0,0,0>: ***use Object Snap Endpoint to select the right corner of the rounded arc*** *identified as A in Figure 15.15*

Enter an option to change [Name/Intensity factor/Status/Photometry/Hotspot/Falloff/shadoW/Attenuation/filterColor/eXit] <eXit>: ***N [Enter]***

Enter light name <Spotlight1>: ***ACCENT [Enter]***

Enter an option to change [Name/Intensity factor/Status/Photometry/Hotspot/Falloff/shadoW/Attenuation/filterColor/eXit] <eXit>: ***I [Enter]***

Enter intensity (0.00 - max float) <1.0000>: ***0.75 [Enter]***

Next, you will set the falloff and hotspot for the spotlight. *Falloff* is the angle of the cone of light from the spotlight. *Hotspot* is the angle of the cone of light for the brightest area of the beam. The angles for the falloff and hotspot must be between 0° and 160°. You cannot set Hotspot to a greater value than Falloff.

Enter an option to change

Enter an option to change [Name/Intensity factor/Status/Photometry/Hotspot/Falloff/shadoW/Attenuation/filterColor/eXit] <eXit>: ***H [Enter]***

Enter hotspot angle (0.00-160.00) <45.0000>: ***15 [Enter]***

Enter an option to change [Name/Intensity factor/Status/Photometry/Hotspot/Falloff/shadoW/Attenuation/filterColor/eXit] <eXit>: ***F [Enter]***

Enter falloff angle (0.00-160.00) <50>: ***30 [Enter]***

Enter an option to change [Name/Intensity factor/Status/Photometry/Hotspot/Falloff/shadoW/Attenuation/filterColor/eXit] <eXit>: ***[Enter]***

Click: ***Render to Size button***

The model is rendered to the render window. Notice that the right side of the model is lit more.

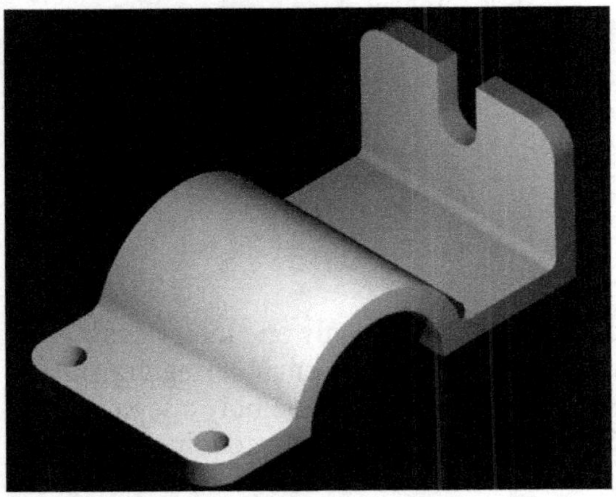

Figure 15.16

Choosing Materials

You can also improve your rendered drawing by selecting or creating realistic-looking *materials* for the objects in it. You can either use the materials that are provided in the Materials Library or create your own materials.

 *Click:* ***Materials Browser button***

Click: ***Autodesk Library*** *from the list at left (if it does not show, click the icon identified in Figure 15.17)*

On your own, click and drag on the right edge of the browser window to make the browser window wider. Click and drag on the titles to fit the names so that you are able to read them as shown in Figure 15.17. You can also sort the items by clicking on the titles.

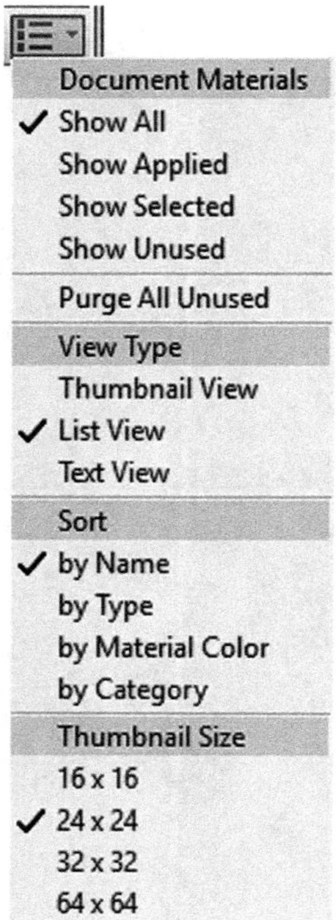

Click: ***menu button*** *from the Library area*

Click: ***24 x 24*** *for the Thumbnail size*

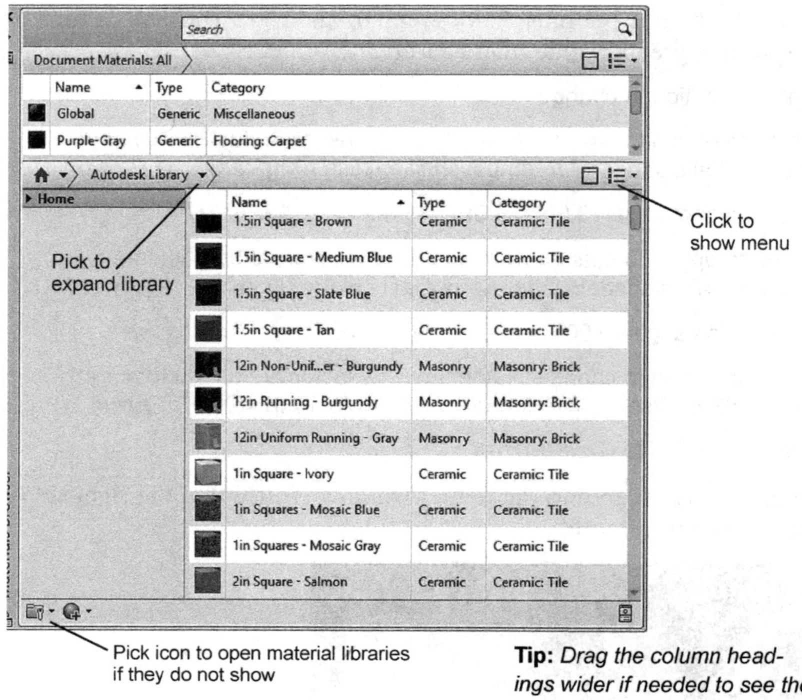

Tip: *Drag the column headings wider if needed to see the entire name.*

Figure 15.17

A single solid object in the drawing can have only one material assigned. This limitation usually isn't a problem in engineering drawings because you will typically make each part in an assembly a separate object in the drawing. Do not use Boolean operators to join parts to which you want to assign different materials.

To select from the library of premade materials,

Click: ***downward arrow next to Autodesk Library*** *to expand the list of material types*

The categories of materials in that library appear.

Click: ***Metal*** *to select it from the list*

Drag and drop Anodized - Red on to your drawing object.

Turn the Grid off. You also may want to turn the Default Lighting back on and adjust the exposure slider.

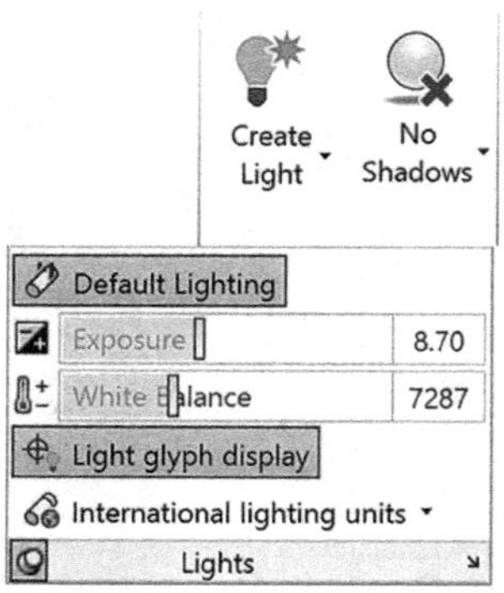

Once the material is used in the drawing it is added to the Document Materials shown at the top row of the Materials Browser. Your screen should look similar to Figure 15.18.

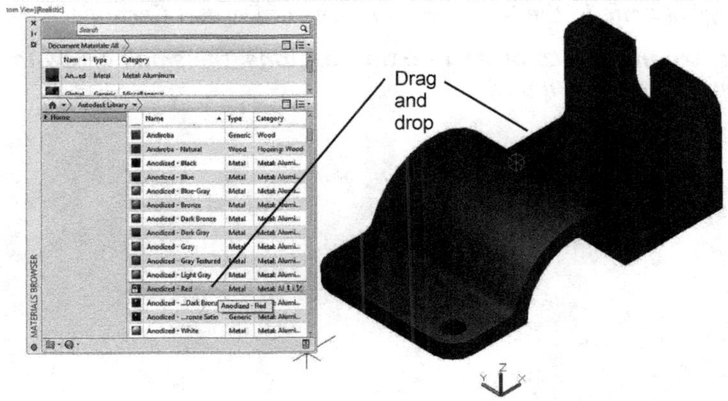

Figure 15.18

The object in the viewport now appears as though it is made of red annodized aluminum.

Creating a New Material

You can create your own materials. Next, you will create a material that looks like copper. Make sure that the Materials palette is still open.

*Click: **Create New Material button** from the bottom left of the Material Browser*

*Click: **Ceramic** from the drop down list as shown in Figure 15.19*

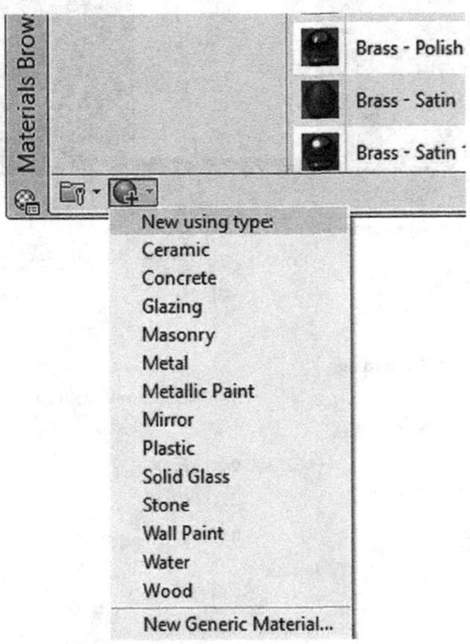

Figure 15.19

The Materials Editor appears as shown in Figure 15.20.

Tip: *An extensive material and texture library is included with AutoCAD.*
Make sure to install the Materials Library. By default, the materials are installed in the File Locations path specified on the Files tab of the Options dialog box. (See Texture Maps Search Path on the Files tab for the location of texture maps.)

Note: *The materials library components are always installed to the default location. If you change the paths before you install the materials library, the new materials may not display on the Material Browser and the texture maps may not be referenced by the materials. Either copy the newly installed files to the location you want, or change the path to the correct location.*

Warning: *If you don't see the list of materials shown in Figure 15.17, you may not have the path set correctly to tell the software where to look for texture files. To change the path, pick Tools, Options. Use the Files tab of the dialog box to set the path to where your texture files are stored. Make sure that you have loaded the materials files.*

Type: ***MyCeramic*** *in the Name box in place of Default Ceramic*

Click: ***to expand the color and texture options*** *(the small arrow to the right of the Color input)*

Click: ***Speckle***

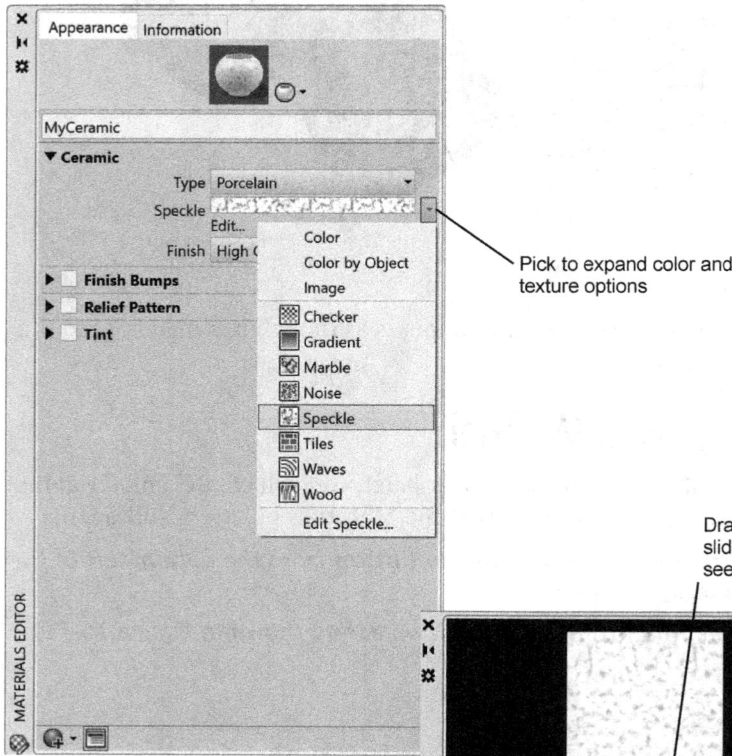

Figure 15.20

The Texture Editor appears similar to Figure 15.21.
You can use it to edit the colors, scale, position and rotation of a pre-selected texture map, such as Speckle, or your own image (by selecting the Image option from the list).

On your own, make changes to the color and scale of the texture image. To access the position offset and rotation, click the arrow to expand the Transformation choices. Make changes if desired.

Click: ***[X]*** *to close the Texture Editor*

Click: ***Tint*** *so it shows a check; choose a color on your own.*

Click: ***[X]*** *to close the Materials Editor*

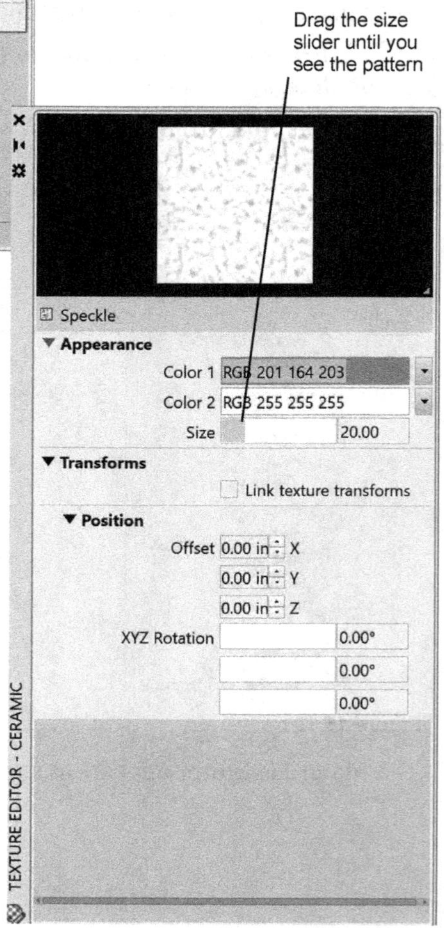

Figure 15.21

The new MyCeramic material now shows in the Materials Browser. To save the materials to your custom library,

Click: ***Material Library button*** *from the lower left of the dialog box*

Click: ***Create New Library***

Use the File dialog box that appears to name your library; for example: ***MyMaterials*** *then click* ***Save***

Drag and drop the material from the Document Materials area into your library.

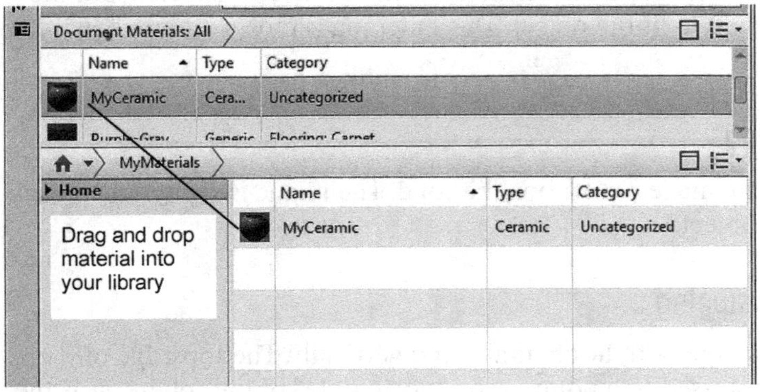

Figure 15.22

To apply the new material to the object it is best to remove the old material first.

Drag and drop: ***Global material*** *onto your object*

The object will return to its original color. Now add the new material.

Drag and Drop: ***MyCeramic*** *onto your object*

Click: ***Render button*** *to see the results of the new material. (If it is washed out, you may need to adjust your lighting/exposure.)*

Next you will use a noticeably patterned material so that you can easily see the results in the next steps.

Click: ***Home button*** *and choose* ***Autodesk Library***

On your own, drag and drop the **Flooring, Checker Black - White** material onto your object. Close the Material Browser. Render the result in the render window with the default lighting. The result should look similar to Figure 15.23.

Figure 15.23

Adjusting Mapping

When bitmaps or materials that use bitmapped patterns are applied to surfaces in your drawing, you can control the type of mapping, coordinates, scale, repeat, and other aspects of the maps' appearance. There are several types of mapping.

Planar Mapping

This maps the image onto the object as if you were projecting it from a slide projector onto a 2D surface. The image is not distorted, but the image is scaled to fit the object. This mapping is most commonly used for faces.

Box Mapping

This maps an image onto a boxlike solid. The image is repeated on each side of the object.

Spherical Mapping

Warps the image both horizontally and vertically. The top edge of the map is compressed to a point at the "north pole" of the sphere, as is the bottom edge at the "south pole."

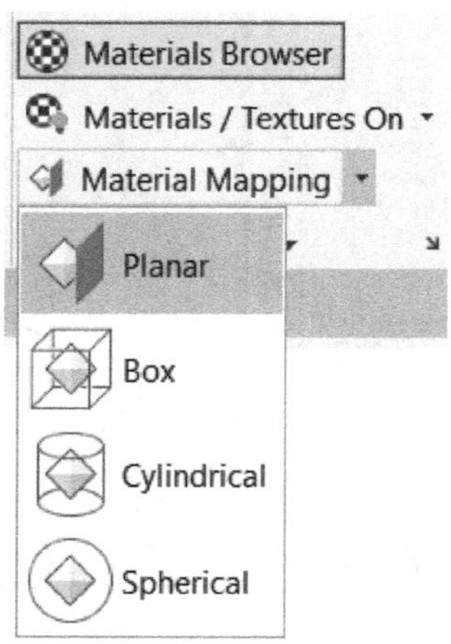

Cylindrical Mapping

This maps an image onto a cylindrical object; the horizontal edges are wrapped together but not the top and bottom edges. The height of the image is scaled along the cylinder's axis.

Click: ***to expand the Material Mapping drop-down list*** *from the Visualize tab, Materials panel*

Click: ***Box button***

Select faces or objects: ***click anywhere on the model [Enter]***

Accept the mapping or [Move/Rotate/reseT/sWitch mapping mode]: ***click and drag on a triangular grip or use the axes of the 3D gizmo to move the pattern*** *(Figure 15.24)*

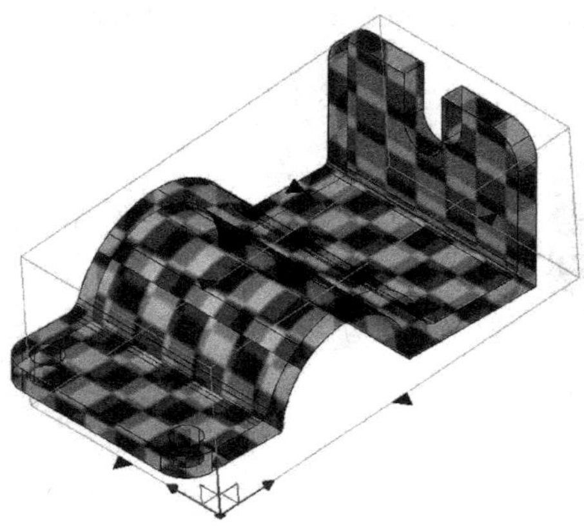

Figure 15.24

***Right**-click on the **3D gizmo** and use the rotation orbits to rotate the pattern. When you have finished experimenting with the rotation, right-click on the 3D gizmo and **click Reset**. (Notice you can type the option letters also.)*

Accept the mapping or [Move/Rotate/reseT/sWitch mapping mode]: ***[Enter]** to end the command*

Using mapped materials is a good way to add detail to your rendered drawing without creating complex models. For example, you could model every brick in a wall as a separate solid and create a different solid for the mortar between them. Doing so would create a very complex solid model with a lot of vertices. Instead, you can create the entire wall as a single flat surface and then apply the appearance of brick to it as a bitmapped pattern. The drawing will look very detailed but will have far fewer vertices and take less file space than the previous example. You can combine bitmaps and bump maps to give a raised appearance to parts of the material.

Adding Backgrounds

You can add a background to your rendering using the View command. Backgrounds can be solid colors, gradient colors (which blend one to three colors), images (bitmaps), or the current AutoCAD image (selected using Merge).

*Click: **View Manager button** from the Named Views panel*

The View Manager dialog box appears as shown in Figure 15.25 left.

*Click: **New button***

The New View dialog box appears, similar to Figure 15.25 at right.

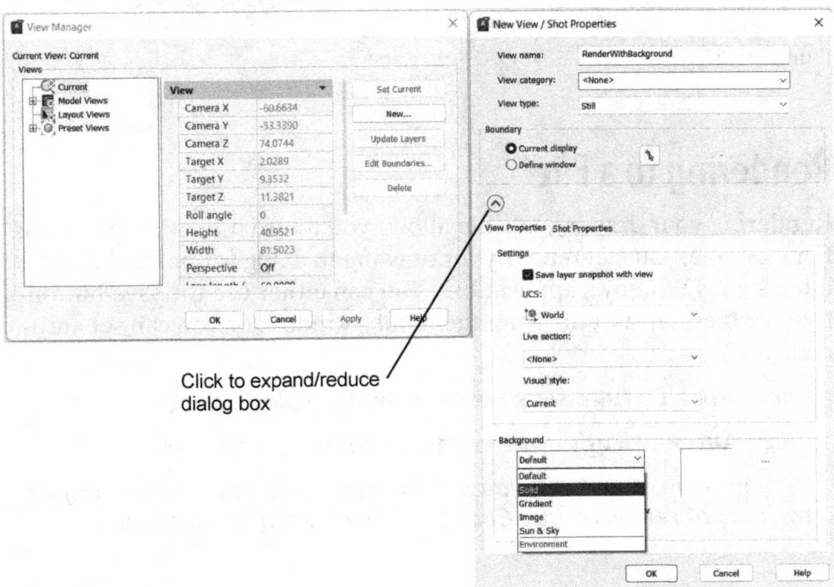

Figure 15.25

*Type: **RenderWithBackground** for the View name*

*Click: **on the small arrow to expand the dialog box options***

Warning: *The AutoCAD software keeps track of the location (path) for the textures and bitmapped materials. If your options do not show this location correctly for where your files are stored, you will not be able to see materials that contain textures (bitmaps) correctly.*

*On your own, use the **Background drop-down** list from the bottom of the dialog box to set a **solid** background. Click the ellipsis (...) and select a color for the background. (Notice that you can also use a gradient or an image for the background.)*

*Click: **OK** to exit the Background dialog box*

*Click: **the RenderWithBackground** view name to highlight it*

*Click: **Set Current button***

*Click: **OK** to exit the View dialog box*

*Click: **Render button***

The drawing in the Render Window now appears with a solid colored background as shown in Figure 15.26.

Figure 15.26

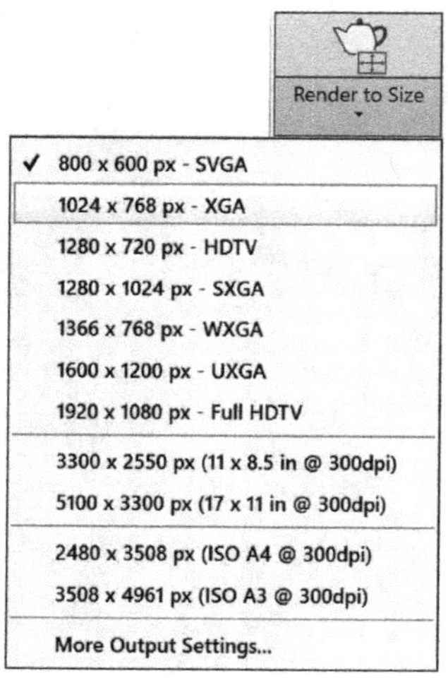

Rendering to a File

Rendering your drawing to a file allows you to use it in other programs. For example, you can render your drawing to a .jpg format and insert it into various Windows applications. You can either use the save button to store the snapshot file from the render window, or you can set automatic.

*Click: **More Output Settings** to show the dialog box*

*Click: **Automatically save rendered image** (check box)*

*On your own, use the dialog box to enter a file name. Click **.jpg** as the type of rendered file. Click the **Save** button to continue.*

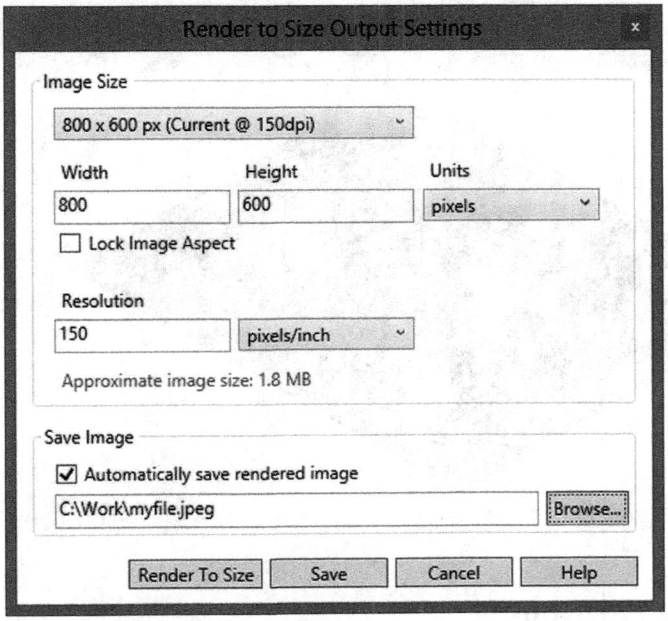

Figure 15.27

Click: ***Render to Size button***

The Render window will appear and the rendering will take place and the file will be written to your desired location. You can use Windows Explorer to locate the file and preview it.

On your own, ***save and close your GuideRender.dwg*** *file.*

Using Sun Properties

Sun properties is a particularly useful feature for creating lighting and doing lighting studies in architectural drawings. You can use it to show the different effects that sunlight has on the rendered view at different times of the day and year. The Sun Properties feature provides this lighting information without laborious information look up from tables. You can even set the geographic location by clicking from the map.

The rays of the sun are parallel and have the same intensity at any distance. Shadows can be on or off. To improve performance, turn off shadows when you don't need them. All settings for the sun except geographic location are saved per viewport, not per drawing. Geographic location is saved per drawing.

Start a ***new*** *drawing* ***from*** *the* ***house3d.dwg*** *provided with the data files.* ***Save*** *your drawing* ***as housesun.dwg****.*

Change the Visual Style to ***Realistic****.*

Turn ***off*** *the* ***grid****.*

Adjust your ***lighting exposure*** *as needed to see the shapes clearly.*

The drawing should look similar to Figure 15.28.

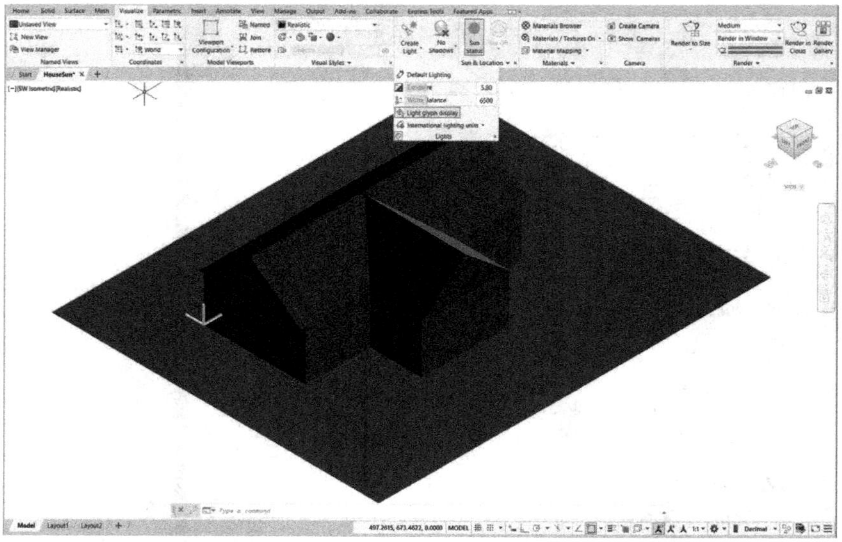

Figure 15.28

Geographic Location

The angle of the sun depends on the geographic location as well as the date and time. You have the options to:

- open Live Map to select a location
- import *.kml* and *.kmz* files (types associated with Google Earth and other mapping software)
- enter location values using the Geographic Location dialog box

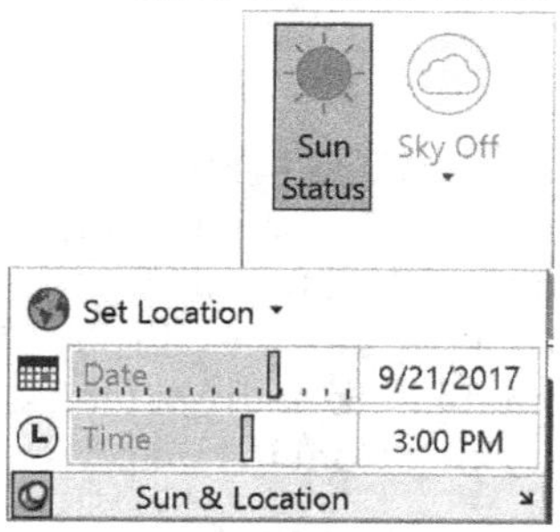

Figure 15.29

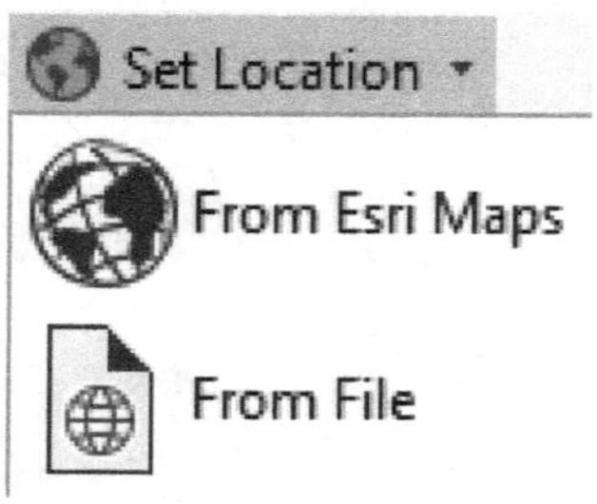

*Click: to expand **Set Location** from the Visuzalize tab, Sun and Location panel*

*Click: **From Esri Maps***

You may have to sign in to your account and choose whether to sync your settings.

The Geographic Location dialog box appears on the screen.

On your own, enter **Bozeman, MT, USA** in the search box near the top of the dialog box. You can also directly enter a latitude and longitude into the box.

On your own, expand the map type options by moving your cursor over the small box in the right corner. Try some of the map styles on your own.

Click: ***Esri OpenStreetMap*** *from the map type choices*

Click: ***Drop Marker Here*** *from the left panel*

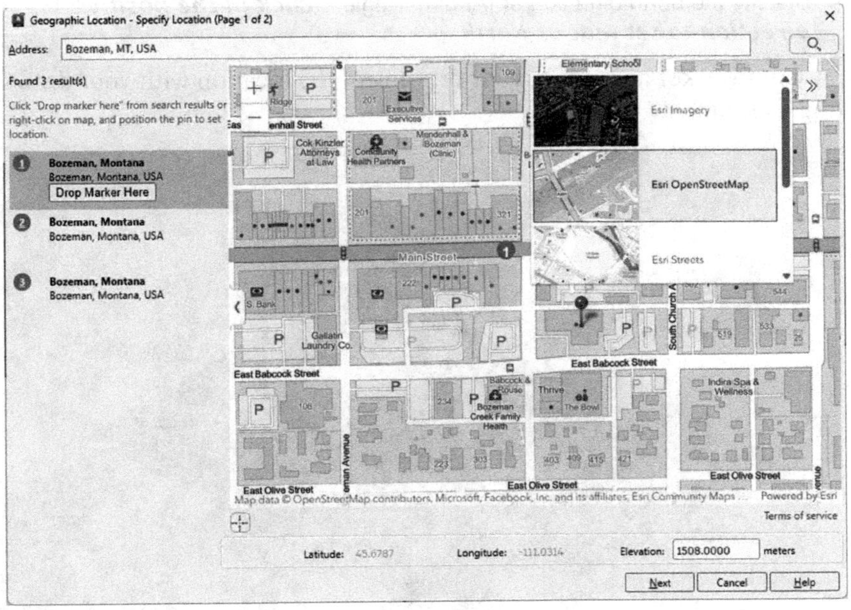

Figure 15.30

You can move the cursor to a different location and then right-click and select Move Marker Here to change the marker position. Of course you can select your location around the globe if you are not near Bozeman, MT (cultural center of the universe).

Type: ***1508*** *into the Elevation input box (in meters)*

Click: ***Next***

The Set Coordinate System page appears on your screen. The one closest to the location you selected is at the top of the list. Notice the units. Select a coordinate system to use. For example, MT83F.

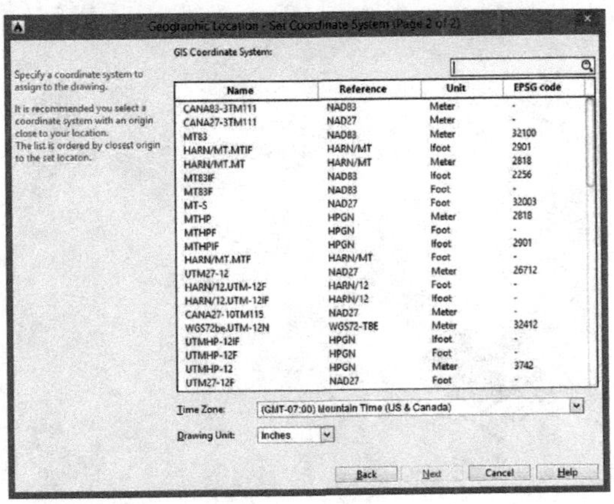

Figure 15.31

Click: ***Next***

You are returned to your drawing for the next selection.

Select a point for the location <0.0000, 0.0000, 0.0000>: ***select near the lower left corner of the building*** *as the marked location*

Specify the north direction or [Angle]<Angle>: ***click in the positive Y direction*** *to set that as North*

A Geo-Marker appears in your drawing at the location with your drawing overlain.

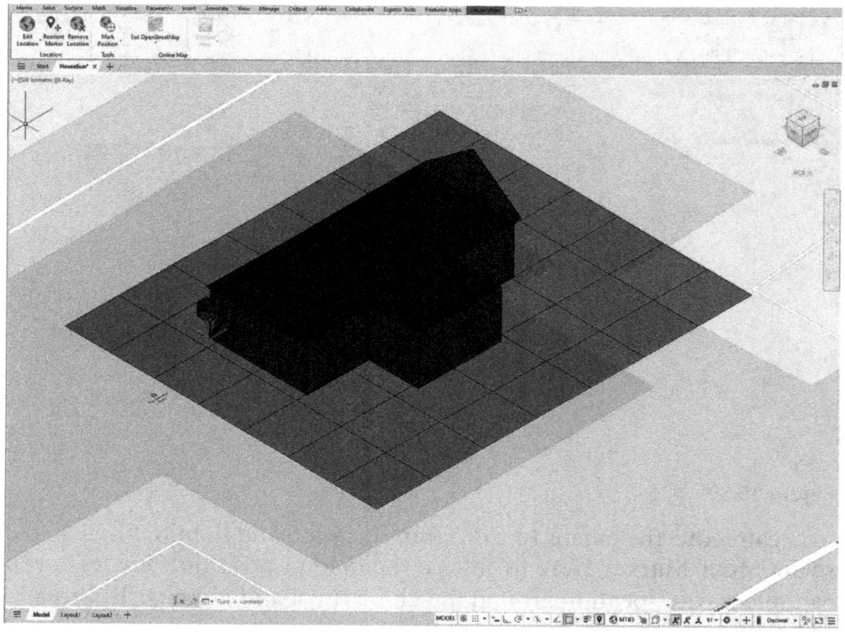

Figure 15.32

Zoom out so that you can see more of the street map with your drawing now located on it.

Figure 15.33

Tip: *Experiment with the map types on your own. To match the next images in the book, use Map Off.*

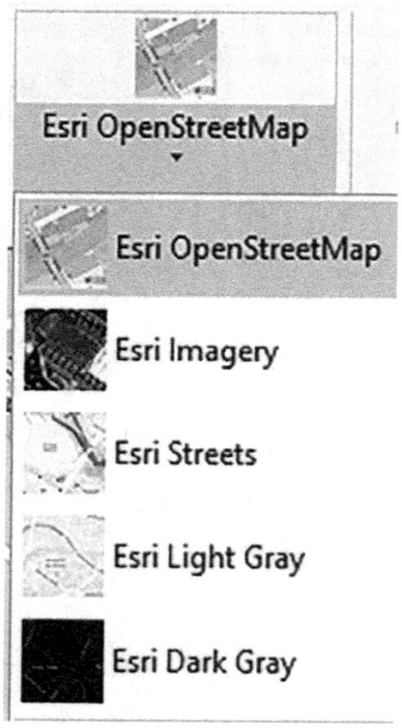

Click: ***Geolocation tab*** *to make it active if it is not*

Click: to expand the map types then select ***Map Off***

Zoom so the drawing fills the screen area.

Sun Status

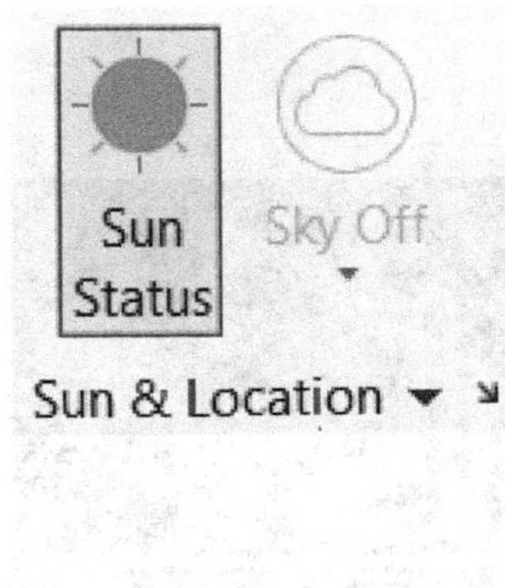

The Sun Status button is a toggle. It switches on and off the use of the Sun lighting feature. Once it is turned on, the lighting in your model is set to reflect how it would appear if lit by the sun on the date and time listed in the Sun and Location panel.

Click: ***Sun Status button*** *from the Visualize tab to turn it on*

The default lighting turns off. The Lighting - Sunlight and Exposure message box appears.

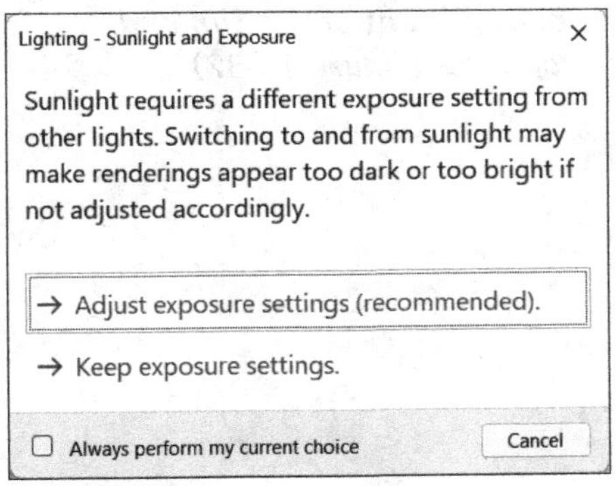

Figure 15.34

Click: ***Adjust exposure settings (recommended)***

The Environment dialog box appears similar to Figure 15.35.

On your own, use the **Exposure slider** to adjust the lighting.

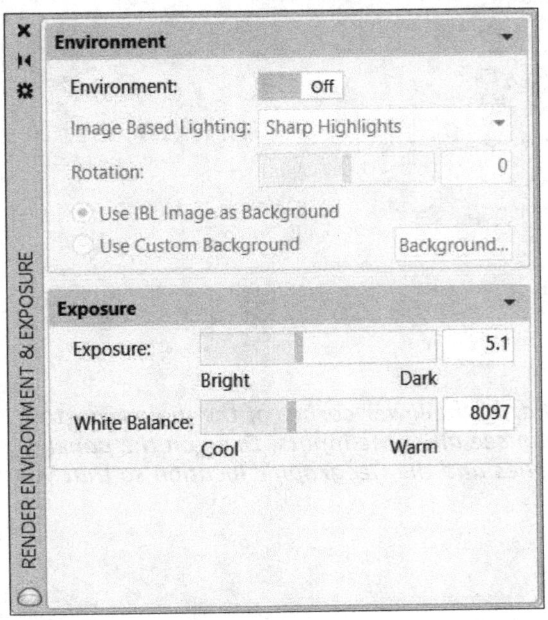

Figure 15.35

Drag the date and time sliders *to see the result of changing the sun angle on your model shading as shown in Figure 15.36.*

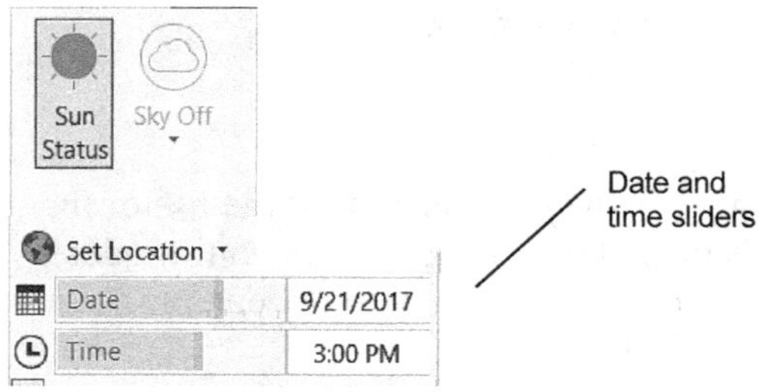

Figure 15.36

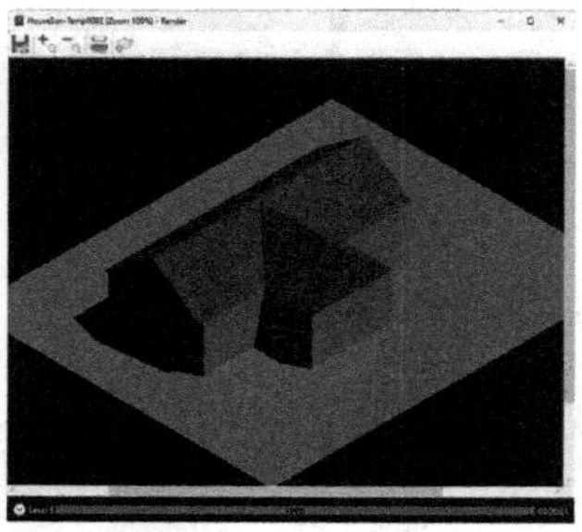

Use ***Render to Size*** *to show a realistically shaded view in the Render Window.*

Click: ***on the small arrow*** *at the bottom right of the Sun and Location panel to show the Sun Properties (Figure 15.37)*

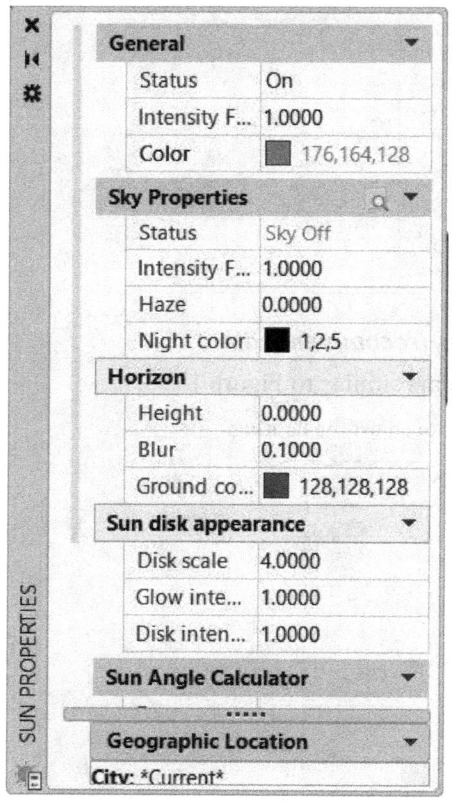

Figure 15.37

On your own, click and drag the lower corner of the dialog box to expand it so that you can see all of the inputs. Drag on the panel between the Sun properties and the Geographic location so that you can see all of them.

The Sun Properties dialog box provides the following inputs:

General

Status turns the sun lighting on and off. If lighting is not enabled in the drawing, this setting has no effect.

Intensity Factor sets the intensity or brightness of the sun. The higher the number, the brighter the light.

Color controls the color of the light.

Sky Properties

Status On makes the sky illumination available for the rendering computation. This has no impact on the viewport illumination or the background.

Intensity Factor magnifies the effect of the skylight.

Haze determines the magnitude of scattering effects appearing like haze in the atmosphere.

Night Color sets the color of the night sky.

Horizon

Height determines the height of the ground plane above WCS zero, formatted in the current length units.

Blur specifies the blurring between ground plane and sky.

Ground Color specifies the color of the ground plane.

Sun Disk Appearance

Disk Scale set the scale for the sun disk (1.0 = normal size).

Glow Intensity set a value 0.0 to 25.0 for the intensity of the sun's glow.

Disk Intensity set a value 0.0 to 25.0 for the intensity of the sun disk.

Sun Angle Calculator

Date shows the current date setting.

Time shows the current time setting.

Daylight Saving shows the current setting for daylight saving time.

Azimuth shows the azimuth, the angle of the sun along the horizon clockwise from due north. This setting is read-only.

Altitude shows the altitude, the angle of the sun vertically from the horizon. The maximum is 90 degrees, or directly overhead.

Source Vector displays the coordinates of the direction of the sun.

Tip: *You can use SaveAs and change the Save As Type area to save your drawing files back to previous AutoCAD versions.*

Tip: *You can create electronic drawing sets using the Publish command found by clicking the Application icon. Other people, such as your clients, can view the published set of drawings using a free download of Autodesk Express Viewer available at www.Autodesk.com.*

You *can also use the Publish to Web menu selection to create a web page to display images from one or more drawing files.*

Geographic Location

Geographic Location shows the current location settings. Cities with no stored latitude and longitude aren't listed.

*When you are finished examining the Sun properties, **close** the dialog box on your own.*

***Save** your file.*

Exporting AutoCAD Files

You can export your AutoCAD drawings to many other formats in addition to the main types you see listed.

Click: ***Application icon, Export***

Click: ***Other Formats** from the bottom of the list*

Figure 15.38

The Export Data dialog box appears on your screen, as shown in Figure 15.38. You will find these file types:

3D dwf	**.dwf*
3D dwfx	**.dwfx*
FBX	**.fbx*
Metafile	**.wmf*
ACIS	**.sat*
Lithography	**.stl*
Encapsulated PS	**.eps*

DXX Extract	**.dxx*
Bitmap	**.bmp*
Block	**.dwg*
MicroStation® V8 DGN	**.dgn*
MicroStation® V7 DGN	**.dgn*
IGES	**.iges*
IGS	**.igs*

Click: ***Cancel***

On your own, ***save and close*** *the file.*

Exit *the AutoCAD program.*

You have completed Tutorial 15 and this tutorial guide! Use what you have learned from these tutorials along with the AutoCAD software's Help files to continue exploring and learning to communicate your designs and ideas. Experiment with the collaborative tools available using Autodesk and the AutoCAD web app. There is still so much more to learn.

Key Terms

ambient
ambient lighting
back faces
bump map
distant light
falloff
hotspot
intensity
materials
normal
point light
reflection
refraction
resolution
scene
spotlight
surface map
transparency

Key Commands

Background
Lights
Mapping
Materials
Publish
Render
Sunproperties

Exercises

Use solid modeling to create the objects shown below or retrieve your files from the exercises you did earlier. Produce three different renderings of the object, varying the type, location, intensity, and color of the light. Experiment with different materials and backgrounds.

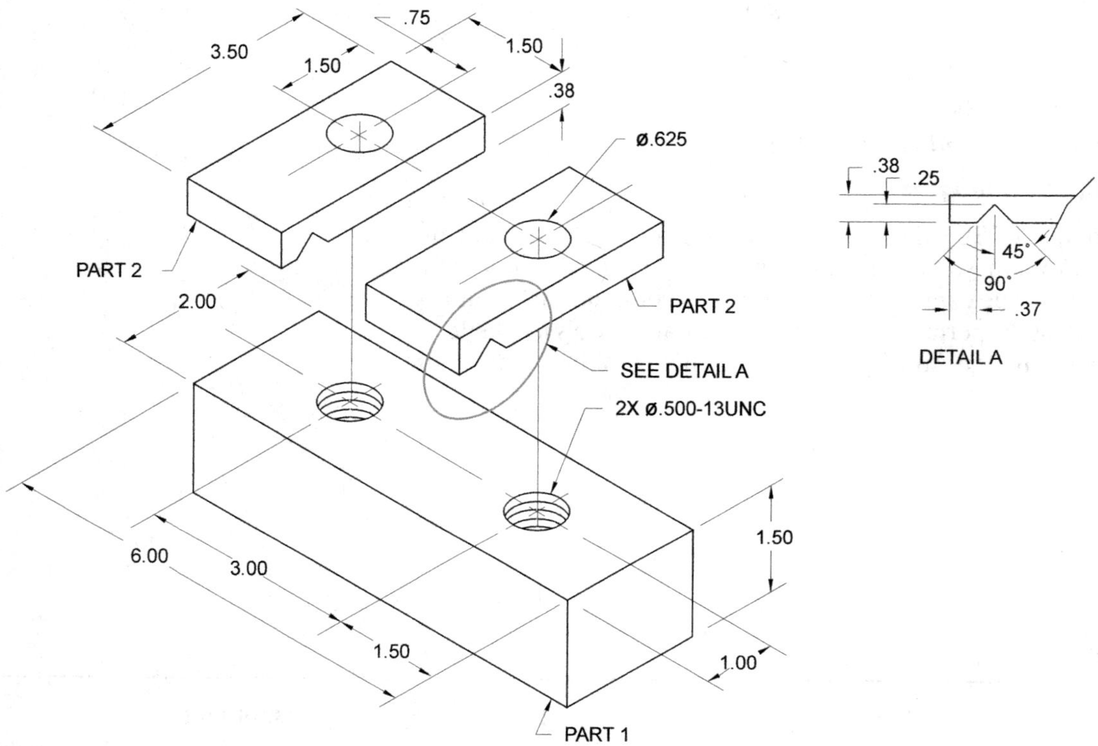

Exercise 15.1 Clamping Block

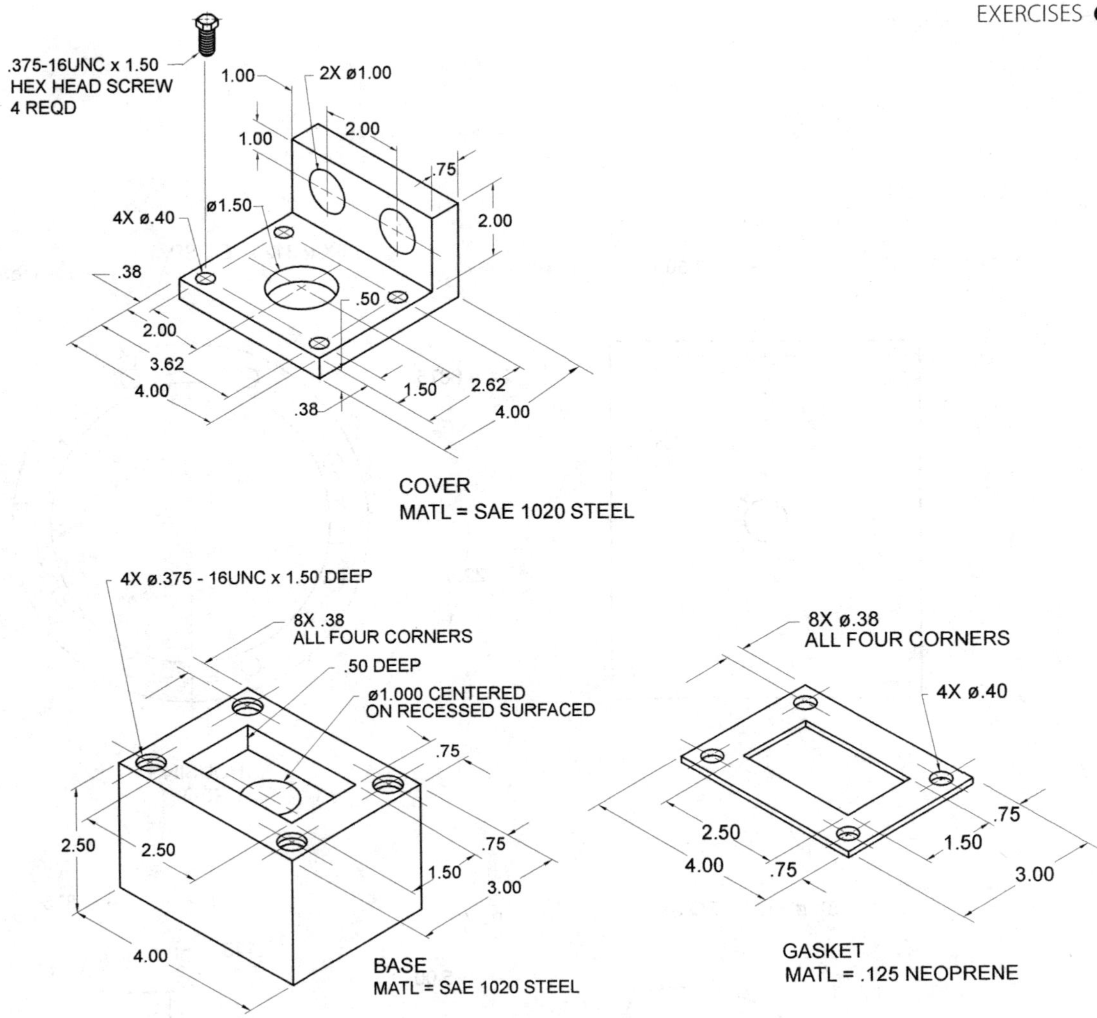

Exercise 15.2 Pressure Assembly

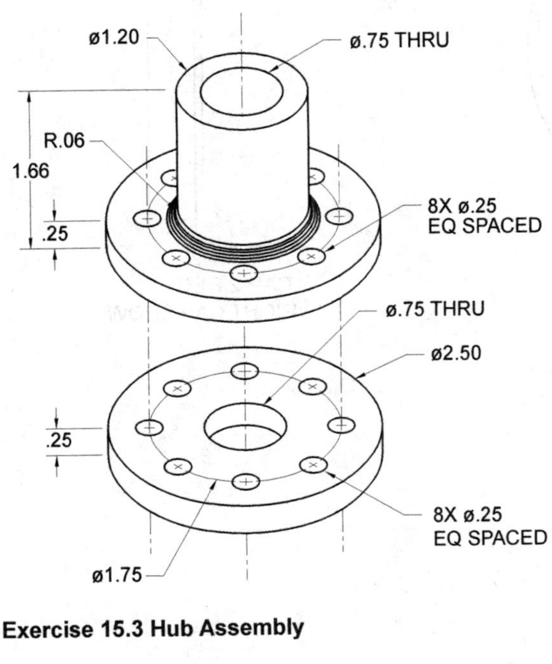

Exercise 15.3 Hub Assembly

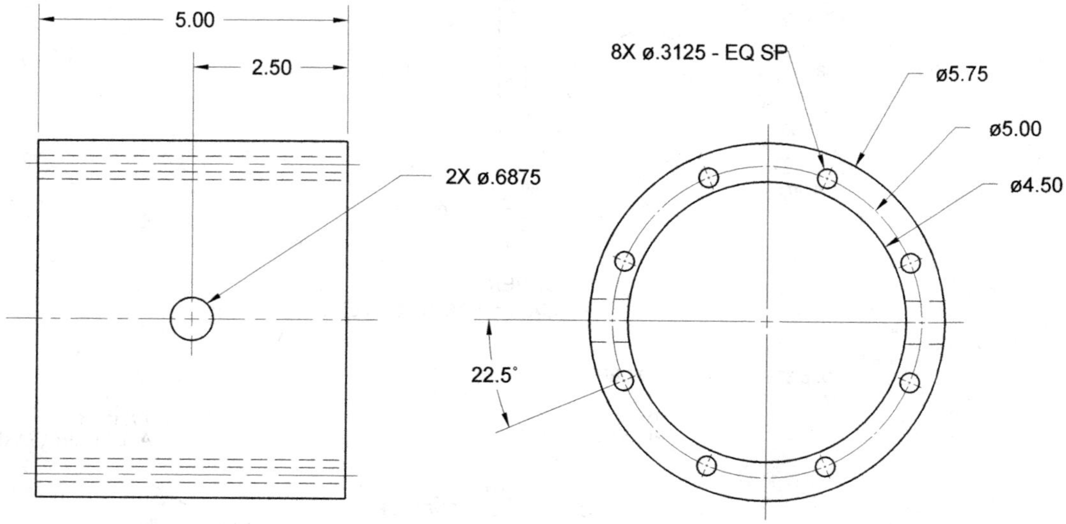

1 HOUSING
1 REQ

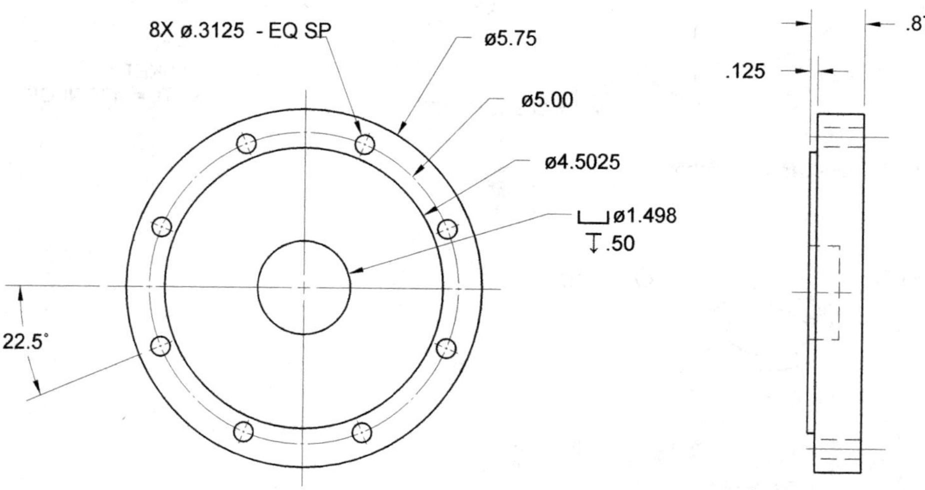

2 CAP-2 REQ
RIGHT CAP SHOWN

Exercise 15.4 Turbine Housing Assembly

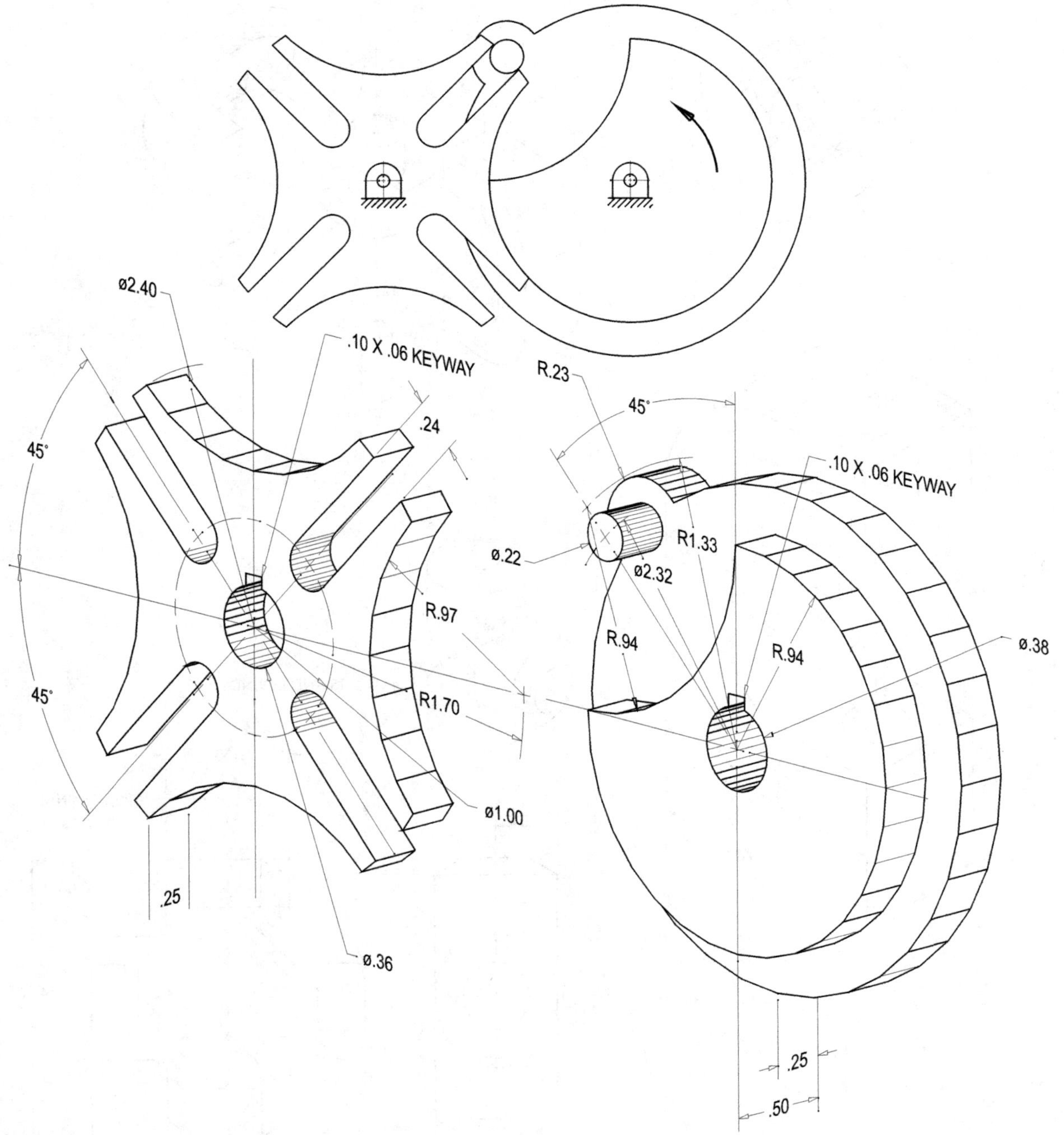

Exercise 15.5 Geneva Wheel Assembly

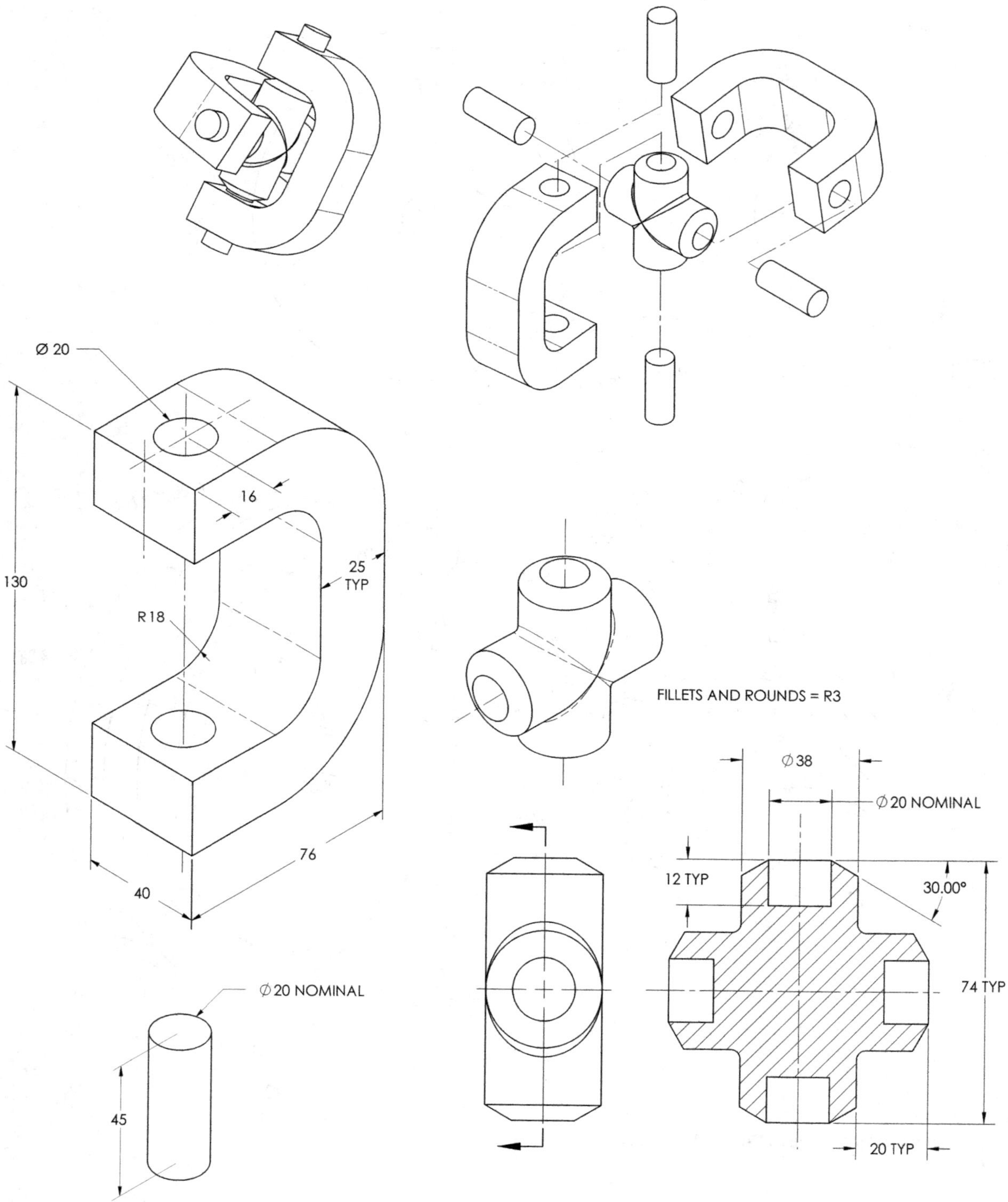

Exercise 15.6M Universal Joint

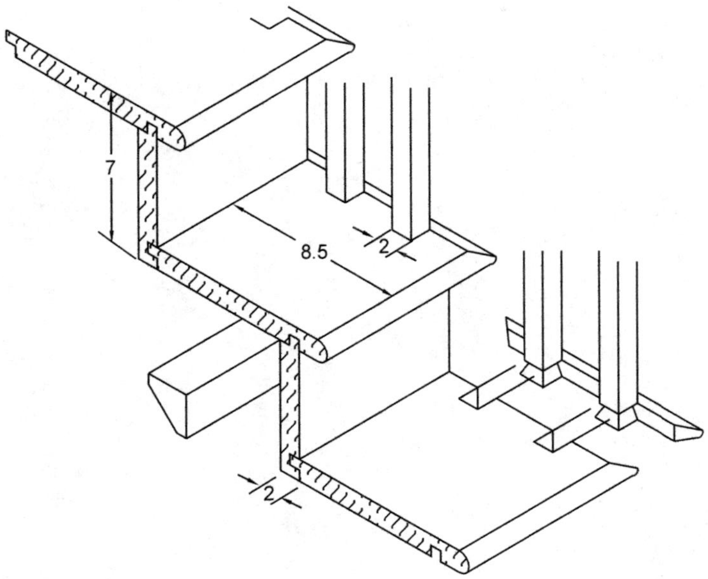

Exercise 15.7 Staircase

Create the staircase or retrieve your file from Tutorial 13 exercise. Render the stairs using wood materials.

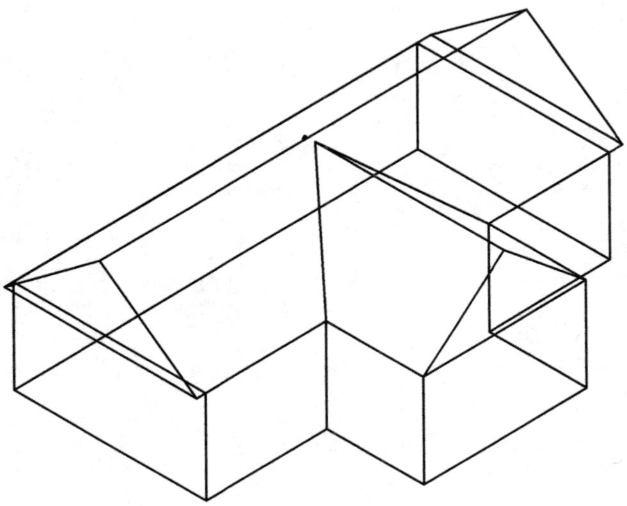

Exercise 15.8 House

Open your file, *housesun.dwg,* from Tutorial 15. Apply different materials and textures to the walls, roof and ground plane. Render the appearance at 10am and 3pm in your local area.

Glossary

absolute coordinates — The exact location of a specific point in terms of x, y, and z from the fixed point of origin.

absolute value — The numerical value or magnitude of the quantity, without regard to its positive or negative sign.

alias — A short name that can be used to activate a command; you can customize command aliases by editing the file *acad.pgp*.

ambient — The overall amount of light that exists in the environment of a rendered scene.

And gate — An electronic logic symbol; if either input is zero, the output is zero.

angle brackets — A value that appears in angle brackets < > is the default option for that command, which will be executed unless it is changed.

aperture — A type of cursor resembling a small box placed on top of the crosshairs; used to select in the object snap mode.

architectural units — Drawings made with these units are drawn in feet and fractional inches.

aspect ratio — The relationship of two dimensions to each other.

associative dimensioning — Dimensioning where each dimension is inserted as a group of drawing objects relative to the points selected in the drawing. If the drawing is scaled or stretched, the dimension values automatically update.

associative hatching — The practice of filling an area with a pattern which automatically updates when the boundary is modified.

attribute — Text information associated with a block.

attribute prompt — The prompt, which you define, that appears in the command area when you insert the block into a drawing.

attribute tag — A variable name that is replaced with the value that you type when prompted as you insert the attribute block.

AutoSnap™ — A feature which displays a marker and description to indicate which object snap location will be selected.

auxiliary view — An orthographic view of an object using a direction of sight other than one of the six basic views (front, top, right side, rear, bottom, left side).

ball tag — A circled number identifying each part shown in an assembly drawing; also called a balloon number.

base feature	In a feature-based model, the main feature from which other features are defined based on the constraints put on the model.
base grip	The selected grip, used as the base point for hot grip commands.
baseline dimensioning	A dimensioning method in which each successive dimension is measured from one extension line or baseline.
basic dimension	A theoretically exact dimension to which no tolerance is applied.
basic view	One of the six standard views of an object: front, top, right side, rear, bottom, or left side.
bearing	The angle to turn from the first direction stated toward the second direction stated.
bicubic surface	A sculptured plane, mathematically describing a sculptured surface between three- dimensional curves.
bidirectional associativity	Describes the link between the drawing and the model. If a change is made to the model, the drawing is automatically updated to reflect the change; if a change is made to the parametric dimensions in the drawing, both the drawing and the model update automatically.
bilateral tolerances	Tolerances specified by defining a nominal dimension and the allowable range of deviation from that dimension, both plus and minus.
blip marks	Little crosses that appear on the screen, indicating where a location was selected.
block	A set of objects that have been grouped together to act as one, and can be saved and used in the current drawing and in other drawings.
block name	Identifies a particular named group of objects.
block reference	A particular insertion of a block into a drawing (blocks can be inserted more than once).
Boolean operators	Find the union (addition), difference (subtraction), and intersection (common area) of two or more sets.
Buffer	An electronic logic symbol.
bump map	Converts color intensity or grayscale information to heights to give the appearance that features are raised above the surface, like embossed letters.
buttons	A method of selecting options by picking in a defined area of the screen resembling a box or push button.
Cartesian coordinate system	A rectangular coordinate system created by three mutually perpendicular coordinate axes, commonly labeled x, y, and z.

chained (continued) dimensioning	A dimensioning method in which each successive dimension is measured. From the last extension line of the previous dimension.
chamfer	A straight line segment connecting two otherwise intersecting surfaces.
chord length	The straight line distance between the start point and the endpoint of an arc.
circular view	A view of a cylinder in which it appears as a circle (looking into the hole).
circumscribed	Drawn around the outside of a base circle.
clearance fit	The space available between two mating parts, where the greatest shaft size always is smaller than the smallest hole size, thus producing an open space.
cloud	A distributed network of internet storage.
colinear constraint	Constrained to remain on the same straight line.
command aliasing	The creation and use of alternative short names for commands, such as LA for Layer.
command prompt	The word or words in the command window that ask for the next piece of information.
command window	The lines of text below the graphics window that indicate the status of commands and prompt for user input.
construction plane	A plane that is temporarily defined during commands for creating new drawing objects.
context sensitive	Recognizes when you are in a command, and displays information for that command.
Coons patch	A bicubic surface interpolated between four edges.
coordinate system locator	An icon to help you visually refer to the current coordinate system.
coordinate values	Used to identify the location of a point using the Cartesian coordinate system; x represents the horizontal position on the X axis, and y represents the vertical position on the Y axis. In a three-dimensional drawing, z represents the depth position on the Z axis.
crosshatching	The practice of filling an area with a pattern to differentiate it from other components of a drawing.
current layer	The layer you are working on. New drawing objects are always created on the layer that is current.

cursor (crosshairs)	A mark that shows the location of the pointing device in the graphics window of the screen; used to draw, select, or pick icons, menu items, or objects. The appearance of the cursor may change depending on the command or option selected.
custom hatch pattern	A design that you have previously created and stored in the file *acad.pat* or another *.pat* file of your own making to use to fill an area.
customize	To change the toolbars, menus, and other aspects of the program to show those commands and functions that you want to use.
cutting edges	Objects used to define the portions to be removed when trimming an object.
cutting plane line	Defines the location on the object where the sectional view is taken.
datum surface	A theoretically exact geometric reference used to establish the tolerance zone for a feature.
default	The value that AutoCAD will use unless you specify otherwise; appears in angle brackets < > after a prompt.
default directory	The directory to which AutoCAD will save all drawing files unless instructed otherwise.
delta angle	The included angular value from the start point to the endpoint.
diameter symbol Ø	Indicates that the value is a diameter.
difference	The area formed by subtracting one region or solid from another.
dimension line	Drawn between extension lines with an arrowhead at each end; indicates how the stated dimension relates to the feature on the object.
dimension style	A group of dimension features saved as a set.
dimension value	The value of the dimension being described (how long, how far across, etc.); placed near the midpoint of the dimension line.
dimension variables	Features of dimensions that can be altered by the user; you control the features by setting the variables using the Dimension Style dialog box.
dimension	Describes the size and location of a part or object so that it can be manufactured.
distance across the flats	A measurement of the size of a hexagon from one flat side to the side opposite it.
docked	Attached to any edge of the graphics window, as a toolbar can be.
draft angle	The taper on a molded part that makes it possible to easily remove the part from the mold.

drag — To move an object on the screen and see it at the same time in order to specify the new size or location.

edge view — A line representing a plane surface shown on its end.

elements — Parts of a multiline, which can be made up of up to 16 lines.

engineering units — Drawings made with these units are drawn in feet and decimal inches.

export — To save a file from one application as a different file type for use by another application.

extension line — Relates a dimension to the feature it refers to.

extension line offset — Specifies a distance for the gap between the end of the extension line and the point that defines the dimension.

extrusion — Creates a long three-dimensional strip with the shape of a closed two-dimensional shape, as if material had been forced through a shaped opening.

falloff — The angle of the cone of light from a spotlight.

feature — Any definable aspect of an object—a hole, a surface, etc.

feature control frame — Geometric dimensioning and tolerancing specification that uses rectangular boxes with symbols to specify allowable variations in the manufactured part.

file extension — The part of a file name that is composed of a period followed by one to three characters that helps you to identify the file type.

fillet — An arc of specified radius that connects two lines, arcs, or circles, or a rounded interior corner on a machined part.

floating — Refers to the toolbar's or command window's ability to be moved to any location on the screen.

floating viewport — A window, created in paper space, through which you can see your model space drawing; very useful for plotting the drawing, adding drawing details, showing an enlarged view of the object, or showing multiple views of the object.

flyout — A sub-toolbar that becomes visible when its representative icon on the main toolbar is chosen.

font — A character pattern defined by the text style.

foreshortened — Appears smaller than actual size due to being tipped away from the viewing plane.

fractional units — Drawings made with these units express lengths less than 1 as fractions (e.g., 15 1/4).

freeze	Make a layer invisible and exclude it from regeneration and plotting.
G2 continuity	The position, tangency, and curvature between the surfaces match.
generated layer	A layer created automatically (instead of by the user) during commands such as SOLPROF.
geometric characteristic symbol	Form, orientation, profile, runout, and locational symbols used to specify allowable variations in the manufactured part.
geometric tolerance	Specialized tolerance symbols based on geometric form.
global linetype scaling factor	The factor of the original size at which all lines in the drawing are displayed.
globe	Used to select the direction for viewing a three-dimensional model.
graphics window	The central part of the screen, which is used to create and display drawings.
grid	Regularly spaced dots covering an area of the graphics window to aid in drawing.
group	A named selection set of objects.
handle number	A unique identifier assigned to each AutoCAD drawing object, including viewports.
heads-up	Entering a command while looking at the screen; by picking an icon, for example, you do not need to look down to the keyboard to enter the command.
hidden line	A line that represents an edge that is not directly visible because it is behind or beneath another surface.
highlight	A change of color around a particular command or object, indicating that it has been selected and is ready to be executed or worked on in some way.
hot grips	A method for editing an already drawn object using only the pointing device, without needing to use the menus, toolbars, or keyboard.
hotspot	The angle of the cone of light for the brightest area of the beam of a spotlight.
image tile	An active picture which displays dialog box choices as graphic images rather than words.
implied Crossing mode	When this mode is activated, the first corner of a box is started when you select a point on the screen that is not on an object in the drawing. If the box is drawn from right to left, everything that partially crosses as well as items fully enclosed by the box are selected.

implied Windowing mode	When this mode is activated, the first corner of a box is started when you select a point on the screen that is not on an object in the drawing. If the box is drawn from the left to right, a window is formed that selects everything that is entirely enclosed in the box.
import	To open and use a file created by a different application than the one being used.
inclined surface	Slanted at an angle, a surface that is perpendicular to one of the three principal views and tipped away from the other principal views.
included angle	The angular measurement along a circular path.
inscribed	Drawn inside a base circle.
inspection	The act of examining the part against its specifications.
instance	Each single action of a command.
intensity	The brightness level of a light source.
intersection	The point where two lines or surfaces meet, or the area shared by overlapping regions or solid models.
Inverter gate	A symbol used to draw an electronic logic circuit; for inputs of 1, the output is 0, for inputs of 0, the output is 1.
layer	A method of separating drawing objects so that they can be viewed individually or stacked like transparent acetates, allowing all layers to show. Used to set color and linetype properties for groups of objects.
leader line	A line from a note or radial dimension that ends in an arrowhead pointing at the feature.
limiting element	The outer edge of a curved surface.
limiting tolerances	Tolerances specified by defining an upper and lower allowable measurement.
lock	To prohibit changes to a layer, although the layer is still visible on the screen.
major arc	An arc which comprises more than 180° of a circle.
major axis	The long axis of symmetry across an ellipse.
manufacture	To create a part according to its specifications.
mass properties	Data about the real-world object being drawn, such as its mass, volume, and moments of inertia.
matrix	An array of vertices used to generate a surface.

menu bar	The strip across the top of the screen showing the names of the pull-down menus, such as File, Edit, etc.
minor axis	The short axis of symmetry across an ellipse.
mirror line	A line that defines the angle and distance at which a reflected image of a selected object will be created.
miter line	A line drawn above the side view and to the right of the top view, often drawn from the top right corner of the front view, used to project features from the side view onto the top view of an object.
model space	The AutoCAD drawing database, when an object exists as a three-dimensional object.
Nand gate	A symbol used to draw an electronic logic circuit; when both inputs are 1, output is 0, when any input is 0, output is 1.
nominal dimension	The general identification for the size of a typical feature, for example a 1/2" diameter hole.
Nor gate	A symbol used to draw an electronic logic circuit; when both inputs are 0, output is 1, any input of 1, output is 0.
normal surface	A surface that is perpendicular to two of the three principal orthographic views and appears at the correct size and shape in a basic view.
noun/verb selection	A method for selecting an object first and then the command to be used on it.
nurb	A cubic spline curve.
offset distance	Controls the distance from an existing object at which a new object will be created.
options	The choices associated with a particular command or instruction.
Or gate	A symbol used to draw an electronic logic circuit; any input of 1 results in output of 1, when both inputs are 0, output is 0.
orthographic view	A two-dimensional drawing used in representing a three-dimensional object. A minimum of two orthographic views are necessary to show the shape of a three-dimensional object, because each view shows only two dimensions.
output file	The file to which attribute data is extracted.
overall dimensions	The widest measurements of a part; needed by manufacturers to determine how much material to start with.
override mode	When the desired object snap mode is selected during each command it is to be used for.

palette	A type of toolbar, usually divided into areas, that allows for quick selection of items. AutoCAD Tool Palettes are used to organize blocks, hatches, and more in a location where they can be dragged into a drawing (similar to the way paint is held on an artist's palette for quick access).
paper space	A mode that allows you to arrange, annotate, and plot different views of a model in a single drawing, as you would arrange views on a piece of paper.
parametric	A modeling method that allows you to input sizes for and relationships between the features of parts. Changing a size or relationship will result in the model being updated to the new appearance.
partial auxiliary view	An auxiliary view that shows only the desired surfaces.
parts list	Provides information about the parts in an assembly drawing, including the item number, description, quantity, material, and part number.
perspective icon	A cube drawn in perspective that replaces the UCS icon when perspective viewing, activated by the 3D Dynamic View command, is in effect.
pictorial full section	A section view showing an object cut in half along its vertical center line.
pin registry	A process in which a series of transparent sheets are punched with a special hole pattern along one edge, allowing the sheets to be fitted onto a metal pin bar. The metal pin bar keeps the drawings aligned from one sheet to the next. Each sheet is used to show different map information.
plan view	The top view or view looking straight down the Z axis toward the XY plane.
plus/minus tolerances	Another name for variance tolerances.
point filter	Option that lets you selectively find single coordinates out of a point's three-dimensional coordinate set.
point light	A light source similar to a bare light bulb that casts light in every direction.
pointer	An indicator established from the current drawing to the original drawing or external reference.
polar array	A pattern created by repeating objects over and over in a circular fashion.
polar coordinates	The location of a point, defined as a distance and an angle from another specified point, using the AutoCAD input format @DISTANCE<ANGLE.
polygon	A closed shape with sides of equal length.
polyline	A series of connected objects (lines or arcs) that are treated as a single object.

precedence — When two lines occupy the same space, precedence determines which one is drawn. Continuous lines take precedence over hidden lines, and hidden lines take precedence over center lines.

primitives — Basic shapes that can be joined together or subtracted from each other to form more complex shapes.

profile — A two-dimensional view of a three-dimensional solid object created using the Solprof (Setup Profile) command.

project — To transfer information from one view of an object to another by aligning them and using projection lines.

projection lines — Horizontal lines that stretch from one view of an object to another to show which line or surface is which.

Properties toolbar — Contains the icons whose commands control the appearance of the objects in your drawing.

prototype drawing — A drawing saved with certain settings that can be used repeatedly as the basis for starting new drawings.

quadrant point — Any of the four points that mark the division of a circle or arc into four segments: 0°, 90°, 180°, and 270°.

ray tracing — The method of calculating shading by tracking reflected light rays hitting the object.

real-world units — Units in which drawings in the database are drawn; objects should always be drawn at the size that the real object would be.

rectangular array — A pattern created by repeating objects over and over in columns and rows.

rectangular view — A view of a cylinder in which it appears as a rectangle (looking from the side).

reference surface — A surface from which measurements are made when creating another view of the object.

reflection — The degree to which a surface bounces back light.

refraction — The degree to which an object changes the angle of light passing through it.

regenerate — To recalculate from the drawing database a drawing display that has just been zoomed or had changes made to it.

region — A two-dimensional area created from a closed shape or a loop.

relative coordinates — The location of a point in terms of the X and Y distance, or distance and angle, from a previously specified point @X,Y.

relative path — File location related to the current folder using designators like \\mynetwork-drive\mydrawing.dwg

rendered	Lighting effects, color, and shape applied to an object in a single two-dimensional view.
resolution	Refers to how sharp and clear an image appears to be and how much detail can be seen; the higher the resolution, the better the quality of the image. This is determined by the number of colors and pixels the computer monitor can display.
revolution	Creating a three-dimensional object by sweeping a two-dimensional polyline, circle, or region about a circular path to create a symmetrical solid that is basically circular in cross-section.
roman	A font.
root page	The original standard screen menu column along the right side of the screen, accessed by picking the word AutoCAD at the top of the screen.
roughness	The apparent texture of a surface. The lower the surface roughness, the more reflective the surface will be.
round	A convex arc, or a rounded external corner on a machined part.
running mode	When the current object snap mode is automatically used any time a command calls for the input of a point or selection.
scale factor	The multiple or fraction of the original size of a drawing object or linetype at which it is displayed.
section lines	Show surfaces that were cut in a section view.
section view	A type of orthographic view that shows the internal structure of an object; also called a cutaway view.
selectable group	A named selection set in which picking on one of its members selects all members that are in the current space, and not on locked or frozen layers. An object can belong to more than one group.
selection filters	A list of properties required of an object for it to be selected.
selection set	All of the objects chosen to be affected by a particular command.
session	Each use, from loading to exiting, of the AutoCAD program.
shape-compiled font	Character shapes drawn by the AutoCAD software using vectors.
sign	Positive or negative indicator that precedes a centermark value.
slicing plane	A plane that is defined for use in slicing a solid object. During the Slice command, the object can be removed on either side of the slicing plane or the selected object can be parted along the slicing plane and both sides can be retained.

solid modeling — A type of three-dimensional modeling that represents the volume of an object, not just its lines and surfaces; this allows for analysis of the object's mass properties.

spotlight — A light source used to highlight certain key areas and cast light only toward the selected target.

Standard toolbar — Contains the icons which control file operation commands.

status bar — The rectangular area at bottom of screen that displays time and some command and file operation information.

style — Controls the name, font file, height, width factor, obliquing angle, and generation of the text.

submenu — A list of available options or commands relating to an item chosen from a menu.

surface modeling — A type of three-dimensional modeling that defines only surfaces and edges so that the model can be shaded and have hidden lines removed; resembles an empty shell in the shape of the object.

swatch — An area that shows a sample of the color or pattern currently selected.

sweeping — Extrusion along a non-linear path rather than a straight line.

takeoff — A detailed list of each item, quantity, and typical price for drawing items in a construction project.

target area — The square area on an object snap aperture, in which at least part of the object to be selected must fit.

template drawing — A drawing with the extension *.dwt* having certain settings that can be used repeatedly as the basis for starting new drawings. Any drawing can be renamed and used as a template.

template file — Specifies the file format for the Extract Attribute command as *.cdf* or *.sdf.*

tessellation lines — To cover a surface with a grid or lines, like a mosaic. Tessellation lines are displayed on a curved surface to help you visualize it; the number of tessellation lines determines the accuracy of surface area calculations.

threshold value — Determines how close vertices must be in order to be automatically welded during the rendering process.

through point — The point through which the offset object is to be drawn.

tiled viewports — Multiple viewports that cannot overlap. They must line up next to each other, like tiles on a floor.

tilemode — An AutoCAD system variable that controls the use of tiled or floating viewports or paper space.

title bar — The rectangular area at the top of the screen which displays the application and file names.

toggle — A switch that turns certain settings on and off.

tolerance — The amount that a manufactured part can vary from the specifications laid out in the plans and still be acceptable.

tool tip — The name of the icon that appears when you hold the cursor over the icon.

toolbar — A strip containing icons for certain commands.

transparency — A quality that makes objects appear clear, like glass, or somewhat clear, like colored liquids.

transparent command — A command that can be selected while another command is operating.

typing cursor — A special cursor used in dialog boxes for entering text from the keyboard.

UCS icon — Indicates the current coordinate system in use and the direction in which the coordinates are being viewed in 3D drawings.

unidirectional dimensioning — The standard alignment for dimension text, which is to orient the text horizontally.

unilateral tolerance — A tolerance that is applied in one direction from a specified dimension.

union — The area formed by adding two regions or solid models together.

units — The type of metric, decimal, scientific, engineering, or architectural measurement scales used in AutoCAD drawings. These are set with the Units command.

update — To regenerate the active part or drawing using any new dimension values or changed sketches.

User Coordinate System (UCS) — A set of x, y, and z coordinates whose origin, rotation, and tilt are defined by the user. You can create and name any number of User Coordinate Systems.

user-defined hatch pattern — A predefined hatch pattern for which you have specified the angle, spacing, and/or linetype.

variance tolerances — Tolerances specified by defining a nominal dimension and the allowable range of deviation from that dimension; includes bilateral and unilateral tolerances.

vector	A directional line. Also, a way of storing a graphic image as a set of mathematical formulas.
Venn diagram	Pictorial description named after John Venn, an English logician, where circles are used to represent set operations.
viewpoint	The direction from which you are viewing a three-dimensional object.
viewport	A "window" showing a particular view of a three-dimensional object.
virtual screen	A file containing only the information displayed on the AutoCAD screen. Used to allow fast zooming without having to regenerate the original drawing file.
Windows close button	A button in the upper right corner of a window that closes the window.
wireframe modeling	A type of three-dimensional modeling that uses lines, arcs, circles, and other objects to represent the edges and other features of an object; so called because it looks like a sculpture made from wires.
World Coordinate System (WCS)	The AutoCAD system for defining model geometry using x, y, and z coordinate values; the default orientation is a horizontal X axis with positive values to the right, a vertical Y axis with positive values above the X axis, and a Z axis that is perpendicular to the screen and has positive values in front of the screen.

AUTOCAD® COMMAND SUMMARY

This grid includes AutoCAD commands used in this book and many others. You should use the AutoCAD on-line Help feature for complete information about the commands and their options. Most commands with dialog boxes can be run at the command line by typing a hyphen (-) in front of the command name. Many commands have keyboard shortcuts.

Command or Icon Name	Description	Command or Alias
2D Wireframe Shade	Displays objects using lines and curves to represent boundaries.	SHADEMODE
2D Solid	Creates solid-filled polygons.	SOLID, SO
3 Point UCS	Selects a user coordinate system based on any three points in the graphics window.	UCS
3D Array	Creates a three-dimensional array.	3DARRAY, 3A
3D Clip	Interactive 3D view and to adjust clipping planes.	3DCLIP
3D Continuous Orbit	Interactive 3D view showing continuous motion.	3DCORBIT
3D Distance	Make objects appear closer or farther in the interactive 3D view.	3DDISTANCE
3D Dynamic View	Changes the 3D view of a point.	DVIEW, DV
3D Face	Creates a three-dimensional surface.	3DFACE, 3F
3D Fly	Interactively changes your view of 3D drawings so that you appear to be flying through the model.	3DFLY
3D Free Orbit	Interactive 3D view showing free movement.	3DFORBIT
3D Mesh	Creates three-dimensional mesh objects.	3DMESH
3D Mirror	Creates a mirror image of objects about a plane.	MIRROR3D
3D Move	Displays the move grip tool in a 3D view and moves objects a specified distance in a specified direction.	3DMOVE
3D Orbit	Controlled interactive 3D viewing.	3D ORBIT, 3DO
3D Polyface Mesh	Creates a 3D polyface mesh by vertices.	PFACE
3D Polyline	Creates a 3D polyline of straight line segments.	3DPOLY, 3P
3D Rotate	Rotates an object in a 3D coordinate system.	3DROTATE
3D Studio In	Imports a 3D Studio® (**.3ds*) file into an AutoCAD drawing.	3DSIN
3D Swivel	Changes the target of the view in the direction that you drag.	3DSWIVEL
3D Walk	Interactively changes the view of a 3D drawing so that you appear to be walking through the model.	3DWALK

Command or Icon Name	Description	Command or Alias
About	Displays information about the AutoCAD software.	'ABOUT, ABOUT
Acadlspasdoc	System variable controlling whether or not the *acad.lsp* file is loaded into every drawing.	ACADLSPASDOC
Acadprefix	System variable that stores the directory path, if any, specified by the ACAD environment variable (read only).	ACADPREFIX
Acadver	System variable that stores the AutoCAD version number (read only).	ACADVER
ACIS In	Imports an ACIS (**.sat*) file into an AutoCAD drawing.	ACISIN
ACIS Out	Saves a file formatted in ACIS (**.sat*).	ACISOUT
Active Assistance	Displays Quick Help about the current command in the Info Palette.	ASSIST, 'ASSIST
Adcclose	Closes the DesignCenter™ window.	ADCCLOSE
Adcenter	Manages and inserts blocks, xrefs, hatch patterns, and more.	ADCENTER
Adcnavigate	Lets you specify a path or drawing file name to load in the Folders tree view of the DesignCenter.	ADCNAVIGATE
Administration	Performs administrative functions with external database commands.	DBCONNECT, AAD
Align	Moves and rotates objects to align with other objects.	ALIGN, AL
Align Dimension Text, Edit	Aligns dimension text to Home, Left, Right or Angle position.	DIMTEDIT, DIMTED
Aligned Dimension	Creates an aligned linear dimension.	DIMALIGNED, DAL, DIMALI
AME Convert	Converts AME solid models to AutoCAD solid objects.	AMECONVERT
Angular Dimension	Dimensions an angle.	DIMANGULAR, DAN, DIMANG
Animation Path	Saves an animation along a path in a 3D model.	ANIPATH
Annotation Reset	Resets the location of all scale representations for an annotative object to that of the current scale representation.	ANNORESET
Annotation Update	Updates existing annotative objects to match the current properties of their styles.	ANNOUPDATE
Aperture	Controls the size of the object snap target box.	'APERTURE, APERTURE
Aperture Box	System variable controlling display of the object snap target box.	APBOX
Application Load	Loads AutoLISP® (**.ads*), and (**.arx*) files.	'APPLOAD, AP

Command or Icon Name	Description	Command or Alias
Arc	Draws an arc based on three points.	ARC, A
Arc Center Start Angle	Draws an arc of a specified angle based on the center and start points.	ARC, A
Arc Center Start End	Draws an arc based on the center, start, and endpoints.	ARC, A
Arc Center Start Length	Draws an arc of a specified length based on the center and start points.	ARC, A
Arc Continue	Draws an arc from the last point of the previous line or arc drawn.	ARC, A
Arc Length Dimension	Dimensions the length of an arc, using the symbol set using Dimension Style.	DIMARC
Arc Start Center Angle	Draws an arc of a specified angle based on the start and center points.	ARC, A
Arc Start Center End	Draws an arc based on the start, center, and endpoints.	ARC, A
Arc Start Center Length	Draws an arc of a specified length based on the start and center points.	ARC, A
Arc Start End Angle	Draws an arc of a specified angle based on the start and endpoints.	ARC, A
Arc Start End Direction	Draws an arc in a specified direction based on the start and endpoints.	ARC, A
Arc Start End Radius	Draws an arc of a specified radius based on the start and endpoints.	ARC, A
Area	Finds the area and perimeter of objects or defined areas.	AREA, AA
Array	Creates multiple copies of objects in a regularly spaced circular or rectangular pattern.	ARRAY, AR
Array, Classic	Displays the legacy Array dialog box.	ARRAYCLASSIC
Array, Path (Path Array)	Evenly distributes object copies along a path or a portion of a path.	ARRAYPATH
Array, Polar (Polar Array)	Evenly distributes object copies in a circular pattern around a center point or axis of rotation.	ARRAYPOLAR
Array, Rectangular (Rectangular Array)	Distributes object copies into any combination of rows, columns, and levels.	ARRAYRECT
Attdia	System variable that controls whether the Insert command uses a dialog box for attribute value entry.	ATTDIA
Attedit	Allows you to change attribute information.	ATTEDIT
ATTIPEDIT	Changes the textual content of an attribute within a block.	ATTIPEDIT
Attribute Display	Globally controls attribute visibility.	'ATTDISP, ATTDISP
Attribute Editor, Enhanced	Edits attributes of a block reference.	EATTEDIT
Attribute Redefine	Redefines a block and updates its attributes.	ATTREDEF

Command or Icon Name	Description	Command or Alias
Audit	Evaluates the integrity of a drawing.	AUDIT
AutoCAD Runtime Extension	Provides information, loads/ unloads ARX applications.	ARX
Autocomplete	Controls what types of automated keyboard features are available at the Command prompt.	AUTOCOMPLETE
Autopublish	Publishes drawings to DWF files automatically.	AUTOPUBLISH
Back View	Sets the viewing direction for a three-dimensional visualization of the drawing to the back.	VPOINT, -VP, DDVPOINT, VP
Base	Specifies the insertion point for a block or drawing.	'BASE, BASE
Baseline Dimension	Continues a linear, angular, or ordinate dimension from the baseline of the previous or selected dimension.	DIMBASELINE, DBA, DIMBASE
Bitmap Out	Saves AutoCAD objects in a bitmap (*.bmp*) format.	BMPOUT
Blend	Creates a spline to fill the gap between two selected lines or curves.	BLEND
Block Attribute Manager	Allows editing of block attribute properties.	BATTMAN
Block Editor	Adds dynamic behavior to blocks.	BEDIT
Block Icon	Generate preview images for blocks created with R14 or earlier.	BLOCKICON
Bottom View	Sets the viewing direction for a three-dimensional visualization of the drawing to the bottom.	VPOINT, -VP, DDVPOINT, VP
Boundary	Creates a region or polyline of a closed boundary.	BOUNDARY, BO, -BOUNDARY, -BO
Boundary Hatch	Automatically fills the area you select with a pattern. Same as HATCH.	BHATCH, BH, H
Box	Creates a three-dimensional rectangular-shaped solid.	BOX
Break	Removes part of an object or splits it in two.	BREAK, BR
Browser	Launches the Web browser defined in the system registry.	BROWSER
Calculator	Calculates mathematical and geometrical expressions.	'CAL, CAL
Calculator, Quick	Performs calculations, converts units, and more.	QUICKCALC
Cancel	Exits current command without performing operation.	[Esc]
Celtype	System variable that sets the linetype of new objects.	celtype
Center Mark	Draws center marks and centerlines of arcs and circles.	DIMCENTER, DCE
Chamfer	Draws a straight line segment (called a chamfer) between two given lines.	CHAMFER, CHA

Command or Icon Name	Description	Command or Alias
Chamfer Edge	Bevels the edges of 3D solids and surfaces.	CHAMFEREDGE
Change	Changes the properties of existing objects.	CHANGE, CH, CHPROP
Check Standards	Checks the current drawing for CAD Standards violations.	CHECKSTANDARDS
Circle	Draws circles based upon center point and radius.	CIRCLE, C
Circle Center Diameter	Draws circles based upon center point and diameter.	CIRCLE, C
Circle Tan Tan Radius	Draws circles based upon two tangent points and a radius.	CIRCLE, C
Circle Tan Tan Tan	Draws circles based upon three tangent points.	CIRCLE, C
Circle 3 Points	Draws circles based upon 3 points.	CIRCLE, C
Circle 2 Points	Draws circles based upon 2 points.	CIRCLE, C
Classic Group	Opens the legacy Object Grouping dialog box.	CLASSICGROUP
Close	Closes the current drawing; prompts to save or discard the changes if it was modified.	CLOSE
Close All	Closes all open drawings.	CLOSEALL
Cmddia	System variable controls whether dialog boxes are enabled during some commands.	CMDDIA
Color Control	Sets the color for new objects.	'COLOR, COLOR, 'DDCOLOR, DDCOLOR, COL
Command Line	Displays the command window when it has been hidden.	COMMANDLINE
Compile	Compiles PostScript font files and shape files.	COMPILE
Cone	Creates a three-dimensional solid primitive with a circular base tapering to a point perpendicular to its base.	CONE
Construction Line	Creates an infinite line.	XLINE
Content Explorer	Finds and inserts content such as drawing files, blocks, and styles.	CONTENTEXPLORER, CONTENTEXPLORER-CLOSE
Continue Dimension	Adds the next chained dimension, measured from the last dimension.	DIMCONTINUE, DIMCONT, DCO
Convert	Converts associative hatches and 2D polylines created in Release 13 or earlier.	CONVERT
Convert Color Dependent Plot Style	Converts color-dependent plot style table to a named plot style table.	CONVERTCTB
Convert Old Lights	Converts lights created in previous releases to lights in AutoCAD 2008 format.	CONVERTOLD LIGHTS
Convert Old Materials	Converts materials created in previous releases to materials in AutoCAD 2008 format.	CONVERTOLD MATERIALS
Convert Plot Styles	Converts the current drawing to a named or color dependent plot style.	CONVERTPSTYLES

Command or Icon Name	Description	Command or Alias
Convert to Solid	Converts polylines and circles with thickness to 3D solids.	CONVTOSOLID
Convert to Surface	Converts objects to surfaces.	CONVTOSURFACE
Copy	Copies an existing shape from one area on the drawing to another area.	COPY, CP, CO
Copy Link	Copies the current view to the Windows Clipboard for linking to other OLE applications.	COPYLINK
Copyclip	Copies objects to the Windows Clipboard.	COPYCLIP
Copyhist	Copies all text in the command line history to the Clipboard.	COPYHIST
Count	Highlights all instances of the selected object or block and displays the counted number.	COUNT
Customize	Allows customization of toolbars, buttons, and shortcut keys.	CUSTOMIZE
Cutclip	Copies objects to the clipboard and erases them from the drawing.	CUTCLIP
Customize	Customizes tool palettes and tool palette groups.	CUSTOMIZE
Customize User Interface	Manages the customized user interface elements.	CUI
Cylinder	Creates a three-dimensional solid primitive similar to an extruded circle, but without a taper.	CYLINDER
Data Base Close	Closes the dbConnect Manager and removes dbConnect menu from the menu bar.	DBCLOSE
Data Base Connect	Interfaces with external database tables.	DBCONNECT
	Extracts drawing data and merges data from an external source to a data extraction table or external file.	DATAEXTRACTION, -DATAEXTRACTION
Database List	Lists database information for drawing objects.	DBLIST
Define Attribute	Creates attribute text.	ATTDEF, -AT, DDATTDEF
Delay	Adds a timed pause (33 seconds maximum) within a script.	'DELAY, DELAY
Delobj	Controls whether objects used to create other objects are retained or deleted from the drawing database.	DELOBJ
DesignCenter	Manage drawing content.	ADCENTER
DesignCenter Navigate	Controls path for AutoCAD DesignCenter.	ADCNAVIGAT,
Detach	Removes an externally referenced drawing.	XREF, XR, -XREF, -XR
Detach url	Removes hyperlinks from a drawing.	DETACHURL
DGNADJUST	Changes the display options of selected DGN underlays.	DGNADJUST
DGNATTACH	Attaches a DGN underlay to the current drawing.	DGNATTACH

Command or Icon Name	Description	Command or Alias
DGNCLIP	Defines a clipping boundary for a selected DGN underlay.	DGNCLIP
DGNEXPORT	Creates one or more V8 DGN files from the current drawing.	DGNEXPORT
DGNIMPORT	Imports the data from a V8 DGN file into a new DWG file.	DGNIMPORT
Diameter Dimension	Adds center marks to a circle when providing its diameter dimension.	DIMDIAMETER, DIMDIA, DDI
Diastat	System variable that stores the exit method of the most recently used dialog box (read only).	DIASTAT
Dimalt	System variable that enables alternate units.	DIMALT
Dimaltd	System variable that sets alternate unit precision.	DIMALTD
Dimaltf	System variable that sets alternate unit scale.	DIMALTF
Dimalttd	System variable that stores the number of decimal places for the tolerance values of an alternate units dimension.	DIMALTTD
Dimalttz	System variable that toggles the suppression of zeros for tolerance values.	DIMALTTZ
Dimaltu	System variable that sets the units format for alternate units of all dimension style family members, except angular.	DIMALTU
Dimaltz	System variable that toggles suppression of zeros for alternate units dimension values.	DIMALTZ
Dimapost	System variable that specifies the text prefix and/or suffix to the alternate dimension measurement for alternate types of dimensions, except angular.	DIMAPOST
Dimaso	System variable that controls the creation of associative dimension objects.	DIMASO
Dimassoc	System variable which controls the associativity of dimensions. Set to 0, it creates dimensions with no association between dimension elements—lines, arrows, etc. are all separate objects. Set to 1, it forms elements into non-associative dimension objects, whose values update. Set to 2, it creates fully associative dimension objects.	DIMASSOC
Dimasz	System variable that controls the size of dimension line and leader line arrowheads.	DIMASZ
Dimaunit	System variable that sets the angle format for angular dimensions.	DIMAUNIT
Dimblk	System variable that sets the name of a block to be drawn instead of the normal arrowhead at the end of the dimension line or leader line.	DIMBLK
Dimblk1	System variable that, if Dimsah is on, specifies the user-defined arrowhead block for the first end of the dimension line.	DIMBLK1

Command or Icon Name	Description	Command or Alias
Dimblk2	System variable that, if Dimsah is on, specifies the user-defined arrowhead block for the second end of the dimension line.	DIMBLK2
DIMBREAK	Adds or removes a dimension break.	DIMBREAK
Dimcen	System variable that controls the drawing of circle or arc centermarks or centerlines.	DIMCEN
Dimclrd	System variable that assigns colors to dimension lines, arrowheads, and dimension leader lines.	DIMCLRD
Dimclre	System variable that assigns colors to dimension extension lines.	DIMCLRE
Dimclrt	System variable that assigns color to dimension text.	DIMCLRT
Dimdec	System variable that sets the decimal places for the tolerance values of a primary units dimension.	DIMDEC
Dimdle	System variable that extends the dimension line beyond the extension line when oblique strokes are drawn instead of arrowheads.	DIMDLE
Dimdli	System variable that controls the dimension line spacing for baseline dimensions.	DIMDLI
Dimension, Arc Length	Dimensions the length of an arc, using the symbol set using Dimension Style.	DIMARC
Dimension Edit	Edits dimensions.	DIMEDIT, DIMED, DED
Dimension Status	Shows the dimension variables and their current settings.	DIMSTATUS
Dimension Style	Controls dimension styles.	DDIM, D, DIMSTYLE, DST, DIMSTY
Dimension, Update	Updates the dimensions based on changes to the dimension styles and variables.	DIM (w/update), STYLE
Dimexe	System variable that determines how far to extend the extension line beyond the dimension line.	DIMEXE
Dimexo	System variable that determines how far extension lines are offset from origin points.	DIMEXO
Dimfit	System variable that controls the placement of text and attributes inside or outside extension lines.	DIMFIT
Dimgap	System variable that sets the distance around the dimension text when you break the dimension line to accommodate dimension text.	DIMGAP
Dimension, Inspect	Creates or removes inspection dimensions.	DIMINSPECT
Dimension Jog Line	Adds or removes a jag line to a linear or aligned dimension.	DIMJOGLINE
Dimjust	System variable that controls the horizontal dimension text position.	DIMJUST

Command or Icon Name	Description	Command or Alias
Dimlfac	System variable that sets the global scale factor for linear dimensioning measurements.	DIMLFAC
Dimlim	System variable that, when on, generates dimension limits as the default text.	DIMLIM
Dimoverride	Allows you to override dimensioning system variable settings associated with a dimension object but will not affect the current dimension style.	DIMOVERRIDE, DIMOVER, DOV
Dimpost	System variable that specifies a text prefix and/or suffix to the dimension measurement.	DIMPOST
Dimrnd	System variable that rounds all dimensioning distances to the specified value.	DIMRND
Dimsah	System variable that controls the use of user-defined attribute blocks at the ends of the dimension lines.	DIMSAH
Dimscale	System variable that sets overall scale factor applied to dimensioning variables that specify sizes, distances, or offsets.	DIMSCALE
Dimsd1	System variable that, when on, suppresses drawing of the first dimension line.	DIMSD1
Dimsd2	System variable that, when on, suppresses drawing of the second dimension line.	DIMSD2
Dimse1	System variable that, when on, suppresses drawing of the first extension line.	DIMSE1
Dimse2	System variable that, when on, suppresses drawing of the second extension line.	DIMSE2
Dimsho	System variable that, when on, controls redefinition of dimension objects while dragging.	DIMSHO
Dimsoxd	System variable that, when on, suppresses drawing of dimension lines outside the extension lines.	DIMSOXD
DIMSPACE	Adjusts the spacing equally between parallel linear and angular dimensions.	DIMSPACE
Dimtad	System variable that controls the vertical position of text in relation to the dimension line.	DIMTAD
Dimtdec	System variable that sets the number of decimal places to display the tolerance values for a dimension.	DIMTDEC
Dimtfac	System variable that specifies a scale factor for the text height of tolerance values relative to the dimension text height.	DIMTFAC
Dimtih	System variable that controls the position of dimension text inside the extension lines for all dimension types except ordinate dimensions.	DIMTIH

Command or Icon Name	Description	Command or Alias
Dimtix	System variable that draws text between extension lines.	DIMTIX
Dimtm	System variable that, when Dimtol or Dimlim is on, sets the minimum (or lower) tolerance limit for dimension text.	DIMTM
Dimtofl	System variable that, when on, draws a dimension line between the extension lines even when the text is placed outside the extension lines.	DIMTOFL
Dimtoh	System variable that, when turned on, controls the position of dimension text outside the extension lines.	DIMTOH
Dimtol	System variable that generates plus/minus tolerances.	DIMTOL
Dimtolj	System variable that sets the vertical justification for tolerance values relative to the nominal dimension text.	DIMTOLJ
Dimtp	System variable that, when Dimtol or Dimlim is on, sets the maximum (or upper) tolerance limit for dimension text.	DIMTP
Dimtsz	System variable that specifies the size of oblique strokes drawn instead of arrowheads for linear, radius, and diameter dimensioning.	DIMTSZ
Dimtvp	System variable that adjusts text placement relative to text height.	DIMTVP
Dimtxsty	System variable that specifies the text style of a dimension.	DIMTXSTY
Dimtxt	System variable that specifies the height of the dimension text, unless the current text style has a fixed height.	DIMTXT
Dimtzin	System variable that controls the suppression of zeros for tolerance values.	DIMTZIN
Dimunit	System variable that sets the units format for all dimension family members, except angular.	DIMUNIT
Dimupt	System variable that controls the cursor functionality for User Positioned Text.	DIMUPT
Dimzin	System variable controlling the suppression of the inch portion of a feet-and-inches dimension when distance is an integral number of feet, or the feet portion when distance is less than a foot.	DIMZIN
Disassociate Dimension	Removes associativity from selected dimensions.	DIMDISASSOCIATE
Dispsilh	System variable that controls the display of silhouette curves of body objects in wire-frame mode.	DISPSILH

Command or Icon Name	Description	Command or Alias
Distance	Reads out the value for the distance between two selected points.	'DIST, DIST, DI
Divide	Places points or blocks along an object to create segments.	DIVIDE, DIV
Donut	Draws concentric filled circles or filled circles.	DONUT
Double-click Edit	Turns on and off double-click editing mode used to automatically launch the Properties palette and other editing features.	DBLCLKEDIT
Drafting Settings	Sets Snap mode, grid, polar and object snap tracking.	DSETTINGS
Drafting Settings	Sets the drawing aids for the drawing.	'DSETTINGS
Dragmode	Controls the way dragged objects are displayed.	'DRAGMODE, DRAGMODE
Drawing Adjust	Changes the display options of selected DGN underlays.	DGNADJUST
Drawing Attach	Attaches a DGN underlay to the current drawing.	DGNATTACH
Drawing Bind	Binds DGN underlays to the current drawing.	DGNBIND (-DGNBIND)
Drawing Clip	Defines a clipping boundary for a selected DGN underlay.	DGNCLIP
Drawing Convert	Converts drawing format version for selected drawing files.	DWGCONVERT
Drawing Export	Creates one or more V8 DGN files from the current drawing.	DGNEXPORT
Drawing Import	Imports the data from a V8 DGN file into a new DWG file.	DGNIMPORT
Drawing Properties	Set and display properties of the current drawing.	DWGPROPS
Draworder	Changes the display order of images and objects.	DRAWORDER, DR
DWF Out	Saves drawing objects in Drawing Web format (*.*dwf*).	DWFOUT, PLOT
DXB In	Imports coded binary files (*.*dxb*).	DXBIN
DXF In	Imports drawing saved in DXF™ Drawing Interchange (*.*dxf*) format.	DXFIN
DXF Out	Saves drawing objects in DXF™ Drawing Interchange (*.*dxf*) Format.	DXFOUT
DWG Props	Sets and displays properties of the current drawing.	DWGPROPS
Edge	Changes the visibility of three-dimensional face edges.	EDGE
Edge Mesh	Creates a three-dimensional polygon mesh.	3DMESH
Edit Attribute	Edits attribute values.	EATTEDIT, ATTEDIT, -ATE
Edit Attribute Globally	Edits attribute values.	DDATTE, ATTEDIT, ATE

Command or Icon Name	Description	Command or Alias
Edit Hatch	Modifies an existing associative hatch block.	HATCHEDIT, HE
Edit Links	Updates, changes, and cancels existing links.	OLELINKS
Edit Multiline	Edits multiple parallel lines.	MLEDIT
Edit Polyline	Changes various features of polylines.	PEDIT, PE
Edit Scale List	Modifies the list of scales displayed in view and plot scale lists.	SCALELIST-EDIT
Edit Spline	Edits a spline object.	SPLINEDIT, SPE
Edit Text	Allows you to edit text inside a dialog box.	DDEDIT, ED
Electronic Transmit	Creates a set of drawings and related files for transmittal.	ETRANSMIT
Elev	Sets elevation and extrusion thickness of new objects.	'ELEV, ELEV, ELEVATION
Ellipse	Used to draw ellipses.	ELLIPSE, EL
Ellipse Axis End	Used to draw ellipses.	ELLIPSE
Ellipse Arc	Used to draw ellipses.	ELLIPSE
End Startup Dialog	Turns off use of the Startup dialog box.	N/A
Erase	Erases objects from drawing.	ERASE, E
Explode	Separates blocks or dimensions into component objects so that they are no longer one group and can be edited.	EXPLODE, X
Export	Exports a drawing to a file of type DXF so that another application can use it.	EXPORT, EXP
Export Links	Exports link information for selected objects.	DBCONNECT
Express Tools	Activate Express Tools if needed.	EXPRESSTOOLS
Extend	Extends the length of an existing object to meet a boundary.	EXTEND, EX
Extract Attributes	Extracts attribute data to an external file.	EATTEXT, ATTEXT, DDATTEXT
External Reference	Attaches, Detaches, Reloads, Unloads, Binds, etc. other drawings as external references, without really adding them to your current drawing.	XREF, XR, -XREF, -XR
External Reference Attach	Uses another drawing as an external reference, without really adding it to your current drawing.	XATTACH, XA
External Reference Bind	Binds symbols of an xref to a drawing.	XBIND, XB, -XBIND, -XB
External Reference Clip	Defines an xref clipping boundary.	XCLIP, XC
External Reference Clip Frame	System Variable that controls visibility of clipping boundaries.	XCLIPFRAME
Extrude	Extrudes a two-dimensional shape into a three-dimensional object.	EXTRUDE, EXT
Facetres	System variable that adjusts the smoothness of shaded and hidden line-removed objects.	FACETRES

Command or Icon Name	Description	Command or Alias
Filedia	System variable that suppresses the display of the file dialog boxes.	FILEDIA
Fill	Controls the filling of multilines, traces, solids, and wide polylines.	'FILL, FILL
Fillet	Connects lines, arcs, or circles with a smoothly fitted arc.	FILLET, F
Fillet 3D Edge	Rounds and fillets the edges of solid objects.	FILLETEDGE
Filter	Creates a list of requirements that an object must meet to be included in a selection set.	FILTER
Find	Finds, replaces, selects, or zooms to specified text.	FIND
Flat Shot	Creates a 2D representation of all 3D objects in the current view.	FLATSHOT
FREESPOT	Creates a free spotlight, which is similar to a spotlight without a specified target.	FREESPOT
FREEWEB	Creates a free weblight, which is similar to a weblight without a specified target.	FREEWEB
Front View	Sets the viewing direction for a three-dimensional visualization of the drawing to the front.	VPOINT, VP, ddvpoint, -VP
Global Linetype	System variable that sets the current global linetype scale factor for objects.	LTSCALE
Graphics Screen	Switches from the text window back to the graphics window.	'GRAPHSCR, GRAPHSCR, [F2]
Grid	Displays a grid of dots at desired spacing on the screen.	'GRID, GRID, or toggle off and on with [F7]
Grips	Enables grips and sets their color.	'grips, grips, 'ddgrips, ddgrips, GR
Group	Creates and manages grouped objects.	GROUP
Group, Classic Legacy	Opens the legacy Object Grouping dialog box.	CLASSICGROUP
Group Edit	Adds and removes objects from the selected group, or renames a selected group.	GROUPEDIT
Handles	System variable that displays the setting for the use of handles in solid models.	HANDLES
Hatch	Automatically fills the area you select with a pattern.	HATCH, -H
Helix	Creates a 2D or 3D spiral.	HELIX
Help	Displays information explaining commands and procedures.	'HELP, '?, HELP, ?, or toggle on with [F1]
Hide	Hides an object.	HIDE, HI
Highlight	System variable that controls object highlighting.	HIGHLIGHT
Hyperlink	Attaches/modifies a hyperlink to an object.	HYPERLINK
Identify Point	Displays the coordinate of a location.	ID
Image	Opens the Image Manager.	IMAGE, IM, -IMAGE, -IM

Command or Icon Name	Description	Command or Alias
Image Adjust	Controls the fade, contrast, and brightness of a selected image.	IMAGEADJUST, IAD
Image Attach	Attaches a new image to the drawing.	IMAGEATTACH, IAT
Image Clip	Creates clipping boundaries for image objects.	IMAGECLIP, ICL
Image Frame	Controls whether an image frame is displayed or not.	IMAGE-FRAME
Image Quality	Controls the quality of images.	IMAGEQUALITY
Image Transparency	Controls whether the background of an image is opaque or clear.	TRANSPARENCY
Import	Imports many different file formats.	IMPORT, IMP
Insert Block	Places blocks or other drawings into a drawing via the command line or via a dialog box.	INSERT, -I, DDINSERT, I
Insert Multiple Blocks	Inserts multiple instances of a block in a rectangular array.	MINSERT
Insert Objects	Inserts a linked or embedded object.	INSERTOBJ, IO
Interfere	Shows where two solid objects overlap.	INTERFERE, INF
Intersect	Forms a new solid from the area common to two or more solids or regions.	INTERSECT, IN
Isolines	System variable that specifies the number of isolines per surface on objects.	ISOLINES
Isometric Plane	Controls which isometric drawing plane is active: left, top, or right.	'ISOPLANE, ISOPLANE, or [Ctrl]-E or [F5]
Join	Joins the endpoints of lines, 2D and 3D polylines, arcs, elliptical arcs, helixes, and splines to create a single object.	JOIN
Jpeg out	Saves selected objects to a file in JPEG file format.	JPEGOUT
Justify Text	Changes the justification point of text.	JUSTIFYTEXT
Layer Properties Manager	Creates layers and controls layer color, linetype, and visibility.	'LAYER, LAYER, 'LA, LA, 'ddlmodes, ddlmodes, -Layer, -LA
Layer Translator	Changes a drawing's layers to specified layer standard.	LAYTRANS
Layout	Create, rename, copy, save, or delete layouts for managing plotted views.	LAYOUT
Layout Wizard	Starts the layout wizard which you can use to create and control layouts.	LAYOUTWIZARD
Leader	Creates leader lines for identifying lines and dimensions.	LEADER, Lead, LE, QLEADER
Left View	Sets the viewing direction for a three-dimensional visualization of the drawing to the left side.	VPOINT, -VP, DDVPOINT, VP
Lengthen	Lengthens an object.	LENGTHEN, LEN
Light	Controls the light sources in rendered scenes.	LIGHT

Command or Icon Name	Description	Command or Alias
Light List	Opens the Lights in Model window to add and modify lights.	LIGHTLIST
Limits	Sets up the size of the drawing.	'LIMITS, LIMITS
Line	Draws straight lines of any length.	LINE, L
Lineweight	Sets the line thickness for objects.	LWEIGHT, 'LWEIGHT, Right-click LWT button, pick Settings
Linear Dimension	Creates linear dimensions.	DIMLINEAR, DIMLIN, DLI
Linetype	Changes the pattern used for new lines in the drawing.	'LINETYPE, LINETYPE, -LT 'DDLTYPE, DDLTYPE, LT
Linetype Scale	System variable that changes the scale of the linetypes in the drawing.	'LTSCALE, LTSCALE, LTS
List	Provides information on an object, such as the length of a line.	LIST, LI, LS
List Variables	Lists the values of system variables.	'SETVAR, SETVAR, SET
Load	Makes shapes available for use by the Shape command.	LOAD
Locate Point	Finds the coordinates of any point on the screen.	'ID, ID
Loft	Creates a 3D solid or surface by lofting through a set of two or more curves.	LOFT
Log File Off	Closes the log file.	LOGFILEOFF
Log File On	Writes the text window contents to a file.	LOGFILEON
Make Block	Groups a set of objects together so that they are treated as one object.	BMAKE, B, BLOCK, -B
Make Slide	Creates a bitmapped slide file of the current viewport or layout.	MSLIDE
Mapping	Lets you map materials onto selected geometry.	MATERIALSMAPPING
Markup Set Manager	Displays and allows you to add notes to markup drawings.	MARKUP
Match Properties	Copies the properties of one object to other selected objects.	'MATCHPROP, MATCHPROP, MA, PAINTER
Materials	Controls the material a rendered object appears to be made of, and allows creation of new materials.	MATERIALS
Mass Properties	Calculates and displays the mass properties of regions and solids.	MASSPROP
Measure	Marks segments of a chosen length on an object by inserting points or blocks.	MEASURE, ME MEASUREGEOM
Menu	Loads a menu file.	MENU
Menu Load	Loads partial menu files.	MENULOAD

Command or Icon Name	Description	Command or Alias
Menu Unload	Unloads partial menu files.	MENUUNLOAD
Mesh, Cap	Creates a mesh face that connects open edges.	MESHCAP
Mirror	Creates mirror images of shapes.	MIRROR, MI
Mirror3d	Creates mirror images of shapes with options for 3D.	MIRROR 3D
Multileader, Align	Organizes selected multileaders along a specified line.	MLEADERALIGN
Multileader Collect	Organizes selected multileaders containing blocks as content into a group attached to a single leader line.	MLEADERCOLLECT
Multileader, Style	Defines a new multileader style.	MLEADERSTY- LE
Model Space	Enters model space.	MSPACE, MS
Modify Properties	Controls properties of existing objects.	PROPERTIES, DDMODIFY, MO
Move	Moves an existing shape from one area on the drawing to another area.	MOVE, M
Mtprop	Changes paragraph text properties.	MTPROP
Multileader	Creates a line that connects annotation to a feature.	MLEADER
Multiline	Creates multiple, parallel lines.	MLIne, ML
Multiline Style	Defines a style for multiple, parallel lines.	MLSTYLE
Multiline Text	Creates a paragraph that fits within a nonprinting text boundary.	MTEXT, MT, T, -MTEXT, -T
Multiple	Repeats the next command until canceled.	MULTIPLE
Multiple Redo	Reverses the effects of previous UNDO commands.	MREDO
MV Setup	Helps set up drawing views using a LISP program.	MVSETUP
Mview	Creates viewports in paperspace (when Tilemode = 0).	MVIEW, MV
Named UCS	Selects a named and saved user coordinate system.	UCSMAN, DDUCS, UC
Named Views	Sets the viewing direction to a named view.	'VIEW, VIEW, -V, 'DDVIEW, DDVIEW, V
NE Isometric View	Sets the viewing direction for a three-dimensional visualization of the drawing.	VPOINT, -VP, DDVPOINT, VP
New Drawing	Sets up the screen to create a new drawing.	NEW
NW Isometric View	Sets the viewing direction for a three-dimensional visualization of the drawing.	VPOINT, -VP, DDVPOINT, VP
Object Group	Creates a named selection set of objects.	GROUP, G, -GROUP, -G
Object Scale	Adds or deletes supported scales for annotative objects.	OBJECTSCALE

Command or Icon Name	Description	Command or Alias
Object Selection Filters	Creates lists to select objects based on properties.	'FILTER, FILTER, FI
Object Selection Settings	Defines Selection Mode.	'DDSELECT, DDSELECT, SE
Object Snap Settings (Running Object Snap)	Sets running objects snap modes and changes target box size.	'OSNAP, OSNAP, 'DDOSNAP, DDOSNAP, OSNAP, -OS, OS
Object UCS	Selects a user coordinate system based on the object.	UCS
Offset	Draws objects parallel to a given object.	OFFSET, O OFFSETEDGE
OLE Properties	Allows you to control properties of linked objects.	OLESCALE
Online Collaboration	Starts an online session with AutoCAD WS so you can invite people to simultaneously view and edit your current drawing.	ONLINECOLNOW
Online Documents	Shows your Autodesk 360 documents list and folders in a browser.	ONLINEDOCS
Online Sharing	Lets you specify users who can access the current document from your Autodesk 360 account.	ONLINESHARE
Online Synchronization	Starts or stops syncing your custom settings with your Autodesk 360 account. Can also use Options dialog box.	ONLINESYNC
Online Synchronization Settings	Displays the Choose Which Settings Are Synced dialog box. Can also use Options dialog box.	ONLINESYNCSETTINGS
Online to Mobile	Sends a notice to your smart phone or other mobile device to let you find and open the current drawing on it.	ONLINETOMOBILE
Oops	Restores erased objects.	OOPS
Open Drawing	Loads a previously saved drawing.	OPEN
Options	Customize the AutoCAD software for your use.	OPTIONS
Ordinate Dimension	Creates ordinate point dimensions.	dimordinate, DIMORD, DOR
Origin UCS	Creates a user-defined coordinate system at the origin of the view.	UCS
Ortho	Restricts movement to only horizontal and vertical.	'ORTHO, ORTHO, or toggle with [F8]
Page Setup	Specifies the layout page, plotting device, paper size, and settings for new layout.	PAGESETUP
Pan Down	Moves the drawing around on the screen without changing the zoom factor.	'PAN, PAN, 'P, P
Pan Left	Moves the drawing around on the screen without changing the zoom factor.	'PAN, PAN, 'P, P
Pan Point	Moves the drawing around on the screen without changing the zoom factor.	'-PAN, -PAN, '-P, -P

Command or Icon Name	Description	Command or Alias
Pan Realtime	Moves the drawing around on the screen without changing the zoom factor.	'PAN, PAN, 'P, P
Pan Right	Moves the drawing around on the screen without changing the zoom factor.	'PAN, PAN, 'P, P
Pan Up	Moves the drawing around on the screen without changing the zoom factor.	'PAN, PAN, 'P, P
Paper Space	Enters paper space when TILEMODE is set to 0.	PSPACE, PS
Paper Space Linetype Scale	System variable that causes the paper space LTSCALE factor to be used for every viewport.	PSLTSCALE
Paste From Clipboard	Places objects from the Windows Clipboard into the drawing using the Insert command.	PASTECLIP
Paste Special	Inserts and controls data from the Clipboard.	PASTESPEC, PA
PC In Wizard	Displays a wizard to import PCP and PC2 configuration file plot settings into the Model tab or current layout.	PCINWIZARD
Perimeter	System variable that stores the last perimeter value computed by the Area or List commands. (read only)	PERIMETER
Plan	Creates a view looking straight down along the Z-axis to see the XY coordinates.	PLAN
Planar Surface	Creates a planar surface.	PLANESURF
Plot Stamp	Places information on a specified corner of each drawing and logs it to a file.	PLOTSTAMP
Plot Style	Sets or assigns current plot style.	PLOTSTYLE
Plotter Manager	Allows you to add or edit plotter configurations.	PLOTTERMANAGER
Point	Creates a point object.	POINT, PO
Point Cloud	Provides options to create and attach point cloud files for generating 3D models from sampled 3D point data.	POINTCLOUD
Point Filters (.X, .Y, .Z, .XY, .XZ, .YZ)	Lets you selectively find single coordinates out of a point's three-dimensional coordinate set.	(used within other commands) .X or .Y or .Z or .XY or .XZ or .YZ
Point Light	Creates a point light.	POINTLIGHT
Point Style	Specifies the display mode and size of point objects.	'DDPTYPE, DDPTYPE, PDMODE
Polygon	Draws regular polygons with 3 to 1024 sides.	POLYGON, POL
Polyline	Draws a series of connected objects (lines or arcs) that are treated as a single object called a polyline.	PLINE, PL
Polyline edit (Pedit)	Edits polylines and three-dimensional polygon meshes.	PEDIT
Preferences	Customizes the AutoCAD settings.	PREFERENCES, OPTIONS

Command or Icon Name	Description	Command or Alias
Preset UCS	Selects a preset UCS.	DDUCSP, UCSMAN
Press or Pull	Presses or pulls bounded areas.	PRESSPULL
Previous Layer	Undoes the last change or set of changes to the layer settings.	LAYERP
Previous Layer Mode	Enables/disables the tracking of layer changes.	LAYERPMODE
Previous UCS	Returns you to the previously used user coordinate system.	UCS
Print/Plot	Prints or plots a drawing.	PLOT, PRINT
Print Preview	Previews the drawing before printing or plotting.	PREVIEW, PRE
Projmode	System variable that sets the current projection mode for trim or extend operations.	PROJMODE
Properties	Used to change the properties of an object.	PROPERTIES, CHPROP, DDCHPROP, CH
PS Drag	Controls the appearance of a PostScript image as it is dragged into place.	PSDRAG
PS Fill	Fills a 2D outline with a PostScript pattern.	PSFILL
PS In	Imports a file in PostScript (*.*eps*) format.	PSIN
PS Out	Saves drawing objects in PostScript (*.*eps*) format.	PSOUT
Publish	Creates multi-sheet drawing sets for publishing to a single multi-sheet DWF™ (Design Web Format) file, a plotting device, or a plot file.	PUBLISH
Publish to Web	Includes images of selected drawings in HTML page format.	PUBLISHTOWEB
Purge	Removes unused items from the drawing database.	PURGE, PU
Qtext	Controls the display and plotting of text and attribute text.	'QTEXT, QTEXT
Quick Calculator	Performs calculations, converts units, and more.	QUICKCALC
Quick Dimension	Quickly creates dimensions.	QDIM
Quick Leader	Quickly creates leaders and annotations.	QLEADER
Quick Select	Quickly creates selection sets based on filtering criteria.	QSELECT
Quit	Exits with the option not to save your changes, and returns you to the operating system.	QUIT, EXIT
Radius Dimension	Adds centermarks to an arc when providing its radius dimension.	DIMRADIUS, DIMRAD, DRA
Ray	Creates a semi-infinite line.	RAY
Reassociate Dimension	Associates dimension to drawing object.	DIMREASSOCIATE
Recover	Repairs a damaged drawing.	RECOVER
RECOVERALL	Repairs a damaged drawing and xrefs.	RECOVERALL
Rectangle	Creates rectangular shapes.	RECTANG, REC

Command or Icon Name	Description	Command or Alias
Redefine	Restores AutoCAD internal commands changed by the Undefine command.	‘REDEFINE, REDEFINE
Redefine Attribute	Redefines a block and updates associated attributes.	ATTREDEF
Redo	Reverses the effect of the most recent UNDO command. MRedo has multiple redo capability.	MREDO, redo, [Ctrl]-Y
Redraw All	Redraws all viewports at once.	‘REDRAWALL, REDRAWALL, RA
Redraw View	Removes blip marks added to the drawing screen and restores objects partially erased while you were editing other objects.	‘REDRAW, REDRAW, ‘R, R
Reference, Close	Saves back or discards changes made during in-place xref editing.	REFCLOSE
Reference Edit	Selects a reference for editing.	REFEDIT
Refset	Adds or removes objects from a working set during in-place editing of an xref or block.	REFSET
Regenauto	Controls the automatic regeneration of a drawing.	‘REGENAUTO, REGENAUTO
Regenerate	Recalculates the display file in order to show changes.	REGEN, RE
Regenerate All	Regenerates all viewports at once.	REGENALL, REA
Regenerate Dimensions	Updates the locations of associated dimensions.	DIMREGEN
Region	Creates a two-dimensional area object from a selection set of existing objects.	REGION, REG
Reinit	Reinitializes the digitizer, input/output port and program parameters.	REINIT
Remove Duplicate	Removes duplicate or overlapping lines, arcs, and polylines. Also, combines partially overlapping or contiguous ones.	OVERKILL
Rename	Changes the names of objects.	RENAME, DDRENAME, REN, -REN
Render	Creates a photorealistic or realistically shaded image of a three-dimensional wireframe or solid model.	RENDER, RR
Render Environment	Provides visual cues for the apparent distance of objects.	RENDERENVIRON-MENT
Render Exposure	Provides settings to interactively adjust the lighting global for the most recent rendered output.	RENDEREXPOSURE
Render Presets	Specifies render presets, reusable rendering parameters, for rendering an image.	RENDERPRESETS
Render Window	Displays the Render Window without invoking a render task.	RENDERWIN

Command or Icon Name	Description	Command or Alias
Restore UCS	Restores a saved user coordinate system.	UCS, UCSMAN
Resume	Continues an interrupted script.	'RESUME, RESUME
Revision Cloud	Creates a polyline of sequential arcs to form a cloud shape.	REVCLOUD
Revolve	Creates a three-dimensional object by sweeping a two-dimensional polyline, circle or region about a circular path to create a symmetrical solid.	REVOLVE, REV
Revolved Mesh	Creates a rotated surface about a selected axis.	REVSURF
Right View	Sets the viewing direction for a three-dimensional visualization of the drawing to the right side.	VPOINT, DDVPOINT, VP, -VP
Rotate	Rotates all or part of an object.	ROTATE, RO
Rscript	Creates a continually repeating script.	RSCRIPT
Ruled Surface	Creates a polygon mesh between two curves.	RULESURF
Save	Saves a drawing using Quick Save.	QSAVE
Save	Saves a drawing to a new file name without changing the name of the drawing on your screen.	SAVE
Save As	Saves a drawing, allowing you to change its name or location, or to a previous version.	SAVEAS
Save Image	Saves a rendered image to a file.	SAVEIMG
Save Slide	Creates a slide file of the current viewport.	MSLIDE
Save Time	System variable that controls how often a file is automatically saved.	SAVETIME
Save UCS	Saves a user coordinate system.	UCS, UCSMAN
Scale	Changes the size of an object in the drawing database.	SCALE, SC
Scale Text	Changes the scale of text objects without changing location.	SCALETEXT
Script	Executes a sequence of commands from a script.	SCRIPT, SCR
SE Isometric View	Sets the viewing direction for a three-dimensional visualization of the drawing.	VPOINT, DDVPOINT, VP, -VP
Section	Uses the intersection of a plane and solids to create a region.	SECTION, SEC
Select	Selects objects with a selection method listed below. Commands must be typed following the Select command.	'SELECT, SELECT
Select Add	Places selected objects in the previous selection set (default method).	ADD (at Select Objects: prompt)
Select All	Places all objects in the selection set.	ALL (at Select Objects: prompt)
Select Auto	Selects objects individually, objects within a left-to-right window, and objects crossing and within a right-to-left window (default selection method).	AUTO (at Select Objects: prompt)

Command or Icon Name	Description	Command or Alias
Select Box	Selects objects within a left-to-right window, and/or objects crossing and within a right-to-left window (default selection method).	BOX (at Select Objects: prompt)
Select Crossing	Selects all objects within and crossing the selection box (default selection from right to left).	Crossing (at Select Objects: prompt); C
Select Crossing Polygon	Selects all objects within and crossing a user-defined polygon boundary.	CPolygon (at Select Objects: prompt); CP
Select Fence	Selects objects crossing a user-defined polyline.	Fence (at Select Objects: prompt); F
Select Group	Selects all objects within a specified group.	Group (at Select Objects: prompt); G
Select Last	Re-highlights last selection.	Last (at Select Objects: prompt); L
Select Multiple	Selects objects without highlighting them.	Multiple (at Select Objects: prompt); M
Select Previous	Places previously selected objects in the selection set.	Previous (at Select Objects: prompt); P
Select Remove	Removes selected objects in the previous selection set.	Remove (at Select Objects: prompt); R
Select Single	Selects a single object.	Single (at Select Objects: prompt); S
Select Undo	Cancels the selection of the most recently selected object.	Undo (at Select Objects: prompt); U
Select Window	Selects all objects within a user-defined window.	Window (at Select Objects: prompt); W
Select Window Polygon	Selects all objects within a user-defined polygon.	WPolygon (at Select Objects: prompt); WP
Set Variables	Changes the values of system variables.	'SETVAR, SETVAR, SET
Setup Drawing	Generates Profiles and sections in viewports created with SOLVIEW.	SOLDRAW
Setup Profile	Creates profile images of 3D solids.	SOLPROF
Setup View	Creates floating viewports for orthographic projection, section views, and multi-views of 3D solids.	SOLVIEW
Shape	Inserts a shape into the current drawing.	SHAPE
Sheet Set Manager	Organizes, displays, and manages named collections of sheets.	SHEETSET
Shell	Accesses operating system commands.	SHELL
Single Line Text	Adds text to a drawing.	DTEXT, DT
Sketch	Creates a series of freehand line segments.	SKETCH
Slice	Slices a set of solids with a plane.	slice, SL

Command or Icon Name	Description	Command or Alias
Snap	Limits cursor movement on the screen to set interval so objects can be placed at precise locations easily.	SNAP, SN, or toggle off and on with [F9]
Snap From	Establishes a temporary reference point as a basis for specifying subsequent points.	'osnap, osnap, 'ddosnap, ddosnap, OS, -OS, OSNAP
Snap to Apparent Intersection	Snaps to a real or visual three-dimensional intersection formed by objects you select or by an extension of those objects.	'app, app, Eappint, appint
Snap to Center	Snaps to the center of an arc, circle, or ellipse.	'cen, cen
Snap to Endpoint	Snaps to the closest endpoint of an arc, elliptical arc, ray, multiline, or line, or to the closest corner of a trace, solid, or three-dimensional face.	'endp, endp, end
Snap to Insertion	Snaps to the insertion point of text, a block, a shape, or an attribute.	'ins, ins
Snap to Intersection	Snaps to the intersection of a line, arc, spline, elliptical arc, ellipse, ray, construction line, multiline, or circle.	'int, int
Snap to Midpoint	Snaps to the midpoint of an arc, elliptical arc spline, ray, solid, construction line, multiline, or line.	'mid, mid
Snap to Nearest	Snaps to the nearest point of an arc, elliptical arc, ellipse, spline, ray, multiline, line, circle, or point.	'nea, nea
Snap to Node	Snaps to a point object.	'nod, nod
Snap to None	Turns object snap mode off.	'none, none
Snap to Parallel	Aligns new drawing vector parallel to an acquired object.	PAR
Snap to Perpendicular	Snaps to a point perpendicular to an arc, elliptical arc, ellipse, spline, ray, construction line, multiline, line, solid, or circle.	'per, per
Snap to Quadrant	Snaps to a quadrant point of an arc, elliptical arc, ellipse, solid, or circle.	'qua, qua
Snap to Tangent	Snaps to the tangent of an arc, elliptical arc, ellipse, or circle.	'tan, tan
Solid Edit	Edits faces and edges of 3D solid objects.	SOLIDEDIT
Space Translation	Converts length values between model space and paper space.	SPACETRANS
Spelling	Checks spelling in a drawing.	'SPELL, spell, SP
Sphere	Creates a three-dimensional solid sphere.	sphere
Spline	Fits a smooth curve to a sequence of points within a specified tolerance.	spline, SPL
Spotlight	Creates a spotlight.	SPOTLIGHT
Standards	Manages CAD standards files associated with AutoCAD drawings.	STANDARDS
Status	Displays drawing statistics, modes, and extents.	'STATUS, status

Command or Icon Name	Description	Command or Alias
STL Out	Stores solids in an ASCII or binary file.	STLOUT
Stretch	Stretches the objects selected.	STRETCH, S
Style	Lets you create new text styles and modify existing ones.	'STYLE, STYLE, ST
Styles Manager	Uses dialog box to manage plot styles.	STYLESMANAGER
Subtract	Removes the set of a second solid or region from the first set.	SUBTRACT, SU
Sun Properties	Opens the Sun Properties window and sets the properties of the sun.	SUNPROPERTIES
Surface Blend	Creates a continuous blend surface between two existing surfaces.	SURFBLEND
Surface, Extract Curve from	Extracts isolines curves from a surface so that you can use them in creating additional model features.	SURFEXTRACTCURVE
Surface Patch	Creates a new surface by fitting a cap over a surface edge that forms a closed loop.	SURFPATCH
Surftab1	System variable that sets the number of tabulations to be generated for Rulesurf and Tabsurf.	surftab1
Surftab2	System variable that sets mesh density in the N direction for Revsur and Edgesurf.	surftab2
Sweep	Creates a 3D solid or surface by sweeping a 2D curve along a path.	SWEEP
SW Isometric View	Sets the viewing direction for a three-dimensional visualization of the drawing.	VPOINT, ddvpoint, VP, -VP
Synchronize Attributes	Updates all instances of specified block to current attributes.	ATTSYNC
System Windows	Arranges windows and icons on screen.	SYSWINDOWS
Tablet	Calibrates the tablet with a paper drawing's coordinate system.	tablet, TA
Tabmode	System variable that controls the use of tablet mode.	tabmode
Tabulated Surface	Creates a tabulated surface from a path curve and direction vector.	TABSURF
Target	System variable that stores location (in UCS coordinates) of the target point for the current viewport (read only).	target
Target Point Light	Creates a target point light.	TARGETPOINT
Text	Creates a single line of user-entered text.	TEXT
Text Screen	Switches from the graphics screen to the text screen.	'TEXTSCR, or toggle back and forth with [F2]
Thicken	Creates a 3D solid by thickening a surface.	THICKEN
Thickness	Sets the current 3D solid thickness.	THICKNESS, TH

Command or Icon Name	Description	Command or Alias
Tiled Viewports	Divides the graphics window into multiple tiled viewports and manages them.	vports
Tilemode	When set to 1, allows creation of tiled viewports in model space; when set to 0, enables use of paper space.	tilemode, TI or pick model/ layout tabs
Time	Displays the date and time statistics of a drawing.	'TIME, TIME
Tolerance	Creates geometric tolerances and adds them to a drawing in feature control frames.	tolerance, TOL
Tool Palettes	Opens the Tool Palettes window.	TOOLPALETTES
Toolbar	Displays, hides, and positions all toolbars.	toolbar, TO
Tooltips	System variable that controls the display of Tooltips.	tooltips
Top View	Sets the viewing direction for a three-dimension-al visualization of the drawing to the top.	vpoint, ddvpoint, VP, -VP
TPNAVIGATE	Displays a specified tool palette or palette group.	TPNAVIGATE
Torus	Creates a donut-shaped solid.	torus, TOR
Trace	Creates solid lines.	trace
Transparency	Controls transparency of background in a bitmap image.	TRANSPARENCY
Treestat	Displays information on the drawing's current spatial index.	treestat
Trim	Removes part of an object at its intersection with another object.	TRIM, TR
UCS	Manages User Coordinate Systems.	UCSMAN, ucs, dducs, UC
UCS Follow	System variable that allows you to generate a plan view of the current UCS in a viewport whenever you change the UCS.	UCSFOLLOW
UCS Icon	System variable that repositions and turns on and off the display of the UCS icon.	UCSICON
UCS Manager	Manages defined user coordinate systems.	USCMAN
Undefine	Allows an application-defined command to override an AutoCAD command.	UNDEFINE
Undo	Reverses the effect of previous commands.	UNDO, U
Ungroup	Explodes a group.	UNGROUP
Union	Adds two separate sets of solids or regions together to create one solid model.	UNION, UNI
Units	Controls the type and precision of the values used in dimensions.	'UNITS, UNITS, -UN 'ddunits, ddunits, UN
View	Saves views of an object to be plotted, displayed, or printed.	'view, view, 'ddview, ddview, -V
View Component	Selects drawing view components for editing when using views extracted from 3D models.	VIEWCOMPONENT
View Detail select	Used to select the existing drawing view for creating a detail view.	VIEWDETAIL

Command or Icon Name	Description	Command or Alias
View Section select	Lets you specify the view to cut during the creation of a section view from a 3D model.	VIEWSECTION
View, Detail Style	Sets or modifies the style of detail view created from a 3D model.	VIEWDETAILSTYLE
View, Section Style	Sets or modifies the style of section view created from a 3D model.	VIEWSECTIONSTYLE
View, Sketching constraints	Used to enter model space "view sketching" state to edit and constrain a section line or detail boundary.	VIEWSKETCH
View, Sketching constraints Exit	Used to exit the model space "view sketching" state.	VIEWSKETCHCLOSE
Viewport Clip	Clips viewport objects.	VPCLIP
View Resolution	Sets the resolution for object generation in the current viewport.	VIEWRES
View Slide	Displays a raster-image slide file in the current viewport.	vslide
View UCS	Selects a user coordinate system aligned to a specific view.	ucs
Viewport Layer	Controls the visibility of layers within specific viewports in paper space.	VPLAYER
Visual Basic Editor	Display the Visual Basic Editor.	VBAIDE
Visual LISP	Display Visual LISP® interactive development environment (IDE).	VLISP
Visual Styles	Creates and modifies visual styles and applies a visual style to a viewport.	VISUALSTYLES
Visual Style in Current Viewport	Sets the visual style in the current viewport.	VSCURRENT
Walk and Fly Settings	Specifies walk and fly settings.	WALKFLYSETTINGS
WEBLIGHT	Creates a weblight that is a 3D representation of the light intensity distribution of a light source.	WEBLIGHT
Wedge	Creates a three-dimensional solid with a closed face tapering along the X-axis by specifying the center.	wedge, WE
Who Has	Display ownership info. for open drawing files.	WHOHAS
WMF In	Imports a file saved in Windows Metafile (*.wmf) format.	WMFIN
WMF Options	Sets options for importing a Windows Metafile.	WMFOPTs
WMF Out	Saves drawing objects in Windows Metafile (*.wmf) format.	WMFOUT
World UCS	Selects the world coordinate system as the user coordinate system.	ucs
Write Block	Saves a block as a separate file so that it may be used in other drawings.	wblock, W

Command or Icon Name	Description	Command or Alias
X Axis Rotate UCS	Selects a user coordinate system by rotating the X-axis.	ucs
Xplode	Breaks a component object into its component objects; see also Explode.	xplode
Y Axis Rotate UCS	Selects a user coordinate system by rotating the Y-axis.	ucs
Z Axis Rotate UCS	Selects a user coordinate system by rotating the Z-axis.	ucs
Z Axis Vector UCS	Selects a user coordinate system defined by a vector in the Z direction.	ucs
Zoom All	Resizes to display the entire drawing in the current viewport.	'zoom, zoom, 'Z, Z
Zoom Center	Resizes to display a window by entering a center point, then a magnification value or height.	'zoom, zoom, 'Z, Z
Zoom Dynamic	Resizes to display the generated portion of the drawing with a view box.	'zoom, zoom, 'Z, Z
Zoom Extents	Resizes to display the drawing extents.	'zoom, zoom, 'Z, Z
Zoom In	Resizes areas of the drawing in the screen to make it appear closer or larger.	'zoom, zoom, 'Z, Z
Zoom Object	Resizes display to fit one or more selected objects centered in drawing area.	'zoom, zoom, 'Z, Z
Zoom Out	Resizes areas of the drawing in the screen so that more of the drawing fits in the screen.	'zoom, zoom, 'Z, Z
Zoom Previous	Resizes to the previous view.	'zoom, zoom, 'Z, Z
Zoom Realtime	Resizes the view in a real-time fashion.	'zoom, zoom, 'Z, Z
Zoom Scale	Resizes to display at a specified scale factor.	'zoom, zoom, 'Z, Z
Zoom Vmax	Resizes so that the drawing is viewed from as far out as possible on the current viewports virtual screen without forcing a complete regeneration of the drawing.	'zoom, zoom, 'Z, Z
Zoom Window	Resizes to display an area specified by two opposite corner points of a rectangular window.	'zoom, zoom, 'Z, Z

INDEX

Symbols

A

B

C

9781630578213